I0821571

The Urban Design Legacy
of Colin Rowe

Published by Applied Research and Design Publishing,
an imprint of ORO Editions.
Gordon Goff: Publisher

www.appliedresearchanddesign.com
info@appliedresearchanddesign.com

Editors: Steven W. Hurtt and James T. Tice
Book Design: Pablo Mandel / CircularStudio,
with Steven W. Hurtt and James T. Tice
Illustration Consultant: Richard Bosch
Project Manager: Jake Anderson

10 9 8 7 6 5 4 3 2 1 FIRST EDITION

ISBN: 978-1-940743-51-6

Prepress and Print work by ORO Editions Inc.
Printed in China

AR+D Publishing makes a continuous effort to minimize the overall carbon footprint of its publications. As part of this goal, AR+D, in association with Global ReLeaf, arranges to plant trees to replace those used in the manufacturing of the paper produced for its books. Global ReLeaf is an international campaign run by American Forests, one of the world's oldest nonprofit conservation organizations. Global ReLeaf is American Forests' education and action program that helps individuals, organizations, agencies, and corporations improve the local and global environment by planting and caring for trees.

STEVEN W. HURTT AND JAMES T. TICE

EDITORS

THE URBAN DESIGN LEGACY OF COLIN ROWE

DEDICATION

Colin Rowe

and

Alex Caragonne
Wayne Copper
Don Duncan
Klaus Herdeg
Lee Hodgden
Fred Koetter
John McDermott
Bill McMinn
John Reps
Piero Sartogo
Thomas Schumacher
Werner Seligmann
John Shaw
Roger Sherwood
Terrance Williams

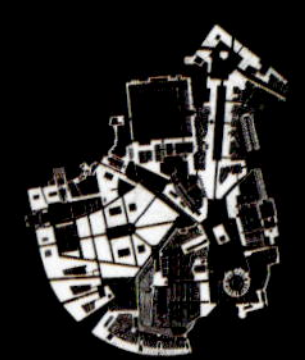

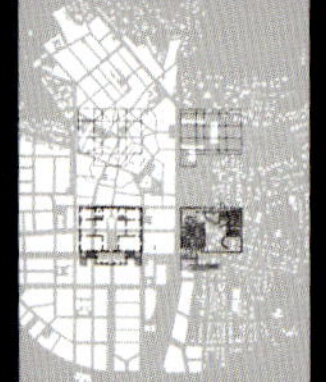

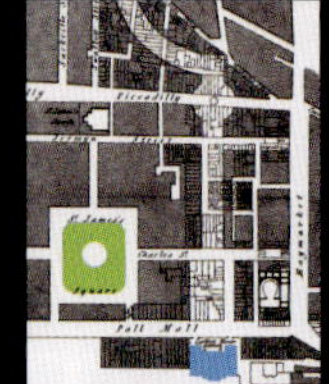
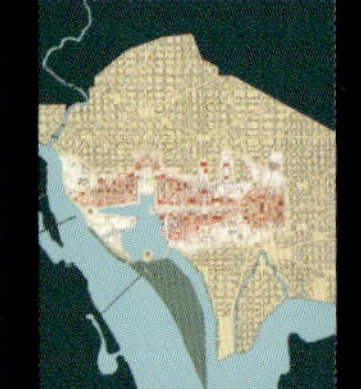

I. Colin Rowe & Urban Design

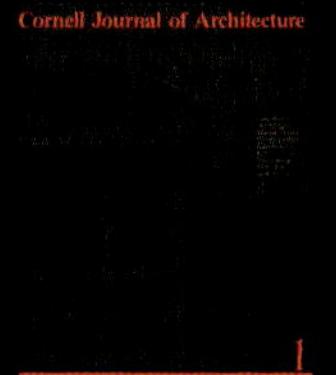

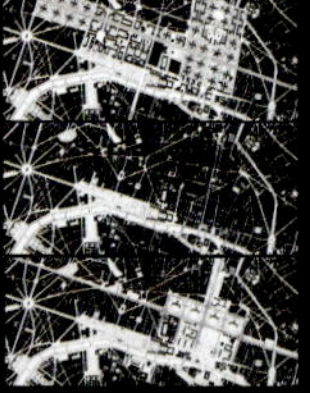
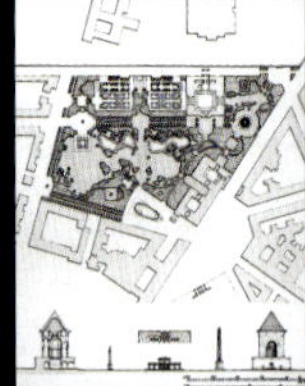
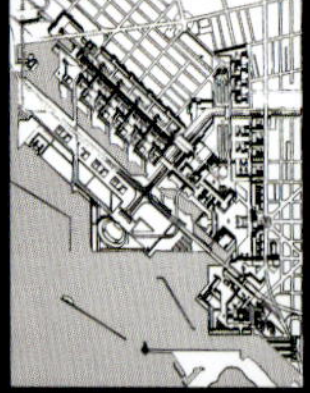
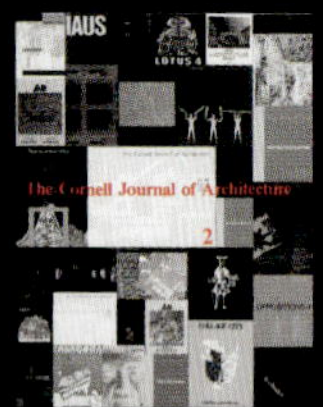

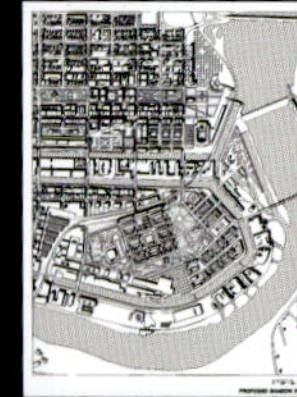

II. Pedagogy

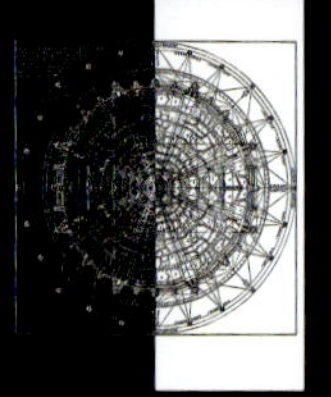
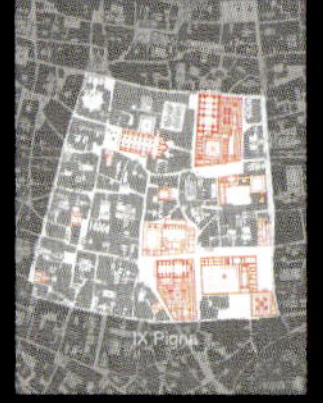

III. Rome

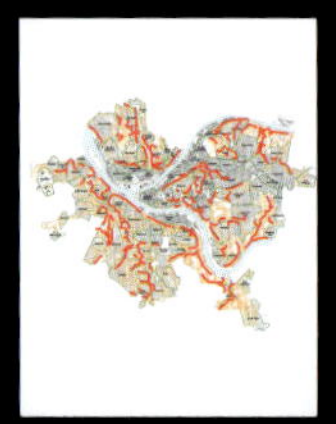
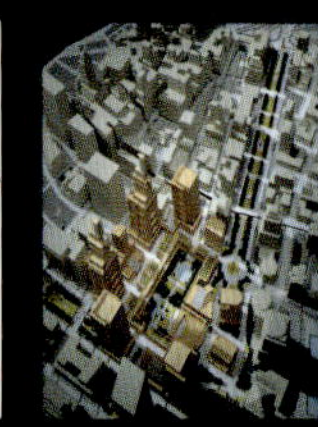

IV. Praxis

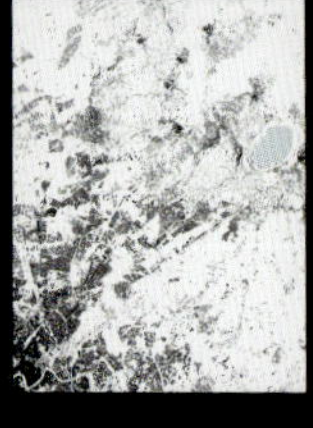
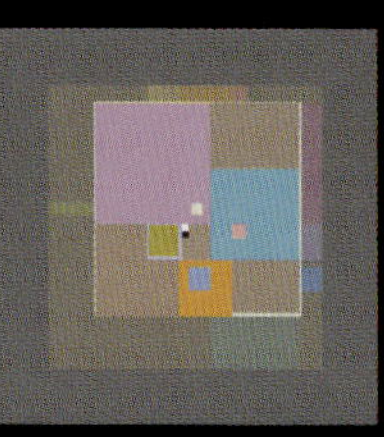

V. Diagnosis /Prognosis

Contents

Foreword

frontispiece:
Rowe Interrotto, detail
(original 102cm × 148 cm) oil on canvas, courtesy of Carl Laubin, 2002, collection of Eve Happold.

The Urban Design Legacy of Colin Rowe explains how and why the field of urban design developed coincident with Rowe's long and influential career, the contributions that he, his students, and his colleagues made to it, how those ideas were disseminated, how they have impacted theory, and have been realized in practice. Rowe's exceptional influence began with a series of essays published between 1947 and 1963. That influence was greatly expanded during the years he initiated and taught the Urban Design Studio at Cornell from 1963 until 1988. This collection of essays focuses on and elucidates the ideas that Colin Rowe bequeathed to us and how he did so; ideas that radically challenged what had become the Modernist catechism by mid-century.

Colin Rowe was among the first in his generation to call attention to the degradation of the physical environment of the city which he attributed to Modernism. He argued that Modernist forms of architecture and planning were based on an ideological attack on the city that amounted to an existential threat to democracy itself. He provided both a diagnosis of the underlying causes of the contemporary city's ills, and a prognosis for its return to good health.

A legacy is defined as something of enduring value or as a gift to posterity. Colin Rowe's enduring gift to our discipline and to prosperity has been acknowledged multiple times. In 1985 the American Institute of Architects awarded Rowe the Topaz Medal for his contributions to architectural education. A decade later, in 1995, the Royal Institute of British Architects conferred on Rowe the Royal Gold Medal, recognizing him as "the most significant architectural teacher of the second half of the 20th century". In 2011, the Congress for the New Urbanism posthumously conferred the Athena Medal, in recognition of Rowe's highly influential contribution to urban design theory and practice.

Our contributors, distinguished educators, scholars, and practitioners, many of whom were Colin Rowe's former students, present his ideological admonishments about, and design aspirations for, a healthy future for the city, for society, and for the planet.

SWH and JTT

Preface

Rowe's influence has been in two arenas of design during two different periods of his academic life: the first focused on architecture, the second on urban design. The former has been accorded much critical attention; the latter, despite its notoriety, remains less well known. And while theoretical and historical texts often reference Rowe's contributions to urban design, no book to date explains, explores, and demonstrates his thoughts, methods, values, and their continuing influence. As both a retrospective and prospective that is intended to explain and honor Rowe's legacy, some might consider this book a Festschrift.

It was an 'outsider's' prompt and persistence that started and sustained this book. Antonio Pietro Latini, Italian architect, educator, editor and scholar asked: "What of the Colin Rowe diaspora? Rowe, so famous, the work of the Studio so influential, what of his students? Where did they go, what have they accomplished? What impact have they had?" Latini suggested that the journal *Urbanistica* might publish a group of essays addressing these questions. Texts were solicited and drafts prepared on the topics of theory, pedagogy, and multiple forms of practice, but this proposed project for *Urbanistica* was not realized. Two years later, Latini proposed an international conference devoted to Rowe's influence on the discipline and profession of urban design. It would be held, quite appropriately, in Rome, acknowledging Rowe's 'adopted' city that he often referenced as a guide to good urban form, hence "Rowe/Rome". Latini insisted that we three should organize the event, building on the unrealized *Urbanistica* project.

A conference date was set for June 18–22, 2014, to be held in Rome, titled "Urban Design and the Legacy of Colin Rowe" ("La progettazione urbana e il lascito di Colin Rowe"). The event was sponsored by Università Roma Tre Architettura, to be held in their revitalized and splendid ex-Mattatoio campus in the Testaccio district of Rome. The three-day event was both an academic conference about Colin Rowe and a reunion of sorts for his students. It attracted over 200 participants from the U.S., Italy, and other European countries. The conference generated a great deal of enthusiasm and left no doubt in the editors' minds that there was abundant material for a book. Complete recordings for the conference, which are preserved in a private archive, served as a guide for structuring the book and enlisting essays from most contributors. We are pleased to have been able to include several other contributors as well.

Latini proposed that "Rowe/Rome" should be an annual event, and, in fact, four conferences followed:

"The Best of Both Worlds: Urban Design and the Regeneration of the Light City", "sulla rigenerazione della "città leggera", sponsored by the Ordine degli Architetti PPC di Roma e provincia, Casa dell'architettura. Camera dei Deputati, Rome. October 15–16, 2015.

"Urban Design Matters", sponsored by the Facoltà di Ingegneria della Sapienza Università di Roma, Sala Grande del Chiostro di San Pietro in Vincoli, Rome, June 2016.

"Cities of Good Intentions" ("Le città delle buone intenszioni"), Rome, sponsored by Sapienza Università di Roma, Facoltà d'ingegneria, Sala Grande del Chiostro di San Pietro in Vincoli, Rome, June 2017.

"Urban Design: Colin Rowe", sponsored by the School of Architecture, Planning, and Preservation, University of Maryland, April 2019.

Most of the essays for the book emerged from the first conference, a few from the second, and those that followed served to keep us mindful of ongoing developments in the discipline. It was after the 2016 conference that a commitment to making a book took shape. A few days after that event, Latini, Michael Schwarting, Steven Hurtt, and Jim Tice met for an afternoon aperitif in Trastevere. Inevitably, the discussion turned to the book. Could we commit ourselves to it? Caravaggio's *The Calling of St. Mathhew* came to mind. Such a book would give us, and others, the opportunity to express our gratitude to Rowe for shaping and enriching our intellectual growth, careers, and lives. More importantly, it would fill a gap in the knowledge about Rowe's contribution to the development of the urban design discipline making some aspects of that history more fully available to future students, practitioners, and scholars.

Contributors to one or more of the conferences, as well as others aware of our efforts, responded to our invitation to provide essays. The 31 essays in this book represent the efforts of 25 authors who are practitioners, educators, or scholars. Almost all were personally involved with Rowe, most as former students, a few as colleagues, some as both. A few others were influenced by his ideas, and in that more general sense made themselves his students as well. As Rowe would be quick to say, it worked both ways, that is, he prompted students and colleagues, but they likewise prompted his developing ideas.

A Guide to this Book

We have divided the following essays into thematic divisions which collectively treat multiple aspects of Rowe's legacy. Brief descriptions follow.

Colin Rowe & Urban Design provides an immersion into the related worlds of urban design and Colin Rowe: the problems for the city created by Modern architecture; Rowe's shift in his scholarly focus from architecture to urban design; and the foundational language, design processes, and conceptual frameworks Rowe developed for the Studio. The initial essays in this grouping are followed by others, each devoted to exploring or applying one of the many ideas nurtured by Rowe.

Pedagogy primarily describes Rowe's form of teaching. It includes his belief in the unique value of studio education; the importance of the 'presence of the past' for both a liberal and a design education; and in the diverse, broadly informative readings that challenge conventional thinking. It describes the dissemination of his ideas and teaching through Studio projects; through articles written by former students; as demonstrated by the "Roma interrotta" exhibition of 1978; and essays in *The Cornell Journal of Architecture*, 1981–91. Finally, it demonstrates how these resources can be applied in teaching urban design today.

Rome, particularly the historic core of that city, figured prominently in Rowe's life, career, and teaching. It was a source of empirical knowledge that prompted his theories on urban design and served to illustrate them. It grounded and placed in context the study of Giambattista Nolli's 1748 *Pianta di Roma* and Paul Letarouilly's *Édifices de Rome Moderne*. It explained the relationship of building typologies and iconologies interlocked with urban morphology. These resources, and Rowe's delight in elaborating them, inspired further research and documentation of urban design subtleties and accomplishments, and a basis for speculations on alternate histories and design outcomes.

Praxis reveals the global reach and extraordinary breadth of Rowe's impact on the profession of architecture and urban design. The illustrated examples vary widely in scale from single buildings and related spaces to college and business campuses, entire neighborhoods and city districts. They illustrate diverse manners of selectively relating to their setting, context, or circumstance. Executed projects also include critiques of, innovations in, and applications of, design codes. As with design projects, these codes range widely in intent and form. They may be dependent and/or independent of related building uses, types, locales, and histories and may serve to prompt or sustain good urban form for multiple reasons: social, economic, and aesthetic.

Diagnosis/Prognosis recalls Rowe's cautionary assessment of the ills impacting our cities and their consequences to civilization. Among these is a uniquely Modern fixation on the building as an object rather than as a participant in city making. Ideological ills include unhealthy preoccupations with utopianism, millennialism, positivism, *zeitgeist* propensities, and the perpetual declarations of crises. The single crisis that presciently concerned Rowe was climate change. As early as 1988, he recognized the potentially horrific consequences and declared himself an ecological partisan. Rowe's prognosis, however, remained optimistic. He imagined that we not only should, but could, engage the emerging complexities of our urban world, think dialectically about our alternatives, respect opposing arguments, seek ameliorations, and by doing so, change our current course for the better.

While these divisions have logical consistencies and affinities, other thematic structures might have served equally well. Rowe himself might have suggested alternative alignments. Or, disinclined to think along rigid lines and preferring accidental possibilities, he might have suggested no thematic divisions at all! Nonetheless, we hope these groupings serve to further an appreciation of Rowe's complex persona, his originality, the breadth and complexity of his understanding of urban form as representative of the complexity of human nature, and the overriding importance of good city form in sustaining civilization.

Introduction

John Reps

The first period in Rowe's teaching and writing career had been devoted almost exclusively to architectural criticism. His incisive critique of architectural form was well known through essays written between 1947 and 1961—later gathered in *The Mathematics of the Ideal Villa and Other Essays*, the title recalling his first essay. In 1962 Colin Rowe's career took a dramatic turn when he accepted a position in the Department of Architecture at Cornell University. He was assigned to lead a new graduate program. Following a suggestion by John Reps, professor in the Department of City and Regional Planning, Rowe decided to devote the program to urban design—the intersection of architecture and planning. The subject had been largely abandoned in the post-WWII era, overwhelmed by early 20th century developments in Modernist architecture and a new world vision promoted primarily by Le Corbusier. In urban design terms, the shortcomings of the Modernist movement, in essence an attack on the traditional city, had become painfully evident by the mid-century. Rowe, otherwise a devotee of the good intentions of much of the Modern movement, had become acutely aware of its inadequacies. Seizing the opportunity to address them, Rowe focused the Studio on that very subject. Thus began a new chapter in his intellectual life. It revitalized Rowe's career with a new passion and sense of urgency, which also contributed to a rebirth of the field of urban design.

For centuries, ideality in architecture had been good for the city. It had given hierarchy and meaning to special buildings and institutions, elevating them within and above a dense fabric of more commonplace structures. But Modern architecture was replacing that paradigm with a radically different one. It was composed of three related parts: all buildings to be regarded as equally important, idealized objects; hygienic improvements made possible by engineering technologies and vast resources; all buildings to be surrounded by park-like open spaces also related to hygiene concerns of sunlight and air circulation *soleil, espace, verdure.* Together, these also had a moral authority derived from the assumption of significantly improved living conditions for all people. Le Corbusier had modelled all this with compelling images and arguments. As these became increasingly real, the new paradigm replacing the old one, its shortcomings became increasingly obvious: the destruction of the old city, its fabric, and its culture. With typical insight Rowe was able to reduce the problem to the simplest of terms: the old paradigm, the city as a solid with voids, public spaces carved in it, versus the new paradigm, a city of idealized objects, spaced well apart. The architectural object that Rowe had validated with exceptional insight, albeit at a modest scale, was now looming large. Implemented at a vast scale, it threatened the very life of the city. If Le Corbusier had offered the best of what we might imagine for Modern architecture, he had also promoted the worst we might imagine for the city.

Rowe would address the conflict between the idealized architectural object and the traditional city in multiple ways: through his teaching, students' projects, public lectures, writings, and exhibitions. He searched for a *détente* between Modernist enthusiasms with the counter position: respect for the existing city as a repository and emblem of Western civilization and its venerated ideals. He summed up the problem in his quip "How to reconcile the Mod with the 'trad' city?" He called it a 'conundrum' for architecture and for civilization and, throughout his career at Cornell and beyond, he stressed the importance of resolving it. Could these opposite architectural realities be reconciled? Could the traditional city be either a background for the *avant-garde* object or a co-equal partner in a form of collage? Or would the traditional city be overwhelmed and displaced by it? Finding answers to these questions became the driving theme of the Studio for several generations of his students and the entire architectural culture. How Rowe's students developed ideas, how these matured in the Studio, how they were disseminated, further developed, and influenced the urban design discipline, is the crux of this text.

The Mod/'trad' conundrum

This introduction sets the stage for Rowe's transition into his Urban Design Studio. It describes the milieu of the 1960s, the decade during which the fundamentals of the Rowe–Koetter critique of the contemporary city were incubated, and most completely described in *Collage City*. It sketches the 1960s–'80s duration of Rowe's tenure at Cornell leading the Studio, and records interactions with other 'influencers' primarily in the U.S., but also the U.K. and Western Europe. It comments upon the further development of the urban design discipline through the 1990s and from 2000 to 2022. It describes the field of urban design as it evolved, incorporating Rowe's critique to address a full range of urban design issues—social, political, cultural, and environmental, but focusing on his passion for the formal-spatial design of the city.

In *The Texas Rangers: Notes from an Architectural Underground* of 1995, Alex Caragonne notes that, during Rowe's University of Texas appointment, 1953–56, there was already evidence of his dialectical architecture–urban design thinking, that is, buildings occupying space versus buildings defining space. His fundamental urban design solid/void and figure/ground argument was emerging, but the focus was still architecture. After Texas, Rowe held a series of short appointments at U.S. schools, including Cornell, then at Cambridge. During his four-year appointment at Cambridge, 1958–62, he remained focused on architecture. However, his response to an exhibition of Le Corbusier's work in London in 1959, and a BBC program devoted to it, provoked an off-the-cuff article by Rowe in the *Listener*, "Le Corbusier: Utopian Architect", followed by the more comprehensive "The Architecture of Utopia", published in *Granta* a few months later—an historical account of utopia, with a nod to Platonic and Judaic-Christian influences, assumptions about the perfectibility of society, and illustrations of ideal cities from the Renaissance forward. The thrust of that essay had a lasting impact on all of Rowe's subsequent thinking. He concluded that any of these 'idealities'

Utopia and Le Corbusier

are only reasonable as fragmentary achievements. Otherwise, he viewed utopia as a 'monstrosity'. However, Rowe gave no evidence that his devastating critique of utopia would become the foundation of the urban design theory he later developed at Cornell, or that it would place him among a handful of intellectuals who likewise chose to challenge the 'monstrosity' in a theoretical conflict that continues to rage, eviscerating the city as it does so.

Peter Eisenman and Jaquelin Robertson

Rowe says of his time in Cambridge that he "wrote quite a lot … . However, in 1960 this was changed by the arrival of Peter Eisenman from Cornell-Columbia, and Jaquelin Robertson from Yale-Oxford-Yale; and thenceforward … it was conversation that usurped the role of writing". Subsequently, Eisenman and Robertson relocated to the U.S., where they became professionally involved in architectural and urban design. Some of their initiatives significantly contributed to Rowe's career trajectory and the notoriety of his urban design work at Cornell. In a general sense, the Eisenman–Robertson duality personifies the extremes of Rowe's interests and influences. Eisenman, through the Institute for Architecture and Urban Studies (IAUS) in New York, primarily emphasized architecture as an ideal autonomous discipline in alignment with the Modernist avant-garde: Robertson emphasized the city as the context of architecture, shaping the urban environment and shaped by it, physically and culturally. Robertson promoted urban design as one of the central policies of John Lindsay's campaign for Mayor of New York City and subsequently led the Office of Midtown Planning and Development (OMPD). We will return to the Eisenman–Robertson duality to illuminate Rowe's conundrum. But what world did Rowe encounter in 1960? How did he respond to it then and throughout his career?

Joseph Hudnut and Sigfried Giedion

In his prescient 1952 essay, "The Three Lamps of Modern Architecture", Joseph Hudnut, former dean at Harvard, implicitly took Walter Gropius and Sigfried Giedion to task in his critique of the underlying assumptions of Modernism. The Hudnut essay was one of many readings Rowe frequently recommended to his students. Hudnut's lamps, "progress", "nature", and "democracy", equate approximately to Rowe's critique of Modernism: *zeitgeist* worship, natural landscape, *vox populi* and the infallibility of social 'science'. Rowe and Hudnut saw these Modernist forces threatening tradition, history, the humanities, and the city as a cultural endeavor and work of art.

Giedion had been promoting Modernism. His *Space, Time and Architecture* of 1941 was based on the Charles Eliot Norton Lectures at Harvard for 1938–39 and republished in sixteen printings and five separate editions until 1966. The book's section "Space—Time in City Planning" celebrated 1930s superhighways and traffic interchanges. Robert Moses was the driving force behind such initiatives in New York City. Having consolidated his authority as New York City's principal "Power Broker", he was realizing his visionary equivalent of the Le Corbusier–CIAM Ville Radieuse as promoted by Giedion and recast in the Norman Bell Geddes short film *Futurama* presented at the 1939 World's Fair. It projected 'highways' of brain power that would produce 'highways' of free-flowing vehicles serving and connecting a New World in which, by 1960, the Old World with all its problems will have been swept away. New York City had become the recognized theater in which these Modernist forces were being played out in high relief. It was the site of the wanton razing of New York City's magnificent Penn Station between

1963 and 1968, which signaled to the editors—one of whom witnessed the demolition of Penn Station firsthand—that something had gone terribly wrong with our society, our culture, and the profession. The razing of Penn Station gave a renewed impetus to the historic preservation movement nationwide.

Robert Moses and Jane Jacobs

By 1960, the former U.S. city of blocks, buildings, squares, streets, and boulevards was being systematically and intentionally destroyed by the combined forces of power brokers and visionaries like Robert Moses, aided and abetted by dedicated gasoline taxes, an interstate highway system that too often cut through cities and towns with devastating effect, and government subsidized suburbs. The traditional city, the *polis*, was dying as it morphed into a metropolis and then into a sprawling megalopolis. Protests by a handful of critical thinkers had begun, and a reappraisal of Modernism was underway throughout the U.S. and Europe.

In 1959, Henry Hope Reed had made a powerful visual argument by juxtaposing monumental late 19th and early to mid-20th century Beaux-Arts buildings with their Modernist counterparts in *The Golden City*. Reed's argument was much like Hudnut's. But the most effective argument for the traditional city was made by Jane Jacobs in *The Death and Life of Great American Cities* of 1961. Jacobs stood up to Robert Moses. She challenged his ideas, and all those responsible for the ongoing and highly destructive incursions being made into the very heart of neighborhoods in New York City and nationwide. She emphasized the importance of the fact that the physical fabric of the traditional city affords the opportunity for social well-being. Similar sentiments had begun to emerge from multiple quarters and disciplines. Reportedly, Rowe wrote an approving letter to Jacobs about her book.

Beyond the world of architecture and a nascent urban design discipline, profound environmental problems were emerging as central, not only to the city, but to the planet. In 1962 Rachel Carson's *The Silent Spring* sounded the alarm about the chemical poisoning of the environment. Carson's book had an impact. The Environmental Defense Fund was established in 1967, and in 1970, with President Nixon's approval and all but one vote in Congress, the U.S. Environmental Protection Agency (EPA) was created.

Kevin Lynch and Edmund Bacon

In *Image of the City* of 1960, Kevin Lynch proposed five everyday terms to talk about the form of the city and cognitive mapping—landmark, node, pathway, edge and district. These everyday and stylistically neutral terms equated readily with the Rowe Studio use of *gestalt* terminology—figure, contour or edge, and field. It was likewise in the early 1960s that architectural historians turned their attention to the 'problems of the modern city' resulting in *The Historian and the City* of 1963 edited by Oscar Handlin and John Burchard. Similarly, in 1963/67 Leonardo Benevolo published *L'orgini dell'urbanistica moderna – The Origins of Modern Town Planning*. Next came Giulio Carlo Argan's *Europe of the Capitals* of 1964, followed by Aldo Rossi's *L'architettura della città – The Architecture of the City* in 1966. The same year Robert Venturi challenged the stylistic strictures of Modernism in *Complexity and Contradiction in Architecture*. He penned his famous "Mainstreet is almost all right" which called for a re-evaluation of the existing city and the 'high and low' of architectural culture. In 1967 Edmund Bacon published *Design of Cities*, its breadth of examples and graphic sophistication inspired the Studio and validated the study of traditional cities. And, as at Cornell, fledging urban design programs could be found in a handful of other schools of architecture nationwide.

Robert Venturi and Aldo Rossi

In Europe, where the contrast between the traditional and Modernist city was more stark than in the U.S., *contextualism* had a half-century antecedent unknown to the Studio. With a meaning similar to *contextualism*, or what Rowe and Koetter called the *psycho-cultural field*, Gustavo Giovannoni (1873–1947) had promoted *ambientismo*. This paralleled Rowe's interest in the 'prevalent fabric' of the city. In post-war Italy a new generation of architects, members of *La Tendenza*, challenged the basic tenets of Modernism and the avant-garde. Better known to the Studio was the work of Giancarlo de Carlo, particularly his 1964 town plan for Urbino and Law School embedded in the fabric of that city. Likewise, the Studio was aware of Saverio Muratori's early "typo-morphology" studies in 1959 that included detailed building-by-building city plans of Venice and the Campo Marzio of Rome in 1963—the latter based on the 1748 map of Rome by Giambattista Nolli. Related typological studies by Gianfranco Caniggia in 1963 and later with Gian Luigi Maffei, *Composizione architettonica e tipologia edilizia,* although not well known in the studio, were to influence urban housing research in the 1970s by Rowe's students, Sherwood and Tice.

Giancarlo de Carlo and Saverio Muratori

Alan Colquhoun: Typology

Rowe referenced building types or 'paradigms' to describe the ideal/circumstantial phenomenon. Otherwise, he directed attention to types and their formal variation by referencing such texts as Giulio Carlo Argan's essay "On the Typology of Architecture" of 1962–63, Allan Colquhoun's "Typology and Design Method" of 1967, Paul Marie Letarouilly's *Édifices de Rome Moderne* (three volumes, 1840–55), Carl L. Franck's 1966 *The Villas of Frascati, 1650–1750*, and the text *Strada Nuova* of 1970, a study of the Genovese palazzo and its aggregation along its most famous street. While Rowe made no such studies himself in types or urban morphology, he seems to have inspired them among colleagues and former students, as exemplified by Wayne Copper's thesis, "The figure/grounds", Klaus Herdeg's "Formal Structure in Indian Architecture", and Michael Dennis's "The French Hôtel Plans" in 1974, which was "inspired by concurrent research into French hôtels of the 17th and 18th centuries ... to develop an expanded and more flexible architectural vocabulary ... which, in contrast to Modern architecture, could deal with contextual issues of the city". In a similar vein, a typological study of a unique urban housing tradition titled *Courtyard Housing in Los Angeles* was published in 1982 by Rowe's former students, Roger Sherwood and James Tice, along with Stefanos Polyzoides. Among other things, it was intended as a counterpoint to Reyner Banham's hip, 1971 book, *Los Angeles: The Architecture of Four Ecologies*, which was an apotheosis of the city as an auto-utopia.

Wayne Copper: The Figure/Grounds

In this same 1960–70 decade, a reappraisal of Modernism was underway throughout the U.S. and Europe. At Cornell, Rowe was directing the Studio's attention to the possibility of reconciling the Modernist and traditional city, primarily using 19th century America cities to do so. In the spring semester of 1966, the Buffalo Waterfront project (displayed at the Albright-Knox Gallery in Buffalo in 1969), made the possibility of such a reconciliation look promising. Students were adopting design strategies and operational processes that they began describing with terms like *collision city*, *collage city*, and *contextualism*, words that would later become well-known in the lexicon of urban design. The Buffalo project was followed by another group Studio project that was part of the 1968 MoMA "The New City: Architecture and Urban Renewal" exhibition. It was one of four schemes executed by Cornell, Columbia, MIT, and Princeton. Rowe notes that he, Eisenman, and Robertson met with Arthur Drexler at MoMA to propose, plan, and select areas for which each school would provide schemes—the Cornell Studio's portion included East Harlem.

Meanwhile, Robertson, as director of OMPD and a member of the planning commission, and Eisenman, through the IAUS, promoted contractual academic urban design studies. In 1969, the Rowe Studio provided an IAUS study of NYC zoning. These combined factors resulted in Rowe's students being invited to work in Lindsay's urban design offices. Their work had major impacts: initiating and contributing to policies that continue to the present. They also produced early studies of Lower Manhattan, some of them fundamental to the later Battery Park City achievement. These studies were more specific to the relation of urban morphology and architectural typology—typo-morphology—than had been common to Studio work.

Rowe: Collage City

In 1967, Rowe wrote a book review for the *New York Times* referencing both Reyner Banham's *The New Brutalism* and Venturi's *Complexity and Contradiction in Architecture*, titled "Waiting for Utopia". That same year, Rowe lectured in Berlin on "Collage City". For the symposium "The Provincial City" of May 1970 at Cornell, Rowe's talk was "Utopia or Collage City". The same topic once again was presented later that summer at the first International Institute of Design (IID) at the Architectural Association (AA) organized by Alvin Boyarsky. Rowe describes their first meeting at Cornell when he was a visiting faculty member and Boyarsky a graduate student in the Department of City and Regional Planning doing a thesis on Camillo Sitte. Boyarsky went on to act as director of the AA from 1971–90. That Rowe presented the utopia-collage theme so frequently during the years of 1967-70, combined with a fall 1969 sabbatical leave and his statement in the *Collage City* "Acknowledgements" that the text was completed by the end of December 1973, suggests that he began to write it with Fred Koetter in the spring of 1970—Koetter was on the faculty from 1968 to 1973.

Studio Texts

There were only a few basic urban design reference books known in the early Studio years. Primarily these referencess included *City Planning According to Artistic Principles* of 1889 by Camillo Sitte, *The American Vitruvius: an Architects Handbook of Civic Art* of 1922 by Werner Hegemann and Albert Peets, *The Urban Pattern: City Planning and Design* by Arthur B. Gallion of 1950, and *Towns and Buildings* of 1951 by Steen Eiler Rasmussen. *Design of Cities* of 1967 by Edmund Bacon was a welcome addition, as was, a few years later, *History of Urban Form Before the Industrial Revolution* of 1974 by A.E.J. Morris. In sharp contrast, the rich intellectual aura that Rowe subtly created for the Studio was nurtured by Studio projects he selected and his frequent recommendations of books to read, these often in response to an interest a student asked about or innocently blundered into. These books ranged through philosophy, anthropology, music, the arts, and, of course, art criticism. These readings in turn contributed significantly to *Collage City*. Many were fundamental themes that Rowe returned to throughout his life. The breadth of these subjects can best be appreciated with reference to what became a non-mandatory 'great books' bibliography for the course (see the appendix to "The Best of Both Worlds" in this volume).

Buffalo: Collision, Collage, Contextualism …

Rowe described the 1966 Buffalo Waterfront project as "an early super-climax for the Studio". It sparked discussions among some students about the ideas and processes being used: *collision*, *collage*, and *contextualism* primary among them. They first emerged in a more mature state in Tom Schumacher's "Contextualism: Urban Ideals and Deformations" for *Casabella* in 1971, followed by Stuart Cohen's "Physical Context, Cultural Context: Including It All" for *Oppositions* in 1974. The following year, Rowe and Koetter published what was essentially a long, abridged version of *Collage City* in *The Architectural Review*, making it generally available prior to the publication of the book three years later.

While writing *Collage City*, Rowe also wrote the "Introduction" for *Five Architects: Eisenman, Graves, Gwathmey, Hejduk, Meier*, published in 1972. That book rekindled an exploration of, and debate about, early Modernist themes and styles, especially those promoted by Le Corbusier. The book featured ten built and unbuilt private residencies in suburban settings, half of which were located on Long Island or Long Island Sound. Without mentioning *Five Architects*, Robertson authored an article for *Architectural Forum* saying the profession had abrogated its responsibility to society by turning inward to a hermetic architecture disconnected from contemporary problems of the larger environment. He wrote of Long Island, and places like it, as having once been beautiful landscapes with attractive towns and beach communities cared for by those living there. He now saw these environments as dilapidated and unkempt, the epitome of a society devoted to the self rather than community, and an architectural profession obsessed with the singular building and oblivious to the ongoing deterioration and ruination of the surroundings.

Education for Urban Design

A decade later, for *Education for Urban Design*, Robertson recalled his earlier *Forum* article and its conclusion: that urban design was regarded as a peripheral add-on to either architecture or planning when it should be central to both, and that, ten years later, the problem continued to persist. As articulated by Robertson, there was an urgent need for a change in societal and professional values. Rowe likely shared Robertson's view; however, Rowe thought about and described such positions dialectically—Self/Community, Architecture/City. As previously noted, these choices, viewpoints, and values were personified by Eisenman/Robertson: architecture promoted as foreground autonomous object versus architecture as contributing to a city's complex fabric and cultural iconography. For Rowe, having turned his attention to urban design, the Modernist erosion of this object/fabric polarity and associated meanings deserved investigation.

Other similar studies of the architecture of traditional cities were also underway in Europe. Robert-Louis Delevoy and Maurice Culot led studies at the architecture school of La Cambre in Brussels. Exhibitions of context influenced professional work began to appear with regularity. Aldo Rossi organized the 1973 xvth Triennale of Milan along the thematic lines of architectural types and forms derived from the traditional city, argued as 'rational architecture.' It was followed two years later in a London and Barcelona exhibition of the same name. Organized by Léon Krier, it proposed to rebuild the European city along historic, traditional lines. In 1975, *Architectural Design Profile* 59, regularly edited by Andreas C. Papadakis, and guest edited by Luciano Sermerani, was devoted to the "School of Venice", home to such personages as Bruno Zevi, Saverio Muratori, Carlo Aymonino, and Manfredo Tafuri. The list of consultants for volume 59 includes 'all of the usual suspects' including Rowe. The main chapters are devoted to the city, territory, type, and figuration. As might be said of *Collage City*, the text is comprehensive, questioning, and well-reasoned in arguing for learning from the past. The architectural projects reflect an 'in-between', more Modernist than not struggle in attempting to continue to make a Modernist architecture imbued with historic types and forms of figuration—what should or should not be figural, when, where, and why. Thus, one sees a U.S.-European attempt to revive the most important qualities of traditional architecture as wedded to either iconic-types, or as markers of significant city locations. Just as Rowe was influencing others, parallel work in Europe was having a strong influence on the Studio. And, just as Rowe was discrediting Modernism, so did Brent Brolin in *The Failure of Modern Architecture* of 1976. Brolin traced the many cultural roots of 20th century Modern architecture's tenets to the 19th century, describing and discrediting the rationale of each.

The Failure of Modern Architecture

The U.S. Bicentennial year of 1976 was the cause for exceptional reflections on U.S. cultural history, creating a new level of public interest in various forms of preservation from buildings to districts and landscapes, associated guidelines, and tax credit incentives to encourage both rehabilitation and preservation efforts. Ray and Charles Eames's acclaimed exhibition, "The World of Franklin and Jefferson", traveled in the U.S. and Europe, and later became the basis for a book and film. As the title suggests, the exhibition focused on people and events that shaped the intellectual life and times of Jefferson and Franklin. References to urbanism of the colonial and post-Revolutionary era were included: Oglethorpe's ingenious plan of Savannah, Penn's ideal city plan for Philadelphia, and the L'Enfant and Ellicott plans for Washington, D.C. It also featured visions of continental development with canals linking East Coast waterways to those of the Midwest. The Eameses attempted a balanced cultural history that included U.S. participation in the worldwide institution of slavery, very early abolition efforts, and legislative restrictions of trade and slavery beginning with the Continental Congress.

École at MoMA

In 1975–76, MoMA featured a major architectural exhibition, "The Architecture of the École des Beaux-Arts". That landmark show reappraised the contribution of the École to architecture and city design that had been assailed and displaced by Modernism. From an urban design perspective, the main impact of the show was to rescue the City Beautiful movement from the jaws of CIAM. Rowe noted that the reviled Beaux-Arts had provided many American cities with their most memorable places, citing examples like San Francisco, Chicago, Philadelphia, and Washington, D.C. When Modernist achievements were compared to those of the École, they were found wanting. If, since 1966, Venturi-like architectural projects had been nibbling away at the roots of Modern architecture that Brolin discredited, the MoMA "École des Beaux-Arts" show seemed to deliver a *coup de grace*. It implicitly refuted the Modernist construct, and pointedly did so, on the same stage that had debuted the "Modern Architecture: international exhibition" in 1932, proclaimed to be the new 'International Style'.

In the decade between the publication of Venturi's *Complexity and Contradiction in Architecture* in 1966 and the MoMA "École des Beaux-Arts" show, architects on both sides of the Atlantic attempted to understand, reconstitute, reinvent, or simply find ways to apply lessons drawn from the forms of both traditional architecture and the traditional city. Modernist architectural tenets were poked and prodded through irony and wit, literary references, pop art, super-graphics, the reintroduction of elements of traditional architectural styles, and collage. Any subversion of Modernist conventions was of interest. In 1977, these heterogenous efforts were packaged by Charles Jencks as *The Language of Post-Modern Architecture*. As Jencks noted, there was no unifying theory other than challenges to Modernist architecture. Nor did Jencks recognize a rationale related to urban form. Many others had identified urban themes and been engaged in a dialogue along those lines. Rowe wrote the "Foreword" to Rob Krier's *Stadtraum /Urban Space* first published in 1975 followed by an English translation in 1979.

Roma interrotta

A significant prompt to this dialogue occurred in 1977 when Piero Sartogo proposed an ideas exhibition that became the *Roma interrotta* show held in the Markets of Trajan the following year. A dozen architects were invited to participate, four from the U.S.—Romaldo Giurgola, Michael Graves, Robert Venturi, and Colin Rowe—eight from Europe—Sartogo, Constantino Dardi, Antoine Grumbach, Paolo Portoghesi, Rob Krier, Léon Krier, Aldo Rossi, and Rowe's friend and former student at Liverpool, James Stirling. Using the Nolli map of Rome, each participant was assigned one of its twelve plates and asked to imagine how the city might have developed from the mid 18th century to the present.

The Rowe team included Steven Peterson, Judith DiMaio, and Peter Carl. Their submission was a *tour de force*. It outshone the other 11 submissions with its radical embrace of, and elaboration on, Rome's historic urban structure and Rowe's accompanying fictive libretto. 18th and 19th century Rome was reimagined as it might have evolved without the benighted influence of Modernism, creating a compelling counterfactual history. The project bestowed on Rowe and the Studio an elevated status among the leaders of the developing anti-Modernist campaign. That status was further enhanced by the publication of *Collage City* the same year, 1978. The Rowe team's "Roma interrotta" submission provided a demonstration of what could be achieved by deploying what seemed the forgotten wisdom of the traditional city strategically applied. Team member Steven K. Peterson provided a detailed explanation of the "Roma interrotta" scheme in "Urban Design Tactics" published in AD in 1979. Peterson Littenberg provided a second demonstration with their "Les Halles, Paris Competition" of the same year. Broadly speaking, the temporal *zeitgeist* was being routed by the atemporal *genius loci*.

Place / Time

In *Collage City*, the Modernist universal *zeitgeist* tenet had been counterposed with the *genius loci*: of-our-time versus of-this-place. The word *place* had become the everyday, all-inclusive term that could convey all things opposed to the universalizing tenets of Modernism—the new international style. Kevin Lynch wrote *What Time is This Place* in 1972. Rowe and Koetter had used *psycho-cultural field* to fully embrace the interactive dynamics of the *genius loci* and the *zeitgeist*. Christian Norberg-Schulz, author of *Intentions in Architecture*, and partner with Paolo Portoghesi for the "Roma interrotta" exhibit, published *Genius Loci: Towards a Phenomenology of Architecture* in 1980. The journal *Places* would be created in 1983. Whereas for Koetter *zeitgeist/genius* loci was an idea to be observed in *Collage City*, in professional practice it was a conflict to be resolved. That conflict was bannered in the title of their monograph, *Koetter Kim & Associates: Place|Time*, and resolved decidedly in favor of *place* and the *genius loci*. Essays by Koetter explain how the *genius loci* influenced their work from the macro-scale of the region, culture, and city, to the micro-scale of the street, block, and neighborhood, thereby to make *place*.

By the 1980s, all that had taken place in the 1960s and 1970s seemed to manifest a new seriousness of purpose in the dialogue about urban design. Possibilities which were previously only imagined were being made real.

Battery Park City and Seaside

In 1980, an Eisenman – IAUS lecture series brought "The New Wave of European Architecture" through Miami with Massimo Scolari, Rem Koolhaas, Rob and Léon Krier. Listening to Léon Krier were Andrés Duany and Elizabeth Plater-Zyberk (DPZ), who had been generating alternate plans for a Florida beach community for developers Robert and Daryl Davis. Impressed with Krier's argument, DPZ made major revisions to the Seaside plan and developed a straightforward, clearly illustrated, architectural code. Plan and code were based on regional typo-morphological studies. This process is well documented in Dhiru Thadani's retrospective *Visions of Seaside* of 2013. In 1984 the annual *Progressive Architecture* awards recognized both Seaside on the Gulf in Florida and Battery Park City on the Hudson River in Lower Manhattan with citations in recognition of their regulating plans and architectural codes. Otherwise radically different in scale and setting, each was based on traditional urban typo-morphological studies relevant to their region and their unique environments, each an affirmation of 'place'. Was it possible that urban design considerations were beginning to regulate architecture and achieve admirable results?

Andrés Duany and Elizabeth Plater-Zyberk had begun their practice about the same time as Fred Koetter and Susie Kim began theirs. Both firms were developing urban design plans and related codes governing building form and clearly and simply illustrating those forms. Dhiru Thadani recalls prompting an exchange between the two partnerships about coding. The two firms were at the forefront of a broader urban design movement advocating the visual continuity of place and seeking the means to achieve it. When DPZ was working out Seaside, Koetter Kim was undertaking their urban design work for Miller Park and Miller Park Plaza in Chattanooga, Tennessee, followed by University Park in Cambridge, Massachusetts—developing codes governing the work was essential for both firms and became central to their future practices. In *Urban Design Since 1945 – A Global Perspective*, of 2011, David Grahame Shane called these 'contextual codes' with diverse origins including the work of Ernesto Rogers as editor of *Casabella* in the 1950s, and the Gordon Cullen 1960s 'Townscape' critique of the Ville Radieuse. He specifically references Rowe, the Cornell Contextualists, and Koetter Kim design and coding at the Canary Wharf, East London docklands.

Architecture School Journals

If, as appeared to be the case, U.S. architectural journals were not going to deal with urban issues in a substantive manner, a group of university based architectural journals would step into the breach, promote the dialogue, and publish supporting visual material. Rowe's former Studio students contributed essays to journals issuing from at least Columbia (*Precis*), Cornell (*The Cornell Journal of Architecture*), Harvard (*The Harvard Architecture Review*), University of Illinois at Chicago (*Threshold*), University of Miami (*The New City*), University of Minnesota (*Midgård*), UVA (*Modulus*), Yale (*Perspecta*), and *Oppositions*. At Cornell, under the leadership of Jerry Wells, the school published four issues of *The Cornell Journal of Architecture* between 1981 and 1991, essentially a guide to a contextual, historically aware approach to architecture and urban design illustrated with student work and essays by faculty, students, and others. Rowe contributed essays to three of those four issues. The *Journal* 2 of 1983 focused on urban design. It was edited by Blake Middleton, with essays by Rowe, Grahame Shane, Wayne Copper, Steven Hurtt, and a "Foreword" by Léon Krier.

Colin Rowe and Léon Krier

Rowe and Krier wrote about meeting each other. Rowe states that he considered the Kriers 'quasi-allies', an exceptional statement. They shared and debated ideas. Both Rowe and Robertson contributed essays to Léon Krier's *House, Palaces, Cities* of 1984. While Rowe and Krier were close theoretically, Krier increasingly rejected the Modernist city and Modernist iconography, making his position clear in *Rational Architecture, The Reconstruction of the European City* of 1978. Rowe, on the other hand, had left open the *possibility* of accommodating both the Modernist City and its iconography in *Collage City*, a position that remained consistent throughout his career. In a conversation with a strident partisan in another setting, Rowe remarked, perhaps thinking of Utopia, "there is room for you in my city, but no room for me in your city".

Some of the Krier – Rowe and European – U.S. dialogue was aided by teaching assignments Rowe enjoyed in Italy from the late 1970s through the 1980s in Venice and Florence but primarily in Rome, at both Cornell and Notre Dame. For Cornell, these were aided and abetted by department chair Jerry Wells (1980–89), deans William "Bill" McMinn (1983–96) and Kent Kleinman (2008-2019) and the first director Roberto Einaudi (early '60s–1992). Together they stabilized Cornell's long-running but previously fragile program in Rome and strongly supported Rowe's role in it. Likewise, McMinn and Wells assured continuity of the Studio with regular and visiting faculty including former Rowe students.

Jaqueline Robertson served as dean of the School of Architecture at the University of Virginia from 1980 until 1988, while also partnering in practice with Eisenman. As dean, Robertson promoted a dialogue across the architecture/urban design divide. When young faculty member Neal Payton showed him Melville C. Branch's 1978 *An Atlas of Rare City Maps: Comparative Urban Design, 1830–1842*, Robertson selected a dozen or so of the book's 40 city plans, had them copied, framed, and prominently displayed. As visiting faculty, he engaged Rowe, and also Michael Dennis, whose firm won a major design competition for development of the Carnegie Mellon University campus. The firm's multiple buildings for the campus over the next decade honored the earlier planning and architecture of Henry Hornbostel, whose own planning had been likewise embedded in the cultural landscape of Pittsburgh.

Robertson hosted a symposium of 25 leading architects across several generations resulting in *The Charlottesville Tapes* of 1985. In 1986, Robertson and Joseph Riley, the highly effective, long-serving mayor of Charleston, South Carolina, convinced the National Endowment for the Arts and the U.S. Conference of Mayors to create the Mayors' Institute on City Design. That program brought urban design expertise together with city mayors in small groups, insulating them from partisan politics and special interests to focus on urban design problems unique to their city or town. In 1988, Robertson returned to New York, ending his partnership with Eisenman and beginning a new partnership with Alex Cooper, as Cooper-Robertson, to focus on urban design. That same year, Rowe retired from Cornell. Meanwhile, MoMA gathered a miscellany of avant-garde architects to exhibit their work under the label of 'Deconstructivists', among them Peter Eisenman. Seen by many as a promotional ploy rather than a serious critical contribution to the discipline, it continued analogies being drawn between architecture and linguistics, analogies that had shifted from Claude Lévi-Strauss (structuralism) to Jacques Derrida (deconstruction), the first of which Rowe and Koetter had critiqued earlier in *Collage City*. The second, called 'Deconstructivism' or 'DeCon', was of no interest to Rowe. He remarked that 'reconstruction' would be preferable to 'deconstruction'.

1980s and 1990s

The late 1980s and early 1990s seem remarkable as a great summing up and illustration of the previous two decades of work by urban designers and historians who were now seriously contending with the city. Jonathan Barnett, in *The Elusive City: Five Centuries of Design, Ambition, and Miscalculation* of 1986, credits Rowe for simultaneously reviving principles of the 'monumental' city while emphasizing the street, the block, well-defined urban space related to the fabric of the city, and the value of the figure-ground as a didactic technique for which the Nolli Plan served as a prototype. Roger Trancik, in *Finding Lost Space: Theories of Urban Design* of 1986, describes the unique spatial qualities of the traditional city contrasted with the 'lost space' of the Ville Radieuse-type high-rise offices served by vast surface parking lots. Trancik describes, illustrates, then combines and applies three emerging urban design strategies: 'Figure/ground' (Rowe); 'Linkage' (Fumihiko Maki): and 'Place' (Ian McHarg; Aldo Van Eyck, Herman Hertzberger, Kevin Lynch, Ralph Erskine, Gordon Cullen, Léon Krier). An extensive review of urban design work of the 1960s through the 1980s was provided by Geoffroy Broadbent's *Emerging Concepts in Urban Space Design* of 1990. Also, in 1990, Andreas Papadakis & Harriet Watson edited the comprehensive *New Classicism, Omnibus Volume*, an elaborately illustrated text arguing for the enduring vitality of classical architecture and its relevance to urban form. Rowe, the Kriers, Robertson, Duany, Plater-Zyberk, and historians Giulio Carlo Argan, Alan Colquhoun, Giorgio Grassi, John Summerson, Manfredo Tafuri, and Carroll William Westfall were among the many contributors. Rowe provided two essays: "Urban Space" and "Comments on the IBA Proposal", which included diagrammatic plans for Berlin. Historian Spiro Kostof provided an in-depth analysis of cities and their interrelated parts, past and present, in his comprehensive, 1991 *The City Shaped: Urban Patterns and Meanings through History*, followed by its 1992 companion, *The City Assembled: The Elements of Urban Form through History*. Like Rowe, architectural historians had shifted their focus to include the city and the role of architecture in it—a major shift in historiography. Through the 1980s, Rowe's ideas continued to spread, enjoyed wide influence, and comingled with those of others similarly inclined, who also illustrated and explained them.

Soon after retiring from Cornell, Rowe took up residence in Washington, D.C., where he began a new highly productive period. With Leon Satkowski, he co-authored *Italian Architecture of the 16th Century*. Rowe's *The Architecture of Good Intentions: Towards a Possible Retrospect* was published in 1994. Decades earlier, in a letter to Robert Slutzky and, as recorded in Daniel Naegele's *Letters of Colin Rowe: Five Decades of Correspondence*, Rowe noted that he had overcome his "inhibition about doing a demo job on modern architecture" with an intended book and had even projected the title as *The Architecture of Good Intentions*. Rowe also produced, with Alex Caragonne as editor, an extensive record of his essays and Studio projects in the three-volume *As I Was Saying: Recollections and Miscellaneous Essays* of 1996. As author of *The Texas Rangers, Notes from an Architectural Underground*, published the year before, Caragonne had tabulated and graphed the many graduates of the Studio who were or had been teaching, and/or serving as program director, chair, or dean in schools of architecture. With what result?

Our assessment is that most often Studio graduates acted as the lone faculty member in a school, and even with the authority of leading a program, the Rowe argument has rarely if ever been more than partially embraced. This appears to hold true even at schools which, at least for some years, harbored more than one Rowe Studio graduate. To our knowledge this includes Arizona State, Catholic University, Columbia, ETH, Harvard, University of Illinois in Chicago, University of Kentucky, Maryland, Miami, MIT, NYIT, Notre Dame, Oregon, Princeton, Syracuse University, University of Tennessee, USC, and UVA. Caragonne's book provides an extensive tabulation. An entrenched focus on the *zeitgeist* and building as object continues to collude to defeat the Robertson argument that urban design ought to be central to architectural education—and we think how easily that could be accomplished: start with the city.

The gap between the academy and the profession was partially filled by rare instances where faculty established studios that regularly and seriously served in the public interest. It was one of those, associated with the University of Tennessee but located in Chattanooga and led by Stroud Watson, that brought Koetter Kim to Miller Park, Miller Park Plaza, something of a leap forward for their practice. In that same vein, and at the same institution, Studio grad Tom Davis led public service studios for several cities, and through such initiatives as radio programs has carried urban design into the public arena in a way that is rare and a model worthy of emulation.

Make UD Central to the Profession

Nationwide, the lessons provided by Battery Park City and Seaside were being absorbed by developers and architects. Placing emphasis on community, place, connectivity, a mix of uses, and walkability, they became part of a larger movement to reform suburban sprawl and redress the erosion of cities. The means to achieve that reform also found support among citizens living in older city neighborhoods and towns when those places began to erode due to the Modernist vision, related zoning, and unrestrained capitalist enterprises.

One can see in this work that Rowe's critique had matured from theory into practices that included planning principles and illustrated directives, including codes governing form, and they had achieved *de-rigueur* status. That is, it had been shown that among the best means to achieve at least some semblance of visual continuity in either new or old 'places' was 'form-based codes' as either alternative to, or overlays on, 'use-based codes'. A backlash among many professionals ensued. Modernist platitudes were once again invoked—not of our times, historicist, merely copying and repressing creativity—and, as Post-Modernism had evolved, architectural *pastiche* was added to the older invectives. Andrés Duany, who had been debating Modernist avant-gardists, concluded that their conversion was impossible, and instead rallied reformist-minded architects and urban designers to common cause. In 1993, the Congress for the New Urbanism, 'CNU', ironically alluding to 'CIAM', its antithesis, was founded. Directly or indirectly, the Rowe emphasis on the traditional city as a font of exemplary models to apply to urban design problems had led to linking urban design plans with form-based codes. Using that model, Koetter Kim was practicing worldwide, most notably in East London docklands, Canary Wharf. Fred Koetter also served as dean at Yale, 1993–98. DPZ was practicing nationwide and Elizabeth Plater-Zyberk served as dean at the University of Miami 1995–2013. Many other firms followed the DPZ and Koetter Kim practice model that included the iteration of many possible solutions to sort through complex issues involving multiple stakeholders to determine a widely agreed-upon plan and an accompanying set of architectural codes that typically changed the codes in place or were provided with variances.

Koetter Kim and DPZ

Invited with a handful of others to a review and critique of Seaside, Rowe, as usual, expressed enthusiasm and skepticisms. He 'contextualized' Seaside as a Garden City, which he said he had been taught to despise. But equally broadly speaking, in terms of implementation, regulatory reform, and innovation in the face of an intractable bureaucracy, Rowe was deeply impressed with the DPZ achievements in Seaside, finding them to be "… of a very high order". And as he said of Poundbury, "… now one must look for the next installment of the saga". Rowe's comments leave one wanting more. It intensifies, for many of us, the sense of loss we have that Rowe did not leave to us his imagined series of essays on small American towns, including his reveries on their landscapes, exemplified by just one, "Lockhart, Texas" of 1957, in *Architectural Record*. The light such a series would have shed on similar achievements found in the saga of American towns and their unique landscapes remains a challenge.

9 / 11

Colin Rowe died in 1999. The millennium passed without the anticipated apocalypse. But then, it was 9/11. In the aftermath of the terrorist attack, a memorial was called for. In some quarters, it was also seen as an opportunity to improve a part of the Lower Manhattan urban fabric traumatized decades earlier by the World Trade Center's anti-urban superblock. Could the fabric of Lower Manhattan be healed or restored? If so, how best to do it? Studies done in 1994 by Peterson Littenberg were recalled, and based on their previous work, they were again commissioned by the Port Authority of New York to study the reintegration of the World Trade Center superblock site with the surrounding city fabric, including memorial concepts. They vetted many schemes with the public. Initial support for their work by the popular press, *The New York Post*, and the public at large was overwhelmingly positive. But the Peterson-Littenberg effort was undercut by the architecture critic Herbert Muschamp at *The New York Times*. And *The New Yorker* art critic Joseph Giovannini likewise panned the Peterson-Littenberg schemes. They promoted their favored architects, most of whom had exhibited in the 1988 MoMA 'Deconstructivists' show. In the highly emotional and politically charged post-9/11 atmosphere, Daniel Libeskind's individualistic, discordant scheme defeated the Peterson-Littenberg alternatives. For us the fact that the humane and contextual urban design scheme inspired by Rowe's former students was not realized added to the tragedy of 9/11.

2000s

The early 1960s marked a time when both historians and architects redirected their attention from a focus on the building as an object independent of its surroundings to include its physical context, most importantly, the city—the intersection summed up as urban design. By the 1990s, architectural historians had begun to produce literature on city form. The traditional city was being rediscovered and valued anew. The architecture profession, which initially seemed incapable of shedding mega-building 'urban design' solutions, had begun to shift toward more nuanced urban typo-morphological strategies. Battery Park City and Seaside had marked a seismic shift in profession-wide thinking, making a point of the value of a regionalist point of departure and form-based coding. A developing architecture *plus* urban design profession was beginning to enshrine and build on principles developed in Rowe's 1960–1980s Studios. The Studio had deliberately embarked on the study of traditional city morphologies and related architectural typologies at all scales. Citizen groups effectively opposed the Modernist, technologically driven infrastructure projects that had encouraged sprawl and eviscerated cities, particularly in neighborhoods of poor and marginalized populations. The long-term detrimental cost to the city and the planet of such patterns was becoming abundantly clear with early warnings about a carbon-based economy and sprawl.

Conclusion

Professionals across the full range of disciplines that determine urban form began to change their thinking and the standards they followed. Together, informed citizens and professionals were having significant success, from neighborhoods and main streets to national policy. These movements have adopted typological approaches ranging from the region to the neighborhood or city district. Sample publications would include *The Urban Design Handbook* of 2003, authored by lead partner Ray Gindroz. Major books that have provided comprehensive surveys and illustrations of cities, parks, plazas, urban districts, garden cites, and their buildings at all scales are represented by *The New Civic Art* of 2003, authored by Andrés Duany, Elizabeth Plater-Zyberk, and Robert Alminana, and *Paradise Planned: The Garden City and the Modern Suburb* of 2013 by Robert A.M. Stern, David Fishman, and Jacob Tilove. In 2007, *Sustainable Urbanism: Urban Design with Nature*, was written by Douglas Farr. Most recently, the focus on the resiliency of many urban building types has led to a movement that has proposed jettisoning functional zoning as the primary regulatory basis for urban development in favor of form-based codes. Similarly, attention to housing shortages has produced a renewed focus on a richer range of types. This was under the banner of "missing middle housing" coined by Dan Parolek in 2010 and published in book form in 2020. The progress that has been made in the professional realm can be more readily seen in the monographs that firms published on their work than what is found in the architectural journals where object buildings still reign supreme. Occasionally one finds a book that collects and illustrates the professional work of dozens of firms, such as *Increments of Neighborhood: A Compendium of Built Types for Walkable and Vibrant Communities* by Brian O'Looney, published in 2020. The objective is well understood by the architect: urban design leaders in these offices are convincing communities and developers to build forms that encourage functional and social diversity, economic heterogeneity, integration, and even beauty.

Rowe's former students and colleagues who have contributed significantly to the evolution of urban design through diverse forms of work, practice, teaching, and publications would include several by Michael Dennis: *Court and Garden: From the French Hôtel to the City of Modern Architecture* of 1986; *Architecture and the City: Selected Essays* of 2022; and *Temples and Towns: A Study of the Form, Elements, and Principles of Planned Towns* of 2020. By David Graham Shane, *Recombinant Urbanism* of 2005 and *Urban Design Since 1945 – A Global Perspective* of 2011. By James Tice, *The Interactive Nolli Map Website*, co-authored with Allan Ceen and Erik Steiner, initiated in 2005, and revised in 2020 as the Interactive Nolli Map Website 2.0 with Nicola Camerlenghi and Giovanni Svevo [https://web.stanford.edu/group/spatialhistory/nolli//index.html]. By Charles Graves, *The Genealogy of Cities* of 2009. By Norman Crowe, *Nature and the Idea of a Man-Made World* of 1997 and *Building Cities* of 1999, co-edited with Richard Economakis and Michael Lykoudis. By Jon Michael Schwarting, *Rome: Formation and Transformation* of 2017. By Dhiru Thadani, *The Language of Towns and Cities, a Visual Dictionary* of 2010; *Visions of Seaside*, 2013; and *Reflections on Seaside* of 2021. By Steven Peterson and Barbara Littenberg, *Space and Anti-Space* in 2020.

Colin Rowe: a continued presence

As interest in the form of the traditional city has grown internationally, so has a scholarly interest in Rowe's voice. In 2009, *L'architettura come testa e la figura di Colin Rowe* was published by the Istituto Universitario di Architettura di Venezia (IUAV), edited by Mauro Marzo, recalling that the Venetian School was headed by Saverio Muratori, whose devotion to the urban fabric as early as 1959 aligned with Rowe's. In 2014, there was a retrospective exhibition of "Roma interrotta". The exhibit, curated by Piero Sartogo, was held in Rome at the MAXXI, and included the Rowe team entry to the original exhibition. By coincidence, the MAXXI exhibition coincided with our first of four conferences on Rowe and his legacy, "Urban Design and the Legacy of Colin Rowe" ("La Progettazione urbana e il lascito di Colin Rowe"). In 2016, two books emerged. First, *Reckoning with Colin Rowe*, a collection of essays edited by Emmanuel Petit was published. Then, that same year, Daniel Naegele published *The Letters of Colin Rowe: Five Decades of Correspondence*. He followed with *I Almost Forgot* in 2022. In both books, Naegele contextualized Rowe's letters and other writings with introductory descriptions explaining Rowe's many references to people, authors, and events. Naegele also explains the role of some of the writings as preludes to or initial drafts of intended articles, whether published or not. And, most recently, *Colin Rowe's Gospel of Modern Architecture* by Braden R. Engel of 2022. This renewed interest in Colin Rowe over the last two decades in the U.S. and abroad continues to expand his global presence, and the enduring relevance of his ideas, as we increasingly understand that the health of cities and the planet are as inseparable as the eye and the mind.

SWH and JTT

I. Colin Rowe & Urban Design

... the tradition of Modern architecture has tended to produce objects rather than spaces, has been highly involved with the problems of the built solid and very little with the problems of the unbuilt void ... just how to make a city if all buildings proclaim themselves as objects? ... [and] any idea of facade, and any idea of necessary interface between the res publica *and the* res privata *is a final and terrible dissimulation.*

... attack upon facade and permeation of building as object can only become attack on the street.

The Present Urban Predicament, The Cornell Journal of Architecture, 1, 1981.

"Colin Rowe & Urban Design" provides an analysis of the contemporary city and articulates principles that could guide the design of cities toward a more humane, livable future. It provides a basic lexicon that expands Rowe's multi-layered critique, connecting the perfunctory to the profound. The visual world of the architecture of the city—urban design—is explained in terms: figure/ground; *parti*, precedent, and paradigm; ideal type, the circumstantial and resulting deformations; contextualism, type, transformation; and collision and collage. One moves rapidly from the abstractions of *Gestalt* psychology to concrete architectural examples, and from these to the city described metaphorically, whether as museum or theater emblematic of human nature and culture and, therefore, as an instrument of education. As Rowe's own ideas and understandings of the city developed along these lines, his early enthusiasm for Modern architecture, and even the notion of a reconciliation of the Modernist City with the Traditional City, began to wane. Described dialectically as the Mod/'trad' problem, exploring that speculative possibility was the leitmotif of Studio investigations and Rowe's writing for much of his later career. Could *rapprochement* between the Modernist city and the Traditional city be achieved? Could the Modernist free-standing towers and slabs in park-like settings and the Traditional City of streets, blocks, and squares complement each other, reducing the liabilities of each? Over time, as successive Studio attempts at reconciliation proved less than satisfactory, he edged closer and closer to a complete rejection of Modernist ideology and urban forms. By 1970 Rowe saw, as clearly as any of the critics of the Modernist City, the problem of the Machine metaphor coupled with Natural Man ('noble savage') that resulted in the skewed idea of towers in a park linked by the automobile. Rowe understood that the resulting impoverishment of cities posed a threat to civilization and to democratic freedoms. The unremediated Modernist city not only eliminated a sense of place but also erased the real and existential space of the *polis* and the possibility of civic identity.

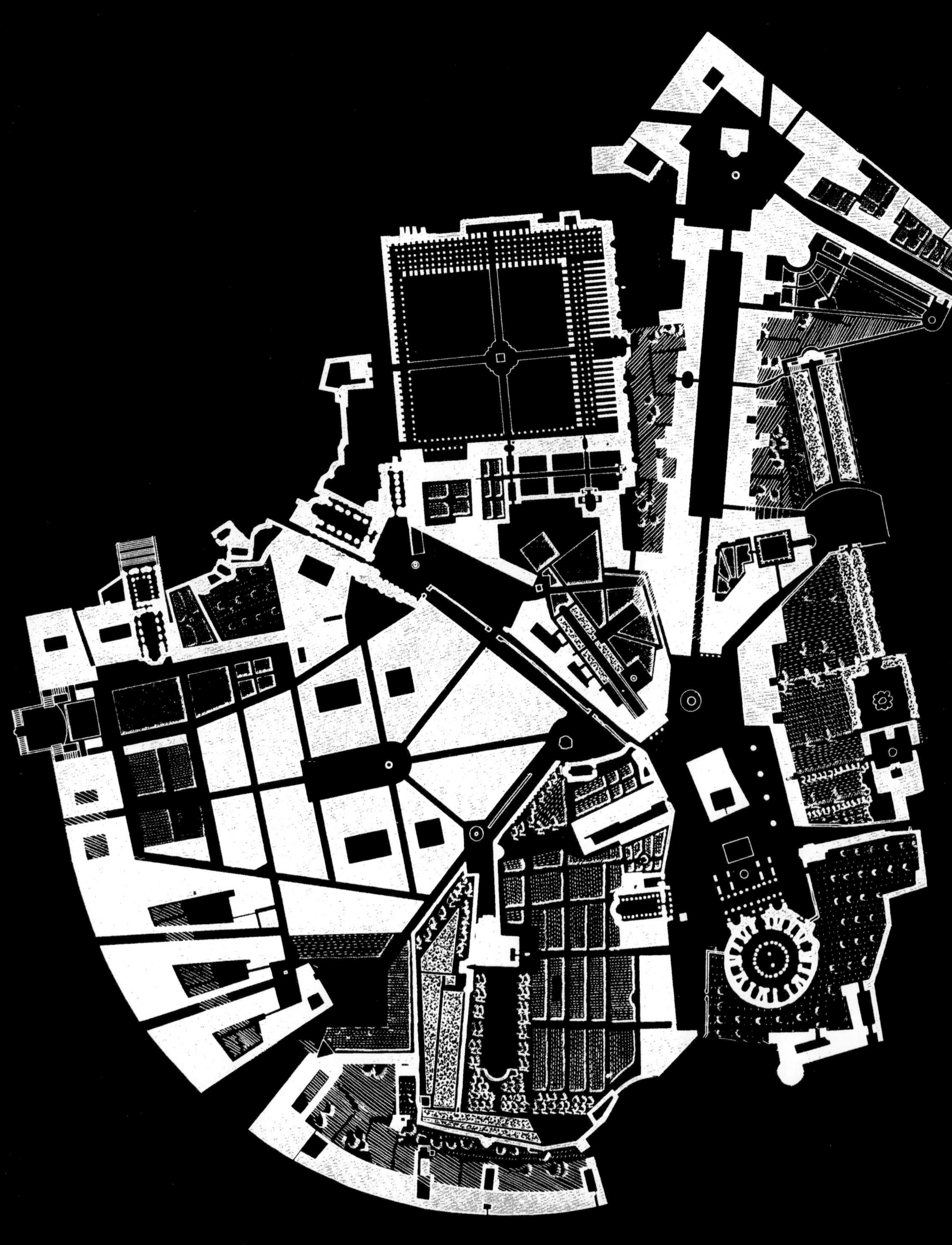

The Colin Rowe Model of Urban Form: "Just How to Make a City"

Steven K. Peterson

frontispiece:
The Celio Hill as hill town; final plan detail from Sector 8 of "Roma interrotta".

Colin Rowe spent much of his adult life criticizing Modern architecture for its destructive attack on the city. He argued that the very existence of the 'traditional city' was considered anathema to Modern architecture's central premise: that everything would be better if it were made over new, from scratch. The existing city posed an existential contradiction which threatened the idea of a cleaned-up, orderly future. A better world would only result if the new architecture stood alone, unencumbered, clean, and free, with no messy streets, no awkward blocks with hidden backyards and dark alleys, no gloomy courts, no confined public places, no facades or false fronts to confuse things; just gleaming architectural objects in an unrestricted, free, and open void. This idea still holds with the resulting consequence that the new 'cities', and city projects being built all over the world today, are not really urban. They are filled with extravagant dramatic buildings, but the essence of what constitutes the city has been discarded and lost.

Colin Rowe recognized this problem early on, first addressing it as "Crisis of the Object: Predicament of Texture" in *Collage City*, written in 1970–1973, and he reiterated it in "The Present Urban Predicament" in 1979, where he said directly:

> *the tradition of modern architecture has tended to produce objects rather than spaces, has been highly involved with problems of the built solid and very little with problems of the unbuilt void, that the inner angle which cradles space has scarcely been among its concerns. Which further statement may introduce the pressing question:* just how to make a city, *if all buildings proclaim themselves as objects and how many object-buildings can be aggregated before comprehension fails?*[1]

The predicament that Colin identified remains in contemporary city projects today. There is no identifiable urban space on the ground and scaled down to a human comprehension; there is no aggregate pattern of streets and blocks, no network of interconnecting public spaces. There is just a proliferation of wizardly designed objects, clustered towers in picturesque *Ozian* skylines. The new global city has no urban fabric (Fig. 1).

1 Rowe, Colin, "The Present Urban Predicament: Some Observations", (lecture delivered at The Royal Institution, London in 1979), in *The Architectural Association Quarterly* 11 (4), 1979, then in *The Cornell Journal of Architecture* 1, 1981: 17. Republished in Rowe, Colin, *As I Was Saying: Recollections and Miscellaneous Essays 3, Urbanistics*, , Caragonne, Alexander, ed., MIT Press, Cambridge, MA, and London, 1996: 153, (emphasis mine).

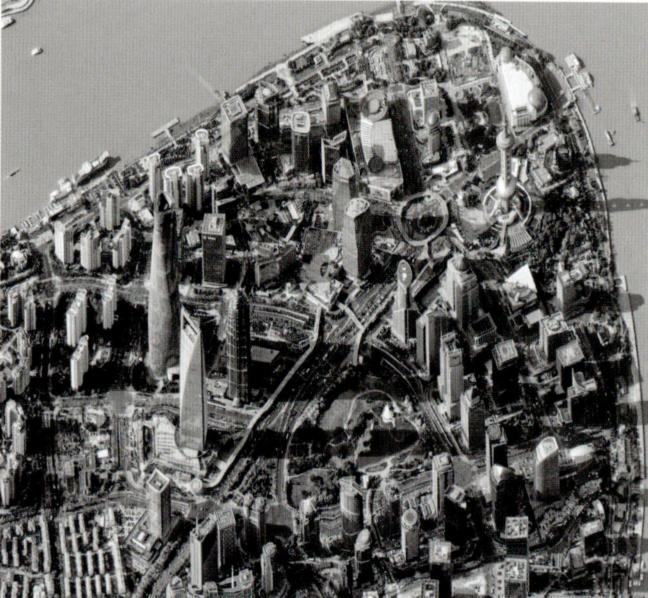

Fig. 1. This is an amazing comparison (only made possible by Google Earth). Lower Manhattan is on the left and the Pudong area of Shanghai is on the right. Each image shows one square mile. Both are printed here at the same scale along with the Pudong skyline. It is a warning. The richness of Manhattan's streets and blocks has been erased, leaving just the towers in a melancholy emptiness.

This is a problem for both the city and architecture, because, without context, architecture can only express itself in a vacuum. Without a broader responsibility for the urban fabric and the city, architecture will be forced to continue its pointless competitive quest for novelty. So, "just how to make a city?" is a crucial issue. It is my contention that through the Urban Design Studio at Cornell and in his writings, Colin Rowe set out the fundamental framework to answer this question. He was the first to provide an explicit diagnosis that explained the limitations of the contemporary city. He developed the familiar techniques and strategies now used to describe the nature of urban form: figure/ground, solid/void, contextualism, transparency, collage, and the spatial field, all of which are attributes of the urban fabric, which he identified as the most essential component of city structure. In effect, Colin Rowe provided the basis for what could be called "A Standard Model of Urban Form".

The Standard Model

This model is not explicitly stated, but Colin's work does address all the elements of a descriptive morphology of urbanism in the scientific sense. Colin identifies the city's constituent urban forms and explains their characteristics, relationships, and structures. The implication is that, while the city is created as a human invention, it must exist within certain limited spatial and geometric constraints; it is a logical physical phenomenon that can be observed and explained formally. All cities are constituted of specific similar elements in consistent interacting patterns.The paradigm for this idea of a standard urban model derives from the general climate of scientific discovery in the 1960s and 1970s and, in particular, Richard Feynman's contemporary work on The Standard Model in nuclear physics. Feynman (1918–1988) was just two years older than Rowe (1920–1999). They both taught at Cornell University at different times, but overlapped in 1964 when Feynman gave the Cornell University Messenger Lectures. Rowe's Urban Design program had just started the year before, in 1963. Both were beloved and famous teachers—brilliant, personable, and equally irreverent.

Their early contrarian works made each of them famous: Rowe publishing "The Mathematics of the Ideal Villa" in 1947; Feynman publishing "A Relativistic Cut-Off for Classical Electrodynamics" in 1948, called Quantum Electrodynamics or, with a bit of irony, QED.[2]

Feynman was the key figure in completing the "Standard Model of Quantum Mechanics", which explained the sub-nuclear order of things. Like Rowe, Feynman was concerned with reconciling two conflicting ideas. For Feynman, it was the particles (objects) of Quantum Theory in contrast with General Relativity's cosmology. For Rowe, it was the objects (particles) of Modern architecture in contrast with the city's general connective continuity.

The essential concept shared by both is the presence of a continuous medium spread over a large area, acting as an interactive *field*. The concept of the field had been explored by Michael Faraday beginning in 1847.[3] In modern physics, a field is defined as an entity acting independently from its parts, "A region of space and time that manifests the interaction of different things woven together". Electromagnetism can only be understood as a field, an extended fabric of double forces woven together, each inseparable, and operating on the other. The urban fabric is also a field, "a region of space" that is occupied as a pattern of interactions between solids and voids, interwoven, bonded, and acting together as a continuous fabric.

Colin's brilliance here was to deploy this notion of the field as an interdependency of elements to describe city form. Derived from painting and perception psychology, Colin's experiments with the phenomena of figure/ground is after all the study of spatial fields and their components. The duality of a figure/ground field is conceptually necessary for all the other elements of an urban model, for *Contextualism*, for *Phenomenal Transparency*, and for *Collage*.

Feynman made visual quantum diagrams that explained particle interactions, a drawing explaining a mathematical formula. He thought visually and with humor. He titled one of his popular books on physics, *Surely You're Joking, Mr. Feynman!* For comparison, Colin treasured the fantasy drawings of the German architectural student Rainer Jägals (Fig. 2). He was always bringing out a book of Jägals' work to display an attitude toward the city, a suggestive drawing of its potential narrative poetry. I have often wanted to say, "Surely you're joking,

2 Feynman, Richard P., "A Relativistic Cut-Off for Classical Electrodynamics", *Physical Review* 74 (8), 1948: 939-46.

3 Faraday, Michael, "Ein Und Zwanzigste Reihe Von Experimental - Untersuchungen über Elektricität", *Annalen Der Physik* 146 (1), 1847: 24-59.

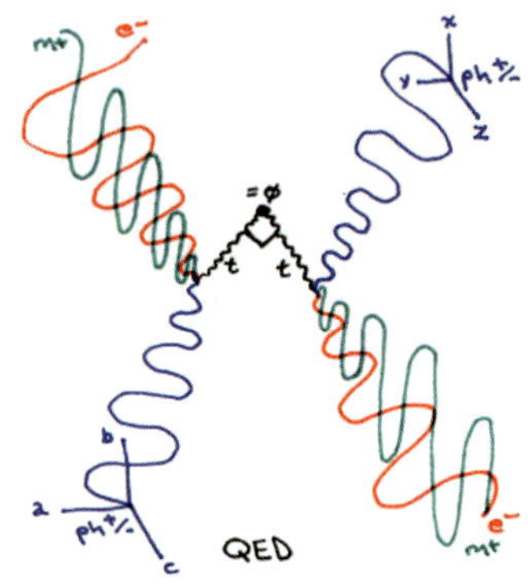

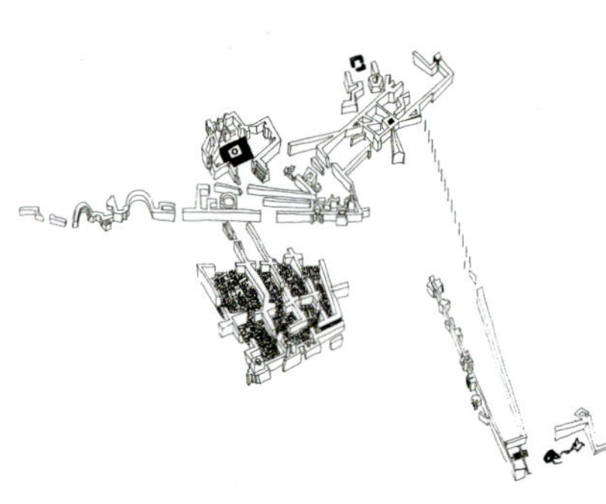

Fig. 2. Diagrams of interaction: above, Richard Feynman; below, Rainer Jägals.

Mr. Rowe!" How does this explain urbanism? Perhaps it was more like a scan of Colin's brain at work.

The Colin Rowe Urban Model

What are Colin Rowe's analytic strategies for studying urban form? There are four, each one a distinct analytical filter through which different aspects of the city's urban form can be described and compared.

The Analytic Strategies

1. *Figure/ground*
2. *Contextualism*
3. *Phenomenal Transparency*
4. *Collage*

Then there are the two operational viewpoints that Colin recognized as essential for the design method, as a source of knowledge and reference.

The Operational Viewpoints

1. The use of *Precedent*
2. The recognition of *Parti*

These two operational viewpoints apply to anything designed, including furniture, architecture, and urban design. They are not elements as such, but are mental operations, part of the underlying method of its creation. Each of the six terms described above is familiar as a separate item of his lexicon (Fig. 3).

How did Colin arrive at these? What was his method? He was often preoccupied with esoteric subjects apparently unrelated to architecture: the history of the popes, silver candlesticks, or furniture auction catalogs. (You must be joking. No?) His face was in a constant expectant state of delight. In fact, he usually appeared to be in a ceaseless, internal conversation, which would erupt audibly if he were encountered: "Steven, you know, I was just thinking…"

The constant element of Rowe's work and thought is the dialectic in his conversation; the unexpected conjunctions that are presented as covalent: Le Corbusier and Palladio, solid and void, past and present, Mannerist complexity and Modernist minimalism, the ideal and the contingent. It is Barbara Littenberg's penetrating observation that the idea of conversation was the key to Colin's rich intellectual manner. Conversation is, of course, talk, yes, but it means other things too. Significantly, it is also about opposites, as in the *converse*; it is about persuasion, as in *converting* someone; and it is about translation, as in a *conversion* factor, equating things from different times or different places, from one field of endeavor to another.

A MODEL OF URBAN FORM

Colin Rowe's Urban Dialogs

Characteristics of The Urban Field

FIGURE/GROUND	Urban SPACE is in dialog with enclosing BLOCKS in a balanced equilibrium. The SOLIDS and VOIDS of an urban fabric are both palpable forms.
CONTEXTUALISM	Urban ARCHITECTURE is in dialog with its city CONTEXT. Architecture is responsible for both itself and its background.
TRANSPARENCY	MULTIPLE FIGURES of urban space and block patterns can overlap to appear SIMULTANEOUSLY.
COLLAGE	JUXTAPOSITION is a unique urban method to accommodate different solutions. Multiple intersecting fragments can form a legitimate dense urban context.

Viewpoints of Reference

PRECEDENT	Reference to existing places and historical forms are the primary source of formal knowledge in urban design and architecture.
PARTI	Diagrammatic formal arrangements underlie most urban patterns - grid, radial, linear, axial, etc.

Fig. 3. The Standard Model of Urban Form.

In this sense conversation is not linear, but a Mannerist method, a play on and a critique of orthodoxy, an indirect peripheral approach to get a fresh view on issues. Colin's talk was integral to his method of thought because he was conversant in so many topics.

Evidently, Colin's pursuit of conversational practice and his delight in the English language were both an amusement and framework for serious pursuit, especially since he usually did most of the talking. We know from long phone calls from him and endless evenings with "drinks" that it served as a primary source of his own amusement. He practiced conversation, in all its iterations. It was surely the chief mechanism for his extraordinary intellectual achievements and the essence of his charisma. The concept of comparative interacting parts is manifest in each of these analytical categories. Each is a kind of dialogue.

Analytic Strategies in Dialogue

First is *figure/ground*, the dialogue of solids and voids in an x-ray plan view revealing its essential bones. It describes any *urban fabric* in black and white. The most potent *urban fields* occur when both space and solids are palpable figures, covalent with each other and interdependent. For a place to be urban, it must first establish and maintain this field of created spaces in an urban fabric—*il tessuto urbano*. Colin's conjecture (explored through his student Wayne Copper's figure/ground thesis)[4] was that true urban city plans could be viewed in reverse; that the balanced weaving of space and solid would not break down if drawn as a negative image. Figure/ground describes the essential condition of an urban field. Its presence is the precondition for all the other elements of urbanism.

Second is *contextualism*, the dialogue of architecture with its city fabric. Contextualism is commonly misrepresented as just facades mimicking adjacencies. However, the broader idea of contextualism is really a proposition about the interdependence of architecture and city form, its context. It recognizes that architecture is both an object of special interest and an element in the background of urban fabric. In urban and city design, contextualism is not just about the adaptive responses of architecture to a pre-existing surrounding; it is about its participation in forming the presence of that continuity.

Third is *phenomenal transparency*, the dialogue between the reality of form and its multiple appearances. The concept of perceptual overlapping and nearly simultaneous reading of different figures is usually thought of as relating primarily to vertical surfaces in art and building elevations, as in shallow painterly space. It is clearly a key ingredient in the blending of facades on the surface of a block through implicit connections and overlapping readings. The illusion of a unified wall depends on it. Colin lectured about the overlapping qualities of adjacent Venetian facades. Phenomenal transparency also exists in urban plans and 3D space. The several different spatial readings of the interpenetration of different street grids and block orientations can be perceived nearly simultaneously. For example, every street intersection is an overlapping presence of two spaces created by intersecting streets. The essence of phenomenal transparent reading is a fluctuation of spatial location or reading: the dominant or figural reading of the street intersection can fluctuate between one street or the other, the intersection itself, or the cross shape made by their combination. The basic illusion of a continuous urban field of spatial closure is imagined, not actual. In an urban fabric things seem joined and extended when, in fact, they are not.

Fourth is *collage*, the dialogue between fragments and a uniform whole. The invention of Modern collage derives from Cubism's composition of fragmented forms, overlapping partial figures, and the incorporation of the found object. Colin showed that it was a useful model for an urban design to incorporate diversity. Collage is a method of joining different things through juxtaposition. It is a more recent aesthetic attitude that can tolerate history, incorporate eclectic references, revel in context, and categorically reject the tyranny of an urban design that suggests a uniform total systemic order.

Methods and References

The first method refers to *precedent,* the dialogue of knowledge, old and new. Precedent is by definition anathema to Modern and contemporary architects who insist on being original and therefore unprecedented. But Colin's conception of precedent is not the Beaux-Arts idea of a historical model to be copied as

4 While Copper's thesis was produced in 1967 with Rowe as advisor, it was published much later: Copper, Wayne W., "The Figure/Grounds", *The Cornell Journal of Architecture* 2, Urban Design, 1983.

Fig. 4. "The Financial Center of the World", postcard, ca. 1939; *The Temptation on the Mount*, Duccio di Buoninsegna, detail. The basic forrm of 'city' stays the same no matter the time or place. To label it as historical or traditional is misleading.

a source of authenticity. His principle is about the transformation (as in a conversion) of historical formal knowledge, bringing it into the present to inform design solutions for current problems.

Second is the reference to *parti*, the dialogue between ideal concept and circumstantial contingency. The *parti* is the diagram underlying every formal arrangement encapsulating its descriptive armature. It is independent of style, place, and time. *Parti*, although typically used as an architectural term, applies equally to cities. Urban *partis* define types of urban order: gridded, radial/concentric, axial, irregular, etc. Colin felt that, in the end, there were only a limited number of organizational *partis*.

A city's urban fabric is revealed through the four analytic strategies: a systemic web of streets, buildings, and blocks in a figure/ground balance of solids to voids; a continuity of connected elements in a dense overall context of buildings; patterns of spaces and streets that interlock and overlap, producing a phenomenal transparency; and conjunctions of different buildings, styles, and eras, 'stuck together' in blocks like a collage.

Colin always used the term, "The City of Modern Architecture", instead of, "The Modern City". This allowed him to hope for a resolution of the impossible.

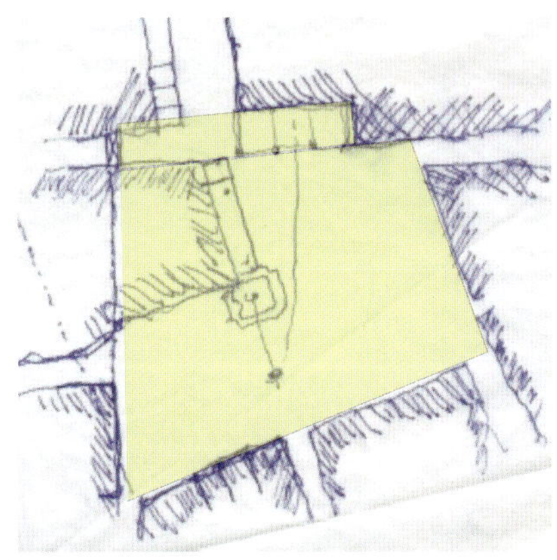

Fig. 5. Sketch of the overlapping spaces in Piazza della Signoria seen from the north. The Palazzo Vecchio seems to be standing in a completed rectangular space. (See Trachtenberg, Marvin, *Dominion of the Eye: Urbanism, Art, and Power in Early Modern Florence*, Cambridge University Press, Cambridge, 1997).

It suggested that a city could emerge out of the new architecture, in spite of its revolutionary premise that demanded the elimination of the city as it had been known. The Ville Radieuse has none of the city characteristics put forward above; it is a rigid, large-scale architectural layout that can't grow, can't be changed or added to, and has no variety of scale or apparent use. It defies the fundamental basis for the city, the on-the-ground urban fabric that allows the content of the block to change and vary over time. The very elements of urban fabric and contextual continuity that determine the definition of cities were removed from the Ville Radieuse and were never replaced by Modern architecture.

However, these city elements are all clearly present and alive in Lower Manhattan, and are all clearly missing in Shanghai's new Pudong district where no urban fabric is made. 'Manhattanization' was initially a derogatory term in the 1970s referring to the clustered skyline of towers. Ironically, it has become the inspiration and general precedent for the image of a contemporary city. The skylines are there, but New York's rich urban fabric is missing. The Pudong district does not make a new type of city; it just eliminates all the necessary urban elements on the ground. The postcard imagery of Wall Street in Lower Manhattan represents a Modern city built on a 17th century plan. It is one of the densest places in the world, an urban place also made of early 20th century architecture. It is not that much different from the image of Duccio's city in the 14th century (Fig. 4). They share the common order of city forms.

Objections to the Rowe Model

Colin probably would not have approved of these characterizations, but I suspect he would also have been amused by the conversation it implies. He would accuse me of "physics-envy" for sure, and gross oversimplification. Surely this conjecture would likely have a Feynman title, *Surely You're Joking, Mr. Peterson!*

Over the years, some of my colleagues have registered objections to parts of the proposition that I have advanced here. I think it is fair to cite these reservations in order to continue the conversation.

Precedent

Steven Hurtt, in a long email to me this year, said that Colin's early articles that focus on architecture, not urban design, could not be read as part of an urban theory. He felt it all started with the Urban Design Studio at Cornell. Of course, it is literally true that "The Mathematics of the Ideal Villa" from 1947 is not about cities, but its underlying and shocking message was that even Le Corbusier, the quintessential Modernist, used *precedents* from the past and followed an underlying Palladian *parti*. The argument here is that reference to precedent is intrinsic to the design of cities as a continuous process.

Phenomenal Transparency

Michael Dennis has objected that transparency cannot be an urban phenomenon, because you can't see through solid blocks. Although initially I agreed, I had changed my mind while preparing my text for the 2014 conference, "Rowe Rome". This was based on my observation of the overlapping spatial readings in the Piazza della Signoria in Florence. From the north, the Palazzo Vecchio clearly occupies the corner of an L-shaped space, which is subdivided in two by a line of statues. Then, because of spatial proportions, the massing of the building and the viewpoint, the palazzo seems to be standing in a larger, virtual, rectangular space that is completed behind it. The Loggia dei Lanzi itself is part of three spaces: the piazza, the extension of a back street, and its own covered space (Fig. 5). In addition, surely transparency exists at every urban intersection when two streets intersect and overlap.

Fig. 6. Colin Rowe as the master detective, Nero Wolfe (seated) and the author as his loyal assistant, Archie Goodwin discussing *The Case of the Missing City*.

Contextualism

Fred Koetter told me long ago that when he and Colin were writing *Collage City*, he rejected contextualism because you might find yourself working in a bad neighborhood where imitation and blending-in would not be good. He assured me that the word could not be found anywhere in their book, *Collage City*, and it is not. But this is only a passive misinterpretation. Urban form depends on a continuous context of connected elements. Contextualism in this definition is the essential means of integration not imitation. Tom Schumacher's essay "Contextualism: Urban Ideals and Deformations", published in *Casabella*, describes Sant'Agnese in Agone as both participating in the walled definition of Piazza Navona and erupting from that same urban fabric. Sant'Agnese retains all the iconic characteristics of the centralized church while it is also modified or 'deformed' so as to participate fully in the continuity of the facade-wall that gives spatial and figural definition to Piazza Navona. The architectural conventions of the centralized church type and architectonic language shared by both church and palazzo are transformed in a slightly unconventional manner to achieve the result.

Collage

As for Barbara Littenberg and myself, although we appreciate Hadrian's Villa, like everyone else, we have never used a conscious *collage* technique of juxtaposed, fragmented, incomplete parts, such as the Piazza d'Italia in New Orleans by Charles Moore. Although interpreted more broadly, every city eventually becomes an accidental collage as it accumulates changing architectural volumes and styles. It could also be argued that the unresolved conjunctions between the Palazzo della Signoria, the Uffizi Galleria and the Loggia dei Lanzi are all in a collaged state of composition.

Colin Rowe, the Master Detective

Barbara remembers that Colin loved detective stories, especially Rex Stout's fictional character Nero Wolfe, the famous armchair detective, with his confidential assistant Archie Goodwin—who did all the actual legwork and took all the risks. Wolfe was a brilliant investigator; born abroad, he was a naturalized U.S. citizen who had traveled widely before settling into his West 35th Street townhouse in New York City to investigate crime. Nero Wolfe never left this house but sent Archie out to do everything, and bring everybody back to his carefully ordered and decorated environment, where all was explained. This was Colin's fantasy: that the architectural mysteries could be solved from his study in Ithaca, New York.

I was able to find a picture of Rowe playing the master detective in his later years wearing the long anticipated and much debated mustache. Colin is joined by

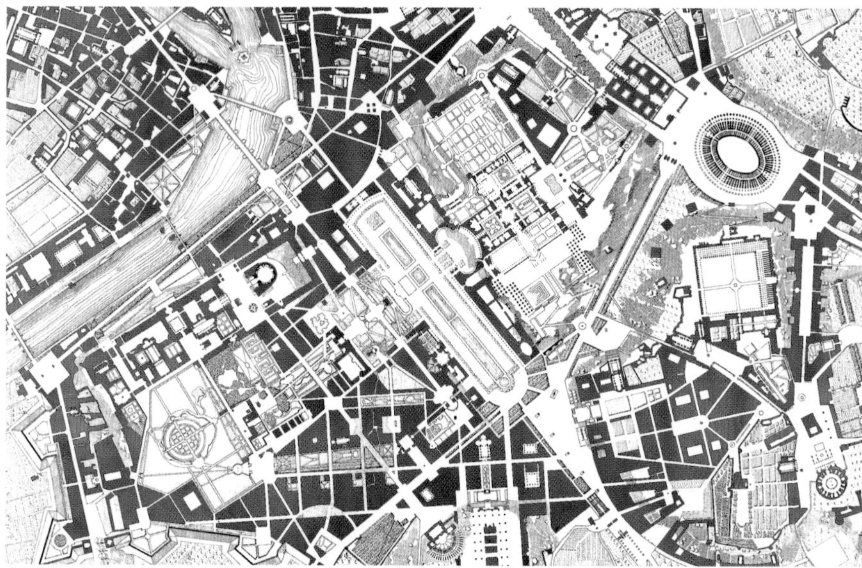

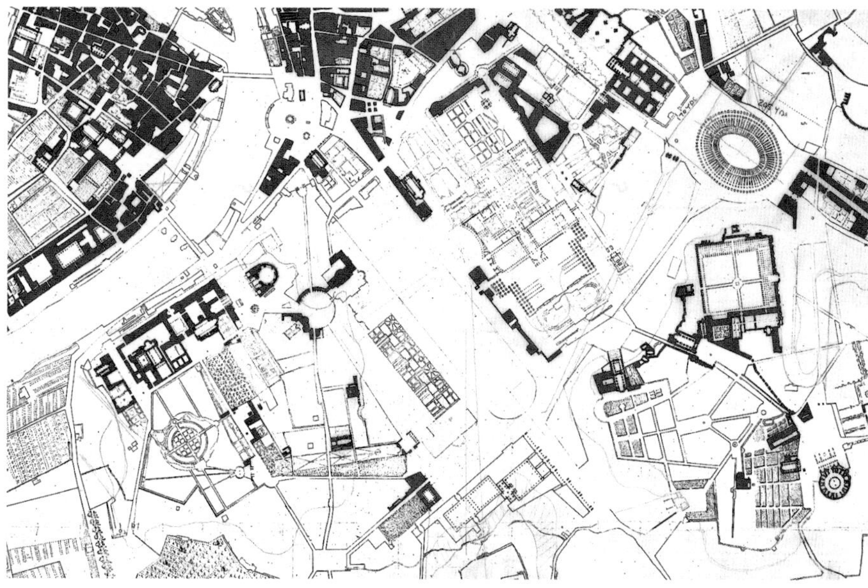

Fig. 7.
top:
Roma interrotta, the completed plan.

below:
The empty site before we started, there was no city at this point.

me, sitting at his side playing his assistant detective, Archie (Fig. 6). The crime of course, is *The Case of the Missing City,* the perpetrator is the usual suspect, Modern architecture, which has hopefully been subdued, and will be brought in for lengthy questioning.

The investigation seeks to find the missing victim, the traditional city, and see if we can rescue it from an otherwise uncertain future. Both Wolfe and Archie are clearly a bit anxious in this murky period photograph. They seem to be waiting for someone or something to arrive in the frame, and are trying to anticipate what will happen next.

Let's join them to visit the suspected 'crime scene of design' where the traditional city was last seen. Is there still evidence of an urban presence? Has the urban fabric been kidnapped and killed off, or is it just in hiding, hoping for rescue?

Fig. 8. The end run: completing the fortifications from the Gianicolo at the Porta Portese in Trastevere so that the Nolli urban fabric can enter the site.

The Crime Scene

The scene to be investigated is "Roma interrotta", where the two detectives worked closely investigating the *modus operandi* (MO) contained in the Nolli Plan of Rome of 1748. The 1978 "Roma interrotta", exhibition was held at Trajan's Market. Colin's innovative method of studying cities with figure/ground mapping was a primary inspiration for the exhibit, which was organized after Piero Sartogo had been a visiting critic in the architecture schools at Cornell and Princeton. The original map was divided into twelve sectors; Colin was assigned the central, mostly empty section of the map, just south of the historic center.

The sector was designed in two phases, the first with Judy DiMaio and Peter Carl when they were teaching at the University of Kentucky with Colin. Then, after they left (Peter to teach in Cambridge, England, Judy to become a fellow at The American Academy in Rome), I joined Colin to complete the project. At the time, I was teaching at Columbia University and Colin would come down to New York City every week to work on it in my apartment on 72nd Street. This site was largely empty with minor interventions when we began working together in the fall of 1977. Over time, we eventually filled in that large 'emptiness' with an invented city fabric that grew out of the historic center. The result is what was displayed at the Rome exhibition in January (Fig. 7). In 1978 there was a renewed interest in the city on both sides of the Atlantic: *Rational Architecture* and *Collage City* were both published the same year.[5]

The "Roma interrotta" project was somewhat unfamiliar territory for Colin because now he would have to participate as a principal designer, not as a teacher/critic. So, even before doing the design work, Colin had invented a written history about the place, people, and events as an elaborate little tourist *Baedeker* guide for him to use as support. Those of us who worked on it were a little baffled by this. I never paid any attention to it myself, but he would be forced to update it each week as we changed things around and settled on different design

5 Delevoy, Robert L. ed., *Rational Architecture Rationnelle: The Reconstruction of the European City*, Archives d'Architecture Moderne, Bruxelles, 1978.

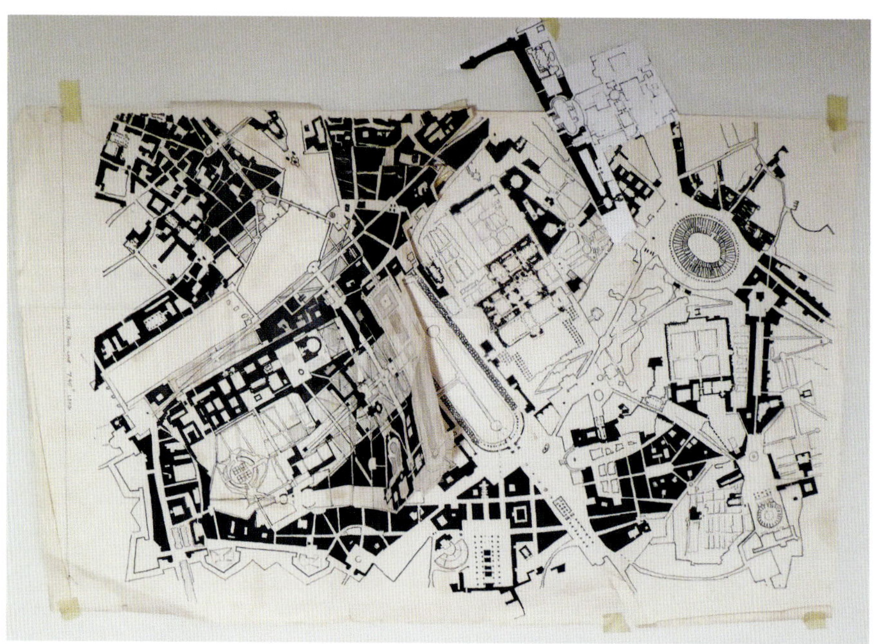

Fig. 9. Work in progress: literally pasting it up and gluing it together.

solutions. I think now he was substituting the missing 'windmill' of Modern architecture by locating the narrative in the 19th century. There was no battle to be waged here. It was all about understanding Nolli's paradigmatic mapping technique and exploring the essence of the pre-Modern city. We approached it as a controlled experiment and a test of ideas. The problem with the site, at the point we started working together, was that there was no 'Nolli' on the site, no black and white, no solid and void, no city. It was all bits of architecture and gardens and villas carefully drafted with lines and details, some of it quite nice: Peter's classicism on the Palatine, Judy's Orto Botanico park on top of the Aventine Hill, and Colin's Baroque blocks built over the garden parterres of the Villa Mattei on the Celio.

But, essentially there was no *parti* or strategy for the connections between the various pieces and no urban fabric. So Colin and I slowly changed the focus of the work from individual pieces to a larger strategy of urban continuity. How to get the Nolli city fabric to grow and move down from the center into this area? It was more like military tactics. How do we get around the barriers at the river-bend to outflank the antiquities? How do we get the Nolli fabric from the center city of the Campus Martius through the bottleneck at the end of the Circus Maximus, past the steep terrain of the Aventine, and down to the south, so it can link up with the Celio, and then drive on south to reach St. John Lateran?

Instead of struggling with the particulars of site, we executed a quick General Patton flanking maneuver through Trastevere, crossed the river with a new bridge from the Porta Portese, and occupied the whole south end of the Aventine with a new line of urban growth connecting all the way from the Tiber to the base of the Celio. The existing fortifications, coming down from the Gianicolo to the west of the river, were extended across it to form a southern flank to our site and the whole city (Fig. 8).

Fig. 10. Trying out the Paris Opera in Rome, high and low. Left on the Aventine, right in the valley south of the Palatine.

After that, it was all about city forms using the urban texture, not individual architectural designs. The primary question was how to make a plausible pattern of urban growth which might be imagined to have spread over this large area of complex terrain as an extension of the original Nolli Plan. We worked with the Nolli representational method and started to invent fields of urban texture.

Looking back at these drawings now, the process we used involved a shift in thinking for Colin in his approach to urban design; it certainly was for me. Instead of the Cornell Urban Design Studio problems of the time, made of recognizable architectural elements, slabs, point blocks, etc., we were obliged by our interpretation of the exhibition's purpose to ignore individual buildings and imitate the Nolli technique, where few buildings are described within the undifferentiated mass of solid blocks. The Nolli Plan is, in Colin's terms, a figure/ground map of *space.* It is the drawn representation, the plan as the essence of Rome's urban fabric. We adopted Nolli as the medium of our solution and invented connective patterns of urban tissue and began to discover the identity of the missing city. The provocation for the exhibition was the reemergence of a new interest in the city. The unstated question for the participants was, "What is the city?"

To find the city again, the Nolli Plan implied three things: first, that the *context* had to be designed; second, that the city spaces and its solids had to be in a *figure/ground equilibrium;* and third, that in order to hold together, the *fabric* had to be *continuous and establish a complete context.*

It was an experiment in which the process we used is interesting in itself. Instead of drafting individual objects, we made freehand outlines of whole areas of blocks and streets on tracing paper, photocopied them, blackened them in, cut them out, and then pasted them on the map, which we hung on the wall (Fig. 9). By not drawing, we went faster and were able to try a lot of approaches without full commitment. Obviously this was a literal *collage* process—more like painting a

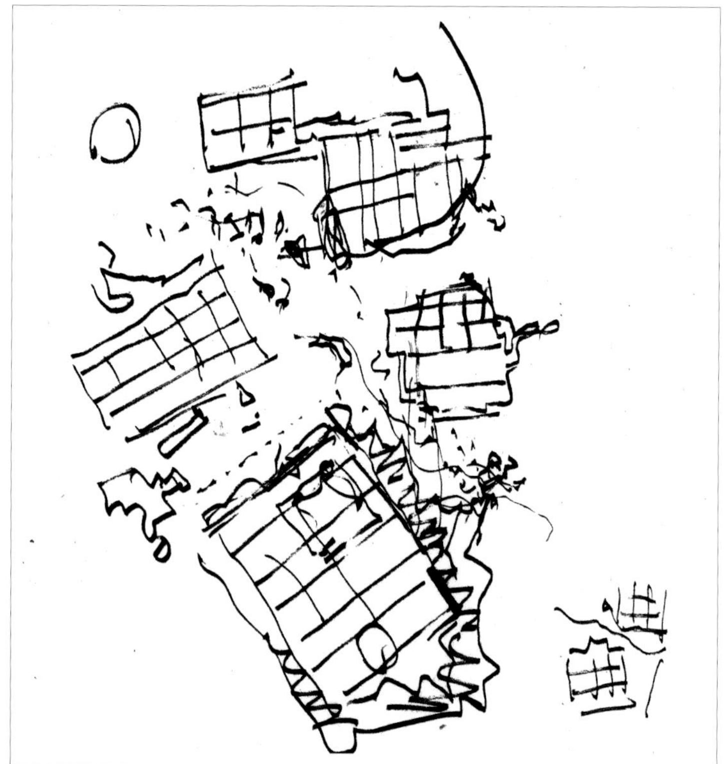

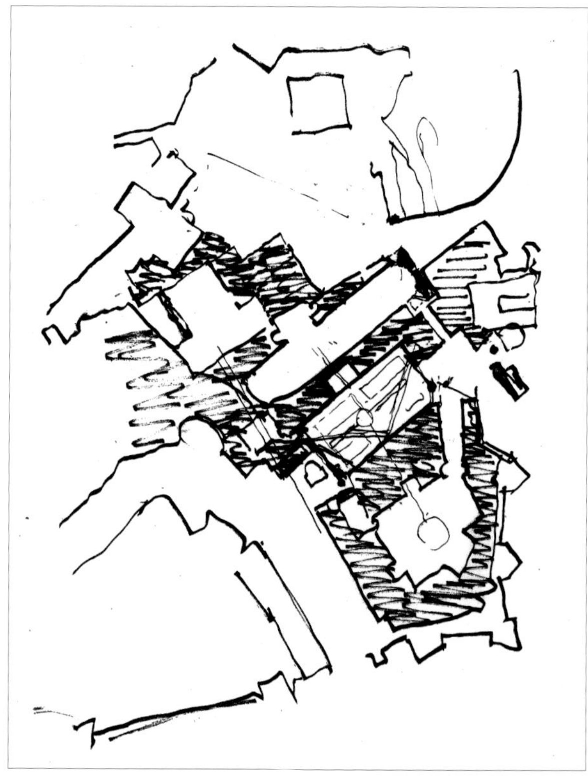

directly above:
Fig. 11. Note at the bottom of Colin's "Opera Plan" that it was OK and done. Things changed the next week.

top row:
Fig. 12. Two sketches that try to define the larger strategy and so guide the particulars. On the left, a collision of set piece fields on each hill with unresolved 'interstitial loose debris'.
On the right, a solid/void continuous fabric.

surface or pasting fragmented areas together than drawing outlined edges. The first rule of painting is to cover the whole canvas from the beginning and try not to work from one corner to the other. So, we just put a lot of city down on paper and then began working to manipulate it.

At one point the need for monumental objects did seem to return briefly, as Colin became interested in importing a copy of the Paris Opera into Rome. I think this emerged from his history text.

One drawing by Colin for the Aventine slope shows a grand *piazzale* solution containing the Paris Opera above the Circus Maximus. A second sketch tries again to include the Paris Opera, but over in the valley between the Palatine and the Celio (Fig. 10). It diverts another axis onto the side of the Colosseum. I can't remember why he wanted Garnier's opera house in Rome, but, isn't this great, a very skilled bi-axial, symmetrical performance from the man of *Collage* and *Collision City*? It makes you smile. It was also, strangely, an architectural composition of objects rather than an urban concept. One lesson that I learned from this exercise was that a monumental object seemed to require a lot of backup in the form of a contextual setting to justify its presence and establish its location.

There is a note from Colin about streets being too wide (Fig. 11). This was because I had drawn the plan of Rockefeller Center at the same scale of the Nolli Plan at the bottom of the plan in order to compare the site to a 20th century piece of urbanism. The streets actually were too wide because they were New York City dimensions transposed to the Nolli Plan scale. I drew the RCA Building at the south-east corner of the Circus Maximus stripped of its walls so the plan

Fig. 13. Exploring solutions for the Circus Maximus. On the left, a floating figure of trees replicating the original stadium. On the right, a built-in piazza.

mimics a big temple with the elevator cores as the *cella* (Fig. 14). It was deliberately placed at the end of the central Corso axis where it would be visible from the Piazza del Popolo—it was part of the game, a *precedent* used in a reversal of time for "Roma interrotta".

For some reason, Colin never wanted to understand this part of the plan, perhaps because it couldn't fit the narrative of his history. The whole south slope area of the Aventine Hill, beginning from the temple plan of Rockefeller Center, is based on the size and spacing of the blocks up 5th Avenue from the RCA Building to Central Park. As Colin wrote in Volume 3 of *As I Was Saying: Urbanistics*, "...to the south of the Circo Massimo (which Steven always insisted is a version of Rockefeller Center—though I don't understand why), I believe we were elegantly lucid."[6]

There was always an issue of how to relate the four hills conceptually. It was discussed frequently and remained a question right until the end. Two sketches (Fig. 12), one by Colin and one by me, show the two opposite strategies that we discussed: a continuous connected solid or a collision of disconnected fields. One was a continuous, blended, contextual fabric with large public spaces, the other a collage-like juxtaposition of four independently designed areas on top of each hill. The choice was more a question of what was logically possible given the steep slopes. In the end, because of the introduction of the garden and French *allées*, we did neither one exclusively, as you will see.

The huge empty space of the Circus Maximus was, of course, the inhibiting elephant in the plan for our sector. It was strangely hard to reconcile its size and placement, because it was too big to simply be built over with buildings like

6 Rowe (1996/3): 153.

Fig. 14. The final plan of pasted-up pieces just before we drew it up. Several things didn't make it into the final: the solid buildings around the Colosseum over Nero's house; the confusing multiple roads in the valley between the Palatine and the Celio; and the French hôtel on the Aventine.

the Piazza Navona, and too close to the adjacent hills to accrue a sufficient surrounding fabric of blocks and streets to back it up. The sequence of options we explored is illustrated in these working studies that show the dilemma. The earliest version of the Circus Maximus recreates it as a detached object but made of trees, a *precedent* used in reverse, a larger version of the Prato della Valle in Padua (Fig. 13). In the next version, the Circus is actually constructed as a building but is not freestanding. It tries to grab onto the hills behind, with a kind of zipper of building links. This was also the point at which we realized the large set-piece squares (or the Paris Opera Place) on the lower Aventine Hill would not work because of the terrain. Note the hatching of the actual slope drawn through the two square areas that indicates an unwieldy drop-off across the square forms. Obviously, whatever we decided here would be the key link to the larger strategy for connecting, or not connecting, all the hills on the whole site.

Our breakthrough discovery was that we could construct a second road parallel to the Circus Maximus uphill on the Aventine that aligns directly with the cupola of St. Peter's, thus visually connecting the Vatican at the far end of Rome down to the Circus Maximus in this distant sector (Fig. 14).

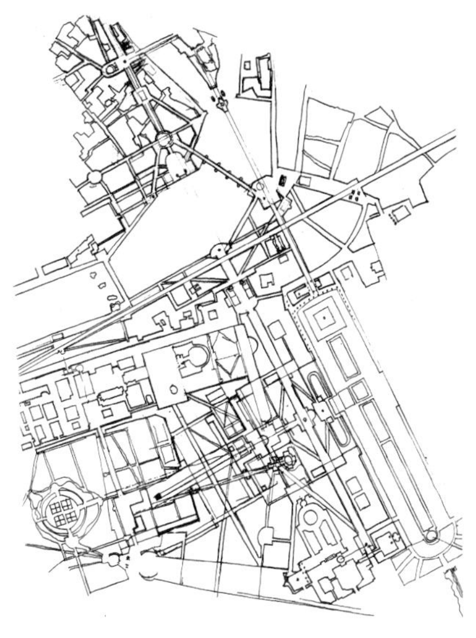

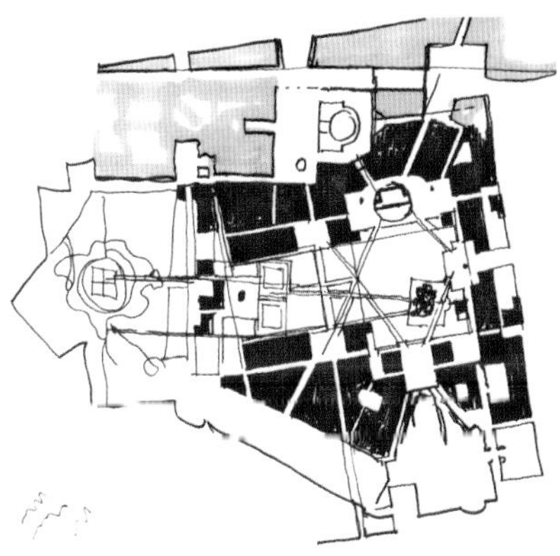

top to bottom:
Fig. 15. A line drawing of the uphill axis, parallel to the Circus Maximus, that is aligned with the dome of St. Peter's. It shows the multiple effects of the French Garden technique in expanding the local space to break out of the set piece blues.

Fig. 16. Last version of the set piece space: the Villa Pia has replaced the Paris Opera.

With this change the solution on the site could be shifted. Everything became layered up from the Circus Maximus as a center. Instead of a separating gap between, it became the connecting generator. The ancient Roman circus space, which had been a static stadium enclosure, now expands and breaks out of its valley to reach clear across Rome in a dynamic, symbolic axis (Fig. 15). This linear expansion of space doubled the effect of the Circus Maximus alignment, opening up the site, which allowed us to break free of the burdensome closed monumental symmetry we had been struggling with (Fig. 16). The linear extension of the Circus Maximus orientation links the two quintessential periods of Roman history by expanding and projecting the visual space to reveal a relationship that is not apparent in reality, not even today.

At the immediate surrounding site, the new duplication of parallel lines seemed to open up the possibility that the sides of the Circus could be treated differently. The relationship of the adjacent hills could be resolved in the form of a cross-axis between them. The Aventine hillside was opened up to a grand public garden flowing down from the Botanical Garden on the Palatine Hill into the Circus Maximus as the last parterre at the lowest level. The Palatine hillside could be closed and defined by a new facade of buildings backed up to the steep slope. The Circus Maximus footprint is animated and pulled apart into pieces expanding its spatial influence, but still retains its presence as a static, spatial 'ghost'. The simultaneous reading of the Circus space, as both a cross-axis and a linear form, is an example of Colin's *phenomenal transparency*. Because its sides are asymmetrical, it is also defined by large fragments, an aspect of collage.

So all is now urbanized. The far wall of Nash-like residential terraces provides a facade to the Palatine Hill, and also connects to the central Campus Martius, south through the tight gap of the Forum Boarium. It is as if our first flanking movement is now finished, joined in a frontal assault backing up the center of the plan. Following on the French garden theme, the Tiber is marked off by bridges and banks to form a series of geometric lagoons. Note, too, how the central axis of the Circus Maximus terminates at the Tiber Island Statue of Liberty sculpture. This drawing makes clear how flexible, adaptive, and complex the urban-fabric can be, especially as an interacting expansive geometry of garden forms.

The final sketch (Fig. 14) shows all the characteristics of the Rowe strategies integrated into an actual design.

Figure/Ground Field
There are multiple, different fields of urban fabric, overlapping, interpenetrating, establishing boundaries to neighborhoods and identifiable districts.

Contextualism
Essentially the whole problem, as we defined it on this complex site, was to create spreading fields of invented contexts, each with distinct character.

Phenomenal Transparency

Overlaps appear at all scales: the interpenetration of the Circus Maximus in a cross-axis up the terraced gardens of the Aventine Hill and the cross-graining of the New York field of blocks up the Aventine. On the Celio Hill, the square at the bottom of the Uffizi piece, behind the Colosseum, is a transparent overlapping of two twisted voids (*frontispiece*).

Collage

Collage appears in two ways: as a method of inserting partial quotations that are pasted in from other places—the botanical garden of Padua, Nash's London terraces, and Rockefeller Center—in the colliding fragments of each hill (as determined by each local context) and so on. Collage is also implicitly evident in the intentional strategy that no single formal solution could suffice for the whole area. Patterns from different places are not resolved or integrated with each other, but left in juxtaposition.

Precedent

Certainly, this is the key point of the exhibition, to treat the Nolli Plan as precedent for the whole exercise. The Rowe plan contains many amusing references (precedents) including literal scale copies of city plans and pieces of architecture as measured and to-scale instigations for further development. I'll point some of them out. Others you can find, if you want to look. There is the Statue of Liberty on the main axis to the Tiber Island (imitating the copy in Paris); the Villa Madama; the Villa Pia; the Palazzo Borghese; Asplund's Chancellery in Stockholm; the botanical garden from Padua; the château at Compiègne in France; the Nash terraces of Regents Park; the Uffizi Gallery; all of Rockefeller Center, with its channel gardens and skating rink; Saint Patrick's Cathedral; even Radio City Music Hall as a Greek theater. Drawn across the bottom of the plan, there is a 10-block stretch of 5th Avenue leading from 50th Street at Rockefeller Center up to the botanical park entrance to Central Park, and similar to it.

Parti

Yes, there are multiple *partis*; each hill develops its own *parti*—a fortified city, a hill town, a classic acropolis, etc. The whole composition has a *parti* of connecting landscape lines. Note the unexpected cross-axis line from the Tiber into the heart of the Roman Forum at the base of the Capitoline Hill.

The Line and The Garden

The garden's straight lines of axial extension are a long-range antidote to the local containment of an urban fabric. The geometry of the garden is a spatial field-form too. It is also connected to Rome's history. Long straight streets were always important in Rome, starting with the antique Via del Corso, the Renaissance Via Giulia, and then the Sixtus V Baroque expansions to the south. In France these lines, bordered with trees, become *allées* and boulevards, asserting the public garden structure as a virtual city.

Léon Krier speculated on what "Roma interrotta" had meant for Colin saying in *The Cornell Journal*, "The all too mechanical and academic diagrams had at last matured into well-measured and well-composed cities. ... After nineteen years of relentless struggle with the dragon, the Cornell Urban Design Studio seems finally to have freed itself from the indelible grasp of modern planning

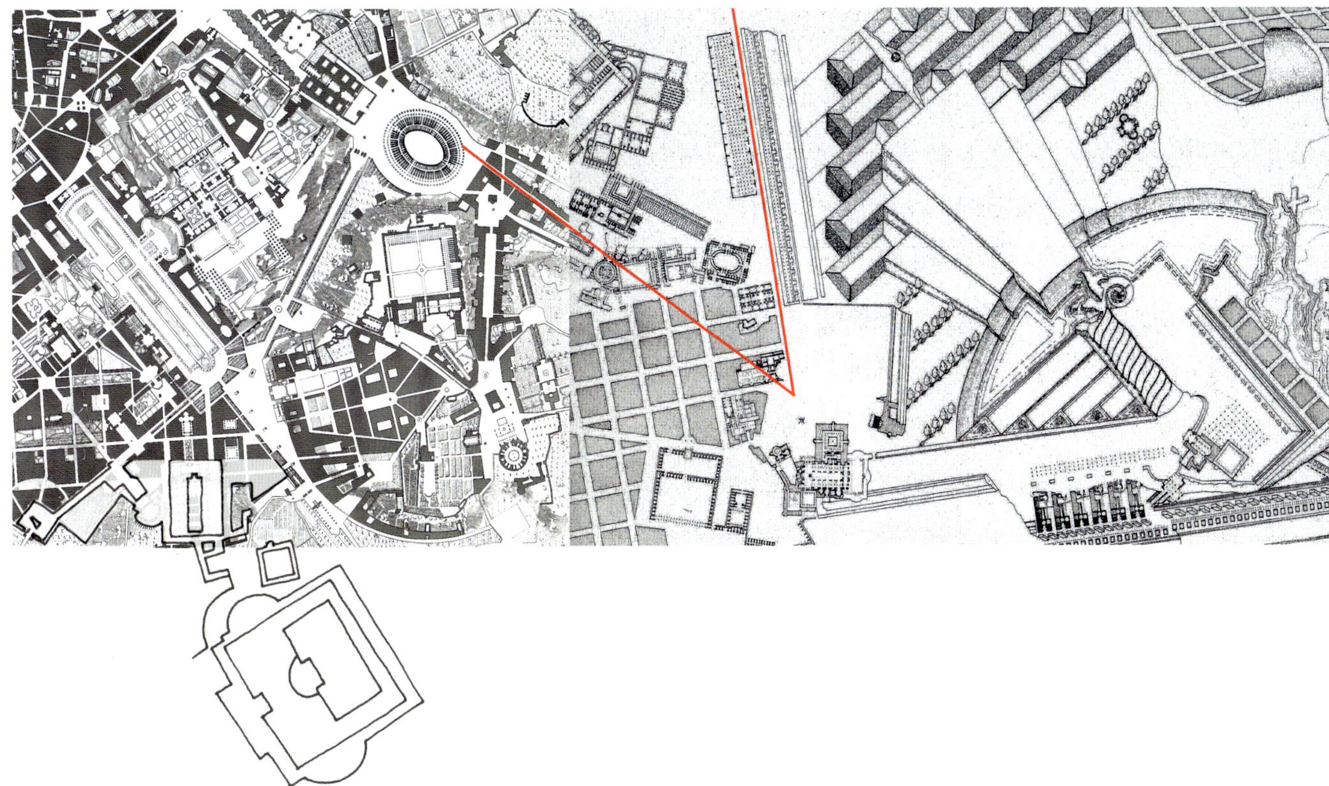

Fig. 17. Relationship of Sector 8 by Colin Rowe team (left), Sector 9 by Michael Graves (right), and the Baths of Caracalla in Sector 11 (below).

and fragmentation" and abandoned "the hypothetical synthesis between the Traditional City and the City of Industry which for a while had been the declared goal of Rowe…".[7]

The Exhibition

It turns out that the urban approach, which I have just described, was totally unique and distinct from the other contributors to the exhibition. When we arrived at the exhibition and saw the other schemes, we were shocked. We expected urban plans, but no one else had tried to use the Nolli Plan as a precedent, or to explore its language as a planning medium of city design. No one else had tried to design a plausible piece of Rome that took into account their adjacent map sections and anticipated connections.

Michael Graves, who had the sector connected directly east of ours, ignores most of what was present on the site and its surroundings to produce a collage graphic organized around a giant Postmodern keystone shape (Fig. 17). In the Graves submittal, the Sixtus V axis, which potentially connects to the Rowe site and leads from the Colosseum up to St. John Lateran, is covered over and obliterated with an arbitrary square grid. The other axis in the Graves site, the axis related to Santa Maria Maggiore, is not retained as an urban boulevard, but reduced to a slot between buildings. The carefully proportioned existing piazza, north of St. John Lateran, is willfully enlarged, leaving the church complex floating like a leaf in the wind.

7 Krier, Léon, "Foreword", *The Cornell Journal of Architecture* 2, 1983.

A PARTIAL MODEL
of
URBAN FORM

Based on The Rowe Strategies, an urban city must consist of two essential elements:

AN ESTABLISHED URBAN FABRIC
Made of palpable FORMED SPACE and its enclosing BLOCKS, in a congruent, continuous, figure/ground FIELD
and

A CONTEXTUAL ARCHITECTURE
That simultaneously makes the foreground and the background, shaping public space, and forming continuous urban walls.

COLIN: "I regard the revival of the city as far more important than any survival of Modern Architecture ..." because "the object building interpreted as a universal proposition represents the demolition of Public Life".

Fig. 18. A Partial Model of Urban Form.

In all the sectors adjacent to ours, those by Michael Graves, Robert Venturi, and Aldo Rossi, the architects did not make plausible plans or build on the content of their sites. Their proposals were more like posters of the author's particular style and reputation, literally collaged graphic images pasted on the map. This is the normal, literal interpretation of collage as a two-dimensional method of composition, relating things through juxtaposition of fragments. As David Grahame Shane points out in his book *Recombinant Urbanism,* "Roma interrotta" exposed the weakness of a total collage strategy.[8] No contributors on the project related to their neighbors. Each became an isolated display case with no overall composition of the city, even a fractured one. This is the mistaken idea that collage is just an excuse for free play, that it eliminates the obligation for integration. The exhibition as a whole did not recognize urbanism as Nolli intended. The panels taken as a whole had no overall *gestalt;* they became an excuse to disregard context, avoid urban continuities, and ignore each other.

Crime Scene Report

We have done our detective work at the crime scene of design (or at least viewed the forensics lab of drawings). We can report back to the master detective with our assessment of *The Case of the Missing City.* From the evidence shown in Rome, it

8 Shane, David Grahame, *Recombinant Urbanism: Conceptual Modeling in Architecture, Urban Design, and City Theory,* Wiley-Academy, Chichester, 2005: 132.

would seem that the Missing City *can* be found, albeit in the realm of the hypothetical. As Colin wrote in "The Present Urban Predicament", to achieve this is only a matter of having a continuous urban fabric, from which spaces are carved and objects erupt.[9] Nothing could be clearer, or more difficult to achieve. This is because it involves a radical change in the relationship and purpose of both urban design and architecture. Colin again: "I regard a *revival* of the city as far more important than any *survival* of modern architecture".[10] Because, "... the object building, when interpreted as a universal proposition, represents nothing more than a demolition of public life...."[11]

Fig. 19. From the left: Archie Goodwin (aka Steven K. Peterson); Nero Wolfe (aka Colin Rowe); Pope Leo X (aka Giovanni de'Medici) and his nephew Cardinal Luigi Rossi.

This 'demolition' has already begun in many places. Look down at the new Pudong district in Shanghai and compare it with Lower Manhattan. Where in the Pudong district would you walk? How would you get from one building to another? Where would you find a shop? Where would you catch a cab? Could you live around the corner from your office? How would you give someone directions? Where in Pudong would you have a ticker-tape parade or other public events or celebrations?

I want to go back to the concept of a *field*, the idea that is common to both Rowe and Feynman. If the urban fabric is analogous to a cloth that is spread out over an area in a continuous, connected pattern, then it becomes a medium of design, where the strings and gaps can be woven into different patterns with a variety of textures, densities, grains, scales, and multi-directional networks. This is the most important defining ingredient of the urban condition. It is the central binding force in any overall model of urban form without which the city cannot exist. It is the key to Colin's legacy that he recognized its critical necessity in the very definition of what is urban (Fig. 18).

Back to the Master Detective

Finally, I would like to imagine asking Colin's opinion of this conjecture, he who seems to be quite enjoying the role of master detective, "Does he agree with my fieldwork searching for a standard model of urban form"? He does look wary, and, as always when asked a direct question, he avoids a straight answer, so to change the subject, he mumbles something about another of his favorite topics: the Renaissance popes, which somehow conjures up Leo X and his nephew who appear in front of us (Fig. 19). Leo is clearly about to confront me while Colin looks back at him with astonishment and relief. For the first time I sensed that Colin Rowe was truly speechless.

Some Thoughts on Colin Rowe

I want to end with some thoughts about Colin himself, while we observe him doing what he often did, fantasizing about the popes and the amusing folly of human behavior.

It is probably a mistake to define Colin as a teacher in the conventional sense, as if he gave instruction or tried to codify information or technique, or to prescribe a method. To be a student of Colin's in the Urban Design Studio was not an organized pedagogical experience, but rather an ongoing engagement with

9 Rowe (1981): 25.

10 Ibid.: 32.

11 Ibid.: 24.

Colin as a person. You became a witness to his state of curiosity, which was in a mode of constant inquiry, conjecture, and wit. At the same time his personal vivacity and openness allowed you to interact on casual and equal terms. This is why one can't pull out a definable theory from his words.

Colin taught implicitly by setting standards through the example of his own attitudes and behavior. There was a sense that he was working on the problem with you. He was curious, passionate, discovering things right beside you. You were all in the same game.

Colin didn't teach a class and go home. He was always around. He would pop into the studio at midnight, or early in the morning, with an idea or an example of something. He would show you amazing things in books or give 'crits' by drawing suggestive sketches in wiggly lines. However, it is the example of his intellect that always seemed to hold the key to things. You had to understand, to read everything he had written (even though he never assigned any of it), and to try to participate in his unique way of seeing things.

The standards he set were also not conventional in method or behavior. His basic attitude was to combine passion with doubt, a passionate appreciation of things of excellence or an idea with an amused skepticism about theories to explain them. He would say, "It is not very useful to try and establish definitions". Colin as a teacher always assumed the best of you, even going beyond reality to fantasize about your abilities and background. There was never any patronizing or any sense of being intimidated by his knowledge; if anything, he had a way of giving you credit for knowing more than you actually did.

He would say, "Steven, of course you know that painting by Pontormo in the Santa Felicita chapel in Florence, with all that green, etc." After he had finished, since you didn't know what he was talking about, and couldn't admit it, you were left with a new puzzle, something new to look up.

He engaged in a wide range of subjects without pedantic explanations. His manner left things deliberately ambiguous and open-ended. Ideas could, like books and pictures, be dropped on your table for easy access.

Colin, like many of us, didn't want to finish anything, but for him it was a preference for the open-ended condition. He was always content to let the Studio work go on forever, even if the end product would never really be finished as a result. He was this way even in casual habits, leaving conversation open and unfinished, deliberately changing subjects or finishing a statement by saying, "Boom, boom, boom", implying that all was known, but would be tedious to explain.

There was a time when he would end phone conversations, not by saying, "Goodbye", but rather, "Steven let's stop talking now", then just as the receiver left your ear, on the way to be hung up, you would hear him go, "Uh, uh", as if he was actually going on without you anyway. To Colin, teaching architecture was only one possibility. He would say, "I would just as soon deal with other objects: silverware, china, furniture or paintings as architecture or cities". In an evening at his house, one was as likely to discuss, or rather hear about: furniture, European genealogy, engravings, philosophy, Hilaire Belloc's *Cautionary Tales*, Giulio Romano, mustaches—sometimes a lot about mustaches—boom, boom, boom!

The conjunction of so many topics was like a conversational collage. All the bits were part of the same flow, a diversity that comes from a sense of wit, a genuine enjoyment of ideas. Once, he was listening to a serious and impossible argument among several faculty about the first-year design curriculum. Colin broke in to say, "Well, you know, it doesn't really matter. We are all just in the business of seducing students—pause—about architecture". This statement was what finally explained to me the famous test of furniture books. Everyone came to study architecture with Colin. At some point, you went to his house for drinks. He then would bring out a very thick auction catalogue filled with furniture. He would say, "Steven, just have a look".

Then, while he is mixing drinks in the other room you start turning pages. There are chairs, tables, chaises-longues, etc., all in different styles, periods and types. What in the world are you supposed to think? Some of it is hideous, some you recognize. Colin, from the other room shouts, "Now just keep going". It turns out he knew the book by heart and how long it takes to get to certain pages, but you were not aware of this at the time. As you got to the 10th page or so, and starting to get a bit nervous, Colin returns to the room as if on cue, and says, "Ja, ja, ja, now just look at that. Isn't that something?" You are staring at a double page with eight different pieces of "furn". Which one does he mean? You make a gesture toward one, but he saves you from making a mistake, suggesting a piece at the top of the opposite page. Well, it's a chair, with exaggerated pieces, resembling parts of animals. The whole thing is unusual, with rather squat, slightly-flared proportions. Quickly you survey all the other pictures, but, no, this piece is clearly distinguished and unique in a way you can't define.

Now with drink in hand, more pages are turned, more books come out. You are getting a little better at seeing which ones are going to be right. Eventually you actually get one ahead of him. Something has begun to happen to you, but you're not sure what. You have begun to encounter a new sense of what constitutes quality and the idea of taste. All this happens without a word of theory or explanation. Nothing is said about architecture. I ran across a statement by Jaques Barzun which explains this initiation:

> *Genuine learning, whether physical as in learning an instrument, or intellectual … proceeds just so: awkward excessive awareness is followed by a forgetting that leaves one in possession of a new power.*[12]

At the end of my two graduate years studying with Colin, we evolved into friends and I stayed on in Ithaca for another year. One day driving together, I told him I was taking a job with Wells/Koetter/Dennis Architects, saying that I thought I could learn something there. He arched his eyebrows in sympathy and said, "Oh, Steven, don't you know, you can't learn from anyone else; you can only do it by yourself."

So, with his permission and hopefully, no offense, I write this article to show part of what I learned by myself with Colin Rowe.

12 Barzun, Jacques, *The Use and Abuse of Art*, Princeton University Press, 1975: 139.

Colin Rowe: The Rediscovery of the City

Michael Dennis

Rome

The population of Imperial Rome was about 1,000,000. By the 6th century, however, the city had shrunk to a small area within the Aurelian walls and contained barely 20,000 inhabitants. By the mid-18th century, Renaissance and Baroque Rome had been rebuilt over the ancient Roman core and the population had risen to nearly 150,000 inhabitants. This was the Rome depicted in the famous 1748 plan by Giambattista Nolli. It was also nominally the extent of the city until the late 19th century and is still the heart of the city today. It is the Rome revered by architects and the part of the city where students and teachers go to study architecture and urbanism. (No one goes to Prati for example).

frontispiece:
Aerial plan of Rome, 2019. *Centro storico* from *Pianta di Roma* by Giambattista Nolli, 1748, superimposed (M. Dennis).

This, the *centro storico*, is distinct in a contemporary aerial plan. Its dense urban fabric of mostly irregular blocks and very narrow streets contrasts sharply with the surrounding gridded neighborhoods planned during massive urban expansion in the late 19th and early 20th centuries. These surrounding areas generally have bigger, more regular blocks, and notably wider streets (*frontispiece*).

Rowe

Colin Rowe had a 'good eye'. His visual acuity, coupled with extensive historical knowledge, total recall, and verbal dexterity, enabled him to imbue inanimate forms with a vitality that rendered complex ideas visible even to the uninitiated. This was his true talent. He was interested in ideas—complex ideas. He was interested in talking about them, sharing them, and promoting them. He was also interested in the city, but he was not an urbanist.

Consequently, it is ironic that today he is arguably best known for his contribution to urbanism. Indeed, in the second half of the 20th century, Rowe was a major figure in the rediscovery of the city—the traditional city—in contrast to the so-called Modernist city. This is especially remarkable since he never designed a plan, never drew a plan, and, prior to 1963, there was virtually no evidence of his interest in urban design. He accomplished everything by teaching, lecturing, and writing. But, while Colin Rowe's contributions to both architecture and

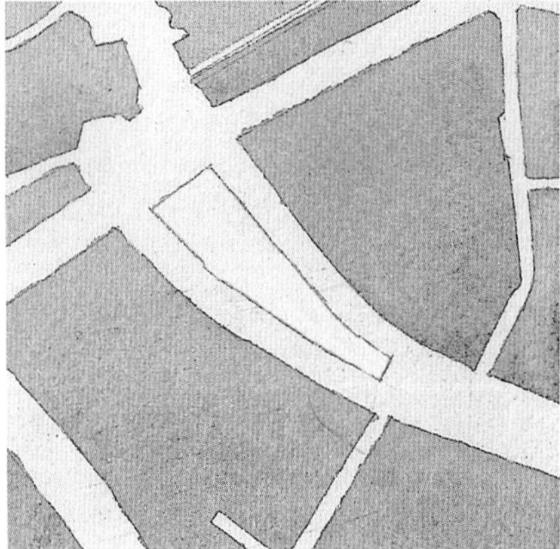

Fig. 1. Urban element diagrams after M. R. G. Conzen.

urban design must be acknowledged, his real interests were not applicable to town planning—the physical design of cities and major urban expansions. Rowe never developed a comprehensive idea of urban form and its elements and principles. (Neither did Aldo Rossi, Rob Krier, Venturi/Scott Brown for that matter). That would fall to Léon Krier. Rowe's interests were in the particular, the inconsistent, and the contradictory, thus his fascination with Italian Mannerism, Cubism, and Le Corbusier. Le Corbusier the architect was, like Rowe himself, complex, discontinuous, and idiosyncratic. On the other hand, Le Corbusier the town planner was relentless, simplistic, and ruthless. But, Le Corbusier's architecture—like Cubism—does not easily lend itself to town planning.

Rowe's Rome

Rowe was in love with the historic center of Rome, with its picturesque, irregular plan and its dense accumulation of architectural and urban episodes, and he passed his knowledge and enthusiasm for the city to countless students and colleagues. But the historic core of Rome is not applicable to town planning. No one in history ever made a plan like central Rome. Architects and town planners may add to the cumulative city, but they do not design it. In fact, the majority of Rome, the part outside the ancient core, is regular and gridded. This is obviously the problem: the planned town versus the cumulative city. In the whole history of cities, there are no irregular planned towns.

Today, there is great confusion between architecture and urban design, as too many architects see urban design as large-scale architecture. I am therefore using the term 'town planning' instead of 'urban design', because the term urban design is too often used for any design in the city. The urban geographer, M.R.G. Conzen is clear: "urban fabric" is comprised of three interlocking elements: 1) the town plan of streets, blocks, and spaces; 2) the land use patterns of parcels; and, 3) the three-dimensional building fabric (Fig. 1). The first, and possibly the second, of Conzen's elements are the realm of town planning. Conzen's third element is the realm of architecture. Accordingly, for 2,500 years, town planners or urban designers designed and drew city plans and pieces of cities, while architects designed and drew buildings that fleshed out the plans.

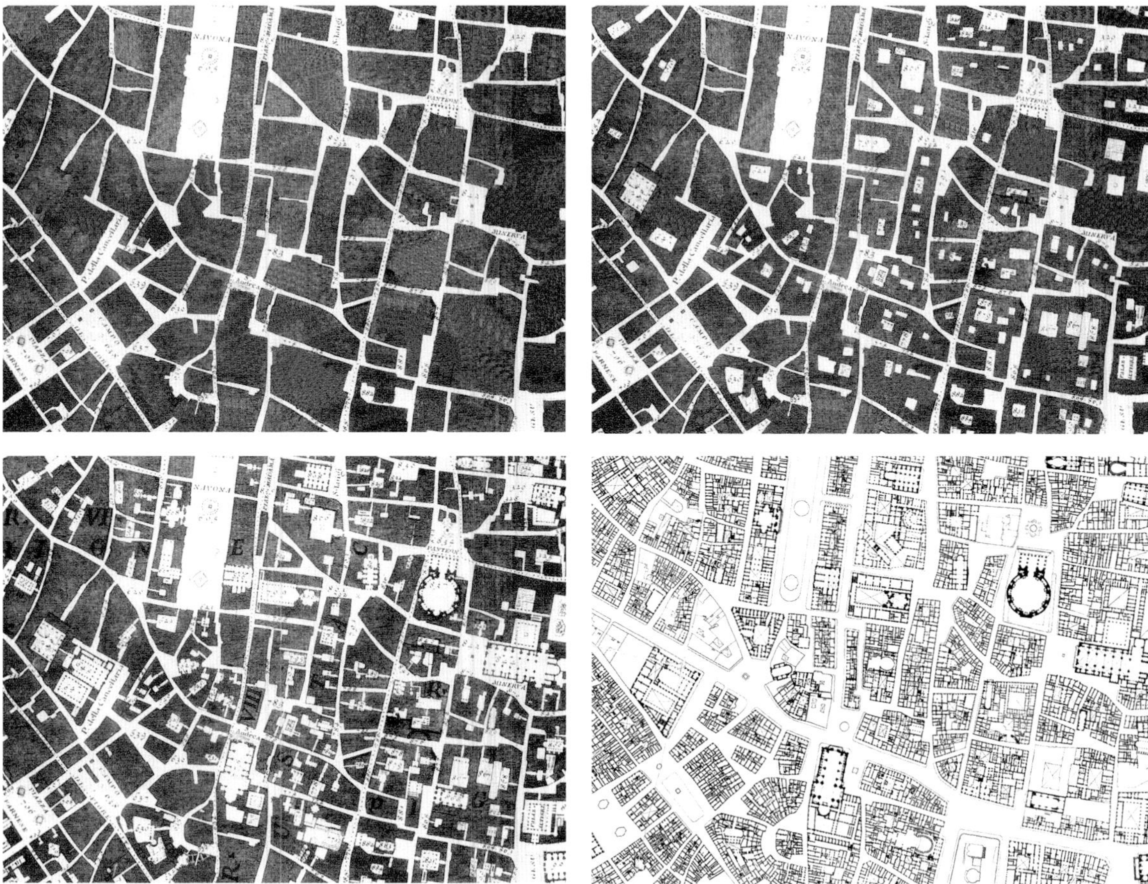

Nolli's Rome

Four detail plans of Nolli's Rome illustrate why it is not applicable to town planning. The detail plans cover the area of the Piazza Navona, the Pantheon, and the Gesù.

The first detail plan shows only the streets, blocks, and urban spaces (Conzen's first element) (Fig. 2). In other words, this would correspond to a town or urban design plan for the area. Obviously, no one could design such a plan. This plan is the end result—not the beginning—of a myriad of local, particular decisions. It is a cumulative plan.

The second detail plan shows the semi-public building courtyards in addition to the streets, blocks, and urban spaces (Fig. 3). Again, it is obvious that no designer could foresee this level of urban and architectural detail.

The third detail plan adds major interior spaces to the area (Fig. 4), while the fourth detail plan by Muratori adds the ground plans of most of the area's buildings (Fig. 5).

Thus, the Nolli Plan is a beautiful record plan, but not a design plan. This may be the most beautiful part of Rome, filled with endless urban lessons, but not applicable to town planning.

above left to right:

Fig. 2. Central Rome showing block structure (M. Dennis).

Fig. 3. Central Rome showing block structure and semi-public courtyards (M. Dennis).

Fig. 4. Central Rome showing block structure, semi-public courtyards, and major interior spaces (Nolli Plan, 1748).

Fig. 5. Central Rome showing block structure, semi-public courtyards, major interior spaces, and building ground plans (Muratori plan, 1963).

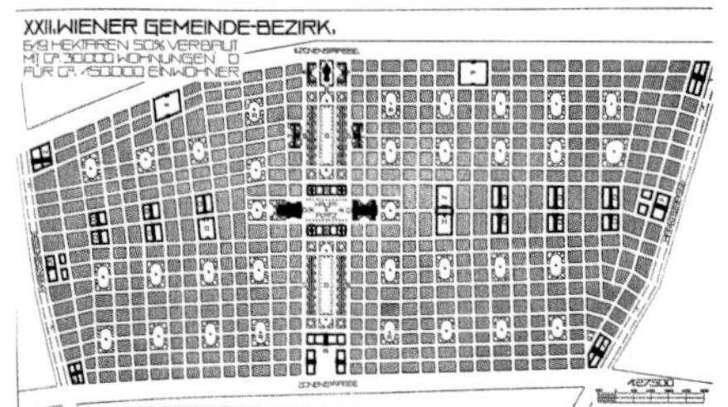

above:
Fig. 6. Aerial perspective of the District XXII Civic Center for Vienna, by Otto Wagner 1911.

below:
Fig. 7. Comparison of Central Vienna and Grosstadt plan for Vienna, District XXII, by Otto Wagner at the same scale.

Planned Towns

Planned towns and cities used to be regular, and they were usually grid plans. This was true of Greek and Roman towns, of Bastides, of the Great Estates of London, and of the 1811 "Commissioners' Plan" for Manhattan Island. Architecture was never illustrated.

But, around 1890, architects and town planners began to draw buildings rather than streets, blocks, and squares—to illustrate the architecture of the plan. Otto Wagner's 1911 plan for Vienna (Fig. 6) was traditional, uniform, and of limited height, but he illustrated what he imagined to be the architecture of the plan—not only the public buildings, but the private buildings as well (Fig. 7).

Eugène Hénard's 1910 "City of Tomorrow" also illustrated his idea of the architecture of the plan, and it was prescient in the celebration of tall buildings (Fig. 8). The ground-level city fabric was still there, but it would soon disappear, paving the way for what Danish urbanist Jan Gehl—referring to Dubai— calls the city of "Birdshit" buildings dropped by architects flying over (Fig. 9).

The tradition of iconic, detached buildings that began in the 18th century finally came to fruition in the early 20th century, and architecture became divorced from the city (Fig. 10). Pick up any book on the history of Modern architecture, and you will (almost) not find a single urban building. The demise of the traditional city was imminent (Fig. 11).

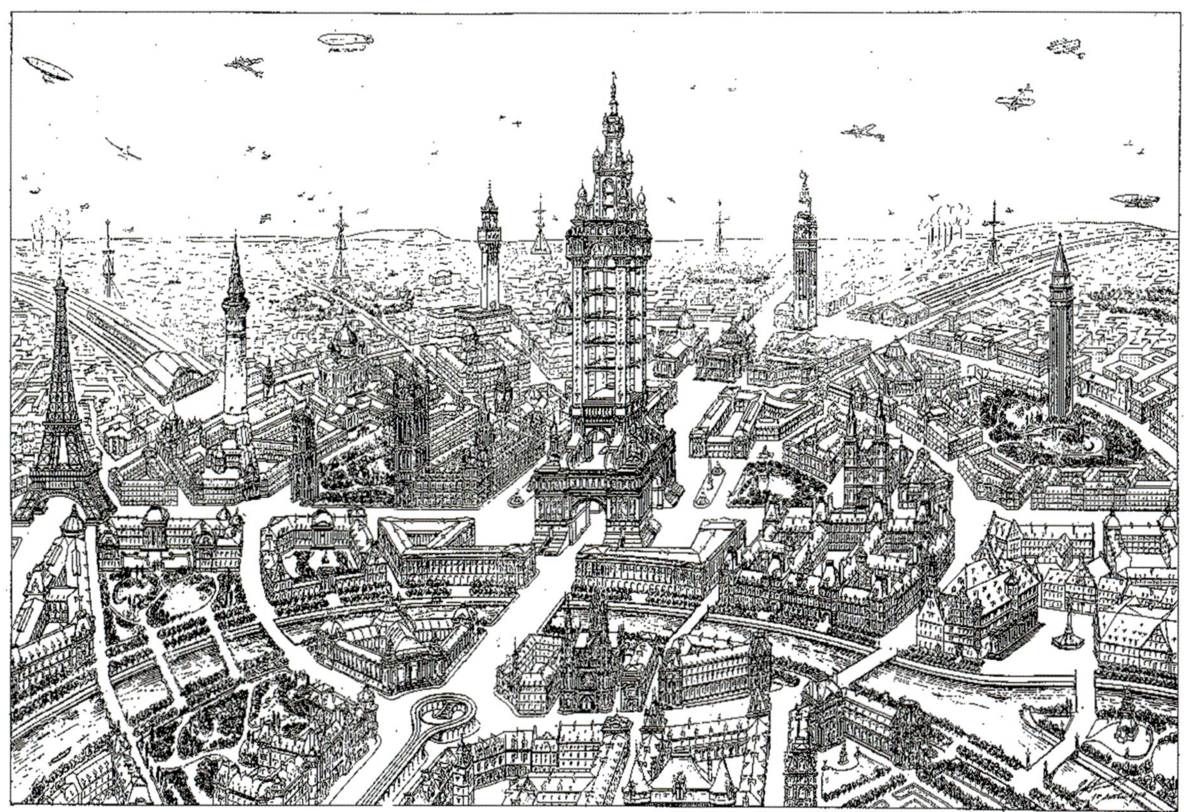

above:
Fig. 8. Aerial perspective of "The City of the Future," by Eugène Hénard, 1910.

below:
Fig. 9. Proposed center of Dubai.

Fig. 10. Aerial perspective of towers from "The City of the Future," by Eugène Hénard, 1910 (M. Dennis).

Two Strains of Modern Architecture

Despite Modernism's anti-urban consensus, there were profound differences within architecture. Indeed, there are two strains of Modern architecture. One of these strains can be found in the work of Wright, Van Doesburg, Gropius, and Hannes Meyer. The work of this group was most related to Russian Constructivism, and favored axonometric drawings, deep diagonal space, and unity of form and ideas—total design. Together, these architects formed what might be called the "Taliesin-Amsterdam-Dessau-Moscow axis". For Colin Rowe, these architects were the "hedgehogs". They saw the world according to a unitary vision. On the other hand, the work of Le Corbusier (the architect), Alvar Aalto, early Mies, and perhaps Giuseppe Terragni was different. Their work was related more to Paris and Cubism, and they presented a more complex and contradictory view of the world—one where total unity had no place, one where both the rational and the relative were simultaneously entertained. They favored perspective, and the frontal, shallow, layered space of Cubism. For Rowe, they were most certainly the "foxes". Of all these Modernist architects, however, only Le Corbusier produced genuinely urban buildings.

These two strains of Modern architecture were introduced into American architectural education: the first group by Mies's later work at IIT, and by Gropius at Harvard; the other group by Aalto at MIT, and by Rowe and the "Texas Rangers" at the University of Texas and at Cornell University.

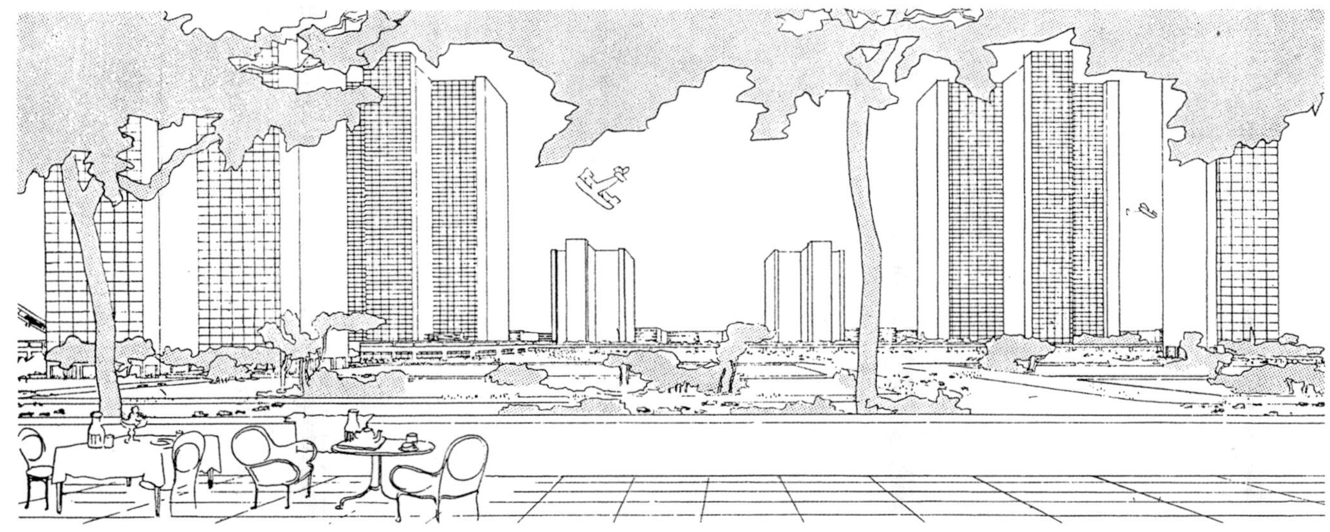

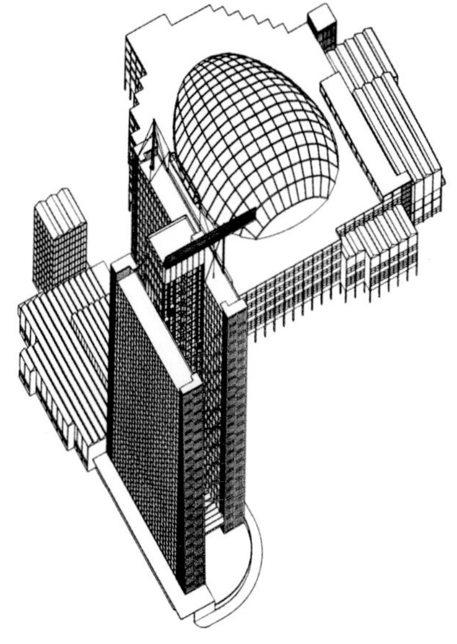

Modern Architecture and the Destruction of the City

The story of Modernist architecture's anti-urban characteristics and the resultant destruction of the city is now well known, but it might just be good to remember how insidiously destructive and arrogant the post-WWI architects and town planners were, as well as how long their ideas persisted. This was the status quo—the background against which the rediscovery of the city appears in sharp relief (Fig. 11, 12).

If Le Corbusier (the town planner) has become the common whipping boy for the sins of Modernist planning, surely Walter Gropius deserves at least equal flogging. Since he dominated the Harvard Graduate School of Design in 1937, Harvard has had a more or less continuous tradition of being the East Coast distributor of anti-urban teaching and practice—a tradition that continues to this day. Gropius brought Martin Wagner to teach at Harvard, and an early example of his "urban design"—one that still boggles the mind—was Wagner's 1942 Boston Center proposal, in which he proposed the destruction of the entirety of downtown Boston, and its replacement with a gigantic megastructure in the form of a question mark (Fig. 13, 14).

above:
Fig. 11. Perspective view of proposed Ville Contemporaine, Le Corbusier, 1922.

below:
Fig. 12. Axonometric view of League of Nations competition entry by H. Meyer, 1927.

below left to right:
Fig. 13. Plan of downtown Boston, 1950.

Fig. 14. Plan of Central Boston, M. Wagner, 1942.

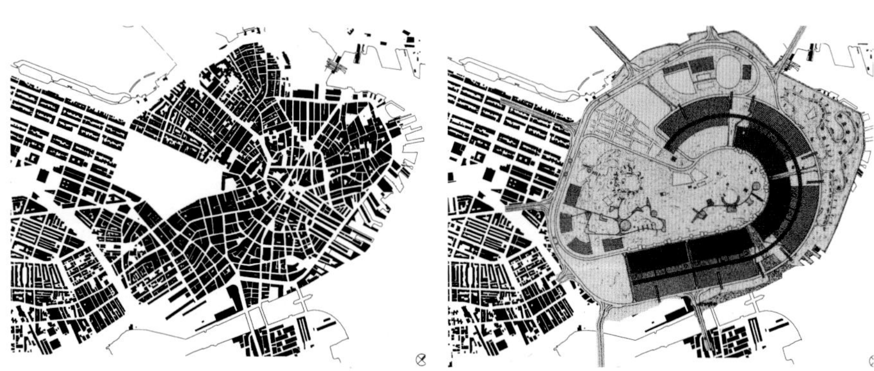

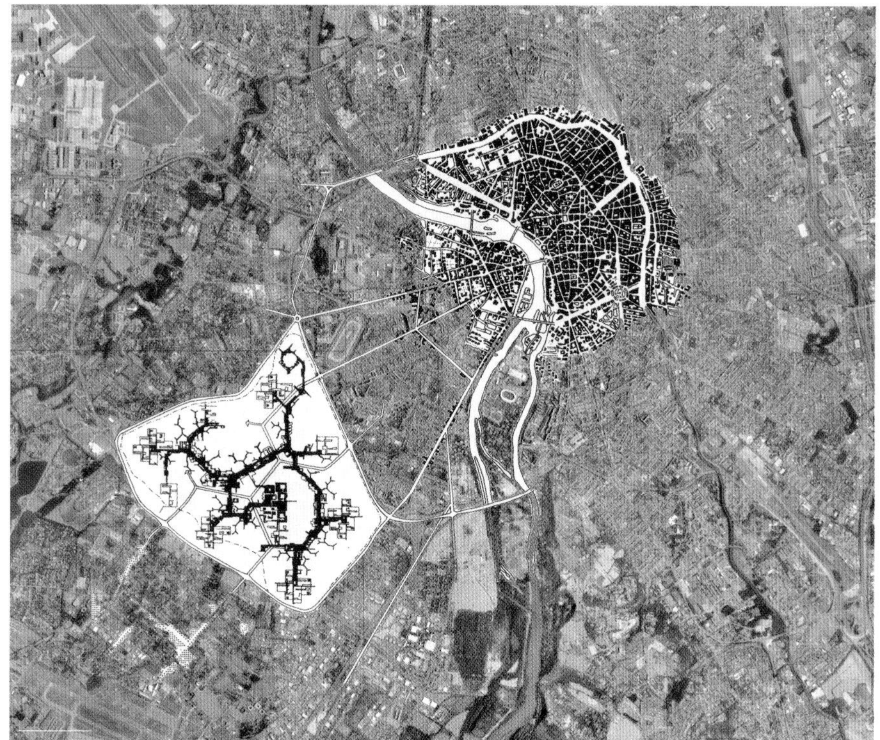

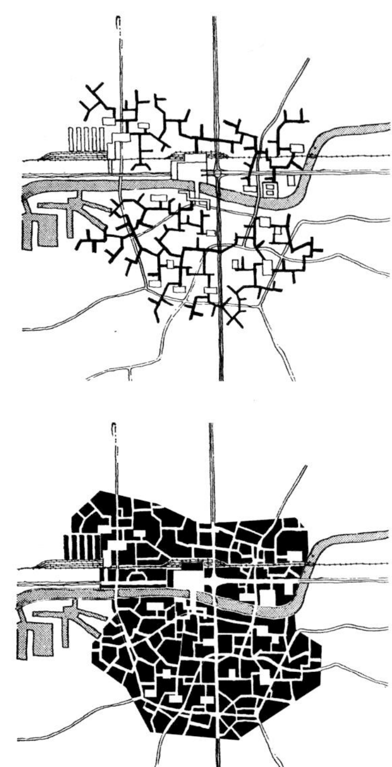

right inset:
Fig. 15. Plan of Toulouse Le Mirail, Candilis-Josic-Woods, 1961 (M. Dennis).

above:
Fig. 16. Cluster Plan, A. and P. Smithson, 1952

Fig. 17. Cluster Plan Reversed, 2017 (M. Dennis).

Team X and the Reversal of the Street

The work of Team X, the successors to CIAM, seems equally inexplicable today. Modernist ideas about the city were becoming increasingly discredited after WWII, but they were still being prominently promoted by Team X and others. Indeed, Mathias Ungers, who became the chair of Architecture at Cornell in 1968, brought many of the members of Team X to Cornell in 1972. Their arrogance was matched only by their righteous certainty about their ideas, despite their bizarreness.

The sectional rationalization of the street had been around for a long time, as had the idea of the building as a street. But, in 1952, Allison and Peter Smithson proposed an urban network of continuous buildings with "streets-in-the-air". This so-called "cluster plan" for the replacement of the city—as preposterous as it seems today—infected not only their colleagues, but students as well. It is as if the streets of a medieval town were made solid, and the blocks made voids. The pattern is irregular and picturesque, but, unfortunately, it doesn't work to reverse the traditional city (Fig. 16, 17).

Picking up the theme of "streets-in-the-air", in 1961, Candilis-Josic-Woods won the Toulouse Le Mirail competition for a community of 100,000 people outside Toulouse, France (Fig. 15). The scale of the project was immense. It was as large as the dense historic core of Toulouse. Only a portion of the project was included in the first phase of design, and only a portion of that was actually built. The project was an almost immediate failure for many reasons, and now much of the built portion has been demolished, leaving only remnants of the original idea. Today, it is a confusing mess.

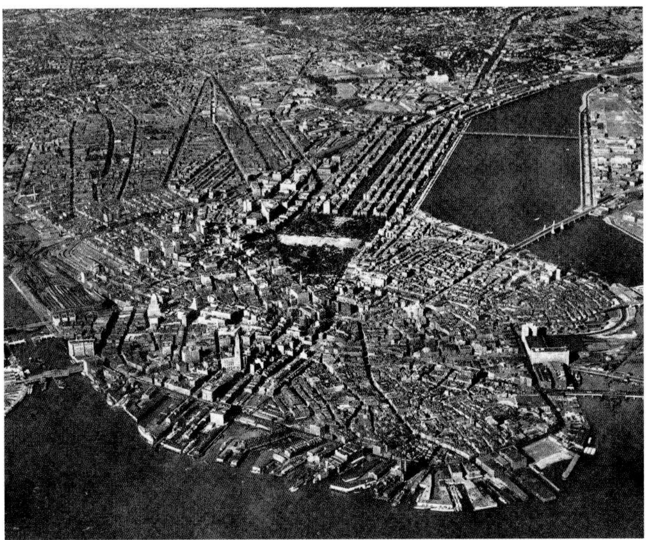

above left to right:
Fig. 18. Aerial view of Boston, 1930.

Fig. 19. Aerial view of Boston, 1960s.

opposite above left to right:
Fig. 20. Model of proposed plan for Boston, S. Minsk, K. Lynch and J. Myer, 1962.

Fig. 21. Hôtel de Beauvais, A. Le Pautre, 1654.

opposite below:
Fig. 22. Plan of Villa Malcontenta, A. Palladio, 1558–60.

Fig. 23. Plan of Villa Stein, Le Corbusier, 1927.

The Rediscovery of the City

American cities were largely intact following WWII, but a combination of Modernist urban theory fueled by urban "renewal" accomplished massive urban destruction that bombs did not. In contrast to the anti-urban Modernist principles of Le Corbusier, CIAM, and Team X, however, the traditional city was being rediscovered on several fronts.

Early contributors in the late 1950s and early 1960s were Kevin Lynch and Jack Myer, whose Boston urban design projects tried to repair the urban fabric ripped apart by urban renewal (Fig. 20), as well as Jane Jacobs, whose now-famous 1961 book, *The Death and Life of Great American Cities*, called attention to the human value of mixed-use neighborhoods of streets, blocks, and squares, and the destructive nature of freeways that cut through existing urban fabric.

During this period, Colin Rowe and the Cornell School emerged as one of three major centers of urban design revision—i.e., the "rediscovery of the city". The other two were Denise Scott Brown and the Philadelphia School, and the Krier brothers and the European Rationalist School.

Rowe and the Cornell Urban Design School

Colin Rowe established the Urban Design Studio at Cornell University in 1963 and continued to explore urban design ideas there until the 1980s. His seminal urban publication, *Collage City*, co-authored with Fred Koetter, was published in 1978. This was an auspicious period for urbanism, and for twenty years Rowe's urban studio was a fertile laboratory of urban design explorations, beginning with early attempts to make Modernist building types urbanistically biodegradable, and ending with more normative architectural and urban types. Throughout, there was an attempt to apply the complexities of Le Corbusier's architecture, and of Cubism, to urban design. Therein lies the dilemma, *and it is a fundamental one.*

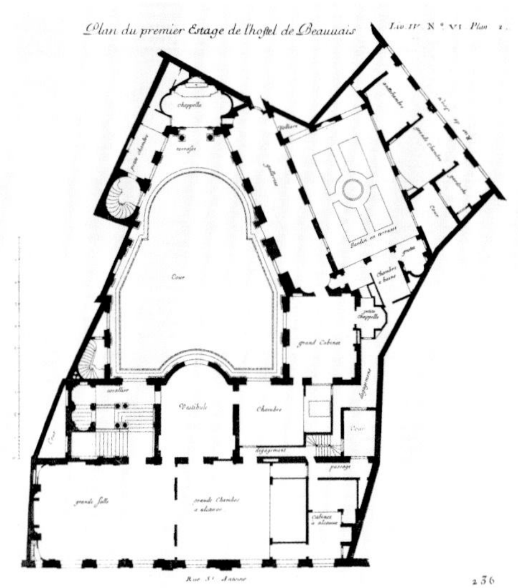

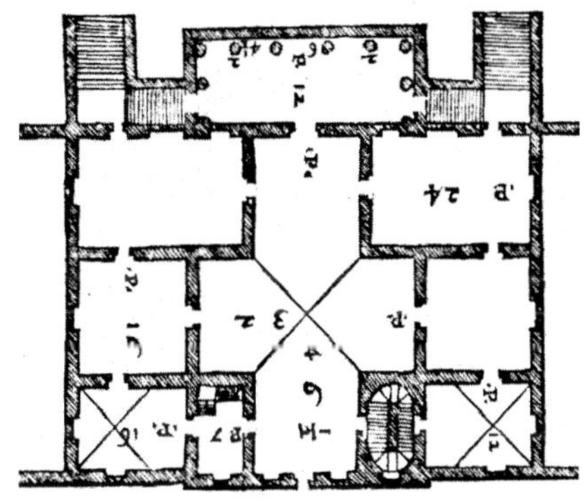

It can be argued that the things in which Rowe was most interested may perhaps be utilized in urban interventions, but not that they are appropriate for town planning. Rowe's most significant contribution, other than focusing attention on the city, may be a contribution to architecture and architectural theory, rather than town planning. Between 1947 and 1961, Rowe wrote eleven articles—some of seminal importance. Of these, only one, "Lockhart, Texas" (1955–56), written with John Hejduk, had even a glancing relationship to urbanism. His first article, "The Mathematics of the Ideal Villa" (1947) (Fig. 22, 23), illuminated a connection between Modern architecture and the past—the classical past— while his second, "Mannerism and Modern Architecture" (1950), was at the core of his thought. In Le Corbusier's architectural work, Rowe saw a Modern version of the relative, non-absolute, anti-canonical position of 16th century Italian Mannerism.

The late 17th century "Quarrel Between the Ancients and Moderns"—an argument for the timeless absolute canon of classicism versus its relativity—might now be seen as the rehearsal for the 20th century quarrel between the two strains of Modernism: between the canon of unified consistency of total design exhibited in the work of Wright, Van Doesburg, Gropius, and Hannes Meyer, and the simultaneous juxtaposition of rational and relative order in the work of Le Corbusier and Alvar Aalto. Those familiar with Rowe will of course recognize the parallel to Isaiah Berlin's "Hedgehog and Fox". If Le Corbusier the Architect was, for Rowe, a "fox", Le Corbusier the Town Planner was most certainly a "hedgehog". Thus, when Rowe's quest to rediscover the traditional city began in 1963—perhaps serendipitously—it should not be surprising that the techniques deployed to produce urbanism were largely derived from Cubism and the architectural complexities of Le Corbusier. Rowe also admired the tantalizing complexities of the French hôtels and recognized their relationship to the "highly sophisticated vestibules and boudoirs" of Le Corbusier's plans (Fig. 21). The hôtels have an inextricable relationship to irregular plans, however, and though they are not necessarily excluded from grid plans, they do not inherently produce them.

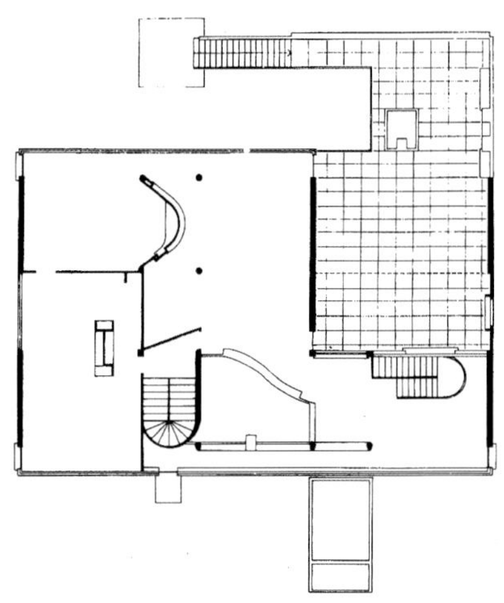

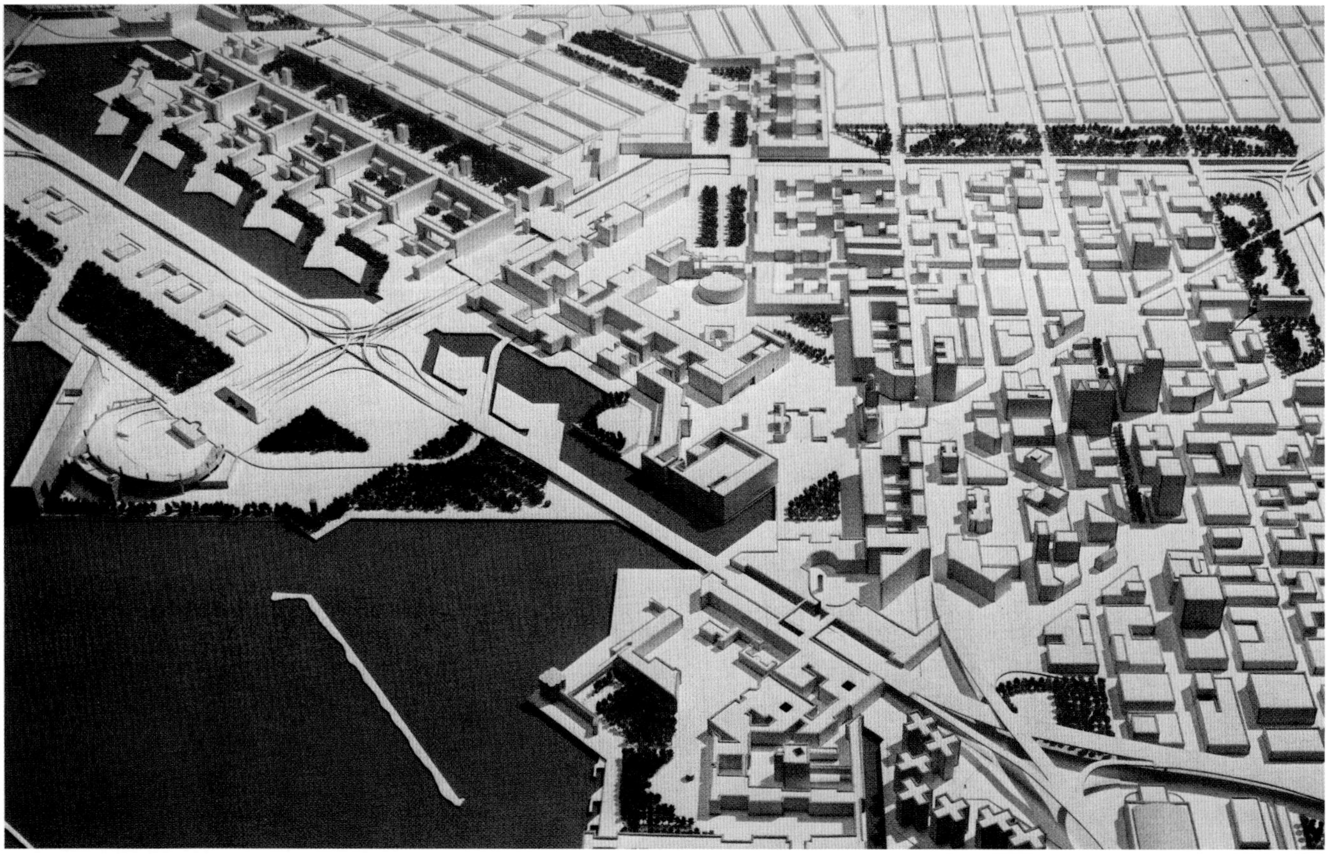

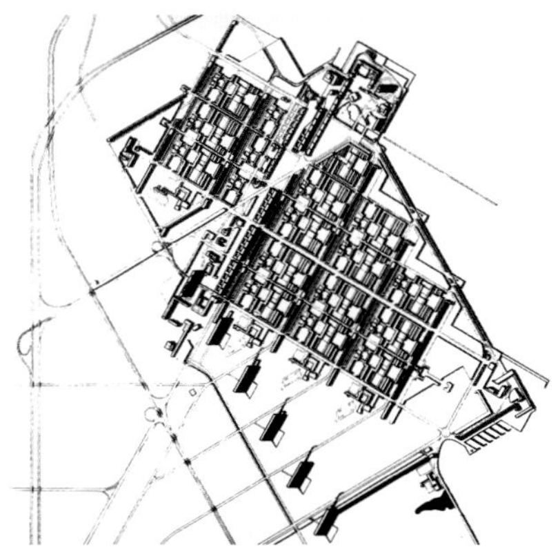

The Cornell Urban Design Studio

In many ways the 1966 project for the reconstruction of the Buffalo Waterfront was a watershed for Rowe's urban studio (Fig. 24). Prior to this project, the prevailing architectural language in the studio used the high-Modern typologies of slabs, wall buildings, and towers to produce urban fabric. The 1966 thesis project for a new town in South Amboy, New Jersey, by Tom Schumacher, is an early example (Fig. 25). Highly reminiscent of Le Corbusier's plan for Chandigarh, Schumacher's project gives no clues to future work in the studio.

The Buffalo project also used Modern, thin wall buildings to define courtyards and establish urban fabric to connect to the existing neighborhood, but, near the center, it used irregularly shaped blocks to form a coherent pattern of spaces, rather than a continuous pattern of urban blocks. A decade later, the Modernist buildings had disappeared from studio projects, and irregular buildings shaped a virtuoso display of urbanism. Around the same time—the late 1970s—the "Roma interrotta" project, described by Steven Peterson in "Urban Design Tactics", was an inspired explosion of urban ideas and tactics in the midst of mildly embarrassing performances by others (Fig. 26). Had the Cornell Studio continued, it is uncertain how it would have evolved, but one thing is certain: Rowe would never have developed a comprehensive idea of town design, such as Léon Krier did later.

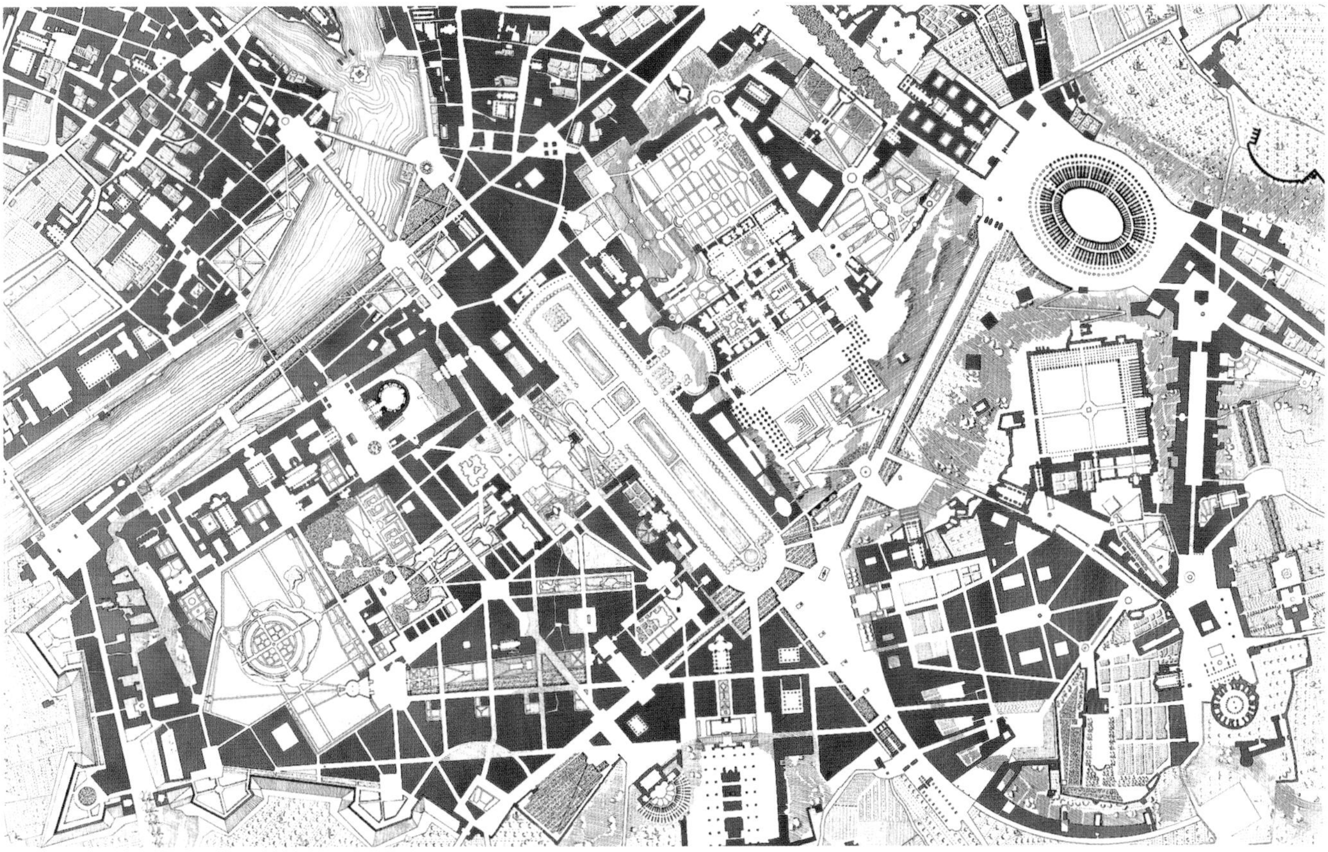

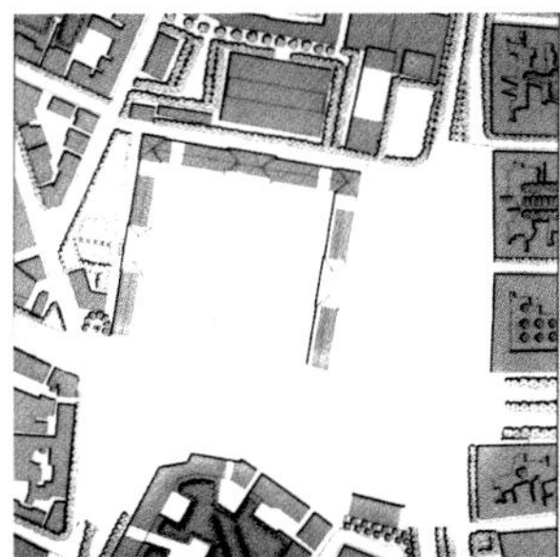

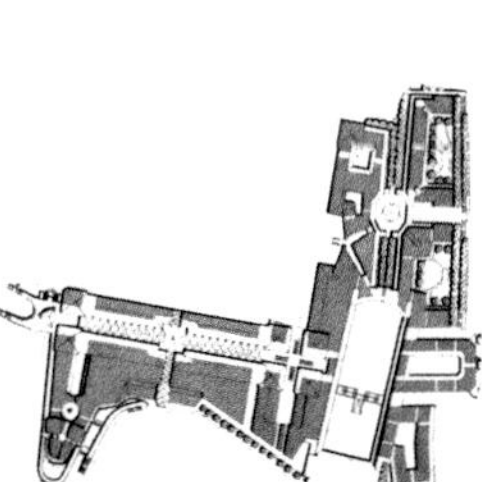

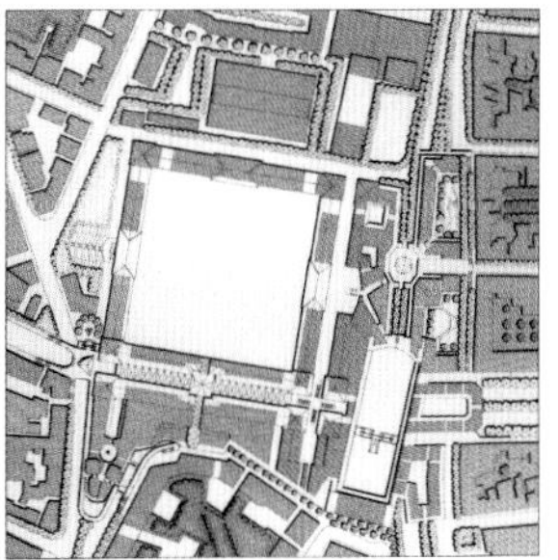

opposite above:
Fig. 24. Model view of Buffalo Waterfront, Colin Rowe Urban Design Studio, Cornell University, 1966.

opposite below:
Fig. 25. Thesis project, South Amboy, T. Schumacher, 1966.

above:
Fig. 26. Plan for "Roma interrotta", C. Rowe, S. Peterson, J. Di Maio, and P. Carl, 1978.

below:
Fig. 27. Proposed plan for Rotebühl Platz, Stüttgart, R. Krier, 1975.

Rob Krier and Stüttgart

At that time at Cornell, there was a strong affinity for the work of Rob Krier, and it is difficult to overstate the impact of his publication of *Stadtraum* in 1975 (published in English as *Urban Space* in 1979, with a foreword by Colin Rowe). Therein were illustrated a series of urban interventions that reconstructed the tattered city of Stüttgart (Fig. 27). The Stüttgart sites were irregular and fragmented, and the urban design techniques were those cherished at Cornell. The tactics were more appropriate to European cities than to American ones, but we were envious of that as well. Rob's Stüttgart projects used regular spaces and irregular blocks to engage the city. Thus, his projects were at once set-pieces and urban fabric at the same time.

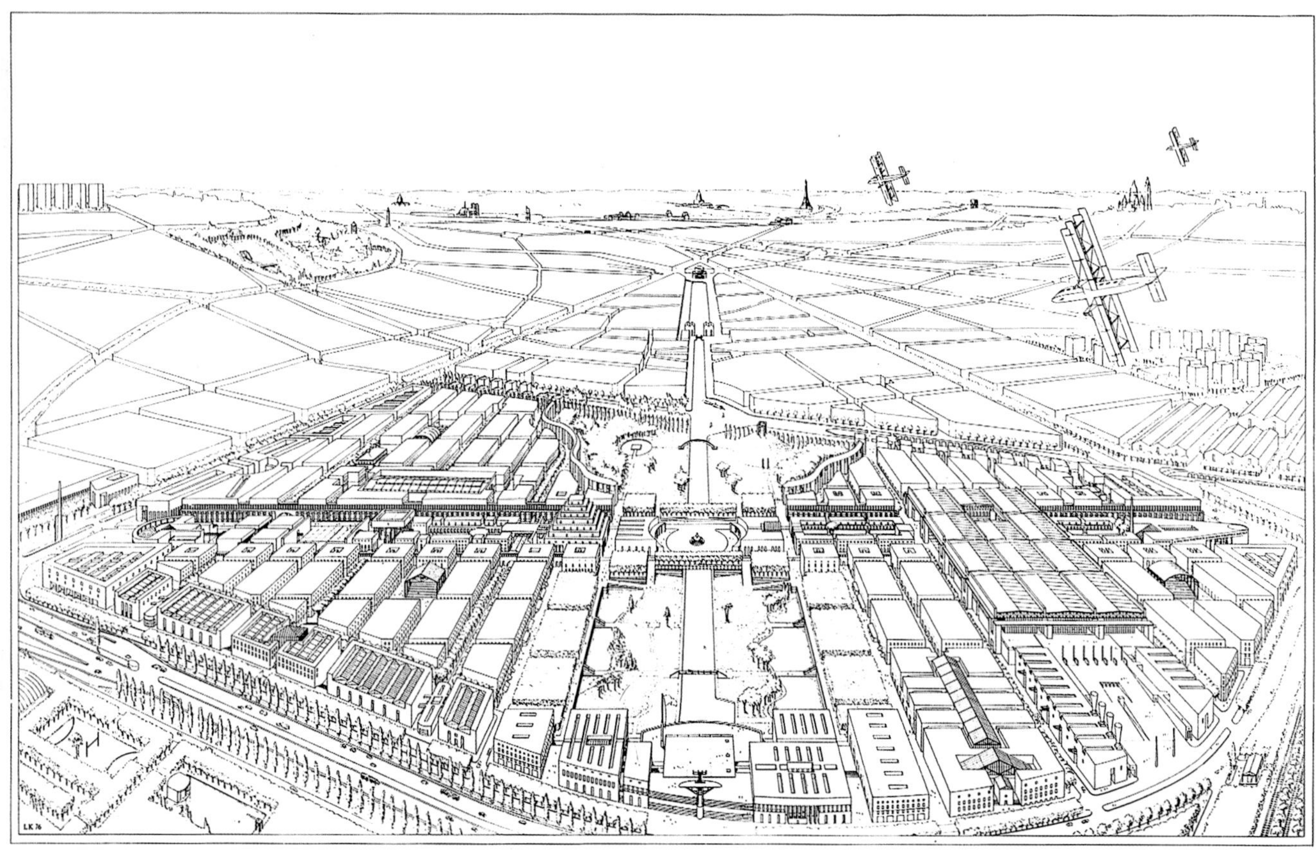

Fig. 28. Aerial perspective of La Villette, Léon Krier, 1976.

The Rationalist movement in Europe was massively important, but with the passage of time, the clearest urban voice to emerge was that of Léon Krier. Others, such as Maurice Culot and the School of La Cambre in Belgium, were—like Rob Krier—involved with reconstruction through "urban interventions". Aldo Rossi reexamined architecture's role in the city. But it was Léon that attacked the idea of the whole city. As Andrés Duany observed:

> *What Leo actually did at the crucial point in the '60s and early '70s was that he pulled the trigger and actually drew the entire city. No one for 40 years had drawn the city. The project at La Villette was the first time that all of the elements of the city—the streets, the roads, the civic buildings, the mixed-use, the places to work—first appeared.*

The project for La Villette was urban design on the level of town planning, not urban intervention, and Léon went on to outline the revisionist principles of the city (Fig. 28). These early projects adhered to the time-honored principles of grid planning that had existed for at least 2,500 years. Up until this time, there were no irregular planned towns, but that was about to change.

To reiterate: there have been planned towns (grids), and cumulative cities. But there have also been composite cities such as Jaipur and Palermo, and these are inspiring. If Jaipur is a grid plan that gradually became a composite city, Palermo is a city of circumstance that became a composite city.

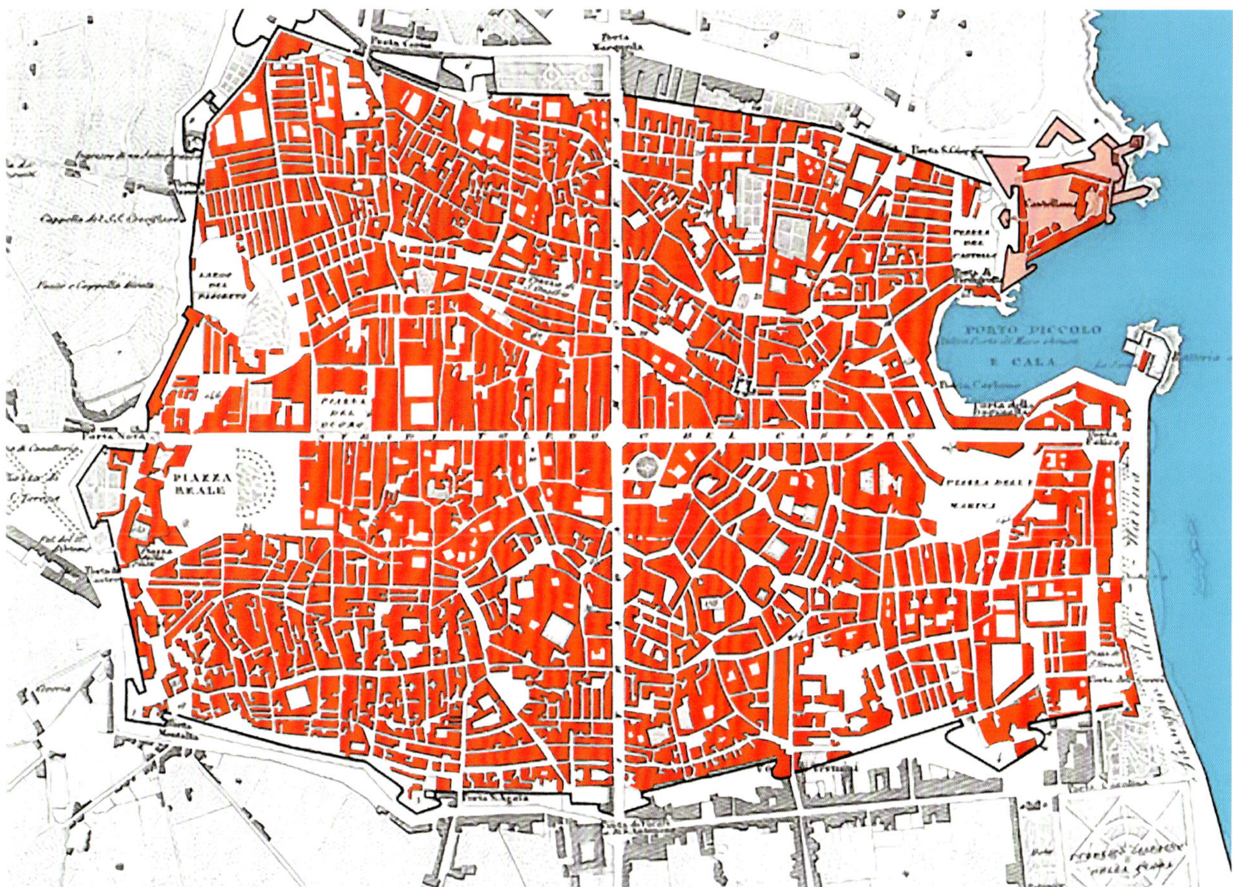

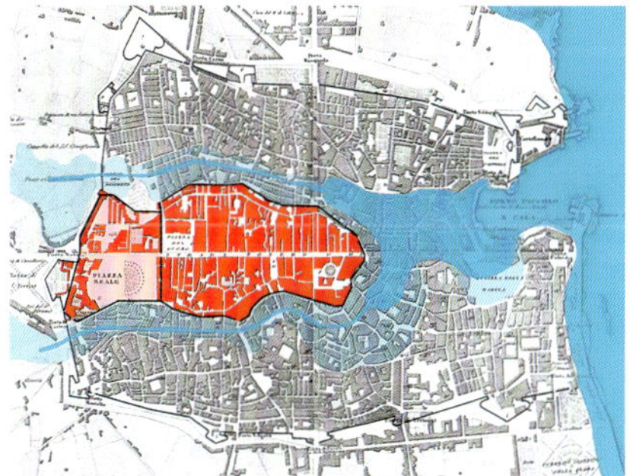

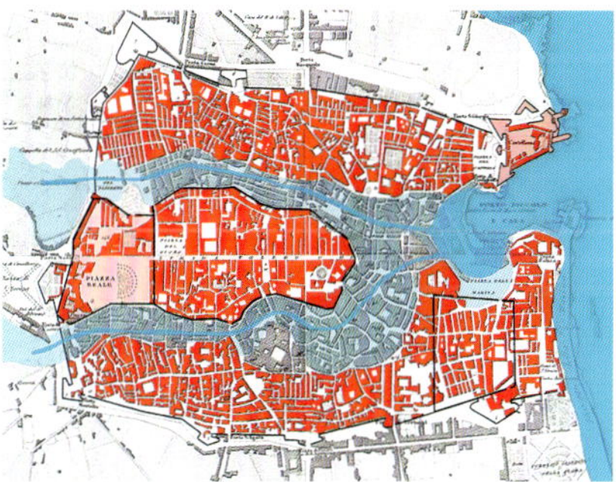

above:
Fig. 29. Palermo, plan of the 19th century city.

below left to right:
Fig. 30. Palermo, plan of the Phoenician city of Neapols.

Fig. 31. Palermo, plan of the Arab city.

Before there was the city of Palermo, there was a lake, two rivers, and a harbor. The original Phoenician settlement was a fortified area on the high ground between the rivers. This settlement was extended down to the harbor, and the expanded city became known as "The Phoenician Foot" (Fig. 30). This was the extent of the city throughout the Roman Empire. After the Arabs conquered Sicily in the 9th century, they began to have trouble with the native population and established a fortified area near the harbor. Gradually, the areas outside the rivers were built up (Fig. 31). In the 15th century, the rivers were diverted or channeled, and the valleys were filled in. The central spine was extended to the sea in the late 16th century, and in 1605, the cardo was cut through. This was the extent of the city until the mid-19th century (Fig. 29).

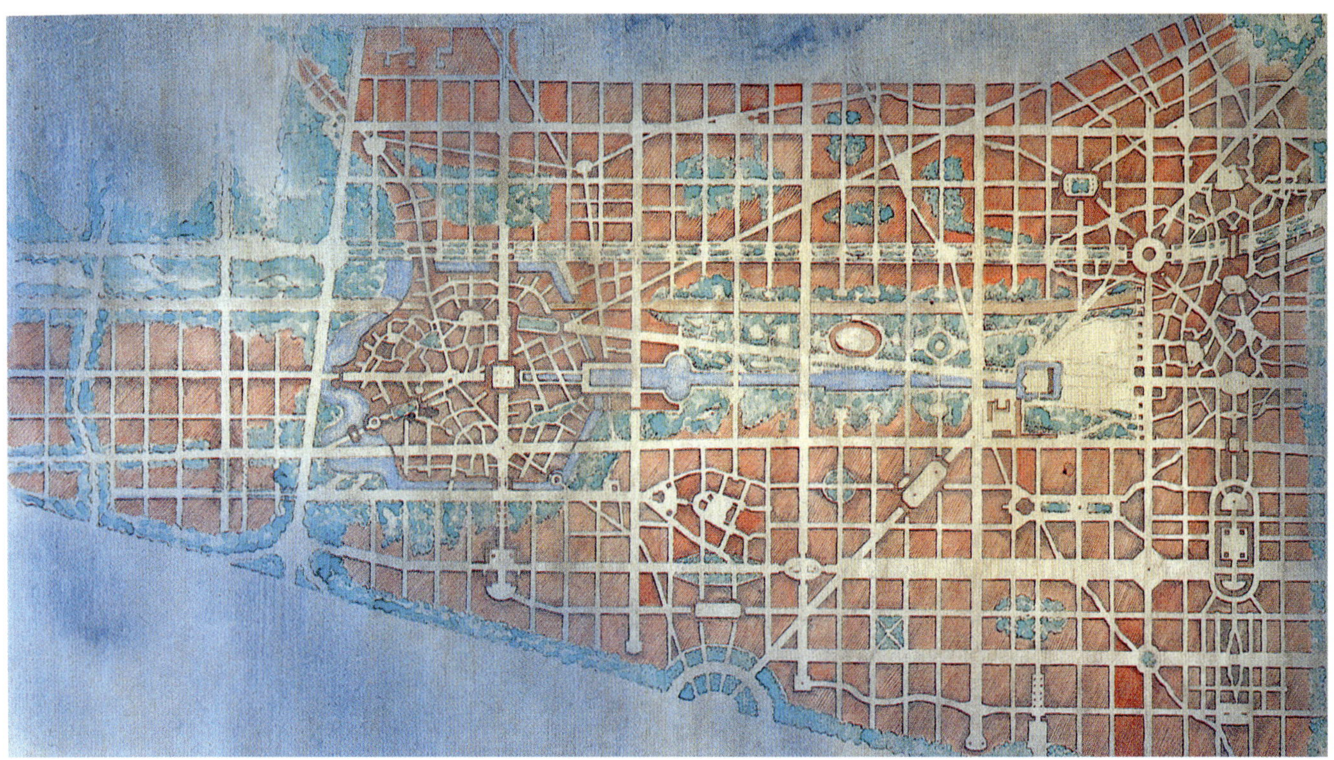

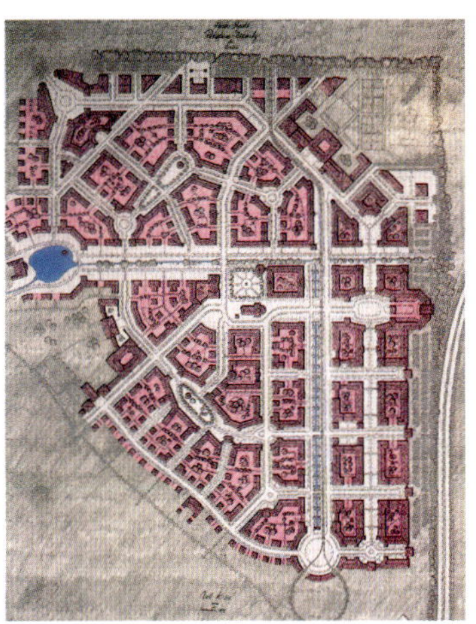

Irregular Plans

Rob Krier's plan for Bussy-Saint-Georges is surprising (Fig. 32). A large-scale grid had already been established by the planning authority when Rob entered the process. In order to articulate and enliven the mega-grid, he established distinct districts by making smaller blocks, reintroducing site paths and diagonals, and expanding the water system. Two districts in particular were planned as a quasi-medieval fabric of irregular blocks and picturesque streets, crossed and stabilized by a cardo and decumanus.

The same formal strategy was initially used for the Kirchsteigfeld competition for a new community outside Potsdam. The first concept plan was, like Palermo, an irregular plan crossed by a cardo and decumanus (Fig. 33). As the competition workshop developed, the plan became more regular, and the cardo and decumanus disappeared. In the final plan, the streets are wider, and the blocks are more regular, with the interiors of the blocks more open to the streets (Fig. 34). Somehow, one wishes that the sequence was reversed, but contemporary demands for the automobile still dictate planning strategy. Much of this project was built out—with buildings by Krier, Kohl, and other architects—but the project was stopped by the financial crisis of 2008.

The rediscovery of the city shortly after WWII, has engendered countless planning efforts that continue today, but, as in that post-war period, the anti-urban hegemony of architecture over urbanism also continues. Indeed, today, it may again be the norm.

Contemporary Urban and Environmental Issues

Despite our fantasies about Rowe and cities, evidence suggests that not much has really changed in the last hundred years—unless things have gotten worse. Even (perhaps especially) famous architects vie for producing the most vulgar anti-urban buildings. The term "urban" has not only been articulated away from architecture, but from the city as well. Urban used to be synonymous with "city", but now city is defined by population, not by character. Too many "cities" are not urban at all. Just look at China, or Dubai. Contemporary urbanism is the result of the current status quo—of 100 years of increased population, vehicular circulation, resource consumption, and waste. But the parameters of the near future will be radically different from the parameters of the past century, and the present.

The world is facing unprecedented environmental challenges, and urbanity and density are the solution, not the problem. Cities like Rome, Paris, and Manhattan are the most ecologically efficient forms of human habitation on a per capita basis. We should not need an excuse for this kind of urbanity, but very soon we will be forced to live smaller, closer, and more simply. Otherwise, human and animal life on our planet will likely become extinct, making the disintegration of the Roman Empire seem like a pleasant interlude.

No one knows what the future city will be like, but just possibly, it might look a lot like Rome—dense, compact, irregular, and with urban architecture and public spaces (Fig. 35).

opposite above:
Fig. 32. Marne-la-Vallée plan, Paris, Rob Krier, 1989.

opposite below:
Fig. 33. Preliminary plan for Kirchsteigfeld, Rob Krier, 1991.

Fig. 34. Final plan for Kirchsteigfeld, Rob Krier, 1991.

above:
Fig. 35. Panoramic view of Rome from St. Peter's dome.

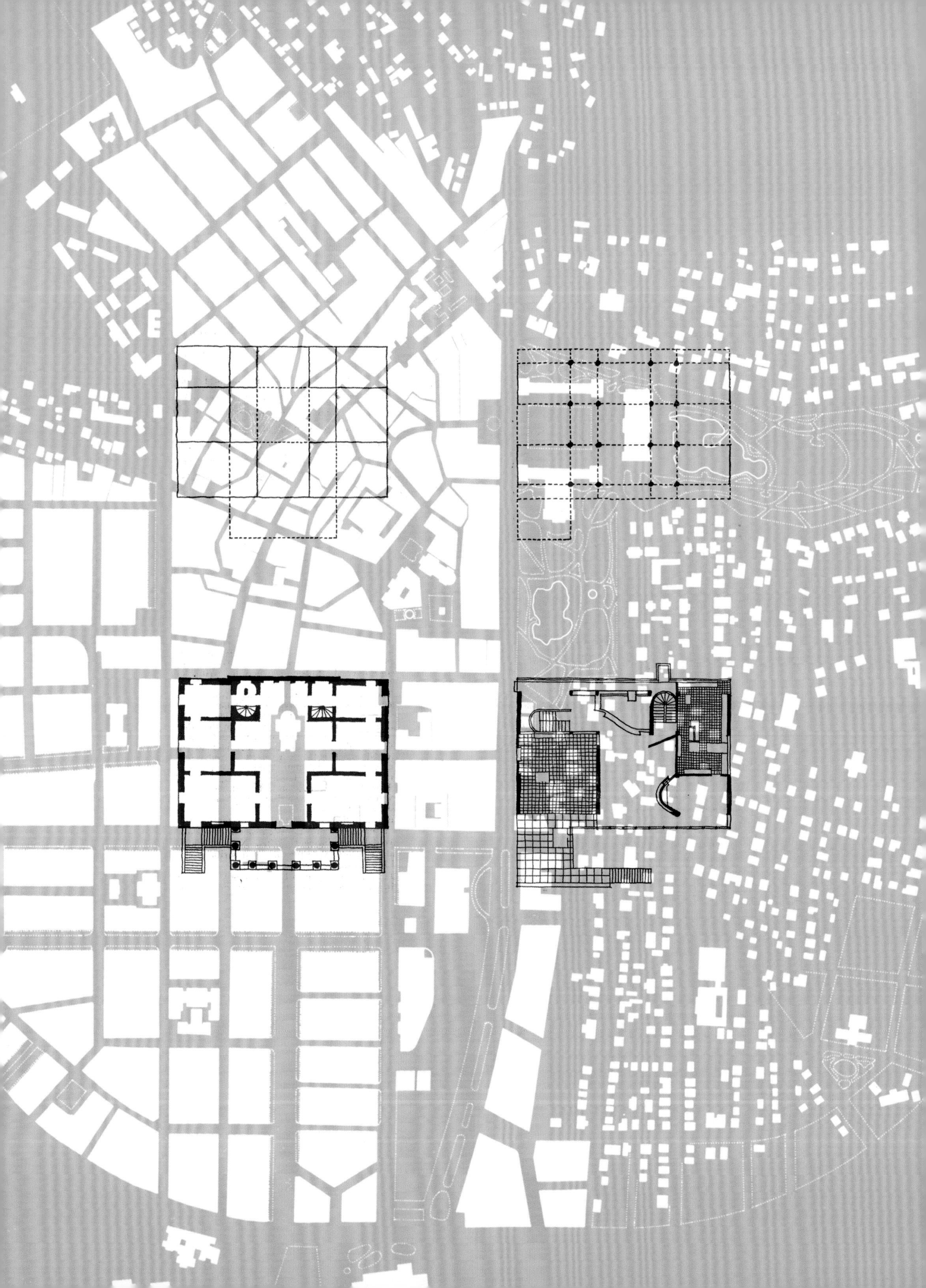

From "Mathematics" to "Urbanistics"

Antonio Pietro Latini

alla memoria di Paolo Avarello

frontispiece:
Superimposition of diagrams from the "The Mathematics of the Ideal Villa" and figure/ground reversal drawing of Wiesbaden by Wayne Copper. Graphic design by J. Tice.

The disciplinary development of Colin Rowe and the various but remarkably consistent production of the "creative group"[1] that consolidated around him, starting in the 1960s, were among the main factors of a broadly shared and largely successful disciplinary attempt. A recognizable structure was restored to the urban design praxis; values and methodological tools were provided and effectively deployable for use in a wide range of applications.

Principles and design rationales, both products of this development, are elements of a system that starts emerging in the late 1940s and is transformed by addition during the next twenty-five years. Like the neck of an hourglass, Rowe and his circle seem to have been able to accumulate, select, and use for reference a generous and yet complex and contradictory tangle of ideas, concepts, methods, and models, variously available in a world of cultural dynamics. Cleverly compared, combined, and conflated, and despite their resistance to a linear reading, these ideas were subsequently spread through the multiple forms and geographies of physical, academic, and professional venues.

Thus, Rowe's extraordinary stand seems to rest, not on the originality of his inventions, but on his exceptional ability to contribute to the needs of design—and especially urban design—by making a system out of different pieces of knowledge, of combinations and of rationales found in the disciplinary and broader cultural debate. He was not a counter-current intellectual, then. Rather, he was unique in funnelling the vigor of the theoretical turbulence of the time to the use of design.

"Mathematics"

Colin Rowe published his first essay, "The Mathematics of the Ideal Villa", in the March 1947 issue of *The Architectural Review*[2] (Fig. 1). It was destined to have multiple impacts: on a new way of looking at Modern Architecture, on

1 Here I adopt the expression "creative group" in the sense described in De Masi, Domenico, ed., *L'emozione e la regola. I gruppi creativi in Europa dal 1850 al 1950*, Editori Laterza, Roma – Bari, 1989, because it seems to me particularly apt to indicate the collective activity and the dynamics of Rowe's group before, during, and after his tenure at Cornell University.

2 Rowe, Colin, "The Mathematics of the Ideal Villa. Palladio and Le Corbusier compared", *The Architectural Review* CI (603), Mar 1947: 101-04, also in Rowe, Colin, *The Mathematics of the Ideal Villa and Other Essays*, MIT Press, Cambridge, MA, and London, 1976: 1-27.

The Mathematics of the Ideal Villa

Palladio and Le Corbusier compared

"There are two causes of beauty—natural and customary. Natural is from geometry consisting in uniformity, that is equality, and proportion. Customary beauty is begotten by the use, as familiarity breeds a love to things not in themselves lovely. Here lies the great occasion of errors, but always the true test is natural or geometrical beauty. Geometrical figures are naturally more beautiful than irregular ones: the square, the circle are the most beautiful, next the parallelogram and the oval. There are only two beautiful positions of straight lines, perpendicular and horizontal; this is from Nature and consequently necessity, no other than upright being firm." *SIR CHRISTOPHER WREN*

By Colin Rowe

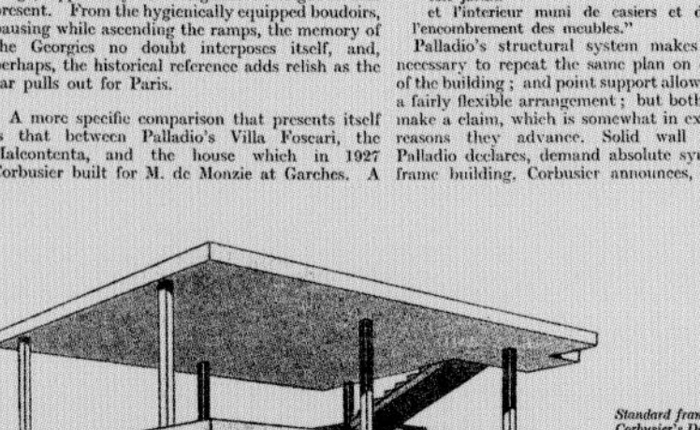

Standard framework, of Le Corbusier's Domino House, designed in 1914 for mass-production, which shows how the quality of partial paralysis inherent in the plan of solid wall buildings such as Palladio's Villa Malcontenta is in reinforced concrete structure transferred to the section.

Villa Malcontenta

The modular grid, plan and section of Palladio's Villa Malcontenta below provide a revealing comparison with those of the villa by Le Corbusier opposite. For all their differences of style and construction, in the mathematical basis of their design these two buildings have an important factor in common.

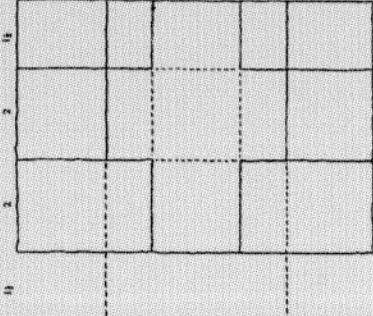

modular grid

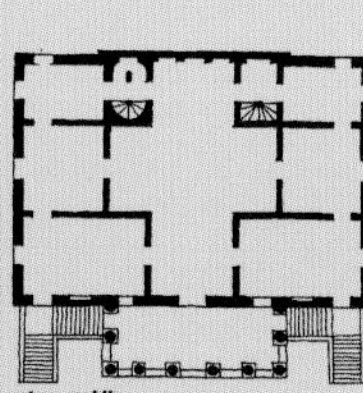

piano nobile

elevation

the development of architectural culture, and on the making of architecture itself, particularly English architecture.[3] Of course, it was bound to cause much disappointment in opposing theoretical camps as, for example, testified by the influential critic Reyner Banham.[4]

"Mathematics" was nurtured in the cradle of the Warburg Institute where, beginning in the 1920s, neo-Platonic inclinations had developed, and architecture was seen as science. It had been fertilized by the crystalline theoretical construction of Rudolf Wittkower, Rowe's advisor, and preceded by Wittkower's essays which had been published in the organ of the Institute and, after two years, would be collected in *Architectural Principles in the Age of Humanism*[5] (Fig. 2).

The most direct effect of "Mathematics" seems to have been as a formidable tool to strengthen and give profundity to that deep-rooted inclination of architecture's theory and methodology based on modulation, proportion, and essential geometry. Jean Nicolas Louis Durand, Ludwig Mies van der Rohe, and Le Corbusier had pursued different paths with this approach. Le Corbusier published his first book on the *Modulor* in 1948,[6] the result of an active interest since at least 1942[7] (Fig. 3). His lecture in which the Modulor system was given its name was held on December 18th, 1947, at the Architectural Association in London.[8] Its philosophy was disclosing the rationale for architecture structured around geometry and nature (Fig. 3).

3 Jencks, Charles, *Modern Movements in Architecture*, Anchor Books Edition, Garden City, 1973: 249-52.

4 Caragonne, Alexander, "Editor's note", in Rowe, Colin, *As I Was Saying, Recollections and Miscellaneous Essays* 1, "Texas, Pre-Texas, Cambridge", (Caragonne, Alexander, ed.), MIT Press, Cambridge, MA, and London, 1996: ix-x.

5 Out of the four chapters of which *Architectural Principles* is made, three had substantially been published as articles between 1940 and 1945. Wittkower, Rudolf, "Alberti's Approach to Antiquity in Architecture", *Journal of the Warburg and Courtauld Institutes* 4 (1/2), Oct 1940 – Jan 41: 1-18; Idem, "Principles of Palladio's Architecture", *Journal of the Warburg and Courtauld Institutes* 7, 1944: 102-22; Idem, "Principles of Palladio's Architecture-II", *Journal of the Warburg and Courtauld Institutes* 8, 1945: 68-106. Payne, Alina A., "Rudolf Wittkower and Architectural Principles in the Age of Modernism", *Journal of the Society of Architectural Historians* LIII (3), Sep 1994: 325n; Idem, *Rudolf Wittkower*, Bollati Boringhieri editore, Torino, 2011: 16 and 50n (orig. "Rudolf Wittkower", in Pfisterer, Ulrich, ed., *Klassiker der Kunstgeschichte* II, C. H. Beck, München, 2008: 107-23).

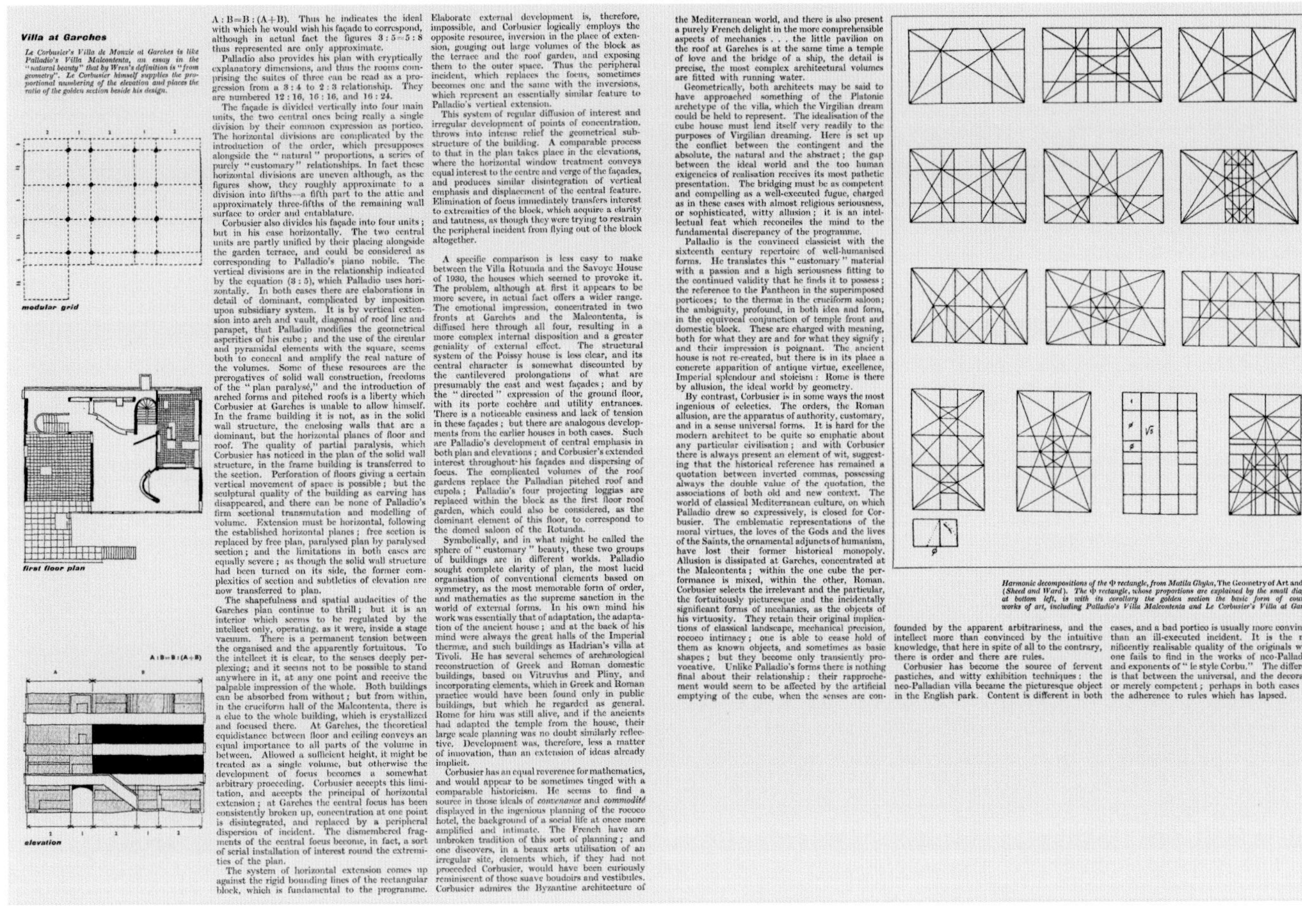

Villa at Garches

Le Corbusier's Villa de Monzie at Garches is like Palladio's Villa Malcontenta, an essay in the "natural beauty" that by Wren's definition is "from geometry". Le Corbusier himself supplies the proportional numbering of the elevation and places the ratio of the golden section beside his design.

A : B=B : (A+B). Thus he indicates the ideal with which he would wish his façade to correspond, although in actual fact the figures 3 : 5=5 : 8 thus represented are only approximate.

Palladio also provides his plan with cryptically explanatory dimensions, and thus the rooms comprising the suites of three can be read as a progression from a 3 : 4 to 2 : 3 relationship. They are numbered 12 : 16, 16 : 16, and 16 : 24.

The façade is divided vertically into four main units, the two central ones being really a single division by their common expression as portico. The horizontal divisions are complicated by the introduction of the order, which presupposes alongside the "natural" proportions, a series of purely "customary" relationships. In fact these horizontal divisions are uneven although, as the figures show, they roughly approximate to a division into fifths—a fifth part to the attic and approximately three-fifths of the remaining wall surface to order and entablature.

Corbusier also divides his façade into four units; but in his case horizontally. The two central units are partly unified by their placing alongside the garden terrace, and could be considered as corresponding to Palladio's piano nobile. The vertical divisions are in the relationship indicated by the equation (3 : 5), which Palladio uses horizontally. In both cases there are elaborations in detail of dominant, complicated by imposition upon subsidiary system. It is by vertical extension into arch and vault, diagonal of roof line and parapet, that Palladio modifies the geometrical asperities of his cube; and the use of the circular and pyramidal elements with the square, seems both to conceal and amplify the real nature of the volumes. Some of these resources are the prerogatives of solid wall construction, freedoms of the "plan paralysé," and the introduction of arched forms and pitched roofs is a liberty which Corbusier at Garches is unable to allow himself. In the frame building it is not, as in the solid wall structure, the enclosing walls that are a dominant, but the horizontal planes of floor and roof. The quality of partial paralysis, which Corbusier has noticed in the plan of the solid wall structure, in the frame building is transferred to the section. Perforation of floors giving a certain vertical movement of space is possible; but the sculptural quality of the building as carving has disappeared, and there can be none of Palladio's firm sectional transmutation and modelling of volume. Extension must be horizontal, following the established horizontal planes; free section is replaced by free plan, paralysed plan by paralysed section; and the limitations in both cases are equally severe; as though the solid wall structure had been turned on its side, the former complexities of section and subtleties of elevation are now transferred to plan.

The shapefulness and spatial audacities of the Garches plan continue to thrill; but it is an interior which seems to be regulated by the intellect only, operating, as it were, inside a stage vacuum. There is a permanent tension between the organised and the apparently fortuitous. To the intellect it is clear, to the senses deeply perplexing; and it seems not to be possible to stand anywhere in it, at any one point and receive the palpable impression of the whole. Both buildings can be absorbed from without; but from within, in the cruciform hall of the Malcontenta, there is a clue to the whole building, which is crystallized and focused there. At Garches, the theoretical equidistance between floor and ceiling conveys an equal importance to all parts of the volume in between. Allowed a sufficient height, it might be treated as a single volume, but otherwise the development of focus becomes a somewhat arbitrary proceeding. Corbusier accepts this limitation, and accepts the principal of horizontal extension; at Garches the central focus has been consistently broken up, concentration at one point is disintegrated, and replaced by a peripheral dispersion of incident. The dismembered fragments of the central focus become, in fact, a sort of serial installation of interest round the extremities of the plan.

The system of horizontal extension comes up against the rigid bounding lines of the rectangular block, which is fundamental to the programme.

Fig. 1. Facsimile of the original text, "The Mathematics of the Ideal Villa", *The Architectural Review*, Colin Rowe, 1947.

Meanwhile, Wittkower was highlighting and articulating the geometric roots of historic architecture in its highest representation: that of the 'white' Renaissance of Alberti, Leonardo, and Palladio. Relying on the solidity of geometry and on the authority of history, Wittkower was implicitly legitimizing the transformation that had long been completed by Modern architecture into an *autonomous* product.[9] As Renaissance architecture before it, Modern architecture could very well be organized around its internal *mathematical* relations and thus arguably be exempt from having to represent "place and occasion": in principle, it could be beyond both *Zeitgeist* and *genius loci*, and therefore at least partly sempiternal and fully *international*.

The *rapprochement* between the field of the historians and the field of the designers under the flags of architecture's autonomy—of both Renaissance and Modern architecture—was already solid and tangible in Rowe's 1947 synthesis in which architecture could reclaim authoritativeness and independence. So, the "peculiar discrepancy between theory and the so-called 'modern movement'", as Paul Zucker would later phrase it,[10] could be partially reconsidered. While architects declared they were expressing functionalist ideas, in reality it was conceptual forms that were the deep principle underlying their designs. This was analogous to what had been claimed by aestheticians—mainly those from the German tradition of the first quarter of the century.

6 Le Corbusier, *Le Modulor. Essai sur une mesure harmonique à l'échelle humaine applicable universellement à l'architecture et à la mécanique*, Editions de l'Architecture d'Aujourd'hui, Boulogne, 1948.

7 Tentori, Francesco, *Vita e opere di Le Corbusier*, Laterza, Roma – Bari, (1979) 1980: 117 and Payne (1994): 341n.

8 Payne (1994): 338n.

9 Payne's (2011) argument on this subject, especially: 23-24.

10 Zucker, Paul, "The Paradox of Architectural Theories at the Beginning of the 'Modern Movement'", *Journal of the Society of Architectural Historians* 10 (3), Oct 1951: 8-14.

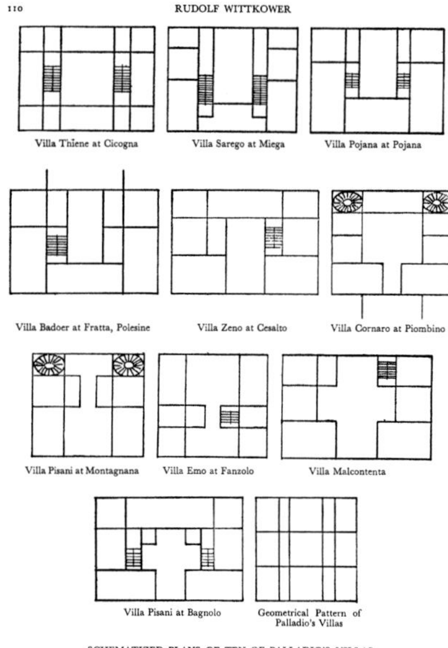

Fig. 2. Schematized plans of ten of Palladio's villas, Rudolf Wittkower, 1944.

"Mathematics" was providing a cultural backbone and intellectual *allure* to the stereometric Modernist production by showing its connection to the noblest of disciplinary historical periods. At the same time, its reliance on Palladio's legacy and on the whole sequence of geometric composition in architecture after Vitruvius, Leonardo, and Alberti, was asserting the immanent validity of Modern architecture. By disclosing Le Corbusier's intellectual genealogy, Rowe was adding to the equipment of Modern Architecture's logic and offering an effective methodological reference for architectural design. Most of all, while revealing the compositional watermarks of architectural plans and elevations, Rowe was defending the Modern Movement from charges of blandishments and reductionist arbitrariness. In this case architectural significance was relying on an activity of abstraction rather than inclusion—analogously attributed to both the Renaissance's and the Modern Movement's stylistic choices. His reading would unveil the complexity—interpreted as phenomenological depth—of Modern design, even though such complexity was confined to the realm of a scholarly culture of forms. Thus, the freedom of the *plan libre* was neither random nor wanton.

—

"Mathematics" not only placed Rowe in a partisan standing, supporting *de facto* Modern orthodoxy, but also made him the prime mover of a resurgent spirit of neo-classicist, neo-Platonic, neo-geometrical, neo-rationalist rigor. Nothing could be more antithetical than the English neo-Palladians, leaning on Rowe's theory, to the Townscape vulgate which, after appearing in the 1930s, was being consolidated in *The Architectural Review* and in general in Britain beginning in the mid-1940s. While the *Review* and its conceptual strongmen, Nikolaus Pevsner and James Maude Richards, were representing the architectural establishment, Rowe—together with Alison and Peter Smithson, Alan Colquhoun, and Reyner Banham—was the younger alternative avant-garde, as depicted by Banham himself while describing the "English architectural polemics" of those years.[11]

Conversely, looking more broadly, nothing seems more distant than Rowe's influential standing from the reformist attitude producing the accolade for the Scandinavian neo-empiricism, variously sponsored in and out of CIAM, notably by English teams,[12] and, on the Italian side, from Bruno Zevi's organic, pro-Wright and neo-humanist position. Nothing could be further away than Rowe's intellectual demonstrations from the concern about the lack of attractiveness of Modern Architecture for "the man in the street" expressed by Hubert de Cronin Hastings and Richards in the *Review* from the 1940s on and treated in the CIAM discourse in the 1947 VI congress in Bridgwater and again in the 1953 IX congress in Aix-en-Provence.[13]

A dualistic interpretation of the English architectural scene along these lines was to be proposed a decade later, in a 1957 article by James Stirling, "Regionalism and Modern Architecture". This is especially relevant to this argument if Colin Rowe had some role in its formulation.[14] In Stirling's text, two "styles or minor movements" are considered. "The first style, *which probably reached its peak about 1950-54*, has been termed 'neo-Palladian'" and derives from Wittkower's theories and from Le Corbusier's Modulor. Rowe is not mentioned. "This style is in

11 Banham, Reyner, "Revenge of the Picturesque: English Architectural Polemics, 1945-1965", in Summerson, John, ed., *Concerning Architecture: Essays on Architectural Writers and Writing Presented to Nikolaus Pevsner*, Allen Lane, London, 1968: 265-73. Also, Macarthur, John, "'The revenge of the picturesque', redux", *The Journal of Architecture* 17 (5), 2012: 643-53.

12 Richards, J[ames] M[aude], "The New Empiricism. Sweden's Latest Style", *The Architectural Review* CI (606), Jun 1947: 199-204.

13 For an inclusive reference on humanization of Modern Architecture, on the New Empiricism, and on the critiques advanced by Zevi, Mumford, Eric, *The CIAM Discourse on Urbanism, 1928-1960*, MIT Press, Cambridge, MA, and London, 2000, in particular: 163-68, 198-200.

14 Stirling, James, "Regionalism and Modern Architecture", *Architects' Year Book* 7, 1957: 62-68, now in Ockman, Joan, *Architecture Culture 1943-1968: A Documentary Anthology*, Columbia Books of Architecture/Rizzoli, New York, 1993: 243-48 and in Canizaro, Vincent B., ed., *Architectural Regionalism: Collected Writings on Place, Identity, Modernity, and Tradition*, Princeton Architectural Press, New York, 2007: 327-30. Here: 451, Thomas Muirhead's hypothesis of Rowe's involvement in this article is reported (italics are mine). Dualisms analogous to the one represented in this article were fairly common, with multiple labelling and variations, in the post-WWII architectural debates. As an example, in the U.S. environment, during the MoMA February 11, 1948 symposium, referred to below, the two "points of view" were labeled "International Style" and "New Empiricism/Bay Region".

decline in some of the schools ...", Stirling specifies. Regarding the second style: "*The more recent trend* in many ways is a reaction from the former and could be considered a reassessment of indigenous and usually anonymous building ...". An example of this inclination can be found in "Le Corbusier's assimilation of Mediterranean domestic and native Indian architecture" and in the "anonymous architecture of Italy" as depicted in "Kidder Smith's recent book, *Italy Builds*".[15]

Fig. 3. Modulor Man, *Poem of the Right Angle*, Le Corbusier, 1955.

Rowe's availability to be used as figure-head for the neo-Palladians is actually uncertain from the very beginning if we consider the close of "Mathematics" and the tone of some of his letters.[16] Also, the parallel development of the growing disciplinary interest in traditional, common architecture and in the historic fabric, and of the Townscape agenda, can be variously interpreted. Nonetheless we cannot be surprised by the increasing frequency with which the group of designers who associated themselves with Rowe's theories are seen to be antithetical to the members of the Townscape group, particularly in the English disciplinary debate of the following years.[17]

The relevance attributed by Rowe to this dichotomy between two opposite approaches seems to be implicitly confirmed from the onset of his first published work.

> *There are two causes of beauty—natural and customary. Natural is from geometry consisting in uniformity, that is equality and proportion. Customary beauty is begotten by the use, as familiarity breeds a love for things not in themselves lovely. Here lies the great occasion of errors, but always the true test is natural or geometrical beauty. Geometrical figures are naturally more beautiful than irregular ones: the square, the circle are the most beautiful, next the parallelogram and the oval. There are only two beautiful positions of straight lines, perpendicular and horizontal; this is from Nature and consequently necessity, no other than upright being firm.*
> Sir Christopher Wren[18]

Christopher Wren's epigram on natural and customary beauty (Fig. 4) opening "Mathematics" is not intended to anticipate a dualism between Palladio's and Le Corbusier's architectural schemes and, by synecdoche, between classical and Modern architecture.[19] Rather, it reflects the ideological polarization of the time. It simply offers authoritative tutoring on a major, topical question: the desirable role for contemporary architecture and architecture *tout court*. In Le Corbusier's design, as in Palladio's before him, geometry generates "natural" beauty, which is the "true" one. As Wren stated: "Geometrical figures are naturally more beautiful than irregular ones" and, after Rowe's examination, not only Palladio but also Le Corbusier confirmed this principle through their masterpieces.

In "customary beauty", generated by "use" and "familiarity", "lies the great occasion of errors". Here "customary beauty" should stand for "an aesthetic of the familiar, the close-at-hand, the appropriable" as Uvedale Price, according to Macarthur, had proposed for the Picturesque Movement.[20] And, in turn, picturesque stands for Townscape. A standard for both picturesque and Townscape is irregularity—or, rather, a more complex form of regularity—and, of course, a search for the organic, vernacular, ordinary, and anonymous.

15 Smith, G[eorge] E[verard] Kidder, *Italy builds: Its modern architecture and native inheritance*, Reinhold, New York, 1955. (My note).

16 As an example, the February 7, 1956 letter to Louis Kahn: Naegele, Daniel, ed. *The Letters of Colin Rowe: Five Decades of Correspondence*, Artifice Press, London, 2016.

17 Macarthur, John; Aitchison, Mathew, "Pevsner's Townscape", in Pevsner, Nikolaus, *Visual Planning and the Picturesque*, (Aitchison, Mathew, ed.), Getty Publications, Los Angeles, 2010: 5: "The politics of architectural discourse in Britain in the 1950s was largely divided between the neo-picturesqueness of the *AR* and a classicist/modernist tendency in the work of Rudolf Wittkower and applied to contemporary architectural issues by Colin Rowe".

18 Rowe (1947).

19 This aspect has been well clarified by Paolo Berdini. Berdini, Paolo, "Introduzione", in Rowe, Colin, *La matematica della villa ideale e altri scritti*, Zanichelli Editore, Bologna, 1990: XVI. A partial translation in English in: "Introduction to *La matematica della villa ideale*", *AA Files* 72, 2016: 109: "... this theorised dichotomy between nature and custom ... is not even presented as the great historical *caesura* dividing the world of Palladio, anchored in the metaphysical certainties of the treatises, from that of Le Corbusier, caught in the coils of a dialectic between the certainty ensured by the norm and the uncertainty inherent in form."

20 Macarthur (2012): 647.

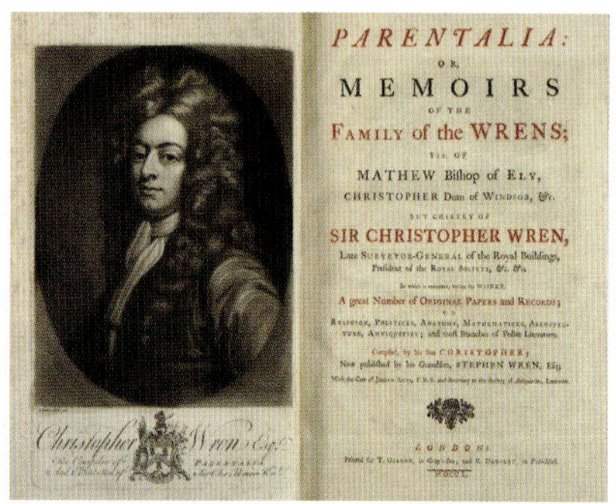

Fig. 4. Frontispiece of *Parentalia*, Sir Christopher Wren, 1750.

As in Stirling's synthesis above, this argument was made with equal passion, if not always with the same elegance and scholarship as in Rowe, by several contemporaries under various standards, post-WWII CIAM, including Team 10, organic architecture, regionalism, new empiricism being some of them, which for the sake of simplicity, I refer to as 'Modern Reform'. The *Review* environment provided plenty of examples. In 1946, the year before the publication of "Mathematics", Richards, who was one of the editors of *The Architectural Review*, had delivered a series of talks for the BBC on "English architectural tastes" in which "intellectual" and "vulgar" inclinations were contrasted. "Vulgar" here means dear to common people. The "charm of the familiar" is, according to Richards, one of the factors that, supported by a desire for stability, "shaped ordinary people's judgment in architecture".[21]

Two months before the appearance of "Mathematics", the *Review* had published "The Second Half Century", an editorial manifesto for a desirable development of Modern Architecture in which the historical roots of the functional tradition are shown, an appreciation of anonymous architecture is confirmed, and, in order to humanize architecture, "a recovery of ornament, colour, texture and a consciousness of history in relation to place" is argued for.[22]

A few months earlier, Richards had published *The Castles on the Ground* (Fig. 5), a controversial book in which it was argued that the "suburban environment is the choice of people who know what they like, and the architecture of the suburb may even be called a true contemporary vernacular".[23]

Suburbia is, for sure, the vulgarized version and, supposedly, the irreconcilable antithesis of both villas of late 16th century nobles in the Veneto and of the trendy, well-to-do vacationers in Poissy.[24] Both Villa Rotonda and Villa Savoye are displayed and surrounded by a dignifying natural context that merits attention in the very first paragraphs of "Mathematics". However, in neither case are the surroundings said to carry design implications other than the opportunity to take advantage of the views. And while in both cases, as with the English Augustan progenitors of the picturesque landscape tradition, the Virgilian nostalgia relies on the dialectic between classical architectural volumes and bucolic irregular context, in both Villa Rotonda and Villa Savoye, the "disengaged cube" is the absolute protagonist of this dialectic. In turn, both architectural volumes seem to make a deliberate effort to keep their natural setting as intact as possible. This is most evident in the floating structure of Le Corbusier's masterpiece.

Thus, a dichotomy between high versus low culture, authorial versus anonymous, aristocratic versus popular architecture is implied in both Rowe's argument and the contemporary discursive activities and, for the time being, Rowe places the natural, history-proven, and desirable destiny of architecture in the former field. Therefore, the ultimate message of "Mathematics" is that architecture must be aiming for the natural, geometry-based beauty. And although Rowe's reasoning is too complex and multiple to be effectively summarized as a single concept, it seems safe to assume that, at first glance, the most powerful effect of "Mathematics" was to give authority to the prospect of an aristocratic architecture bound to internal relations and emancipated from external dependencies, free

21 Kelly, Jessica, "Vulgar Modernism: J. M. Richards, Modernism and the Vernacular in British Architecture", *Architectural History* 58, 2015: 247.

22 Erten, Erdem, "The Hollow Victory of Modern Architecture and The Quest for the Vernacular: J.M. Richards and the Functional Tradition", in Guillery, Peter, ed., *Built from Below: British Architecture and The Vernacular*, Routledge Press, London and New York, 2011: 146. Richards, J[ames] M[aude]; Pevsner, Nikolaus; Lancaster, Osbert; Hastings, H[urbert] de C[ronin], "The Second Half Century", *The Architectural Review* CI (601), Jan 1947: 21-26.

23 Richards, J[ames] M[aude], *The Castles on the Ground: The Anatomy of Suburbia*, The Architectural Press, London, 1946: 13 and Erten, 2011: 148.

24 For a much-needed reframing of the role of vacation housing: Romano, Marco, "Una libera casa di vacanza", in *Liberi di costruire*, Bollati Boringhieri, Torino, 2013: 119-31.

25 Rowe, Colin, *As I Was Saying: Recollections and Miscellaneous Essays* 3, "Urbanistics", (Caragonne, Alexander, ed.), MIT Press, Cambridge, MA, and London, 1996.

26 Argan, Giulio Carlo; Fagiolo, Maurizio, *Guida alla storia dell'arte*, Sansoni, Firenze, (1974) 1981: 35. (My translation).

27 The psychology of architecture is the topic of Wölfflin's dissertation: Wölfflin, Heinrich, "Prolegomena to a Psychology of Architecture", in Mallgrave, Harry Francis; Ikonomou, Eleftherios, *Empathy, Form, and Space: Problems in German Aesthetics, 1873–1893*, Getty Center for the History of Art and the Humanities, Santa Monica, 1994: 149-92 (orig. *Prolegomena zu einer Psychologie der Architektur*, 1886) and in his *Renaissance and Baroque* he deals extensively with the relationship between architecture and psychology. The position of Wittkower is however ambiguous and evolving and, for him, psychology seems to be mostly the evidence of man's need for order and harmony. See: Payne (1994): 325 and n. 14 (on Wittkower's standing and on psychology in the last addition of *Architectural Principles*), 332-33 (on a comparison with Scott), 338 - n. 106 (on his temporary juvenile interest in psychology), 340 and n. 112 (on different nuances of his interpretation of the role of psychology). The whole argument in Payne (1994) is a useful reference on the polarization between abstract conceptualization and perceptual psychology.

from duties to relate even with its specific cultural, figurative, social contexts: indifferent, that is, to 'urbanistics'.

Fig. 5. J. M. Richards holding a copy of *The Castles on the Ground*, Peggy Angus, 1947.

From "Mathematics" to "Urbanistics"

The intellectual journey that led Rowe from the positions he expressed in the late 1940s to the disciplinary construction that would later have so much influence over the field of urban design—mostly collected in "Urbanistics", the third volume of *As I Was Saying*—is rich, adventurous and fascinating.[25] It's hardly an exaggeration to say that, with its connotations, this journey connects two antipodal extremes, since for Rowe, architecture will be invested with three additional tasks, able to revolutionize its statute. One is the responsibility for an identity other than itself: the identity of the place. Second, consequently, is the undertaking of a reciprocity of conditioning with the adjacent spatial and architectural surroundings. Third, finally, is the responsibility for the psychological projection of its own form on the perceiving subject, the viewer, and of the cultural connotations of this relationship. In so doing, Rowe's design rationale would gradually shift from an emphasis on autonomy to that of complex heteronomy.

In some respects, the enzymes for overcoming the 'mathematical' autonomy of architecture were provided by the cultural environment of the Warburg Institute itself. Firstly, and quite simply, because of the role that form had for the iconological tradition, strongly relying on the psychological *medium*. This had been the case in very important components of the Bauhaus and of the Modern Movement. In fact, for that tradition, form is not relevant for its absolute value but for its ability to respond to and evoke "the deepest impulses, at the individual and collective unconscious level".[26] Well before the foundation of the Institute, Aby Warburg himself, after receiving his doctorate in art history in the mid-1890s, had spent some time at the Medical School of the University of Berlin studying psychology. Ernst Gombrich, a friend of Rowe and author of numerous essays on the relationship between psychology and art, had been at the Warburg Institute after it moved to London from Germany, in 1936. In 1951 Gombrich became its director. Heinrich Wölfflin, who was Wittkower's master for one season in Munich before he moved back to Berlin to study with Adolph Goldschmidt, certainly had a major influence on his disciplinary evolution. Wölfflin must have provided a base for Wittkower's recognition of the Baroque, but might also be credited for the importance that he would attribute to psychology in architecture starting with his earliest studies.[27]

Although the distinction between form as pure geometrical reference for architectural design and form as a *medium* of perception may appear rather elusive, it seems in fact an essential element in the shift from orthodox Modernism (masters) to Modern Reform developing in the architectural culture between the 1950s and the 1960s. This shift, recurrent in historiography and in the contemporary critical debate, from reason to feeling and emotion, from conception to perception and, therefore, from project autonomy to heteronomy[28] echoes the evolution from Renaissance to Baroque as highlighted by Wölfflin.[29]

For Modern Reformists, the field of psychology could now contribute to overcoming the limitations of a superficial rationalism and the complexity revealed

28 As a support to this interpretation: Smith, C. Ray, *Supermannerism: New Attitudes in Post-Modern Architecture*, E. P. Dutton, New York, 1977: 77-79. "... architects began to design the forms of buildings according to the users' actual living patterns and to their psychological requirements. ... The major change in architecture from the 1950s to the 1960s was, in fact, from rationalism to concentration on feelings and emotions, from pure design to human concerns ... 'It doesn't make much difference what is out there so much as the way you can see it, how you perceive it', Joseph Esherick said. In Tim Vreeland's view, the difference between the architecture of the 1950s and the 1960s was the difference between the 'Architecture of Conception and the Architecture of Perception'. ... Colin Rowe had said it was a distinction between the thing as it *is* and as it *appears*. ... Tim Vreeland could distinguish the 'architecture of conception' from the 'architecture of perception'. He pointed out that Renaissance architecture also had been one of conception, ... Then, Dr. Rudolf Wittkower pointed out, that view gave way in the following century to Guarini's view that the only important thing is what man can see".

29 Wölfflin, Heinrich, *Principles of art history: The problem of the development of style in later art*, Dover Publications, Inc., New York, 1956 (1915, originally published in English in 1932 by G. Bell and Sons, Ltd.).

by psychology could provide architecture with a scientific support to what otherwise would be considered derogatory concessions to the irrational. In fact, the reformists' propositions and solutions could be argued to be more objective than those provided by the orthodox 'functionalists'.[30]

Along this trajectory, if Wittkower was gaining notoriety and sympathy in the world of architectural practice for his studies on Renaissance architectural principles, his expertise in Baroque art and architecture was certainly more significant and well-grounded.[31] Baroque was central to the attention of the Warburg Institute precisely because it was the quintessential 'culture of the image'.

The Warburg Institute's attraction to Italy, projected on Rowe during his studies there, may have had a substantial role in consolidating his sensitivity to a dialectical interplay of apparently irreconcilable attitudes. This interest of the Institute had been made explicit by the itinerant exhibition "English Art and the Mediterranean" which was familiar to Rowe because it had been shown in Liverpool, where he was studying, as early as in 1942.[32]

One can find affinities between English and Italian cultures not only in the Palladian borrowings of English architecture but also in the critiques converging on Modern orthodoxy, mentioned above. Empathies could be also discovered in that "spirit of the Gothic" which, as proposed by Karl Scheffler, unites aspects of antiquity, the Middle Ages, Baroque, and Rococo and arrives at certain expressions of the present:[33] that spirit, that is, which leads to a regulation of complexity, rather than to its reduction. This could be seen in the urban design of historic city centers and villages, both Italian and English, that were used as illustrations—certainly vulgarized in Rowe's opinion—in the pages of *The Architectural Review*, in the 1940s and 1950s. Later, these would become the subject of study by Italian typo-morphologists, Saverio Muratori and followers, and by geographers such as Michael Robert Günter (M.R.G.) Conzen, yet another German emigrant in England. One can argue that the same spirit could be found more frequently in urban spaces than in buildings, commonly illustrated with Italian and often Baroque examples. Publications and exhibitions showed the growing interest in the *piazze*, in 'streets for people' and in the 'spontaneous' architecture of historic city centers. In 1963, Hubert de Cronin Hastings, the 'disguised' leader of the Townscape movement and impresario of the *Review*, would, under the pseudonym Ivor de Wolfe, dedicate an entire book to the celebration of Italian historic centers.[34]

—

In 1947, when "Mathematics" was published, Rowe delivered his thesis at the Warburg Institute in November[35] and visited Italy, probably for his first time, during the summer. He returned to Italy in the late summer of 1950, the year of the publication of his second essay, "Mannerism and Modern Architecture".[36] In this article his contribution to the debate, opened in England by Pevsner and Anthony Blunt as well as by Wittkower himself,[37] seems to mark the beginning of Rowe's itinerary towards the coexistence and contamination of opposites, which I try to describe here.

30 Richards (1947) and Mumford (2000): 167.

31 Consider, as an example, the fundamental *Die Zeichnungen des Gianlorenzo Bernini*, published as early as 1931. Engl. trans.: Bernini, Gian Lorenzo, *Bernini's Drawings*, (Brauer, Heinrich; Wittkower, Rudolf, eds.), Römische Forschungen Der Bibliotheca Hertziana, 9-10, Collectors Editions, New York, 1970.

32 Mazzucco, Katia, "1941 English Art and the Mediterranean. A photographic exhibition by the Warburg Institute in London", *Journal of Art Historiography* 5, Dec 2011.

33 Scheffler, Karl, *Der Geist der Gotik*, Insel Verlag, Leipzig, 1923, and Payne (1994): 341n.

34 De Wolfe, Ivor, *The Italian Townscape*, Architectural Press, London, 1963, republished, (Ertem, Erdem; Powers, Alan, eds.), Artifice, London, 2013.

35 Francesco Benelli anticipates the date of Rowe's graduation to 1946 (Benelli, Francesco, "Rudolph Wittkower e Colin Rowe. Continuità e frattura", in Marzo, Mauro, ed., *L'architettura come testo e la figura di Colin Rowe*, Marsilio, Venezia, 2010: 97) while Molly Claypool states that Rowe's thesis, "'The Theoretical Drawings of Inigo Jones: Their Sources and Scope', was submitted in 1948". Claypool, Mollie, "The Consequences of Dialogue and the Virgilian Nostalgia of Colin Rowe", *Architecture and Culture* 4 (3), Nov 2016: 362.

36 Rowe, Colin, "Mannerism and Modern Architecture", *The Architectural Review* 107 (641), May 1950: 289-300, then in Rowe (1976): 29-58.

37 Rowe (1976): 34 and Vidler, Anthony, "Mannerist Modernism: Colin Rowe", in *Histories of the immediate present: Inventing architectural modernism*, MIT Press, Cambridge, MA, and London, 2008: 87-97.

During the 1950 trip to Italy, a triangulation with England, Italy, and the United States began that was destined to mark the Englishman's academic career, his studies, and his entire life. In Italy, he met the American eclectic architect, Arthur Brown, famous for both his Beaux-Arts and Arts and Crafts work. This encounter, and especially the visit they made together to two Baroque masterpieces in Rome, Santa Maria in Campitelli and the Oratorio dei Filippini, contributed to convincing Rowe to move to the United States. This is at least proposed in the novelized reconstruction of the events as Rowe himself has written of them.[38]

The other declared reason for his American adventure was the desire to study with Henry-Russell Hitchcock. Rowe had met Hitchcock, contributor to *The Architectural Review*, in London through the circle of the Warburg.[39] This decision has some significance in Rowe's intellectual journey. Firstly, Rowe's teacher Wittkower would have preferred that he study with Sigfried Giedion.[40] After all, Giedion was the secretary general of CIAM and a major player in the Modernist orthodoxy; he was lecturing at Harvard,[41] which had become the new Bauhaus, and he had begun his career as a scholar with a thesis on the late-Baroque and romantic classicism.[42]

Hitchcock, on the other hand, while on the faculty at Smith College and director of the Smith College Museum of Art, was also teaching at Yale. A scholar of Richardson and Wright, in 1929 Hitchcock had published *Modern Architecture: Romanticism and Reintegration*.[43] Albeit this may be to oversimplify and strain my argument, but to suppose yet another polarizing dialectic, Giedion was attracted by the *classicist* "shade of colour" (Färbung) in late-Baroque and romanticism,[44] whereas Hitchcock highlighted the *romantic* roots of Modern Architecture.

By the time of Rowe's travel to Yale, Hitchcock certainly had provided clues that his adherence to Modern orthodoxy was not as uncritical as one might have expected from one of the two scholars responsible for the MoMA exhibition of 1932 and the book, *The International Style*.[45] At this point in Hitchcock's arguments, Modern architecture was still a solid basis for design but its definition could not be limited and had to include a broader range of expressions (for example, the Swedish, Swiss, and Dutch contributions) and be able to convey the idea of 'monumentality' as per Giedion. Frank Lloyd Wright and his 'Organic Architecture' had become an unparalleled reference for Hitchcock.[46]

—

Officially, Colin Rowe went to study at Yale to attend the courses of the brand new, two-year program of City Planning directed by Christopher Tunnard.[47] We do not know the nature of the relation between Rowe and Tunnard before 1951. A list of invitees included in Tunnard's archive, perhaps for a lecture delivered at the Institute of Landscape Architecture during a journey in England on July 1, 1947, includes several protagonists of the establishment: among others, Maxwell Fry, Jim Richards, Sir Leslie Martin, Sir Hugh Casson, Geoffrey and Susan Jellicoe, Nikolaus Pevsner, John Betjeman, Ian Nairn, Reyner Banham, as well as Henry-Russell Hitchcock and Colin Rowe.[48] Nor do we know how much time Rowe actually devoted to urban issues and to contacts with Tunnard while at Yale, probably very limited. Rowe rarely mentions Tunnard in his memoirs or in correspondence.[49]

38 Rowe (1996/1): 6-10.

39 One further reason, the stories of Jim Stirling returning from his travels in the United States, is mentioned in Rowe (1996/1): 344 and in Rowe, Colin, "James Stirling: A Highly Personal and Very Disjointed Memoir", in Arnell, Peter; Bickford, Ted, *James Stirling: Buildings and Projects*, Rizzoli, New York, 1984: 18.

40 Rowe (1996/1): 21-23.

41 In 1951, Giedion was teaching at MIT and lecturing at Harvard, having been appointed professor at Harvard in 1938. He had returned from Europe after being appointed head of the Federal Polytechnic School in Zurich in 1947. "Giedion, Sigfried", in "Dictionary of Art Historians", [https://arthistorians.info/giedions/]. A thorough analysis of Giedion's production is in Georgiadis, Sokratis, *Sigfried Giedion: An Intellectual Biography*, Edinburgh University Press, Edinburgh, 1993.

42 His thesis, "Spätbarocker und romantischer Klassizismus", followed by Wölfflin as his advisor, was discussed in 1922. Georgiadis (1993): 11-32.

43 Hitchcock, Henry-Russell Jr., *Modern Architecture: Romanticism and Reintegration*, Payson & Clarke Ltd., New York, 1929.

44 Georgiadis (1993): 17.

45 Hitchcock, Henry-Russell, Johnson, Philip, *The International Style: Architecture since 1922*, W. W. Norton & Co, New York, 1932.

46 "What is Happening to Modern Architecture?", proceedings of the symposium held at the MoMA on February 11, 1948, *The Bulletin of the Museum of Modern Art* XV (3), Spr 1948, now in Canizaro (2007): 293-309, and Hitchcock, Henry-Russell, "The International Style Twenty Years After", *Architectural Record* 110 (2), Aug 1951: 89-97, now in Hitchcock, Henry-Russell; Johnson, Philip, *The International Style*, (2nd ed.), W. W. Norton & Co, New York, 1966: 237-55 and in Ockman (1993): 138-48.

47 Ockman (1993): 205; Wong, Colby, "A Continuing Chronology: Colin Rowe", in Somol, R[obert] E., ed., "Form Work: Colin Rowe", *ANY* 7/8, 1994: 36, and Stern, Robert A. M.; Stamp, Jimmy, *Pedagogy and Place: 100 Years of Architecture Education at Yale*, Yale University Press, New Haven, CN, 2016: 150-54.

48 Jacques, David; Woudstra, Jan, *Landscape Modernism renounced: The career of Christopher Tunnard (1910–1979)*, Routledge, London and New York, 2009: 60.

49 Tunnard and wife appear in Rowe's letters to his parents of February 5 ("a delightful person who is Professor of Town Planning over here") and May 11, 1952. Naegele, Daniel J., "The Letters of Colin Rowe: Five Decades of Correspondence", *Architecture Books* 2, 2015. [http://lib.dr.iastate.edu/arch_books/2] now in Naegele (2016).

The mere fact that Tunnard's book, *Gardens in the Modern Landscape*, appears among the readings that Rowe advised to his students at the University of Texas, in the mid-1950s,[50] is not sufficient to assume a disciplinary debt (Fig. 6). However, the presence of Tunnard at Yale in a key position adds to a picture revealing the eclectic and inclusive atmosphere in that university, also favored by the chairman of the Department of Architecture, George Howe, beginning in January 1950.[51] That atmosphere was fertile ground for a coetaneous of Rowe, Vincent Scully, who would contribute to turning the spotlight of historiography and criticism on minor, ordinary and vernacular architecture.[52] Also, Harwell Hamilton Harris, who was an advocate at this point of the 'regionalism of liberation' in architecture, was a visiting critic at Yale immediately before his moving to Austin in the fall of 1951, to become director of the new architecture program at the University of Texas, and again in late 1952.[53] It is not unlikely that Rowe, arriving at Yale in September 1951, became aware of Harris' presence.

Tunnard was a Canadian landscape designer educated in a British Arts and Crafts environment. After his articles that had been published in the *Review* were collected in the 1938 book *Gardens in the Modern Landscape*,[54] he had been invited by Dean Hudnut and Gropius to teach at Harvard, where he had remained until the end of 1942.[55] During that period, however, "Tunnard came under the influence of Joseph Hudnut—both men were increasingly disillusioned with Modernism and opposed to Gropius' view of urbanism".[56] His new position, starting in 1945 at Yale, marks not only a change of interest from landscape to city planning—but this is, in fact, an urban design that echoes Townscape modes. Tunnard moves away from Modernist orthodoxy towards a *milieu* of a more complex sensitivity that is closer to the themes of the Modern Reform.

Interestingly enough, in one of the founding texts of the Townscape movement, Tunnard had been credited by Hubert de Cronin Hastings with having reintroduced the Picturesque term *sharawaggi*, which later became one of the buzzwords in the Townscape architectural vocabulary.[57] In 1950, Tunnard was the editor of a special issue of *The Architectural Review*[58]—including an article

50 Caragonne, Alexander, *The Texas Rangers: Notes from an Architectural Underground*, MIT Press, Cambridge, MA, and London, 1995: Appendix 7.

51 Ockman, Joan; Sachs, Avigail, "1945-1968. Modernism Takes Command", in Ockman, Joan, ed., *Architecture School: Three Centuries of Educating Architects in North America*, MIT Press, Cambridge, MA, and London, 2012: 139, and Stern and Stamp (2016): 97-99.

52 In 1952, Scully and his co-author, Antoinette Downing, won the Alice Davis Hitchcock Award for their book *The Architectural Heritage of Newport*.

53 Germany, Lisa, *Harwell Hamilton Harris*, University of California Press, Berkeley, Los Angeles, and London, 1991: 217n.

54 Tunnard, Christopher, *Gardens in the Modern Landscape*, Architectural Press, London, (1938) 1948.

55 Jacques and Woudstra (2009): 42-43, 48-70.

56 Stern and Stamp (2016): 150.

57 The editor, "Exterior Furnishing or Sharawaggi: The Art of Making Urban Landscape", *The Architectural Review* XCV (565), Jan 1944: 5. Tunnard (1948): 61. As Pevsner's *Pioneers of Modern Design* [Pevsner, Nikolaus, *Pioneers of Modern Design: From William Morris to Walter Gropius*, The Museum of Modern Art, New York, (1936) 1949] had derived the beginning of the Modern Movement from the English Arts and Crafts, Tunnard's book (illustrated by Gordon Cullen) described the English Picturesque roots of Modernism.

58 Tunnard, Christopher, ed., "Man Made America", a special number of *The Architectural Review*, Dec 1950. Subject and title will be resumed in a successful book that he later wrote with Boris Pushkarev: Tunnard, Christopher; Pushkarev, Boris, *Man-made America: Chaos or Control? An Inquiry into Selected Problems of Design in the Urbanized Landscape*, Yale University Press, New Haven and London, 1963.

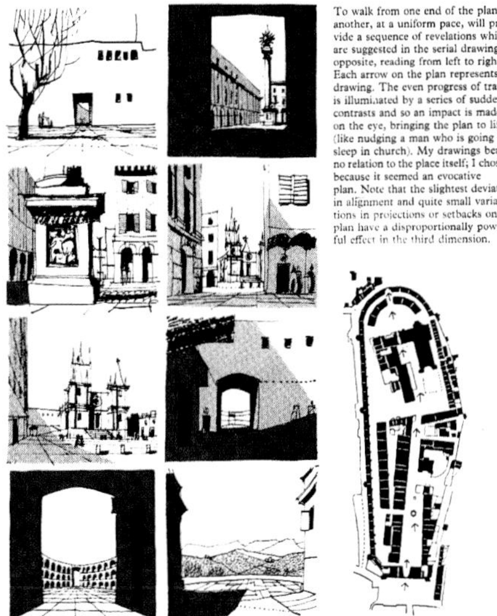

CASEBOOK: SERIAL VISION

To walk from one end of the plan to another, at a uniform pace, will provide a sequence of revelations which are suggested in the serial drawings opposite, reading from left to right. Each arrow on the plan represents a drawing. The even progress of travel is illuminated by a series of sudden contrasts and so an impact is made on the eye, bringing the plan to life (like nudging a man who is going to sleep in church). My drawings bear no relation to the place itself; I chose it because it seemed an evocative plan. Note that the slightest deviation in alignment and quite small variations in projections or setbacks on plan have a disproportionally powerful effect in the third dimension.

opposite left to right:
Fig. 6. Book cover of *Gardens in the Modern Landscape*, Christopher Tunnard, 1938.

Fig. 7. Journal cover of "Outrage", *The Architectural Review*, 1955.

Fig. 8. Journal cover of "Counter-Attack against subtopia", *The Architectural Review*, 1956

inset:
Fig. 9. "CASEBOOK: SERIAL VISION", from *Townscape*, Gordon Cullen, 1961.

by Hitchcock—that resulted in a heated disciplinary debate and would be a reference for the most well-known special issues of the *Review*, "Outrage" and "Counter-Attack", produced by the Townscape group five and six years later[59] (Fig. 7, 8). Both the form and contents of that 1950 issue reinforce the interpretation of Tunnard as one fully involved in the Townscape movement.[60] His activity is an important testimony to the influence of the British Townscape culture on the birth of American urban design as an academic and disciplinary field.[61]

In an article of the same year, Tunnard defended the City Beautiful tradition which he believed had been undeservingly denigrated in the recent past. He praised it for its ability to express "collaboration", "coordination", and "sense of unity".[62] And in another lengthy article published in October 1951,[63] he argued for a renewed "creative urbanism", an artistic, visual, three-dimensional civic design, looking for beauty, variety, and decoration, and based on care for the relationship among buildings, history, and continuity with the past. Tunnard's contribution to the 1948 MoMA symposium "What is Happening to Modern Architecture?" indicated his interest in public taste and historical precedents as correctives to the course of Modern Architecture.[64] If we had to assign Tunnard to one of the two parties in play, we would, indeed, opt for including him in the Modern Reformist party.

All things considered, it is not surprising that Rowe's stay at Yale, along with his subsequent North American journey prompted by Hitchcock[65] to look at Wright's houses, may have been a stimulus to his shift in interest from the "linear" towards the "picturesque", to use Wölfflin's categories. This assumption seems to be supported by Rowe's essay "Character and Composition", completed in 1953–54 but set and matured in the Yale period.[66] This essay, rather than a reprimand of the picturesque "Englishness" that Pevsner and the Townscape movement had started promoting, seems a re-appropriation of picturesque issues through a more profound interpretation, *sub specie historiae*.

59 "Outrage" was published in June 1955, "Counterattack" in December 1956. For an account of the surrounding dynamics: Gosling, David, *The Evolution of American Urban Design*, John Wiley & Sons Ltd., Chichester, 2003: 42-47.

60 Macarthur and Aitchison (2010). 16.

61 Orillard, Clément, "Tracing urban design's 'Townscape' origins: some relationships between a British editorial policy and an American academic field in the 1950s", *Urban History* 36 (2), 2009: 284-302, offers an account of the evolution of Townscape, the beginnings of urban design in the U.S. and their cross-fertilizations.

62 Tunnard, Christopher, "A City Called Beautiful", *Journal of the Society of Architectural Historians* 9, (1/2), Mar – May 1950: 31-36.

63 Tunnard, Christopher, "Creative Urbanism", *The Town Planning Review* 22 (3), Oct 1951: 216-36.

64 Canizaro (2007): 293.

65 Eisenman, Peter, "The Rowe synthesis", in Marzo (2010): 49. Eisenman reminds us that in that period, Hitchcock himself was preparing his book on English Victorian architecture: Hitchcock, Henry-Russell, *Early Victorian Architecture in Britain*, Yale University Press, New Haven, 1954.

66 Rowe, Colin, "Character and Composition or Some Vicissitudes of Architectural Vocabulary in the Nineteenth Century", *Oppositions* 2, Jan 1974, also in Rowe (1976): 59-87, where it is said to have been written in 1953-54. References to this text are in Rowe's letters to his parents of May 11, 1952 and to Hitchcock of May 6, 1953 and of December 29, 1953, where it is said to have been completed about six weeks before: Naegele (2016).

above left to right:
Fig. 10. Lockhart, Texas: aerial view of the courthouse with the project site in the background.

Fig. 11. Context showing street elevation for "A small bank in Lockhart", Lee Hodgden. Black and white inverted.

If it is possible that, for Rowe, Yale's cultural environment was able to build up an archive of memories of urban space and townscape on the one hand and of the *Malerisch* spirit on the other, the next period, spent in Austin, Texas, from January 1954 to summer 1956,[67] seems to mark Rowe's intellectual route in many respects, at least three of which are decisive in the transformation that interests us here: the value of place as 'identity' which often translates into the 'imageability' or 'figurability' of the defined spatial void,[68] the contextual character of architectural design, and the role of psychology in the interpretation of form and in the formulation of the design project.

The projects for Lockhart, Texas, and Losoya Park are examples of attention to both place identity and contextual character in the Austin faculty circle. Alexander Caragonne describes these projects in detail in his book on *The Texas Rangers*[69] (Fig. 10–12). In this respect, the Lockhart studio exercise seems to imply an advancement toward an 'urban' sensitivity greater than the well-known article, written by Rowe and John Hejduk, on "Lockhart, Texas". However, "Lockhart, Texas" is a clear sign of Rowe's growing inclination to cast minor works of architecture as important players in constructing the larger urban stage.[70] While Rowe was in Austin, the interest in "planning"—in fact urban design, again—the concept of architecture as space, the relevance of the "surrounding setting", i.e. the context of architecture, are all part of the pedagogical structure designed by Bernhard Hoesli and Rowe, together with their young colleagues.[71]

Harris' reformist position must have been of some relevance too. His asserted regionalism and liberalism were expressed, even though in a vague, cloudy way, in a conference delivered on August 22, 1954 at the Northwest Regional Council of the AIA in Eugene, Oregon and published in 1958 as "Regionalism and Nationalism in Architecture".[72]

The interest in the psychology of form, which was to have such an essential and fundamental role in setting Rowe's and the Cornell school's methodological approach to urban design and architecture, materialized in "Transparency",[73] written with Robert Slutzky, during the Austin period. It was probably supported by Slutzky and Lee Hirsche, who both had come to Austin from Yale,

67 A detailed account of Rowe's period at the University of Texas at Austin is provided in Caragonne (1995) and a synthetic one, complementary to that and, somehow, contradictory, in the September 23, 1955 letter to Hitchcock. Naegele (2016): 97-106.

68 I am encouraged to assume here the equivalence between 'imageability', a term used by Lynch in *The Image of the City*, and 'figureability', of the the figure/ground system by the choice of Lynch's Italian translator, Giancarlo Guarda who translates 'imageability' as 'figurabilità' and 'image' as 'immagine'. Lynch, Kevin, *L'immagine della città*, Marsilio, Venezia, (1960) 1964: 31n.

69 Caragonne (1995): 214-31 (Losoya Park) and 249-54 (Lockhart).

70 Rowe, Colin; Hejduk, John, "Lockhart, Texas", *Architectural Record* 121 (3), Mar 1957: 201-06, also in Rowe (1996/1): 55-71, where the intention of publishing a series on American small towns is mentioned.

The interest in the architecture of the urban fabric and in the preservation of historic centers are intertwined in several disciplinary products, during this period. In these years, the Italian culture consolidates a certain primacy on the question of historic centers. After Gustavo Giovannoni's early contribution and the plans for Bergamo Alta and Bari Vecchia, before the war, the plan of Assisi is designed by Astengo in the mid-1950s and the Charter of Gubbio is a product of 1960. *(cont.)*

inset:
Fig. 12. Sketches from Bernhard Hoesli's notebook drawn during the final jury of the Losoya Park projects. Black and white inverted.

recommended to Harris by Rowe and their professor Josef Albers.[74] It is also possible that Rowe himself had had direct relations with Albers in 1951-52, as Albers had been at Yale since 1950. It is also likely that Lee Hodgden contributed to Rowe's interest in the psychology of form since Hodgden[75] had studied at MIT, where György Kepes had been teaching since 1947. Kepes' contribution to urban design and in particular to the research of Lynch's circle is well known.[76]

Two evocative and premonitory figure/ground drawings, taken from Bernhard Hoesli's notebook and published by Caragonne, show opposite situations (Fig. 12): objects as figures in space as opposed to space as figure defined by buildings—an extraordinary anticipation of the fertile solid/void interplay on which Cornell Urban Design would build its own methodological architecture.[77]

It would be problematic, however, to argue that Rowe's production in the 1950s is full of references to urban issues. Urban design seems to take on a significant presence in Rowe's thinking only in 1963 when Rowe had just taken responsibility for the Cornell graduate program and John Reps, head of City and Regional Planning, suggested to Rowe that he deal with this subject of growing disciplinary interest. Between the Texas period and this time, there appear to be only two episodes of relevance. During Rowe's first temporary stay at Cornell—late 1957—he suggested to Alvin Boyarsky, then a student of planning at Cornell, that he study Camillo Sitte as his thesis topic. Sitte, who in the late 1950s, and at least until the mid-1970s, was not a preferred reference in the dynamics of the urban discourse—except in the Townscape circle—will be, more or less explicitly, an important presence in the evolution of the design system of Rowe's school.[78]

Finally, the essay on "The Architecture of Utopia",[79] crafted during the hostile English interlude in Sir Leslie Martin's pseudo-scientifically-inclined Cambridge,[80] is possibly Rowe's first public reflection on urbanistics. It seems to establish a solid conceptual basis in support of a new idea of a complex, rich and inclusive city as would be developed over time in the Cornell Urban Design Studio. "The

(cont.) On this subject: Ertem, Erdem; Powers, Alan, "Introduction" to De Wolfe (1963): xv-xvi. The Situationist International, for an architecture without architects, was held in 1957: Sadler, Simon, *The Situationist City*, MIT Press, Cambridge, MA, and London, 1998. The same year Moholy-Nagy, Sibyl, *Native Genius in Anonymous Architecture*, Horizon Press Inc., New York, 1957, is published. The Townscape debate is, obviously, sensitive to these issues: Ertem; Powers, "Introduction". It is worth noting that issue 32 of *Urbanistica* (1960), which deserves a reprint, is dedicated to two themes: historical centers and 'the face of the city'.

71 For the occasions during those Austin years that seem relevant to this discussion and for some precedents, Caragonne (1995): xi, xviii, xx, 39, 42, 157-64, 214-31, 253, 275, 344, Appendix 5.

72 Harris, Harwell Hamilton, "Regionalism and Nationalism in Architecture", *Texas Quarterly* 1, Feb 1958: 115-24, now in Canizaro (2007): 57-64.

73 Of the essay "Transparency: Literal and Phenomenal", by Colin Rowe and Robert Slutzky, there are two parts and several versions. Part I, written in 1955-56, published in *Perspecta* 8, 1963: 45-54, and later in Rowe (1976): 159-83, and Part II, written in 1956, published in *Perspecta* 13-14, 1971: 287-301, and later in Rowe (1996/1): 73-106. Both are published again in different book versions. Among these, an updated version in English, edited by Bernhard Hoesli: Rowe, Colin; Slutzky, Robert, *Transparency*, Birkhäuser, Basel, 1997. A third part "exists in fragments and has never been published". Ockman, Joan, "Form without Utopia: Contextualizing Colin Rowe", *Journal of the Society of Architectural Historians* 57 (4), Dec 1998: 445 and n. 4.

74 Germany (1991): 142; Rowe's September 23, 1955 letter to Hitchcock and July 14 and 24, 1995 to Lisa Germany in Naegele (2016): 97-106, 435-38.

75 Caragonne (1995): 299.

76 Also, Oechslin, Werner, "'Transparency': the Search for a Reliable Design Method in Accordance with the Principles of Modern Architecture", in Rowe and Slutzky (1997): 12.

77 Caragonne (1995): 228.

Architecture of Utopia" is a measure of Rowe's increasing distance not only from geometric reduction but also from the position that in 1947 Wittkower had expressed in his review of the recent English edition of Sitte's *Art of Building Cities*.[81] There, Rowe's advisor had boldly argued: "Sitte cannot nowadays be regarded as a satisfactory guide" because "he cannot see and interpret [a town] as an entirely integrated whole—an interest which for us lies at the heart of town planning".[82] Wittkower's position was rather commonplace in Modernist orthodoxy: the best known proponents such as Le Corbusier and Hilberseimer had created images of Cartesian cities designed by one hand only. But, to use a more contemporary example, the flexible multiplicity of British new towns was rather limited as well.

In Rowe's "The Architecture of Utopia" an entire system of well-grounded and recent values and their consequences look weary: the utopian impulse of Modern Architecture, the conceptual bases of the neo-Platonic 'image' of the ideal city, its intentional elimination of variety, its problematic relationship with the plural aspects of reality and, finally, the long-lasting illiberal inclinations of urbanistics, theory and practice.

"Urbanistics"

Rowe's first travel to the U.S. was in 1951, to spend one academic year at Yale on a Fulbright Fellowship.[83] Beginning in the summer of 1952, Rowe's American *grand tour* took place 'on the road',[84] which reportedly included visits to forty houses by Frank Lloyd Wright[85] and a prolonged period of work in Bakersfield, starting in September.[86] Details of Rowe's itinerary can be inferred from the fascinating account in Rowe's letters to his parents and to Hitchcock, gathered by Daniel Naegele. Rowe was in Mexico from January 28 to March 1953, and then, for a while in Houston, partly with Howard Barnstone.[87] In mid-April he would meet Jean Murray Bangs Harris, wife of Harwell, in Norman, Oklahoma when it is possible that the idea of teaching at the University of Texas at Austin was stimulated by Jean Harris and considered by Rowe.[88] By May, Rowe must have visited Harwell Hamilton Harris in his Austin office, as Lisa Germany reports, "got to know the Harwell Harrises rather well" and confirmed "the idea that there would be a job available at Austin", as Rowe writes to Hitchcock.[89] This was the background for a follow-up phone contact with Harwell Harris to communicate his interest and availability to move to Texas and begin his teaching appointment starting the following January 1954.[90] In the meantime, Rowe, after spending a few months in New York, went back to Europe (including London and Paris),[91] where he stayed during the autumn of 1953: the period during which the essay "Character and Composition" is likely to have been developed, to be completed roughly one year later.

1951 is a symbolic year, and not only as the promising and demanding beginning of the second half of the 20th century. In 1951, the supposedly Townscape-oriented Festival of Britain, that Rowe will not miss any occasion to vituperate, took place. The conference "De Divina Proportione" (The Divine Proportion) at the IX Triennale in Milan was held on September 27–29, with the participation of Wittkower, Le Corbusier, and James Ackerman. All of them had recently published on the subject of 'mathematics'.[92] By that time, Rowe was already in the U.S.

78 Sitte's book was published in English (Sitte, Camillo, *The Art of Building Cities*, (Steward, Charles T., ed.), Reinhold, New York and Chapman and Hall, London) in 1945 and, in 1946, was reviewed by Pevsner in the *Review:* Pevsner, Nikolaus, "A Pioneer of Town-Planning", *The Architectural Review* C (600), Dec 1946: 186. In 1947, Wittkower blasted this edition mostly but not only because of the poor, misleading translation. Wittkower, Rudolf, "Camillo Sitte's 'Art of Building Cities' in an American Translation", *The Town Planning Review* 19 (3/4), Sum 1947: 164-69. Besides Sitte, Rowe had suggested to also study other "representatives of proto-Modern urbanism": Geddes, Howard and Burnham but of the four, Sitte, flanked by Nolli as a further precedent, seems to have influenced Rowe's methodology more than any other. Rowe (1996/3): 17, 336.

The work of Camillo Sitte was among the readings for an Urban Design Seminar given in the planning program at Cornell, taught by Kermit Carlyle [K.C.] Parsons and Stuart Stein, that many of the Rowe Urban Design students took. I owe to Steve Hurtt this piece of information as well as so many insights and interpretive keys on Colin Rowe's activity, especially during the 1960s, that it is impossible to single them out.

79 Rowe, Colin, "The Architecture of Utopia", *Granta* LXIII (1187), Jan 24, 1959: 20-26, 41; Rowe (1976): 205-23.

80 Deyong, Sarah, "Colin Rowe, Karl Popper and the Discipline of Architecture", *journal of visual culture* 15 (3), 2016: 373.

81 Wittkower (1947): 164.

82 I treat the question of the 'whole' in my other text included in this volume. Here it is worthwhile highlighting a recurrent ambiguity between 'wholeness' as coherence and harmony, as expressed by Burnham, *infra*, and as homogeneity, as emerging in some of the best-known urban design products of the Modern Movement.

83 The date reported on Rowe's passport is September 19. I owe a great deal to David Rowe, Colin's younger brother, for this and other pieces of information which have clarified a few of Colin's vicissitudes in this period of his life.

84 The journey was made in company with Brian Richards, alumnus of Liverpool and Yale. Right in 1951, Jack Kerouac was completing *On the Road* (published only in 1957).

85 Rowe (1996/1): 22.

86 Rowe and Richards worked for about three months with the firm Wright, Metcalf & Parsons, Architects, dealing with the project of the State College. They also worked, for a shorter period, in Vancouver, with the firm Sharp Thompson Berwick & Platt, designing the Seaman Institute: Naegele (2016): 17 (n. 15); Rowe (1996/1): 22.

87 Rowe (1996/1): 22. Rowe writes from his residence on May 6: Naegele (2016).

88 Naegele (2016). The most likely version of the facts derives from Rowe's letters to his parents and to Hitchcock, then romanticized by Rowe in Caragonne (1995): 7-8 and in Rowe (1996/1): 25-26 and further corroborated by David Rowe, combined with what is reported in Germany (1991): 142-43. However, Germany places these events one year earlier. This is *(cont.)*

Most important to the present argument, the second Colloquium in Darmstadt, held on August 4 to 6 and dedicated to "Man and Space", saw the participation, among many architects, of two philosophers: Martin Heidegger, who contributed with the famous lecture "Bauen, Wohnen, Denken" (Building, Dwelling, Thinking), and José Ortega y Gasset, with the less-known but not less-important lecture "Der Mythus der Menschen hinter der Technik" (The Myth of Men behind Technique).[93]

Ortega was also an indirect protagonist of CIAM 8, which had taken place in Hoddesdon a few weeks before, July 7–14, 1951, and was dedicated to "The heart of the city". President of CIAM, Josep Lluís Sert's opening remarks, as they are reported in the published proceedings, started—or, in fact, ended—citing Ortega's famous passage on the urban square which Rowe and Koetter would later refer to in *Collage City.*

> *For in truth the most accurate definition of the* urbs *and the* polis *is very like the comic definition of a cannon. You take a hole, wrap some steel wire tightly round it, and that's your cannon. So, the* urbs *or* polis *start by being an empty space, the* forum, *the* agora, *and all the rest are just a means of fixing that empty space, of limiting its outlines.*[94]

The similarity of this image of the city square and the concept of *Raum*, discussed in the Darmstadt conference by Heidegger deserves notice.

> *What the word for space,* Raum, *designates is said by its ancient meaning.* Raum, Rum *means a place cleared or freed for settlement and lodging. A space is something that has been made room for, something that has been freed, namely with a boundary, Greek* peras. *A boundary is not that at which something stops but, as the Greeks recognized, the boundary is that from which something* begins its essential unfolding. *That is why the concept is that of* horismos, *that is the horizon, the boundary. Space is in essence that for which room has been made, that which is let into its bounds.*[95]

The space delimited and rescued from formless nature—space as void, that is—is 'place' with its own identity and is *'piazza'* as urban center. CIAM and its Team 10 evolution, as synthesised by Aldo van Eyck's, "Whatever space and time mean, place and occasion mean more" here is more than just embryonic.[96]

I refer to Heidegger and Ortega—void, space as *Raum*, place, *piazza*—to propose that this renewed *episteme* was slowly consolidating into the dynamics of the Modern Reform and becoming a solid conceptual basis for and a stimulating evocation in the development of urban design. The effective planimetric abstraction of solids and voids, present in a long tradition of urban studies in the late 19th and early 20th centuries, could resurface and be made available for design and the methodological and axiological relevance of voids—as equal to or more important than solids—would then be supported and validated.

In urbanistics, this tradition had been presented in two specific subjects and variations: one including the whole urban fabric, made of solids and voids, and the other focusing on the town square or on the binomial square-monument.

(cont.) likely because her report is based on Harris's recalls many years later. A similar but reversed shifting of dates applies to Harris's recall of the year of the Eighth Pan-American Congress of Architects in Mexico City that he (Harris 1958) places in 1953 but, in fact, was held in 1952. Germany also notes that Rowe had been informed of Harris's presence in Austin from John Adams Comstock, a client of Harris' whom Rowe met in Mexico.

89 Rowe's letter to Hitchcock dated May 17: Naegele (2016): 80-81.

90 Rowe (1996/1): 22; Germany (1991): 142-43.

91 Rowe (1996/1): 26.

92 Besides Wittkower's *Principles* and Le Corbusier's *Modulor*, in 1949 Ackerman had produced: Ackerman, James S., "'Ars Sine Scientia Nihil Est'. Gothic Theory of Architecture at the Cathedral of Milan", *The Art Bulletin* 31 (2), Jun 1949: 84-111.

93 The proceedings of the Colloquium were published the following year. Bartning, Otto, ed., *Darmstädter Gespräch. Mensch und Raum*, Neue Darmstädter Verlagsanstalt Gmbh, Darmstadt, 1952. The magazine *Domus* 983, Sep 2014: 153-55 has the merit to have recently referred to Ortega's conference which can be found, together with reflections on the same subject in Ortega y Gasset, José, *Meditazione sulla tecnica e altri saggi su scienza e filosofia*, Mimesis, Milano, 2011. While published in Spanish, Italian, and French, an English translation does not seem to be available yet. Heidegger's conference has been published on several occasions, also on line. In English: Heidegger, Martin, "Building, Dwelling, Thinking", in *Poetry, Language, Thought*, Harper & Row, New York, 1971: 145-61 (orig. *Vorträge und Aufsätze*, 1954).

94 Tyrwhitt, J[aqueline]; Sert, J[osé] L[uis]; Rogers, E[rnesto] N[athan], *The Heart of the City: towards the humanisation of urban life*, Pellegrini and Cudahy, New York, 1952: 3. Ortega y Gasset, José, *The Revolt of the Masses*, W. W. Norton & Company, New York, (1930) 1957: 151. On the difference between the actual lecture by Sert and the proceedings, Mumford (2000): 207. Rowe and Koetter use this quotation at the beginning of a chapter of *Collage City*: "Crisis of the Object: Predicament of Texture", (Rowe, Colin; Koetter, Fred, *Collage City*, MIT Press, Cambridge, MA, and London, 1978: 50) and to conclude its reworking: Koetter, Fred; Rowe, Colin, "Crisis of the Object: The Predicament of Texture", *Perspecta* 16, 1980: 109-41.

95 Heidegger, Martin, "Building Dwelling Thinking", in *Basic Writings from* Being and Time *(1927) to* The Task of Thinking *(1964)*, Harper Collins, New York, (1977) 1993: 356; Heidegger (1971): 154.

96 Smithson, Alison, ed., "Team 10 Primer", *Architectural Design* XXXII (12), Dec 1962: 600.

The growing attention to this immateriality of the object of interest, space, a sort of disciplinary illusionism, had had many well-known contributors. On the side of urbanistics, one could count: Camillo Sitte (Fig. 14), Otto Schlüter, Joseph Stübben, Albert Brinckmann, Raymond Unwin, Gustavo Giovannoni, Paul Zucker but also, more recently, Eliel Saarinen, and Steen Eiler Rasmussen[97] (Fig. 15) as well as, again, the Townscape group with their discursive exchanges.[98]

This line of development was intertwined with a renewed attention to the centrality of space towards which the theoretical contributions of August Schmarsow, mainly in architecture, and, later, of Herman Sörgel and Paul Zucker, including both architecture and urban design, are only the best known of a copious, multi-centered, and long-lasting system supported by physiological and psychological evidence. The studies of applied optics by Hermann Maertens are among the most frequently recorded scientific supports in the early stages of this flow of research that is hardly isolated.[99] During the 1950s, Gaston Bachelard was already working and publishing on the subject that he treated in *La poétique de l'espace* in 1957.[100]

The concept of the centrality of space in architecture and urban design was not as well developed in English-speaking countries. In a footnote to his lecture delivered at the Royal Institution, London in 1979, Rowe observed with dismay that "space-talk made its decisive entry into the critical vocabulary of American and English architects with the publication of Sigfried Giedion's *Space, Time and Architecture* in 1941, and Nikolaus Pevsner's *An Outline of European Architecture* in 1943", well after its development in German speaking countries.

Giedion's book had been prepared as the Charles Eliot Norton Lectures at Harvard University, for the 1938–39 academic year. Rowe regards as no more than exceptions, "Bernard Berenson, his disciple Geoffrey Scott, and, maybe, Frank Lloyd Wright".[101] Bruno Zevi's 1948 *Saper vedere l'architettura* would be published in English as *Architecture as Space* not earlier than 1957.[102]

Space is a co-protagonist in Rowe's 1956 essay "Chicago Frame"[103] and, as anticipated, reference to the concept of space was an essential foundation in the pedagogical reform at Austin, and this applied to both architectural and urban space.[104] The convergence of optics and psychology, of spatial composition, and the multiplication of studies on *piazze* supported the recognition of the identity and figural role of the void in the figure/ground representations of urban fabrics.

It is worth noting the similarity between Heidegger's definition of *Raum*, as "something that has been made room for, something that is cleared and free, namely within a boundary ..." and Rowe's 1966 analogy of the city as "a field of standing corn waiting to have spaces made in it".[105]

In 1967, long before the publication of *Collage City*, the thesis by one of Rowe's earliest students at Cornell, Wayne W. Copper, used the figure/ground technique to reproduce, in black and white, exemplary models of the dialectic interplay of solids and voids making urban fabrics (Fig. 17). Copper, and Rowe with him, could certainly count on far more authoritative precedents than the frequently cited maps by *Baedeker* which, in fact, had been in circulation since 1827 and cover a very large number of examples.

97 Sitte, Camillo, *Der Städte-Bau nach seinen Künstlerischen Grundsätzen*, C. Graeser, Wien, 1889; Schlüter, Otto, "Über den Grundriss der Städte", *Die Erde. Zeitschrift der Gesellschaft für Erdkunde zu Berlin*, 34, 1899: 446-62; Stübben, Joseph, *Der Städtebau, Handbuch der Arkitectur*, Alfred Kröner Verlag, Stuttgart, (1890) 1907; Brinckmann, Albert E., *Platz und Monument. Untersuchungen zur Geschichte und Ästhetik der Stadtbaukunst in neuerer Zeit*, Wasmuth, Berlin, 1908; Unwin, Raymond, *Town Planning in Practice*, T. Fisher Unwin, London, 1909; Giovannoni, Gustavo, *Vecchie città ed edilizia nuova*, UTET, Torino, 1931 (the first essay with the same name was published in 1913); Zucker, Paul, *Entwicklung des Stadtbildes*, Drei Masken Verlag, Berlin – Munich, 1929; Saarinen, Eliel, *The City. Its Growth. Its Decay. Its Future*, Reinhold Pub. Corp., New York, (1941) 1943; Zucker, Paul, *Town and Square: from the Agora to the Village Green*, Columbia University Press, New York, 1959. Rasmussen, Steen Eiler, *Towns and Buildings: Described in Drawings and Words*, MIT Press, Cambridge, MA, 1969 is first published in English right in 1951—after an original Danish edition in 1949—with no fewer than 39 'figure/ground' urban maps, almost all of them at the metric scale 1:20.000.

98 Macarthur and Aitchison (2010): 21.

99 Schmarsow, August, "The Essence of Architectural Creation" (a translation of the lecture "Das Wesen der architektonischen Schöpfung" – Leipzig, November 8th, 1893), in Mallgrave, Ikonomou: 287; Sörgel, Herman, *Einführung in die Architektur Ästhetic*, Piloty & Loehle, München, 1918. Sörgel is quoted in De Fusco, Renato, *Segni, storia e progetto dell'architettura*, Editori Laterza, Roma-Bari, 1978: 28-29. Zucker, Paul, "The Aesthetics of Space in Architecture, Sculpture, and City Planning", *The Journal of Aesthetics and Art Criticism* 4 (1), Sep 1945: 12-19. On this renewed centrality of space: Payne: 330 (n. 31); Schwarzer, Mitchell W., "The Emergence of Architectural Space: August Schmarsow's Theory of *Raumgestaltung*", *Assemblage* 15, Aug 1991: 48-61 (for an inclusive overview); Gullberg, Johanna, "Voids and bodies: August Schmarsow, Bruno Zevi and space as a historiographical theme", *Journal of Art Historiography* 14, Jun 2016: 1-20.

100 Ockman (1993): 110; Bachelard, Gaston, *The Poetics of Space*, Beacon Press, Boston, (1957) 1963.

101 Rowe, Colin, "The Present Urban Predicament: Some Observations", lecture delivered at The Royal Institution, London in 1979, in *The Architectural Association Quarterly* 11 (4), 1979, then in *The Cornell Journal of Architecture* 1, (1981): 16-33, and in Rowe (1996/3): 219 (n. 18). Rowe treats the question of space also in his July 31, 1993 letter to Cynthia Davidson. Naegele (2016).

102 Giedion, Sigfried, *Space, Time and Architecture*, Harvard University Press, Cambridge, 1941. *Architecture as Space* is the title of the 1957 English translation of Zevi, Bruno, *Saper vedere l'architettura. Saggio sull'interpretazione spaziale dell'architettura*, Giulio Einaudi, Torino, 1948. On Rowe's controversial attitude towards architectural space: Schnoor, Christoph, "Colin Rowe: Space as well-composed illusion", *Journal of Art Historiography* 5, Dec 2011: 1-22.

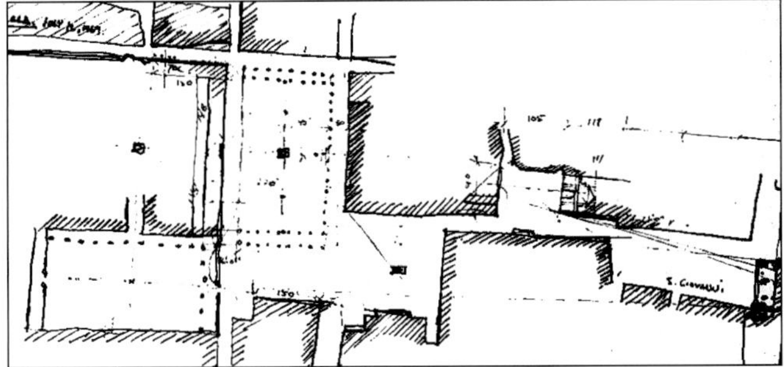

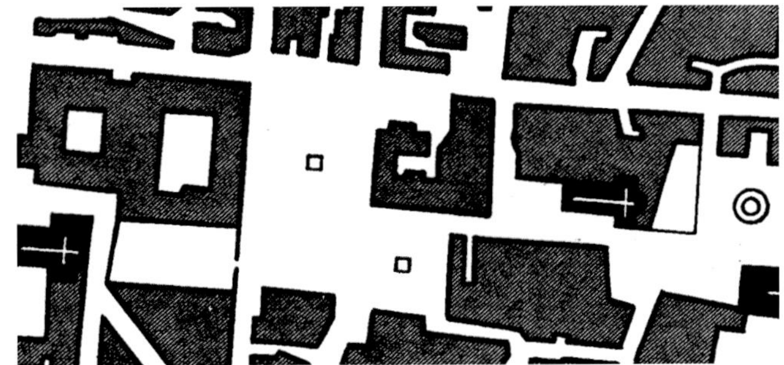

left to right:

Fig. 13. On-site sketch of Lucca, Italy, Steven Hurtt, 1969.

Fig. 14. Sequence of urban squares in Lucca, Italy, Camillo Sitte, 1889 (detail, legend removed).

Copper's argument, published years later,[106] implicitly exhibits one of Rowe's most important contributions to urban design. Urban typological analysis, the rediscovery of the existing city, the relevance of historiographic interpretation, the phenomenology of urban composition, and the psychology of form, all seem to converge to build a solid base and extraordinarily effective means by which to tackle the complexity of the urban project using a rather essential key to read the urban *figura*.

As in its turn-of-the-century development, that interpretive key could rely on a growing understanding of the psychology of form. It would count on the support not only of Gombrich and the Warburg, of Albers at Yale, perhaps of Kepes at MIT, through Slutzky, Hirsche, and Hodgden, as mentioned above, but also of the school of *Gestalt* psychology at Cornell where James Jerome Gibson taught from 1949 to 1972.[107]

In the urban figure/grounds used as both interpretive and design devices, the overcoming of the "paradox" revealed by Zucker,[108] the rift between architects' praxis, striving "for strongest expression of functionalist ideas", and theoretical research focusing on problems of space and volume, seems definitely reconciled. However, contrary to what had happened with "Mathematics", this recomposition does not depend on the revelation of the hidden virtues of Modern architecture. Instead it relies on a reversal of the Modern Movement's attitude towards the relevance and the foundations of urban design.

As Rowe himself would recognize, the 'architecture of the city' that is revealed in the figure/ground studies at Cornell appears simplistic.[109] This is evident, for instance, when compared to the objects of the Italian typo-morphological studies. Nevertheless, the figure/ground studies are often still able to capture the essence of the dialectic between 'monuments' and 'urban fabric', as highlighted by Aldo Rossi.[110] They can portray an 'image of the city' that is more abstract and less guided, in its black and white reduction, than Kevin Lynch's generalized experiential categories—but capable of a wider spectrum of variations.

Yet, the 'architecture of the city' represented by figure/ground maps projects itself as a significant 'image of the city' because the cartographic representation is implicitly an analogous system of the physical and phenomenological reality, of its components and mutual relations, and of their perceptual projections on the observer, in the very sense that a figural element in the cartographic representation

103 Rowe, Colin, "Chicago Frame", *The Architectural Review* 120 (718), Nov 1956: 285-89, also in Rowe (1976): 89-117.

104 Caragonne (1995): 157-64.

105 Heidegger (1971): 134; Maxwell, Robert, "Rowe's urbanism in *Collage City*: a triumph for common sense", in Marzo (2010): 155.

106 Images of Copper's thesis and a text, "The Figure/Grounds", are published in *The Cornell Journal of Architecture* 2, "Urban Design", (Middleton, D. Blake, ed.), Fall 1983. The representation in figure/ground will have a future both within the school, with photocopied reproductions—e.g. Dennis, Michael; Herdeg, Klaus, *Urban Precedents*, Department of Architecture, Cornell University, 1974—and outside it, in various forms, which are still very much alive, in both solid/void and streets/block patterns, and with good reasons. Among them: Jacobs, Allan B., *Great Streets*, MIT Press, Cambridge, MA, 1993; Bosselmann, Peter, *Representation of Places*, University of California Press, Berkeley, 1998; Idem, *Urban Transformation: Understanding City Design and Form*, Island Press, Washington, D.C., 2008; Jenkins, Eric J., *To Scale: One Hundred Urban Plans*, Routledge, Abingdon and New York, 2008; Graves, Charles P. Jr., *The Genealogy of Cities*, Kent State University Press, Kent, OH, 2009; Mayr, Markus; Mayr, René, *Schwarzplan: Open Street Map Basierte Schwarzpläne*, epubli GmbH, Berlin, 2014. Recently, *The New York Times* has dedicated a special section to a figure/ground survey of the U.S. Wallace, Tim; Watkins, Derek, "Where We Live: A Map of Every Building in America", *The New York Times*, October 14, 2018: F1.

107 Gibson was the author of *The Perception of the Visual World* (1950), which was among the texts recommended in the reading list of the Urban Design Studio. In later years, he would be the protagonist of a *querelle* with Gombrich. In more general terms, the importance attributed to the psychology of form in Rowe's program is made evident by the significant presence of texts on this subject among those suggested to his students. Note that a text on this topic, Rudolph Arnheim's *Art and Visual Perception*, *(cont.)*

depicts an element of the reality, represented in the drawing which carries the same figural qualities. Accordingly, the figure/ground approach to urban design, as it is supported by the psychology of form, may constitute a 'scientific' validation and an anchor for the empirical phenomenology-based arguments that had been proposed by Gordon Cullen and Townscape, Steen Eiler Rasmussen and Edmund Bacon.[111]

Because of its grounding, this aspect of Rowe's analytic and design method seems to offer a lesser support in directly solving some facets of present urban design, such as the composition of fields of sparse settlements. But it is likely that this impression stems from its currently limited use, not only as a design tool but even as an analytical device, rather than from an inherent weakness of the figure/ground method itself. Its decreased consideration by the contemporary avant-garde seems to derive from a simplistic disregard for space rather than from its presumed irrelevance.[112] Figure/grounds are, in many cases, still a valid component in the disciplinary toolbox.

The polysemy produced by the dialectical interplay between solid and void, and the potential ambiguities that can be derived from them, seem to apply to urban design the same inclusive and ambivalent solutions that Robert Venturi was valorizing in the composition of the building.[113] As in the "twin-phenomenon" described by Aldo van Eyck, the architectural object is both individual element and part of a greater whole.[114]

With figure/grounds, the situation around the building or the 'surroundings' in the approach by the Austin group in the 1950s becomes protagonist. It is an essential element of the foundational interplay of urban components. It is either the relevant 'ground' essential for the existence of the building as 'figure' or it is 'figure' itself and the building is bound to contribute to it as 'ground'. Thus, the quality of architectural form now depends not only (or not any more) on either its functional program or on its ability to recall Platonic volumes but (also) on its relationships with its context and it is available to be deformed accordingly.[115]

This dependence of the architectural artifact on its context, in fact extended to a broader set of declensions: formal, contiguous, regional stylistic, functional, atmospheric... with different accents in different disciplinary *milieu*, is obviously not something unprecedented.

If one has to be limited to the stylistic and compositional aspects, one might recall as examples: the 'question' of the interventions in historic settings, Eugène Emmanuel Viollet-Le-Duc and Gustavo Giovannoni, the Italian "moderno ambientato", Henry K. Murphy's "adaptive architecture" in China, Trystan Edwards' "good and bad manners in architecture", the traditionalist French reconstruction after WWII, Ernesto Rogers' "pre-existing conditions", the historicist expressions of the Modern Reform, particularly the Italian (the "retreat from Modern architecture" stigmatized by Banham) and English ones (from the London County Council Architects Department's People's detailing to the County of Essex *A design guide for residential areas*) and, once again, the recurring references to the

---

(cont.) although apparently selected by Hoesli and not by Rowe, was already included in the students' bibliography at Austin. Caragonne (1995): 428. For an example of Gibson's influence on urban research: Gosling (2003): 36-37. According to Hurtt and Tice, Laurel Hessler Hodgden, Lee Hodgden's wife, taught in the department of psychology at Cornell University.

108 Zucker (1951).

109 Rowe (1996/3): 24.

110 Rossi, Aldo, "Primary Elements and the Concept of Area", in *The Architecture of the City*, MIT Press, Cambridge, MA, and London, (1966) 1982: 62-101.

111 Reference here is, in particular, to the classics: Cullen, Gordon, *Townscape*, Architectural Press, London, 1961; Rasmussen, Steen Eiler, *Experiencing Architecture*, MIT Press, Cambridge, MA, (1949) 1959 and Bacon, Edmund N., *Design of Cities*, Thames and Hudson Ltd., London, 1967.

112 Petit, Emmanuel, "Rowe after Colin Rowe", in Petit, Emmanuel, ed., *Reckoning with Colin Rowe: Ten Architects Take Position*, Routledge, New York and Abingdon, 2015: 20, has highlighted how "[t]he decreasing usefulness of Rowe's analytic method in the context of the contemporary avant-garde denotes a changed understanding of space today". A recent overall account on figure/ground showing its confirmed validity is in Hebbert, Michael, "Figure-ground: history and practice of a planning technique", *Town Planning Review* 87 (6), 2016: 705-28.

113 Venturi, Robert, *Complexity and Contradiction in Architecture*, The Museum of Modern Art, New York, 1966; Costanzo, Denise, "Text, lies and architecture: Colin Rowe, Robert Venturi and Mannerism", *The Journal of Architecture* 18 (4), 2013: 455-73.

114 Lammers, Harm, "Potentially... Unravelling and reconnecting Aldo van Eyck in search of an approach for tomorrow", masters thesis, Architecture, Building and Planning, Eindhoven University of Technology, 2012: 45-47. It is of some interest registering the similarities between the positions expressed by van Eyck and some ideas emerging from Caragonne's description of the school in Austin and in particular the concept of *Meherdeutige* (ambiguity and multiplicity) expressed by Hoesli. Caragonne (1995): 91.

115 In Rowe's circle, the question of contextualism is especially tackled by some members of the group: Tom Schumacher is the first to publish "Contestualismo: ideali urbani deformati" in *Casabella*, 359-60, 1971. As Schumacher acknowledges in his article, Stuart Cohen and Steven Hurtt were the first to use the term in their Urban Design thesis, 1967. A list of early 'Rowian' texts on this subject is reported in Hurtt, Steven, "Conjectures on Urban Form: The Cornell Urban Design Studio 1963-1982", *The Cornell Journal of Architecture* 2, Fall 1983: 142n.

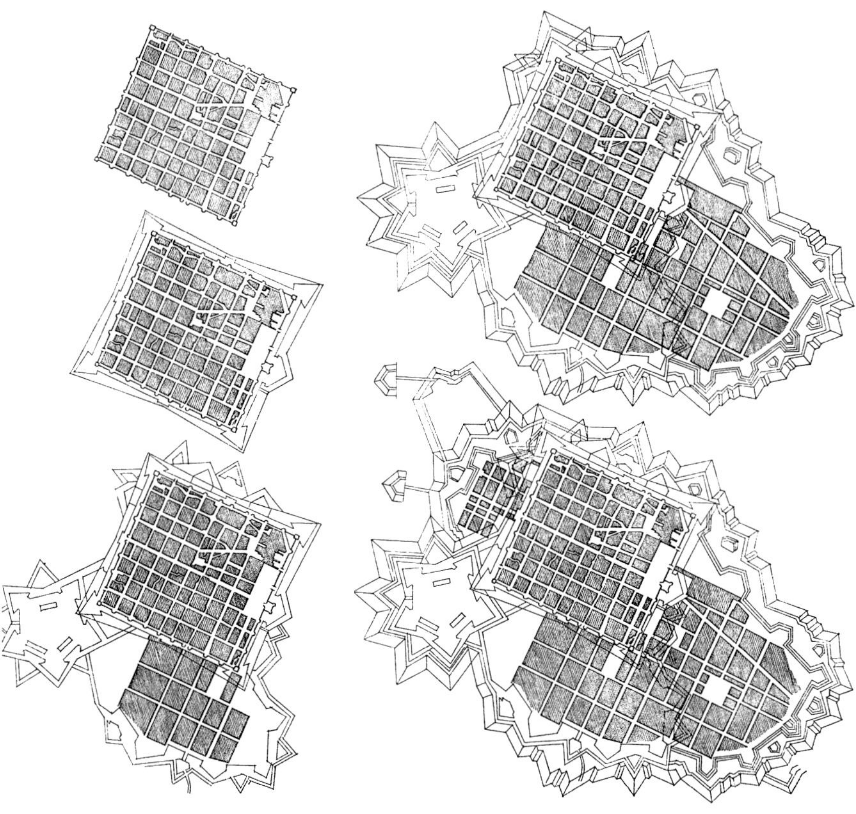

Fig. 15. The city of Turin in five stages, Steen Eiler Rasmussen, 1949.

genius loci and to the picturesque taste of the editors of the *Review* and, above all, of some of their historical references: Uvedale Price and Richard Payne Knight.[116]

This relevance of the harmonious combination of the components of a whole was a widely shared achievement: a foundation of modern urban design at least since Sitte[117] and Daniel Burnham[118] and had been confirmed by the *Gestaltpsychologie*. In the interpretation of Townscape, it is a fundamental concept, as explained in the opening of Cullen's 1961 *Townscape*,[119] (Fig. 9) and, occasionally, it would become radical when the appropriateness of the syntax reached the point of making the aesthetic quality of the single building superfluous. In one of the texts that best represents the Townscape ideology, the editorial "Exterior Furnishing or Sharawaggi", of 1944, Hubert de Cronin Hastings would emphasize: "The aesthetic qualities of the individual items are quite irrelevant. Let them be ugly, let them be incongruous. What matters alone is the unity and congruity of the pattern".[120] The idea would go beyond the discussion among architects. To quote Ortega, from a text of 1953:

> *If an architect creates a project with an impressive personal style, this does not mean, strictly speaking, that he or she is a good architect. ... Imagine a city built by 'brilliant' architects, each working, however, to his or her own personal style. Each of their buildings might be magnificent in and of itself and yet the city as a whole would be bizarre and intolerable.*[121]

116 Macarthur and Aitchison (2010): 25.

117 Collins, George R.; Crasemann Collins, Christiane, *Camillo Sitte: The Birth of Modern City Planning*, Rizzoli, New York, 1986: 217.

118 Burnham, Daniel H., "White City and Capital City", *The Century Magazine* 63, Feb 1902: 619-20.

119 Cullen (1961).

120 The editor [Hastings] (1944): 5 and Macarthur (2012): 650.

121 Ortega y Gasset, José, "On style in architecture", *Domus* 983, 2014: 155 and Ortega (2011): 110.

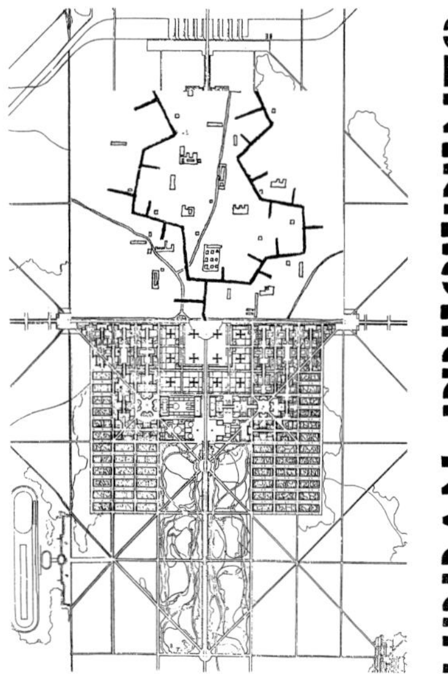

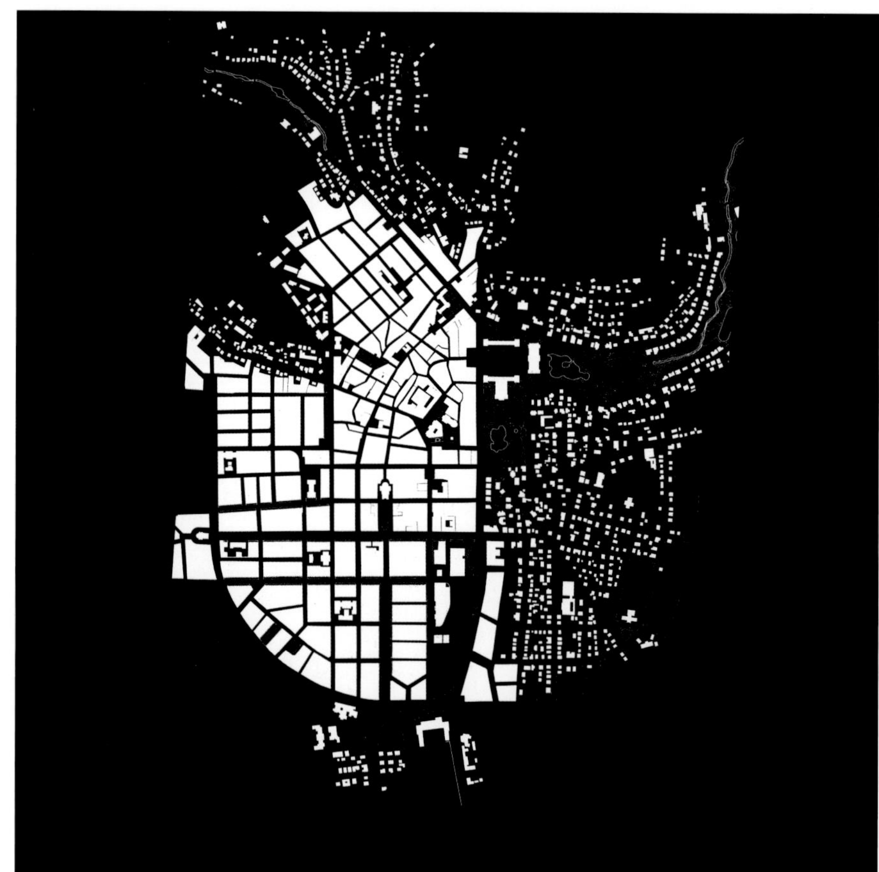

above:
Fig. 16. Front cover of *Urban Precedents*, Michael Dennis and Klaus Herdeg, 1974.

inset:
Fig. 17. Figure/ground reversal plan of Wiesbaden, Wayne Copper.

opposite page:
Fig. 18. *Pianta di Roma* (detail), Giambattista Nolli, 1748, after Leonardo Bufalini, 1551. Black and white inverted.

It must be highlighted, however, that in Rowe's circle contextualism is the appeal to perturbation (a deformation induced from outside) but not necessarily to mimesis; as a concept, it appears ambiguous when one considers the potential results of its application and some of its actual effects in the inclinations of the following decades of Postmodernism, but it is certainly fertile. At the same time, its role in the design process is evident, and it well represents the point of arrival in Rowe's intellectual journey from 'Mathematics' to 'Urbanistics'.

Conclusions

Rowe's "Urbanistics" emerges in the work of his 'creative group', his collaborators, and his students (Fig. 13, 16, 17). It begins to reach maturity in the 1970s with the writing of *Collage City* and with the projects for "Nicollet Island" in Minneapolis and "Roma interrotta", but its yeast is clearly recognizable in the work of his students since the mid-1960s. There seems to be a shift in Rowe's thinking between the late-1940s and the early-1960s, at least in terms of the intensity of the attention and relevance he accords to the architectural object as opposed to the urban fabric;[122] perhaps even from Platonic to Aristotelian, from purity to inclusion, from the hedgehog to the fox, evoked by Archilochus and recalled by Isaiah Berlin in his celebrated essay.

122 The effects of this evolution appear most clearly in the late 1970s and early 1980s in design work as well as in the articles: Rowe "The Present Urban Predicament…"; Koetter and Rowe (1980), which is a reformulation of the core part of *Collage City*, and, partly, in Rowe, Colin, "Foreword", in Krier, Rob, *Urban Space*, Rizzoli, New York, 1979 and in Rowe, Colin, "The Revolt of the Senses", in Porphyrios, Demetri, ed., "Léon Krier. Houses, Palaces, Cities", *Architectural Design Profile* 54, 1984. These last two are republished in Rowe (1996/3). It seems of some interest that, in the very same years the first projects of a new, mature urban design trend appear: theoretical projects like "Roma interrotta" by Peter Carl, Judith Di Maio, Steven Peterson, Colin Rowe, Léon Krier's "Luxembourg" [for a relevant parallelism: Krier, Leon, "Foreword", *The Cornell Journal of Architecture* 2, "Urban Design", (Middleton, D. Blake, ed.), Fall 1983: 6-7] and professional ones: Josef Paul Kleihues's IBA Berlin, Alexander Cooper's and Stanton Eckstut's Battery Park City and Andrés Duany's and Elisabeth Plater-Zyberk's Seaside.

Contextualism well represents the point of arrival of Rowe's conceptual journey, the episodes of which I have tried to piece together here. Thus, on one side, there is geometry conceived as architecture's internal compositional structure or as the embodiment of Utopia. On the other side, one can detect not only the variegated interplay of external and internal formal conditioning elements but also freedom:[123] the uncertain and impervious regulation of complexity rather than its abstraction. The Nietzschean dualism of Apollonian and Dionysian, as well as the aesthetic traditions of *Formwissenschaft* and *Formgefühl,* seem to be reconciled. Having started from the introspection of the 'ideal type', at the end of his journey from "Mathematics" to "Urbanistics" Rowe seems to arrive at the contamination of 'context'.[124] It goes without saying that the purist rigor gradually loses relevance in the composition's rationale and architecture becomes increasingly dependent on urbanistics.

123 Rowe (1976): 216.

124 Hurtt (1983): 67.

The Legacy of Colin Rowe and the Figure/Ground Drawing

Charles Graves

Colin Rowe introduced and continued to advocate the use of the figure/ground drawing as a design tool during his tenure at Cornell University as head of the Urban Design Studio from 1963 to 1990. Even though these characteristic black and white drawings and related versions are well known today, and even though it is a basic tool in the arsenal of urban designers and planners, there remain many unanswered questions surrounding the origins and evolution of this seemingly simple drawing instrument.

frontispiece:
Roma interrotta, detail by Colin Rowe with Steven Peterson, Judith DiMaio and Peter Carl, 1979 (digital image by Charles Graves).

Overview

By 1964 Rowe's students were implementing the figure/ground as a standard tool for presenting their work. In his 1967 Cornell thesis, "The Figure/Grounds", Wayne Copper described its importance for designing at the urban scale. Over the next decade the figure/ground drawing became the standard format in the studio for imparting a particularly cogent understanding of urban settings and site conditions. Meanwhile, research by Rowe and his students revealed new sources to produce meaningful figure/ground analyses. In Rowe's 1971 publication of "Transparency: Literal and Phenomenal Part II,"[1] he first discussed the *gestalt* theory of figure/ground in relation to architectural (facade) analysis. In 1978 Rowe and Fred Koetter published their seminal *Collage City* in which they detailed the use of the figure/ground drawing in urban analysis and design. In the same year, Rowe and his design team published "Roma interrotta". There they further demonstrated how figure/ground could be linked to the conception of public/private space implicit in Giambattista Nolli's famous 1748 plan of Rome. Rowe's later years at Cornell expanded the repertoire to include a broad range of city plans as well as landscape examples, especially those derived from Italian Renaissance gardens. All of these were rendered through the use of black or hatched *poché* for buildings and landscape volumes and white for open space.

By the 1980s and 1990s the figure/ground became an accepted method for both urban analysis and design by many in the profession and the academy. Perhaps the very acceptance of this technique set the stage for a contrarian position

1 Rowe, Colin; Slutzky, Robert, "Transparency: Literal and Phenomenal, Part II", *Perspecta*, 13/14, 1971: 287-301.

1

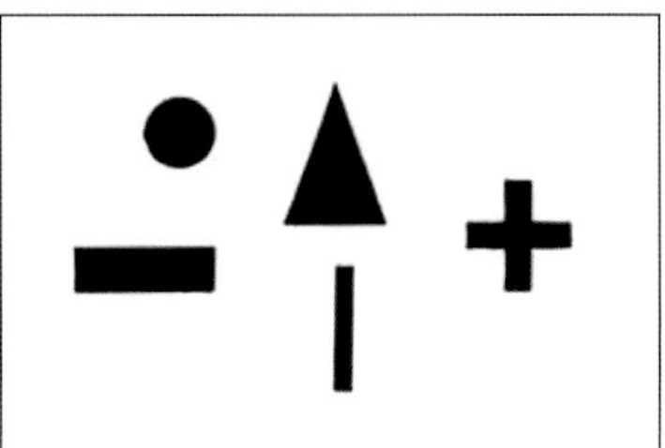

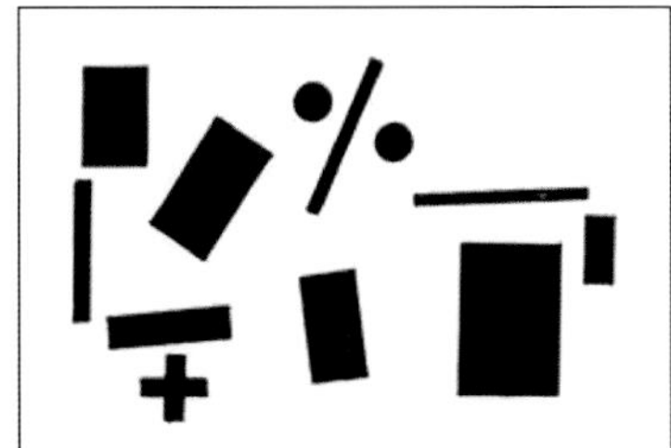

2

Fig. 1. The image on the top is commonly called *Rubin's Vase*, which first appeared in Edgar Rubin's 1915 thesis. The images on the bottom are stimuli used by Rubin in his study of the recognition of figures, flipped as either figure or ground.

Fig. 2. The three frames show a static field of objects (top), a field of two circles offset by similar rectilinear shapes (middle), and a field of rectilinear shapes creating a void area with a cruciform shape placed as object (bottom).

Fig. 3. From left to right; *Composition with Lines*, 1917 Piet Mondrian; *Fox Trot; Lozenge Composition with Three Black Lines*, 1929 Piet Mondrian; *About Two Squares: A Supremicist Tale of Two Squares in Six Constructions*, 1922 El Lissitzky.

Fig. 4. Images from Rudolph Arnheim's *Art and Visual Perception: A Psychology of the Creative Eye* in which he discusses the use of figure/ground in art. Shown from left to right are a woodcut by Hans Arp, *Silent Tension*, with Arnheim's layered analysis and Madame Réjane a print by Aubrey Beardsley

taken by the architectural critic for *The New York Times*, Herbert Muschamp. He complained that both the figure/ground drawing and its progenitor, the Nolli Plan, were "seldom used by contemporary architects and planners for serious purposes".[2]

Muschamp asserted that figure/ground was not the neutral, scientific device it was assumed to be and that it, and the 18th century map upon which it was based, were inextricably embedded in a political and social milieu and, finally, that the drawing had lost any real value, devolving instead into a style:

> *both drawing styles had become instead merely a symbol of pedigree. For one group of American architects, it represents the 'classical' tradition connected with the Rome Prize, the City Beautiful movement and the connotations of social entitlement attached to the firm McKim, Meade, & White* [sic]. *For another faction, it signifies the more recent lineage of figure/ground abstraction associated with Colin Rowe and his students at Cornell University's architecture school.*[3]

Despite this critique, today the figure/ground drawing still remains a widely recognized tool (even if limited) and a valuable method for gathering and displaying urban data. Its use has extended far beyond the schools of urban design in which it was first explored. Urban design schemes using figure/ground representations continue to be generated and exploited in creative ways while also proving to remain useful in their original black and white format. In the last decades computerized drawings, in some cases aided by other forms of digital

2 Muschamp, Herbert, "A Rush to Complete Plans for Downtown", *The New York Times*, October 14, 2001.

3 Ibid.

3

4

visualization techniques, are opening up new and promising possibilities for using figure/ground. We can see that Rowe's figure/ground drawing technique is far from dead, that it is a relevant design tool for urban designers and not the outdated stylistic affectation that Muschamp claimed it to be.

Figure/Ground Makes its Introduction

The investigation of the cognitive approach to art, known as *gestalt* psychology, begins in Germany at the Berlin school in 1887 with the work of Christian von Ehrenfels. The fundamental principle of *gestalt* theory is that the human mind forms a global whole with self-organizing tendencies. This principle maintains that human perception considers objects in their entirety before, or in parallel with, recognition of their individual parts; suggesting the whole is other than the sum of its parts. Gestalt psychology attempts to understand the laws that determine our ability to acquire and maintain meaningful perceptions in a seemingly disordered world.[4]

Within the field of *gestalt* psychology it was Edgar Rubin who first coined the term figure/ground in his doctoral thesis, "Synsoplevede Figurer" (Visually Experienced Figures), which he defended at the University of Copenhagen in 1915 (Fig. 1, 2).[5]

Figure/ground organization is a type of perceptual grouping that is a vital necessity for recognizing objects through vision. In Gestalt psychology it means

4 Erenfels, Christian von, *Ueber Fühlen und Wollen: Eine Psychologische Studie*, C. Gerold's Sohn, Wien, 1887.

5 Pind, Jörgen L., "Figure and Ground at 100", *The Psychologist* 25 (1), Jan 2012, [https://www.bps.org.uk/psychologist/looking-back-figure-and-ground-100].

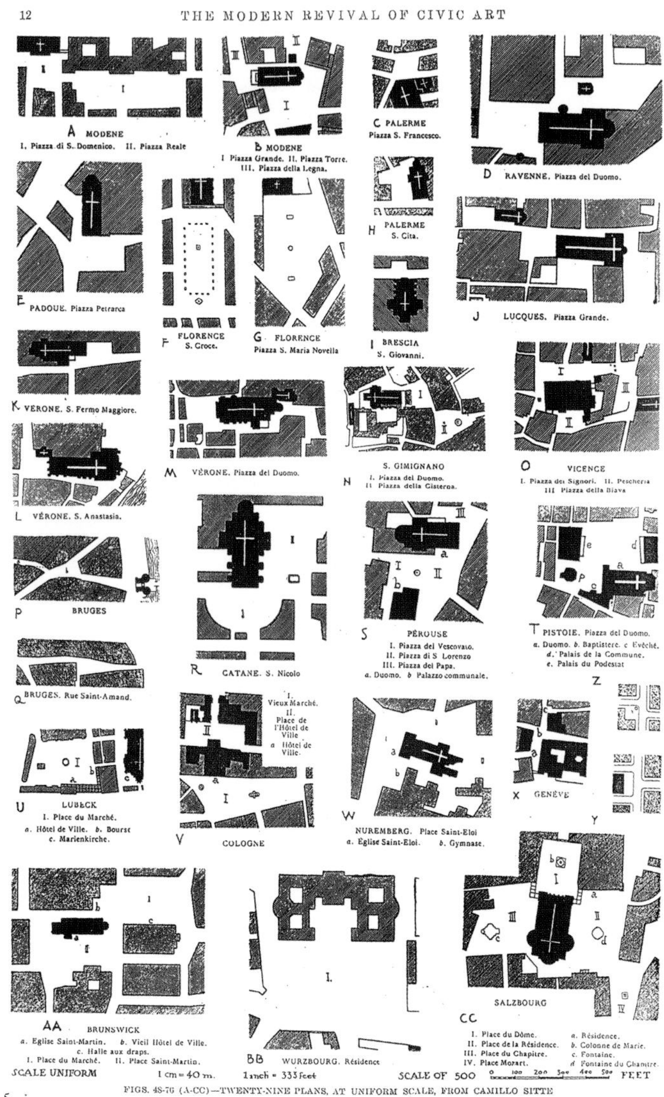

5

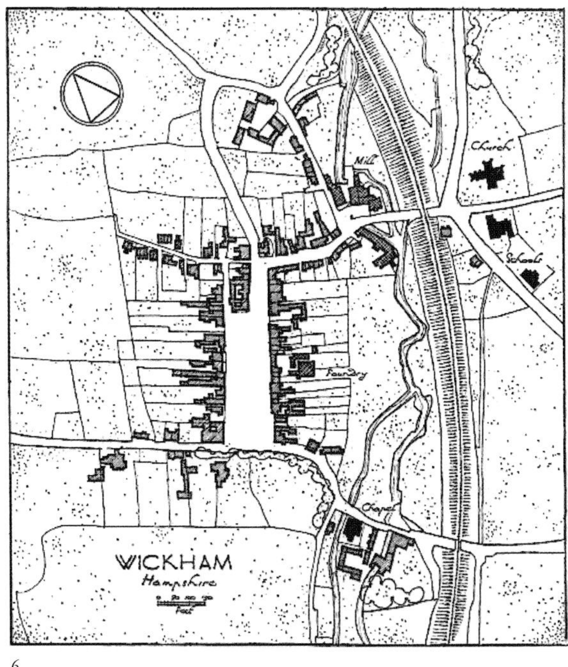

6

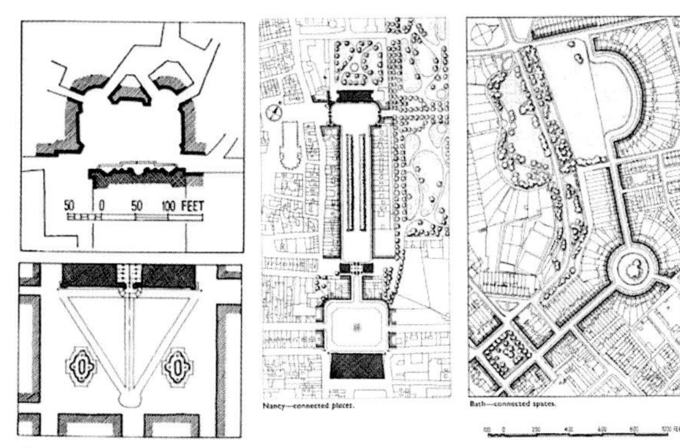

7

distinguishing a figure from its background. For example, one sees words on printed paper as the 'figure' and the white sheet as the 'ground'.[6]

Throughout his life Colin Rowe was an avid reader touching on many subjects but especially those that delve into the world of the visual arts. This, coupled with his razor-sharp memory, suggests that Rowe may have been introduced to *gestalt* principles during the early years of his formal education and then drew on this reservoir of ideas later in his career.

> Collage City *was not Colin Rowe's first interaction with Gestalt psychology….He and Robert Slutzky use the Gestalt framework of figure and ground to analyze architectural form and facades in their* Transparency *essays from the 1960s. In the second essay, the authors express their admiration for the "curious little diagrams" of Gestalt psychologists.*[7]

These diagrams, which follow Rubin's seminal work, are typically found in basic gestalt texts such as Koffka's *Principles of Gestalt Psychology*, Köhler's *Gestalt*

6 Schacter, Daniel L.; Gilbert, Daniel T.; Wegner, Daniel M., "Sensation and Perception, Vision II: Recognizing What We Perceive" in *Psychology,* (2nd ed.), Worth Publishers, New York, 2011: 149-50.

7 Khamsi, James, "Curious Little Diagrams: Gestalt Psychology and the Urbanism of Colin Rowe and Kevin Lynch", *Urban Infill,* 5, "Diagrammatically", Schwarz, Terry; Lewis, Karen (eds.), Cleveland Urban Design Collaborative, College of Architecture and Environmental Design, Kent State University, 2012: 84-89.

8 Köhler, Wolfgang, *Gestalt Psychology*, H. Liveright, New York, 1929 and Hartman, George, *Gestalt Psychology; A Survey of Facts and Principles*, The Ronald Press Company, New York, 1935.

9 Rowe, Colin; Slutzky, Robert, "Transparency, Literal and Phenomenal", *Perspecta* 8, 1963: 45-54.

10 Kepes, György, *Language of Vision*, Paul Theobald, Chicago, 1944.

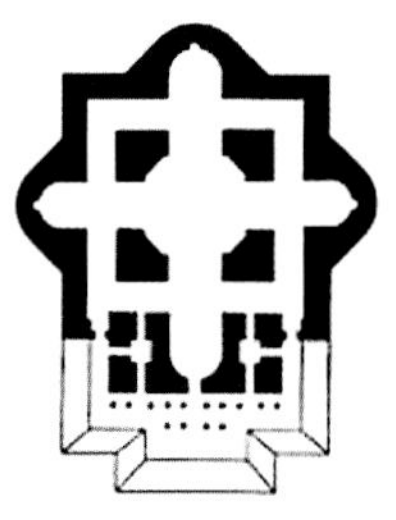

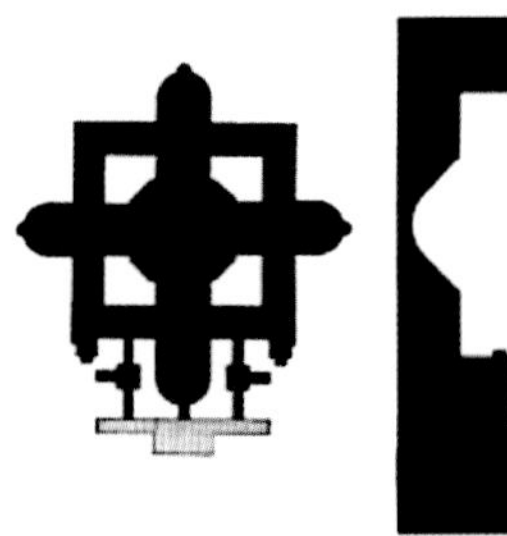
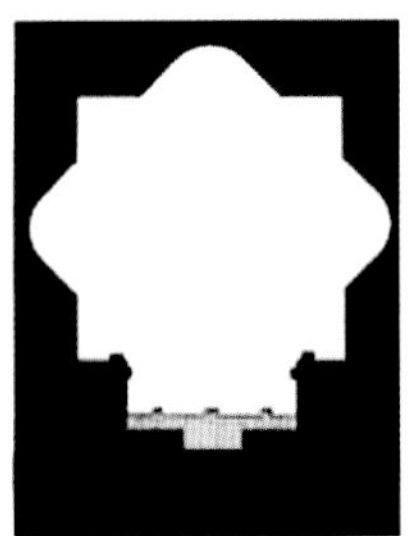
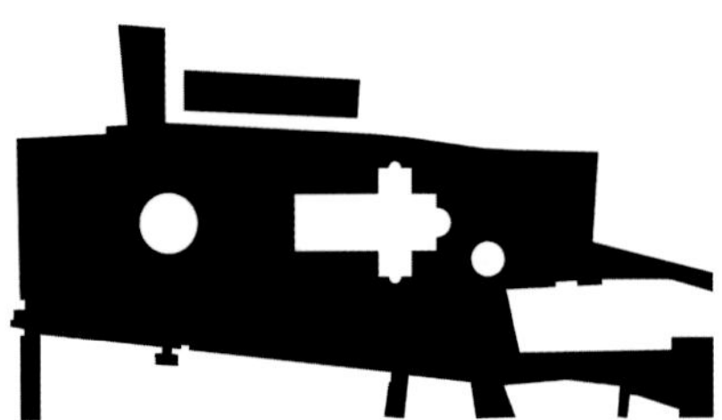
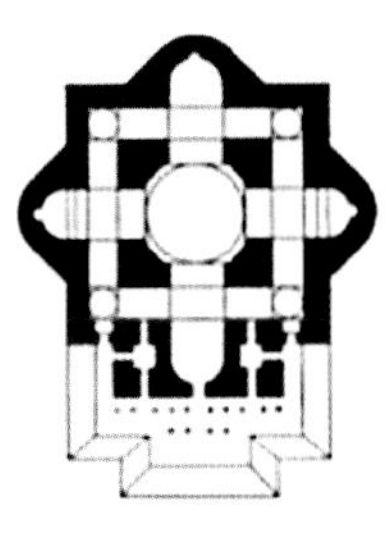
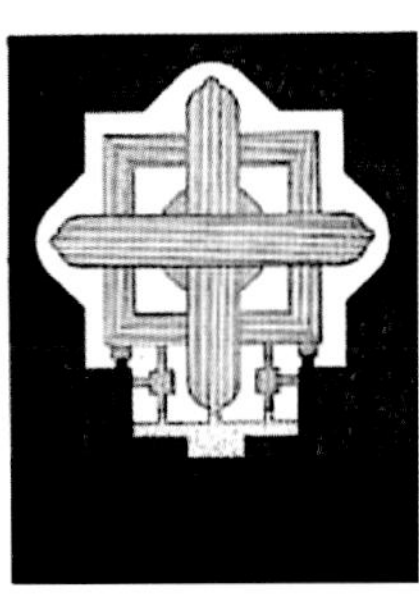
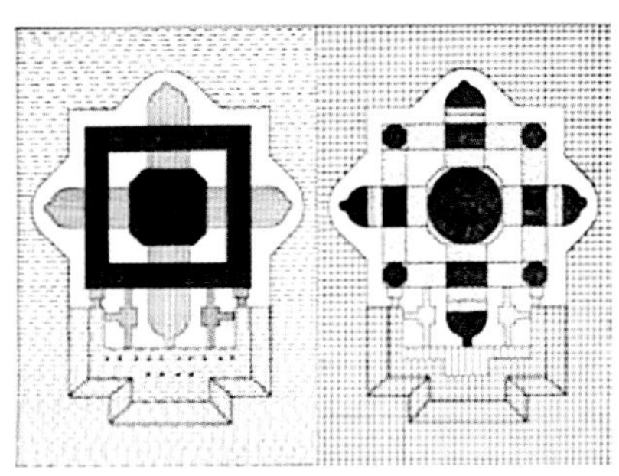
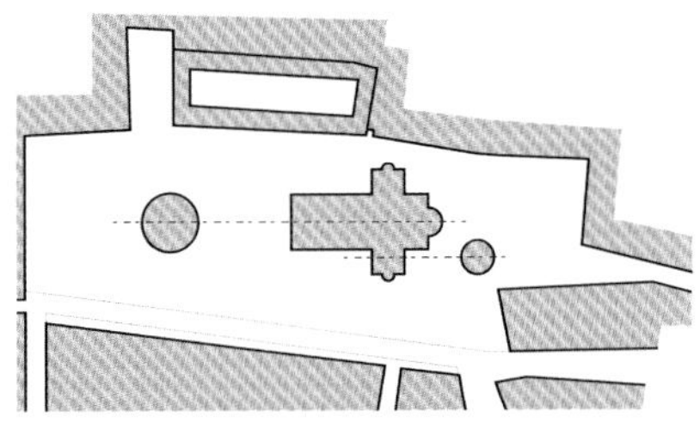

8

9

Psychology, and Hartmann's *Gestalt psychology*.[8] In "Transparency: Literal and Phenomenal"[9] Rowe mentions György Kepes who published *Language of Vision* in 1944. Rowe includes images from his text in "Transparency: Literal and Phenomenal Part ii". Kepes never uses the term figure/ground but he does reference the term *ground* in describing the base field upon which his images are placed.[10]

It is also possible that Rowe might have drawn his own connections to art and Gestalt theory prior to the writings of Kepes and Rudolph Arnheim discussed below. It is an established fact that Colin was preoccupied with certain early 20th century artists such as Mondrian and El Lissitzky. In the early 1900s Mondrian was beginning to investigate the use of space via the use of basic line work and simple planes. His 1917 piece, *Composition with Lines*, is produced with a series of parallel and perpendicular black lines on a white field and his later work *Fox Trot; Lozenge Composition with Three Black Lines* follows suit. There also existed other black and white paintings that related to figure/ground, which Rowe could have seen. El Lissitzky's 1922 book,[11] *About Two Squares: A Suprematist Tale of Two Squares in Six Constructions* illustrates a square divided into halves with the top half being black and the bottom half being white while black and white rectilinear shapes are superimposed and appear to float in space. The overall effect is one of layered depth (Fig. 3).

Figure/ground became adopted by the arts, however, only when Rudolf Arnheim produced *Art and Visual Perception: A Psychology of the Creative Eye*. Published in 1954, Arnhem's *magnum opus* offered the first in-depth description of the artistic principles of the figure/ground relationship.[12] In chapter v, "Space", Arnheim discusses the idea of figure/ground relation in art (Fig. 4). In her review, Marianne L. Simmel describes his book as:

Fig. 5. From Hegemann and Peets's, *The American Vitruvius: An Architect's Handbook of Civic Art*, a series of *piazze* shown at the same scale. The drawings were taken from Camillo Sitte's *City Planning According to Artistic Principles*.

Fig. 6. From Thomas Sharp's *The Anatomy of the Village*, published in 1946.

Fig. 7. See: Sharp, Thomas, Frederick Gibberd, and William Graham Holford, *Design in Town and Village*, H.M. Stationery Off., London, 1953. Holford presents a number of illustrations similar to the urban fabric pieces that Rowe would show his urban design students.

Fig. 8. In 1948 Bruno Zevi published *Saper Vedere L'architettura*. In this text Zevi uses a plan of Michelangelo's design for St. Peter's to discuss his idea of the primacy of space and the process of analysis for determining its key attributes. Although Zevi never uses the term figure/ground, his diagrams are a clear use of both figure/ground and reverse figure/ground.

Fig. 9. A telling image from Frederick Gibberd's *Town Design*, 1953 that depicts figure/ground and reverse figure/ground.

11 El Lissitzky, *About Two Squares: A Suprematist Tale of Two Squares in Six Constructions* (Lodder, Christine, trans.), Tate Publishing, London, 2015.

12 Arnheim, Rudolf, *Art and Visual Perception: A Psychology of the Creative Eye*, University of California Press, Berkeley, 1954: 213-91.

10

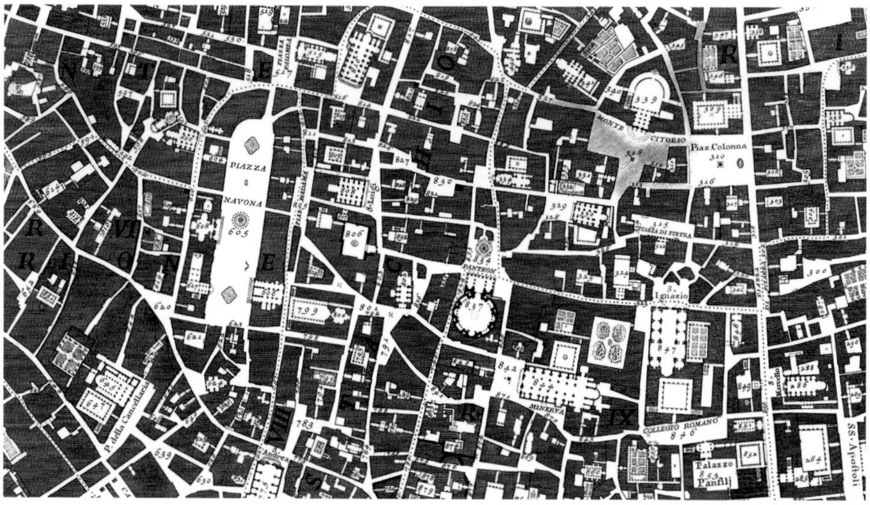

11

Fig. 10. Although Rowe was not a fan of Gordon Cullen's *Townscape* there is a study by Cullen called "Casebook: Serial Vision", which shows a small figure/ground in the lower right corner that offers an abstract synopsis of his perceptual argument.[13]

Fig. 11. Detail of Nolli's *Pianta Grande di Roma.* Note the massing is hatched dark gray, allowing for various building plans to be drawn in black. From *University of Oregon Nolli Map* ©.

> *the first systematic application of our knowledge of perception to problems of the visual arts, and it contains much that is new to psychologists, estheticians, artists, art-historians, and art-educators.*[13]

In 1954, Colin Rowe joined the faculty at the University of Texas, where Bernhard Hoesli was already teaching. Alexander Caragonne writes in *The Texas Rangers: Notes from an Architectural Underground* that the term "figure/ground" crops up in the copious notes Hoesli recorded while at Texas, a system of note taking that Hoesli attributes to Rowe.[14] In the world of urban design theory and practice, there had already existed a number of examples of the simple black and white figure/ground city plan drawing. More than likely, Rowe studied these precedents, which no doubt helped him solidify the critical importance of the black and white figure/ground urban plan.

In 1922, *The American Vitruvius: An Architect's Handbook of Civic Art* was published and included a set of same scale piazze from Camillo Sitte's work (Fig. 5).[15]

There existed other sources with black and white city plans Rowe might have seen such as *The Anatomy of the Village* by Thomas Sharp.[16] Published in 1946, Sharp, in the 1946 work, draws the village plans freehand using black and white values. The buildings are primarily hatched, trees and green space are stippled, while roads and water features are left white (Fig. 6).

In *Design in Town and Village,* "The Design in City Centers", Part Three, 1953 (Fig. 7), W. G. Holford represents a number of illustrations similar to the urban fabric pieces that Rowe would show his urban design students.[17] In 1948 Bruno Zevi published *Saper Vedere L'architettura* (Fig. 8). In this text, Zevi uses a plan of Michelangelo's design for St. Peter's basilica in Rome to discuss his idea of the primacy of space and the process of analysis for determining its key attributes. Although Zevi never uses the term figure/ground, his diagrams are a clear use of both figure/ground and reverse figure/ground. Another telling image is shown in Frederick Gibberd's *Town Design*, 1953, (Fig. 9) which also depicts figure/ground,

---

13 Simmel, Marianne L., "Art and Visual Perception: A Psychology of the Creative Eye by Rudolf Arnheim" (review), *The American Journal of Psychology* 68 (2), Jun 1955: 330-36.

14 Caragonne, Alexander, *The Texas Rangers: Notes from an Architectural Underground*, MIT Press, Cambridge, MA, and London, 1995.

15 Hegemann, Werner; Peets, Elbert, *The American Vitruvius: An Architects' Handbook of Civic Art,* The Architectural Book Publishing Co., New York, 1922: 12; Sitte, Camillo, *City Planning According to Artistic Principles*, Random House, New York, 1965.

16 Sharp, Thomas, *The Anatomy of the Village*, Penguin Books, Harmondsworth, 1946.

17 Holford, H.G., Ministry of Housing and Local Government (Great Britain), "The Design of City Centres" in *Design in Town and Village*, H.M. Stationery Off., London, 1953.

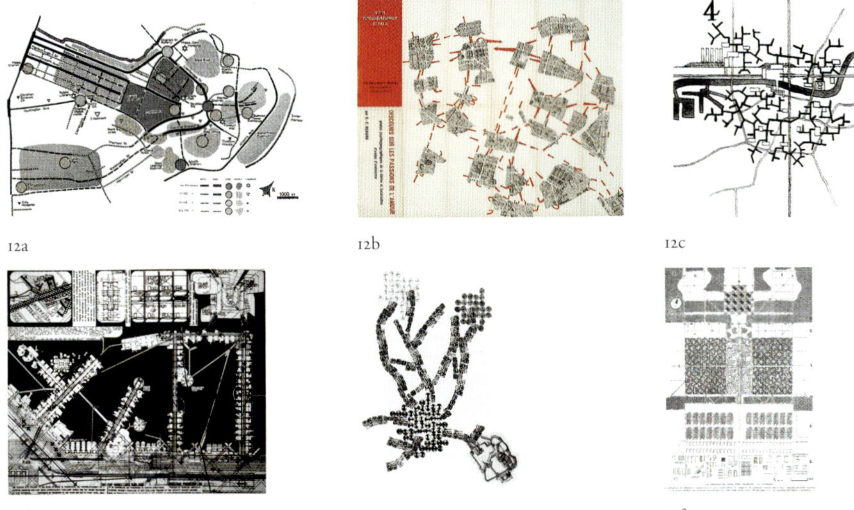

12a 12b 12c

12d 12e 12f

Fig. 12a. Boston from *Image of the City*, by Kevin Lynch, 1960.

Fig. 12b. *Psychogeographic Guide of Paris*, by Guy Debord, 1955.

Fig. 12c. Golden Lane, by Alison Smithson and Peter Smithson, 1952.

Fig. 12d. Plug-In City, by Archigram, 1966.

Fig. 12e. City Helix Project, by Kisho Kurokawa, 1961.

Fig. 12f. Ville Radieuse, by Le Corbusier, 1934.

and reverse figure/ground. It's also interesting to note that even though Rowe was not a huge fan of Gordan Cullen's *Townscape* his "Casebook: Serial Vision" shows a small figure/ground inset which offers an abstract synopsis for his perceptual argument (Fig. 10).[18]

Out of all the figure/ground examples that may have influenced Rowe, the most important is the *Pianta Grande di Roma*, by Giambattista Nolli, published in 1748 (Fig. 11). The question arises, when was Colin Rowe first introduced to this cartographic milestone? Two articles were published in 1925 on Nolli's plan,[20] but it is more probable that Rowe would have been exposed to Nolli's map at the Warburg Institute as a student of the Italophile Rudolf Wittkower during his studies in 1945–46. My research shows that the Institute owned a reproduction of the *Pianta Grande* published in 1932,[21] which would have been close at hand. Although I cannot find any documentation that shows Wittkower having discussed the Rome plan with Rowe, Wittkower does mention Nolli in his 1958 book, *Art and Architecture in Italy, 1600-1750,* Volume 3,[22] so it is likely that the Nolli Plan was at least mentioned by Wittkower during his earlier lectures.

What was 'Out There' Prior to Rowe's Figure/Grounds?

It is understood that the figure/ground tool allows the viewer to quickly process solid to void information. Moreover, Rowe created the conception of the figure/ground in part as a critical response to the perceived inadequacies of other city planning theories and their related graphic techniques that existed in the 1950s and '60s.

For Rowe the figure/ground drawing was a deliberate rejection of Gordon Cullen's perceptually oriented theories articulated in *Townscape*, and the imaginary mega-city designs such as Walking City by Archigram. In contrast to Cullen's *Townscape* process, where the viewer uses the eye in identifying picturesque qualities in a sequence of frames, or Archigram's preference for 3D imagery, Rowe's approach to urban design, represented by figure/ground drawing,

18 Rowe, Colin; Koetter, Fred, *Collage City*, MIT Press, Cambridge, MA, and London, 1978: 32-35.

19 Cullen, Gordon, *Townscape*, Reinhold Pub. Corp., New York, 1961: 19.

20 Craig, Edward G., "Nolli's Plan of Rome, 1748", *The Architectural Review*, 57 (Feb 1925): 86-87.

21 Nolli, Giambattista, *Roma al tempo di Benedetto XIV / La pianta di Giambattista Nolli del 1748*; (riprodotta da una copia vaticana con introduzione di Francesco Ehrle), Biblioteca apostolica vaticana, Città del Vaticano, 1932.

22 Wittkower, Rudolf, *Art and Architecture in Italy, 1600-1750* 3, Penguin Books, Ltd., Harmondsworth-Baltimore, 1958: 12.

13a

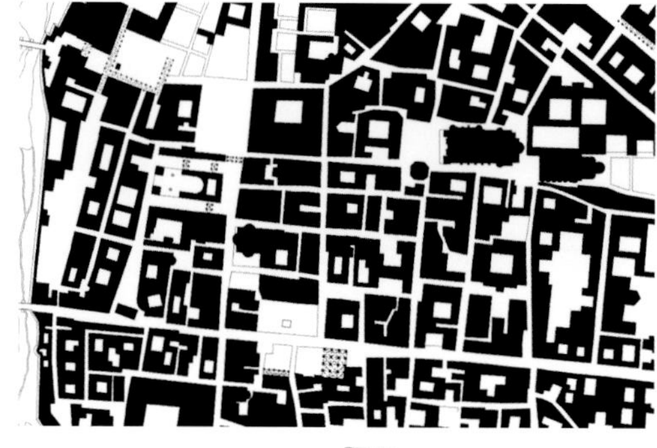

13b

Fig. 13a. Visual notes comparison of the traditional city and the Modern city; by Bernhard Hoesli; from the *Loysoya Park Project* with textual notes, attributed to Rowe.

Fig. 13b. Figure/ground comparison of Parma, Italy and Saint-Dié drawings by Wayne Copper showing the same dichotomy of Modern to traditional urban form.

insisted on viewing the city as a constant conceptual whole—primarily in plan view. The six examples of graphic techniques from the 1950s and '60s contrast with Rowe's preferred mode of representation: graphic techniques that preceeded Rowe's concept of the figure/ground drawing (Fig. 12a–12f).

It is difficult to say when Rowe first actually used the term figure/ground as a critical device. It is alluded to in his writings, but never actually documented. What is documented are some sketches by Bernhard Hoesli using the term figure/ground.[23, 24]

On March 17, 1955, Hoesli, John Hejduk, and Rowe issued an urban design problem at the University of Texas titled the Losoya Park Project (Fig. 13a). During the reviews Hoesli uses the term figure/ground twice while taking notes, and Alex Caragonne states:

> *Rowe's early appreciation of the spatial entourage—the physical environs (as?) a critical element in the formulation of the solution to an architectural/urban design problem——is expressed here for the first time.*[25]

Caragonne goes on to state:

> *Two illustrations … almost certainly have their origins in Rowe's habit of rapidly sketching out his equally rapid formulations and juxtapositions during jury reviews. Significantly, as well, the pair of direct quotations to the right of the illustrations follows Rowe's own speech patterns.*[26]

23 Rowe, Colin, *As I was Saying: Recollections and Miscellaneous Essays* 1, *Texas, Pre-Texas, Cambridge*, Caragonne, Alexander, ed., MIT Press, Cambridge, MA, and London, 1996: 40, "… Bernhard [Hoesli] … was a filing cabinet addict and would never allow any piece of paper to escape his possession; *apologia pro vita sua*, related to the documents."

24 Caragonne (1995): 228-29.

25 Ibid.: 18.

26 Ibid.: 228-29.

14 15a 15b

The two sketches and their notes record the difference between the Losoya Park site and Modern city. Notice the similarities of these two sketches and the figure/ground drawings of Le Corbusier's Saint-Dié and Parma (Fig. 13b) shown in the chapter "The Crisis of the Object: Predicament of Texture", from *Collage City,* where Rowe and Koetter discuss the Modern "object city" versus the traditional city of articulated voids.[27]

Figure/Ground at Cornell

Linear Design Fabric

In *The Cornell Journal of Architecture,* 2, Steven Hurtt writes about Colin Rowe's Cornell urban design studio from 1963–82. He describes Rowe and his students' use of figure/ground as follows:

> *Cities known to be of high experiential quality were examined in terms of figure/ground plan to understand the complex order and experiential richness they represented. In the studio, figure/ground plans became design shorthand that carried rich perceptual potential analogically recalling the exemplary urban conditions....In the early studio years, it was felt that the figure/ground plan carried the crucial information, the genetic code for future design decisions.*[28]

Fig. 14. Figure/ground plan from Roger Sherwood's Cornell thesis of 1964, "The Redesign of a Portion of Downtown Seattle".

Fig. 15a. Although accurate orthogonal city plans generally did not appear until the late 18th century, there were exceptions. Leonardo da Vinci's town plan of Imola32 (upper) is recognized as the first orthogonal city plan drawn in the Renaissance. Graves' figure/ground plan (lower) is based on this plan. The comparison demonstrates a marked degree of abstraction necessary to reveal the basic solid/void dynamic.

Fig. 15b. An important source for Copper, the original SUDK plan of Parma from 1840 (upper), is featured by The Society for the Diffusion of Useful Knowledge (SDUK) published in London from 1830–1844. Copper's figure/ground (lower) is drawn from the same plan.

27 Rowe, Colin; Koetter, Fred, "The Crisis of the Object: Predicament of Texture", *Collage City*, MIT Press, Cambridge, MA, and London, 1978: 62-63.

28 Hurtt, Steven, "Conjectures on Urban Form: Cornell Urban Design Studio 1963-1982", *The Cornell Journal of Architecture* 2, Fall 1983: 56.

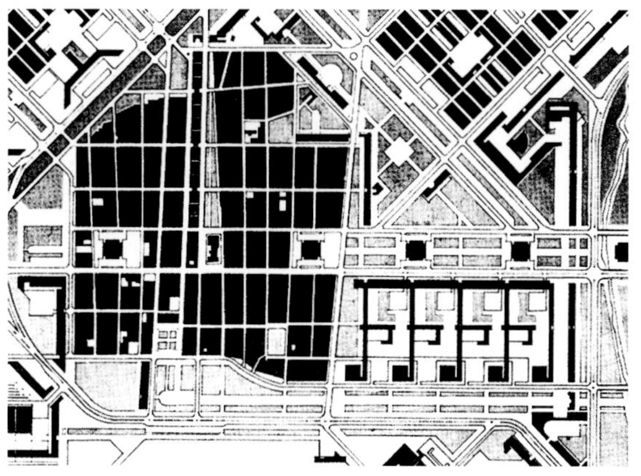

16

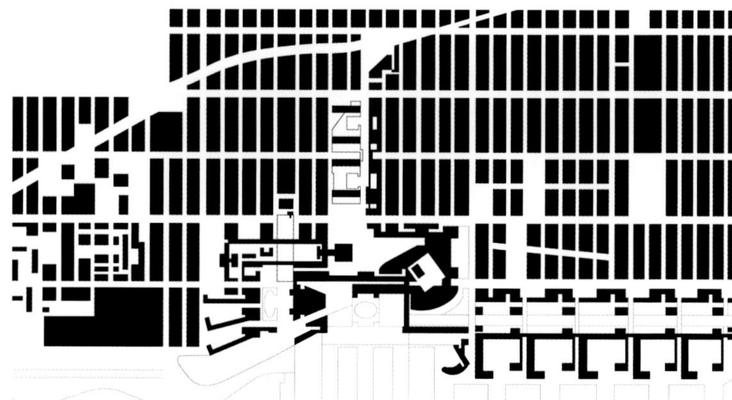

17

Fig. 16. Detail, figure/ground plan from Manuel R. de Vengoechea's thesis of 1968, "Santa Marta: Urban Patterns", Colombia".

Fig. 17. Detail, figure/ground plan from Steven K. Peterson's "Manhattan, West Side Plan" of 1969.

Hurtt continues:

> *The gestalt emphasis and figure/ground methods encouraged the study of figure-field structures, and especially the textures and edges by which such figure-fields are perceived. Correlations were sought and easily established between traditional urban design principles and those of gestalt perception. Hierarchy and focus could be equated to figure, enclosure to closure and modified closure, and edge to contour or good continuation. Applying these correspondences, edge definitions were postulated for each identifiable field of constant texture, pattern, or alignment. Fields were simplified to take on the figure characteristics of simple or good shape.*[29]

Roger Sherwood produced one of the first theses from the new Urban Design Studio at Cornell. His 1964 project for the redesign of Seattle shows the use of a figure/ground plan and linear buildings (Fig. 14). During the early years in the Studio, Hurtt maintains that:

> *The linear building was the principal architectural means for the clarification of fields* [as dominant] .... *The linear building seemed a panacea, the principal mediator between the Modern and traditional city. Inherently non-figural, it could provide enclosure, define traditional figural space, and define the edges of fields, all at the open-space to built-solid ratios typical of twentieth-century urban development.*[30]

In *The Cornell Journal of Architecture,* 2, Wayne Copper writes about his 1967 urban design thesis, "The Figure/Grounds". In this essay he discusses figure/grounds:

> *In order to understand some of the ideas with which this monograph is involved, one must first dissolve various sets—historical, connotational, and otherwise—as well as establish some common level of abstraction in the hope that the familiarity of things known might be overcome. To these ends, the figure/ground phenomenon has been called into play, in an attempt to argue that the roles of solids and voids are somehow conceptually reversible.*[31]

29 Ibid.: 56.

30 Ibid.: 61.

31 Copper, Wayne, "The Figure/Grounds", *The Cornell Journal of Architecture* 2, Fall 1983: 43.

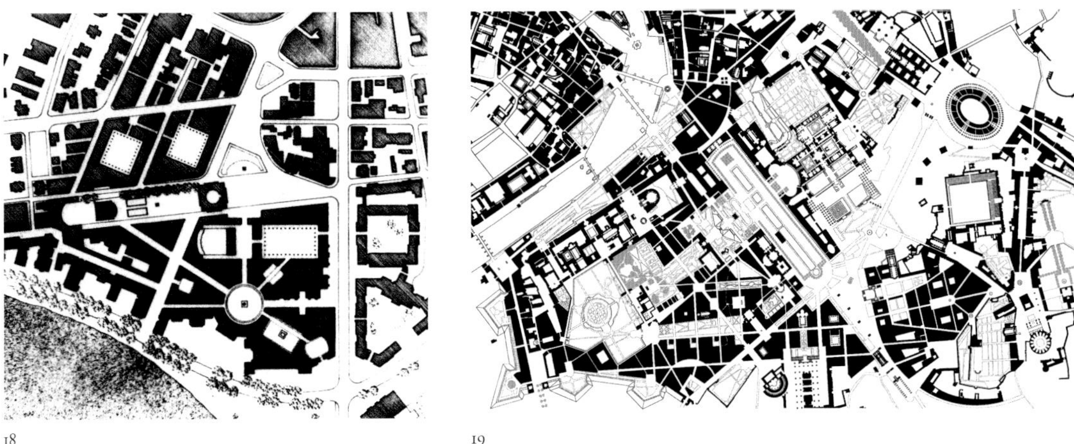

18 19

Fig. 18. Figure/ground plan of the Project for Harvard, by Charles Graves, 1978.

Fig. 19. *Roma interrotta*, by Colin Rowe, with Steven Peterson, Judith DiMaio, and Peter Carl, 1979 (digital image by Charles Graves).

Copper is describing the process of using existing plans as base maps for drawing the finished figure/ground plans, which eventually were included in his thesis. During Rowe's tenure at Cornell, the College of Architecture, Art, and Planning library provided an extensive number of resources of orthogonal city plans needed to produce suitable figure/grounds. The historic city plans that existed, however, often contained superfluous information, which did not always lend itself to a simple solid-to-void investigation (Fig. 15a, 15b).[32]

Contextual Design Fabric

> *Narrowly described, Contextualism is the derivation of form from its context. It depends upon and extends a pre-existing form order. Contextualism is opposed to the utopian aspects of Modern architecture, an architecture derived from new determinants and opposed to the old and traditional. In a broader sense it embraced and valued context of all kinds: natural, man-made, and historical—what Rowe and Koetter have called the* psychocultural field.[33]

Copper's figure/ground drawings were very influential and helped direct investigations into the theory of context. Prior to Copper's production of figure/ground plans, Rowe's reference to urban precedents was usually presented in fragmented form, separate from the larger urban context. In a portion of Manuel R. de Vengoechea's 1968 thesis, "Santa Marta, Colombia; Urban Pattern", his figure/ground illustrates the transition from designing with linear buildings to a denser texture (Fig. 16).

Collision City Design Process

Collision City developed as a shorthand term for identifying a condition in cities, or parts of cities, where 'colliding' grids occurred. Collision City as a process was interested in reestablished the character of both 'figure' and 'archetype' stitched with the 'ground' or 'context'. Lower Manhattan was an early "go-to site" due to its many shifting grid patterns. Steven K. Peterson's Manhattan, West Side Plan from 1969 is one important example (Fig. 17). Hurtt describes the project:

32 See for example, da Vinci, Leonardo, *Piano di Imola*, 1502, (44 x 60 cm.), Royal Library, Windsor Castle, England.

33 Hurtt (1983): 67.

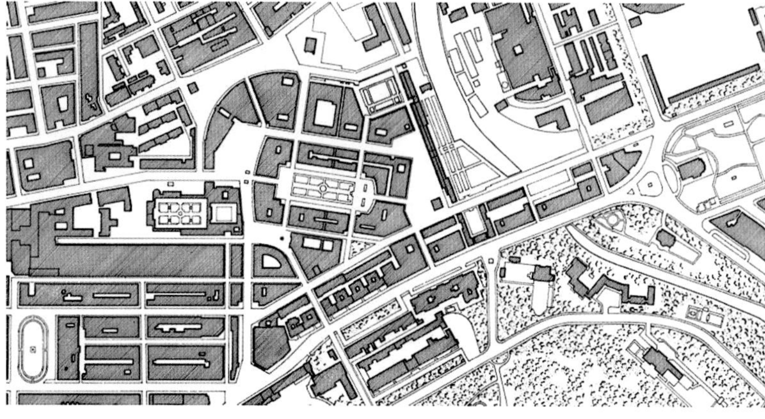

20

21

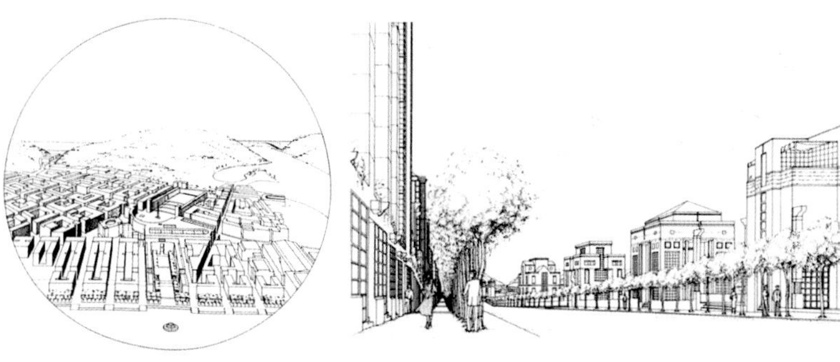

22

23

24

Fig. 20. Detail,"Marylebone Rail Station", near Regents Park, London, thesis, Steven Fong, 1979.

Fig. 21. "Manhattan a Measure", thesis, Charles Graves, 1979.

Fig. 22. "Urban Development for Upper Manhattan", thesis, Michael Manfredi, 1978.

Fig. 23. "Project for Burlington Vermont", thesis, Craig Nealy, 1981.

Fig. 24. "The Milwaukee Lakefront Design Competition", Colin Rowe, Douglas Fredericks, Lee Hodgden, Derek Tynan, 1980.

> *In* [Peterson's] *early 'contextual' work 'figure' is suppressed at the small scale, but established in larger spatio-temporal 'fields'. Collision City debated these assumptions, re-establishing the importance of the* ideal, *the 'figural' space or mass and its* symbolic *role in the cityscape.*[34]

Collage City Design Process

> *Collage City is a Contextualism that embraces culture through history. It is the attitude of Picasso and Eliot, that respects not only the pastness of the past, but also its presence.*[35]

The term *città grassi* appeared in the lexicon of Rowe's Urban Design Studio, 1977–78, as attention shifted to a dense traditional city in contrast to (or opposed to) the sparse Modern city-in-the-park. The figure/ground plan, Project for Harvard by Charles Graves of 1978 went through an early study whereby the graduate student rolled out modeling clay to a standard height and then proceeded to design by cutting away material to develop voids, or fields. This subtractive design process, which readily articulated spatial qualities, was a departure from the more common additive method, which tended to favor solids (Fig. 18).

34 Ibid.: 71.

35 Ibid.: 71.

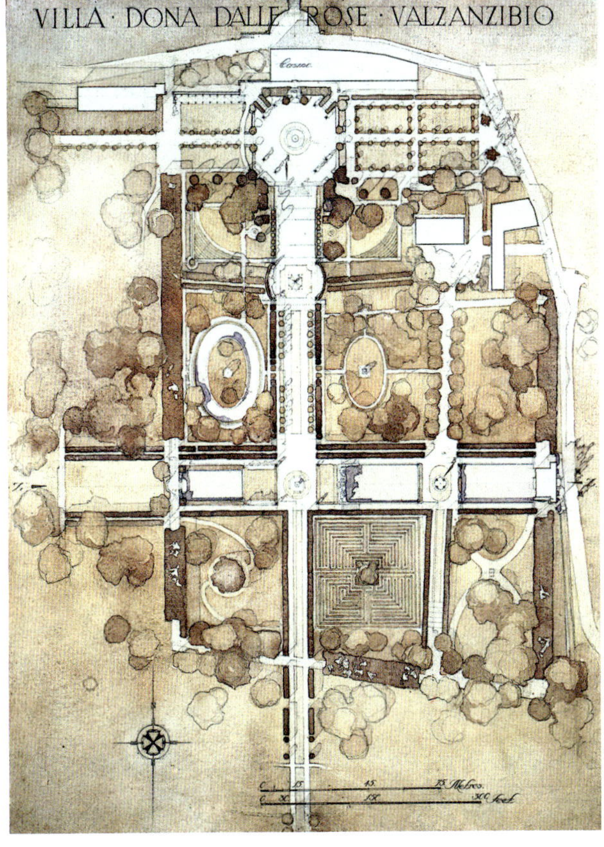

25

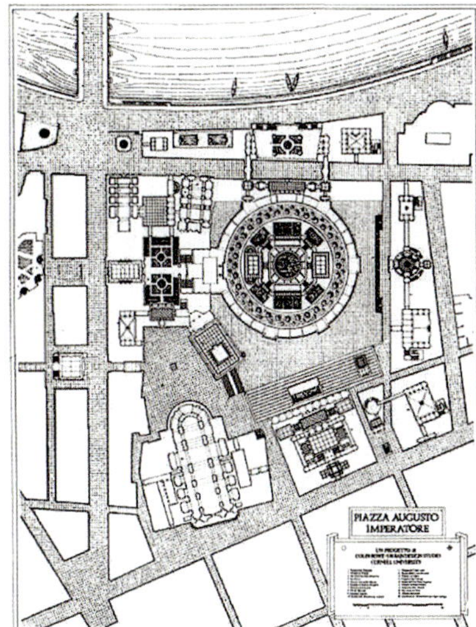

26

Fig. 25. Detail, Villa Donà delle Rose, from *Italian Gardens of the Renaissance* by Shepherd and Jellicoe, 1925.

Fig. 26. "Piazza Augusto Imperatore", Rome, Milano Triennale, *Nove Progetti per Nove Cittá*, by Colin Rowe, Matthew Bell, Robert Goodill, Kevin Hinders, Brian Kelly, Cheryl O'Neil, and Paolo Berdini, 1987.

In 1978 "Roma interrotta" was published.[36] Rowe and his design team, Peter Carl, Judith DiMaio, Barbara Littenberg, and Steven Peterson, worked on plate eight of the Nolli Plan. The results are one of the key achievements of urban design in the second half of the 20th century (Fig. 19).

Another project which depicts the "collage city" design process is Steven Fong's "Marylebone Rail Station" of 1979, near Regents Park, London (Fig. 20). Both projects by Graves and Fong show the building mass as hatched, which more closely emulates the hatching method found in the Nolli Plan.

In 1979 Graves published his thesis titled "Manhattan a Measure" (Fig. 21). This thesis was similar to Copper's figure/ground thesis in that it displayed comparative city figure/grounds, but now at the same scale. The limitations of the figure/ground drawing are readily apparent and have been enumerated by both critics and those sympathetic to this method of representation. Colin is reported to have once quipped when accused of basing his entire urban design theory on figure/ground that, "Figure/ground isn't everything but it's a good place to start". The drawing format does not indicate height of structures, nor change in topography, nor does it readily represent landscape elements, and others have commented that, since it omits facades or more generically the vertical surface, the 'feel' of place is missing from the figure/ground drawing from an experiential point of view. Other drawing types and models are needed to more completely explain

36 Graves, Michael (guest editor), "Roma Interrotta", *Architectural Design* 49 (3/4), Academy Editions, London, 1979.

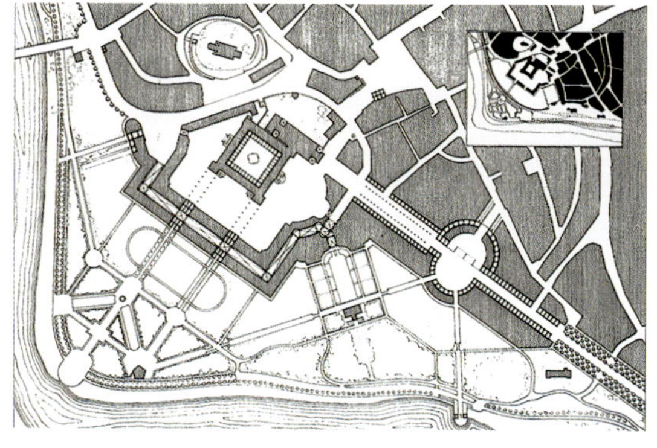

27a

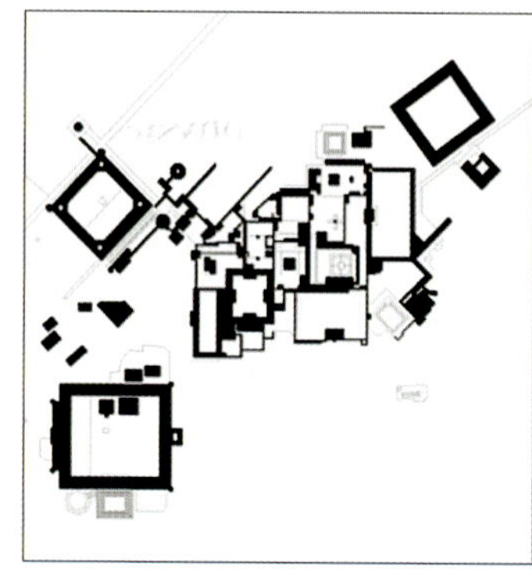

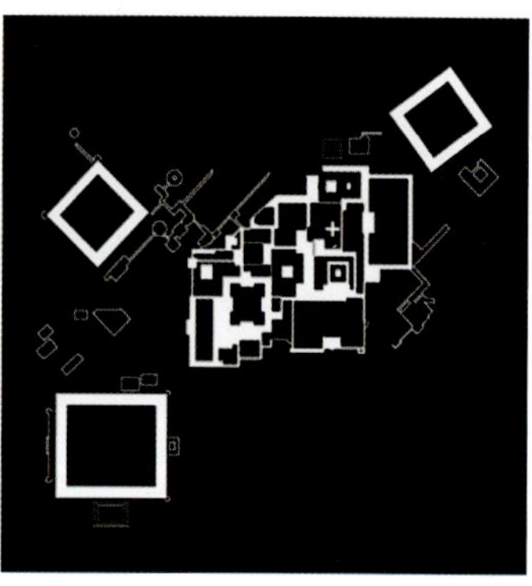

27b

27c

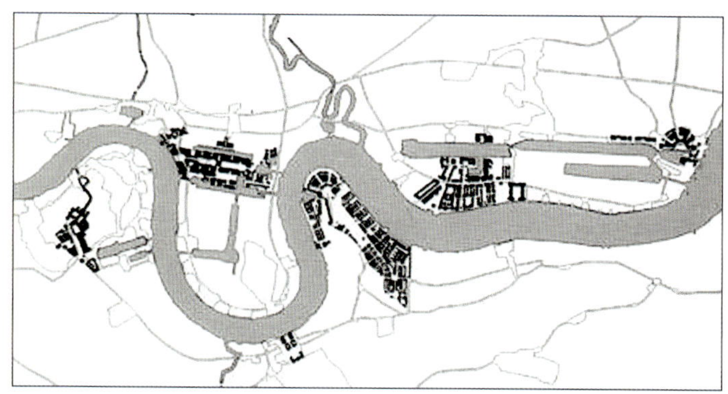

27d

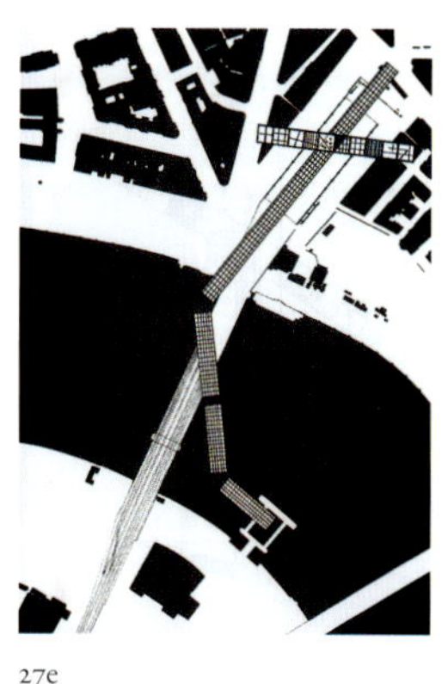

27e

27f

27g

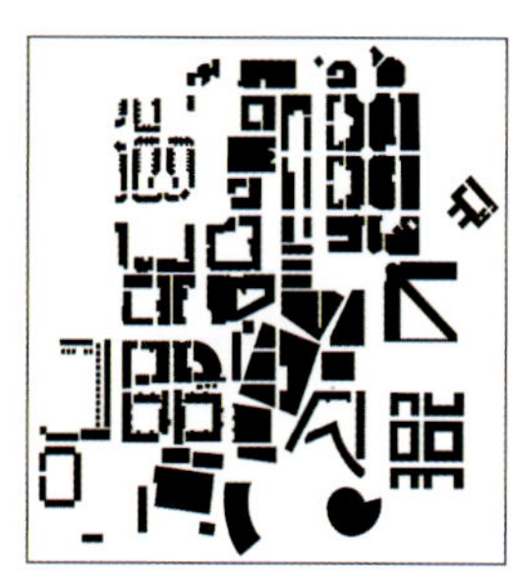

27h

27i

the overall urban project and these methods were eventually incorporated into Rowe's Urban Design Studio. In the early years students would render axonometric drawings of their urban designs and build physical models. This was expanded to include aerial perspectives, as shown in the roundel type drawing in Michael Manfredi's 1978 thesis, "Urban Development for Upper Manhattan" (Fig. 22). It wasn't until Craig Nealy's 1981 thesis, "Project for Burlington, Vermont", however, that the eye-level perspective was finally introduced (Fig. 23).

The Influence of Renaissance Garden Design

Rowe introduced his students to *Italian Gardens of the Renaissance,*[37] one of many books he shared from his private library (Fig. 25). Published in 1926 by two young British fifth-year students, J. C. Shepherd and G. A. Jellicoe, the book would become an influential reference in the design studio for two reasons. First, it reinforced and amplified design principles taken from Italian Renaissance landscape design, a new avenue of exploration. Secondly, it reinforced the studio's figure/ground drawing preoccupations, albeit using landscape elements rather than building mass, streets, and piazze. Shepherd and Jellicoe drew plans and sections of numerous gardens basing their technique on the drawing style of the École des Beaux-Arts. The foliage cut in a tight topiary style is shown in a similar dark figure/ground type fabric while the allées and parterres, rendered as the light void in between, as spatially equivalent to squares and streets. The analogy to the city figure/ground plans already familiar in the Studio facilitated a seamless transition between the two (Fig. 19a).

The Milwaukee Lakefront Design Competition, 1980, designed by Rowe, Douglas Fredericks, Lee Hodgen, and Derek Tynan, illustrates the use of figure/ground incorporating precedents derived from Italian Renaissance gardens (Fig. 24).

A late project from Rowe's Urban Design Studio, "Piazza Augusto Imperatore" in Rome, exemplifies all of the periods of his tenure at Cornell. A contribution to the "1987 Milano Triennale Nove Progetti per Nove Città", the proposal was designed by Rowe, Matthew Bell, Robert Goodill, Kevin Hinders, Brian Kelly, Cheryl O'Neil, and Paolo Berdini; the latter served as the occasional critic. Although small in scale compared to earlier studio projects, the design is quite complex. In the tradition of the Nolli/*Roma interrota* design, the ground floor plans for all interior public spaces have been designed. Primary facades have been rendered, both in aerial and eye-level perspective, and landscape elements, albeit minimal, have been incorporated as well (Fig. 26).

The Profession and Other Urban Design Schools

In the late 1970s and '80s figure/ground drawings began to appear in both the professional design world and other urban design schools, albeit reinterpreted (Fig. 27a–27j). For the 1971 City Centre of Leinfelden Project, Leon Krier shows the urban design plan in figure/ground format with the massing as hatched, similar to the style found in the Nolli Plan (Fig. 27a).[38] In 1977 Klaus Herdeg published *Formal Structure in Indian Architecture.*[39] This is one of the first contemporary figure/ground analyses of urban fabric in regions outside the Western World (Fig. 27b). At the same time the thesis project by Zaha Hadid from the Architectural

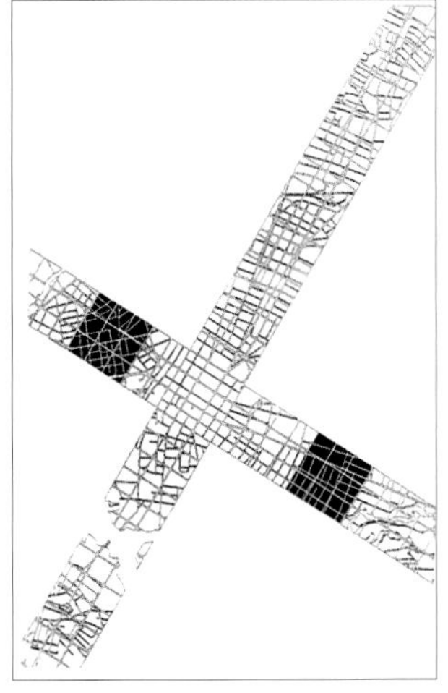

27j

Fig. 27a. City Centre of Leinfelden Project, Leon Krier, 1971.

Fig. 27b. Figure/ground plans of Fathepur Sikri, from *Formal Structure in Indian Architecture*, Klaus Herdeg, 1977.

Fig. 27c. Campus plan study for the Carnegie Mellon campus Dennis, Clark & Associates/TAMS.

Fig.27d. Plan for Canary Wharf, London, Koetter | Kim & Associates, ca. 1985.

Fig. 27e. Thesis project, Zaha Hadid from the Architectural Association, 1977/78.

Fig. 27f. *Suprematism No. 58*, Kazimir Malevich, 1916.

Fig. 27g. Site plan, Vitra Firestation, Zaha Hadid, ca. 1990.

Fig. 27h. Almere, Holland Master Plan, Rem Koolhaas OMA, 1994.

Fig.27i. The Figural City / West L.A., project by Sarah Maansson, faculty of record, Peter Zellner, 2012.

Fig. 27j. Invisible Walls and The Cross from *X-Urbanism: Architecture and the American City*, Mario Gandelsonas, 1999.

37 Shepherd, J. C.; Jellicoe Geoffrey, *Italian Gardens of the Renaissance,* Scribner's, New York, 1925.

38 Porphyrios Demetri, ed., "Leon Krier. Houses, Palaces, Cities", *AD Profile* 54, 1984.

39 Herdeg, Klaus, *Formal Structure in Indian Architecture*, JAAP Rietman Art Books, New York, 1977.

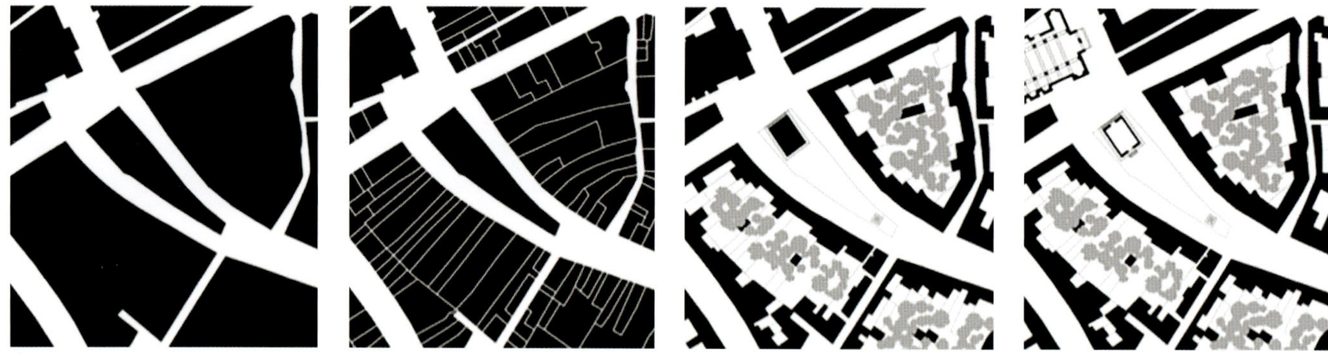

28

29

30

Fig. 28. *The Four Types of Figure Grounds*, by Charles Graves, 2009.

Fig. 29. *Space Syntax*, computer model analysis of Trafalgar Square, "Spatial Accessibility: existing/ proposed". Bill Hillier, Tim Stonor, Mark David Major and Natasa Spende, September 1998.

Fig. 30. Berlin's spatial transformation, in *Schwarzpläne* form, during the 20th century.

Association in 1977–78 was proposed. Later she would produce a figure/ground study drawing in the somewhat classic style for the Vitra fire station, ca. 1990. It's interesting to compare the painting by artist Kazimir Malevich titled *Suprematism No. 58,* 1916, to understand where Hadid may have looked for inspiration, noting the dark and light structure implied by the painting (Fig. 27 e, f, g). Or perhaps she was looking at a page of El Lissitzky's book *About Two Squares*, previously mentioned (Fig. 3).[40] The project by Dennis, Clark & Associates/TAMS for Carnegie Mellon University signals the use of the figure/ground beginning to appear in the work of the architectural profession in the U.S. (Fig. 27c). Around mid-1980s the office of Koetter Kim produced designs for Canary Wharf in London. In both the Dennis and Koetter Kim plans, the figure/ground drawings have been modified from the classic black and white format to include color and entourage but still suggest the spatial dialogue of solid and void (Fig. 27d). Also appearing in figure/ground and reverse figure/ ground is the Almere, Holland Master Plan designed by Rem Koolhaas–OMA in 1994 (Fig. 27h). The project from an urban design studio at SCI-Arc titled The Figural City / West L.A. taught by Sarah Maansson while the faculty of record is Peter Zellner reveals similar graphic design methods (Fig. 27i). Further reinterpretations of the figure/ground can be found in Mario Gandelsonas's 1999, *X-Urbanism: Architecture and the American City.* The image (partial) is titled, "Invisible Walls and The Cross" (Fig. 27j).[41]

New Uses for The Old: The Figure/Ground Today

With the introduction of CADD (computer-aided design and drafting) software into architectural schools and the profession, the production of the figure/ground

40 El Lissitzky (2015).

41 Gandelsonas, Mario, *X-urbanism: architecture and the American city*, Princeton Architectural Press, New York, 1999: 25.

drawing began to change. What took hours to draw could be realized in a fraction of the time. Once the figure/ground plan is produced in a digital format it is then very easy to import the file to a 3D CADD program and then convert the 2D plan to 3D for further study.

The use of figure/ground has also evolved into a design theory called "space syntax". This approach incorporates a set of theories and methods for the analysis of spatial configurations as they relate to social factors. Conceived by Bill Hillier and Julienne Hanson, colleagues at The Bartlett, University College London, in the late 1970s and early 1980s, it was intended to serve as a tool to help architects and urban designers simulate and predict correlations between spatial layouts and social effects likely to result from specific design options. The premise behind space syntax is that it's possible to quantify, describe, and navigate any space at any scale, such as the design of museums, airports, hospitals, and cities where wayfinding is a significant matter (Fig. 29).[42]

One of the most important changes in the world of cartography has been in the introduction of geographic information system (GIS). GIS is a computer system designed to capture, store, manipulate, analyze, manage, and present all types of geographical data. Following are two images from the book, *Schwarzplan: OpenStreetMap basierte Schwarzpläne.*[43] The authors used the open source site OpenStreetMap Project for their base data.[44] The data was then converted to figure/ground plans using GIS software (Fig. 31).

Berlin's spatial transformation is illustrated, in *Schwarzpläne* form, during the 20th century. The plan shows graphically how the connected heart of pre-WWII Berlin was divided by the Berlin Wall and later reconnected after Reunification (Fig. 30).

In Stan Allen's 1999 *Points + Lines,* he depicts a series of diagrams drawn in the manner of figure/ground.[45] Although this example of diagramming is not new, the abstraction differs from earlier uses in city diagrams, in its simplicity and use of only black and white (Fig. 32).

Charles Graves published *The Genealogy of Cities* in 2009.[46] The book is a collection of more than 1,000 historic city plans for comparison and analysis. These plans were drawn in the classic figure/ground style. Influenced by Stan Allen's work, Graves explains the four drawing types used in producing the plans (Fig. 28). The four types illustrate how figure/grounds can be developed to relay increasingly complex and detailed information. The classic format of the black and white block is shown on the left; followed by the outline of the block with a division of property lines; next, the footprint of the buildings with possible property division, and foliage as a gray mass; and on the far right the footprint of the buildings with key public/private buildings shown in ground plan, possible property division, and foliage as a gray mass.

In his book Graves uses simple diagrams to represent urban typologies and their transformation over time. Comparative diagrams illustrate hypothetical alternatives to actual urban design schemes as in the studies of the Blackwall Penninsula in the London Docks by Koetter Kim of 1988 (Fig. 33).

31

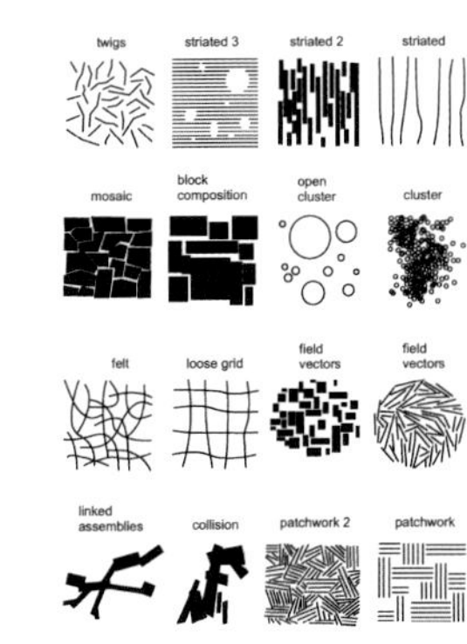

32

Fig. 31. *Schwarzpläne: OpenStreetMap basierte Schwarzpläne*, using *OpenStreetMap Project* for base data.

Fig. 32. "Points and Lines" by Stan Allen in *Points + Lines. Diagrams and Projects for the City*, 1999.

42 Hillier Bill, *The Social Logic of Space*, Cambridge University Press, Cambridge, New York, 1984.

43 Mayr, Markus; Mayr, René, *Schwarzplan: Open Street Map Basierte Schwarzpläne*, Epubli GmbH, Berlin, 2014.

44 *OpenStreetMap* [http://www.openstreetmap.org/about].

45 Allen, Stan, *Points + Lines. Diagrams and Projects for the City*, Princeton Architectural Press, New York, 1999.

46 Graves, Charles P., *The Genealogy of Cities*, Kent State University Press, Kent, Ohio, 2009: 200-01.

33

Fig. 33. *The Genealogy of Cities*, by Charles Graves, 2009 (Studies of 'Blackwall Peninsula', by Koetter | Kim & Associates, 1988).

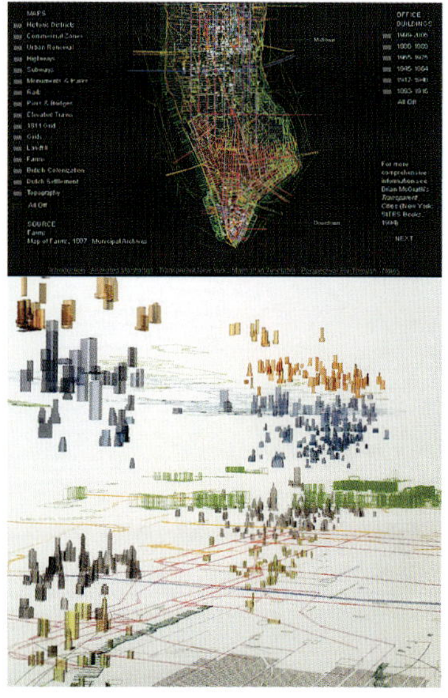

34

Fig. 34. *Manhattan Timeformations*, a digital project by architect Brian McGrath with designer Mark Watkins, originally appeared as hand drawn maps in *Transparent Cities*, 1994.

Manhattan Timeformations, a digital project by architect Brian McGrath with designer Mark Watkins, originally appeared as hand drawn maps in *Transparent Cities,* 1994. In 1999 the work reappears in digital format and is the first to incorporate animated figure/ground into 3D massing.[47] The project maps Manhattan's skyscraper districts through time. The viewer begins in plan mode, and then has the option to rotate the flat image into an aerial perspective. The introduction describes the project's connections to Rowe's use of figure/ground, both literal and phenomenal (Fig. 34).

A more recent figure/ground investigation is *The Interactive Nolli Map Website,* produced in 2005 at the University of Oregon, with James Tice and Erik Steiner as the principal investigators.[48] The website features a digitally mastered, high-resolution Interactive Nolli Map. Layers have been created that focus on particular topics, such as gardens and *rioni* (city districts). Layers may be turned on and off, and blended with the base map to provide a variety of superimpositions (Fig. 36). The map is used to geo-reference information about the city and its history.

As much as I find the new uses and investigations of the figure/ground in conjunction with the computer interesting, I still find myself wandering to my library shelves to peruse those old books with city plans. A colleague of mine once asked, "How did you ever become interested in city plans?" We were in my personal library and I selected a small red book from the shelf, which fit nicely in the hand. "This is called a *Baedeker*, an old travel journal that always contains city plans from the period in which it was written" (Fig. 35). As I handed the book to my colleague I told him, I had a teacher once who took me to our school's library and handed me *Baedeker's Central Italy* and without any explanation as to what it was, told me, "Charles ... I think you might be interested in looking at this." That teacher, of course, was Colin Rowe. Colin firmly believed in research and analysis. So what better way to get to know, or analyze, a city than to trace existing city plans and using those ever so simple yet complex "curious little diagrams" known as figure/ grounds as a paradigm? I've been hooked since the day a *Baedeker* was handed to me. I still study old and new city plans, and, of course, if I really want to fully understand what is before me, I begin to develop the indispensable figure/ground drawing as a kind of *gestalt* overview.

It's interesting to note, beginning design students of architecture are exposed to the term figure/ground almost from day one. The phrase has become so ingrained in the lexicon of architectural vocabulary that it's hard to imagine an informed

47 McGrath, Brian, *MANHATTAN TIMEFORMATIONS. Mapping Manhattan's Skyscraper Districts Through Time:* 1994.

48 Tice, James; Steiner, Erik; Ceen, Allan; Camerlenghi, Nicola; Giovanni Svevo, *Interactive Nolli Map Website* 2.0.

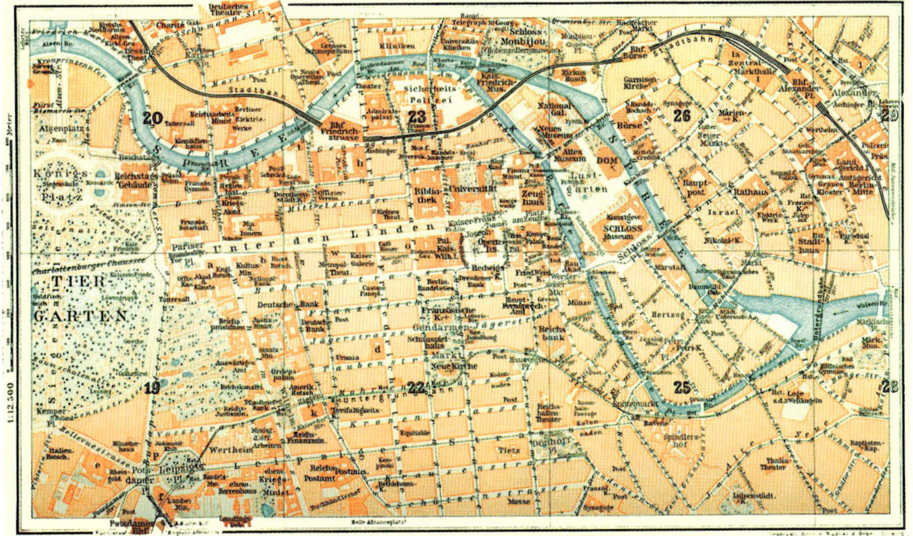

35

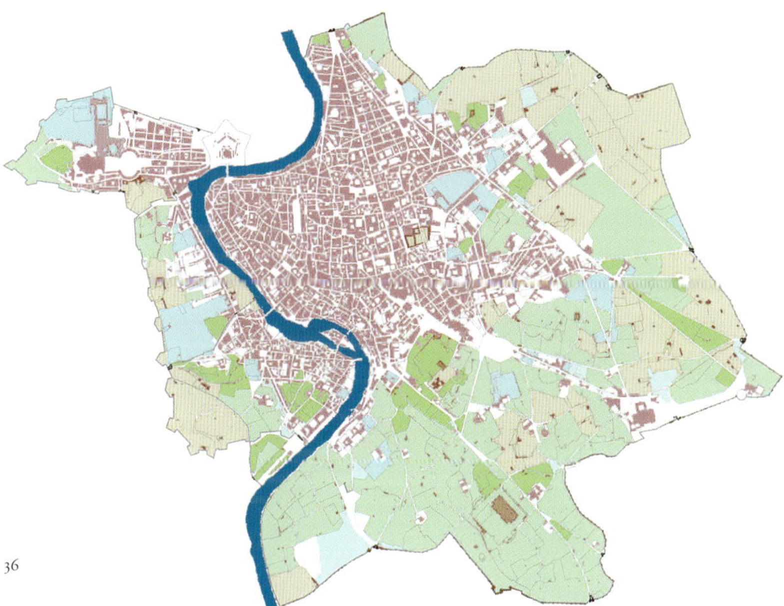

36

design process without it as an indispensable aid. I believe we'll always have a use for the figure/ground plan in some form, although one wonders what will be added to the urban design tools-at-hand in the future. The act of map-making has changed drastically, but the key to figure/grounds is in the actual making. The act of constructing a simple black and white plan through the act of tracing enables you to learn about the city and its fabric intuitively and with an immediacy that is unparalleled. Through these means the figure/ground becomes the *non plus ultra* of urban design and exposes the bare essentials of solid urban mass versus void urban space.

Fig. 35. *Baedeker Guide to Germany*, ca. 1896, cover and plan of Berlin.

Fig. 36. Image from Interactive Nolli Map Website showing superimposition of architectural and landscape layers of Rome in the 18th century. Courtesy of the University of Oregon; update at [https://web.stanford.edu/group/spatialhistory/nolli/].

Type and Transformation

James T. Tice

Prologue: Why not Feathers?

In comparative biology, a philosophical division defines two opposing views: whether dinosaurs are ancestors of birds and hence whether they had feathers, or whether they did not.[1] The debate has highlighted the tension between the idea of type espoused by one camp and the related idea of transformation of type promoted by the opposing group. Because architectural and urban studies have dedicated a great deal of attention to form type and transformation, the debate about the origin of birds as related to formal structure may shed light on our discipline.

frontispiece:
"Transformation of a Square Through Letter Shapes: Figure/Ground Reversal". Student exercise, instructors, Klaus Herdeg and Michael Dennis, Cornell University, ca. 1970.

In the most general sense, typology is the study of types and their taxonomic structure. A form type can be defined as any group or member of a group with shared formal structure. Transformation, as the root word "formation" and qualifying prefix "trans" suggests, is change in form. The essential dichotomy, then, between the two approaches is that the first, the study of types, *defines* boundaries while the second, transformation, *transcends* boundaries. In our example, the strict typologist argues that the type 'bird' is fundamentally different from reptilian species (warm blood vs. cold, brooding vs. non brooding of young and so forth) and, therefore, to propose a link between birds and dinosaurs would violate the fundamental principle of type and its reliance on stable characteristics. The transformation camp argues for fluidity between types, stressing commonalities that may defy otherwise accepted typological conventions, reflecting a belief in the inherent mutability of all things, perhaps channeling Heraclitus who maintained that one never steps into the same river twice. The advocates for transformation ask, if certain fundamental characteristics are held in common, why not others? If birds and dinosaurs share an erect stance and an aerated bone structure, *why not feathers*?

The following essay is the author's reflection on type and transformation and related use and meaning as it was understood in the Urban Design Studio and the encircling undergraduate program at Cornell in the 1960s. Examples follow which demonstrate applications and their relevance for contemporary urban

1 Padian, Kevin and Horner, John R., "Typology versus transformation in the origin of birds", in *TRENDS* in *Ecology & Evolution* 17 (3), Mar 2002.

design and architecture derived from this exchange. Other examples by the author and others expand on this theme. The essay ends with a seminal case-study that first appeared in *Collage City* that treats both urban design and architecture in this context, treating both type and transformation.

Type and Transformation: Purpose and History

The purpose of all typological studies is to facilitate comparisons within a given group and between groups. Thus compared, it is argued, a more profound understanding of phenomena is made possible, and decidedly more so than by studying the same examples in isolation. Whereas the study of types has, as its goal, the differentiation and classification of objects, transformation has as its goal the breaking down of categories, searching for 'similarities in dissimilar things'. It was the premise in the Studio that somewhere between these two poles—one static, one dynamic—there was room to maneuver. It is the author's belief that accepting the dialectical ambiguity between type and transformation describes an essential component of Rowe's approach to teaching in his Urban Design Studio.

A Short History of Type and Transformation

In the natural sciences, grouping examples into types and then into sub-types and then further classifying those groups using sophisticated taxonomies is a set of evolving refinements evident in the history of typology. During the Enlightenment, taxonomic structure in botany was pioneered by the Swedish scientist, Carl Linnaeus (1707–78). As the "Prologue" hints, in very general terms, we can claim that typological studies in the natural sciences moved from a Linnean interpretation of fixed types in the 18th century toward a Darwinian, transformational, or evolutionary, interpretation of types in the 19th and 20th centuries (Fig. 1).

With their *Encyclopédie* of 1751, the editors, Denis Diderot (1713–84) and Jean d'Alembert (1717–83), attempted to catalogue *all* human endeavor as well as natural phenomena, recording everything from types of beehives and beekeeping paraphernalia to military fortifications (Fig. 2). With a similar ambition of creating a comprehensive body of knowledge for architecture, J.N.L. Durand (1760–1834) and Quatremère de Quincy (1755–1849) turned their attention to the study of building types, seeking to establish a systematic method for treating architectural phenomena. For Durand, who taught at the École Polytechnique, it was a way to catalogue architectural examples and architectural components, so that one could pick and choose from amongst the assembled examples, combining them at will to achieve new-but-related architectural compositions (Fig. 4).[2]

In architecture and urban design, the study of types reached a crescendo at mid-20th century, concurrent with the early Rowe Studio years. Severio Muratori's early study of types led to an initiation of typo-morphology as a branch discipline. M.R.G. Conzen, Giulio Carlo Argan, Rafael Moneo, Rob Krier, Anthony Vidler, and others explored formal structure in buildings and cities as types, in large part as a critique of Modernist orthodoxy that saw form as effect, rather than cause.[3]

2 Roger Sherwood characterized this as the 'Frankenstein' approach to design.

3 Vernez Moudon, Anne, "Urban morphology as an emerging interdisciplinary field", in *Urban Morphology* I, (revised manuscript), 27 Mar 1997: 3–10.

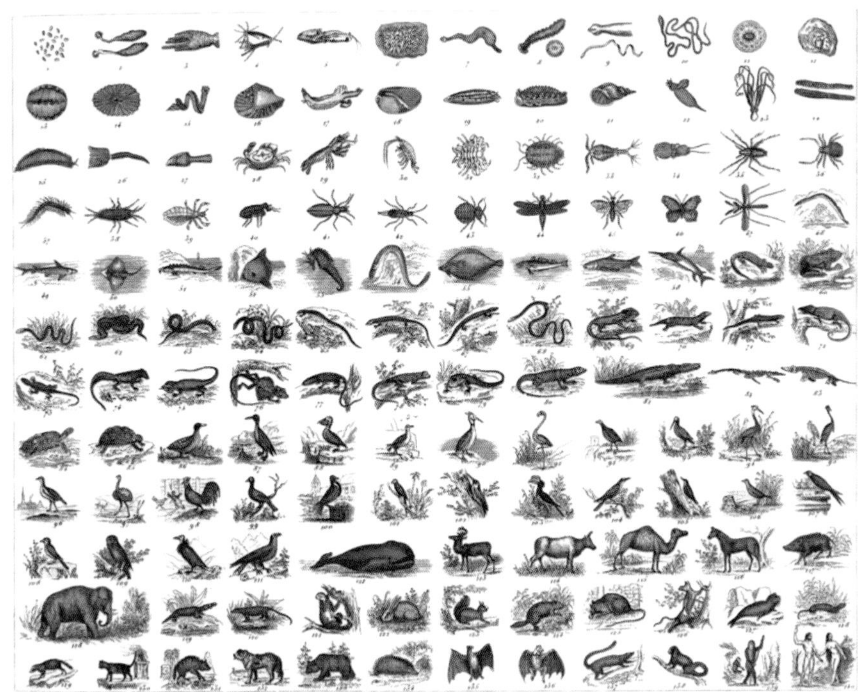

left to right:
Fig. 1. "The Linnaean Classification System", from *Classification of Species*, Henry Winkles, 1851.

Fig. 2. "Agriculture and Rural Economy, Honey Bees", from *Encyclopédie ou Dictionnaire raisonné des sciences, des arts et des métiers*, Diderot and d'Alembert, 1765.

Form Type and Transformation in the Urban Design Studio

This emphasis on form was an implicit critique of the Modernist fixation on function and program which had been proclaimed by Hannes Meyer and others to be the chief, if not only, determinant of all architectural form. In *A History of Building Types*, Nikolaus Pevsner implicitly continues that Modernist argument, defining types based primarily on shared program. Thus, libraries are compared to libraries, schools to schools, and so on. Form type and transformation as an ahistorical endeavor, served as a critique of an antiquarian view put forth by Sir Bannister Fletcher in *A History of Architecture on the Comparative Method.* The English writer presented a historical filter predicated on 'style types', mostly European, but narrowing down the field further by relying heavily on English examples.[4] In *A Pattern Language: Towns, Buildings, and Construction*, Christopher Alexander cautioned against the intrusion of formal decisions into the design process proposing a positivist approach, summed up in the belief that once all the 'facts' were known—those being described largely in terms of use—the resolution of any design problem would automatically follow.[5] Lewis Mumford, in *The History of Cities: Its Origins, Its Transformation, and Its Prospects*, seemed more intent on interpreting urban design, to the extent it was acknowledged at all, as a kind of applied sociology, skeptical that form was a significant contributor to social behavior or general well-being. A bright spot in this cauldron of anti-formal bias was Edmund Bacon's book, *The Design of Cities*, which focused on exemplary urban design examples throughout history based on formal characteristics that invited a comparative, typological understanding.

Since its emergence by the middle of the 20th century, the study of types has been hotly debated, especially its legitimacy in the design process. In his essay, "Typology and the Design Method", Alan Colquhoun draws attention to the

4 Fletcher, Sir Bannister, *A History of Architecture on the Comparative Method*, various editions. This was required reading for all undergraduates at Cornell in 1963. Colin seemed ambivalent about the text, valuing its comparative method, but somewhat embarrassed about its Anglophile tenor and what he considered to be its deplorable graphics. Most problematic was the insistence on the work as an object detached from any physical context.

5 In response to this approach, Rowe remarked, "well, you know, facts do not organize themselves".

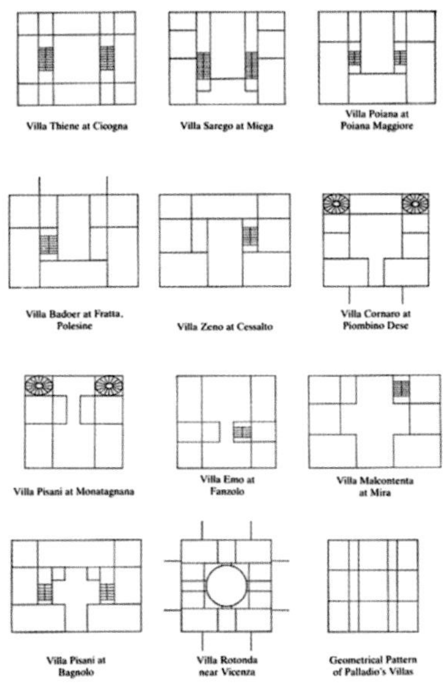

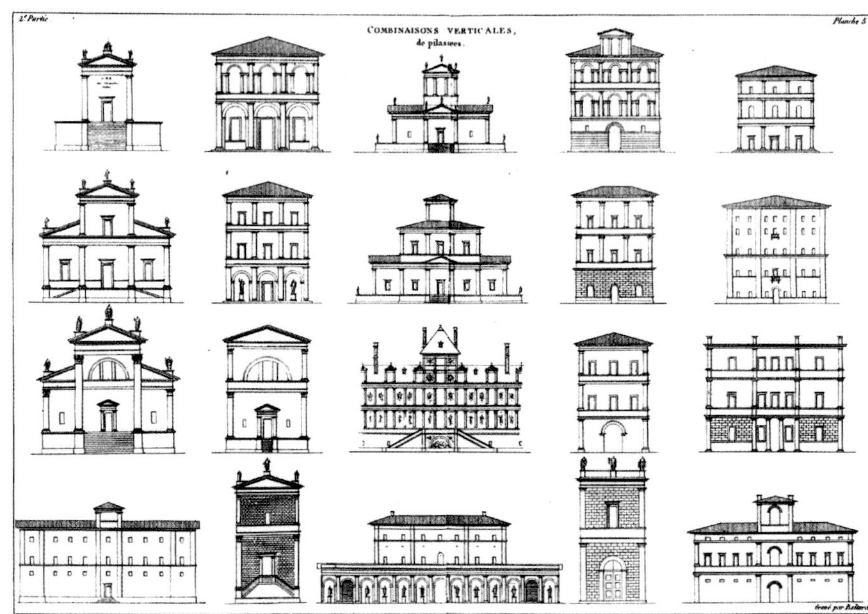

left to right:
Fig. 3. "Schematized plans of 11 of Palladio's Villas", Rudolph Wittkower, ca. 1949.

Fig. 4. "Combinaisons verticales", from *Précis des leçons d'architecture données à l'École polytechnique*, J.N.L. Durand, 1802-5.

benefits of using a systematic approach to architectural precedents organized as types.[6] Colquhoun argues that the value of typological references over individual precedents is that it shifts attention from the specifics of a single example to qualities that can bind diverse examples into a coherent group, and therefore, as a method, it seeks common principles—or essences—over mere 'copying' the one off. Thinking analogically, Colquhoun argues that such an approach embraces, rather than rejects, the collective, historically accumulated wisdom embedded in types. Mimesis, he argues, as does Rowe, is the basis for all creative acts in the visual arts, and so to confront this reality and bring it into the design process through an understanding of types can only be beneficial. Analogies to types provide a foothold for the designer that can move the design process from a given type to its transformation. Confronting programmatic and functionalist design methodologies, the proponents of typology asserted: 1) the 'seat of the pants' intuitive approach was too 'hit and miss'; and 2) a 'scientistic' linear, functionally deterministic approach over-simplified the inherent complexity of design by not recognizing that 'facts' were mutable; and 3) assumptions based on mechanistic analogies or 'innocence of forms' do not recognize architecture as a culturally laden, interpretive endeavor that can convey meaning through formal iconography associated with type. The controversy involving problem-solving recalls Colin's many references to Denise Scott Brown's comment that "architects suffer from physics envy".[7]

At Cornell in the 1960s, type and transformation were both fundamental concepts to be studied as analytic tools as well as aids to design. As ideas focusing initially on formal structure, they were independent of other factors such as program and function. As Colin's student Tom Schumacher noted:

> *... because form need not follow function, building programs and uses need not be expressed in the configuration of buildings and towns. This renders out-of-context comparisons feasible. Hence a church plan and a housing block can be rationally compared.*[8]

6 Colquhoun, Alan, Colquhoun, "Typology and Design Method", *Arena* 83, Jun 1967, later in *Perspecta* 12, 1969, also in *Essays in Architectural Criticism: Modern Architecture and Historical Change*, MIT Press, Cambridge MA, and London, 1981. Colquhoun was a close friend of Rowe. He had a visiting faculty appointment at Cornell in the 60s and was a frequent critic in the Studio. His essay was widely circulated as a photocopy in both the undergraduate and graduate studios.

7 Using the RCA Building as a metaphor, Rowe remarked that American architects imagine themselves as either Yankee Pragmatists in the boiler room or Transcendental Poets in its Rainbow Room—and nothing in between.

Colin's view was simply that, "Since design necessarily results in *some* form, it might as well be a good one". Therefore, the question posed by Rowe: Does the good city require good form? If so, then how does one achieve it? And following that, he posited (as noted above) that function and form could be decoupled so that form could be studied independently. Colin's position was that competent urban design manifest in formal or spatial sophistication in the postwar era was lacking, and that this was a detriment to the city and society at large. This condition was due he believed, in large part, to the hegemony of Modernist theory with its anti-historical *zeitgeist* worship and related 'scientistic' persuasions. Therefore, for the Studio, it was critical that formal and spatial aspects of good urban design should be resuscitated, studied, and further elaborated upon. And it was the study of the traditional city and its components, often grouped into types, which served as the most important conceptual frame of reference by which the Studio could address this shortcoming. It was the transformation of known and recognizable types—precedents—that served as its empirical methodology.

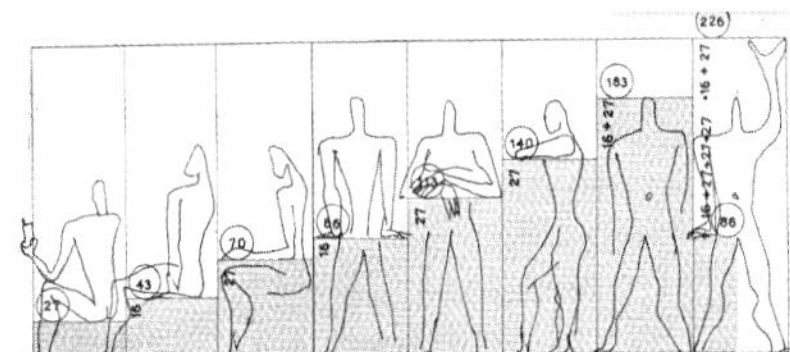

top to bottom:
Fig. 5. "Matrix of Palladian rooms showing the transformations of the seven ideal plans into volumes", by K. Paul Zygas, ca. 1986.

Fig. 6. "Les occupations caractéristiques de l'espace par les corps humain", *Oeuvre complète 1946-1952*, Le Corbusier.

The Study of Types

The notes above describe the context in which type and transformation entered discussions and debates within the Studio. At the outset, typology had two basic interpretations, already noted—one based on program, the other on formal type. Usually these were thought to be antagonistic but possibly reconcilable according to Rowe. Without denying the utility of programmatic groupings, Colin's position was nuanced, accepting formal structure as an important, even decisive, consideration in determining types, a position he made clear in "Paradigm vs. Program".[9] For Rowe, paradigm was a kind of *super type*, that is, type raised to the tenth power. Without ignoring either their history or program, the Italian Renaissance ideal city, the centrally planned church, and the palazzo—the latter discussed below—were three important examples of the super type. Rowe's preoccupations centered on these exemplary paradigms that integrated the functional-pragmatic with the cultural-iconic. Adopting a paradigm could *set the stage* for future transformations and accommodations towards a realization that would account for the pragmatics of program, as well as historical, cultural, and associated meanings. Colin's premise was that, in the end, an equilibrium, even if fraught with internal tensions, could and should, be achieved between the two poles: paradigm and program.

Transformation

In the visual arts, transformation typically describes change in two-dimensional shape or three-dimensional form. It should be evident, however, that its study can aid in understanding architectural and urban form and space as well. In the Studio, and in the undergraduate architecture program at Cornell in the 1960s, transformation and the related idea, 'deformation', were both central to the design discourse and both intersected the study of types.[10]

Transformation was both a method to demonstrate change between and within types and a conceptual construct to explain that change. It involved improbable connections and analogical thinking as described by the mathematician, George Pólya, in *How to Solve It*.[11] With his irreverent delight in words and their

8 Schumacher, Thomas, "Contestualismo: ideali urbani deformati" in *Casabella* 359–60, 1971: 79-86.

9 Rowe, Colin, "Program vs. Paradigm", *The Cornell Journal of Architecture* 2, 1983: 9–19.

10 The terms transformation and deformation are often used interchangeably. However, there is a significant difference. Thus 'formation' is the process of giving form. The two prefixes: 'trans' and 'de' qualify the term. 'Trans', meaning change in the most general sense, is a neutral qualifier. It does not assign value between states of change. But the prefix 'de' is value laden. It suggests moving away from a more idealized state toward a less idealized state.

11 Pólya, G. *How to Solve It*, Princeton University Press, 1945. Lateral thinking in the design process was encouraged, even suggesting to begin at the end, and work backward as recommended by Leonardo. Lee Hodgden required readings of Polya and was perhaps his strongest advocate during the author's time at Cornell. Jean-Luc Godard captured this approach when he noted that all cinema should have a beginning, middle and end: but not necessarily in that order!

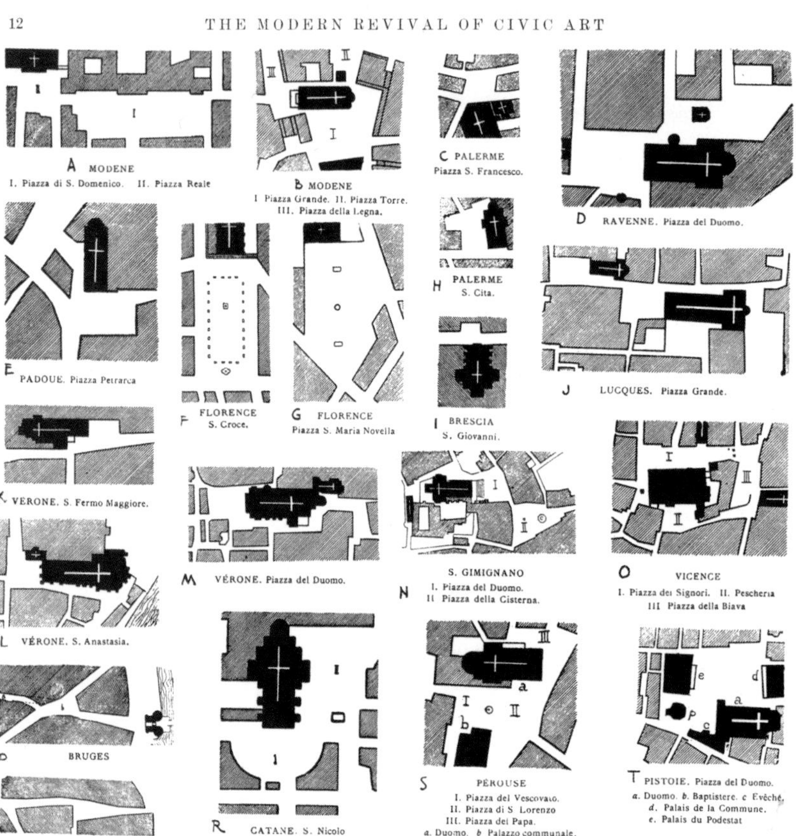

associations, Rowe liked to quote Samuel Johnson's quip, "Wit is the unexpected copulation of ideas". It was transformational thinking used as an analogical framework and heuristic device that could facilitate that 'unexpected coupling'.

Transformation had a double function related to typology. Analytically, it moved backward: how and why an artifact came to be and how it may have changed over time—its origins and evolution. Synthetically, it moved forward as a heuristic device, exploring the form potential of a type through imagined transformation(s) that could lead to discovery and invention. The belief in the inherent mutability of form and its potential for change was effectively unlocked by the process of transformation. It opened new ways of thinking about precedents and types and it helped one imagine whole new worlds that were nonetheless grounded on a bedrock of known, demonstrable precedents (types) or *paradigms*. It challenged a Hegelian view of progress because it found value in the entire body of history treated as a reservoir of ideas that did not obsolesce. Thus, transformation allowed the student to avoid the temporal limits of the antiquarian or the futurist. One could not rely on the conventions of historical orthodoxy nor hide behind highly advertised contemporary work. The freedom to move independently of any historical time frame was exhilarating but also unsettling. It meant that, ultimately, one had to rely on one's own judgement. Perhaps one of the most important lessons from Rowe was that one had to take intellectual and moral responsibility for one's decisions: one had to think for oneself.

12 Tice, James, "Transformation Studies". Unpublished student exercises, ca. 1995. The relationship suggested by Colin between the Altes Museum and the Assembly building in Chandigarh in the revised edition to the *Mathematics of the Ideal Villa* is but one example of over a dozen pairings that were studied, frame-by-frame, by students.

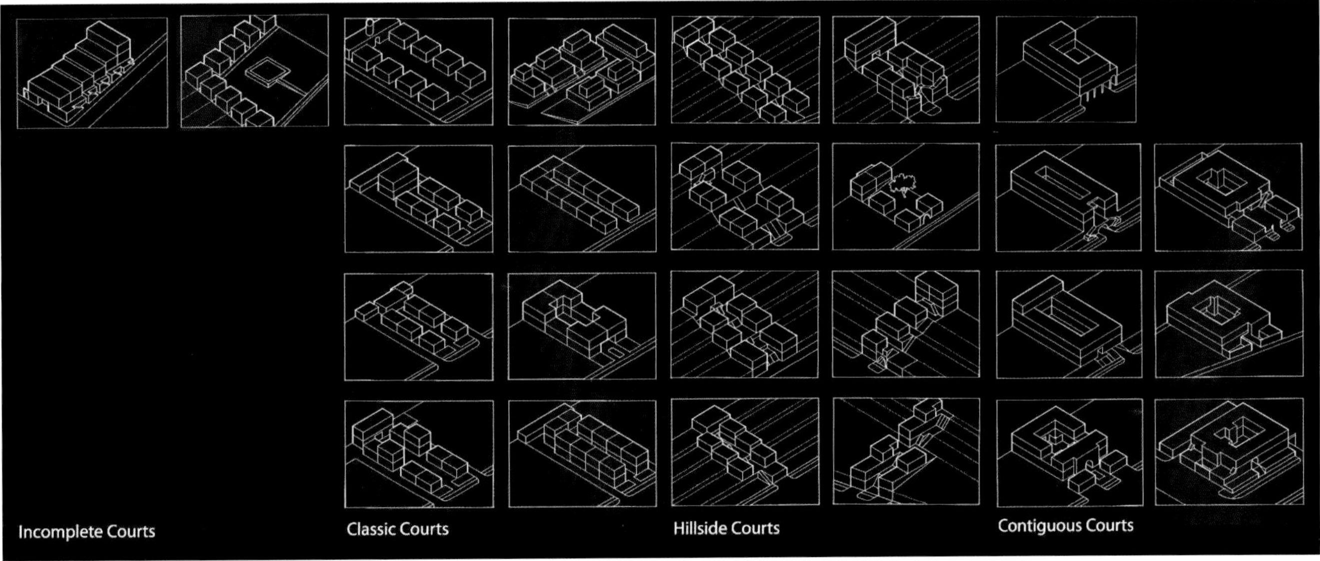

Compelling Visual Examples

A typological construct in the visual arts ultimately relies on images. A question often posed in the Studio: could one demonstrate examples of architectural and urban transformations in a visually compelling manner? For example, could one posit an imagined history of a given work from real to ideal? Could one rewind the process creating a kind of fictional history from ideal to real or vice versa?[12] This way of thinking opened a world of connections between known examples and their possible transformations. Examples of this kind conjured up typological-transformational references for individual buildings, building groups, and the entire city.

Rudolph Wittkower's famous typological matrix of Palladian villas compares their formal structure, implying a transformational relationship among them (Fig. 3). The potential transformation of the group was further expanded by Paul Zygas to include room types as volumes in three dimensions (Fig. 5).[13] And the transformation of the Palladian villas and its planning logic was elaborated by Rowe in his well-known reference to Le Corbusier's Villa Stein.

Le Corbusier's sequential diagram of the Modulor Man was drawn ostensibly to represent anthropometric parameters (Fig. 6). The eight-frame serial moves from a figure, reading in an informal sitting position, to a contemplative figure writing at a desk, to an erect figure standing proud. Thought of as a series of stop-frames, they convey an animator's sensibility, and its serial framing suggests the transformational possibilities of the Modulor itself.

Camillo Sitte's figure/ground study of churches and their piazze in *City Planning According to Artistic Principles*, organized as a matrix by Hegemann and Peets in *The American Vitruvius: An Architects Handbook of Civic Art*, invites a typological comparison (Fig. 8). As Sitte notes, rarely are churches freestanding in this exhaustive study; all others are embedded in the urban fabric. Similarly, the

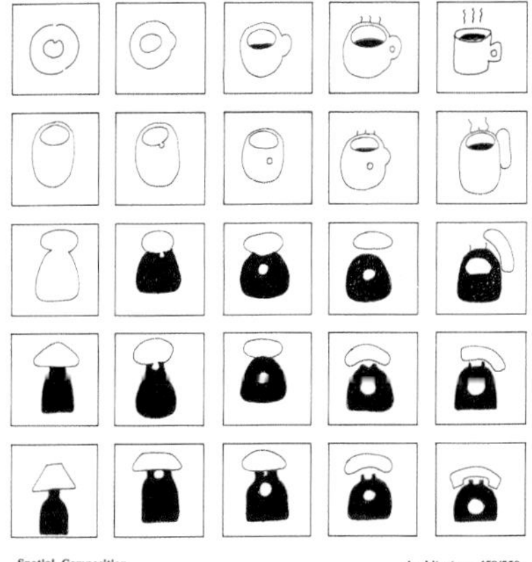

opposite left:
Fig. 7. "Mayan Plan Transformations: Games concerned with formal structure". Student exercise by Paul Buck. Roger Sherwood, instructor, Cornell University, 1968.

opposite inset:
Fig. 8. Detail matrix of comparative city squares by Camillo Sitte, *The American Vitruvius: An Architects Handbook of Civic Art*, Hegemann and Peets, 1923.

above:
Fig. 9. "Typology of Los Angeles Courts", drawing by author, 1976.

below:
Fig. 10. "Transformation of doughnut to coffee cup (with variations)". Student exercise, University of Oregon, 1997.

13 Zygas, Paul K. *Five Strategies for Classical Plans*, unpublished essay, ca. 1986.

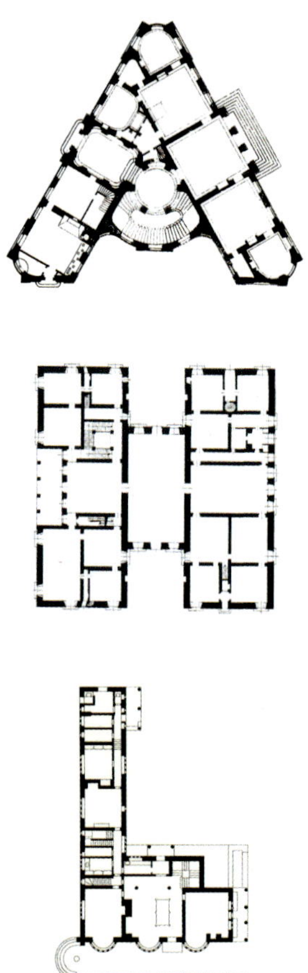

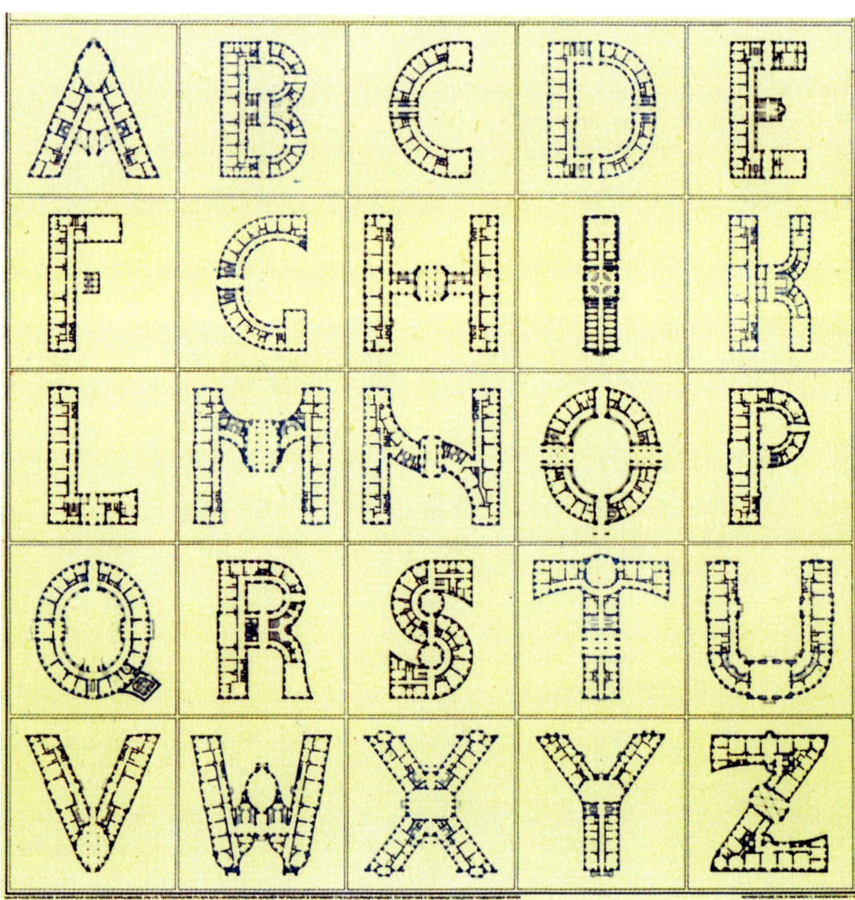

matrix of axonometric drawings in *Courtyard Housing in Los Angeles*[14] displays the variety of residential courtyards extant in that city suggesting their varied contexts (Fig. 9).

Studies in formal and spatial structure enjoyed a dedicated following at Cornell.[15] This was seen as an essential skill that could facilitate the connection to deep meaning. The investigations were a kind of piano finger-exercise intended to hone one's skills by manipulating form, thus developing eye-hand-mind dexterity. Developing these skills meant training the eye to see and think incisively, imagining varieties of form that had potential for any specific design task. In suggesting likely comparisons, it was not necessary to presume, much less to demonstrate, causality, as the exercises relied primarily upon the architectonic potential of abstract patterns. To further aid notions of type and transformation, ingenious design studio exercises were invented by Roger Sherwood, Lee Hodgden, Mike Dennis, and others that served as an inspiration for transformational thinking (Fig. 7, 10).[16] The pursuit was interdisciplinary, not to mention unorthodox. References included painting, music, film, art criticism, mathematics, and science, as well as game theory. These paradigms in other fields of inquiry challenged students in Studio to think outside the 'cube', or in some cases, to think about complexity inherent in the cube. It underscored Rowe's creative interdisciplinary impulse and his impatience with a certain academic rigidity that placed an embargo on the transmigration of ideas across disciplines.

14 Tice, James and Polyzoides, Stefanos, "Los Angeles Courts", *Casabella* 412, Apr 1976: 17–23.

15 For example see Herdeg, Klaus, exhibition, "Formal Structure in Indian Architecture", 1967, and subsequent publication of the same name, Rizzoli International, New York, 1990.

16 Sherwood, Roger, *1 Transformations* published by the Department of Architecture, Cornell University, Fall, 1968: 5–8. Mayan sites have been transformed with the intention of strengthening latent formal structure.

Johann David Steingruber's Architectural Alphabet, 1773

Steingruber's architectural alphabet (Fig. 12) presented an array of possible building configurations as letter shapes, reminding us that 'type' is the root word in 'typography'. In the Studio it served as a kind of periodic chart that could prompt speculations about the relative merits of any given configuration as a *parti* based on a host of parameters: program, site, entry, etc. It explored strategic moves that could enhance latent architectural properties. In the Studio it was important to speculate about real urban sites for which this form types would make sense. For example, the 'A' or 'V' became a natural footprint for a flatiron site, while the 'O' would logically be an object in the round, a *tempietto* or amphitheatre. From an urban design point of view, the 'L' was perhaps the most ambiguous shape of all, as it could complete the outside corner of a city block, serve as the inside corner within the same block, or be free-standing. Several letters shared features that could be easily transformed. The 'C' could be imagined as a simple variant of the 'D', changing the dynamics of entry and site condition, alluding to the difference between the Greek and Roman theater types.

Perhaps inspired by Steingruber, Colin liked to play the "letter game" (Fig. 10). This consisted in imagining a simple letter shape as a building footprint. One was asked to imagine its attendant attributes including entry, circulation, hierarchy of interior spaces, program, and site. The author vividly remembers one such game with Colin. His opening gambit to me: where would one logically enter the letter 'H'? The author's response: naturally, one should enter through one of the courtyards. Colin's reply: this was the typical architect's response, and the annals of architectural history are brimming with this solution. He proceeded to point out that another alternative had strategic advantages. Using the example of Villa Medici at Poggio ai Caiano by Giuliano da Sangallo, he showed that an entrance at right angles to the face of the 'H' established a hierarchical frontal condition, giving representational identity. By penetrating the symbolic temple front of that structure, one had cognition of its importance and time enough to orient oneself to the sequence that followed. Once in the interior it was then possible to proceed to the center of the H, climaxing in the magnificent *salone*, compositionally the heart of the entire composition. This strategy avoided what would have been an abrupt introduction to a central space through the courtyard. Furthermore the central *salone*, with its dual courtyards on either side, could expand horizontally in opposite directions to embrace distant views. On one side, the Villa Medici viewed the distant silhouette of Florence, and on the other side, it provided a prospect of the Certosa di Galluzzo. Thus, with the entry strategically placed, the potential of architectural form and movement was clarified, magnifying its potential into an extended landscape.

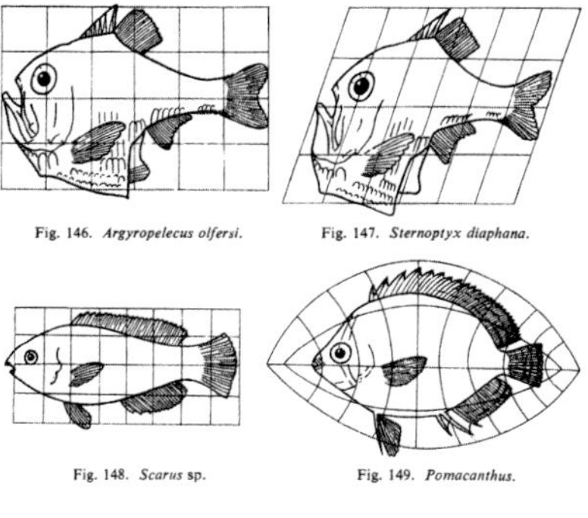

LES POIRES,

Vendues pour payer les 6,000 fr. d'amende du journal le *Charivari*.

opposite:
Fig. 11. top to bottom: Parisian apartment building, late 19th century; Villa Medici, Poggio ai Caiano, ca. 1480; Broad Leys, Lake Windermere, C.F.A. Voysey, 1898.

Fig. 12. "Architectural Alphabet" composite from *Architektonisches Alphabeth bestehend aus 30 Rissen*, Johann David Steingruber, 1773.

above:
Fig. 13. Comparative diagram of fishes illustrating morphogenesis, from *On Growth and Form*, D'Arcy Thompson, 1917.

Fig. 14. "Les Poires" 19th century caricature of Emperor Louis Philippe, from *Art and Illusion*, E.H. Gombrich, 1959.

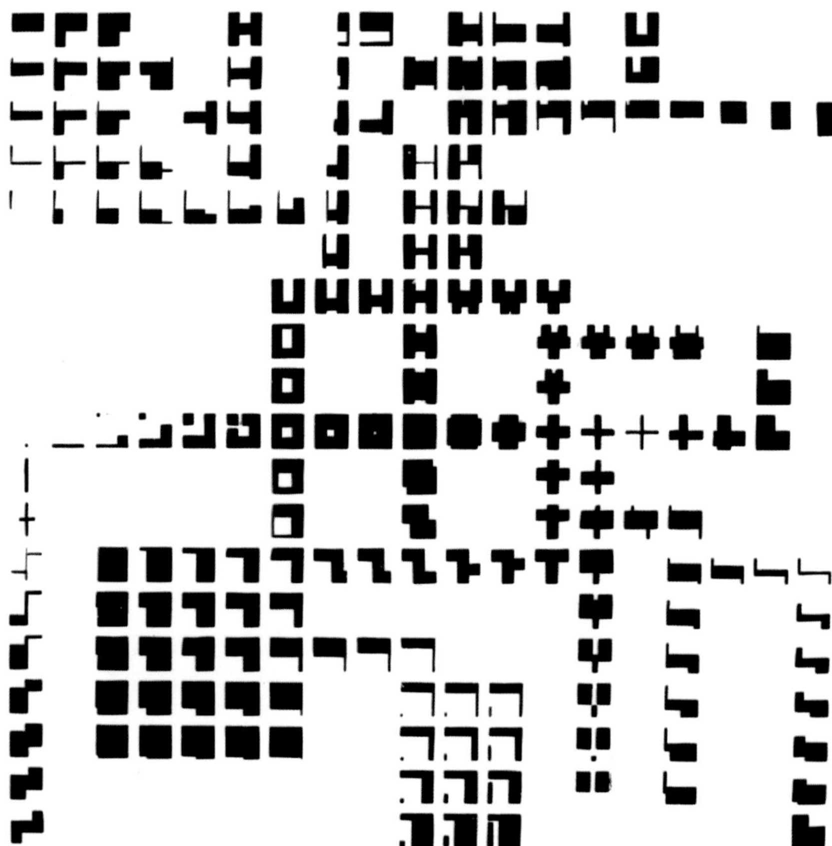

above left to right:
Fig. 15. *Liberation*, lithograph, M.C. Escher, 1955.

Fig. 16. "Transformation of a Square Through Letter Shapes, Figure/Ground". Student exercise, Herdeg and Dennis, Cornell University, ca. 1970.

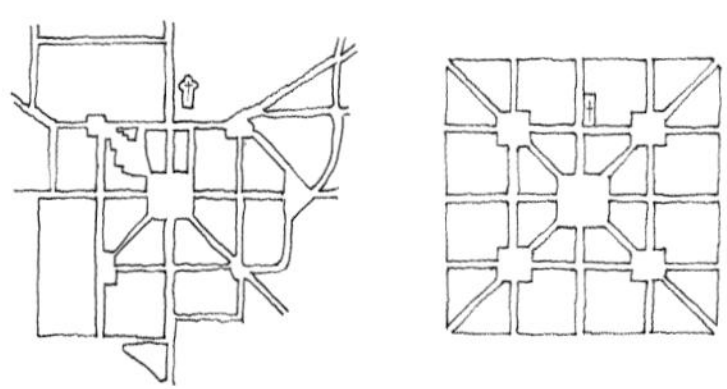

below:
Fig. 17. Henrichemont, city plan, 17th century: actual state and ideal state.

Transformation of the Square: A Graphic Exercise

The graphic exercise "Transformation of the Square Through Letter Shapes" was invented at Cornell by Klaus Herdeg and Mike Dennis to specifically study types and transformation (*frontispiece*, and Fig. 16).[17] It is the quintessential exercise for systematically and rigorously studying the interplay of types; this case based on simple letter shapes and their transformation of the square. The exercise asked students to think in figure/ground terms, consequently, there were two graphic sets required in the problem statement: a figure/ground with black figures on a white ground, and a figure/ground reversal with white figures on a black ground. This reinforced the premise that ideas of form were directly related to ideas of space; solid and void could be interchangeable. In the gridded field of the exercise, all figures transform incrementally from the central solid square to 'key frames'; in this case to letter shapes: 'U', 'H', 'T', 'L', 'Z', 'Y', 'X', and 'O'. The methods for transformation are straightforward: subtraction, addition, and horizontal or vertical shifts of letter parts. The letters in turn transform by stages into their adjacent letter shapes, making sure that every change displays a smooth, visual transition. No 'cold turkey' juxtapositions were permitted. Moving to the outer field, more freedom is apparent. Beyond requiring the boundary of each frame to remain fixed within its square and a smooth transition between frames, no other limits applied. However, ordering of a more inventive sort could be introduced by the designer. For example, one could make constellations or 'clouds' of

17 In animation theory, recognizable figures are called 'key frames' to distinguish them from less stable intervening frames. When executing an animated series, animators recommend beginning and ending with a key frame and interpolating in between. An example would transform from a standing to seated figure.

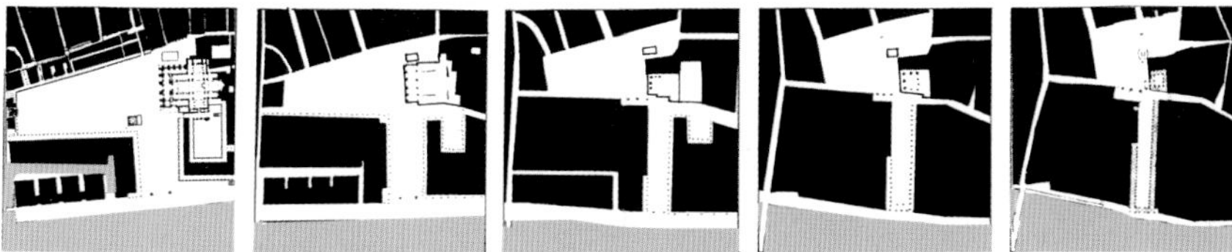

like figures. Or one could choose to code changes with a pivot in direction. For example, one could move along the x-axis with a subtractive process and then, turning at right angles along the y-axis, use addition, rotation, or some other manipulation. These moves established secondary rules of considerable complexity, but in the last analysis, every figure in the field, whether at the center or periphery or in between, had to be visually linked to its neighbors. Amazingly, the entire panoply was centered on the simple square at its center.

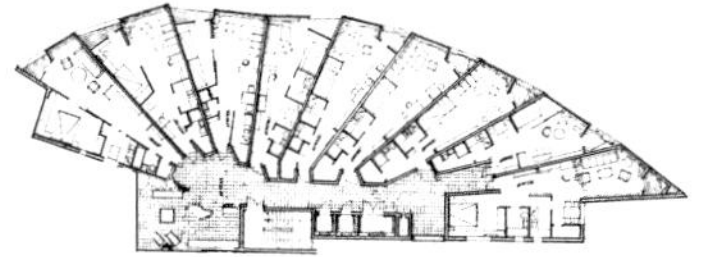

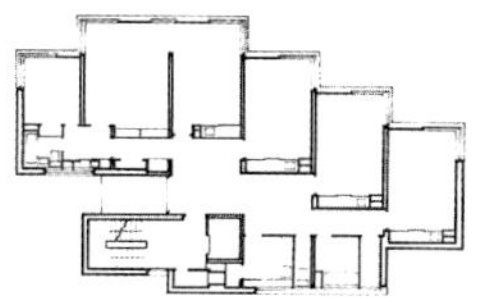

The exercise could expand to include a search for implied precedents, problem solving, ideas about history, and, perhaps, ultimately, about the nature and meaning of change itself. Building on the example of Steingruber's architectural alphabet, the author asked his students which figures in the square transformation exercise are analogous to actual building footprints or urban spaces. Could a 'treasure hunt' reveal built equivalents for *all* the abstract figures or for only a few? And if so, what might the greater or lesser frequency of use reveal about the intrinsic utility of some forms to solve architectural and urban problems? What might we deduce about well-known architects favoring certain form-types challenging the presumed notion of objective, *aposteriori* design over *apriori*, pre-rational formal inclinations? For example, why did Kahn favor the square-doughnut "O" while Frank Lloyd Wright obsessed over the cruciform "X"? Why did Aalto typically embrace the ambiguity of inbetween letter shapes? And, more provocatively, what is the nature of ambiguous shapes? What value, if any, do they have for design since they lack the formal clarity of pure letter shapes? Do they possess a quality that neither of their perfected counterparts possess? In other words, do they possess the *positive* quality of ambiguity being both/and, suggesting ambivalence and double meaning? If so, can lesser stable figures as building footprints or urban spaces solve problems which perfect figures cannot, precisely because of their ambiguity?

above left to right:
Fig. 18. Transformation of Piazza San Marco, Venice to Piazza della Signoria, Florence. Student exercise, instructor, J. Tice, University of Oregon, ca. 1993.

Fig. 19. *Pole Vaulter*, fixed plate chronophotograph. Photo: Etienne-Jules Marey, 1884.

below:
Fig. 20. Above: Alvar Aalto Bremen Apartment, 1958. Below: Sir Leslie Martin and Colin St. John Wilson Cambridge Apartment, 1963 (plan reversed), based on Rafael Moneo's comparison in "On Typology", *Oppositions* 13.

A follow-up exercise asked if it possible to observe ideal-to-real examples in city plans, such as that of Henrichemont (Fig. 17). Could one also invent plausible interpolations—fictional history—of a given work. Klaus Herdeg's study of an Indian palace in Mandu shows the hypothetical transformation of an ideal plan through a series of strategic additions and subtractions (Fig. 21).[18] The process can also illustrate a relationship between related urban examples, such as the Piazza and Piazzetta San Marco and the Piazza della Signoria and Uffizi corridor (Fig. 18). The two examples display an L-shaped piazze. The major space of each addresses an important civic building while the minor space connects to the landscape: the Venetian Lagoon in the former and the Arno in the latter. At the intersection of the two spaces, a vertical axis—a campanile-tower—acts as visual hinge which marks the turning point in the composition while providing a focus and link for both major and minor spaces. Such exercises are not necessarily

18 Herdeg (1990): 41-43.

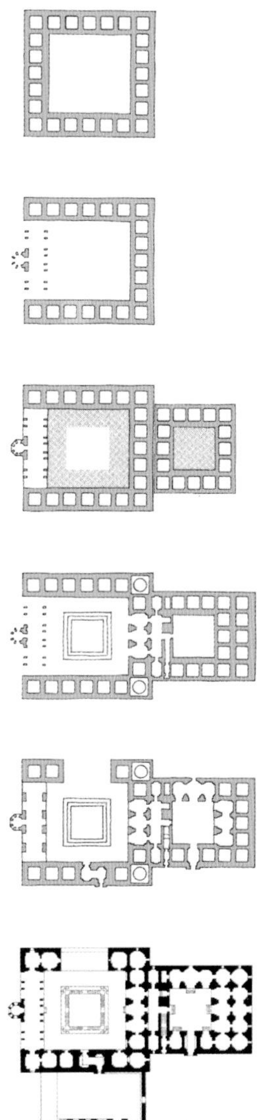

above:
Fig. 21. Plan transformation of Palace of Sultan Baz Bahadur, Mandu, India; from *Formal Structure in Indian Architecture*, Klaus Herdeg, 1967.

right:
Fig. 22. Detail, matrix of arcades; from *Arcades: The History of a Building Type*, Johann F. Geist, 1983.

R Spatial Types	1 Entrance	2 Entrances							3 Entrances		4 Entrances		6 Entrances	8 Entrances
		Straight Parallel	Straight Perpendicular	Angle	Double Angle	Angle/Diagonal	Right Angle	Diagonal	Y Shape	T Shape	H Shape	Cross	Double Cross	Quadruple Cross
	1	2	3	4	5	6	7	8	9	10	11	12	13	14
Street a														
Street and Central Space b														
Central Space c														
Street and Block d														

55
Spatial types

56
Building types

G Building Types	No Facade	1 Facade	2 Facades				3 Facades			4 Facades	
			Straight	Right Angle	1 Corner	2 Corners	1 Corner	2 Corners			
	1	2	3	4	5	6	7	8	9	10	11
Regular a											
Irregular b											
Block Form c											
Connection with Additional Side of Block d											

meant to suggest causality, but rather to establish analogies between precedents that could serve as models for further design investigations.

In *Arcades: The History of a Building Type*,[19] Johann Friedrich Geist catalogues over 300 examples of glass-covered urban streets (Fig. 22). In his diagrams summing up the type, he uses a figure/ground and figure/ground reversal technique to clarify the spatial unit of each example set into an urban block. The graphic yields a compelling picture that suggests how the simple linear arcade may have been transformed into complex spatial structures in a variety of urban settings. His elegant matrix shows an amazing range of sub-types of the basic arcade and its transformations as related episodes of the type. Implicitly, it is a guide for how the type could function as an urban design tool.

Methods to Aid 'Transformational' Thinking

Visual linkage is a key factor in the use of precedents, rendering that 'aha' moment when the unexpected could reveal itself. Some visual methods to facilitate connections could be rather simple. Side-by-side juxtapositions were the most obvious and common. Using the same scale, or, alternately, the same size, similar placement, and orientation could facilitate further connections. Rotating images to align to a common axis or datum could help. Using a common grid or superimpositions could reveal commonalities otherwise overlooked. But it was also possible to see forms transitioning from one state to another using an incremental, step-by-step sequence similar to the square transformations noted above. A more complex version moved from a one-dimensional, linear sequence to a two-dimensional matrix, as we have seen (Fig. 4, 9).

Typological studies[20] in urban form focusing on actual examples were useful. But, as noted above, it was the premise of the Studio that knowledge of types

19 Geist, Johann Friedrich, *Arcades: The History of a Building Type*, MIT Press, Cambridge, MA, and London, 1983.

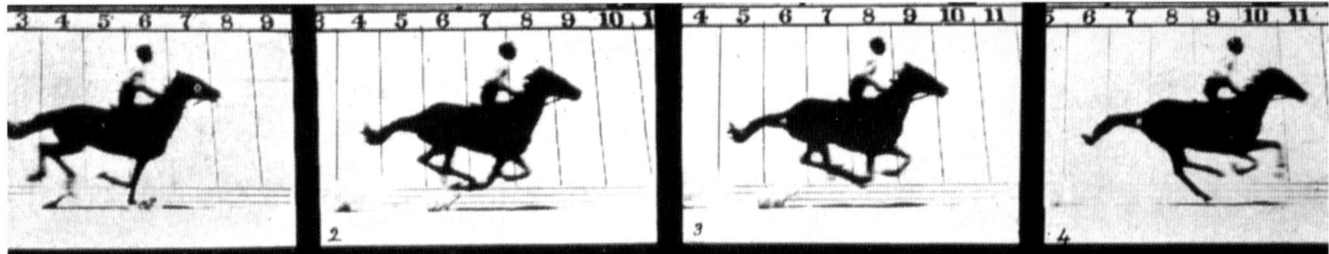

and transformational examples in the sciences and the arts could benefit architectural and urban studies as well. A high premium was placed on graphic techniques used in other fields that communicated related ideas in a compelling visual manner. A paradigmatic example in the sciences using transformation as an aid is D'Arcy Thompson's classic study, *On Growth and Form*.[21] In several striking images he illustrates his premise of how organic structures are formed through "morpho-genesis". In several comparisons, he uses a warped grid to show a topological relationship between certain fishes even though their superficial appearance would suggest otherwise (Fig. 13).[22]

The art historian and critic Ernest Gombrich presents an amusing story from the 19th century as an example of transformation in a political context.[23] The French journal, *Figaro*, referred to then King Louis Phillipe as a "pear head" or colloquially, a "fat head". Outraged, the king's authorities slapped the editors with a 6,000-franc fine. But the newspaper responded by publishing a caricature of the king's visage, transformed in a kind of slow-motion analysis into a pear, thus proving their contention (Fig. 14). A judge sided with the newspaper and the fine was dropped. Gombrich argues that the key to winning the case was the use of a compelling and clever visual argument that showed similarities through incremental change. A simple cold turkey juxtaposition between visage and pear would not have swayed the judge. The smooth visual transformation was crucial for this understanding.

M.C. Escher relentlessly pursued transformation themes in the visual arts. In his black and white print "Liberation" he uses a figure/ground technique that shows change from abstract triangular shapes emerging into highly articulated silhouettes of birds in flight. Even the space in between the figures is an integral part of the composition, transforming along with the figures (Fig. 15). Paul Klee's "Temples by the Water" shows a transformed and mirrored drawing to create a fantasy city (Fig. 25), one that evokes similar variations on a theme in the Strada Nuova in Genova (Fig. 26).[24]

Chronophotography

No other art treats visual transformation as directly as film and cinema evident in 19th century explorations through chronophotography. Not surprisingly, Modernists like Marinetti and Futurist painters were inspired by the new kinesthetics, and the 'creed of speed'. In early experiments, two basic types of chrono-photography emerged, serial plate and fixed plate. The first studied movement using a series of photographic stills in linked sequence, best represented

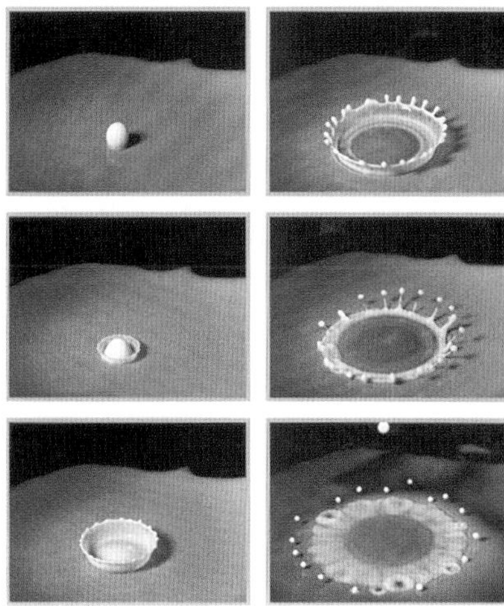

Fig. 23. Detail, *Galloping Horse and Rider*, serial plate chronophotograph.
Photo: Eadweard Muybridge. ca. 1870.

Fig. 24. *Milk Droplet*, stroboscopic photograph.
Photo: Harold Edgerton, 1937. © 2010 MIT.
Courtesy of MIT Museum.

20 For reasons of space this essay does not include other typological studies such as those by Carl Franck, *Villas of Frascati*, Roger Sherwood, *Modern Housing Prototypes*, Michael Dennis, *Court and Garden*, Rob Krier, *Urban Form*, and the author's study with Paul Laseau, *Frank Lloyd Wright, Between Principle and Form: A Typological Study*, and *Courtyard Housing in Los Angeles* with Roger Sherwood and Stefanos Polyzoides.

21 Thompson, D'Arcy, *On Growth and Form*, Cambridge University Press, Cambridge, 1917.

22 In mathematics, topology is used to describe geometric properties and spatial relationships independent of changes in shape or size of figures. Thus, in the warped grid comparisons by Thompson, spatial relationships and formal elements remain constant even though their shape may change through deformations such as stretching, twisting, or bending.

23 Gombrich, E.H., *Art and Illusion: A Study in the Psychology of Pictorial Representation*, Phaidon Press Limited, Oxford, UK, Fifth Ed., 1977: 190–91.

24 *Univesità degli Studi di Genova, Istituto di Elementi di Architettura, e Rilievo dei Monumenti, Genova, Strada Nuova*, Vitali e Ghianda, Genova, 1970: 11.

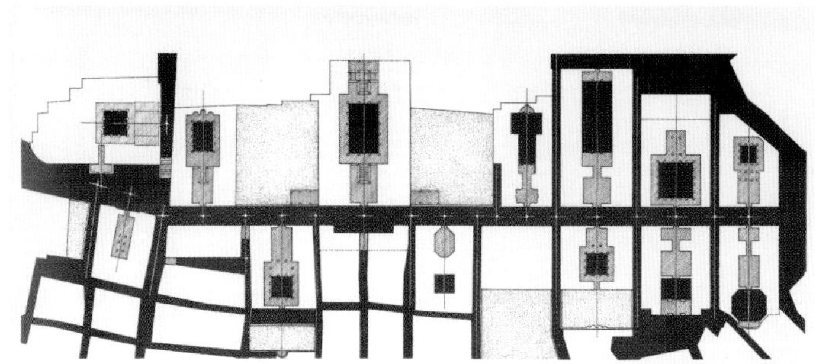

left to right:
Fig. 25. *Temples by the Water*, drawing by Paul Klee, 1927.

Fig. 26. *Strada Nuova*, Genova, figure/ground drawing from *Strada Nuova*, University of Genova, ca. 1968.

by Eadweard Muybridge's studies of animal and human locomotion (Fig. 23).[25] His most famous image in serial format shows horse and rider at full gallop. Conveniently for our purposes, the figures are shown silhouetted in a stark black and white, evoking architectural plans in figure/ground. Ètienne-Jules Marey explored a variety of techniques using chronophotography. In *Walking Soldier* he shows sequential movement using a figure clad in black with white highlights that may have inspired Marcel Duchamp's *Nude Descending a Staircase*. Marey's fixed plate superimposition, *Pole Vaulter* (Fig. 19), seems to be a prevision of Alvar Aalto's Bremen apartment as it fans out to the landscape (Fig. 20).[26] Harold Edgerton photographed at speeds of 1/100,000 of a second using a stroboscope technique that captured movement in humans and objects too fleeting for the human eye to detect.[27] His most memorable serial photograph shows a droplet of milk splashing into a saucer, creating a series of three-dimensional rings that would have made 16th century architects weep with envy (Fig. 24). But it was Edgerton's fixed-plate superimpositions, *Speed Stroke Golfer*, that apparently caught Sigfried Giedion's eye, and was published by him in *Space, Time and Architecture* as an example of 'space time' in the arts (Fig. 42).[28]

The Roman Palazzo: Development of a Super-type.

I believe that for Rowe the seminal example of the relationship between the stable and unstable characteristics of a type, what I have called earlier in this essay, a super-type, is the Renaissance palazzo. It was a key example that he often alluded to in the early Studio and further referenced in *Collage City*. In their text, Rowe and Koetter compare the Palazzo Farnese and the Palazzo Borghese (Fig. 30).[29] The two examples, shown side-by-side, provide a classic visual argument of the ideal palazzo type transformed, or, perhaps more accurately, de-formed.

Some brief notes on the derivation of the palazzo type should prove useful. The Renaissance palazzo, especially its iterations in 16th century Rome, is derived from the ancient Roman *domus* as described by Vitruvius and also evident in the Pompeian courtyard house. The basic type survived and continued to find fertile soil in Italy. It was elaborated by 15th century theorists (Fig. 28) and developed into many regional variations. Antecedents to what was to become the normative Roman type can be seen in the Palazzo Piccolomini in Pienza and the Palazzo Medici in Florence (Fig. 29). Besides those early examples realized in Tuscany, radical variants are to be found in the Veneto witnessed by the three-bay Venetian palazzo. Other regional sub-types occur in Liguria along Genova's

25 Muybridge, Eadweard, *Animals in Motion*, 1899 and *The Human Figure in Motion*, 1901.

26 Moneo, Rafael "On Typology", *Oppositions* 13, June 1978: 23–45. See plan comparisons between the Aalto Bremen apartment, 1958 and Leslie Martin and St. John Wilson Cambridge apartment, 1963.

27 Edgerton, Harold E., *Stopping Time: The Photographs of Harold Edgerton*, H.N. Abrams, New York, 1987.

28 Giedion, Sifgried, *Space Time and Architecture*, Harvard University Press, Cambridge, MA, 4th ed., 1963: 444, 755.

29 Rowe, Colin and Koetter, Fred *in Collage City*. The images are taken from Letarouilly's *Édifices de Rome Moderne* (Farnese, plate 115, Borghese, plate 175) showing site plans and perspectives of each. It is curious that neither of the site plans includes the Tiber, which lies close by.

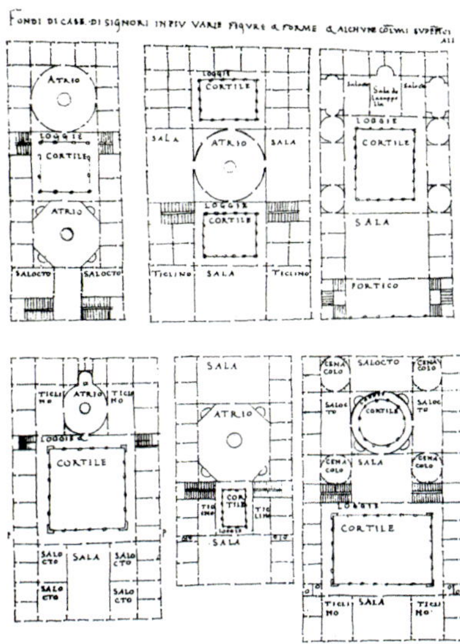

left to right:
Fig. 27. Matrix of Roman palazzi, Paul Marie Letarouilly, ca. 1845, diagram by author.

Fig. 28. "Case dei Signoria", from *Trattato di architettura* by Francesco di Giorgio Martini, 1497-1500.

Strada Nuova (Fig. 26). The elaborate stair compositions of the Sicilian palazzo further testify to the almost infinite transformations of the palazzo type.[30]

In 16th century Rome, the patrician palazzo emerged as one of its chief urban constructs and ornaments of the city. Even though Roman palazzi were realized on a much grander scale than the typical ancient *domus*, they embody much of its formal and spatial structure. The ideal Roman palazzo is basically a courtyard building. It consists of an imposing cubic mass surrounding a cubic volume or *cortile* which functions as its symbolic heart, while also providing a core volume for light and air. The palazzo displays a prominent facade and, as an urban episode, it is strategically located facing a major street, or more ideally a piazza which provides aspect and prospect. Ideally, the palazzo is Janus-like with one facade facing a public piazza and a second facade facing a walled private garden, or *giardino segreto*. The palazzo thus comprises a simple spatial triad: piazza, *cortile*, and *giardino*. Even a modest palazzo features an *androne* (entry hall), *scalone* (grand stair), and *piano nobile* (honorific level) located immediately above the ground floor. Elaborations could be incorporated or added to this basic formal structure. These might include a roof-top belvedere, *altana*, designed to catch Rome's evening breezes and provide a view of the city and landscape.[31] Variants to the palazzo depended on patronage, urban context, and terrain, the latter of which could be highly irregular along the Tiber and the slopes of Rome's hills. The graphic array from Letarouilly's *Édifices de Rome Moderne* shows a morphological transformation of several Roman palazzi (Fig. 27).[32] The spatial nexus

30 Tice, James, "The Renaissance Palazzo: A Typological Study", *Dimensions* 2, College of Architecture and Urban Planning, University of Michigan, Spring 1988 (unpaginated).

31 Zarina, Astra, Balthazar, Korab, *I tetti di Roma: le terrazze, le altane, i belvedere*, Edizioni D'Arte, 1979.

32 In *Édifices de Rome Moderne*, Letarouilly has over 250 palazzi, by far the largest number of plan drawings in his three volumes. No other author has achieved so thorough a tabulation of this building type in Rome or anywhere else.

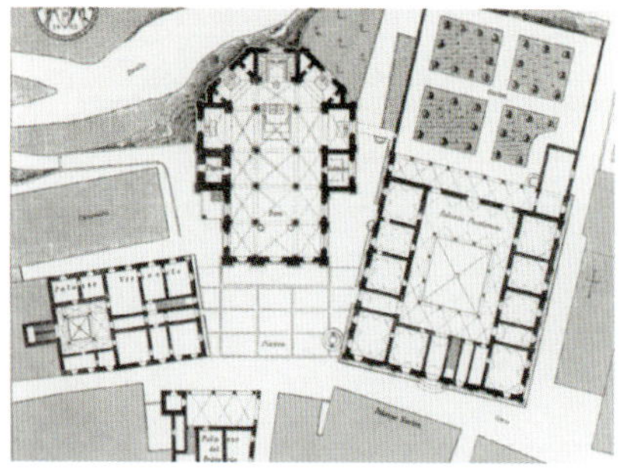

Fig. 29. View and site plan of Piazza Pio II and Palazzo Piccolomini, Pienza, ca. 1485. Photo: Andrea Bertozzi.

which makes this comparison possible and links them as a type is, of course, the *cortile*. In the diagram, axial relationships are maintained as they transform incrementally outward into more complex configurations *of the same type*. From the Renaissance into the 20th century the palazzo type plays an important, and often strategic, role in defining the urban fabric of Rome. It is its versatility, the variations on the type so well illustrated by Letarouuilly, that help make it a super-type.

The Palazzo Farnese (Fig. 33–35)

Beginning in 1515 Antonio da Sangallo the Younger began work on the Palazzo Farnese, leaving his imprint on major aspects of the building proper and related urban space we see today. Michelangelo was entrusted with the design after Sangallo's death in 1546, and continued work on the project, transforming it into a dynamic urban ensemble that the more conservative Sangallo could never have imagined. When Sangallo began his project for Cardinal Farnese, the palazzo was embedded in the dense medieval fabric of the Campo Marzio bordering the Via Giulia but facing the older and more important parallel street, Via di Monserrato (Maior Via Arenulae). With the elevation of the cardinal to Pope Paul III in 1534, the architectural and urban ambitions changed from that of a cardinalate residence to that of a papal domicile. The palazzo was enlarged to 13 bays and the Piazza Farnese was enlarged to accommodate its increased proportions. The new Via dei Ballauri was created to visually link the Farnese to the Via Papalis, the honorific pathway connecting the Vatican to the Lateran for *il Possesso*.

Michelangelo's brilliance as an urban designer, evident in the Campidoglio, was his ability to derive an ideal order by elevating the ad hoc to a higher level of understanding and realization. The existing order in this case included aspects of Sangallo's project. It was Michelangelo's genius, however, to both intensify and transform his palazzo and piazza into a compelling urban ideal. That urban order reverberated beyond the immediate context of the palazzo to its larger urban setting, expanding to embrace the human-made with nature. Ultimately this led to an ambitious but only partially realized proposal by Michelangelo to unify the Farnese holdings with a bridge over the Tiber. The plan was described by Vasari in his *Vite*.[33]

Michelangelo recognized the important dichotomy between the city-palazzo and the country-villa. He sought to connect the two physically and metaphorically. As we have referenced, he had already established the focal point of the Via dei Ballauri on the Palazzo Farnese facade with an oversized heraldic display and benediction balcony. On the garden side, facing the Tiber, he proposed to erode the palazzo block into a 'U' shape configuration that opened into a loggia, recalling the loggia of the Villa Farnesina, but here interpreted as a mere screen. The resultant open-air loggia-belvedere on the *piano nobile* was to be continued as a *giardino pensile* connected by a pair of *cavalacavie* (street overpasses) crossing the Via Giulia.[34] Once over this hurdle the twin connectors would descend via a symmetrical pair of stairs to the Farnese gardens on the eastern banks of the Tiber. From here, a bridge would span the Tiber to the villa gardens on the Trastevere side and further link to the Via della Lungara. Thus the entire Farnese holdings would be united in one deft move.[35] The transition from piazza, palazzo, *cortile*, *giardino*, to villa and gardens—from *urbs* to *natura*—was to be interpreted as a

33 Vasari, Giorgio, *Le vite de' piu eccellenti pittori, scultori ed architetti*, (C.Ricci, ed), Milan, Rome (1550) 1927: VII, 224.

34 Only one of the planned *cavalacavie* was built in 1603, presumably intended to realize Michelangelo's proposal.

35 Salerno, Luigi, Spezzaferro, Luigi, and Tafuri, Manfredo, *Via Giulia*, Casa Editrice Stabilimento Aristide Staderini, SPA, Roma, 1975: 104. An interpretation of Michelangelo's plan uniting the Farnese holdings on both sides of the Tiber is shown in diagrammatic fashion. In the same text, a hypothetical plan drawing of the Palazzo Farnese garden appears based on a manuscript identified by Anthony Blunt at the Metropolitan Museum of Art, 1960–6: 477. It is used as the basis for the drawings by the author.

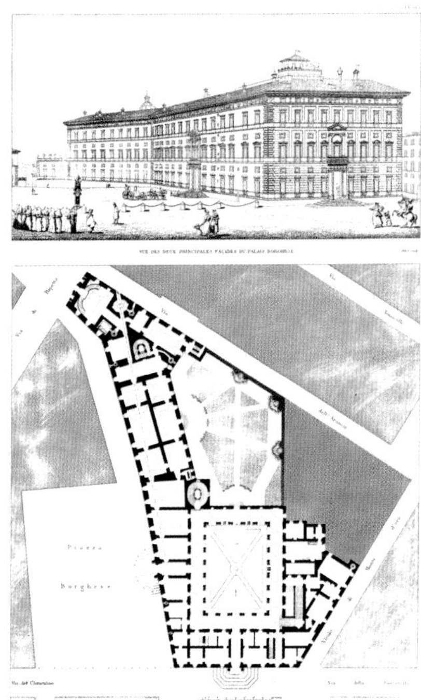

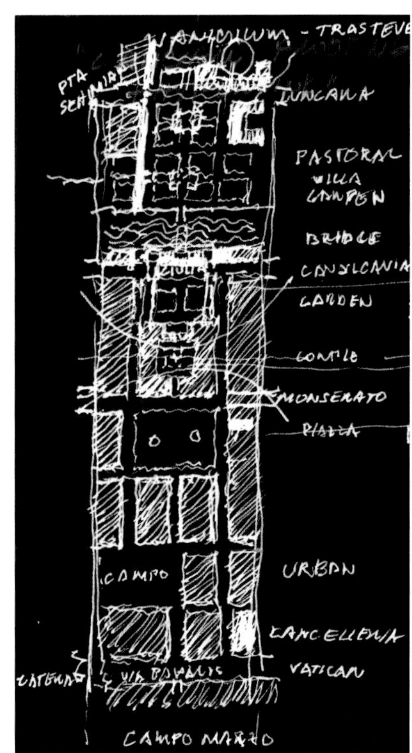

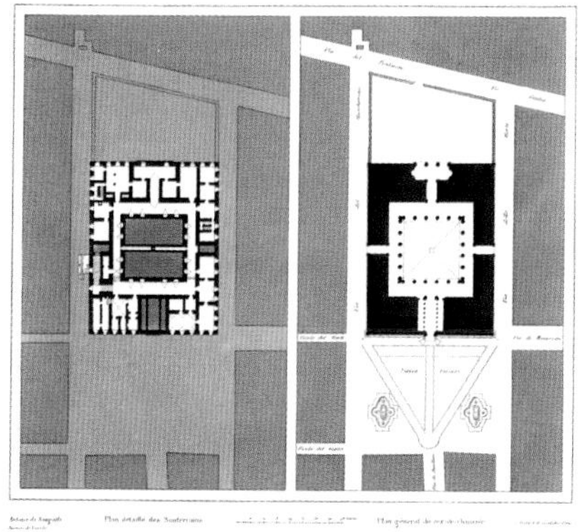

metamorphosis from the worldly cares of the city, *negotium*, to the contemplative life provided by an Edenic landscape, *otium*, embodying the good life as prized by the ancient Romans. (Fig. 31).

The Palazzo Borghese (Fig. 36–39)

The Baroque Palazzo Borghese, and its urban setting, is a brilliant transformation of the ideal palazzo type exemplified by the Palazzo Farnese and its urban complex.[36] Begun almost 75 years after the initial building campaign for the Palazzo Farnese, the Palazzo Borghese was executed for Cardinal Camillo Borghese. Several architects contributed to its realization, most importantly Flaminio Ponzio and Carlo Rainaldi. Although the Palazzo Borghese lacks the compact organization and singular axial composition of its Renaissance predecessor, it is almost identical in size and program, being one of Rome's premier cardinalate palazzi. Just as the Palazzo Farnese is positioned at a strategic juncture in the city, so is the Palazzo Borghese. Like its predecessor, the Palazzo Borghese is a kind of lynchpin that connects to important city's streets—in this case the Via di Ripetta and Via Condotti—and to the landscape across the Tiber. But obvious differences readily emerge.

The exterior perimeter of the Farnese reinforces the quasi rectangular grid in which it is placed. The Borghese, on the other hand, displays a highly elastic perimeter, reflecting the collision of diagonal streets along the Tiber. The palazzo block seemingly stretches to free itself from the regular *cortile* to which it is attached in order to accommodate its context. From an oblique angle of view, the Borghese disengages from the fabric as a volume, as an object in space. From a normal, that is, perpendicular viewpoint, the insistent frontal plane of the facade defines the space of its piazza. Meanwhile, its elongated arm and prow-like

left to right:
Fig. 30. Comparative views and plans of the Palazzo Farnese and Palazzo Borghese; from *Édifices de Rome Moderne*, P.M. Letarouilly. This comparison appears in *Collage City*, by Colin Rowe and Fred Koetter, 1978.

Fig. 31. Site plan sketch of the Palazzo Farnese and its context from the Campo de'Fiori to the Villa Farnesina, diagram by author.

36 Hibbard, Howard, "The Architecture of the Palazzo Borghese", *Memoirs of the American Academy in Rome* 27, 1962.

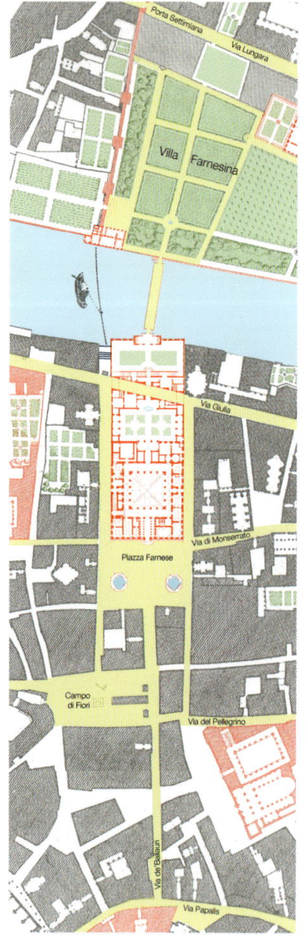

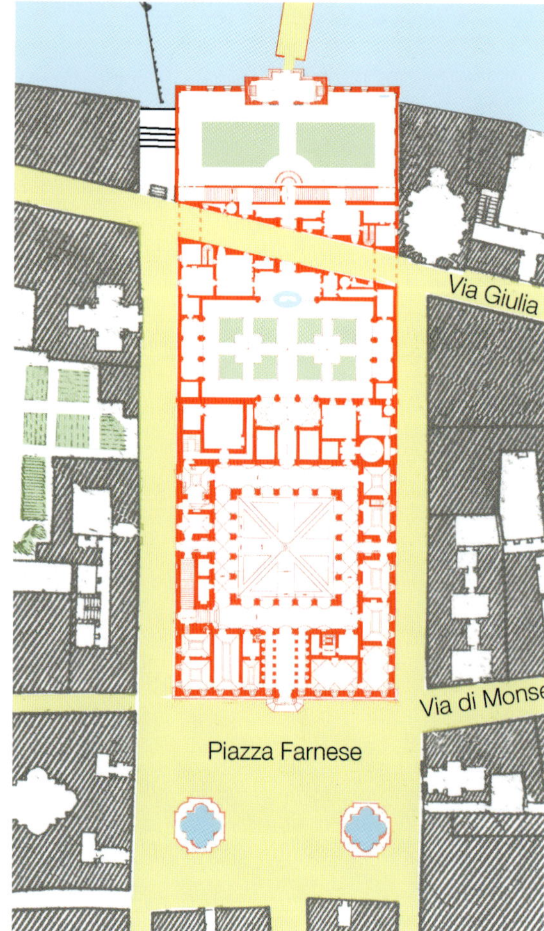

Fig. 32. Palazzo Farnese Site Plan (hypothetical, showing Michelangelo's bridge to the Villa Farnesina).

Fig. 33. Views of the Piazza and Palazzo Farnese (above) and the rear gardens facing the Villa Farnesina and Ponte Sisto (below). Prints by Giuseppe Vasi, ca. 1750.

belvedere overlook the Via di Ripetta and the Porto di Ripetta by Alessandro Specchi, which in turn links to the Piazza del Popolo. From this strategic vantage point, the winding Tiber and open fields of Prati unfold to a distant perspective of the Vatican over a mile away, thus unifying the urban-country ensemble at the scale of the city. From a conceptual and perceptual view, the resulting configuration—ideal-regular-center versus circumstantial-irregular-perimeter—is a rational response that resolves the conflicts between type and context and object and space.

Although each of these two palazzi has a unique set of qualities that sets it apart from the other, both retain the defining characteristics of the type: relationship to a major piazza or piazze, prominent facade or facades, imposing building mass, internal cortile, loggia-belvedere, followed by a walled garden and extended landscape view. Especially significant is that the *cortili* of the Farnese and Borghese retain a simple geometric shape, one square (1:1), the other with the proportions of a square root of 2 rectangle (5:7). Both courtyards establish a stabilizing element with strong figural identity.

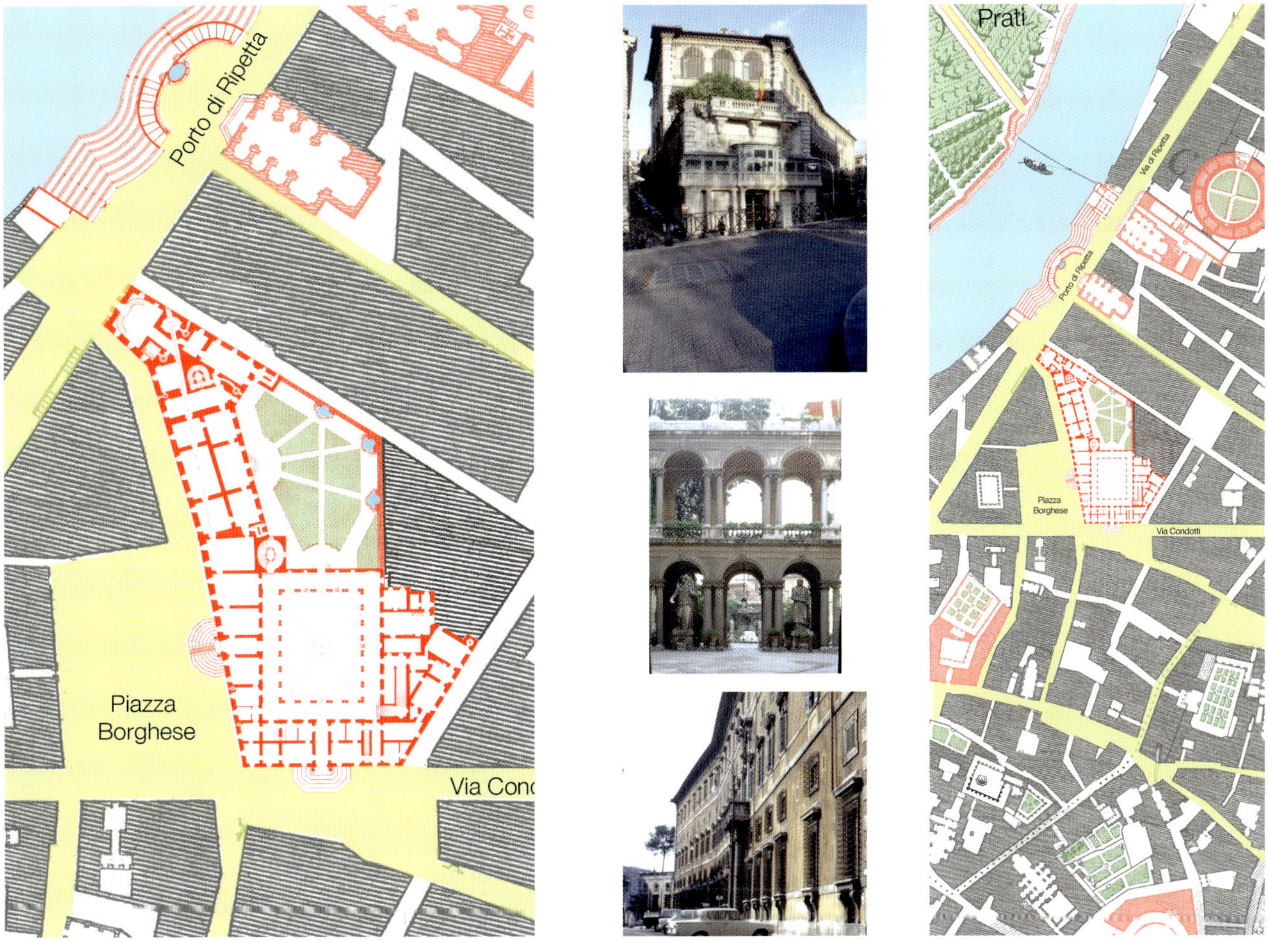

Fig. 34. Palazzo Borghese Site Plan (with Tiber crossing from the Porto di Ripetta to the Prati).

The Palazzo Farnese is essentially a simple compact cube. It has been referred to as a *dado* or dice. Romans fondly refer to the Palazzo Borghese with its more complex configuration as a *cembalo*, or harpsichord. The *dado/cembalo* dialogue follows. Farnese exhibits a nearly perfect state of equilibrium between disengaged object and adjacent space. In fact, the Piazza Farnese is an almost exact Jell-O mold of its palazzo, the palazzo structure measuring 76m by 55m and the piazza measuring approximating 76m by 54m. The Palazzo Borghese, with its irregular configuration, and its less regularized dual piazze, exhibits an imperfect state. Whereas the Farnese is detached on all sides, the Borghese is partially embedded in the urban fabric. One is an *object in space* the other *defines space*. The ideal Farnese provides a powerful urban identity in a design context which reinforces and extends that ideal. The Borghese accomplishes an equally powerful identity, maintaining its core ideal while incorporating complex contingencies on every side. The first strategy continues or absorbs the ideal order into its context; the second thrives on the tension between the palazzo and its misbehaving, contrarian, but ultimately resolved, context.

Fig. 35. Views of the Piazza and Palazzo Borghese (above) and its aspect on the Porto di Ripetta (below). Prints by Giuseppe Vasi, ca. 1750.

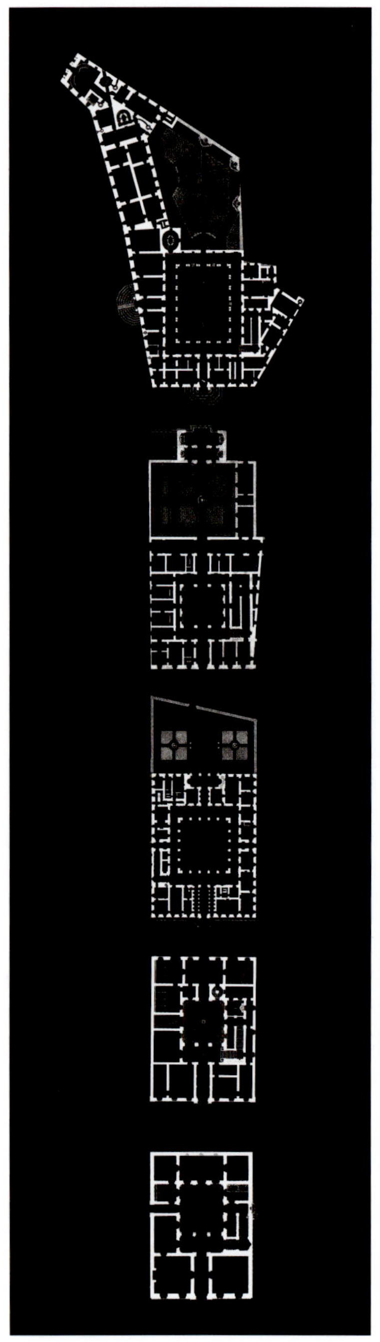

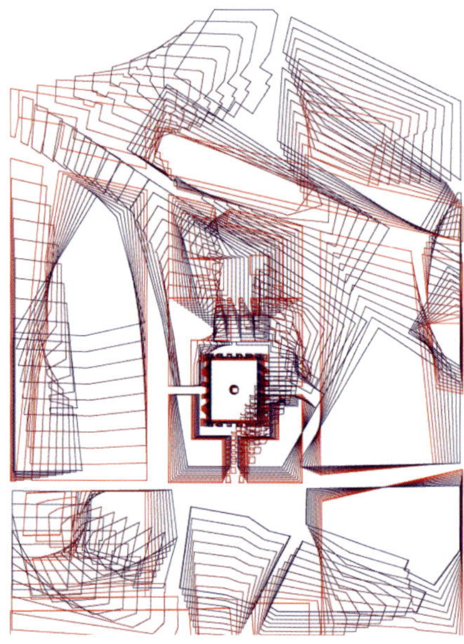

above:
Fig. 36. Palazzi transformations in descending order: Palazzo Borghese, Palazzo Sachetti, Palazzo Farnese, Palazzo Baldassini, and Palazzo Ossoli. Drawings from *Édifices de Rome Moderne*, P.M. Letarouilly.

inset left to right:
Fig. 37. Superimposed digital transformation of the Palazzo Farnese and the Palazzo Borghese. Student exercise by Tony Michaels, instructor, J. Tice, University of Oregon, ca. 1995.

Fig. 38. *Speed photograph of golf stroke.* Photo: Harold Edgerton, 1938. © 2010 MIT. Courtesy of MIT Museum.

In Studio parlance, the Borghese composition was highly valued for its flexibility in treating seemingly intransigent urban forces. It was referred to as a 'fried egg *parti*': the internal courtyard or 'egg yolk', remains intact while the external perimeter or 'egg white', runs freely, potentially responding to an assortment of ad hoc pressures.[37] Because the Borghese shifts between figure/object and ground/wall, it is a paradigmatic example of a both/and urban construct. It demonstrates the principles of type and transformation and its utility as an urban strategy that can effectively deal with the vicissitudes of complex settings employing an ideal as a crucial factor.

Rowian Comparisons and Transformations (Fig. 36–39)

Colin's lectures were of two basic types, often identifiable by the first pair of slides. Regarding the villa as a building type, Rowe used two memorable pairings. In the first, two images are shown that look the same, but by the end of the lecture one is made to realize that they are fundamentally different (Villa Rotunda and Chiswick House). In the second, the reverse occurs: two images are presented that look different, but in the end are shown to be essentially the same (Villa Foscari and Villa Garches). Colin liked to remark with a devilish grin that "things are only interesting when they are not what they appear to be".

What sets the Palazzo Farnese and Borghese apart from the antonyms above is that it invites, nay demands, a reckoning with notions of type and transformation. It would be impossible to compare the Farnese and Borghese palazzi in any meaningful way without recognizing the type to which they both belong. The Borghese design, with all its suave accommodations to context and brilliant innovations in building form, still maintains the essential features of the Farnese. Arguably the Baroque palazzo could not have been realized without the conceptual frame of reference provided by the Renaissance precursor. The ideal Palazzo Farnese acts as a provocation for the deformations that make for the ideal/circumstantial Palazzo Borghese. Paradoxically, it may be that the chief value of

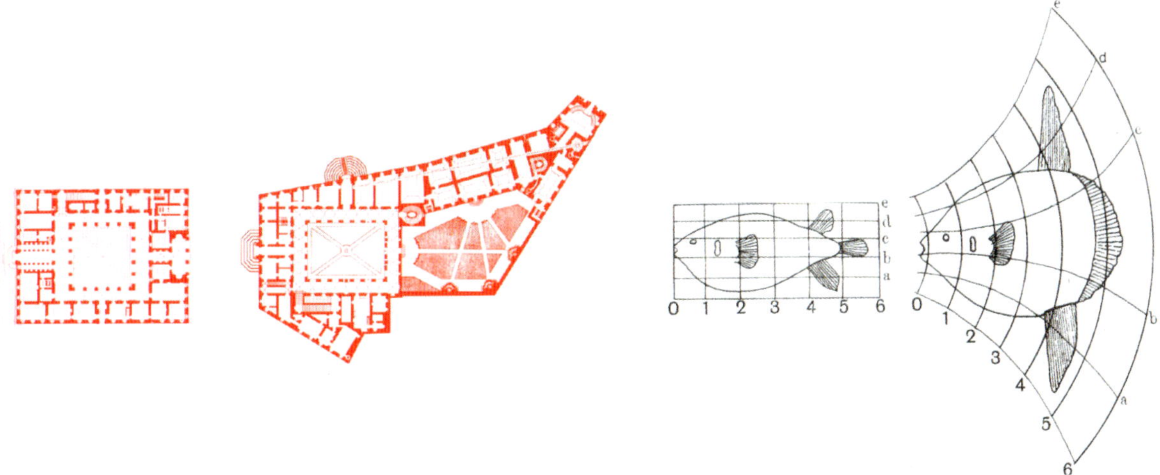

type is that it ignites an impetus for its own 'demise' through transformation: the very definition allows one to know, abide by, or overcome its defining characteristics and boundaries.

Fig. 39. Transformations of the Palazzi Farnese and Borghese compared to fishes by D'Arcy Thompson, Diodon and Orthagoriscus (Giant Sunfish); diagram by author.

The tension between the ideal type and its transformation unfolds like Greek tragedy: constant aspirations toward an ideal are battered down by an unrelenting reality. Just as with Greek tragedy, one can see the variations, deformations, and transformations of the palazzo as a drama that elucidates the tension between the heroic ideal and the compromises and imperfections caused by circumstantial realities. That fraught dialogue is one highly prized by Rowe. It reminds one of his references to Tolstoy who observed that "Happy families are all alike; every unhappy family is unhappy in its own way and are, therefore, always more interesting".

A study of types articulates groups and associated principles. Transformation provides a critical method for manipulating the type without destroying its essential characteristics. Like pursuits in the sciences and the arts, typology provides a conceptual frame of reference in which to work, transform and explore ideas, and solve problems. The duality presented by types and their transformation opens the possibility of moving from a known condition to a new state through a process of rigorous, sustained criticism that can be aided with sophisticated visuals, thus making connections intuitively accessible, resulting in that 'aha' moment. The *modus operandi* in the Studio relied on precedents, types and typologies, and history, but was profoundly *ahistorical*, moving freely in space and time, being both "transcultural and a-temporal".[38] Transformation was seen as a key in the design process that could enhance the creative act, coupling ideas in unexpected ways, as noted by Dr. Johnson. Thinking of types, and especially transformation in these broad terms, could make one believe that, just possibly, *dinosaurs had feathers*.

37 Ceen, Allan, *Roma Traversata: Tracing Historic Pathways through Rome*, Cornell University Press, Ithaca and London, 2022: 36-38. Ceen identifies the important street patterns that determined the urban setting of the palazzo.

38 Rowe, Colin and Koetter, Fred, *Collage City*, MIT Press, Cambridge, MA, and London, 1978: 151.

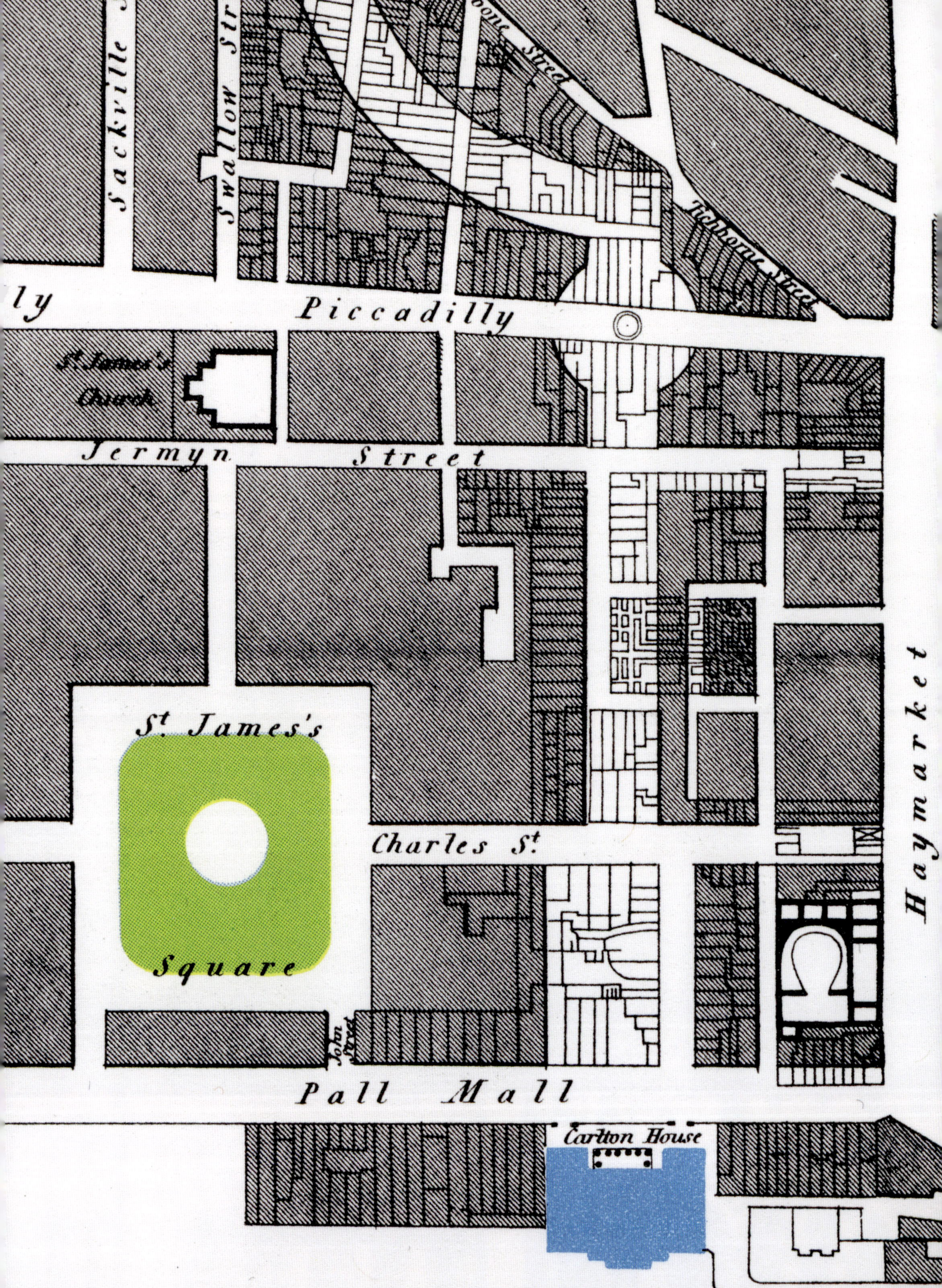

Sackville S
Swallow Str
bone Street
Tichborne Street
ly
Piccadilly
St. James's Church
Jermyn Street
St. James's Square
Charles St.
Haymarket
John Street
Pall Mall
Carlton House

Inland Architect and Contextualism: a Commentary

Stuart Cohen

frontispiece:
Map showing John Nash's Regent Street, London over existing context, Waterloo Place to the Great Quadrant. From John White, *Some Accounts of the Proposed Improvements of the Western Part of London*, 1814. Color emphasis by Bacon.

Contextualism was a term that Steve Hurtt, Tom Schumacher, and I began using while students at Cornell University to describe the design strategies of Colin Rowe's graduate Urban Design Studio in the late 1960s. Tom would subsequently write a description of these urban strategies in a 1971 article in *Casabella*. Steve would, in his 1983 article for *The Cornell Journal,* provide a useful developmental history of these design strategies. I was interested in extending the ideas of the Studio's urban design strategies to the design of individual buildings, with respect to the idea of making additions and interventions based on existing conditions. For me, Contextualism seemed to have relevance with respect to the question of how we determine the starting point for the design of buildings (beyond program). In 1974, the second issue of *Oppositions*, a publication of the Institute for Architecture and Urban Studies in New York, carried my article, "Physical Context, Cultural Context: Including it All". The subtitle was a play on the idea of "inclusivism" being put forward by Charles Moore and Robert Venturi, among others. I wished to point out that their, and Rowe's, positions were not that far apart, although it was clear that the Venturi-Moore group were primarily interested in the inclusion of popular culture and what they celebrated as mundane imagery. Thus my inclusion of cultural context along with physical context in the title of my article.

Author's note: As Regent Street is mentioned in the text, the author chose it as an example of a contexual reconfiguring of a city street that both removes and retains existing buildings while constructing new ones to suggest the street as an idealized condition. All illustrations appeared in Edmund Bacon's, *Design of Cities.*

My article on Contextualism for *Inland Architect* appeared about a decade later and was not intended to add anything new to the argument. At the time, I was teaching at the University of Illinois, Chicago. I taught a design studio and typically gave, depending on the year I was teaching, problems where both unusual site configurations, and adjacent (often party-wall) buildings, were intended to be strong design determinants. I also frequently gave building addition problems, where the existing building to be modified was a significant work of architecture, demanding consideration. In short, I believed that I was teaching the application of Rowe and his design Studio's ideas.

The *Inland Architect* magazine, a storied Chicago publication of the 1890s and first part of the 20th century, had been resurrected in the late 1970s as a publication of the Chicago Chapter of the AIA. Nory Miller, who would later go on to be an editor for *Progressive Architecture* magazine, was *Inland Architect*'s editor. She also wrote architectural criticism for the *Chicago Daily News* (no longer in publication). She believed that trade architectural publications, in addition to reporting building news, should also publish architectural criticism and architectural theory. To that end she invited several of the faculty at the university to write for her. One of my fellow faculty wrote a long essay, published in two parts, which criticized Contextualism as being just another utopian and unrealizable theory about the design of cities. It seemed to me that he had gotten it all wrong. Contextualism wasn't really a fixed theory, but a set of strategies, and it certainly wasn't about the design of entire cities from scratch. I decided to write a letter to the editor, which Nory sent back with a note asking that, instead, I write a short, simple, no architectural jargon allowed, article saying what Contexualism was and what it was not. The result is the brief article below that was originally published in the May/June 1987 issue of *Inland Architect*.

Contextualism, from Urbanism to a Theory of Appropriate Form

In the national best-seller, *House*, author Tracy Kidder describes the book's protagonist, architect Bill Raun.

> *Bill ... loves architecture of all ages, and he embraces what is called the Contextualist branch of the postmodern movement.... He believes that a building should fit its surroundings, both the land around it and other buildings nearby. The Contextualist does not believe in form for form's sake, as many modern architects did, but in appropriate form. The principle is perhaps a variation of the environmentalist's creed. To Bill, Contextualism partakes of a community's character and history. The Contextualist wants to capture some of the spirit of old buildings in new designs...Contextualism suits Bill. He does not like to think of himself arrogantly imposing some wild vision of his own on a client or a neighborhood.*[1]

If the general public understands that contemporary buildings look different from their counterparts of a dozen years ago because of something called Postmodernism, they also know, judging from Kidder's book, that Contextualism in contemporary architecture requires that a building relate to its surroundings. This popular understanding of Contextualism, shared by the architectural profession, suggests that what began as an urban design strategy for reconciling Modern and traditional cities has become a theory of appropriate form in building design.

The term Contextualism refers to the design of buildings by selectively choosing to relate them to their immediate physical context or to their cultural context—the history of a place. Where appropriate, buildings are designed to reinforce the physical characteristics of an area of a city by extending them. The decision to do this presumes a value judgment; that the existing architectural fabric to be extended is believed to be important to the urbanism of a city.

The term Contextualism was first applied to architecture in the mid-1960s by Steven Hurtt and myself. We used it to describe one aspect of the urban design work being done at Cornell University by the students in Colin Rowe's graduate Studio. Rowe and his students questioned several of the basic premises of architecture as it was being taught (and, for that matter, practiced) elsewhere. Rowe's

1 Kidder, John Tracy, *House*, Houghton Mifflin Co., Boston, 1985: 51-52. Contextualism is capitalized throughout, my emphasis.

Fig. 1. Regent Street, The Great Quadrant. From James Elmes, *Metropolitan Improvements*, 1829.

teaching made use of precedent. Although the 'models' he cited were often historical, they were understood to be of relevance as abstractions demonstrating principles worth applying to contemporary architectural designs. Other important educators, such as Vincent Scully, Robert Venturi, and Charles Moore, all associated with Yale in the mid-60s, were delivering a similar message to their students. However, where other architectural educators still stressed the design of individual buildings, Rowe's studio concentrated on the design of public spaces: streets, courts, plazas, greens, and quadrangles. These were to be given shape just like buildings. Defined public space was presented as the object of urban design rather than the result of building design.

One of Rowe's teaching methods was to emphasize the shape of exterior public space by suggesting that students reverse the plan conventions of *poché*, coloring in the spaces as if they were solid forms and leaving the buildings white. Seeing the space first inverts normal perception. This is like the famous drawing which reverses figure and ground, causing us to see the shape of a goblet as the space between the profiles of two faces.

Emphasizing the space in cities as the public domain, Rowe suggested that the construction of freestanding, private, noninstitutional buildings was anti-urban because it tended to destroy the definition of public space, an important physical characteristic of the city. Rowe also suggested that the freestanding buildings of Modern architecture had a meaning that was inseparable from Modernism's utopian aspirations for revolutionizing society. Through its total detachment from the surrounding fabric of the city, the freestanding Modern building was interpreted to symbolically pronounce the coming of a new physical and social

Fig. 2. Regent Street, The Great Quadrant. From James Elmes, *Metropolitan Improvements*, 1829.

order. If this was a radically new meaning for the freestanding urban building, one that interpreted Modernism as if it were history, then Contextualism was conceived by Rowe's students as conveying the opposite: reaffirming the physical experience and social value of a city of defined public spaces. Modernism had swept away history to symbolize progress, technology, and the overthrow of an aristocracy with which the historical styles were associated. However, by favoring a grandiose restructuring of the city, Modernism implicitly suggested the application of political power antithetical to its social program.

The political power required to execute grand schemes at the scale of a Haussmann in Paris or a Speer in Germany seemed not only gone forever, but un-American and un-democratic. What Rowe and his students sought were urban design strategies that were realistic in scope and possible today. Contextualism was one of these formal strategies along with 'collage' and the resolution of 'collisions' between areas of urban fabric. Their development at Cornell University has been described by Steven Hurtt in the second volume of *The Cornell Journal of Architecture.* Of these strategies, only collage saw urban design as the imposition of ideal images on an urban fabric. Each strategy involved interventions which required the designer to think in terms other than those of the closed, idealized composition. These interventions, although independent of one another within a city, were to collectively suggest two important things: first, that they had always been a part of the city; and second, and more importantly, that the city, no matter how random it was in reality, had a larger underlying structure that could be understood from the experience of these parts. Such design interventions were fragments implying the presence of a whole presumed to have once been there. They were fragments not in the sense of being remains, but rather as part of an incomplete order capable of being extended. Thus, the Grand Plan, with its untenable political implications, was no longer perceived as a prerequisite for attempting to achieve cognitive order in a city. Order, it was believed, could be implied by the location of important parts—like cornerstones—rather than by the construction of the whole. Further, and perhaps more subtly, cities were to have the best of all possible worlds: order and variety.

Any discussion of the meaning of Contextualism or its role in contemporary architecture must understand that it was never intended as a theory for the design of cities; it was conceived as a set of strategies for building in cities. Its interpretation as a theory for the complete redesign of cities suggests a misunderstanding of its intended scope and of the body of explanatory writing about it. The criticism of Contextualism as fragmentary suggests a view of urban design only as the history of ideal form imposed on cities. The term Contextual literally means "of or pertaining to the context", from the Latin *contextus*, or connection. To speak of a Contextual city or a Contextual environment confuses the idea of Contextualism. There is no such thing as a Contextual city, or a Contextual environment. We cannot speak of Contextual appearance and assume we know what this means without knowing what context is being referenced. To be Contextual cannot by definition suggest an *a priori* preference for any set of architectural or urban forms. Contextualism proposes the establishment of physical continuities between adjacent buildings. Many models that satisfy this dictate come to mind, from the picturesque buildings of medieval towns to Regent Street, London. In London, Nash's buildings and new street alignments were clearly 'imposed' on the fabric of the city. The measure of their Contextualism or anti-Contextualism is not the degree to which they actually reconfigured the city, but the degree of their physical integration into the resulting form. Do they suggest that they had always been a part of the city, and do they suggest that they are part of a larger underlying order?

Crucial to the agenda of Contextualism is the understanding that the legibility of the city depends on the clear hierarchy of its parts. The biggest, tallest, or most prominently located buildings were always the most important buildings in a city. These were usually the public institutions. Uniqueness of construction, materials, or architectural form also reinforced a building's importance. Cities were understandable in these terms when only the most important buildings, such as the cathedral, stood out. In a city where all the buildings were attached to one another, freestanding buildings took on a great importance. If this is our typological understanding of the city (as opposed to the town or the suburb), then the freestanding building or otherwise uniquely distinguished buildings should house the most important public institutions. However, this is no longer the case, and our ability to understand the city in these terms has been undermined by the use of Modern architecture's preferred building types: the point block, the tower, and the slab. These freestanding structures were the building blocks not just of Modern architecture's theoretical "City of Tomorrow", but of the urban renewal projects and subsequent commercial development that disfigured the space of most American cities. Thus, the first step in re-establishing urban sense in the practice of architecture is to teach architects to see the city as spaces as well as buildings, and to ask themselves, Am I really building the most important building on the block? Am I really building in the most important location? Should my building rightfully differ from the buildings around it in its urban type or should it continue the fabric of the city? Once these questions are correctly answered, architects can go on unfettered in their creativity. Surely 'blending in' does not mean that everyone must wear gray flannel suits; it means that if everyone has agreed that the occasion calls for a suit, to arrive in shorts and a t-shirt is either an act of ignorance or of arrogance.

By referring initial decisions of a building's configuration to the larger frame of reference offered by the building's place in the city, architects are once again addressing the difficult issues of determining appropriate architectural form. Before Modernism, design proceeded in one of two ways. Aesthetic choices were made consciously by reference to precedent. The aesthetic system used, comprised of an architectural language and compositional strategies, was the result of social and cultural forces. These led architects to argue for the appropriateness of reviving Classical, Gothic, or some other style of architecture which was thought to best represent the aspirations of a society and its institutions. Design began with the selection and study of the appropriate model from within an already agreed upon system of forms. At other times architects employed a theory of eclecticism which prescribed the appropriate choice for each type of building and for each situation. Unlike each of the historical revivals which argued for a single architectural style, eclecticism argued for the appropriateness of a style to a particular use. This depended on an understanding of the shared associations of different architectural forms and the establishment of rules for their use. These rules were based on the belief that associative meaning could allow us to identify a church as a church, a bank as a bank, and a city hall as a city hall. Thus, for each building use-type, the designer had a clear starting point for considering aesthetic choices.

Current changes in architectural thought have reintroduced the study of building typology into architecture. Unlike Modernism, which believed every building should be considered as a new problem, contemporary architects wish to see the problems of formal choice in the broader context of history. However, architectural theory does not address the issue of the choice of architectural language, creating a dilemma for the contemporary designer. The study of typology—an examination of 'use of types', 'organizational types', and 'structural/spatial types' is devoid of aesthetic and associational values. Like the program of a client's requirements or the materials of construction which Modernism believed would yield the appropriate form for each building, the study of history is now expected to somehow magically yield the idea for a building's appropriate form. Today we acknowledge that it was not technology that gave form to Modernism, but the desire to express progress and modernity through visual associations that created a 'machine aesthetic' or led to the use of abstract form. Thus, in the absence of rules governing the visual appearance of buildings, the Modernists were able to build because they shared a common belief in the appropriateness of the forms they employed. Today, we share no such common belief, nor do we deal with architecture as a compendium of aesthetic rules. Today we live in a culture and at a time when both practical and theoretical disciplines seem to have rejected the use of rules in favor of proceeding from first principles, the intellectual legacy of scientific method.

Fig. 3. Waterloo Place from Carlton House. James Elmes, *Metropolitan Improvements*, 1829.

Contextualism suggests that one of the methods for determining appropriate form and architectural language is based on the recognition of institutional and urban hierarchy. The more civic in importance a building is, the more distinctly different it may be from its context. Conversely, the less important the difference between buildings, the less different their architectural form and expression should be. Contextualism suggests that these less important buildings can be seen as dependent additions to their immediate surroundings. This offers the opportunity to determine forms, materials, and details as extensions of the visual characteristics of a building's surrounding context. In the absence of an immediately adjacent built context, Contextualism urges the architect to look to local building traditions, vernacular forms, and indigenous materials and techniques; in short, to look to the dominant architectural history of a place. In the absence of an architectural history or tradition, Contextualism proceeds by analogy, selecting the forms of an architecture appropriately associated with a similar environment, climate, or terrain. In this way, Contextualism, like the rules of usage that accompanied eclecticism, can constitute an empirical and authentic method for determining appropriate architectural form. Like the historical concept of appropriate building character, responding to a context provides a focus to the range of formal choices offered by history and typology. At a time when fixed rules for the use and selection of historical models for new buildings would seem hard to accept, it is not surprising that a theory of Contextual response, like the "environmentalist's creed", has arisen to accompany our new interest in the study and use of architectural precedents in design.

The Influence of Colin Rowe on My Urbanism and Architecture

Dhiru A. Thadani

For many not fortunate to have studied at Cornell under Colin Rowe and benefited from his enormous intellect, his writing could be inspirational as well as difficult. I had struggled to read his essays in *The Mathematics of the Ideal Villa*[1] and they introduced me to architectural thought unlike anything that I had been exposed to in my undergraduate and graduate education. For me it was a wake-up call. I realized that my studies had not ended at graduation, for there was an infinite world of architectural and urban theory to be investigated, analyzed, and shared.

What ignited my curiosity while researching Rowe was the figure/ground graphic representation of cities and the urban theories extracted from the examination of these drawings. The black and white figure/ground depiction of solid objects and voids appealed to my visual sensibility. Prior to my undergraduate and graduate architectural studies in Washington, D.C., I had come of age in Bombay, a walkable city of five million residents. The suburban landscape of America was somewhat foreign to me, for although I had experienced it first hand, I didn't understand the widespread attraction to this environment that was so antithetical to my own background. Using the representational technique promoted by Rowe, I was able to read, analyze, and comprehend placemaking within a town or city in very different environments that were both spatially and culturally diverse.

I began teaching in 1980 at Catholic University of America (CUA) with Peter Hetzel, who later became my professional partner. Teaching proved to be an opportunity for structured reflection of my beliefs regarding architecture and urbanism. From 1983 to 1986, I was fortunate to teach in the CUA Summer Program in Architecture alongside several faculty and scholars who were well-versed in Rowe's teachings on urban design and the city.[2] I had already been exposed to Andrés Duany and Elizabeth Plater-Zyberk's contextual investigations of Southern towns used by them in designing the traditional town and implementing form-based coding for Seaside, Florida. Duany and Plater-Zyberk were resurrecting strategies to make buildings behave responsibly within the urban fabric. While employing a set of prescriptive rules that dictated the building morphology and disposition on the site, form-based codes were proving that they could foster predictable built results and high quality public realms.

frontispiece:
Léon Krier's 1985 Completion of Washington, D.C. plan superimposed on Pierre Charles L'Enfant's area map.

1 *The Mathematics of the Ideal Villa and Other Essays*, by Colin Rowe, was published in 1976. These essays were written decades ago but they're still enormously valuable and relevant. The first essay, from which the book takes its title, is an analysis of the geometrical and proportional similarities between Le Corbusier's Villa Stein at Garches and Palladio's Villa Malcontenta.

2 The CUA Summer Program faculty between 1983 and 1986 included: Jonathan Barnett, Tom Beeby, Alan Chimacoff, Steven Hurtt, John McDermott, Alan Plattus, Tom Schumacher, and Roger Sherwood.

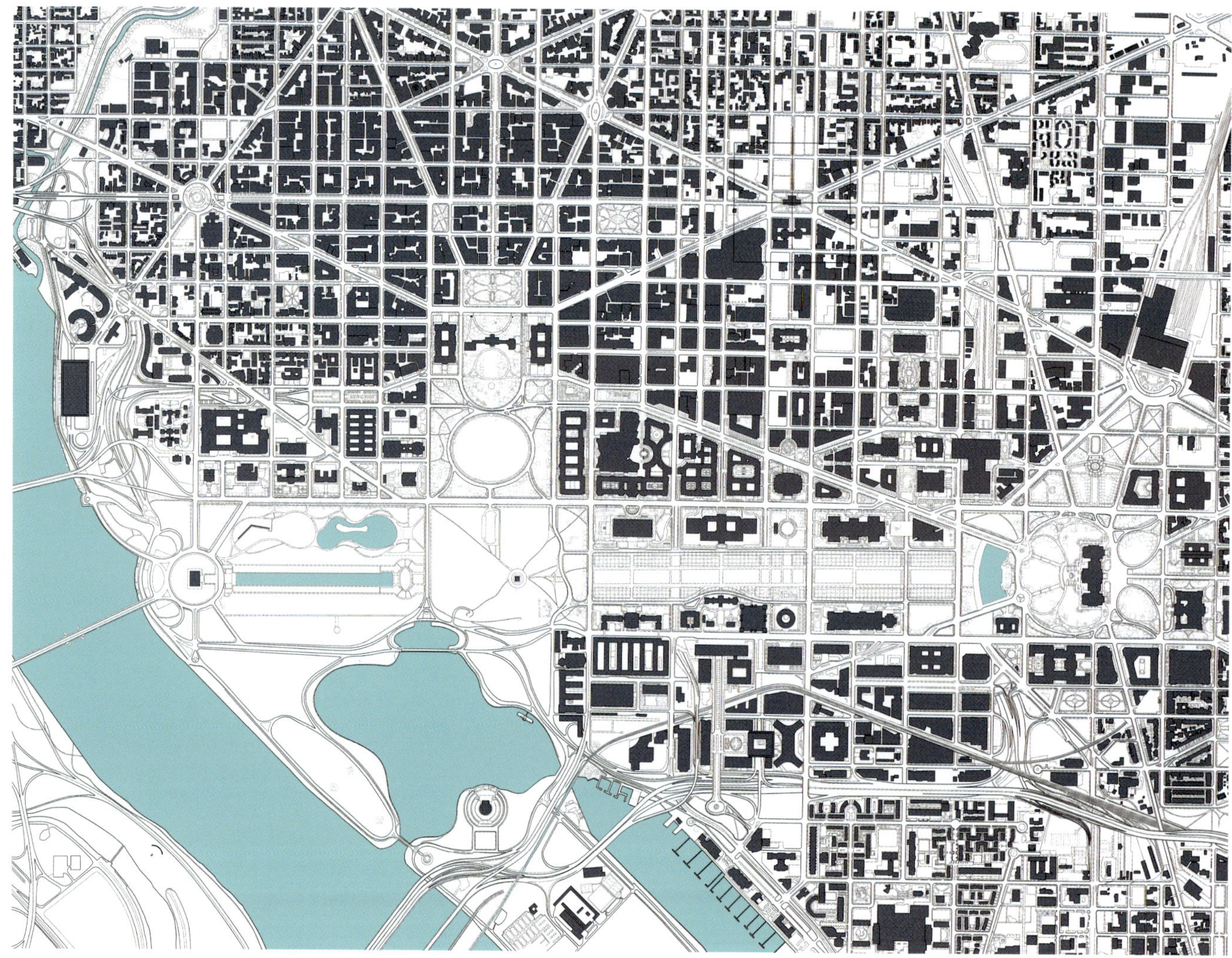

Monumental Core of Washington, D.C.

The two parallel enquiries by Rowe, and by Duany and Plater-Zyberk, sought to build meaningful urban realms focused on architecture that contributed to the making of legible places within the city. This was in dramatic opposition to my architectural education, which had focused on object-buildings devoid of context. Rowe's proposition that Modern object-buildings were partial to making outside corners, promoting the idea of the free-standing object, while urban-responsive buildings made inside corners to define and contain space in courtyards and the public realm, was an early revelation.

At the same time, I was exposed to the plan of Rome drawn by Giambattista Nolli, a heroic effort that was begun in 1736 and required 12 years to complete. The map identified the public and private realms of the city using a figure/ground representation of built space with blocks and buildings shaded in as hatched *poché*. Major enclosed semi-public spaces such as the Pantheon, the colonnades in St. Peter's Square, and church interiors such as St. Peter's, are drawn as floor plans representing open civic spaces. Surprisingly, the convention up to Nolli's time was to orient maps to the east. Nolli broke this convention by reorienting his plan to magnetic north, reflecting his reliance on the compass, a scientific instrument used to get his bearings.

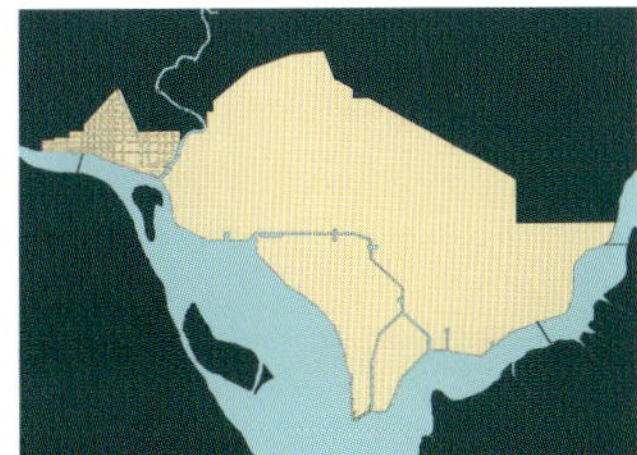
1790 Georgetown, pre-Washington, D.C.

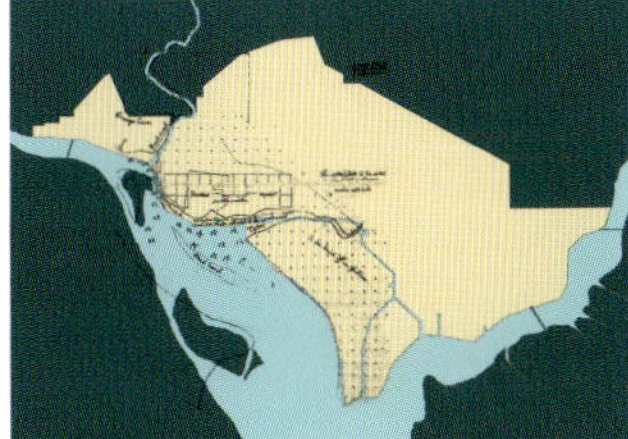
1791 Thomas Jefferson

1791 Pierre Charles L'Enfant

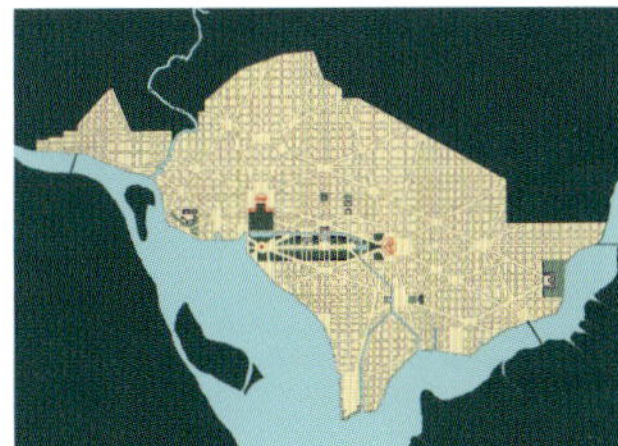
1792 Andrew Ellicott

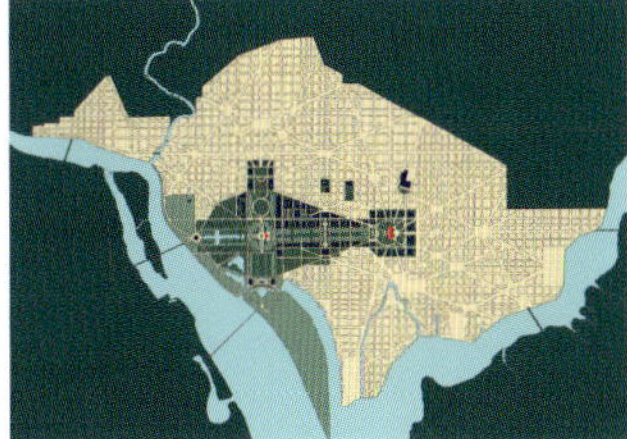
1902 McMillan Plan / Senate ParkCommission

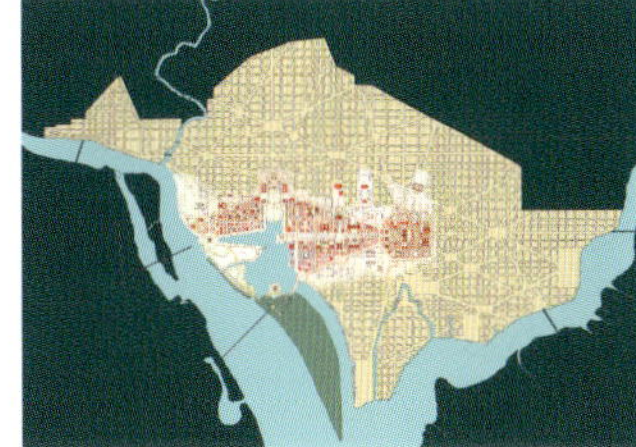
1985 Léon Krier

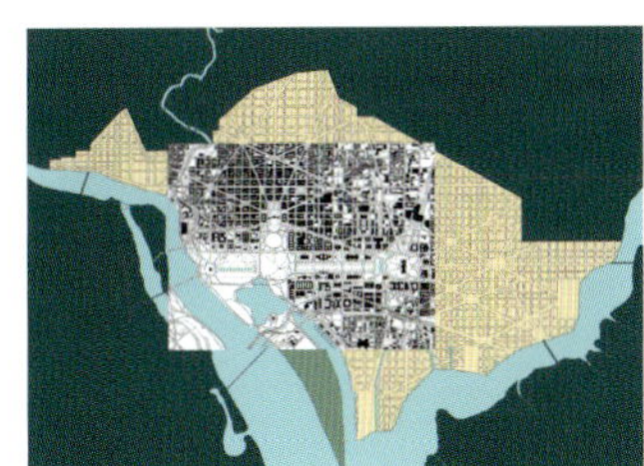
1991 Thadani building footprint plan

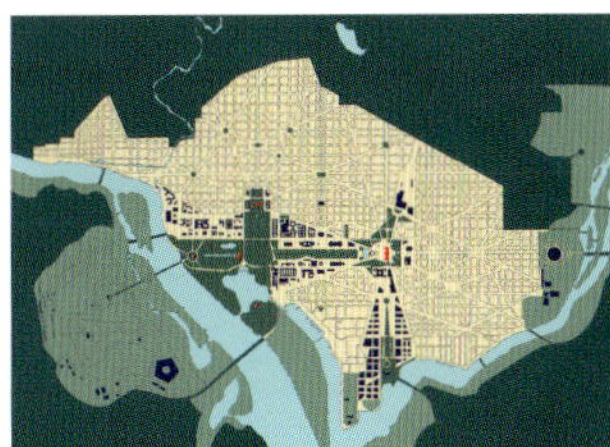
2000 Legacy Plan

Various plans for Washington, D.C., superimposed on Pierre Charles L'Enfant's area map.

Appalled by several new object-buildings and street closures that were proposed for Washington, D.C., where I had chosen to live, I embarked on a project to make a modified Nolli-type plan of the city. My goal was to highlight the relationships between the city's many civic buildings and the public spaces that they defined. Unlike European cities, American cities did not have a robust culture of making and updating city maps. And Washington, D.C., unlike most American cities, was deliberately planned with a large percentage of land dedicated to the public realm, making this a unique and particularly interesting challenge to document. While teaching at CUA from 1980 to 1986, my interest in urbanism and Washington, D.C. led me to assign several design studio projects that analyzed architectural typologies and addressed urban issues.

With a sense of increasing alarm at the lack of cohesiveness between architecture and urbanism, a cadre of young architects[3] volunteered their Saturdays to help make the Washington, D.C. 'Nolli Plan'. These weekend work sessions initiated a discourse on urban design. As the city of Washington, D.C. developed, there had been egregious errors and deviations from the L'Enfant plan. The working map that we were making permitted the Saturday crew to discuss strategies for both representation and urban repair.[4] Intrigued by the Nolli representation of both interior and exterior public and semi-public space, we selected a plan cut at the level that would also show selected interior spaces of Washington, D.C.'s major public buildings. The end-goal of the endeavor was to aid designers and decision makers in evaluating new proposed buildings within their urban context, to provide constructive criticism and to help restore the original vision for the city.[5]

The economic downturn in the late 1980s was a devastating period for the building industry and allied professions. At this low point, many who were concerned with the built environment began self-supported research. And as a consequence, a coalition formed of architects and planners who started to share information about urbanism. By 1990, many design professionals across the U.S. were discouraged by the prevailing development patterns that focused

3 Architects who volunteered to help with the Washington plan included Phil Eagleburger, Tom Hofman, Bill Hutchins, Tom Johnson, Glenn MacCullough, and others.

4 Energized to discuss urban issues, the group of young, D.C.-based architects, organized three, two-day symposia for the Smithsonian Institution in the summers of 1987, 1988, and 1989, titled "Building in the City". Speakers included Diana Agrest, Jonahan Barnett, Michael Dennis, Andrés Duany, Steven Hurtt, J. L. Sibley Jennings Jr., Léon Krier, Steven Peterson, Patrick Pinnell, Joseph Rykwerk, Thomas Schumacher, Michael Schwarting, Lawrence Speck, Bill Westfall, and several others.

5 The Washington plan drawing was digitized and the figure/ground was made available to the public through the Washington, D.C., Chapter of the American Institute of Architects (AIA).

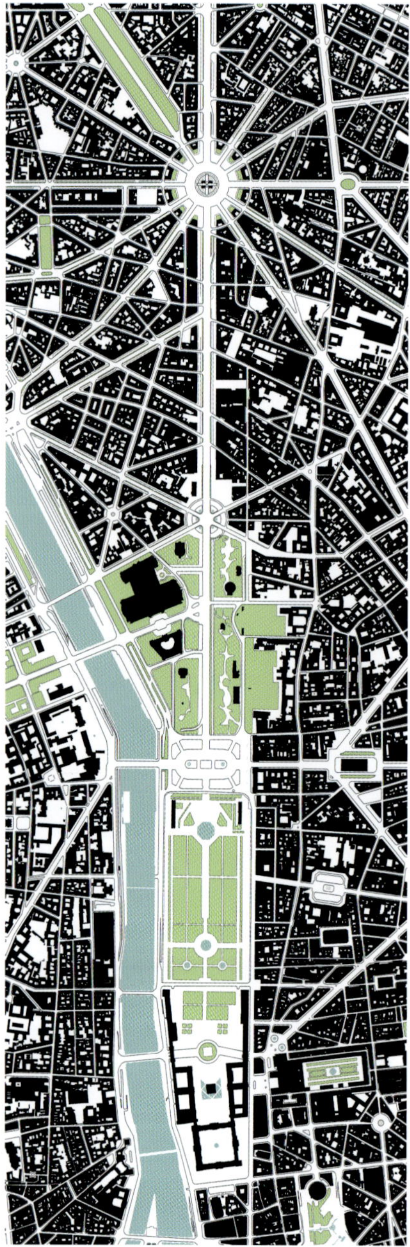

Paris - Champs-Élysées

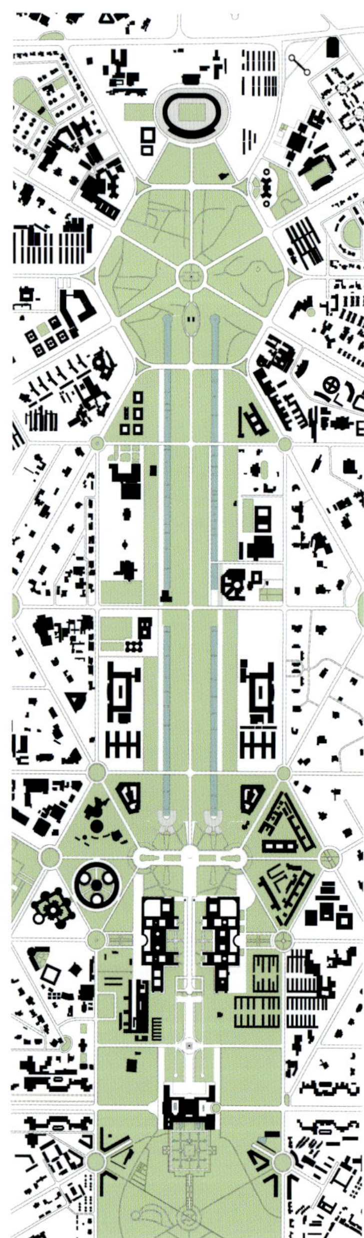

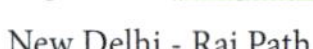

New Delhi - Raj Path

Washington, D.C. - National Mall

Note: All plans on this spread are drawn at the same scale

on segregation of uses and dependence on private automobiles for mobility. Historic downtowns and Main Streets had been disinvested, urban renewal had destroyed many neighborhoods and these historic neighborhoods and previously thriving communities were losing populations.

In the spring of 1993, I was a visiting critic at the University of Miami and I spent my non-teaching hours at Andrés Duany and Elizabeth Plater-Zyberk's office in the Little Havana neighborhood. The two partners were in conversation with four West Coast architects[6] who were equally concerned about the proliferation of suburban sprawl and failing cities across the U.S. Encouraged by Léon Krier to emulate the International Congress of Modern Architecture

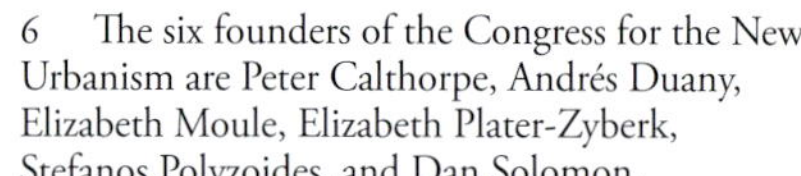

6 The six founders of the Congress for the New Urbanism are Peter Calthorpe, Andrés Duany, Elizabeth Moule, Elizabeth Plater-Zyberk, Stefanos Polyzoides, and Dan Solomon.

7 The Congrès Internationaux d'Architecture Moderne (CIAM), or International Congress of Modern Architecture, was an organization founded in 1928 and disbanded in 1959. The organization's main objective was spreading the principles of the Modern Movement. It was responsible for a series of events and congresses arranged across Europe by the most prominent Modernists architects of the time and focused on all the main domains of architecture—landscape, urbanism, industrial design, construction, and city planning, among others.

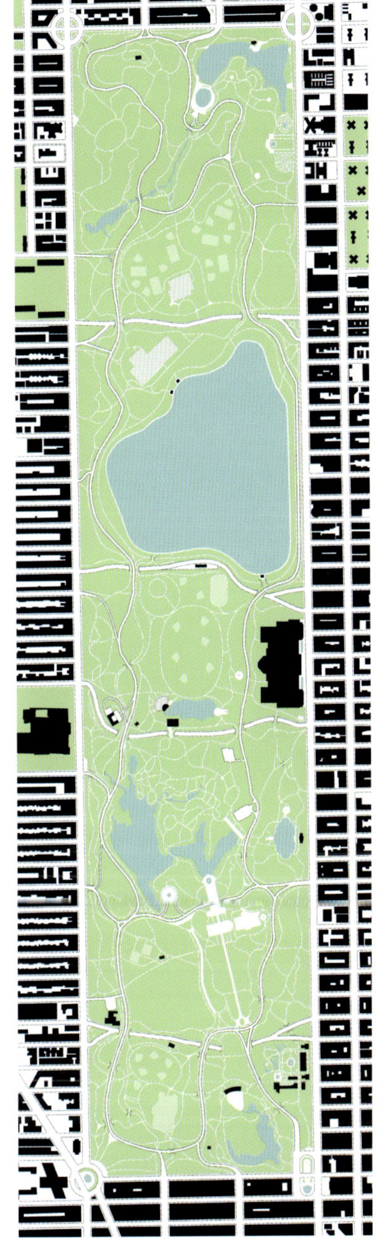
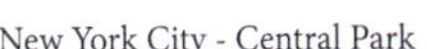
New York City - Central Park

Chandigarh - Leisure Valley

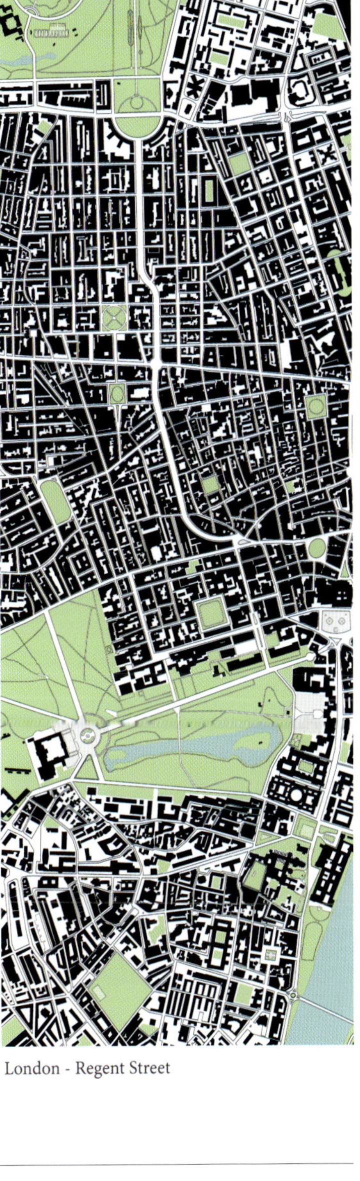
London - Regent Street

(CIAM),[7] the Congress for the New Urbanism (CNU) was founded mid-year. I was able to help organize the first CNU Congress in Alexandria, Virginia that was held in August 1993.[8] It is interesting to note that there was much cross-pollination between the early new urbanists and students or colleagues of Colin Rowe. These included Michael Dennis, Steve Hurtt, and Steven Peterson, who presented at the first congress.[9]

The New Urbanism movement united urban designers, architects, planners, developers, and engineers around the belief that the physical environment had an impact on the quality of life. The built environment affected everyone's chance to thrive, be safe, happy, healthy, and live a prosperous life. It was clear to the New

8 Shortly after the first CNU Congress, in November 1993, the first book on New Urbanism titled *The New Urbanism: Toward an Architecture of Community* by Peter Katz was published. Among the projects included was Lake West, designed by Cornell graduates Steven Peterson, Barbara Littenberg and Blake Middleton. The essay by Vincent Scully ties in the Yale School of Architecture connection to New Urbanism.

9 Like many of Rowe's students who have presented at CNU congresses, Tom Schumacher taught a single-speaker session on the design of facades at CNU XI held in Washington, D.C., in 2003.

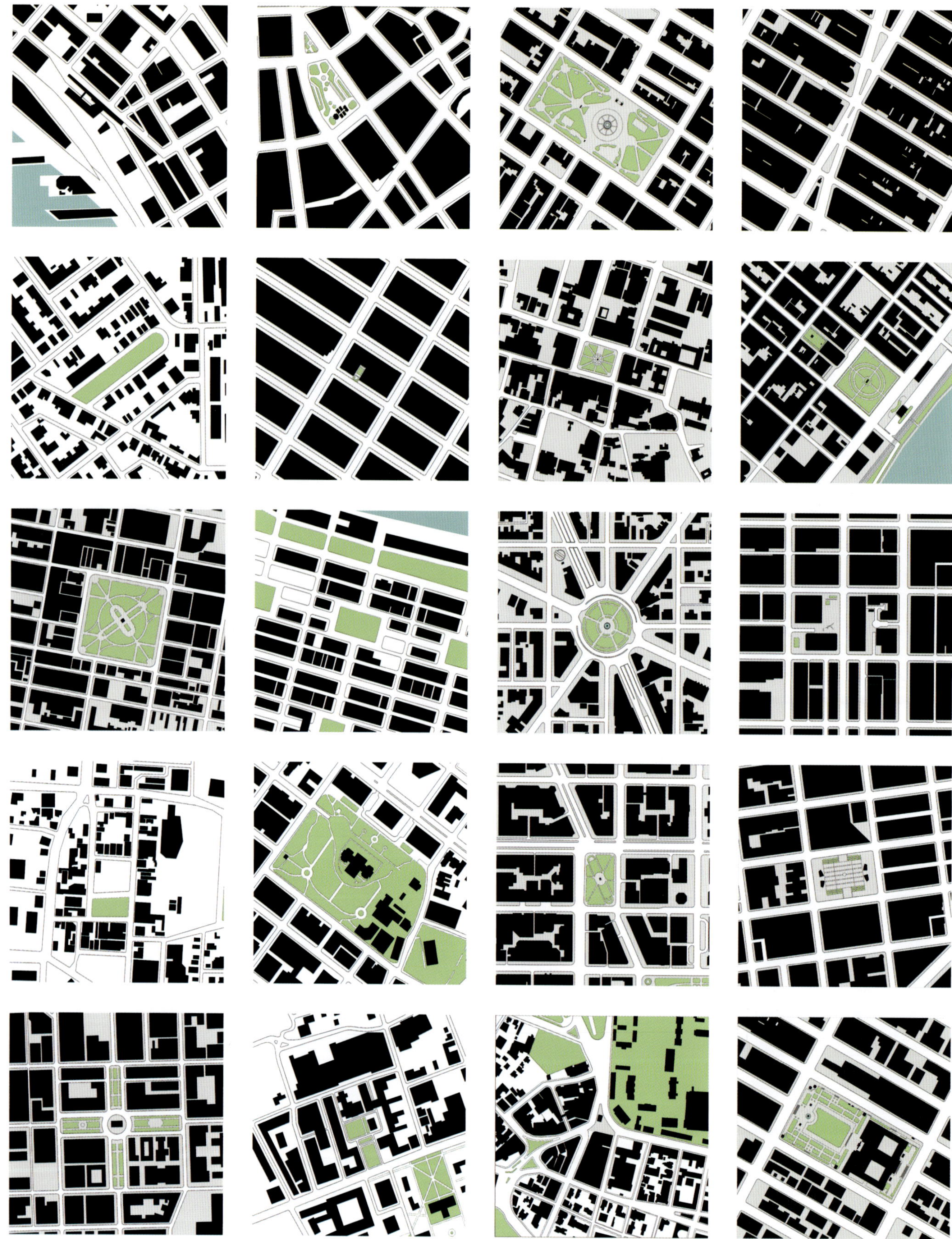

opposite page left to right:
Row 1
Pike Place Market, Seattle
Post Office Square, Boston
Washington Square Park, New York City
Times Square, New York City

Row 2
Days Park, Buffalo
Paley Park, New York City
Santa Fe Plaza, Santa Fe
Jackson Square, New Orleans

Row 3
Rittenhouse Square, Philadelphia
Johnson Square, Savannah
Dupont Circle, Washington, D.C.
Federal Center, Chicago

Row 4
Old Town, Albuquerque
Capitol Square, Richmond
Farragut Square, Washington, D.C.
Union Square, San Francisco

Row 5
Mount Vernon Square, Baltimore
Palmer Square, Princeton
Harvard Square, Boston
Bryant Park, New York City

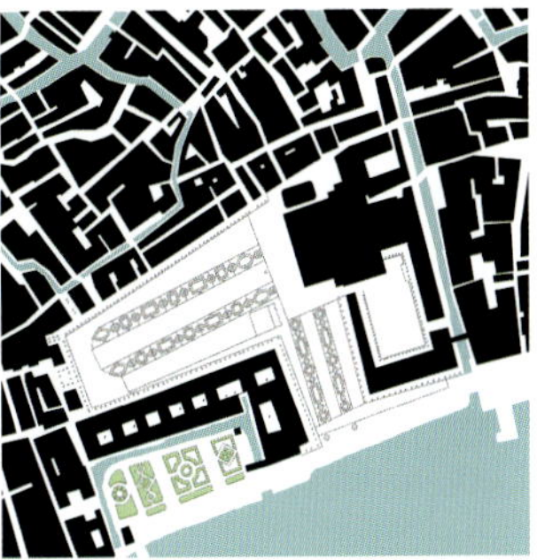
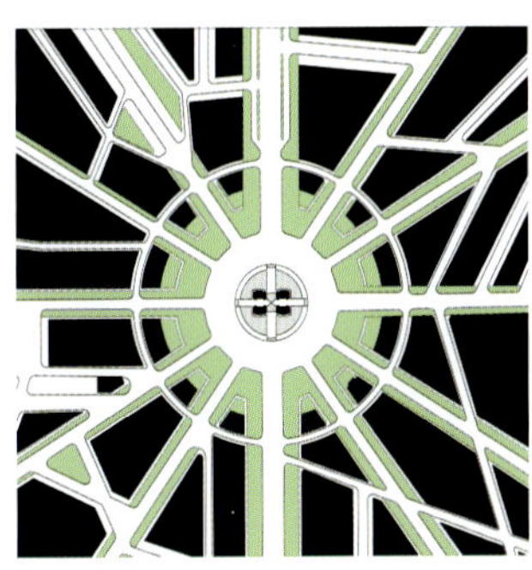

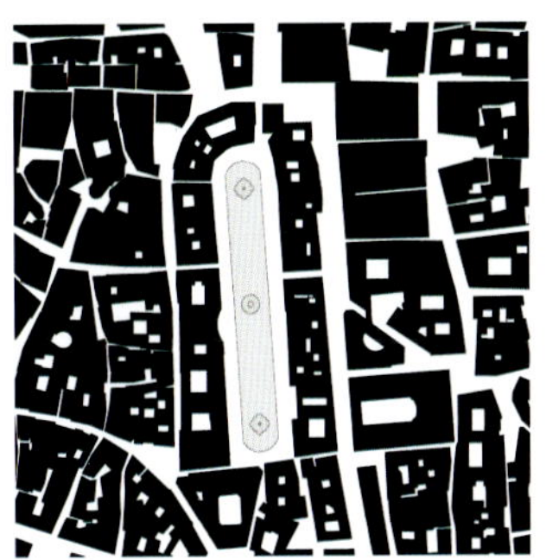

above left to right:
Row 1
Royal Crescent and Circus, Bath
Piazza San Marco, Venice
Étoile Charles de Gaulle, Paris

Row 2
Place Vendôme, Paris
Piazza Navona, Rome
Campidoglio, Rome

Note: All plans on this spread are drawn at the same scale and oriented north.

Urbanists that the public realm is essential, that every individual is entitled to a well-designed public realm within their neighborhood, town or city, and that civic life fosters community. In achieving these goals it was useful to seek out and analyze precedents to emulate, using the figure/ground drawing as a tool. This graphic device helps identify figural or readily identifiable public spaces within the urban fabric, including streets that are the umbilical cords connecting public spaces to one another. The tools promoted by Rowe had a direct bearing on what New Urbanists were striving to achieve.[10]

The values of CNU and its core principles are articulated in the *Charter of the New Urbanism*. The charter promotes mixed-use developments instead of segregated zoning, and walkable neighborhoods over auto-dependent suburbs. In the past 29 years, the CNU community has risen to the challenge of building on past successes by establishing new design and development standards, accelerating the pace of change to land-use zoning, and striving to make places people enjoy and where businesses can thrive.

In 1995, encouraged by the CNU Charter and a healthy dose of optimism, I started to work on several master plans in India.[11] An early realization working overseas was that mapping of cities had been, and was still, a low priority. Accurate data was hard to find in my homeland, just as it was in the U.S. This led to an effort to make a digital figure/ground drawing of my other hometown, Mumbai, to aid my design efforts and make scale comparisons to spaces that we were proposing within our master plans. Additionally, my Indian clients were unfamiliar with a wide range of global public squares and plazas; this made it important to show them comparative scale drawings of local examples with which they were familiar. These efforts led me to make drawings of public spaces

10 Recognizing the contribution of the Cornell Urban Design Studio, Colin Rowe, Fred Koetter, Michael Dennis, Steven Peterson, and Barbara Littenberg were recipients of CNU's Athena Medal. CNU bestows the Athena Awards to honor those who have cast a lasting and enduring influence on the practice and thought of New Urbanism. Named after the goddess "defender of the city and weaver of fabric", the Athena Awards recognize the pioneers who laid the groundwork for the CNU movement.

11 My overseas planning work started in 1995 when I was a partner with Peter Hetzel in Thadani Hetzel Partnership. THP operated an office in Bombay from 1995 to 1999. I continue to work overseas when the opportunity arises.

Figure/ground drawing of South Bombay, India.

as a normal operating procedure within whatever country or context that I was fortunate to be working in.

Just as others who have been interested in making comparative collections of urban forms and spaces, so was I.[12] As that interest developed, I became fascinated with two aspects of cartography: better representation of the spatial qualities of the ground plane, and development of constant scale dimensions for accuracy of comparison.

It is hard to question the efficacy of representation of the black and white graphic technique of either those related to Colin Rowe or the hatched version that

12 Others who have made comparative plan studies include Wayne Copper, Jean-Nicolas-Louis Durand, Sir Banister Fletcher, Charles Graves, Werner Hegemann and Elbert Peets, Allan Jacobs, Eric C. Jenkins, Léon Krier, Rob Krier, Eduardo Sacriste Jr., and Camillo Sitte.

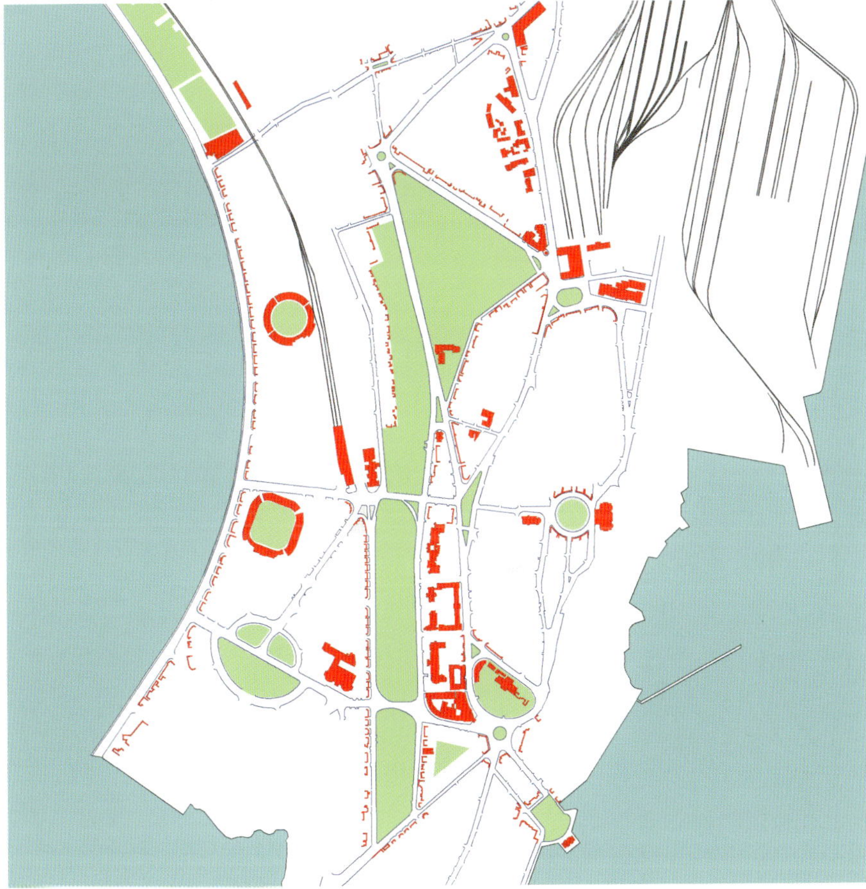

Plan identifying civic buildings and public spaces in South Bombay, India.

Nolli employed. Both are well-suited to places like the historic center of Rome or many European towns and cities. These places, however, have little or no vegetation within the public realm of their urban centers and they favor a homogeneous ground plane. But many great public spaces have a variety of ground surfaces and materials including landscape features, water elements, and so on. Several critics[13] have opined that the Cornell urban design figure/ground black and white graphics do not adequately convey the nuances of detail embodied in some of the more canonical public spaces.[14] By 1999, in response to this critique, I had started to explore the use of color to illustrate the various ground planes: white for hardscape, light green for vegetation, and light blue for water bodies.

Regarding comparative dimensions, New Urbanism promoted a shared standard and settled on a numeric dimension of 1,320 feet, or 400 meters, to promote a walking distance achievable within five minutes. Today the ¼-mile radius is commonly used on maps, especially on transit maps to depict the catchment area of transit stops. Responding to this standard, I chose a 1,320-foot square as the frame dimension for comparative drawings of memorable public spaces from around the world. For monumental axial public spaces, such as the Champs-Élysées in Paris, the Mall in Washington, D.C., or Raj Path in New Delhi, I chose a frame of three miles by ¾-miles, multiples of the basic ¼-mile module.[15]

13 Waldheim, Charles, ed., *The Landscape Urbanism Reader*, Princeton Architectural Press, New York, 2006, reiterates the criticism on the reliance of black and white figure/ground drawings to understand public space. Without the rigor of New Urbanism, Landscape Urbanism hopes to organize space to address concerns such as decentralization of population and sprawling cities.

14 By the early 1980s, Rowe studio projects had begun to move away from the stark black and white drawing toward the softer hatch technique of Nolli; trees and other landscape elements were being drawn. Steven Hurtt and others had also started to encourage and incorporate the use of color in studio projects for anaylsis and design representation. Inexpensive tracing paper and magic markers facilitated the making of multiple design alternatives to clarify and test design ideas.

15 Starting in 1999, I printed and distributed eleven 24" by 36" double-sided color posters of comparative plans of towns and cities. The posters were distributed free-of-charge at the annual CNU congresses, to share the information and encourage the discourse on urbanism.

Inspired by the Charles Eames film *Powers of Ten*,[16] I chose a viewport of one-mile square for small towns and city centers. For their regional context the frames were ten-miles square and 100-miles square. Using a fixed dimension for the drawing frame permitted digital projection of these drawings, while enabling direct comparison by always having a known dimension.

Most of the documentation and analysis that I have completed has been driven by real-world projects. I believe that the role of the urban designer and architect has morphed into that of being an educator for stakeholders and decision makers who control the purse strings and often determine urban design decisions for good or for bad. Without their buy-in and support nothing of real value can be implemented. At the beginning of the projects I have led, the drawings are made to inform the design team. However experience shows that the layman and non-planner are comfortable accepting a design proposal if a direct comparison can be made with an existing place with which they are familiar. Comparative plan drawings of local examples have become essential in convincing stakeholders that what is being proposed is time-tested and that the actual dimensions have worked successfully before in similar applications. After all, the human body is globally universal. Humans can only walk a certain distance comfortably before getting fatigued and it is the rare individual who can climb four or five flights of stairs before exhaustion sets in. Cities need to be designed or retrofitted to accommodate the most sustainable means of movement—walking. Drawing comparative and scale plans of places that have these characteristics is an indispensable tool in achieving this goal.

There is a symbiotic relationship between what I have learned from Colin Rowe and my discourse with his former students and that same engagement with fellow New Urbanists. The study and making of cities is a complex task, requiring teamwork, persistence, and fortitude. Ideas should not be proprietary or presumed to be limited by the boundaries of style; they must be shared if we are to make desirable quality-of-life places for a sustainable future.

opposite:
Brasov, Romania. Freehand plan drawing

16 *Powers of Ten* was produced in 1977 by Charles and Ray Eames. They employed the system of exponential powers to visualize the importance of scale. *Powers of Ten* illustrates the universe as an arena of both continuity and change, from everyday picnics to cosmic mystery. The film begins with a close-up shot of a man sleeping near the lakeside in Chicago viewed from one meter away. The landscape steadily moves out in increments, until it reveals the edge of the known universe. Then, the film takes us towards Earth again, continuing back to the sleeping man's hand and eventually down to the level of a carbon atom. The concept of the film was derived from Kees Boeke's 1957 book, *Cosmic View: The Universe in Forty Jumps.*

Scena Comica.

Three Stage Sets in Search of a City: An American Perspective

James T. Tice

"All the world's a stage."
As You Like It
William Shakespeare

It is the premise of this essay that the Renaissance stage and the three stage sets—the Comic, Tragic and Satyric—conceived, described, and depicted by Sebastiano Serlio represent the first crystallization of a spatial and iconographic construct that presaged the development of Western cities from the Renaissance to the mid-20th century.[1] First evident in Europe, that construct also arrived in the Americas with colonizing settlement. In the U.S. it survived, almost as a subconscious referent, in countless cities and towns through the 19th century. Then it burst forth into full consciousness and deliberate expression with the Chicago World's Fair of 1893 and then spread as a national movement for 'civic' improvement. By the mid-20th century, it had shaped U.S. cities, towns, parks, and suburbs at every scale from small buildings to entire cities and national parks. However, the Modern movement, with its attendant attitudes toward architecture and planning, brought about a new paradigm antithetical to any defined spatial structure in the city and seemingly immune to iconography. Its anti-urban bias and its attack on 'meaning' swept aside the Serlian construct. As a reassessment of a Modernist hegemony is underway, a new pluralist and interpretative understanding of our cities makes room for Serlio. His three stage sets can serve as a critical commentary, one which benefits the ongoing debate about contemporary architecture, urban design, and landscape and, indeed, the very nature of all three as contributors to the city. This essay is a reappraisal of a tradition that had informed the act of making cities for 400 years. It suggests that the U.S. can be thought of as an illustration—a 'theater of realization'—of Sebastiano Serlio's stage sets with deep relevance for contemporary urban design.[2]

The idea of theater, whether real or metaphorical, requires space for both spectacle and spectator. During the Renaissance, architects conceived and built architectural and landscape settings for plays, spectacles, and other forms of pageantry. In some cases, this could mean transforming the city or landscape into a temporary theater that might last a day. In some instances, it meant building a dedicated performance space in classically inspired salons, theater houses, or

frontispiece top to bottom:

Scena Comica
U.S. Strip Highway, ca. 1970.
Photo: Luke Sharrett.

Scena Tragica
Washington, D. C. McMillan Plan, 1902.

Scena Sayrica
The Mall, Central Park, Maurice Prendergast, 1901.

1 Serlio uses the word *scena* or scene for stage set, rather than *strada*, street. I use 'stage set' or simply *scena* as it seems to be more spatially expansive with references to *piazze* and *piazzette*. John Onians, in *Bearers of Meaning*, asserts that Sansovino's library in the Piazzetta San Marco was inspired by a Venetian stage set attributed to Serlio, ca. 1535. Stage sets by Peruzzi, Serlio's mentor, and Serlio himself are less uniform than the narrow corridor streets designed in 1580 by Scamozzi for the Teatro Olimpico. It seems we are so accustomed to the dramatic perspectives realized by Scamozzi in Vicenza that we have tended to impose the designation "street" on the more ample spaces depicted by Serlio. All images by Serlio in this essay are from the original 1545 French edition, courtesy of the Metropolitan Museum of Art. Later editions deviate from the original in some details, especially in the satyric scene.

2 I am indebted to Grahame Shane for his insights on this topic. For more extensive acknowledgments, see the *Epilogue* at the end of this essay. See also Krautheimer, Richard, "The Tragic and Comic Scenes of the Renaissance; the Baltimore and Urbino Panels", *Gazette des beaux-arts* 33, 1948.

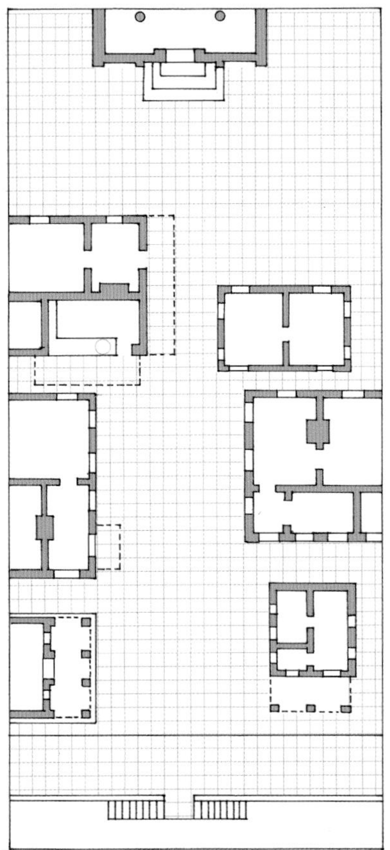

above left to right:
Fig. 1. Scena Comica, plan. Diagram by J. Tice

Fig. 2. Scena Comica, Sebastiano Serlio, 1545.

below:
Fig. 3. Stage Design, Baldassare Peruzzi, ca. 1535; Roman landmarks are recognizable: the Colosseum, Torre delle Milizie, Augustan obelisk in Piazza Montecitorio (although not erected in place until the late 18th century), the Pantheon, Castel Sant'Angelo, the Temple of Castor and Pollux, and Trajan's Column.

opposite left to right:
Fig. 4. Scena Tragica, Serlio 1545.

Fig. 5. Scena Tragica, plan. Diagram by J. Tice

gardens where perspectival representation of places, both real and imagined, provided the setting. In further developments it meant conceiving the city itself as theater that would become, almost imperceptibly, the setting for everyday life as well as the stage for public drama.[3] In the process of designing theatrical stage sets, reality, illusion, and allegory merged into one seamless experience that gave profound meaning to actual places in the European city, especially in Italy. These stage sets, with their forays into imagined cityscapes and landscapes, can be broadly interpreted as a preview of urban places realized throughout Europe and in American cities centuries later. The continuities—and discontinuities—of this atemporal comparison bring to light how the 'image of the city' and its capacity to embody and express the 'the human condition' has contributed to the quality and livability of Western cities.

Sebastiano Serlio (1475-1554)

The first published account of the modern theater appears in Book II of Sebastiano Serlio's 1545 illustrated treatise, *Architettura*, in which he offers extensive instructions on the three-dimensional theatrical construct, including an amphitheater for the audience, proscenium, stage machinery, lighting design, and stage sets. He presents his famous three stage sets with attendant scenes for three different dramatic modes: Comic, Tragic, and Satyric (Fig. 2, 4, 8). Each is rendered in linear perspective. Each features a brief description by Serlio who based his commentary on Vitruvius, who in turn derived his three dramatic modes from Greek sources, most prominent among them being Aristotle in his *Poetics*.[4]

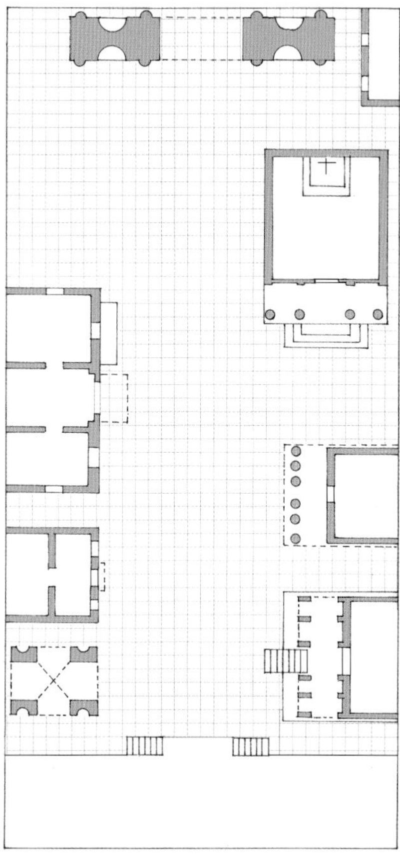

In discussing the dramatis personae for classical theater, Giulio Argan notes:

> *The characters of tragedy are historical figures, whose actions and sufferings are of interest to everyone, to the* polis, *and they can be the cause of happiness or sadness to all. The characters of comedy are ordinary people, whose doings depend upon chance, not upon supreme laws; if they are to be of any interest, this is only because they represent ordinary people as the playthings of chance. This explains why 'historical' art aims at the ideal and 'genre' art the characteristic. The first imitates the best, the second the ordinary, even the inferior.*[5]

The characters of the satyr set are distinct from the former two. They are simple, innocent folk, shepherds, and shepherdesses, who share the stage with satyrs—lusty half-human, half-goat creatures who enjoy wine, music, and dance. The satyric characters inhabit a mythic, pastoral woodland where historic dimensions of time and place are dissolved into a timeless fantasy world.

These scenes reveal the Renaissance belief in decorum, espoused by theorists such as Serlio, which stipulates that outward appearance and inner being are inextricably linked and that appropriate character should be manifest in our environment no less than it is apparent in the individual. An imposing palace would be fit for a prince, while the shopkeeper-merchant would be at home in a conventional domicile, and shepherds and satyrs would find the rustic hut, among trees and tangled vines, to be a fitting place of repose. At once the natural order

below:
Fig. 6. Uffizi Corridor, Giorgio Vasari, ca. 1565, drawn by Giuseppe Zocchi and etched by Giuseppe Vasi, 18th century.

3 Sarah McPhee notes that the Italian term *teatro* was used by 17th and 18th century artists who depicted urban landscapes or *vedute* in Rome. Examples include: Giovanni Battista Falda's *Il nuovo Teatro di Roma* for Alexander VII, and Giuseppe Vasi's *delle Magnificenze di Roma*. Contemporaneous views in other Italian cities were commonly imagined as theatrical settings. Joseph Connors describes the Piazza Sant'Ignazio in theatrical terms in "Alliance and Enmity in Roman Baroque Urbanism", *Römisches Jahrbuch der Bibliotheca Hertziana* 25, 1989: 279.

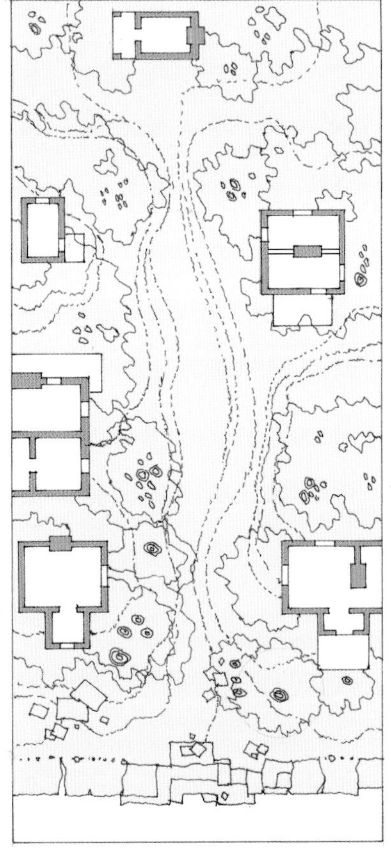

above left to right:
Fig. 7. Scena Satyrica, plan. Diagram by J. Tice.

Fig. 8. Scena Satyrica, Sebastiano Serlio, 1545.

below:
Fig. 9. *A Home in the Wilderness*, Currier & Ives, New York, 1870.

and its appropriate setting is established in urban terms: from the existing city to the ideal city, and a pastoral escape from both.

Serlio's three stage sets are more than painted scenes: they are built, three-dimensional representations of a world view. They encompass actual urban places, their psychological underpinnings, and the architectonic stagecraft required for their realization. They act as three-dimensional surrogates for a possible reality. They are remarkable for their display of linear perspective in the aid of a nascent stagecraft that would dominate Western theater for the next 400 years.[6] These scenes depict visions of city streets and public places, as well as landscape vistas, that would have an uncanny and persistent presence in the architecture, urbanism, and landscape of Europe and the Americas, particularly in the U.S.

A comparative analysis of Serlio's woodcuts: the comic, tragic, and satyric—and the sequence in which he presents them in his text—can clarify further their highly differentiated meanings.[7]

4 Tofani, Annamaria Petrioli, "From Scenery to City: Set Designs." in *The Renaissance from Brunelleschi to Michelangelo, The Representation of Architecture*, (Millon, Henry A. and Lampugnani, Vittorio Magnago, eds.) Milan: RCS Libri & Grandi Opere S.p.A., 1994. 15th and 16th century stage design is discussed at length, including Serlio's contribution.

5 Argan, Giulio Carlo, *The Europe of the Capitals 1600–1700*, Editions d'Art Albert Skira, Geneva, 1964: 135.

The Comic Scene (*Fig. 1, 2, 3*)

Serlio tells us that the comic scene depicts "houses appropriate to private persons, as citizens, lawyers, merchants, parasites, and other similar persons. Above all, the scene should have its house of the procuress, the *ruffiana*, its tavern, and its church".[8] Serlio thus illustrates a lively urban street. The bordering structures are a heterogeneous mix of Gothic and ordinary buildings with pointed arches, assorted wood brackets, and picturesque chimneys. It is further enlivened with gay waving pennants, heraldic signs, and other traces of everyday life: note the open flame and victuals within the Tavern of the Moon positioned midway on the left. Along with the Gothic portico in the foreground, the *ruffiana*, or bordello, defines an embryonic *frons scaena* set back from the flat proscenium. The deep perspective recess is rendered as a tilted upward street, rather like a piazza in its broad proportions, which runs perpendicular to the frontal plane. The scene is raised on a podium with stairs that descend to the orchestra and place for the audience. Serlio advises us that the stage designer must render the near buildings lower than the distant ones to show those in the distance advantageously, like the partially ruined campanile, a prominent vertical axis which punctuates the skyline. While the resulting composition is contrived to appear ad hoc the key elements are arranged giving a 'carefully careless' picturesque quality organized on a simple grid clearly shown on the ground plane. The partially ruined church-temple, which is located precisely on axis with the central vanishing point of the composition, is the only apparent classical structure. It provides a stabilizing element to the otherwise ad hoc scene. The church terminates the vista just as the bordello introduces it: the moral pendulum swings from the spatially and metaphorically distant sacred to the all too human profane in the foreground, with the tavern as a stopping off point in between. Serlio skillfully stages his images and their placement as an emotional and moral dialectic.

The Tragic Scene (*Fig. 4, 5, 6*)

As Rowe and Koetter note in *Collage City*, the tragic scene is an "icon of the good society, the terrestrial shadow of an idea".[9] Its setting, we have been informed, is for "those great persons because amorous adventures, sudden accidents, and violent and cruel deaths… have always taken place in the house of lords, dukes, grand princes and particularly kings".[10] Serlio depicts his urban scene, a rather broad street, with near formal symmetry framed by a rudimentary triumphal arch on one side and an arcaded palace elevated on a plinth on the other. The august tragic set replaces the ad hoc, and a formal classical language upstages the less noble picturesque Gothic. Antique statuary, rather than banners, enliven the silhouetted roofs. The *frons scaena* is cut by an even deeper spatial cleft than the comic; the space recedes in a more uniform fashion to a prominent triumphal arch, perhaps a city gate. The street continues through the arch and beyond to an extended landscape featuring obelisks and pyramids. The latter is a likely reference to the Porta San Paolo in Rome with its tomb of Caius Cestius nearby. The obelisk as the major vertical accent in the background corresponds to the vertical medieval campanile in the comic. It may be a premonition of Sixtus V's late 16th century plan for Egyptian obelisks positioned as urban *foci*. Throughout, regularity, uniformity, and sobriety of the tragic contrast with the variety, informality, and gaiety of the comic.

6 Oenslager, Donald, *Stage Design: Four Centuries of Scenic Invention*, The Viking Press, New York, 1975. 30. The three scenes described by Vitruvius and represented by Serlio were likely inspired by ancient Greek stagecraft that used painted scenes on devices called *periaktoi*. These triangular prisms were mounted on either side of the performance space and could easily be rotated on their vertical axes to reveal one of the three scenes. These devices are the distant precursors of the common flat wings used especially by Baroque stage designers and adopted universally thereafter. See Hewitt, Barnard, ed., *The Renaissance Stage: Serlio, Sabattini, Furttenbach*, University of Miami Press, Coral Gables, FL, 1958: 10–11.

7 It is my contention that the sequence of stage scenes in *Architettura* is significant, that is, comic, tragic, followed by satyric. Commentators on Serlio's stage sets have tended to omit one or more of the scenes or ignore this order. I believe the complete triad is important and that the ordering sequence is deliberate. The ideal tragic is seen as a mediator between the chance comic and the 'untutored' natural. The tragic serves as the ideal in between the two, from which we either aspire, or to which we hope not to descend. The original sequence suggests a kinesthetic, spatial, and topographic structure, a discussion of which follows.

8 Hewitt (1958): 27.

9 Rowe, Colin and Koetter, Fred, *Collage City*, MIT Press, Cambridge, MA, and London, 1978: 14.

10 Hewitt (1958): 29.

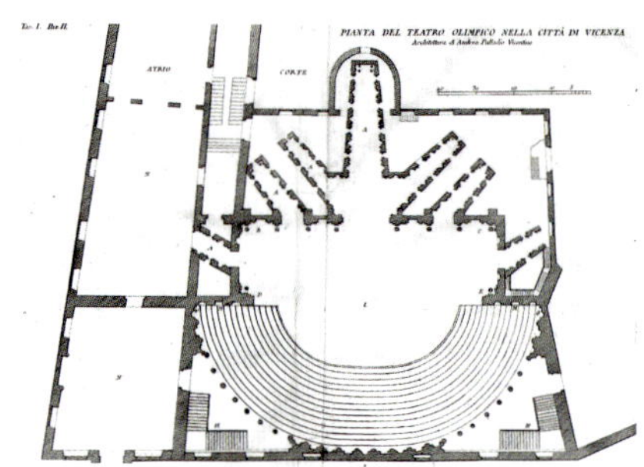

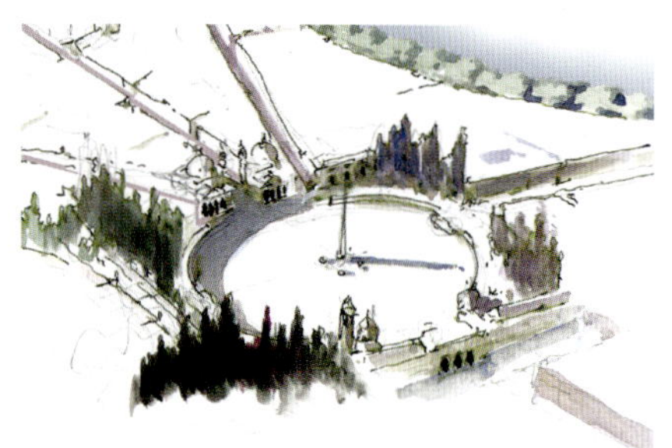

left to right:
Fig. 10. Section view, Teatro Olimpico, Vicenza, Palladio and Scamozzi, 1580.

Fig. 11. Plan, Teatro Olimpico.

Fig. 12. Piazza del Popolo, Rome, by Giuseppe Valadier and others, 1811-22.
Watercolor by J. Tice.

The Satyric Scene (Fig. 7, 8, 9)

The satyric scene is composed exclusively of modest dwellings. Serlio recommends, after Vitruvius, that it "be composed of trees, rocks, hills, mountains, herbs, flowers, and fountains, together with some rustic huts".[11] He notes that the role of the ancient satyr play was one of reproving and castigating contemporaries for licentious and evil behavior. The innocence of the rustics allows them to speak freely without fear of custom's rebuke. As the satyric scene evolved during the Renaissance, it came to represent a pastoral retreat, an Arcadian home for the sub-human and super-human alike, a land populated by shepherds, shepherdesses, satyrs, and nymphs as well as gods and goddesses. Perhaps embedded in this duality is a premonition of the sublime pastoral scenes by Poussin with their mythical landscapes on the one hand and Rousseau's Noble Savage and Laugier's Primitive Hut on the other. Trees screen the rustic dwellings that are constructed with thatched roofs and wattle and daub, innocent of any architectural style or architectural pretensions.[12] The satyric scene retains, however, a measure of the architectonic-spatial structure found in the comic and tragic scenes. The trees on either side of the stage are analogous to the forward buildings of the previous stage sets and act as the *frons scenae*. A somewhat winding *allée* cuts a deep spatial recess into the forest, recalling that of the comic and tragic streets. And if one looks carefully, one can see a doorway and window nearly on axis at the far end of the scene. A crumbling stair descends from the rustic proscenium to the orchestra and a place for the audience. Despite their primitive construction, the simple rectangular dwellings conform to the implied grid of the one-point perspective. Nature is revealed as a distant, but nonetheless related, spatial phenomenon. There is no evidence of the city, no aspects of the urban-comic nor the urban-tragic, all is rustic and human artifice remains in a near complete state of nature.[13] Despite their obvious differences, all three stage sets clearly provide ample breathing room to establish "a place of public appearance".[14] The spatial corridor-like vista is common to all, whether regular or irregular, whether urban or wooded: a 'stage within a stage'. With its windowed eyes and framed space, it is a physical and spatial construct that provides a place for the spectacle to unfold.

The Renaissance Theater and the Renaissance City

As we shall see, since the 16th century, these three scenes, representing the human psyche and attendant fantasies, have insinuated their way into urban and natural landscapes with surprising regularity. In cities, their specific manner of

11 Hewitt (1958): 32.

12 Perhaps with a touch of irony, some have found the rustic structures to be a premonition of the 19th century Shingle and Stick Style promoted by the 'gray' architects of the '60s.

13 Dennis, Michael, *Court and Garden: From the French Hôtel to the City of Modern Architecture*, MIT Press, Cambridge, MA, and London, England, 1984: 237–240.

14 Here I use Louis Kahn's apt phrase.

15 Rudofsky, Bernard, *Streets for People*, Van Nostrand Reinhold, (1969) 1982: 128–29. Rudofsky maintains, "The identification of the street with the theater, and vice versa, corresponds precisely to the Italian's idea that the street is the supreme stage. Never before had artists been so much intrigued by the street as during the Renaissance. The modern avenue that usually leads nowhere in particular was born, quite fittingly, in the make-believe atmosphere of the stage ... in other words, the illusionistic street preceded the real one". He notes that Shakespeare favors the street in his stage directions and that 11 street scenes appear in *The Merchant of Venice*. Shakespeare's stage sets were derived from the less formal 'inn yard' type and not the Renaissance perspective stage type by Serlio. Inigo Jones is credited with having introduced the perspective stage in England, having visited Italy and Palladio's Teatro Olimpico.

16 Kernodle, George R., *From Art to Theatre: Form and Convention in the Renaissance*, University of Chicago Press, Chicago, 1944: 178.

treatment is a telling index of changing sensibilities, both psychologically and culturally. Significantly, the *dramatis personae* of each—or their avatars—the People (Sociologist), the Hero (Architect), and the Noble Savage (Engineer)—have populated their respective stages with just as much determination. The staying power of the three scenes in dramatic productions from the Renaissance to the current day is also well substantiated in the literature of theatrical design.[15] The appearance of these stage sets in both venues could be attributed to the tradition of stage architecture transformed into reality, or it could be that the psychic dimensions embodied in the Renaissance theater—a kind of 'collective unconscious' via Jung—has been culturally internalized only to erupt as tangible manifestations. Whatever the case may be, their interpretation provides a measure of the implicit or explicit preoccupations and values of any given age.

Teatro Olimpico: Stage Architecture

The first permanent materialization of Serlio's guidelines for the stage was realized in the Teatro Olimpico by Palladio in 1580 (Fig. 10, 11). As prescribed by Serlio, and in keeping with the classically minded Olympian Academy for which the structure was built, Palladio used a triumphal arch-inspired *frons scenae* and proscenium. These are housed within a large audience hall along with recessed orchestra and oval amphitheater. After Palladio's death, Vincenzo Scamozzi completed the perspectival scenes. His five streets cut into the *frons scenae* with two additional flanking passages at either side for the players. Scamozzi's streets (and here they are really linear streets) in the proscenium stage provide key elements of the tragic scene: streets fronted by classically inspired structures rendered in linear perspective which represent a further refinement of Serlio's tragic stage set. As per Serlio's instructions, they are literal constructions that can be likened to constructed prisms of space, modeling and achieving real depth with wood lath, plaster, and painted fabric. This example realizes the stage set as described by stage historian, Kernodle: it is more than two-dimensional painted scenography; it is truly three-dimensional 'stage architecture'.[16]

Rome

In Rome, Renaissance and Baroque era stage sets were rehearsals for real interventions in the city. Beginning with Via Giulia for Julius II by Bramante, a 400-year program began for the transformation of Rome. The intention was to transform the comic scene of the medieval city in the Campo Marzio and the peripheral satryic scene in the *disabitato* to become the exalted tragic scene, befitting the

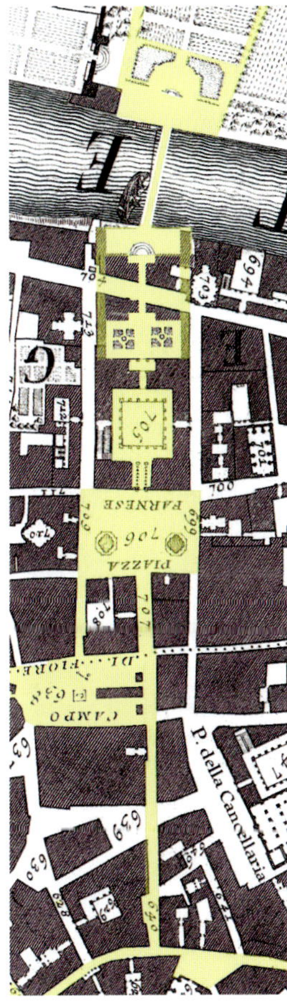

top row left to right:
Fig. 13. Campo de'Fiori as "Comic" set by G. Vasi.

Fig. 14. Piazza and Palazzo Farnese as "Tragic" set by G. Vasi.

Fig. 15. Ponte Sisto and Villa Farnesina gardens as "Satyric" set by G. Vasi.

below:
Fig. 16. Detail, *La Pianta Grande di Roma* by Giambattista Nolli, 1748. Yellow highlights show the link between Via Papalis, Campo de'Fiori, and Piazza and Palazzo Farnese. Note the Farnese bridge, proposed by Michelangelo, that connects to the Villa Farnesina. Diagram by J. Tice.

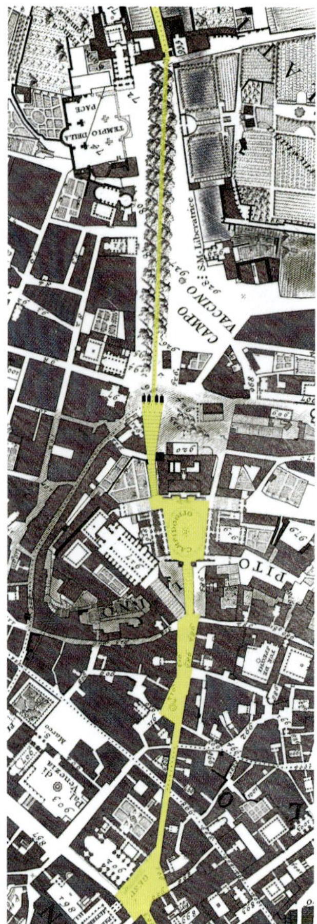

above left to right:
Fig. 17. Campidoglio, anon., ca. 1517.

Fig. 18. Campidoglio, Etiénne Dupérac, ca. 1569.

Fig. 19. Campo Vaccino and Via Sacra with Campidoglio in the distance, ca. 1650.

below:
Fig. 20. Detail, *Pianta di Roma*. Yellow highlights show the link between Via del Gesù, the Campidoglio and the Roman Forum, known as the Campo Vaccino, or cow fields. The passage descends from the Campidoglio, through the Arch of Septimius Severus, along the Via Sacra to the Arch of Titus. Diagram by J. Tice.

epicenter of Christendom. Piazza del Popolo, realized by Sixtus V in 1589, with later interventions by Bernini and Valadier, is a realized example of the stagecraft of Palladio and Scamozzi. The earlier tragic stage set has become a reality—illusory space has become real (Fig. 12).

The pope and clergy of Rome began a transformation of the city in the 16th century that would continue through the 19th century. Aspects of the ideal city would emerge from the medieval fabric or be inserted into it, often complementing the natural terrain. This conflation of the Serlian triad became a permanent *modus operandi* in the city. Its linked spatial sequence gave added meaning to processional episodes, real or implied. It is instructive to view these relationships in the 1748 *Pianta Grande* by Gambattista Nolli. Michelangelo's initiatives for the Palazzo and Piazza Farnese, including his proposed bridge to the Villa Farnesina, can be seen as an illustration of Serlio's three stages unfolding spatially along a defined axis. That intervention linked the comic scene of the Campo de'Fiori to the tragic scene of the Piazza Farnese, to the satyric scene of its gardens crossing the Tiber to the Villa Farnesina (Fig. 13–16).[17] The axis continues upward climaxing in the green hills of the Janiculum: another invocation of the satyric world.

The Campidoglio

In an even more dramatic fashion, the Campidoglio follows a similar pattern, using the three stage sets in sequence that follows the papal procession, *il Possesso*, from the Vatican to the Lateran. As designed by Michelangelo, the Campidoglio was clearly meant to present a public space, the *res publica*. This is the setting for Argan's historical figures, "whose actions and sufferings are of interest to everyone, the *polis*". The Campidoglio rises above the emerging modern city on the Capitoline Hill set into the saddle of the ancient Roman acropolis between the Temple of Jupiter and the Arx. It occupies a strategic 'in between' place: rising, Janus-like, it faces both the revived urban core on one side and the ancient Roman Forum on the other.

Before-and-after views by Duperac and his predecessors invite comparisons with Serlio's comic and tragic scenes (Fig. 17, 18). It is an extraordinary transformation: the ad hoc contingencies of the site and assorted medieval buildings yielding to Michelangelo's almost miraculous transformation of it into an ideal. In comparing Duperac with Serlio's tragic set one can see how Michelangelo recast the Capitoline, and elevated it as Caput Mundi, the center of the world's stage,

left to right:
Fig. 21. Stage Design for a pastoral, *Florimène*, Inigo Jones, 1635.

Fig. 22. The University of Virginia Lawn, Charlottesville, Thomas Jefferson, 1817.

the tragic scene par excellence. Michelangelo's masterpiece is an example of 'the best' over 'the inferior', a universal model with implications far beyond Rome.[18] In its topographic context, readily shown in the Nolli map, the Campidoglio can be seen as the tragic mediator inferred as a sequential relationship between the comic medieval city and the satyric scene of the Forum, then comprised of cow pastures and rustic huts (Fig. 19, 20). On the Forum side, the ancient trace of the Via Sacra appears as a tree-lined allée on Falda's map, stretching between the Arch of Septimius Severus and the Arch of Titus. The resulting triad—existing, comic city; ideal, tragic city; and natural, satryic world—conveniently parallels Serlio's three stage sets as an interrelated, mutually dependent set. The lesson may be that all three stage sets are available to give order and meaning to the city that can, in concert, establish a cosmic order.

England, Continental Europe, Paris and Haussman

The profound influence of Serlio's scenes on the later Renaissance and Baroque stage appears, not only in Italy, but in numerous theatrical venues in Continental Europe and England. As a theatrical designer, Inigo Jones[19] is credited with replacing the Elizabethan inn-type stage represented by the Globe Theater with the Italian perspective stage with its *frons scenae* and proscenium specified by Serlio. During the Restoration and in collaboration with Ben Johnson, Jones furnished numerous masques for the Royal Court (Fig. 21). These productions and other theatrical displays demonstrate his debt to Serlio's classical understanding of the Vitruvian stage prominently featuring both tragic and satyric sets. Jones's realized classical Covent Garden was set into the existing fabric of London, now, coincidentally, near the heart of the contemporary theater district. It established an urban prototype for future development throughout central London. Could his piazza and church—a tragic impulse—be likened to the Serlio tragic set through his developed theatrical sensibility? The French theater embraced a more formal landscape formula for the satyric along with uniform building alignments for the tragic. Could these stage sets be an 'audition' for real landscapes and real urban interventions in Paris and its hinterland? Le Notre's garden allées and, a century later, Haussmann's monumental boulevards, with a 'green' assist by Adolphe Alphand, slicing through medieval Paris seem to confirm this notion. The Opera by Garnier and its Boulevard might be seen, then, as the ultimate realization of Serlio's tragic scene with a French accent. Could the 'informal' Latin Quarter on the Left Bank, 'formal' Louvre, Tuilleries, Place Vendôme on the Right Bank, and the vast gardens of the Bois de Vincennes and Bois de Boulogne to the east and west be interpreted more broadly as a vast theater?

17 Michelangelo proposed a bridge to connect the Palazzo Farnese with the Farnesina gardens which would have made this connection explicit. The extant Farnese bridge over the Via Giulia, although built later, is often cited as evidence of his plan.

18 The ceremonial context for the Campidoglio is underscored by the Via Papalis that connects the three stage sets into one sequential drama as the papal entourage processed from the Vatican to the Lateran. The passage through these 'sets' was central to one of Rome's most important religious processions, *il Possesso*. The processional route of the Via Papalis required a journey through the city, up the Via d'Aracoeli to the Capitoline and down its slopes to the Via Sacra and through the forum and Via Sacra (shown tree lined by Falda) and onto the Lateran, where the pope would symbolically take possession of his throne or cathedra as bishop of Rome.

19 Peacock, John, "Inigo Jones's Stage Architecture and Its Sources", *The Art Bulletin* 64 (2), College Art Association, Taylor & Francis, Ltd., London, 1982: 195–216. See also Strong, Roy and Wragg, Thomas eds., *Festival Designs by Inigo Jones, An Exhibition of Drawings for Scenery and Costumes for the Court Masques of James I and Charles I,* International Exhibitions Foundation, The Meridian Gravure Co., 1967–68: figure 71.

left to right:
American street scenes of the 19th century from *Main Street* by Carole Rifkind, 1977:

Fig. 23. Main Street, Eureka, CO, settled ca. 1849.

Fig. 24. State Street and Chase County Courthouse, Cottonwood Falls, KS, ca. 1872. Photo: Charles Phelps Cushing.

Fig. 25. Elm Street (Main Street), Stockbridge, MA, 1880.

Colonial and Post-Colonial America

In Colonial America, early urban plans conformed to Italian ideal cities: Penn's plan for Philadelphia's four-square grid is reminiscent of Scamozzi's plans for an ideal city with major north-south streets, the *decumanus* linking the Schuylkill and Delaware rivers. Colonial Williamsburg's urban layout similarly shows a classical structure. The Duke of Gloucester Street as *decumanus* connects the Capitol on the east with the College of William and Mary on the west. At the center, Market Square represents a kind of forum with the Governor's Palace at the 'head' of the *cardo-decumanus* layout. Post-colonial America witnesses Jefferson's Monticello a la Palladio, but the plan for the University of Virginia exhibits a theatrical manner that hybridizes the tragic and satyric in a uniquely American manner (Fig. 22). Finally, L'Enfant's plan for Washington, D.C., with its grand axial mall, epitomizes the self-conscious classical impulse in post-colonial America. The idea was to elevate the new nation to the status of a classical Roman Republic, that not coincidentally, threw off the tyranny of kings. The Mall was intended as a place for the *polis*, a vision, by way of Le Notre, that has an unmistakable affinity to Serlio's tragic stage set hybridized with the satyric.[20]

Serlio in 19th Century America: Main Street, State Street, and Elm Street

With these three dramatic modes in mind, urban America in the late 19th and early 20th centuries can be imagined as a reincarnation of Serlio's three stage sets (Fig. 23–25). In their purist form, Main Street is equivalent to the Comic Set, State Street evokes the Tragic Set, and Elm Street is a domesticated version of the Satyric Set.[21] As John Reps has pointed out, the grid is the distinguishing characteristic of the American city. The ubiquitous Cartesian ground plane facilitates the idea of a measured, perspectival space for the typical street. The Serlian perspective sets, therefore, seem to be a natural invitation for exploitation in this vein. Examples of this kind include many towns in which the three stage sets appear with exceptional clarity, side by side, and others where they are hybridized or collaged in almost endless variations of comic-tragic-satyric.

In her book, *Main Street*, Carol Rifkind demonstrates the historic role of the street in 19th century America.[22] Rather than treating Main Street as a thoroughfare serving utilitarian interests, Rifkind argues for the social and spatial significance of the street as 19th century America's most successful public realm, one imbued with profound symbolic meaning. Her astonishing array of photographs from the 1860s onward focuses on the nominal title of the text, *Main Street.*

20 By analogy, what better embodiment for the form of the new American republic than to take those of Republican Rome? Like the American revolt against the Georgian kings, hadn't the ancient Romans overthrown the tyranny of their kings in order to install a new democratic republic? The author is indebted to Allan Ceen for this insight.

21 Grahame Shane used this felicitous analogy. Michael Dennis makes an analogy between Serlio's satyric stage set and Elm Street in his essay "Excursus Americanus" in *Court and Garden.*

22 Rifkind, Carol, *Main Street: The Face of Urban America*, Harper & Row, Publishers, New York, Hagerstown, San Francisco, London, 1977. I am reminded of Upton Sinclair's novel, *Main Street*, published in 1920, which satirizes the banality of the Midwestern small town. The protagonist declares, "I do not admit that Main Street is as beautiful as it should be!"

However, Rifkind also makes clear that, as an urban phenomenon, the dimensions and meaning of Main Street became as varied and complex as the people who created them: Main Street as an urban 'set piece' seemingly had an infinite number of variations. It could be a public space that was exclusively dedicated to commerce and quotidian transactions. Or it might transform in character to State Street with the strategic siting of city hall, grange, or Masonic temple. The placement of such elements could terminate an axis or step back from the street edge or dominate a corner intersection. By upping the ante in this way, civic institutions were symbolic of civic responsibility and higher aspirations. The streets they adorned became fitting representations for a tragic State Street and a plausible representation of the *res publica*.

Fig. 26. Lincoln's funeral cortege, Philadelphia, PA, 1865.

The most ordinary Main Street could be temporarily transformed for special occasions with a profusion of ephemeral embellishments, flags, and hundreds of yards of bunting. Adding to the theatricality were marching bands and the inevitable speech by the mayor. Specific examples represent only a few of the variations: Fourth of July parade in Nantucket, Massachusetts, Founders Day in Dayton, Ohio, Bicycle parade in Hartford, Connecticut, Rodeo Day in Pendleton, Oregon, Lincoln's funeral cortege in Springfield, Illinois (Fig. 26). Not to be forgotten are suffragette marches and abolitionist rallies that used Main Street as a public forum. All attest to multiple forms of public display and celebration, all contributing to and defining the Main Street-State Street dynamic.

The Edenic character of the American continent was celebrated by writers and painters such as the Transcendentalists and the Hudson River School. The extension from Main to Elm, either in alignment with, or perpendicular to, was facilitated by the ubiquitous grid. Elm Street was a place where the treeless Main Street, which seemed to abhor the wilderness, could now embrace nature once it had been tamed and domesticated. Thus, the street was transformed into the tree-lined Elm Street, the Serlian satyric, a *res privata,*[23] a place of quiet repose, a place for the hearth and family. But like those of Main, the best American examples of Elm could possess a profound spatial-aesthetic dignity. As Michael Dennis has pointed out, Elm Street retains its identity with amazing tenacity. That uniquely American landscape structure carries with it a communal meaning beyond the individual private dwellings which line its edges with well-kept lawns and porches.[24] Even in a setting that was predominantly suburban, the vaulted arboreal canopy of 19th century American Elm Street symbolized a higher order, one that was also integral to the idea of an idealized public realm.

Finally, there occurred from time to time a 'split' image where one side of the street could be urban-tragic and the opposing side could contrast as urban-satyric. Great urban examples come to mind in Europe: the Rue di Rivoli overlooking the Tuileries and Princes Street in Edinburgh opposite the green North Loch. In the U.S., Fifth Avenue opposite Central Park, and Nassau Street in Princeton opposite the university campus are striking examples of this split-screen urban phenomena.

23 Léon Krier is one of the few architects of his generation who is attuned to the psychological dimensions of urban space. He uses this apt term in a slightly different context but does not treat the satyric landscape component provided by Serlio.

24 Dennis (1984): 237–241.

Serlio in Big City America

In post-Civil War America—aptly termed the "Brown Decades" by Lewis Mumford in his book of the same name—a national malaise became almost palpable. America's lost innocence was exacerbated by social and economic upheavals. According to Modern architectural historiography, Chicago became the mythic theater where America's Manifest Destiny would be tested: either strong and virile in its New World role or weak and servile to Old World masters. In Serlian terms, the three stages that emerge in Chicago in the 1890s are: the 'comic' Loop (William Le Baron Jenney and Holabird and Root); the 'tragic' 1893 Columbian Exposition (Daniel Burnham and Charles Follen McKim); and the 'satyric' suburbs such as Riverside (Frederick Law Olmsted, Calvert Vaux).

Chicago: From the Fire to the Fair (Fig. 27, 28, 29)

above left to right:
Fig. 27. The Loop, Chicago, ca. 1890.

Fig. 28. Court of Honor, World's Columbian Exposition, 1893.

below:
Fig. 29. General Plan of Riverside, IL, Frederick Law Olmsted and Calvert Vaux, 1868.

After the devastating fire of 1871, Chicago's urban center was being rebuilt in the rough and tumble arena of unbridled commercial interests of the salesman and entrepreneur. It had essentially two theaters of architectural production. One was the central business Loop dedicated to commerce and nearby industry; the other was the streetcar suburb, without much in between. And here we might again interject Serlio's stage sets: the comic being the Loop; the satyric being the suburbs pushing against the former "Indian Territory" into newly settled agricultural land. What was missing, of course, was the tragic set. Indeed, the civic or aspirational identity of Chicago was hard to find except for a succession of modest city halls. The other exception was Sullivan's Auditorium Building, but it was only made possible because it was embedded in a larger commercial enterprise. There were few prominent civic buildings in which Chicagoans could take pride: no concert halls, museums, or libraries could match those of Boston, Philadelphia, or New York.[25]

25 Another exception is the Newberry Library which was founded in 1887 and opened in 1893.

The Fair as Three Stage Sets: Midway, Court of Honor, Wooded Isle (Fig. 30, 31, 32)

After a modest display of America's achievements at Philadelphia's 1876 Centennial Fair, it was the 1893 World's Columbian Exposition that presented the opportunity to prove to the world that America was 'first among equals'. Chicago's civic leaders and its architects had to convince the dubious East Coast power structure and their architects that they could 'pull it off'. Their task was nothing less than to make America's coming-of-age tangible in architectural and urban terms. Rather than individual buildings loosely related to one another, as was the case in Philadelphia, the Chicago Fair was planned as a complex urban landscape grouping with services, sophisticated infrastructure, and distinct places within its larger structure. Montgomery Schuyler notes, "The success [of the Fair] is first of all a success of unity, a triumph of ensemble".[26]

The Fair's reception on the national stage was a resounding popular success.[27] The Fair provided an idealized urban vision that demonstrated that the host city of Chicago could be elevated to be more than, in Burnham's words, "a place for sticking pigs". The Fair was quite literally a stage set made of plaster and paint, as several of its critics declared with pejorative intent. As was typical of such events of the day, the buildings were temporary. But, unlike any previous spectacle of its kind, it was arguably the Serlian theatricality of the Chicago World's Fair that was one of the primary reasons for its tremendous popular success. Its impact on American architecture and urbanism lasted for the next fifty years. The three parts of the Fair, the Midway Pleasance, the Court of Honor, and the Wooded Isle, created an uncanny realization of Serlio's Renaissance stage sets conveying their attendant meanings ranging from the urban formal-informal to the wooded pastoral.[28] In short, the Chicago Fair, over 130 years ago, gave America a dazzling example of the stage architecture of Serlio, an immense theater, a city within a city, in the semi-permanent context of an international exposition.

Chicago World's Fair, 1893 by Burnham and Root, et al.

above left to right:
Fig. 30. Midway Plaisance.

Fig. 31. Court of Honor.

Fig. 32. Wooded Lagoon Promenade.

below:
Fig. 33. Iroquois dwellings near the Wooded Lagoon.

Given the Serlian categories above, the three parts of the Fair fall neatly into place. First, the Court of Honor-tragic is the appropriate setting for the heroic civic leader and architect. Lined with classical temples, it is populated by respectable citizens hungry for cultural enlightenment, or perhaps, less generously, the country bumpkin or recently arrived immigrant, overwhelmed by the trappings

26 Quoted by Fitch, James Marston, *American Building: The Historic Forces that Shaped It*, Second Edition Revised and Enlarged, Houghton Mifflin Company, Boston, The Riverside Press, Cambridge, MA, 1966: 213.

27 According to Wikipedia, the Fair hosted 27 million visitors during its six-month run. Even more remarkably, the Fair occurred during an economic recession. [https://en.wikipedia.org/wiki/World%27s_Columbian_Exposition].

28 For a general discussion, see Rowe, Colin, "Chicago Frame" in *Mathematics of the Ideal Villa and Other Essays*, MIT Press, Cambridge, MA. and London, 1976.

above clockwise:
Fig. 34. Alaska-Yukon-Pacific Exposition, Olmsted Brothers and Galen Howard, Seattle, WA, 1909. The magnificent axis terminating in Mt. Rainier is now incorporated into the University of Washington campus as 'Rainier Vista'.

Fig. 35. Palace of Fine Arts, Bernard Maybeck, Panama Pacific International Exposition, San Francisco, CA, 1915. The structure and artificial lagoon provide a landmark for the Marina District.

Fig. 36. Puente Cabrillo, Cram, Goodhue and Ferguson, Panama California Exposition, San Diego, CA, 1915. The exposition grounds in Balboa Park were later transformed into a center for civic institutions.

of culture, and finding them here in abundance. Second, it was the carnival-like Midway-comic that stole the show with the world debut of the Ferris Wheel and its popular and sometimes bawdy entertainment such as Little Egypt, the "hootchy-kootchy" girl. Lastly, perhaps mirroring Chicago's suburbs, the Wooded Isle-satyric paralleling Lake Michigan was a place of informality and opportunity to enjoy nature. The park-like setting featured a variety of primitive huts constructed by Native Americans and other indigenous peoples from a time and place untainted by European culture (Fig. 33).[29]

The Fair was a promise that art and beauty could enhance everyday life. It gave birth to a national enthusiasm for the conscious design of places in American cities that came to be called, appropriately, The City Beautiful movement. But 'beauty' was a reference not only to the urban grandeur of the city associated with the tragic; it also embraced public parks and gardens: the satyric. After all, Frederick Law Olmsted was one of the primary designers of the Fair. The impulse to ameliorate the 'ordinary city' by consciously creating an intentional tragic and satyric component coursed through hundreds of U.S. cities after the Fair. It was a movement that went beyond crass commercialism and private self-aggrandizement toward higher aspirations of community, elevating the public realm in both moral and physical-spatial terms. As components of the Serlian triad, the hodge-podge comic was to be transformed into an acropolis of civic virtue and the extra-urban boundaries were to be transformed into an idyllic virtuous Arcadia. The impulse of the Fair took two forms. One was the proliferation of grand national and international expositions throughout the country—from Buffalo to San Diego—each seemingly trying to outdo those that came before. The other influence, the City Beautiful movement, had a more lasting impact on cities.[30] This aspect of American urban design was almost totally ignored by orthodox Modernist historiography. The early decades of the 20th century were arguably the only time in American history when aesthetic urban planning on a large scale had a beneficial impact on the design of its cities.

29 We seem to have an American incarnation of Serlio's stage sets taken through a French-American filter with a decidedly Victorian twist. Colin remarked that the Court of Honor was a kind of tragic front room or parlor for polite talk and tea with the parson; the Midway Plaisance was the comic back room for cussin', drinkin', and smokin' with reprobate friends; and the Wooded Lagoon was the satyric garden, a place for an afternoon idyll or, alternatively, a setting for an assignation.

30 Just as the three stage sets had been present during the U.S. Colonial period, it has also been a factor in the development of college campuses. This exceptional presence of the satyric scene is the defining quality of the U.S. campus that separates it from its European counterparts. See Turner, Paul Venable, "The University as City Beautiful" in *Campus: An American Planning Tradition*, MIT Press, Cambridge, MA, and London, 1984: 163–213.

After the Fair: The Great American Expositions

The American expositions that followed Chicago were numerous: Pan-American Exposition, Buffalo, New York, 1901; Louisiana Purchase Exposition, St. Louis, Missouri, 1904; Lewis and Clark Exposition, Portland, Oregon, 1905; Trans-Mississippi and International Exposition, Omaha, Nebraska, 1908; Alaska-Yukon-Pacific Exposition, Seattle, Washington, 1910; New York State Fair, Syracuse, New York, 1910; the Panama-Pacific International Exposition, San Diego and Pan Pacific International Exposition in California, 1915. The West Coast examples, in particular, were brilliant in the manner in which they incorporated the natural landscape (Fig. 34, 35, 36). Another consequence of the Fair was the proliferation of amusement parks throughout the U.S. and Europe—the comic stage writ large—often appropriating the name "Midway" derived from the Midway Pleasance. One prominent example was Coney Island's Luna Park, opened in 1903, replete with Ferris wheel, amusement rides and other popular diversions.[31] As we shall see, these national fairs and amusement parks set the stage for theme parks in America, most notably Disneyland.

left to right:
Fig. 37. Michigan Avenue, *Plan of Chicago*, Burnham and Bennet, 1906.

Fig. 38. Fairmount Parkway (Benjamin Franklin Parkway), Philadelphia, PA, Jacques Gréber, Philippe Cret, 1917.

Many of the expositions have become part of an American mindscape, fondly remembered as an important legacy of early-20th-century culture, celebrated in song and cinema.[32] Without the impetus of the Fair and its aftermath in the form of permanent structures, some of the most beloved places in U.S. cities would not have been realized: in San Francisco, the Palace of Fine Arts by B. R. Maybeck; in Chicago, Grant Park, the Art Institute, and the Field Museum; and many university campuses such as the University of Washington campus plan by John Charles Olmsted. Only a few years after the last of these Fairs, in 1922, and one year before the French publication of *Vers une Architecture* by Le Corbusier, *The American Vitruvius: An Architects' Handbook of Civic Art* by Hegemann and Peets documented what is surely a golden age in American urban design in detail.[33] As these authors show in their profusely illustrated book, the great American expositions created fertile ground for "civic art", inclusive of the three stage sets (Fig. 37, 38).

31 With the appearance of the Millennium Eye, with its tribute to the Ferris Wheel, rampant development, and the giant "Gherkin", some believe London is threatening to become a vast Luna Park, perhaps a sympathetic gesture in line with Pop sensibilities and Archigram?

32 Popular songs like "Meet Me in St. Louis, Louis, Meet Me at the Fair" coincided with the opening of the St. Louis Exposition of 1904.

33 *The American Vitruvius: An Architects' Handbook of Civic Art* was originally published in 1922, a year before *Vers Une Architecture*. It provides a radically contrary position to Le Corbusier's idea of the Modern city.

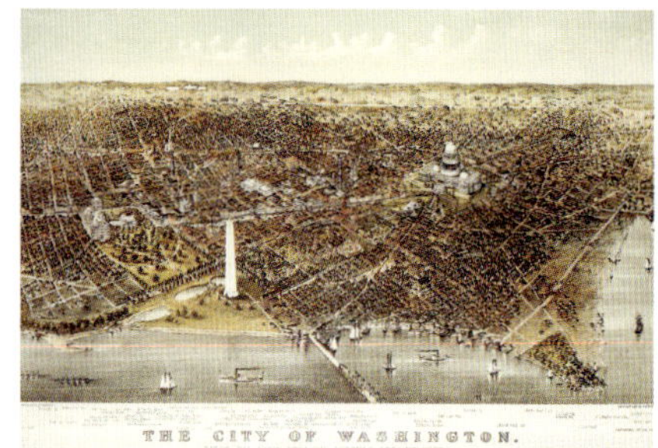

left to right:
Fig. 39. Washington, D.C., The Mall, ca. 1850.

Fig. 40. The Mall, Washington, D.C., McMillan Plan, 1902.

Fig. 41. "Piscataway People", "View of Washington D.C. from The Heights", 17th century.

The Cities Beautiful and the McMillan Plan for Washington, D.C.

Among many others, two direct results of the Chicago Fair were the partially realized, tragic plan of Chicago by Burnham and Bennett in 1909, and the plan of Philadelphia's Fairmount Parkway by Gréber and Cret realized in 1917. Their grand esplanade extended Penn's 17th century plan from the city hall to the Schuylkill River promontory, replete with civic plazas, fountains, gardens and Beaux-Arts museum (Fig. 37, 38).[34] Earlier, the McMillan Commission, led by Burnham, McKim, St. Gaudens, and Olmsted, successfully resuscitated and expanded L'Enfant's 18th century Baroque plan for Washington, D.C., transforming the National Mall into "America's living room" (Fig. 39, 40, 41). It replaced the Victorian Baltimore and Ohio railway station and 130-foot train shed that effectively divided the Mall. Picturesque English gardens reached from the base of the Capitol building to the edge of the Potomac River (called the "Tiber" in early drawings) just beyond the Washington monument. The McMillan Plan doubled the length of the Mall with formal gardens and parterres lined with classically inspired buildings. The pre-existing Italian Gothic Smithsonian castle, however, was retained and its presence on the Mall was preserved. The McMillan Plan is the *ne plus ultra* of the City Beautiful movement. It remains the most successful marriage of urban design and formal landscape design in America at a grand scale. Sometimes criticized for its overt formality and its alleged imperial pretentions, it has served splendidly as a setting for national expressions for public celebration, mourning and protest: Marian Anderson sang from the steps of the Lincoln Memorial; the 'Poor Peoples' March culminated on the Mall; Martin Luther King Jr.'s "I have a dream" speech was also broadcast from the Lincoln Memorial at the height of the Civil Rights Movement; and Vietnam anti-war protests stood vigil. More recently the Mall saw the AIDS Memorial Quilt project realized and the recent installation of thousands of flags representing those who have died of the Covid virus.

The plan of Washington, D.C., by L'Enfant was certainly intended as a tragic scene, but also what we have called a domesticated version of the satyric, as it was also imagined as something akin to a grand suburban domicile serving a legislature away from their home constituents. The comic scene was well-established in the town of Georgetown just upriver. The natural version of the satyric was present a little farther north at Great Falls. And slipping between the intended tragic scene of Washington, D.C. and the comic scene of Georgetown was the

34 Colin Rowe remarked to me that although the City Beautiful movement is vilified by Modernists, it generated some of the most memorable urban places in the U.S.

left to right:
Fig. 42. Times Square, New York, 1953.

Fig. 43. Rockefeller Center, New York, 1931-39.

Fig. 44. The Mall, Central Park, New York 1853. Photo: Dave Deckerman, 1994.

outfall of Rock Creek. Its heavily forested and winding ravines became designated as a National Park in 1870. Washington, D.C. is only one example of civic improvements created during the years of the City Beautiful movement across the U.S. when the tragic set became ascendant, with planned formal compositions replacing the unplanned and ad hoc character of the commercial city. At the same time, the Olmsted brothers were complementing the City Beautiful with parks and park systems in Boston, Indianapolis, Milwaukee, Minneapolis, Buffalo, Louisville, San Francisco, and countless other cities.

Serlian Stage Sets through the Great Depression: Rockefeller Center

With the economic collapse of 1929, Main Street declined in the face of twenty-five percent unemployment. The City Beautiful lost much of its popular support, effectively dampening its momentum. But Roosevelt-era Works Progress Administration (WPA) sustained many of the City Beautiful era projects and created new ones. These ranged in scale from embellishments of Main Street that buoyed up the tragic scene in the form of U.S. post offices complete with murals celebrating historic events to major Federal courthouses. The satyric scene received similar attention from the Civilian Conservation Corps (CCC). Overseen by the Forest Service and U.S. National Parks Service, the CCC enhanced access to parks and recreational mountain eyries such as Timberline Lodge on Mt. Hood. But the influence of the great expositions, the City Beautiful, and the three stage sets it epitomized, was waning.[35]

Times Square, Rockefeller Center, and Central Park (*Fig. 42, 43, 44*)

New York City has three memorable places which invite comparison to Serlio. Central Park is a fitting stand-in for the satyric, but it is the juxtaposition of Times Square comic and Rockefeller Center tragic that brings into sharp focus the contrast between the ad hoc with the planned, and the ordinary with the extraordinary. Like the Renaissance Palazzo Farnese with its formal piazza, fountain, and other monumental embellishments contrasted with the adjacent medieval market, Campo de'Fiori, the tragic Rockefeller Center contrasts admirably with the comic Times Square.

35 Exceptions to the demise of the national fairs in the U.S. included the Chicago Fair of 1933 and the New York World's Fair of 1939. While the site plans suggested a formal order, the buildings themselves were conceived as independent objects with no space-making role nor relationship to one another. The resulting effect might be likened to an architectural zoo.

Fig. 45. Aerial view, Campidoglio with the Palazzo Nuovo and Palazzo dei Conservatori flanking the central piazza. The ancient Republican Forum appears immediately behind the central Palazzo Senatorio.

Broadway at Times Square is an exuberant cacophony of human desire and competitive private interests vying for advantage. Analogies to Serlio's comic stage may be especially warranted as this is the traditional heart of the city's theater district and had long been associated with seedy movie theaters and peep shows, not to mention its theatrically raucous New Year's Eve celebration. On the other hand, the more dignified Rockefeller Center was made possible by a unified set of values combining public funding with the resources of New York's elite and the singular philanthropy of John D. Rockefeller. Rockefeller Center, built during the Depression (1931-39), seems an unlikely success story given that it was undertaken by a nation beset by economic, social, and political uncertainties on the eve of another world war.[36]

Rockefeller Center is remarkable on several counts. It elevates the mundane 'business of business' from crass commercialism and infuses it with the tragic. Except perhaps for Radio City Music Hall, there are no civic buildings featured in Rockefeller Center, yet there is a magnificent set of civic spaces. It is the sophisticated urban design of the Center that is crucial to its success. Although the RCA building is the iconic 'figure' of the composition, it is the spatial matrix or 'ground' of the Center itself that is the primary unifying idea, or *gestalt*. The Center was inserted into the heart of Manhattan grid adjoining and amplifying one of America's great streets: Fifth Avenue. It is a rare urban intervention that both respects the existing context—mid-town Manhattan with its unrelenting neutral grid—and elevates it into an ideal with exceptional visibility and meaning.

The composition features the Channel Gardens, recalling the Palazzo Nuovo and Palazzo dei Conservatori (Fig. 45, 46), a short, highly defined urban passage, which links Fifth Avenue to the sunken plaza cum amphitheater. The slender RCA skyscraper reinforces the same axis, its exhilarating verticality dramatizing the tight spatial matrix and urban fabric of Manhattan. The ensemble's spatial formality is enlivened with fluttering flags, monumental sculpture, and seasonal activities and events such as its popular ice-skating rink and Christmas tree. The Center includes Radio City Music Hall, with its illuminated marquee wrapping the northwest corner of the block at 6th Avenue. Existing landmarks are drawn into the composition: Saks Fifth Avenue, a venerable New York emporium, lies on axis with the RCA building connected by the Channel Gardens. St. Patrick's Cathedral, located slightly to the north on 5th Avenue, is directly across from the Center's monumental statue of Atlas. Each of these elements is an independent and self-contained event, but each acts in concert with its neighbors, thus achieving greater intensity and continuity.

Arguably the last hurrah of the City Beautiful movement, Rockefeller Center is without the usual classical garb, but is rather in the guise of a somewhat severe, abstracted Art Deco. The architecture still retains the formality and grandeur of the tragic, leavened by the comic and demonstrates that a successful urban ensemble can transcend a particular architectural style. Rockefeller Center constitutes one of the rare urban design triumphs of the 20th century, and perhaps the greatest in the U.S. It is an example of *détente* between private enterprise and public support resulting in the common good. Presumably this is the philosophical underpinning of any enlightened capitalism, useful in any body politic but essential in a liberal democracy. It represents a struggle to balance entrepreneurial

36 The capitalist underpinnings of Rockefeller Center have tended to shift the critique of the Center's urban design contribution toward a narrower one based on ideology. See Frampton, Kenneth, *Modern Architecture, A Critical History*, Oxford University Press, New York and Toronto, 1980: 221–222. While praising Raymond Hood for his design acumen—ironically referred to as a member of a design "troika"—Frampton describes Rockefeller Center in terms of real estate development, functional programming, and political ideology. Commenting on Diego Rivera's controversial Marxist inspired mural for the Center, he states that the episode was emblematic of, "This contradictory New Deal gesture of monopoly capital". Debates about the questionable 'good intentions' for creating the Center could be interpreted in light of Bernard Mandeville's 1714 satirical classic, *The Fable of the Bees or Private Vices and Publick Benefits*.

self-interest with social responsibility. Its continued celebrity helps to counter the otherwise dark image of Gotham City as New York's primary dramatic reference.

Fig. 46. Aerial view, Rockefeller Center, showing the Channel Gardens on axis with the RCA building.

Erosion and Displacement of the Comic, Tragic, and Satyric Sets, and the City Beautiful

The demise of the City Beautiful in the U.S. accelerated after WWII. Gone was any coherent aesthetic approach to civic design the tragic purpose of which was to represent and inspire civic participation by the body politic. This idealism was being replaced by a blind Modernist belief in progress—a utopian faith in science and technology unrelieved by tradition or historical precedent.

As is now being recognized and argued here, the City Beautiful movement can be understood as a realization of the three Serlian stage sets, a movement that helped to create some of the most memorable urban spaces and public parks and gardens realized in the U.S. The City Beautiful seemed to peak and die with the end of WWII. It is as if a series of divergent forces suddenly coalesced and overwhelmed it. The Serlian tripartite paradigm as a subconscious frame of reference was displaced by a new bipartite paradigm at war with itself: the old, concentrated city versus the new dispersed city. Such a formulation continues to have destructive consequences for the American city.

The Rise of Stradaphobia and the Demise of the Street

Modern architecture's formal preoccupations had their origins in abstraction. It paralleled the non-figurative art advocated by Modern painting, and the tendency to treat all buildings as art objects to be viewed in the round, thus removed from any urban context or space-defining role. One sees these effects in Russian Constructivism, Futurism, De Stijl, and the Bauhaus, culminating in the International Style and CIAM. Le Corbusier's Plan Voisin and the Ville Radieuse saw the Modern city as a network of highways linking a grid of sixty-story office buildings in the middle of super-blocks, and a zigzag pattern of apartment buildings. The projected urban pattern no longer defined the street, the primary public space of the traditional city. Colin Rowe described this urban neurosis as "stradaphobia".[37] The Modernist vision arrived with explosive force after the Depression and WWII and became the dominant urban paradigm in the U.S.

The emerging profession of planning laid claim to all but the physical form of the city. Its focus was on economics, statutory regulations, resource management, and demographics. It has been criticized for advocating social engineering as a solution to urban problems. A variety of utopian theorists from Patrick Abercrombie to Le Corbusier, happily supported experiments in alternatives to the traditional city, such as dispersed settlements like the Garden City movement. One example, Radburn, New Jersey, was realized in 1929 by Clarence Stein and Henry Wright. It was championed by Lewis Mumford largely on the grounds of pedestrian safety (Fig. 47). Radburn had no Main Street or State Street. Even though it had an extensive landscape it had no real Elm Street. It separated movement systems providing cul-de-sac access to housing for the automobile and pedestrian paths through the landscape that extended under or over roads

37 The elimination of the corridor street would logically cancel venerated urban institutions such as the Parisian sidewalk cafe, the American penchant for parades, the Italian *passeggiata*, and the running of the bulls in Pamplona.

top to bottom:
Fig. 47. Merritt Parkway, CN, 1938.

Fig. 48. "Aerial view of a complex of Long Island highways that provide access to New York City", Robert Moses, 1946.

to reach common areas. Its core concept eliminated the spatial–civic structure of the street. It enshrined the road—not the street. Begun as a theory about the ideal ex-urban neighborhood, it laid the foundation for the cul-de-sac world of sprawl. And Frank Lloyd Wright's Broadacre City, from the same era, was promoted in his related text, originally titled *The Disappearing City* (Fig. 50). It too lacked any street as a defined public realm. This well-intended but devastating separation of people and streets, ensconced individuals in their automobiles, preventing any public interaction.[38] Elm Street in the traditional city was abandoned as an aesthetic, spatially intact, public realm that could resolve the mutually beneficial existence of the car and pedestrian.

Robert Moses

At the scale of the entire city, Robert Moses's automobile Parkway emerged as a kind of hyper-Elm Street for the automotive age, a world with people in cars but no pedestrians. Scenic roadways snaked through designed landscape corridors modelled on carriage ways and walkways through 19th century romantic gardens. Moses idealized these combined landscapes and roads projecting that they would eventually displace the New York City street grid. To be sure, some of the resulting suburban roadways were beautifully scenic, such as the 1938 Merrit Parkway, inspired by Moses, which connects Manhattan with Connecticut's Gold Coast (Fig. 47). But the *parkway* was soon transformed into the *freeway* where efficiency and speed replaced any aesthetic ambitions or social values (Fig. 48). Traffic engineers became the undisputed arbiters of an entirely new transportation system. Proffering progress, they became an unassailable authority. Citing statistics—just the facts—they overrode protests of citizen groups, whether rich or poor, who were often defending the places they lived in historic neighborhoods. Robert Moses's worst ideas for New York were not realized, but Dwight Eisenhower's National Interstate and Defense Highways Act of 1956 brought the same idea to the entire nation, making little or no distinction between city, suburb, or open landscape—whether cultivated or natural. As is well-known, this development had disastrous effects. The economic energy concentrated on Main Street was dispersed to peripheral areas, a fatal, or near fatal, blow to countless towns and cities. *Laissez faire* capitalism and benign neglect led to the abandonment of Main Street and its Serlian triad—arguably the existential soul of many American towns and cities.

Sigfried Giedion versus Joseph Hudnut

By 1938 Sigfried Giedion had joined the faculty at Harvard as historian at the behest of Walter Gropius. As the first secretary general of CIAM, he was also a polemicist for Modernism. Former leaders of the Bauhaus and CIAM had already arrived at Harvard, including Gropius and Josep Lluís Sert. Giedion's *Space, Time and Architecture: The Growth of a New Tradition* was initially presented as The Charles Eliot Norton Lectures at Harvard for 1938–39. It was first published in 1941 followed by no less than four editions (1949, 1954, 1962, 1967). While primarily a history of architecture and city planning, the treatment of Modernism is highly selective, and judgmental. His book, which touched upon some of the most notable chapters in American urban history, was instrumental in painting a compelling but very biased history of the past and an equally biased assessment

38 Except, it seems, for road rage.

of the present, along with a highly questionable prognosis for the future. He acknowledged the role played by Frederick Law Olmsted in designing landscaped parks for the city, but reserved special praise for architects and their individual buildings. He idolized the three greats in the Pantheon of Modern American architecture: Henry Hobson Richardson, Louis Sullivan, and Frank Lloyd Wright[39] without a word about their urban impact.

Giedion echoed the negative assessment of the Chicago World's Fair that had been promulgated by Sullivan and Wright. For Giedion, the White City, with its false plaster fronts and the foreign classical language, were dissimulating of the true American aesthetic represented by the rational commercial architecture of Chicago's Loop. His drama unfolds accordingly: the heroes were the no-nonsense American architect-engineers of the Loop with their technological innovations. The villains were the debauched East Coast architects, who had been infected by the European academicism of the École des Beaux-Arts. While approving historic urban paradigms earlier in his text, from the Rome of Sixtus V to the Paris of Baron von Haussmann, it seems contradictory that Giedion would later ignore the Fair and its urban achievements that had continued the very urban traditions he had celebrated earlier.

Rockefeller Center: Encore

In his 1949 edition, Giedion devotes his penultimate chapter to "The New Scale in City Planning", featuring Rockefeller Center as his last word on the subject. Oddly, he is unwilling to connect this urban masterpiece to its obvious historical antecedents, such as Michelangelo's Campidoglio (Fig. 48, 49). He goes on to discuss three components of the Modern city: "The Parkway", "Tall Buildings in Open Space", and "A Civic Center".[40] About the parkway he writes:

> *the first necessity in the development of the future town: the abolition of the rue corridor. There is no longer any place for the street with its traffic lane running between rows of houses; it cannot possibly be permitted to persist. And the parkway is the first realized step in this clear separation of traffic and housing. It looks ahead to that time when, after the necessary surgery has been performed, the artificially swollen city will be reduced to its normal size. Then the parkway will go through the city as it does today through the landscape, as flexible and informal as the plan of the American home itself.*[41]

About tall buildings he writes:

> [certain European architects] *have seen that, in order to achieve in densely populated districts the placement of living quarters, amidst greenery which is imperative, there must be concentration in groups of high buildings which will stand in parks or, at any rate, in open spaces. Only in such a way can the necessary distances between buildings be secured. Thus the basic principle on which they have worked has been to condense great dwelling units into high buildings so as to gain free open spaces and thus be able to place them in gardens and recreation grounds.*[42]

About civic centers in general he states that "According to the highly differentiated requirements of present-day social life, this center will be concentrated in tall buildings freely placed in open spaces surrounded and defined by greenery".[43]

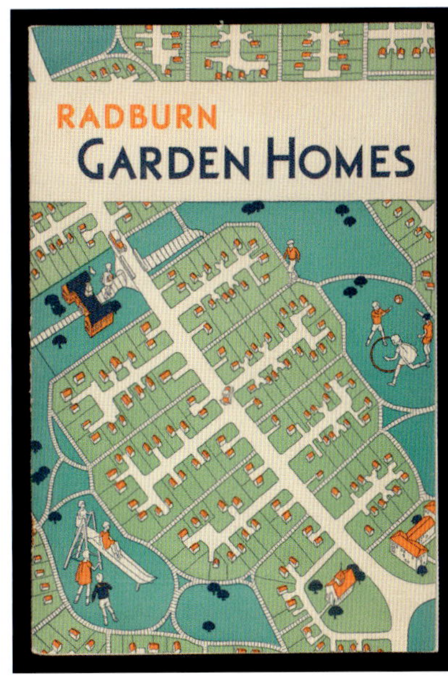

top to bottom:
Fig. 49. Radburn Garden Homes, promotional poster, ca. 1930.

Fig. 50. Book cover of *The Disappearing City* by Frank Lloyd Wright, 1932.

39 Rowe noted wryly that this eschatological narrative neatly cast Richardson as Moses, Sullivan as John the Baptist, and Wright as Jesus Christ.

40 Giedion's proposal reminds me of Ken Kesey's nurse Ratchet, in *One Flew Over the Cuckoo's Nest*. Her solution to cure the ills of the patient: perform a frontal lobotomy. A similar erasure of the past, inducing urban amnesia, seems to be part of a more general Modernist tendency.

41 Giedion (1949): 623.

42 Ibid.: 623.

43 Ibid.: 633. Emphasis is mine.

left to right:
Fig. 51. Lincoln Center, New York City, Philip Johnson and others, ca. 1965.

Fig. 52. Los Angeles County Museum of Art described as "art acropolis" and "floating campus", William Pereira, ca. 1965.

As the ultimate civic center he praises Rockefeller Center, but not as an urban ensemble. He extolls the RCA building, but then complains that both the building and the Center are hemmed in by the city:

> *Rockefeller Center simply is in advance of its period in the urban scale. What must change is not the Center but New York itself. The city must adopt the new scale which is identical with that of its bridges and parkways. Only then will the civic center stand amidst greenery. Until then it will stand as a reminder that the structure of the city must be transformed, not in the interest of single individuals but for the sake of the community as a whole.*[44]

Although his commentary on Rockefeller Center is effusive, he fails to acknowledge its refined connection to the streets and urban fabric of Manhattan. He downplays its urban-spatial role. Instead, a full-page photomontage dematerializes the buildings, fracturing them into an art piece, presumably to expresses the new space-time aesthetic. The civic center that he does praise unequivically is the Project for Back Bay in Boston by The Architects Collaborative (TAC) (Fig. 54). In reality the Gropius civic center has a stronger affinity to the object-oriented civic center at Saint-Dié by LeCorbusier (Fig. 53). Giedion's mandate influenced high profile but isolated 'civic centers' that were to emerge in the 1960s, including Lincoln Center in New York and the Los Angeles County Museum (Fig. 51, 52). The essence of Rockefeller Center, as an urban ensemble inserted within, and elevating the existing city integrated with its urban fabric, is missing, in all these examples. This progeny bears no resemblance to the tragic Serlian stage sets and the urban complexity that they historically engendered. It is ironic that from his podium at Harvard, and in *Space, Time and Architecture*, Giedion was replacing one European paradigm, the École des Beaux-Arts with yet another, the European inspired CIAM Modernism. He had hoped, and largely succeeded, in helping replace what had been, by and large, a successful urban tradition that had flourished in the U.S. from the late 19th century through WWII.[45] CIAM with Giedion's support, has proven to be destructive of both City Beautiful ideals and the fabric of countless historic cities in America.[46]

44 Ibid.: 643. He also notes that "... the Center dominates, indeed tyrannizes over, the entire vicinity ...". A counter opinion is offered by Geoffrey Broadbent, "For the first time ever, anywhere, skyscrapers were to be grouped with consciously designed urban spaces between, a practice which, even now, has rarely been emulated. ... The plaza itself with its fountain, sunken skating rink, and shopping mall is one of the most loved, and most used urban spaces, not just in New York, but in the world." Broadbent, Geoffrey, *Emerging Concepts in Urban Space Design*, Van Nostrand Reinhold (International) Co. Ltd, London and New York, 1990: 70–71.

45 Rowe commented, "I think that one has to recognize that [in the U.S.] a period from the late 1800s to somewhere in the mid-1930s was a period which possessed a high sense of order. This is evidenced in the U.S. by the Chicago Columbian Exposition of 1893 and the City Beautiful movement and lots of American campuses". "Interview: Design Book Review", 1989, Rowe, Colin, *As I Was Saying* 3, *Urbanistics:* 322.

46 Joseph Hudnut's essay, "The Three Lamps of Modern Architecture", was a rebuttal of the Hegelian position taken by Gropius and Giedion. His three lamps are: The Lamp of Progress, The Lamp of Nature, and The Lamp of Democracy. Rowe seems to be following this line of thought in a more theatrical mode relevant to my essay when he states, "I would like to imagine an opera in which Zeitgeist, Volksgeist and Genius Loci would all be among the dramatis personae" in *Koetter Kim and Associates: Place | Time*, Rizzoli International Publications, New York, NY, 1997: 13.

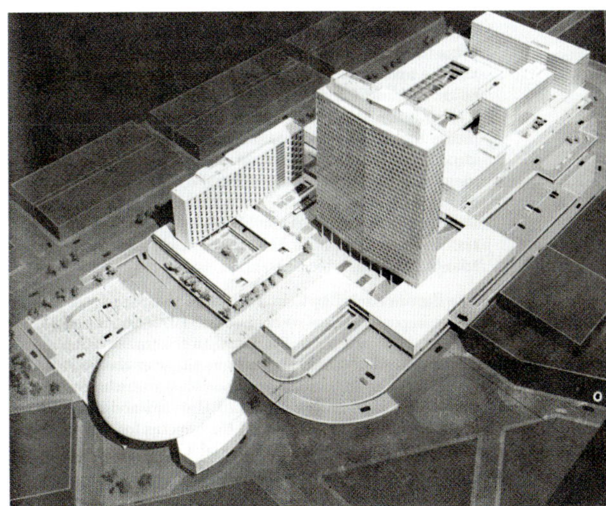

left to right:
Fig. 53. Sketch for the Ciivic Center, Saint-Dié Le Corbusier, 1945, 18413. ©FLC-ADAGP.

Fig. 54. "Project for Back Bay Center", Walter Gropius, The Architects Collaborative, Boston, MA., 1953. This image appears in *Space, Time and Architecture*, Sigfried Giedion, 1967 ed. , p. 513. Giedion goes on to say, "If this project had been implemented it would have been the finest American urban center".

Post-War Modernism and Postmodernism

After WWII, the triumph of Modernist architecture, including its anti-urban and anti-space doctrines, was nearly universal. For at least the next twenty years, that unquestioned bias contributed to the demise of the American public realm, thrusting the traditional Main, State, and Elm streets into further decline. In the 1967 edition of *Space, Time and Architecture*, Giedion had not changed his views on the Modern city he had promoted two decades earlier. He did include a new section consistent with his earlier views, "Changing Notions of the City", that focused on building groups and megastructures.

City Planners, developing their new field, were less and less interested in the physical and spatial form of the city and increasingly concerned with policy centered on issues of social and economic well-being—as if these issues were not intrinsically interrelated.[47] For a time, they dismissed the idea that physical form had social impact, or that there was any psychological need for tangible evidence of a sense of place. All of these had been served rather well by iterations of the Serlian triad in the traditional city.

Jane Jacobs, Walt Disney, Robert Venturi, and Colin Rowe

It was Jane Jacobs in *The Death and Life of Great American Cities*, published in 1961, who resurrected the street as the single most important social-spatial unit in the life of the American city, one that acted as an incubator for community values and democracy. Mulberry Street, in Little Italy in Lower Manhattan, is the realization of the comic set (Fig. 53). Although such streets were lambasted by CIAM as insalubrious, which they often were, they provided social cohesion, identity, and community. They were the scene of ordinary lives of ordinary people. Often these locations were captured on Broadway and in film epitomized by *West Side Story*, *The Godfather*, or *Do the Right Thing*. Whereas Mulberry Street could be complemented by Church, Synagogue, or Union Hall, the city promoted by Giedion segregated housing, offices, and civic centers, that placed them in a spatial ether connected by parkways or vast, undefined space. By creating

47 Antipathy toward urban design understood as a formal problem is not uncommon in academia. Dan Solomon commented on this to the author, noting the tendency of architecture faculty in planning-oriented programs to cast off any design role and imagine themselves as practicing a species of "applied sociology". In my experience, political commentaries have insinuated themselves as well. Ideologically inspired criticism has been leveled at urban design plans which show any formal affinity to classically inspired design principles, suggesting, without proof, that Burnham and Speer were somehow ideological soul mates.

Fig. 55. Mulberry Street, Little Italy, New York City, ca. 1910.

a homogeneous landscape predicated on spatial isolation, it promoted social isolation as well. Giedion's prescribed utopia had a demonstrably bad effect on the good city. His city could not support the daily lives of its citizens with the instruments of a defined comic set. Nor could it serve, even marginally, as a scene for tragedy. However, its towers in the park could be imagined as an emasculated version of the satyric scene, now, however, beset with immense parking lots.

Main Street as Nostalgia: Disneyland

Enter the entrepreneur and salesman, Walt Disney. Almost 60 years after the Chicago Fair, Disney cartooned diverse theatrical modes into a new vision: Disneyland. He acknowledges that Disneyland owes an enormous debt to the Fair, and by extension, to the dramatic possibilities of the Renaissance stage. In a promotional film highlighted at Disneyland in the 1970s, he relates that his father worked as a carpenter at the Columbian Exposition in Chicago and shows a movie clip of the Court of Honor under construction for emphasis. Young Disney visited the Fair and acknowledges that it made a profound impression on him. The fact that a fantasy could become a constructed reality seems to have been a key that emboldened his efforts. His remarks confirm, beyond any doubt, that it was the Fair that provided the inspiration for his 'Magic Kingdom'. And like the Chicago Fair, the original Disneyland consisted of a variety of reminiscent places. A prominent Main Street (Court of Honor) acts as the threshold and primary promenade leading to all attractions (Fig. 54). These include displays such as Fantasy Land (Midway Plaisance) and Adventure Land (Wooded Isle). If sufficiently inclined to invoke Chicago—and Serlio—one can see echoes of the comic, tragic, and satyric. Although one may be mesmerized, amused, and at times even enchanted by an ersatz Victorian Main Street with some semblance

left to right:
Fig. 56. Disneyland, Main Street, ca. 1955.

Fig. 57. Main Street, from *Complexity and Contradiction in Architecture* by Robert Venturi. Photo: Wallace Litman, ca. 1971 .

of the tragic, there is no real courthouse or city hall, no memorial to the Fearless Fireman, nor a monument to those who gave the last full measure of their devotion to country in time of war, and certainly no indication of human mortality unless portrayed in the Haunted House. In other words, no representation of tragedy unless sanitized and completely drained of its moral content. Disneyland manipulates in service to a dominant economic imperative. Reality lies in its bowels, not on the surface. Below is a vast machine, both inanimate and animate, designed to ensure the success of the commercial enterprise above.

Robert Venturi

By the 1960s there was increasing awareness that the city of Modern architecture was a disaster. It prompted critiques from academics and professionals, including Edmund Bacon, Vincent Scully, Colin Rowe, and, more polemically, Robert Venturi. In *Complexity and Contradiction* Venturi famously declares in the concluding pages that "Main Street is almost all right".[48] He takes Peter Blake to task for his call to "beautify" the public realm as promoted in *God's Own Junkyard*. The two opposing images that terminate Venturi's treatise are surprisingly Serlian: the University of Virginia Lawn recalls the tragic, and the ordinary Main Street recalls the comic (Fig. 22, 55). Curiously, Jefferson's heroic model is regarded as unattainable or, at least, irrelevant as a paradigm for contemporary America. But the image of his Main Street was 'real'. It portended a future that included the commercial strip and a hip architecture favored by Pop art, promoted by contemporary artists such as Warhol and Oldenburg. The comic attitude adopted by these artists attempted to raise the banal commercial world to the level of high art, paving the way for Robert Venturi's apotheosis of Main Street and the "ordinary". Venturi's approach represents an attempt to supplant the tragic with the comic.

Venturi's message is reprised in *Learning from Las Vegas* with Denise Scott Brown and Steven Izenour. To his credit, Venturi may be the first practicing architect of his generation to call attention to the values of the street. But, the Las Vegas Strip, a gigantic version of Main Street, inflates the anti-heroic comic rather than

48 Venturi, Robert, *Complexity and Contradiction in Architecture*, New York: Museum of Modern Art, 1966: 104–105.

left to right:
Fig. 58. Las Vegas Strip, ca. 1970.

Fig. 59. Lincoln Center Collage attributed to Charles Moore, ca. 1965.

Fig. 60. Typical Suburb, ca. 1970.

monumentalizing the tragic (Fig. 56). Perhaps Las Vegas is America's comic stage par excellence, replete with a pastiche of styles, bawdyhouses, tavern-casinos, and wedding chapels. A startling reincarnation of Serlio's comic stage, specified over 400 years ago? Sounding a bit like Serlio's incantation for the comic stage, Venturi argues that the strip, like Main, is "almost alright". But his suggestions about how to improve the strip are vague. Bigger signs? Supergraphics? More billboards? Less architecture? The larger question that arises from Venturi's paradigm is whether the emerging anti-city in postwar America should be resisted or embraced: Route 66 or *West Side Story*? Is the underlying message in *Learning from Las Vegas* a fatalistic acceptance of the status quo, the fatalism of historical inevitability that was famously criticized by Isaiah Berlin?[49] The optimistic philosophy of Dr. Pangloss satirized by Voltaire's *Candide* comes to mind: "all is for the best" in this "best of all possible worlds"!

The lack of conviction in the possibility or necessity for accommodating tragedy is poignantly illustrated in the gulf that separates Rockefeller Center from its diluted imitation, Lincoln Center, lampooned by Charles Moore (Fig. 57).[50] Perhaps Marx was right: history repeats itself, first as tragedy and then as parody. Whereas the civic, social, and spatial dimensions of the tragic set are maintained and even amplified in Rockefeller Center, the limited and narrow values and spatial isolation of the Modernist civic center, commercial strip, and suburbs (Fig. 58) have made it difficult to believe in any of them. Their realities do not measure up to the promise of Serlio's spatial-theatrical vision of the city where urban gaiety, dignity, and pastoral fantasy could inform and structure human experience. Meanwhile, something like the satyric mode, perhaps the most elastic vision of the three, became the pervasive scene for both imported Modernist European architecture via Le Corbusier's notorious towers in the park and Frank Lloyd Wright's anti-urban Broadacre City. The garden is no longer an event within the city but rather its replacement. The garden in the city, realized in Central Park, becomes the city in the garden—Broadacre City.

The linkage between the 19th century American Main Street, State Street, and Elm Street and the Renaissance comic, tragic, and satyric could take on epic proportions on the North American continent. By the last quarter of the 20th century this formulation had become the dramatic coda for America: the comic stage as

49 See *Historical Inevitability* by Isaiah Berlin, London: Oxford, University Press, 1954, and "Unchanging Change" in *Ktisma Journal* 4, by J. Tice, University of Oregon, School of Architecture and Allied Arts, 2015: 1–8.

50 See *Architectural Record*, ca. 1972.

Times Square, Coney Island, or Las Vegas; the tragic stage as Rockefeller Center, Washington, D.C., or City Beautiful; the satyric stage as 19th century Elm Street, Central Park, or Yosemite Valley (Fig. 59, 60, 61).

left to right:
Fig. 61. Strip highway, Route 66, Gallup, N.M., 2020. Photo permission: Luke Sharrett.

Fig. 62. Reverend Dr. Martin Luther King Jr. at the Prayer Pilgrimage for Freedom, Lincoln Memorial, Washington D.C., 1957. Photo: Paul Schutzer.

below:
Fig. 63. Half Dome, Yosemite Valley, CA. Photo: Craig Wolfe.

Colin Rowe

Colin Rowe was better attuned to the metaphor of the city as memory theater than anyone in his generation. In his lectures, Studio, and writing, he promoted that idea as a pluralistic alternative to the city of Modern architecture. He argued that, like the theater, the city should be able to have many different identities that change and transform over time even while retaining aspects of its structure. Sebastiano Serlio, with his specifications for three fundamentally different stage sets and attendant dramatic modes, provided an apt vehicle for Rowe to explore his expansive view of the city as a theater of provocative memories. These speculations suggested connections between the landscapes of Italy and America as described in his early essay with John Hejduk, "Lockhart, Texas". These landscapes underscored a collective unconscious that transported Rowe to Italy, recalling the 15th century Ideal City.[51] For his students, these were poignant lessons about illusion and reality and how the power of certain ideas and images could transcend time and space. Rowe's references to Renaissance urbanism, stage sets, and scenography had profound relevance because they opened a window into psychological and cultural dimensions, the "household of the mind".[52] His students began to understand the potential of these ideas as beneficial to the contemporary city.

51 "Lockhart, Texas" resonated with me. That a new American city in a vast landscape on the edge of Western civilization could be compared to an Italian city with its three thousand years of dense urban development was a radical proposition. Rowe makes a convincing case for their affinity—spatially and symbolically. The Texas courthouse, centered in its dedicated square, was seen as analogous to the 15th century city with its centrally planned church and central square. The courthouse in the U.S. is an icon of a nation of rational laws and democracy, an approximate icon of the Church with its revealed laws and divine right.

52 This recalls E. H. Gombrich, Rowe's mentor and colleague, who said that the Warburg Institute "bent its efforts ... for the purpose of finding out what role the image may play in the household of the mind". Gombrich, E. H., *Meditations on a Hobby Horse*, Phaidon Press Ltd, London, 1963: 127.

letf to right:
Fig. 64. *Cliff Dwellers*, detail, George Bellows, Los Angeles County Museum of Art, 1913.

opposite left:
Fig. 65. *Allies Day Parade on Fifth Avenue*, Childe Hassam, National Gallery of Art, 1917.

right:
Fig. 66. *Central Park, New York*, detail, Maurice Prendergast, Whitney Museum of American Art, ca. 1901.

Conclusion

Beginning in the 1960s, historians and critics had begun to shift their attention from the single building to the city. What has emerged in some quarters is a more comprehensive view of architecture as a contributor to the rich complexity of a healthy, resilient, endearing urbanity. The 19th century American city with its memorable streets has been the subject of an ongoing re-evaluation. The positive influence of the "White City" on American urbanism has become better known and its story has re-entered the popular consciousness as a positive episode in American urbanism and history.[53] The City Beautiful movement is beginning to be more objectively considered and appreciated. And a new generation of historians has begun to address the shortcomings of Modernist historiography.[54]

These developments suggest that the time may be ripe to consider the city again as theater, informed by the three Renaissance stage sets. As models for the city, the Serlian stage hosts a variety of dramatic modes and an infinite cast of dramatis personae. Both the stage and the city require coherent spaces that can accommodate spectator, performer, and spectacle. The argument presented here for the city as theater, and its varied dramatic manifestations, is that it should include, at least, comic Main Street, tragic State Street, and satyric Elm Street. These ideals have infused the American city with an imaginative vitality that springs from deep human emotions and aspirations, frequently captured by artists (Fig. 62, 63, 64). In contrast, Modernist architects, whether rejecting or simply being ignorant of the power and flexibility of the three stage sets, have

53 See Larson, Erik, *The Devil in the White City*, Crown Publishers, Chicago, 2003.

54 Kostof, Spiro, *The City Shaped*, Little Brown and Company, Boston, Toronto, London, 1991. See especially "The Grand Manner as Theater", where Kostof invokes two of Serlio's three stage sets, and "The Grand Manner and Landscape Design": 222–28.

Epilogue

As an undergraduate at Cornell in the mid-'60s, I was introduced to Serlio's three stage sets by Colin Rowe in his course on the Italian Renaissance. In another course on Modern architecture, Rowe drew analogies between Serlio's sets and Chicago's World's Fair. As a graduate student in Rowe's

embraced a singular vision of progress with self-limiting possibilities. Modernism has been incapable of change despite its advertised efforts to create novel forms and utopias. As a movement, it has basically remained static in its promotion of discredited urban values for the last hundred years.

The intellectual capital evident in the Western dramatic tradition with its almost infinite, varied, contrasting, and even contradictory tenets, was captured by the 16th century architect, Sebastiano Serlio. This essay is a call to revitalize and concretize the Serlian triad, to make these stage sets—and their many hybridizations—formally, spatially, and culturally tangible, intuitively accessible, and intellectually comprehensible. It is becoming increasingly clear that of the three, it is the tragic stage that is the most necessary, and most impoverished. If democratic institutions are to have a presence in the collective consciousness in our everyday and civic lives, they must be made evident and elevated in the public realm so they can contribute to the *polis*. The appreciation and application of the Serlian triad may just be the vehicle to accomplish that goal.

Studio, references to the Renaissance stage appeared in class discussions and over the drafting board. Versions of this paper were presented at ACSA conferences: "Stage Sets into Landscapes" in 1993, and "City as Theatre: Rome, Chicago, New York" in 2003 for the session, "The City as a Work of Art" and published in the International ACSA conference proceedings. An earlier study was funded by the John Yeon Foundation at the University of Oregon in 2000. Rowe and Koetter refer to Serlio's stage sets in *Collage City*. Former students and colleagues of Rowe have written on the subject. I would like to thank Grahame Shane for sharing his notes on this subject, many years ago, which primarily treats European developments. Anthony Vidler's "Scenes of the Streets" in *On Streets*, edited by Stanford Anderson, refers to Serlio in his critique of 18th and 19th century Parisian urbanism. In "Excursus Americanus", in *Court and Garden*, Michael Dennis argues that Elm Street as an urban type can be found in virtually every 19th century North American town, and that it is a plausible incarnation of Serlio's satyric scene. Steve Hurtt encouraged me to develop this essay for this volume. I am indebted to him for his helpful suggestions and careful editing.

II. Pedagogy

I presume architectural education to be a very simple matter; and the task of the educator I am convinced can be quite simply specific as follows: 1) to encourage the student to believe in architecture and Modern architecture; 2) to encourage the student to be skeptical about architecture and Modern architecture; and 3) then to cause the student to manipulate, with passion and intelligence, the subjects or objects of his conviction and doubt.

Architectural Education: USA, Lotus international, 27, 1980.

Is not precedent, and are not its connotations, the primary cement of society?
Is not their recognition the ultimate guarantee of legitimate government, legal freedom, decent prosperity, and polite intercourse?

Precedent and Invention, The Harvard Architecture Review, 5, 1986.

Colin Rowe regarded the teaching of studio design and its concomitant learning to be a highly effective, rare, and unique form of education. He argued its potential for other disciplines, as did the 1996 Carnegie Foundation study *Building Community* by Ernest Boyer and Lee Mitgang.

The common theme for these essays is a 'contextual' or 'site specific' design approach. Rowe cast doubt on *tabula rasa* and utopian alternatives, for where to begin? How to generate possibilities, evaluate, and proceed? The existing city as precedent was the primary instrument for studio learning *par excellence*. It was the medium used as a source of ideas and the medium in which design performance was tested. The ideal, the abstract city, the city of the utopian philosophers, the city as idea with or without definite form, could little instruct. Even Le Corbusier's utopian proposal for Paris shows it to have been responsive to the city's deep structure. Contextualism can be seen as an ethical and practical mandate and means for re-examining cities. Any city with a 'loaded' context, like Buffalo, NY, was the operative paradigm for investigations into topographies and histories at once unique and commonplace allowing the student to invent designs both general and particular, moving backward and forward in history.

Dissemination of this Studio 'method' was given voice by the student work shown, described, and accompanied by essays in *The Cornell Journal of Architecture* from 1981 to 1991. It is illustrated in projects for 19th and early 20th century towns with canal systems and railway infrastructures in Illinois and Tennessee. This method has also been taught in seminars and in the domains of community service.

Rowe's teaching was not limited to the Studio or lecture hall and could be highly personalized and impromptu. Questions asked by students prompted suggestions by Rowe: books to read, architectural or urban exemplars to study. His apartment, his 'salon', displayed prints, books, and furnishings that opened doors to worlds of ideas, material culture, and matters of taste, both temporal and timeless. Traveling with Rowe, the landscape became a font of historical incidents, related biographies, and a critique of regional character.

The Studio was central. It could appear vague, ill-defined, and ad hoc to outsiders but it radiated a mystique and the students always had a sense that they were on to something 'big'. The exceptional work effort was undeniable. The University set the meeting time. Otherwise, standard course accoutrement was absent: no syllabus, goal statement, grading standards typical of formal architectural studios. What was evident were maps, aerial photographs, tracing paper, and flurries of intense activity. An *esprit de corps* was palpable, the productivity remarkable.

Circumstantially, a minimum three-semester program over two regular academic years assured overlapping classes, advanced students acted as mentors and guides to all things Rowe. Each new class was partly accidental. But Rowe's colleagues directed students to him, and Rowe recruited others, many from the undergraduate program at Cornell. Most intentional was project site selection and absence of 'program' specifics. Rowe was skeptical of city planning, social science 'facts', and bureaucratic zoning standards. By contrast, the Studio operated in the thick of things, in the messy crucible of an evolving culture, specific to place, bringing history and identity to the fore.

Cornell Journal of Architecture

Colin Rowe
Lee Hodgen
Michael Dennis
Werner Goehner
Kenneth Schwartz
Steven Fong
John Shaw
O.M. Ungers

1

Colin Rowe: My Personal Recollections

Jerry A. Wells

I have written in *The Cornell Journal of Architecture* that there has been a tradition at Cornell that is fundamental to its unique success:

> *That architecture is greater than a single part, that it is not a stylized object existing on its own but is a product of its context and a contributor to that context; that architecture exists in history and that the history of architecture should therefore be taught as a discipline in conjunction with design, creating real respect for architecture and a context for ideas.*[1]

frontispiece:
The Cornell Journal of Architecture 1, 1981.

That special tradition has been summarized most concisely over the years by the graduate Urban Design Studio under the direction of Colin Rowe. The body of work from that studio is highly theoretical and in many instances full of fantasy. I believe in facts. However, I believe that fantasy plays a parallel role with fact in most fields where design and creativity are involved. In his introduction to *Five Architects,* Colin wrote:

> *When, in the late Nineteen-Forties, modern architecture became established and institutionalized, necessarily, it lost something of its original meaning. Meaning, of course, it had never been supposed to possess. Theory and official exegesis had insisted that modern building was absolutely without iconographic content, that it was no more than the illustration of a program, a direct expression of social purpose. Modern architecture, it was pronounced, was simply a rational approach to building: it was a logical derivative from functional to technological facts; and—at the last analysis—it should be regarded in these terms, as no more than the inevitable result of twentieth century circumstances. There was very little recognition of meaning in all this. Indeed the need for symbolic content seemed finally to have been superseded; and it was thus that there emerged the spectacle of an architecture which claimed to be scientific but which—as we all know—was in reality profoundly sentimental. For very far from being as deeply involved as he supposed with the precise resolution of existing facts, the architect was (as he always is) far more intimately concerned with the physical embodiment of even more exacting fantasies.*[2]

Fantasies—exacting fantasies—so much of life is like that and we can all be grateful.

1 Wells, Jerry A., "Preface", *The Cornell Journal of Architecture* 1, 1981: 2.

2 Vv. Aa., *Five architects: Eisenman, Graves, Gwathmey, Hejduk, Meier*, Oxford University Press, New York, (1972) 1975: 3.

To understand Cornell Architecture for the last 50 years, one has to start at the University of Texas in the 1950s. The new dean of the school was Harwell Hamilton Harris, a fairly renowned architect at the time with a commitment to Modern architecture with a Wrightian influence. He was hired to bring the school out of the College of Engineering and make it an independent school of architecture. He faced an old guard of tenured faculty, steeped in the Beaux-Arts and a misunderstood influence of the Bauhaus. Harris brought in a group of young faculty in their late 20s and early 30s to rebuild and reinvigorate the school. The group included Colin Rowe, Bernhard Hoesli, John Hejduk, Robert Slutzky, John Shaw, Lee Hodgden, Lee Hirsche, and Werner Seligmann. Hoesli and Rowe became the ring leaders.

Bernhard Hoesli had worked with Le Corbusier as an assistant at the Rue de Sèvres. He had worked on the Villa Curutchet at La Plata in Argentina. He was later assigned as project architect for the Unité d'habitation and he relocated to Marseilles to manage and oversee the construction of that project. Despite working for Le Corbusier, he was also interested in the work of Frank Lloyd Wright and came to this country to see that work when he met Harris and was hired to teach at the School of Architecture at the University of Texas. He was the first of the reformers to arrive in Austin and the last to leave. Later he was Dean of the ETH in Zurich and was in charge of the building of the Heidi Weber Pavilion in Zurich, one of the last of Le Corbusier's buildings.

Colin Rowe had arrived after having studied at the Warburg Institute, London, with Rudolph Wittkower and Yale with Henry Russel Hitchcock. Colin had already written essays of importance including "The Mathematics of the Ideal Villa".[3] Hoesli and Rowe were the primary proponents in developing the architecture curriculum at Texas.

Robert Slutzky arrived a year later from his education with Josef Albers at Yale and initiated a first-year drawing course and a second-year color course both influenced by Albers. Robert Slutzky, John Hejduk, and Lee Hirsche taught the drawing course. The course was so effective that, when I became chairman at Cornell, I re-introduced it at Cornell with an ex-Texan, Mike Dennis, teaching it. We still teach it at Cornell today. Rowe and Slutzky produced the famous article "Transparency: Literal and Phenomenal" the following year.

This group of teachers put together an experimental program that revolutionized the way architecture was taught. They researched new ways of teaching with an emphasis on architectural space and its definition. After a few short years, they were all fired when Harris abruptly left because of conflicts with the university and the tenured faculty. The old guard reclaimed the school.

The Texas faculty dispersed around the world. Colin went to Cambridge University in England. Bernhard Hoesli and Werner Seligmann went to Switzerland and started teaching at the ETH. Lee Hodgden went to the University of Oregon and John Shaw to North Carolina State. John Hejduk went on to Cooper Union and Bob Slutzky entered the I. M. Pei office.

3 Rowe, Colin, "The Mathematics of the Ideal Villa. Palladio and Le Corbusier compared", *The Architectural Review* CI (603), Mar, 1947: 101-04.

After a brief stay at Cornell during the 1957–58 academic year, Colin Rowe returned to Ithaca and Cornell University in 1962, where he remained until his appointment as A.D. White Professor Emeritus in 1994. Andrew Dickson White, a great expounder of architecture and humanism at Cornell, would have been delighted with Colin's appointment to a professorship in his honor.

The Cornell students, some of whom were very clever, invented songs about this group of Texas faculty, and thus the reference "The Texas Rangers" was born:

> *Oh I am a ranger and I come from Texas,*
> *Oh I am a ranger and I am teaching you,*
> *We are Lee, John, and Werner and we are all rangers,*
> *Just get you an outfit and you will be one, too.*
> (sung to the tune of *The Streets of Laredo*)

There were many, many more songs in this vein, mostly by Alan Chimacoff and Tom Schumacher. Alex Caragonne wrote, quoting Colin Rowe:

> *But should it not be obvious that the term 'the Texas Rangers' belongs to the theater of New York Jewish irony; and that it could scarcely have originated in Texas itself. It is a kindly, though sardonic,* ex post facto *designation applied by Jewish wit, to the Cornell faculty members who were at the University of Texas.*[4]

After I graduated from the University of Texas, Bernhard Hoesli and Werner Seligmann recruited me to come to Switzerland to work for Bernhard and attend graduate school at the ETH in Zurich where they were teaching. I stayed in Switzerland several years. I returned to the United States where I soon learned that the old Texas faculty had re-assembled at Cornell University, including Colin Rowe, Werner Seligmann, Lee Hodgden and John Shaw. Hejduk and Slutzky were there briefly before returning to New York.

Upon my return, I was working for John Johansen in Connecticut when I went to visit my college roommate at the University of Texas, Irving Phillips, who was a student in the first graduate program at Cornell Architecture, the Urban Design Studio that Colin Rowe and John Reps had created. Irving was, in fact, the initial and only student in that studio. On that trip I reestablished my connection with Colin Rowe and the other ex-Texas faculty at Cornell. It was not long before Colin Rowe and Werner Seligmann recruited me for a teaching job at Cornell in 1965. It was a learning experience: my first appointment was after the faculty had flunked the entire thesis class. I was assigned to that group as their critic. I had never taught before! Trial by fire was their *modus operandi*. The next few years were the equivalent of one of the greatest graduate schools I could have ever attended. Colin, Martin Dominguez, and I taught third year together and Colin and I taught in the Urban Design Studio, while John Reps had dropped out of teaching that studio. In the following years the Urban Design Studio produced a project on Buffalo, New York, that put Cornell's Urban Design program 'on the map'. For several years after that I taught both third year and the Urban Design Studio with Colin and sometimes Werner Seligmann.

4 Caragonne, Alexander, *The Texas Rangers: Notes from an Architectural Underground*, MIT Press, Cambridge, MA, and London, 1995: 68-69.

Colin's strategy for studying cities was an intense observation of the *gestalt* patterns that city structures make in a very abstract way. He initiated the figure/ ground drawing as a means of studying these particular analyses. It allowed one to see things one would not ordinarily see. It was primarily an analysis tool that related to cities, and of course related to the historical Nolli Plan of Rome. That means of analyzing cities was unique in schools of architecture at the time and allowed one to deal with abstract issues of cities in a way that was revolutionary. It also allowed one, if you knew about the patterns cities make, to understand cities' historical evolution. In fact, we practiced analyzing cities we'd never even visited or seen by discussing the patterns they made and figuring out the dates. It was a fascinating time of my life—and I only understood that years after it happened.

Colin and I were friends for our entire adult lives. Therefore, I have a much different perception of him from most people. I knew him as a close personal friend and a colleague. I've read only a few of Colin's finished books but I read almost everything Colin wrote as a manuscript that he was working on, before it became a finished book. Colin would arrive at my house at 2:00 or 3:00 in the morning. "Hi, Jerry, what do you think about this?" And he would start reading what he'd written on yellowed paper on his old typewriter. When you tried to explain to him that it was 3:00 in the morning, he would simply go on reading, disregarding your concern. He would return a few nights later with the revised version of what we'd discussed a few nights before. Of course, there were also many late nights at his house just discussing things. Most of Colin's students know what I am talking about and cherish these memories. Being a student-friend of Colin was a 24–7 experience, one that I remember fondly.

When Mathias Ungers was named as chair at Cornell, Colin was at first a great supporter. In time they became disenchanted. I left Cornell in 1977 and went to USC in California. I came back in 1979 and was named chairman of the Department of Architecture in 1980 (in one's absence one's reputation grows larger). My first job was to make peace between Rowe and Ungers. To get them to talk to each other was a struggle, but in time they buried the hatchet. Ungers was still running one of the graduate studios for some time when I was chair. I ended up presiding over Ungers's retirement.

As chair, I established a curriculum very similar to the curriculum at the University of Texas:

- The design studios primarily deal with demonstration and application of knowledge.

- The parallel courses would concentrate on the teaching of skills, technology, and history. These parallel courses relate to the expectations of the design studios and run parallel to them.

- Design teaching is based on five fundamental ideas:

    1) That architectural space and its definition are important aspects of architecture.

View of Sibley Dome,
Cornell College of Architecture Art and Planning. Cornell University archive.

2) That architecture is greater than a single part; that it is not a stylized object existing on its own but a product of its context and a contributor to that context.

3) That architecture exists in history and that the history and understanding of architecture and its analysis should therefore be taught as a discipline in conjunction with design, creating knowledge of precedents and real respect for architecture and a culture and context for ideas.

4) That 'how'? and 'why'? are still important questions.

5) That we cannot teach architecture, but we can teach students how to learn about architecture.

I created *The Cornell Journal of Architecture*, which proved that there was a pretty good school of architecture in upstate New York. I was amused to learn that at one point there used to be a *Cornell Journal of Architecture* on every desk at Harvard.

In all the complexity and chaos of an architectural education, two very simple principles made an education in Cornell Architecture unique and valuable. The first was that the individual building is part of a greater whole: it exists in a context. A building would then be designed in a manner that is not only affected by this physical context, but that also simultaneously responds to that context and contributes to it. Thus, the building would not be a decorated object standing alone, but would be a part of the city, part of the landscape. The second principle was that history is important (not a particularly obvious concept in a Modernist endeavor that considered itself to be founded on continuous invention) and that students should be made aware of their place in a philosophical and historical context. The persons who made these two principles the foundation of Cornell's architectural pedagogy were the Texas Rangers and, primarily, Colin Rowe.

Colin Rowe saw the teaching of architecture differently from most. He taught students, colleagues, and architectural scholars around the world that Modern architecture in particular was not revolutionary, as it was supposed to be, but evolutionary and connected to history. In his first great essay, "The Mathematics of The Ideal Villa" (first published by *The Architectural Review*, 1947), he brilliantly and conclusively demonstrated the influence of Palladio's Villa Foscari (the Malcontenta of c. 1550–60) on Le Corbusier's Modernist manifesto, the Villa Stein (1927) at Garches. In this one essay, he reunited Modern architecture with a past that, according to the polemic of the time, it was never supposed to have had. However, far from criticizing Modern architecture's inherent ideas, Rowe was pointing out its inevitable relationship to historical precedent. Many years later, Colin wrote:

> *While I am constantly moved by the magnificence of the original idea of Modern architecture and while I can scarcely think except in terms of its repertory of forms, I cannot really believe in it any longer.*[5]

With statements like this, many have credited (or blamed) Rowe for setting the stage for Postmodernism and the New Architecture. This is, in many respects, more a critique of Modern architecture's execution than its inherent principles—in particular of second generation Modern architects. Characteristically Rowian, it professes an enthusiasm that is both faithful and filled with doubt.

As a teacher and a muse, Colin Rowe constantly crossbred an extensive knowledge of architectural history with equally extensive erudition in the arts, as well as in political and cultural history. All were combined with one of the most perceptive set of eyes ever cast in the direction of a building or a drawing. More than retellings, more than reconstructions, Rowe's writings and lectures were biographies of architecture. Chronology and documentation can provide only skeletal information; the mind and the eye would provide the organs and flesh. He conveyed a conviction that speculation was the mind's most intimate engagement with a work. And that designing was the flirtation of mind through eyes. With his brilliant insights he was able to enlighten students to the notion that many ideas in architecture are universal; that by studying the history of architecture, the arts, politics, and culture, they could liberate their ideas, and, through a process we call transformation, apply them to contemporary problems.

5 Rowe, Colin, "Architecturaal Education: USA", in *As I Was Saying: Recollections and Miscellaneous Essays* 2, *Cornelliana*, Caragonne, Alexander, ed., MIT Press, Cambridge, MA, and London, 1996: 53-54.

Colin Rowe went on to write many more important essays and books. His most influential work, "Transparency: Literal and Phenomenal", was written as two essays with Robert Slutzky; the first in 1955, published in 1963, and the second published in 1971. The essays related analytical Cubist painting and *gestalt* perception psychology to architecture. Alex Caragonne, in *The Texas Rangers*, wrote:

> *Credit both of them for discerning a new perception and conception of architectural space, a reemphasis of the relationship of the plan to architectural space, and most importantly the recognition of phenomenal transparency as a means of conceptually organizing architectural space.*[6]

Colin was best known by colleagues and students at Cornell for creating the Graduate Urban Design Studio, which drew students from around the world and produced more educators in the field than any other such program. Colin's lectures on the architecture of the Italian Renaissance drew not only students, but also many faculty members from all corners of the campus. For all of his intellectual contributions, Colin will be best remembered and loved by many of us for his conversations—amazing conversations—late into the night. I am the very last of the Texas types at Cornell. I miss them all.

6 Caragonne (1995): 173.

The 1967 Cohen-Hurtt Master's Thesis (abridged)

Steven W. Hurtt

Introduction

With our first discussions about *The Urban Design Legacy of Colin Rowe*, Antonio Latini insisted on inclusion of the 1967 urban design Master's thesis by Stuart Cohen and Steven Hurtt,[1] abridged or in full, and accompanied by an introduction. Latini had seen our thesis footnoted in Tom Schumacher's 1971 article in *Casabella* "Contextualism: Urban Ideals and Deformations", then found and read the thesis in the early 1980s.[2]

Latini claims the thesis is an important historic document, influenced other Rowe students, is fundamental in the history of ideas emanating from the Rowe Studio including Contextualism, and contributes to understanding Rowe's impact on the developing urban design discipline. He further argues the thesis ought to be made more easily accessible through inclusion in this book, whether abridged or in full.[3]

The abridgement form I used maintains the structure, order, ideas, and voice of the original, while eliminating wordiness with minor rewriting and reordering for clarity.[4] The Introduction and Part One represent our 1966–67 understanding of Rowe's critique of Modern architecture's questionable rationales and imperatives; its millennial fervor, messianic tone, promise of salvation to humankind, and a new architecture based on faith in advancing technologies, mass production, and related utopian urban propositions and architectural iconographies, as evidenced specifically in Le Corbusier's writing and projects. Rowe's broad critique included the 1959 article "The Architecture of Utopia".[5] In the first sentence he writes, "…if, as we might suppose, Utopia does find one of its roots in Jewish millennial thought …", which prompted, "Colin, what's millennialism"? His indirect answer was four book titles, all read, three footnoted in our thesis and below.[6] Rowe returned to these millennial, messianic, and utopian themes many times, culminating in his *The Architecture of Good Intentions* in 1994.[7] Beyond his 1959 essay, Rowe recalls that the earliest public presentation of these, and related or developing themes, was in the same year as our thesis, 1967.[8]

frontispiece top to bottom:

Plan Voisin, 1925, Le Corbusier.

Paris, extant, ca. 1925.

Plan for Paris, 1937, Le Corbusier.

Figure/ground drawings by Stuart Cohen & Steven Hurtt, 1967.

1 Cohen, Stuart E. and Hurtt, Steven W., *Le Corbusier: The Architecture of City Planning*, thesis, Master of Architecture, (urban design), Department of Architecture, College of Architecture, Art, and Planning, Cornell University, June 1967.

2 Schumacher, Thomas, "Contextualism: Urban Ideals and Deformations", *Casabella* 359-360, 1971: 79-86. This article by our Studio colleague introduced the word 'contextualism' into the architectural discourse. Latini knew the article, then researched and read our thesis. Within weeks of his arrival in the U.S., Latini also found and purchased a copy of *The Cornell Journal of Architecture* 2, 1983, devoted to urban design in general and Rowe's Urban Design Studio and his ideas, including my "Conjectures on Urban Form: The Cornell Urban Design Studio 1963-1982".

3 Co-editor Jim Tice, Stuart Cohen and I agreed, with the proviso that I take responsibility for abridging the thesis and these introductory remarks.

4 I adopted this abridgement form after trying several others including varied deletion and explanatory additions. Generally, footnoted citations are updated and more complete in the bibliography.

5 Rowe, Colin, "The Architecture of Utopia", *Granta* 63, Jan 24, 1959: 20-26, 41.

Part Two focused on a formal analytic understanding of Le Corbusier's highly influential work including ideal city plans and their application to historic contextual conditions, primarily central Paris: the 1922 *Ville Contemporaine* as the basis for the 1925 Plan Voisin, and the 1933-34 *La Ville Radieuse* as the basis for the 1937 Paris Plan. In 1966, given Rowe's essays on Le Corbusier, many in the Studio were desperate to find evidence of contextual references in our Modernist – Le Corbusier inheritance. That effort led to a study model and, for our thesis, the three frontispiece figure/ground drawings: top to bottom: the Plan Voisin, extant Paris, and the 1937 Plan. They are published together here for the first time.[9] Excised from Part Two is the text and related drawings for sections subtitled "ILOT No. 6; Tokyo Museum; League of Nations; Saint-Dié; Chandigarh [the Capitol Complex]" that illustrated Le Corbusier's work as it moved increasingly toward what Rowe had identified as Le Corbusier's evolving preference for *acropolean* open spatial compositions epitomized by the Athenian Acropolis. Detail descriptions of these projects seemed tangential to the urban design emphasis of this book.[10] Except for the figure/grounds related to Paris, none of the other illustrations included here were part of the original thesis.

Part Three, the Conclusion, expresses our dismay at the erosion of the traditional city due to the widespread adoption of the spatial tenets of Modernist architecture and planning, and our proposal of an alternative architectural-urban theory, *contexturalism*,[11] fundamentally opposed to Modernist tenets. Contextualism is a theory of architecture that is probably at least vaguely familiar to readers of this volume, as the related words, *context, contextual, contextualist,* and *contextualism* entered the theory, literature, and every-day language of architecture fifty years ago and remain commonplace today.[12]

Regarding the figures that accompany this essay, the figure/ground drawings were originally prepared as part of the thesis. The other figures included with this abridged version were not included in the 1967 thesis. Regarding footnotes, as with the original thesis text there is a bibliography at the end, now updated. In the footnotes a short form cites author, title, and page number.

6 Cohn, Norman, *The Pursuit of the Millennium*, Harper and Row, New York, 1961; Mannheim, Karl, *Ideology and Utopia*, Harcourt Brace and World, New York, 1936; Tuveson, Ernest Lee, *Millennium and Utopia*, Harper and Row, New York, (1949) 1964. These three Rowe recommended texts are cited in our thesis; he also suggested, and likely imagined that it would be amusingly relevant to a doubting Christian with a Unitarian background (me), to read Schonfield, Hugh J., *The Passover Plot*, Hutchinsin, 1965. It is not included in the bibliography of our thesis, nor do I believe Rowe references it elsewhere.

7 Rowe, Colin. *The Architecture of Good Intentions: Towards a Possible Retrospect*, Academy Editions, Academy Group Ltd. London, 1994: 9-10. By way of introducing the millennial theme, Rowe cites Focillon, Henri, *The Year 1000*, Frederich Ungar, 1969: 39: it was published two years after our thesis.

8 Rowe (1994): 6. " … offered at a symposium sponsored by Mathias Ungers at the Technical University of Berlin as long ago as 1967". Rowe casually suggested readings to different students, part of his manner of teaching. Shared readings contributed to the intellectual excitement of the Studio. Without presuming that Cohen and I influenced Rowe's thinking rather than the other way round, it has been rewarding to find parallel commentary and the same or similar citations referenced in our thesis and in *The Architecture of Good Intentions.* I believe Rowe's 1967 presentation was in the Fall following our thesis submission in the spring (1967). Additionally, I recall Rowe inviting me to a reading-discussion of these ideas at his apartment sometime between 1967-70, a characteristic of his manner of working.

9 Formal analysis was unusually rigorous at Cornell and in clear contrast to most of my previous undergraduate and graduate architectural educational experiences at Princeton.

10 Rowe, Colin, "Dominican Monastery of La Tourette, Eveux-sur-Abresle, Lyons". *The Architectural Review* 129, Jun 1961.

11 Cohen and I struggled with whether it should be 'contexturalism' or 'contextualism', and opted for the more specific reference to the 'texture' of the traditional city rather than the more inclusive contextualism. Elsewhere in this book, I describe our discussions including physical and cultural contexts. Rowe commented to us, "It should have been contextualism"—as it became.

12 For example, an essay sent to me by Antonio Pietro Latini by Zhou, Shangyi; Zhang, Shaobo, "Contextualism and Sustainability: A Community Renewal in Old City of Beijing-*Sustainability,* 2015, 7. 7, 2015: 747-66. Two of the conclusions in the article affirm a national level phenomenological understanding of contextualism; another assertion extends contextualism into the realm of social planning: My co-editor and I think that Colin Rowe would be dubious of these conclusions: the first leading to 'blood and soil'; about the second conclusion, Rowe was skeptical of social engineering as a basis for city or community planning.

LE CORBUSIER: THE ARCHITECTURE OF CITY PLANNING

Stuart E. Cohen, Steven W. Hurtt

This paper and the original drawings accompanying it are presented in partial fulfillment of the requirements for the degree of Master of Architecture at Cornell University. It has provided an invaluable learning experience for its authors.

We would like to thank Colin Rowe, K. C. Parsons, Thomas Schumacher, and Henry Moses for their encouragement and criticism, and our wives for their patience. The model of the Voisin plan illustrated in photographs was prepared by the authors and the following: Alexander Caragonne, Frederick Hammann, and Michael Schwarting.

Preface

Tradition is a matter of much wider significance. It cannot be inherited, and if you want it you must obtain it by great labor.[13]

T. S. ELIOT

As the products of modern historicism, our predilection toward historic causality produces a desire to understand our traditions in order that we may use them with awareness and purpose. This study is intended as an architectural criticism. If it seems a history, it is that to "regard all things in their historical setting appears, indeed, to be an instructive procedure of the modern mind. We do it without thinking because we can scarcely think at all without doing it".[14]

The subject of this criticism is Le Corbusier's work. The first chapter gives a sketch of the ideas and intellectual milieu that influenced him. The second chapter is primarily a discussion of the formal characteristics of his work but inclusive of relevant meanings. The conclusion deals briefly with the relevance Le Corbusier's architecture has for urban design today.

Le Corbusier represents only one of a number of people who have had an influence on the shape of Modern architecture. Our exclusive treatment makes it possible to miss other influences. But it is preeminently Le Corbusier who has both directly and indirectly dominated the architectural thought of this century. His work stands as *the* example of Modern architecture most firmly rooted in the past, and simultaneously most cognizant and expressive of contemporary ideas.

13 Eliot, T. S., "Tradition and Individual Talent," *The Sacred Wood:* 49.

14 Becker, Carl, *The Heavenly City of the Eighteenth Century Philosophers:* 19.

Part One (I)

> *Human consciousness is in need of a revelation ... (182). Architecture: decisive demonstration of our creative powers. It concerns a human voice; with the profundity of time, permanent and carrying a message forward, eagerly ... (201). I was forced to pick up my pilgrim's staff and journey forth, often for great distances. Preaching a crusade? Who knows! Already there are many premonitory signs on the horizon ... (173). This age is heavy with portent. By building, you can direct events toward the solution and toward joy for some time to come ... (248). Total city planning .... Already we are hurtling forward into the modern adventure. You think the time is not yet ripe? What terrible sounds, what rending, what avalanche must assail your ears then, before they will hear? The thunder now rolling around the world fills the heart of the coward with fear and hearts of the brave with joy .... And to you, the idlers, the pleasure-seekers and the liars, you in your niches, conservatives and robbers, I say tomorrow will see the necessary task accomplished ... (343). A simple decision of the mind, a simple movement of the pendulum towards the side of GOOD instead of the side of EVIL. Simply choosing CONSTRUCTION rather than accepting DESTRUCTION... (345). Let us make our plans, plans on a scale with twentieth century events, plans equally as big as Satan's. Plans to trample Satan back into dust ... (185).*[15]
>
> LE CORBUSIER

above:
Fig. 1. Holy City of the New Jerusalem, Julius Goltzius, 1646.

opposite top to bottom:
Fig. 2. Isaac Newton, portrait by John Vanderbank, 1725.

Fig. 3. René Descartes, portrait by Frans Hals, 1649.

Fig. 4. Auguste Comte, engraving by Johan Hendrick Hoffmeister, 1851.

Fig. 5. Georg Wilhelm Friedrich Hegel, portrait, Bollinger engraving after Christian Xeller, ca 1825.

Underlying the above quotation is the resounding tone of millennial messianism. Colin Rowe has suggested that Le Corbusier's work is predicated on the expectancy of a utopia and that it was in a messianic role that Modern architecture cast itself at the beginning of this century,[16] the millennial myth having undergone what George Kubler refers to as "deforming pressures"... the "rejuvenation of myths a case in point: when an ancient version becomes unintelligibly obsolete, a new version, recast in contemporary terms, performs the same old explanatory purposes".[17]

Millennialism is a complicated body of myths that grew in complexity. In its original form millennialism was literal in intent. It had as its essence the ultimate defeat of evil and the establishment of the City of God on earth. While a utopia is common to many faiths, its Judaic form, the millennium, is removed from reality in time rather than space. This temporal removal accounts for the expectancy of a utopia and the need for its construction at some moment in time. The expectancy implies a teleological view of the universe that, when secularized under the influence of humanism, becomes historicist in character. It requires an 'authority' on which it can be based, 'grace' by which it can be determined who it should benefit, and a 'power' by which it can be brought about.

During the 14th century, the church, due to the failure of the millennium to occur, and the resulting increase in anti-clerical chiliasm, expediently removed the expected millennium to a non-terrestrial sphere. But as millennialism had long served man's need to believe in the possibility of a better world, it also underwent "deformation" into a secular rather than an ecclesiastical ideology. Theologically, millennialism presented no difficulties in its rationalization. Belief in God provided the necessary 'authority,' the 'power,' and the 'grace' to bring it about. But the secularized millennium required a new *raison d'etre* and detail attention to

15 Le Corbusier, *Towards a New Architecture.* Page numbers indicated in parentheses.

16 Rowe, Colin, "Le Corbusier: Utopian Architect", *The Listener*: 287, and "The Architecture of Utopia", *Granta* 63: 20-26, 41 .

17 Kubler, George, *Shape of Time*, 1962: 22.

its form. Quattrocento humanism provided for these considerations: the continued persistence of millennialism is the result of Christianity's simultaneous accommodation of Judaic and Platonic thought.

Colin Rowe has pointed out that the idea of utopia enjoyed architectural crystallization a full century prior to its literary expression by Sir Thomas More. Both the architectural or physical images of utopia and the literary forms have undergone "deformation". The ideal cities of the Renaissance, images of utopia, were an outgrowth of quattrocento humanism to which the papacy and church played host. The formal attributes of these cities rest on ideal or God-given geometries. Their central squares are sometimes occupied, not by churches, but by their humanist counterpart, temples. This somewhat heretical activity was embraced by the Church of Rome until after the first tremors of the Reformation. But then an ideal city only tacitly conveys its utopian implications, that its construction work as a panacea on the world, and it therefore represents no threat to the existing order. As the image of ideal cities found no opposition, it remained virtually static until the early part of this century. Even then, the dependence of Le Corbusier's Ville Contemporaine and Ville Radieuse on their Renaissance predecessors attests to the stasis of the image.

The same generalizations can hardly be made about the literary counterpart of the utopian theme. Based on social criticism, and therefore subject to philosophic speculation, it is to these literary utopias that we owe the changes the millennial myth has undergone. As a reflection of 16th century thought, it seems pertinent that the publication of More's famous book, *Utopia*, and the Reformation were coincidental. Arguably, both were precipitated by the church's liberal accommodation of humanism during the previous century. The subsequent reaffirmation of the transcendental nature of Catholicism and its authority led to the determinist tendencies of the later 16th and 17th centuries. But no increase in the coercive presentation of doctrine could stem the rise of interest in non-ecclesiastical interpretations of the universe the church had engendered by removing itself from the basis of earthly utopianism. A Cartesian view of the universe governed by discoverable natural laws enjoyed wide popularity; God was still recognized as the creator of the system, but no longer thought necessary to the continuation of its workings. This neo-classical view was handed down through Newton and Descartes to those two philosophers to whom Le Corbusier's and our own age owe so much: Auguste Comte and Georg Wilhelm Friedrich Hegel. They, in turn, seem indebted to the philosophers of the Age of Reason who Carl Becker regards as having "merely demolished the Heavenly City of St. Augustine only to rebuild it with more up-to-date materials".[18]

Comte and Hegel "deformed" our contemporary version of the millennial myth rooted in Judaic-Christian traditions. First, they ejected philosophy from the realm of science and embraced a positivist empiricism seeking 'authority' in science: but this has given only passing satisfaction because many of the so-called sciences are inexact; refuge is found only in the absolutes of mathematics. Second, they attempted to base history on a scientific teleology that presumed an orderly progression towards a pre-established end seeking 'grace' in the judgments of history, in the future.

18 Becker, *Heavenly City:* 31.

Fig. 6. Le Corbusier, portrait, Photo: Philippe Halsman, 1935.

While these versions of 'authority' and 'grace' were a part of Le Corbusier's inheritance, 'power', was contemporaneous to him. The power of technology stands out on the first pages of *Towards a New Architecture:*

> *A great epoch has begun.*
>
> *There exists a new spirit.*
>
> *Industry overwhelms us like a flood which rolls on towards its destined ends, has furnished us with new tools adapted to the new epoch, animated by the new spirit.*
>
> *Economic law inevitably governs our acts and our thoughts.*
>
> *The problem of the house is the problem of the epoch. The equilibrium of society depends upon it.*
>
> *The primordial instinct of every human being is to assure himself of a shelter. The various classes of workers in society today no longer have dwellings adapted to their needs; neither the artisan nor the intellectual.*
>
> *It is a question of building which is at the root of social unrest today: architecture or revolution.*[19]

The words and phrases pile up: economic law, classes of workers, social unrest, and revolution; the new epoch, the new spirit, the engineer, and industry. Le Corbusier is enmeshed in the catchwords and ideas of the late 19th century. He begins the first chapter of *La Ville Radieuse* with the slogan of the French Revolution—*Liberte! Egalite! Fraternite!*

While for the Romantic the will of man represented 'authority', the social and economic failure of the French Revolution aroused a need to find a more substantial basis for inevitability than man's will. A neo-classical return to 'natural' law was in order. The Realists found 'authority' in the 'science' of economics and shared with romantics, utopians, and communists, an aim and quest for a theory of history that would make the millennium inevitable. Le Corbusier praises the collective spirit, eulogizes the engineer, heralds the new technology and industry, and idolizes the machine, as harbingers and symbols of a better society. Whether to accept the machine, as a means to achieve a better way of life, for him is a "question of morality".

Twenty-three years before the publication of *Vers une Architecture*, Henry Adams found himself also in Paris, "lying in the Gallery of Machines at the Great Exposition of 1900; his historical neck broken by the sudden eruption of forces totally new".[20] Adams, seeking the same unity of history that Le Corbusier embraced, wrote skeptically of his confrontation with technology:

> *To Adams the dynamos became a symbol of infinity ... he began to feel the forty-foot dynamo as a moral force, much as the early Christians felt the cross.... Before the end, one began to pray; inherited instinct taught the natural expression of man before silent and infinite force.... For Adams... its value lay in its occult mechanism ... the nearest approach to the revolution of 1900 was in 310 when Constantine set up the cross. Symbol of energy, the Virgin had acted as the greatest force the Western world ever felt, and had drawn man's activities to herself more strongly than any power, natural or supernatural, had ever done.*[21]

19 Le Corbusier, *Towards a New Architecture:* 14.

20 Adams, Henry, *The Education of Henry Adams:* 382.

21 Ibid.: 380-88.

Fig. 7. Gallery of Machines, Paris Exhibition, 1900.

Was Adams, a man of the 19th century, a man who understood the power of the Virgin, seeking a generative force potent enough to replace her? He doubted technology would do so. Another historian, Charles A. Beard, writing in 1932, exhibits neither the skepticism of Adams nor that of any to whom WWI revealed the obverse side of the technological coin. Neither did Beard exhibit the objectivity one might expect of an historian of his stature.

> *A hundred years after the so-called "industrial revolution"... technology was evidently only at the opening of its career. By that time it had undone many of the effects brought about by the crude steam engine and started another "revolution" with the internal combustion engine and the dynamo... What then is this technology which constitutes the supreme instrument of modern progress?... technology has a philosophy of nature and a method... and hence is a subjective force of high tension. It embraces within its scope great constellations of ideas... Technology by its intrinsic nature transcends all social forms... Universal in its reach, it cannot be monopolized by any nation, class, period, government, or people. In catholicity it surpasses all religions. It is... [the] dynamic character of technology that makes it so significant for the idea of progress. What was once Utopian becomes actuality.*[22]

Le Corbusier and his contemporaries were not exclusively indebted to the thought of the late 19th and early 20th centuries. While they accepted the determinism of 'natural' and historic law, they reasserted a faith in individual will, a faith that can be traced first to the Romanticism of the early 19th century and finally to the Platonic ideal of quattrocento humanism.

> *As the man, so the drama, so the architecture. We must not assert with too much conviction that the masses give rise to their man. A man is an exceptional phenomenon occurring at long intervals, perhaps by chance, perhaps in accord with the pulsation of a cosmography not yet understood.*[23]

22 Beard, Charles A, "Introduction" to Bury, J.D., *The Idea of Progress:* xxii-xxiii.

23 Le Corbusier, *Towards a New Architecture:* 153.

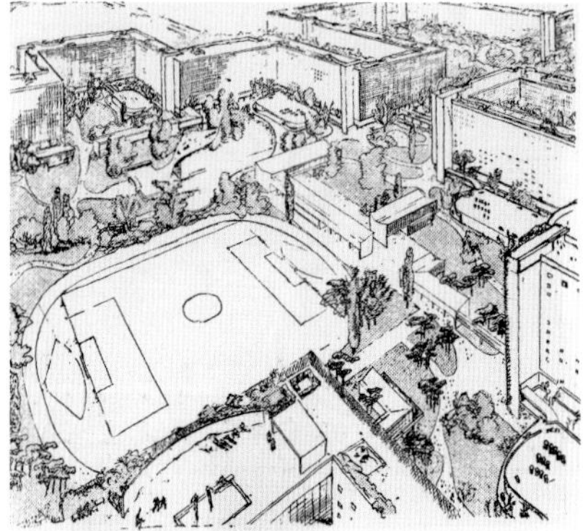

top to bottom:
Fig. 8. *Maison redent* housing showing athletic fields, sun, space, greenery, ca. 1922-34, Le Corbusier.

Fig. 9. "Immeuble Pour Artistes", housing unit type, *Oeuvre Complète: 1910–1929*, Le Corbusier.

In a series of lectures given at approximately the same time as the publication of the excerpts from Beard, Carl Becker said:

> *Since our supreme object is to measure and master the world, we can make relatively little use of theology, philosophy, and deductive logic—the three stately entrance ways to knowledge erected in the Middle Ages. In the course of eight centuries these disciplines have fallen from their high estate, and in their place we have enthroned history, science, and the technique of observation and measurement.*[24]

We have suggested that science, technology, and history are the basis of a contemporary millennium, but to identify the meaning of certain formal aspects of Le Corbusier's work, it is imperative that we have some notion of what he imagined "eternal bliss" to be:

> *As soon as production is reorganized, the leisure time made available by the machine will suddenly emerge as a social danger; an imminent threat.... The necessity of transforming this still vague notion of "leisure time" as quickly as possible into a disciplined function is therefore immediately evident.... Having reached a clear awareness of these things, there came a day when I expressed my conclusions in the following formula: sport should be a daily matter and IT SHOULD TAKE PLACE DIRECTLY OUTSIDE THE HOME.*
>
> *I will explain what I mean: the notion of "sport" has penetrated deeply into the contemporary consciousness; it contains a diversity of elements all of which are well worth our interest; the element of aggression first of all, then that of performance, of competition; strength, decision, flexibility, and speed; the elements of individual contribution as well as that of team-work; a discipline freely accepted by the individual.*
>
> *To a healthy body, to a mind kept in a continual state of activity and optimism by daily physical exercise, the city, if the right measures are taken, can also provide a healthy mental activity.*
>
> *Yet when I look about me, I see city authorities ... planning towns that will deprive men of the BASIC PLEASURES!*
>
> *The basic pleasures, by which I mean sun, greenery, and space, penetrate into the uttermost depths of our physiological and psychological being. They bring us back into harmony with the profound and natural purposes of life.*
>
> *But we must not forget a second group of basic pleasures; action,* participation *in collective work....*[25]

While the origins of the second group of "basic pleasures" are embedded in the ideals of communism, the first group owe their derivation to a late 19th century interest in a Hellenic way of life, the development of mind and body related to the competitive implications of Darwinism.[26] Among the "deforming pressures" of the late 19th and early 20th centuries, any city that could provide the physical environment for the cultivation of mind and body would be a "Heavenly City".

Regarding Le Corbusier's formal architectural education, he is the product of no known architecture curriculum. But despite his recurring attacks on the academies, it is clear from the breadth of material he calls upon and publishes, that Le Corbusier owes his respect and liberal accommodation of the past to that same 19th century historicism, that same self-consciousness about style, that allowed the academies to flourish. He is careful to distinguish himself from those who reject the lessons of history, as well as from those who use them in a rote manner.

24 Becker, *Heavenly City:* 17.

25 Le Corbusier, *The Radiant City:* 88.

26 Ibid.: 112. "Competition, the struggle for life, the necessity for earning our daily bread have accomplished miracles. The book, the newspaper and the magazine can truly be said to have transformed the world. And I don't mean Gutenberg's book, I mean the books printed on the printing machines of 1850." In 1859 Darwin published *Origin of Species*, and in the same year Marx published *Critique of Political Economy*.

> *I know that the word 'art' is execrated by the younger generation, which believes that to give voice to this detestation is the best way of overcoming the hydra-headed monster of academicism. Though I have to admit that my own hands are soiled by the scourings of the past centuries, I prefer washing them to having to cut them off. Besides, the centuries have not soiled our hands. Far from it they have filled them.*[27]

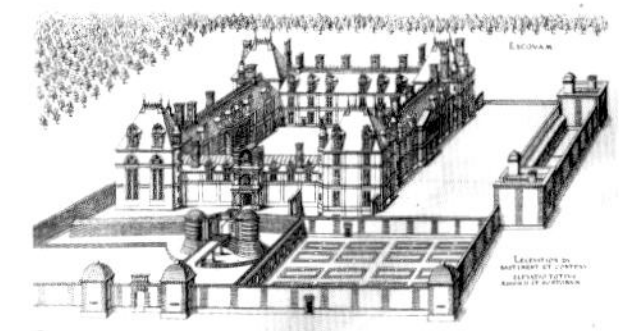

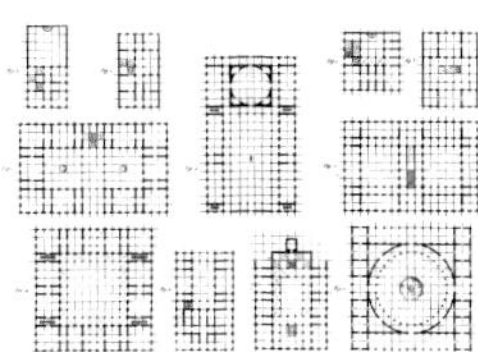

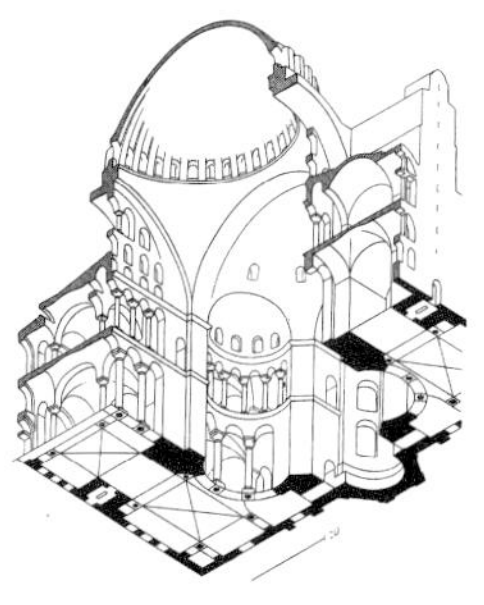

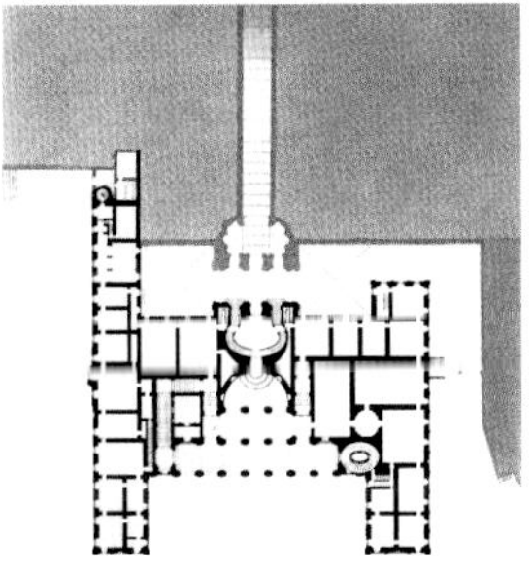

top to bottom:
Fig. 10. Du Cerceau, *Les Plus Excellents Bastiments de France*, 1576.

Fig. 11. J.N.L. Durand, *Recueil et Parallèle: L'Architecture*, 1799-1801: Plate 15.

Fig. 12. Auguste Choisy, *Histoire de l'Architecture*, 1899, Hagia Sophia.

Fig. 13. Letarouilly, Paul, *Édifices de Rome Moderne*, 1860, Palazzo Barberini.

Le Corbusier must have known the work of Viollet-le-Duc, who sixty years earlier had reproached the École des Beaux-Arts for its lack of attention to modern and rational methods of construction. But Le Corbusier was very much in sympathy with the basic ideas underlying Beaux-Arts teaching.

> *The virtue of the plan, the elegance of the solution, eminently French values, are unknown everywhere else. Such a lack of spirituality saddens me. The practical spirit dominates. The École de Beaux-Arts in Paris would emerge victorious if its aims were other than constantly striking effects reached by graphical methods....*[28]

His sketchbooks, laden with notes and drawings from both his travels and studies, bear witness to the astuteness of his observations, and their assimilation into his work.

> *When one travels and works with visual things—architecture, painting—one uses one's eyes and draws, so as to fix deep down in one's experience what is seen. Once the impression has been recorded by the pencil, it stays for good, entered, registered, inscribed.... To draw oneself, to trace the lines, handle the volumes, organize the surface... all this means first to look, and then to observe and finally perhaps to discover....* [29]

His travel sketches indicate a fascination with the hierarchical massing of primary volumes, the spatial intricacies of Eastern floor plans, and an acute awareness of the wall as a surface. These, along with other annotated sketches copied from books, suggest his familiarity with architectural history: French Renaissance gardens; du Cerceau's Pont Neuf and his *Les Plus Excellents Bastiments de France*; drawings from Auguste Choisy's *Histoire de L'Architecture* appear in *Towards a New Architecture* as does Blondel's Port Sainte Denis. He quotes Blondel suggesting he knew his drawings of Parisian *hôtels*, supported by his references to the "eloquence" of French plans, and his preoccupation with *promenade architecturale.* The style of Choisy's sectional axonometric drawings, both volumetric and constructional, have an analytic quality that made them 'scientific'; distinct from the pictorial quality of Beaux-Arts perspective, they evidently appealed to Le Corbusier. He likely knew the two great building catalogues of the 19th century, those of Durand and Letarouilly illustrating antique and Renaissance Roman architecture that exemplified the use of axes and local symmetries in plan arrangement. *Towards a New Architecture* is couched in the maxims of the Beaux-Arts. For Le Corbusier's architecture is composed of a system of *elements,* generated by a plan that is the result of an arrangement and grading of *axes*, and refined by a use of *regulating lines*, that is, *proportions.* His debt to the entire history of architecture and to the 19th century view of it is clear.[30] Le Corbusier stands apart from many of his contemporaries, not in a rejection of the past, but in his manner of using it. Herein was his greatness. Embracing the main currents of thought in his own time, he possessed what T. S. Eliot calls the "historic sense", a perception, not only of the pastness of the past, but of its presence.[31]

27 Le Corbusier, *Oeuvre Complète: 1910–1929*: 11.

28 Le Corbusier, *When the Cathedrals Were White:* 141.

29 Le Corbusier, *Creation is a Patient Search:* 37.

30 Le Corbusier, *The Radiant City:* 129. "Nineteenth century architecture is underestimated. It was discovery, it was change.... The nineteenth century was a time of fervor: new discoveries were made each day".

31 Eliot, *Sacred Wood:* 49.

Fig. 14. Purist painting. *Still Life,* Le Corbusier (Charles-Edouard Jenneret-Gris), The Museum of Modern Art, 1920.

As the influence most contemporaneous to him, Cubism, like technology, was the most recognizable. Cubist concepts of space were the first real departures from Renaissance concepts of perspective space since the Mannerist paintings of the early 17th century. It shared its era's fascinations with science. Albert Einstein had just published his first text on the theory of relativity (1905) and the Cubists developed multiple views, time sequential views, simultaneous depictions of profile and contour, simultaneous station points, and various ways of suggesting the fourth dimension. Cubism was as potent a force in Modern architecture as analytic perspective had been to the architecture of 15th century Italy.

With hindsight, Le Corbusier and Ozenfant set forth in *L'Esprit Nouveau* a critique of Cubism and their related tenets for Purist painting. While asserting the romantic role of the individual and intuition in making "pure creations of the mind", art could be thought of as a science: state the question properly, establish standards, and apply a scientific method of selection to arrive at a solution. This attitude assisted their critical proposition. Purism embraced many Cubist spatial inventions but opposed the empirical nature of Cubist subject matter. Purism proposed principles by which to establish a more universal and pure vocabulary of form-meaning subject matter. Some of the formal characteristics of Analytic Cubism are found in Le Corbusier's Purist painting, and architecture; these generally include: frontality of surfaces and their presentation; layering or spatial zoning relating objects and elements; and emphasis on peripheral rather than central composition.

Le Corbusier's Purism, both a romanticizing of the scientific process and an idealization of the universality of primary form, is more ancient and more modern than the purist movement of Blondel's students Boullée and Ledoux, although Le Corbusier surely knew of their romanticist rejuvenation of 'natural geometries'. Cubism, to all outward appearances, represented a break with what had been considered the proper and customary subject matter of art (the depiction of the visual world). This attitude was likewise shared by Modern architecture, which in its outward appearances was rejecting its customary subject matter, 'the orders' and 'the styles'.

Although the writings of Ozenfant and Le Corbusier deal almost exclusively with painting, the approach could be applied to architecture as well. Le Corbusier's purist disposition was continually manifest in his desire to reach a distillation, a poetic statement of fact. We will be tracing some of these tendencies in the subsequent chapter as they develop and reach culmination.

Part Two (II)

> *Cassirer's partial definition of art as symbolic language has dominated art studies in our century. A new history of culture anchored upon the work of art as a symbolic expression thus came into being. By these means art has been made to connect with the rest of history. But the price has been high, for while studies of meaning received all our attention, another definition of art, as a system of formal relations, thereby suffered neglect.*[32]
> *We are discovering little by little all over again that what a thing means is not more important than what it is; that expression and form are equivalent challenges to the historian; and that to neglect either meaning or being, either essence or existence, deforms our comprehension of both.*[33]

As George Kubler, in *The Shape of Time*, so adequately notes, the separation of meaning from form, while perhaps necessary to verbal analysis, is a false dichotomy. Our primary task in this chapter will be to examine the formal principles and characteristics of Le Corbusier's architecture and city planning, and the symbolic meaning of his work where pertinent to the discussion. That is, while it is often customary to speak of his architecture and his city planning as if they were separate, this too is a false dichotomy detrimental to understanding the part or the whole of his work. Le Corbusier confirms this:

> *architecture and urbanisme (planning for town and country) are, in fact, one problem only and are not separate questions. They demand one solution only and this is the work of one profession only.*[34]

For this reason, individual buildings and building types, when mentioned, will be discussed as they meaningfully relate to Le Corbusier's planning work. It is our central thesis to show Le Corbusier's work as a continual development, which moves from a preference for the closed spatial characteristics of the courtyard of the Palais Royale and Louvre to the open spatial characteristics of the Acropolis, a preference partially explained by Le Corbusier's interest in Cubist space and by his purist leanings towards primary forms of "universal meaning".

Le Corbusier's early work may be categorized according to what we have called 'Spatial Strategies'. Their origin and development are partially dependent upon archetypes Le Corbusier also chose to represent them. Two of them, the Roman aqueduct and the Athenian Acropolis, are extroverted in nature, that is, they depend on elements outside of them for their realization and spatial completion: they combine with geographic features (aqueduct) or other buildings or both (acropolis). The third archetype is represented variously by the Place Vendôme, the Place des Vosges, the Palais Royale, and the Louvre. It is fundamentally introverted in nature, represented by the enclosed courtyard independent of anything outside of it. These buildings are presented by Le Corbusier as analogous to his *immueble villa* and *maison redent* housing types. As his preference for open rather than closed spatial composition develops, the Louvre with its open-ended partially defined court is increasingly emphasized, as are the *maison redents*.

The Roman aqueduct is referenced as an archetype in relation to Le Corbusier's proposal that combines elevated highways with multi-story housing below them; the highway like the aqueduct seen as a continuous horizontal line in a hilly

32 Kubler, *Shape of Time:* vii.

33 Ibid.: 126.

34 Le Corbusier, *Creation is a Patient Search:* 300.

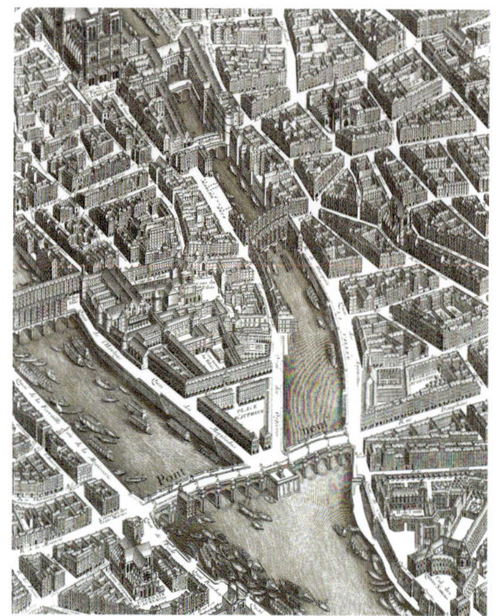

Fig. 15. Paris, detail showing Île de la Cité and Pont Neuf, Michel-Étienne Turgot, 1739.

landscape, the housing below the highway adjusting to changing contours. "Will the aqueduct, on a scale so much larger than that of the houses, destroy the site? Of course not! The aqueduct has created the site!"[35] Le Corbusier identifies the aqueducts as extrapolations of the linear housing structure he uses to make *maison redents* and explains their adaptation:[36]

> *The redent is curving because on an uneven terrain, the curved form means that the lowest point can be found and that consequently, the highest volume of structure can be attained. Curved, the redent, is better able to embrace distant horizons, curved it contributes architectural eloquence and supple power, crowning the landscape with dignity.*[37]

All the plans dependent upon the aqueduct for their inception were created between 1929 and 1934: Sao Paolo, Rio de Janeiro, and Buenos Aires 1929; Algiers, project A, 1930; project B, 1931-34. Although Le Corbusier never denies their validity, they drop from his repertoire after 1934.

Returning to those archetypes that enjoyed a more constant influence in his work, Le Corbusier wrote of the courtyard early in his career:

> *History has left us objects of admiration whose scale and dimensions have become for us an inexhaustible source of delight and contentment; the Place Vendôme, the courtyard of the Louvre, the Place de la Concorde… the proposals of modern town planning have led to the adoption of precisely this same scale in the dimensioning of architectural ensembles and ground plans. This happy coincidence must signify some deep relationship to the human scale. Within such a framework we may hope to attain to beauty by working with the highest ideals towards the attainment of unity.*[38]

Accepting Le Corbusier's initial dependency on architectural precedents, his early planning ideas show the influence of planner M. Patte.[39] From the tradition of Baroque planning comes the concept of organizing a city by creating grand public spaces. In this traditional way Le Corbusier begins his work, creating building types that make courtyard-like spaces.

In the creation of "the prototype of a classless city of men busy with work and leisure in surroundings that made these possible,"[40] the Louvre is the prototype for Le Corbusier's courtyard building types. It is symbolic of placing power and authority in the hands of the people of a new "classless" society, of providing "palaces for the people," amidst gardens, in which all men can live royally; imbuing each man with the state of mind that the Louvre, as the symbol of Paris, represents to Le Corbusier, "enterprise, belief and action".

But, while Paris figures so strongly in Le Corbusier's work, while it is a symbol of "foresight and the radiance of a pure mind," a symbol of "mathematical expression, and a pure profile, a line," while it is the city which had the "temerity" to build those "great outlines created by Louis XIV" and "those canon-straight avenues blasted by Napoleon-Haussmann,"[41] while it is "the Cartesian city," Paris was still second best to the formal lessons and cultural symbolism represented by the Athenian Acropolis, the baptismal experience of Le Corbusier's architectural self-education.

35 Le Corbusier, *The Radiant City:* 58.

36 *Redent* derives from the word *redan* meaning a fortified wall.

37 Le Corbusier, *The Radiant City:* 246.

38 Le Corbusier, *Concerning Town Planning:* 100.

39 Le Corbusier *Oeuvre Compléte 1910-1929:* 20. See Le Corbusier's sketch of Patte's plan for Paris from *Monumens Eriges en France a la Gloire de Louis XV*, 1765.

40 Le Corbusier, *The Radiant City:* 13.

41 Ibid.: 101.

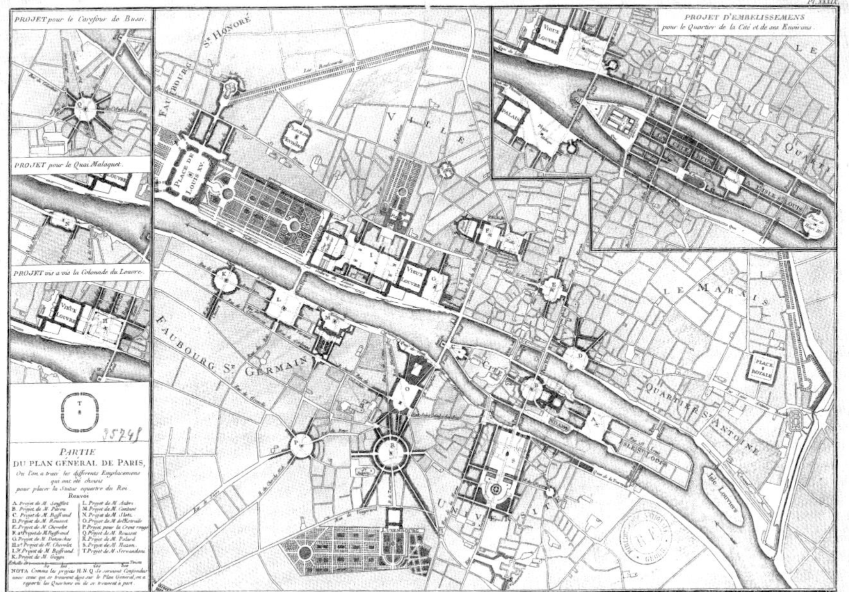

clockwise:
Fig. 16. Plan of Paris, Pierre Patte, 1765.

Fig. 17. Arc Carrousel, Nicolai Wolpert, 1900; view from Tuileries Garden toward the Louvre.

Fig. 18. *Rue de Castiglione*, W. Price, 1831.

> *Athens, Acropolis, six weeks. The columns of the north facade and the architrave of the Parthenon were still lying on the ground. Touching them with his fingers, caressing them, he grasps the proportions of the design.*[42]

In the writings and work of Le Corbusier, the Acropolis is used symbolically—representing the highest achievements of man; and metaphorically—with respect to those formal principles toward which his architecture and planning evolved. But there was also Paris. Le Corbusier spent most of his adult life in Paris. The city occupied his mind for years. It was the source of many of his architectural ideas. And their testing ground. Paris was also the best of European cities, the archetype of the "eminence of French scientific planning," and the constant reaffirmation of his architectural beliefs:

> *At twenty I had covered Paris in all directions.... Paris an assembly of clear, bold, organs, sane, rational, and proportioned: the cathedral, scintillating technique, miraculous statute; the Sainte Chapelle, an entire glass facade. The Chatelet, and shop-lined bridges; and the great Pont Neuf, yes n-e-u-f, the word giving pleasure on its baptism, and repudiating with its style in a superb and thankless gesture, four centuries of Gothic.*[43] *Here then is Paris, where all live happily together.*[44]

In the planning of the architects of Louis xv, Le Corbusier saw order imposed upon the irregular "donkey's way", the accidental plan. "The right angle is the primordial sign of the ordering and organizing spirit. One sees, appearing in the heart of the outlandish town, a pure geometry."[45]

Le Corbusier prepared two plans for the rebuilding of the center of Paris, the city of his affection, one in 1925, the other in 1937. The sacrificial nature of their preparation and presentation, and their martyred rejection, while undermining their historical importance, detracts nothing from their value: their similarities and differences provide a vehicle for examining Le Corbusier's early work.

42 Le Corbusier, *Creation is a Patient Search:* 20.

43 The "shop-lined" bridges existed in the 18th century but had disappeared by the early 19th. Those bridges originally having shops were the Pont Marie to the Île St. Louis and the Pont Notre Dame and the Pont Au Change to the Île de la Cité. They are pictured in the plan of Paris prepared by Michel Etienne Turgot in 1739 and it is possible that Le Corbusier knew them from this source.

44 Le Corbusier, *Concerning Town Planning:* 15.

45 Ibid.: 20.

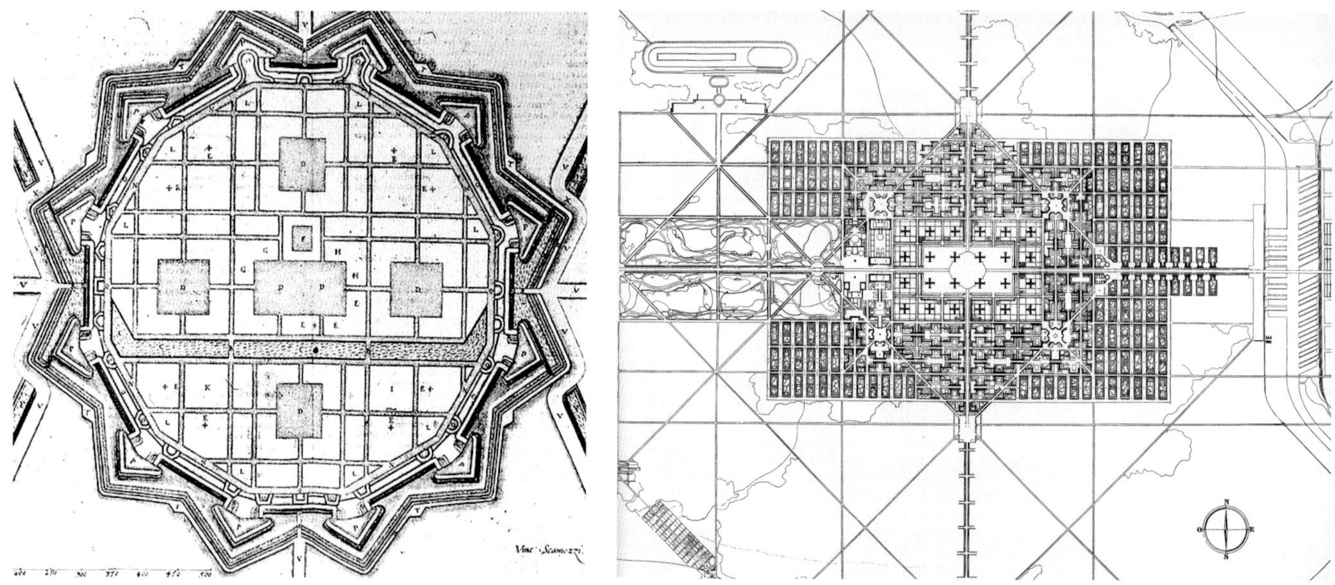

left to right:
Fig. 19. Ideal City, Vincenzo Scamozzi, 1615.

Fig. 20. Ville Contemporaine, Le Corbusier, 1922.

The Ville Contemporaine and the Plan Voisin

> *The 'Voisin' scheme does not claim to have found a final solution to the problem for the centre of Paris; but it may serve to raise the discussion to a level in keeping with the spirit of our age.... It sets up* principles *as against the medley of silly little reforms with which we are constantly deceiving ourselves.*[46]

The 1925 Plan Voisin is dependent in both a particular and a general way upon its ideal predecessor the Ville Contemporaine. Presented in 1922 at the Salon d'Automne, the Ville Contemporaine is based on a transportation network of two grids, the larger of which is rotated forty-five degrees, that is diagonally, to the first. The primary grid, with its major north-south and east-west axes, references the *cardo* and *decumanus* of early Roman military camps and earlier Middle and Far Eastern city plans as they were absorbed into Western traditions. The central square, occupied by a transportation center, and the four subsidiary open spaces are reminiscent of the ideal cities of the Italian Renaissance. The overlay of the two grids, while recalling L'Enfant's plan for Washington, D.C., seems to represent a conflation of the opposing theories of the linear and the radial-concentric growth and form of cities. The diagonals, beyond offering a convenience to transportation, tend to activate the ordering orthogonal grid which might otherwise be regarded as sterile and uninteresting.

Fundamentally, the Ville Contemporaine is made up of three building types: the cross-shape office towers, sixty stories in height; and two types of housing; *Immeuble Villas* and *Maison Redents*. The cross-shape office towers, of which there are twenty-four, stand in the center of the Ville Contemporaine. Surrounding these office buildings are the two housing types that Le Corbusier had developed because, "The problem of the house is the problem of the epoch. ... The equilibrium of society depends upon it." He was equally concerned with the relation of these parts to the whole, the architecture to city planning:

46 Le Corbusier, *The City of Tomorrow:* 288.

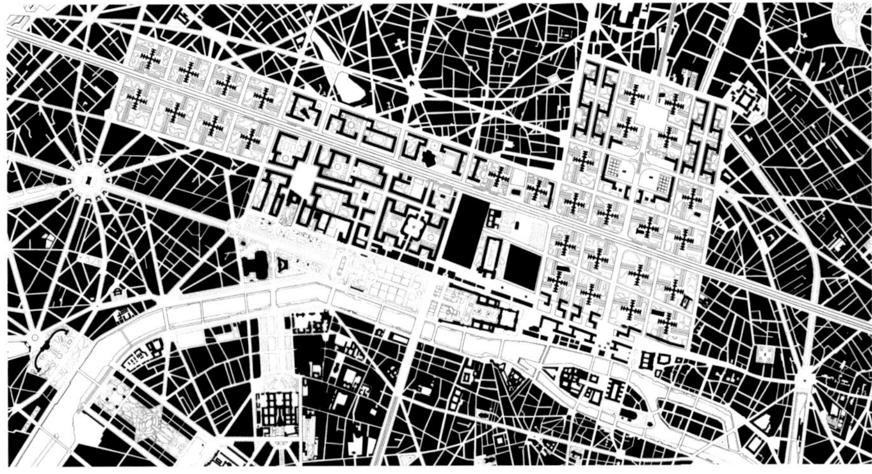

Fig. 21. Plan Voisin, Le Corbusier, 1925.

> *My role has been a technical one, to discover exactly how the development of a city takes place and to find a formula which should give the rules for classification on which all modern planning must rest.*[47]

The formal origins of the two housing types are closely linked to the archetypes previously cited as exemplars of the courtyard idea, the Place des Vosges, the Place Vendôme, and the Louvre. The closed courtyard *immeuble villas* play the same role as the block in a grid city; they create corridor streets and act as a texture, the edges of which can define spaces or fields.

The *maison redents* form open-ended enclosures rather than the closed spaces made by the *immeuble villas*. When used as repetitive units, they also have a textural quality and define a field. But due to their open form they cannot produce the hard-edged fields made by the *immeuble villas*. As used in the Ville Contemporaine, the *maison redents* also allow for the accommodation of a secondary grid, that of the diagonal.

The Ville Contemporaine, Le Corbusier's ideal city, is clearly his utopia, a city in a park arrayed with schools and stadiums, libraries and tennis courts, museums and running tracks, theaters and swimming pools. Physical culture as an aspect of the 'good life' is further implied in the conversion of the roofs of buildings: they are treated like the decks of ships where the body may be offered in ritual nudity to the glory of the elements of city planning—the 'sun, sky, trees, steel, and concrete'.

At the center of the city, standing foursquare, in that position formally reserved for ecclesiastical authority, is a city of towers symbolizing the power of the technological and economic forces which are now to bring about the millennium.

Turning to an examination of the Plan Voisin, an application of the ideal elements of the Ville Contemporaine to the non-ideal site of Paris, a number of things are immediately obvious. The ideal is at least partially derived from Paris; the ideal is then modified in application to Paris. There is accord with the primary, if approximate, east-west and north-south orientations and axes of historic Paris, including much of its roughly orthogonal street and block structure, but

47 Le Corbusier, *The City of Tomorrow*: 298.

Fig. 22. Paris, Turgot, 1739. Note the north-south axis crossing the Île de la Cité, a major axial 'contextual' reference in both the Plan Voisin and the 1937 Plan.

without the field-activating diagonals of the ideal. An elevated superhighway runs through the center of Paris from and into the countryside in both directions. This superhighway affirms the major east-west axis that lies roughly parallel to the Seine as the river passes the Île de la Cité and the Louvre, as well as the Rue de Rivoli and the Champs-Élysées.

The cross-shape towers are not uncompromisingly disposed according to the ideal geometry of the Ville Contemporaine. Their grid is slightly skewed to accommodate the not quite perpendicular axes of Paris. Otherwise, they are organized according to the several north-south axes of the various zones they occupy. Located to reinforce what was inherent in the plan prior to their placement, they also adjust with respect to the whole plan through insertion or deletion. The *maison redents* are used in a similar manner. They are slightly racked and skewed forming not-quite right angles allowing for a high level of accommodation to the plan irregularities of Paris.

The building types from the Ville Contemporaine are disposed in a series of zones along the east-west axis. Proceeding east to west, the first zone is formed by the cross-shape office towers axially focused on the Île de la Cité; the second zone by a transportation center east of the Palais Royale; the third zone by *maison redents*; and the fourth zone by additional cross-shape towers. Examining these zones makes it evident that the Plan Voisin was designed with more care at both large and small scales than a cursory glance reveals.

Considering each zone, now from west to east, the westernmost zone is made up of a field of eight cross-shape towers, four on each side of the east-west highway. This field of towers references a larger field related to the Rond Point on the east, the Arc de Triomphe on the west, and more generally the Trocadéro.

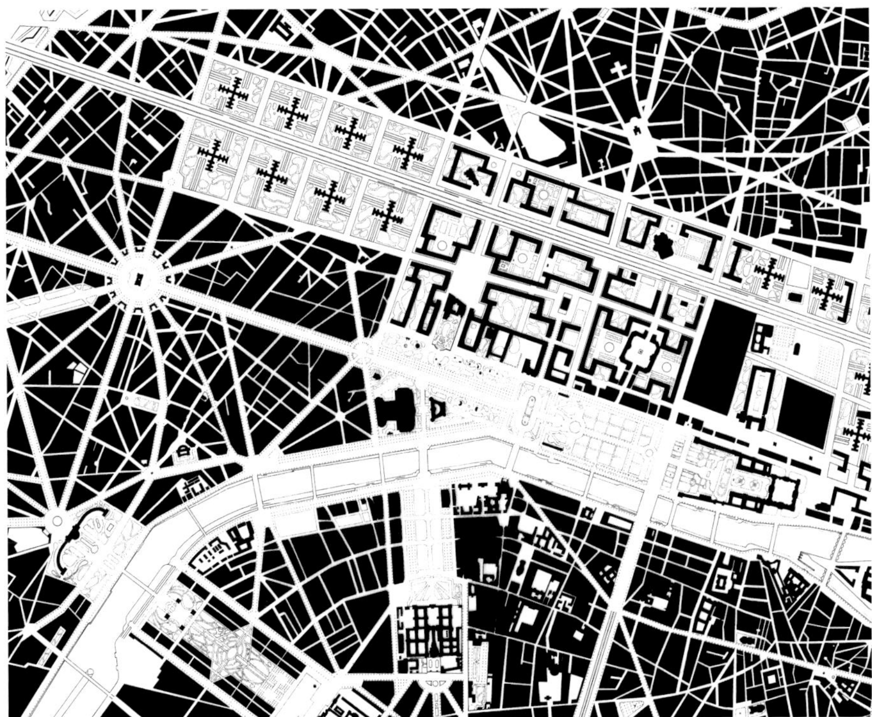

Fig. 23. Plan Voisin, detail.

The second zone is occupied primarily by *maison redents*. This field extends east-west from the face of the Louvre to the Rond Point. It is organized around three secondary north-south axes. One axis extends from the gardens of the Tuileries through the Place Vendôme to the Place de l'Opera. The Opera sits in a new courtyard space formed on three sides by *maison redents* and on the fourth by the colonnade-like structure of the elevated superhighway. A second north-south axis is that of the Rue Royale as it leads from the Place de la Concorde to the Madelaine. The Madelaine, and the new space around it, receive and shift an opposing axis created by the *redents* running between and through the transportation center on the east and extending west to continue along the south side of the second field of eight towers. At the Palais de l'Élysée, a new grand space is defined by the *redents*. Together they anchor the third north-south axis. The Palais de l'Élysée, on its opposite and south face, culminates a shifted axis from across the Seine that is created by the Esplanade and Gardens of the Hôtel des Invalides as it passes between the Grand Palais and Petit Palais. The south-facing buildings along the Rue de Rivoli and facing the Tuileries continues past the Place de la Concorde to the Rond Point. Their continuity is reinforced or reestablished by continuous *redent* housing, only interrupted when historically or architecturally expedient.

Stretching beneath the *pilotis* of all these flexible *maison redents*, and making the base plane to the fields of cross shape towers, is a carpet of green so that:

> *The Tuileries might be continued over the whole quarter of Paris in the form of parks, whether the formal French kind or in the undulating English manner and could be combined with the purely geometrical architecture.*[48]

48 Le Corbusier, *The City of Tomorrow:* 236.

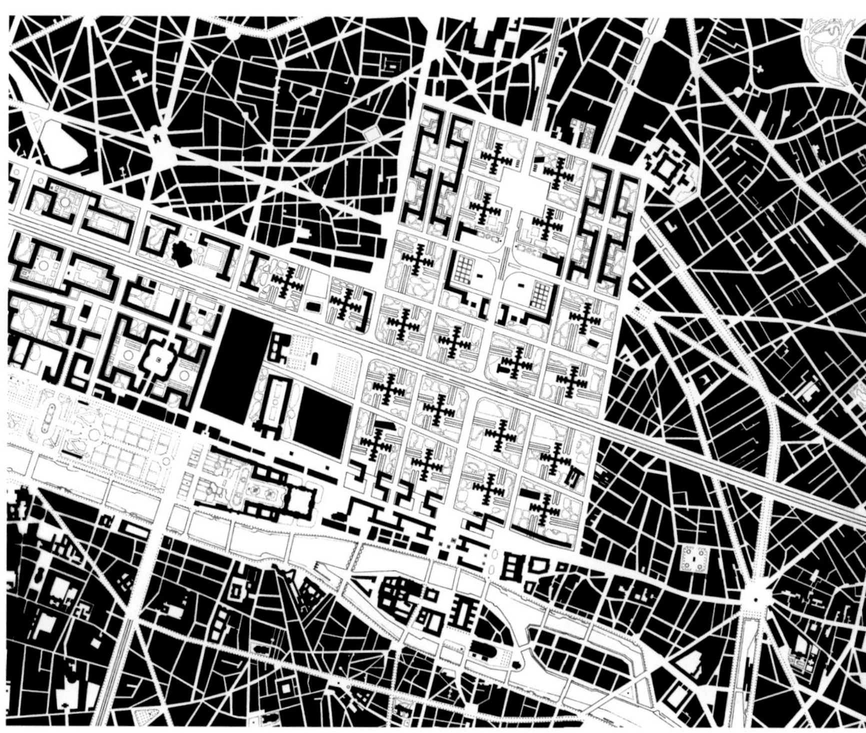

Fig. 24. 1925 Plan Voisin, detail, Le Corbusier.

The third zone is referred to as the Transportation Center. It references the Louvre on the south, two cross-shape towers on the north, and between them the Palais Royal and National Library. It is approximately centered on a north-south spatial axis that passes to the east of the Palais Royal. The two towers located just north of the super-highway reinforce the north-south axis. West of the Palais Royal is the new multi-level transportation center from and to which a new major southern highway crosses the Seine on a wide bridge passing directly in front of the wings of the Louvre as it opens to the Tuileries.

The fourth zone is the large field of eighteen office towers. It is centered on the north entrance road to the city and references the Île de la Cité. Approaching from the north, one proceeds above the tracks of the replaced Gare de l' Est through a forespace created by the four northernmost towers, and then into a larger open square marked by the Port St. Denis and the Port St. Martin. Once the northern portals of Paris, Le Corbusier described them as symbolizing arrival at its new center. Continuing south one encounters layers of elements making spatial zones perpendicular to the path of travel: past a row of four towers, beneath the superhighway, and past two more rows of four towers. Arriving in a space formed by *redent* type buildings at the east-west Rue de Rivoli, the axis is visually focused by a new obelisk and paired with another obelisk—such that the axis of the space shifts slightly to the east while the route along the edge of the space crosses the Seine and the Île de la Cité to the left bank.

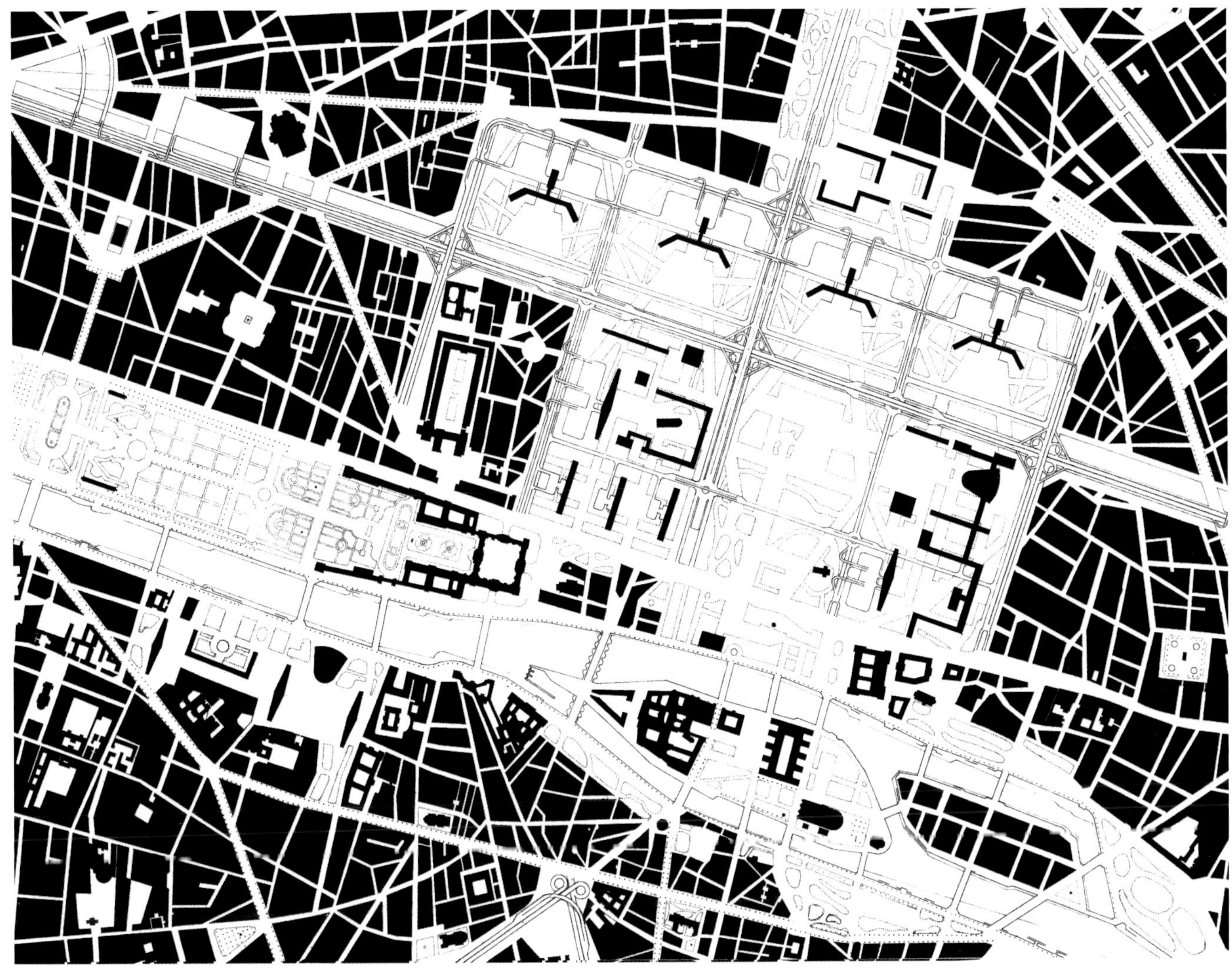

Fig. 25. 1937 Plan, detail, Le Corbusier.

Taken in its entirety the Plan Voisin, like the buildings contemporaneous to it, was offered as a polemic on the methods of architecture and city planning. When interpreted as a real proposition it was roundly criticized with justification. But it is well to recall Le Corbusier's comment that "The 'Voisin' scheme does not claim to have found a final solution to the problem for the center of Paris; but it may serve to raise the discussion to a level in keeping with the spirit of our age". We imagine Le Corbusier intended the 1937 Plan in the same spirit.

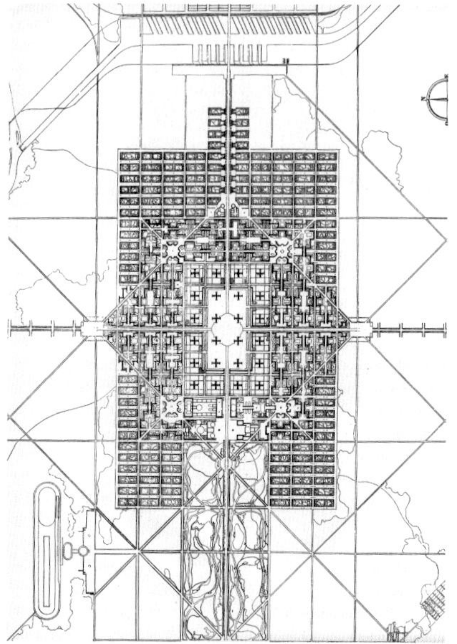

Fig. 26. Ville Contemporaine, 1922, Le Corbusier.

Le Corbusier's 1937 Plan for Paris

The 1937 Plan for Paris represents an appreciable condensation of the area to be rebuilt and a change in Le Corbusier's spatial preferences. Just as the Plan Voisin was dependent upon the ideal proposals of the Ville Contemporaine, the 1937 Paris Plan is dependent upon the further development of these ideas, as seen in the 1933 publication of *La Ville Radieuse.*

With but few changes the Ville Radieuse is made up of the same building types as the Ville Contemporaine. The transportation grid of streets remains the same, but the Ville Radieuse is linear as opposed to the more centralized organization of the Ville Contemporaine. In order, it consists of 14 cross-shape office towers, a transportation terminal (rail and air), and *redent* housing with a central axial green in which civic, governmental, and service facilities are located. Separated from the *redent* housing by a strip of park, there is an area of factories, warehouses, and heavy industry.

The *immeuble villa* housing type has disappeared. No direct explanation is given. But they created corridor streets that had become anathema to Le Corbusier's planning goals because of their association with narrow streets, crowded tenements, stagnant air, limited sunlight, lack of sanitation, and consequent poor health and the resulting axiom: 'sun, space, greenery'.

Comparing the Ville Radieuse and the Ville Contemporaine at first seems difficult. But it appears that the Ville Contemporaine was thought of as a real city plan, albeit ideal and utopian, while the Ville Radieuse was put forward as a generalized zoning scheme. The Ville Contemporaine, a city for "three million inhabitants", has geometries that recall the ideal and abstract centralized cities of the Renaissance, but it also has a great sense of locale or place. Supplementing the areas of offices, housing, and industry, there are forests, parks, and large athletic fields as well as formed spaces referencing Rome and Paris; its eastern entrance an adaptation of the Piazza del Popolo, its western terminus an adaptation of the Gardens of the Tuileries and the Champs-Élysées. For all these temporal references, the Ville Contemporaine is still clearly utopian. To paraphrase Karl Mannheim, it is a physical orientation transcending reality, bursting the bounds of the existing order.[49]

The Ville Radieuse appears to be put forward less as a coherent plan for an ideal city than as a generalized zoning scheme, a sorting out or compilation of ideal building types. Arguments about zoning and function, circulation, and housing types abound.[50] Was this perhaps a realization by Le Corbusier that there is a basic conflict between the fixed and static character of an ideal city and the maxim of change basic to the 'new epoch'? In 1933 Le Corbusier wrote that the architectural revolution was over[51] and the elements of the new order (Modern architecture) were generally accepted. As a means for realizing the ideals of the new order, the utopian Ville Contemporaine had been offered as a revolutionary manifesto, intended to transcend reality and break the bounds of the existing order. A few years later, the Ville Radieuse was offered for the institutionalization of the ideals of a revolution in a post-revolutionary period.[52]

49 Mannheim, Karl, *Ideology and Utopia:* 192-104.

50 Translated as *The Radiant City.*

51 Le Corbusier, *The Radiant City:* 96; "Architectural revolution? *Already accomplished.* Industry, practical production techniques? They already exist."

52 Ibid., 154; "And this plan is your despot: a tyrant a tribune of the people. Without other help it will plead its cause, reply to objections, overcome the opposition of private interest, thrust aside outworn customs, rescind outmoded regulations, and create its own authority."

With the publication of the *Ville Radieuse*, there is the appearance of several new building types, and their spatial dispositions. They define space, not by surrounding, enclosing, or even forming the corners of it: they have come to have an acropolean presence, occupying and channeling space. One building, referred to by Le Corbusier as a "spine building" is a slab with origins in his Pavillion Suisse and Salvation Army. A second is a "lens" building of varying heights that first appears in Le Corbusier's 1933 second scheme for Algiers and then in the 1937 plan for Paris. A third is a 'Y' shape tower with a plan geometry that shares the orthogonal and diagonal geometries of the transportation grid. Its rectilinear cupped face "seems to pick up by its concave surface the whole surrounding landscape and to establish a relationship that carries its effect far beyond the actual bounds of the architecture itself"[53]. This quality gives it a frontality the cross-shape towers did not have.

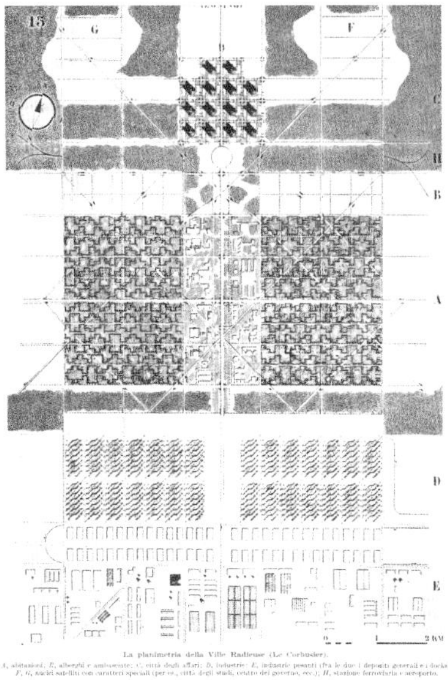

Fig. 27. Ville Radieuse, 1933-34, Le Corbusier.

In the 1937 Plan, the major east-west highway of the Voisin scheme remains in its original position. The primary north-south axis shifts slightly to just west of the Boulevard de Strasbourg. This road, as it enters Paris from the north, passes between the Gare de l'Est and the Gare du Nord, but instead of stopping as in the Plan Voisin at the Rue de Rivoli, it continues underground, tunnels beneath the Seine about halfway between the Pont Neuf and the Pont au Change, to resurface in a space created just south of the Boulevard St. Germain. There it interchanges with two new elevated highways, one toward Orleans, Toulouse, Lyon, and the Mediterranean, the other towards Rennes, Brest, Bordeaux, and Biarritz.

Approaching Paris from the north, the entrance condition, previously created by two of the cross-shape towers of the Voisin Plan, is now signified by the penetration of a plane which is stipulated by the long surfaces of the 'Y' towers aligned in super-blocks just north of the highway; they all stand facing the Seine. The four 'Y' towers are symmetrical about the north-south axis of the scheme, but the central axis of the municipal area lies in the center of the zone stipulated by the 'Y' tower immediately to the east of the north-south axis. Each tower is the northern terminus of a north-south zone of civic buildings, the westernmost of which contains the Palais Royale. To the south of these towers and new highway, Le Corbusier's scheme stretches nearly to the banks of the Seine. This area, like the rest of the plan, is composed of east-west zones or layers of space.

As in the Plan Voisin, the entire scheme is under-laced with gardens, in this case geometrized like those of the Louvre. On the left bank of the Seine, running parallel to the gardens of the Louvre is a new "*cité governementale*". Like the royal garden it faces, this area is a park containing the buildings from which 20th century France would be ruled.

We might debate whether Le Corbusier's Plan Voisin and 1937 Plan were intended only, as he said, "to raise the discussion to a level in keeping with the spirit of our age" or much more: to again paraphrase Mannheim, to serve as utopian models transcending reality for the purpose of bursting the bounds of the existing order.[54] It can little be debated that they did so: and such were the intentions of the *Ville Radieuse*; Le Corbusier's many subsequent illustrated planning schemes, and the arguments and proposals made by CIAM.

53 Le Corbusier, *The New World of Space:* 50.

54 Mannheim, Karl, *Ideology and Utopia:* 192-104.

Conclusion (III)

Images are not arguments, rarely even lead to proof, but the mind craves them...[55]

HENRY ADAMS

The Ville Radieuse, the child of Modern architecture, was to have delivered human kind from the evils of the city just as the Jewish Messiah was to have delivered the children of Israel from this earthly life. The *Ville Radieuse* has proven a great disappointment. No longer an infant, having reached adolescence, its mystical newness no longer veils its shortcomings. It has been reproached for its demonstrated lack of precociousness, spanked by politicians, economists, and sociologists, and suffered public derision by aestheticians proud to point out the blemishes of what was to have been a most beauteous child.

Whether the outcry is directed against the child or the shortcomings of its all-too-earthly parents, no one denies the justice of the criticism. Despite claims to the contrary, the manner by which we have been 'renewing' our cities has been cavalier and we are distressed with the outcome. If we were to create a potpourri or collage of all the areas of U.S. cities that have been 'renewed' since WWII and put this creation on public display, it would elicit disheartening reviews. The constancy of the image created would bespeak a lack of experimentation and an over-dependency on some vague notion of what a city, or the parts of a city, ought to be like. It would, in all likelihood, look like a higher density Garden City as envisioned by Ebenezer Howard and/or like a bastardized version of Le Corbusier's Ville Contemporaine. It would include building types reminiscent of the early projects of Modern architecture, more recent versions of slab building of which Le Corbusier's Marseille Block is the prototype, and the new darling of urban designers, the linear building including variations on the 'aqueduct'.

This constancy of solutions, while partially dependent on the proliferation of Modern building types, can hardly be the result of a constancy presented by each site and programmatic facts, thereby making the results inevitably the same. One has a feeling some psychic force is mysteriously producing these results. One is neither truly surprised nor truly alarmed as yet by this fictive construct because, despite the banners of functionalism and technocracy paraded by Modern architecture, at any moment in time there are a few who have the ability to create new things or new ideas, in short to lead, and the rest quite naturally tend to follow or to mimic that lead.

Genuine alarm does not occur until mentally comparing the fictive collage or potpourri with the real item, the existing city. The rapidity with which the reality is approaching the condition of the potpourri gives pause. The result of utopian ideas warped by reality, it manifests the worst of both conditions and little of their best. But this has not been the target of most verbal barrages fired at our misguided attempts at city renewal. The fault-finding has been specific rather than general, as if, having made one false turn at the start of a maze, we might correct our course by numerous correct turns from that point forward. This is not the case. Rather than being dissatisfied with some specific aspects of attempts at 'renewal' we are, in fact, terribly dissatisfied with the entire image and the results.

55 Adams, Henry, *The Education of Henry Adams:* 498.

Since the process of continual renewal is as old as cities themselves, our dissatisfaction does not stem from the nature of renewal. To what might we attribute the constancy of the collage? Practical rationales are unconvincing. Such consistency requires the tacit or unconscious acceptance of an idea or image by a great many people. Such broad acceptance must be founded on faith. The faith may be based in fact or fancy, but in either case it is faith. And while particularized criticism of the faith may be questioned, its foundations remain unaltered. Upon the realization that the existence of such a mystical faith in a particular image was having a profound effect on the physical shape of our cities, we felt moved to inquire into its origins and its values, for in its misappropriation it has made great strides in banishing from our cities what we have come to define and value as urbanism itself.

If the reader remains skeptical of whether an image held in the collective unconscious of a people could affect to a large degree what they do, one has merely to consult history. The creation of the ideal city of the Renaissance had a profound effect on the shape of city growth that followed. One could not critique the suburban counterpart of our topic without mentioning Ebenezer Howard's Garden City or Frank Lloyd Wright's Broadacre City. Living, as we are, in the middle of the 20th century, and influenced by these 20th century ideas, our inclination is to accept our condition as fact, caused by things, events, or ideas, except that if these influences are uncovered the unhappy condition may be remedied. This is the task we took on. Disenchanted with the results that entertainment of a particular image, the Modernist city inspired by Le Corbusier, has brought about, because minor alterations have not remedied the situation, we have examined the image we believe has so influenced the shape of our cities in the hopes that, by bringing that image to a conscious level, we may fully appreciate both its potentials and limitations, and create a new one more in conjunction with the exigencies of our own time.

Although the acceptance of his architecture has been limited, even in a period that institutionalized progressive architecture, Le Corbusier created the most powerful image of the 'new city' of the 20th century. That image, readily absorbed into the unconscious of an era, perhaps indicates a deep resonance with an image of the city already present in what Jung would call our racial [cultural] unconscious. Like the city of the New Jerusalem promised in the Book of Revelations,[56] Le Corbusier's city would sit, foursquare, glittering in the distance. The other architectural utopias of this century, those of Wright, Hilberseimer, Mendelsohn, the Goodman brothers, and even the futurist, St. Elia, have provided no mental image that has stuck in the collective mind with the force of Le Corbusier's city of towers—the unacknowledged faith and force that architecture and physical planning operate under today, secularized with little awareness of the original.

The cross-shaped housing towers of Harlem or the lower east side of New York, and the dismal *Unités* of Chicago's south side, bespeak of Le Corbusier and his Ville Contemporaine. We are in the presence of an image whose pervasive misuse can only be compared in its damage to the Clarence Perry–Frank Lloyd Wright image of suburban America. We are impressed that the work of Le Corbusier, particularly the later work, is suburban in intent. In this respect Le Corbusier and Wright are surprisingly close together. Both men, in their reaction to the

56 See especially Bible verses 10-25.

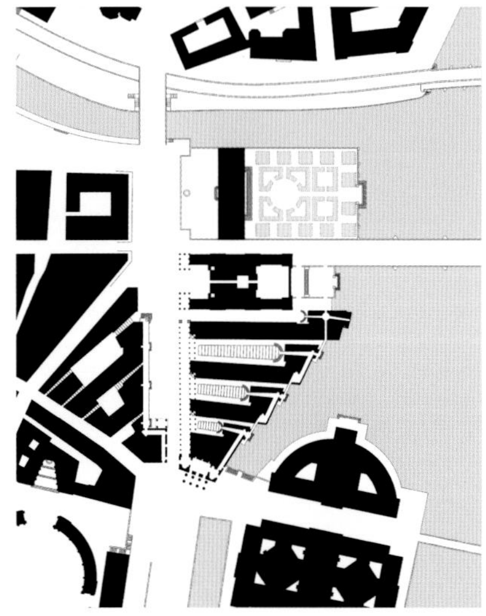

above:
Fig. 28. "Competition for the Royal Chancellery", Stockholm, Sweden, Gunnar Asplund, 1922, Charles Graves, *Looking @ Cities* [https://lookingatcities.info/].

opposite:
Fig. 29. The Long Meadow, Prospect Park, Brooklyn, NY, Frederick Law Olmsted and Calvert Vaux, 1866; a large urban park landscape designed to appear naturalistic.

horrors that industrialization had wrought on the 19th century city, hoped to secure for the collective society, the family, and each individual, their modicum of 'sun, space, and greenery'. While the concept of the city in the park is somewhat rural in building density and spatial definition, Le Corbusier, in his later work, directed attacks at the conventional garden city because its ideal sacrificed the distinction between city and country. In contrast, he employed the principles of his Radiant City to produce designs for agrarian towns.

For Paris, particularly the 1937 Plan, two things are done. A large void is carved in the texture of the old city, a Haussmann-like move carried out at the scale of the entire city. Then the old parts of Paris are reordered by the new ideal pieces added. Ultimately a problem arises; when the old urban texture, the context for the 'new', has been replaced, then the building on *pilotis,* the new order, becomes the context for the older relics of urbanism. Likewise, these new idealized forms lose their power to reorganize the old city, for everything has become too thin. Perhaps Le Corbusier's town of *Unités* is a desirable alternative to suburban sprawl, but in our city centers?

The alternative would appear to be some form of contextural approach, or strategy of local response. Such a method precludes any possible dialogue between the real and the ideal, although the contexturally derived building or space can allude to idealized prototypes. Contexturalism, however, could profit from a vocabulary of slightly more idealized pieces than those which it can locally derive. Such idealized pieces could be used not to superimpose order, but to imply that order had always existed, to convert the random into the ordered without undergoing a change in scale. The whole process is one of completion. An incomplete order is intuited and then either strengthened or completed. Implicit in such a method is a value judgment: that the existing scale and type of architectural order (status quo) are worth preserving. What is needed is a synthesis of the utopian and the contextural, a synthesis of change and status quo.

One wonders what might have resulted had Le Corbusier been commissioned to rebuild portions of cities as he was commissioned to build buildings. It is possible that his work might have taken on either the contextural/ideal aspects of the *Ilot Insalubre #6* through the development of new building types, or that the contextural adjustment of the ideal parts, as in the Voisin Plan where the *maison redents* are racked to absorb irregularities in the grid, would have been developed further to put the 'new' on a meaningful continuum with the 'old'.

Author's Note:

This thesis researched, drawn, and written with Stuart Cohen also provided the basis for later related publications on Le Corbusier, the first, on Ronchamp, was likewise co-authored.

"The Pilgrimage Chapel at Ronchamp: Its Architectonic Structure and Typological Antecedents", *Oppositions* 19/20, MIT Press, Win/Spr 1981: 42-157.

"Le Corbusier: Type, Archetype, and Iconography", College of Architecture and Landscape Architecture, University of Minnesota, *Midgard Monograph* 2, Princeton Architectural Press, 1991: 51-89.

"Le Corbusier: Symbolic Themes at Chandigarh", *Marg, A Magazine of the Arts,* Marg Publications, Mumbai, India,1999: 94-106.

BIBLIOGRAPHY

Adams, Henry, *The Education of Henry Adams,* Houghton Mifflin, Boston (1919) 1964.

Barzun, Jacques, *Darwin, Marx, Wagner,* Doubleday, New York, (1942) 1958.

Barzun, Jacques, *Classic, Romantic and Modern,* Doubleday, New York, (1943) 1961.

Becker, Carl, *The Heavenly City of the Eighteenth Century Philosophers*, Yale University Press, New Haven, (1932) 1966.

Bury, J. L., *The Idea of Progress,* Dover, New York, (1921) 1955.

Cohn, Norman, *The Pursuit of the Millennium,* Harper and Row, New York, (1957) 1961.

Eliot, T. S., *The Sacred Wood*, Barnes and Noble, New York, (1920) 1966.

Gray, Christopher, *Cubist Aesthetic Theories*, The John Hopkins Press, Baltimore, (1953) 1961.

Hayek, F. A., *The Counter-Revolution of Science*, The Free Press, Glencoe, (1952) 1967.

Herbert, Robert L., ed., *Modern Artists on Art*, Englewood Cliffs. Prentice-Hall, Englewood Cliffs, 1964.

Kahnweiler, Daniel-Henry, *The Rise of Cubism*, Wittenborn, Schultz Inc., New York, 1949.

Kubler, George, *The Shape of Time*, Yale University Press, New Haven, 1962.

Le Corbusier. (pseudonym of Charles Édouard Jeanneret-Gris).

The City of Tomorrow, John Rodker, London, 1929.

Concerning Town Planning, The Architectural Press, London, 1947.

Creation is a Patient Search, Frederick A. Praeger, New York, 1960.

Modulor 2, Harvard University Press, Cambridge, 1958.

The New World of Space, Reynal and Hitchcock, New York, 1948.

Les Plans Le Corbusier de Paris, Les Editions de Minuit, Paris, 1956.

The Radiant City, Orion Press, New York, (1933, trans. 1964) 1964.

Towards a New Architecture, Frederick A. Praeger, New York, (1923, trans. 1927) 1959.

When the Cathedrals were White, McGraw-Hill, New York, (1937, trans. 1946) 1964.

Le Corbusier et Pierre Jeanneret, *Oeuvre Compléte*, 7 volumes, W. Boesiger-Editions Girsberger, Zurich, 1910-1965.

Mannheim, Karl, *Ideology and Utopia*, Harcourt, Brace and World, n.d. New York, (1929) 1936.

Ozenfant, A., *Foundations of Modern Art*, Dover, New York, (1925) 1952.

Rowe, Colin.

"The Architecture of Utopia", *Granta*, 1959.

"Chicago Frame," *The Architectural Review*, Nov 1956.

"Le Corbusier: Utopian Architect", *The Listener*, Feb 12, 1959.

"Dominican Monastery of La Tourette, Eveux-sur-Abresle, Lyons", *The Architectural Review*, 129, Jun 1961.

Rowe, Colin and Slutzky, Robert, "Transparency: Literal and Phenomenal", *Perspecta* 8, 1963.

Scully Jr., Vincent, *Modern Architecture*, George Braziller, New York (1961), 1965.

Tuveson, Ernest Lee, *Millennium and Utopia: A Study in the Background of the Idea of Progress*, Harper and Row, New York, Evanston and London (1937, trans. 1946) 1964.

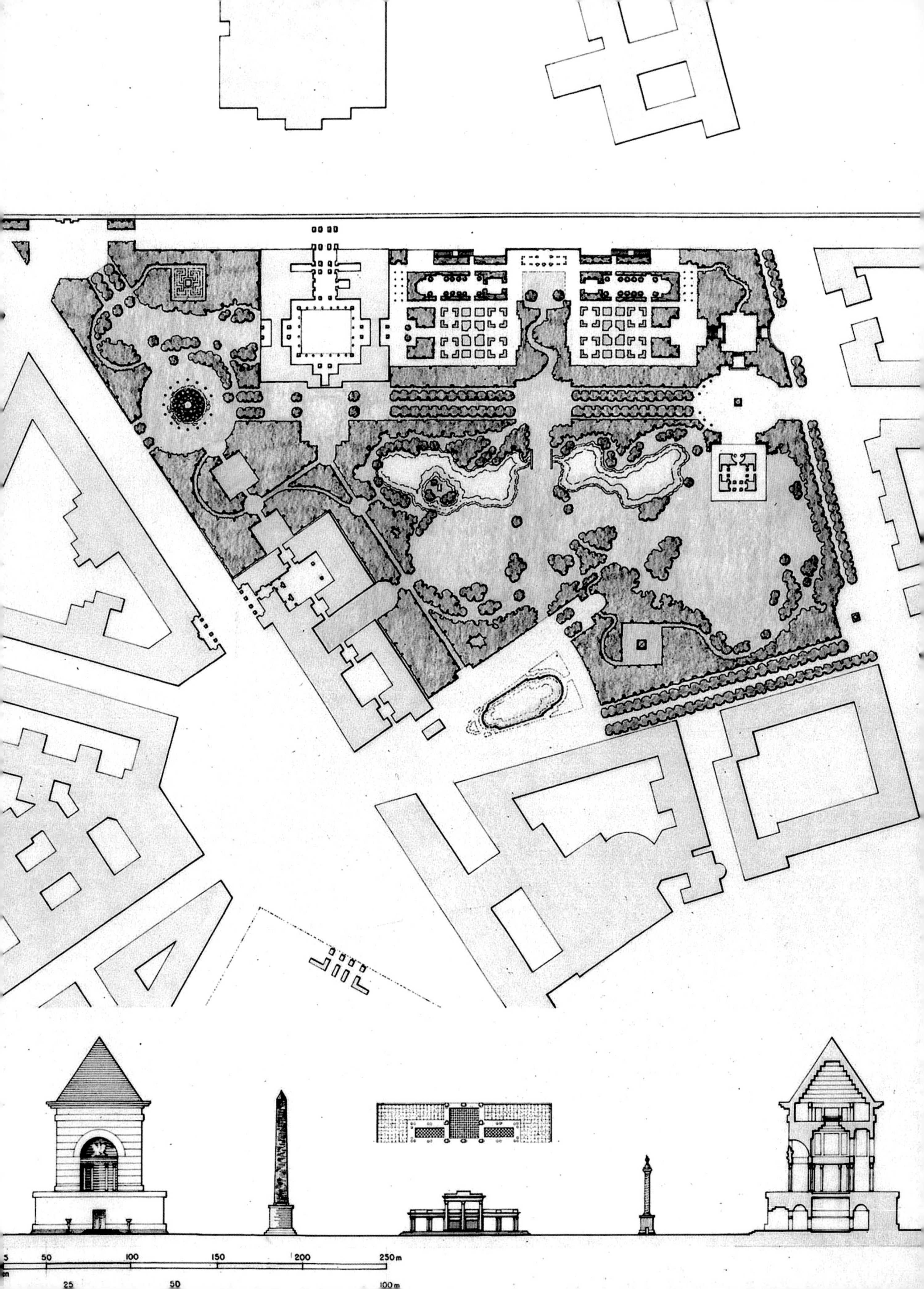

5
50
100
150
200
250 m
25
50
100 m

Contextualizing Contextualism

Brian Kelly

In the course of history, man has occupied himself more frequently with objects transcending his scope of existence than with those immanent in his existence and, despite this, actual and concrete forms of social life have been built upon the basis of such ideological states of mind which were incongruent with reality. Such an incongruent orientation became utopian only when in addition it tended to burst the bonds of the existing order.[1]

KARL MANNHEIM

What is needed is a synthesis of the utopian and the contextural [sic], *a synthesis of change and status quo.*[2]

STUART COHEN AND STEVEN HURTT

Contextualism is often associated with the theories of Colin Rowe and his Urban Design Studio at Cornell University. The term originated among students in studio discussions and was shared with a broader academic and professional audience by Tom Schumacher in his 1971 *Casabella* article, "Contextualism: Urban Ideals and Deformations". Contextualism proposed new ways to deal with the utopian overtones of Modern, specifically Corbusian, urbanism. This paper posits that in the 1960s students in the Rowe Studio (and Rowe himself) were working through the implications of Corbusian urbanism attempting to find some form of *rapprochement* with the traditional city. The working process of the early years was one in which the modes of Le Corbusier's Ville Contemporaine or Ville Radieuse were taken as a starting point and efforts were made to tame or domesticate this utopian model to work in traditional contexts, implicitly valuing the Corbusian model before the traditional city. Schumacher's 1971 article signaled a change in direction for the Studio, which over time abandoned Corbusian urbanism as its starting point and concentrated more on the existing character of the traditional city into which interventions could be made to elevate the circumstantial to the ideal. The shift in focus from the city of Modern architecture to that of the traditional city required the studio to reassess its own methods and tools.

frontispiece:
Prinz Albrecht Museum & Garden, Berlin.
Brian Kelly, Studio project, 1982.

1 Mannheim, Karl, *Ideology and Utopia: An Introduction to the Sociology of Knowledge*, Harcourt, Brace, (London 1936), New York, 1954: 173.

2 Cohen, Stuart E.; Hurtt, Steven W., "Le Corbusier: The Architecture of City Planning", Master's thesis, Cornell University, mimeo, 1967: 70.

Utopia First, Then Contextualism

Contextualism first entered the contemporary architectural and urban design lexicon in the mid-1960s. The term is widely recognized to have its initial connection to these disciplines by means of a 1967 master's thesis authored by Stuart Cohen and Steven Hurtt.[3] Cohen and Hurtt, who were graduate students in Colin Rowe's Urban Design Studio at Cornell, introduced the concept in the closing arguments of their thesis titled, "Le Corbusier: The Architecture of City Planning".

As one might intuit from the title of the thesis, Contextualism was perhaps the by-product, or at best, a subordinate theme of their investigations rather than a central hypothesis. Cohen and Hurtt tell us in their abstract that they intend to focus on "the formal aspects of Le Corbusier's work"[4] but the thesis engages much more than that. The thesis extends utopian themes introduced by Colin Rowe in two 1959 articles, "Le Corbusier: Utopian Architect" and "The Architecture of Utopia"[5], through analysis of Le Corbusier's urban and architectural projects.

Prior to the two 1959 articles engaging the topic of utopia, Rowe's writings focused largely on architectural issues. With the exception of the article "Lockhart, Texas" written with John Hejduk and published in *Architectural Record* in 1957, Rowe offers little published writing as evidence of his insights into the topic of urbanism until the 1978 publication of *Collage City* with Fred Koetter. In his introduction to "Lockhart, Texas", in *As I Was Saying*, Rowe asserts that the article was intended as an installment in a series on small-town America that never came to fruition.

Lockhart recounts Rowe's direct encounter with a real American urban landscape. In contrast to the later utopia articles, Lockhart, a paradigmatic Texas courthouse town, really exists, and although its architectural origins are, with a certain amount of tongue-in-cheek, assigned to a lost "Master of Lockhart", the urban situation was in Rowe's mind contrived by customary means to serve as a representation of a social order:

> *...the American courthouse town.... A completely normal and widely distributed type, scattered throughout the northern states and consistently reoccurring throughout the South, it is scarcely the product of any deliberately expressed taste—and yet one assumes its repetition was inspired by more than mere habit. For patently this is a town dedicated to an idea, and its scheme is neither fortuitous nor whimsical .... There is hence a curious decorum about these towns which, however run-down they might often be, are apt to display an air of generality. Urbanistic phenomena they palpably are, but they are also emblems of a political theory .... They are the foyers of a republican ceremonial, and their uncompromising form neatly condenses all the imponderables of republican principles. It is the almost classical typicality, the emblematic significance, and the completely adequate symbolism of these towns that is responsible for their seeming antiquity.*[6]

Lockhart and its American courthouse town cousins provide diagrams in built form supporting republican *virtu* and casting urbanism as a quintessentially political undertaking. Importantly these manifestations of urbanism seem to have little preoccupation with the utopian, and they are of a genre of urbanistics that Rowe would return to in later writings. They constitute Rowe's broader interest

3 While there may be some dispute regarding whether the term "context" was first used at Cornell, or perhaps earlier at Princeton (specifically by Robert Venturi) it is to the Rowe Studio that we must credit much of the development and dissemination of Contextual theory and practice.

4 Cohen and Hurtt (1967): 1.

5 Cohen and Hurtt (1967) cite Colin Rowe's "Le Corbusier: Utopian Architect", *The Listener*, Feb 12, 1959, but do not cite Rowe's, "The Architecture of Utopia", first published in *Granta* 63, Jan 24, 1959: 20-26, 41, reprinted in Rowe, Colin, *As I Was Saying: Recollections and Miscellaneous Essays* 1, *Texas, Pre-Texas, Cambridge*, Caragonne, Alexander, ed., MIT Press, Cambridge, MA, and London, 1996. Though the latter essay is not referenced in the Cohen and Hurtt thesis, the themes it presents are pervasive throughout the document, so might the content of that article have naturally influenced discourse between Rowe and his students?

6 Rowe, Colin; Hejduk, John, "Lockhart, Texas", *Architectural Record*, Mar 1957. Cited in Rowe (1996/1): 57.

in the *psycho-cultural field* that contributes to the formulation of any architectural or urban proposition.

In contrast to "Lockhart, Texas", "The Architecture of Utopia" traces the origins of architectural utopias to the Italian Renaissance. Utopia, in its Renaissance incarnation, is a fusion of Jewish millennial thought and neo-Platonism. Filarete's centralized town plan for Sforzinda, although never built, provides Rowe with the ideal paired with the built specimen Palmanova (1593), which owes its realization as much to military planning as utopian thought. Rowe continues his narrative by brokering an overview of utopian appearances in architectural discourse through the 17th, 18th, and 19th centuries that variously distinguish between formal propositions and ideological imperatives. In the 19th century, Rowe suggests utopian themes remained untouched by any significant architectural talent, having become a "somewhat provincial idea" and because "Utopia seems now to have descended the social scale; for it is apparently no longer concerned with the redemption of the society as a whole, but only with the redemption of its lower strata".[7]

Utopian thought returns full-force in the 20th century and the utopian impulse in modern architecture is in Rowe's mind "indisputable".[8] He identifies the dynamic cities of Futurism as evidence of this utopian mindset, but focuses on Le Corbusier's Ville Radieuse as the most vivid example of a contemporary utopian expression. Although the discussion of Le Corbusier's urbanism is admittedly brief in the essay, Rowe offers a glimpse at his opinion regarding Le Corbusier's utopian vision, "in reality the Ville Radieuse would be *almost* as boring as Sforzinda, before it, if it has a similar schematic monotony",[9] but he offers little more critique of Corbusian urbanism or of utopia itself in a present-day context.

"The Architecture of Utopia" is fueled in part by Karl Mannheim's *Ideology and Utopia* (1936), which asserts "a state of mind is utopian when it is incongruous with the state of reality in which it occurs ... [and] tends to shatter, either partially or wholly, the order of things prevailing at the time".[10] Then it is curious to find Rowe proceeding rather cautiously in his assessment of Le Corbusier's utopian urbanism. Considering the Plan Voisin proposed to "shatter" and upset the prevailing Parisian order of 1925, one must imagine that Rowe was still getting his footing in the arena of urbanistic critique and perhaps was not yet ready to take on Le Corbusier's legacy. Likewise, it was perhaps too early for an all-out critique of the misguided application of Corbu-inspired urbanism in post-WWII Britain and urban renewal in the United States. "Le Corbusier: Utopian Architect" offers no additional resistance to the implications of contemporary utopian thought and little substantive critique of Le Corbusier's role as its agent of implementation. In later life, Rowe himself was aware of this and in his postscript to the article, as it appears in *As I Was Saying,* he simply writes, "But how quickly I changed my mind about Utopia ...".[11]

Critiques of Modern urbanism began to appear in the early 1960s, most notably with Jane Jacobs' *The Death and Life of Great American Cities* (1961) leading the way. Gordon Cullen's *Townscape* (1961) provided a counter-argument to large-scale Modern urbanism, but Cullen was too preoccupied with the picturesque and lacked the kind of intellectual grounding necessary to capture Rowe's interest.

7 Rowe, Colin, "The Architecture of Utopia", in *The Mathematics of the Ideal Villa and Other Essays*, MIT Press, Cambridge, MA, and London, 1976: 210.

8 Ibid.: 211.

9 Rowe dedicates only nine lines of text to a discussion of Le Corbusier in "The Architecture of Utopia".

10 Mannheim (1954): 173.

11 Rowe (1996/1): 142.

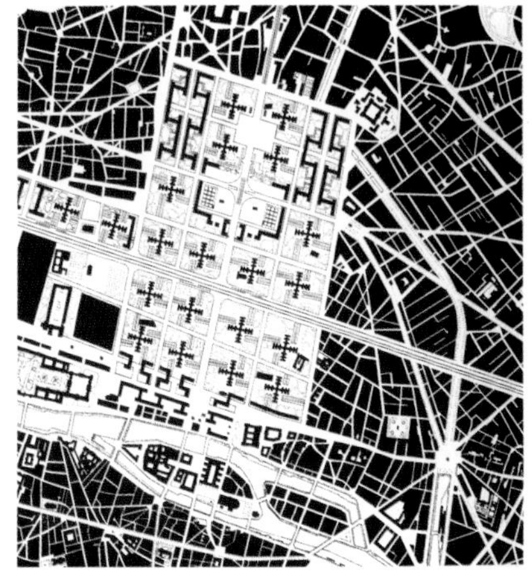

Fig. 1. Detail, Plan Voisin, Le Corbusier 1925. Drawing by Stuart E. Cohen and Steven W. Hurtt.

Consequently, we can see the work done in Rowe's Urban Design Studio (including the studio projects, theses, and essays by his students) in the early 1960–70s as a laboratory of ideas that helped Rowe develop his urbanistic posture empirically. These projects tested the waters and allowed Rowe the time to provide substantive arguments based on observations of design processes and actual design alternatives rather than on *a priori* conjectures. In the two 1959 essays, Rowe set the stage for the Cohen and Hurtt thesis (and much of the work in the Urban Design Studio) by having articulated that there was a problem with utopia and that Le Corbusier was a Utopian architect. That is, utopias tended to obliterate the *status quo* (not good for the city) and the *enfant célèbre* of Rowe's theoretical fortress was one of its champions (not good for Rowe).

Contextualism or Contexturalism

Cohen and Hurtt offer the Ville Contemporaine (1922) as an articulation of Le Corbusier's urban principles in an idealized form, uncompromised by pre-existing site circumstances:

> *The primary grid, with its major north-south and east-west axes, clearly makes reference to the cardo-decumanus of early Roman military camps and earlier Middle and Far Eastern city plans as they were absorbed into Western traditions of ideal cities. The central square, occupied by a transportation center, and the four subsidiary open spaces are reminiscent of the ideal cities of the Italian Renaissance.*[12]

The Ville Contemporaine is employed to represent the ideal, the utopian city in the garden, which later became deformed by the pre-existing urban texture of Paris in the 1925 Plan Voisin (Fig. 1) as could also be said of Le Corbusier's 1937 Plan for Paris. The dialectic between the traditional city and the city in the park, between the existing texture or context and the idealized utopian order, is offered as the basis for their argument.

In their discourse, however, neither the Ville Contemporaine nor the Plan Voisin are vilified as might have been the case in later commentaries emanating from Rowe Studios, particularly after the publication of *Collage City*. Cohen and Hurtt acknowledge that the Plan Voisin was poorly received in its 1925 debut, but they counter:

> *The general reaction to Le Corbusier's proposal was that he had brashly dropped his Ville Contemporaine, an ideal city for three million inhabitants, into the center of Paris with little regard for what already existed. Although we will argue that the Voisin scheme is far from insensitive to Paris, it is clearly dependent in both a particular and a general way upon its ideal predecessor.*[13]

The authors methodically work through the implications of the Plan Voisin and other Le Corbusier projects related to city planning. They acknowledge a give-and-take between the existing city and the imposition of a new order that becomes problematic "when the old urban texture, the context for the 'new', has been replaced ... these new idealized forms lose their power to reorganize the old city for everything has become too thin".[14]

12 Cohen and Hurtt (1967): 31-32. If we can allow the images that Le Corbusier crafted to count as much as his words, then the great central square, the transportation center, contains a reading that establishes an explicit connection between the Ville Contemporaine and Renaissance site planning. At the core of this city is a double square field, populated by eight Cartesian towers, and anchored at its center by the *cardo-decumanus,* which appears to slip beneath a large quatrefoil form–the transportation center. This constitutes an almost direct quotation of Michelangelo's scheme for St. Peter's, in which the edges of the field substitute for the colonnades at the edges of the great piazza and the profile of the transportation center itself replaces the profiles and contours of St. Peter's basilica. Le Corbusier's fascination with Michelangelo's plan is to be found in the almost contemporaneous *Vers une architecture* (1923), in the chapter "The Lesson of Rome", in which Le Corbusier presents his drawing of Michelangelo's intentions, after a painting in the Vatican. Simply put, the central component of the Ville Contemporaine is a direct quotation of Michelangelo's unbuilt version of St. Peter's.

13 Ibid.: 31.

14 Ibid.: 69

Cohen and Hurtt seem to struggle with whether the term should be "contextural" as in a derivative of texture, such as the warp and weft of an urban fabric, or "contextual" as in pertaining to context—the set of circumstances that surround a particular event, situation, or in this case, site. Both the idea of urban texture and context have long-standing and nuanced usage in Rowe's Studio. However, if there was any doubt over "contextural" versus "contextual", it was settled by others operating in the Urban Design Studio at Cornell.[15] As for the idea of the "thinness" resulting from the imposition of the new order upon the old, Cohen and Hurtt did not reject Corbusian urbanism, rather they were asking if its forms and principles could be tempered to better address the situation of pre-existing sites. Similarly, the early Rowe Studio projects do not reject Corbusian urbanism, rather they sought to understand the malleability of its forms and principles. There seems to have been a strategy to reform the *Ville Radieuse*, to find a middle-ground or a *rapprochement* between the Modern city and its traditional counterpart, but importantly, starting with Corbusian principles as a given.

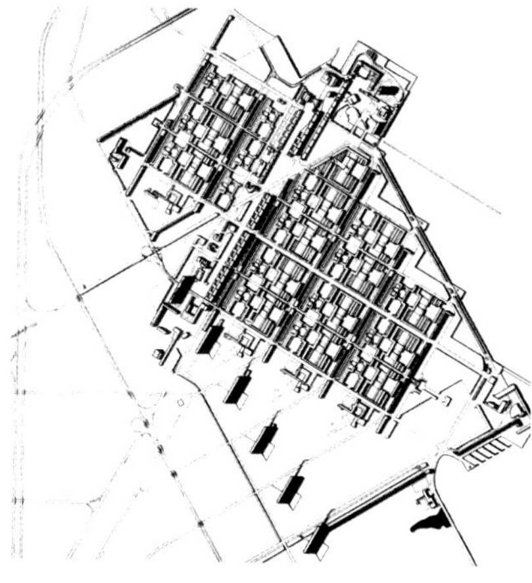

Fig. 2. South Amboy New Town, Schumacher, Cornell Master's thesis, 1966.

Tom Schumacher: Utopian Architect

Tom Schumacher's 1966 thesis for South Amboy, New Jersey, is an experiment in utopian urbanism (Fig. 2). While it has been described as a new town on an open site, South Amboy is today, and was in the early 1960s, clearly not a remnant cow-pasture or backwater New Jersey marsh awaiting development. South Amboy was more than just an exit on the Garden State Parkway, and the working class inhabitants of this unpretentious settlement (established in 1798) would have found Schumacher's plan as unsettling and explosive as the 1950 ammunition plant disaster that rocked their small enclave and propelled it onto the front pages of newspapers everywhere.[16] While the proposal recognized major lines of movement (the Garden State Parkway, railroad lines, and major arterial roads), acknowledged its proximity to the mouth of the Raritan River, and even provided a relocated port on land that was an undeveloped tributary to the Raritan Bay, the scheme can hardly be described as contextual. Its implementation would have required the erasure of the existing urban pattern of streets and blocks, demolition of nearly all building fabric, and the surrender of land ownership. To recall Mannheim's characterization of utopia, South Amboy New Town would "shatter, either partially or wholly, the order of things prevailing at the time".

Luckily for the inhabitants of South Amboy, this experiment in utopian urbanism was conducted in the relative safety of Cornell's Urban Design Studio. Schumacher's thesis is the first of the Cornell projects to fully invoke the Corbusian model of urbanism and is more like the Ville Contemporaine or the Ville Radieuse than the Plan Voisin, in that there is little actual concern for existing South Amboy. The plan is more about the ideal than it is about circumstance. South Amboy New Town is a large-scale intervention characterized by a field rotated approximately 30 degrees east of due north. Its *cardo* is a remake of South Amboy's main street complete with a new civic center at its northerly extent. The *decumanus* stretches from the relocated port area on the eastern edge of the site, crossing the *cardo*, passing a school, to what appears to be a hospital complex located at considerable distance from the port, which, should it explode again (and it most certainly might) is buffered from the town by plenty of open space. The civic center on the north end recalls elements of Le Corbusier's Tokyo

15 Steven Hurtt recounted, in a conversation with the author in May 2014, that there was some debate in the authors' minds as to whether the term might be "contextural", as in texture, or "contextual", as in context. Because Cohen and Hurtt's thoughts on contextualism came in the form of an unpublished thesis it served mostly as a working-paper for further discourse at Cornell and can be taken to represent an aspect of the intellectual milieu of the Urban Design Studio in the mid–60s.

16 "South Amboy, New Jersey", Wikipedia, [http://en.wikipedia.org/wiki/South_Amboy,_New_Jersey]. South Amboy was the site of two munitions explosions, the first in 1918 and the second in 1950. Both incidents killed many people and injured hundreds of local victims. Perhaps the volatility of South Amboy caught Schumacher's attention and suggested it as a place for his urban experiment.

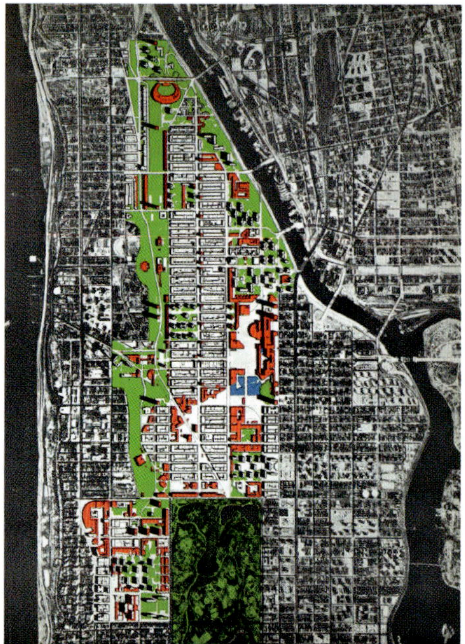

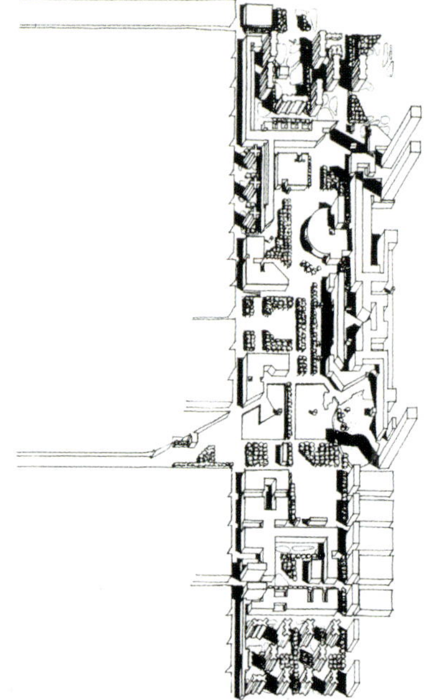

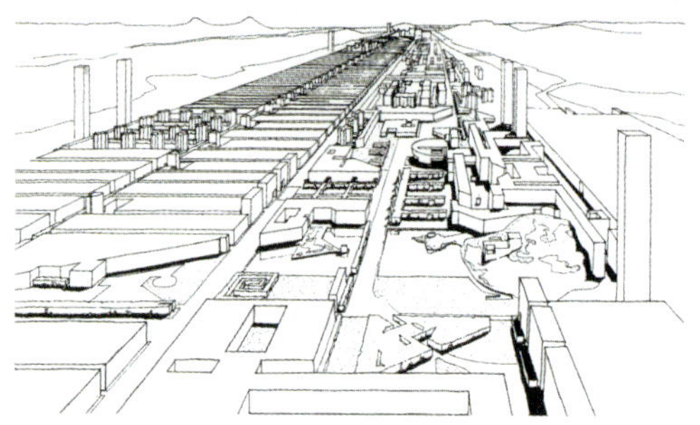

Fig. 3. Rowe, Schumacher et al., Harlem Redevelopment Plan, MoMA, 1967.

Museum or Chandigarh's Center, while a series of six Unité d'habitation-like slab buildings mechanically anchor the southern extent of the city. Throughout the scheme one finds examples of continuous buildings, which are sometimes over several thousand feet long and would make the Corviale in Rome[17] seem *staccato* in comparison.[18] The continuous buildings are further evidence of Schumacher's utopian study, for nowhere in the conventional fabric of South Amboy can one find this type of prolonged architectural extrusion.

Steven Hurtt has said that in South Amboy New Town Schumacher "uses the building types of Modern architecture to make a traditional city; defined edge, dense texture, and regular enclosed spaces".[19] While indeed the scheme has many of these attributes, it is difficult to ascribe the designation "traditional city" to this project. What is clearly innovative (and at the same time tending toward the more traditional) in Schumacher's proposal was the exploration of low-rise housing, descendants of Le Corbusier's *redent* housing, but with more substantial *poché*, and step regularity of pattern, and more discrete open spaces (including a higher premium placed on street as spatial figure) than the Corbu model. The 'thicker' substance of Schumacher's 'grid housing' suggested that the Ville Radieuse could be tamed and brought into some form of *rapprochement* with its traditional counterpart. But this would not take place in South Amboy, where

17 Though the Corviale post-dates the Schumacher thesis, it is mentioned because it captured Schumacher's attention. Often on bus rides that skirted the Roman periphery, Schumacher would be on the lookout for the Corviale and would proclaim any citing to students and colleagues alike.

18 Schumacher often remarked toward the end of his undergraduate years at Cornell, that Rowe asked Tom if he would join "me in my continuous building studio?" This story was retold several times over many years in conversations between Schumacher and the author.

19 Hurtt, Steven, "Conjectures on Urban Form: The Cornell Urban Design Studio 1963-1982", *The Cornell Journal of Architecture* 2, Urban Design, Fall 1983: 64.

the existing context had been largely dismissed; even if it had been accepted, the intensity of urbanism suggested by the new town would have overwhelmed the existing fabric.

The Traditional City and the City in the Park

While Cohen and Hurtt were completing their thesis in 1967, a team led by Colin Rowe and Tom Schumacher presented a project for Harlem at the Museum of Modern Art in an exhibition titled "The New City: Architecture and Urban Renewal". The text describing the Harlem project offers a similar dialectic involving the circumstantial realities of the traditional city and the utopian ideals represented by the city in the park that were cited in the Cohen and Hurtt thesis:

> *There are at present two major urbanistic conceptions: the traditional city–a solid mass of building with spaces carved out of it; and the city in the park–an open meadow within which isolated buildings are placed.*[20]

The designers clearly used these conceptions in the formulation of the plan, but the city in the park and the traditional city are largely kept at bay from one another, forming a kind of urbanistic *détente* between the two (Fig. 3). The text describes the compositional strategy as being divided into three zones, with two developed as a city in the park, and the third retaining the traditional grid plan of Manhattan. Rowe's intention was to connect Central Park to the Harlem River by means of a city in the park intervention that worked primarily with the abrupt topography of upper Manhattan and linked a number of existing parks. Here the natural features of Upper Manhattan take precedence over the 1811 Commissioner's Plan for the city. The landscape connection exists in a fragmentary and discontinuous form reading from south to north including Morningside Park, St. Nicholas Park, Jackie Robinson Park (originally Colonial Park), and Highbridge Park. This preoccupation with the topographic features of Upper Manhattan renders a plan that today could almost be interpreted as a prefiguration of contemporary urban issues, possibly a proto-Landscape Urbanist intervention.

The exuberance of the grand gestures of the Harlem Redevelopment Plan easily override the more subtle explorations of contextual design, particularly in the interventions within the "third zone" that retained the original street and block structure of the city. Text and diagram call out the precision of the surgical interventions in this area, illustrating the Cornell team's ability to work directly within the existing context of Upper Manhattan, without having to resort to radical intervention. Some radical interventions are present, of course, and consist of continuous linear buildings and composite buildings (some stretching a shocking ten blocks in the north-south direction) all called out in red on the plan should we happen not to notice them. *Redent* housing, which informed the 'grid housing' in the South Amboy project, has largely been sidelined for this scheme.

Like South Amboy, Harlem is a field composition. In this case, however, the field is ready-made. It consists of the pre-existing street and block texture of the Commissioner's Plan into which are collaged parks and buildings that become distinct. If we think of Schumacher's thesis as a form of "Juan Gris Urbanism",

20 Schumacher, Tom, "Modification of the Grid Plan", in Drexler, Arthur, ed., *The New City, Architecture and Urban Renewal*, MoMA, New York, 1967: 24-29. This phrase becomes a sort of invocation to be found at the beginning of literature from the Urban Design Studio for nearly two decades.

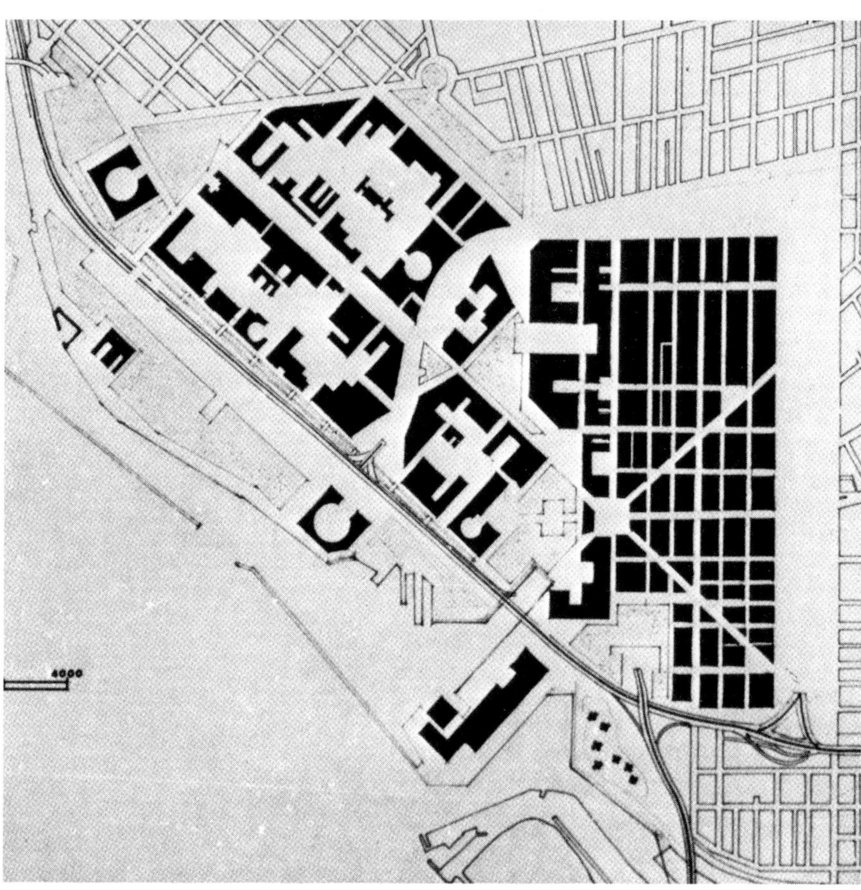

Fig. 4. Cornell Urban Design Studio, Buffalo Waterfront, Scheme 1, 1966/1969.

complete with the requisite rotated fields, overlapping and interpenetrating figures and peripheral emphasis, then the collage of parks and set pieces in Harlem is more a form of collage that we could characterize as "Still Life with Chair Caning Urbanism", with the Manhattan grid substituting for caning. The shift is significant because it signifies a transition from Analytic Cubism to Synthetic Cubism, which began first as a formal observation of the compositional similarities between more complex plans and Synthetic Cubist painting, then transitioned to become one among alternate design strategies, and quickly took on the socio-political meanings that Rowe would come to call "...contending powers". These were presumed to be associated with democracies on one hand, which supported the idea of collage, rather than autocracies, which any of the grand scale Modernist proposals troublesomely implied.

The link between Urban Design Studio language and the compositional strategies found in Cubism arises naturally out of Rowe's own work on Modern architecture. The connection between architecture and Modern painting is solidly grounded in the work of Le Corbusier, so Rowe himself would clearly have had that as a starting point. In addition, Rowe was most certainly influenced by Henry-Russell Hitchcock's book *Painting Toward Architecture* (1948) and was an avid reader of Clement Greenberg's work as well. The language used to describe this genre of painting was borrowed from *gestalt* perceptual psychology, and the use of *gestalt* terms in the Urban Design Studio was pervasive. This is not surprising because between 1963 and 1971, the two "Transparency"[21] articles

21 The "Transparency" articles were: Rowe, Colin; Slutzky, Robert, "Transparency: Literal and Phenomenal", *Perspecta* 8, 1963. Rowe, Colin; Slutzky, Robert, "Transparency: Literal and Phenomenal, Part II", *Perspecta* 13–14, 1971. The book authored by Hoesli, Bernhard; Rowe, Colin; Slutzky, Robert, *Transparenz*, Birkhäuser Verlag, Basel and Stuttgart, 1968.

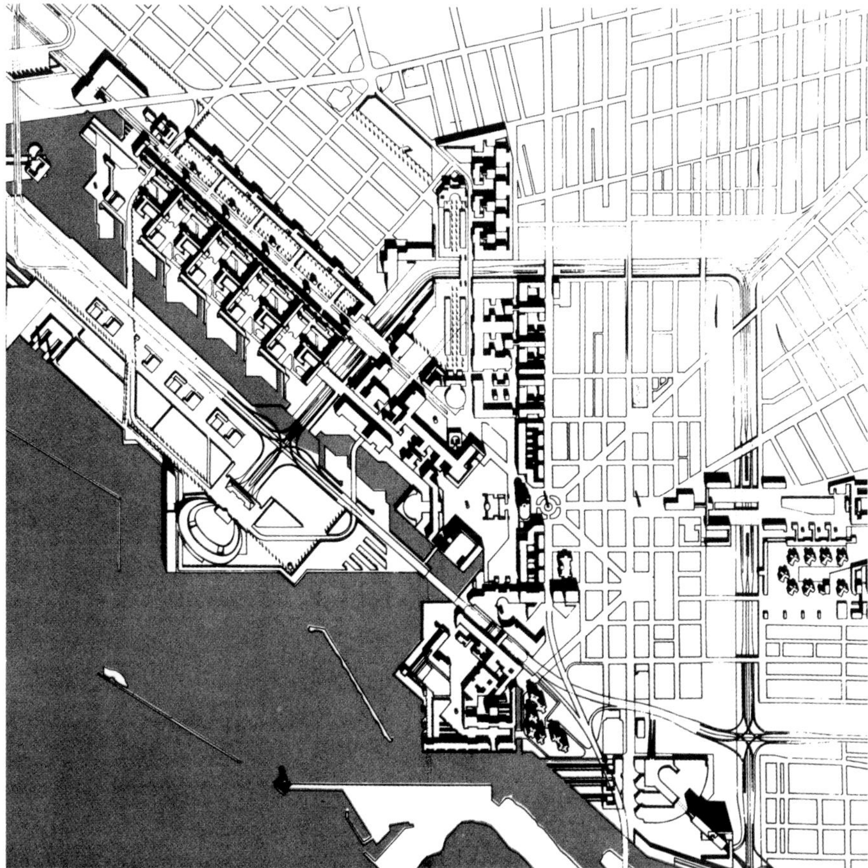

Fig. 5. Cornell Urban Design Studio, Buffalo Waterfront, Proposed Plan, 1966–69.

and a book authored by Bernhard Hoesli, *Transparenz*, appeared in print, providing students with Rowe's most current writings. Sibley Hall[22] was awash with Braque, Picasso, and Juan Gris. The figure/ground vocabulary adopted by the studio and codified by Wayne Copper in his 1967 thesis[23] became the basis for both the design process and presentation of its products.

The abstract language of Cubism lent itself well to a depiction of the concerns for a utopian urbanism, but required a more tangible source in order to find its grounding in the traditional city. The work of Camillo Sitte was to provide that impetus and was preeminently compatible with the figure/ground vocabulary of the studio because Sitte used a plan graphic that depicted building masses as black and open spaces as white. In 1965, George Roseborough and Christiane Crasemann Collins reintroduced Sitte to the American intellectual scene in their book, *Camillo Sitte and the Birth of Modern City Planning.*[24] Rowe's connection to Sitte originated at Liverpool, where Professor Sir Patrick Abercrombie, along with others, began publishing the *Town Planning Journal* in 1910, which was to eventually feature several articles focusing on Sitte's work. Additionally, Rowe worked from 1945 to 1947 in Abercrombie's London office, during roughly the same period that he was a Junior Fellow at the Warburg Institute.[25] So the taste for urbanism, if not fully implanted in Liverpool, must have received further nurturing in Abercrombie's London studio. Compounding the contact with Sitte, Rudolf Wittkower, Rowe's advisor, wrote a book review for *The Town Planning Review* of the 1945 translation of Sitte for an American audience, by Charles T.

22 Sibley Hall was the home of Rowe's Urban Design Studio at Cornell's College of Architecture, Art, and Planning.

23 Copper, Wayne William, "The Figure/Grounds", Master's thesis, Cornell University, June, 1967.

24 Collins, George Roseborough; Collins, Christiane Crasemann, *Camillo Sitte and the Birth of Modern City Planning*, Random House, New York, 1965.

25 Rowe, Colin, "CV", prepared after 1995 by Matthew Bell and Brian Kelly under the direct supervision of Rowe in advance of the RIBA Gold Medal and revised in 1995 after the medal was conferred.

Stewart.[26] Wittkower panned the book, writing "that it falls short of our expectations in almost every respect".[27] But Wittkower's 1947 review of the book provides some significant insight into the topic of Le Corbusier, urbanism, and Sitte, that deserves some examination at length:

> *By a curious paradox no single man has contributed more than Le Corbusier to Sitte's reputation as a hopeless sentimentalist who turned his face back to the past. Yet Le Corbusier incorporated Sitte's ideas into his Urbanisme though, admittedly, much disguising his debt by new emphasis and new viewpoints; he replaced Sitte's nineteenth-century level-headedness by a pseudo-mechanistic twentieth-century romantic enthusiasm. Thus we see the Sitte-Corbusier relationship in a light which the latter would hardly have expected. But whether we are attracted or repulsed by Le Corbusier, we cannot throw him off and return whole-heartedly to Sitte. For it was Le Corbusier and not Sitte who gave us, once and for all, a sense for the unity and indivisibility of the complex phenomenon of the modern town. I regard it therefore as a danger signal that Ralph Walker in his "Introduction to the English Translation" interprets Le Corbusier as wrongly as Le Corbusier interpreted Sitte. "The 'monotonous cells' of Le Corbusier's City of Tomorrow", he declares, "belong to the dictatorship of the 'little men' who occupy them." Here, indeed, is logic untempered by humanity." It seems rather that Le Corbusier's enthusiastic humanity has lost its audience. Retrogression from Le Corbusier to Sitte appears consistent with the general intellectual reaction which we have witnessed these last few years. If our alternative lies between Sitte and Le Corbusier, and we choose Sitte, then, indeed, a translation of Sitte is timely and almost assumes a symbolic quality.*[28]

Wittkower provided Rowe with the link between Le Corbusier and Sitte, that, in and of itself, was not the first time that the two urbanists had been connected. S. D. Adshed's 1930 essay in *Town Planning Review* titled "Camillo Sitte and Le Corbusier" laid the groundwork for this avenue of thought.[29] And, at Cornell, Alvin Boyarsky's 1959 thesis, "Camillo Sitte: City Builder", formed another connection between Sitte and the work in the Urban Design Studio.

The Buffalo Waterfront project of 1966 extended the idea of the traditional city and the city in the garden by developing new approaches to further the interplay between the pre-existing urban situation and Corbusian utopian ideals (Fig. 4). As was the case in the Harlem Redevelopment Plan, the surrounding urban fabric was of sufficient magnitude and density, such that it was not as easily dismissed as it had been in South Amboy. Unlike Harlem however, the Buffalo waterfront was an edge condition, a post-industrial zone set between the lakefront and the city's downtown. The ambiguity of the site's edge condition, a common problem that designers encounter in urban propositions, afforded significant opportunity to interpret the extent and nature of the intervention.

Like South Amboy, the Buffalo project used Corbusian principles as an overall compositional strategy, however schemes were developed that illustrate that the team was wrestling with other strategies to create urban form (Fig. 5). The possibility that "Scheme 1", as it is identified in *The Cornell Journal of Architecture,* 2, is a primitive experiment in Sittesque urbanism provides some intellectual relief from the mechanism of Modernist urbanism. Was this the beginning of a more direct encounter with the traditional city and perhaps an attempt to further distance the authors from the tyranny of the *Ville Radieuse*? Could this have been

26 Wittkower, Rudolf, "Camillo Sitte's art of building cities in an American translation", *Town Planning Review*, 19, 3-4, Sum 1947: 164-169. [https://www.jstor.org/stable/40101896].

27 Ibid.: 165.

28 Ibid.

29 Adshead, Stanley Davenport, "Camillo Sitte and Le Corbusier", *Town Planning Review* 14 (2), Nov 1930: 85-94. [https://www.jstor.org/stable/40100984].

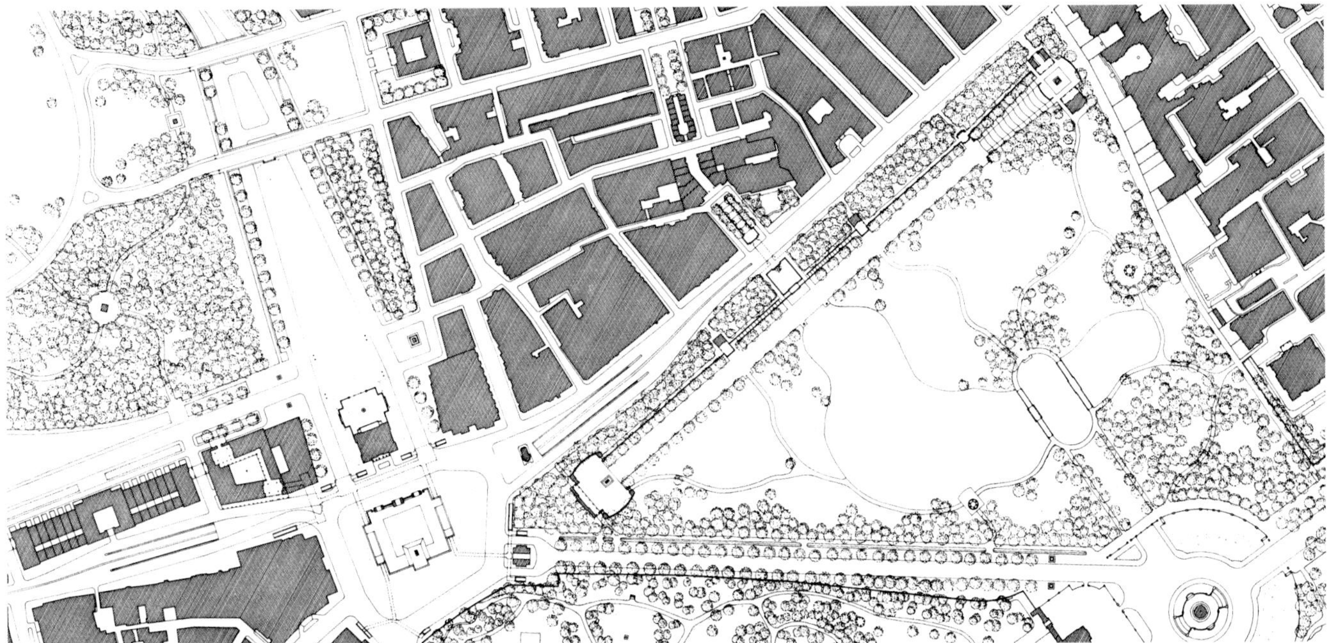

Fig. 6. John Chadwick, London West End, Cornell Master's thesis, 1980.

an indication of a shift to equally value the principles of the existing context and the reformative potential of the utopian paradigm? For Contextualism to be fully operational as a design strategy, must both the traditional city and its alternative be given equal presence? An examination of Urban Design Studio projects from the 1960s to the 1980s will illustrate that ultimately the large-scale strategic field projects like those in South Amboy and Buffalo gave way to smaller-scale tactical interventions that emphasized the continuity of urban spatial figures. Over time in the Urban Design Studio, there would be less concern for making the Ville Radieuse behave in a traditional context and more emphasis on parity between the old and the new.

Contextualism: Urban Ideals and Deformations

> *The twentieth century town is physically a combination of two simple concepts: the traditional city of corridor streets, grids, squares, etc., and the city in the park. ... So far, modern theories of urbanism and their applications have tended to devalue the traditional city. ... Obviously some middle ground is needed. To retreat to a hopelessly artificial past is unrealistic, but to allow a brutalizing system to dominate and destroy traditional urbanism is irresponsible. Contextualism, professing to be a reconciliation of the above ideas, has attempted such a middle ground.*[30]

In the mid-1960s, Schumacher enjoyed extensive intellectual exchanges with Rowe, traveling almost daily to the latter's house to discuss architecture and urbanism. Michael Schwarting recalled that Rowe would talk while Schumacher would furiously take notes, offer a critique, and engage in the kind of witty discourse that he was known for. In 1969 Schumacher was awarded the Rome Prize, removing him for a period of time from the direct orbit of Rowe.[31] By his own admission, the American Academy was a profoundly transformative experience for the Bronx native. The abstractions of urbanism offered by Corbusian

30 Schumacher, Thomas, "Contextualism: Urban Ideals and Deformations", *Casabella* 359-360, 1971: 79-86.

31 Conversation between Jon Michael Schwarting and the author, May 15, 2014.

Fig. 7. *Baedeker's Great Britain*, Cambridge, 1927.

Utopianism and the generalizations offered by the American grid were countered by the rich history and particularized urban fabric of Rome. During his second year at the academy, Schumacher was joined by Cornell classmate Michael Schwarting—eventually even Rowe himself was "in residence" at the American Academy during 1969.[32]

"Contextualism: Urban Ideals + Deformations" was the first important, widely disseminated writing to come from the Cornell Studio. Many of the ideas and images presented in Schumacher's article would be further amplified in *Collage City*, but, perhaps since the essay itself sufficiently addressed the idea of contextualism, the topic was hardly referenced in Rowe and Koetter's book. Importantly, Schumacher worked beyond utopian urbanism of which he was now skeptical and observed that, 'big ball' renewal projects have created a chasm between the existing and the new preventing either from offering any reasonable amenity".[33] Schumacher advocated for the traditional city with exuberance and with the knowledge he gained first-hand in Rome. In addition to providing the dialectical tools of the ideal versus the circumstantial, Schumacher allows an understanding of the 'ideal' in a broader sense than that of the utopian city alone. The 'ideal' in Schumacher's mind could operate at a variety of scales permitting a divorce, or at least amicable separation, between utopia and urban operations. Analytical pairings such as object building versus figural space, idealized type versus accommodation of circumstance, programmatic imperatives versus formal logic and sensibilities, and architecture as a vehicle of both

32 American Academy in Rome, Society of Fellows, Member Directory. [https://aarome.org/society-of-fellows/directory]. With Rowe and Schwarting in Rome, Schumacher could reconstitute much of the discourse that had taken place in Rowe's apartment in Ithaca.

33 Schumacher (1971): 79-81.

Fig. 8. Wayne Copper, Cambridge, 1966.

reality and representation become themes that broadened the operational idea of contextualism. The result was that this dialogue allowed the traditional city to occupy an equivalent position within the 'order of things' that the city in the garden had previously enjoyed in the collective urban design studio mindset.

After Contextualism:

Several articles follow after Schumacher's work. In 1974, Stuart Cohen's "Physical Context/Cultural Context: Including it All" attempted to expand contextualism beyond its perceived formalist limitations.[34] Grahame Shane's 1976 essay "Contextualism" provides a methodical overview of the topic, complete with definition of its tools and processes, as well as its affinities outside of Ithaca, specifically in the context of the Italian Rationalists.[35] A series of virulent critiques of Contextualism offered by Wojciech Leśnikowski, a faculty member at the University of Illinois Chicago, appeared in *Inland Architect* in 1986. A brief letter to the editor accusing Leśnikowski of falling "into a category of postmodern criticism which is concerned more with personal taste than operative critical theory and history", was offered by Greg Lynn, then a student at Princeton who would later go on to coin the term "Blob Architecture" a stance quite far from Contextualism. Promted by Leśnikowski's essays, both Stuart Cohen and Steven Hurtt wrote rebuttals, also published in *Inland Architect.*[36]

34 Cohen, Stuart, "Physical Context / Cultural Context: Including it All", *Oppositions* 2, 1974: 1-40.

35 Shane, Grahame, "Contextualism", *Architectural Design* 46 (11), 1976: 676-79.

36 Leśnikowski, Wojciech; Windmiller, Jifat, "Contextuality Historic & Modern Perspectives", *Inland Architect*, Jul/Aug 1986: 41-60. Lynn, Greg, "Context for Contextuality", "Letters", *Inland Architect*, Sep/Oct 1986: 2. Leśnikowski, Wojciech; Windmiller, Jifat, "Contextualism Today", *Inland Architect*, Nov/Dec 1986: 49-59. Cohen, Stuart E. "Contextualism, from Urbanism to a Theory of Appropriate Form", *Inland Architect*, May/Jun, 1987: 68-69. Hurtt, Steven, "Contextualism: of Paradigms, Politics, and Poetry", *Inland Architect*, Sep/Oct 1987: 66-75.

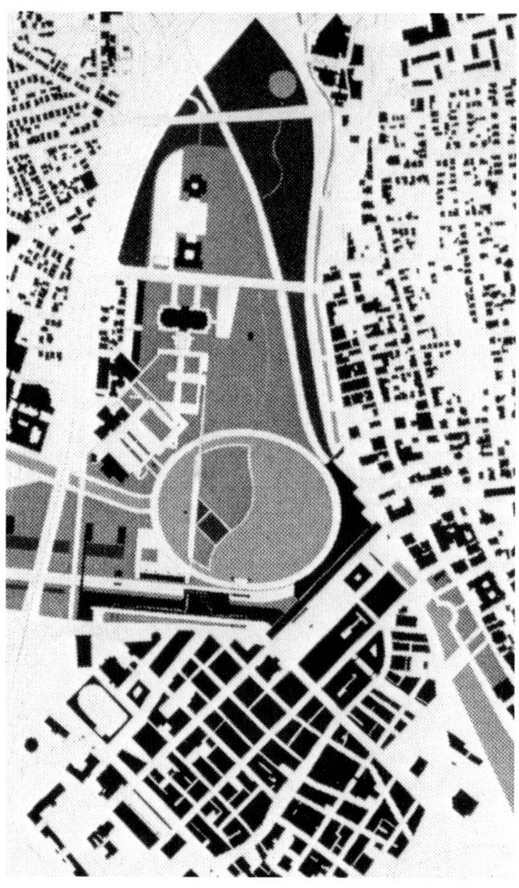

Fig. 9. Joel Bostick, Providence, RI, Cornell Master's thesis, 1973.

By the mid-1970s, projects in the Cornell Urban Design Studio began to signal a change in design strategy. This evolutionary approach challenged the idea of first superimposing a utopian order upon existing sites in favor of beginning with the existing circumstantial order and *then* intervening in order to elevate site conditions toward the ideal. The shift in project scale from large-scale strategic projects to smaller-scale tactical interventions, mending collisions and negotiating field discrepancies, is also evident during this period. By the time of the publication of Schumacher's article on Contextualism, urban renewal in the United States had run its course and no longer were its large-scale projects politically palatable, nor were they economically feasible. This trend paralleled the Studio projects' tendency to move away from definition of edges of broadly articulated fields to concentrate instead on more discretely defined spatial figures; in a sense the move was from city as object (utopian) to the city as a series of interconnected spatial events. Finally, the realization of limits to figure/ground, which was noted in Schumacher's article, led the studio to look for more conventions to portray massing, topography, and importantly, landscape. John Chadwick's 1980 thesis for London's West End skillfully weaves urban fabric and landscape (Fig. 6). The project would have been inconceivable without a convention for depiction of plant materials, walls, gates, walks, monuments, fountains, and all the other appointments of an urbane landscape. Copper's otherwise useful figure/ground drawings serve as an example of the limitations with regard to landscape. *Baedeker's* 1927 guidebook to Britain shows a more robust and highly developed graphic for representing the interplay of buildings, landscape, and topographic

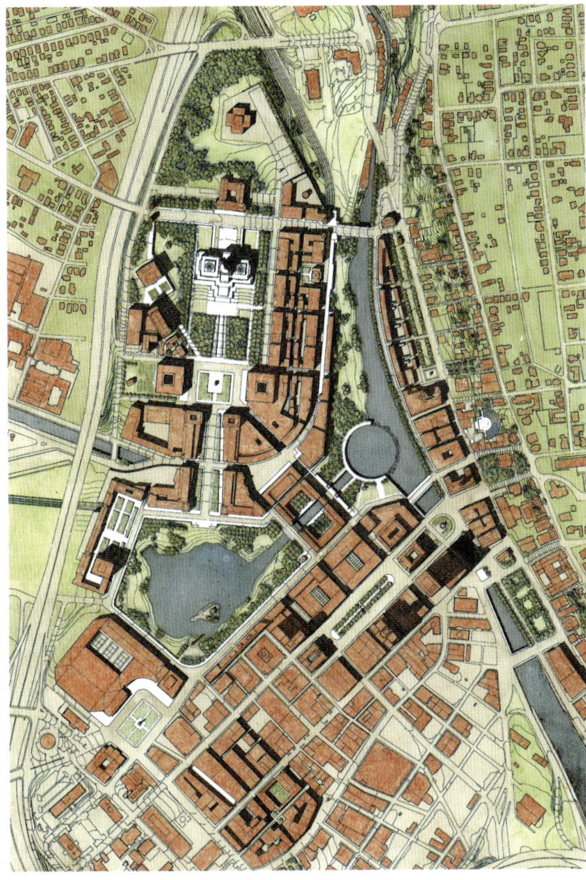

Fig. 10. Blake Middleton, Providence, RI: Capital District Development Strategy, Cornell Master's thesis, 1980.

features than the Copper figure/ground drawing from the 1960s. As evidence, a comparison of two plans of Cambridge, UK, one appearing in the *Baedeker* guidebook for Great Britain, and the other from the Copper series, aptly illustrate a general anemia at Cornell with regard to depictions of landscape in an urban setting (Fig. 7, 8).

Without a suitable graphic method for representing landscape, there was only so much play between solid and void and between building and open space that could be achieved. Two projects for Providence, Rhode Island, can illuminate this condition. Joel Bostick's 1973 thesis for Providence took up the problem of resolving multiple discrepancies between the orientation of the State Capitol building, its axis, the general orientation of the city, the river's edge, intervening railroad lines, and, of course, the usual array of streets and squares already existing in the city (Fig. 9). A large oval park was proposed as a hinge between the several geometries at play on the site. The big oval figure overlapped with additional spaces to the north and south, presumably with spurs of the parkland. Zipatone (an adhesive film adhered to the drawing) was used to signal the idea that this zone was to be a landscape intervention and the oval figure is an icon for a generalized resolution of the conflicting circumstances of the site. By contrast, in Blake Middleton's 1980 thesis for the same site, a full vocabulary of landscape elements have come into the scene allowing a finer-grained resolution to the site (Fig. 10). Emphasis was placed on the centers of spaces, which were sometimes irregularly formed, in contrast to the Bostick scheme where the perimeter of the

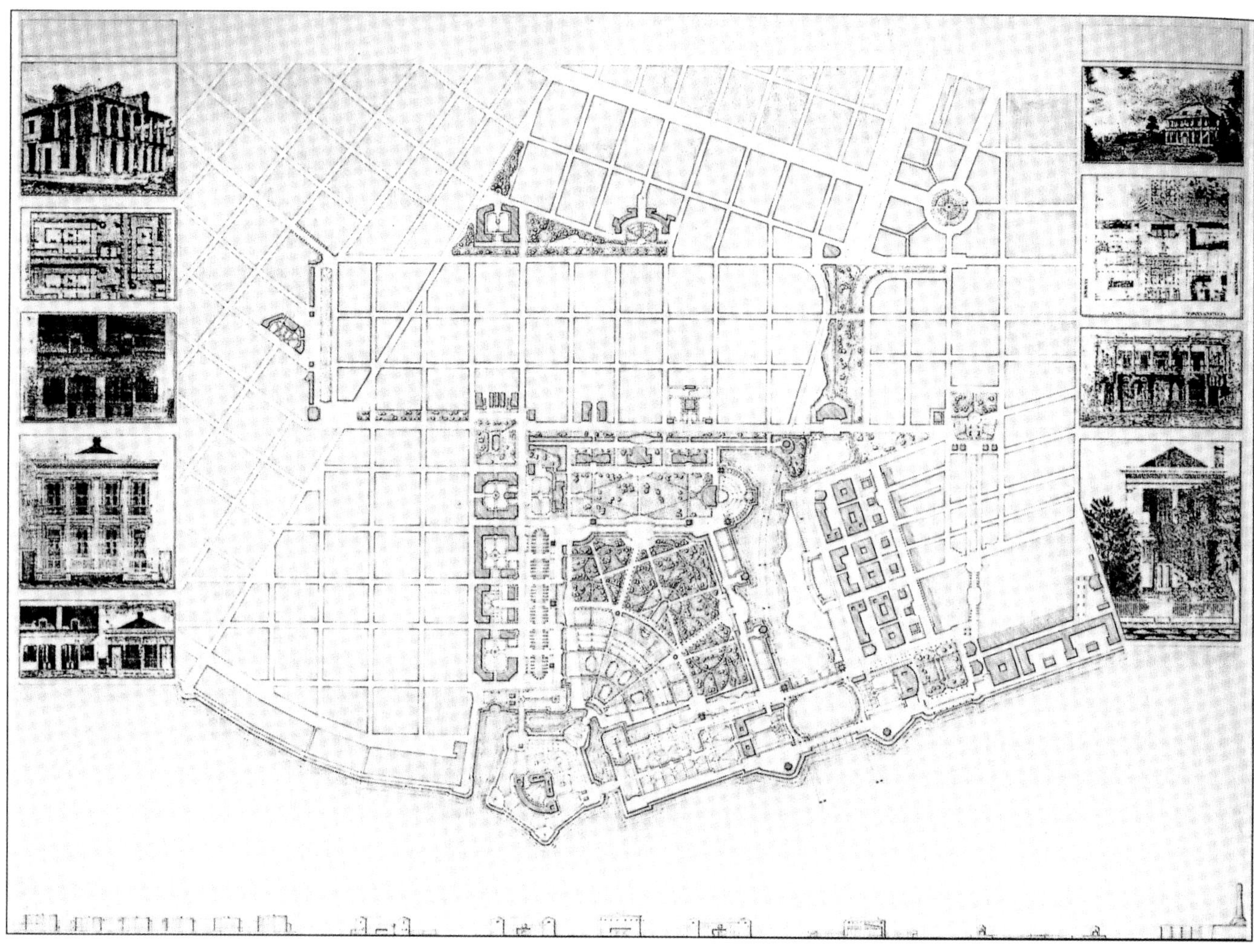

Fig. 11. J. Carey McWhorter, New Orleans: Lower Garden District, Cornell Master's thesis, 1985.

regular oval form was of necessity designed to hold back the multiple orientations surrounding the site. Bostic's resolution of the site relies on the abstract form of the oval and its implications as a landscape boundary. Middleton's scheme relies on localized resolution of conflicting geometries through implementation of a landscape vocabulary that simply was not present in Bostick's work. Bostick's proposition continues to employ aspects of the Ville Radieuse (big-field geometries, continuous buildings, overlapping and interpenetrating spatial zones), which one could argue still participates in the effort to find *rapprochement* between the modern and the traditional city. Middleton's scheme, importantly, invites landscape into the dialogue between figure and ground, at once providing a more concrete grounding of the proposal and an ability to place his solution into the finer-grain of existing site conditions. Middleton's scheme appears to start with the circumstance of context and elevate it to ideal while Bostick's scheme appears to superimpose an ideal order that is tailored to the context.

By the 1980s it was common for students in the Urban Design Studio to look back over previous studio projects and theses in an effort to offer fresh perspectives to old problems. In the case of projects in an American context, the additional ability to convincingly represent landscape issues was a necessity. Perhaps no other project better supports this assertion than J. Carey McWhorter's 1985 thesis located in the Lower Garden District of New Orleans (Fig. 11). His designs for an "Audubon College" located between the Garden District and the levee provide more park than building, as is often the case with small campuses.

Over time the definition of Contextualism broadened from a mediation between the traditional city and the city in the park to a more inclusive meaning that accommodated the city, the park, the ideal, the circumstantial, figural space as well as the figural object, all without a threat of destruction by utopian agendas. In a sense, Contextualism came to provide the kind of reassurance suggested by Karl Mannheim:

> *The relationship between utopia and the existing order turns out to be a dialectical one. By this is meant that every age allows to arise (in differently located social groups) those ideas and values in which are contained in condensed form the unrealized and the unfulfilled tendencies which represent the needs of each age. These intellectual elements then become the explosive material for bursting the limits of the existing order. The existing order gives birth to utopias which in turn break the bonds of the existing order, leaving it free to develop in the direction of the next order of existence.*[37]

In the 1950s Rowe identified the problem of utopian urbanism and its major proponent, Le Corbusier. In the 1960s and 1970s his Urban Design Studio at Cornell, beginning with the work of Cohen and Hurtt, worked directly with the utopian urban models championed by Corbu in order to see if there might be further accommodation of the traditional city. Schumacher's article, "Contextualism: Urban Ideals + Deformations" gave the traditional city equal footing with its Modern counterpart and helped to facilitate a gradual shift from tailoring Modern paradigms to fit traditional contexts to beginning with the circumstances already present on a site and attempting to discover how those circumstances might accommodate a notion of the ideal.

37 Mannheim (1954): 179.

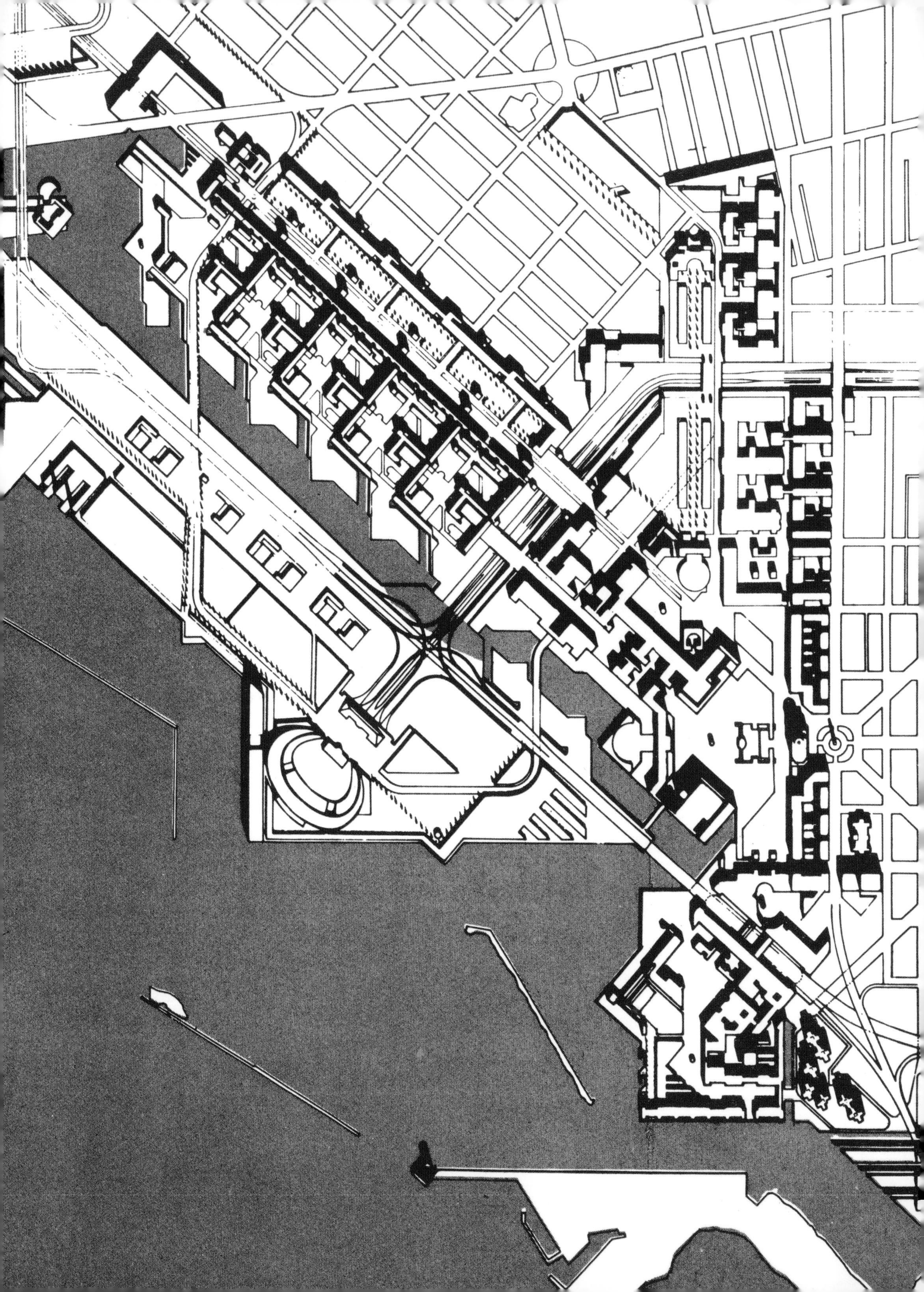

Buffalo and Beyond: The Cornell Urban Design Studio, Theory and Practice 1962–1988

Steven W. Hurtt

Introduction

This essay examines the 'theory' and 'practice' that is the urban design legacy of Colin Rowe, as developed and illustrated by the Cornell Urban Design Studio during Rowe's leadership of that Studio for a quarter century, 1962–1988. In 1965, Rowe remarked that the Studio was "totally devoid of theory", but within a year some Studio students were suggesting otherwise. By 1973, Rowe and former student Fred Koetter had written a propositional urban design 'theory' known to us from their book *Collage City*. It was published in 1978. The work of the Studio is the closest thing we have to a representation of Rowe's continuous related 'practice'. In 1996, for the third and final volume of his *As I Was Saying: Recollections and Miscellaneous Essays*, subtitled *Urbanistics*,[1] much of the Studio work was published or republished with commentary either by Rowe himself or with descriptive commentary he endorsed. These two publications offer an opportunity to examine something of the back and forth between 'theory' and 'practice' over twenty-five years of activity. Following a few introductory remarks consisting of cautions about theory/practice, notes about Rowe's teaching mode, and Rowe's surprising 1965 "devoid of theory" take on the Studio, the body of my essay has two distinct parts. The first part focuses on the import of the 1966 Buffalo Waterfront project to the development of 'theory' through early Studio 'practice'. The second part is structured by Rowe's 1996 characterization of the "Cornell Studio Projects and Theses" in his "Introduction" to them. I expand on Rowe's brief remarks, point-by-point, for purposes of further explanation, clarification, and occasional correction.

frontispiece:
The Buffalo Waterfront project, shadow plan, Studio project, 1966.

Theory / Practice, and Cautionary Notes: The fundamental proposition here is that Rowe's urban design legacy exists in both verbal and visual forms, and that these can be roughly equated to theory and practice as categorical conveniences for discussion. The first caution is that if the same meaning could be conveyed by words as by images, there would be no need for both. The one may help us understand the other, but they are neither equivalent nor do they necessarily occur simultaneously.[2] Practice may lead to, explore, or demonstrate theory. Theory might prompt, promote, or explain practice, at least partially. Second, for our

1 Rowe, Colin, *As I Was Saying: Recollections and Miscellaneous Essays* 3, *Urbanistics*, Caragonne, Alex, ed., MIT Press, Cambridge, MA, and London, 1996. See footnote 16.

2 I cannot recall the art critic I am paraphrasing who said as much about writing and painting.

purposes, Studio work represents Rowe's practice, but this is student work. It is influenced by Rowe, but it is not by him.[3] What Colin Rowe has written, himself or collaboratively, we can call theory. It can be extracted from his numerous essays, but here it is primarily sourced in two places, *Collage City* (1978) and *As I Was Saying* (1996). In the "Introduction" to *Collage City*, the first sentence says of theory, "... it might be possible to construct a theory of society and even a theory of architecture: but if modesty restrains the attempt, there are also pragmatic reasons which make the same insistence".[4] And on the relation of theory to practice, in Rowe's "Introduction" to *As I Was Saying*, 3, he says of the Studio: "the content of this course is extensively written about in Colin Rowe and Fred Koetter, *Collage City*, and is presented in condensed form ... as 'The Present Urban Predicament' ". He notes that the essay began as a 1979 lecture that was published in 1980 and 1981.[5] Notably, while *Collage City* represents theory as of 1970–73 when the text was written, no Studio design projects were shown, whereas in 1996 they are profusely illustrated.[6] It seems reasonable to assume that the Studio practice of 1963–73 supported development of the theory as described in *Collage City*, but the inclusion of Studio projects was imagined as possibly distracting from, or appearing contradictory to, the theoretical argument.[7] Whereas, approximately two decades later, among the purposes of the third volume of *As I Was Saying* was linking image with word, practice with theory, "a display of studio projects and theses executed between 1963 and 1988" followed by a collection of Rowe's thematically related essays.[8] A selection of Studio projects published in *The Cornell Journal of Architecture*, 2, (1983) are republished in *As I Was Saying* along with captions, descriptions, and the introduction by Blake Middleton. Some are supplemented with brief comments by Rowe. For the later 1982–88 projects previously published in *The Cornell Journal of Architecture*, 4, (1991), Rowe provides longer commentary. Most projects are theses authored by individuals. They are presented chronologically. A few, by small groups and usually for exhibitions, follow the theses.

Rowe's teaching mode: Rowe's mode of teaching and the resulting milieu of the Studio is worth noting as having a substantial impact on both theory and practice. Studio reading was potentially extensive, none of it required. Books or articles Rowe suggested to individuals got around informally. Others were introduced from elective courses. Perception psychology was fundamental to understanding and provided a shared Studio language. Photocopies of Rowe's published articles seemed always available and reading them helped one understand Rowe's comments and placed his approach into a critical philosophical and aesthetic framework. The readings also sponsored ad hoc seminar-like student discussions on perception, painting, architecture, landscape, and urban form. After a few years many of these readings constituted a shared but still non-mandatory reading list.[9]

Dialectics permeate Rowe's writings. Some pairings helped us understand architectural-urban form: figure/ground; solid/void; formal/informal; classical/anticlassical (romantic); ideal/circumstantial or ideal/real. Others helped us understand the world of ideas.

Rowe's charge to the Studio: solve the Mod/"trad" city problem, provided a unifying theme and focus. The 'Mod' was described as all 'objects' surrounded by open space, primarily represented by Le Corbusier, *the* architect who had gathered

3 This is true even of projects typically credited to Rowe such as *Roma interrotta* and Rowe's combined engagements with Berlin, see "Comments on the IBA Proposals" and "A Student Project: Berlin" in Rowe (1996/3): 221–42; 254–60.

4 Rowe, Colin and Koetter, Fred, *Collage City*, MIT Press, Cambridge, MA, and London, 1978: 2. Rowe might have preferred his work described as criticism, connoisseurship, and psychobiography (his essays on Léon Krier, Robert Venturi, and James Stirling) rather than as theory.

5 Rowe (1996/3): 164–220. Rowe states the lecture was given in London in 1979, first published in *The Architectural Association Quarterly* in 1980 and again in *The Cornell Journal of Architecture* 1, Cornell University, Ithaca, NY, 1981.

6 Only Studio research projects were illustrated in *Collage City:* Griffin-Kollhoff, 'City of composite presence'; Cohen-Hurtt figure/ground of the Plan Voisin; Copper figure/grounds of Saint-Dié, Parma, Louvre, Tuileries and Palais Royal, Wiesbaden, Munich, and others; and Shane's 'field analysis of London'.

7 Rowe, Colin and Koetter, Fred, *The Architectural Review*, 1975; this earlier abridged text with illustrations was likewise published without Studio projects.

8 For the *Cornell Journal of Architecture* 2, Cornell University, Ithaca, NY, 1983, I wrote "Conjectures on Urban Form: The Cornell Urban Design Studio 1963–82". Blake Middleton wrote the introduction and copious explanative captions. That issue included a forward by Léon Krier, and essays by Rowe, Grahame Shane, and Wayne Copper's thesis, "The Figure/Grounds" including some in loose leaf form, a boon to teaching.

9 See Antonio Pietro Latini's "Mathematics to Urbanistics" essay in this volume for the reading list.

and synthesized into coherent wholes the ideas and related forms of the 'Heroic' period of Modern architecture and presented them most completely.[10] Rowe's articles that featured Le Corbusier's architecture intensified the Studio interest in all Le Corbusier's work. In contrast, the 'trad' city, described as primarily a textural solid with occasional figural spaces and figural buildings located in and/or emerging from that solid, was represented by portions of pre-Mod cities: Rome, Paris, London, Vienna .... Rowe's sweeping characterization of these dialectically opposite urban extremes, the hyper-contrast between them, clarified 'the problem' otherwise muddied by lesser examples.[11]

Rowe's formal analysis that associated Cubism and Collage with Modern architecture prompted the Studio to find similar associations in the field/figure characteristics of U.S. cities, the Studio's primary study areas, 1963–78.

In *Collage City*, Rowe and Koetter describe the architect as a *bricoleur* gathering things that *might be* useful. Rowe too was a *bricoleur* gathering exemplars independent of the immediate problem. They were primarily Western, post-Renaissance, but rarely Modernist. They were not lectured about, only pointed out.[12] Rowe thought of them as atemporal. To the Studio, they embodied elusive lessons to be learned. Sometimes they served as analogies susceptible to transformation in the design process.[13]

Providing students with the opportunity of discovery was essential. Rowe introduced projects without including clear boundaries. Goals were vague, 'Let's look at Buffalo'. 'Looking' became a source of knowledge, opportunity, and speculative design. To paraphrase Yogi Berra, 'You can see a lot by just looking'. But you had to *see* it when you looked, then try to master and apply it. It wasn't easy. It could be intimidating. It was highly stimulating.

1962–65: "I really have quite a hot shot urban design thing going... totally devoid of theory": Rowe had begun teaching at Cornell in 1962, been given responsibility for the fledgling graduate program, and called the program Urban Design at the suggestion of Professor John Reps.[14] Urban design was new, and Rowe was new to it. There was little supporting disciplinary literature.[15] In the post-depression, post-WWII period the Modernist urban-architectural visions of CIAM and Le Corbusier had become built realities. Enough so that doubts had emerged. In that milieu, urban design had been conceived to fill a widening gap between architecture and planning. Architecture was preoccupied with single, generally isolated buildings; urban planning was preoccupied with applying sociology, economics, and management to its evolving field with little or no relation to or interest in the intentional design of 'trad'-like urban form. While Rowe later critiqued those problems, he clearly thought that whatever urban design was to be, it was primarily about the relationship between city form and architecture. Excited to explore that relationship, he wrote of it to Alvin Boyarsky in a 1965 letter dated March 14, barely two years after the real start-up of the program:

> *I really have got quite a very hot shot urban design thing going. It's a composite of Ducerceau, Aalto, Corbu, Mexican sites, Chantilly, the Hofburg, etc. It's entirely empirical, pragmatic and accommodating. It is totally devoid of theory. But it is waiting to be publicized and bought.*[16]

10 Le Corbusier's *Oeuvre Complète* and the *Ville Radieuse* were ever present in Studio discussions. In a theory course, faculty (Lee Hodgden, Werner Seligmann) gave numerous analytic lectures on the work of prominent architects, primarily Aalto, Wright, Le Corbusier.

11 This 'problem' was later described in "Crisis of the Object: Predicament of Texture", Rowe and Koetter, (1978): 50–85.

12 Many analogic exemplars known to the 1966–67 Studio were later illustrated in Schumacher, Thomas, "Contextualism: Urban Ideals and Deformations", *Casabella* 359-360, 1971: 79-86, and later in *Collage City*, 1978.

13 I believe the *bricoleur* descriptive analogy first appeared in writing in *Collage City*, but, as Rowe says, the writing was complete by 1973, Rowe (1978): 186.

14 "It all began with John Reps." is the first sentence in Rowe (1996/3): 1. Historians had seen value in expanding their studies to the city; see *The Historian and the City*, Handlin, Oscar; Burchard, John, eds., MIT Press, Cambridge, MA, and London, (1963), 1977. The architectural profession was similarly inclined. The AIA promoted 'urban design' to fill the gap between architecture and planning. I believe the AIA commissioned a series of articles for the *AIA Journal*, which became Sprieregan, Paul, *Urban Design: The Architecture of Towns and Cities*, McGraw-Hill Book Company, New York, 1965. Isolated architecture academics like Holmes Perkins at Columbia and Harvard had been attempting to create an urban design discipline for years with little success.

15 In the early years, a Department of Planning seminar available to us introduced some of the scant readings on urban design: Kevin Lynch, Camillo Sitte, and so on.

16 Naegele, Daniel, ed., *The Letters of Colin Rowe: Five Decades of Correspondence*, Artifice books on architecture, London, 2016: 152.

Despite this inauspicious beginning, little over a year later, by June of 1966, the Buffalo Waterfront project had been completed, "totally devoid of theory", except for one thing. Rowe had described the conflict between the characteristic *forms* of the Modernist (CIAM) architectural urban vision and those of pre-Modernist, Western cities, described in characteristic synoptic Studio lingo as the Mod/"trad" problem.[17] Rowe simply pointed this out as *the* urban design problem to be solved. Described dialectically, the problem seemed obvious, the charge to find 'reconciliation' a reasonable one: general problem/specific site. By the spring semester of 1966, the Studio was 'looking at' central downtown Buffalo and that city's Lake Erie waterfront.

1966 and The Buffalo Waterfront Project

"... an early super-climax for the Studio": Little over a year after Rowe's "totally devoid of theory" remark to Boyarsky, the Buffalo Waterfront project had been completed. About it, in 1996, Rowe made what is for him an exceptionally unqualified and effusive remark:

> *Buffalo Waterfront is the first of what the French would probably call the* grands projets *to be associated with the U.D. Studio; and, to me, it still appears to be the best, the most extensive, the most conclusive. It represented an early super-climax for the studio. It was grand and its orchestration was beyond the capacities of that date (1966)...*[18]

Buffalo appeared to demonstrate that a Mod/"trad" reconciliation was possible. It even had a few of us thinking the Studio not only had "a very hot shot urban design thing going", but that it was not "totally devoid of theory". Weren't we exploring a theory counter to that of Modernism? The possibility of an intelligent subversive counterattack on the seriously flawed Modernist establishment was intoxicating. That excited sentiment produced the first discussions about a nascent theory and names for it: Contextualism, Collision City, Collage City were in contention.[19] How had this happened? If Rowe's selection of Buffalo as a Studio project contributed to the level of design resolution achieved, how?

The Buffalo Waterfront project, an Instrument of Education: Nine students melded individual efforts to produce The Buffalo Waterfront project. The brochure prepared for the 1969 exhibition at the Albright Knox Gallery in Buffalo mentions Buffalo's history and several cultural landscapes.[20] Given Rowe's analogical teaching mode, any of these cultural landscapes might have been *seen* or discovered, studied, and applied to achieve the practical and aesthetic-cognitive goals of the project. Rowe's *ex post facto* brochure comment is that Buffalo's most obvious cultural landscape is "Joseph Ellicott's original plan ... an ideal city", and that it has the greatest presence in the scheme. Because ideal/circumstantial conditions were high among Rowe's interests, later amply described in *Collage City*, his selection of Buffalo as an instrument of teaching appears more deliberate in retrospect than it did in 1966, independent of how well that construct might have been understood by the Studio. As Rowe's description in the brochure makes evident, he had further directed Studio attention:

17 The *zeitgeist* honored the 'trad' but only by placing it in the past, making it 'of its time' and therefore irrelevant and illegitimate because not 'of our time'.

18 Rowe (1996/3): 10. The Buffalo Waterfront project was completed in the spring semester of 1966 and briefly exhibited in Buffalo. It was exhibited in the Albright-Knox Gallery in Buffalo in 1969 with a descriptive brochure included in this essay. See footnote 20.

19 These naming discussions included primarily Stuart Cohen, Steven Hurtt, Fred Koetter, but also, importantly, Franz Oswald, and Tom Schumacher, and quite probably Alex Caragonne, among others.

20 The brochure illustrated in this essay was provided by James Tice. See also Rowe (1996/3): 97–119.

> *This project... is offered as a commentary upon the potential of Buffalo's waterfront. It assumes that a basic strategy... must, first of all, recognize the real and symbolic significance of Niagara Square and must attempt to place this space in some explicit relationship with Lake Erie and the mouth of the Buffalo River... that the entry from Canada and the diagonal of Niagara Street are among the valuable determinants of any significant solution... that Symphony Circle... ought to be recognized as an important urbanistic achievement... Analysis of Buffalo discloses a composite of complementary and conflicting elements, of deliberate acts of will and of incongruous accidents... evident in Joseph Ellicott's original plan... a clear indication of a conflict between an ideal city model and specific circumstances... the ideal model... is equipped with a central square and is penetrated by major orthogonal and minor diagonal axes... generally reminiscent of Washington D.C. and is ultimately derivative from the Utopian speculations of Renaissance theorists.*[21]

Knowing more about "Joseph Ellicott's original plan" and "a conflict between an ideal city model and specific circumstances" enhances appreciation of Ellicott's plan, the Studio's scheme, and Rowe's teaching.

The Ideal and the Circumstantial: Joseph Ellicott's "New Amsterdam" plan, Buffalo 1804: Rowe's comment on Buffalo's ideality being "generally reminiscent of Washington, D.C.," implied much that he surely knew but did not say. Joseph Ellicott assisted his older brother, Andrew Ellicott, and Benjamin Banneker make the final survey and detailed plan of Washington, D.C.[22] The younger brother became a surveyor and later spent many years responsible for the survey and sale of much of New York State's 'western land'. Joseph Ellicott also developed plans for several towns including Buffalo, initially named New Amsterdam.[23] Ellicott's 'New Amsterdam' plan suggests lasting effects far beyond its size and simplicity.[24]

Ellicott's central "Public Square" became Buffalo's *axis mundi*, now Niagara Square. Surrounding blocks made a larger 'ideal' square city with radiating orthogonals and diagonals. He located the ideal plan at the edge of an escarpment close to, but safely above, Lake Erie. The plan suggests the influence of 'Renaissance theorists' and Penn's 'five-square' plan for Philadelphia that Ellicott knew.[25] For 'New Amsterdam', the ideal form is complemented with a measure of social utopianism: the north corners are marked, "DD, Situation for Churches and School-houses". Another "D" block occurs adjacent to the south axis, where it joins a street along the escarpment labeled "Busti Terrace", a potentially prominent location.[26]

While ideal and centralized, Ellicott's plan faces eastward. Radial streets fan out overland to the northeast and east across upper New York State. Most significant are two east-facing street axes. One of these, now Court Street, extends from the "Public Square", aligned with a mound labeled "B, Elevation suitable for a Public Building forty-five feet perpendicular height above the surface of the Water in the Lake", making the mound central to what is today a three-block-long area of public parks and accompanying memorials.[27]

The other east-facing axis extends from the southeast corner of the ideal figure. Tinted green, it combines a semicircular space, an 'urban exedra', with a one-block-wide mall that extends to the edge of the plan, implying continuation

21 "Buffalo Waterfront", brochure, Albright-Knox Art Gallery exhibition, 1969.

22 Andrew Ellicott followed L'Enfant's scheme, surveyed the perimeter, and made the final determination of the dimensions of streets, blocks, sites for major buildings and important spaces. Benjamin Banneker was a highly educated free Black man who owned a farm on the Patapsco River near where Philadelphia Quaker George Ellicott established a mill (later Ellicott City, near Baltimore). George Ellicott helped Banneker expand his already prodigious knowledge, including timekeeping and astronomy essential for survey. George Ellicott's cousin Andrew was commissioned to make the survey; Banneker was hired to provide essential assistance.

23 Joseph Ellicott had surveyed land in Western Pennsylvania and New York for the Holland Land Co. He became their agent supervising land sales for several decades ca. 1800–20. He encouraged settlement and growth, including promotion of the Erie Canal.

24 To explore Rowe's interest in the symbolic power and the practicality of simple 'ideal' city plans, see his "Lockhart, Texas" essay. Also "Program vs. Paradigm: Otherwise Casual Notes on the Pragmatic, The Typical, and The Possible", *Cornell Journal* 2, 1983: 8–19.

25 From Bucks County, PA, north of Philadelphia, Joseph and Andrew Ellicott certainly knew Philadelphia's 'ideal' five-square plan.

26 Busti, from Milan, was among the lead investment group from the Netherlands, Ellicott's clients. And "terrace" suggests Ellicott imagined something like Adelphi Terrace in London built 1768–72.

27 Now Five Flags Park, a Civil War memorial, and Fireman's Park.

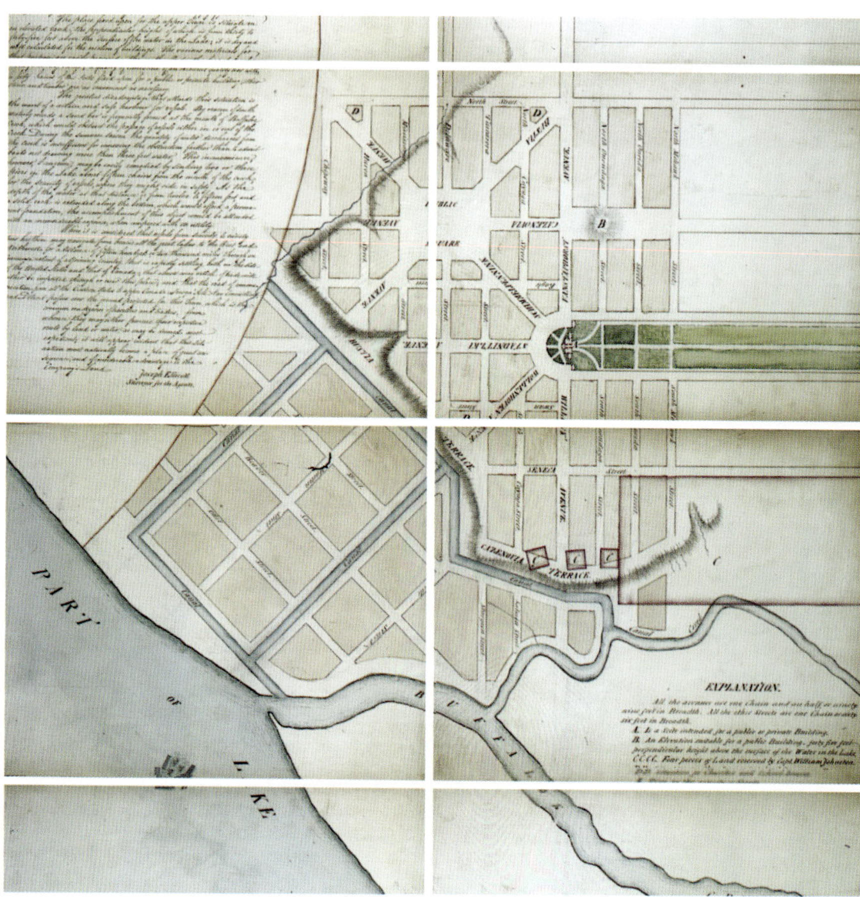

Fig. 1. Joseph Ellicott's first plan for Buffalo, NY, or "New Amsterdam", ca. 1800–04. New York Heritage Digital Collection, SUNY Fredonia.

for a greater distance. Subsequent and multiple city plans drawn between 1800 and 1849 confirm that intention, indicating both a wider and much longer axial mall.[28] The urban exedra is connected by a diagonal street back to the Public Square. The sole building indicated on the entire plan is located precisely where the urban exedra and axial mall join:[29] "A. Is a Scite [sic] intended for a public or private Building", most probably Ellicott's projection of a seat of authority.[30]

Ellicott's plan is presented as though his ideal central figure is in alignment with the cardinal directions, and at forty-five degrees to the Lake Erie shoreline. The alignment is closer to magnetic north. The reason why is hinted at by the arc inscribed in the upper-left corner of the plan, a boundary of a town named Black Rock surveyed prior to Ellicott's "New Amsterdam" plan. It seems reasonably certain that the pre-existing Black Rock street grid was aligned with both magnetic north and the 'circumstance' of Lake Erie's shoreline. Ellicott then aligned the northwest diagonal of his 'ideal' plan, the future Niagara Street, with the 'circumstance' of the street grid of Black Rock. Ellicott's 'ideal' plan was thereby integrated with Black Rock and the shoreline. This alignment and the Niagara Street diagonal prompted Rowe's brochure statement, "the entry from Canada and the diagonal of Niagara Street are among the valuable determinants of any significant solution, this area is a major feature of the Studio's plan". It is as if Ellicott anticipated it.

28 A half dozen maps 1800–49 show variations on this 'mall'. They support a speculation that Ellicott's ideal plan included an extension as far as the tributaries of Buffalo Creek that in 1800 was still within a Native American Reservation. Washington, D.C., and Mt. Vernon were likely in Ellicott's thoughts.

29 The building's plan is a 1700s symmetrical central hall type with flanking dependencies. The grand landscape axis extends through the central hall and leads to a radial room or porch facing the urban exedra. The layout recalls Stratford Hall, Mt. Vernon, and the 'Wren' building in Williamsburg. Continuation of the axis to the west extends to a dimple in the escarpment, suggesting ceremonial development in the future.

30 We might imagine public and private interests aligned for the common good, cities as both economic and socio-political constructs, this building as a 'Governor's Mansion' recalls others known from the colonial period.

Fig. 2. Buffalo, composite plans ca. 1800–49. To the northwest note the alignment of Niagara Street with the earlier surveyed Black Rock. To the east, note Ellicott's green tinted mall as likely envisioned to reach Buffalo Creek.

Ellicott had idealized the form of the working waterfront area as well. Below the escarpment and between the ideal city and the circumstantial shoreline, Ellicott planned a canal wrapping around a two-by-four rectangle of eight blocks with at least four more blocks to either side of the canal. Of the canal segments perpendicular to the lake, one canal is an extension of the Genesee Street diagonal from the Public Square, while the other is an extension from the corner of the urban exedra. With a canal connection between them at the escarpment, the foundation for the later development of ceremonial arrival spaces is established and was likely envisioned.

Water from the Buffalo Creek and Buffalo River feeds the canals. Ellicott's canal branches northwest along the lake, no doubt in anticipation of the Erie Canal. While Buffalo was being surveyed, the Erie Canal was being imagined, and Ellicott was among its promoters. That massive project, built between 1817 and 1824, was completed just twenty years after Ellicott's 'New Amsterdam' plan. The canal would arrive from the northwest along Lake Erie and the Niagara River, resulting in the commercial trade and industrial area Ellicott had imagined, but the elegance of his plan for the port area was lost to its overwhelming commercial success.[31] Rowe would have only suggested this history be investigated thereby setting in motion discoveries made by the Studio.

31 The Erie Canal linked the Great Lakes water transport system to the Hudson River, the first canal linking the East Coast to the Midwest, a great economic engine for New York City, Buffalo, and the Great Lakes Midwest region.

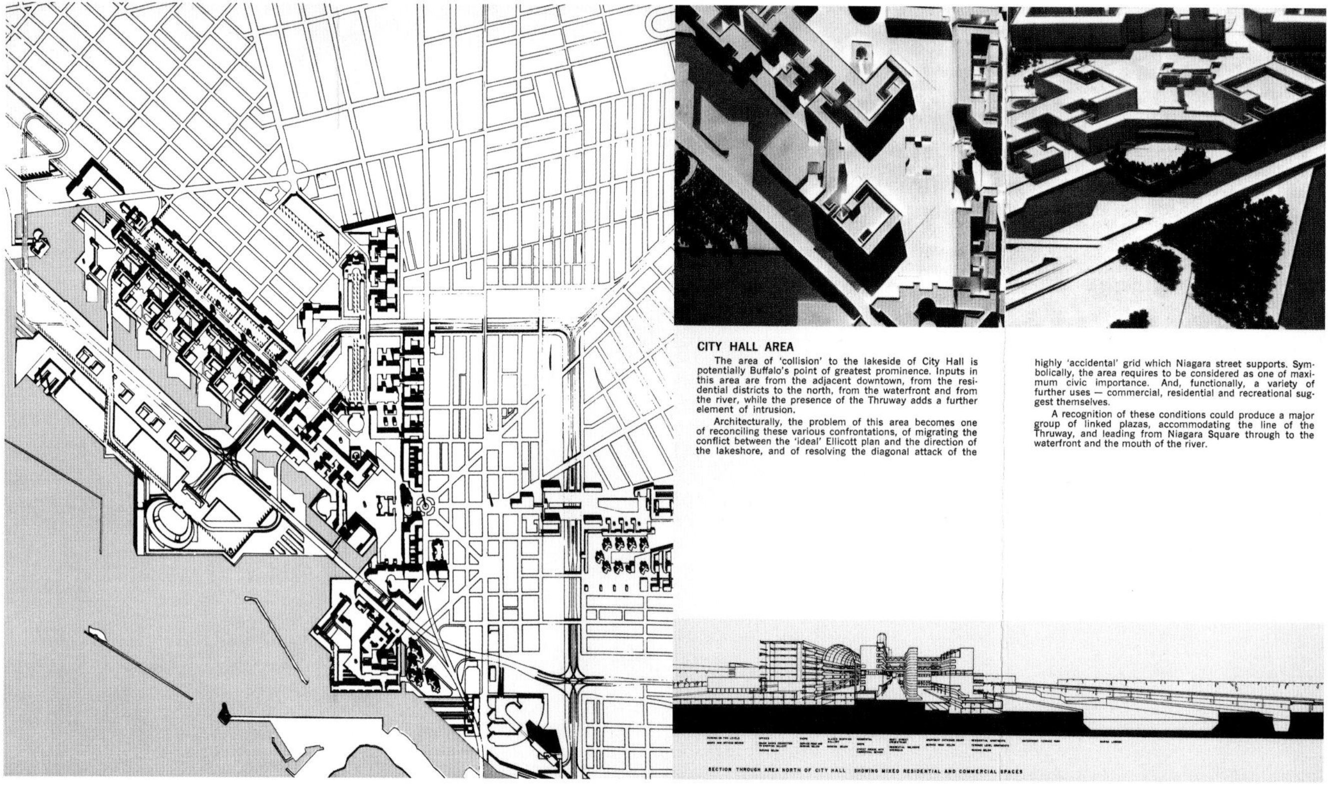

CITY HALL AREA

The area of 'collision' to the lakeside of City Hall is potentially Buffalo's point of greatest prominence. Inputs in this area are from the adjacent downtown, from the residential districts to the north, from the waterfront and from the river, while the presence of the Thruway adds a further element of intrusion.

Architecturally, the problem of this area becomes one of reconciling these various confrontations, of migrating the conflict between the 'ideal' Ellicott plan and the direction of the lakeshore, and of resolving the diagonal attack of the highly 'accidental' grid which Niagara street supports. Symbolically, the area requires to be considered as one of maximum civic importance. And, functionally, a variety of further uses — commercial, residential and recreational suggest themselves.

A recognition of these conditions could produce a major group of linked plazas, accommodating the line of the Thruway, and leading from Niagara Square through to the waterfront and the mouth of the river.

Fig. 3a. "Buffalo: Waterfront", exhibition brochure, Albright-Knox Art Gallery, Buffalo, 1969.

Affirming the Cultural Landscape of Ellicott's plan: The 1969 brochure included diagrams of the ideal/circumstantial conditions mentioned by Rowe. Ellicott's "Public Square" had become Buffalo's *axis mundi*. Niagara Square features a monumental central fountain. On the west side of the square the 32-story Buffalo City Hall rises above the square, facing eastward down the Court Street axis. The Studio scheme recognizes, reinforces, and expands on the ideal geometries first established by Ellicott's plan, addressing both ideal and various circumstantial conditions mentioned by Rowe, expanding the central ideal figure, giving emphasis to Buffalo's east-facing frontality, and, most prominently, creating a significant connection to the Lake Erie waterfront.[32]

Examining the eastern half of the Studio plan, Ellicott's ideal plan, including the corner public squares, is maintained. That ideal plan figure is extended east and north to the proposed depressed highway. As limited access highways were newly being imposed on and disrupting cities in the 1960s, the Studio response was to depress it, formalize it, and accompany it with a block-wide greensward that rings the expanded ideal figure.[33] This greensward, possibly suggested by the Vienna Ringstrasse, falls far short of what that exemplar could have inspired.[34] However, where Court Street reaches the depressed highway, a broad plaza extends over it and four slab type buildings mark the plaza's corners, making a symmetrical Modernist urban gateway. A cluster of existing cross-shape towers, anachronistically named Ellicott Town Center, is incorporated into this new urban event.

Examining the western half of the plan, the Studio built out Buffalo's central figure from the Buffalo City Hall. Flanking it north and south, buildings extend

32 In 1965–66, more of the ideal central figure of Ellicott's plan had survived than is evident today. The southeast and northeast diagonals have been sacrificed to create large north-to-south parcels and buildings.

33 In the 1960s, depressing highways in cities seemed reasonable; the Buffalo Waterfront team designed this one with much attention to urban form and parking terminals.

34 The Vienna Ringstrasse was well-known to the Studio, as were other cities with rampart or walled surrounds converted to areas for parks, civic buildings, and boulevards; however, the 1966 Studio was not equipped with a handful of civic building types, such as those built in Vienna or the U.S. during the City Beautiful era, with which to complement the proposed greensward.

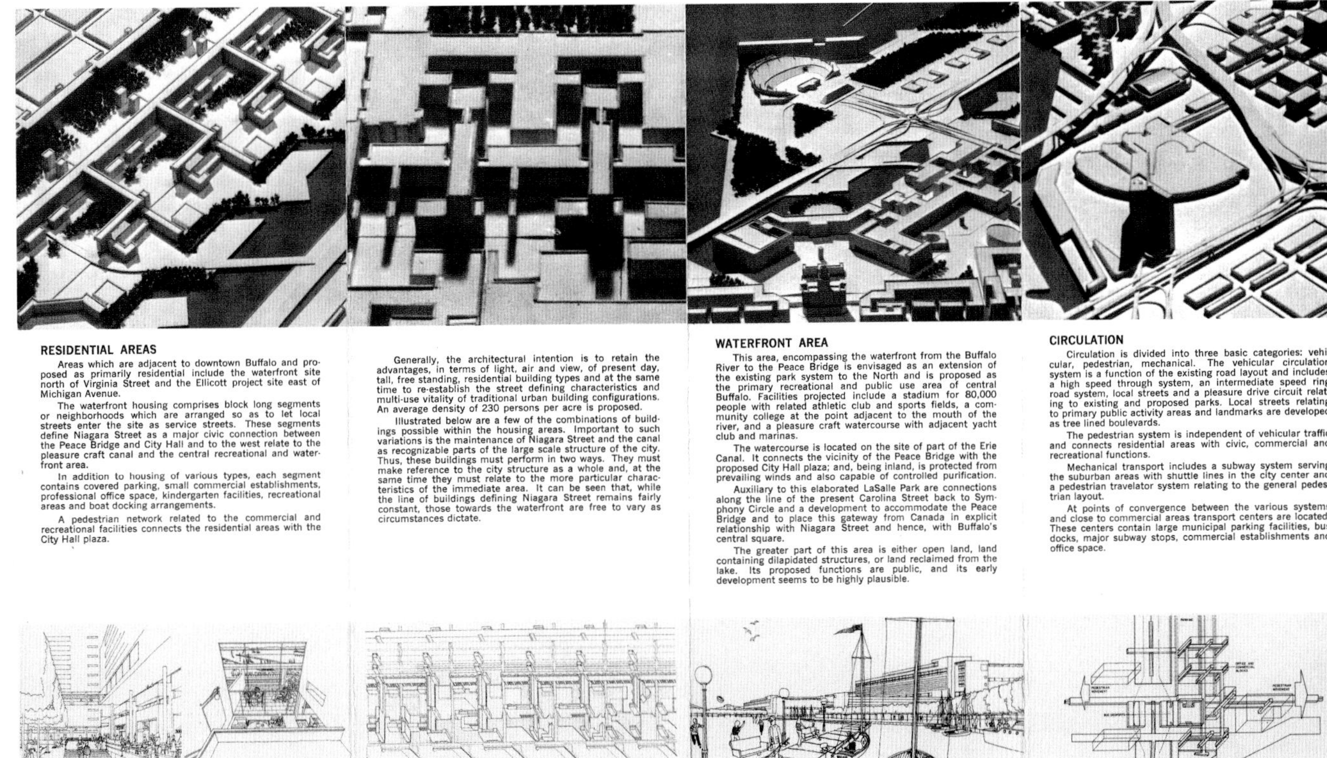

RESIDENTIAL AREAS

Areas which are adjacent to downtown Buffalo and proposed as primarily residential include the waterfront site north of Virginia Street and the Ellicott project site east of Michigan Avenue.

The waterfront housing comprises block long segments or neighborhoods which are arranged so as to let local streets enter the site as service streets. These segments define Niagara Street as a major civic connection between the Peace Bridge and City Hall and to the west relate to the pleasure craft canal and the central recreational and waterfront area.

In addition to housing of various types, each segment contains covered parking, small commercial establishments, professional office space, kindergarten facilities, recreational areas and boat docking arrangements.

A pedestrian network related to the commercial and recreational facilities connects the residential areas with the City Hall plaza.

Generally, the architectural intention is to retain the advantages, in terms of light, air and view, of present day, tall, free standing, residential building types and at the same time to re-establish the street defining characteristics and multi-use vitality of traditional urban building configurations. An average density of 230 persons per acre is proposed.

Illustrated below are a few of the combinations of buildings possible within the housing areas. Important to such variations is the maintenance of Niagara Street and the canal as recognizable parts of the large scale structure of the city. Thus, these buildings must perform in two ways. They must make reference to the city structure as a whole and, at the same time they must relate to the more particular characteristics of the immediate area. It can be seen that, while the line of buildings defining Niagara Street remains fairly constant, those towards the waterfront are free to vary as circumstances dictate.

WATERFRONT AREA

This area, encompassing the waterfront from the Buffalo River to the Peace Bridge is envisaged as an extension of the existing park system to the North and is proposed as the primary recreational and public use area of central Buffalo. Facilities projected include a stadium for 80,000 people with related athletic club and sports fields, a community college at the point adjacent to the mouth of the river, and a pleasure craft watercourse with adjacent yacht club and marinas.

The watercourse is located on the site of part of the Erie Canal. It connects the vicinity of the Peace Bridge with the proposed City Hall plaza; and, being inland, is protected from prevailing winds and also capable of controlled purification.

Auxiliary to this elaborated LaSalle Park are connections along the line of the present Carolina Street back to Symphony Circle and a development to accommodate the Peace Bridge and to place this gateway from Canada in explicit relationship with Niagara Street and hence, with Buffalo's central square.

The greater part of this area is either open land, land containing dilapidated structures, or land reclaimed from the lake. Its proposed functions are public, and its early development seems to be highly plausible.

CIRCULATION

Circulation is divided into three basic categories: vehicular, pedestrian, mechanical. The vehicular circulation system is a function of the existing road layout and includes a high speed through system, an intermediate speed ring road system, local streets and a pleasure drive circuit relating to existing and proposed parks. Local streets relating to primary public activity areas and landmarks are developed as tree lined boulevards.

The pedestrian system is independent of vehicular traffic and connects residential areas with civic, commercial and recreational functions.

Mechanical transport includes a subway system serving the suburban areas with shuttle lines in the city center and a pedestrian travelator system relating to the general pedestrian layout.

At points of convergence between the various systems and close to commercial areas transport centers are located. These centers contain large municipal parking facilities, bus docks, major subway stops, commercial establishments and office space.

Fig. 3b. "Buffalo: Waterfront", exhibition brochure, Albright-Knox Art Gallery, Buffalo, 1969.

for several blocks. Their east face affirms the north-south Delaware axis through Niagara Square. Their west face combines with a one-block-wide park that extends north-south along Elmwood Street to the edge of Ellicott's ideal plan. Elmwood Street to the north is continued as a corridor street until interrupted by the depressed highway. Elmwood Street to the south is interrupted by a diagonal highway, I-90, where a proposed building formalizes its passage. Elmwood reemerges below I-90 as a boat-slip with a proposed slab building paralleling the canal and making a bounding edge to the existing cross-shape towers of the Busti Terrace housing complex.[35]

The Studio maximized the west-facing second front of the Buffalo City Hall by developing an axis to the west that extends across a large, rotated square or diamond.[36] The large square is modulated with a smaller orthogonal and lowered square within it beyond which an obelisk marks a continuation of the axis which extends to the broad facade of a framing building.[37] Behind it, at the water's edge, a landscape exedra implies the continuity of this west axis to the stadium where it could have been marked by the single mast of a cable-stayed fabric roof suggested by the stadium's form.[38]

Given Rowe's prompt that, "Symphony Circle … ought to be recognized as an important urbanistic achievement", the Studio scheme meets this objective with two linked axes. One axis extends northward from approximately the northwest corner of Ellicott's ideal plan and continues north past the depressed highway to an area where three city grid geometries 'collide'. This axis is capped north and south by figural civic buildings with multiple frontages. At the northern cap,

35 In the Buffalo Waterfront brochure, Rowe listed three residential "textures", finding all unsatisfactory: dense city, sparse suburbs, towers. Each was lacking either adequate air and light or adjacent supporting functions. Cross-shape towers like Busti Terrace, icons of the Corbusian object building surrounded by open space, were never used by the Studio. Slabs and point towers were used.

36 Height-to-width calibrations to achieve visual closure were familiar from Hegemann and Peets, *Civic Art*. This large square was possibly calibrated relative to the 32-story height of City Hall.

37 In the brochure Rowe invites us to imagine numerous civic buildings; imagine here a version of a Rowe favorite, the Altes Museum with its stately colonnade.

38 The open-sided, 'C'-shaped stadium is common in projects by Le Corbusier and early Studios. Jim Tice suggested this one was influenced by Frei Otto's with the single mast of its cable-stayed roof structure terminating the east-west axis.

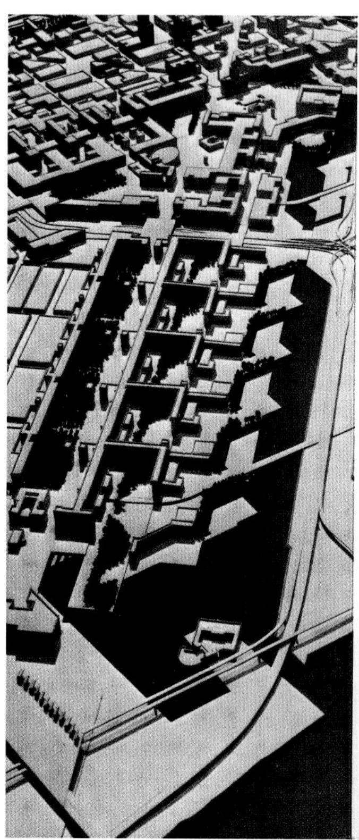

BUFFALO: WATERFRONT

This project, prepared by members of the urban design class at Cornell, is offered as a commentary upon the potential of Buffalo's waterfront.

It assumes that a basic strategy for the area must, first of all, recognize the real and symbolic significance of Niagara Square and must attempt to place this space in some explicit relationship with Lake Erie and the mouth of the Buffalo River; it further assumes that the entry from Canada and the diagonal of Niagara Street are among the valuable determinants of any significant solution; while, in addition, it implies that Symphony Circle with the layout to which it relates ought to be recognized as an important urbanistic achievement which, of necessity, must modify any immediately adjacent new developments.

These issues are here considered as being vital ones if the waterfront area is to be in any way integrated with the Buffalo city center as it at present exists; but, obviously, no less vital must be the nature and constitution of the area itself and, in this connection, a variety of recreational, residential, commercial and civic facilities are proposed. These, which are intensively inter-related, include: a stadium with adjacent installations for athletic activities; public and private docking for pleasure craft; a diversity of high and low rise housing; a provision for a full range of shopping and hotel possibilities; and office space for the use of both private and public establishments.

Further to these are supplied a community college, a convention and exhibition center, a library, an opera house, and an international museum.

In the absence of a specific program of requirements, projects such as these are proposed as possible but, by no means the only developments which might occur within the waterfront area; and obviously, they are not presented as the rigidly definitive components of a static and unchangeable plan. Instead they are introduced as the variable details of a model which now requires to be submitted to empirical criticism. It is a physical model; but, while it is primarily envisaged as a logical development of factors inherent in the site, it is believed that the generalisations which it suggests need not be in contradiction with conclusions derived from sociological, economic, and other criteria.

CREDITS

The initial project was prepared by the following:
Richard A. Baiter, Richard H. Cardwell, David W. K. Chan, Wayne W. Copper, Harris N. Forusz, Alfred H. Koetter, Makoto Miki, Elipidio F. Olympio, Franz G. Oswald.

Critics were:
Colin Rowe, Werner Seligman, J. Alan Wells.

This exhibition has been prepared under the supervision of Alfred H. Koetter of Wells/Koetter Architects, Ithaca, N. Y. and has been organized by Stephen K. Peterson.

The following have assisted:
Paul A. Curtis, Harris C. Feinn, Richard K. Gelber, Jerry W. Kreider, Henry W. Richardson, Terence R. Williams, Priscilla L. Wilson.

Advice on graphics has been given by Klaus Herdeg.

Model photographs are by C. Hadley Smith, Ithaca, N. Y.

Historical photographs are by courtesy of the Buffalo Historical Society.

This exhibition has been made possible through the interest of the President and Board of Directors of The Buffalo Fine Arts Academy and Mr. Gordon M. Smith, Director, Albright-Knox Art Gallery.

1810

In 1804 James Ellicott established the plan for the town of New Amsterdam which took the name of Buffalo in 1813. The centralized plan with its radial streets was extended by the linear common and was intercepted by the boundary of the New York State Reservation, later incorporated into the city as Black Rock. The immediate area of the central square early became highly developed while the outlying lands to the east were planned as farm lots. (See Diagram A to right.)

1910

The general grid of the city, after various twists, has aligned itself along a north-south axis. Intensive development remains at the original core and continues along the radials in a linear fashion; but, as early as the 1850's, a park and boulevard system had been proposed to the north of the core and it was this system which became the setting for further residential development. The Pan-American Exposition of 1900 was an extension of this park system. It was planned according to the principles of the City Beautiful Movement wtih an emphasis upon such civic amenities as fountains, symmetry and monumentality of structure.

Meanwhile an extension of the Erie Canal has penetrated the city and, as the transportation of goods switches from barge to train, it has shortly been followed by the arrival of railyards. Buffalo c. 1910 shows an area of apparently self-conscious urbanistic activity — the city core and the park system — in the grip of a seemingly uncontrollable transportation happening.

Below are shown images of Buffalo at the turn of the century.

1969

The self-conscious urbanistic initiative of 1910 has scarcely been maintained though the strangle hold of the railroad has signficantly diminished. Transportation by rail is now supplemented by auto and truck and arterial highways penetrate the city along the old canal and rail lines. The need to replace decayed housing and to provide more open space has resulted in the construction of large tower complexes set in open lots. The linear definition of the street is thus destroyed, while the steady sprawl of the suburbs has consumed the open land once existing between subsidiary rural centers and the city proper. As the city has expanded the memorable Buffalo of the early twentieth century has been reduced in importance and, correspondingly, has entered into a process of decay.

Below are shown images of the contemporary city.

Analysis of Buffalo discloses a composite of complementary and conflicting elements, of deliberate acts of will and of incongruous accidents — all of which factors are evident from the very beginning in Joseph Ellicott's original plan, Diagram A.

Evident in Ellicott's plan are not only a highly ambitious orchestration of streets and spaces, but also the clear indication of a conflict between an ideal city model and specific circumstances which this model cannot accommodate.

The ideal model which seems to be implied is presented in Diagram B. A distinct and self-contained community is equipped with a central square and is penetrated by major orthogonal and minor diagonal axes. It is generally reminiscent of Washington, D.C. and is ultimately derivative from the Utopian speculation of Renaissance theorists.

Diagram C illustrates certain topographical conditions of the site which necessarily acted to modify what we might call Ellicott's Platonic idea. The grid of Ellicott's layout is neither aligned with the Lake Erie waterfront nor with the course of the Buffalo River. Also the closeness of his central square to both lake and river suggests that any major expansion of his community will result in lopsidedness and a consequent erosion of its basic centralized theme.

Diagram D indicates some other factors which promoted further distortions of an ideal state. To the northwest the presence of the New York State Reservation prohibits a logical development; to the northeast, the lines of the present Genesee and Broadway introduce still more elements of disturbance.

As a diagonal axis in Ellicott's layout, Genesee is conceptually of less significance than the 'major' axes of Court and Delaware, but, as an important entry into town and as a street leading directly to the lake, Genesee competes in importance with the 'ideally' more prominent Delaware. Thus its functional values are wholly at variance with the status assigned to it, and this is a condition which seems destined to render still further ambiguous the southeast quarter of the scheme where Busti Terrace (see Diagram A) has already introduced an entirely erratic condition.

Some of these conflicts between ideal concept and empirical conditions Ellicott was able to resolve; but some issues he could not. Diagram E, showing Buffalo c. 1900, reveals the continuing importance of his dispositions — and the insufficiency.

Primarily through the agency of Delaware, Main and Genesee, his city has been able to extend itself throughout the nothern sector; but, along the waterfront, the confusion which might have been anticipated has now come to prevail. Thus this area preserves itself as both major opportunity and problem.

The nature of the opportunity is suggested by the examples of waterfronts elsewhere, but the solution to the problem can only be derived from the fabric of Buffalo itself; and the panels which follow are presented as a minimum examination of this fabric.

Fig. 4a. "Buffalo: Waterfront", exhibition brochure, Albright-Knox Art Gallery, Buffalo, 1969.

another landscape axis extends on a northwest diagonal to the Kleinhans Music Hall and Symphony Circle. From Symphony Circle, a new road cuts through the grid making a connection to Niagara Street at a new land-water edge.[39]

Erie Canal, Resurrection of a Cultural Landscape: Before rail and highway severed Buffalo from its land-water edge, Ellicott's plan, together with the Erie Canal, created and maintained psychological and practical connections between the lake and the city. In the brochure, Rowe describes the phases of industrial development that obliterated that connection:

> *the Erie Canal has penetrated the city and, as the transportation of goods switches from barge to train, it has shortly been followed by the arrival of railyards... the city in the grip of seemingly uncontrollable transportation happenings... rail is now supplemented by auto and truck and arterial highways that penetrate the city along the old canal and rail lines.*

He describes re-establishing the relationship with the regional landscape:

> *... some explicit relationship with Lake Erie and the mouth of the Buffalo River... the entry from Canada and the diagonal of Niagara Street.*

39 The Kleinhans Music Hall is outlined in the Studio plan, but not the nearby First Presbyterian Church. Nor are other figural buildings. It later became common practice to distinguish significant religious, social, or civic structures, seen as 'figural'.

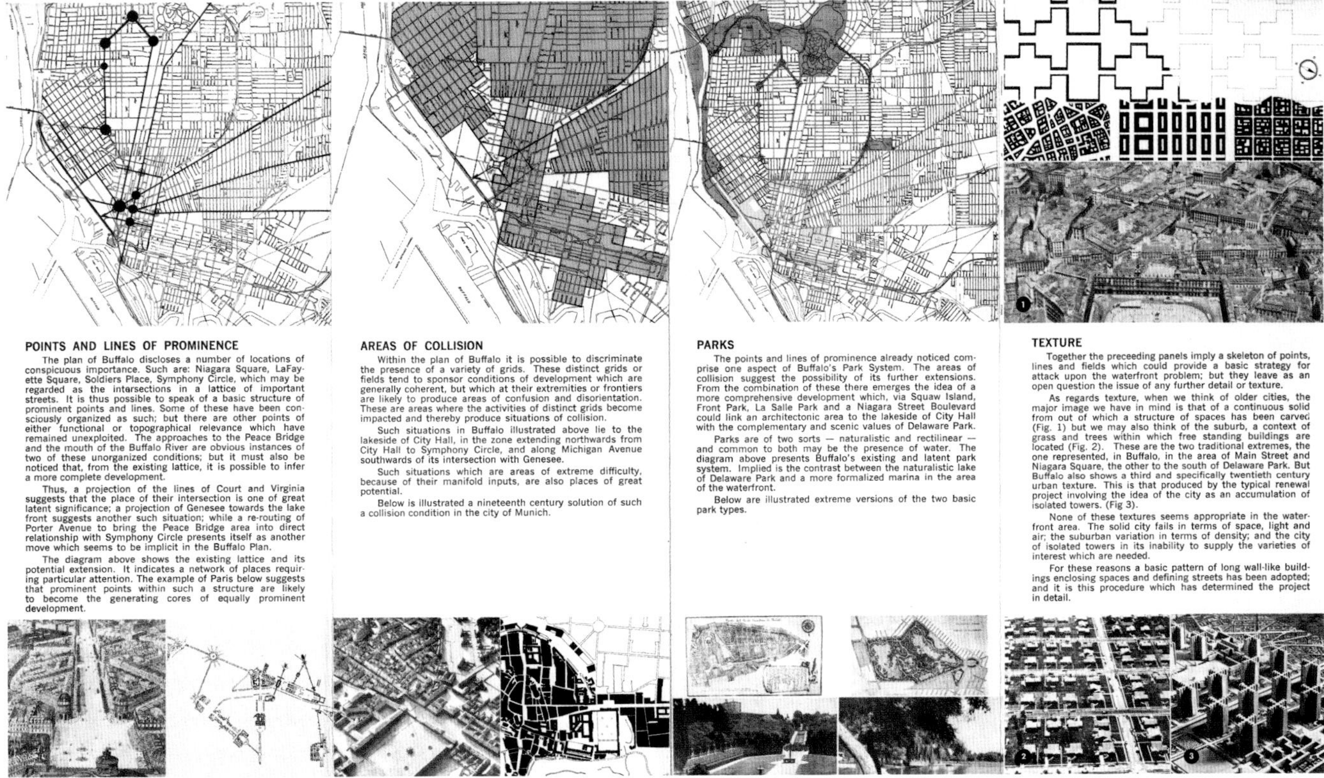

POINTS AND LINES OF PROMINENCE

The plan of Buffalo discloses a number of locations of conspicuous importance. Such are: Niagara Square, LaFayette Square, Soldiers Place, Symphony Circle, which may be regarded as the intersections in a lattice of important streets. It is thus possible to speak of a basic structure of prominent points and lines. Some of these have been consciously organized as such; but there are other points of either functional or topographical relevance which have remained unexploited. The approaches to the Peace Bridge and the mouth of the Buffalo River are obvious instances of two of these unorganized conditions; but it must also be noticed that, from the existing lattice, it is possible to infer a more complete development.

Thus, a projection of the lines of Court and Virginia suggests that the place of their intersection is one of great latent significance; a projection of Genesee towards the lake front suggests another such situation; while a re-routing of Porter Avenue to bring the Peace Bridge area into direct relationship with Symphony Circle presents itself as another move which seems to be implicit in the Buffalo Plan.

The diagram above shows the existing lattice and its potential extension. It indicates a network of places requiring particular attention. The example of Paris below suggests that prominent points within such a structure are likely to become the generating cores of equally prominent development.

AREAS OF COLLISION

Within the plan of Buffalo it is possible to discriminate the presence of a variety of grids. These distinct grids or fields tend to sponsor conditions of development which are generally coherent, but which at their extremities or frontiers are likely to produce areas of confusion and disorientation. These are areas where the activities of distinct grids become impacted and thereby produce situations of collision.

Such situations in Buffalo illustrated above lie to the lakeside of City Hall, in the zone extending northwards from City Hall to Symphony Circle, and along Michigan Avenue southwards of its intersection with Genesee.

Such situations which are areas of extreme difficulty, because of their manifold inputs, are also places of great potential.

Below is illustrated a nineteenth century solution of such a collision condition in the city of Munich.

PARKS

The points and lines of prominence already noticed comprise one aspect of Buffalo's Park System. The areas of collision suggest the possibility of its further extensions. From the combination of these there emerges the idea of a more comprehensive development which, via Squaw Island, Front Park, La Salle Park and a Niagara Street Boulevard could link an architectonic area to the lakeside of City Hall with the complementary and scenic values of Delaware Park.

Parks are of two sorts — naturalistic and rectilinear — and common to both may be the presence of water. The diagram above presents Buffalo's existing and latent park system. Implied is the contrast between the naturalistic lake of Delaware Park and a more formalized marina in the area of the waterfront.

Below are illustrated extreme versions of the two basic park types.

TEXTURE

Together the preceeding panels imply a skeleton of points, lines and fields which could provide a basic strategy for attack upon the waterfront problem; but they leave as an open question the issue of any further detail or texture.

As regards texture, when we think of older cities, the major image we have in mind is that of a continuous solid from out of which a structure of spaces has been carved (Fig. 1) but we may also think of the suburb, a context of grass and trees within which free standing buildings are located (Fig. 2). These are the two traditional extremes, the one represented, in Buffalo, in the area of Main Street and Niagara Square, the other to the south of Delaware Park. But Buffalo also shows a third and specifically twentieth century urban texture. This is that produced by the typical renewal project involving the idea of the city as an accumulation of isolated towers. (Fig 3).

None of these textures seems appropriate in the waterfront area. The solid city fails in terms of space, light and air; the suburban variation in terms of density; and the city of isolated towers in its inability to supply the varieties of interest which are needed.

For these reasons a basic pattern of long wall-like buildings enclosing spaces and defining streets has been adopted; and it is this procedure which has determined the project in detail.

Fig. 4b. "Buffalo: Waterfront", exhibition brochure, Albright-Knox Art Gallery, Buffalo, 1969.

And how the Studio scheme accomplished that objective:

> *... at the point adjacent to the mouth of the river... a pleasure craft watercourse with adjacent yacht club and marinas... is located on the site of the Erie Canal. It connects the vicinity of the Peace Bridge with the proposed City Hall plaza, and, being inland, is protected from prevailing winds and is capable of controlled purification.*

Between the new and expanded Erie Canal watercourse and the Niagara Street boulevard, streets and spaces are defined by numerous linear buildings. Subtle differences in building width imply differences in use related to location. In the City Hall vicinity, the buildings are wide implying institutional or commercial office uses consistent with prevalent center-city zoning. Away from the City Hall area, northwest of the depressed highway and along the waterfront, narrower courtyard buildings represent housing. They are scaled to the adjacent blocks such that the streets perpendicular to Niagara extend through the new courtyards. These pedestrian and service lanes connect the entire neighborhood to the "pleasure craft watercourse" and waterfront.

The area between the new City Hall Plaza and the Peace Bridge extends approximately ten city blocks along Niagara Street toward the Peace Bridge, and from the edge of Lake Erie inland to just past Niagara Street. Parallel to the waterfront and Niagara Street, the Erie Canal is expanded to become a "pleasure craft watercourse". Thereby, the Buffalo Waterfront project is contextually grounded in two of Buffalo's historic-cultural landscapes: Ellicott's ideal plan, and the resurrection, expansion, and elaboration of the Erie Canal.

left to right:
Fig. 5. Buffalo's Niagara Square and 1932 City Hall looking northwest along Niagara Street. Postcard 1933. Fairchild Aerial Surveys.

Fig. 6. Buffalo's industrial waterfront, *Harper's Weekly* illustration, 1877. Buffalo's resounding economic success resulted in a waterfront that displaced Ellicott's ideal plan proposed for it.

Studio Reflections on the Buffalo Waterfront project and Early Impacts: The Studio was reflecting on the Buffalo Waterfront project and looking ahead before it was finished. Most obviously, it had been inspired by the history of the 'place'. Grounding the proposal in Buffalo's history made for drawing parallels between the Mod/"trad" and what T.S. Eliot had called 'the presence of the past'.[40] Hadn't the past been accorded a greater presence by the Studio's Buffalo Waterfront scheme than other contemporary projects of its type, built or unbuilt, known to us? Didn't the design make what Elliot called something wholly new from a past/present alloy: compositionally a *gestalt* derived from Cubism integrated with and expanding on the ideal geometry of Ellicott's historic plan; and a Modernist palette of building types integrated with, rather than opposed to, historic urban patterns?

The Buffalo Waterfront project, while not perfect in our eyes, suggested that new urban design developments could and should be guided by the method used, one that could be applied almost universally, and therefore, possibly serve as a theory of both urban design and architectural practice.[41] That notion led to discussion of the proto-theories of *collision city*, *collage city*, and *contextualism* that emerged in the architectural literature a few years later—Studio practice had prompted the development of theory. Meanwhile, Rowe and the Studio suddenly seemed part of a broader theoretical discussion: with other schools, with displays of projects at MoMA and in Buffalo, with students going to New York City for a combination of academic and contractual urban design work, and with a major Studio project for Baltimore getting underway.[42] Rowe became part of a U.S. and European exchange of ideas and work which, over time, had some discernable impacts on the Studio.[43] However, the central concern of the Studio remained Rowe's charge: "reconciliation" of the Mod/"trad" city.

Recollections and Assessments: 1983, 1996, and 2022

As previously noted, there are two comprehensive presentations of the student projects executed in Rowe's Urban Design Studio at Cornell, *The Cornell Journal of Architecture*, 2, of 1983, and Rowe's *As I Was Saying: Recollections and Miscellaneous Essays*, 3, *Urbanistics* of 1996. The *Journal* presentation explained, illustrated, and assessed the 1963–82 Studio work. For the 1996 publication, many projects from the *Journal* were republished along with later Studio projects of 1983–1988. These projects were followed by approximately a dozen of Rowe's essays, as well

40 Elliot, T.S., "Tradition and the Individual Talent", *The Sacred Wood: Essays on Poetry and Criticism*, Methun & Co. Ltd., London, 1920.

41 There is a past/present theme in most of Rowe's essays.

42 My notes indicate Baltimore was a contracted IAUS study involving Studio students ca. 1968–71.

43 Primarily the work of Léon and Rob Krier.

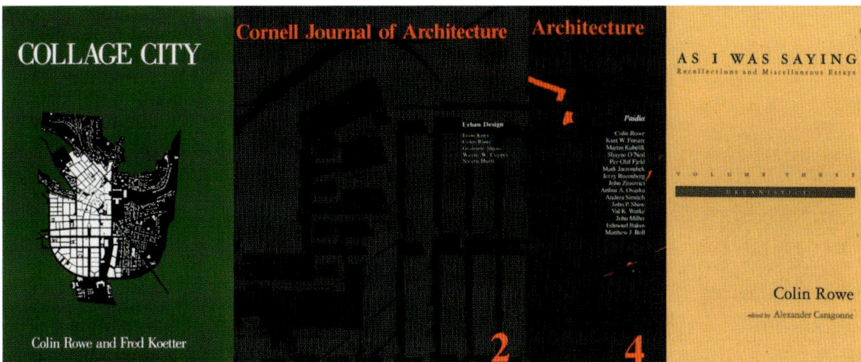

Fig. 7. Composite image of *Collage City, The Cornell Journal of Architecture* 2 and 4, *As I Was Saying* 3.

as "recollections". The structure of the three volumes of *As I Was Saying* is both chronological and thematic, such that the correlation of Studio-as-practice and essays-as-theory is both intended and indirect, as are Rowe's synoptic comments on the Studio projects and exhibitions. But, in Rowe's "Introduction" to the 1996 *Urbanistics* volume, cited below, Rowe describes what the Studio "believed", did or did not "tolerate", what it "preferred", its "ideal", and some of its "passions", all of which we can reasonably take as constituent parts of the theory driving Studio practice. I take up Rowe's points one by one, treating them in something like a true/false or confirmation/correction manner for the purpose of clarification. I see his statements as mostly true; where they are misleading, it is primarily because by the early 1970s and thereafter, theory for Rowe was running well ahead of Studio practice—not at all a trivial matter. As an immediate indication of possible confusions between the state of Studio practice and Rowe's remarks about it, note that Rowe conflates himself with the Studio: "The Studio was.... The Studio believed...."[44]

> *The Studio was never tolerant of the urbanistic proposals of Le Corbusier and Ludwig Hilberseimer. It was never able seriously to regard either Townscape as proposed by* The Architectural Review, *or Science Fiction as proposed by Archigram and others. If not conservative, its general tone was radical middle of the road. It believed in dialectic, in a dialectic between the present and the past, between the empirical and the ideal, between the contingent and the abstract. It believed in the virtues and the values of Synthetic Cubism. Simultaneously it was classical/anticlassical. It preferred what it called "Hadrianic disarray" to the classical set piece. In terms of specifics, presented with the plans of Vaux-le-Vicomte and Chantilly, it invariably opted for Chantilly. Its ideal was a mediation between the city of Modern architecture—a void with objects—and the historical city—a solid with voids. It also displayed some sort of passion, aided and guided by Wayne Copper, for the irregular and palatial megastructures of small princely German cities… it presumed that all would benefit from a good gestalt. The word contextualist, so frequently used nowadays, probably first erupted in Studio conversations—always very loud—between Tom Schumacher and Stuart Cohen in 1966. In spite of the hostility to Le Corbusier and Ludwig Hilberseimer, in its early years the studio was accustomed to long skinny buildings; but this* Zeilenbau *fixation seems absolutely to have disappeared as a result of the revolutions of Paris 1968/Cornell 1969… when, after a few months in Rome at the American Academy, I returned to Ithaca in January 1970, it was to an entirely different body of students… they had become determined that* Zeilenbauen *were no longer their thing; and that from then on, it was to be trad city with trad city blocks. A big*

44 Regarding confusion of self with Studio, given my comments, I might be similarly accused.

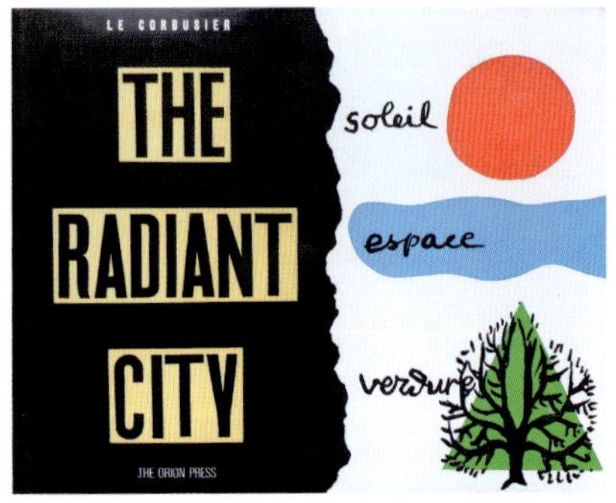

Fig. 8. *The Radiant City*, Le Corbusier, 1933/1967. Book jacket.

> reversement? *But of course; and of course, it wasn't all that traumatic. Although myself quite liked the* Zeilenbau *as presented by the Manica Lunga of the Quirinale and the Hofgarten of the Munich Residenz, there was no reason to remain exclusively attached to these prototypes, and so we continued with some change of style and with some attrition of quality which is always to be associated with a revolutionary aftermath.*[45]

In proceeding, keep in mind that Studio theory and practice are, at best, what is in the mind and eyes of a single student, or an amalgamation of the minds and eyes of various Studio students at different times, approximately half of whom changed each year, and that this collective Studio mind is almost always playing catch-up with Rowe's.

"The Studio was never tolerant of the urbanistic proposals of Le Corbusier and Ludwig Hilberseimer": This is true of Hilberseimer but not Le Corbusier. Le Corbusier may have had little influence on Rowe's own urban inclinations and therefore his intentions regarding the Studio enterprise, but Le Corbusier cast a huge shadow over all Modernist architecture and the Studio for at least a decade after the Buffalo Waterfront project. Le Corbusier's architecture was held up as exemplary in Cornell's five-year professional degree program, used as an instructive model and much emulated. That influence carried into Rowe's Studio. Rowe's articles on Le Corbusier were more positive than pejorative, leading us to conclude that Le Corbusier's work merited study, even emulation. To investigate the Mod/"trad" dialectic, where better to find the Mod? Le Corbusier had codified and thoroughly illustrated it. Sites Rowe selected for study mostly displayed 'trad' urban and suburban formal orders and architectural styles. Thus, the Mod often had to be introduced to meet Rowe's challenge. In the *Cornell Journal* of 1983, Blake Middleton astutely observed about Buffalo that subsequent "Studio projects were inspired by this project's resolution of edge, contour, and tactical design *within a generally Modernist palette of architectural elements*".[46] The italics are mine: The "Modernist palette" focused Studio attention and exploration but also created a drag on Studio investigations of the "trad".[47] Rowe's invocation of 'a willing suspension of disbelief', which wonderfully made all past architecture available as exemplars, also rationalized the rigorous study of the Modernist palette, whether believed in or not. In 1974 Rowe expressed his own doubt/belief in Modern architecture, but rested a heavy thumb on the Mod side of the Mod/"trad" scale. I paraphrase and quote Rowe: encourage the student to believe in architecture and Modern architecture, to be skeptical of them, "to manipulate, with passion and intelligence, the subjects or objects of his conviction and doubt".[48] Middleton's "tactical design *within a generally Modernist palette of architectural elements*" conveys both the expansive possibilities and consequential limits of such a palette. Little wonder that through the 1960s and 1970s Studio projects, particularly those with much open space to infill, appear governed by the Cubist *gestalt* combined with a limited "Modernist palette" of building types.

"It [the Studio] was never able seriously to regard either Townscape, as proposed by *The Architectural Review*, or Science Fiction as propounded by Archigram and others": Notice the qualifiers to both Science Fiction and Townscape. About Science Fiction, "whether propounded by Archigram and others". True, none of these kinds of proposals were of interest to the Studio. They were regarded as too *zeitgeist*, making the Mod/"trad" problem worse, anathema to our interests.

---

45 Rowe, "Introduction" (1996/3): 2-3.

46 *Cornell Journal* 2, 1983: 88.

47 Earlier drafts of this essay examined various Studio struggles in attempting to reconcile the "Modernist palette of architectural elements" derived from Le Corbusier with more traditional urban forms and exemplars. I also drew parallels between the phrases physical/cultural and Rowe's literal/phenomenal.

48 Rowe, lecture, 1974, MoMA; "Architectural Education: USA", *Lotus international* 27, 1980; and Rowe (1996/2): 54.

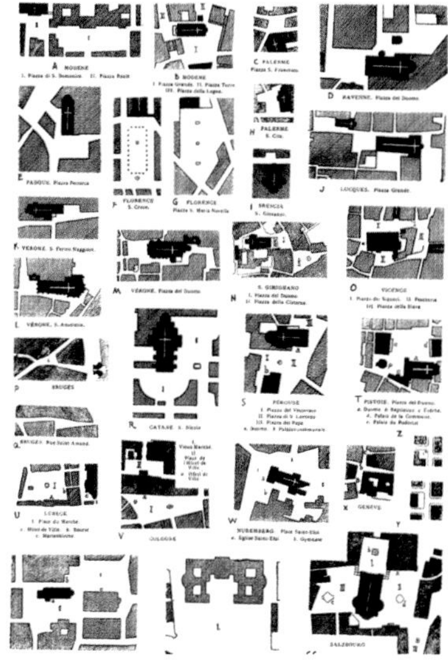

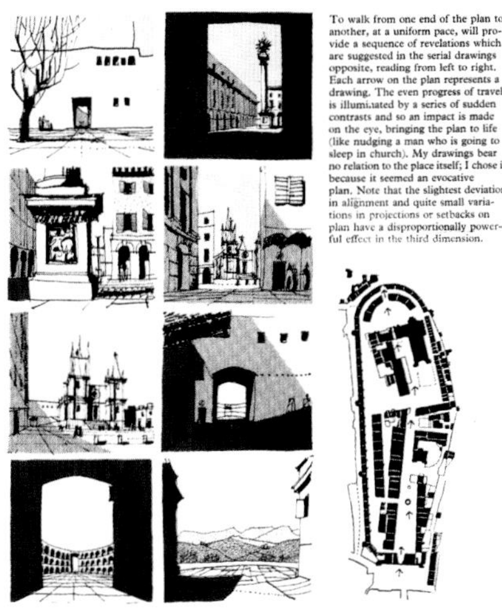

left to right:
Fig. 9. Camillo Sitte's documentation of urban spaces in Europe, as illustrated by Hegemann and Peets in *The American Vitruvius: An Architects' Handbook of Civic Art*, 1922.

Fig. 10. Serial Vision, illustrated by Gordon Cullen for his book *Townscape*.

How initially surprising that in *Collage City*, 'science fiction' images are included among "Nostalgia producing instruments" and rationalized because "fundamentally, the city of composite presence is too pervasive an idea to become outdated".[49] *Collage City* argues that iconoclast and iconophile are psychological types inevitably present in society, and, therefore, an inclusionary balance of both manifestations is possibly the optimal reality, resulting in a "city of composite presence".[50]

About Townscape, "as proposed by *The Architectural Review*", Townscape alone could not provide "a good *gestalt*" for the city. But this did not mean the dismissal of Camillo Sitte, the sequential vision aspects of urban design illustrated on the first page of Gordon Cullen's book *Townscape*, or similarly in Edmund Bacon's *Design of Cities*. Sitte's analytic studies of medieval squares and buildings were highly regarded because what otherwise could have been dismissed as accidentally picturesque conditions were grounded in practical and visual logic, possibly intentional, potentially serving as exemplars, and easily related to some of Copper's figure/ground studies of "trad" cities, which were both abstractions and representations of 'place' known from related studies and direct experience. What Sittesque Townscape lacked as an adequate *gestalt* was compensated by the hierarchic visual prominence of societally important buildings, sometimes not evident in figure/grounds but known from other related studies. Sittesque exemplars were highly relevant to mending and converting 'collisive' vacant ruptures in fractured U.S. grids in attempts to make them meaningful 'places'.[51] Regarding lessons in composing building complexes, *The American Vitruvius: An Architects' Handbook of Civic Art* by Hegemann and Peets was a highly instructive urban design discovery. It made it easy to equate Civic Art with Urban Design. We wondered at the coincident publication year, the same as Le Corbusier's Ville Contemporaine exhibition, 1922.

"If not conservative, its general tone was radical middle of the road": Studio projects were always grounded, located on sites in existing and very real cities. Given the Modernist polemic of past versus present fueling the Mod/"trad" and either/or standoff, a both/and reconciliation did seem "not conservative" and

49 Rowe (1978): 172-73 & 181.

50 Ibid.

51 I doubt many of us knew of the Rowe – Boyarsky interest in Sitte.

above:
Fig. 11. *The Theory of the Avant-Garde*, Renato Poggioli. Book cover.

opposite left to right:
Fig. 12. *Mont Sainte-Victoire*, Paul Cézanne, 1902–04, oil on canvas, Philadelphia Museum of Art.

Fig. 13. *The Portuguese*, Georges Braque, 1911–12, oil on canvas, Kunstmuseum, Basel, Switzerland.

Fig. 14. *Bouteilles et Couteau*, Juan Gris, 1912, oil on canvas, Kröller-Müller Museum, Otterlo, Netherlands.

quite "radical middle of the road". While sites were real, they were often located in city areas in serious need of repair: large, abandoned, or vacant, somewhat marginal, but not isolated. This made for an ideal studio practice, neither restrained by realities that would inhibit "manipulation" nor isolated from circumstantial conditions to respond to. It avoided the problems of both irrelevant utopianism and preservationist paralysis. It might explain Rowe's 1965 comment to Boyarsky, cited above, that the Studio was "empirical, pragmatic, and totally devoid of theory". Theory *per se* seemed neither a necessity nor a goal. While an unavoidable Modernism was prominent in the Studio's manipulation of the "subjects or objects of ... conviction and doubt", Rowe nurtured or introduced doubt by recommending Renato Poggioli's *Theory of the Avant-Garde* which tended to nip avant-gardism in the bud. Rowe simply encouraged looking at historic cities. *Seeing* patterns of city changes over time fostered a willingness to manipulate urban form as a means of discovery while gaining design skill and knowledge. It fostered respect for, tolerance of, and deference to what existed while also legitimizing the introduction of seemingly alien exemplars into contention. The result was to seek the existing formal structures and redeeming qualities of a place and enhance them in multiple ways. The goal was a significantly improved environment. While the results in the early Studio years often shared the problematic Mod qualities of large areas of undefined open space and too great a reliance on the "Modernist palette of architectural elements", such results were partially related to attempts to deal with large, quite vacant city sites otherwise so useful to encouraging wide ranging formal manipulation.[52] As the Studio built a body of work, what were imagined as the best urban exemplars, considered independent of time, increasingly became the standard against which to measure one's work.

"It believed in dialectic, in a dialectic between the present and the past, between the empirical and the ideal, between the contingent and the abstract": Dialectical thinking was all Colin Rowe. It was how he presented arguments, clarified problems and theoretical positions. His dialectic pairings are legion and found throughout his writings. "A dialectic between the present and the past" evokes T.S. Elliot. It is always present in urban-architectural city form—whether acknowledged or not, whether "between the empirical and the ideal, between the contingent and the abstract", whether physical and/or cultural. It is what we have seen above in the Buffalo Waterfront project and is a leitmotif of Studio work. There is more to observe on this, but it is best described below related to Rowe's comment about Wayne Copper's 1966 passion for documenting a collection of "irregular and palatial megastructures of small princely German cities".

"It believed in the virtues and the values of Synthetic Cubism": The Buffalo Waterfront project had demonstrated a melding of the compositional properties of a 'trad' ideal city with those of a Mod geometric order born partially from Cubism. Rowe's references to Cubism in relation to the structure and experience of architecturally defined space gave Cubism a high profile in the Studio. It provided an analogic demonstration of how one might extrapolate higher levels of order out of disorderly 'collisive' grids, particularly those evident in U.S. cities. And Cubism was Modern, psychologically important to most students in the 1960s and 1970s, as might be understood through the *Cabaret* song lyric, "If you could see [it] thru my eyes, you wouldn't wonder at all". We could be and were critical of the Mod, but with reconciliation the goal, it could not be rejected.

52 *Cornell Journal* 2, (1983): 88.

Gaining credible mastery was a necessity. We were still learning to *see* and *do* the Mod. Cubism was part of it. Our understanding of Cubism came from multiple sources: from Rowe's essays, his descriptions of "phenomenal transparency" as he saw it in select pre-Cubist and Cubist paintings and select architectural works; from the analysis by other faculty of Cubist, Purist, and post-Purist paintings in which contour, fields of texture, and color, independent of each other, make superimposed and overlapping fields or figures. These analogies provided useful ways to *see*, analytically, forms of urban order and enabled us to strengthen and/or integrate them.[53] For the visual artist, lines and planes and fields are composed in relation to the gravitational field.[54] For the urban designer, lines and planes and fields represent the cognitive order of the landscape-cityscape, as experienced and remembered in real space through time.[55] Le Corbusier's *oeuvre* bridged the worlds of painting, architecture, and the city, again making his work seem particularly relevant. Through our eyes, the opposing orthogonal/diagonal grids of his 'ideal' cities shared form characteristics with Renaissance ideal cities, Cubism, Buffalo, and most U.S. gridded cities. "The virtues and the values of Synthetic Cubism" informed numerous Studio projects in need of what Rowe later called "a good *gestalt*". That was the upside: a readily applicable, discernably Modern, formal design technique that combined a Cubist *gestalt* with a palette of Modernist building types. The downside was that mastering that technique tended to be all consuming. It inhibited *seeing* other available good *gestalts*, even as the Rowe-Koetter atemporal attitude became more influential and interest in the 'presence of the past' more compelling.[56] Rowe referenced alternate *gestalts*, as is indicated in the Buffalo Waterfront project brochure:

> *as early as the 1850s, a park and boulevard system had been proposed to the north of the core and it was this system which became the setting for further residential development. The Pan-American Exposition of 1900 was an extension of this park system. It was planned according to the principles of the City Beautiful movement with an emphasis upon such civic amenities as fountains, symmetry and monumentality of structure… Buffalo's Park System. The areas of collisions suggest the possibility of its extension… a more comprehensive development which via Shaw Island, Front Park, La Salle Park and a Niagara Street Boulevard could link an architectonic area to the lakeside of City Hall with the complementary and scenic values of Delaware Park. Parks are of two sorts – naturalistic and rectilinear – and common to both may be the presence of water*

53 Rowe, Colin, "Transparency: Literal and Phenomenal" with Robert Slutzky, *The Mathematics of the Ideal Villa and Other Essays*, MIT Press, Cambridge, MA, and London, 1976: 158–83. Published earlier in *Perspecta*, 1963 and in Hoesli, Bernhard, *Transparenz*, 1968. Rowe extended the description of phenomenal transparency provided by György Kepes in *The Language of Vision* to selected Cubist paintings and selected works of architecture. The related aspects of matrix and grid, figure and field, run through many of Rowe's essays. See "Giulio Romano's Palazzo Romano and the Sixteenth Century Grid/Frame/Lattice/Web", Rowe (1996/2): 104–169.

54 Mondrian's last paintings, *Broadway Boogie Woogie* and *Victory Boogie Woogie*, are said to have been influenced by his experiences of Manhattan. Rowe references both and illustrates *Victory Boogie Woogie*. He relates the suppression of figure in these paintings to the similar suppression of buildings as figure by the Manhattan grid. Further, he suggests this phenomenon can be related to socio-democratic politics comprised of a multitude of contending powers, none of which are defeated by the others. See Rowe and Koetter (1978): 107-117; and "The Present Urban Predicament", Rowe (1996/3): 165-220.

55 We were trying to think of our lines and planes and textures as highly satisfactory urban places full of lives and livelihoods, places like many remembered from our own childhoods and young adulthoods, places where 'life' was to be realized to the fullest by the many, as Jane Jacobs would have it, but also contributing to a clarified comprehensive spatial order. Quite the opposite of the arrogance assumed to be the métier of the Studio by its critics.

56 This atemporal attitude can be seen as similar to the espousal of sentiments later called Postmodernism.

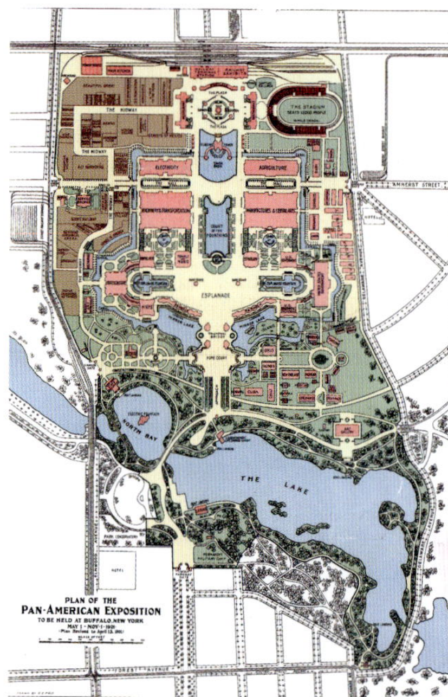

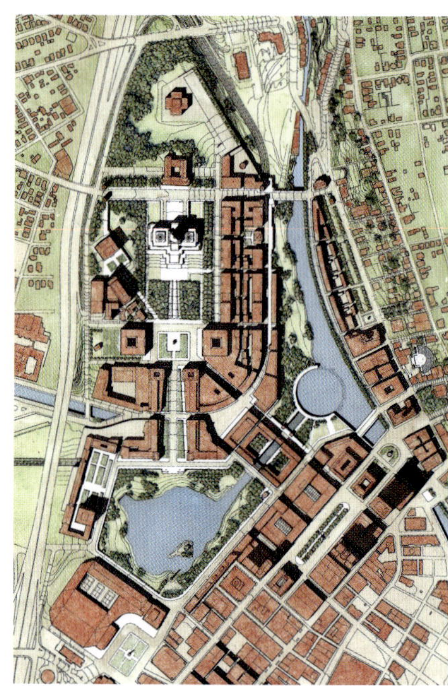

left to right:
Fig. 15. Pan-American Exposition 1901. Drawn by C.E. Pelz, 1901, Harvard Map Collection.

Fig. 16. Providence, RI, Capital District Development, site plan, Blake Middleton, thesis 1980.

> .... *Implied is the contrast between the naturalistic lake of Delaware Park and a more formalized marina in the area of the waterfront. Below are illustrated extreme versions of the two basic park types.*[57]

The brochure illustrations are of the Boboli Gardens at the Palazzo Pitti in Florence (rectilinear), and Prospect Park in Brooklyn, NY (naturalistic), the latter designed by Olmsted, who also designed numerous parks for Buffalo. These park types had been informing city plans for several hundred years. They could have been among the good *gestalts* useful to the Studio but would not be *seen* and applied in Studio projects for another decade.[58]

"Simultaneously it was classical/anticlassical": True. The 'Mod' had been partially defined as anticlassical and most decidedly anti Beaux-Arts, against which it railed. But in Mod practice, classical ordering was commonplace, as Rowe described in his two essays on "Neo-'Classicism' and Modern Architecture".[59] Axial composition, axis/cross-axis and radial/concentric orders are universals and fundamental to the classical. The classical informed Ellicott's plan for Buffalo. Compositionally, the Buffalo Waterfront project expanded on that classical order; in fact, it is far more classical, axial, and figural, than anticlassical. Most of Copper's figure/grounds are of cities that combine the classical/anticlassical. So do many Studio projects. But classical is not Classical, Neo-Classical or Beaux-Arts. It is not until Blake Middleton's 1980 Providence, Rhode Island, Capitol District thesis that an unequivocally Classical, Beaux-Arts, City Beautiful *gestalt* is embraced and extended. Even after Middleton's project, such explicit embrace of the City Beautiful *gestalt* is rare.[60]

---

57 From the brochure republished in Rowe (1996/3): 103, 108.

58 In the early 1970s, I began introducing these rectilinear (classical) and naturalistic (romantic) landscape *gestalts* as complements to figure/ground studies, as initially informed by Reps, *The Making of Urban America*, followed by Barzun, Jacques, *Classic, Romantic and Modern*, Collins, Peter, *Changing Ideals in Modern Architecture*, and Fein, Albert, *Fredrick Law Olmsted and the American Environmental Tradition*. These developed traditions, good *gestalts*, await rediscovery by both architecture and landscape architecture.

59 Rowe, Colin, "Neo-'Classicism and Modern Architecture I, and II", *The Mathematics of the Ideal Villa and Other Essays*, MIT Cambridge, MA, and London, England, 1976: 119–38; 139–58.

60 In history/theory classes, Louis Sullivan's claim that the Chicago World's Columbian Exposition of 1893 set back architecture for half a century or longer, was cited as an authoritative rejection of all things Beaux-Arts and City Beautiful, part of our 'Mod' indoctrination.

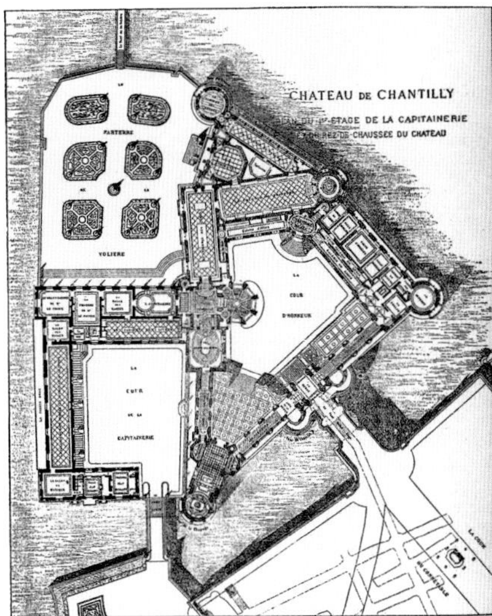

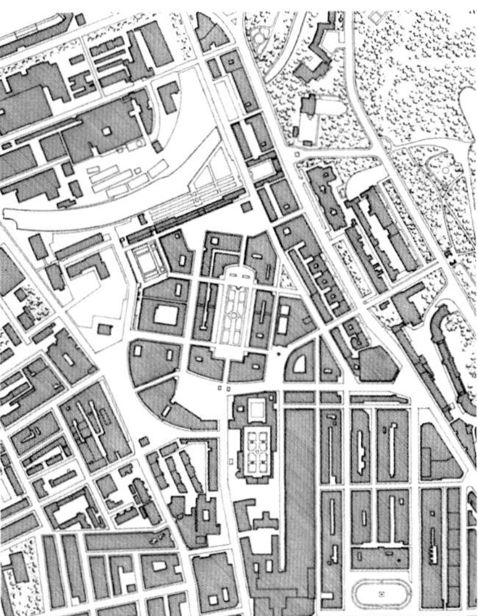

left to right:
Fig. 17. Château, Chantilly, France.

Fig. 18. Marylebone Rail Station, Regents Park, London, Steven Fong, thesis, 1979.

"It preferred what it called "Hadrianic disarray" to the classical set piece. In terms of specifics, presented with the plans of Vaux-le-Vicomte and Chantilly, it invariably opted for Chantilly": This preference for compositional complexity was shared by Rowe and Koetter. In 1966 Rowe was pointing out examples such as Chantilly and the Vienna Hofberg without much comment. As the Buffalo Waterfront project developed, Koetter promoted Studio interest in "collisions" of architectural and urban form. Florence exemplified such conditions: the orthogonal Roman encampment grid surrounded by fragmentary grids with different orientations, the areas of collision often marked by important spaces and buildings resulting in multiple picturesque conditions, and above all the Piazza della Signoria, Palazzo Vecchio, Uffizi Gallery achievement.[61] The Studio's compositional interest in 'collision' and 'collage' later served Rowe and Koetter as the basis for their expanded theoretical use of those terms and ideas in *Collage City*.

About Vaux-le-Vicomte and Chantilly, both are châteaux with accompanying landscape gardens. Vaux-le-Vicomte appears simple, the bilaterally symmetric landscape a setting for the bilaterally symmetric château. Chantilly appears complex, a crush of buildings seemingly compacted together by the forces of a gigantic and overwhelming formal landscape. Ignoring whether the settings are landscapes or cityscapes, Chantilly and Hadrian's villa can be grouped with the Hofburg in Vienna and Asplund's project for the Royal Chancellery in Stockholm, qualifying in *Collage City* as "ambiguous and composite buildings". 'Ambiguous' as to whether their shape derived from their surroundings or vice versa. And a 'composite' of multiple somewhat discernible building types, adding to their ambiguity. "Hadrianic disarray" in Studio projects surely resulted primarily from challenging sites often selected by Rowe,[62] and Studio efforts to create a higher level of complex order rather than an intended orderly 'disarray'. It is typical of Studio projects that some existing 'orders' are downplayed, while others are emphasized and reinforced. Related or new orders are sometimes introduced.

61 As the intentional picturesque qualities of the Piazza della Signoria/Uffizi Gallery were being appreciated, Koetter also recognized the figure/ground and solid/void reversal quality of the Marseille Unité d'habitation/Uffizi Gallery, the ship/the dock, illustrated in *Collage City*.

62 Others who shared related compositional interests and assisted or led the Studio in Rowe's absence, I think, included at least Michael Dennis, Fred Koetter, Lee Hodgden, Franz Oswald, and Steven Peterson.

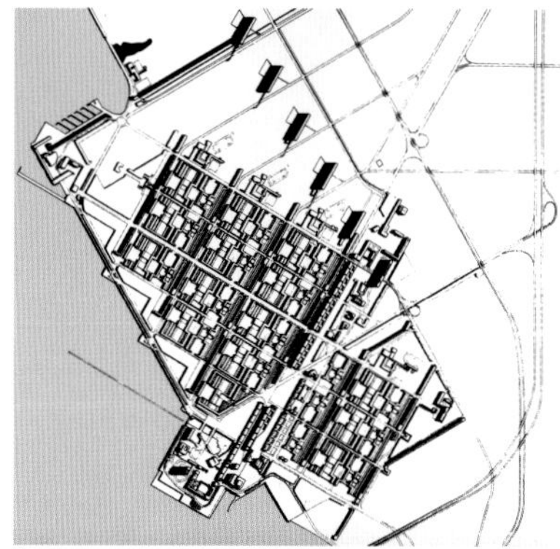

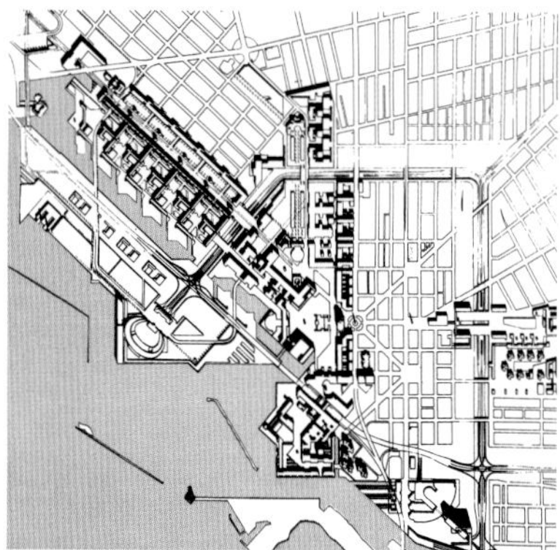

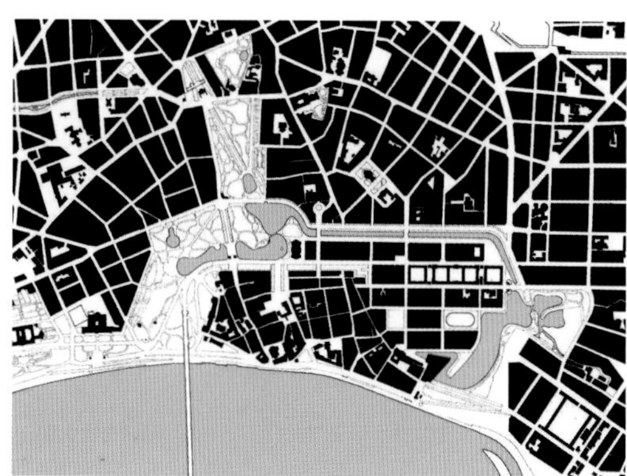

left to right:
Fig. 19. 'Mod Cubist gestalt': South Amboy Newtown, Thomas Schumacher, thesis, 1967.

Fig. 20. 'Mod/ 'trad' reconciliation: The Buffalo Waterfront project, 1966.

Fig. 21. Trad City documentation: Düsseldorf figure/ground, Wayne Copper, thesis, 1967.

"Its ideal was a mediation between the city of Modern architecture—a void with objects—and the historical city—a solid with voids": True. "Mediation"... reconciliation... etc. If the Studio was driven by a single shared sustained interest and enthusiasm, this was the governing idea. It appears repeatedly in Rowe's essays and books. The void with objects standing in it has little presence in the Buffalo Waterfront project. No new towers are added, but two existing groups of them are acknowledged. However, the idea that Mod towers could be located as ordering elements, rather than random visual events, was a proposition of note in Studio projects. Typically, towers or slabs are aligned and located at regular intervals along major roadways or paired as 'gateways', in either case seen against the sky in contrast to a lower, quite continuous building height.[63] "Mediation" was most continuously an effort to bend the arc of the Mod city toward that of the 'trad', an ongoing David versus Goliath effort, until "Roma interrotta", when the emphasis shifted decidedly away from the Mod to a greater focus on the 'trad' and a comparative promotion of the classical and demotion of the Cubist *gestalt*.

"It also displayed some sort of passion, aided and guided by Wayne Copper, for the irregular and palatial megastructures of small princely German cities": Absolutely true. I joined the one-room Studio in January 1966. Wayne Copper was making carefully drawn figure/ground and figure/ground reversal drawings of numerous 'trad' cities as well as the Palais Royal and two Mod urban projects by Le Corbusier. Across the room, Tom Schumacher was developing his plan for "South Amboy Newtown". It included combining two of Le Corbusier's housing types—his *maison redents* and his step section 1933–34 Durand Housing project for Algiers—to make a new, dense, Mod urban texture of blocks and squares, a goal contrary to Le Corbusier's anti-trad, anti-corridor street urban vision.[64] All these years later, I can see these Schumacher/Copper investigations as a model of Mod/"trad" dialectical argumentation, thesis/antithesis. At desks between them, nine students were making schemes for central Buffalo and its lakefront, a middle ground 'reconciliation'. How deliberate or circumstantial was this? Rowe selected Buffalo. He helped Copper select cities to 'look at'. What might Rowe have said to Schumacher? I wondered but never asked Tom why he was working so hard at what seemed such an impossible task.[65] In *As I Was Saying*, 3, Rowe comments about my *Cornell Journal*, 2, comparison of Schumacher's South Amboy project with Le Corbusier's proposal for Antwerp: "I find this a very gratifying opposition to contemplate. Though much alike the two proposals are very

63 *Cornell Journal* 2, (1983), "Harlem Redevelopment, The New City: Architecture and Urban Renewal", MoMA (1967); Baltimore Master Plan, D. Duncan, F. Hammann, A. Valk, (1968).

64 Schumacher's "South Amboy Newtown" can be associated with the post-WWII British 'Newtowns' movement that exudes Modernist utopian ideality. Its geometry, a Cubist *gestalt*, is strikingly like Le Corbusier's project for Antwerp, about which Le Corbusier's remark seems to apply: an "occasion for a MODEL CITY, because the city could be built according to a coherent plan, free of the historical contingencies which make older cities hard to transform". See Le Corbusier, *La Ville Radieuse*, Vincent, Fréal & Cie, Paris, 1933, *The Radiant City*, (trans, 1967): 285. The building types that Schumacher used as a basis for the housing were the *maison redent* and a step-section housing scheme Le Corbusier proposed for the "Oued-Ouchala plot in Algiers", *The Radiant City:* 51.

65 In most of his studio design teaching, Schumacher claimed *zeitgeist* neutrality while using 'trad' exemplars in lecture and exploring 'trad' design parameters in seminar classes. See "The Palladio Variations", *The Cornell Journal of Architecture* 3, Cornell University, NY, 1988: 12–29. In later years, teaching together, Schumacher and I often invented studio projects that emphasized 'trad' site planning and/or 'trad' buildings.

different".[66] Rowe does not elaborate, but "very different" is the dense interlocking streets, buildings, and courtyards in Schumacher's project. How striking that the Schumacher/Copper, Mod/"trad" investigations were bracketing the Buffalo Waterfront project exploration of the middle ground between those dialectical extremes.[67] And that so many other students, like Manuel de Vengoechea (Fig. 25), would so earnestly try to relate the Mod to the 'trad' through such strategies as a shared geometry and calibration of block and field sizes, relation of axes to landscape vistas, and making large scale spatial enclosures in conjunction with the hills and mountains of the surrounding landscape.[68]

"The word contextualist, so frequently used nowadays, probably first erupted in Studio conversations—always very loud—between Tom Schumacher and Stuart Cohen in 1966": "Always very loud", Schumacher and Cohen were, indeed, outspoken. Both had developed a comfort level with Rowe in undergraduate studios. Schumacher had also served as an assistant to Rowe. Several years later, Schumacher wrote the first essay describing 'Contextualism' (1971), and Cohen wrote the second (1974). In 1966, four of us had promoted and debated names and rationales for what we imagined was the Studio's developing theory. Fred Koetter and I were the other two. Koetter was promoting 'collision city'; I was promoting 'contextualism'. 'Collage' was in the mix. My argument was that Robert Venturi was making a 'contextual' argument related to American culture and architectural iconography parallel to our Rowe-inspired 'contextual' responses to the physical form of cities.[69] 'Contextualism', 'collision city', 'collage city' remained in discussion for the next several years. In the fall of 1969, both Rowe and Schumacher were at the American Academy in Rome.[70] They surely picked up the Studio discussions of 1966–67 while there. Two years later, "Contextualism: Urban Ideals and Deformations" by Schumacher was published. Rowe gave lectures referencing the idea of 'collage city' as early as the late 1960s and, for a May 1970 conference at Cornell, Rowe's lecture title was 'Collage City'.[71] Most likely, Rowe and Koetter had begun discussions about *Collage City* and writing may have commenced about that time concluding in 1973 (publication in 1978).[72] Meanwhile, Cohen, working in New York City, developed his essay, "Contextualism: Physical Context, Cultural Context: Including It All", published in 1974.[73] The words *including it all* referenced Robert Venturi. The words *physical context* and *cultural context* have provided the defining parameters of Contextualism or simply *context* in much of the subsequent literature.

"... it presumed that all would benefit from a good *gestalt*": True. The Studio objective was creating a higher level of cognitive order to be understood through the experience of the visual world, specifically the city, the town, the suburb, or their combination—a good *gestalt*. How? Identify latent orders to reinforce them. And/or introduce new orders to complement or better organize those already present. Apply lessons from urban exemplars, particularly those exhibiting clear edges, developed land-water interfaces, field continuity, spatial foci and/or linked sequences of spaces, extensive axes, and alignments with important vistas. Study drawings that documented changes to cities over time to see examples of both extending existing patterns and the introduction of entirely new forms—the latter encouraging parallels with collage. The visual association of fractured U.S. grids with the formal properties of Cubism heightened interest in the completions, extensions, clarifications, overlaps, and interpenetrations of

66 Rowe (1996/3): 14–16. And *Cornell Journal* 2, 1983: 65, two full pages illustrate Schumacher's project including six preliminary schemes, the final scheme, and a detail of the dense blocks with a caption: "Housing systems have been invented to form a grid matrix, or field of blocks, with a hierarchy of public to private use. The housing blocks are also ... a modification of Corbusian *redents*, made denser and with a more elaborate section."

67 Copper's figure/grounds enjoyed an influential photocopy circulation before and after their *Cornell Journal* 2, 1983 publication.

68 The importance of reference to landscape was supported by Rowe's description of Le Corbusier's 'Acropolitan complex', by Le Corbusier's poetic descriptions of the Athenian Acropolis in *Towards a New Architecture*, by Vincent Scully's *The Earth, the Temple, and the Gods* of 1962, and by Rowe's numerous descriptions of landscapes in his essays.

69 It was challenging to make this Venturi – Rowe argument in the Le Corbusier – Aalto world of Cornell. Rowe's formal analysis of Renaissance Mannerism aided my argument that the Vanna Venturi house exhibited Mannerist and Cubist compositional characteristics and emblematic references, both Italian and American.

70 Rowe on sabbatical, Schumacher having received a two-year Rome Prize fellowship.

71 Rowe likely used the 'Collage City' idea as early as 1967. In Rowe, Colin, *The Architecture of Good Intentions*, Academy Editions, London, 1994: 6, Rowe states, "previous versions of this material were offered at a symposium sponsored by Mathias Ungers at the Technical University of Berlin as long ago as 1967". James Tice attended a 1970 "Provincial Cities" conference at Cornell and has the brochure in which Rowe's lecture title is "Collage City".

72 Rowe, "Acknowledgements", (1978): 186.

73 Cohen, Stuart, "Contextualism: Physical Context, Cultural Context: Including It All", *Oppositions* 2, The Institute for Architecture and Urban Studies, MIT Press, New York, 1974.

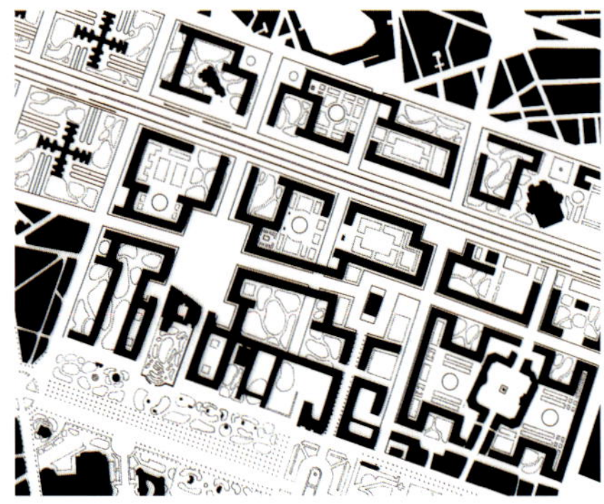

left to right:
Fig. 22. Louvre, Paris, aerial view. Google Maps.

Fig. 23. Plan Voisin, Paris, Le Corbusier. Figure/ground, Stuart E. Cohen and Steven W. Hurtt, thesis, 1967.

Fig. 24. Quirinale Palace, Rome, aerial view. Apple Maps.

these formal orders. In all cases the idea of making a good *gestalt* was well understood. But, why the nearly exclusive use of the Cubist *gestalt* for more than a decade in Studio projects? The reasons pile up: 1) Rowe's unwavering interest in the properties of Cubism beginning in the mid-1950s, 2) that interest shared by a half dozen itinerant faculty and former students then gathered at Cornell,[74] 3) Rowe's lengthy leadership of the Studio, 4) his selection of many of the 'collisive' sites for pre-thesis Studio study and team projects, 5) for new students wondering 'how-to-do-it', the Cubist *gestalt* was the obvious model to adopt and explore,[75] 6) the Modernist indoctrination that continued to suppress pre-Mod *gestalts*. There were some exceptions. Where other good but not stylistically 'trad' *gestalts* existed and could be identified, they were typically reinforced. Tom Davis's thesis project for the industrial town of Holyoke is representative. The industrial area was being abandoned, but it possessed a good *gestalt*. Revitalization might be realized through selective removals and renewals, a strategy that had begun to show success in the world of practice.[76]

"… in its early years the Studio was accustomed to long skinny buildings … Zeilenbauen": Yes, as evidenced in the Buffalo Waterfront project. This remains true well into the 1970s. They flowed as lines from Rowe's felt-tip marker, and his suggestive lines were developed into long skinny buildings. He would say, "look at" the *Manica Lunga* of the Palazzo Quirinale in Rome or the *Residenz* in Munich, but early on 'Mod' versions got more attention. As Rowe said, the urban proposals of Hilberseimer were of no interest, they were too mechanical, too bureaucratic. Alvar Aalto's long skinny buildings were of greater interest because they were site specific and space defining, but as most were in landscape and campus settings, they seemed not big-city enough. Le Corbusier's *immeuble villas* and *maison redents* looked more relevant to the big city. The *immeuble villas* made grids of streets, defined them, and enclosed courtyards. The *maison redents*, set back from the street, were modelled on historic 'long skinny buildings'. Both Le Corbusier and Colin Rowe saw the Louvre as an exemplar of the long skinny building. Le Corbusier illustrated numerous patterns that could be made with the type. In the Studio, they seemed particularly relevant when treated less ideally, more circumstantially.[77] About the type, Rowe fundamentally endorsed it. He says in the 1969 Albright-Knox Gallery Buffalo Waterfront brochure:

74 This group included John Shaw, Jerry Wells, and, via Oregon Lee Hodgden. And as students previously from Oregon, at least, Norman Crowe, Tom Davis, Michael Dennis, Don Duncan, Fred Koetter, Roger Sherwood, and Terry Williams.

75 The Texas-Oregon-ETH contingent of students, Roger Sherwood, Franz Oswald, Fred Koetter, most with prior office experience, established the compositional model and graphic standard emulated in other early Studio projects and sustained until at least 1976.

76 Embrace of the 'trad' as seen in the 1962–64 Ghirardelli Square, San Francisco, transformation of industrial buildings, and John Carlo de Carlo's work in Urbino represented contextual projects. See Davis's essay in this book.

77 Wayne Copper's figure/ground drawing of the Louvre – Palais Royal appear equivalent to Le Corbusier's *redent* – immeuble villa. His Swiss Pavilion in Paris; Immeuble Clarté in Geneva; and Unité de Habitation in Marseille made some *redent* proposals seem believable.

Fig. 25. Santa Marta, Colombia, Manuel R. de Vengoechea, Master's thesis, 1968.

The solid city fails in terms of space, light and air; the suburban variation in terms of density; and the city of isolated towers in its inability to supply the varieties of interest which are needed. For these reasons a basic pattern of long wall-like buildings enclosing spaces and defining streets has been adopted; and it is this procedure which has determined the project in detail.

A brief research project contemporary with the Schumacher/Copper theses illustrates the Studio's interest in the circumstantial use of long skinny buildings as seen in Le Corbusier's 1925 Plan Voisin for Paris. That Plan, by 1966, had lost its luster, but with Modernism still in full swing it had not yet gained the status it holds today: icon of everything wrong with Modernism.[78] Moreover, Rowe's descriptions of Le Corbusier's work induced the Studio to sacralize, study, and rationalize his work rather than reject it. That high regard was challenged one day by John Reps who pointed out the absurdities of the Plan Voisin. While his remarks were consistent with Rowe's critique of the Mod, they drew our attention to the relationship of the Ville Contemporaine / Plan Voisin as an ideal / circumstantial condition at a dimension much greater than most exemplars Rowe was referencing.[79] Contextual deformations appeared numerous. What lessons might be *seen* in this ideal/circumstantial example? Of greatest interests were the very flexible *redents* playing multiple spatial roles. They make axial spaces; link figural spaces; define corridor streets, courtyards, the edges of fields; and infill gaps in street walls.[80] They perform similarly in the Buffalo Waterfront project. Typically, Rowe's felt-tip lines were simply indications of the important edges of

78 Brasilia had been recently built (1956–60). Le Corbusier was still *the* heroic Modern architect, highly productive until his unexpected death (1965). Le Corbusier's staff continued his work and/or gravitated to the U.S., making a loosely affiliated group of highly respected Modernists in various U.S. institutions, including at Cornell and U. Kentucky, where Anthony Eardley was dean. Guillermo Jullian de la Fuente and Jose Oubrerie both taught at numerous U.S. schools of architecture including Cornell.

79 The linear building housing type plus open space had a worldwide impact, whether 'ideal' or 'deformed', whether autonomous or context sensitive. It met multiple housing hygiene goals with updated infrastructure, fresh air, and sunlight. Post-WWII European housing needs fueled industrial-scale housing. Projects like the Golden Lane and Robin Hood Gardens by Alison and Peter Smithson of 1952 were still a fascination in the 1960s.

80 Evidently the 'ideal' Ville Contemporaine had been adjusted to the 'circumstance' of historic Paris. A few of us built a study model of the Plan Voisin. That study inspired the Cohen-Hurtt thesis the next semester (abridged in this book). Later, the model was mounted on a wall in the architectural office of Wells and Koetter. Possibly, it contributed to *Collage City*, as did the Cohen-Hurtt, Plan Voisin figure/ground.

streets and fields that, when translated into three dimensions by students, took on the Mod and mega-structure quality seen in early Studio projects. While anathema to the scale of the 'trad' city, they persisted in Studio work until ca. 1978 and "Roma interrotta." But Rowe dates the waning of interest in these *Zeilenbauen* nearly ten years earlier?

"... but this *Zeilenbau* fixation seems absolutely to have disappeared as a result of the revolutions of Paris 1968/Cornell 1969": Yes and No. Yes, the studio was accustomed to long skinny buildings, but the "*Zeilenbau* fixation" remained in place 1964–78. Then they almost disappeared. Why would Rowe collapse the time frame by a decade and reference the "revolutions of Paris 1968/Cornell 1969"? At Cornell, racial insensitivities led to a Black student sit-in/occupation of the student union: violence was threatened but averted; it was memorable to anyone there, but, among disturbing national and international events or 'revolutions' around that time, those of Paris/Cornell were minor.[81] It was a dark period for the nation, understandably magnifying the events at Paris/Cornell. But for Rowe, Paris/Cornell was personal. The student protests that shut the École des Beaux-Arts in Paris led to the coming of Mathias Ungers to Cornell as department chair in 1969, an appointment Rowe had supported.[82] The results were intrusions on his Studio budget and urban design arena by Ungers and the departure of Rowe's untenured faculty colleagues, including friend and co-author Fred Koetter.[83] Additionally, the stimulus provided by writing *Collage City*, 1970–73, had ended. Rowe's frustrations during this time might partially explain his remark in the text of *As I Was Saying*, 3, inserted between the work prior to 1976 and the work of 1977 and afterwards:

> *A hiatus or marking time in the Studio.* Zeilenbauen *remain persistent though reduced. However, city blocks have become decisive.*[84]

Rowe did not supplement Middleton's description of projects between 1966–76. What one *sees* is that in that period, the Studio continued to wrestle with the Mod/"trad" problem, and that the Cubist *gestalt* and the Modernist palette of elements continued to be deployed. A preponderance of long skinny buildings, many of which can also be read as megastructures, is quite constant. Therefore Rowe's "hiatus or marking time" assessment is basically true but undervalues a determined and continuous Studio investigation of resolving the Mod/"trad" problem. Afterall, *Collage City* was not published until 1978, no doubt also a frustrating "marking time" for Rowe, but this also meant the 'theory' developed in such a complete form by Rowe and Koetter was not readily or so completely available to the Studio. Meanwhile the Studio continued the inquiry into the Mod/"trad" problem, often addressing particularly challenging sites that varied considerably in size. No, the "*Zeilenbau* fixation" did not disappear with the "revolutions" of 1968–69. Rowe's interest in the type had not waned. After declaring that the Studio "fixation" on the type had ceased, he said, "Although myself quite liked the *Zeilenbau* as presented by the Manica Lunga of the Quirinale and the Munich Residenz".[85] Rowe's continued interest sustained Studio interest. So, simply change Rowe's 1968–69 date in his "Introduction" to the 1977–78 date in the body of the text and his contention that the Studio students "*had become determined that* Zeilenbauen *were not their thing*" is far more accurate.

81 It seemed the nation entered a dark period in 1963 with the assassinations of Medgar Evers (June 1963) and John Kennedy (Nov. 1963), followed by the hopeful Civil Rights Act (July 1964), the Black Power movement, the assassination of Malcom X (Feb. 1965), the Vietnam War and mounting resistance to it, the student sit-ins at Columbia University (March 1968), the assassination of Martin Luther King (April 1968), related protest riots, the assassination of Bobby Kennedy (June 1968), the Poor People's Campaign and March on Washington (1968), and Nixon's 'secret' bombing of Cambodia (March 1969), provoking more anti-war protests. The 'revolutions' at Cornell included an occupation of the Student Union by an aggrieved group of Black students that resulted in a three-day suspension of classes and multiple teach-ins.

82 Rowe (1996/2): 5. Rowe contributed to Ungers becoming department chair. He apparently suggested to Ungers that he apply for the position and must have remarked in favor to the search committee, chair, and dean, to his later regret.

83 Columbia, Princeton, and Yale seem to have been the early beneficiaries of this exodus of faculty from Cornell, later and less noticeably, at least the universities of Southern California, Virginia, Miami, Notre Dame, Maryland, and Catholic in D.C.

84 Rowe (1996/3): 34.

85 Ibid.: 3.

left to right:
Fig. 26. Richmond, Virginia, plan of existing at the State Capitol and waterfront area, Steven Muse, thesis, 1976.

Fig. 27. Richmond, Virginia, proposed plan, Steven Muse, thesis, 1976.

"... from then on, it was to be trad city with trad city blocks": True: but primarily after approximately 1977–78. Street/anti-street is the great divide between the 'trad' and Mod city. Rowe's interests in Le Corbusier and Modernism continued to result in some Mod/"trad" ambiguities, but there was never ambiguity about Rowe's pro-street position. He frequently remarked on the social-cultural importance of streets and the related physical manifestations of public versus private space and property.[86] He likely influenced the 1978 book edited by Stanford Anderson, *On Streets*.[87] In the 'trad' city the legally defined street occasionally expanded into an agora, forum, piazza, square, green, or common, that is, a related part of the public realm and place of public assembly. The Studio's earliest definitive departure from the Mod city is its preference for defined street space. That preference led inevitably to greater and greater attention to the "trad city and the trad city block" and associated defined urban spaces.[88] While Rowe and the Studio embraced Léon Krier's generalized description of the *res publica + res privata = civitas*, Rowe paid considerable attention to the relation of street and block.

> *The perimeter block is a highly ambiguous construction which can only present the question: does one walk along the streets or through the courtyards? ... the answer... via the courtyards* [but then]... *the streets will remain residual... barely capable of arresting focused attention. But if this is a criticism of the perimeter block as a general proposition, it must be noticed that as an occasional strategy and embedded within a contrary fabric, it may sometimes be productive of most satisfying results. For what... is the Hofgarten... the Palais Royal... the Inns of Court, in Oxford and Cambridge what are the colleges, unless examples of a highly specific use of perimeter block? However, all of these are places of restricted entry. Their security is elaborate.... Many hybrid blocks both in Paris and Rome combine a quantity of* hôtels particuliers, *or* palazzi, *and often other items too.... Their primary relationship is to the street, and with regard to each other, relationship is little more than casual... a city of perimeter blocks must, of necessity, be better than a city of* Zeilenbauen, *but it is far from good enough.*[89]

86 Rowe (1978): 66–68. Rowe asked, how could such large-open spaces be policed? "...almost certainly it would be more satisfying to be presented with the exclusions—wall, railings, fences, barriers—of a reasonably constructed ground plane".

87 Anderson, Stanford, ed. *On Streets*, Institute for Architecture and Urban Studies, MIT Press, Cambridge, MA, and London, 1978. Rowe's circle included Stanford Anderson, and many contributors to *On Streets:* Kenneth Frampton, Robert Gutman and Anthony Vidler, and, among former students at least, Peter Eisenman, William C. Ellis, Thomas L Schumacher, and Peter Wolf. In 1965 "Anderson had asked Rowe to become a member of an organization he was initiating called CASE (Consortium of Architects for the Study of the Built Environment)", see Naegele, Daniel, *Letters of Colin Rowe: Five Decades of Correspondence*, Artifice books on architecture. London, 2016: 156–157.

88 Former Rowe students who undertook teaching encouraged studio projects on urban sites, hoping to challenge the object building paradigm and suggest design responses to historical, environmental, and cultural contexts.

89 Rowe, "The Vanished City", (1996/3): 248–49. The essay seems prompted by the IBA proposals for Berlin but is used to discuss general urban issues. The citation is from two short sub-sections titled 'Block or Street' and 'Immensely Large Blocks'. See similar points about Amsterdam South in Rowe and Koetter (1978): 52.

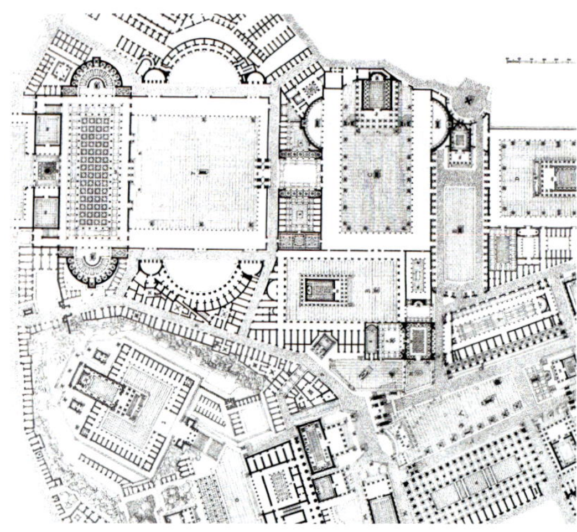

Fig. 28. Dragon featured at the annual St. Patrick's Day celebration. Courtesy Department of Architecture, Cornell University.

Fig. 29. Imperial Fora, Rome. From *Grandes Compositions Executees*, Georges Gromort, 1910.

Having declared the change in Studio thinking from *Zeilenbauen* to "trad city with trad city blocks", Rowe asks, How big a change, how traumatic was this?

"... trad city with trad city blocks. A big *reversement*? But of course; and of course, it wasn't all that traumatic": Yes, and No. Rowe's 1996 observation was likely prompted by Léon Krier's statement in the "Forward" to the 1983 *Cornell Journal of Architecture*, 2:

> *After nineteen years of relentless struggle with the dragon, the Cornell Urban Design studio seems finally to have freed itself from the indelible grasp of modern planning and fragmentation. The hypothetical synthesis between the Traditional City and the City of Industry which, for a while, had been the declared goal of Rowe and his peers has been recognized as being at an impasse and abandoned for good.*[90]

Krier's view was based on his experience of Cornell's architectural culture, his participation in *Roma interrotta*, his reading of *Collage City*, and his review of the Studio projects published in the 1983 *Journal*. Rowe says, Yes, "A big reversal? But of course", followed by, No, "it wasn't all that traumatic". Yes: ca. 1977–78, the Studio appears to abandon the 'Mod city' in favor of the 'trad' alternative; deliberate efforts at 'reconciliation' appear to cease in favor of greater attention to 'trad' city characteristics, seemingly a traumatic change.[91] But not so traumatic in Rowe's mind because the Studio had been concerned with the street and block all along, as exhibited in the Buffalo Waterfront project, the Copper and Schumacher theses, and, in those same years, in projects like Manuel R. de Vengoechea's thesis for Santa Marta, Colombia, in which the blocks and buildings of the historic center are preserved, and a Mod texture of blocks similar in size and reminiscent of Spanish plaza traditions is invented.[92]

And "it wasn't all that traumatic" because, likewise, in Rowe's mind, during the writing of *Collage City* 1970–73, the Mod/"trad" balance shifted in favor of the 'trad'.[93] In *Collage City*, a juxtaposition of plan images of the Athenian Acropolis and the Roman Imperial Forums is said to represent "a debate between two models ... typified as acropolis and forum",[94] illustrated on opposing pages, and preceded by:

---

90 Krier, Léon, "Foreword", *The Cornell Journal of Architecture* 2, 1983: 6.

91 Books and projects by the Kriers provided a critique and exemplars assimilated by the Studio in the late 1970s.

92 The block systems invented by both de Vengoechea and Schumacher may also have been influenced by Savannah's system of wards familiar from Rep's course and book, and Edmund Bacon's *Design of Cities* (1967).

93 Rowe and Koetter (1978): 186. The *Collage City* text was written 1970–73; the publication delay was due mainly to illustrations.

94 Rowe and Koetter (1978): 83–85. Or the entire chapter "Crisis of Object: Predicament of Texture": 50–85.

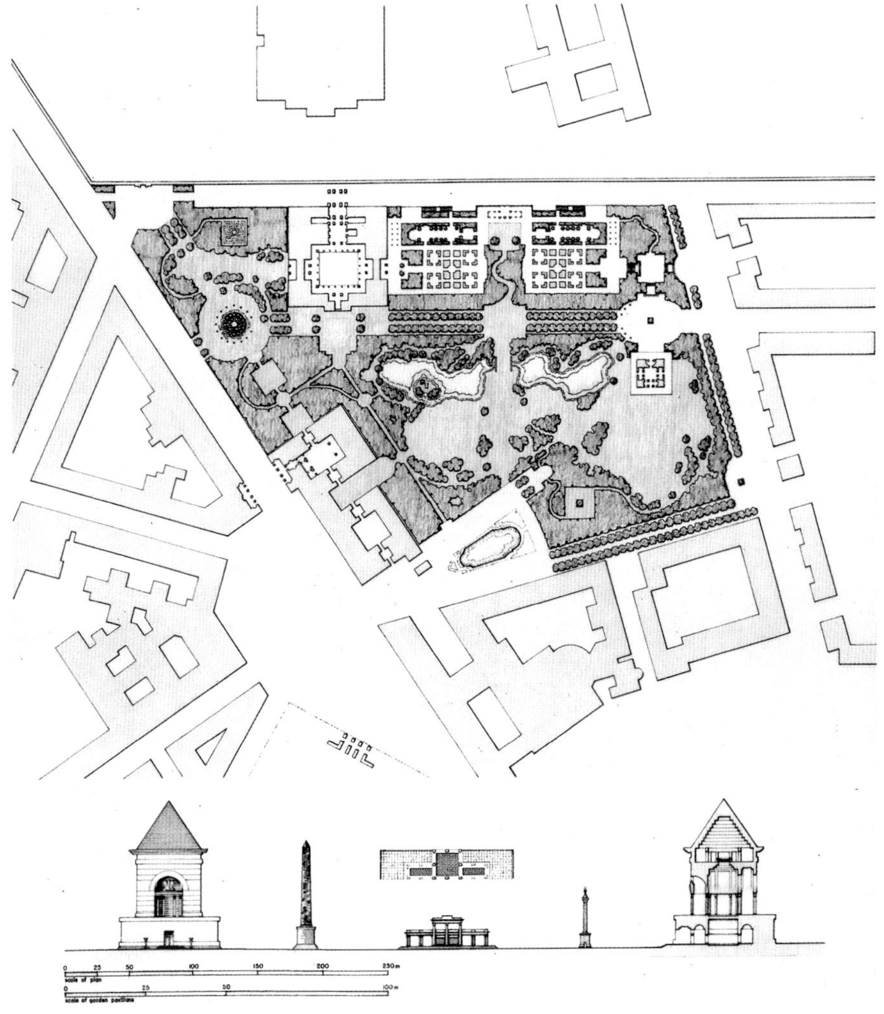

Fig. 30. Prinz Albrecht Museum & Garden, Berlin. Brian Kelly, Studio project, 1982.

> *To summarize, it is here proposed that, rather than hoping and waiting for the withering away of the object... it might be judicious, in most cases, to allow the object to become digested in the prevalent texture or matrix, one in which both buildings and spaces exist in a quality of sustained debate... which might allow for the joint existence of the overtly planned and the genuinely unplanned, of the set-piece and the accident, of the public and the private, of the state and the individual.... Crossbreeding, assimilation, distortion, challenge, response, imposition, superposition, conciliation....*[95]

And Ancient Rome has a greater visual presence in *Collage City* than any other urban exemplar. It is represented by ten photos of the model of Ancient Rome executed by Italo Gismondi.[96] Does the Studio by 1982 appear to have "freed itself from the indelible grasp of modern planning and fragmentation" and the "hypothetical synthesis between the Traditional City and the City of Industry"? The answer is, 'Yes', making Krier prescient in signaling a change in the Studio's direction consistent with his own view, and noting the need for the same trauma in the larger world of architecture and planning. Yes, in the 1977–87 Studio projects displayed in the 1983 and 1991 *Journals* 2 and 4, there is less and less evidence of the Mod palette or Cubist *gestalts*. Yes, a wider range of building types and forms is exhibited. The emphasis on abstraction and aversion to entourage and

95 Rowe and Koetter (1978): 83. Some of the language used to describe 'reconciliation' found here and elsewhere in *Collage City* echoes language related to phenomenal transparency and Cubism.

96 Rowe and Koetter (1978): iv–v; 108-111. From 1933–71 Italo Gismondi executed the model of Ancient Rome. Whether viewing the drawing or the model, the eye is drawn to the 'figures', the temples, but we are intended to equally note the compactness of the buildings; the abundant public and private 'courtyards'; the variety of the streets, irregular and regular, both modest and magnificent. It represents the 'trad' city *par excellence*.

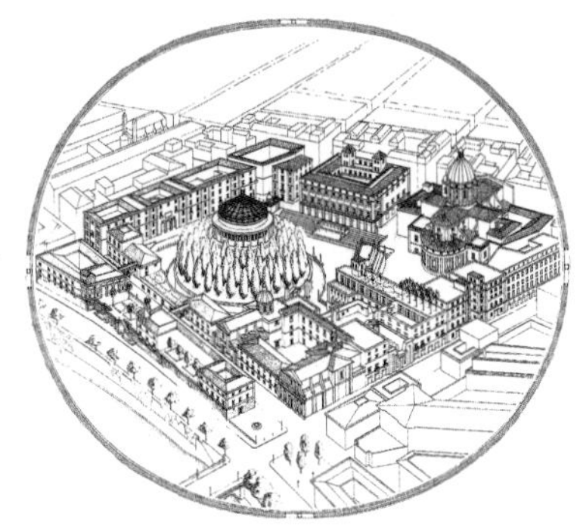

Fig. 31. Piazza Augusto Imperatore, Rome: Milan Triennale, 1987. Colin Rowe, Matthew Bell, Robert Goodill, Kevin Hinders, Brian Kelly, Cheryl O'Neil.

developed building masses and elevations has been replaced by indications of them as seen in thesis projects by Carter Hord, Brian Kelly, Carey McWhorter, Blake Middleton, Paul Mortensen, Craig Nealy, Jerri Smith, Derek Tynan, and others. And there is little-to-no aversion to the 'trad'. Quite the opposite. In most Studio theses, and in group projects based in Rome, the emphasis has become 'of their place', not 'of their time'. In *Journal* 4, Matt Bell describes the reintegration of landscape and architecture exhibited in the late Studio work as a logical and next step for the architect in the recovery of the city.[97]

Summary and Conclusions

Among schools of architecture that focused on urban design beginning in the early 1960s, the Cornell program appears to have been uniquely successful due to a combination of the following: the critique of Modern architecture Rowe had previously formulated, his dialectical framing of ideas and forms, his emphasis on form over program, his exceptional openness to Studio design testing of alternative form possibilities applied to real city sites at a variety of scales, and rediscovering and/or creating exemplary analogical material as a core body of knowledge. More specifically, Rowe's critique of Modern architecture included exposing its utopian, millennialist, *zeitgeist*, and futurist propensities that, together, falsely induced a state of perpetual crisis and the equivalent of an architectural and city design book burning. His essays demonstrated the opposite approach, exploring connections between Modernist architecture and works drawn from previous centuries and eras. His dialectical framing clarified competing ideas and prompted their deeper investigation through Studio design conjectures and proposals. Rowe's selection of real city sites for study was a deliberate mode of teaching that enabled discovery, encouraged form manipulation, and supported the possibility of learned application that was carried into professional practices. His approach combined liberal and professional educations by allowing questions about urban form and the design of cities to lead to the ideas that shaped them. As a model of architectural education and of urban design and architectural practice, it could be and was transported and recreated elsewhere, in whole or part, by anyone who understood and valued it. In the evolution of Rowe's own thinking, by 1979, he definitively stated, "I regard a revival of the city as far more important than any survival of Modern architecture".[98]

We can be grateful for the fortunate coincidence of Rowe's interests, mode of teaching, and the beginning of a field of inquiry—urban design—that was suited to his expansive but focused and critical thinking. The Studio environment he created and the Buffalo Waterfront project inspired a handful of us ca. 1965–67 to believe the Studio was not "devoid of theory", but that we were onto something big—a theory in the making, and underdeveloped or not, by whatever name, Collision City, Collage City, or Contextualism, that theory could challenge the Modernist juggernaut. Subsequently, several generations of students joined one another in Rowe's Studio to continue exploring the expanding field of urban design, its theory, and practice it under the near-ideal circumstances of Rowe's Studio. Subsequently, exploring a wide range of individual interests in that developing field, many of them have been able to make important contributions to the quality and endurance of our built city environments and spatially well-defined public realm.

97 Bell, Matthew, J., "Urbanism, Landscape and The City", *The Cornell Journal of Architecture* 4, Cornell University, 1991: 178–91.

98 Rowe, "The Present Urban Predicament", *Architectural Association Quarterly* 11 (4), 1979; *The Cornell Journal of Architecture* 1, 1981; *As I Was Saying*, (1996/3): 216.

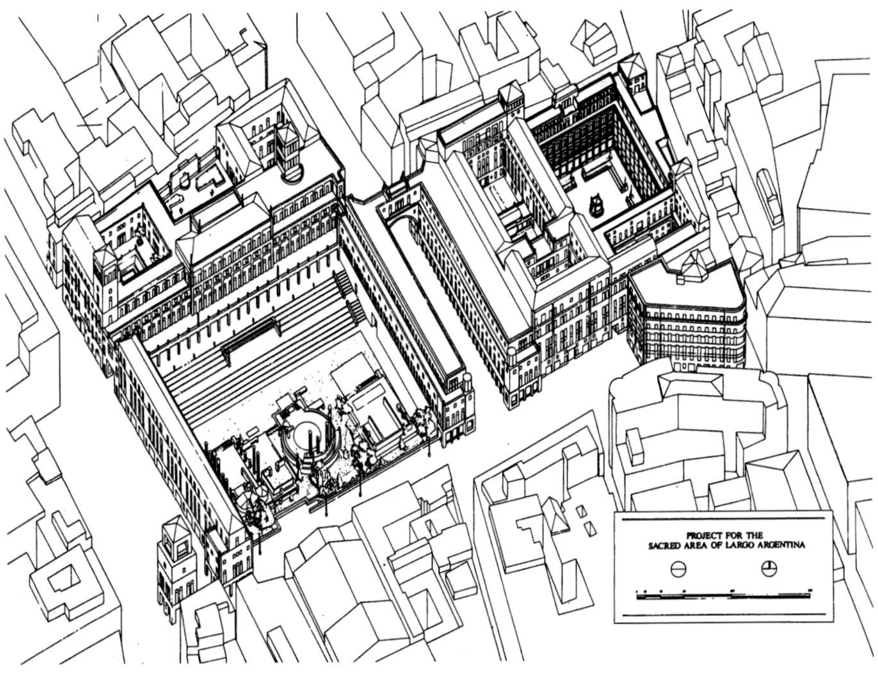

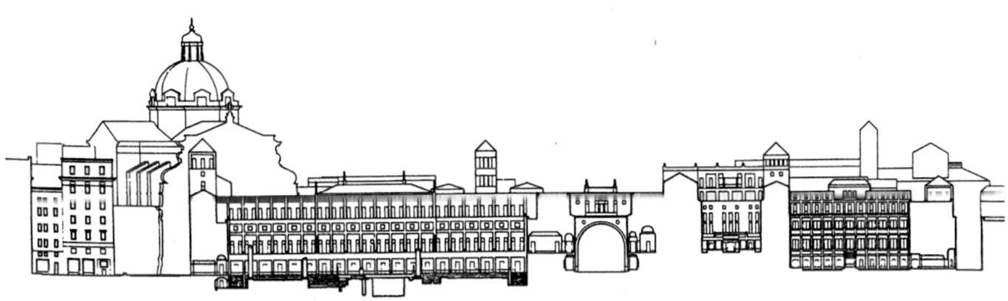

Fig. 32, 33. Largo Argentina, Rome. Cheryl O'Neil, thesis, 1987.

The Cornell Journal of Architecture
2
Roma interrotta
The Cornell Journal of Architecture
French Hôtel Plans
City Segments
27 Lotus International
LOTUS 4
RATIONAL ARCHITECTURE RATIONNELLE
IAUS
THE INSTITUTE FOR ARCHITECTURE AND URBAN STUDIES
The Texas Rangers
AS I WAS SAYING
Beyond the Modern Movement
The Mund Plan
RECKONING WITH COLIN ROWE
COLLAGE CITY
Colin Rowe and Fred Koetter
OPPOSITIONS
the letters of Colin Rowe five decades of correspondence
casabella
ROMA INTERROTTA
E URBAN VILLA
GOTHAM CITY
LUXEMBOURG
Design Quarterly
Modulus The University of Virginia School of Architecture Review

Disseminating an Idea: *The Cornell Journal of Architecture 2*

Blake Middleton

For a man of extraordinary intellectual range—who, through his influential writing, stimulated a cogent and considered critique of Modern architecture and the traditional city, who influenced the entire curriculum of a school of architecture, increasing its stature along the way, and who for 28 years led a graduate studio devoted to fundamental problems of contemporary "urbanistics"—Colin Rowe was unusually ambivalent about seeking the academic limelight.[1] For years his writings found a quiet outlet through a smattering of professional and scholarly magazines and publications. These articles, however, quickly established his reputation as an original thinker of great acuity, erudition, and passion. Yet the work of his graduate students in the Urban Design Studio at Cornell University, so fundamental to the research and development of his ideas on urbanism postulated in his writings, so unusual for its consistent quality of thought, formal exploration, presentation, and persistent focus on a singular and vexing issue of urban design, was not well known outside a small circle of like-minded colleagues. This is a chronicle of how and why the work of the Urban Design Studio—and that of the Department of Architecture so heavily influenced by it—was published and disseminated to a wider audience.

Among the few publications that have attempted to represent the design work emanating from Rowe's Studio, *The Cornell Journal of Architecture*, 2 entitled "Urban Design" is the most thorough and informative. As a graduate student in Rowe's studio, I had the good fortune to be the editor for this issue, and in concert with fellow students and faculty at Cornell, brought this publication to print in 1983. My retrospective focuses on a certain time and place, on those who were responsible for making it happen, and the impact the *Journal* had at that time. The role that printed media and articles of that period played to inspire Cornell students to create an architecture journal, and the subsequent pivotal position the "Urban Design" issue had in disseminating the work of the Studio, is unpacked within the context of a turbulent period of reaction to the evident failures of Modernist urbanism in the middle to late 1970s.[2] The essay concludes with a brief survey of recent publications that continue to describe, analyze, critique, and finally judge Rowe's extraordinary contribution to urban design theory and practice.

frontispiece:
"*The Cornell Journal of Architecture* 2 in context". Collage by J. Tice.

1 This is a reference to the Italian term *urbanistica* and relates to both the elements and principles of urban design, as well as the idea of urbanism. Rowe used it in his title, *As I Was Saying: Recollections and Miscellaneous Essays* 3, *Urbanistics*, MIT Press, Cambridge, MA, and London, 1996.

2 The mainstream architectural press included *Architectural Record*, *Progressive Architecture*, *Casabella*, *Architectural Forum*, *Architectural Design*, and *L'Architecture d'Aujourd'hui*. *Design Quarterly* was produced by the Walker Art Center in Minneapolis. *Lotus international* by Electa Editrice in Milan. a+u, *Architecture and Urbanism*, in Japanese and English. *Casabella* in Italian and English. *Architectural Design* was a British publication featuring a mix of professional work and academic theory. *Architectural Forum*, a vehicle for commentary, and several of Rowe's early articles, ceased printing in 1974. Some sporadic publications, small in circulation or even format, had their own audiences, such as *Pamphlet Architecture*, edited by Columbia's Stephen Holl.

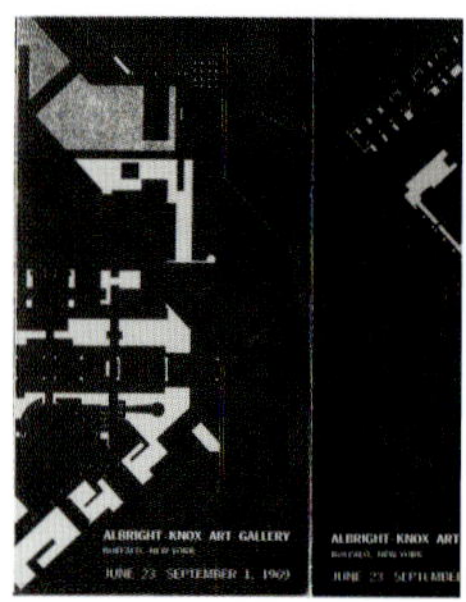

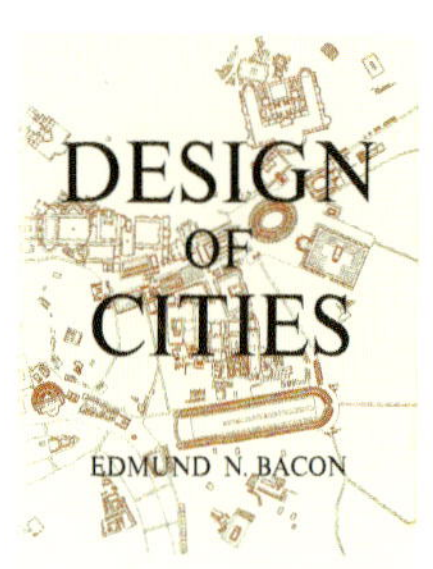

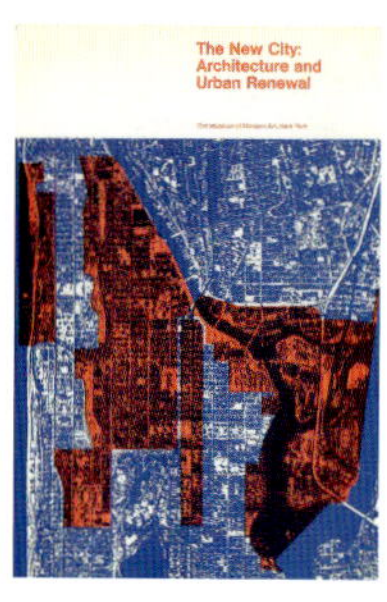

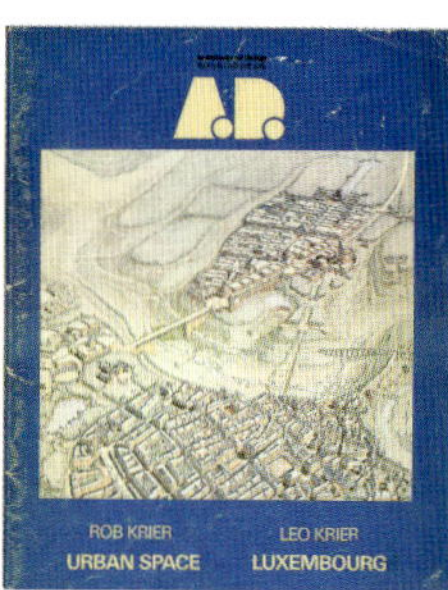

Collage City, Colin Rowe and Fred Koetter, 1978.

top row left to right:
"Buffalo: Waterfront", exhibition brochure, 1969.

Design of Cities, Edmund Bacon, 1967

The New City, MoMA, 1967

Casabella, The City as Artifact, 1971

Architectural Design, R. Krier, L. Krier, 1979

The Mund Plan, Cornell University, Roger Sherwood, 1970

Oppositions 4, IAUS, 1974

Arhitecture Rationelle, Rob Krier, 1978

Urban Space, Rob Krier, 1979

Stimulus

In the 1970s there was an intense debate in architectural design schools about how to address the shortcomings of urban renewal in the U.S. as well as Europe. It was a period of an uncertain, but sometimes exhilarating, search for an architectural syntax that might move past what was seen, in some quarters at least, as the inability of orthodox Modern architecture to rise to the challenge of relevance in a post-industrial society. This conversation played out not just in architecture schools, Cornell among them, but also in academic and professional journals. Before the advent of the Internet, other than books, which involve enormous time and resources to produce, the only medium available to disseminate current architectural and urban design theory and criticism was printed journals. Through the 1960s these would be regularly published professional organs with broad distribution and advertising. Complementing these were the better-known academic publications, issued somewhat regularly or in annual intervals, like *Design Quarterly*, *Perspecta*, *Lotus international*, and *Oppositions*. In this context the appearance of several publications in the late 1970s had a powerful influence on the students and faculty at Cornell who were instrumental in creating *The Cornell Journal of Architecture.*

In early 1978, the controversial "Roma interrotta" exhibition occurred, followed by its accompanying catalogue printed in English in early 1979. The show, curated by Michael Graves and Piero Sartogo, used the 230th anniversary of the publication of the Nolli Map of Rome as the pretext for twelve prominent architects and critics to each use one of the map's twelve plates as a canvas for commentary on urban architecture during the height of the Postmodernist debate.[3] On its heels came a partial translation in English of Rob Krier's *Stadtraum* (*Urban Space*) printed in *Architectural Design.*[4] This edition allowed anglophone students to read the narrative accompanying the elegant systematic analysis of typology and morphology Krier had published several years earlier. Around the same time, *Architecture Rationnelle* (*Rational Architecture*), a compendium subtitled *The Reconstruction of the European City* was released. This book, to which Léon Krier broadly contributed, was edited by Robert Delevoy. It contained descriptive text in English and illustrations staking out a European perspective on strategies for reconstituting the traditional morphology of the European city.[5]

The Fall of 1978 saw the launch of *Collage City.*[6] Many critics have remarked on the import of this publication by Rowe and Fred Koetter. For the architecture community it provided, for the first time in hardback book form, a comprehensive polemic addressing the ideological failures of Modern urbanism, while

3 Cerruti, Marisa, ed., *Roma interrotta*, Incontri Internazionali d'Arte, Officina Edizioni, Roma, 1978.

4 Krier, Rob, *Stadtraum in Theorie und Praxis*, Karl Krämer, Stuttgart, 1975. English translation: *Urban Space*, Academy Editions, London, 1979. Also Krier, Rob, "Typological and Morphological Elements of the Concept of Urban Space", *Architectural Design* 49 (1), 1979.

5 Delevoy, Robert, ed., *Rational Architecture Rationnelle: La reconstruction de la ville européenne*, Éditions des Archives d'Architecture Moderne, Bruxelles, 1978. The book is based on a 1975 exhibit of the same name.

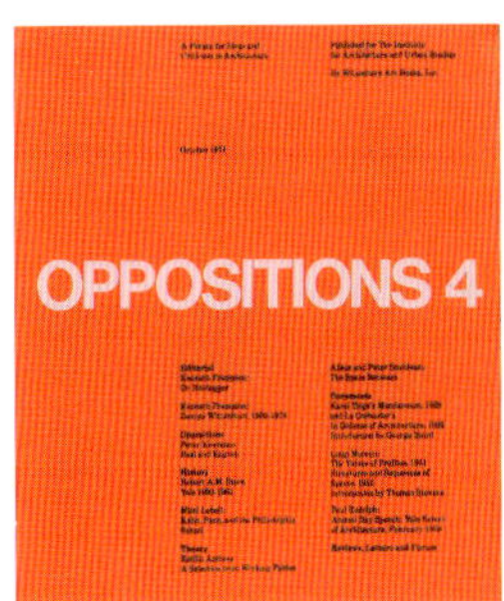

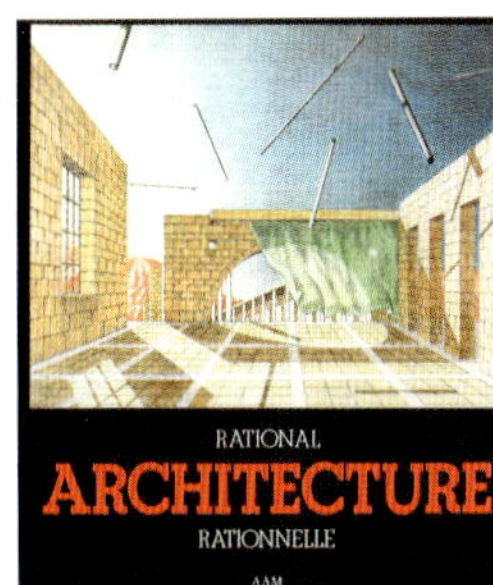

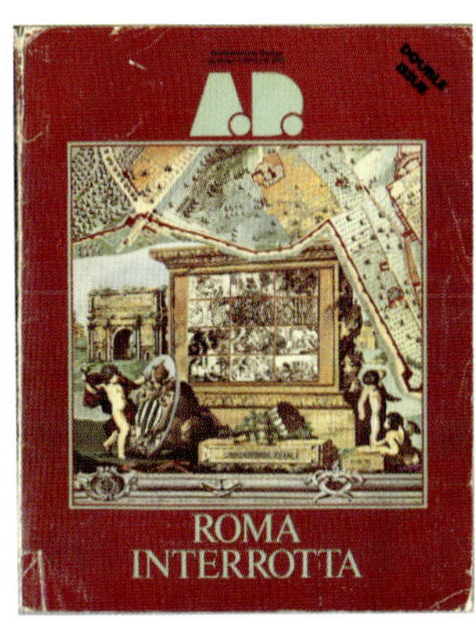

Architectural Design, ROMA INTERROTTA, 1979.

offering a possible conceptual path forward. *Collage City* also provided a window, albeit a slightly misty one, into many of the design principles that underlay the projects of Rowe's graduate program. At about the same time, Rem Koolhaas published *Delirious New York*, a thought-provoking "retrospective manifesto" celebrating urban density. Among other ideas in this original take on urban development in Manhattan, and pertinent to the discussions in the Urban Design Studio, was Koolhaas's observation about mixed-use urban buildings with unusual combinations of "program", a term he notes as an invention of the Modern era.[7] These remarks were not unfamiliar to those in the Studio who had been for some years examining the potency of 'composite' buildings—structures amalgamating multiple functions and typological form—in order to accommodate local contingent planning issues.

The fifth publication to arrive on student drafting tables was the *ROMA INTERROTTA* issue of *Architectural Design* in the summer of 1979. An abridged reprint of projects from the exhibition, it contained a much-reproduced and influential article by Steven K. Peterson titled "Urban Design Tactics".[8] Having collaborated with Rowe on the "Roma interrotta" submission, Peterson used the design to structure a template for the design tactics of city making, at least applied in this fictive setting of 18th century Rome. Dispensing with Rowe's elaborate narrative, Peterson used components of the project to describe clearly articulated principles with concise analytic illustrations.[9] For some years at Cornell, Edmund Bacon's *Design of Cities* had been a popular introduction for undergraduates to build their 'urban design literacy'. However, focused primarily on the historical development of urban form, it did not delve deeply into the 'mechanics' of what Peterson considered constituent elements and spatial imperatives of urbanism: streets, squares, and blocks. More importantly, Bacon saw no deficiency with contemporary urban design examples (e.g. his work in Philadelphia) deploying towers that, among other questionable tactics, eschewed street wall definition.[10] Finally, in the early spring of 1980, the first issue of the *Harvard Architecture Review* arrived in the Fine Arts Library at Cornell. Thematically titled *Beyond the Modern Movement*, and elegantly laid out, the maiden issue contained what proved to be a highly influential polemic: Peterson's article "Space and Anti-Space".[11] A sequel of sorts to "Urban Design Tactics", this essay added analytic heft to his previous article and was a foundational primer for civic design based on the typological components of the 'traditional city'.

---

6 Rowe, Colin; Fred, Koetter, *Collage City*, MIT Press, MA, and London, 1978. The authors published a condensation of *Collage City* in *The Architectural Review* 158, 1975: 66-77. Rowe presented a public lecture at Cornell titled "Utopia or Collage City" in May 1970 at the symposium "The Provincial City". O.M. Ungers, Kenneth Frampton, Josep Lluís Sert, Alvin Boyarsky, Henry Milllon, and Werner Seligmann, among others, participated.

7 Koolhaas, Rem, *Delirious New York*, Oxford University Press, New York, 1978. Koolhaas spent several months in the early 1970s at Cornell studying with O.M. Ungers. In 1973 he became a Fellow at the IAUS in New York City providing an opportunity to research his book.

8 Peterson, Steven K., "Urban Design Tactics", *Architectural Design* 49 (3-4), 1979: 76-81.

9 Finding Michael Graves's image pastiche for the Lateran sector in "Roma interrotta" lacking, Rowe assigned a fictional urban intervention to his first-year students in the Fall of 1978. Each project in the Studio had to stitch into the Rowe–Peterson–DiMaio–Carl scheme in a sort of "exquisite corpse" exercise.

10 Bacon, Edmund N., *Design of Cities*, Viking Press, New York, 1967.

11 Peterson, Steven K., "Space and Anti-Space", *The Harvard Architecture Review*, MIT Press, Cambridge, MA, 1980: 89-113.

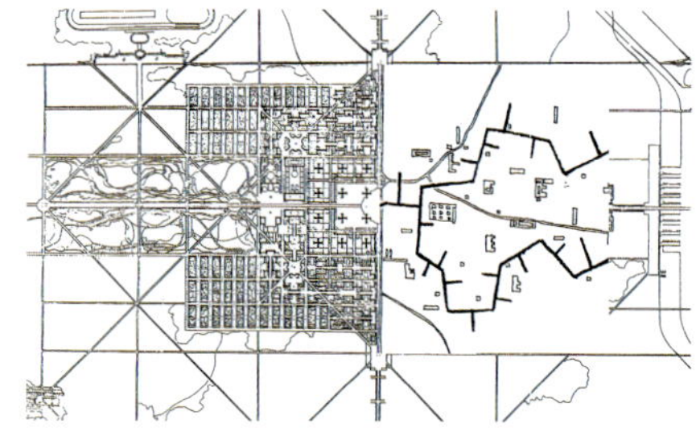

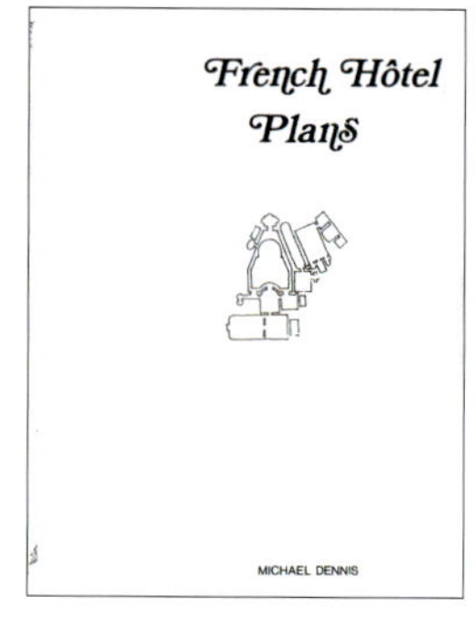

top row left to right:

Urban Precedents, Michael Dennis, Klaus Herdeg, 1974

The Paris Architectural Center, Michael Dennis, 1977

The French Hôtel Plans, Michael Dennis, 1974

Court and Garden, Michael Dennis, 1986

Gotham City, Cornell, O.M. Ungers, 1976

The Urban Villa, Cornell University, 1978

Delirious New York, Rem Koolhaas, 1978

Modulus, The University of Virginia, 1979

The Harvard publication added something substantial to the pedagogic debate (literally, it weighs in at 1.5 lbs.) and possessed the same 'brand prestige' as Yale's *Perspecta.* In 1979, both Columbia University and the University of Virginia began publications, *Précis* and *Modulus*, respectively.[12] And all the while, *Oppositions*, produced by the Institute for Architecture and Urban Studies (IAUS) seemed to operate on another plane altogether, oscillating between cogent criticism and obtuse theory.[13] Prominent schools of architecture seemed to have their distinct voice. But there were few design studio projects to be seen in any of these publications. For students at Cornell, far from the academic I-95 corridor stretching from Boston to Washington, D.C. or even Charlottesville, these new journals stimulated us to act. Feeling under-appreciated, full of pride in the rigor of the design and theory program, the school's long history and distinguished alumni,[14] and looking for validation among our peer group of schools, students asked: Where is the voice of Cornell?

For younger professors looking to make their mark the opportunity for commissions of substance in upstate New York in the late 1970s was pretty thin. The economic recession triggered by the oil embargo of 1973 had put the brakes on the late 1960s building boom. Other than some Urban Development Corporation (UDC) housing projects and the occasional small city bank headquarters, the declining industrial economy offered few opportunities for young architects to establish a practice.[15] In this setting, it is easy to imagine Cornell faculty being as eager as the students to have a proximate outlet for their own scholarly efforts.

Creating the 'Soap Box' for Cornell Architecture

Outside of Ithaca, beginning in 1976, an interesting culture of architectural *samizdat* percolated to the surface at Cornell, involving several of the faculty. "Urban Precedents" was prepared by students under the direction of Michael Dennis and Klaus Herdeg. Oswald Matthias Ungers, nearing the end of his tenure as chair of the Department of Architecture, produced a compendium of student design projects from his graduate studio called "The Urban Block and Gotham City: Metaphors and Metamorphosis".[16] By the following spring, Michael Dennis had produced two photocopy volumes: one based on the design work of his undergraduate fourth year studio, and the other an analysis of the Parisian *hôtel particulier*, titled "French Hôtel Plans".[17] Shortly thereafter in 1977, Ungers' summer studio published a massive analytic study of building typologies titled "The Urban Villa".[18] Each publication was conveniently printed on U.S. letter format, bound in a white cover. They were narrowly distributed at nominal cost mostly

12 *Précis* was produced by Columbia graduate students with faculty advising, and was, as the name implies, "a précis – or summary – of student and faculty work" of a given year. *Modulus: The University of Virginia School of Architecture Review*, contained mostly articles by faculty or invited writers. "Roma interrotta" by Rowe, Peterson, DiMaio and Carl was reproduced in its entirety around the same time in *Architectural Design* 49. Syracuse University's School of Architecture began publishing *Catalogue* in 1978. An annual of undergraduate student work.

13 The IAUS was founded in late 1967, and the first issue of *Oppositions* appeared in September 1973 and continued until 1984. For an account of the founding of *Oppositions:* Frank, Suzanne, *IAUS: An Insider's Memoir*, AuthorHouse, Bloomington, IN, 2011.

14 Notable Cornell architecture alumni include Nathaniel Owings, Edmund Bacon, Richard Meier, Peter Eisenman, Arthur Gensler, Werner Seligmann, and Thomas Schumacher, to name only a few.

15 The New York Urban Development Corporation (UDC) 1968–75 was set up by Nelson Rockefeller in 1968 to create new housing and other civic improvements on a statewide scale. It would have extraordinary powers of imminent domain. Edward Logue ran the operation; he and his staff would select rising star architects for new projects. Several Cornell alumni or affiliated professors would benefit from this patronage including Meier, Seligmann, and Wells/Koetter/Dennis. The UDC disbanded in 1975, a casualty of the same recessionary economic pressures elsewhere in the nation.

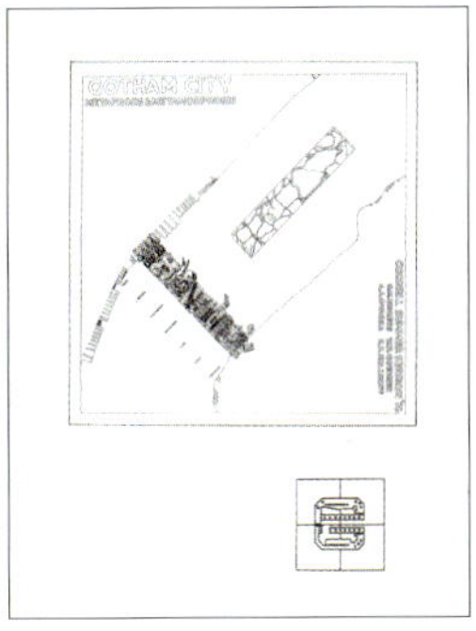

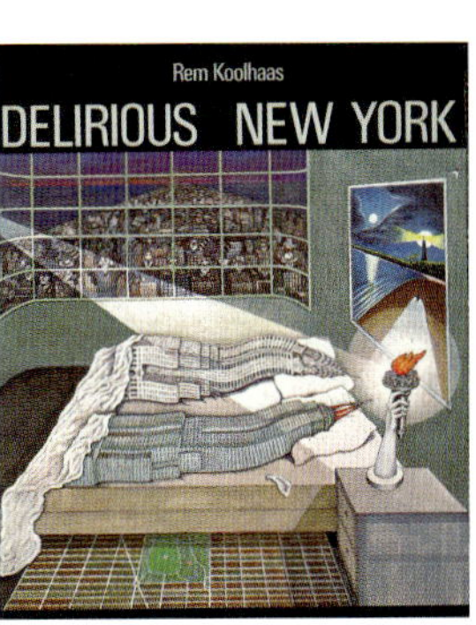

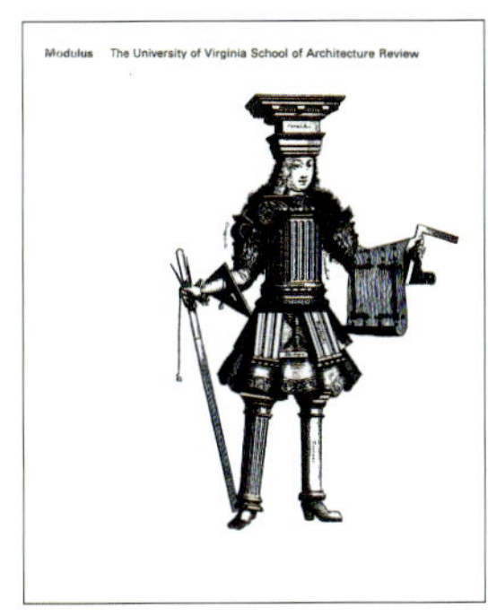

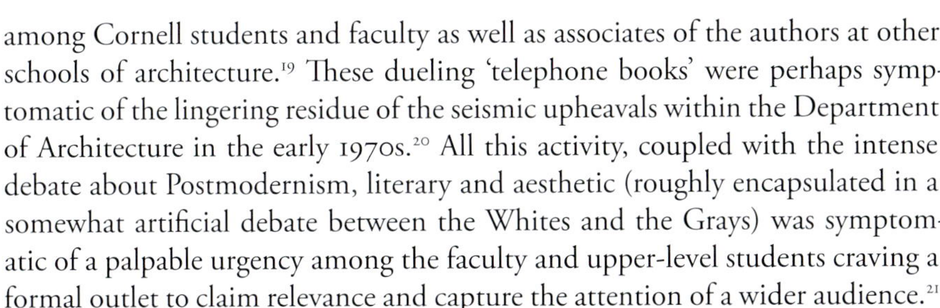

among Cornell students and faculty as well as associates of the authors at other schools of architecture.[19] These dueling 'telephone books' were perhaps symptomatic of the lingering residue of the seismic upheavals within the Department of Architecture in the early 1970s.[20] All this activity, coupled with the intense debate about Postmodernism, literary and aesthetic (roughly encapsulated in a somewhat artificial debate between the Whites and the Grays) was symptomatic of a palpable urgency among the faculty and upper-level students craving a formal outlet to claim relevance and capture the attention of a wider audience.[21]

Thus a group of high-spirited and talented students, mostly advanced undergraduates, felt compelled to join this critical dialogue through mainstream architectural journals. Without any prior experience, they got it into their heads to create a student-edited architectural publication.[22] Commandeering an unused office in the bowels of Sibley Hall, they set about testing layouts, typeface, and format. Most importantly, there were intense speculations and fantasies about what to publish. They wanted to have drawings for sure, since what was being produced in the design studio seemed, to their parochial eyes, to be superior to most of what they were seeing published elsewhere. But then lots of head scratching about writing. What would augment the graphic work? What were they going to say? And just who was going to contribute articles to this fledgling operation? At this point architecture faculty began to take notice, agreeing to write articles or curate student work while Jerry Wells, chair of the Department of Architecture, organized course credit around the efforts.[23]

At my behest, and surely nudged by Wells, Rowe pledged to yield up a revised version of a lecture he had recently given in London in the summer of 1979 titled "The Present Urban Predicament". Armed with a Colin Rowe essay as a headliner for this nascent publication, the student editorial board began to give shape to what evolved into *The Cornell Journal of Architecture*. After reaching out to several publishers, Rizzoli agreed to publish and distribute this new addition to the academic dialogue on architecture and urban design.

16 Ungers, Oswald Mathias; Goehner, Werner H.; Ovaska, Arthur A., *The Urban Block and Gotham City: Metaphors and Metamorphosis: Two Concurrent Projects*, Studio Press for Architecture, Cologne, 1976.

17 Dennis, Michael, "French Hôtel Plans", mimeo, Ithaca, NY, 1977. Dennis's fourth year Cornell students made this analytical compendium of Parisian *hôtel particulier* plans of the late 17th and early 18th centuries. It was a prelude to designing a Paris Architectural Center on the site of the Hôtel d'Evry.

18 Ungers, Oswald Mathias; Kollhoff, Hans F., Ovaska, Arthur A., *The Urban Villa: A Multi-Family Dwelling Type*, (Cornell Summer Academy 77 in Berlin), Studio Press for Architecture, Cologne, 1977. First printed in Ithaca, it was intended to be part of a series on urban design.

19 As the original publications by Ungers and Dennis were quickly out of print, they were unofficially copied by eager students. "French Hôtel Plans" enjoyed a robust circulation at many other architecture schools. As a student in both the Ungers and Dennis studios I became accustomed to the rigors of analytic drawing while researching these building types.

20 "OMA RE: OMU", Interview with Jeremy Alain Siegel, et al., *The Cornell Journal of Architecture* 8: 161-63, in which Rem Koolhaas reflects on the brief Rowe-Ungers 'bromance' and subsequent antagonism.

21 The "White" schools included Cornell, Columbia, and Cooper Union. The "Gray" schools were Yale and the University of Pennsylvania and possibly Princeton. Because of his "Introduction" to *Five architects*, and maybe for his appreciation of Le Corbusier's architecture (but clearly not his urbanism), Rowe was perceived to be the flag bearer for the Whites: Meier, Gwathmey, Graves, Hejduk, and Eisenman. *The Architectural Forum* "Five on Five" (May 1973) published the work of Romaldo Giurgola, Jacquelin Robertson, Robert A. M. Stern, Allen Greenberg, and Charles Moore to represent the Grays with Robert Venturi and Denise Scott Brown as standard bearers. The appellation also referenced the preferred color of each camp's architectural models.

22 The initial posse of 'journalistas' included Michael Markovitz, Ken Gruskin, Marla Glazner, Daniel Kaplan, Craig Nealy, Edward Siegel, and me. Kaplan, Siegel, and Barnes had been my students in the freshman class. Nealy was my classmate. Markovitz and Gruskin provided the lion's share of the energy, stamina, and perseverance to bring the first issue to fruition.

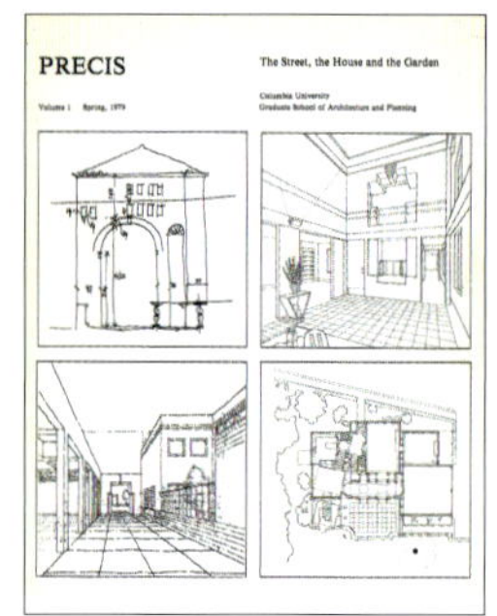

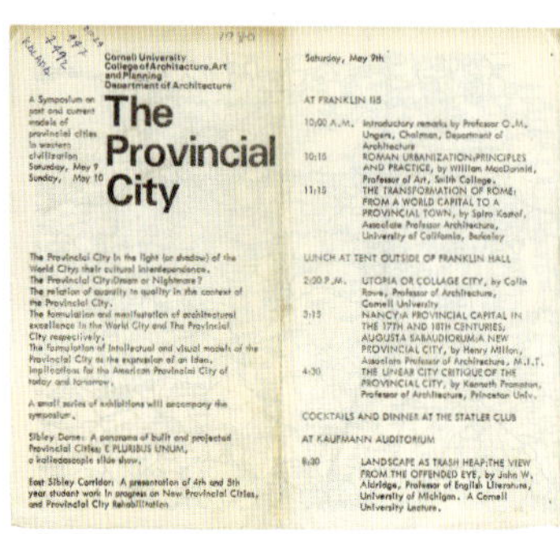

top row left to right:

Precis 1, Columbia University, 1979

Perspecta 16, 1980

"The Provincial City", symposium brochure, 1970

The Architectural Review 158, "Collage City", 1975

Collage City, Colin Rowe, Fred Koetter, 1978

Roma interrotta, exhibition catalogue, 1978

Architectural Design 49, "*ROMA INTERROTTA*", 1979

Harvard Architectural Review 1, 1980

The Cornell Journal of Architecture 1, 1981

Conceiving an Exhibition

With all this stimulation around the school—*Collage City* being published, the influential images of "Roma interrotta", Krier's *Urban Space*, the Peterson articles, the proliferation of French *hôtel* plans in the design studios, participating in Ungers' summer studio on building typology and morphology, and helping to start the *Journal*—the idea of making an exhibition of the Rowe Urban Design Studio work kept percolating in my mind. Furthermore, as first year undergraduates, *our* teachers were the students of Rowe and Ungers. While immersed in their own work making elaborate drawings and site models, these graduate students were themselves often referencing earlier Urban Design Studio work seen in pamphlets such as the "Buffalo: Waterfront" exhibition (1966–1969), "The New City" at MoMA (1967), the MUND design proposals for Baltimore (1971), and the 50 to 60 thesis books then available in the library. Indeed, the slightly decaying Buffalo model, a good six-feet square, sat in the corner of the UD Studio in the mid-1970s. It was an inspiring relic for both a freshman visiting for a 'crit', and for the graduate students toiling on their own theses. So, why had all this effort gone unnoticed and why had the work remained unknown to a wider audience?

During the fall of 1978 in my first year of the Urban Design Studio, it became apparent to me that this collective body of work amassed by faculty and students had not been published in any significant forum. The work predated much of the recent urban design theory emanating from Europe. Notably it had persistently applied certain principles, broad in scope, diverse in the geography of application. We all had read articles like Schumacher's "Contextualism: Urban Ideals and Deformations",[24] or William Ellis' "Type and Context in Urbanism: Colin Rowe's Contextualism",[25] which hinted at the character of the Studio work. Other than Arthur Drexler's overview in the MoMA exhibit catalogue, no one in a visible critical capacity had made any public review or assessment of the Urban Design Studio work as a whole.

Motivated to rectify this situation, in the spring of 1979 I resolved that an exhibition of the Urban Design Studio should be mounted and consequently set to work. My initial resource was in the Fine Arts Library, where all the graduate theses could be found.[26] Collecting images via photocopies, I began making a rough chronological catalogue of projects. The diversity of locale, consistency of graphics, and quality of presentation were remarkable. At first, Rowe was ambivalent about assembling this material into an exhibit. Nevertheless, persistence, and possibly some pleading, led him to endorse the enterprise. He suggested

23 In "My Personal Recollections of Colin Rowe" presented at the 2014 Rowe/Rome conference, Wells states that, "I created The Cornell Journal of Architecture, which put the school on the map and proved that there was a pretty good school of architecture in Upstate New York". Naturally we students involved at that time have a slightly different recollection of how the *Journal* came to be.

24 Schumacher, Thomas, "Contextualism: Urban Ideals and Deformations", *Casabella* 359-360, 1971: 79-86.

25 Ellis, William, "Type and Context in Urbanism: Colin Rowe's Contextualism," *Oppositions* 18, 1979: 3-27.

26 Judith Holliday, Cornell Fine Arts Librarian who has held this position for more than two decades, generously provided me with guidance throught the thesis collection classified under NA39.

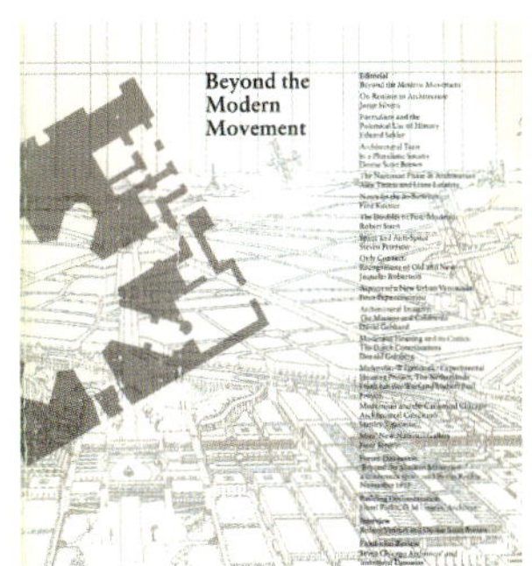

I contact Carter Manny Jr. at the Graham Foundation for funding, which resulted in a grant to accomplish our goal.[27] Original drawings, or archival negatives, were collected from former students or unearthed from Rowe's spotty collection, and then reproduced in large format, high contrast prints for display. The exhibit was mounted in March 1980 in the Hartell Gallery in Sibley Hall and stayed up for a brief three weeks. Unfortunately plans for a catalogue and traveling venue did not materialize.[28]

Lotus international 27, "Architectural Education in the USA", 1980.

Lotus to the Rescue

Lotus magazine learned of the exhibit and reached out to say they were planning an issue focused on American architectural education and invited our participation. This was either through the initiative of the editor of record, Pierluigi Nicolin, or, more likely, Kenneth Frampton, who had past London associations with Rowe. We were asked to submit projects from the exhibition for the edition. This dialogue evolved into Rowe's essay about American architectural education that Nicolin included, along with essays by Frampton with Alessandra Latour at Columbia, Rafael Moneo and Robert Slutzky from Cooper Union, and Richard Plunz also from Columbia.[29] Though still a graduate student, the *Lotus* editors invited me to write a brief introduction about the Studio work.

The opportunity to present the Cornell student work on a larger stage, with a prestigious publication like *Lotus*, validated our intuition that there was an audience for learning about the Urban Design Studio and introducing it into the larger conversation about urban design and architectural education. Struggling with how to condense and frame the material and connect it to a larger polemic, I felt obliged to get Rowe's take on the matter. He made a few corrections and suggestions. And then, as usual, he brilliantly condensed an entire argument into a single phrase upon which I could then summarize the Studio work for a wider audience: "Somewhere or another, Cézanne is supposed to have said that he would 'like to make of impressionism something solid like the art of the museums'". To this he added in his capitalized, slightly shaky scrawl on my essay draft, "Blake: substitute for impressionism 'Modern architecture', and for museums 'the traditional city', and you have an argument to make".[30] Only later did I discover Rowe's penchant for this type of preparatory statement that combines two rhetorical devices for literary references: crediting an author's quote while circumventing the drudgery of confirming the exact source and the analogy by

27 If memory serves, the grant was awarded in mid-1979 and yielded about $7,500. An additional grant was secured from the National Endowment for the Arts.

28 The exhibition coincided with Rowe's 60th birthday—March 27. Opening night was not unlike the Marx Brothers' "Night at the Opera"; over-caffeinated students running about all night into the next afternoon, frantically framing prints still damp from the Sibley dark rooms half an hour before the doors opened for the public.

29 Since Rowe was participating in the *Lotus* 27 issue (1980) perhaps he had suggested to *Lotus* that they include the Cornell Studio work recently exhibited in Ithaca.

30 Middleton, Blake, "The Combining of the Traditional City and The Modern City", *Lotus international* 27, 1980: 47.

"City Segments", *Design Quarterly* 113-114, 1980.

substitution. Colin began one well-known essay thus: "Bernard Berenson somewhere describes himself as being 'a Christianity graduate'", or elsewhere, as in "Somewhere or other, Wordsworth said something about 'emotion recollected in tranquility'". The original text of Wayne Copper's 1967 thesis starts with this line: "Somewhere or other, Ezra Pound once described literature as language charged with meaning. By simple substitution, one might even define architecture as building charged with meaning".[31] I mention these examples because it demonstrates how Rowe inspired his students not only to hone critical design thinking skills but also to creatively harness the use of language to describe design ideas.

The *Lotus* publication came out in late 1980, handsomely produced. It served temporarily as the *de facto* catalogue for the 1980 exhibition; it enjoyed a wide circulation. Frampton and Latour's astute assessment of American architecture education compared the programs of Cornell, Columbia, and Cooper Union. While a little parochial in its selection of schools, their observations and critique of the Cornell program focused on the work of the Rowe Urban Design Studio as the intellectual heart of the entire program. Its mission, they note, was driven by Karl Popper's *Open Society:*

> *The Rowe school has argued with conviction that the large-scale urban interventions projected during the heroic phase of the Modern Movement were not only anachronistic but also an anathema. In its stead, they posited the contextual idea of bricolage.*[32]

But the authors, in their overview of the Cornell program, concluded with a trenchant statement:

> *That Rowe's influence has foundered somewhat in the last few years is due largely to two factors: 1) to the strength of the opposed populist approach stemming from the Philadelphia School and from Yale—that is to say, the influence represented by the work of Robert Venturi and Charles Moore; and 2) to the loss of direction and method within the Cornell school; its failure to continue to pursue the shallow-space aesthetics and its own growing disbelief in the 'collage' approach. The current exhibition recently staged at Sibley Hall ... would seem to indicate that a certain moment in American architectural education is drawing to a close.*[33]

This seemed to me a premature closing of the door on an important recalibration and synthesis of various ideas motivating the research of Rowe and his students in a new, fruitful direction. Conflating the activities of the graduate studio with the overall program at Cornell was inappropriate, as the critique had not accounted for the depth, breadth, and quality of the design work of the undergraduate students, which would surely warrant a reevaluation. This would become amply evident in the publication of the first *Cornell Journal of Architecture* the following year.[34]

Coincidentally, other publications appeared in 1980 solidifying the Cornell position on urban design. One was *Perspecta,* 16 in which Fred Koetter and Rowe published "The Crisis of the Object: The Predicament of Texture". Here they developed in more depth an argument found in *Collage City* addressing the problem of "two distinctly different and usually antagonistic conditions of urbanism" (that is, Modern Architecture versus the Traditional City), but in this case looking closely at how this dilemma manifested itself in the composition

31 These examples can be found in Rowe's "Architectural Education in the USA", *Lotus international* 27 1980; in the "Introduction" of *As I Was Saying* 2 Caragonne, Alexander, ed., 1996; and in Wayne Copper's "Introduction" to his unpublished Cornell thesis, "The Figure/Grounds", 1967: 1. Copper rewrote his thesis for the *Journal* 2.

32 Frampton, Kenneth; Latour, Alessandra, "Notes on an American Architectural Education", *Lotus international* 27, 1980: 29. In referencing bricolage, Frampton is alluding to a Cubist painting device and, perhaps, to Rowe and Slutzky's articles on "Transparency: Literal and Phenomenal", *Perspecta* 8, 1963: 45-54.

33 Frampton and Latour (1980): 31.

34 Distributed in Fall of 1981, *The Cornell Journal of Architecture* 1 included design projects and competitions by undergraduates, and work of graduate students from Ungers's studio. Rowe contributed "The Present Urban Predicament". Faculty essays were contributed by Lee Hodgden, Michael Dennis, Werner Goehner, John Miller, John Shaw, O.M. Ungers, along with a joint student essay by Kenneth Schwartz and Steven Fong. The black cover format became a recurring signature of the *Journal*, perhaps an ironic counter-statement to the 'white' neo-Corbusian imagery associated with the school.

of city blocks, or the urban texture. In the same issue, Michael Dennis, having developed an abiding interest in the predicament of spatial coherence in urban building typology when confined only to the orthodox Modernist 'tool kit' of the *plan libre,* wrote a penetrating analysis called "The Uffizi: Museum as Urban Design".[35] In this article he articulated the tension between internal programmatic exigencies and external urban contextual coherence.

"Urban Design at Cornell", 1980. Drawing by the author for the exhibition of the graduate Urban Design Studio. In a Vasari-like gallery of Studio work Le Corbusier and Rowe warily scrutinize one another.

Another publication on the Studio work, "City Segments", appeared in *Design Quarterly,* 113–114. This was the result of an invitation by the Walker Art Center in Minneapolis in late 1979 for Rowe to submit a project for a travelling exhibition on urbanism. Rowe engaged his first-year students, myself among them, to develop a series of schemes for parts of Baltimore. This was well-trod territory; at least four Studio students in the previous 12 years had made thesis proposals for this city. Eschewing the high-contrast figure/ground plans of those projects, we employed color axonometric and site plans with a robust deployment of landscape features. Five different districts were developed, and true to the *bricolage* sensibility, stitched into an overall master plan. Both *Perspecta,* 16 and *Design Quarterly,* 113–114 contributed to the sporadic dissemination of Rowe's argument about urbanism. It was yet another reminder that a catalogue of the work of the Urban Design Studio was still missing.[36]

An Exhibition Catalogue and The Cornell Journal of Architecture *2*

Following the exhibition in Sibley Hall, the editors and I decided to use the exhibition work as the content for the second issue of the *Journal* to be completed the following year. Having established connections with former Rowe students while I was curating the exhibition, several promised to support this effort with articles. They included: Grahame Shane, who was completing his PhD dissertation under Rowe's guidance; Steven Hurtt, who along with Stuart Cohen coined the term "contextualism";[37] and Wayne Copper, whose figure/ground drawings and thesis of the same name, were repeatedly referenced for the last 15 years but had not been published. Shane suggested, and likely Rowe persuaded, Léon Krier to write a foreword to this compendium of Urban Design Studio projects. This was vital because Krier was the first contributor to the *Journal* not affiliated with Cornell, and of course he was establishing his own reputation as urban design theorist.

By 1981 I had graduated and left Ithaca, so Elliott Barnes and Edward Siegel, along with Ken Gruskin and Daniel Kaplan, assumed a major role in editing documents, illustrations, obtaining drafts from the authors, and generally maintaining the continuity of the *Journal.* Continuing as "Guest Editor" of *Journal* 2, my task was to frame the concept of the issue, introduce each article and write a synopsis for each project or thesis published. This proved to be more demanding than initially anticipated and coupled with the editing process for the various authors' contributions, delivery of the final draft stretched out over a year's time.[38] *The Cornell Journal of Architecture,* 2 was finally published in 1983, 20 years after Rowe started the Urban Design Studio.

35 Dennis, Michael, "The Uffizi: Museum as Urban Design", *Perspecta* 16, 1980: 62-72. The editorial theme was museums. It included an appendix of 30 museum plans from the Renaissance to the mid-1970s. It inspired the urban figure/ground plans in *Journal* 2. Projects by Stirling and Wilford significantly impacted the evolution of Cornell pedagogy.

36 Friedman, Mildred S., ed., "City Segments", *Design Quarterly* 113-114, 1980: 34-36. This exhibition featured 30 international academics and practitioners. Proposals ranged from work in construction to the visionary. Rowe, the team leader for the Nicolette Island competition, credited Cornell University. Introductory essays were provided by University of Minnesota faculty including former Rowe student, Garth Rockcastle.

37 Cohen, Stuart; Hurtt, Steven, "Le Corbusier: The Architecture of City Planning", Master's thesis, Cornell University, 1967.

38 *Journal* 1 had 3,500 copies printed, and *Journal* 2, 3,000. The cost of volume 2, with the expensive Wayne Copper figure-ground inserts, may have reduced the publisher's appetite for the same print run as *Journal* 1. But these high contrast, black-and-white city plan plates, 26 in all, made *Journal* 2 a highly desirable reference document. Elliot Barnes and Edward Siegel were the editors, with me as guest editor, a singular, and perhaps dubious, distinction in the annals of the *Journal.*

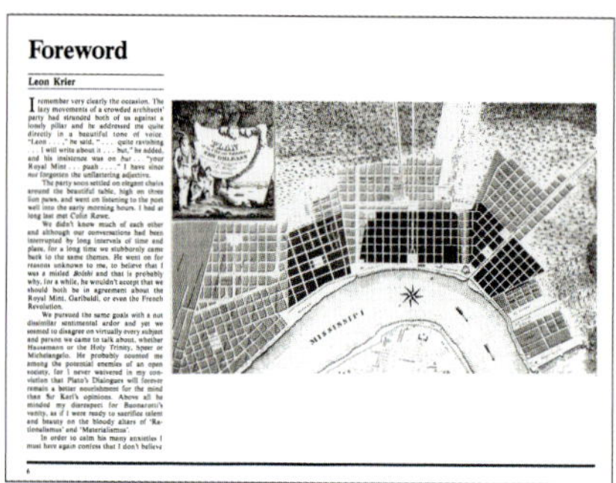
Foreword

Léon Krier

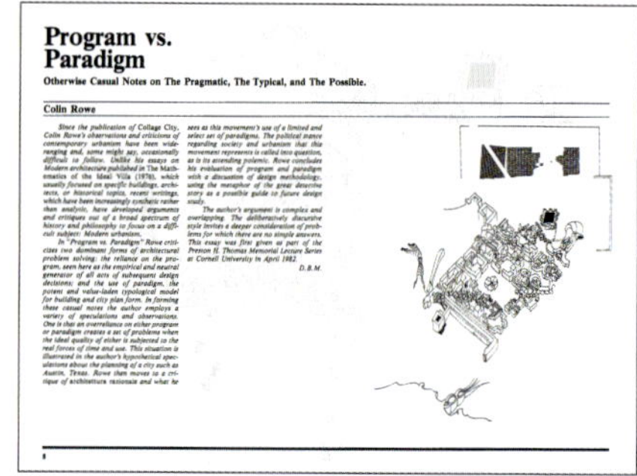
Program vs. Paradigm

Otherwise Casual Notes on The Pragmatic, The Typical, and The Possible.

Colin Rowe

Cornell Journal of Architecture 2, 1983.

Essays from the *Cornell Journal* 2 left to right:

"Foreword", Léon Krier

"Program vs. Paradigm", Colin Rowe

"The Street in the Twentieth Century", Grahame Shane

"The Figure/Grounds", Wayne Copper

"Conjectures on Urban Form", Steven Hurtt

Impact of The Cornell Journal of Architecture 2

Distribution of the *Journal* was mostly to students and faculty at various schools of architecture, university bookstores and libraries, and interested individuals. As for the Cornell design community, *Journal* 2 was a validation of the Urban Design Studio and a belated recognition of the importance and influence of those who had studied with Rowe or his associates. Both *The Cornell Journal of Architecture,* 2 and the *Lotus,* 27 articles made a strong impression on younger minds, people who might be considering which graduate school to attend, or who wanted to know what the Rowe Studio was all about, or found utility in Wayne Copper's figure/ground documentation. Within the regulatory environment of city planning, where agencies were already adopting zoning that absorbed the broad tenets of Contextualism, there may have been some substantiation conferred from an academic journal, although given the *Journal's* lack of prescriptive solutions or empirical data, it isn't likely the work was perceived as much more than ivory tower theoretical posturing. But the discourse about urban space-making was, for many, a refreshing shift from what by then seemed the superficial arguments of the Postmodernist debate.

Regarding architecture *cognoscenti* at other universities or the critical media, *Journal* 2 does not appear to have garnered much notice. However, this did not mean it was without influence. Jerry Wells, familiar with the GSD, noted that "there used to be a *Cornell Journal of Architecture* on every desk at Harvard".[39] Typical of a host of younger designers coming from similar backgrounds who may have purchased or borrowed a copy of the *Journal,* Bryan Shiles, while in his fifth year at the University of Tennessee and before matriculating to the Harvard GSD, had this to say recently on the impact of the *Journal* 2:

> *It was about urbanism, naturally. As I recall this was a time when much of the discourse about architecture in school centered around language. Signs, signs everywhere. The designed object was the point of reference and concern. Edmund Bacon's book was around and there were stirrings of urban conversations but they were quite unformed. I don't think my mates had heard of the Nolli Map at the time. So here comes this beautiful book and the most compelling figures we saw were the spaces between buildings. I'm likely collapsing some memory points but the shift in emphasis from object to space and from composition of the vertical surface to consideration of the public realm, at least in my academy, coincided with* The Cornell Journal's *popularity. There was both an exoticism and at the same time a grounding about the promise of the city we saw in* The Cornell Journal 2. *In the South most privileged kids, so therefore the architecture students, grew*

39 Wells, supra. By 1982 Fred Koetter had been teaching for several years at Harvard, and likely informed Wells of his observations on popular student source material.

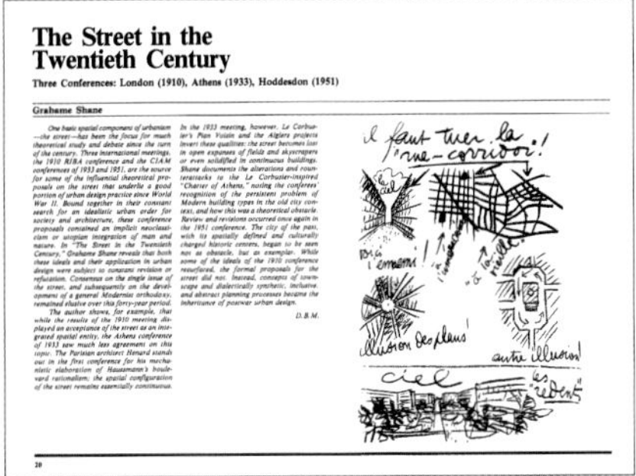

The Street in the Twentieth Century

Three Conferences: London (1910), Athens (1933), Hoddesdon (1951)

Grahame Shane

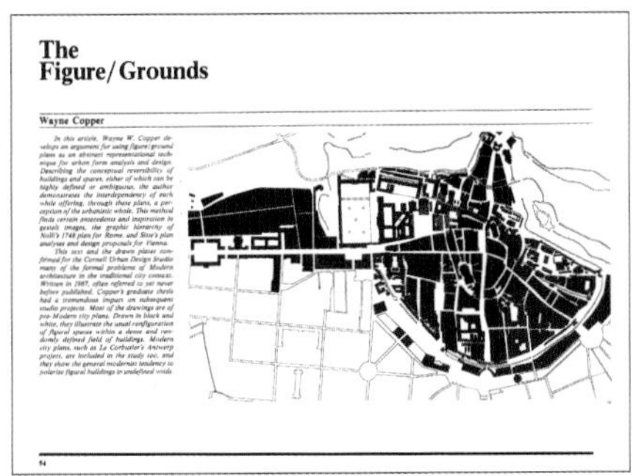

The Figure/Grounds

Wayne Copper

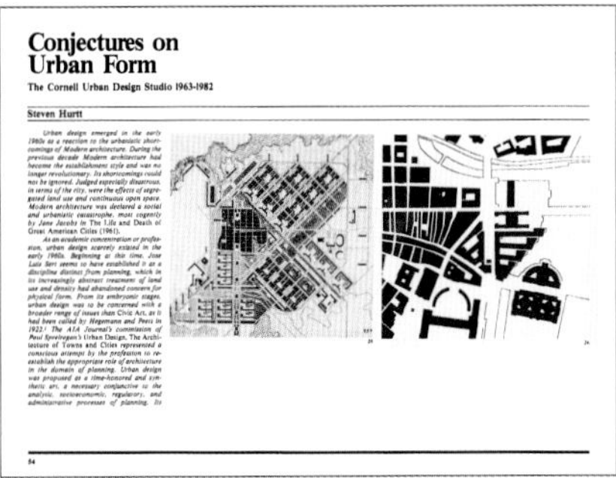

Conjectures on Urban Form

The Cornell Urban Design Studio 1963-1982

Steven Hurtt

> *up in the suburbs. We had no urban frame of reference in our everyday lives and yet we knew NYC was the center of the universe and therefore cities were good. So what we saw in* The Cornell Journal *was an exotic and compelling urbanism rich with complexity and promise. At the same time, it was Europe! The European DNA grounded this urbanism in our shared past, somehow.*[40]

Léon Krier's appraisal of the Urban Design Studio work published in *Journal* 2 managed to both recognize its import while pointedly stating that no one could assume (in the 1980s) the battle to implement constructive urban design had been won. With respect to the projects illustrated, he had this to say:

> *But let us have no illusions. However elegant the graphics, however learned the manuscripts, however clever the critics, I dare say that the main work is not yet done. An operative synthesis [between the Traditional City and the Industrial City] may be within reach, but it requires another even more formidable effort. To be all too triumphant at this stage would be to underestimate the candid brutality of the enemy who has dethroned our art and craft.*[41]

These statements were startling to an American student not yet familiar with a European sensibility filtering almost all formal design issues through a political lens. In hindsight, I see how right he was, and—despite the significant progress in how urban design has advanced in many cities—how ceaseless the vigilance and political effort needs to be to prevent the spatial chaos characteristic of contemporary urban developments.

Of course, Rowe was still active in his Studio. The 1980 exhibition "Urban Design at Cornell" and the *Cornell Journal of Architecture,* 2 may be considered an important milestone. By the mid-1990s Rowe, having officially retired from Cornell, was working assiduously with Alexander Caragonne, as his editor and persistent nudge, to complete the revisions and editing of his various writings covering almost 50 years. Having just traced in detail Rowe's indelible imprint on architectural pedagogy in *The Texas Rangers*, Caragonne now effectively played Boswell to Rowe as Dr. Johnson, helping shepherd this extensive compilation of Rowe's writings into the three-volume, *As I Was Saying.*[42]

40 Shiles to Middleton, email, September 2018. Bryan Shiles is a founding partner in WRNS Studio, an architecture firm in, San Francisco and New York designing many distinctive urban projects.

41 Krier, Léon, "Foreword", *The Cornell Journal of Architecture* 2, 1983: 6.

42 Caragonne, Alexander, ed., *The Texas Rangers: Notes from an Architectural Underground*, MIT Press, Cambridge, MA, and London, 1995. Also see Rowe, Colin, *As I Was Saying*, Caragonne, Alexander, ed., MIT Press, Cambridge, MA, and London, 1996. The 'Rangers' were Bernhard Hoesli, John Hejduk, Robert Slutzky, Lee Hodgden, Werner Seligmann, and John Shaw. Hodgden, Seligman, and Shaw were teaching at Cornell by the early 1960s. Michael Dennis, Jerry Wells, Alex Caragonne, Texas natives and students in the late 1950s, were by the mid-1960s teaching at Cornell. Rowe, in a 1965 letter to Alvin Boyarsky, said, while sympathetic, he was "not a member of their party". See *The Letters of Colin Rowe*, Daniel Naegele, editor (2016). With Rowe's health rapidly deteriorating during his work with Caragonne, one could not help but recall the exertions of U.S. Grant writing his famous memoirs of the Civil War.

The Texas Rangers, Alex Caragonne, ed., 1995

top row left to right:

As I Was Saying, 1996:

Volume 1: *Texas, Pre-Texas, Cambridge*
Volume 2: *Cornelliana*
Volume 3: *Urbanistics*

ANY: "Form Work", Colin Rowe, 1996

L' architetettura come testo e la figura di Colin Rowe, IUAV, 2009

Reckoning with Colin Rowe, Emmanuel Petit, ed., 2015

Appraisal and Re-appraisal

A growing commentary on the topic of Rowe's influence on architectural pedagogy and practice had already begun. The 1994 issue of *ANY*, 7/8 magazine, edited by Cynthia C. Davidson, includes an "interview" and essay by Rowe along with an appraisal by others including R.E. Somol, guest editor. Commentaries on Rowe's work continue to inspire more than 20 years after his death. Kenneth Frampton recently offered me his assessment of the work published in the *Journal*. Frampton had, after all, helped put the Rowe Studio work 'on the map' through his 1980 article on American architectural education. Looking back some 35 years later, he responded to my query by noting that:

> *In the mid-1960s Colin Rowe's teaching of urban design at Cornell University was one of the most lively and pragmatic approaches to this relatively young discipline. It touched on Le Corbusier at the level of taste and* modus operandi *but invariably was referential to the fertile Sitte-esque tradition with its emphasis on poché as a device for adapting to existing conditions. This was fully elaborated as a design strategy in Rowe's influential book* Collage City *of 1978, written in collaboration with Fred Koetter, who was teaching with Rowe in the Cornell program.*

I asked Frampton what, after so many years, he thought most impressive about the *Journal* or the work of the Urban Design Studio. Musing on the topic for a few moments, what unfolded was thirty minutes of spontaneous, enthusiastic, and rapid recollections, the gist of which was that:

> *the* Journal *2 remains unusual: it's the most concrete record of Colin Rowe's teaching, and was very beautifully reproduced... no school could come near this level of work today... the Studio work showed an unusual intensity of effort, working in an almost suspended reality, with a romantic belief in the idea of fragmented urban form.*

Warming to the subject, Frampton went on to describe that Rowe's political position "was in alignment with Karl Popper's *Open Society*, and antithetical to both Krier's 'Rationalist' concept of reconstructing the city and the humanistic rationalism espoused in Chermayeff and Alexander's *Community and Privacy*". He concluded his observations by noting that "Rowe's acolytes were interesting and accomplished people in their own right, and many have gone on to have a significant impact in teaching or practice".[43]

43 Conversations and emails between Frampton and the author, 20–26 September and 6 November 2018. The author is indebted to Professor Frampton for sharing his recollections about Rowe in this context.

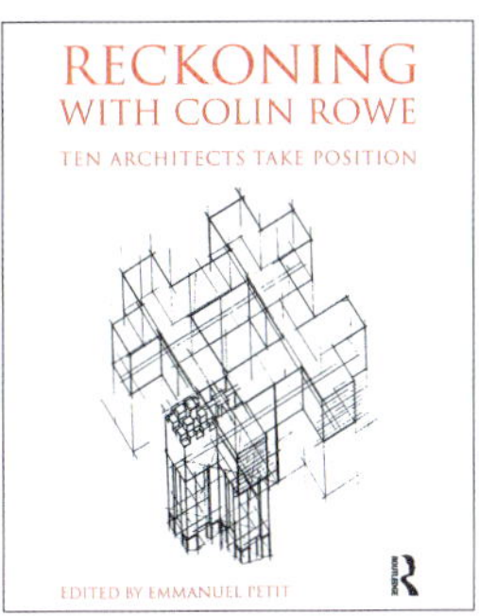

Around 2010, new critical appraisals, primarily of Rowe's architectural design theory, began to appear, less so of his urban design theory. In 2009, the Istituto Universitario di Architettura di Venezia (IUAV) held a colloquium devoted to the writing and architectural theory of Rowe. The presentations were published in *Architecture as Text and the Figure of Colin Rowe,* which contains articles by several prominent scholars, as well as early students or contemporaries of Rowe, notably Peter Eisenman (his student at Cambridge University) and Robert Maxwell (his contemporary and close friend).[44] Carlo Magnani writes in the introduction about the importance of the new course of study at the IUAV, the doctor of philosophy in architectonic composition, perhaps ushered in through the influence of Rowe—at a university that has been historically dedicated to the *cultura del progetto*. This is literally the "culture of the project" semantically something closer to "importance of the architectural making" implying a refined balance between theory and practice as the two main domains of architecture.[45]

The Letters of Colin Rowe, Daniel Naegele (ed.), 2018.

In 2011 a related publication appeared, *The Institute for Architecture and Urban Studies: An Insider's Memoir* by Suzanne Frank. Frank outlines the foundational story of the IAUS in the late 1960s, when Rowe and his Cornell students made a brief but lasting impression on the program. The book is supplemented with interviews of many of these students and a few of the surviving teachers, several of whom described Rowe's influence. They also recounted the appearance of *Oppositions* and the Institute's role in disseminating architectural theory outside mainstream academic and professional institutions. Emmanuel Petit organized and edited a publication of essays reviewing Rowe's theoretical work in *Reckoning with Colin Rowe: Ten Architects Take Position* published in 2015.[46] In a recent publication already opening new avenues of scholarly inquiry and analysis, *The Letters of Colin Rowe: Five Decades of Correspondence* was released in late 2018.[47] A Herculean effort of collecting, assembling, and editing by Daniel Naegele, this is an exhaustive and revealing compilation of letters by Rowe to his many students, family, and colleagues.

Something significant is missing, however, in these recent anthologies about Rowe. For example, in the Marzo and Petit publications, quite typically, there is scarcely any mention of, nor a single illustration regarding, the work of the Urban Design Studio or the contributions of its graduates. It is as if the substantial portion of Rowe's endeavors as a consummate teacher who inspired an

44 Robert M. Maxwell, born in 1922, was a fellow architecture student at the University of Liverpool and a life-long close personal friend of Rowe. In the 1980s he was the dean of the Princeton Architecture School.

45 Translation kindly provided by Marta Tonelli, a graduate of the IAUV. Paraphrasing of Magnani's "Introduction" from *Architecture as Text and the Figure of Colin Rowe.*

46 Petit, Emmanuel, ed. *Reckoning with Colin Rowe: Ten Architects Take Position*, Routledge, Abingdon, and New York, 2015.

47 Naegele, Daniel, ed., *The Letters of Colin Rowe: Five Decades of Correspondence*, Artifice Press, London, 2016.

international cadre of dedicated and accomplished academics and practitioners was somehow beside the point. The 'presence of absence' of such a critique indicates that this long 'laboratory experiment' has been under-appreciated. One correction to this omission has been a series of conferences, 2014–2017, held in Rome with a concentration on the "Urban Design Legacy of Colin Rowe", to which this volume is a testament.

As Kenneth Frampton recently observed, the formation of a studio of urban design, with one person overseeing a group of students almost continuously for over a quarter century, producing a consistent stream of high-quality design studies, is unlikely to be repeated.[48] There are probably few similar precedents. If, for example, one looks at architecture programs in the 20th century, the Bauhaus, for all its intensity and notoriety, lasted 15 years (1919–1934) with three architect-directors.[49] Among the most influential educators in the U.S., both Joseph Hudnut at the GSD and Eliel Saarinen at Cranbrook presided for 16 and 14 years, respectively, as deans for those schools. Walter Gropius taught at the GSD for 14 years, departing in 1952. This doesn't compare to Rowe's 28 years at the helm of the Cornell Urban Design Studio from 1963 to 1990 when he officially retired.[50]

A more fitting model of duration and lasting influence might be the 20th century symphony orchestra or dance ensembles. These organizations tended to be led by long-tenured maestros presiding over a talented and ever-changing cast of performers, such as Eugene Ormandy (Philadelphia Orchestra, 44 years), George Balanchine (New York City Ballet, 35 years), or Martha Graham (Graham Dance Company, 65 years). In such a setting, the maestro and the ensemble of artists have a symbiotic relationship: both are invested in their public reputation, producing the 'art' requires both parties, and the teacher-student relationship is reciprocal during the act of making art.[51] In the realm of design pedagogy and research, a similar relationship existed between Rowe the 'professor-maestro' and the 'student-performers' of the Cornell Urban Design Studio.

Coda

Regarding the idea of legacy there is not any one single measurement that can be used to assess the influence of the Urban Design Studio. My experience, which I believe many shared, was that the Studio was a highly collaborative and inclusive learning environment. Rowe fostered a rich cultural and intellectual

48 Frampton to Middleton, supra.

49 The Bauhaus directors were: Walter Gropius from 1919 to 1928; Hannes Meyer from 1928 to 1930; and Ludwig Mies van der Rohe from 1930 until 1933.

50 During the 1980s Michael Dennis, Val Warke, and Steven Peterson, would step in to oversee the Studio and supervise graduate students during Rowe's more frequent absences in the last decade of his tenure. Rowe would continue as an advisor for several students after 1990.

51 The typical tenure of architecture school deans is less than 10 years, 15 at best. College deans usually have significant administrative and development duties, diffusing the amount of direct design studio contact with students, let alone strictly controlling faculty interests or the curriculum. Other notable orchestra conductors have had similar tenure at the helm of 'their studios': Charles Munch (Boston Symphony, 16 years) and Arturo Toscanini (NBC, 17 years).

ambience. And we learned from each other: this was often a necessity because interacting with Rowe at the drafting table required osmotic skills to absorb the ideas and concepts he might only hint at when sketching a plan or section. Students who were self-motivated and possessed of an intense intellectual curiosity could thrive. In this respect, the Studio was very much a 'laboratory', a place where students might apply and test concepts underpinning the theory of Contextualism as it incrementally evolved and become adept at employing the strategy of urban *bricolage* for approaching civic form making. Like any worthy research endeavor, there would also be the inevitable false starts or occasional shortcomings. And in his quirky, typically self-effacing way, Rowe encouraged students to take the argument for this approach to urban design beyond the basement walls of the Studio.[52]

The 1983 *Cornell Journal of Architecture,* 2, was, in essence, a mid-term lab report, a demonstration of an iterative process, the result of a particular point in time and in a particular context lasting more than 15 years. There was more to say as the Studio would continue for almost a decade more. Rowe would continue to inspire students to excel at the *art of city-making* that is the fundamental component of urban design. The formation, dissemination and impact of the *Journal* provides a compelling visual testament and remains a significant part of Rowe's legacy as arguably the most important urban design theorist of his generation.

opposite left to right:

Letter to the World, 1940, Martha Graham. Photo: Barbara Morgan.

Eugene Ormandy and the Philadelphia Orchestra.

New Criterion, George Ballanchine and the New York City Ballet. Photo: Nancy Lassalle/Eakins Press.

below:
Colin Rowe, *in critque,* Florence, Italy, ca. 1986.

52 'Taking action' included conjuring up the "Buffalo Waterfront" project with the students in 1966 and making an exhibition at the Albright-Knox Gallery in 1969; moving the Studio to New York for a year (1967-68); participating in the founding of the IAUS; sponsoring the Studio members to work with the NYC Department of Planning (1968-70); encouraging students to work for the Baltimore City Department of Planning (1968); participating in the "City Segments" travelling exhibition (1980); and encouraging former students like Schumacher, Cohen and Hurtt, Ellis, and others to publish.

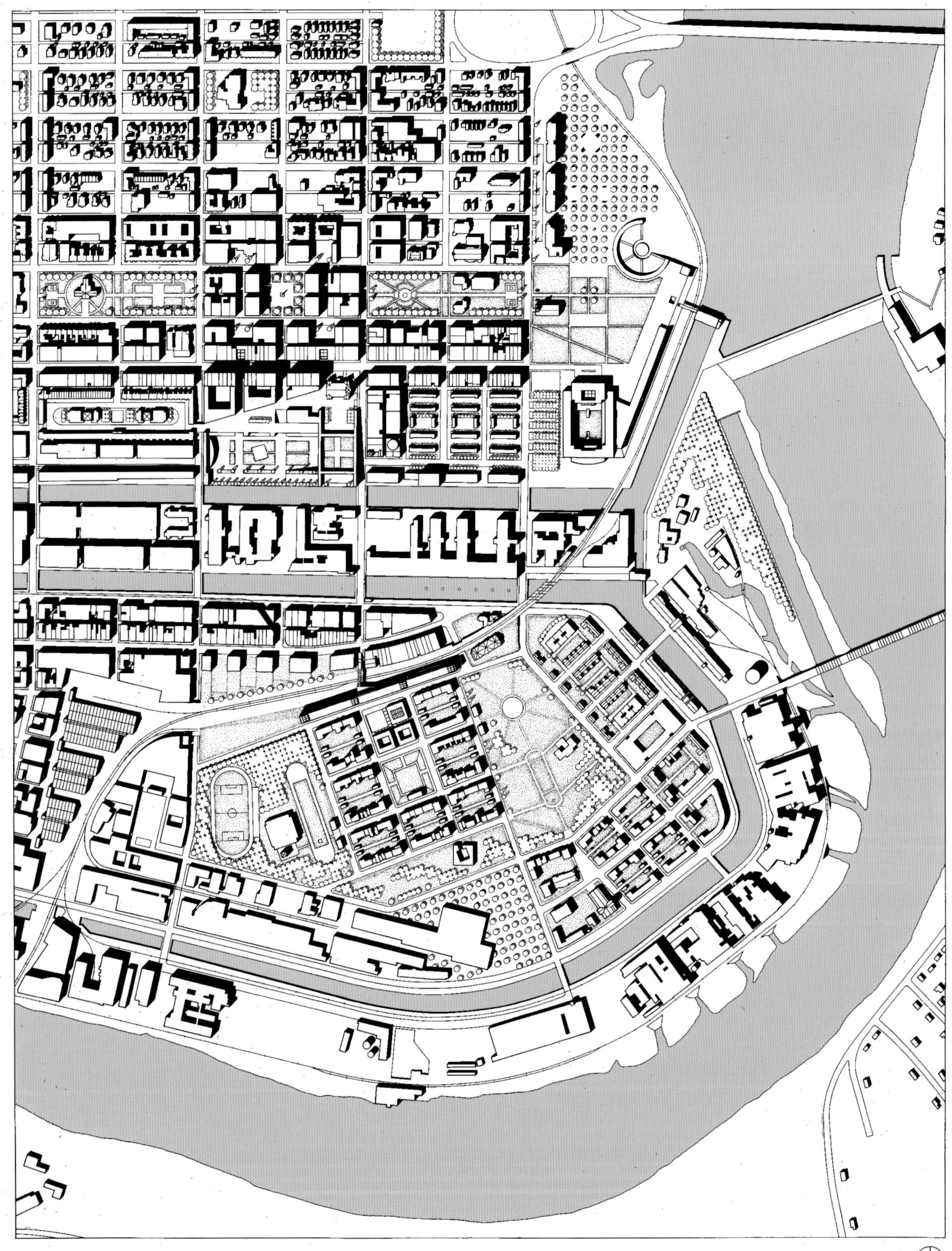

0 200 400

PROPOSED SHADOW PLAN

Reflections on Colin Rowe, Three Decades Hence

Thomas K. Davis

Cornell Undergraduate Days

frontispiece:
Proposed plan of Holyoke, MA, East Side. Drawing by T. K. Davis, Cornell University Master's thesis, 1983.

When I arrived at Cornell as an innocent undergraduate in August 1972, coming from an insular New England prep school, I had no idea of the intellectual intensity I would encounter during my subsequent five-year curriculum in architecture. Undergraduate studio teaching had been led for years by the legendary Texas Rangers—Werner Seligmann, John Shaw, and Lee Hodgden, and a little later by Jerry Wells and Michael Dennis—those who had, in effect, followed Colin Rowe to Ithaca from the University of Texas, Austin. Past students of the Rangers seemed to make up much of the balance of the design faculty, such as Fred Koetter, Steven Peterson, Alan Chimacoff, and Roger Sherwood, and there was Klaus Herdeg from Zurich where Bernhard Hoesli, another Texas Ranger, was his colleague and the director of the ETH. Collectively, the faculty's teaching focus was inspiring, which accounts, in part, for the significant percentage of graduates who went into teaching as a career.[1] While Colin had little direct contact with undergraduates during my period at Cornell, and indeed was rarely sighted on undergraduate juries, it was clear that his influence was enormous on the design faculty, and thereby indirectly, on all students in the program. His elective courses were popular with undergraduates, and his thesis student presentations were major events. Colin was the headliner in a six-week summer program in 1974 in Venice, with over twenty undergraduate students and five other faculty.

Colin had a guru status enveloped in mystique—he once told me he considered Hermann Hesse's *The Glass Bead Game* as an analog to the Cornell Architecture Department, with himself in the novel's Magister Ludi role, or "The Master of the Game". His alternative novel paralleling departmental politics was Stendahl's *The Charterhouse of Parma*, with Colin in the role of Count Mosca, the Prime Minister of Parma, and Fred Koetter playing the young Italian nobleman Fabrice del Dongo. While Colin was seldom seen in the undergraduate curriculum, pirated photocopies of his writings and voluminous dual reading lists—one on intellectual and cultural history and the other on architecture and urbanism—were a very visible and highly valued *de facto* 'great books' reading program for

1 The following fulltime teachers of architecture were fellow Cornell undergraduates during the author's studies in Ithaca: Edgar Adams, Dean J. Almy III, Ann Cederna, Andrew Cohen, Marleen Kay Davis, Judith DiMaio, Adam Drisin, Tom Fisher, Steve Fong, Jose Gelabart-Navia, Miriam Gusevich, Denis Hector, Judith Kinnard, Michael Lykoudis, Evelyn McFarlane, Blake Middleton, Vince Mulcahy, Jonathan Ochshorn, Arthur Ovaska, Ann Pendleton-Jullian, Ken Schwartz, Andrea Simitch, Julia Smyth-Pinney, Simon Ungers, Wilvan Van Campen, Val Warke, and John Zissovici.

Fig. 1. Colin Rowe: 1992 (Source: Valerie Bennett [https://valeriebennett.com/]).

the most motivated undergraduates. These documents were surreptitiously obtained in post-midnight weekend visits to his graduate Urban Design Studio located in the catacomb *cum* subway-like basement of Sibley Hall.

I developed a *modus operandi* for learning in the studio. First, one learns a remarkable amount from one's classmates; Val Warke, who has gone on to a distinguished career teaching, first at Harvard and in recent decades at Cornell. On virtually any given Monday, Wednesday, or Friday design studio afternoon, I would get a desk critique at the outset of the studio, and then leave to sit-in and observe pin-up design reviews of any studio at my level or higher in the undergraduate curriculum. My objective was to intensely observe the proceedings, seeking to anticipate what the faculty panel would critically disclose or ideas they might suggest. Those members of the Texas Rangers, and their extended progeny on the faculty, were the critical protagonists on these reviews. These events often brought with them a rather theatrical dimension. This was particularly true of the charismatic, intense, and sometimes volatile Werner Seligmann, whom I once observed on a design review get into a shouting confrontation with a student whose modest offering on the wall was matched only by the student's immodest tennis attire. In my experience, Werner Seligmann, John Shaw, Lee Hodgden, and Jerry Wells were particularly influential studio critics. In my second-year studio with Seligmann we did 13 individual projects—the last of which was a six-week problem. We would be issued a project on Monday for a Friday pin-up and on Friday for a Monday pin-up. Werner brought a discourse focusing on space, drawing quality, conceptual diagramming, program interpretation, and *parti*. Werner saw this eight-week boot-camp as a remedial corrective to the teaching we had been exposed to during the previous year with other faculty.

By my second year, inspired by this dynamic faculty and coupled with my design review attendance, I knew I wanted, ultimately, to be a teacher. Little did I anticipate that a civil war over faculty politics would break out between a Rowe faculty-student camp and Department Chair Oswald Mathias Ungers (aka OMU) and his faculty-student entourage. Ironically, Ungers had been recruited from Berlin by Colin to lead the department, based on Colin's admiration for Ungers and his projects that had become known to a wider audience through Aldo Rossi's publication in *Casabella* and elsewhere.

The political drama and stress at that time, as I recall, was triggered by Ungers declining tenure to Alan Chimacoff, Fred Koetter, and Roger Sherwood. Ungers believed that the department faculty was "over-represented" by its alumni and verging on a Corbu academy. Of course, the resulting purge was one manner in which Cornell pedagogy flowed outward to other schools: Chimacoff to Princeton, where he would partner with Steven Peterson, Koetter to Harvard and then to Yale as dean, Sherwood to USC, and Herdeg to Columbia. Herdeg left Cornell as a show of solidarity with his colleagues even though he had received tenure. Later, Seligmann became dean at Syracuse in 1975.

In retrospect, it is remarkable how much, philosophically speaking, Colin and OMU shared regarding dialectical thinking, typology, collage, and the use of historical precedent as a creative catalyst in design work. They also shared an abiding interest in reconciling the Modern city and the traditional city through

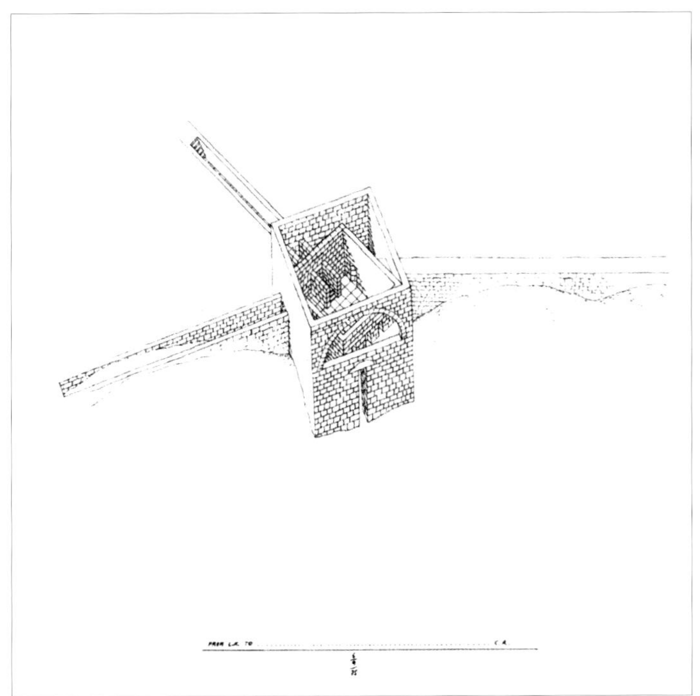

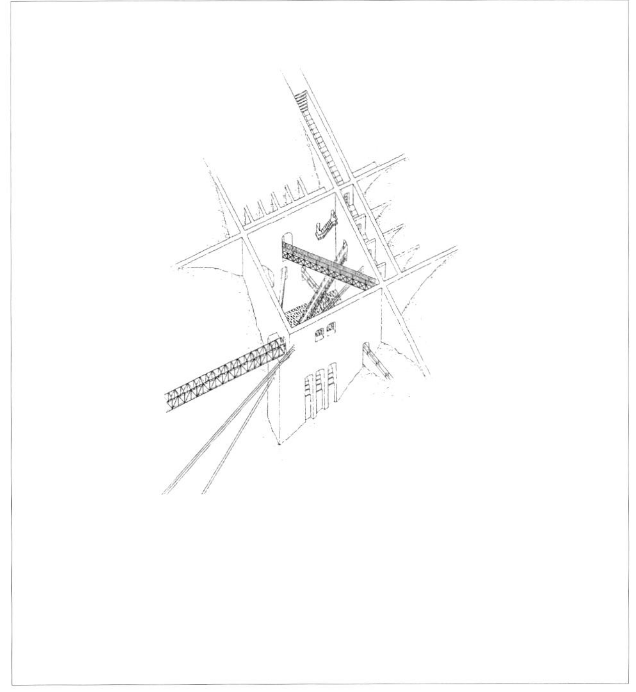

left to right:

Fig. 2. "Difficult Access to O.M.U.", drawing by Léon Krier, 1975.

Fig. 3. "House for Colin Rowe", drawing by Léon Krier, 1975.

the potential of simultaneous presence, which is to say through 'collage'. I concur with Arthur Ovaska's 2009 observations at the Preston Thomas Memorial Symposium, "Shaping Architects = Shaping Architecture". Ovaska observed that where Colin's thinking was foremost about space and its composition, Ungers's foremost concern was concept, i.e. metaphors, transformation, and dialectics.[2] Colin was also fascinated by the juxtaposition and reconciliation of traditional and Modern urban spatial definition, and in this regard he shared Ungers's interest in dialectic analysis/synthesis. For both, their thinking was grounded in context and the transformation of latent patterns of order, within and inflected by a larger realm of ideas.[3]

Berlin architect Hans Kollhoff recently recalled Cornell in the mid-70s this way:

> *You must not forget that Colin Rowe brought Mathias to the States and Cornell. Obviously, Mathias was offered projects there that did not materialize. So their relationship was troubled by conditions that were unexpected. But when you look at the symposium that Ungers had organized in Berlin, and when you read the lecture that Rowe had given there, you cannot but notice how amazingly close their positions were. After a short while in Cornell, I did not understand why there was this fight between a Rowe camp and an Ungers camp. Of course they came from very different backgrounds, but they were extremely close in their criticism of Modernist opinions in architecture and urbanism. I know that Rem (Koolhaas) did not see it that way. I think he hated Colin Rowe, because Colin was explicitly involved with history, whereas Mathias was discovering fascinating images. These images were charged with meaning and could somehow be reinterpreted. For Colin, the issue was less a questioning of reinterpreting history than developing it further, analyzing an urban figure/ground abstraction is still a very efficient tool today. Sometimes too abstract, of course, because you don't know whether the building is one story or fifty stories high. Mathias also used figure/grounds at the time. But for Colin, it*

2 Ovaska, Arthur, "Shaping Architects = Shaping Architecture", the Preston Thomas Memorial Symposium, 2009.

3 For the larger framework of Rowe and Ungers's respective theoretical positions regarding urbanism: Rowe, Colin; Koetter, Fred, *Collage City*, MIT Press, Cambridge, MA, and London 1978, and Ungers, O. M.; Vieths, Stefan, *Oswald Mathias Ungers: The Dialectic City*, Skira, Milan, 1997.

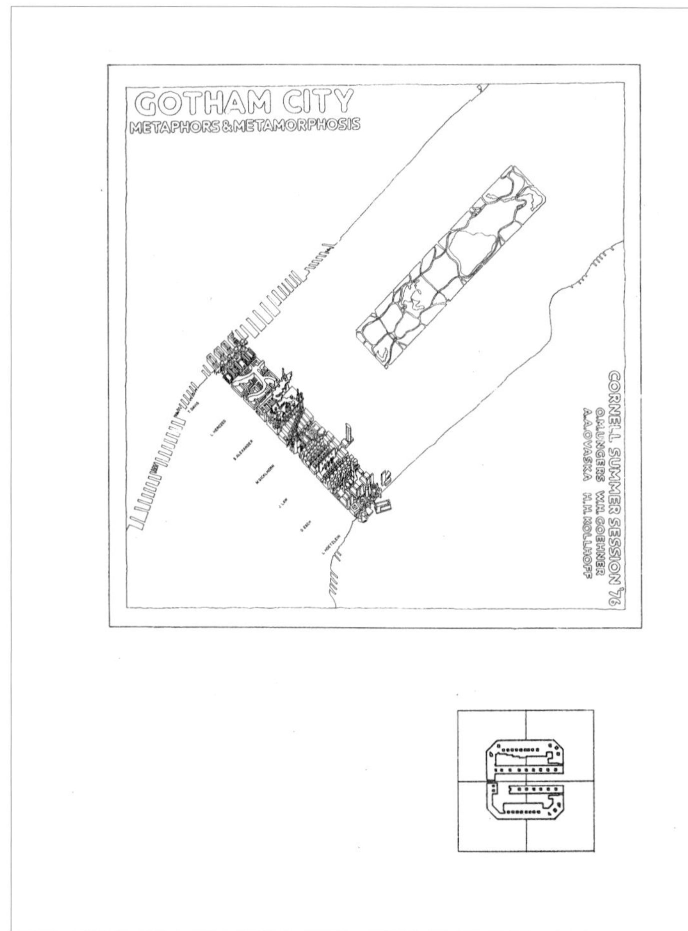

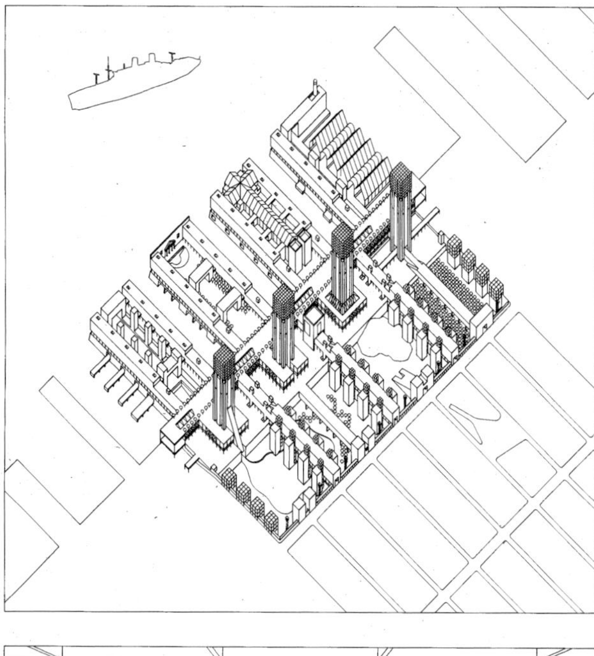

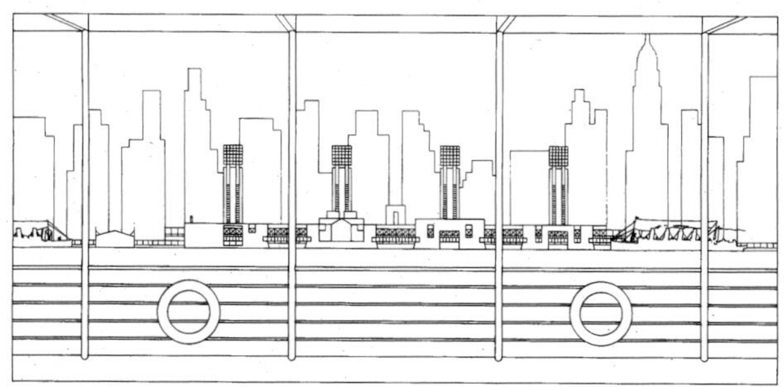

left to right:

Fig. 4. *The Urban Block and Gotham City: Metaphors and Metamorphosis: Two Concurrent Projects*, publication cover, 1976.

Fig. 5. Gotham City project, T.K. Davis, 1976.

was material to be treated, changed, and developed further, whereas Mathias saw it as a field into which one could creatively project images in the same way you read the zodiac configurations in a starry sky. The design was the hypothesis of what you saw.

After a while, I got closer to Colin Rowe. There was a period when Mathias and Colin were also able to talk to each other again, feeling that they had much more in common than their audience expected. They even made an attempt to forget about the past and the situation that had initiated the split in earlier times at Cornell.[4]

The energy and tension in the program were intense. Ungers invited a series of Neo-rationalist architects, visiting critics, lecturers, or researchers. If my memory serves, this included Georg Heinrichs, Ed Jones, Josef Paul Kleihues, Rem Koolhaas, Léon Krier, Aldo Rossi, and Jürgen Sawade. It was during Léon Krier's visit in 1975 that he made his two freehand, enigmatic caricatures entitled "Difficult Access to O.M.U." and "House for Colin Rowe".

I found myself, by fifth-year, an admirer of the Neo-Rationalist competition projects being produced by Ungers and his adroit graduate students, including Rem Koolhaas, Arthur Ovaska, Hans Kollhoff, and Jeffrey Clark. And so I enlisted in the special graduate-undergraduate overlap program, which put me in OMU's graduate studio as a fifth-year undergraduate. One product of this engagement

4 Kollhoff, Hans (in conversation with Florian Hertweck and Sébastien Marot), "An Exciting Exercise", in Ungers, Oswald Mathias; Koolhaas, Rem, (with) Riemann, Peter; Kollhoff, Hans; Ovaska, Arthur, *The City in the City. Berlin: A Green Archipelago*, Hertweck, Florian; Marot, Sebastien, eds., Lars Muller Publishers, Zurich, (1977) 2013: 157.

was my design contribution documented in the 1976 summer school dual publication *The Urban Block and Gotham City: Metaphors and Metamorphosis: Two Concurrent Projects.*[5] It is of some interest to note that OMU was the first to introduce the use of colored pencils in the ink line drawing regimen at Cornell.

Graduation and Graduate School

After five years, and having been issued a Bachelor of Architecture degree in 1977, I determined to leave academia, temporarily, and to proceed toward professional licensure. I subsequently returned to Cornell in 1981 for my Master of Architecture and for 'rehabilitation' with the exciting prospect of joining Colin's Urban Design Studio. Mathias had since effectively left to practice in Germany, only returning annually for cameo appearances on final reviews. As a graduate student, I also received my first real taste of design teaching in the first-year undergraduate architectural design studio. At that time, most of Colin's Urban Design Studio was populated by graduates of the Cornell undergraduate curriculum, and most served as design teaching assistants. While there was little urban design content in first-year studios, the teaching emphasized spatial concepts, diagramming, and rigorous thinking as an evolution of the problem types invented earlier at the ETH in Zurich and the University of Texas, Austin. This served as a strong platform from which to launch a teaching career.

When it came time to choose a project for my urban design graduate thesis, I selected Holyoke, Massachusetts, because of the intriguing formal characteristics that resulted from its topographic setting, unique planning history, and subsequent architectural development. Owing to the construction of a hydropower dam and canal system to support manufacturing mills, Holyoke was one of the first comprehensively planned industrial cities in America. Growing up in Western Massachusetts, I had first encountered Holyoke as a nearsighted child on the day when I obtained my first pair of glasses. That memorable day was visually unforgettable. Colin had never heard of the city, but was immediately intrigued with this 'discovery'.

The city's relationship to the Connecticut River, its varied topography and the ring of 4.5 miles of canals that separate the older city from newer development are quite provocative features, more reminiscent of European than American towns and cities. Unusual typologies of built form are found in Holyoke, including the long narrow mill structures, the Holyoke Dam, a variety of bridges, perimeter block and row housing types, and numerous distinguished civic buildings. The original 1853 plan remains intact today, albeit suffering from severe deterioration of its urban fabric. Therefore, in that the city's *parti* exists, the intention of the thesis was to transform and enhance the existing latent formal order, rather than to superimpose any alien organization onto the city.

During my period in the Urban Design Studio (1981–83) most of Colin's students were working on more limited scale ensembles of new buildings. Rather than examine the city incrementally with discreet, limited, and sequential modifications, my study addressed the city as a whole. This was appropriate because the city was planned comprehensively and still retained clearly defined boundaries. If a comprehensive plan is a carefully comprised series of semi-autonomous

5 *The Urban Block and Gotham City: Metaphors and Metamorphosis: Two Concurrent Projects* was an in-house publication of the Cornell Architecture Summer School 1976. The six students enrolled in the *Gotham City* studio, including the author, were taught by O. M. Ungers, Werner Goehner, Hans Kollhoff, and Arthur Ovaska. After compiling a pan-historical documentation and analysis of urban blocks, the studio focused on speculative ideas for transforming the band of Midtown Manhattan between 34th and 42nd Streets, from river to river. Each of the six students focused on a separate 16-block precinct within this zone, with metaphoric thinking as a creative stimulant.

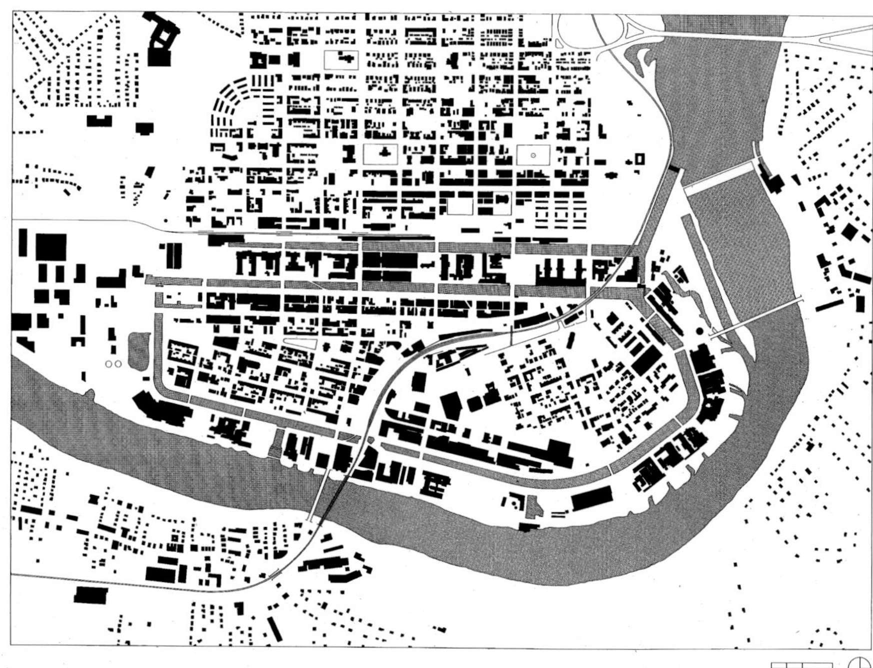

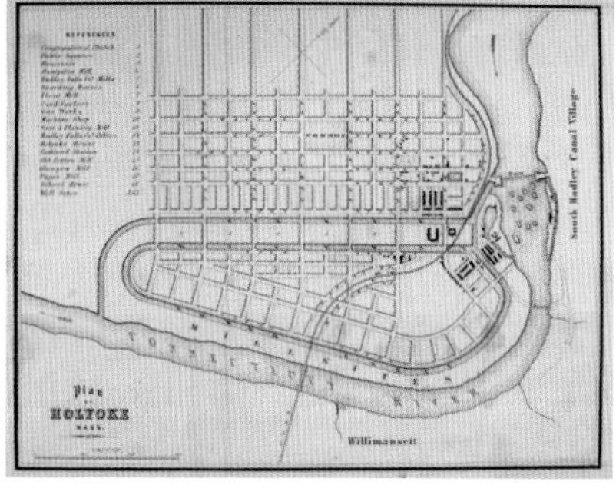

above:
Fig. 6. "Plan of Holyoke, Mass., drawing by S. Chase, 1853". The original grid plan for the downtown area of the City of Holyoke, when it was a planned industrial community of the Hadley Falls Company, under the patronage of the Boston Associates.

left inset:
Fig. 7. Existing figure/ground of Holyoke, drawing by T.K. Davis, 1983.

'interventions' then these urban proposals are not dependent upon each other for their individual efficacy. They may occur, in a formal sense, independent of each other, or as isolated events, and still contribute to an improved condition. What is important is to view the proposed plan not as something which could, or even should, occur in its totality. Rather, the plan is seen as an agenda, subject to change over time; it is in place to suggest growth and development that happens in all corners of a typical downtown in a non-sequential rather random way, driven by the vicissitudes of real estate markets.[6]

In looking at the city more broadly, I suggested a variety of moves at the scale of buildings or urban blocks that would not be contingent on each other. The plan was projected as a model to organize the randomness and flux of development and policy and would be subject to change over time. As an academic exercise in 'urban architecture', it was intended to serve as a catalyst for ideas. And one must concede that one technique shared by Colin and Mathias was the figure/ground drawing as an invaluable analytic/synthetic device in visualizing the *gestalt* spatial qualities of the city. I was no doubt also influenced by the unpublished, but widely copied and distributed, collection of urban figure/grounds produced by Wayne Copper, Colin's former student. These were readily available as photocopies and were soon to be published in *The Cornell Journal of Architecture,* 2.

After study of Holyoke's original plan and history, the primary urban design moves in the thesis were subtractive in nature, in part for reasons of economy. An attempt was made to consolidate that fabric within the city that could be retrieved and which offered tactical advantage or historical significance. The solid-void polarization of the fabric clarified and enriched the plan spatially, while at the same time heightening identity and hierarchy through public space. Several secondary, larger scale insertions of urban architecture were proposed,

6 Davis, Thomas K.; Davis, Marleen Kay, "Holyoke, Massachusetts: An Urban Design Study", *The Journal of Architectural Education* 39 (2), Win 1985: 17-27.

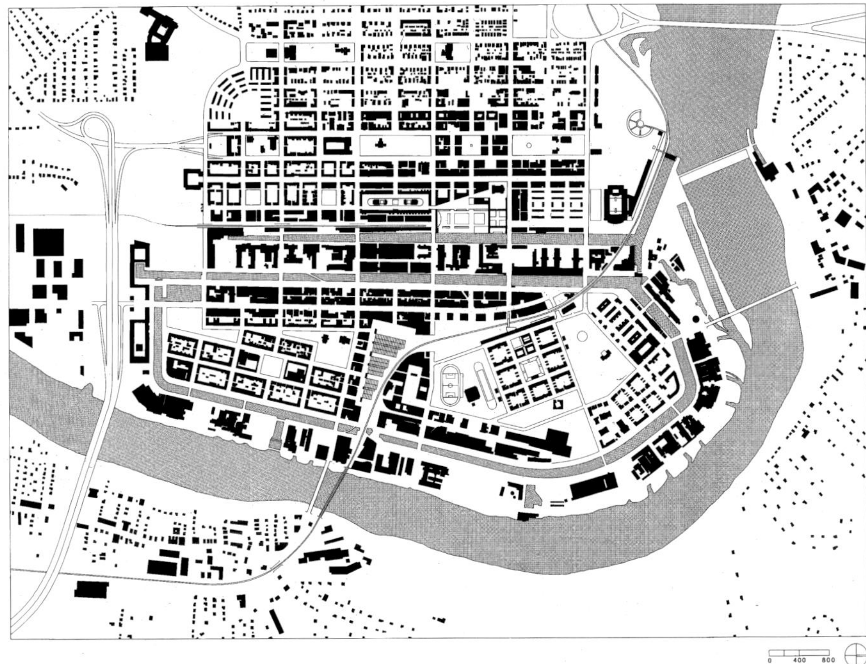

right inset:
Fig. 8. Proposed figure/ground of Holyoke, drawing by T.K. Davis, 1983.

the intent being to produce a maximum effect with minimum means. Clearly, this design approach, that of a tactical subtractive consolidation of fabric, owes something to Ungers's and Koohhaas' Berlin Archipelago project, which had been previously published in *Lotus international*.[7]

John Reps, whose lecture courses were very popular with Colin's urban design students and who was the author of *The Making of Urban America: A History of City Planning in the United States* served on my thesis committee. Colin and John seemed to get along very well. Colin was fascinated by Reps's particular discovery, noted in his book, of the French Azilum, a town of refuge for French aristocrats seeking a new life in America in the wake of the French Revolution. Acreage was secured in Northeast Pennsylvania by several distinguished Philadelphians sympathetic to the plight of the French monarchists. The land was located in Luzerne County, along a picturesque bend in the Susquehanna River, not far from the New York State border. Settlers began arriving in 1793, although they eventually moved on to cities like New Orleans and Charleston. Remains include the town square, shops, a chapel, a distillery, and the largest built residence, called La Grande Maison, that was apparently intended for Queen Marie Antoinette and her children, allowing that they were able to escape France. This was just the kind of *arcana,* the confluence of which linked early American town planning with European history, that Colin found irresistible, all of them well within a modest drive from Ithaca.[8]

Colin loved to go touring throughout upstate New York on weekends, often driven by one of his students, foraging for antiques, books, and 'vernacular' architecture. He delighted in obscure findings, such as the Seneca County Courthouse complex in the village of Ovid, also known as 'The Three Bears'. As described in the website *Exploring Upstate:* "Architectural Gems in Ovid":

7 For a thorough discussion of this 1977 manifesto by Oswald Mathias Ungers and Rem Koolhaas with Peter Riemann, Hans Kollhoff and Arthur Ovaska: Ungers et al. (2013).

8 Reps, John, *The Making of Urban America: A History of City Planning in the United States*, Princeton University Press, Meriden, CN, 1965: 475-76. John Reps always had a ready wit. Colin was to deliver the first of several 1984 Preston Thomas lectures. Throughout the entire first lecture, Colin was stroking his hands up and down the sides of the lectern with considerable intensity, all of which was picked up audibly by the microphone, unbeknownst to Colin. When John Reps introduced Colin at the subsequent lecture, he remarked that he had enjoyed Colin's first talk, but he was concerned that the lectern might have been impregnated!

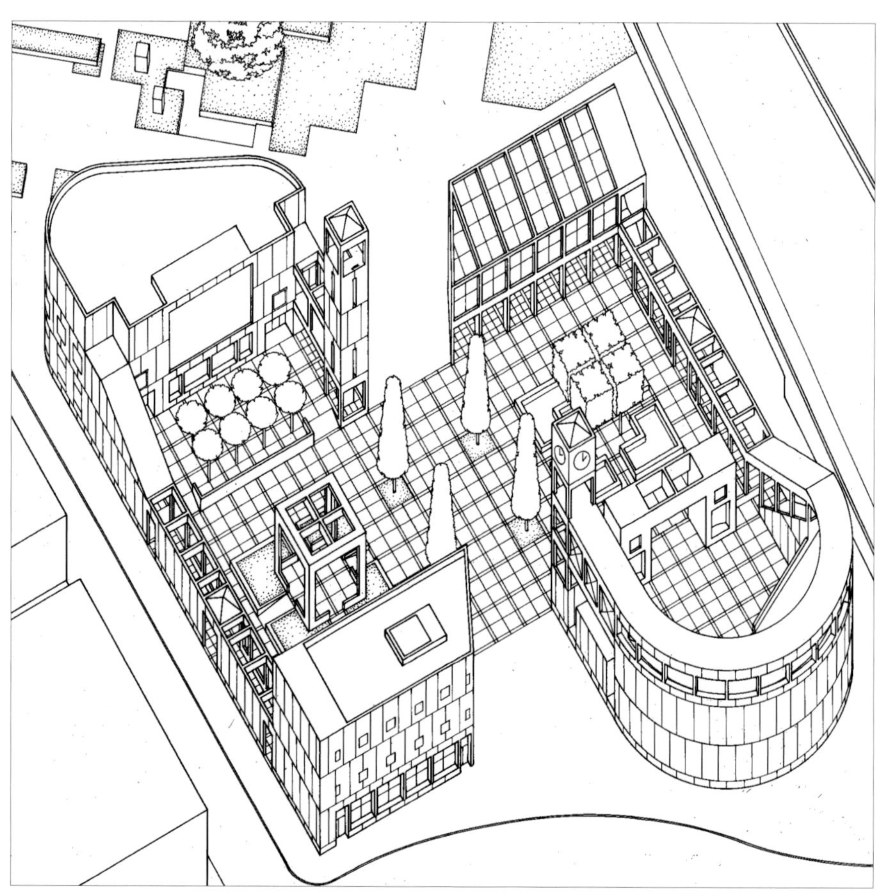

Fig. 9. Fort Lauderdale Riverfront Plaza Design Competition, Third Place Award, axonometric drawing by T.K. Davis and M. K. Davis, 1983.

> *The affectionately named 'Three Bears' are unique in that they are believed to be the only three adjacent Greek-Revival style public buildings that remain standing in the entire United States. Their small, medium and large sizes earned them the nickname long ago, and they're still often cited as an outstanding piece of local history.*[9]

Colin urged all his urban design students to take the two-semester lecture sequence in intellectual history taught by the brilliant Dominick LaCapra, a well-respected Cornell professor, covering the historiography of ideas during the 19th and 20th centuries. LaCapra also brought to his lectures the history of literary studies, aesthetics, post-structuralism, and psychoanalytic techniques of analysis and close reading. My graduate school immersion in critical thinking, cultural theory, and comparative literature, through LaCapra's teaching, was indirectly one of Colin's greatest gifts to me.

Before I advance this narrative, perhaps a few observations about Colin's manner of studio teaching would be of interest. Colin would often bring books into the studio to inspire. His knowledge was encyclopedic, and in cultural realms well beyond architecture and urbanism. For Colin, you could not *not* know architectural history. So design without precedent was scarcely possible, and the acquisition of such knowledge was an essential virtue in the designer. As Christian F. Otto wrote of Colin in his essay "Orientation and Invention: Teaching the History of Architecture at Cornell":

9 Clemens, Chris, "Architectural Gems in Ovid", *Exploring Upstate*, April 20, 2016. [https://exploringupstate.com/architectural-gems-ovid/].

Fig. 10. University of Miami Campus Master Plan Competition, Grand Prize Award, T.K. Davis and M. K. Davis, 1984.

> *Rowe promoted the history of architecture on the basis of his belief in precedent as invention, a heuristic position ... To Rowe, history comprised the very core of architecture, the fulcrum of the design process. "I am not able to comprehend how anyone can begin to act (let alone to think) without resorting to precedent." He then summarized his position: "(Is) it possible to conceive of any society, any civilization or any culture without the provision of precedent?" Historic precedents for him were evocative objects that promoted invention; they stimulated the mind and the eye, they could be mined and transformed. Without history there could be no architecture.*[10]

Colin wouldn't say very much at your desk during a critique, but he was both an extraordinary visual thinker and an incandescent intellect. For all I know, he may well have had a photographic memory. Colin would invariably conclude a desk critique with an aphoristic observation on the design problem at hand, often revealed in an astute diagram, which profoundly reconfigured the circumstantial variables being addressed. His visual acumen was astonishing. His silences, though often expressed in a world-weary demeanor, could at times be misconstrued by an insecure student as boredom. Former students of Mies van der Rohe have said that Mies's long, pregnant silences during student pin-up reviews, sometimes minutes at a time, concentrated one's mind on your drawings to an intense degree, and you would come to see ways the drawing(s) could be improved. Colin's oracular presence and extended silences during desk critiques had a similar effect.[11]

10 Otto, Christian, "Orientation and Invention: Teaching the History of Architecture at Cornell", in Parks, Janet; Wright, Gwendolyn . eds., *The History of History in American Schools of Architecture, 1865-1975*, Princeton University Press, New York, 1990: 115. The embedded quote in Rowe, Colin, "Letter to the Editors", *The Harvard Architectural Review*, 5, 1986: 188.

11 See the James Ingo Freed interview where he talks about Mies's "teaching by silence" in the documentary film *Mies* (1986) by Director Michael Blackwood.

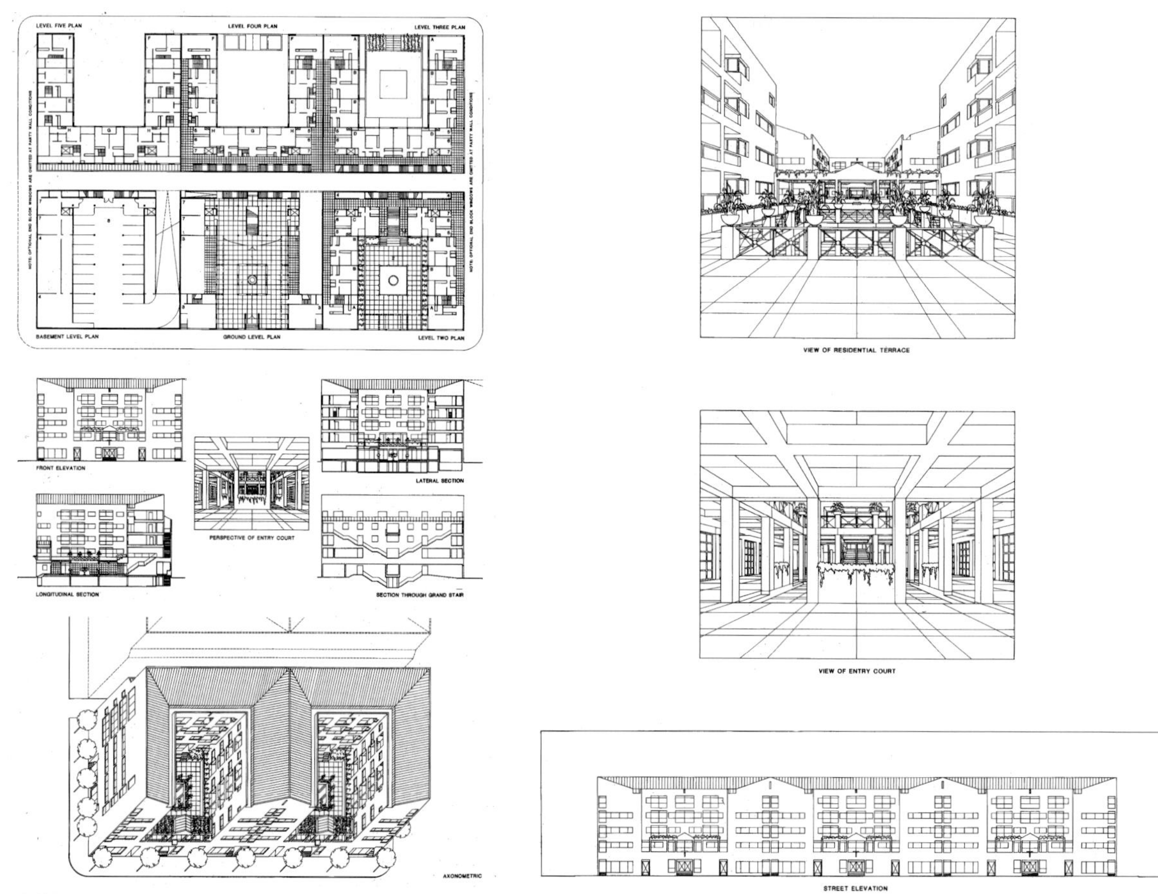

Fig. 11. Seattle Urban Housing Competition submission by T.K. Davis and M. K. Davis, 1988.

With the help of Colin's recommendations and upon receiving my Master of Architecture degree, I was awarded a Fulbright grant in Italy and the National Institute for Architectural Education Traveling Fellowship at the American Academy in Rome. Colin suggested I spend the year studying the *Sacri Monti* of Northern Italy, which was a joy to pursue, both in the library and in the field. The *Sacri Monti* are thematic pilgrimage chapels built in the 16th and 17th centuries to depict various aspects of Christianity and the Bible. Colin's sharing of his ongoing fascination with all things Italian, and his history lectures on Italian Renaissance architecture and gardens, set up great expectations for my 'Italian Journey', expectations that were richly rewarded. During that year, my Cornell classmate and spouse, Marleen Kay Davis, served as director of the Syracuse University Architecture Program in Florence, all of which made for a compelling and memorable *wunderjahr* for the two of us in 1983–84.

Academic Career: Design and Outreach

Upon returning to the United States, I began teaching at Syracuse University, ultimately receiving tenure. I served on a faculty led by Dean Werner Seligmann, who was explicitly building a cohesive school modeled on his own experience in Texas working with Colin Rowe and later at Cornell. In addition to studio teaching, I developed a lecture course titled "The History and Theory of Urban Form". Our demanding dean strongly encouraged faculty to participate in design competitions as a vehicle for creative work and research, and several of my urban design projects (in collaboration with my partner, Marleen Kay Davis) subsequently received international recognition: the Fort Lauderdale Riverfront Plaza Design Competition (Third Place Award), the University of Miami Campus Master Plan Competition (Grand Prize Award),[12] and the Forum Quebec Competition (Second Prize Award).

In 1994, Marleen Kay Davis was appointed dean of the College of Architecture and Planning at the University of Tennessee in Knoxville, and I was concurrently awarded tenure. As Colin's student, I recall his admiration for the work of John Nolen, 'The Father of American Town Planning', whose planned city of Kingsport in northeast Tennessee, was located nearby. Indeed, in speaking to his student from Tennessee, John O'Brien, Colin had often spoken of his arrival at dawn in Kingsport. Colin related that he was riding in an MG sports car with faculty colleague Jerry Wells, and they had come to see Nolen's town as built.[13] Colin always maintained that early morning was the best light with which to view architecture *in situ* and apparently the quality of light added to this experience being a highly memorable one. In moving to Tennessee, I knew I had a rendezvous with Kingsport as well, but little did I know that my thesis on the planned industrial city of Holyoke would foreshadow my work with the planned industrial city of Kingsport.

It was my admiration for Nolen's prolific work and distinguished career that led to my formation of the Kingsport Regional Urban Design Studio. From 1995 through 2002, Kingsport became my laboratory for urban design ideas. In Ithaca and at Syracuse University, my urban design work and teaching was perhaps more conceptual and focused on hypothetical ideas and competitions. When I moved to Tennessee, I realized that, with careful faculty framing of a real urban design challenge, the student work could prove valuable to other cities in the state as citizens tried to identify potential transformations of their communities. This built on a tradition at the University of Tennessee, when in 1981, Stroud Watson had used his student work to inspire change and new development in one such city: Chattanooga. Following his lead, faculty identified urban design advocacy strategies for cities and towns throughout the state as a part of the school's mission, conceived as a collaborative academic outreach engagement. In fact, Stroud Watson was instrumental in securing one of the first major urban design built commissions for Koetter Kim Architects, Miller Park, which included a multi-block building scheme as well as design guidelines.

Working with city leaders, the Kingsport studio enabled me to offer a broad spectrum of expertise, while the students generated a wide variety of ideas for the community—sparking interest, debate, enthusiasm, and subsequent development. The studio provided not only a fine educational experience to its students, but also a special and imaginative form of public service to the citizens of Tennessee consistent with the University's historic Land Grant mission.

Kingsport represented a unique urban context for the study of issues involving urban architecture. The historic downtown was comprehensively designed by Nolen. Seen as an example of a model industrialized City Beautiful, the planned city was considered to be essential to recruit and maintain a stable workforce

12 Davis, Thomas K.; Davis, Marleen Kay, "The University of Miami Campus Master Plan Competition", *The Journal of Architectural Education* 43 (4), Sum 1990: 8-15.

13 Conveyed to the author by my colleague John O'Brien in multiple conversations ca. 1995.

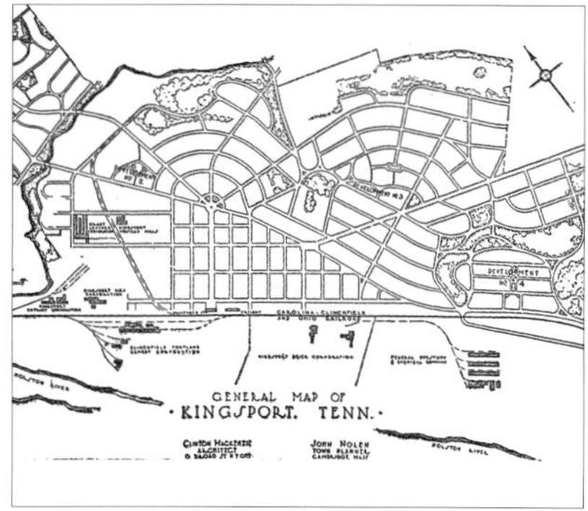

Fig. 12. "General Map of Kingsport, Tennessee" by Clinton MacKenzie and John Nolen ca. 1919, from "An Industrial City Made to Order: Kingsport, Tennessee".

with which industrial capitalism would thrive. Indeed, Kingsport was the largest planned new town built in North America between the years 1915 and 1965. Nolen's plan, reflecting the aspirations of the city's founders, is a brilliant example of visionary thinking and design. The downtown was conceived as the center and heart of the community.

I am sure this sense of vision, made physically manifest, appealed to Colin. But there are many other formal characteristics of Nolen's design sensibility that likely would resonate with Colin as well. Kingsport's circulation spine was a classic American Main Street, with added enhancements of a train station at one end and Church Circle at the other. Drawings of multiple street sections promoted street hierarchy, incorporating the extensive deployment of trees, green belts, and sidewalks throughout the city. Above-ground utilities in the downtown were confined to its comprehensive alley system. Party wall buildings conformed to 25 x 100-foot lot lines, or multiples thereof, providing a proportional repetitive unity to the street facades. Urban parks were an essential component of the city's plan. Buildings that constituted civic, institutional architecture were designed by the best architectural talent available, not only by distinguished figures such as Clinton MacKenzie of New York City, but also by gifted local architects such as Alan Dryden, Sr.

In John Nolen's 1927 book *New Towns for Old*, the opening paragraph of the chapter "An Industrial City Built to Order: Kingsport, Tennessee", reads:

> *Kingsport, Tennessee is in various respects one of our most remarkable examples of modern city planning. It began as a new town, its site, though hardly a wilderness, was an out-of-the-way agricultural region, remote from the world's activities. In 1912, the only human habitations there were two farmhouses. As late as 1915, only a few months after the outbreak of the World War, when it had started to grow in an entirely different way from the course destined for it, it was merely a small agricultural community of about nine hundred inhabitants. In four years ... it had become a flourishing city of more than ten thousand people.*[14]

Elizabeth Plater-Zyberk has acknowledged that John Nolen's Kingsport plan contributed to a rethinking of town planning in "The New Urbanism".[15] The principles in *The Charter of the New Urbanism*, inspired by historic town planning, are entirely consistent with Nolen's plan, and they formed a departure point for communicating urban design values and principles with local citizens.[16] In working with students, I make a clear distinction between enduring urban design principles and typologies, which were applicable to the *genius loci* of Kingsport, and their reconciliation with contemporary languages of architecture. Architects such as Dan Solomon, Michael Dennis, Fred Koetter, and Susie Kim have demonstrated that traditional typologies of urban streets and blocks can coexist very successfully with the deployment of innovative, neo-Modernist architecture.

Kingsport's forty-four-block downtown suffered from many of the problems of neglect facing other small American cities. And while the city had maintained its integrity as an urban plan, its downtown was in serious decline. Thus, Kingsport provided a unique urban context for the study of urban architecture.

14 Nolen, John, "An Industrial City Built to Order: Kingsport, Tennessee", in *New Towns for Old: Achievements in Civic Improvement in Some American Small Towns and Neighborhoods*, University of Massachusetts Press, Amherst MA, (1927) 2005: 50-65.

15 Robert B. Church Memorial Lecturer, Elizabeth Plater-Zyberk observation to Marleen Kay Davis on September 16, 1996.

16 *Charter of the New Urbanism*. [https://www.cnu.org/who-we-are/charter-new-urbanism].

Fig. 13. Proposed composite plan: "Six Strategic Projects to Revitalize Downtown Kingsport" by T.K. Davis with Curtis Lesh, 1998.

The Kingsport studio, inspired by Colin, advocated the center city as the heart of the community, a heart whose health is essential to the community's social, cultural, economic and environmental sustainability—in sum, the downtown as the face of the community and representing its values. Through a self-questioning examination of conventional practices, the studio argued that Kingsport could do better than accept the status quo greenfield development of the city's periphery as the only plan for growth. Re-establishing the center city was argued as an urgent priority for revitalization.

In many ways, working with Kingsport was an evocation of my Holyoke thesis; both were planned industrial cities of a similar, small scale, with a balance of traditional repetitive urban block fabric and sophisticated civic buildings, juxtaposed with large-scale adjacent industrial architecture. I found that my strategy in leading the Kingsport studio was similar to the non-contingent strategy I had adopted with Colin's encouragement for Holyoke. We focused on the figure/ground clarity of the city and its public spaces, while also identifying six "strategic sites" for individual buildings as 'urban architecture'. My belief was that strategically located, appropriately programmed projects, designed and constructed with adequate budgets, would be a long-term civic investment—and could make a significant difference in recovering Kingsport's founding vision.[17] This strategic plan was published in a 50,000 circulation copy Sunday insert as the first comprehensive update of John Nolen's plan.

17 "Six Strategic Projects for Kingsport", in *Kingsport Times-News*, 1998. Urban design by Thomas K. Davis assisted by Curtis Lesh. "Proposed Composite Plan: Six Strategic Projects to Revitalize Downtown Kingsport", 1998.

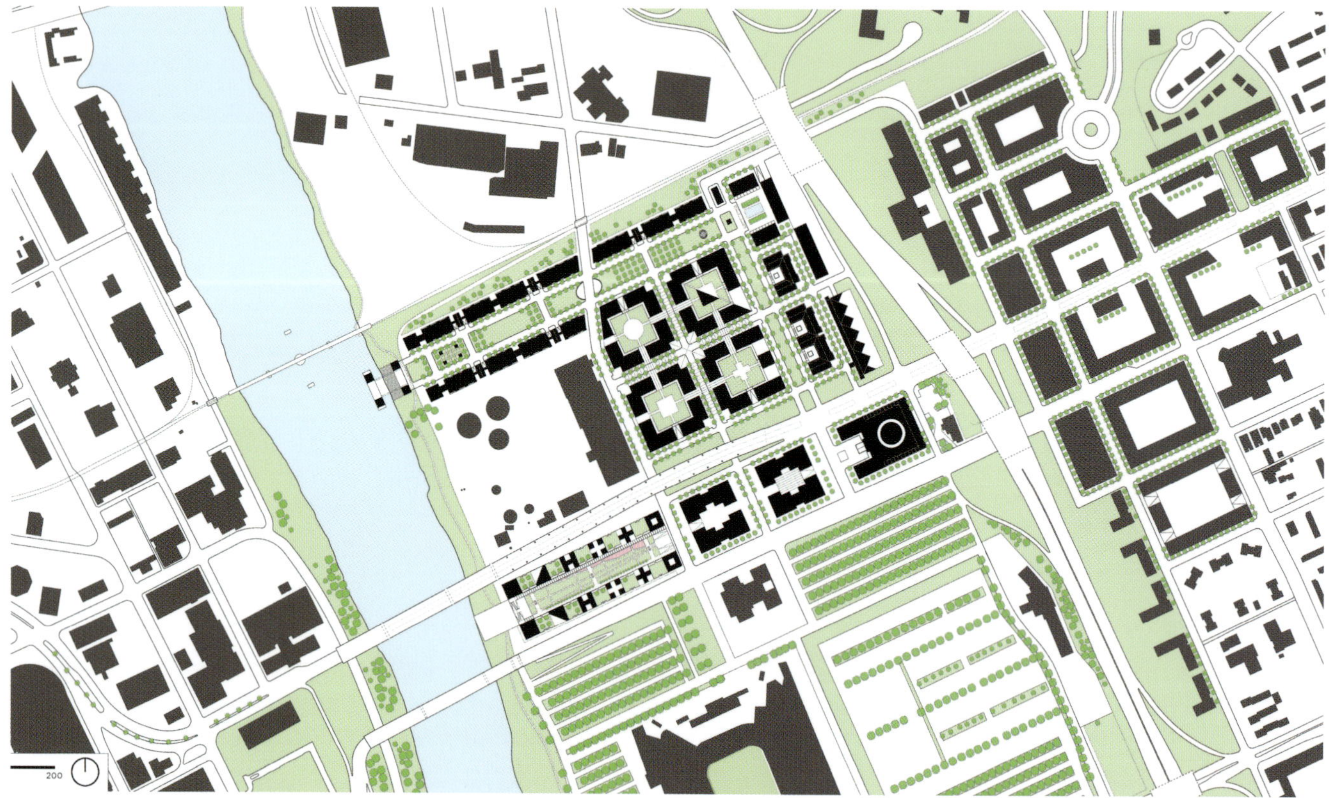

Fig. 14. "A New East Bank Neighborhood for Nashville Urban Design Study", figure/ground drawing by T.K. Davis with Adam Buchanan, 2016.

Meeting frequently with city leaders and stakeholders, I worked with over 140 students during fourteen semesters focusing on Kingsport and its region. I believe these students came to see the value of Colin's formal ideas of urban spatial composition within the context of a small American city with a unique history, located 'in our own backyard' in Northeast Tennessee. And over time, the Kingsport urban design studio and my students' projects led to a community re-appreciation of Nolen's legacy and his unique vision for the city. While we held that holistic vision in mind, our focus on public space and different strategic sites helped city leaders understand the potential inherent in their city. Today, downtown Kingsport's slow but steady revitalization continues as a consequence.

In addition to Kingsport, numerous other projects in Tennessee and Virginia were efficacious in leading to a revitalization of their downtowns. Because of numerous semesters devoted to Bristol, Tennessee, I received "The Keys to the City" in 2003. Although I focused on the urban spaces of Kingsport and Bristol, two other studio semesters were memorable departures: a proposal for a United Mine Workers of America (UMWA) Memorial Park in the town of Appalachia, Virginia, and in another semester, a proposed "Phipps Bend New Town" in Tennessee on the site of an aborted construction project for two nuclear reactors. The premise of Phipps Bend New Town was to use the abandoned structures on the site, including two unfinished reactors and cooling towers, as well as two oval settling basins, as 'set pieces' to form the primary public spaces and civic institutions of a high-density, compact, walkable, mixed-use urbanism.

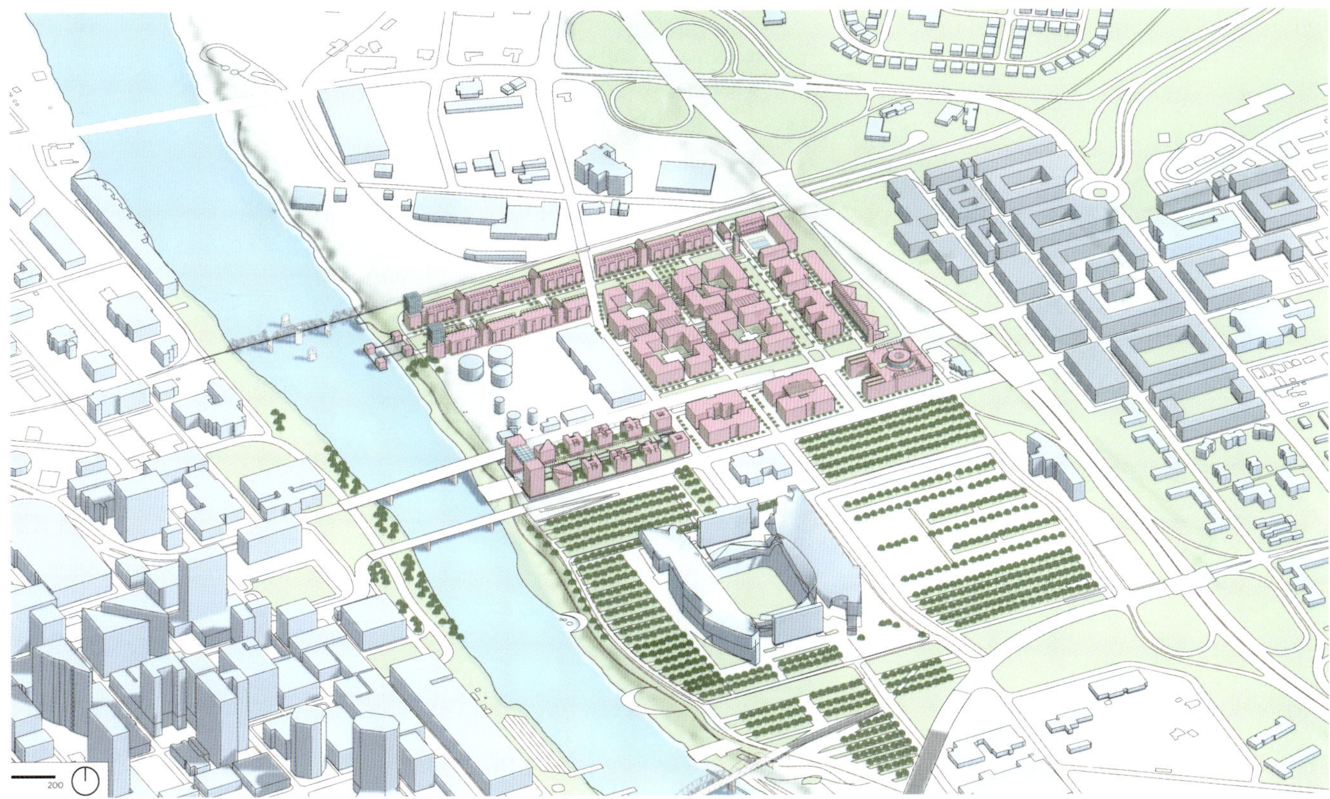

Urban Design and Strategic Sites in Nashville

Fig. 15. "A New East Bank Neighborhood for Nashville Urban Design Study", axonometric drawing by T.K. Davis with Adam Buchanan, 2016.

Nashville's leading architects had witnessed the profound revitalization of downtown Chattanooga over a long period led by University of Tennessee faculty member Stroud Watson along with his Urban Design Center. The Center was later housed in a new building and plaza designed by Koetter Kim & Associates. Beginning in 1981 Stroud Watson's studio began to guide urban redevelopment in Chattanooga, transforming the city as a consequence. This work was the subject of an AIA video and resulted in Stroud Watson receiving the Thomas Jefferson Award for Public Architecture in 2001. Could Nashville benefit from a similar initiative with the School of Architecture?

With the arrival of Marleen Kay Davis in 1994 as dean of of the School of Architecture, Nashville architects, and alumni of the University of Tennessee, actively sought the participation of faculty in planning efforts for the city. Initially, the local profession created an 'Urban Design Forum' with paid membership, classes, events, and monthly lectures. Mayoral candidate Bill Purcell established the Civic Design Center as a component of his successful election platform.

In 2000, the Nashville Civic Design Center (NCDC) was created in partnership with the city, the University of Tennessee, Vanderbilt University, and the Frist Foundation. The NCDC is essentially an independent, non-profit think tank located in the downtown, which sponsors frequent events and outreach activities for local professionals and the general community. The formation of the NCDC was motivated by a general perception that the city's planning department lacked

Fig. 16. Student Transit-Oriented Development Proposal for Lebanon, Tennessee, 2010.

vision and that the city needed more public participation in planning for the growth of downtown and its surrounding inner-ring neighborhoods. Over the years, hundreds of citizens have taken the NCDC's Urban Design 101 course, and hundreds of individuals, local architects, faculty members, elected officials and others have contributed to the success of the NCDC.

The first NCDC Design Director Mark Schimmenti was a University of Tennessee architecture faculty member and charter member of the Congress for the New Urbanism. He led a four-year community assessment and visioning process involving over 50 public meetings and 800 citizens. This process, inspired by Daniel Burnham's *Plan of Chicago*,[18] culminated in *The Plan of Nashville: Avenues to a Great City*. Written and edited by Christine Kreyling and published by Vanderbilt University Press, this 250-page document contained not only "Ten Principles and Related Goals" to guide public policy, development practice, urban planning and design, but also a plethora of site-specific ideas and illustrated proposals.[19]

From 2004–08, following Mark Schimmenti's initiatives, I served as NCDC's Design Director. My role was to promote public education, participation, and advocacy for the value of excellence in civic design in Nashville. Developer and design review and consultation was significant, as was our inclusion on designer selection committees and revitalization studies on various underserved neighborhoods. During my four years we operated a number of programs, including monthly Urban Design Forums, the already established Urban Design 101 course, over 130 presentations to academic, civic, and professional groups, and an Architecture and Urbanism Exhibition and Film Series. Perhaps the most

18 Burnham, Daniel H.; Bennett, Edward H., *Plan of Chicago*, Princeton Architectural Press, New York, (1909) 1981.

19 Kreyling, Christine, *The Plan of Nashville: Avenues to a Great City*, Vanderbilt University Press, Nashville, TN, 2004: 43-45.

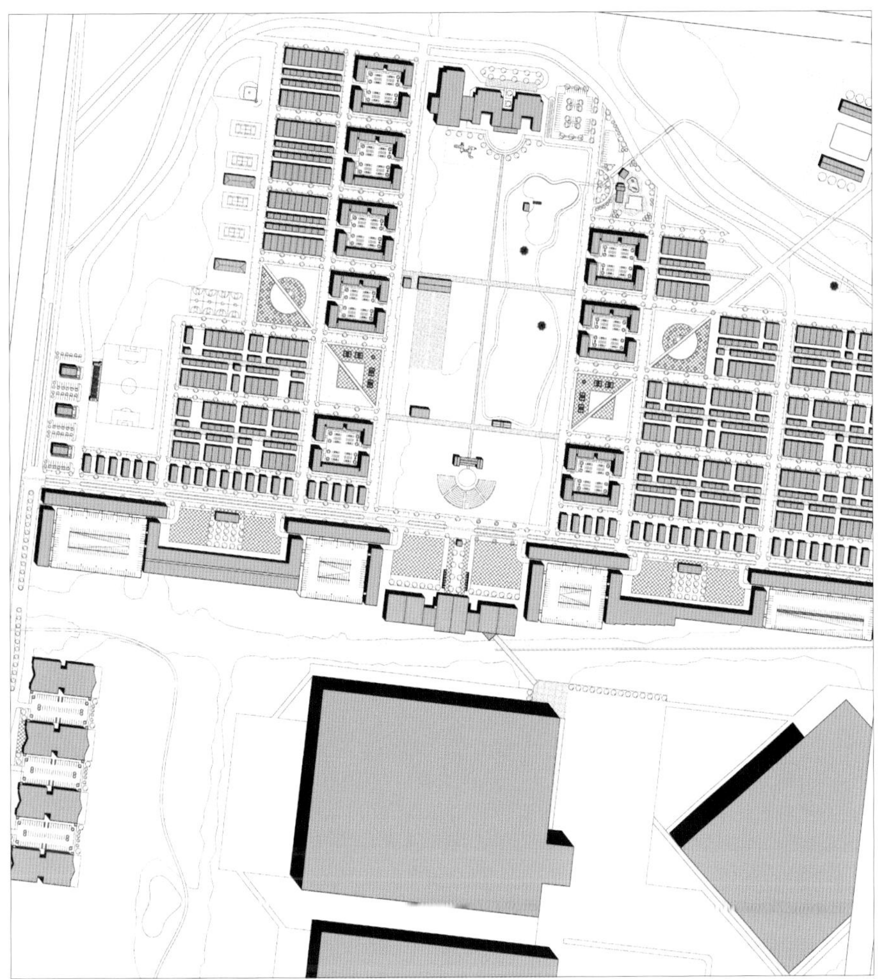

Fig. 17. Student Transit-Oriented Development Proposal for Gallatin, Tennessee, by Aaron Grohol, 2010.

important role we played was to facilitate public workshops at the request of the mayor on major projects which were potentially controversial: a Nashville Riverfront Concept Vision Plan to be designed by Hargreaves Associates, a new downtown AAA ballpark, and a new downtown multi-block convention center. Regarding the latter, the mayor asked us to weigh in on where the convention center should be located and how design criteria could produce a 'state-of-the art' facility. In addition, Christine Kreyling and I developed a local television program with 15 episodes titled *Cityvisions*, available to 275,000 households in metropolitan Nashville. The program had an interview format, inviting key people on topics ranging from civic space design to urban homelessness.

I can't imagine Colin ever having the patience for such participatory engagement, but today it is both desirable and important in order to build educated, informed consensus on public projects. In 1982, Colin was invited by Josef Paul Kleihues to Berlin for a week-long consultation on the planned IBA housing exhibition. Upon his return, Colin confronted me in the hallway of the architecture school with one of his typical, startling questions. "Tom, do you suppose there's much wife-beating in Berlin?" How does one respond? I took it to mean that this comment was Colin's elliptical way of conveying that he had been subjected to a painful number of under-structured, discursive, open-microphone public forums where Berlin citizenry vented political and social frustrations on everything from bad urban planning and inadequate housing, to concerns of domestic violence. Keeping Colin's experience in mind, during my four years in Nashville we developed a series of format techniques in public workshops to first educate, then brainstorm, and then find consensus while neutralizing the inevitable few at the meeting who arrive with a rigidly problematic agenda.

Although I returned to Knoxville for full-time teaching in 2008, I continue to stay strongly involved with the NCDC. With my knowledge of issues, sites, and players in Nashville, I realized that my urban design studios could be an important form of public outreach engagement, connecting students with the leaders and stakeholders in Nashville. For 28 semesters, including summers, I have worked with my students on issues and opportunities confronting Greater Nashville. We have public design review events monthly at the NCDC with students presenting their work to city officials and distinguished architects, many of whom are our alumni on the lookout for design talent.

My typical teaching *modus operandi* is to consult with Nashville's city planning office to select a relevant topic or location for investigation, one which I think would meet the pedagogical goals of the studio. Before the start of the semester, I would outline a basic urban design concept for the area, testing assumptions of public spaces, streets, and urban blocks. Then, during the semester, I would have my students refine this urban design study as 'urban architecture'. As with my own thesis, we look at city districts as a whole, then focus on strategic sites, and finally on the urban architecture. Much of this work is explored and illustrated with axonometric drawings, but my students are also encouraged to use perspective drawings as a vehicle to convey the perceptual experience of spaces as places.

This work has been done with modest financial support from the Metro Planning Department as well as the Metro Planning Organization of Nashville. Post-semester work is documented in the form of "Urban Design Research Reports", achieved in partnership with the NCDC, and displayed on various websites as educational advocacies. We have two design reviews monthly, one in Knoxville with faculty and one in Nashville with city officials, architects, and planners serving as reviewers. This is a win-win-win program for the students, faculty, and community as it serves as an academic outreach in our state's capital city, with its enormous alumni base and our state legislators. It is also entirely consistent in its deployment of civic design as a vehicle for engaging the public advocated by Ernest Boyer and Lee Mitgang's *Building Community: A New Future for Architectural Education*,[20] as well as Donald Schon's *The Reflective Practioner*.[21] The challenge is framing complex problems that offer both critical, exploratory academic content, as well as rigorous credibility in the community.

My studio work for Nashville has advocated transit-oriented development as a strategy to address three key, overlapping challenges facing the city—extremely rapid growth needing densification of centers and corridors, totally inadequate public transit, and a lack of affordable urban housing. The importance of public space and streets has been embedded in all our work with its reference to the "Ten Principles" of *The Plan of Nashville*. In 2012, the NCDC published *Moving Tennessee Forward*, an analysis of transit needs in Nashville and its region, a

20 Boyer, Ernest L.; Mitgang, Lee D., *Building Community: A New Future for Architectural Education,* Jossey-Bass, Inc., San Francisco, (Second printing edition), 1996.

21 Schon, Donald A., *The Reflective Practitioner: How Professionals Think in Action,* Basic Books, Inc., New York City, 1983.

compendium of best practices related to transit-oriented development and ten project proposals with sixty images by University of Tennessee architecture students. This kind of work helps the community visualize potential solutions, generating interest and support for new ideas.

I have worked with numerous students on many different proposals over the years. I believe two in particular might have been intriguing to Colin. The first was a comprehensive urban design study for the town of Lebanon, 25 miles east of Nashville. With its centralized town square, Lebanon is similar to the Texas courthouse-square towns (such as Lockhart, Texas) that Colin visited, admired, and about which he wrote in the *Architectural Record*. Our urban design proposal involved the basic 'urban dentistry' involving infill in order to clarify the urban spaces of the town square and primary streets. Additionally, we proposed different concepts for transit-oriented development within a quarter-mile radius of the existing commuter rail station, with each student developing a different schematic proposal. Based on these proposals, the first transit-oriented development in the state of Tennessee is now approaching full build-out in Lebanon.

A second strategic site design proposal that might have appealed to Colin was for a new walkable community in Gallatin, located twenty miles northeast of Nashville. Gallatin's agrarian landscape could have succumbed to sprawl in the typical form of disaggregated suburban subdivisions or big box development. Instead, students produced schemes for a transit-oriented development proposal with pedestrian-scaled, differentiated block typologies with related diverse housing options, mixed uses, and public spaces and streets anchored by a proposed new commuter rail stop inspired by the student team's study of historic Savannah.

The value of the NCDC efforts can best be appreciated by attending its annual fundraising luncheon: it features a report to the community regarding annual accomplishments and keynote addresses from the mayor and an invited national speaker. Attendance continues to grow, with over 800 in 2018.

So for all those who encountered Colin in the Cornell Urban Design Studio, his influence continues to percolate decades later through our work, values, and Sisyphean resolve. I was extremely fortunate in the educational path onto which I stumbled, a path on which I encountered many extraordinary mentors leading to a career in teaching and public advocacy in urban design. For me, it somehow all leads back to Colin. It has been over four decades since I left Colin's Urban Design Studio and departed for a year in Italy with my master's degree in hand.

I recall Colin, surrounded by students, leafing through Hegemann and Peets's *Civic Art: The American Vitruvius.*[22] While doing so, he observed, "Tom, isn't it remarkable—to look at a plan for thirty seconds—and remember it for thirty years?" Indeed, it is.

22 Hegemann, Werner; Peets, Elbert, T*he American Vitruvius; an Architect's Handbook of Civic Art,* Architectural Book Pub., New York, 1922, (republished by De Facto Publishing, San Francisco, 2008).

Teaching Urban Design and the 'Reconquest of Time'

Kevin Hinders

frontispiece:
Example of Phenomenal Transparency at the Architecture Building.

Numerous opportunities have arisen for me to teach urban design based on the teaching of Colin Rowe and his followers. Working from the general to the specific, I will describe my approach to the teaching of urban design at the University of Illinois Urbana-Champaign (UIUC) in four different venues. While each of the venues is distinctly different in multiple ways, all are informed by Rowe's legacy. One of the venues is offered university wide, the other three are part of the architecture program. The courses are: 1) Design of the Built Environment offered to non-architecture students; 2) an architecture design studio that is part of the regular undergraduate studio sequence based in Urbana-Champaign; 3) a seminar titled Urban Morphology and Design; and 4) The Chicago Studio, a graduate level studio taught in Chicago, now paired with the Urban Morphology and Design seminar. Each of these courses has given me the opportunity to engage and teach the relationships between landscape, urbanism, architecture, and culture to students at a variety of levels within the university and the school, and all have been informed by Rowe's thinking and writing.

Design of the Built Environment

The Design of the Built Environment course is an elective offering for students enrolled in the UIUC Campus Honors Program. Created specifically for students in other majors who are interested in architecture, the course uses the university and its surrounding context, that is, its various urban environments, as a vehicle to explore architecture, landscape architecture, planning, and urban design. The class incorporates eighteen to twenty walks and site visits over the course of a fifteen-week semester. The walks are somewhat determined by the weather or scheduling and necessarily have only a loose correspondence to the four conceptual themes that otherwise order the course's four parts. Each part is described below.

PART 1- Approaches to the Design of the Built Environment

Design of the built environment is presented as a complex combination of both art and aesthetics on one hand, and technical aspects on the other. The designer must evaluate the needs of the owners, the occupants, and the needs of the general

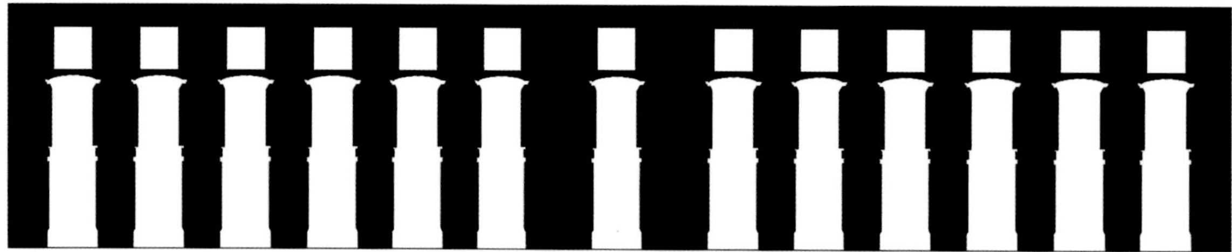

Fig. 1. Figure/ground study of the Architecture Building.

public. Codes and regulations are used by the public to protect the health, safety, and welfare of the community, while the owner and occupant needs must be considered in order to satisfy those who fund construction. The walks explore aspects of design while introducing aesthetic and technical principles. They introduce basic architectural concepts, including concepts readily associated with Rowe: *parti, poché,* figure/ground, literal and phenomenal transparency, and hierarchy. Sometimes the principles are explained in the classroom prior to visiting sites but more often I use the buildings or sites to explain the concepts.

PART 2 - The University Campus and the Public Realm

The university campus is now a product of over 150 years of planning and development. From the early years of land acquisition to the present, ideas about what a university can and should be have helped shape the campus. Thus, the campus can be seen to represent themes one finds in Rowe's writing: the interaction between the ideal and the circumstantial, the importance of a defined

Fig. 2. Aerial view of campus looking North (Main Quadrangle).
Photo: Mike Bohlmann, protomaker.io.

public realm, the need for both figural solids and figural voids to create order, and changes in imagery and iconography over time.

A Campus Plan Commission, headed by Daniel Burnham, created numerous designs for the campus between 1909 and the early 1920s. The common thread for these plans was the need to integrate some existing structures and eliminating others while creating an idealized vision of campus: clear, powerful, and strong enough to maintain its authority when confronted with the realities of 'circumstantial' university decision making. These plans eventually led to a series of plans created by Charles Platt during the 1920s that provided a strong framework for subsequent generations to contribute structures and designs to meet the needs and aspirations of their time.

The visitor to the University of Illinois is inevitably brought to the primary campus spaces, its public realm: the South Quad, Liberal Arts Quad, the Engineering Campus, and Campustown. The walks explore the principles used by designers

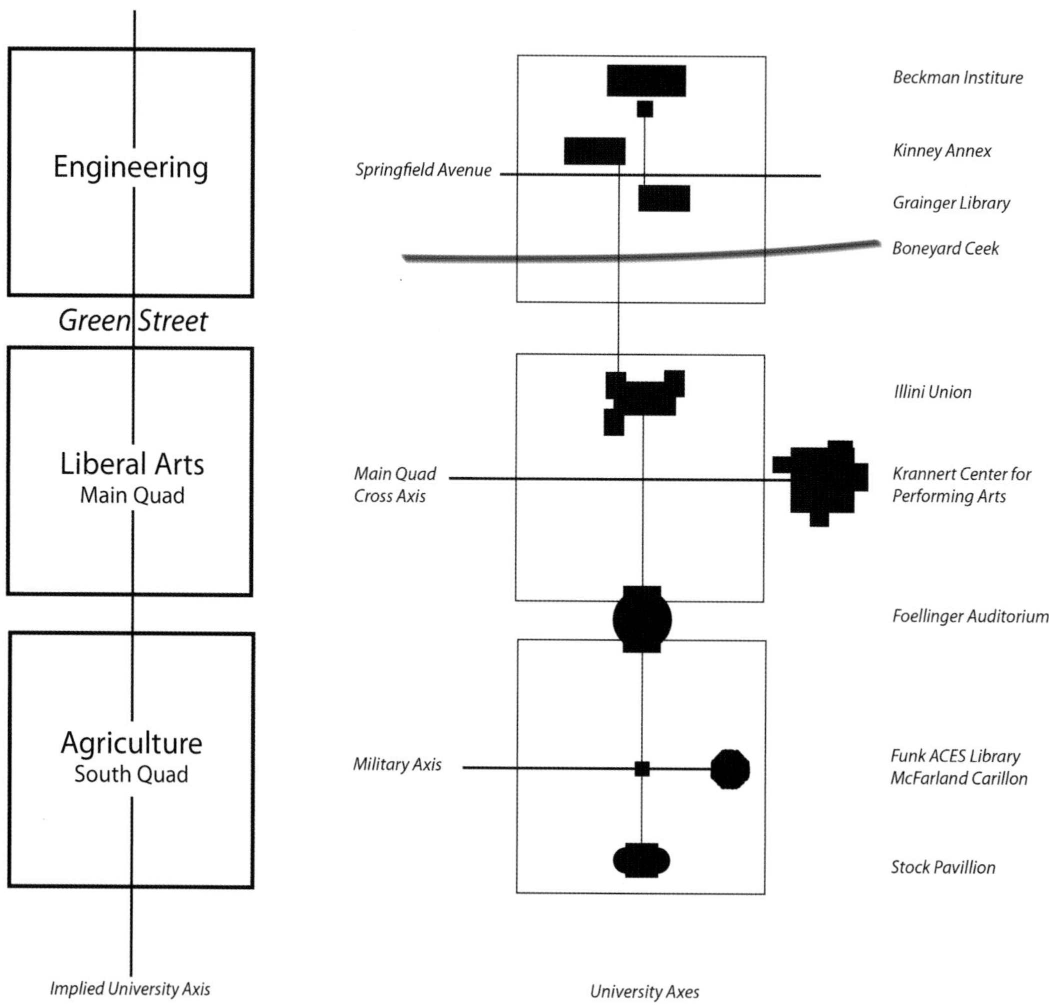

Fig. 3. Diagrams of the University of Illinois Campus.

in the creation of the public realms of the university. The students come to understand that buildings, if organized collectively, can create something far greater than the sum of their parts, contributing to an ordered and ideal vision. This is symbolically understood with reference to what Cardinal John Newman meant when he said:

> *If I were asked to describe as briefly and popularly as I could, what a University was, I should draw my answer from its ancient designation of a Studium Generale, or "School of Universal Learning." This description implies the assemblage of strangers from all parts in one spot;—from all parts. Else, how will you find professors and students for every department of knowledge? And in one spot; else, how can there be any school at all?* [1]

Likewise, reference to Serlio's Tragic and Comic scenes and the related idea of 'vest pocket utopias', helps to explain campus growth and change over time.

1 Newman, John Henry, *The Idea of a University*, Yale University Press, New Haven, 1996, quoted in *Bartleby.com* [https://www.bartleby.com/28/2.html].

PART 3 - The Context Surrounding the University

These walks explore the urban development of Champaign, Urbana, and Philo through major phases of their development. They include: the era of the continental grid, a one-mile square agricultural development oriented to the cardinal points, mandated by the U.S. Land Ordinance of 1785; the subsequent stages of town, city, and campus planning consistent with the continental grid; other planning and grid orientations related to the development of the railroads and towns that served them; patterns of civic buildings typical of many U.S. towns and cities; and finally the development of the suburbs and sprawl.

Each walk or tour looks at issues that are local, regional, and national in their scope with an emphasis on the way that physical, economic, and social contexts play an enormous role in determining the form of the built environment. Traversing these environments reinforces general concepts while providing specific examples of how buildings, landscapes, and cityscapes can be integrated to create cohesive sets of spaces and places.

The grid is the single greatest determinant to the design of the built environment in the campus and its surrounds. From the manner in which the area was sold and settled, to the Illinois Central Railroad's contrasting overlay on this midwestern grid, the insights of Rowe, and others, inform these walks.

The continental grid is the underlying geometry of Champaign. University Avenue runs parallel with Springfield Avenue, one of the mile-by-mile roads that marks this grid. This mile-by-mile grid is marked by roads that extend south with Florida/Kirby Avenue, Windsor Road, Church Street and so on, and likewise extend westward marked by Prospect Avenue, Mattis Avenue, Duncan Road, and Staley Road. Beyond these, in the rural countryside, the grid is simply marked by a numeric system of county roads. One can trace the agricultural and urban development of the U.S. through Urbana-Champaign as the continental grid, a Cartesian regulator of land sale and settlement, became a physical reality that seems to unite much of the nation.

The town of Champaign is part of a system of railroad towns created by the Illinois Central Railroad (ICR) laid out twelve-to-fifteen miles apart so that farms would be within one-half day's journey.[2] Due to the topography and cost of land acquisition, it was decided to locate the railroad several miles west of Urbana and the town was originally 'sponsored' by Urbana residents. At first, this town was called West Urbana. Later, in 1861, the then residents asserted themselves and Champaign was incorporated as a separate local government.

New towns along the Illinois Central share numerous characteristics. Due to the need for the railroads to connect and move through the landscape with the greatest ease, their tracks rarely align with the continental grid. As it was the necessity of regular water, wood, and coal replenishment to propel the engines and the speculative potential of land development that might occur in these locations, standard railroad towns were mapped in alignment with the railroad and were often skewed to the continental grid. As such there often exists an interesting, and often awkward, relationship between the railroad town grids

2 The ICR was granted approximately 10% of the Federal land in Illinois in exchange for creating two new lines which connected existing rail lines through the midsection of the state. The Federal Land Grant of 1850 granted 2.5 million acres in Illinois to the state to hire a railroad corporation. Mississippi and Alabama also received land grants in their states as part of this grant. Senator Stephen Douglas was instrumental in passing the legislation. The rationale given by Douglas was that Illinois (and Alabama and Mississippi) property would be worthless unless rail lines were introduced to open up the territory and get crops from Illinois to market. In Illinois, these lines connected Chicago to Centralia, Illinois, and LaSalle, Illinois, to Centralia. The Centralia line then connected to Cairo, Illinois, at the junction of the Ohio and Mississippi Rivers. Douglas's involvement in this legislation may have led to his defeat by Abraham Lincoln in the 1860 presidential election, as many northerners disapproved of Douglas's relationship with the south. The ICR employed Abraham Lincoln in its legal negotiations beginning in 1853 and lasting almost a decade. It is thought Lincoln represented the ICR in over 50 cases. Lueckenhoff, Sandra K., "A. Lincoln, a Corporate Attorney and the Illinois Central Railroad", *Missouri Law Review,* 61 (2) Spr 1996: 393-428.

and their interfaces with the continental grid. The resulting conditions of these different gridded 'fields' colliding with each other were among the formal fascinations of the early Rowe studios and eventually informed both the formal and sociopolitical views expressed in "Collision City and the Politics of Bricolage" found in *Collage City*.[3]

In my course, I also reference the real and symbolic impacts of the railroad in our history and culture whether locally or nationally, including a host of songs. And, not to be missed, is the lesson of the public/private development inherent in national development of the rail system serving agriculture, industry, and town and city development. And that public/private development remains common and critical today.

In the towns of Plano, Champaign, and Urbana, Rowe's discussion of the important role of figural-iconic buildings in the urban strata that both forms and informs a democratic society comes to be seen in the hierarchical relationship of different kinds of buildings, from rudimentary industrial and commercial buildings through a panoply of modest to grand houses to the more decorous and monumental civic buildings. The grid forms the framework for all of them; the more rudimentary buildings form a background of sorts for the civic buildings. Yet again, whether church, post office, theater, school, or grand house, the grid seems to assure that no one of them seems to dominate over all others. These town patterns are emblematic of the concepts of equality, the rights of both the individual and the collective, and of the freedoms of expression and assembly.

Among the more prominent civic buildings, if one marks the center of community in both physical and social terms, it is usually the courthouse, or, if lacking a courthouse, it is typically the city hall. A succession of courthouses for Champaign County, with their clock towers and cupolas, marked the *axis mundi* of each of these social-political settlements and their urban centers. Urbana was founded as the county seat of Champaign County. Near the end of the 19th century, the city of Champaign was thwarted in its 'hostile' attempt to have the county seat moved from Urbana to Champaign. To compensate, the city of Champaign built a City Hall at the main intersection of the railroad and continental grids.[4] The building occupies a wedge-shaped lot and skillfully uses a hexagonal copper dome to accommodate the site irregularity. The dome sits adjacent to the intersection of the two main streets in the city. It was one of Rowe's studio assignments I encountered as an undergraduate, and his article, co-authored with John Hejduk, "Lockhart, Texas,"[5] that first drew my attention to this nationwide expression of our political values made manifest. The students are quick to grasp it. We start one of our walks at the Urbana County Courthouse, built of red sandstone in the Romanesque style and completed in 1901, located at 101 East Main Street. Another walk begins near the Art Deco-style Champaign City Hall, completed in 1937, at 102 North Neil Street.

These town walks also provide the opportunity to discuss the rather extraordinary stylistic range that many older buildings display along with the fantasy/reality that this imagery and iconography play in architecture. Influencing these observations and discussions are certainly Rowe's idea of the city as a didactic instrument of education and his reference to "nostalgia-producing instruments".

3 Rowe, Colin; Koetter, Fred, *Collage City*, MIT Press, Cambridge, MA, and London, England, 1978: 86-117.

4 Champaign County board officials feared that the population growth of the city of Champaign had outstripped Urbana and thus a county vote could move the county seat to the city of Champaign. The board, wanting to retain the county seat in Urbana devised a plan. The board called for the 'renovation' of the existing courthouse so that this would not go to a public vote. Eventually this met with state approval and the decision on moving the county seat became a moot point. The 'renovation' retained a small portion of one wall that was built into the new structure. From: Huang, Jing; Labrosse, Violet; McCormick Thomas, "Champaign County Courthouse", *ExploreCU.*

5 Rowe, Colin; Hejduk, John, "Lockhart, Texas", *Architectural Record* 121 (3), Mar 1957: 201-06.

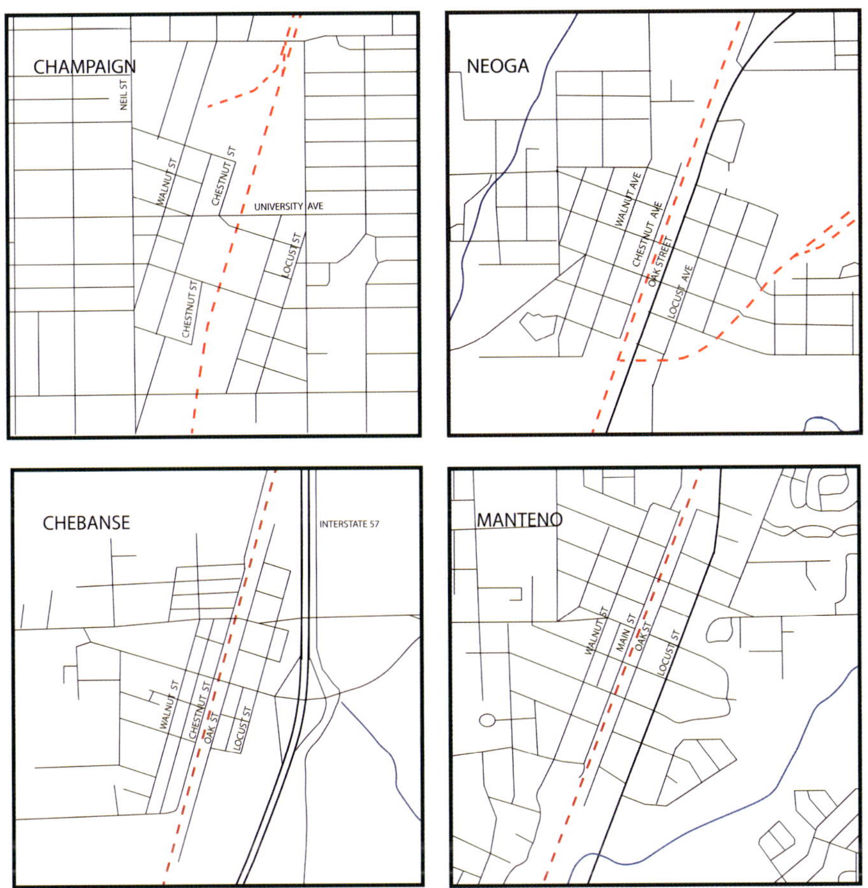

Fig. 4. Diagrams of four Illinois Central Railroad towns in Illinois.

I also related the values and beauty found in these towns including their residential streets to Serlio's Tragic, Comic, and Satyric scenes, drawing on another of Rowe's references.

The urban street of the 1920s, and its idyllic small-town American condition that Rowe appreciated so much, is then contrasted with the post-WWII suburban condition. The students begin to see the impact on urban form of changes in both values and technology that began to hold sway after WWII: functionalism and dependence on the automobile, inventions such as air conditioning and television, and a shift towards less iconic structures. New banks, fast food restaurants, post offices, and other governmental buildings all began to look alike. Their location in the city was increasingly based more on convenience of vehicular access than symbolic presence. The city began to lose the hierarchical patterns that had previously given it the layered richness of a finely woven quilt. The landscape of Serlio's Satyric scene became the paradigm for the earlier American suburb realized in so many upstate New York and Midwest towns, was being transformed into the automobile suburb. Instead of a walk, a bus tour is needed to explore the flight from 'downtown' to the suburbs, with the ever increasing size of single family lots, the movement of religious institutions from town to the suburbs, the rise of strip malls, and the development of enclosed mall shopping centers located at the periphery of the city and accessible via the developing freeway system. The students see that the town morphed into the suburbs and sprawl, made up of discreet use centers, and that this has changed the physical form of community. All these points resonate with many of the Illinois students for whom such places have been the daily experience of their lives.

PART 4 - Exploring Concepts in Individual Buildings

Visits to a number of different campus buildings allow students to understand the cause and effect of a variety of architectural principles and their application, as well as gaining an understanding of structures and mechanical systems at the scale of both the building and campus. Touring individual buildings allows for the exploration of a wide range of specific topics such as the ideas of precedent, functional expression, construction, formal expression, structure, mechanical systems, synthesis, and sustainability. Each visit is themed to concentrate on one aspect while still allowing the opportunity to explore the building holistically. Access to campus buildings and infrastructure is critical to the success of this part of the course. Students learn how infrastructure supports buildings and influences design. A brief outline of some of these building visits includes: a visit to the campus power plant and one of the chiller plants; followed by a trip through one building to look at mechanical systems and life safety issues such as egress requirements; a visit to three different buildings to compare material significance and construction with the building's concepts and aesthetics; a visit to Krannert Center for the Performing Arts to see front of house/back of house and the form/function relationship exemplified by the building; and a tour of three sports facilities and the armory provides a look at long span structural systems to discuss structural principles and characteristic construction. The landscape is brought into prominence with walks that include the University Arboretum and the nearby Mount Hope Cemetery also touching on the primary landscape modes of Western civilization: classical, pastoral, romantic, and sublime.

Raising the awareness that buildings, infrastructure, and landscape must work together to form a greater presence is a simple idea, but one that surprises most of the course participants, particularly regarding all the complexities involved and the roles that values and ideas play in these explorations. The questions raised include: What values were dominant in each building, cityscape, and landscape we experienced? How do design choices manifest those values and ideas?

In all four parts of this Design of the Built Environment course, I explain and emphasize to the students that, in the very near future, they may have important roles to play in the creation of the built environment, and that they have a responsibility, not only to themselves and to others they may be serving directly, but to the public as well. In fact, they are being educated to be better 'citizen-clients' for the architects in our school and elsewhere around the world.

Undergraduate and Graduate Design Studios

In the School's architecture degree courses, it is evident that Rowe's approach to design and context left a lasting impression upon generations of architects. At Illinois the typical undergraduate studio projects are architecturally focused, but the legacy of Rowe asserts itself early in the design studio processes as students are encouraged to absorb the contextual issues that sites provide.[6] Our School

6 I had the good fortune of having Professor Rowe as both an undergraduate and a graduate student. While in Rome, second semester, Rowe gave his studio two projects. The first, the Armenian Embassy, was a fictitious new embassy for a country that did not exist. At that time Armenia was a part of the Soviet Block. The site was located off the Via Giulia, near the Ponte Giuseppe Mazzini. The project allowed us to study the public/private aspects of the program while exploring how to assert a presence in the city fabric. It was the second project that was particularly remarkable to me. Rowe asked us to choose between two contexts. Design a county courthouse for one of two imagined sites: Hudson, Texas (named after fellow student, Jane Anne Hudson), or Hinders, Ohio. Rowe was certainly displaying his admiration for Texas courthouses but, as my grandfather had been a judge in Mercer County, Ohio, I chose the latter. The imaginary context was fairly familiar to me. Rowe received more than a little second guessing for his choice of project. I admire his choice. He understood that most of us might never practice in Rome, but we were going to have a difficult transition upon our return to the US. His choice to have us thinking about a 'future context' while absorbing the one we were occupying appears to have been an act of genius. The courthouse program was similar in size and scope to the embassy. The former, very much a part of a larger context and organized by its surroundings, while the latter demanded a figural presence, a set piece, which organized the town.

has four Program Areas: Health and Well Being; Detail and Fabrication; Building Performance; and Urbanism. Each Program Area takes responsibility for an early design course in the first two years (freshman, sophomore) and a design studio in the next two years (junior, senior). Thus, Urbanism has two explicit design courses at the undergraduate level.

The first four lower level courses introduce the basic concepts that serve as the foundation for the four upper level studios. The Urbanism Program Area is responsible for the first of these design studios. This urban studio focuses on designing a credible structure while exploring the building's role in a larger environment. As Rowe pointed out to his students: "It is absurd to assume that every building must command the foreground. Why is it not logical to teach students to design background buildings?" This studio seeks to do just that: to balance the production of the architectural edifice with the needs of the larger urban environment.

In undergraduate studios the physical and social context become the primary sources for the determination of building form. Students become aware of three of Rowe's critical points. First that, socially, the physical clarity of public versus private realms in the urban construct is of great importance, a concept that is also useful in thinking about the interior spatial ordering of the building. Second is the awareness of balancing paradigm with program.[7] Third is including the value of precedent to learning and to design, as lessons in synthesis and the knowledge of best practices in the creation of new buildings. The importance of precedents has seemed to increase with awareness of sustainability issues. Emphasis on these three concepts assists the students in making the design decisions that inform their work.

As a student progresses into graduate studies these aspects, along with the economic context, inform their work. A recent graduate studio might serve as an example.[8] In St. Louis, the site of the Lemp Brewery provided a rich, albeit dilapidated, context in which to explore both new construction and the renovation of existing structures. The studio sought to reinforce the existing context while also designing new buildings that modified the site to simultaneously meet the changing needs of the developer and the people of St. Louis. The project was modeled on Rowe's exploration of the ideal and the circumstantial, each giving greater prominence to the other. The students were encouraged to strive for the ideal while reinforcing the rich, existing condition. Students were assembled in groups, and each group determined an overall strategy for the design. Then each student began to design smaller, individual insertions into the site consistent with their group's overall strategy. At both a practical and a socially ideal level, these projects proposed infrastructure improvements to connect an existing rail right-of-way to the city's light rail system. The area could then be developed as a Transit Oriented Development (TOD). This approach allowed for a greater density of uses and an enhancement of the quality of life for the entire neighborhood. The result: in Rowe's terms, a collage of sorts, consisting of a complex of existing and new structures and public spaces that at once honors a time past by preserving and repurposing existing buildings while introducing the new and the contemporary. The collage of architectural events symbolic of different traditions, times, and even places, becomes manifest.

7 Rowe, Colin, "Program vs. Paradigm", *The Cornell Journal of Architecture* 2, Fall 1983: 9-19.

8 This studio was undertaken in collaboration with a studio taught by Paul Kapp. His studio investigated the preservation and adaptive reuse of existing structures.

Seminar: Urban Design/Urban Morphology

I have offered an urban design/urban morphology seminar for over two decades. Since 2014, this course has been offered as one in a set of three related courses for upper level students who live and learn in Chicago, remote from the Champaign-Urbana campus. The three related courses are: a studio, a professional practice course, and the seminar described below.

The Urban Design/Urban Morphology seminar begins with a reading and analysis of Colin Rowe and Fred Koetter's seminal work, *Collage City*, which contextualized Modern architecture and urban design through a social, political, and philosophical exploration, critical assessment, and recommendations. The 1978 text revealed the 'evolution' of Modernism and its underlying forces. And it convincingly argued for a city that balances figure and ground, solid and void. The fundamental conclusion, however, was that in order to truly *proceed* as urbanists, we needed to realize this fundamental truth: we exist in time, a time which is inherently no better and no worse than other times but is simply part of a continuum. Rowe and Koetter reject the Hegelian positivist idea of continuous progress that, by inference, if not declaration, regards what is in the past as inferior to what is in the present or the future.[9] At the same time, Rowe's view is that, as designers, we have a responsibility to design for the here and now with an obligation to respect the past and maintain hope for the future. We must design with all the ideality possible in order to imbue our own work with the aspirations of our generation, and for those generations of the future, and that what we do today will be relevant and valued tomorrow, just as the great works of the past remain relevant and valued today. This is the intensely poetic ideology and legacy of Fred Koetter and Colin Rowe's, *Collage City*. Rowe emphasizes an inclusive memory precisely because Modern architecture had such a selective memory that it rejected almost everything before Modernism. Rowe emphasizes the need for prophecy to restate the need for hope:

> *The mass of mankind is likely to be, at any one time, both conservative and radical, to be preoccupied with the familiar and diverted by the unexpected: and, if we all of us both live in the past and hope for the future (the present being no more than an episode in time), it would seem reasonable that we should accept this condition. For, if without prophecy there can be no hope, then, without memory there can be no communication.*[10]

Rowe Pleads for Balance

The seminar's teaching draws directly on the legacy of Colin Rowe and uses his writings as the texts for the course. But, Rowe is not an easy read. Having read Rowe's texts repeatedly and a number of the texts written by his former students,[11] and having lived and worked with him and a number of those students, I have had the privilege of learning both first and second-hand from him, eventually gaining an understanding of this material. I also found an effective method for doing so and use it to assist my students with their reading and comprehension.

I have identified three areas that most students at this level find difficult: *language*, *content* and *structure*.[12] I use a set of Rowe essay readings to help them

9 Rowe sets up his argument by referring to Serlio's *Scena Tragica* and *Scena Comica*, concluding that the former is an ideal and the latter is the reality of man's undertakings. Rowe insists that striving for the ideal is a noble act that elevates human existence. Serlio also included a third scene, the *Scena Satyrica*, which Michael Dennis discusses explicitly in "Excursus Americanus", *Court and Garden: from the French Hotel to the City of Modern Architecture*, MIT, 1986: 230-243, and to which Rowe alludes (see footnote 10).

10 Rowe and Koetter (1978): 49.

11 In a discussion with Steve Hurtt I stated my opinion that there were three basic generations of Rowe's Cornell students. I would categorize them as: the generation that dealt with Modernism and the city, another that responded to the crisis of the object/predicament of texture, and, finally, the group of us that then manipulated and integrated the vertical dimension: massing, perspective, facade, etc. All three generations attempted to insert a level of the ideal into the reality of the context. And I find that it is this ideality that needs underscoring in today's academic and professional climate. It is the need, desire, and necessity of reaching for the unattainable goal that results in our greatest achievements.

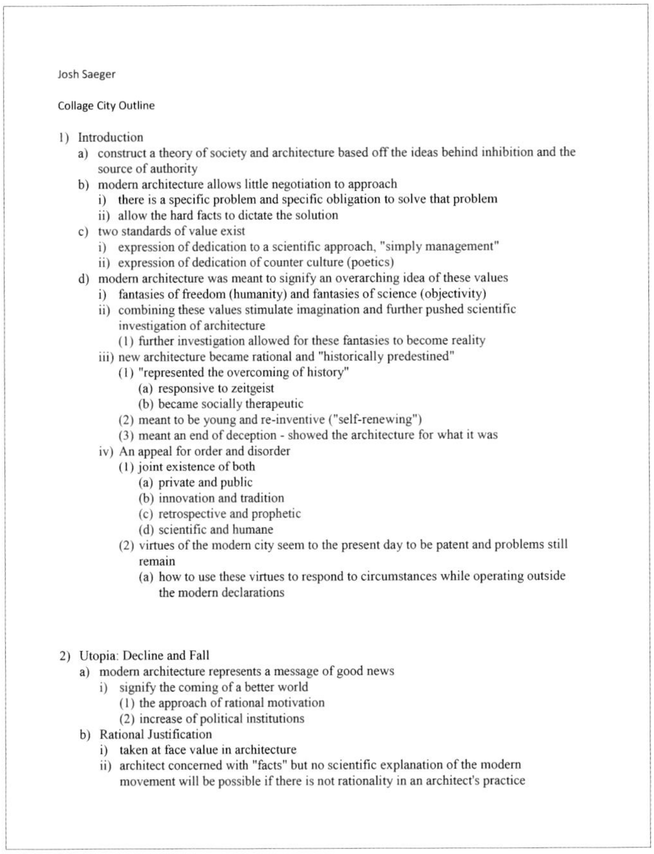

Josh Saeger

Collage City Outline

1) Introduction
- a) construct a theory of society and architecture based off the ideas behind inhibition and the source of authority
- b) modern architecture allows little negotiation to approach
  - i) there is a specific problem and specific obligation to solve that problem
  - ii) allow the hard facts to dictate the solution
- c) two standards of value exist
  - i) expression of dedication to a scientific approach, "simply management"
  - ii) expression of dedication of counter culture (poetics)
- d) modern architecture was meant to signify an overarching idea of these values
  - i) fantasies of freedom (humanity) and fantasies of science (objectivity)
  - ii) combining these values stimulate imagination and further pushed scientific investigation of architecture
    - (1) further investigation allowed for these fantasies to become reality
  - iii) new architecture became rational and "historically predestined"
    - (1) "represented the overcoming of history"
      - (a) responsive to zeitgeist
      - (b) became socially therapeutic
    - (2) meant to be young and re-inventive ("self-renewing")
    - (3) meant an end of deception - showed the architecture for what it was
  - iv) An appeal for order and disorder
    - (1) joint existence of both
      - (a) private and public
      - (b) innovation and tradition
      - (c) retrospective and prophetic
      - (d) scientific and humane
    - (2) virtues of the modern city seem to the present day to be patent and problems still remain
      - (a) how to use these virtues to respond to circumstances while operating outside the modern declarations

2) Utopia: Decline and Fall
- a) modern architecture represents a message of good news
  - i) signify the coming of a better world
    - (1) the approach of rational motivation
    - (2) increase of political institutions
- b) Rational Justification
  - i) taken at face value in architecture
  - ii) architect concerned with "facts" but no scientific explanation of the modern movement will be possible if there is not rationality in an architect's practice 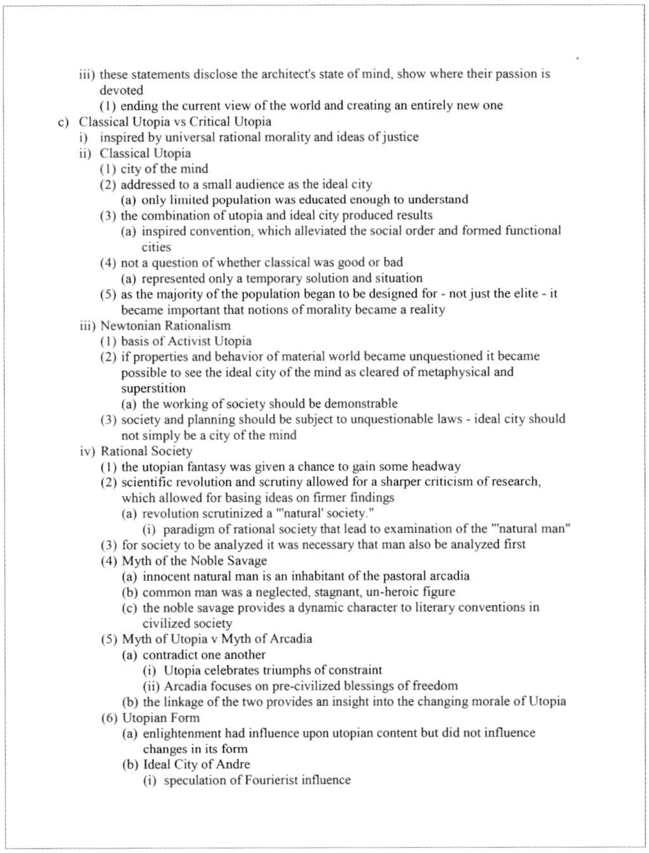
  - iii) these statements disclose the architect's state of mind, show where their passion is devoted
    - (1) ending the current view of the world and creating an entirely new one
- c) Classical Utopia vs Critical Utopia
  - i) inspired by universal rational morality and ideas of justice
  - ii) Classical Utopia
    - (1) city of the mind
    - (2) addressed to a small audience as the ideal city
      - (a) only limited population was educated enough to understand
    - (3) the combination of utopia and ideal city produced results
      - (a) inspired convention, which alleviated the social order and formed functional cities
    - (4) not a question of whether classical was good or bad
      - (a) represented only a temporary solution and situation
    - (5) as the majority of the population began to be designed for - not just the elite - it became important that notions of morality became a reality
  - iii) Newtonian Rationalism
    - (1) basis of Activist Utopia
    - (2) if properties and behavior of material world became unquestioned it became possible to see the ideal city of the mind as cleared of metaphysical and superstition
      - (a) the working of society should be demonstrable
    - (3) society and planning should be subject to unquestionable laws - ideal city should not simply be a city of the mind
  - iv) Rational Society
    - (1) the utopian fantasy was given a chance to gain some headway
    - (2) scientific revolution and scrutiny allowed for a sharper criticism of research, which allowed for basing ideas on firmer findings
      - (a) revolution scrutinized a "'natural' society."
        - (i) paradigm of rational society that lead to examination of the "'natural man"
    - (3) for society to be analyzed it was necessary that man also be analyzed first
    - (4) Myth of the Noble Savage
      - (a) innocent natural man is an inhabitant of the pastoral arcadia
      - (b) common man was a neglected, stagnant, un-heroic figure
      - (c) the noble savage provides a dynamic character to literary conventions in civilized society
    - (5) Myth of Utopia v Myth of Arcadia
      - (a) contradict one another
        - (i) Utopia celebrates triumphs of constraint
        - (ii) Arcadia focuses on pre-civilized blessings of freedom
      - (b) the linkage of the two provides an insight into the changing morale of Utopia
    - (6) Utopian Form
      - (a) enlightenment had influence upon utopian content but did not influence changes in its form
      - (b) Ideal City of Andre
        - (i) speculation of Fourierist influence

Fig. 5. A partial example of a student outline of *Collage City*.

gain access to Rowe's texts. I require the students to do three things while they read these essays. From my syllabus:

1. To assist with *language* difficulties. Use a dictionary, OFTEN.

2. To assist with *content* issues: Use an encyclopedia and annotate all texts. If you are unfamiliar with a person or a concept, you MUST stop and teach yourself; you cannot rely on the surrounding words, sentences, and paragraphs to provide what you need to know. Rowe used these figures and concepts to create the context for his points.[12] Rowe always provided space for the insertion of notes by the reader, use the opportunity provided to make your own marginal notes.

3. To assist with *structure:* Create an outline of the text: first read through it, then on the second pass, outline the article.

As *Collage City* is studied, I use the 1978 book, but I provide the 1975 introduction:

> *It was not so many years ago that the Graduate School of Design at Harvard issued a brochure entitled* Crisis. *It was an opulent production, blood-red letters on a white ground, and its message was not at all oblique. There exists an environmental crisis but the Graduate School of Design possesses most of the know-how to be able to propound the solution; and, therefore, in order that it may realize its mission, give, give to the Graduate School of Design.*

12 When talking with Rowe it was not uncommon for him to make a statement followed by "Boom, boom, boom!" Each 'boom' was like an unstated mathematic axiom or a corollary that needed to be followed to reach his conclusion. His students spent considerable time learning those unexplained 'axioms'.

> *The strategy, of course, begins to be ancient, but it continues, apparently to be irresistible and the notion of impending and monstrous cataclysm would now seem to be ingrained in the psychology of Modern architecture. Apocalyptic catastrophe, instant millennium. The threat of damnation, the hope of salvation. Irresistible change which still requires human co-operation. The new architecture and urbanism as emblems of the New Jerusalem. The corruptions of high culture. The bonfire of the vanities. Self-transcendence towards a form of collectivized freedom. The architect, divested of his cultural wardrobe and fortified by the equivalent of religious experience, may now revert to the virtues of his primal condition.*[13]
>
> *This is to caricature, though not seriously to distort, a complex of sentiments which might be designated the Savonarola syndrome, sentiment often lying just beneath the threshold of consciousness; and, therefore it should not surprise that one observes a recent RIBA (Royal Institute of British Architects) Journal—yet again Crisis (this time red letters on a black background), and this time not an appeal for money but rather an incitement to self-flagellation.*
>
> *... and it certainly should not be understood as condemning a missionary enthusiasm or intimating that convictions of crisis are in any way illusory. It may be presumed that a crisis exists; but it must also be insisted that peddling of crisis by the architect begins to become an objectionable platitude that is now one of those retarded gambits of criticism which any sense of obligation should feel obliged to avoid.*[14]

Thus, at the beginning of the seminar and by way of introduction, the students are challenged: "What has changed? Are we already too late? Perhaps the crisis we now face is an economic crisis? Perhaps the environmental crisis must give way to yet another, more pressing concern, or in the classic mystical manner, do we merge our many crises to create a mega-crisis?"

This course's objectives are to assist students in gaining a clearer understanding of the period referred to as Modern architecture and subsequent developments in the areas of Design Theory, Urban Design, and the Built Environment. The course focuses, of course, on the role of architecture in the creation of the urban environment. Rowe's text is essentially the benchmark for all subsequent readings. The course explores whether, in the face of a post-Modern condition, any new paradigms have been made that supplant Rowe's theory of the temporal utopian collage or whether newer paradigms are regressions to a 'comical' neo-Modernist condition bereft of any idealism.

The syllabus states: "This is a unique opportunity to learn from one another and to utilize one another's insights to enhance our own understanding of the writings, theories and policies that create the urban environment. Scrutiny and discussion are imperative in one's attempt to understand and build upon these writings." Students agree to produce a deliverable for internal consumption. This is an attempt to connect the words with their counterpart, the actions of design. Within reason, the course attempts to recreate an attitude for inquiry that mimics that of Rowe's residence at Renwick Place in Ithaca, where Rowe and his students would sometimes retire from the studio to explore aspects of interest and discuss selected topics.

13 Rowe uses the 'Natural Man/Noble Savage' in two manners. The first as shown above (elaborated upon in Rowe and Koetter (1978): 16-17.) and the second on p. 50-51 when he states: "In intention the modern city was to be a fitting home for the noble savage. A being so aboriginally pure necessitated a domicile of equivalent purity: and, if way back the noble savage had emerged from the trees, then, if his will transcending innocence was to be preserved, his virtues maintained intact, it was back into the trees that he must return." He includes associated illustrations of the Ville Radieuse, 1930 with a Le Corbusier sketch of a wooded park-scape with cross-shape high-rise towers in the near and far distance. The *Scena Satyrica* incarnate!

14 Rowe, Colin and Koetter, Fred, "Collage City", *The Architectural Review* 158, Aug 1975.

In my seminar the readings are typically divided into four groups or sets. The first set is made up of texts from *The Cornell Journal of Architecture,* 2, including Rowe's "Program vs. Paradigm" and Wayne Copper's "The Figure/Grounds". These are followed by a second set of material that includes "Roma interrotta" by Rowe, et. al, and two related articles by Steven Peterson, "Urban Design Tactics" and "Space /Anti Space".[15] These texts are what I have referred to elsewhere and, borrowing from Rowe's introduction to *Five architects,* as the "word made flesh". These texts both explain and illustrate the general principles of *Collage City* and provide a follow-up to Wayne Copper's figure/ground city plan drawings as well.

The third set of texts focus on the American scene. They include: "Excursus Americanus"[16] by Michael Dennis, "The Highway and the City"[17] by Lewis Mumford, *Measuring America*[18] by Andro Linklater, and "The American Continental Grid: Form and Meaning"[19] by Steven Hurtt. Many of our students are international students and these readings help ground them in their present physical context as well as assist in explaining how the local environment has evolved. Even American students are often unaware of the history that has formed the physical contexts they experience and design for in their studios.

These readings are followed by a variety of viewpoints on urbanism and provide introductions to the subsequent developments following the *Collage City* manifesto. These include: "The Way is the Goal"[20] by Gert Mattenklott, *Home from Nowhere*[21] by James Howard Kunstler, *Houses, Palaces, Cities*[22] by Léon Krier, "Rome, its Region and the Regeneration of the 'Light' City"[23] by Antonio Latini, "Between the Crusader's Jerusalem and Piranesi's Rome: Conflicting Ideals for the City"[24] by Alex Kreiger, and "Whatever Happened to Urbanism?"[25] by Rem Koolhaas and Bruce Mau.

A fourth set of readings includes more recent articles and excerpts from *Temples and Towns: A Study of the Form, Elements, and Principles of Planned Towns*[26] by Michael Dennis, "The Ecology Question, Sprawltown as a Second Nature"[27] by Richard Ingersoll, *Resilient Cities: Responding to Peak Oil and Climate Change*[28] by Newman, Beatley, and Boyer, and *Sprawling Places*[29] by David Kolb.

These readings have a counterpart: a series of analysis projects are undertaken in order to gain insights into the role of texture, figure/ground, zoning practices, density, and typology in the built, urban environment. Students created and analyzed selected American cities, or parts thereof, to make a set of collective urban comparisons. For example, in one of the semesters, students were responsible for documenting, analyzing, and presenting a selected city. Their analytic resources included contemporary GIS, aerials, Sanborn Insurance Maps, and other current and historic resources, like zoning and land use maps. This assignment was discussed in class as it developed.

More recently, as this course has become coupled with a Chicago Studio investigation, the projects involved comparative analyses of different sections of that city. For example, figure/grounds, zoning, and land use maps of one-mile by one-mile square sections of the Wrigleyville, Ogden Slips, Englewood, and Logan Square areas were created. A selected area within each section was then looked at with respect to street types, housing and commercial building types,

15 Peterson, Steven Kent, "Urban Design Tactics", *Architectural Design* 49 (3-4), 1979: 76-81; Idem, "Space and Anti-Space", *Harvard Architecture Review* 1, Spr 1980: 88-113.

16 Dennis, Michael, "Excursus Americanus", *Modulus* 16, 1983: 110-25; Idem, *Court and Garden from the French Hôtel to the City of Modern Architecture,* MIT Press, Cambridge, MA, and London, 1986.

17 Mumford, Lewis, *The Highway and the City,* Greenwood Press, Westport, CT, (1909) 1981.

18 Linklater, Andro, *Measuring America: How the United States Was Shaped by the Greatest Land Sale in History,* Walker & Co., New York, 2002.

19 Hurtt, Steven, "The American Continental Grid: Form and Meaning", *Threshold* 2, "America", Journal of the School of Architecture, University of Illinois at Chicago, Rizzoli, New York, 1983.

20 Mattenklott, Gert, "The Way is the Goal", *Daidalos* 47, Mar 1993: 28-35.

21 Kunstler, James Howard, *Home from Nowhere: Remaking Our Everyday World for the Twenty-first Century,* Simon & Schuster, New York, 1996.

22 Porphyrios, Demetri, ed., "Léon Krier: Houses, Palaces, Cities", *AD Profile* 54, 1984.

23 Latini, Antonio Pietro, "Rome, its region and the regeneration of the 'light' city", *City Safety Energy Journal* 2, 2015: 78-98.

24 Krieger, Alex, "Between the crusader's Jerusalem and Piranesi's Rome: Conflicting ideals for the city", in Hoffman, Alexander von, ed., *Form, Modernism, and History: Essays in Honor of Eduard F. Sekler,* Harvard University Graduate School of Design, Cambridge MA, 1996: 151-64.

25 Koolhaas, Rem; Mau, Bruce, *S, M, L, XL,* Monacelli Press, New York, 1998.

26 Dennis, Michael, *Temples and Towns: A Study of the Form, Elements, and Principles of Planned Towns,* manuscript.

27 Ingersoll, Richard, *Sprawltown: Looking for the City on Its Edges,* Princeton Architectural Press, New York, 2006.

28 Newman, Peter; Beatley, Timothy; Boyer, Heather, *Resilient Cities: Responding to Peak Oil and Climate Change,* Island Press, Washington, D.C., 2008.

29 Kolb, David, *Sprawling Places,* University of Georgia Press, Athens, GA, 2008.

Fig. 6a, 6b. Noble Square figure/ground and Zoning Map comparison. See [https://www.chicagostudio-uiuc.com/urban-morphology].

and square footages. These areas were then examined at a larger scale and eventually individual building types were compared at 1" = 20'. The individual studies gained value through comparison and contrast. Graphically, they were modeled on the Ayers Saint Gross comparative campus studies[30] and on examples found in Melville C. Branch's *Comparative Urban Design.*[31]

Chicago Urban Design Studio

The final course described here is an urban design studio that is now interwoven with two others. These are the Urban Design/Urban Morphology seminar described above, a professional practice seminar, and the Urban Design studio, which is based in Chicago. All benefit from collaborative endeavors with communities, the office of the Chicago Mayor, the Department of Planning and Development, citizens groups, and practicing professionals.

> *A strategic alliance between academia and practice has been established in downtown Chicago. This unique 'intersection' of collaboration has yielded a new program: the*

30 Ayers Saint Gross, "Comparing Campuses – Ayers Saint Gross", [asg-architects.com/ideas/comparing-campuses//].

31 Branch, Melville Campbell, *Comparative Urban Design: Rare Engravings, 1830-1843*, Arno Press, New York, 1978.

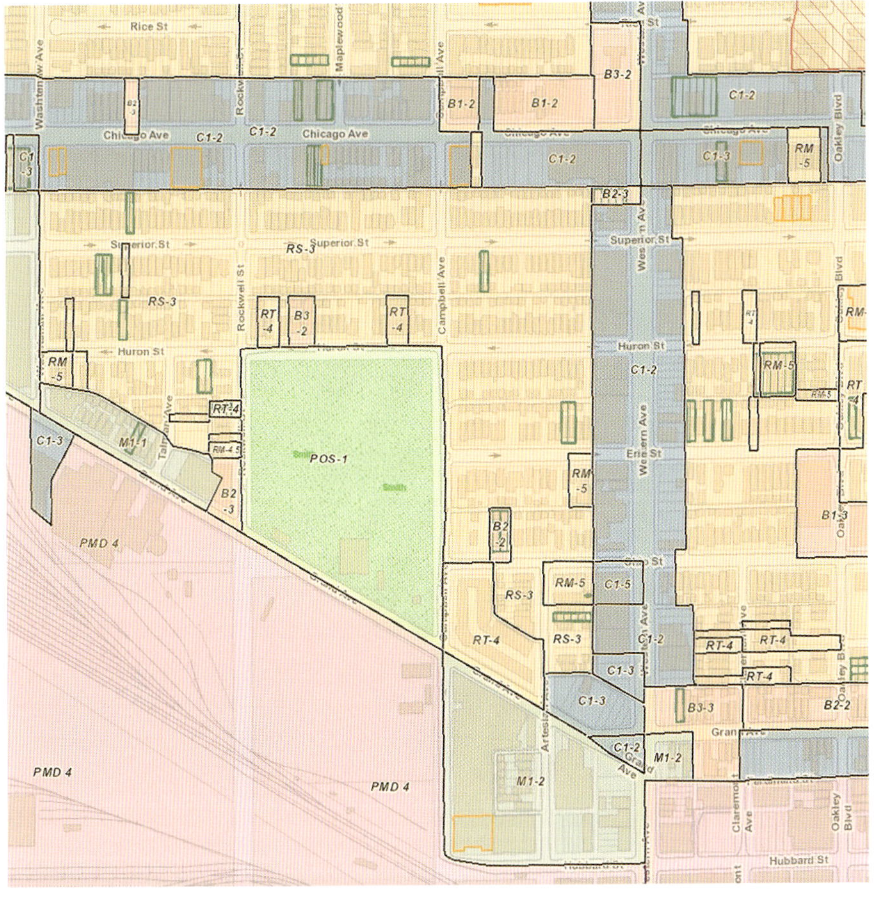

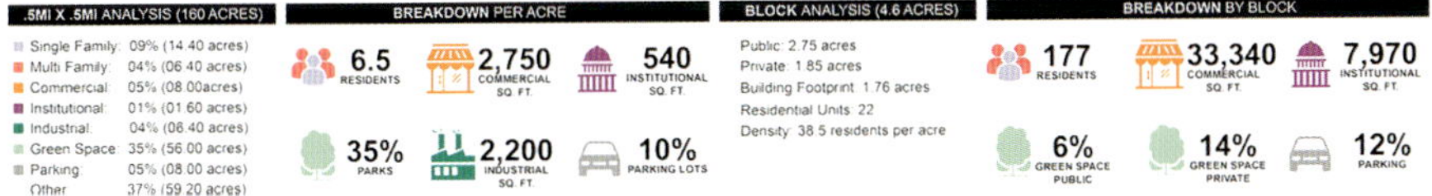

Chicago Studio of the University of Illinois at Urbana-Champaign. This collaborative alliance resulted in a more meaningful project and a more significant experience for students and professionals compared to traditional studio approaches.[32]

In the summer of 2013 Deputy Mayor Steven Koch and members of the Chicago Department of Planning and Development met with faculty from UIUC's School of Architecture and the Department of Landscape Architecture in Chicago. I suggested that the City of Chicago would be a tremendous venue for student urban design investigations and that a partnership might be of value to both the university and the city. Koch replied, "We don't have any money for this but we have plenty of problems". He then suggested that the city might have space available in a closed firehouse, police station, or school. I asked for a firehouse thinking that the building type would make an ideal venue for our purposes. The large firehouse doors could provide access to the community and engagement, while the offices and living spaces could be converted for classroom use and provide housing for a faculty member who could commute to Chicago to provide instruction.[33] Unfortunately, the city was not able to make this work and other

32 Hinders, Kevin; Loganbill, Michael, "The Urban Studio: Intersection Between the Academy and Practice", unpublished paper delivered at the 2015 AIA/ACSA Conference "Intersections", May 13, 2015.

33 The author really wanted to be able to slide down the firepole to studio each day.

spaces suggested proved less desirable as student safety could not be assured. In the end, the Illinois School of Architecture accepted a very generous offer from VOA Associates, Inc. (now Stantec), to provide approximately 2,000 square feet of office space on Michigan Avenue. This venue was made available with a five-year lease agreement, the term remaining on VOA/Stantec's lease agreement.

With the studio location set, the Chicago Studio began the task of establishing a full set of enrollment courses expected at the graduate level and that could be delivered off the main campus. Three courses have become regular offerings: 1) the Urban Design/Urban Morphology seminar described above; 2) a Professional Development course in which students research and visit the offices of 12–15 architecture firms with the required objective of learning the stated values of these offices and how the offices deliver these values to the general public and their clientele; 3) the Studio investigation, the focus of the description that follows.

Since the fall of 2014 my Chicago Studio offerings have included: a design for the area near the United Center which has suffered ever since the fires of 1968 following the assassination of Martin Luther King Jr. (2014); urban designs for areas near proposed new "L" stops,[34] one in the Cabrini-Green Area and the other adjacent to the Illinois Medical District (2015); and interdisciplinary studies for Chicago's Central Manufacturing District (2017). These projects were selected such that each required the reprogramming of existing structures, the selective removal of others, and new insertions into the existing context. The overarching theme, consistent with the mayor's office, the Planning Department, and most citizen groups, was an integrated approach to renewal as well as the survival of the historical context of the city. This approach, while political and practical, also touches on a psychological level that connects us with our past while searching in the present for ways to secure a better future. It is with excerpts from the very last paragraph in *Collage City* that I use as the starting point for this studio.

> *Habitually utopia, whether Platonic or Marxian, has been conceived of as axis mundi [Platonic] or as axis istoriae [Hegelian]: but, if in this way it has operated like all totemic, traditionalist and uncriticized aggregations of ideas, if its existence has been poetically necessary and politically deplorable, then this is only to assert the idea that a collage technique, by accommodating a whole range of axis mundi … might be a means of permitting us the enjoyment of utopian poetics without being obliged to suffer the embarrassment of utopian politics … which is further to suggest that collage could even be a strategy which, by supporting the utopian illusion of changelessness and finality, might even fuel a reality of change, motion, action and history.*[35]

As lofty as my ambitions for this course may be, grounding it in the Rowe and Koetter thinking of *Collage City*, the Chicago Studios are designed to give students the opportunity to work on real projects identified by Chicago's Department of Planning and Development. These projects allow the students to gain insights into the social, economic, and political aspects of urban design. They immerse themselves in the rich Chicago environment. Faculty and students from nearby Roosevelt University's Marshall Bennett Institute of Real Estate Program have run courses in tandem with my Chicago design studios. This partnership provides economic background and insights that help inform the studio projects. Roosevelt's real estate students also benefit from seeing design options as projects

34 Chicagoans affectionately refer to the Chicago Transit Authority's rail system as "The L". A portion of this rail system is elevated above street grade.

35 Rowe and Koetter (1978): 149.

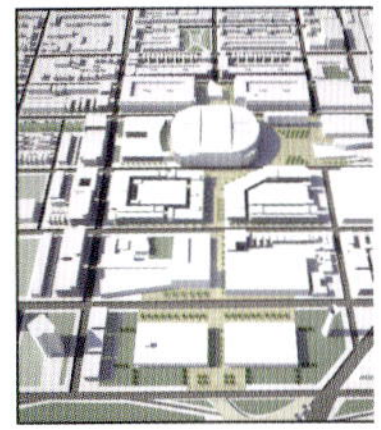

Fig. 7. Plan showing three projects inserted into the Chicago plan, projects from 2014 and 2015.

develop. The combined efforts that include design proposals coupled with real estate financing and exploring planning incentives such as Tax Increment Financing (TIF) districts, and other possible government programs, enhances the value of the projects for the city while greatly increasing the education of both student groups.

Professionals engage the students and their projects in many ways. Some aspects have been institutionalized while others change from semester to semester. Every semester since establishing the program, each student has a mentor from VOA/Stantec. The students are also provided the opportunity to have a mentor from a different Chicago architecture office. These mentors often take students to lectures and lunch-and-learns and stop by the studio after hours to help the students. By engaging the profession the students are able to learn from knowledgeable people outside the typical studio course offerings, and network. It should be noted that VOA/Stantec, and the other firms providing mentors, value the opportunity for these interactions as well. VOA/Stantec sees the engagement as a means to stimulate its employees and keep abreast of academia. Students are encouraged to visit the firm's design studios and engage its architects and interns.

Many government agencies have been involved in past investigations as well. The Chicago Transit Authority has assisted studios and helped select new "L" station locations for the city. These student investigations were, in part, a way for the city to explore the cost/benefit of these proposed new stations. Several projects sought to assist the city in its bid for substantial grant funding from the Transportation Investment Generating Economic Recovery (TIGER) program.[36] The investigations relied upon working with local community groups to explore solutions satisfactory to them, as well as the landowners, including the Chicago Housing Authority, the largest single land-owner in Chicago. The studio regularly

36 TIGER grants were a part of the United States Federal Government's American Recovery and Reinvestment Act of 2009. TIGER Grants were replaced in 2018 by Federal Build Transportation Grants ($1.5 Billion for 2018 was made available from The Consolidated Appropriations Act of 2018).

Fig. 8. Sustainability strategies from the Central Manufacturing District projects.

engages city aldermen and developers to gain their insights and opinions. In this way, no single political or economic voice is given exclusive authority. Hearing different sides and opinions is the educational goal.

In 2017, the University of Illinois Urbana-Champaign's College of Fine and Applied Arts, which is home to the School of Architecture, sponsored an interdisciplinary investigation for the Central Manufacturing District in Chicago. Students from the Departments of Urban and Regional Planning and Landscape Architecture joined the Chicago Studio in interdisciplinary teams to explore the

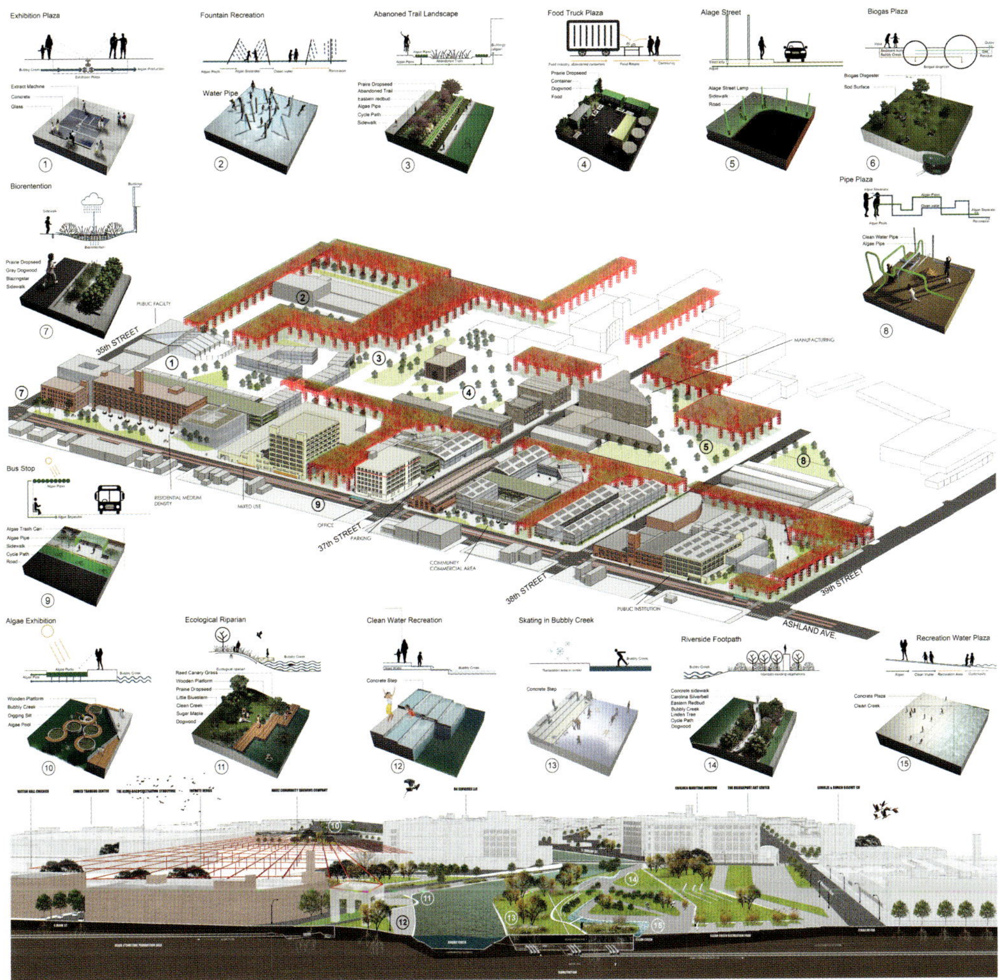

Fig. 9. Axonometric of the Central Manufacturing District project.

area near the former Chicago stockyards. The planning and landscape students worked at the Urbana-Champaign campus while the architecture students worked in Chicago. Students communicated and worked together both digitally and over the table. On five occasions the students from Urbana-Champaign came to Chicago to work and present their investigations. This interdisciplinary strategy enhanced the student experience and the projects themselves.

These Chicago Studio offerings continue to evolve. Each semester I seek to engage our students with meaningful projects that will both enhance their knowledge and assist the people of Chicago. These service-learning exercises prepare the students for their professional engagements as they near graduation and have proven to be extremely rewarding for all involved.

Summary

In summary, I am fortunate to be teaching in an architecture program that values urbanism enough to make it one of four areas of emphasis that structure our curriculum, and to have had the opportunity to develop the four courses described here. Themes drawn from the Rowe legacy that run through his writings

Fig. 10. Area Plan of the Central Manufacturing District projects.

and the writings of his students undergird these courses. Primary among them is Rowe's high regard for knowing history and making it useful to the present, both as a critical frame of reference and as a resource for use in the design process.

While that idea is fundamental to much of what Rowe has written, he made it quite explicit in both *Collage City* and later in *The Cornell Journal of Architecture,* 2, as "Program vs. Paradigm". In this oppositional pairing, "program" refers to a methodology where empirical facts are assembled and the design solution for the building or the city is based upon this so-called objective compilation of information. Contrasted with that approach, "paradigm" refers to a methodology where form, and particularly forms that have been well tested over time, that is historically, are accessed and tested for their efficacy in addressing the complexities of a given architectural or urban design opportunity. For Rowe, the paradigm may be, and often is, an abstract and ideal geometric form, a particular morph, but it may be derived from examples that illustrate accommodation to a specific circumstance. But in either case, his preference seems to be that the ideal form is in evidence, whether distorted by context or not. This is underscored by the final essay, "Excursus", in *Collage City* where almost sixty *objets trouvés* are provided for consideration.

I share, with Rowe, a concern that since the rise of Modernism, the preference for "form ever following function"[37] and the subsequent manipulation of program as

37 Sullivan, Louis, "The Tall Office Building Artistically Considered", *Lippincott's Monthly Magazine,* Mar 1896: 403-09.

the primary determinant of form has been a design studio constant to the general exclusion of reference to a repertoire of historical form precedents as well as urban and architectural morphologies. The role of program (programming, data sets, digital technology, and more and more empirical knowledge and the like) has greatly supplanted the use of precedent and typology that had guided architectural design prior to the advent of Modernism. This has included a Modernist assumption that, with the rise of new building types that address new 'modern' conditions, all conditions must be considered anew, an assumption that again sets aside existing precedents and working typologies.

Of course, new building types based upon human needs will certainly arise. New materials and building technologies will be developed and incorporated into the construction of our buildings and cities in the future. But the little that is typologically 'new' should not be presumed to supplant the great quantity of that which is 'old' and contributes to an environmental and culturally sustainable future.

Program and paradigm are not exclusive of one another. And if the student, or the architect, has in mind to extract the ideal from a deep dive into program complexities that is all to the good. But, particularly for the student, an emphasis on paradigm seems required to plant the aspiration toward the ideal. Paradigm and precedent offer more than ready solutions to the practical issues of program. They provide the basic material for the designer to use to explore a range of possible building and city solutions in search for *appropriate form* for a particular circumstance or context that is inclusive of communicating the values of a culture and its unique place.

Longstanding building traditions, an understanding of place, materials, and climate as understood and utilized by a culture, convey the past into the present and project it into the future. With my students I seek to help them understand and achieve a balance in their work that is accepting of our ever-changing world, that balances paradigm with program, that reclaims and reprograms existing structures, that achieves a fundamental understanding of typology and morphology in order to root new structures in their contexts and thereby provide adaptable, culturally significant structures that will lead to sustainable cities that are prized by their inhabitants. It is balance that is needed:

> *... if we all of us both live in the past and hope for the future (the present being no more than an episode in time), it would seem reasonable that we should accept this condition. For, if without prophecy there is no hope, then, without memory there can be no communication.*[38]

These four course offerings have been, and are, my attempt at teaching urban design to both non-architecture and architecture students, and to teach it at multiple levels of the curriculum. The courses described here all draw from experiences with Rowe and his continuing legacy in seeking to educate the next generations of designers and others who will determine the shape and form of our cities. Each course seeks to champion the nobility of the search for the ideal. The Platonic idea that the ideal is abstract and cannot be attained in the real world must not allay the aspiration for perfection. It is that aspiration that has rendered the best that exists in the products of mankind, and that, as urban designers, it is in attempting to attain perfection that we make the good and great city.

38 The authors continue: "Obvious, trite and sententious though this may be, it was –happily or unhappily–an aspect of the human mind which the early proponents of Modern architecture were able to overlook–happily for them, unhappily for us. But, if without such distinctly perfunctory psychology, 'the new way of building' could never have come into being, there cannot any longer be excuse for the failure to recognize the complementary relationship that is fundamental to the processes of anticipation and retrospection. For these are inter-dependent activities; and since, quite literally, we cannot perform without exercising them both, no attempt to suppress either in the interests of the other can ever be protractedly successful. We may receive strength from the novelty of prophetic declamation; but the degree of this potency must be strictly related to the known, perhaps mundane and, necessarily, memory-laden context from which it emerges."

III. Rome

What better or more obvious exhibit is there available than an overview of Rome? For here we are presented with the greater part of the story; a more or less uniform building height; a dense matrix, tissue, or texture, from out of which relatively neutral field certain spaces are subtracted and certain objects allowed to erupt … and, once looking into the streets from the rooftops, one may begin to discern how certain phenomena propounded up top as objects, ultimately relinquish any such ambition and, finally, present themselves as a mediation between object and prevailing tissue/texture.

The Present Urban Predicament, The Cornell Journal of Architecture, 1, 1981.

The studio language, which belongs to the process of architectural education as it relates to the drawing board, is of necessity, the voice of immediacy and enthusiasm. It is the voice of excited critics and intelligent students … . But the art historical language is something other. It is the voice of caution and aspires to erudition; and if the studio language, always vivacious, is prone to be the language of uncriticized tradition, then the art historical language, often still attempting to show how it really was … will operate to separate and divide … .

Two Italian Encounters, As I Was Saying, 1, 1996.

Rome's importance for Rowe cannot be overstated. Renaissance and Baroque architecture studies with Wittkower initiated "interminable trips to Italy". In "Two Italian Encounters", he describes life-changing visits to Rome in 1947 and 1950. Meeting Arthur Brown revealed the operative presence of Mannerist composition in 20th century architecture. His 'encounters' clarified how he reconciled his competing interests: the studio, architectural design speculation—"pics" and drawings versus the library, archival research—facts dominating ideas.

Rowe's interests included biographies which prompted speculations unchained from historical determinism. Ideas and forms could be freed from their history-bound time and place. Counterfactual histories allowed speculative what-ifs by both designer and historian. He delighted in noting that chance and minor facts could radically alter events, discrediting notions of historical inevitability. Such speculations amused, enlightened, and instructed. Consequentially, city form appeared less rigid, more circumstantial, prompting a cascade of Urban Design Studio what-ifs. Treating forms and ideas as mutable, however, did not free them from rigorous analysis, critical intent, or purposeful discovery and instruction. Prominent in "Lessons of Rome", Rowe's technique was Socratic, dialectical—physique/morale or flesh/word, a stimulant to thinking:

1) Morale: image or icon bearing specific and general meaning—the dome, archetypal symbol and cultural emblem of sacrality, religious or secular.

2) Physique: self-regulating rules of transformation described by Jean Piaget in Structuralism include an ideal wholeness, relationship of part to parts, and part to whole.

3) Physique/Morale: independently or together, they allow speculations about forms/meanings, whether comic, profound, or both.

Living and teaching in Rome inspired former Rowe students to levels of integration and interpretation that would recall the Proustian observation that real creativity is seeing the old with new eyes. Drawing related spatial constructs led to new interpretations of the city's forms, typological origins, and relation of urban form to power, politics, pilgrimage, and pomp. The intersection of architecture and urban design in Rome—the realm of the 'in-between'—was studied under the rubric of micro-urbanism. The 1748 Nolli map with its figure/ground representation showed this phenomenon in detail and was arguably the central vehicle for all Rome studies in the Studio. It became the foundation for the "Roma interrotta" exhibition and the influential Rowe team's speculative 'physique' while Rowe's fictive narrative provided its 'morale'.

Rowe helped revitalize Cornell's Rome program. He argued its centrality to architectural education. Rome was seen as the quintessential theater of debate between Renaissance ideality and messy Medieval reality. Rome, equally exemplifying fine-grained spatial constructs and the grand plan. Rome, inexhaustible resource for ideas.

VUE GENERALE DE LA COUR DU PALAIS PIETRO-MASSIMI,

Baldassarre Peruzzi. Prise sous le portique du fond. _ VI. 25. *Penel et Lecoq sculp.*

Colin Rowe: Rome and Cornell

Roberto Einaudi

This is an updated version of a talk by Roberto Einaudi presented on June 19, 2014 at the Palazzo Lazzaroni in Rome, as part of the conference, "Rowe Rome 2014: Urban Design and the Legacy of Colin Rowe". His remarks follow those given by David Rowe on the same occasion.

frontispiece:

Perspective view of the courtyard of the Palazzo Pietro-Massimi by Paul Marie Letarouilly.

Well, David Rowe's memories of Colin clearly go much further back than mine! I heard Colin speaking through his words.

I finished my undergraduate studies at the College of Architecture, Art, and Planning at Cornell in 1961, a year before Colin arrived, so our paths did not cross at that time. I first met Colin in Rome on the occasion of the exhibition "Roma interrotta" in 1978. I know that many of you present here today worked with Colin on that project, Judy DiMaio for sure, others? Many, I see. The exhibit at the Mercati di Traiano was an extraordinary event for Rome, and Colin's participation was in great part the result of his pioneering studies on the urban fabric, as expressed, for instance, in the book *Collage City*, written with Fred Koetter, who is with us today.

Editors' Note: The images which accompany this essay show the Palazzi Pietro and Angelo Massimo by Baldassare Peruzzi as recorded in Paul Marie Letarouilly's *Édifices de Rome Moderne*, one of Rowe's favorite sources for documenting the architecture and urbanism of the city. Located in the *centro storico*, the Palazzo Angelo Massimo was the center for the Cornell Department of Architecture's Rome Program during Rowe's period as a teacher in the program.

Rome for Colin well expressed his interest in both the complexity and unity of the urban texture and its individual monuments. Colin was inevitably attracted to the Eternal City. Cornell at that time had no Rome program, so Colin was forced to emigrate to other universities in order to enjoy and study Rome. He started teaching at the University of Notre Dame's Rome School of Architecture in the early '80s, and I frequently would be called upon to give crits to his students.

We would also exchange visits to our respective apartments, his in via Monterone, and mine overlooking the Campo de'Fiori. I remember well on one of his visits to our apartment for drinks, when my wife said, "I'm afraid we don't have a coffee table for the glasses". Colin replied: "It's better that way, the coffee table represents the beginning of the end of Western culture". Colin always had a wonderful wit, a sense of understatement that made him irresistible.

In 1986, the then Dean of the College of Architecture, Art, and Planning at Cornell, Bill McMinn, decided to open a program in Rome. I was asked to help find a location and assist in setting up the program. When I proposed the Palazzo Massimo alle Colonne as the location, the previous building that had been identified in Parioli was quickly abandoned.

Colin was a strong supporter of the new program in Rome and of the Palazzo Massimo location. I became the first director of the program, working hard on all aspects, from restoring the palazzo for our use; finding the local faculty, the staff, and housing for the students; programming site trips; teaching; etc. Colin was the shadow behind the program, helping support it, first from Ithaca, then directly by teaching in Rome.

The program had a tough life initially. It was not supported by many of the Ithaca faculty, who thought it was inappropriate and too costly. Colin wrote a long memorandum to the faculty strongly supporting the program and suggesting improvements and greater commitment and involvement. With his usual wit and sarcasm, he ended by saying: "There used to be a graffito in the New York subway: 'Jesus saves, but Moses invests'. So are we to emulate Jesus (in terms of a Wall Street holding operation)? or are we to emulate Moses and place reasonably conspicuous venture capital in Rome? The dividends are reliable, sometimes brilliant and, never, have they been less than good".

I had found an apartment for Colin, available for other Cornell faculty when he was not there, at the Palazzo Massimo di Pirro right next door. We could even talk to each other from adjacent windows, he from his apartment, I from my tiny office.

Colin and I taught together at Palazzo Massimo for several years. He loved the Palazzo, he loved its architect, Baldassarre Peruzzi, and he loved Giulio Romano. He knew all about the many palazzi designed by them. But he was surprised when he learned about my discoveries during the restoration of the Palazzo Massimo. Peruzzi's palazzo was superimposed on the earlier one by Giulio Romano, burnt during the Sack of Rome in 1527, but not destroyed. When Peruzzi had rebuilt it after the Sack, he had kept many of the spaces designed by Giulio, including one with a magnificent fresco, which I uncovered and managed to partially restore with funds from the Kress foundation.

Further thoughts on Giulio Romano: Colin's favorite building in Rome was perhaps Giulio's Palazzo Maccarani, near the Senate, a few blocks away from Palazzo Massimo. I remember well Colin's anguish when, on the day scheduled for his lecture on the Palazzo, his slides were not to be found. I suggested he could make the best of the situation by taking the students directly to the Palazzo and give the lecture on site. After all, were we not in Rome and should we not take advantage of it? Colin retorted with an avalanche of objections: the Palazzo was badly restored, had a *sopraelevazione*, or addition, on top, there was too much traffic and other distractions, he wouldn't be able to show his diagrams, etc., etc. Colin did manage to find his slides and I attended his lecture. Of course he was right, his beautiful drawings illustrating rhythm, proportions, and details—all were essential for a complete understanding of the building.

The Rome program proceeded very well at the Palazzo Massimo location; the students were enthusiastic, but there was mounting opposition in Ithaca. During the first Iraq crisis of 1990, the College wanted to shut it down, but five students were already in Europe and one of the Ithaca faculty, Roger Trancik, was also committed. So we remained open with five students for the semester, but of course all the fixed costs remained and the program lost more money than usual. When, subsequently, the dollar lost value and everything in Rome became relatively more expensive, the College decided to close the program, despite Colin's and my objections. The students in Ithaca staged a sit-in, in front of the dean's office, until that decision was revoked.

Since then, the Rome program has prospered, enrollment has increased, Palazzo Massimo became too small, and the program was moved here to Palazzo Lazzaroni.[1] Now, even here, the facilities have become small, and the College is looking for larger and better spaces. This semester, the Rome program has 90 students, a record, because Dean Kent Kleinman, whom we are fortunate to have with us today, has made it obligatory for all architectural students to attend a semester in Rome.

I retired as director of the Rome program in 1992, but my contacts with Colin remained. In 1993, when Colin was in the U.S. recovering from an illness, I interviewed him for an article to be published in the catalogue for the Richard Meier/Frank Stella exhibition in Rome. I asked Colin whether he thought his article "Transparency: Literal and Phenomenal", written during his teaching at the University of Texas, Austin (1954–56), had directly influenced Meier, as many critics had observed; here is some of our conversation:[2]

CR: "Of course it was written a long time ago and published later. I haven't the faintest idea of whether it influenced Richard or not, I mean, it happened."

1 The Cornell program is now located in the Palazzo Santacroce.

2 The article was written with Robert Slutzky between 1954 and 1956 and published in 1963.

RE: "You wrote that article with Slutzky—he was teaching at Cooper Union at that time, as was Meier. Did you get any feedback?"

CR: "I think you have to assume that during that period from about 1963 onwards Peter Eisenman is desperately trying to put groups of people together. Like Richard, Michael Graves and others."

RE: "Was that how the MoMA exhibit and book *Five architects* came about? Was it Eisenman, was it you?"

CR: "I was merely asked to write an intro. How did it get started? I would imagine it would be Peter, wouldn't you?"

RE: "Your article for the book *Five architects* was, as you stated, a sort of negative article, 'an attack upon an attack'. You avoided saying anything specifically about any of the five architects but rather gave different contexts in which their work could be viewed and analyzed. In hindsight, how would you describe or how would you criticize their work and particularly Meier's?"

CR: "I have always been a little surprised that they remained so attached to a version of the 1920s, if you like, cardboard Corbu. They never had, I feel, any sense of that Corbu that is, say, La Tourette or things of that sort. Surely Richard and Michael in different ways—Michael going off on a different tack—were the most accomplished".

RE: "Do you think the 'New York Five' actually existed as a unit?"

CR: "It was a political and polemical convenience I would say."

RE: "Do you feel that Meier was close to Le Corbusier?"

CR: "The frontality which you get in something like Garches seems to me basic for an understanding of Corbu. This doesn't really seem to have played a great influence in Richard's development."

RE: "Meier's work has a very unmistakable identity, perhaps more so than any other of the five."

CR: "I would think that is probably the case. Richard's houses can't quite manage Corbu, because they are fundamentally too big for the style. Also Richard's planning is rather more Gropius than Corbu ...."

I could go on and on, but time is running out. Anyone interested in pursuing this conversation can read my article in the exhibition catalog for "Richard Meier Frank Stella: Art and Architecture" held at the Palazzo delle Esposizioni, Rome, in 1993.

It is a wonderful occasion to be here together in Rome, to remember our friend and colleague, Colin Rowe. It is exciting to see old friends and acquaintances, all inspired by Colin's teaching. Thank you for this occasion.

Pl. 280.

Vue extérieure des deux Palais et des habitations voisines, prise de la rue di S. Pantaleo.

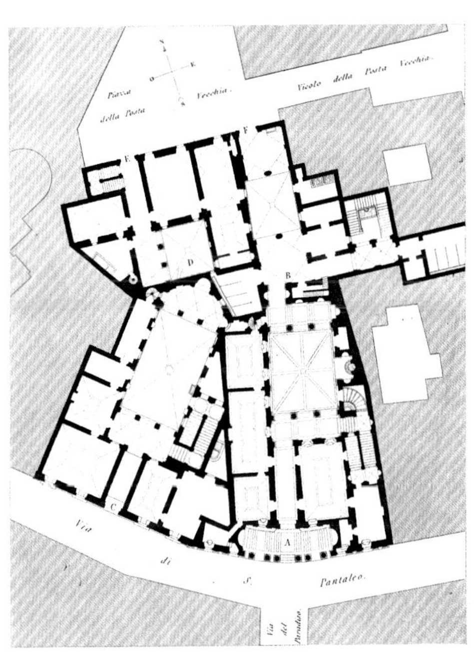

Plan du Rez-de-chaussée des deux Palais.

Echelle de 2 mill. pour mètre.

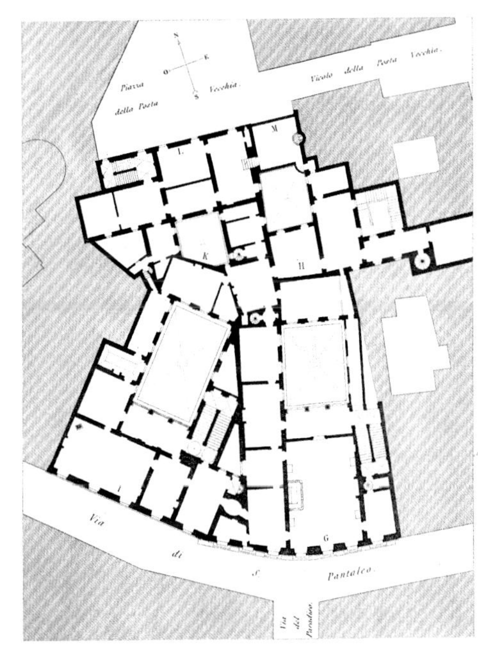

Plan du Premier Etage des deux Palais.

A. B. _ Palais Pietro-Massimi.

C. D. _ Palais Angelo-Massimi.

B.D.E.F. _ Partie conservée du Vieux Palais.

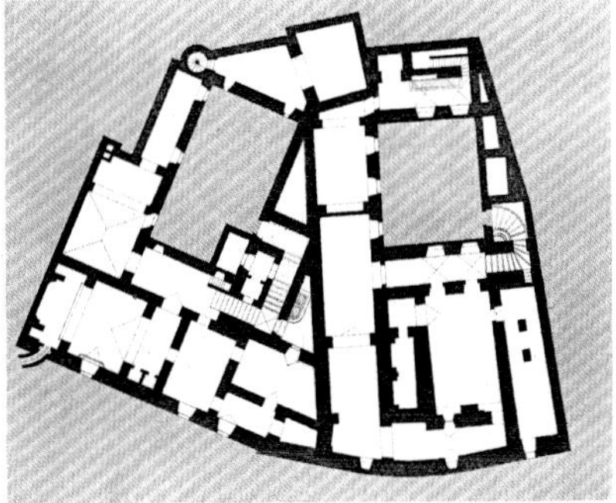

Plan de la partie principale des Souterrains.

G. H. _ Palais Pietro-Massimi.

I. K. _ Palais Angelo-Massimi.

H.K.L.M. _ Partie conservée du Vieux Palais.

Baldassarre Peruzzi.

PALAIS PIETRO-MASSIMI ET ANGELO-MASSIMI. _ VI. 23.

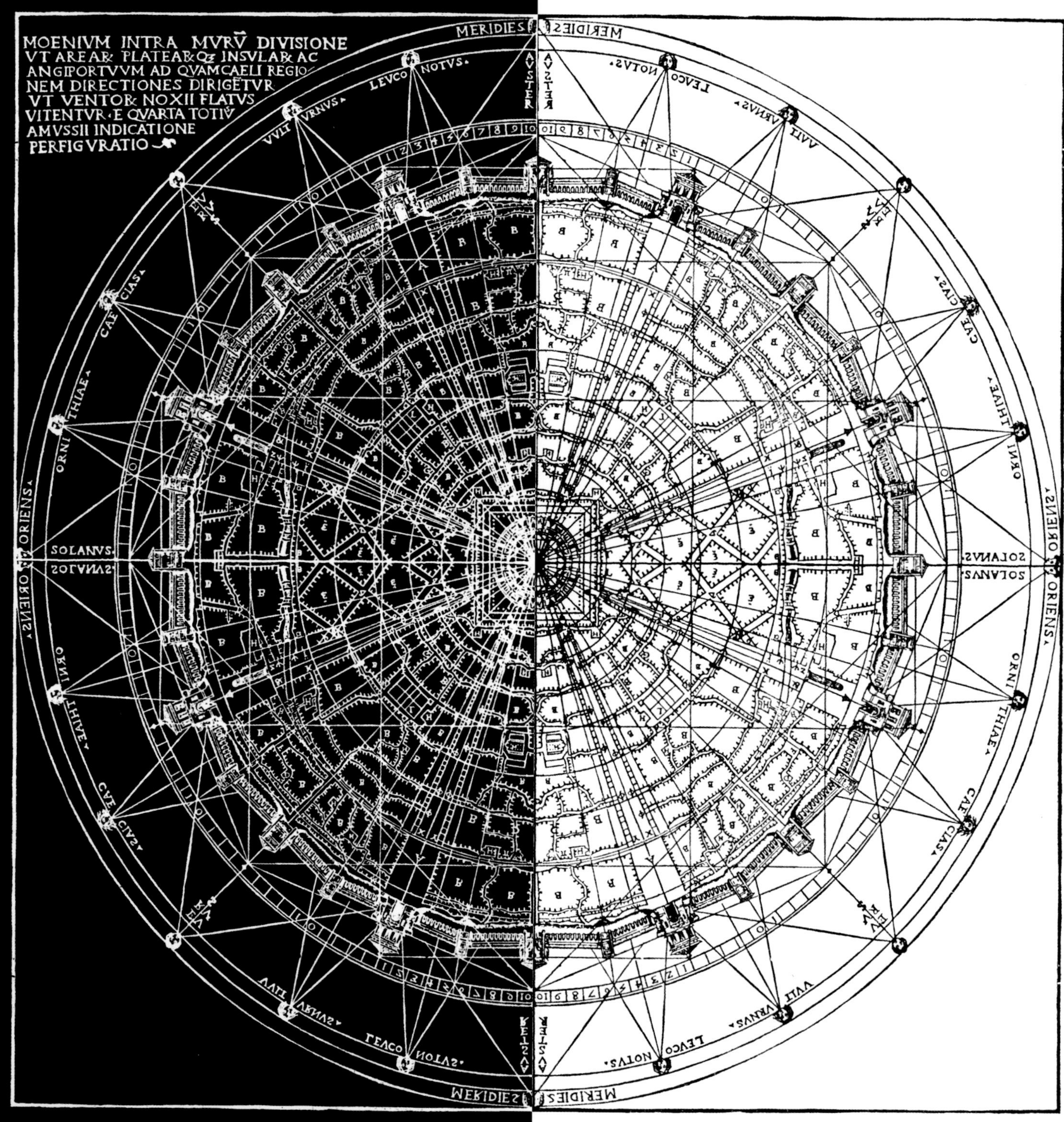
MOENIVM INTRA MVRV̄ DIVISIONE
VT AREAR& PLATEAR&Q; INSVLAR& AC
ANGIPORTVVM AD QVAMCAELI REGIO
NEM DIRECTIONES DIRIGĒTVR
VT VENTOR& NOXII FLATVS
VITENTVR. E QVARTA TOTIV̄
AMVSSII INDICATIONE
PERFIGVRATIO
MERIDIES
AVSTER
LEVCO NOTVS
VVLTVRNVS
CAECIAS
ORNITHIAE
SOLANVS
ORIENS

Rome: A Study in Urban and Architectural Formation and Transformation

Jon Michael Schwarting

Introduction

frontispiece:
"City of Vitruvius", Cesare Cesariano, 1511, graphic interpretation by author. All drawings in this essay by the author and his students unless otherwise noted.

Colin Rowe meant many things, sometimes contradictory, to his students and other followers. He was complex, prolific, and polymorphous, and he changed over time. Most of us were able to grasp and work with some aspect of Colin's vast array of thinking. When something resonated in some way with us, it permitted us to connect with him. It could be about urbanism, architecture, theory, philosophy, and even occasionally politics. When I was studying with him, Colin didn't want to talk about politics directly, even in the mid-'60s during the student 'revolution'. But I did find a way to engage Colin with ideas. I was taken with his then interest with Karl Popper and Karl Mannheim and Colin's long-standing preoccupation with the *ideal* versus the *real,* and with *utopia.*

The material presented here are topics selected from a book that I recently completed, *Rome: Formation and Transformation.*[1] It was first presented at the conference, "Rowe Rome 2014: Urban Design and the Legacy of Colin Rowe". I had been working on this material periodically since I was a Fellow at the American Academy in Rome (AAR) from 1968–70. This was after being in the Cornell Urban Design Studio and connecting again with Colin when he came to the Academy as a resident in 1969. Based on my research and work at the AAR, as well as the teaching from Colin in his Urban Design Studio, I first published this work as "The Lesson of Rome".[2] The work was continued primarily through teaching Columbia architecture students in summer programs in Rome, instructing and demonstrating a particular way to think and work with the city. It is an argument based on my observations about a process of *formation* and *transformation* or *ideal* and *real* in urbanism and architecture.

I begin my argument with the word 'idea' related to Plato's discussion of *idea* as the *ideal* and its relation to things which are 'real' or imperfect examples of it. *Ideal* is defined as, "a concept of what is perfect, existing in the imagination, desirable or perfect but not likely to become reality".[3] The dialectical opposite of *ideal* is the *real,* "the *real* existing as things—not imagined, the empiricism of Aristotle: real ideas are derived from sensation and reflection, not imagined

1 Schwarting, Jon Michael, *Rome: Urban Formation and Transformation*, ORO Editions, Gordon Goff, Novato, 2017.

2 Schwarting, Jon Michael, "The Lesson of Rome", *The Harvard Architectural Review* 2, "Urban Architecture", 1981: 22-47.

3 Murray, James A. H., *The Compact Edition of the Oxford English Dictionary*, Clarendon Press, Oxford, 1971.

opposite left to right:
Fig. 1. Rome at the time of Servius Tulius, 1527 engraving.

Fig. 2. Rome at the time of Augustus, 1527 engraving.

Fig. 3. Rome, fresco by Tadeo di Bartolo, 1414.

opposite lower:
Fig. 4. Diagrams of Rome from top to bottom a. hills; b. hills and roads; c. hills, roads and walls; d. radio-concentric schema.

or presupposed—knowledge directed or guided by experience without knowledge of principles".[4]

The notion of the ideal, as something imagined, is also related to the concept of a utopia defined as, "an imagined place or state of things where everything is perfect. It employs the imaginary to project the ideal, a perfect social, legal and political system, or place, state or condition".[5] A utopian proposition is thus quite different from an ideal notion in a significant way: utopia can enter into the realm of the physical, of architecture, or of the urban. In the *The Story of Utopias*, Lewis Mumford states:

> *Almost every Utopia is an implicit criticism of the civilization that served as its background: likewise, it is an attempt to uncover potentialities that the existing institutions either ignored or buried beneath the ancient crust of custom and habit. They most often indict existing society by showing alternatives, sensing both intolerable conditions and enormous possibilities.*[6]

Colin had an early interest in these matters, and they persisted in different ways throughout his life. In 1959, he published "The Architecture of Utopia", and the first chapter of *Collage City*, written with Fred Koetter and published in 1978, is titled "Utopia: Decline and Fall?" In the 1959 article he stated, "Architecture serves practical ends; it is subjected to use; but it is also shaped by ideas and fantasies; its rationale is cosmic and metaphysical and here of course lay its particular ability to impose itself on the mind".[7]

Colin did not express interest in Mumford's 1922 essay but rather in Karl Mannheim's 1937 *Ideology and Utopia*. Here Mannheim defined utopia, "Only those orientations transcending reality will be referred to by us as utopian, which when they pass over into conduct, tend to shatter partly or wholly the order of things prevailing at the time".[8] One of the characteristics of utopianism is its intent to replace an existing presumed 'reality' with another. It "becomes increasingly bound up with the process of becoming ...".[9] The critique of utopian propositions is that they cannot simultaneously become real and remain ideal. Rowe goes on to say,

> *It may instruct, civilize, and even edify the political society that is exposed to it. It may do all this, but for all that, it cannot become alive. It cannot, that is, become the society which it changes; and it cannot therefore change itself.*[10]

Mannheim expressed a dialectical relationship with reality where a utopian proposition can achieve a reconciliation on another level of truth, requiring a re-evaluation or redefinition of itself. If it has an effect, it is changed by its acceptance. This proposes a dynamic, evolving condition, rather than a static notion of utopia.

---

4 Ibid.

5 Ibid.

6 Mumford, Lewis, *The Story of Utopias*, Viking Press, New York, 1962: 2.

7 Rowe, Colin, "The Architecture of Utopia", *Granta* 63, Jan 24, 1959: 20-26 41.

8 Mannheim, Karl, *Ideology and Utopia*, Harvest Books, Harcourt Brace and World, New York, 1954: 26.

9 Rowe (1959): 20.

10 Ibid.: 41.

11 Marcus Vitruvius Pollio lived from approximately 80 or 70 BC until 15 AD after Rome's Republican era Servian wall had been built in the early 4th century BC, and well before the Imperial Aurelian wall was built ca. 271–75 AD. He wrote the *Ten Books of Architecture*, 1st c. BC. Marcus Vitruvius Pollio, *Ten Books of Architecture*, Dover Publications, New York, 1960: 31.

12 Ibid.: Book 1, Chap. VI: 6, 7, 12.

13 Vitruvius is credited as having designed at least one military *castrum*.

14 The flat-topped hills projecting as promontories toward the center of the city were characteristic of the 'hills of Rome'. It is a feature that can be still seen here and there on the outskirts of the older city. The long, thin hill formations were useful for making walls along their sides and making settlements with linear streets in their valleys or on their tops.

15 This, of course, is reinforced by the well-known saying, 'All roads lead to Rome'.

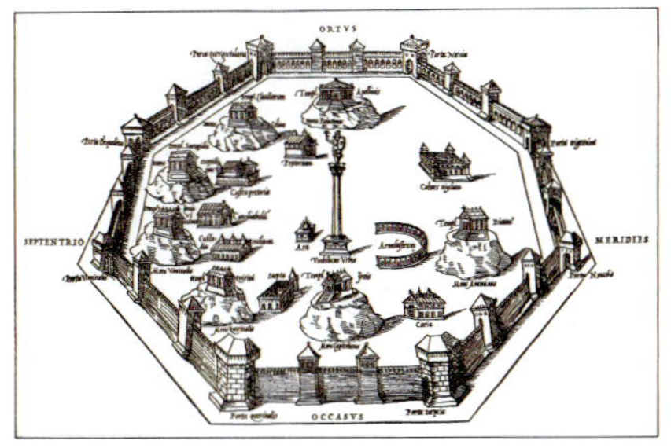

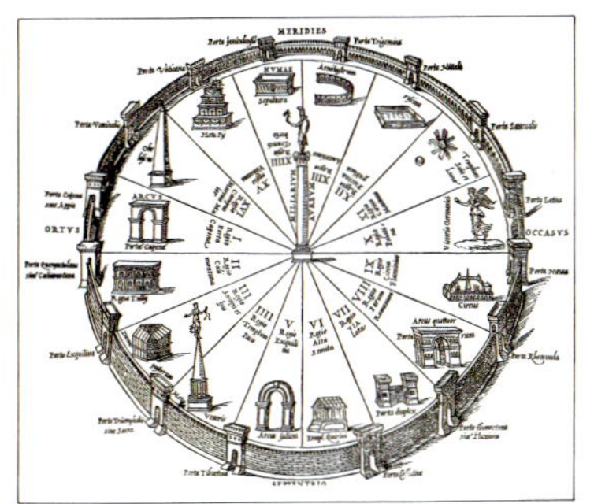

Vitruvius

Vitruvius wrote *The Ten Books of Architecture*, dedicated to the emperor Augustus.[11] In discussing the making of a city,[12] he described an ideal radio-concentric organization (*frontispiece* and Fig. 1, 2), a form that seems to have been outside his direct experience as an engineer-architect. Grid forms dominated cities within the Roman Empire. These cities followed Greek and Etruscan patterns, as did their military new towns or *castra*. Vitruvius had served in Julius Caesar's army as a military engineer, and as such he surely knew these examples.[13] The question arises: What might have inspired Vitruvius, a practical author writing a pragmatic book, to describe a radio-concentric city unrelated to existing practice?

In thinking about how best to make a city, Vitruvius could very likely have thought about Rome as it was conceived in late medieval maps (Fig. 3), imagining it as an imperfect version of an ideal radio-concentric form that is suggested by the topography, the famous 'Seven Hills' or promontories that radiate from the focal area of the Republican Forum.[14] Similarly, the consular roads and even local roads followed the topography as they too radiate out from the forum zone through the valleys and along ridges of the hills. The Rome Vitruvius knew was enclosed by the 4th century BC Servian wall, which had expanded the earliest wall circuit on the Palatine Hill, the *Roma Quadrata*, in a roughly concentric fashion. The Imperial Aurelian Wall had not yet been built as it was only realized ca. 173 AD but possibly it was already imagined. All 'encircled' the city of Rome as it evolved from its core outward (Fig. 4). The city of Rome could be seen, then, as a microcosm of its vast empire in which 'all roads' lead to an undisputed center.[15]

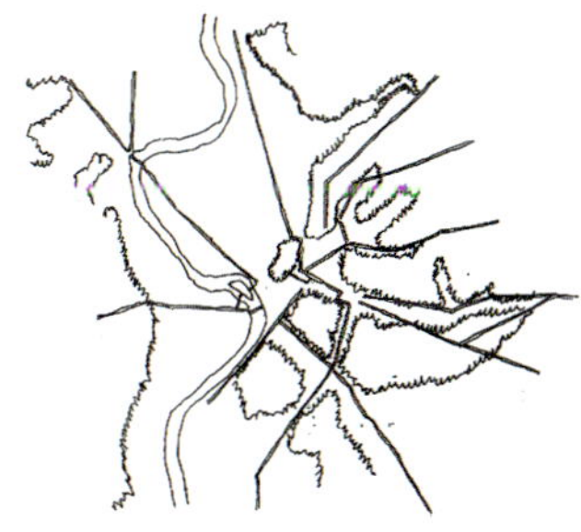

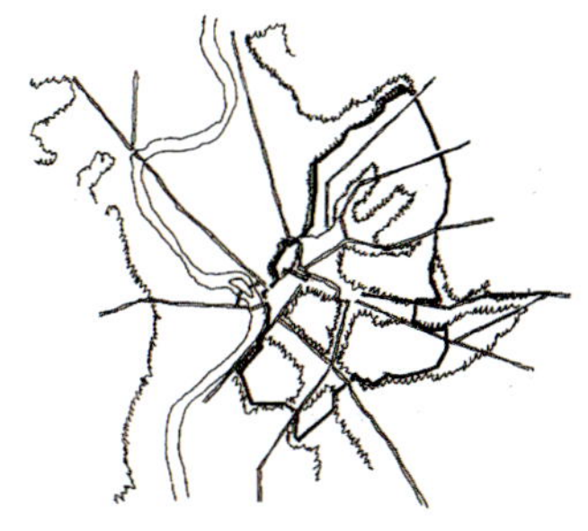

It seems plausible therefore, that based on his direct experience of Rome, Vitruvius thought of the ideal city as a real but imperfect version of an ideal form found in Rome. From this observation he could have derived a perfect model from it leading to his proposition of a radio-concentric ideal city. One aspect of making my analytic diagrams for this study has been to investigate, construct, and possibly assert the dialectic between Rome the *ideal* and Rome the *real,* both at the city scale and its subcenters. This is my starting point in the examination that follows.

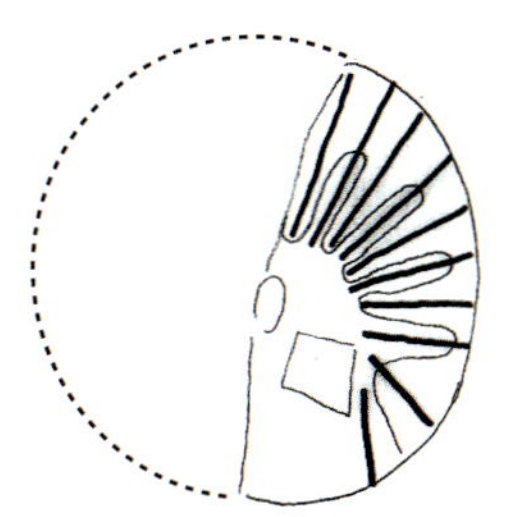

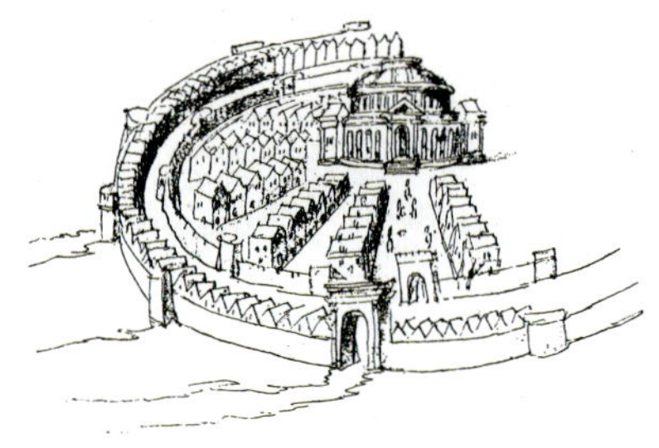
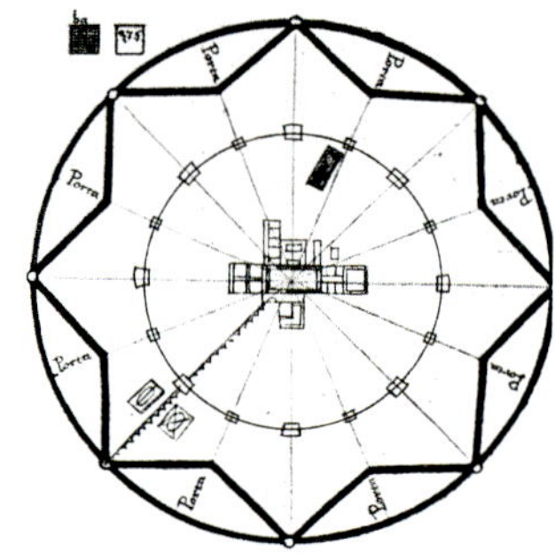
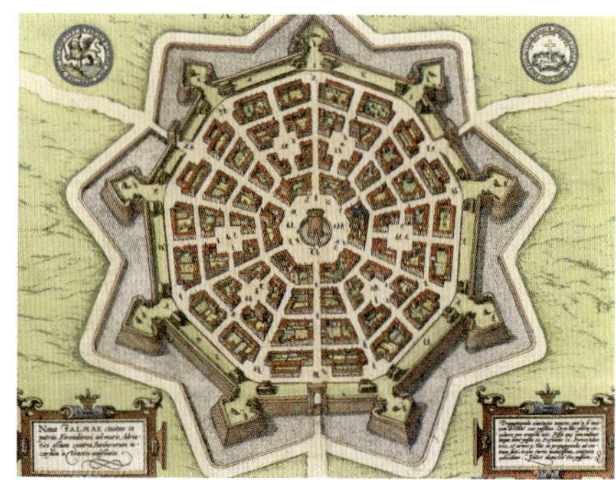
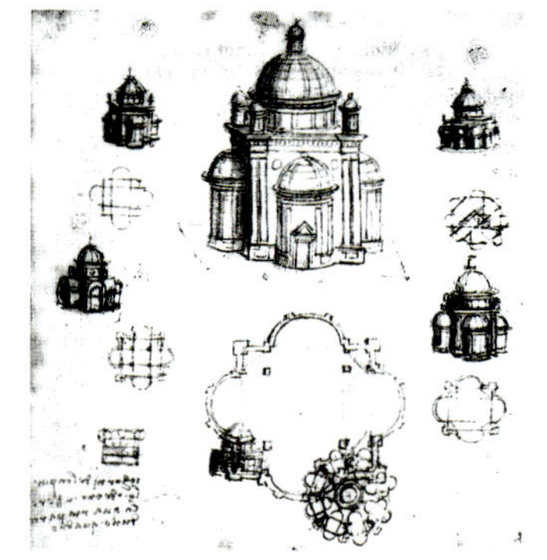

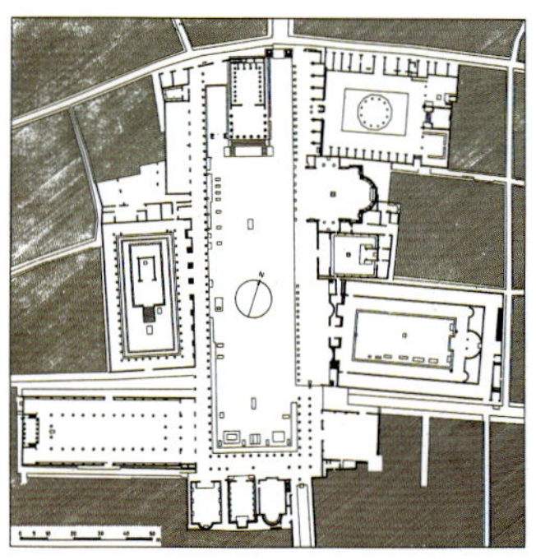
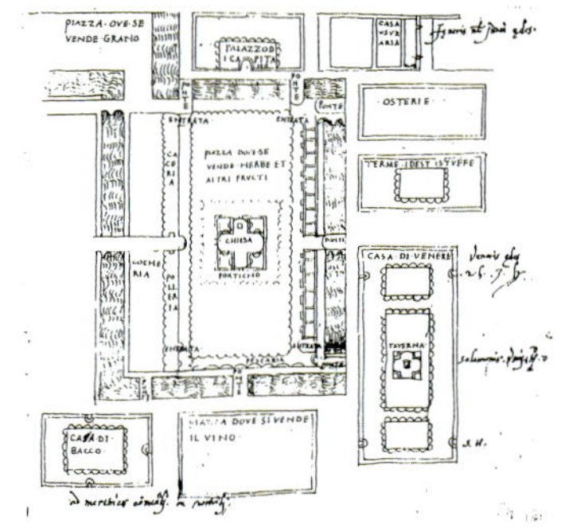

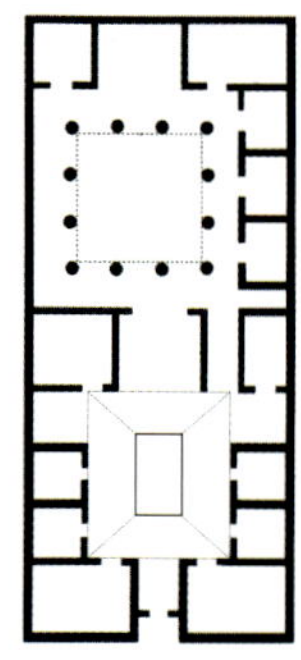
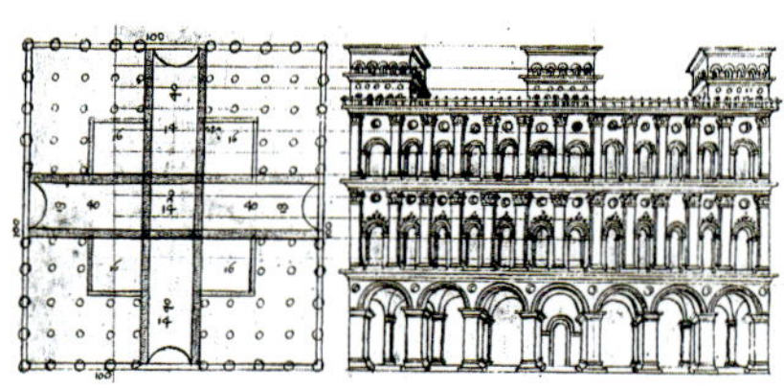
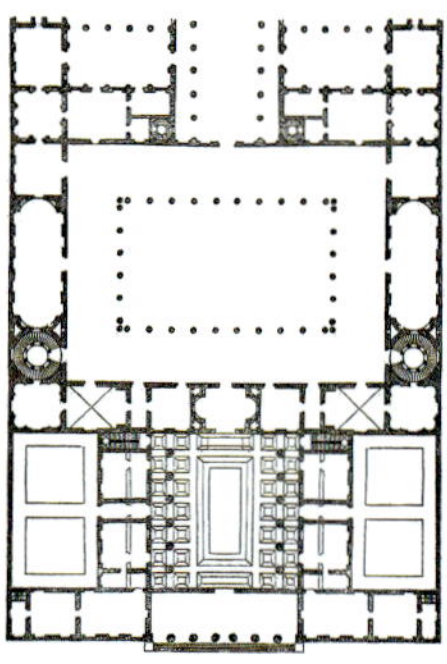

Fig. 5. Ideal City, Fra Giocondo, 1511.

Fig. 6. Sforzinda, Filarete, 1457–64.

Fig. 7. Palmanova, Vincenzo Scamozzi, 1593.

Fig. 8. Centralized plan church studies, Leonardo da Vinci, ca. 1487.

Fig. 9. Santa Maria della Consolazione, Todi, begun 1508.

Fig. 10. San Pietro proposal by Michelangelo, fresco, Vatican Library, ca. 1560.

Fig. 11. Forum at Pompeii.

Fig. 12. Piazza Centrale, Sforzinda, Filarete.

Fig. 13. Piazza del Popolo, Faenza, archival photo.

Fig. 14. Diagram of a house based on Vitruvius.

Fig. 15. Palazzo at Sforzinda, Filarete, ca. 1460.

Fig. 16. 'House of the Ancients', Palladio, 1540.

Fig. 17. Ideal City, School of Piero della Francesca, Urbino, ca. 1480.

The Ideal City of the Renaissance

The ideal city of the Renaissance is made of ideal elements, shown in the Urbino panel as a piazza defined by palazzi with a free-standing circular church as an object in the center (Fig. 17). The ideal city and its early Renaissance interpretations[16] were typically represented abstractly as a centrally planned composition with radiating streets emanating from the center (Fig. 5–7). Beyond this basic diagram, street geometries, blocks, and intersections usually appear. Some plans show not only a primary piazza, church, and palazzi at the center but also secondary events shown as nodes articulated at street intersections.

The ideal Renaissance church is the best-known example of a Renaissance ideal building type (Fig. 8–10). Some combination of a hierarchic system of cross-arms and chapels are arranged around a central vertical space that rises to a dome, symbol of heaven. It was a form well-known in ancient Rome from the monumental Pantheon to Santa Costanza. In the Renaissance, both Greek cross and circular types enjoyed renewed interest from sketches by Leonardo da Vinci and multiple proposals for the 'new' San Pietro. The centrally planned church was imagined as a microcosm of the city and the cosmos.

The ideal Renaissance piazza might logically be thought of as a perfect square, but in practice it was realized as a rectangular space with well-defined longitudinal proportions (Fig. 11–13). Vitruvius described the forum in these terms and this seems to have guided Renaissance practice. The longitudinal shape with covered arcades on its sides also appears in numerous medieval cities and afforded another readily available model. The form is adopted by Filarete as both central piazza and marketplace for Sforzinda. In Rome, it appears in the Piazza della Cancelleria, the Piazza Navona, and the pre-Valadier Piazza del Popolo.

The ideal Renaissance palazzo originates in the Greco-Roman world. As described by Vitruvius, the Roman house, or *domus,* is a rectangular building formed around one or more courtyards, arranged axially and bilaterally symmetric (Fig. 14–16). We see the aspiration to this form in the slightly irregular *domus* plans at Pompeii. Similarly, Renaissance and Baroque palazzi grow vertically while still maintaining their rectangular geometry, axiality, bilateral symmetry, and colonnaded circulation around courtyards. The ideal palazzo consists of an entrance hall, or *androne*, a paved courtyard, or *cortile*, and, if space was available, a second 'green' courtyard, or *peristyle*. Palazzo Medici and Palazzo Strozzi in Florence, and the Palazzi Farnese, Borghese, Barberini, etc. in Rome, exhibit aspects of this ideality, as does Palladio's reconstruction of an "ancient house", shown when he cites Vitruvius.

16 Palmanova was built in the late 16th century by Vincenzo Scamozzi based on early Renaissance models.

Fig. 18. *Pianta di Roma,* Giambattista Nolli, 1748, after Leonardo Bufalini, 1551.

Renaissance and Baroque Rome

During the Middle Ages, Rome had shrunk to the size of a village of less than 20,000 people. The inhabitants lived primarily in the ancient Campo Marzio, referred to as the *abitato,* the area at the bend of the Tevere with the only fresh water source being the Acqua Vergine (later designed as the Trevi Fountain) (Fig. 18). With the return of the papacy from Avignon, an extraordinary program began for rebuilding the city. It was initiated by Nicholas V (1447–55) and extended from the early years of the Renaissance through the papacy of Sixtus V (1585–90) and the Baroque period.

As noted, Renaissance architects imagined the ideal cities as a radio-concentric plan with their focal point featuring an ideal church in an ideal piazza at the center further formed by ideal palazzi. There is evidence that the papal rebuilding projects for Rome referenced the radio-concentric ideal city. Their interventions transformed the medieval fabric in the Campo Marzio toward an ideal city image by insinuating, rather than imposing or destroying, the existing fabric (Fig. 19). Developing radial and concentric elements pulled the primary church, San Pietro, which was located across the Tevere at the edge of the city, into the composition, making it conceptually, if not literally, the central focus of the city. San Pietro was connected to the *abitato,* via a visual axis to the Castel Sant'Angelo, from where it crossed the Ponte Sant'Angelo to the Piazza di Ponte, where a trident of streets continued into the dense center of the medieval city. These trident

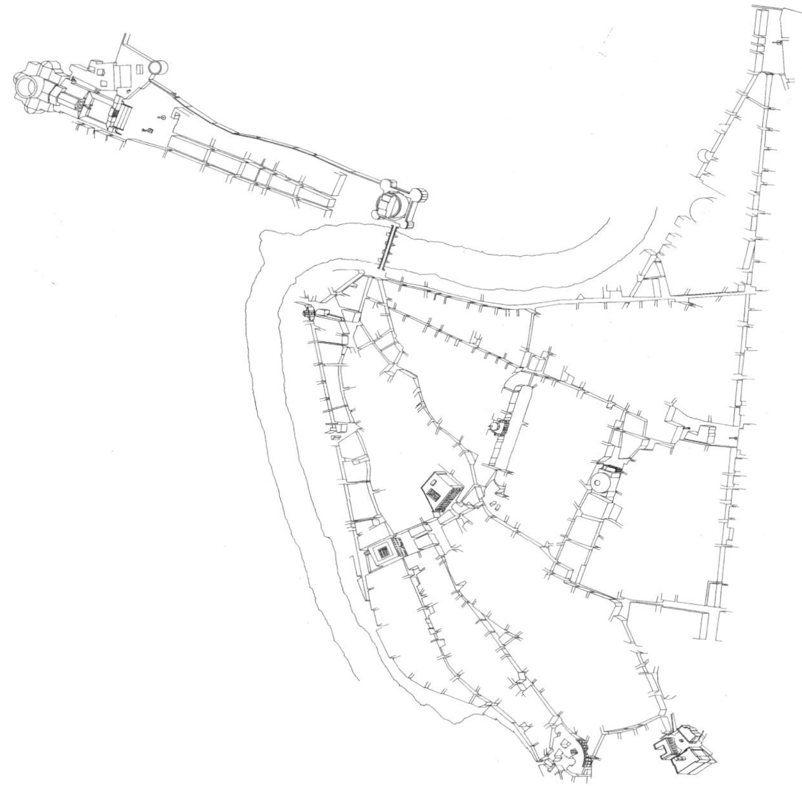

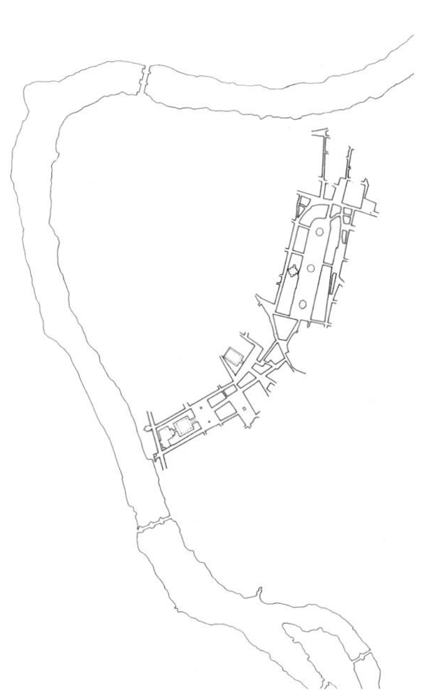

left to right:

Fig. 19. Radio-concentric diagram of the Campo Marzio.

Fig. 20. Concentric diagram of the Campo Marzio.

streets connected various routes of pilgrimage, pageantry, and procession. The most significant of these is the Via Papalis (Via del Governo Vecchio), which sponsored the ceremonial papal procession, or *il Possesso,* from San Pietro and the Vatican to San Giovanni in Laterano. In addition, the Via Peregrinorum (Via del Pellegrino) connected the Piazza di Ponte with the Campidoglio, while the Via dei Banchi Vecchi, continued as the Via di Monserrato, also connected to the Campidoglio. The Via Giulia by Bramante also connected the Piazza di Ponte with the Forum Boarium. The ancient Via Recta (Via dei Coronari) further connected to significant monuments and places in the urban fabric to the east.

In the Renaissance, important families built their palazzi in association with piazze along these routes. These nodes included the Piazza Farnese, Campo de'Fiori, Piazza della Cancelleria, Piazza Navona, and Piazza Sant'Apollinare. Together they created a concentric, arcing sequence of spaces, the center of the arc focusing on the Piazza di Ponte and conceptually, by extension, on San Pietro (Fig. 20). The palazzi associated with these spaces include Palazzo Farnese for Cardinal Alessandro Farnese, later Pope Paul III, Palazzo Cancelleria for Cardinal Raffaele Riario, Palazzo Massimo alle Colonne for its ancient family, Palazzo Pamphilj in Piazza Navona for Pope Innocent X, and Palazzo Altemps for Girolamo Riario at Piazza Sant'Apollinare.

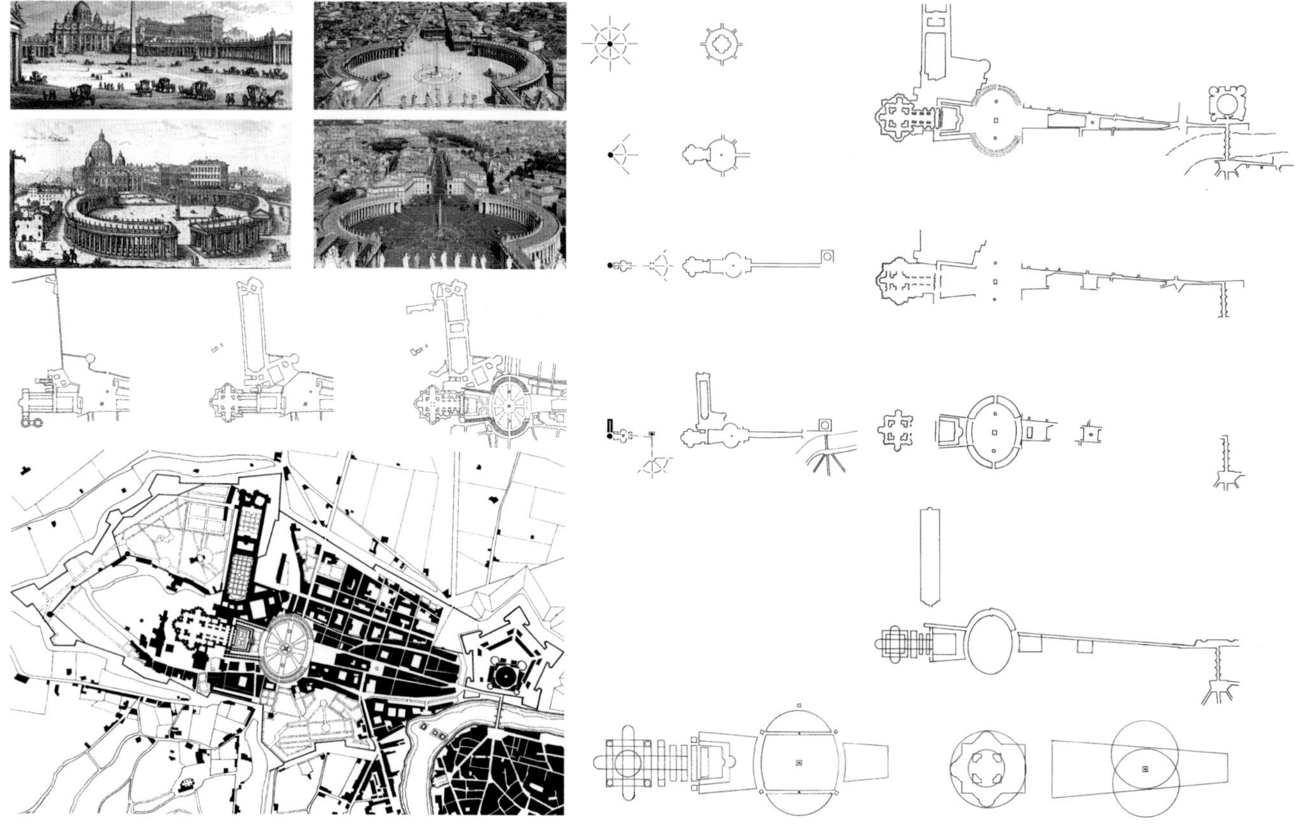

San Pietro – Piazza San Pietro – Ponte Sant'Angelo – Piazza di Ponte

Fig. 21. San Pietro and the Vatican.

San Pietro is the primary church of Christendom and Rome as it is recognized as the tomb of the first pope, Saint Peter.[17] If San Pietro were imagined to be the primary church in an ideal city, it would be central to it: an ideal church form in a central piazza from which streets would radiate to a circular or regular polygonal perimeter, passing through successive concentric streets. Numerous plans by architects from Bramante to Michelangelo proposed a 'temple' at St. Peter's tomb, each imagined as an idealized centralized church; and both Bramante and Michelangelo proposed an ideal piazza surrounding it. Actually, on the edge of Rome, San Pietro nonetheless had become its symbolic center during the Renaissance. Consequently, numerous architects, spanning nearly 500 years and many styles, modified both San Pietro and Rome to make the high altar and its dome seem to be, conceptually, the center of the city. A linear, axial sequence beginning at the altar of San Pietro was extended into, and eventually through, the Campo Marzio over a 500-year span.

Carlo Maderno added a longitudinal nave to San Pietro reinstating the extent of the Early Christian basilica while also acceding to liturgical mandates. Bernini's Piazza San Pietro, which followed this program, is a critical urban spatial element in a sequence, linking his *cathedra* and *baldacchino* inside the church with an axis and promenade outside the church that connects to the city. The design of the piazza overlaps a trapezoid with an oval. At the face of San Pietro, the trapezoidal space widens, featuring broad ramped steps descending a hill. Viewed from

17 Bramante's Tempietto on the Janiculum is sited based on what was believed to have been the place of St. Peter's martyrdom.

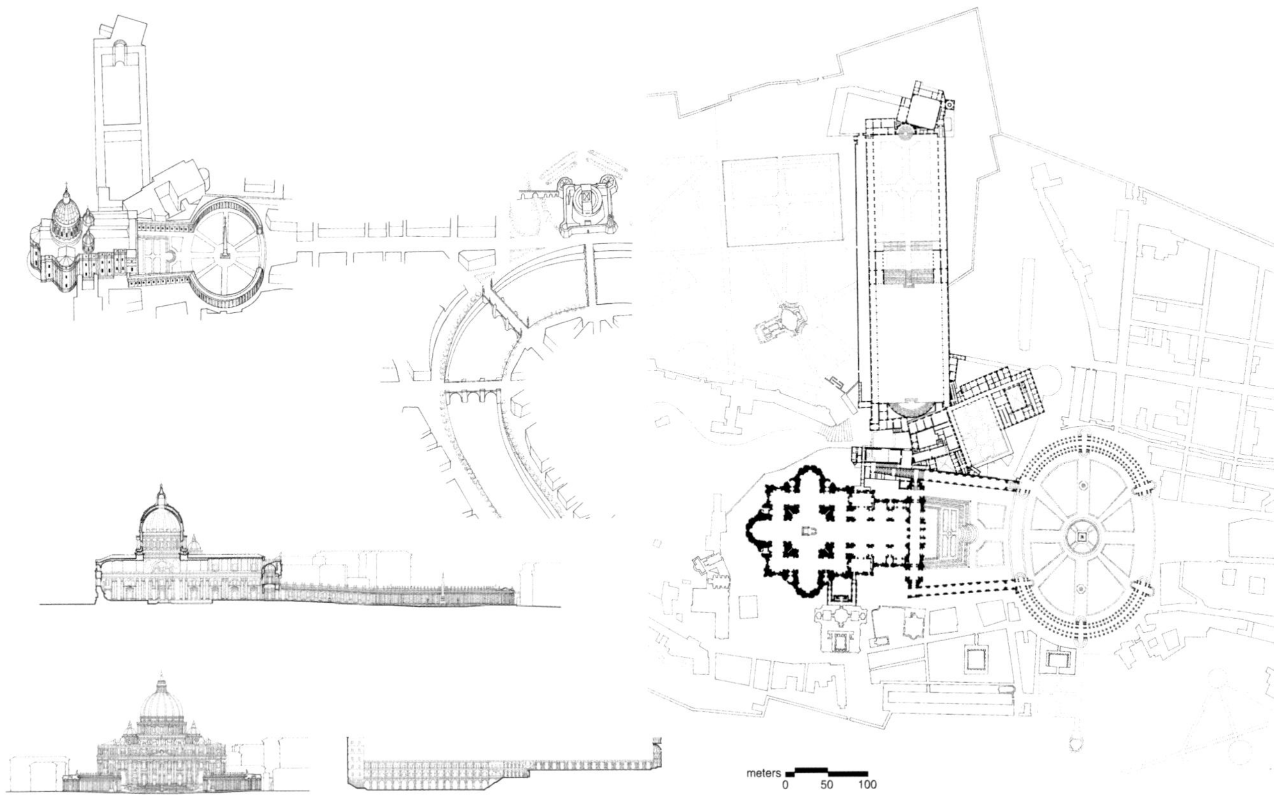

Fig. 22. San Pietro, details.

the foot of the steps the resulting space thereby creates a false perspective effect bringing the church closer to the observer. At the narrow end of the trapezoid, the flanking arms open to the oval Piazza San Pietro. Bernini's design consists of an oval design of two circular colonnades, focused on paired fountains and an obelisk.[18] The colonnades were intended to represent Saint Peter's arms embracing pilgrims in the piazza. The open side of the oval permitted the spatial sequence to continue to the Castel Sant'Angelo by way of the straight Via Borgo Novo created by Pope Alexander IV. Turning back to San Pietro, this street aligned with a tower-portal that Bernini replaced with one of the trapezoidal arms. A monumental stair, the *scala regia*, ascends to the *Cappella Sistina*, which served as the formal Vatican entry vestibule: an honorific space that acts as an interface between the public piazza and church and the private Vatican residences.

The piazza takes into account the existing context of Vatican buildings, the obelisk erected by Sixtus V, and the orientation of the Via Borgo Novo that aligns the *scala regia* Vatican entrance with the space in front of the Castel Sant'Angelo and the Ponte Sant'Angelo.[19] At the Castel Sant'Angelo, Hadrian's bridge was refurbished as the Ponte Sant'Angelo. The bridge, adorned by Bernini's ten angels which represent the Passion of Christ, provides a crossing to the Piazza di Ponte, or Foro Pontis. From this piazza a trident of streets radiates into the urban fabric of the Campo Marzio with links to important spaces and buildings. *Ponte*, like the honorific *Pontif*, symbolizes a bridge between heaven and earth and thus a critical link in the process of making San Pietro both conceptually and experientially the central focus of Rome.

18 Bernini designed a so-called 'third arm' or *terzo braccio* to enclose the eastern edge of the piazza. It was never built but a space defined by the existing fabric did provide enclosure and complete the sequence. Carlo Rainaldi's 17th century plan for the *spina*, the zone between Via Borgo Novo and Via Borgo Vecchio, was effectively achieved when the area was demolished and the Via della Conciliazione was constructed (1936–50).

19 The Castel Sant'Angelo was formerly Hadrian's mausoleum. It was converted into a fortification in the Middle Ages for the Vatican and was connected by way of the *passetto* or secret escape route embedded in the Leonine walls by order of Pope Alexander IV.

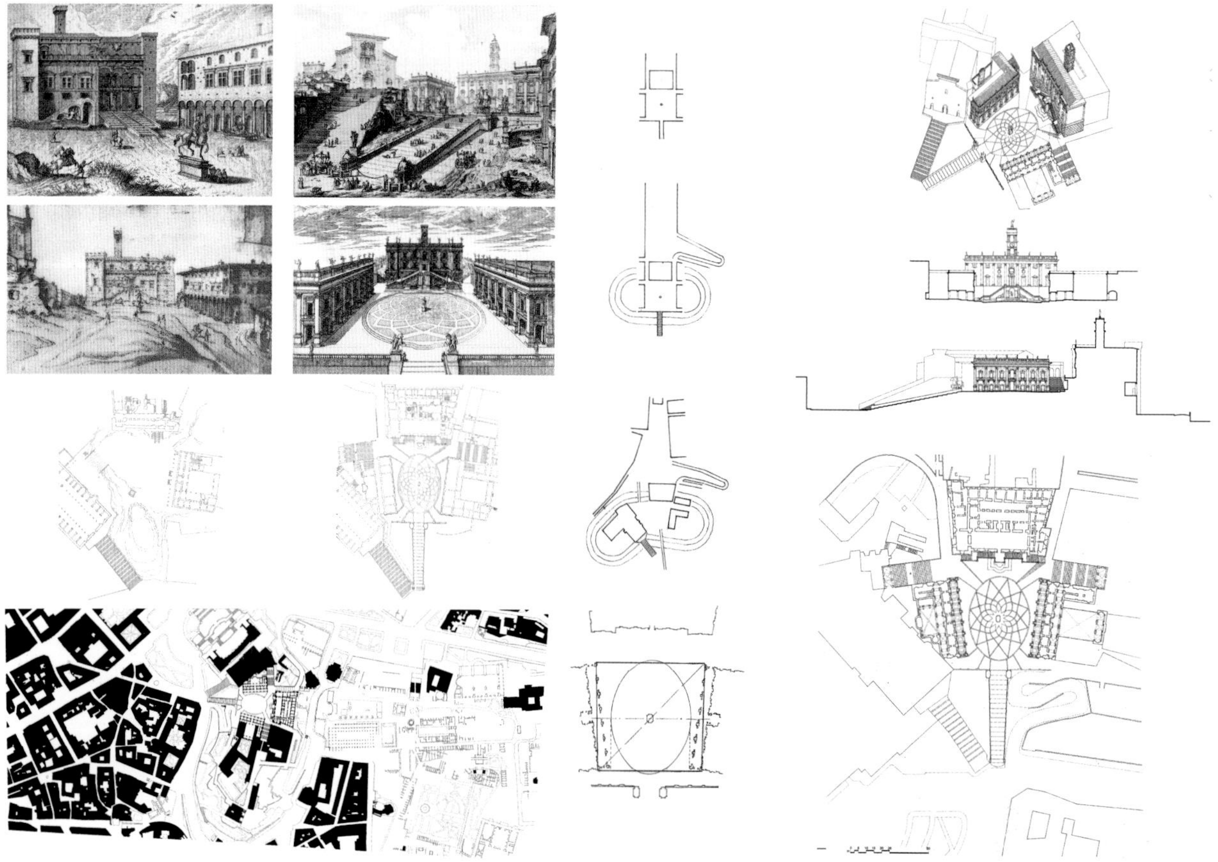

The Campidoglio

Fig. 23. The Campidoglio and environs.

In the Renaissance, the rebirth and revival of learning was built on a belief that ancient Rome was a lesson in perfection. Incorporating the remains of that civilization into the organization of the new city symbolically joined its history and power to further reconcile complex meanings, a discourse on church and state, old and new Rome, connection and disconnection, monumental scale and human scale. The Campidoglio is a paradigmatic example of these principles.

The Campidoglio, or *municipio,* is located on the Capitoline Hill, the acropolis-like center of ancient Rome. In an ideal radio-concentric city, the *municipio,* with its piazza, would be located at the city center along with the primary church. But in Rome, the seat of public governance, the Campidoglio and San Pietro are distant; the Tevere and a broad section of the Campo Marzio standing between them. While symbolically important, during the early Renaissance, the Campidoglio site consisted of a haphazard grouping of three buildings. Its elevated height further separated the *municipio* from the Campo Marzio and from San Pietro.

In the Middle Ages, the ancient Roman *tabularium* on the edge of the hill overlooking the Roman Forum had been converted into the Senatorio or Senator's

20 The 'Senator' was in effect the head secular official or mayor of the city.

21 The symmetrical stairs begin at each of the building's corner projections and ascend over a fountain and statuary of river gods representing the Tevere. The river gods flank Minerva, goddess of Rome, symbol of wisdom, art, trade and strategy. The stairs meet at a projected porch above Minerva, on axis. According to a Dupérac engraving, the porch was originally to have been covered similar in design to the way loggias shelter the entries of the adjacent buildings.

22 This move ensured the practical accessibility and symbolic role of the Campidogio by enabling the papal procession, *il Possesso,* to traverse the Capitoline hill in relative ease.

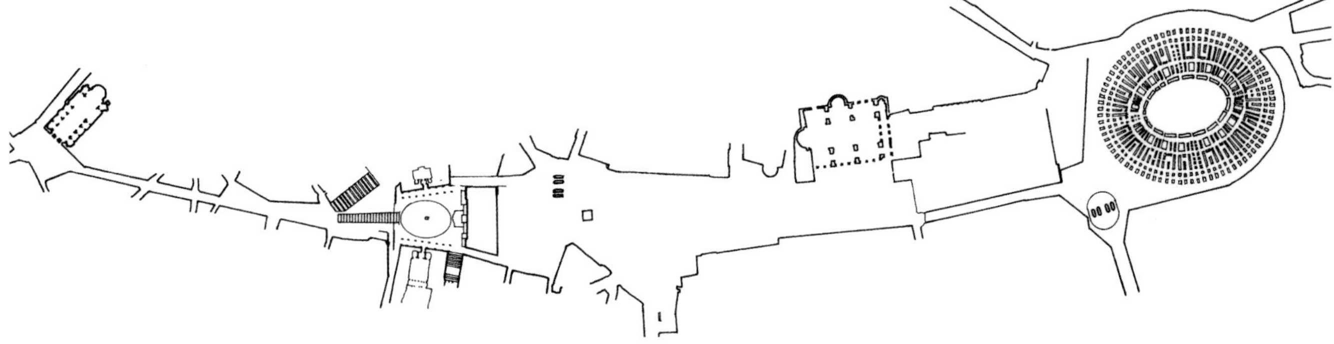

Fig. 24. Passage sequence from Il Gesù, Campidoglio, Via Sacra to the Colosseum.

Palazzo[20], a highly irregular building with a curiously asymmetric facade. Nearly perpendicular to it but slightly skewed was the medieval guild hall, later the Palazzo dei Conservatori. On the opposite side, higher up the hill, the 7th century church of Santa Maria Aracoeli angled away from the Senatorio. It presented a rustic side to the ill-defined space that the three buildings only partially enclosed.

Just as San Pietro and its connections into and through the city were undergoing complex transformations during the Renaissance, the Campidoglio was undergoing a similar metamorphosis. Michelangelo's genius guided it. His axial and symmetrical design for the Campidoglio features a trapezoidal piazza centered on the equestrian statue of Marcus Aurelius. The Senatorio's new symmetrical facade with a grand stair rises above a fountain to its entry porch.[21] Axial symmetry is emphasized by matching colonnaded facades for the refurbished guild building, the Palazzo dei Conservatori, and the Palazzo Nuovo, while the *cordonata*, a perspectival stair-ramp also on axis, descends into the city.[22] From here the axial movement leads down the Via Aracoeli linking it with the Gesù,[23] making this street part of the important radials in the Campo Marzio and an important link between the Campidoglio and the city.[24]

The splayed arms of the composition results in subtle perspectival effects which, in concert with the *cordonata*, seem to bring the distant city closer while at the same time diminishing its apparent height. Thus, from the Campidoglio, overlooking the Campo Marzio toward Castel Sant'Angelo and the dome of San Pietro, the urban space is foreshortened, resulting in a perspectival distortion that symbolically closes the distance between Church and State. The Palazzo dei Conservatori's loggia frames a view in the opposite direction toward the Palatine Hill, while the Palazzo Nuovo's loggia is on axis with the Colosseum. Passing along the Senatorio's flanks, views open on one side across the Foro Romano,[25] Via Sacra, and, on the other side, to the ancient *Roma Quadrata*, the mythical first settlement of the city. The Piazza Campidoglio thus connects *Roma prima* to *Roma seconda.* The sacred hill, dramatized by the *cordonata,* the upward swelling design of the oval paving, as well as the rusticated base and paired stairs to the Senatorio, complete this reading.[26] With the creation of the Campidoglio as *caput mundi,* the papal *Possesso* could practically and metaphorically partake in this mythical, historical, urban narrative.

23 Michelangelo offered to design the Gesù while working on the Campidoglio, but it was designed by Vignola and Giacomo della Porta. The Senatorio, Palazzo dei Conservatori, and Palazzo Nuovo are multi-scalar, displaying both colossal and human scaled elements at the same time. Similar to false perspectives of contrasting scales, old and new statues of varying sizes deliberately disguised one's sense of distance making the far seem near and the near seem far.

24 As part of the choreographed visual sequence starting in the Via Aracoeli, the equestrian statue of Marcus Aurelius, popularly thought to be Constantine, seems to be riding out of the door of the Senatorio.

25 The Roman Forum was called the Campo Vaccino or 'cow field'.

26 Vignola added a cross axis connecting one side of the saddle to the upper site of the ancient Temple of Jupiter on one side and the Arx citadel on the other, now giving entry to the transept of Santa Maria in Aracoeli.

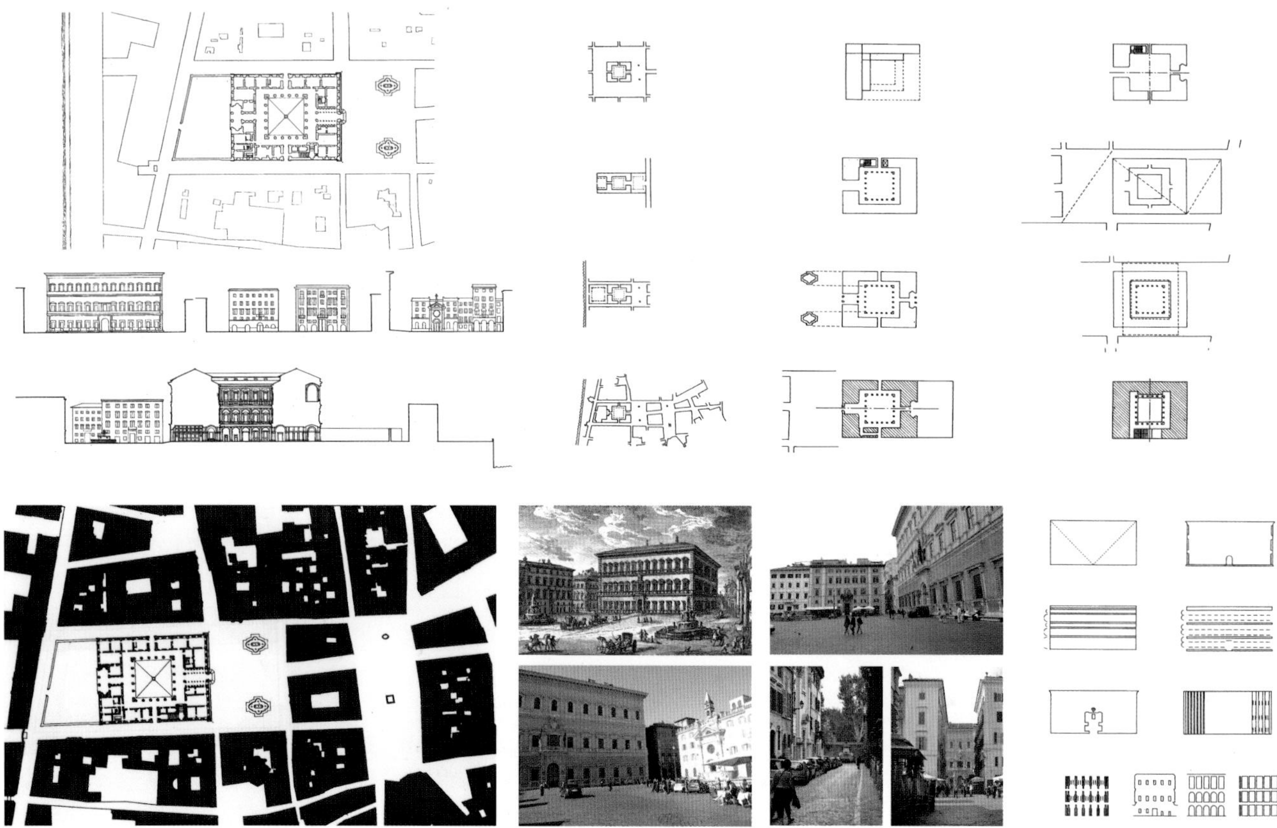

Fig. 25. Piazza and Palazzo Farnese.

Piazza Farnese – Palazzo Farnese

The Palazzo Farnese and its piazza constitute an important subcenter in the larger radio-concentric order of Rome. It acts as a node, an urban event on a continuous street, a radian that connects San Pietro and the Piazza di Ponte to the Capitoline and the ancient Roman Forum.[27] The Farnese palazzo and piazza are one of multiple such nodes in a sequence forming a concentric arc that crosses the Campo Marzio. Generated from the Piazza di Ponte, the arc extends from the Tevere at the Ponte Sisto and the Via Giulia area behind the Palazzo Farnese through the Via dei Baullari and the Piazza Navona to the Via dei Coronari. Numerous major palazzi and related piazze make other nodes where radial streets intersect, or nearly intersect, piazze in this general sequence.[28]

Vitruvius described the Greek house with its forecourt, atrium–*cortile*, and *peristyle* court–*giardino* as an ideal house-type. It is similar in concept to many distinguished Renaissance palazzi interpreted as grand Vitruvian 'houses' which included a piazza-forecourt as civic public space. During the Renaissance, the Palazzo Farnese and its piazza were interpreted as a realization of the Vitruvian ideal. The palazzo is a rectangular block which faces its piazza-forecourt as a civic public space. Inside the building mass is a perfect square *cortile* followed on axis with a *giardino* reflecting the Vitruvian model. The Palazzo Farnese has a double reading: that of an object in space standing between the Tevere and the Via Giulia on one side and as a 'wall-facade' defining the Piazza Farnese. The resultant design adds a private/public complexity into the urban sequence.

27 This radian begins at the Piazza di Ponte and continues through the streets of the Via dei Banchi Vecchi, Via Giulia, and Via Monserrato. The Palazzo Farnese connects to the Tevere, the Teatro di Marcello, and the Forum Boarium.

28 Some of the major piazze and palazzi comprised in this concentric arc from south to north and beginning at Palazzo Farnese include the Campo de'Fiori, Piazza Pollarola, Piazza and Palazzo della Cancelleria, Piazza Navona and Palazzo Pamphilj, Piazza Sant'Apollinare, and Palazzo Altemps at Via dei Coronari.

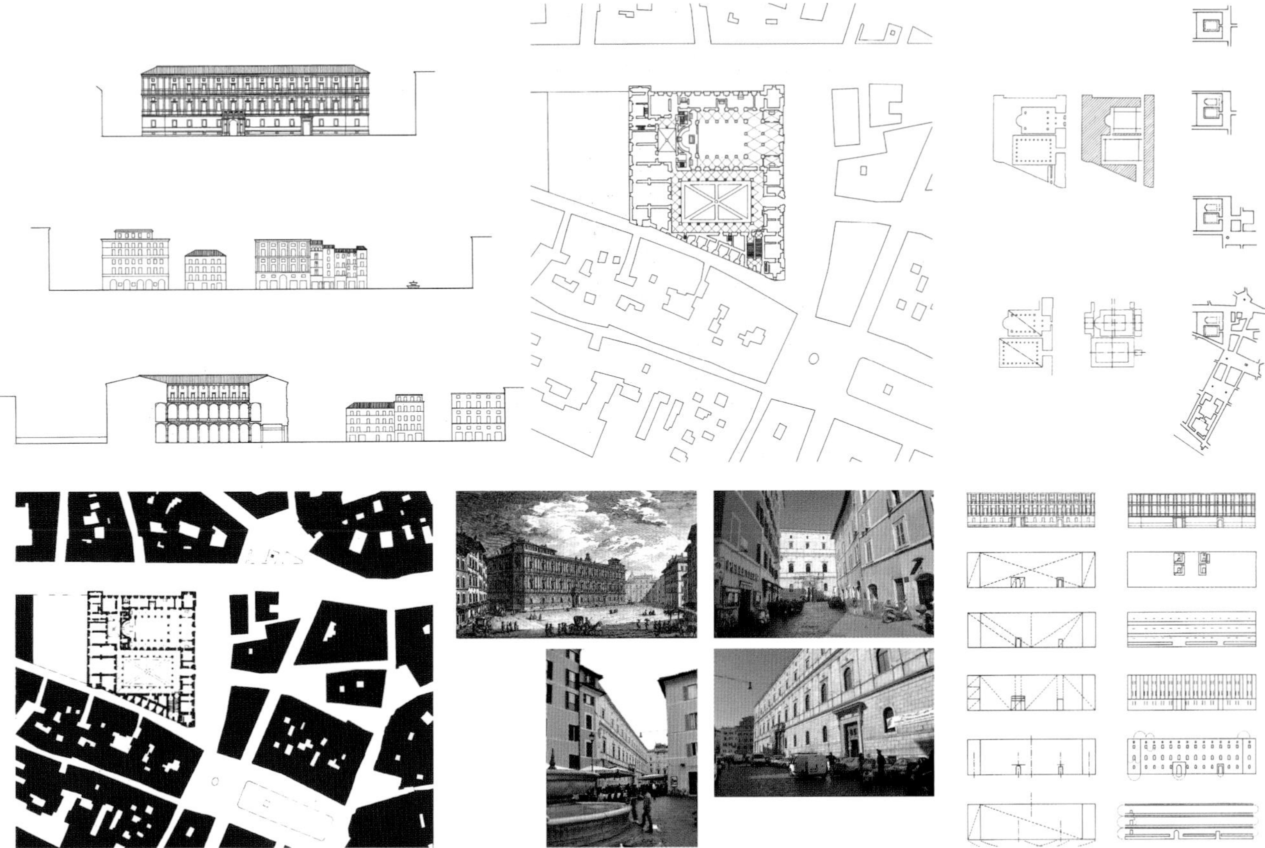

Piazza della Cancelleria – Palazzo della Cancelleria

Fig. 26. Piazza and Palazzo della Cancelleria.

Similar to its neighbor, the Palazzo Farnese, the Palazzo della Cancelleria and its piazza could be interpreted as a building and space in the radio-concentric order of the ideal city. It is located on the Via del Pellegrino (Via Peregrinorum), a radian described by the Piazza di Ponte through the Campo Marzio to the Campo de'Fiori and Teatro Pompeo, which then continues on to Via Giubbonari and to the Capitoline and Campidoglio. It is one of the events in a concentric sequence between the Piazza Farnese and the Piazza Navona. The main portal and *cortile* of Palazzo della Cancelleria align with Piazza Pollarola intersecting at right angles with Via dei Balluari, which presents a cross axial sequence to Palazzo Farnese to the south.

Palazzo della Cancelleria is a contextually transformed version of the Vitruvian Greek house. The Vitruvian element of forecourt as forum and public space is the Piazza della Cancelleria. The character of the piazza is derived from the continuous white travertine facade wall of the palazzo that extends along the entire west side of the piazza. The facade is about as high as the piazza is wide and is a complex composition using the golden rectangle at several scales, creating a statement of geometric perfection. The *cortile* of the Palazzo Cancelleria is similarly composed of proportioned ratios creating a strong interior-exterior continuity and its contextual relationship to the Piazza Pollarola. The *cortile*, as an open void, is juxtaposed next to an enclosed void of approximately the same size—San Lorenzo in Damaso.[29]

29 San Lorenzo in Damaso has an Early Christian foundation but the church was restructured many times. The fact that it could be retained and encased in a late iteration into the new palazzo is a testament to the versatility of the Renaissance architect to treat a complex program and existing context.

Fig. 27. Piazza Navona.

Piazza Navona – Sant'Agnese

Piazza Navona is a highly visible node in the concentric arc sequence focusing on Piazza di Ponte. The arc includes the piazze Farnese, Cancelleria, Navona, and Sant'Apollinare at the Via dei Coronari and stretches nearly from one part of the Tevere to another. Radians from the Piazza di Ponte intersect with the Piazza Navona. The Via del Governo Vecchio, the Via Papalis, passes the south end of Piazza Navona. This is the primary street of the papal *Possesso*, the coronation route connecting San Pietro with San Giovanni in Laterano. Passing at the north end is Via dei Coronari,[30] which leads to and crosses important streets that lead to Santa Maria del Popolo and Via di Ripetta and, farther eastward, to Santissima Trinità dei Monti and Via Condotti.

The long rectilinear form of Piazza Navona is an example of an adaptive re-use or re-purposed space, attesting to purposeful reinterpretations of an urban form. It has changed from an ancient stadium to a medieval market, then to a Baroque 'theater', and now a modern *passeggiata*. But it also realizes the Vitruvian ideal: a rectangular piazza serving as a forecourt to a major 'house'–Palazzo Pamphilj. And it conceptually fits the ideal Renaissance city construct: a secondary radio-concentric intersection with an ideal piazza, a grand palazzo, and a church fronting the space. Borromini reacted to the rectangular piazza by pushing the undulating facade inward for Sant'Agnese to better reveal the dome. Bernini formalized the center '*spina*' of the ancient running track with the Fontana dei Fiume in the center. Together with Giacomo della Porta's two fountains at the ends of the piazza, one of which Bernini restored and enriched, the fountains created secondary 'places' within the primary 'place'.[31]

30 Via dei Coronari was built atop the ancient Via Recta that led to the column of Marcus Aurelius (now Piazza Colonna).

31 A short, arcaded street is a modern reminder of an axis of the Medici's plan by Sangallo to construct a palazzo with a forecourt between Piazza Navona and their palazzo, now Palazzo Madama. The planned forecourt was never constructed. The existing relationship results in a short street into the piazza and a pin-wheel relationship to Sant'Agnese around the Fontana dei Fiume. From Piazza Navona, a conceptual axis continues through Palazzo Madama to the Piazza della Rotonda and the Pantheon. Directly behind Palazzo Madama is the Via della Scrofa which leads north to Via di Ripetta and Piazza del Popolo.

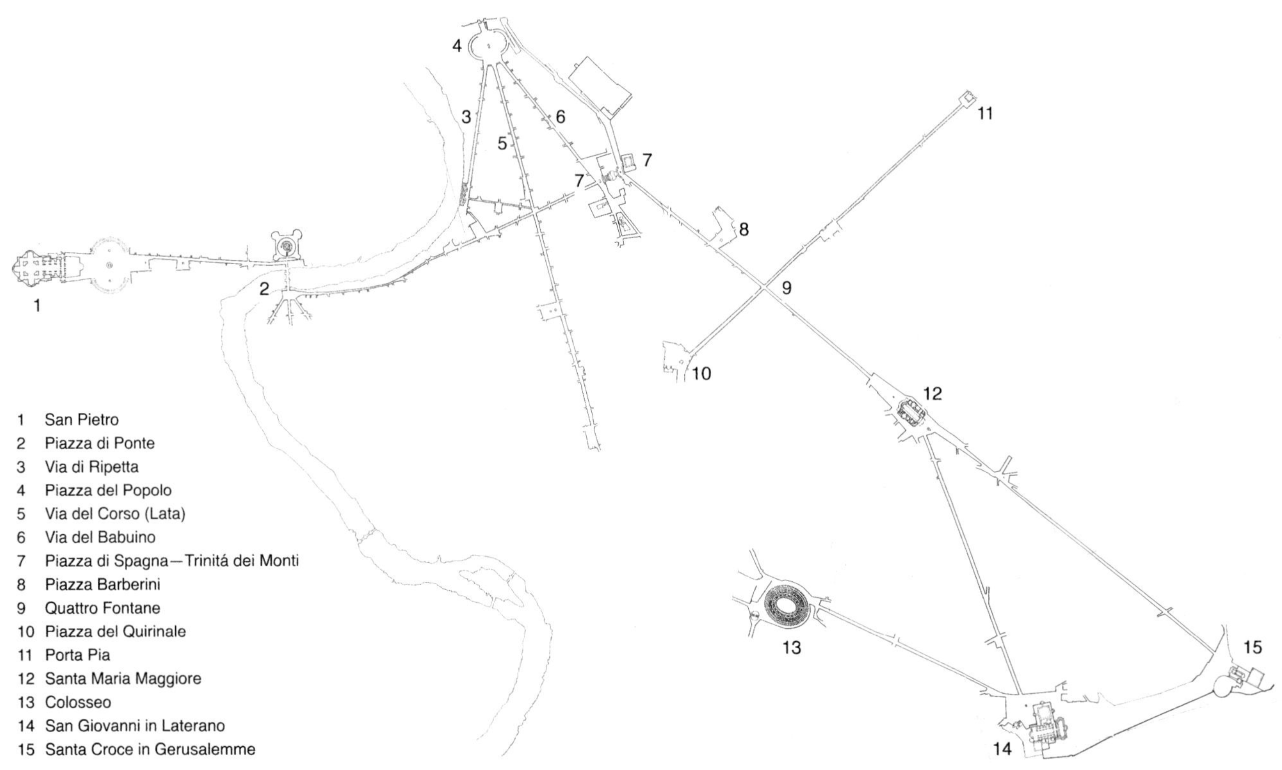

Fig. 28. Key urban interventions and pilgrimage routes in the Vatican, Campo Marzio and the Hills (15th thru 19th century).

Pilgrimage Connections to Early Christian Churches

Early Renaissance restructuring of the Campo Marzio focused on the Piazza di Ponte and San Pietro. Prominent Early Christian churches, however, were located on the periphery of Rome outside the central urban core. But they were eventually connected to the radio-concentric ideal-city ordering concept through subsequent urban interventions, especially by Sixtus V.[32] The location of these Constantinian era churches was dictated by the political imperative of the time requiring Christian spaces to be located outside the Imperial 'pagan' city center. Therefore, these early churches have been purposefully and intentionally oriented away from the center of the ancient city and the Campo Marzio and even remain remote from San Pietro on the opposite side of the Tevere.

With the fall of Rome and the destruction of the aqueducts, the hills had remained undeveloped as they lacked fresh water. In addition to providing new water sources, later Renaissance and Baroque papal urban projects created sequenced connections to these remote but important pilgrimage churches. Sixtus V had several of these churches restructured, providing them with urban piazze. He erected Egyptian obelisks that had been brought to Rome in antiquity and used them as visual markers to emphasize their importance. These papal projects extended radial connections to Santa Maria Maggiore, San Giovanni in Laterano, and Santa Croce in Gerusalemme, linking them together. These radials connect toward the center of Rome and thereby fulfill the expectations of the Renaissance ideal city by serving as secondary urban places and local nodes at intersections of the radio-concentric street system generated from important places in or adjacent to the Campo Marzio, the conceptual center.

32 Connections to the churches of Santa Maria del Popolo and Santissima Trinità dei Monti preceded the work of Pope Sixtus V, who had intended to eventually connect the Seven Pilgrimage Churches: San Pietro, San Giovanni in Laterano, Santa Maria Maggiore, Santa Croce, San Lorenzo, San Sebastiano, and San Paolo, the latter three being *fuori le mura*. Papal projects of this kind as well as other interventions were timed with the *Giubileo* or Jubilee every half century, a practice for urban and architectural projects begun in 1300 by Boniface VIII, now celebrated every quarter century.

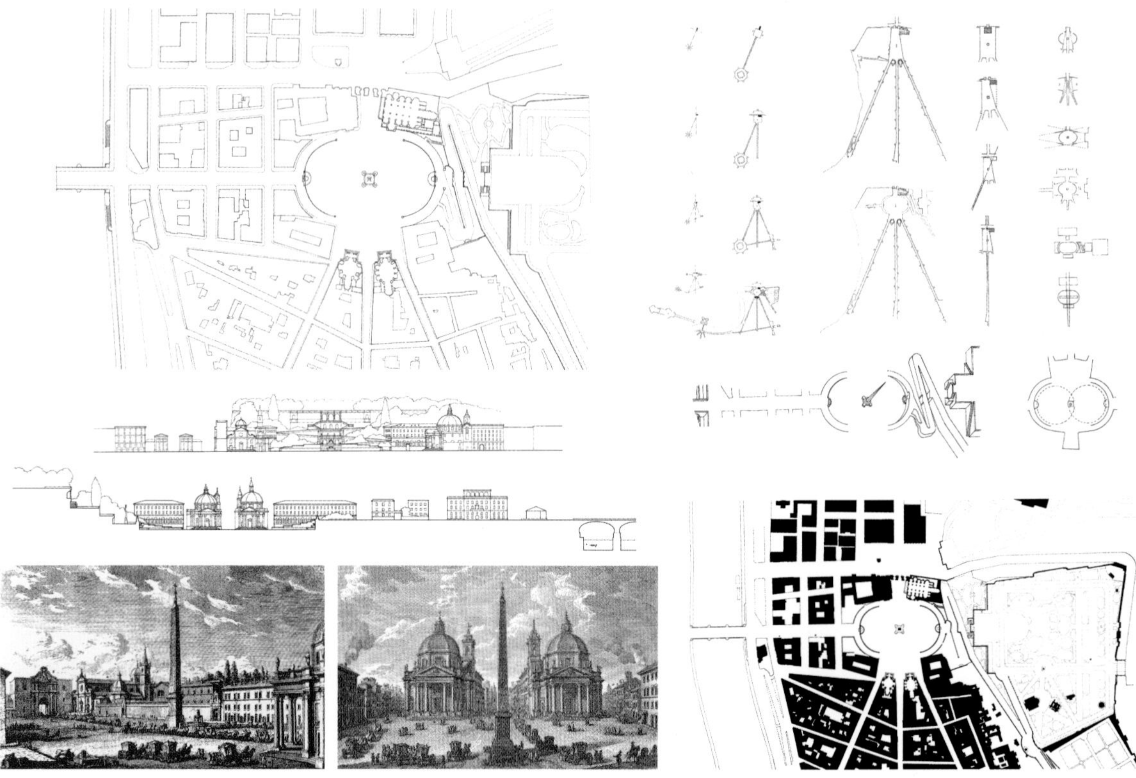

Fig. 29. Piazza del Popolo.

Piazza del Popolo – Santa Maria del Popolo

Piazza Santa Maria del Popolo, its church, city gate, and obelisk mark the traditional arrival point into the city from the north. Located just inside the Aurelian Walls at the end of the ancient Via Flaminia and Corso or Via Lata, the piazza with its trident of streets connects to virtually all the major monuments in the city. The piazza and related structures are therefore a major node in the radial concentric pattern of the city. During the Renaissance, Domenico Fontana created a long, thin, nearly rectangular piazza based on the Vitruvian ideal model.[33] The east side angled in toward Santa Maria del Popolo giving it prominence. He aligned the church facade with Sixtus V's obelisk and the Via di Ripetta. The Baroque twin churches, Santa Maria dei Miracoli and Santa Maria in Montesanto, reinforce the ideal trident: the Via di Ripetta route leading to Piazza di Ponte and San Pietro; the central street, the Via del Corso,[34] connecting to the Capitoline and Roman Forum; the Via del Babuino alongside the Pincian Hill, leading to the Piazza di Spagna and Piazza della Trinità dei Monti; and then to the 'hills' and other pilgrimage churches.

In the early 19th century Giuseppe Valadier created the modern oval piazza and park cascading down the Pincian Hill, making a cross axis aligned with the obelisk.[35] Santa Maria del Popolo lost some of its former prominence in the space, for Valadier's intervention reoriented the directionality of the piazza from north-south to east-west, connecting the Pincian Hill visually to the Tevere and San Pietro.

33 The San Pietro-Vatican connection to Santa Maria del Popolo and S. Trinità dei Monti was initiated by Sixtus IV as part of the restructuring of the Campo Marzio. These works preceded the urban connections by Sixtus V that link the Seven Pilgrimage Churches.

34 Also during the Renaissance, Raphael developed the ancient Via Lata as the Corso connecting the ancient Porta Flaminia and the Via Flaminia to the Capitoline Hill.

35 Valadier had proposed continuing the axis toward the west from the Piazza del Popolo through an urban park to the Tevere.

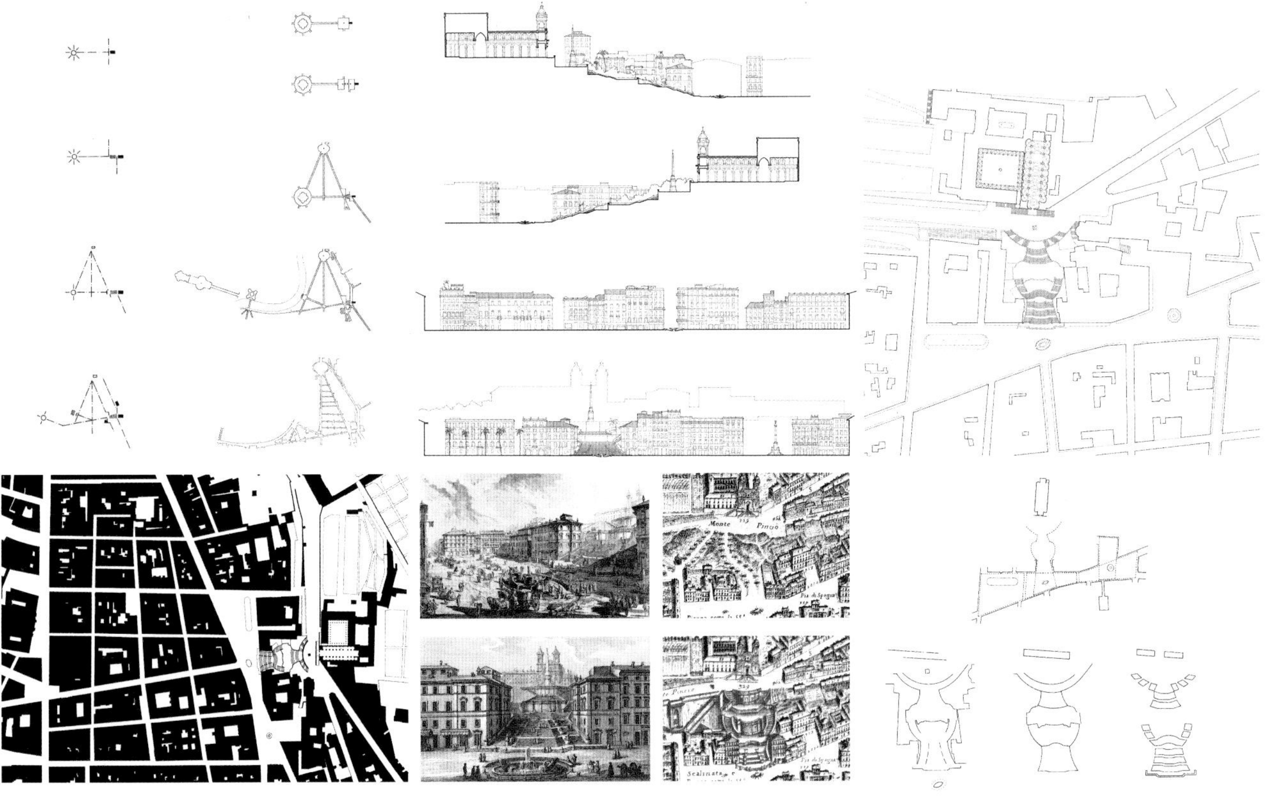

Fig. 30. Scalinata di Spagna.

Piazza di Spagna – Scalinata di Spagna – Santissima Trinità dei Monti

As with the nearby Santa Maria del Popolo, the Piazza di Spagna, Scalinata di Spagna, and Santissima Trinità dei Monti can collectively be thought of as a secondary event in an ideal city located at the intersection of radial and concentric streets. The 'bow tie' shape of the Piazza di Spagna derived from the street grids related to the Corso and the diagonal generated by the Via del Babuino, one of the trident of streets from the Piazza del Popolo that follows the edge of the Pincian Hill.

Providing a continuous route for the faithful, moving from the Piazza del Popolo to the pilgrimage churches beyond, was complicated by the steep hillside. Positioned between the Piazza Trinità dei Monti and Piazza di Spagna below at the level of the Campo Marzio, the Scala di Spagna resolves this by inserting an urban stair. The cascading flight, designed by Francesco de Santis, fluctuates from concave to convex as it rises within a tripartite lateral division, large at the center and small at the sides, creating an architectonic, rhythmic metaphor of 'hill'. The obelisk at the top of the hill is on axis with the Via Condotti which continues to the Via di Ripetta, Piazza di Ponte, and San Pietro.[36]

From the Piazza della Santa Trinità dei Monti, a *passeggiata* leads north along the edge of Pincian Hill to the Villa Medici and formal gardens of Valadier. In the other direction, the Via Sistina leads south down the Pincian slope, continuing the pilgrimage route over the Quirinale Hill to Santa Maria Maggiore on the Esquiline Hill.

36 Alessandro Specchi designed the Porto di Ripetta, which preceded the building of the Scalinata di Spagna by two decades. Both design forms suggest flowing water, one at the river's edge the other at the hillside. They are spatially connected by way of the Via Condotti and the street that leads to the Porto di Ripetta. See the essay in this volume "The Micro-Urbanism of Rome" for further discussion.

Fig. 31. Santa Maria Maggiore.

Santa Maria Maggiore – Piazza Santa Maria Maggiore

In an ideal city plan, Santa Maria Maggiore would be an event in the larger composition with its piazza as a secondary urban center. As bishop of Santa Maria Maggiore, the future Sixtus V had engaged Domenico Fontana to build his Villa Montalto next to the basilica. In his desire to give importance to his favored church, now as Pope Sixtus V, he disentangled the structure from the surrounding urban fabric, conceiving the church as an object in space. Being analogous to a piazza in an ideal city, Santa Maria Maggiore was realized as an object at the center of multiple axes and converging streets.[37]

Via Sistina continues from Santissima Trinità dei Monti to Santa Maria Maggiore, operating as a datum linking three ancient hills and valleys in between. The street axis created by Sixtus V aligns with the obelisk placed in 1587 by his architect, Domenico Fontana, and the central axis of the church, but the church's major entry faced away from the city. The solution by Carlo Rainaldi in the 1670s resolves the problem by treating the rear apse as a frontal facade with paired entries, which access the side aisles of the basilica. He negotiated the hill with an elaborate staircase which mimes the curvature of the apse. In 1614, Paul V continued this urban dialogue by placing a monumental column in the Piazza Santa Maria Maggiore in the front of the basilica. From here the Strada Felice continues to Santa Croce in Gerusalemme while the Via Merulana leads to San Giovanni in Laterano and its obelisk.

37 The site evokes the ideal radiating pattern, treating this secondary node as if it were primary and central. Streets (some no longer extant) emanated to Porta San Lorenzo and San Lorenzo *fuori le mura*; Via Panisperna leading to the Colonna Traiano and the Capitoline hill; the Via Urbana to San Pietro in Vincoli and the Colosseo; and the Via Torino leading to the Piazza S. Bernardo defined by S. Susanna, Santa Maria della Vittoria, and the Acqua Felice.

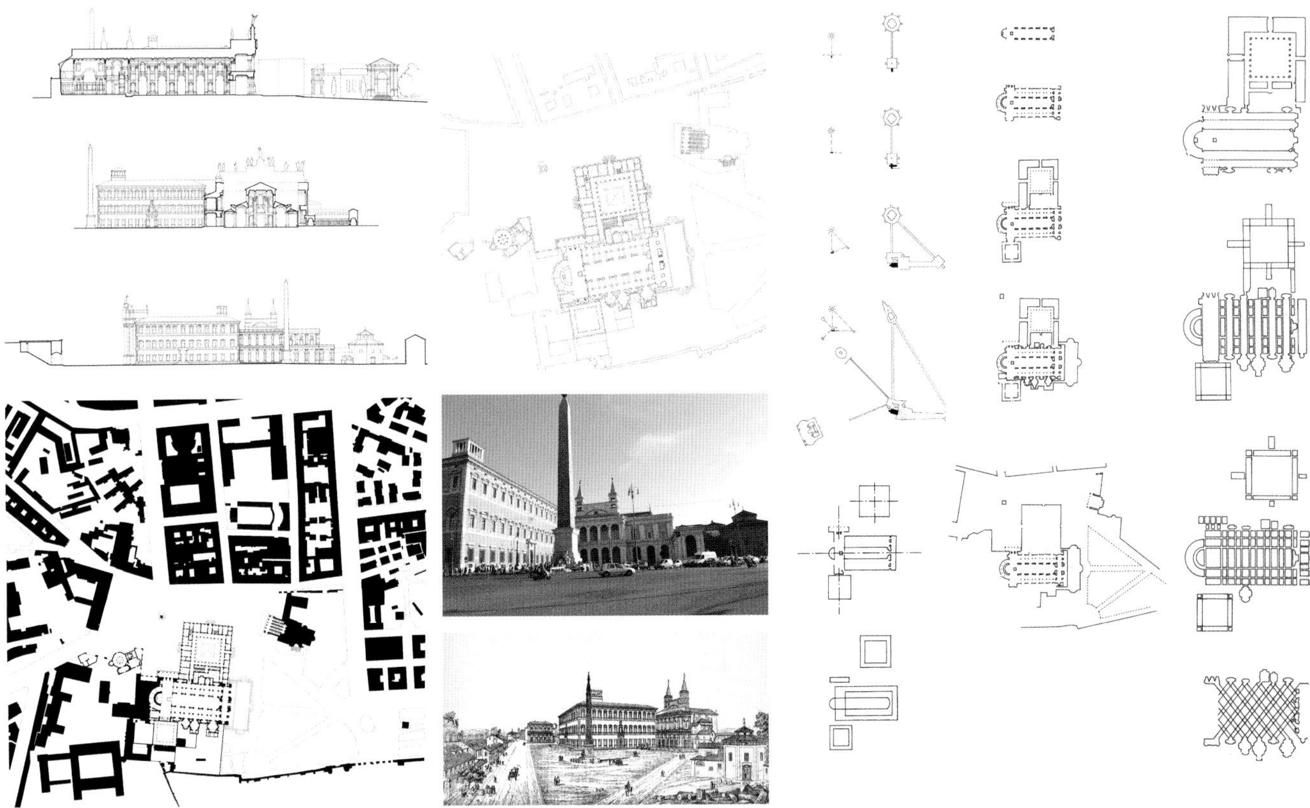

Piazza San Giovanni in Laterano - San Giovanni in Laterano

Fig. 32. San Giovanni in Laterano.

The 4th century basilica of San Giovanni in Laterano was the first of the seven pilgrimage churches to be built; it is designated the First Church of Rome. As a Christian enclave in pagan Rome, it is on the periphery of the city, located adjacent to the Aurelian Walls facing away from the city toward the ancient city gate. As the Cathedral of Rome, San Giovanni was the primary destination of the elaborate *Possesso,* or procession of the popes, from San Pietro in the coronation ritual to take 'possession' of the Lateran, "the mother church of Rome and of the world". Coupled with it being a major pilgrimage destination was Sixtus V's wish to link the church and its two piazze to the city with three radial streets and towering Egyptian obelisk.[38]

The early church presented a dilemma not unlike Santa Maria Maggiore for it included two entrances: the nominal front which aligned with its nave to the east; the other on the north side, with its axis aligned with the transept[39] and facing the city, the latter used as primary entry during the Middle Ages. The dual entries accept the radiating Renaissance streets to connect with other pilgrimage churches: the front toward Santa Croce in Gerusalemme[40] while the 'side' piazza connects with Santa Maria Maggiore. This entrance was given prominence with a benediction loggia and porch by Sixtus V's architect, Domenico Fontana, who further consolidated the piazza by erecting the obelisk and framing it and the entry porch with the Palazzo Pontificio and existing Lateran baptistery refurbished by Borromini.

38 The obelisk, the tallest Egyptian obelisk in the world, was brought to Rome in 357 AD where it stood in the Circus Maximus but collapsed in the 5th century. In 1588, under Sixtus V, it was restored and erected by Domenico Fontana in its current location.

39 The transept cross-axis extends across the nave, concluding in a minor chapel altar and cloister beyond. The main altar and baldacchino are slightly forward of the cross axis, making a closure to the nave and allowing for the visual connection.

40 This piazza is defined by the Scala Santa on one side and Porta San Giovanni and the Aurelian Wall on the other.

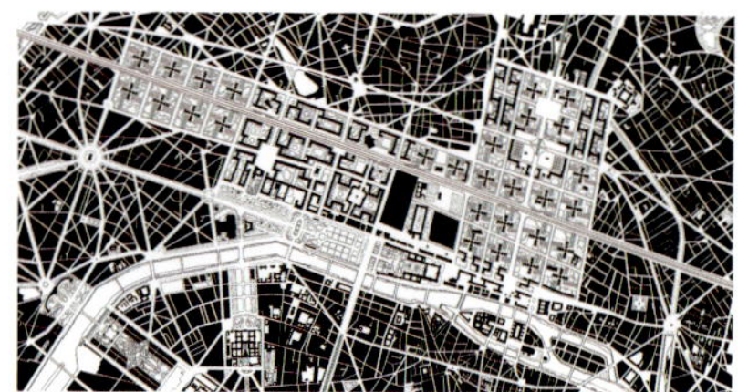

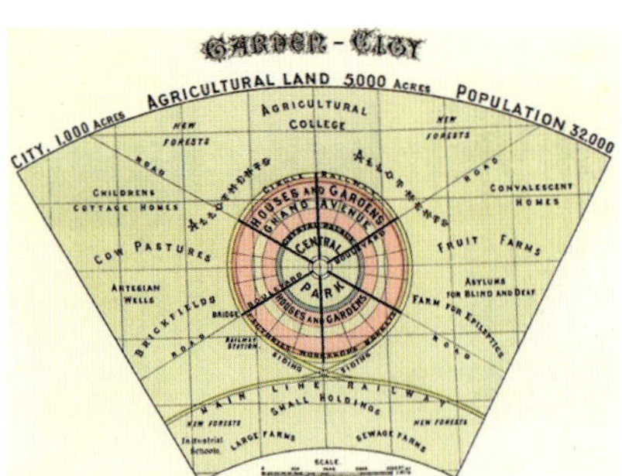

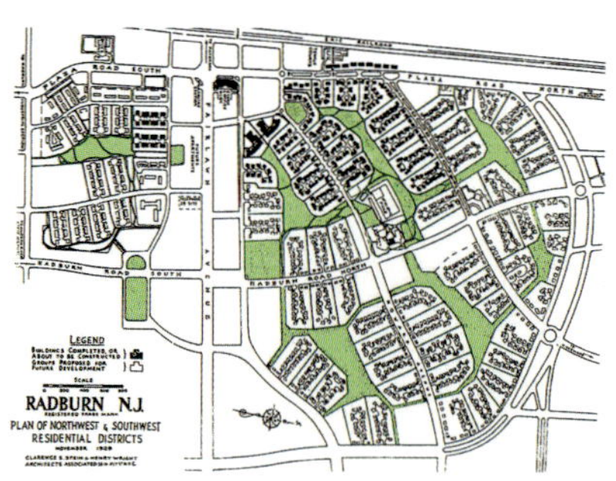

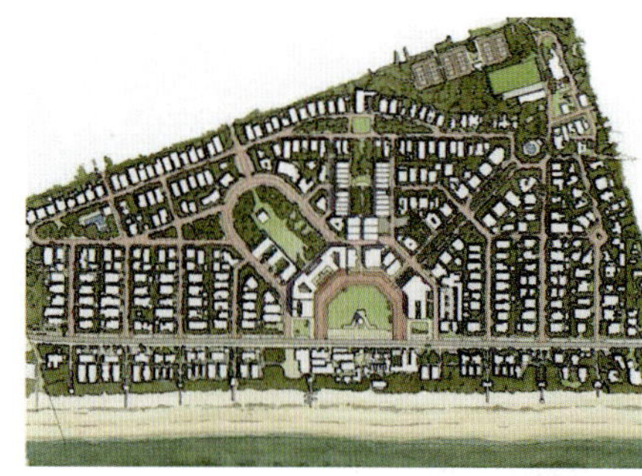

top row left to right:
Fig. 33. Voisin Plan, Paris, Le Corbusier, 1925; drawing by S. Cohen and S. Hurtt.

Fig. 34. Back Bay Urban Renewal Plan, Boston, The Architects Collaborative, 1954.

Fig. 35. Euralile project for Lille France, OMA, 1988.

bottom row left to right:
Fig. 36. Garden Cities of Tomorrow, diagram, Ebenezer Howard, 1902.

Fig. 37. Radburn, "a town for the motor age", Fairlawn NJ, Clarence Stein, Henry Wright & Marjorie Sowell Caultey, 1929.

Fig. 38. Seaside FL, Andrés Duany, Elizabeth Plater-Zyberk, 1985.

Conclusion

The Roman Renaissance and Baroque projects that are illustrated here demonstrate the dialectical idea of *formation* and *transformation.* If one interprets the Renaissance and Baroque utopian proposals as 'diagrams', which were not intended to be built, but rather were meant to "instruct", "civilize", and "edify" the growth, change, and transformation processes in Rome, then the urban events presented can be viewed as dialectical formations—the ideal concept—into transformations to empirical reality. It is argued that these ideas were pursued in Rome and achieved extraordinary results. The premise is that these achievements and methods can inform the urban design of cities today.

These Roman examples demonstrate an approach to remaking the city that is very different from the ideas and theories that have been proposed in the 19th to 21st centuries. This approach was advocated by members of International Congress of Modern Architecture (CIAM), and strongly influenced by Le Corbusier, as evidenced in the 1925 Plan Voisin for Paris (Fig. 33). That idea was to plant a radically new city project into the existing city. This implied the eventual replacement of the historical city with a new city. These projects were made real globally, as exemplified in the clearance and redevelopment projects of the U.S. Federal Urban Renewal program that had deleterious effects on countless American cities (Fig. 34). This form of 'renewal' has continued with deconstuctivist-inspired ideas of the 1980s and '90s and continues to the present day (Fig. 35). On the other hand, the late 19th century proposal by Ebenezer Howard, *Garden Cities of Tomorrow, a Peaceful Path to Real Reform* (Fig. 36), was to replace the existing city on new sites to avoid the problems of the historical city. The subsequent New Town movement, globally as well as in the U.S. (Fig. 37), and much of the early New Urbanism continued this idea (Fig. 38). They essentially imply abandoning the existing city.

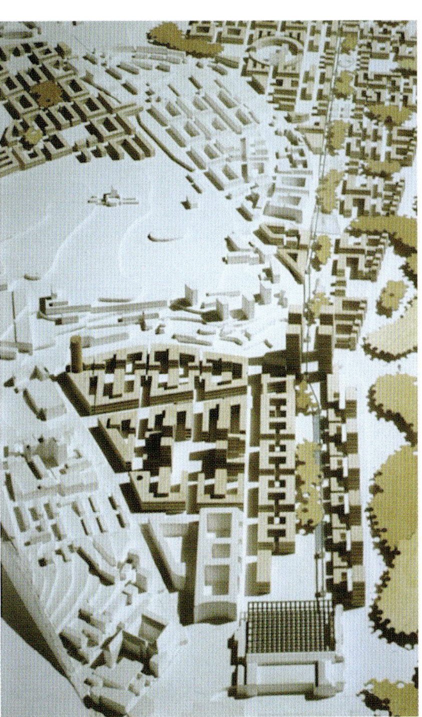

left to right:
Fig. 39. Derby Civic Center, figure/ground before and after, competition entry, James Stirling, 1970.

Fig. 40. Stüttgart Rail Yards plan, figure/ground, and model. Gerkan, Marg and Partners, ca.1995.

But there has been a third alternative view of urbanism. It is exemplified by an approach that promotes adding to the existing city by understanding its underlying structure and insinuating or imposing sympathetic extension and growth. It is an urban design strategy that insists on incremental change by evolution rather than radical change by wholesale destruction. (Fig. 39, 40).

The Renaissance and Baroque city insinuated and, to various degrees, sympathetically imposed the utopian ideas into the existing city of Rome in such a way as to maintain the life and character of the existing while creating a new image of utopia, and thus a new order and meaning. In his early Urban Design Studio at Cornell, Colin Rowe proposed a similar approach and an investigation of how the Modern city might be reconciled with the traditional city, achieving a complex integration of new and old. The lessons illustrated and described here are indebted to Rowe. They exhibit both a way of thinking and a range of strategies by which a more "contextual" architecture and urbanism might be accomplished, without being limited to either historical replication or stark contrast with what exists. This was the basis of Colin Rowe's "Cornell School of Contexualism".

This work is my connection to Colin. It is this aspect of his thinking, what I believe was his progressive side, that resonated with me. I believe that it can continue to 'instruct, civilize, and edify' as I have tried to do in my research, teaching, and practice.

S. Luigi
PANTEON
PIAZZA DI PIETRA
S. Ignazio
PIAZZA DI SCIARRA
S. Marcello
IX

IX Pigna

The Micro-Urbanism of Rome

James T. Tice

Introduction

Although never using the term 'micro-urbanism,' [1] Colin Rowe's teaching in the Cornell Urban Design Studio recognized and engaged this scale of urban design with passion. And it was the *Pianta Grande di Roma* of 1748, by Giambattista Nolli, that served as a wellspring for these ideas. As an antidote to the limits of Modernist architectural practice and theory that favors large scale interventions, micro-urbanism describes a set of ideas, especially manifest in Rome, that treats the small-scale interface and interaction between architecture and city. Fred Koetter referred to this as "the art of the in-between".[2] Micro-urbanism examines the relationship between a building, or group of buildings, and their immediate setting, including the constructed space of streets, squares, courtyards, and curated landscapes. As an urban design strategy, it favors a dialectical approach that addresses the inevitable contradictions and complex relationships of the city and its architecture. It attempts to address the competing forces of an existing empirical reality and the notion of ideal type. It posits how a resolution between the two could be achieved through a process of accommodation and transformation. Beyond being a useful design tool and frame of reference for historical studies, it has proven to be an effective instrument for articulating contemporary urban design principles—all revealed in hundreds of small-scale urban interventions in Rome—*micro-utopias*—each one a perfect fragment within an imperfect whole.

Rowe's interest in Rome and the Nolli map sparked my own interest, particularly at the "in-between" scale of city and building, for nowhere does this twin phenomenon appear with such regularity and stunning brilliance as it does in the city of Rome.[3] This interest has led to an extended study of the graphic and cartographic means by which Rome has been recorded over the millennia and how these techniques contribute to our understanding of Roman urbanism. These methods include a) cartography, which has a rich 2,000-year tradition in Rome; b) *vedutismo*, the art of perspectival rendering of urban landscapes, which reached its peak in the 18th century during the age of the Grand Tour; and c) accurate orthographic drawings first developed in the 15th century by Renaissance architects, climaxing in the early 19th century under the influence of pensioners at the French Academy in Rome. The author focuses on the great documentarians

frontispiece:
Detail, Rione IX Pigna, *Pianta Grande di Roma*, by Giambattista Nolli, 1748. Red inserts from *Édifices de Rome Moderne* by Paul Marie Letarouilly, ca. 1850. All graphics and photographs by the author unless otherwise noted.

1 The term "micro-urbanism" was suggested to the author by Leon Satkowski.

2 Koetter, Fred. "Notes on the In-Between" in *The Harvard Architecture Review* 1, "Beyond the Modern Movement", MIT Press, Cambridge, MA, Spr 1980: 62–73.

3 This paper adapts an earlier essay, "Revealing the Micro Urbanism of Rome: A Posthumous Collaboration between G.B. Nolli and P.M. Letarouilly", *Giambattista Nolli and Rome, Mapping the City before and After the Pianta Grande*, Verstegen, Ian and Ceen, Allan, eds., Studium Urbis, Rome, 2013. These themes continued in various venues for the author, including the Rowe Rome Conferences from 2014 to 2018 and related online publications and interactive websites described below.

Tice, James, ""Tutte Insieme" Giovanni Battista Falda's Nuova Pianta di Rome of 1676". After Falda's death, his maps were published by De Rossi. The complete editions are: 1676, 1697, 1705, 1730 and 1756. See also Latini, Antonio Pietro, "Urbanistica a Rome nelle piante del Falda", for a discussion of the changes recorded for each edition. Both essays are in Bevilacqua, Mario and Fagiolo, Marcello, eds., *Piante di Roma, dal Rinascimento ai Catasti*, Editoriale Artemide, s.r.l., Roma, 2012: 244–271.

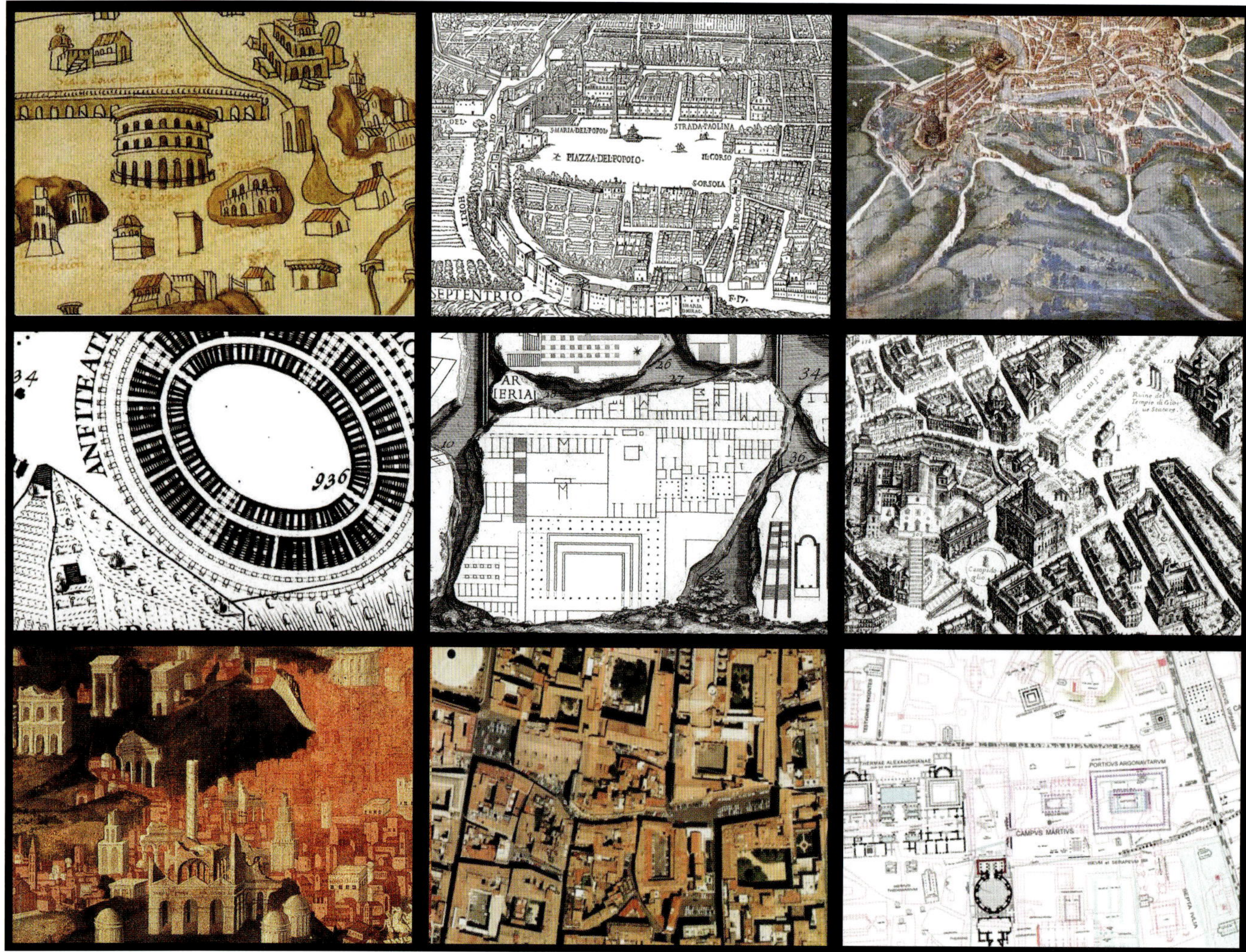

Fig. 1. Details of Roman cartography.
left to right top to bottom:

Veduta di Roma, Pietro del Massaio, 1469.

Pianta di Roma, Giovanni Maggi, 1625.

View of Rome, Vatican, 16th century.

Pianta Grande, Giambattista Nolli, 1748.

Forma Urbis, Severan marble map of Rome, 203–2011 AD, print by Piranesi, 1756.

Nuova Pianta di Roma, Giovanni Battista Falda, 1676.

View of Rome, Mantova, Anon., 1538.

Atlante di Roma, Commune di Roma, Eugenio Baldari and others, 1991.

Forma Urbis Romae by Rodolfo Lanciani, 1901; digital version by University of Oregon, 2014.

of the late Baroque and Neo-classical periods: for cartography, Giovanni Battista Falda (1630–78) and Giambattista Nolli (1695–1752); for *vedutismo*, Alessandro Specchi (1668–1729) and Giuseppe Vasi (1710–83); for drawings and prints, Paul Marie Letarouilly (1795–1855). Architects and artists frequently operated in more than one representational mode, so Falda created his map at the same time that he published his *vedute* and building plans. The combined body of work of these masters—especially when cross-referenced—provides a comprehensive reading of the city-building dialectic.

When geo-referenced—that is cross-referenced topographically—the three types provide a comprehensive picture of the city at its micro-urban scale. The techniques for which Rome is rightly famous coupled with innovations in digital media explore the 'spatial history' or 'spatial logic of place'. Many of the methods and principles embedded in this approach reinforce, overlap, and elucidate ideas that were presciently explored by Rowe's Studio in the 1960s. A summation of the key documentary traditions along with a series of case studies illustrate how their combined use can illuminate the urbanism of Rome. Finally, I list my 'lessons' for urban designers interested in micro-urbanism.

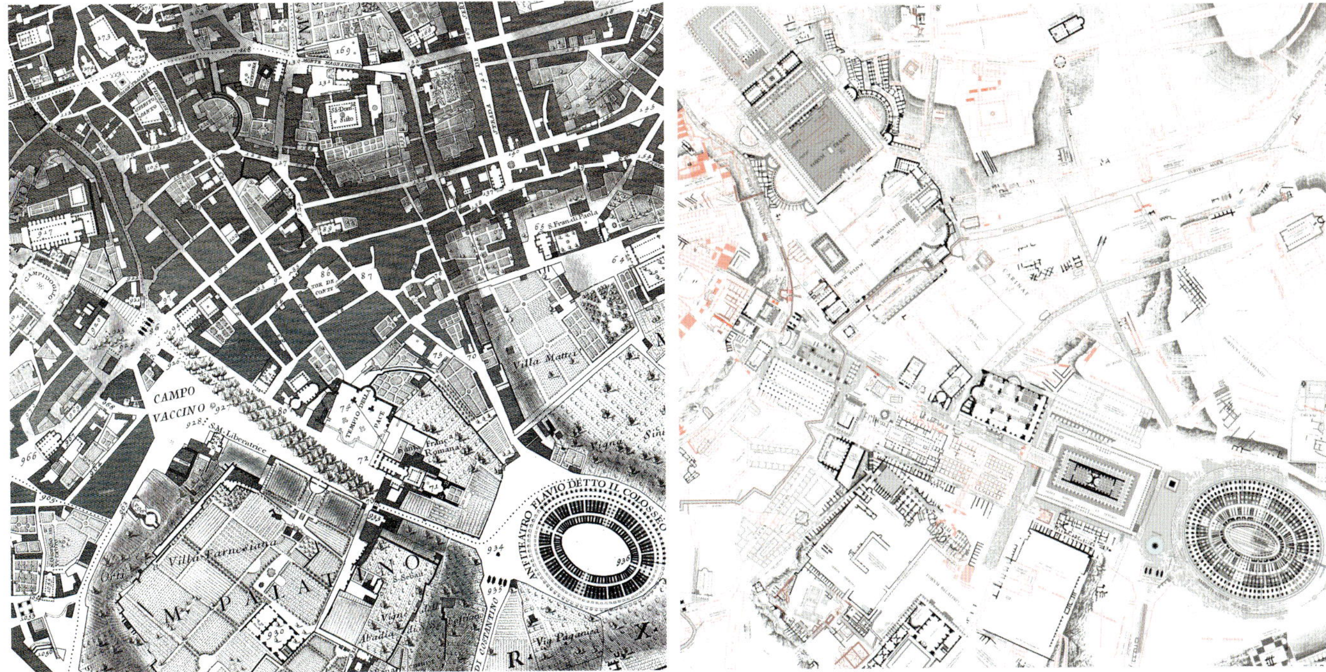

Cartography

The cartography of Rome follows one of two modes: the *volo-d'ucello*, bird's-eye view, or the ichnographic, plan view (Fig. 1). The late 16th century map of Rome by Tempesta is rendered as seen from the air, pictorially (Fig. 3). It represents the entire city of Rome and was the most detailed and accurate map up to that time. But it was the Nolli map as an ichnographic, plan view that became the dominant mode of map making for the city for the next 200 years, with broad influence throughout Europe and America continuing to this day (Fig. 2). The *Nuova Pianta di Roma* of 1676, by Falda, occurring almost exactly midway between Tempesta and Nolli, links both traditions. It is the immediate precursor to the *Pianta Grande*, both for its comprehensive treatment of the city and for its accuracy. As Falda advertises, his plan is a *pianta alzata*, that is, an 'elevated plan' of the city. As it is a paraline drawing, in this case an axonometric, all linear measurements are true, even if shown obliquely. Falda's only concession to his otherwise exacting standards is that he widens streets to better show facades. Maps showing the Vatican and St. Peter's by Falda, Nolli, Letarouilly, and Lanciani[4] trace the development of the pictorial and ichnographic map in Rome (Fig. 4).

Pictorial representations of the bird's-eye type often obscure information due to overlapping features. And, because of the distortion introduced by the nature of perspective rendering, such as diminution in size based on proximity to the picture plane, detailed comparisons with other maps and documents are difficult to realize. The more abstract, ichnographic type overcomes these challenges because it is possible to measure buildings and spaces accurately, thus facilitating comparisons with other similarly constructed examples. The first record of the ichnographic map is the huge Severan marble map of Rome measuring 18 × 13 m. The *Forma Urbis*, as it is called, was erected near the Forum and probably used for

above left to right:

Fig. 2. Comparison of the *Pianta Grande di Roma*, Giambattista Nolli, 1748 and the *Forma Urbis Romae*, Rodolfo Lanciani, 1901. Maps digitally remastered by the University of Oregon.

below:

Fig. 3. Detail, *Pianta di Roma*, Antonio Tempesta, 1593 (1645 edition).

4 Lanciani, Rudolfo, *Forma urbis Romae*, Mediolan: U. Hoepli, Milano, 1893–1901.

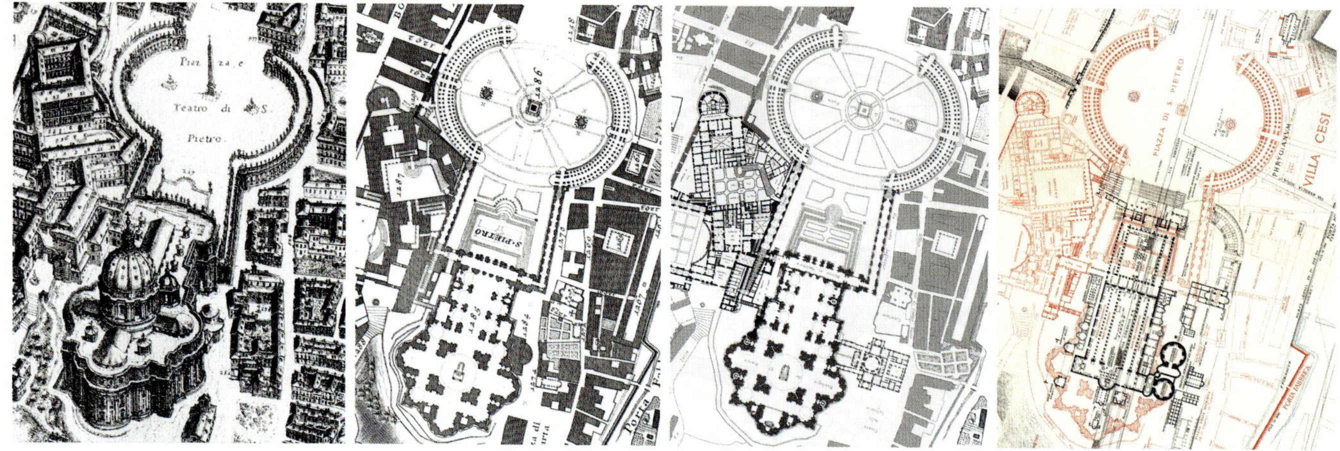

Fig. 4. Detail axonometric and plans of St. Peter's, left to right: *La Pianta et Alzata della Cittá di Roma* by G.B. Falda; 1676; *La Pianta Grand*e by G.B. Nolli, 1748; *Le Vatican et la Basilique de Sainte-Pierre* by Paul Marie Letarouilly, 1882; and *Forma Urbis Romae* by Rodolfo Lanciani, 1901.

administrative purposes.[5] Leonardo Bufalini's map of Rome of 1551 revived the plan type map that was also reproduced by Nolli 200 years later as an *omaggio*. Nolli's *Pianta Grande*, as a scientifically measured plan view map, follows in the footsteps of both. Summing up, the *Pianta Grande* is the consummate example of Roman cartography in the ichnographic mode and is a milestone in the history of cartography. It was a major innovation in Roman mapmaking, as it had superseded the pictorial map that had been the norm up till then.[6]

The plan view map projects the salient features of the city onto a flat plane while the pictorial map renders the city in three dimensions. The plan captures significant features such as building footprints, relative size of features—streets, bridges, walls, and gardens—and the distances in between. Necessarily, this mode has disadvantages. For example, it obviously cannot render the heights of buildings, and can only hint at domes or towers, nor does it easily represent the varied terrain of the city. But it also has advantages. The orthographic plan is most valuable for understanding size, organization, and orientation. It can be scaled and measured accurately, providing a useful scientific instrument for detailed information that can facilitate comparisons with other similarly measured documents. Plan view maps are potentially scalable, that is, whatever the dimensions of given maps, they can be blown up or shrunk down to be commensurate with other maps, even though they may have been rendered at different scales and produced hundreds of years apart. Using Geographic Information Science (GIS), the ichnographic map can be geo-rectified or 'rubber sheeted' so that it can precisely align with historic maps and be brought into real geographic space. This point-by-point documentation allows the map to serve as a geo-database to record vast amounts of information that can be transmitted precisely using latitude and longitude coordinates.[7]

Due to limits of 18th century printing technology, the original Nolli map was printed in twelve separate plates. An important step in the process of making the map more useful has been to digitally remaster the *Pianta Grande* into one seamless document, eliminating the distracting borders. Next in importance was to geo-rectify the map (already extremely accurate) using GIS software and satellite imaging as a guide to bring it into accord with real geographic space.

5 Nolli exhibited the remaining marble fragments of the *Forma Urbis* on the Campidoglio. Piranesi made engravings of the same fragments underscoring the importance of this map for mid-18th century contemporaries.

6 Ceen, Allan, "Introductory Essay," in *La Pianta Grande di Roma di Giambattista Nolli in Facsimile*, ed. J.H. Aronson, Highmount, New York, 1991.

7 Tice, James; Camerlenghi, Nicola; Ceen, Allan; Steiner, Erik; and Svevo, Giovanni. For the revised *Interactive Nolli Map Website 2.0*, published 2021. [https://web.stanford.edu/group/spatialhistory/nolli//index.html]

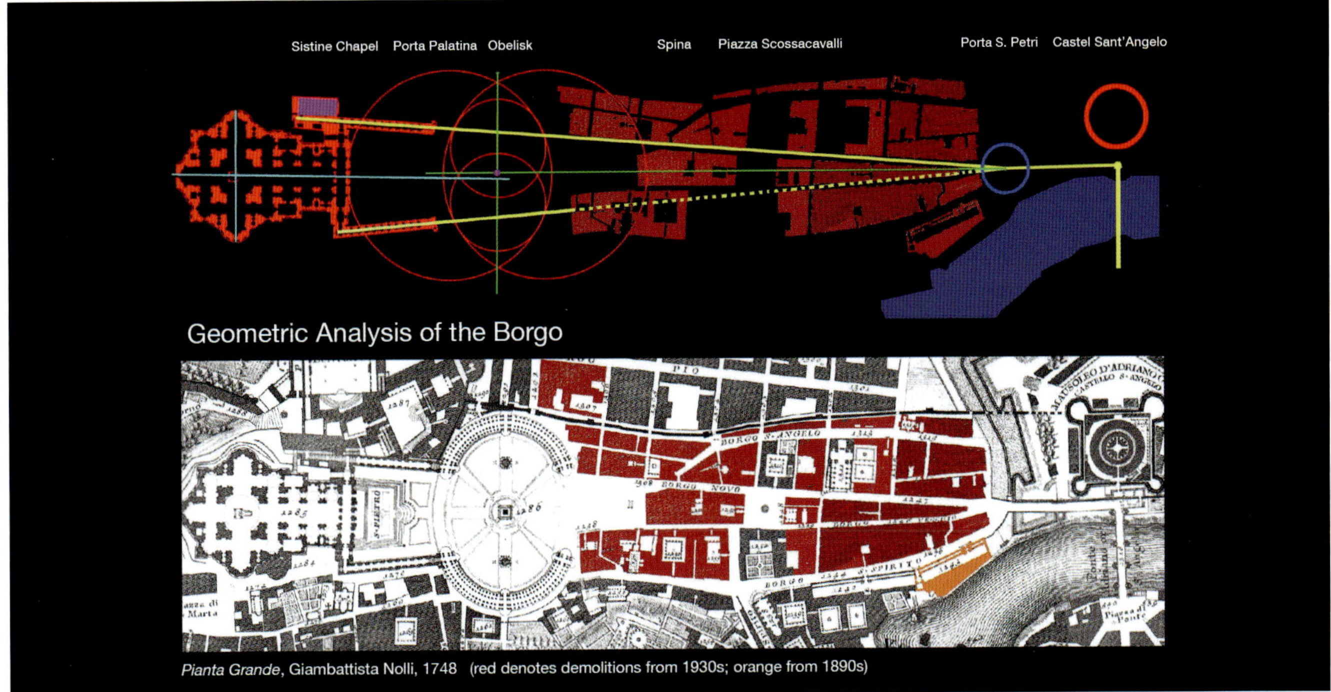

Fig. 5. *The Borgo and its Modern Transformations*, by Allan Ceen and James Tice, from "The GIS Forma Urbis Romae Project: Creating a Layered History of Rome", 2013. Red fabric shows buildings demolished by Mussolini, ca. 1935; yellow indicates major axes.

The Nolli map, as the focus for many of Rowe's critical observations about the nature of urbanism in Rome and the nature of urban structure more generally, was facilitated by Nolli's unique method of graphic representation: the figure/ground. At the urban scale, solid buildings were hatched in dark gray while streets and piazza were left white. Nolli uses this same figure/ground technique at the architectural scale—drawing over a thousand building plans that render walls as black and space as white, achieving a 'microscopic' view of the city. Taken as a section cut at the ground plane, the map shows the habitable public space of streets and piazze between buildings, and the semi-public space found inside many of those same buildings. The void, therefore, represents places where one can move in and through the city. With this graphic mode, the map has a transparent, almost luminescent quality that invites one to explore the city's dense fabric, showing hundreds of building interiors and semi-public interiors such as churches, monastic cloisters, and palace courtyards. The rendition of solids and voids communicates the spatial and formal essence of the city and establishes the context for its many celebrated structures, demonstrating their intimate interrelationship and micro-structure. Nolli's map brings interior and exterior and the public and the semi-public realms intuitively within reach: it is, after all, on the ground plane that the city is typically experienced. Because of its accuracy, the Nolli map can be used as an analytical tool to reveal recent urban interventions, such as those changes wrought to the Vatican and Borgo during the 20th century (Fig. 5).

left top to bottom:
Fig. 6. Comparative views of Castel Sant'Angelo and St. Peters: *Vedute del Tevere a Castel Sant'Angelo,* G. Vanvitelli, ca. 1720; *Ponte e Mole Adriana,* G. Vasi, ca. 1754; and *Veduta del Ponte Castello Sant'Angelo,* G.B. Piranesi, ca. 1750

right:
Fig. 7. The Nolli Plan showing station points and view sheds of *vedute* inserted from *delle Magnificenze di Roma, Antica e Moderna* by G. Vasi, 1747-61.

Vedutismo

Vedutismo reached its height during the 18th century, the Age of the Grand Tour.[8] It is allied to the pictorial tradition in cartography, and artists such as Falda and Vasi practiced in both modes. It is perhaps best exemplified by masters such as Gaspare Vanvitelli, Giovanni Paolo Panini, Giuseppe Vasi, and his student, Giovanni Battista Piranesi. These artists represented the city topographically, primarily through eye-level perspectives that rendered panoramas of the city on canvas or incised on copper plates. *Vedute* typically convey the character of 'place', capturing lighting effects and the ephemeral *genius loci* of the city more than the abstract ichnographic map. The subjects typically highlighted were well-known landmarks such as St. Peter's and the Forum, but, as we shall see, Vasi not only included famous sites, but documented well over a hundred lesser-known places throughout the city. Although views were based on actual places, they were prone to exaggeration to enhance their inherent drama and beauty, recalling Picasso's dictum that "art must lie to tell the truth".[9] A comparison of three views of Castel Sant'Angelo and Vatican by Vanvitelli, Giuseppe Vasi, and Piranesi show the varied emphasis that each artist could bring to the same subject (Fig. 6).

Giuseppe Vasi was the most prolific *vedutista* of Rome during the 18th century. He contributed 236 views in this vein in his ten-volume *delle Magnificenze di Roma antica e moderna* (1747–61). The unique aspect of Vasi's *vedute*, and the reason for his significance to the study of the micro-urbanism in Rome, is that he places *all* his buildings, monuments, fountains, gardens, and other features in their spatial context, making clear important adjacencies and historical continuities.[10] Unlike Piranesi, who focused on the monumental architecture of Rome, especially in its archaeological zones, Vasi was interested in the entire metropolis. His views

8 Tice, James T. and Harper, James G., eds., *Giuseppe Vasi's Rome: Lasting Impressions from the Age of the Grand Tour* (exhibition catalogue) University of Oregon Press, 2010.

9 Tice (2010): 67–76.

10 Curiously, there is only one exception: one of his small plates, or *rametti*, of the Collegio di Propaganda Fide in book 9.

Fig. 8. Views from *delle Magnificenze di Roma* by G. Vasi.

left to right top to bottom:

Piazza del Popolo
Isola Tiberina
Santa Maria Maggiore
Campo Vaccino (Forum)

Piazza San Pietro
Piazza della Rotonda
Fontana di Trevi
Piazza San Giovanni in Laterano

Piazza Santa Maria in Trastevere
Porta San Paolo
Piazza del Quirinale
Campidoglio

show its buildings, *piazze*, streets, and gardens throughout the city, capturing imposing monuments and humble neighborhoods, *tutto insieme*.

The scenographic quality of Vasi's *vedute* is underscored, for it seems each is represented as a stage for spectacle. Vasi was profoundly attuned to the space between buildings as it was lived in by its populace—from the nobility and the clergy to beggars, thieves, and miscreants—rendered with a sympathetic and sometimes humorous eye. Vasi has provided a mini-drama for us to enjoy in each—noisy celebrations, the cacophony of the market, solemn processions, military encampments, and spontaneous musical displays with dancing revelers (Fig. 8).

In surveying his ten books, each of which is dedicated to a building type or topographic theme, it becomes evident that the views were distributed in a pattern facilitated by an intimate knowledge of the *Pianta Grande*. Vasi had produced a small map of Rome at the end of his first book, *delle Magnificenze,* acknowledging Nolli, thereby demonstrating a link between the two masters. So precise are his renderings of city gates, palazzi, churches, bridges, monasteries, *ville*, and *piazze* that each view could be geolocated precisely on the Nolli map with station point and view shed for each (Fig. 7). By situating Vasi's *vedute* into the Nolli map, one is given an immediate sense of the ubiquity of his views, and thereby provided a valuable complement to the map. Furthermore, Vasi regales us with hills, domes, towers, and other three-dimensional features, compensating, we might say, for the absence of such information on Nolli's two-dimensional map.

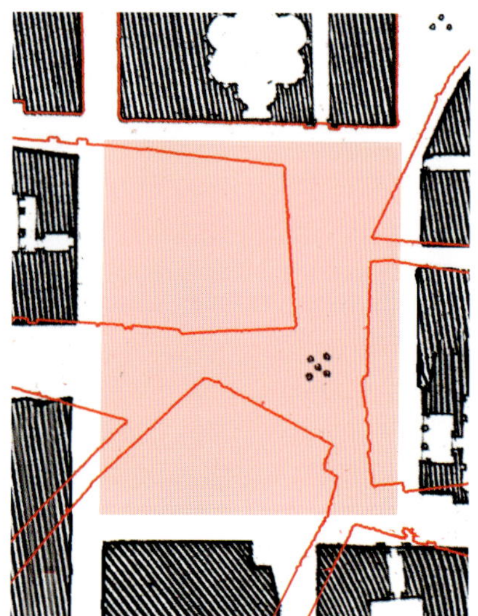

above clockwise:
Fig. 9. View Piazza Sant'Eustachio, G. Vasi, ca. 1756.

Fig. 10. Photo of Piazza Sant'Eustachio, 2009.

Fig. 11. Hypothetical diagram of Piazza Sant'Eustachio based on G.B. Falda.

Fig. 12. Piazza Sant'Eustachio, G.B. Falda, ca. 1676.

Vasi's view of Piazza Sant'Eustachio provides insights into Vasi's method (Fig. 9). It shows the 17th century church of Sant'Ivo by Borromini dominating the piazza of the same name being framed by the 16th century Palazzo Maccarani on one side and the 12th century medieval tower, and later 18th century church facade of Sant'Eustachio on the other. The photograph makes clear that Vasi has widened the piazza like opened pages of a book (Fig. 10). By enlarging the space, he underscores that this ensemble was spatially organized about the piazza: it was not a random collision of buildings. Even more emphatically, Falda's 17th century fictive view shows Sant'Ivo at the head of an enlarged piazza while the buildings on either side are absorbed into the fabric (Fig. 11, 12). By moving buildings and reshaping the space, Falda transforms the empirical situation into an ideal piazza, whereas Vasi's version more subtly suggests the ideal with a distorted but believable perspective view that is very close to a modern photograph.

Unlike Piranesi, whose majestic views of the city betray a longing for the vanished glory of antiquity that result in his tragic outlook, Vasi embraced the contemporary city as it is, with a highly developed sense of the comic shown here in the Campo Marzo (Fig. 14). The social-cultural goings-on of the existing city are Vasi's métier,

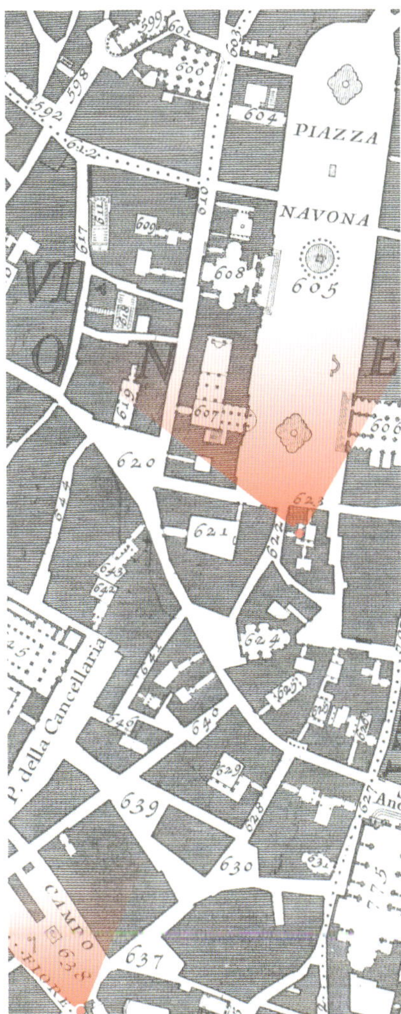

above clockwise:
Fig. 13. View of Piazza Navona, G. Vasi, ca. 1752.

Fig. 14. Detail of the Nolli Plan with view sheds of the Piazza Navona (above) and the Campo de'Fiori (below).

Fig. 15. View of the Campo de'Fiori, G. Vasi, ca. 1752.

depicting a full range of the lives of the people who lived in the city and the micro-urban architecture that frames them.

The view of Piazza Navona is one of Vasi's splendid Baroque representations of the city (Fig. 13). It shows the facades of the Palazzo Pamphilj and the church of Sant'Agnese as background to Bernini's Four Fountains at mid-distance. As if to reiterate the water theme of the fountain, he captures the piazza during the summer festival of the *freggio,* or flooding of the piazza, replete with children splashing about to their heart's content with their parents and others looking on approvingly. A poignant view of the Campo de'Fiori shows the medieval market as a large outdoor room surrounded by a heterogenous mix of buildings. It includes the late 15th century Cancelleria peering above the corner of the market to the east (Fig. 15). The activity of the space is animated with buyers and vendors trading and haggling over their livestock. Meanwhile, layabouts, indolent worthies, and a surprisingly large number of dogs are overshadowed by a postern, reminding us that the piazza was a notorious place for public executions.[11]

11 The Campo de'Fiori was the site of Giordano Bruno being burned at the stake as a heretic on February 17, 1600. A commemorative statue from 1889 marks the site and reflects anti-papist sentiment of the district to this day.

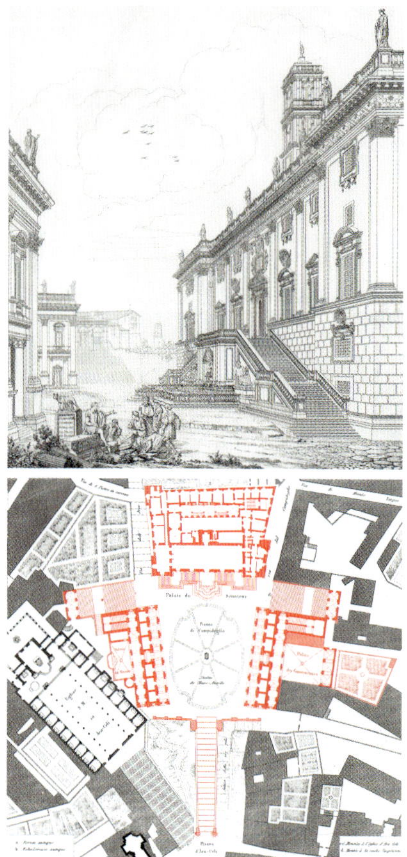

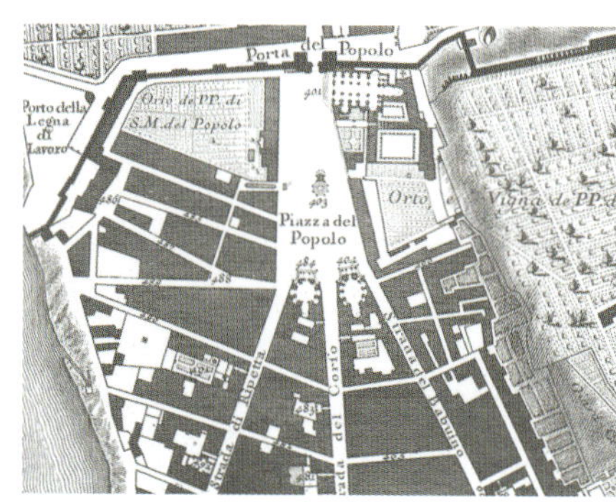

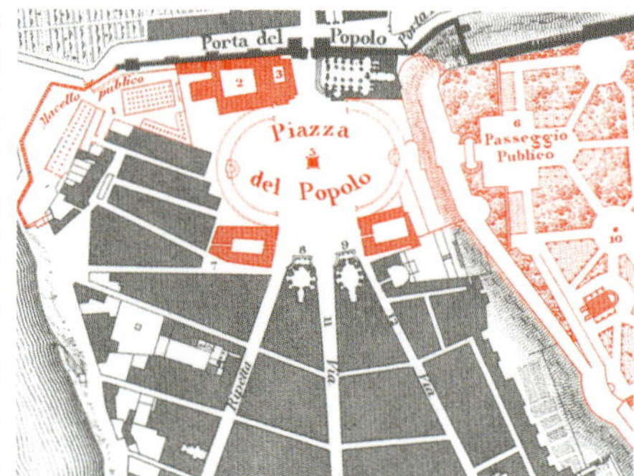

Fig. 16. View and composite plan of the Campidoglio showing *piano nobile* of the Palazzo Senatorio. This is the final plate from *Édifices de Rome Moderne*. Letarouilly appears in the lower left corner of the perspective regaling his students.

Orthographic Drawings

Orthographic drawings—especially architectural plans—are obviously related to the ichnographic plan view maps. There is a highly developed tradition of this practice in Rome reaching back to the Renaissance by architects such as Alberti, Pirro Ligorio, and Palladio, who recorded ancient ruins. The tradition was continued in the 18th century by Piranesi, who transformed his investigations into elaborate architectural and urban fantasies. The documentation and hypothetical reconstruction of ancient ruins became a highly developed rite of passage for Prix de Rome pensioners at the French Academy. Charles Percier and Pierre François Léonard Fontaine, however, departed from this tradition for they documented Rome *moderne*, not Rome *ancien* as had been the practice. In their 1798 *Palais, maisons et autres édifices modernes dessinés à Rome*[12] they included scores of Renaissance and Baroque examples—a departure of considerable consequence for the history of 19th century Neoclassical architecture in Europe and America.[13]

Paul Marie Letarouilly (1795–1855) was a student of Charles Percier and author of his own monumental three-volume *Édifices de Rome Moderne*, published from 1840 to 1856 (Fig. 16–19).[14] Following Percier and Fontaine, he claims his intention to concentrate on 'modern' architecture, that is, the great Renaissance architects: Bramante, Raphael, Peruzzi, Michelangelo, among others. His work, however, was less time bound than is typically assumed, for in addition to his treatment of 16th through 18th century architecture, he also rendered Early Christian churches and

12 Percier, Charles and P.F.L. Fontaine. *Palais, Maisons, et autres édifices modernes, dessines a Rome*. Paris: 1798.

13 Letarouilly's presentation style of drawings can be seen in the highly influential portfolio of McKim, Meade, and White. See McKim, Mead & White: *A Monograph of the Work of McKim, Mead & White*, 1879–1915, 4 volumes, Architectural Book Publishing Co., NY, 1915–1920. Beaux-Arts architects in America in the late 19th and early 20th centuries owe a debt to Letarouilly and his volumes. Penn Station in New York City by McKim, Mead and White is modeled after the baths of Diocletian also shown as Santa Maria degli Angeli as drawn by Letarouilly, not the baths of Caracalla as is sometimes supposed. See plate 316 in *Édifices*.

14 Letarouilly, Paul Marie. *Édifices de Rome Moderne ou recueil des palais, maisons, églises, couvents, et autres monuments publics et particuliers les plus remarquables de la ville de Rome* (three volumes), Morel, Paris, 1868–74.

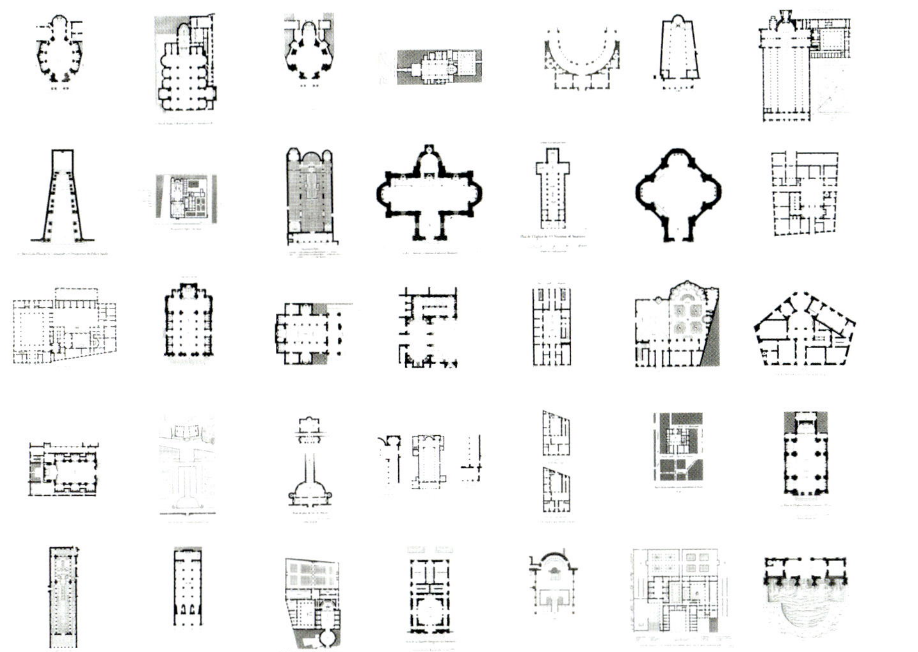

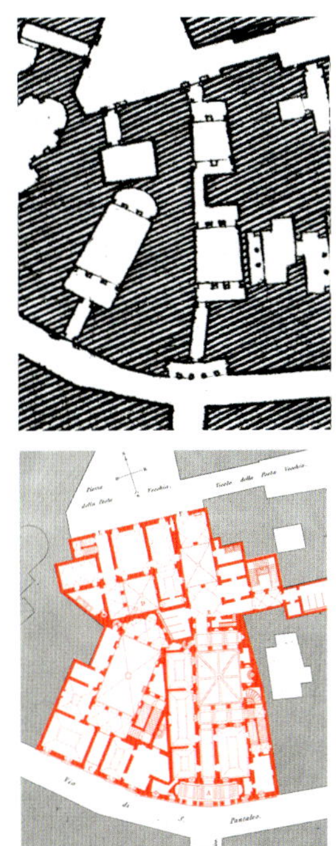

medieval structures. He showed a sophisticated taste for design even amongst lesser-known works: humble houses clinging to the banks of the Tiber and half-forgotten monasteries and churches hidden in the city's vast uninhabited district or *disabitato*. His affinity to Vasi and his *vedute* is most striking in terms of its catholicity, quantity, and ubiquity. There are over 1,700 detailed plans, sections, and elevations and almost two hundred perspectives—many showing interiors and some devoted to interior furnishings—most depicted with extraordinary accuracy. Several of his perspectives were executed with such verisimilitude that suggests he may have used a *camera obscura* (Fig. 17), while at other times he simply copied views by printmakers such as Falda, Specchi, and Vasi. While most of his effort is devoted to buildings, he expanded his repertoire to include over a dozen site plans—those of the Campidoglio, Vatican, and Lateran are the most detailed—using the readily available Nolli map as a base. The three-volume *Édifices* establishes Letarouilly as one of the greatest, if not the greatest, documentarian of Roman architecture of all time.

Letarouilly's prodigious effort went beyond documenting buildings and urban site plans. He produced his first of two maps of Rome in 1841, at about one quarter the size of the *Pianta Grande*. He literally copied Nolli's map in minute detail, while updating those few portions of the city that had changed by mid-19th century, such as the Piazza del Popolo by Giuseppe Valadier (Fig. 18). The posthumous publication, in 1882, of his tomes on the Vatican and St. Peter's expanded his oeuvre with over 1,000 drawings using color lithographs.[15]

As noted, the *Pianta Grande* was an important source of inspiration for Rowe and informed his teaching and urban design theory which focused on Rome. And close behind in importance was his enthusiasm for Letarouilly, citing his

opposite left inset:
Fig. 17. Santa Maria di Monte Santo and Santa Maria dei Miracoli from *Édifices*, ca. 1848 compared to contemporary photo, 2009.

Fig. 18. Piazza del Popolo, with the Nolli Plan, 1748 (left) compared to Letarouilly's *Plan Topographique de Rome Moderne*, 1841 (right) showing the transformation by Giuseppe Valadier, ca. 1822.

inset:
Fig. 19. A random selection of 35 drawings from the over 1,700 drawings in the three volumes from *Édifices*. Plates include site plans, architectural plans, sections, elevations, perspectives, details, and furnishings.

above:
Fig. 20. Comparative plans of the Palazzi Massimi from the Nolli Plan (above) and *Édifices* (below).

15 Letarouilly, Paul Marie, *Le Vatican et la basilique de Saint-Pierre*, Morel, Paris, 1882, and Aversa, Antonella di Luggo. *Paul Letarouilly, Il Vaticano e la Basilica di San Pietro*, Istituto Geografico De Agostini S.p.A., Novara, 1999.

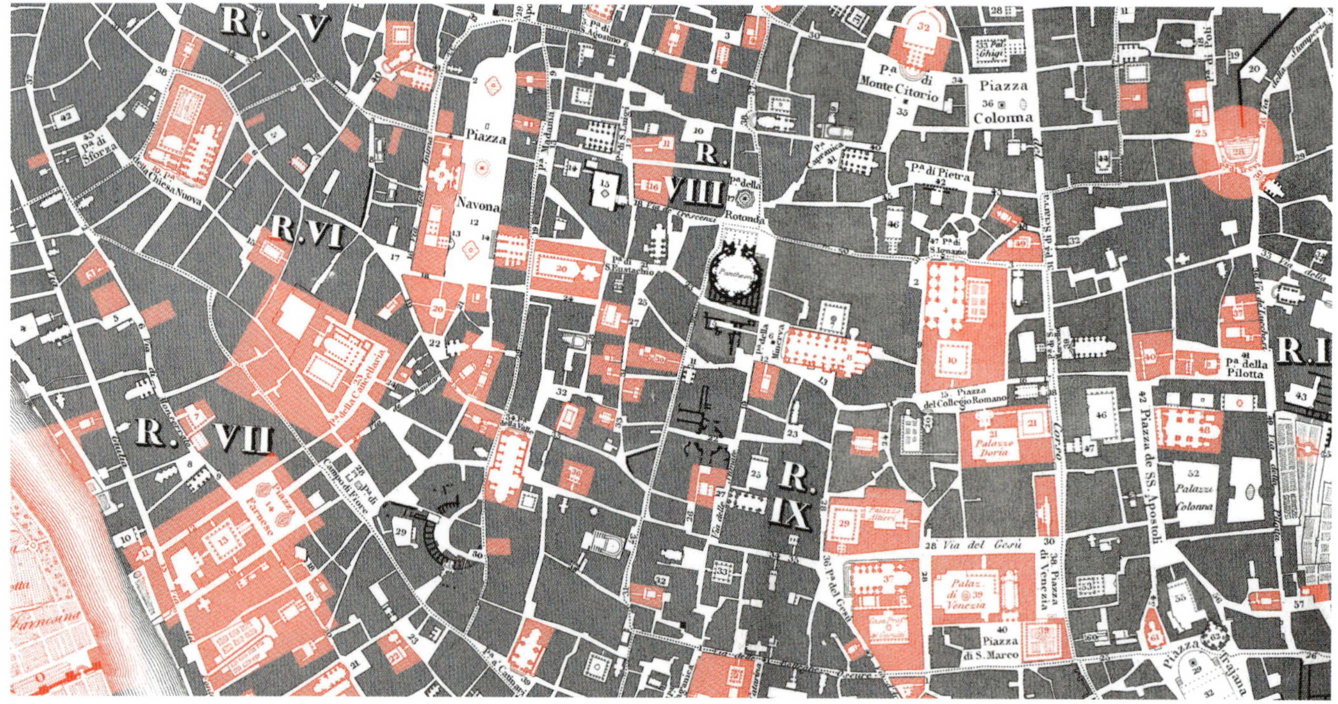

above:
Fig. 21. Detail plan of *Rome Moderne* by Letarouilly with insertions in red from *Édifices* showing the ubiquity of his drawings.

opposite inset:
Fig. 22. Detail of the environs of il Gesù and the Piazza Venezia from the Nolli Plan with station points and view sheds from *delle Magnificenze* in red.

opposite right:
Fig. 23. Vasi's station points and view sheds referenced from *delle Magnificenze.*

exquisite drawings in the Studio and in his lecture courses. For Rowe, the two sources constituted a mutually reinforcing proposition. For example, *poché* and figural space at the urban scale were shown to be analogous to *poché* and figural space at the building scale. Letarouilly's detailed drawings of the Palazzi Massimi is one prime example (Fig. 20). In *Collage City*, Rowe and Koetter would use Letarouilly's plans and views of the Palazzo Farnese and Palazzo Borghese to illustrate how the ideal is deformed as it responds to context of the city. Their comparison includes both plan and perspective documentation by Letarouilly, reinforcing the argument that the orthographic plan can be usefully complemented by the pictorial view.

Rowe would muse "how useful it would be" to construct a composite Nolli map by inserting Letarouilly's plans. Typically, such comments by Rowe were a tacit challenge for his students to realize his idea on their own initiative. Ultimately Rowe's challenge—to combine map and drawings—became the basis for the author's extended investigations into the urban development of Rome. The premise was that the measured drawings by Paul Marie Letarouilly in *Édifices Moderne*, with their minute attention to detail at the architectural scale, could be directly related to the *Pianta Grande* at the urban scale, to the great benefit of both architectural and urban studies of Rome, one that would enable an appreciation of the micro-urbanism of Rome.

The author has geo-referenced the complete building plans of Letarouilly, numbering over 200, into Letarouilly's version of the Nolli map, showing their reach across the entire city (Fig. 21). Importantly for future investigations, it was proof that the Nolli map could serve to geo-reference vast amounts of information, both visual and textual that could be useful and readily accessible.

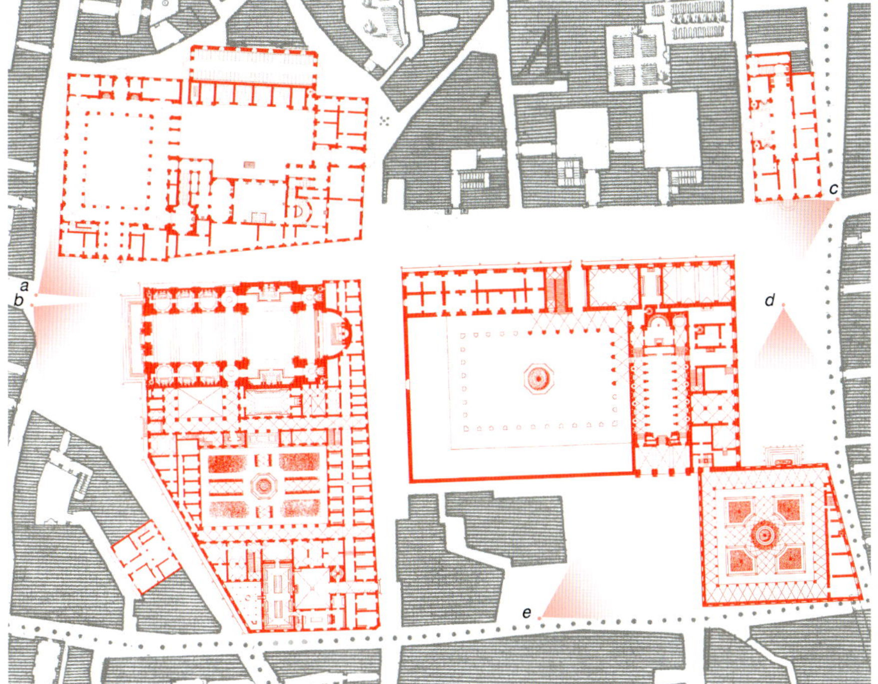

a. Palazzo Altieri

b. Piazza del Gesù

c. Palazzo Venezia

d. Piazza Venezia and Palazzetto Venezia

e. Piazza San Marco

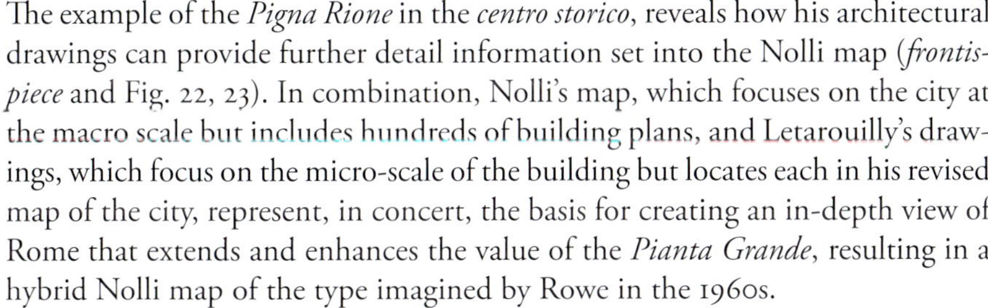

The example of the *Pigna Rione* in the *centro storico*, reveals how his architectural drawings can provide further detail information set into the Nolli map (*frontispiece* and Fig. 22, 23). In combination, Nolli's map, which focuses on the city at the macro scale but includes hundreds of building plans, and Letarouilly's drawings, which focus on the micro-scale of the building but locates each in his revised map of the city, represent, in concert, the basis for creating an in-depth view of Rome that extends and enhances the value of the *Pianta Grande*, resulting in a hybrid Nolli map of the type imagined by Rowe in the 1960s.

The four examples of Roman urbanism that follow are masterworks of micro-urbanism. If the genius of Roman urbanism is to be fully appreciated, these small-scale set-pieces deserve to be as well-known as the great large-scale urban triumphs of the city. The first two examples, Santa Maria della Pace and its piazza and the Piazza of Sant'Ignazio, are concentrated insertions in the dense medieval fabric of the Campo Marzio. Although they are connected to the city by way of important streets, their influence is local and centripetal in nature, especially when compared to the latter two examples. The Porto di Ripetta and the Scalinata di Spagna are to the north of the city in a district defined in large part by rectilinear street networks introduced in the 16th century. While both the Porto and the Scalinata exhibit a defining nucleus and type—the urban staircase—their force-field expands outward in a centrifugal manner to latch onto nearby and even distant events. All four examples exhibit the supreme capacity to transform the ad hoc and contingent into a highly recognizable *gestalt*, creating unforgettable places in Rome.

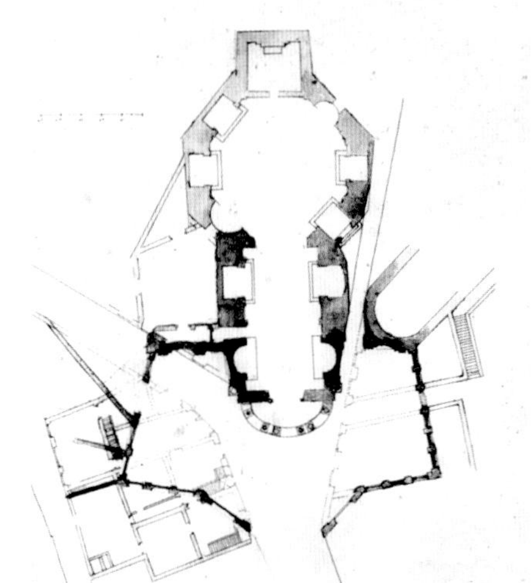

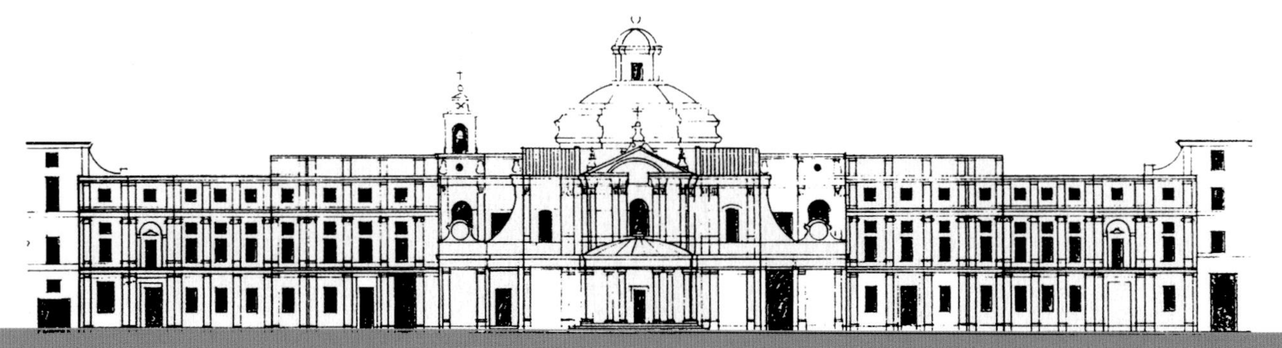

above:
Fig. 24. View of Santa Maria della Pace, G. Vasi, ca. 1756.

Fig. 25. Plan showing alterations by Pietro da Cortona to the pre-existing piazza.

Fig. 26. Elevation of Santa Maria della Pace 'unfolded'. Analysis by Teresa Shannon and Sharone Tomer, University of Oregon.

Santa Maria della Pace, 1656–67

Santa Maria della Pace and its piazza lie hidden in a tangle of medieval backstreets in Rome (Fig. 24–29). The ensemble, referred to as *teatro* in contemporary prints, alludes to its scenographic character. Its diminutive size is such that it could fit into the water basin of the Fontana di Trevi. The significance of this urban ensemble is not its 15th century church or its 16th century dome. It is rather its 17th century portico and faceted facade by the artist-architect Pietro da Cortona. He invokes the idea of a free-standing, centrally planned church, inserted into a regular piazza, recalling the 15th century ideal city while also referencing Bramante's Tempietto and intended placement into a regularized cloister. His solution was to capture the ideal urban type by using his illusionistic skills as an artist and architect, modeling solid and void to give the *appearance* of the ideal while simultaneously respecting the reality of the context.

In his design, Cortona abandoned conventional orthogonal planning, instead following a more nuanced approach, one that employs latent geometries, spatial manipulations, and scenic devices. Located at the juncture of a Y-shaped street intersection, or *trivium*, the church is balanced in plan by Bramante's monastic complex on one side and Santa Maria dell'Anima, the German national church, on the other. The flanking buildings appear to be organized in a near-symmetrical

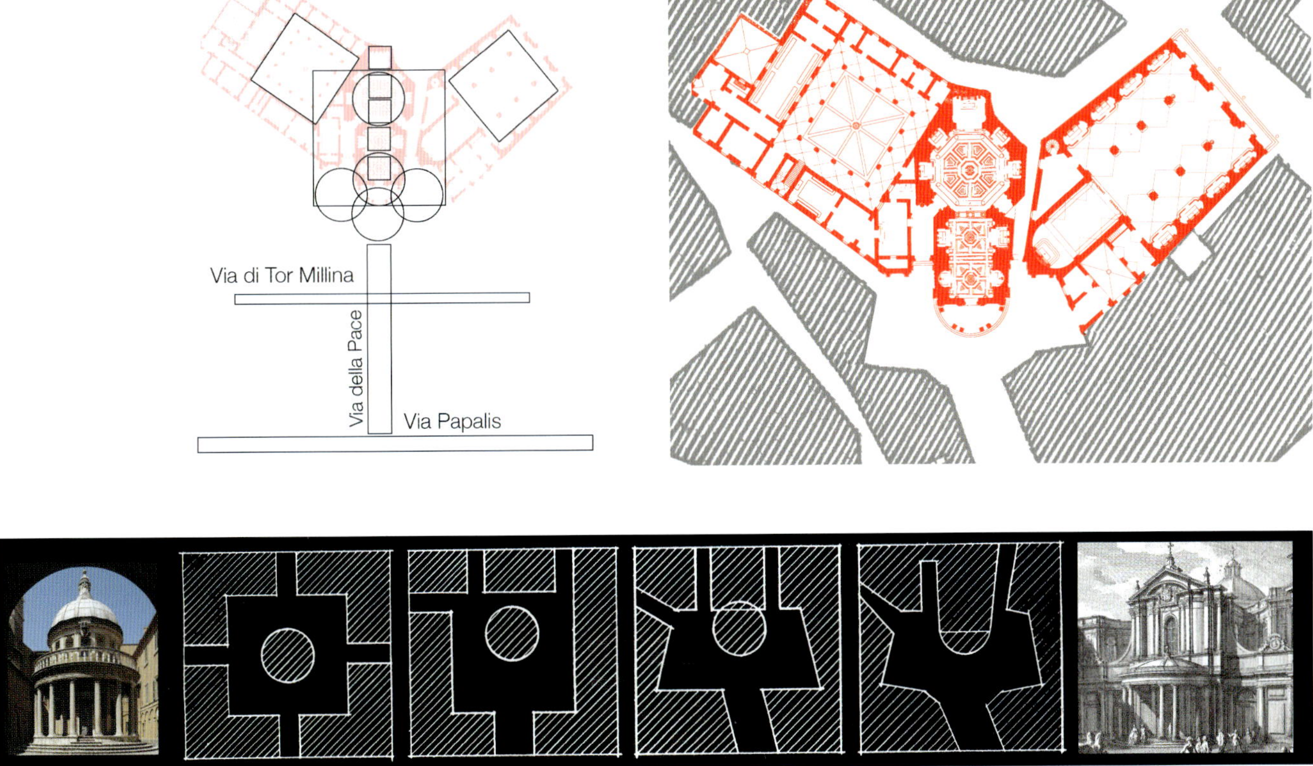

manner responding to the 45-degree grid generated by the church's octagonal plan. The colliding forces that ensue compress the church and facade along a strong central axis that acts as the controlling datum for the composition and visual terminus for the Via della Pace.

Cortona carved away the residences on either side of his facade and portico to give the appearance of a regular space. We are told this move helped ensure room for a carriage turnaround for those approaching from the *Via Papale*. The resultant space, although relatively shallow, was given additional depth by the perspectival treatment of the flanking wings, which tilt inward toward the portico. When projected onto a continuous flat plane, however, the entire facade is revealed to be a nearly perfect symmetrical composition. The flanking portions blend seamlessly into the existing context that act as transitional, flattened surfaces or as a neutral field against which the rotund portico, dome, and its sculpted convex-concave dependencies emerge as the undisputed figures. The oval-like portico is therefore thrust forward as a foil in front of the side wings which recede even farther in space, implying the larger centralized piazza as intended. The flanking wings bridge over the two existing side streets, adding to the sense of enclosure. On the left, a second passageway leads to the monastery. On the right, the street continues as an alleyway. Here, a hidden entrance leads to Santa Maria dell'Anima. The modest dimensions of Santa Maria della Pace and its piazza belie the fact that it is one of the most notable urban achievements in 17th century Rome and a paradigm of micro-urbanism.

above:
Fig. 27. Analysis of Santa Maria della Pace and Santa Maria dell' Anima and environs. It shows the Via della Pace centered on the church entry which in turn leads to the Via Papalis.

Fig. 28. Site plan of Santa Maria della Pace with its monastic dependencies by Bramante and the adjacent church Santa Maria dell'Anima, from *Édifices*.

Fig. 29. Hypothetical transformation of Santa Maria della Pace from the ideal Tempietto and its proposed cloister by Bramante to the real church and its piazza by Cortona. Analysis by Teresa Shannon and Sharone Tomer.

above:
Fig. 30. Panoramic photo of the Piazza Sant'Ignazio, Filippo Raguzzini, 1727-36. Photo: J. Tice.

below right to left:
Fig. 31. Photo of Piazza Sant'Ignazio and church, 2009.

Fig. 32. View of Sant'Ignazio, G. Vasi, ca. 1759.

Fig. 33. View of Sant'Ignazio and its piazza (reversed by the artist) prior to Raguzzini's interventions, Lievin Cruyl, 1665.

Piazza Sant'Ignazio, 1727–36

Occurring on Via del Seminario, the street that leads from the Piazza della Rotonda to the Corso, the Counter-Reformation church of S. Ignazio and its late Baroque piazza are a case study in micro-urbanism (Fig. 30–36). Filippo Raguzzini transforms a random confluence of medieval streets into a stunning outdoor salon, one that invites comparison to stage designs of the period, replete with subtle colors, proscenium, side wings, and stage.[16] The integration of interior architectural space with exterior urban space is without equal in the city of Rome and is, perhaps, one of the most important examples of this urban-spatial-type ever contrived. The new piazza acts as a complement to Sant'Ignazio, expanding its presence in the city and its attached monastic complex, the Collegio Romano.

The early view by Lievin Cruyl (as is typical for this artist, he renders his scenes in reverse) from 1665, shows the church facade and a small flanking piazza with an obelisk. Using his artistic license, Cruyl removes buildings to provide 'breathing room' for the church, similar to Falda's idealized view of the Piazza Sant'Eustachio. Although Cruyl did not anticipate the unique design by Raguzzini, his depiction suggested the desirability of releasing the church from its nondescript surroundings. Wanting a setting worthy of their church, while also wishing to enhance the value of their real estate, the Jesuits endorsed the idea of transforming their 'front room' into an enlarged and carefully orchestrated piazza. Vasi shows the piazza and church at mid-18th century from an oblique angle but barely suggests Raguzzini's unique geometric solution.

16 Connors, Joseph. "Alliance and Enmity in Roman Baroque Urbanism." In *Romisches Jahrbuch der Bibliotheca Hertziana*, Ernst Wasmuth Verlag, Tubingen, 1989: 279–93. Connors provides insightful history and analysis.

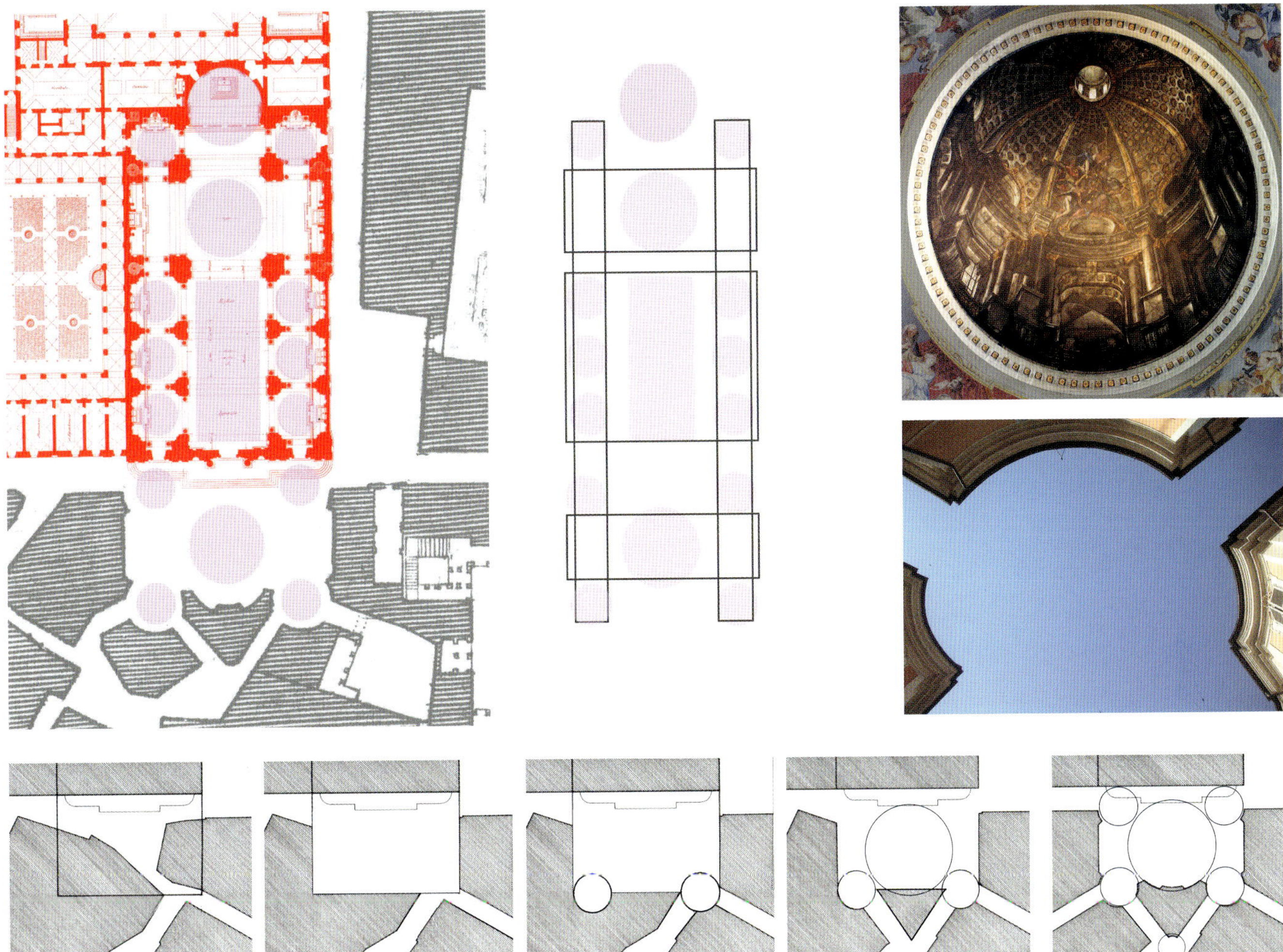

The Piazza Sant'Ignazio is not a case of wiping the slate clean but rather a case study in transforming the existing into an ideal. The solution strategically maintains some streets, straightens others, and inserts new ones to mime those that existed. Joseph Connors provides a hypothetical before-and-after diagram of the piazza, here elaborated upon by the author, that displays the ingenuity of the final solution. It was an inspired decision for the composition of the piazza to follow the tripartite organization of the church. The size and configuration of side chapels and nave establish a measured rhythm that is carried precisely from church interior to the piazza.[17]

The transformation of the piazza is a case study of how a nondescript urban event could be rearranged into a coherent whole, where idiosyncrasies could be transformed into balanced components of the whole. The genius of the design by Raguzzini is that the resultant piazza seems like it had aways been part of the church, and, perhaps, *had preceded* it, even though it was executed over half a century later.

above:
Fig. 34. Diagram showing geometries linking interior and exterior space.

Fig. 35. View of the *trompe l'oeil* dome by Andrea Pozzo and reciprocal side niche in Raguzzini's piazza.

below:
Fig. 36. Diagram showing hypothetical transformation of the pre-existing piazza to the final design. (Diagram based on J. Connors).

17 Especially fascinating is the metaphorical completion of Andrea Pozzo's famous *trompe l'oeil* dome mirrored by the dome of the sky in the piazza.

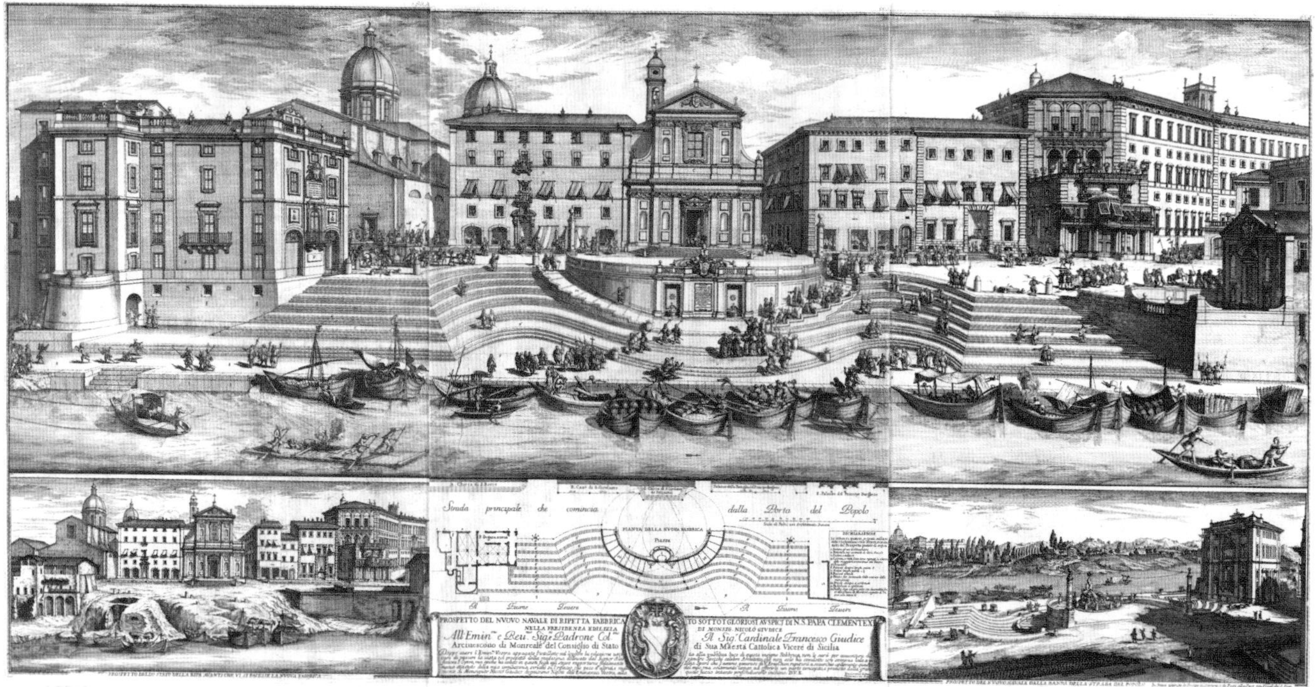

Fig. 37. Porto di Ripetta, Alessandro Specchi, 1695. The print, also by Specchi, shows multiple views: before-and-after as well as aspect-and-prospect.

Porto di Ripetta, 1705

The Porto di Ripetta was located on the banks of the Tiber, sadly demolished in the late 19th century for Rome's new embankments (Fig. 37–40). Designed by the architect and *vedutista*, Alessandro Specchi, the Baroque composition featured graceful, undulating steps that mimed the river current. The port was strategically situated on the Via di Ripetta, the western trident street emanating from the Piazza del Popolo at the point where that street becomes tangent to the river. To emphasize its importance, the port was overseen by the 16th century church San Girolamo degli Schiavoni. The Porto di Ripetta as designed by Specchi had multiple functions, both practical and poetic. Besides serving as a working quay for unloading goods from the hinterland north of Rome, it also served as a 'water piazza' for the church and a convenient place for ferry crossings. As a splendid public terrace and belvedere, it afforded picturesque views upstream and downstream and across the river to the open fields of Prati and Vatican beyond. It served as a reminder of the city's historic and, at times, uneasy relation to the Tiber, which was notoriously prone to flood at regular intervals. As a belvedere, it provided visitors and pilgrims their first distant view of St. Peter's and marked an important pause in their journey along an elaborate promenade from the Piazza del Popolo to the Vatican.

Formally and spatially, the Porto di Ripetta was a marvelous blend of the natural and the built, serving as a kind of urban 'eddy' in the Tiber as it meets the city. The water piazza displays an orthogonal geometry on the land side and a complex curvilinear geometry on the water side, which acts as its effective foil. The composition expands upriver and downriver, caught up, we might say, in the flow of the Tiber, and yet it is tethered or 'docked' effectively by its symmetrical composition centered on San Girolamo. The flanking facades along the Via

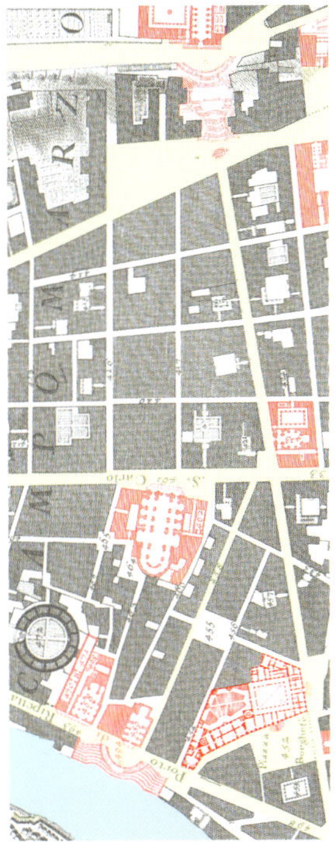

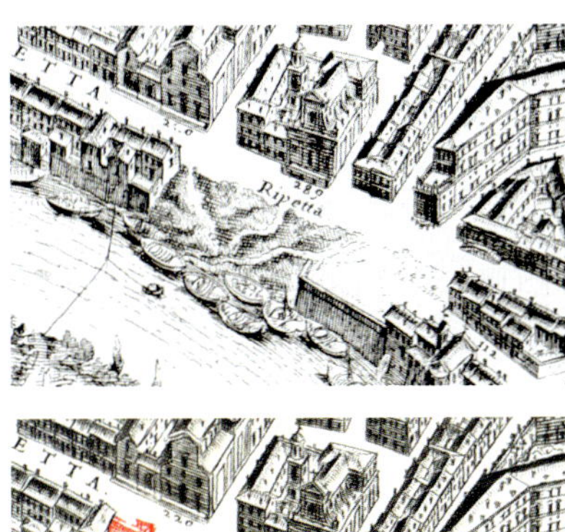

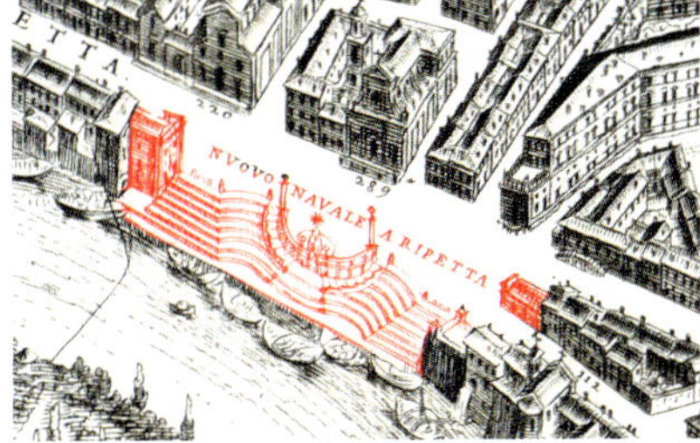

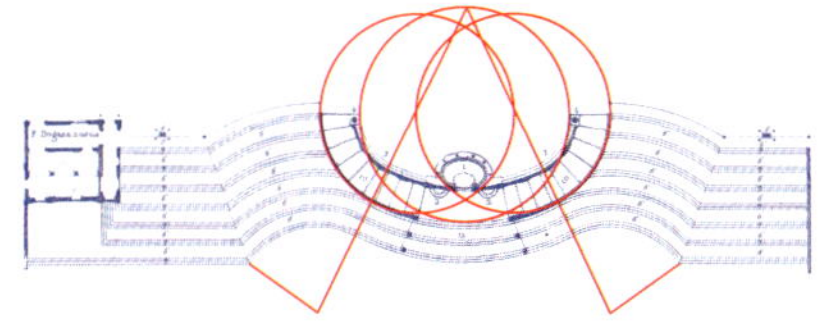

di Ripetta, including the church of San Rocco and the promontory wing of the Palazzo Borghese, act as a large proscenium addressing the landscape, while the dogana and secondary structures on the narrow side bookend the space. The link to the Corso is accomplished by the Strada del Macello which opens into the piazza. At the corso a notch in the street redirects the street, now the Via Condotti, to the Scalinata di Spagna.

The large, magnificent print depicting the Porto di Ripetta was rendered by Specchi, who was equally accomplished as an architect and printmaker. Realized in a composite view, it simultaneously depicts multiple aspects of his design in a virtuoso display unequalled in the history of Roman documentarians. The Porto is, in fact, rendered by Specchi in 'four' dimensions—orthographic plan view and elevations in two dimensions; perspectives in three dimensions showing aspect and prospect; and before-and-after views that show passage of time. His plan diagram, centered prominently on his print, reveals the underlying geometric basis for his design, describing a rational, mathematical underpinning for his flamboyant and seemingly irrational creation. It is his genius for design *and* its graphic representation of it that places Specchi in the forefront of those who may lay claim to be among the masters of micro-urbanism in Rome.

inset:
Fig. 38a. Detail of the Nolli Plan of the Porto di Ripetta and environs. Barely visible on the left are the circular ruins of the Mausoleum of Augusts. San Rocco flanks the piazza on one side while San Girolamo is ostensibly on the axis of the composition. The 'stern' of the Palazzo Borghese completes the quasi-symmetrical ensemble. Note the river ferry or *traghetto* connecting to Prati.

Fig. 38b. The Nolli Plan showing the relationship between the Porto di Ripetta and the Scalinata di Spagna.

above:
Fig. 39. Before-and-after views of the Porto di Ripetta, from prints of *Pianta di Roma* by G.B. Falda: 1676 edition (above); 1705 edition (below).

Fig. 40. Diagram of the geometric structure of Porto di Ripetta by A. Specchi (color enhancements by author).

above:
Fig. 41. Panoramic collage based on Giuseppe Vasi. The combined views show the Scalinata di Spagna (plate 40) with the Piazza di Spagna, and Palazzo di Collegio di Propaganda Fide (plate 40A) from *delle Magnificenze*, ca. 1752.

below right to left:
Fig. 42. *Villa Medici e le pendici del Pincio fino a piazza del Popolo da Trinità dei Monti*, detail, Gaspare Vanvitelli, from the Galleria Nazionale d'Arte Antica, Roma, ca. 1685.

Fig. 43. Proposal for a terrace in front of the Villa Medici. Fresco by Jacopo Zucchi, ca. 1576.

Scalinata di Spagna, 1723–25

Located at the edge of the Pincian Hill and its ancient Sallustian Gardens, the Scalinata di Spagna by Francesco De Sanctis[18] defines a unique place in the city and acts to link to other urban structures and important pathways (Fig. 41–46). The nucleus of the Scalinata complex includes the Renaissance church, San Trinità dei Monti, which presides over the stairway at its summit and the Fontana della Barcaccia by the elder Bernini at its foot. The grand stairway provided a transition for pilgrims as they journeyed from the Piazza del Popolo, along the Via del Babuino, climbing up the steps to the church and then on to the Via Sistina and then to Santa Maria Maggiore. Anomalies of the site abound. They helped to determine the distinctive bow-tie-shaped urban space which expands into the Piazza di Spagna. Colliding geometries, generated by the diagonal slope of the Pincian Hill, confront the rectilinear streets below, primarily inherited from the 16th century grid and the Corso. The forcefield of the stairs expands outward, as we shall see, connecting the Pincian hill along the Via Condotti, eventually leading to the Tiber.

In recognition of the site's importance and extended boundaries, Vasi shows two contiguous views. One displays the Scalinata proper; the other shows the Piazza di Spagna. The two prints are stitched together graphically by the author as one large panorama to show their relationship. The left half focuses on the cascading Scalinata and the church. The right half focuses on the Piazza di Spagna (the modern Piazza Mignanelli) prominently featuring the facade of the Collegio della Propaganda Fide by the younger Bernini. Although there is considerable

18 Alessandro Specchi conceived the initial design for the Scalinata based on his earlier design for the Porto di Ripetta. De Sanctis prevailed in winning the competition using Specchi's ideas.

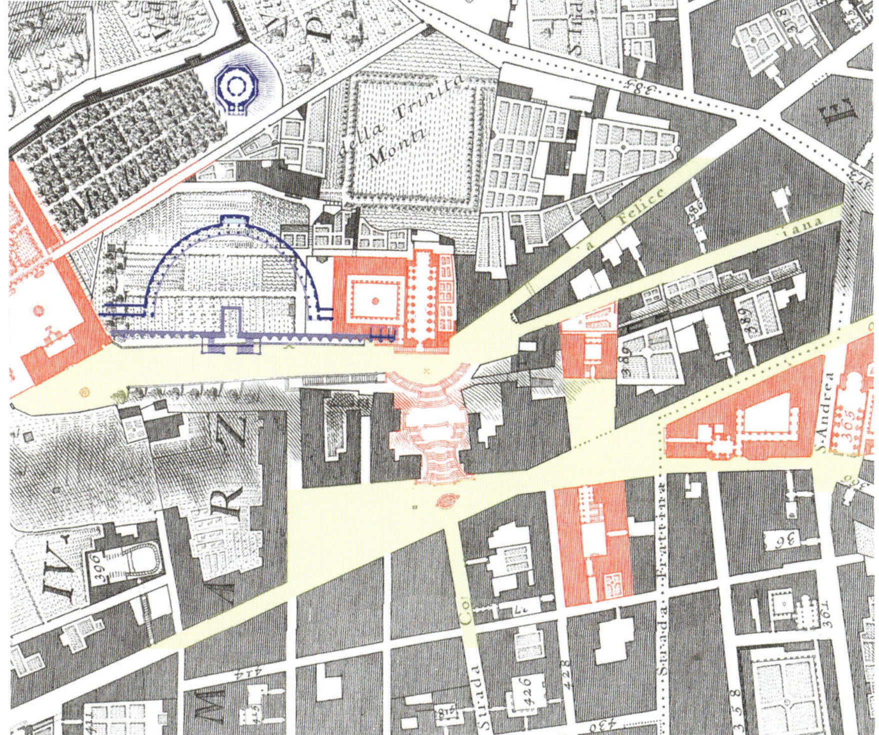

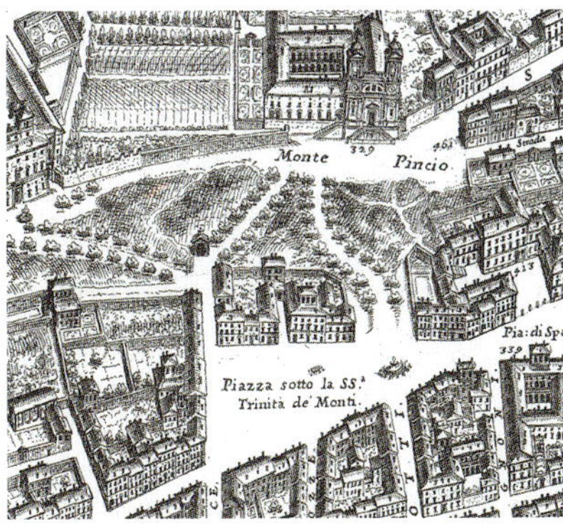

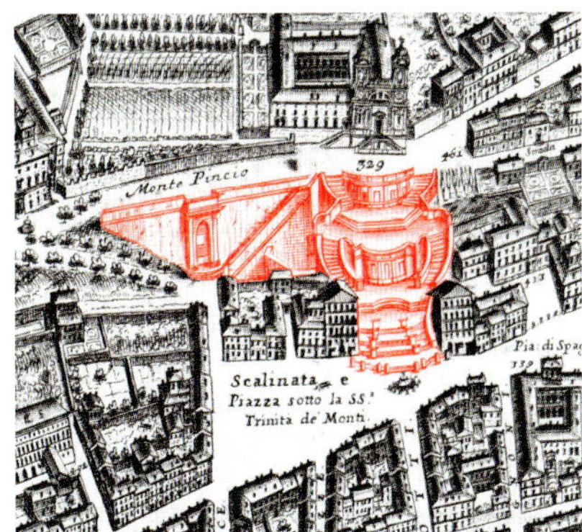

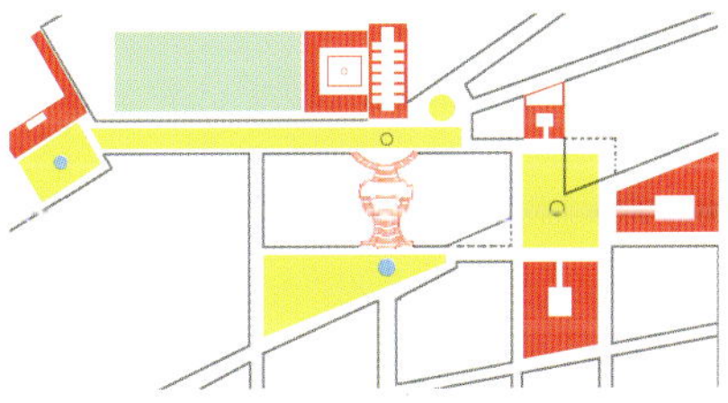

distortion in Vasi's prints—mostly widening the *piazze*—the features of individual structures are accurately rendered. This composite view conveys their actual state with a high degree of verisimilitude.

Nolli shows the *scalinata* and church directly on axis with the 16th century Via Condotti leading to the Corso. From here, the street continues as the ancient Via Trinitatis as it skirts the Tiber, then onward to the Ponte Sant'Angelo, eventually depositing pilgrims on the steps of St. Peter's. At the Via Condotti's juncture at the Corso, a small notch acts as a turning mechanism to redirect one toward the Porto di Ripetta, thus linking that urban trident: Piazza del Popolo, Piazza di Spagna, and Porto di Ripetta. This triangulated structure defines a large part of the Camp Marzio Rione.

By means of a broad, splendid terrace, which Nolli calls the Piazza della Trinità dei Monti, the Villa Medici commands a spectacular view of the city from its position on the Pincio. As the 16th century fresco by Jacopo Zucchi shows, the villa's entry terrace was projected to feature a more prominent, if less probable, lower terrace with fountain. In the early 19th century, Valadier's belvedere and garden terraces will continue the landscape theme of hanging gardens, *giardini pensile*, ultimately linking the Piazza del Popolo, the Villa Medici, and the Piazza di Spagna as an interconnected sequence along the edge of the hill. These episodic urban elements, from Piazza del Popolo to the Pincian Hill to the Tiber, are united as one *gestalt*. These constitute a poignant comment upon the city's topography, which defers in great measure to the Scalinata di Spagna.

inset:
Fig. 44. Detail of the Nolli Plan showing the Pincian Hill and environs from the Villa Medici to the Piazza di Spagna. The large blue exedra and tempietto indicate foundations of an ancient nymphaeum and temple complex according to Lanciani.

above:
Fig. 45. Before-and-after views of the Scalinata di Spagna from *Pianta di Roma* by G.B. Falda; 1676 edition (above) and 1730 edition (below).

Fig. 46. Diagram of the Piazza di Spagna and environs. To the left: Villa Medici and Piazza della Trinità dei Monti; at center and right: San Trinità dei Monti and Scalinata showing the confluence of the Via Sistina and Via Gregoriana; at the foot of the steps is the Fontana Barcaccia; to the right: the Palazzo Collegio di Propaganda Fide and Palazzo di Spagna defines the Piazza di Spagna.

Fig. 47. Comparison of the four case studies at the same scale with views by G. Vasi. The diagram shows the shared strategy whereby the church provides a primary, stable focus for the more heterogenous piazze and other urban elaborations which act as a forecourt.

Four Easy Pieces

These four urban constellations are the result of a dialectical process whereby a given site and its latent structure had been obscured by ad hoc circumstances, only to re-emerge as a new construct with the injection of an idealized, imposed order. To paraphrase Rowe, the genius of Rome's urban dialectic for the examples we have presented in this essay is that "each side of the debate remains undefeated by the other". All the examples share a straightforward formula: symmetrical church with prominent facade facing piazza, which acts as a forecourt that provides aspect and prospect (Fig. 47). As we have seen, however, the way structure and space relate and the ingenious means employed in achieving this relationship is not so straightforward. Each is a nuanced variant of the more general type, one that is highly dependent on the site and its context, and, to a lesser degree, on the specifics of the church which is its focus. For while the church is regular, symmetrical, and contained, the space that sets it off is complex. And although both church and piazza share a common axis (oblique in two instances) the configuration of the piazza is more varied, ranging from the introverted piazze of Santa Maria della Pace and Sant'Ignazio to the extroverted Porto di Ripetta and Scalinata di Spagna. It is exactly this tension between the ideal type and its exceptions that makes this set of examples a remarkable testament to the flexibility of Roman urbanism and the almost infinite possibilities of elevating known types enmeshed in ad hoc urban settings (Fig. 48).

Conclusion

This essay highlights readily available historic documents that can be cross-referenced to benefit the study of Roman urbanism at the micro-scale. The cartographic traditions represented by Nolli, who focuses on the urban structure of Rome but includes its architecture, and Giuseppe Vasi and Paul Marie Letarouilly as masters of the architectural perspective and the orthographic drawing tradition. These architects not only focus on the architecture of the city but place it into its urban context, which can, in concert, illuminate a more transparent Rome from which to learn and from which to reinvigorate the twin disciplines of architecture and urban design.

Fig. 48. Piazza Sant'Ignazio. Watercolor by J. Tice, 1997.

This research has developed into a virtual cascade of related studies that include other maps and documents of Rome—both historic and contemporary—rendered ichnographically and pictorially. These materials have been incorporated, or are now in the process of being incorporated, into interactive websites within the rubric of Spatial History within the Digital Humanities.[19] These efforts have made the author reflect that the disciplinary pursuit that attempts to understand the spatial logic of place—a pursuit that further amplifies the notion of the micro-urbanism in Rome—was anticipated by Colin Rowe.

Lessons of Micro-Urbanism

1. Architecture and urbanism in Rome are interdependent; one cannot be fully understood without the other.
2. The genius of Rome is that design at any given scale is part of a continuum: from room to building to district and to city.
3. Solid and void, form and space are the primary protagonists in urban structure.
4. The empirical and contingent can be transformed into a coherent whole that promotes, rather than denies, the complexities of the city.
5. Context is an important stimulus to design, not a limitation.
6. How a city is represented is crucial to its understanding. Figure/ground representations can reveal its inherent formal/spatial structure.
7. Ichnographic, orthographic, and pictorial representation can, and should, be used to complement one another.
8. Small local urban constellations can be both an aesthetic and practical alternative to master planning, favoring incremental change.
9. Although occurring at a small scale, the principle of treating contextual and complex factors can logically be deduced to include larger-scale interventions.
10. Micro-urbanism, as a method of incremental change over time, can produce a coherent whole that is historically rooted, intellectually complex, accessible, and emotionally engaging.

19 Tice, James, Camerlenghi, Nicola, Ceen, Allan, Steiner, Erik, Svevo, Giovanni, *Images of Rome: The Rodolfo Lanciani Digital Archive*, with the Istituto Nazionale di Archeologia e Storia dell'Arte (INASA). [https://exhibits.stanford.edu/lanciani].

Rome: The Lost and Unknown City *(Roma Ignota e Perduta)*

Judith DiMaio

frontispiece:
Emma Hart afterwards Lady Hamilton as the goddess of health while being exhibited in that character by Dr. Graham in Pall Mall, Richard Cosway, ca. 1775.

In 2014, I was invited to speak at the conference "Rowe/Rome" on the matter of the exhibition, "Roma interrotta," which was displayed in 1978 in Trajan's Market. Our team (that being Colin Rowe, Judith DiMaio, Peter Carl, Barbara Littenberg, and Steven Peterson) was assigned the center plate, or Sector Eight of the 1748 *Pianta Grande di Roma* by Giambattista Nolli, for development.

In his critical remarks to the prelude of 'Urbanistics', the third volume of *As I was Saying*, Colin Rowe states, "The program for the exhibition was based upon the plan of Rome published by Giambattista Nolli in 1748 (Fig. 1) and upon the argument that, after Nolli, the urban tissue of Rome had been 'interrupted', that is, that something assumed to be implicit in the urban texture of Rome had become lost. In other words … the exhibition was an ostensible critique of urbanistic goings-on since the overthrow of the temporal power of the Papacy".[1]

He continues, "Participants—many of whom, I think, failed to understand the message—were each assigned one of the twelve plates which make up Nolli's plan, and from it they were asked to extrapolate their own developments".[2]

He further observes, "... An interesting idea but one that could scarcely lead to any successful issue; and this because Nolli's twelve plates, when they are presented as sites for development, are not equipped with an equivalency of complication",[3] meaning, those 'up north' are dense in tissue and include the Vatican, the Borgo, and the Piazza del Popolo, not to mention the Campus Martius. Whereas, 'down southwest and south', "... since these are occupied by the decorations of the Nolli plan ... except for producing new decorations, just what do you do" (Fig. 2)?[4]

Rowe then focuses, "… ours was the center site, the Palatine, the Aventine, and the Celio, that most difficult theater of ancient Roman debris".[5] His point being, what do we have to grab onto for development (Fig. 3, 4)? He sets the stage by quoting Pope Pius II:

> *half crumbling ruins remain, and traces can be seen of the peristyles, of the grandiose colonnades, and of pools and basins for bathing … Antiquity has deformed it all, and the walls once adorned by painted cloth and golden fabrics are now covered with ivy. You can feel the brambles grow where the tribunes clad in purple sat, and you can see the dwellings inhabited by serpents …*[6]

1 Rowe, Colin, "*Roma Interrotta*", *As I Was Saying: Recollections and Miscellaneous Essays* 3, *Urbanistics*, Caragonne, Alexander, ed., MIT Press, Cambridge, MA, and London, 1996: 127, 129.

2 Ibid.: 129.

3 Ibid.: 129.

4 Ibid.: 129.

5 Ibid.: 129.

6 Piccolomini, Aeneas Silvius, Pope Pius II, *I Commentarii*, lib. V: 138.

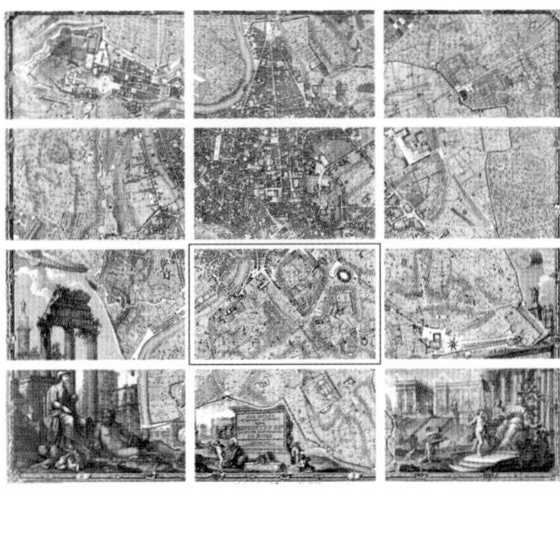

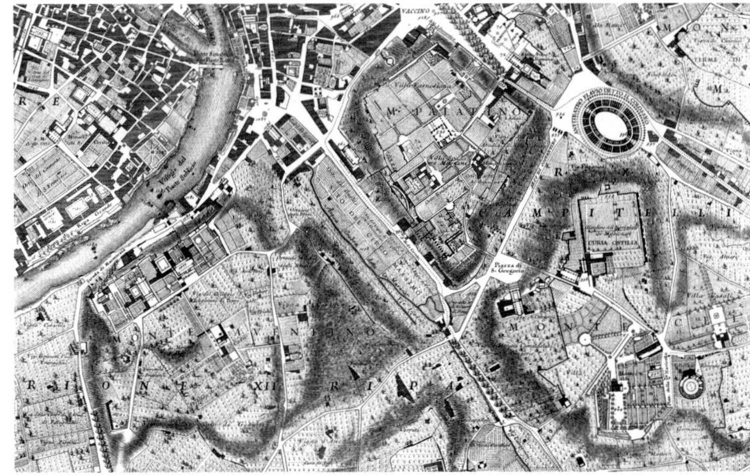

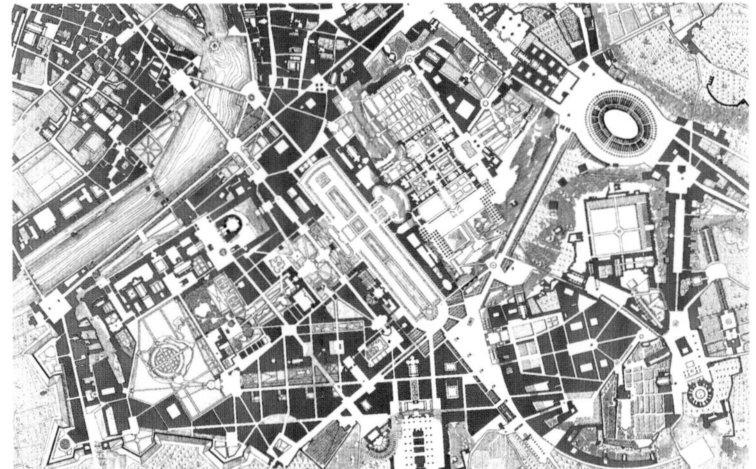

above:
Fig. 1. *La Pianta Grande di Roma* (Large Plan of Rome), Giambattista Nolli, 1748, showing division into 12 plates or sectors. University of Oregon Nolli Map 2004 ©.

Fig. 2. "Roma interrotta," 1978. Sponsor: Incontri Internazionali d'Arte; invited participants: Sartogo, Dardi, Grumbach, Stirling, Portoghesi, Giurgola, Venturi, Rowe (with Carl, DiMaio, Littenberg, Peterson), Graves, L. Krier, Rossi, R. Krier, exhibited at Trajan's Market, Rome, 1978.

inset top to bottom:
Fig. 3. *Plan of Rome,* Nolli, 1748, Sector Eight; existing conditions.

Fig. 4. "Roma interrotta," 1978, based on Colin Rowe's History for Sector 8, ROME: The Lost and Unknown City (*Roma Ignota e Perduta*), Colin Rowe, Judith DiMaio, Barbara Littenberg, Steven Peterson, Peter Carl, 1978–79.

Pope Pius II Piccolomini appears to be of the same opinion as Rowe, albeit ca. 1458. By 1748, things in the center site, our Sector Eight, had not evidenced terribly much change, save more brambles and more serpents, I would suppose (Fig. 5).

Rowe, therefore, presumed that, to advance the supposition of Rome "interrupted" and development for our sector, we required a fake history of Rome to explain the events—an imaginary history to grab onto by way of managing an area of Rome that most certainly provoked Percy Bysshe Shelley to write, "Go Thou to Rome, at once the Paradise, the grave, the city and the wilderness ...."[7]

A consideration for my 2014 presentation and, as I write this essay, is the question, WHY, thirty-six years after the *Roma interrotta* exhibition, was there a resurgence of interest? That interest was first evidenced in 2010 when it was shown at the Venice Biennale. And then again re-exhibited at MAXXI the same year as the 2014 Rowe Rome conference. There has been much critical discussion on Rowe's predisposition for figure/ground, hard to avoid since Nolli's plan is just that, figure/ground. Ada Louise Huxtable, in *The New York Times* critique of the exhibition, "Rome and Artistic Fantasy", observes:

7 Shelley, Percy Bysshe, *Adonais: An Elegy on the Death of John Keats*, Pisa with the types of Didot, 1821, XLIX.

Fig. 5. *Villa Madama*, Rome, Robert Hubert, ca. 1760.

> *Roma interrotta is already a celebrated project in the tight circles of today's international architectural cognoscenti... with instructions to devise 20th century 'interventions' or changes in the plan through insertion of... new buildings. These additions were to be integrated into the historical... frame-work of Nolli's city. It was literally, "Rome Interrupted" at a point in the past for a radical excursion into the 20th century. Billed as an exercise in urbanism, it was, from the start, an elite and erudite game.*[8]

For all intents and purposes, it was, indeed, just that: a brilliant play of places, persons, and events. Since our design and history for Sector Eight were not singled out by Huxtable for acknowledgement as were others in her critique, I often wondered if she merely accessed the formal manipulations and ignored, our text of substantiation without even reading it.[9]

With all this in mind, and realizing that the other invited speakers would most likely treat the formal maneuvering, I delved, once again, into the text. I realized that my interest was not with formal aspects so seductive to those of us concerned with design and form. My fascination was, and still is, centered on the fictive history Colin wrote to accompany our design proposal. I wonder who remembers it, who has read it, and, has anyone actually considered its significance as the

8 Huxtable, Ada Louise, "Rome and Artistic Fantasy", *New York Times*, July 15, 1979.

9 Ibid.

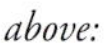

above:
Fig. 6. *The Emperor Napoleon in His Study at the Tuileries*, Jacques-Louis David, 1812.

Fig. 7. *Portrait du Pape Pie VII* (Portrait of Pope Pius VII), Jacques-Louis David, 1805.

inset:
Fig. 8. *La Girandola di Castel Sant'Angelo*, Franz Theodor Aerni, ca. 1874.

counterpart to the design process and proposal? Colin, always the alchemist at heart, conjures Rome —"The Lost and Unknown City"— "a Rome that could have been, but never was; an invented history that might have been, but never was."[10] It is certainly true that our history, more specifically Colin's, was "an alibi for topographical and contextual concerns"[11] which positioned us for design, in both the spirit of Nolli's aesthetic and Colin's interest in figure/ground. But these were the two-dimensional aspirations, and it strikes me that what has been overlooked is the true *raison d' être*; the fictive history, itself. Even though the exhibition posed itself as an "argument" about Rome's urban tissue and implied that something had been "interrupted or lost since 1748", for Rowe the text was not so much about the design *per se*, but an excuse for him to indulge in his favorite game: the 'what ifs' of history. Many of us who were in Colin's orbit know the game well. What if Queen Victoria had been born Prince Victor, a male heir to the throne? What then!? What if Napoleon had been born in Corsica two days earlier? That would have meant he would have been born Italian, not French. What then? What about Waterloo and all the rest?

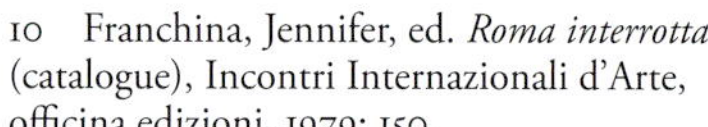

10 Franchina, Jennifer, ed. *Roma interrotta* (catalogue), Incontri Internazionali d'Arte, officina edizioni, 1979: 150.

11 Ibid.: 150.

above:
Fig. 9. *Grand Cascade*, Peterhof Palace and Gardens, detail of the Samson and the Lion Fountain, B. C. Rastrelli, F. Vassu and K. Osner, 1715–1724.

Fig. 10. *Charles Towneley in His Sculpture Gallery*, Johann Zoffany, 1782.

inset top to bottom:
Fig. 11. *The Grand Carousel in Honor of Christina of Sweden*, Filippo Gagliardi and Filippo Lauri, ca. 1656.

Fig. 12. *Ruins of the Temple at Selinunte with Two Figures Seated on the Remains*, Thomas Hearne, 1777.

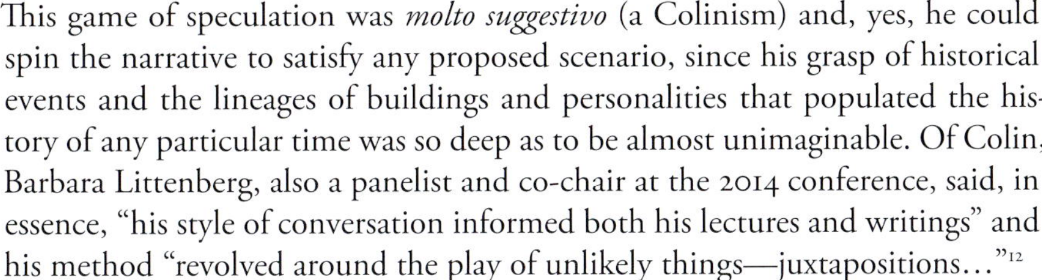

This game of speculation was *molto suggestivo* (a Colinism) and, yes, he could spin the narrative to satisfy any proposed scenario, since his grasp of historical events and the lineages of buildings and personalities that populated the history of any particular time was so deep as to be almost unimaginable. Of Colin, Barbara Littenberg, also a panelist and co-chair at the 2014 conference, said, in essence, "his style of conversation informed both his lectures and writings" and his method "revolved around the play of unlikely things—juxtapositions…"[12]

Thus after many re-reads of our, or, of Rowe's speculative history, I wondered, why has no one translated Colin's imagination and brilliance of memory and visual recall into a 'pictorial exposition' of Sector Eight? The text, an extravaganza of fictive history, is an incisive critique of the exhibition, all couched in the game of 'what ifs' of the late 18th century and 19th centuries, that is, Rome at least up to 1870 or thereabout.

12 Conference: "Rowe Rome 2014 Urban Design and the Legacy of Colin Rowe". Observations and commentary by Barbara Littenberg, Co-chair; Session 3: Rowe/Rome II: Rome for Rowe. Rowe for Rome.

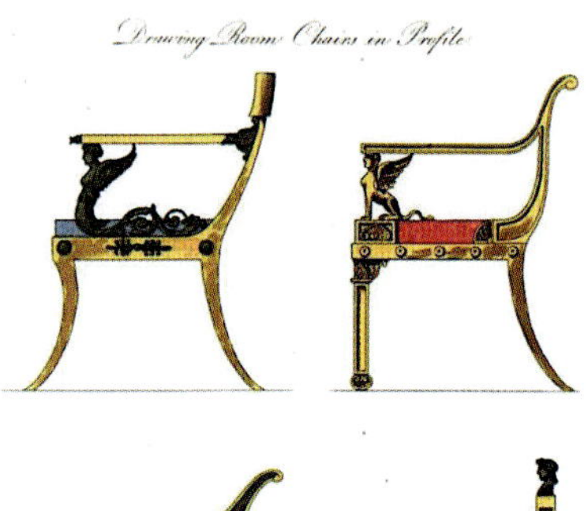

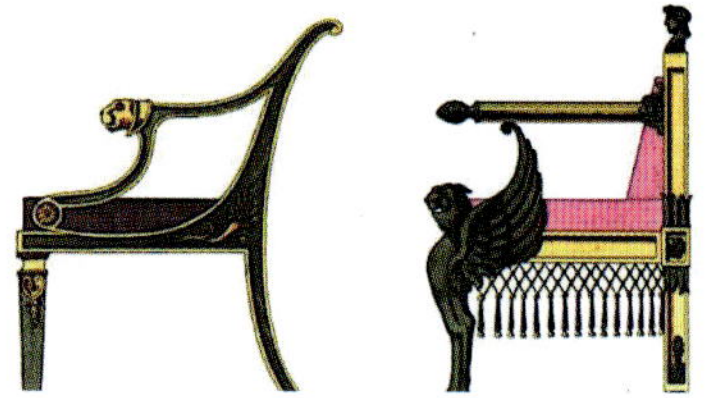

above:
Fig. 13: *Blick vom Alten Museum auf den Lustgarten*, Michael Carl Gregorovius, before 1850.

Fig. 14. *Goethe at the Window of His Apartment by the Corso*, Rome, Johann H. W. Tischbein, 1787.

below:
Fig. 15. *Drawing Room Chairs in Profile*, from *A Collection of Designs for Household Furniture and Interior Decorations in the Most Approved and Elegant Taste*, George Smith, 1808.

To be more specific, for "Roma interrotta" he constructed an entire history replete with a cast of historical figures, all real, save perhaps the Czar's chef, Aldo Rossini, and all played against a stage set made up of 'architectural furniture' or props that could have existed on our site to substantiate our design; a veritable 'word picture' waiting to be properly translated into a visual reality. In other words, where Rowe's stroke of hand was with the written word, my stroke is pictorial, and it is an attempt to paint the visual extravaganza implicit in the imagined history—to bring his history into living color.

Therefore, and effectively, the 'scholarly work' was done by Rowe. Mine is the visual manifestation of Rowe's history. My critique is intended to bring into focus, to conjure the sensibility and atmosphere of 18th century Rome via imagery. Furthermore, though a colleague suggested that I, too, write a scholarly work, I found it rather odd and peculiar to write a scholarly work which is based on a fake history and fake footnotes, albeit believable due to Rowe's genius.

Nevertheless, and with so much said, let me attempt to weave the magician's history with the visuals that could attach themselves to those who frequented his history within the context and topography of our sector.

Delighting in his ability to confound and shake up historical facts—facts, for Colin, were, and I quote, "like cows, if you look them in the eye long enough, they go away"—he created a stage for encounters of both events and personalities, vivid and ostentatious, as well as for the ever-seductive and infamous figure/ground.

As already noted, the topography of our sector included three of the famous Seven Hills of Rome: the Caelian, the Palatine and the Aventine, with the great valleys of the Colosseum and Circus Maximus between. He spins a yarn of fantasy revolving around Napoleon (Fig. 6) and Rome. Not only does he, in his text, conjure up the game plan for the site's architectural gestures, but he subjects his cast of

left to right:
Fig. 16. *A Portrait of Thomas Hope in Turkish Costume*, Sir William Beechey, 1798.

Fig. 17. *The Hon. Mrs. Thomas Hope Full Face in Red Velvet Dress*, Henry Bone, 1813, after Henry Edward Dawe, ca. 1810.

Fig. 18. *Danzatrice con le Braccia sul Capo*, Antonio Canova, 1798–1799.

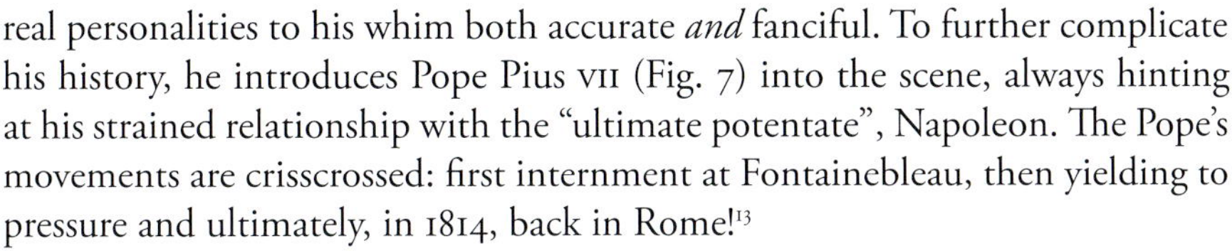

real personalities to his whim both accurate *and* fanciful. To further complicate his history, he introduces Pope Pius VII (Fig. 7) into the scene, always hinting at his strained relationship with the "ultimate potentate", Napoleon. The Pope's movements are crisscrossed: first internment at Fontainebleau, then yielding to pressure and ultimately, in 1814, back in Rome![13]

Rowe heralds Napoleon's triumphant arrival into Rome (did Napoleon ever actually come to Rome?):[14] "Beethoven is to contribute a symphony … there are to be parades, pyrotechnics, fountains running with wine, *feux de joie*, all the rest—and the whole to be conducted in a setting of heroically romantic neoclassical architecture" (Fig. 8, 9, 11). [15]

The stage sets for the history of "Rome: The Lost and Unknown City" include Roman statuary in abundance (Fig. 10).

Lots of "ancient Roman debris" was called for (Fig. 12); and, of course, there was the requisite empire and regency furniture (Fig. 15); not to mention the borrowed bits and pieces of architecture like Canova's 'crib'of the Pantheon for his tomb-temple from Possagno. Rowe was purposeful in his choice for his stand-in for the imperial staircase known to have existed in the Palace of Domitian. It was Schinkel's sublime moment, the staircase of the Altes Museum (Fig. 13) which, as a young man visiting for the first time, Colin confided to me, rendered him to tears of joy as he made his ascent. But returning to Albani, he christened his new and renovated palace, the *Villa Albani al Palatino*. Rowe spared nothing from his experiences and recall for his elaborate stage sets for his sub-plot, the notorious figure/ground.

Now let me introduce the cast-extraordinaire, and "almost always divorced from their proper niche in time".[16] We begin with Mr. and Mrs. Thomas Hope, with their fantasies and eccentricities so much a part of the London of the Prince Regent and the Regency (Fig. 16, 17).

13 Mulcahy, Father Vincent, S. J., *Rome: The Lost and Unknown City (Roma Ignota e Perduta)*, catalogue, Museum of Art, University of Francis Xavier, Great Falls, Montana, 1974: par. 4, 141, par. 1.

14 Ibid.: 139, par. 2.

15 Ibid.: 141, par. 1.

16 Ibid.: 140, n.9.

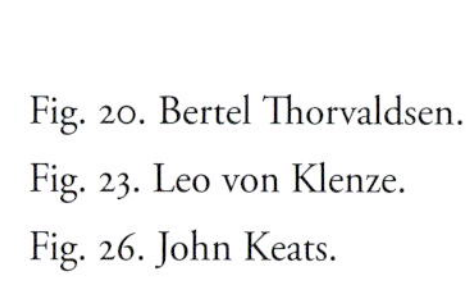

Fig. 19. Angelica Kauffmann.
Fig. 22. Lady Emma Hamilton.
Fig. 25. Lord Byron.

Fig. 20. Bertel Thorvaldsen.
Fig. 23. Leo von Klenze.
Fig. 26. John Keats.

Fig. 21. Sir William Hamilton.
Fig. 24. Karl Friedrich Schinkel
Fig. 27. Percy Bysshe Shelley.

And, in no particular order, we must include Antonio Canova, who made famous those diaphanous dancing muses (Fig. 18) throughout Europe; Johann Wolfgang von Goethe (Fig. 14), who made innumerable visits to Rome and wrote *Italian Journey*; Goethe's great friend, the Swiss painter, Angelica Kauffmann (Fig. 19); and Bertel Thorvaldsen (Fig. 20), who, anxious to be a member of the cast, journeys to Rome from Denmark. The young John Soane undoubtedly made the journey, and Sir William Hamilton (Fig. 21) and Lady Emma Hamilton (Fig. 22) would travel to Rome from Naples bearing gifts of antique vases recently discovered at Pompeii.

Leo von Klenze (Fig. 23) arrives in Rome to share the limelight with his compatriot, Karl Friedrich Schinkel (Fig. 24), whose incisive Prussian hand and mind made him the architect for kings and potentates.

Even the architects Giacomo Quarenghi and Bartolomeo Rastrelli, who had been drawn to Saint Petersburg, returned to Italy to get a piece of the action. Not to be left out, the literary crowd included Lord Byron[17] (Fig. 25), John Keats, and P. B. Shelley (Fig. 26, 27), among others.

Now let us focus on the action as it unfolds on the three hills in question. Using Colin's chronology, the time is approximately 1809, to begin with, but ultimately reaching to 1870.

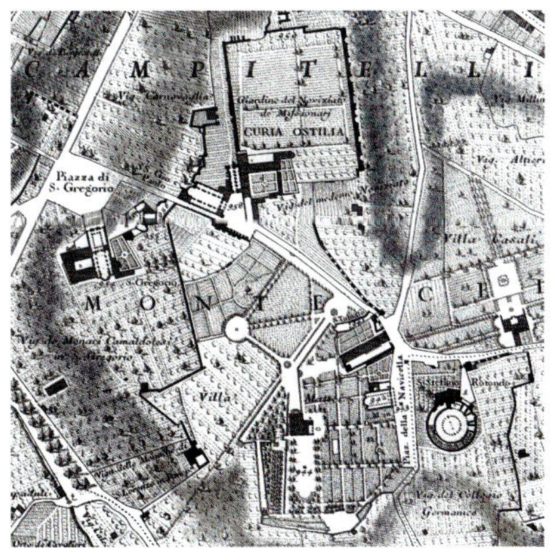

Fig. 28. *View of Santi Giovanni e Paolo, Rome, from the Palatine Hill,* Joseph Mallord William Turner, 1819.

Fig. 29. *Plan of Rome,* Nolli, 1748, Sector Eight; detail of the Caelian Hill.

17 *Roma interrotta:* 144, par. 4.

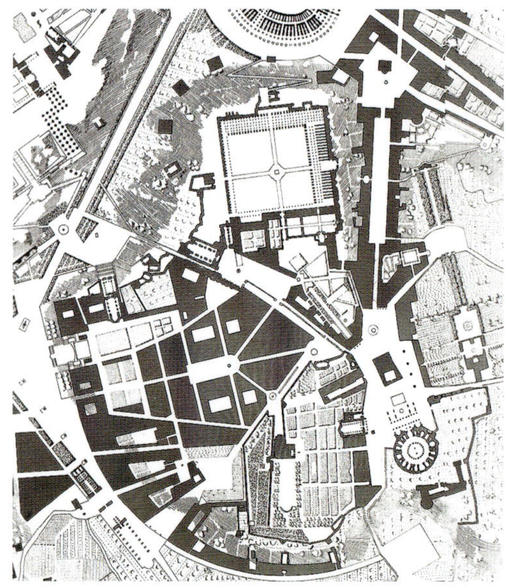

above left to righ:
Fig. 30. Detail: Temple Base for the Temple of the Divine Claudius and the Arches of the Neronian Aqueduct, I. Gismondi, 1933–1955. *Model of Imperial Rome at the Time of Constantine*, Museo Civiltá Romana, EUR, Rome. Photo: Museo Civiltá Romana.

Fig. 31. Detail: Caelian Hill Intervention based upon Rowe's history, *ROME: The Lost and Unknown City (Roma Ignota e Perduta)*, 1978.

Fig. 32. View from the Caelian Hill, Rome - Looking West. Photo: Jeff Bondono.

Stage Set I—The Celio

The Celio, 1748: "... an arid and deserted region of ancient remains, unkempt vineyards, malarial villini, and battered monastic foundations"[18] with the church of Santi Giovanni e Paolo among them (Fig. 28, 29). The dominant debris of the hill was certainly the huge platform built for the Temple of the Divine Claudius, and vestiges of the Neronian aqueduct snaking through and across the Celio to feed the Imperial Palace on the Palatine (Fig. 30).

clockwise:
Fig. 33. Obelisk at the Villa Mattei, Caelian Hill, Rome; *Visit to the Sepulcre of the Scipio*, Robert W. Pilkington, 1818.

Fig. 34. *Portrait of Caroline Murat*, Anon.

Fig. 35. *Caroline Murat, Queen of Naples, in the Silver Salon at the Elysée Palace*, Louis Hippolyte, Lebas, 1810.

Act I

By 1810, the Celio had transformed into a "hill of gentle and brilliant greenness"[19] (Fig. 32), where now there existed a German academy, the Accademia Bavarese, supposedly designed by Leo von Klenze, but no one is sure; for certain, an addition to the once-battered Santo Stefano Rotondo is by von Klenze.[20]

There is the famous *Cimitero for the Uomini Illustrissimi*, a magnificent takeover of the plateau of the Temple to the Divine Claudius—a brilliant reuse of "ancient Roman debris". We cannot ignore the *Quartiere Mattei*,[21] which is so beautifully handled and was careful in its renovation so as not to mutilate the then existing Villa Mattei (Fig. 31) with its upper and lower gardens interconnected by bridges. Imagine the *quartiere*, (Fig. 33) a place where Paolina Bonaparte Borghese and

18 Mulcahy (1974): 138, par. I.

19 Ibid.: 138.

20 *Roma interrotta:* 142, par. 2.

21 Ibid.

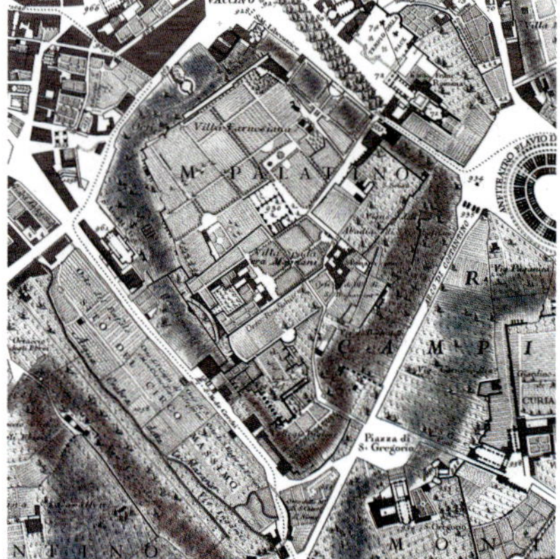

Caroline Bonaparte Murat (Fig. 34) could escape, giving patronage and leading lives of leisure. Undoubtedly there were visitations by Canova to the Villa Paolina—as neoclassical in sensibility as the Silver Salon in the Élysée Palace occupied by Carolina (Fig. 35)—to observe Paolina in anticipation of his transformation of her into white marble, thus immortalizing her forever (Fig. 40).

Stage Set II–The Palatine

above top down:
Fig. 36. *Plan of Rome*, Nolli, 1748, Sector Eight; detail of the Palatine Hill.

Fig. 37. *Posthumous Portrait of Giovanni Battista Piranesi*, Pietro Labruzzi, 1779.

inset:
Fig. 38. *Romeinse capriccio met het Septizodium, de Tombe van Porsenna en de Tempel van Vesta*, Willem van Nieulandt II, early 17th century.

The Palatine, what a world (Fig. 36)! In 1748 so little was excavated, and what was unearthed was being documented by Piranesi (Fig. 37). For sure, he inspected and documented the 'existing furniture' of crumbling remains, including the vestiges of the *Septizodium* (Fig. 38) built by Septimius Severus, a spectacular 'facade' of water heralding Rome as one approached from the south. Only a vestige was standing in 1748, and today nothing of it remains.

Without a doubt, Karl Friedrich Schinkel, drawn to Rome for inspiration, inspected these ruins and what traces of Domitian's palace that remained, or were visible. According to Colin, we owe Schinkel so much, both for his contributions in Rome as well as his master works in Berlin and elsewhere (Fig. 39).

Act II

By 1810, however, the lust for excavating antiquities and with it the passion for collecting made all that change. The Palatine's transformation and build-out is evidenced in the astounding red gauche plan we 'discovered', ca. 1811 (Fig. 43).

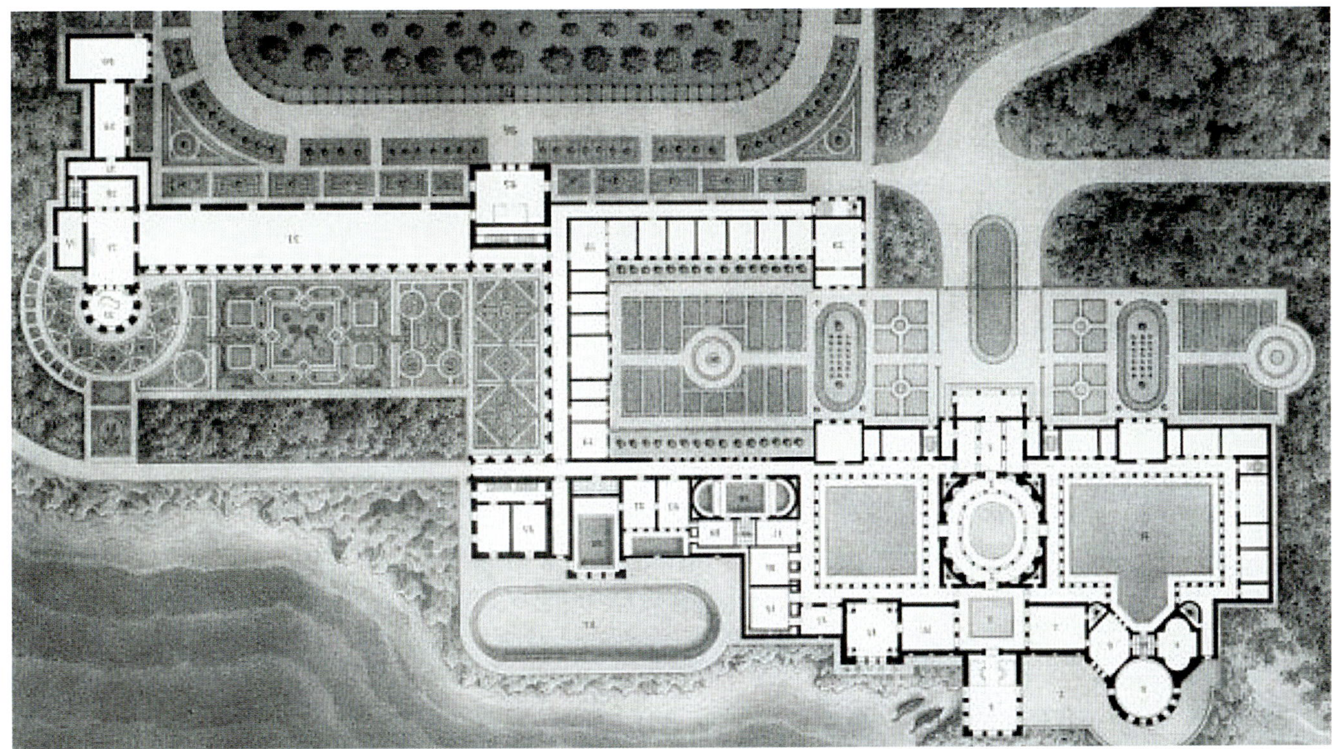

Fig. 39. *Imaginary Reconstruction of Pliny's Villa Laurentina:* plan and view, Karl Friedrich Schinkel, 1833–1841.

Fig. 40. *Paolina Borghese*, Antonio Canova, 1804–1808, Galleria Borghese, Rome. Photo: Architas.

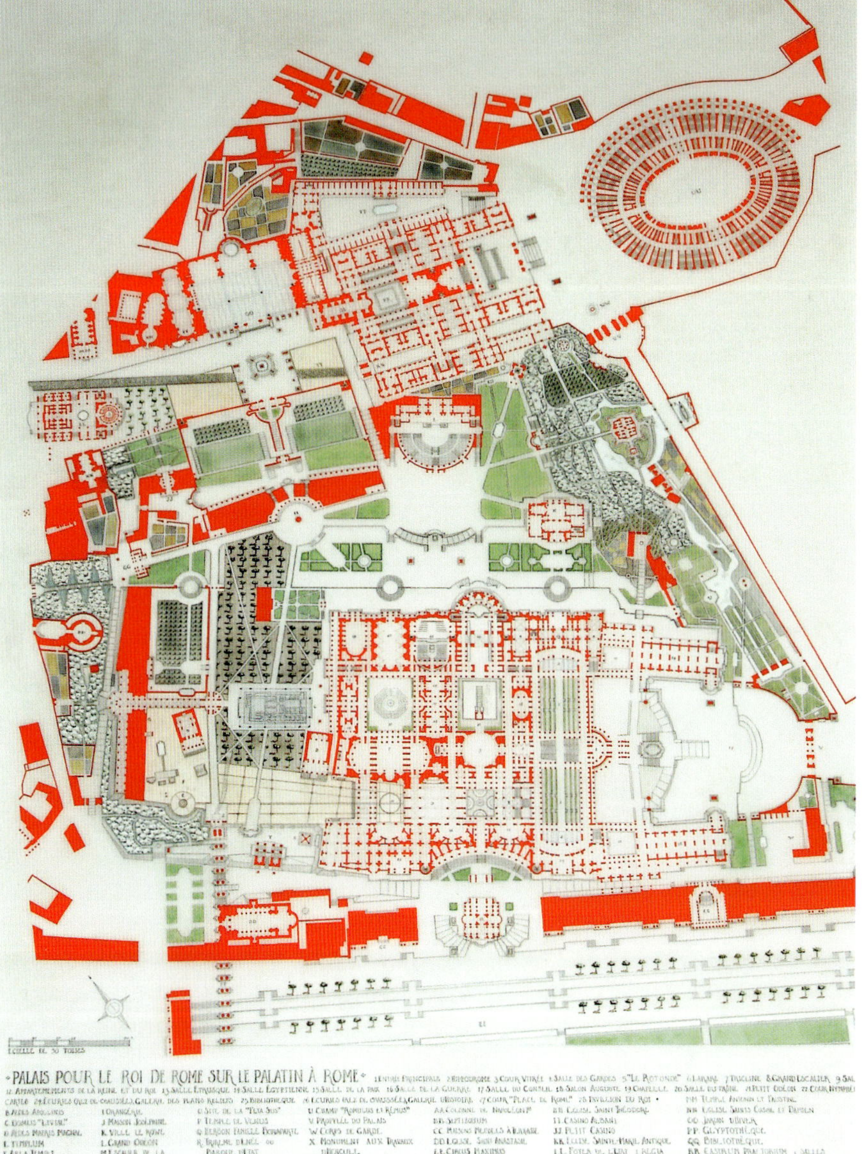

above:
Fig. 41. *Cardinal Pietro Ottoboni*, Francesco Trevisani, ca. 1689.

Fig. 42. *Colonnade of the Casino of the Villa Albani, Rome*, Hubert Robert, 1763–1764.

inset:
Fig. 43. The Palatine Hill 'Rediscovered', Peter Carl, Sector Eight, 1977–1978.

By Colin's determination, the hill's identity began to change much earlier, when Cardinal Alessandro Albani,[22] with Cardinal Pietro Ottoboni (Fig. 41) as his stand-in, purchased the Orti Farnesiani on the Palatine, designed by the 16th century architect Vignola, which remains in ruins to this day. Cardinal Albani already had his 17th century villa on the Via Salaria (Fig. 42), but now he was equipped with "an archeological foyer of unexampled richness".[23] Winckelmann (Fig. 44) came to Rome in 1755, and he and Albani became great friends (for real) and, thus, "provided one of the principal 'forcing houses' in the early history of Neoclassicism; and, as such, was indebted to Goethe for some record of its appearance … on the occasion of his Roman visit of 1786",[24] or so says Colin.

Albani's "hospitality and patronage during his building phases extended, most certainly, to Robert Adam, Jacques Louis Clérisseau, Hubert Robert (Fig. 46),

22 Mulcahy (1974): 138, par. 3, 4.

23 Ibid.: 138, par. 4.

24 Ibid.: 139, par. 1.

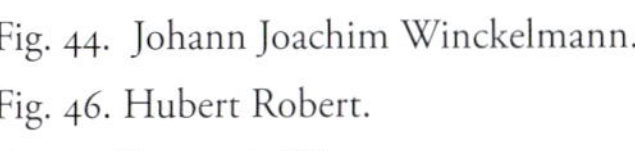

Fig. 44. Johann Joachim Winckelmann.

Fig. 46. Hubert Robert.

Fig. 48. Benjamin West.

Fig. 45. Bust of Sir John Soane.

Fig. 47. Napoleon Receving Queen Louisa of Prussia.

Fig. 49. Giuseppe Valadier.

Fig. 50. *Il Circo Massimio a Roma*, Viviano Codazzi, 1630.

Fig. 51. *Plan of Rome*, Nolli, 1748, Sector Eight; detail of the Circus Maximus Valley.

Raphael Mengs, Antonio Canova, Benjamin West (Fig. 48), and others".[25] Undoubtedly, that obsessive collector of antiquities, John Soane, was among the "others" (Fig. 45).

We are then confronted with an 'intermission' in time and are compelled to wait for Napoleon's 1809 arrival in Rome with his new wife, Maria Louisa, Archduchess of Austria (Fig. 47), to see a later and more splendid building campaign on the Palatine, in the Valley of the Circus Maximus, and on the Aventine.[26] This revelation now known, because the designs by Giuseppe Valadier (Fig. 49), were brought to public awareness only in 1972, after their discovery by the Cabinet des Estampes et Dessins of the Bibliothèque Nationale (Fig. 53)![27] These drawings verified Valadier and Napoleon's collaboration and grand scheme for building out the hill and its splendid belvedere-exedra promenades descending into the Circus Maximus valley.

Stage Set III—Valley of the Circus Maximus

There was not much remaining in the once magnificent Valley of the Circus Maximus, save the debris of the Circus itself, and the southwestern fringes of the Palatine (Fig. 50, 51).

25 Ibid.: 138, par. 4.

26 Ibid.: 139, par. 2.

27 Ibid.: 139, par. 3 and n. 6.

Fig. 52. *Il Circo Massimo a Roma*, Edouardo Ettore Forti, 19th century.

Fig. 53. *Piazza del Popolo, Rome*, Giuseppe Valadier, project, from the Cabinet des Estampes et Dessins of the Bibliothèque Nationale 1816.

Fig. 54. *Departure of the Israelites*, David Roberts, 1829.

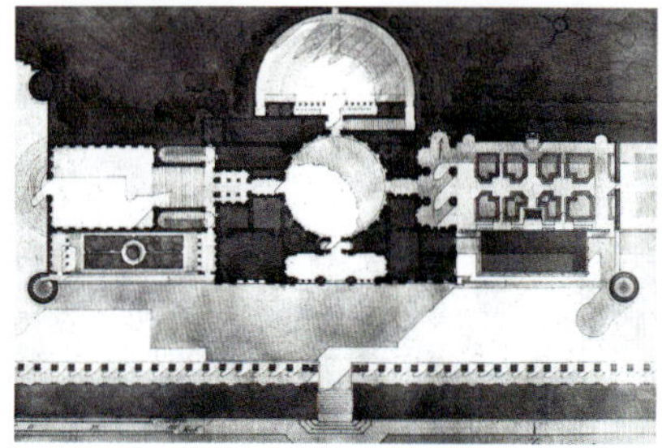

above top to bottom:
Fig. 55. *Il Fontanazzo* or *La Peschiera*, Palazzo Ducale, Sassuolo, Gaspare Vigarani, ca. 17th.

Fig. 56. Medici fountain, Jardin du Luxembourg, Paris, original 16th century by Tommaso Francini, destroyed; new fountain and grotto with fragments of the original by Alphonse de Gisor, 1858–64 with statues by August Ottin, 1866. Photo: Francis Bourgouin.

Fig. 57. *Plan of the Villa Madama,* Rome; Raphael, Antonio da Sangallo the Younger, 1518, *Italian Gardens of the Renaissance*, J. C. Shepherd and G. A. Jellicoe, 1925.

inset:
Fig. 58. *Plan General de la Villa Située dans le Jardin Pontifical*, by Paul Marie Letarouilly. From *Le Vatican et la basilique de Saint-Pierre de Rome*, A. Morel, Paris, 1882.

Act III

The magnificent valley and circus took on many identities. It started out as the Foro Napoleon, where one could find distinguished ladies playing at charioteers (Fig. 52). As time marched on, it was better known as the *Piazza d'Armi del Circo Massimo*, designed with an Egyptian temple (Fig. 54) of a "yet unknown cult (after his Egyptian campaign?)" and later, alas, converted into the present church of Saint Catherine of Alexandria".[28]

But it is to the fantastical nymphaeum-water piece, now in ruins, courtesy of the nymphaeum, from the Palazzo Ducale at Sassuolo (Fig. 55), and its promenades and walkways, to which I wish to draw attention. This extraordinary *grotte rustique* was already celebrated in 1758 by Nicolas Cochin in his *Voyage d'Italie* as a most astounding waterworks. It was surrounded by a canal and tiers lined with trees and "equipped with the apparatus of balustrades, bridges, obelisks, and statues".[29] The scenography of this spectacle suited the wanderings of a decked-out and dignified crowd listening to the sound of water and casting their eyes up to the Imperial Hill and back to the summit of the Aventine. A close approximation, not in a ruinous state, might be the nymphaeum fountain of Catherine de' Medici (Fig. 56) found in the Jardin du Luxembourg, albeit without the tiered levels.

28 Ibid.: 139 and par. 2, n. 8.

29 *Roma interrotta:* 144, par. 2.

above left to right:
Fig. 59. *Veduta di Roma con il Ponte Rotto*, Gaspar van Wittel, 1689.

Fig. 60. *Roma - Pincio, Casina Valadier*, Blick auf Valadier Häuslein, uncredited, historic postcard, ca. 1910.

Fig. 61. *Plan of Rome*, Nolli, 1748, Sector Eight; detail of the Aventine Hill.

The set pieces defining the western edge of the circus-nymphaeum included the formally useful and 'cribbed' plan of the Villa Madama (Fig. 57), and an exact copy of the Villa of Pius IV found in the Vatican gardens (Fig. 58), both extensions of the *quartiere-de-luxe* of the Aventine. The Villa Madama, alternatively as the site developed, became the Villa Monmouth-Bariatinsky, later the Palazzo Letizia, and, somewhere along the line, the Roman establishment of Madame Mère. Ultimately, it became the Canadian Embassy.[30] Even a tea house along the lines of Valadier's Casina Valadier (Fig. 60) found on the Pincian Hill had its place on this western slope facing the Aventine Hill.

Stage Set IV—The Aventine

The Aventine in 1748, aside from the terrace overlooking the Tiber and Rome with its two dilapidated, Early Christian basilicas, Santa Sabina and Sant'Alessio, was dotted with vineyards sloping down toward the south end of Rome with a privileged view of the Tiber and the ancient and broken *Ponte Rotto* (Fig. 59, 61).

30 Ibid.: 150, paragraph 1 (bottom), continued from page 146.

above left to right:
Fig. 62. *Portrait of Robert Adam*, Attributed to George Willison, ca. 1770–1775.

Fig. 63. *The Remains of the Seafront of Diocletian's Palace at Split*, engraving by Paolo Santini, Plate VII from Robert Adam's *Ruins of the the Palace of the Emperor Diocletian at Spalatro in Dalmatia*, 1764.

below:
Fig. 64. *The Adelphi and the Thames Riverside, Looking East*, engraving by Benedetto Pastorini, 1768–70; reproduced in the third volume of the Adam Brothers' *Works in Architecture*, 1822.

Act IV

All that changed with the amplification on the *Terrace* thanks to the embarrassing wealth and foresight of Czar Alexander I of Russia (Fig. 65).[31] Monumental and grand, the sub-structure and super-structure, no doubt, were inspired by the Palace of Diocletian in Split via Robert Adam's transformation of it into the Adelphi Terrace in London (Fig. 62, 63, 64).[32] One cannot overlook the build-out and the addition of Quarenghi's "highly accomplished *Pantheon*",[33] complemented on the opposite end of the *Terrace* by the already existing Knights of Malta precinct with Santa Maria del Priorato, the sole executed building by Piranesi in Rome—or anywhere.

31 Mulcahy (1974): 141, par. 2, 3.

32 Ibid.: 142, par. 2.

33 Ibid.: 142, par. 3.

Fig. 65. Alexander I, Emperor of Russia.

Fig. 66. Bejeweled Russian Woman.

Fig. 67. Prince Alexander Borissovich Kourakin.

Fig. 68. Princess Galitzin.

Fig. 69. Elizabeth Falconer, Mrs. Stanhope.

Fig. 70. Nicholas Boylston.

above left to right:
Fig. 71. *Gli Orti Farnesiani sul Palatino Ripresi dalla Terrazza del Portico di Ingresso*, C. Percier, 1786–90.

Fig. 72. *The Interior of the Palm House on the Pfaueninsel near Potsdam*, Carl Blechen, 1834.

Fig. 73. *Schloss Orianda, Crimea*, Heinrich Mützel, 1846, after Karl Friedrich Schinkel.

The breathtaking enhancement of the *Terrace* was not the only draw for the Russian enclave that congregated here. It was because he, the Czar, brought his famous chef, Aldo Rossini,[34] to Rome, who saw the build-up of the splendid Albergo de Russie (Fig. 71, 72, 73) abounding in Russian excess, making it an irresistible destination for bejeweled Russian men and women (Fig. 66, 67, 68). By 1820 the opulent English society (Fig. 69) and the occasional American (Fig. 70) gravitated here as well, albeit, very different in sense and sensibility.

Defining the south edge of the *Terrace* and proximate to the hotel was the *Parco Luxe* (Fig. 76). The *Parco* was a combination of dreamy landscapes (Fig. 75) amidst Roman ruins, replete with garden follies, water features, topiary, as well as those Hermes-like cypress trees and the spread of the unforgettable Rome umbrella pines, not to mention the shaded rhododendrons beneath.

34 Ibid.: 141, par. 4 and n. 15.

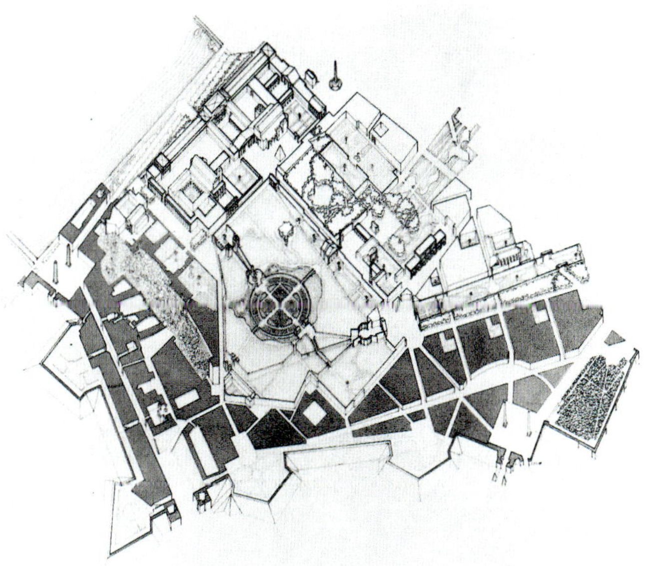

Ascending the Aventine and approaching the *Parco* from the Valley of the Circus Maximus, we encounter more villas, gardens, and the twin neoclassical gateways leading into the park and the island. The gateways were inspired, no doubt, by those of the Villa Borghese (Fig. 74) found just outside of the Porta del Popolo designed by Luigi Canina.

It was, however, the island retreat deftly situated within the park known as the *Isola Segreta Luxe* that was of an irresistible draw and hideaway. No doubt, the *isola's* inspiration and origins were found in the Orto Botanico (Fig. 77)[35] located in Padova, where another neoclassical architect, Giuseppe Jappelli (Fig. 83), was busy at work completing the Caffè Pedrocchi. Rumor has it that he came to Rome to oversee the design of the park and the *Isola Segreta*.

above left to right:
Fig. 74. *Villa Borghese, Gates from the Piazzale Flaminio*, Luigi Canina, 1825–28.

Fig. 75. *Garden of the Palazzo Colonna*, Rome, Giovanni Volpato and Louis Rodolphe Ducros, 1780.

Fig. 76. *The Aventine Hill and the Parco Luxe*, Judith DiMaio, 1977–78.

35 *Roma interrotta:* 142, par. 3.

above: Fig. 77. *Historical Plan of Orto Botanico*, Padova, Andrea Moroni, ca. 1545.

below: Fig. 78. *Isola Segreta*, drawing by Judith DiMaio, 1978.

Perhaps the most stunning moment of the garden-park is the *Isola Segreta*, or circular island, defined by a water canal and reached by four bridges (Fig. 78). The canal and island fountains were fed by a water cascade inspired by Vignola's *giardino segreto* at Caprarola (Fig. 79). The primary approach to the upper level of the cascade was defined by a magnificent pair of aviaries like those found in the gardens of the Villa Borghese (Fig. 80) and on the Palatine in what had been the Orti Farnesiani.

The island retreat is, itself, populated by a thousand marble statues, a fantasy Roman temple made up of 'bits and pieces' of ancient Roman debris, so adored by the likes of Cardinal Albani, who similarly had a sham neoclassical temple in the gardens of his Villa Albani on the Via Salaria, or like the Temple of Aesculapius (Fig. 82) on the artificial lake in the Villa Borghese. There was even a 'rip-off' of Schinkel's sublime *stibadium* found in the park of Schloss Klein-Glienicke (Fig. 81), just outside of Potsdam and Berlin. The *stibadium* of Schinkel was inspired by Pliny the Younger's *stibadium*, or the "curved seat of white marble decked with vines and vine clad columns", found at his Tuscan Villa and described in his famous letters to Gallus.[36] Clipped hedges on the *isola* defined secluded areas for obvious and less obvious clandestine maneuverings, set against a myriad of sounds from the various fountains and *uccelli* singing and flitting about happily in their aviaries.

above left to right:
Fig. 79. *Giardino Segreto*, Palazzo Farnese at Caprarola; design attributed to Jacopo Barozzi da Vignola after 1559; executed by Giacomo del Duca, Giovanni A. Garzoni and Girolamo Rainaldi.
Photo: *Art in Vista Guide, Viterbo.*

Fig. 80. *Uccelleria*, Villa Borghese, Rome, attributed to Girolamo Rainaldi, 1617-19. Photo: Awesome Aviaries.

Fig. 81. *Stibadium*, Schloss Klein-Glienicke, Wannsee, Germany, Karl Friedrich Schinkel, 1823–30, Photo: Andreas F. E. Bernhard.

36 Pliny the Younger, *Letters*, Book V, Letter 6 "The Tuscan Villa"; Lines 36-37: "a curved seat of white marble decked with vines and four vined columns of Carystian marble. From beneath the seat water flows out of … and is caught in a stone hewn out of the rock faced marble …."

Fig. 82. *Vue du Temple d'Esculape et du Lac de la Villa Borghese à Rome*, Louis François Cassas, 1801.

Such was the life of Colin's neoclassical cast: lingering, resting, flirting, romancing, gossiping, engaging in intellectual and philosophical conversation, or, simply stated, enjoying the art of 'lazing' in a dream-like setting. Certainly the Russians visiting the Albergo found their way into the park, making it easy for them to find the great portrait painter Vigée Le Brun (Fig. 85) dressed in flowing, white drapery—with or without her daughter—with whom she enjoyed such a reputation in Saint Petersburg; or even the gorgeous Madame Récamier (Fig. 88) hidden away in a secluded area of the island, reclining and surveying the island park from her sublime neoclassical *stibadium*.

Fig. 83. Giuseppe Jappelli.

Fig. 84. Johann H. W. Tischbein.

Fig. 85. Élisabeth Vigée Le Brun and Daughter.

Fig. 86. Goethe in Repose.

Fig. 87. Lady Emma Hamilton.

Fig. 88 Madame Récamier.

above:
Fig. 89. *Villa Borghese*, Rome, Giovanni Volpato and Louis Rodolphe Ducros, 1780.

below:
Fig. 90. *Triumphal Arch of Pius VI*, Giuseppe Valadier, 1800.

There, too, were the English, who felt the *Parco Luxe* reminiscent of Regent's Park, including, and not to forget, Lady Emma Hamilton (Fig. 87), who, perhaps, found solace in the serenely green garden park and island, pining for her lover, Lord Nelson.

Then again, one could imagine that it was here in this garden park that J. H. Wilhelm Tischbein (Fig. 84) immortalized Goethe in his repose (Fig. 86) contemplating "ruins imposed upon ruins".

Last, but not least, one must cite the occasional visit of Pius VII, servant to Napoleon's aspirations for Rome (ca. 1819); those being "a stage for the ultimate Napoleonic settlement in Europe" (Fig. 90).[37]

But, despite that, even he, when in the *Parco Luxe* with its island precinct, could breathe the "Roman air ... to taste the languid enjoyment of the daydream that they call life ..." (Fig. 89).[38]

Stage Set V—The Giardino Segreto at Caprarola

Act V–Finale

I conclude this excursion of fantasy and imagery with an image of the sorcerer (Fig. 91) in his retreat in the *giardino segreto* at Caprarola (Fig. 92). It was here, "where the beauty of the Pagan world lives again"[39], that Colin always reminded me of Queen Christina of Sweden's strange comment, upon visiting the garden of the whispering Hermes and Caryatids, "I dare not mention the name of Jesus lest I break the spell".[40] And, so, too, one can hear Rowe himself, whispering and conjuring the 'what ifs' of history from his cherished enclave.

Fig. 91. Colin Rowe sitting among the caryatids and cypresses in the gardens of the Palazzo Farnese, Caprarola, spring 1981.

Fig. 92. *Giardino Segreto*, Villa Caprarola from *Italian Villas and Their Gardens* by Edith Wharton, 1904.

37 Mulcahy (1974): 140, par. 4.

38 Hawthorne, Nathaniel, "The Suburban Villa", Chapter VIII, *The Marble Faun or the Romance of Monte Beni:* par. 1. 1859.

39 Masson, Georgina, *Italian Gardens*, Thames & Hudson, London, 1966: 165.

40 Ibid.: 165.

IV. Praxis

Architecture serves practical ends; it is subjected to uses; but it is also shaped by ideas and fantasies; its rationale is cosmic and metaphysical and here of course lay its particular ability to impose itself on the mind.

The Architecture of Utopia, *Granta* 63, Cambridge University, 1959.

"Praxis" presents professional work by Rowe's students, colleagues, and those indebted to his ideas. This work varies enormously from design guidelines to planning proposals and completed projects ranging in scale from micro-insertions of one or two buildings to macro-interventions for campuses, neighborhoods, and entire urban districts. In the background is the Mod/'trad' debate, or, more generally, the *zeitgeist* vs. the *genius loci* conundrum. For these projects, primacy of place is almost always ascendant.

Rowe's involvement in urban design practice was first evident in New York City beginning in 1967. That involvement continued with an exhibition for NYC at MoMA and collaboration with the Institute for Architecture and Urban Studies and the City of New York.These initiatives balanced the requirements and incentives of New York's planning and zoning with community interests, economic development, partisan politics, and social and aesthetic well-being. This laid the groundwork for multiple design proposals for Lower Manhattan by both the Studio and the Office of Lower Manhattan. The success of Battery Park City, and the many commissioned urban designs leading up to the World Trade Center site after 9/11, bear testament to these forays by the Studio.

One begins to appreciate Rowe's global impact, not alone, but in association with like-minded urbanists, some doing extensive professional work. Rowe's influence is found throughout the U.S., South America, Africa, Europe, and Asia. All assume unique attitudes peculiar to their 'sense of place'. This body of work emphasizes the connections between existing city fabrics, environmental-landscape features, and cultural influences. Although there exists a wide range of stylistic variations, one sees a recurring attempt to resolve the *zeitgeist/genius loci* conflict.

Independent of Rowe's ambivalence about city-versus-suburb, practitioners acknowledge that he made them aware that both the Modernist city and the suburb become sprawl are equally deleterious to the city, society, and the environment. Many of their projects consistently make that argument across what has come to be known as the city/suburb 'transect' as described by The Congress for the New Urbanism (CNU), which, more than any other organization, has embraced the Studio's urban design ethic. Following the methods promoted by Rowe, and building on them, New Urbanists have used principles and codes derived from the study and documentation of 'trad' cities and towns, many specific to the U.S. Those documented principles, plans, building types, and exemplars have supplemented the much more prevalent European models. Together they have been applied at multiple scales, from walkable, mixed-use neighborhoods and districts to dense city centers in both the U.S. and Europe. What are now common practices, including the development of form-based codes, were significantly influenced by the innovative exemplars of the coding of form represented at the extremes of scale by Seaside, Florida, and Battery Park City of Lower Manhattan. The 9/11 World Trade Center tragedy in Lower Manhattan should have provided the opportunity to repair the damage done to the urban fabric in the 1970s by the super-block World Trade Center Towers, sadly it did not.

The Impact of Colin Rowe on New York City

Terrance R. Williams[1]

Beginnings

In 1963 Colin Rowe was placed in charge of Cornell's fledgling graduate studio. Following a suggestion by John Reps, he called it Urban Design. Rowe was clearly interested in the evident antithetical and unresolved conflicts between the traditional and Modern city. He presented this problem to successive Urban Design Studio students by asking if these two opposite propositions and manifestations could be reconciled: Can the traditional fabric of blocks, streets, and defined public spaces be reasonably integrated with object and tower buildings that occupy space rather than define it? Only three years later, in 1966, the Museum of Modern Art (MoMA) invited four universities—Princeton, Columbia, Cornell, and later MIT—to prepare urban design proposals for New York City. Not typical studio projects, the teams comprised both students and faculty. The MoMA show, titled "The New City: Architecture and Urban Renewal",[2] opened in 1967, signaling the arrival of urban design in New York City. I joined the studio that same year.

Colin Rowe did not teach a singular view of either the world or architecture. His studio brought together all aspects of design, theory, and history, regarded as a 5,000-year continuum of still relevant design strategies. While highly regarded as a theoretician, Rowe never raised a theoretical issue unrelated to understanding architecture and urban design. He introduced us to the value of ambiguity and to the fact that there is never a single solution to any design problem. Perhaps his most lasting gift to us was to inculcate a design methodology that prepared us to work flexibly at any scale or venue: furniture, architecture, or urban precinct, in either private or public sectors.[3]

Transition

In the spring of 1968 Rowe told the studio that Peter Eisenman, a former student of his at Cambridge and founder and director of the newly created Institute for Architecture and Urban Studies (IAUS) in New York City, had received a contract from the New York City Department of City Planning to review the high-density

Fig. 1. "The New City: Architecture and Urban Renewal", Cornell Team, MoMA exhibition, 1967.

frontispiece: Manhattan Landing Photomontage: Existing and Landfill Option, Office of Lower Manhattan Development Plan, 1973.

1 Terrance (Terry) R. Williams (1938-2015) wrote this essay between 2011-2015. He verified much of the material with his friend and colleague John West with whom he had served in the Office of Lower Manhattan in the early 1970s. In 2020 Steve Hurtt provided the footnotes accompanying this essay. Terry Williams had asked us to extend his thanks to John West. We, the coeditors, likewise thank John West for his editorial help. Any errors are ours. The NYC Department of City Planning website "Special Purpose Districts" was a valuable resource.[https://www.nyc.gov/site/planning /zoning/districts-tools/special-purpose-districts .page].

2 Exhibition catalogue, "The New City: Architecture and Urban Renewal", Museum of Modern Art, Jan 24–Mar 13, 1967. Cornell's team included Rowe, Tom Schumacher, Jerry Wells and Fred Koetter assisted by Steven Potters, Michael Schwarting, and Carl Stearns.

3 FAR stands for Floor Area Ratio. The ratio is the number by which the area of a plot of land treated as a flat plane can be multiplied to establish the maximum floor area for a building; hence FAR of 10 equals ten times the plot area. Other limits such as setback requirements, lot coverage, and height limits also govern the shape and may limit the height of buildings. Bonuses up to 12 means two additional floor areas are allowed as incentives to provide agreed upon amenities.

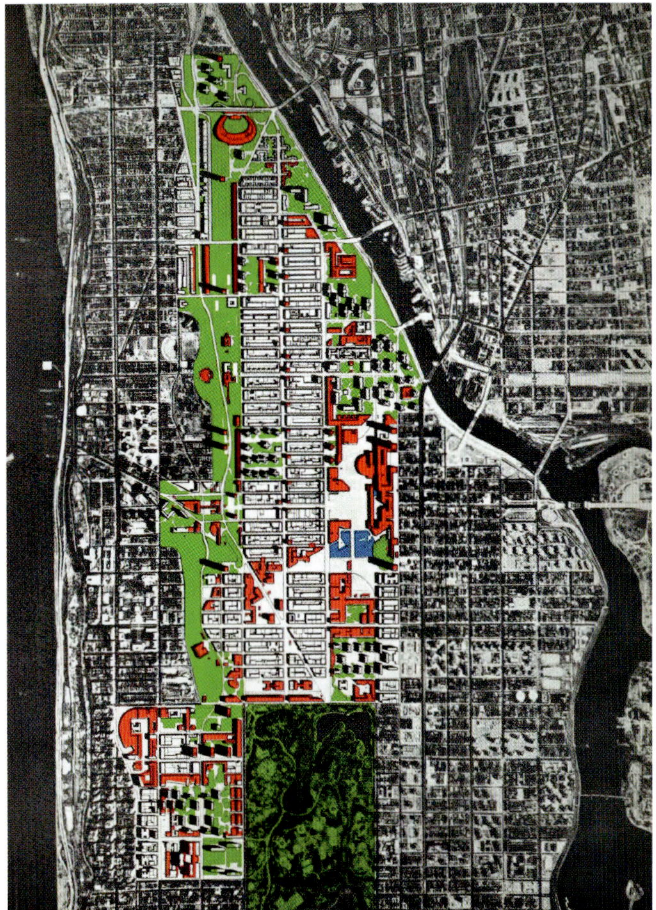

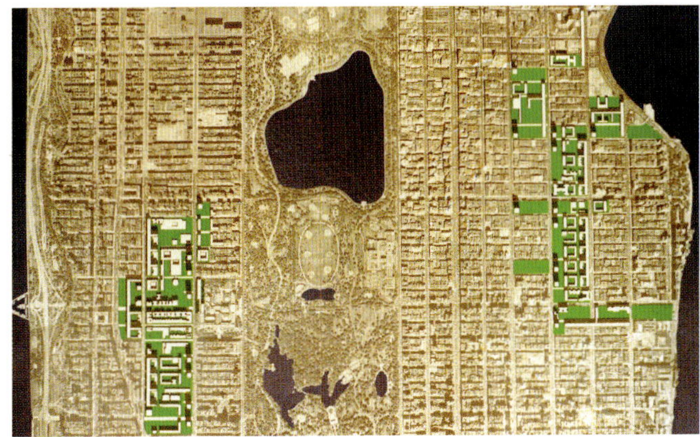

above clockwise:
Fig. 2. Plan of Upper Manhattan from "The New City: Architecture and Urban Renewal".

Fig. 3. Model of "The New City" looking north.

Fig. 4. Proposed plan of Upper East and West Sides of Manhattan, Urban Design Group, 1968.

residential zoning districts R-10/12 (the highest residential zone with an FAR of 10 and bonuses up to 12)[3] of the "1961 Zoning Resolution" that had replaced the original zoning, the "1916 Zoning Resolution". Rowe suggested that some of us might go to New York City and work on the project as part of our Studio experience. Jack Dobson, Stephen Quick, Randall 'Randy' Sandford, Jr., and I agreed to go.

Fellow student Stephen Quick and I were destined to work together for many years. Rowe's teaching assistant, Alex Caragonne, also joined the team a short time later.[4]

Unbeknownst to us, we were about to immerse ourselves and contribute to one of the most innovative urban design experiences in the United States and beyond. A few years earlier, in 1965, when John Lindsay was running for mayor, a group of young New Yorkers offered their assistance in urban issues. The group included Jaquelin Robertson, Richard Weinstein, Jonathan Barnett, Giovanni Pasanella, and Myles Weintraub.[5] They worked under the direction of Donald Elliot who became Mayor Lindsay's chairman of the City Planning Commission and later a major player in the success of Lindsay's economic development corporation.[6] The white papers they had written led the new mayor to establish a commission headed by the president of CBS, William Paley, to study the organization, goals,

4 At this writing, Stephen Quick provided the names of the four students and added that Alex Caragonne, who had been Rowe's teaching assistant and recently had graduated, joined the group at Rowe's urging.

5 Lindsay, John V. "Foreword", Barnett, Jonathan, *Urban Design as Public Policy*, Architectural Record, a McGraw-Hill Publication, 1974: vi.

6 Now called the New York City Economic Development Corporation: previously the Public Development Corporation with seven members appointed by the mayor.

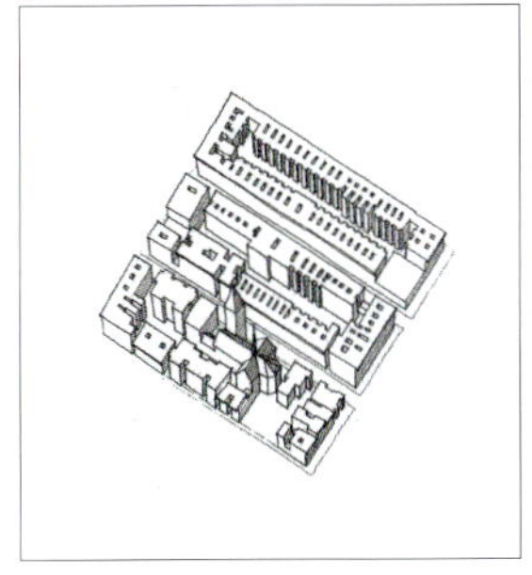
Existing

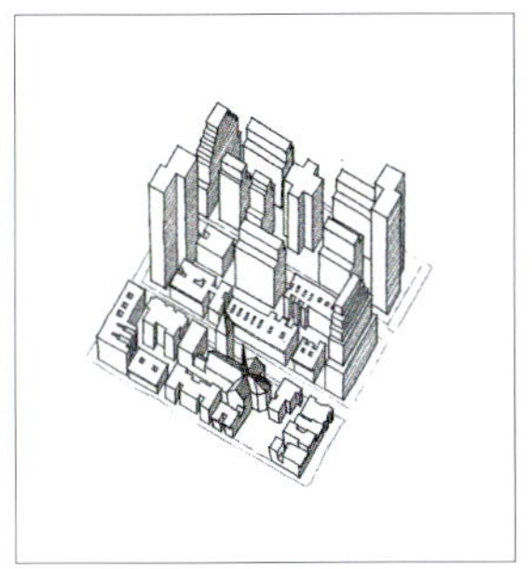
Projected

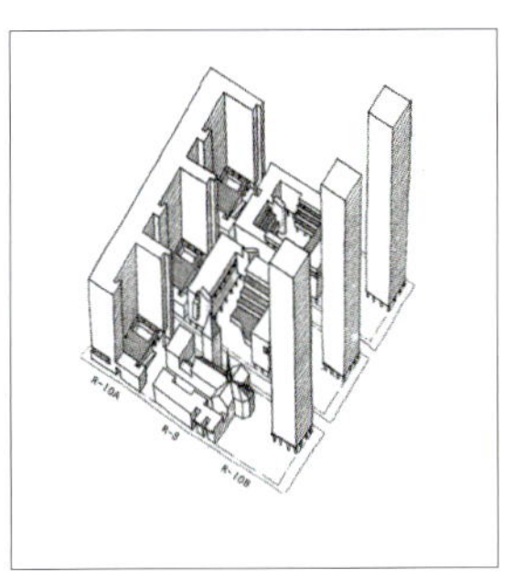
Prototype

left to right:
Fig. 5. Development Block Patterns: Existing, Projected, and Prototype, UDG, 1968.

Fig. 6. Proposed block patterns with infill inserted into existing context from UDG, 1968.

and vision of the Department of City Planning. Formed in 1966, the commission's report of early 1967 advised expanding the department to include a focus on urban design as a vehicle for non-binding community review.[7] The department moved swiftly and the Urban Design Group (UDG) was formed in April 1967.

In January 1968, the UDG was designated the IAUS-Cornell team's client contact. The UDG established the parameters of our work and immersed all of us—including Rowe—in the arcane world of zoning. We were given two study areas in Manhattan, one on the east side of Central Park, and another on the west side. Even though the areas were quite different spatially and in usage, the recently implemented 1961 zoning had been mapped and applied uniformly without exception to all residential areas in Manhattan. No adjustment existed for any special conditions related to use, history, or uniqueness of place. The Cornell team undertook a building-by-building survey of the sites and their surroundings in order to make more site-specific recommendations. These resultant studies helped provide the context and intellectual subject matter for subsequent related projects in the Urban Design Studio at Cornell,[8] where the evolving discussion had been expanded in 1965–66 by two widely regarded texts, "A City is not a Tree" by Christopher Alexander and *Complexity and Contradiction in Architecture* by Robert Venturi.[9]

By December 1968 we were ready to move beyond data collection and analysis into design. Only then did we discover that Eisenman and his group, and Rowe with his Cornell team, held distinctly different views as to how to proceed. Eisenman no doubt saw theory as the primary function of the IAUS, while Rowe and his Cornell cohort tried to remind Eisenman that he had a binding contract with the city requiring a focus on urban design, not theory. We haggled for six weeks, eventually agreeing to disagree. Our space was divided. Eisenman got the front office. We claimed the drafting room.

We returned after New Year's in high spirits and ready to charrette. By late March we were flying! Even Rowe was intrigued by the possibilities of manipulating zoning in accordance with urban design goals.

Special Zoning Districts and "NYC: Rezone"

One of the early successes of the UDG had been passage of the first district overlay zone, the 1967 Special Theater District[10] that literally saved the theater district by

7 The Lindsay administration established 62 community boards where none had existed; they continue to this day making non-binding recommendations to the City on all development projects.

8 Jim Tice recalls that in 1969 Rowe presented a Studio exercise focused on the Upper East Side of Manhattan.

9 Alexander, Christopher, "The City is not a Tree", *Architectural Forum* 122 1: 58-62 (part 1), Apr 1965; 122 2: 58-62 (part 2), May 1965. Venturi, Robert, *Complexity and Contradiction in Architecture: A Gentle Manifesto for a Nonstraightforward Architecture*, Museum of Modern Art, NY, 1966.

10 In 2020, there were two sub-districts, the Theatre Subdistrict Core that extends from 43rd to 50th Streets including most of the area between 6th and 8th Avenues; the Theatre Subdistrict focuses on the 8th Avenue Corridor from 43rd to 56th streets. Both are within the Special Midtown District created in 1982.

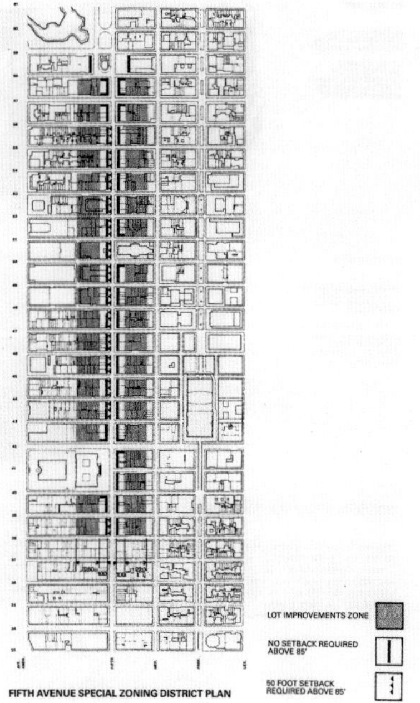

Fig. 7. Fifth Avenue Special Zoning District Plan, Office of Midtown Planning Development, ca. 1968.

adopting the strategy of transferable development rights. We saw that creating special district overlay zones was a significant strategy for preserving, as well as extending, the special qualities of other areas not otherwise protected and indeed threatened by the inflexible 1961 Zoning Resolution. And that, if the overlay zone was well-conceived, a balance between public benefit and private enterprise could be achieved. Our original study area had two clearly defined multi-block sites that could be transformed easily into special districts. While we maintained the current zoning district's FAR, we drew on the conceptual lessons of the earlier 1916 Zoning Resolution, altering the zoning envelopes in accordance with an overall urban design plan and current design and construction methods. The result was a report, "NYC: *Rezone*", which we presented to the City Planning Commission in late May 1969.[11]

Our presentation revealed some of the problems with the 1961 Zoning Resolution and offered solutions. No one had ever shown the city planning commissioners the very serious negative consequences of the new 1961 zoning. The commissioners were stunned. Our study illustrated that increasing open space by applying the new 1961 zoning did not necessarily yield good urban form.[12] Under the existing R-10/12 guidelines, we demonstrated the likelihood that existing and valued character, identity, and overall coherence of distinctive districts would be eroded and irrevocably lost.

The solution we proposed was the use of the recently created "special district zoning" that had been invented for the Theater District. Not only could special district zoning protect uniqueness of place in terms of form, it could also incentivize the protection and creation of desired amenities of all kinds including a positive impact on quality of life, vibrant use, and economic value.

For those of us influenced by Rowe's interest in exploring strategies for reconciling traditional urban fabrics with Modernist 'towers in the park' to create a new urban model, NYC: *Rezone* initiated a range of possibilities through special district zoning—in the most densely developed of U.S. cities. The issue, of course, continued to plague Rowe. A good ten years after "NYC: *Rezone*" in Rowe's lecture, "The Present Urban Predicament", given at the Royal Institute of British Architects in 1979, he questioned:

> *... just how to make a city if all buildings proclaim themselves as objects, and how many buildings can be aggregated before comprehension fails?* [13]

Mayor's Office of Midtown Planning and Development

Following the Cornell team's presentation, two important events occurred. First, the AIA New York[14] exhibited the team's presentation; this helped to establish our bona fides with the professionals with whom we would soon be interacting. In 1967 Lindsay created the Mayor's Office of Midtown Planning Development (OMPD). Most importantly for us, Jaquelin Robertson, the newly appointed director of OMPD, offered to hire us. Alex Caragonne, Stephen Quick and I accepted. This was beyond our wildest dreams. We were immediately placed in the upper echelons of New York City's architectural and development community. On joining OMPD we began preparing the Manhattan volume of the comprehensive

11 The seven-member City Planning Commission was created under the 1936 New York Charter. The commissioners were appointed by the mayor. It began functioning in 1938 charged with creating a master plan.

12 While I have not found explicit reference to NYC: *Rezone* on the official website of the City of New York, there are numerous references to 1969 special zoning districts, special purpose districts, district and sub-district rezoning. The 1961 Zoning Resolution had incentivized plazas and arcades linked to as-of-right bonuses without pedestrian friendly requirements or design review. In 1968 improvements and additional types of privately owned public spaces were added that included pedestrian features and design review, as well as through block arcades (connections) open-air concourses, and covered pedestrian spaces. These were updated and expanded in 1975–77 and again in 2007–09. [https://www1.nyc.gov/site/planning/plans/pops/pops-history.page.].

13 Rowe, Colin, "The Present Urban Predicament", *The Cornell Journal of Architecture* 1, 1981: 16-33. And Rowe, Colin, *As I Was Saying: Recollections and Miscellaneous Essays* 3, Urbanistics, Caragonne, Alexander, ed., MIT Press, Cambridge, MA, and London, 1996: 165-220.

14 New York Chapter, American Institute of Architects, one of 13 chapters in New York State.

Fig. 8. *Plan for New York City*, six volume series by The New York City Planning Commission, 1969-1970.

plan for New York City.[15] This permitted us to state our vision and establish the guidelines to achieve it. It also became an extremely valuable asset for the mayor's economic development office. This was the first ever plan for the City to truly place emphasis on urban design for New York City.[16]

On completion of our Manhattan volume, Robertson assigned Alex Caragonne to direct a design feasibility study of the 48th Street corridor as a potential special zoning district. Stephen Quick and I became part of the team. As it had for NYC: *Rezone*, Rowe's search for the balance between traditional built fabric defining public spaces and the Modernist world of buildings occupying space, clearly inspired the 48th Street study.[17]

Concomitant with the 48th Street study, I was appointed Director of Project Review with Stephen Quick as my teammate. I think we owed our successes to the fact that we had demonstrated three things: we could balance the multiple forces at work in an urban environment; we understood the importance of using zoning districts as a means of inserting a contextual strategy into the generic 1961 Zoning Resolution; and we had mastered how to manipulate zoning as a means of implementing a coherent urban design strategy. This included the use of incentive zoning.

Incentive Zoning

Incentive zoning offered the developer a bonus beyond the allowable buildable area, such as a twenty percent bonus in FAR or an increase in lot coverage if some negotiated public amenity was provided, for example, a new subway entry. In Midtown, 650 Fifth Avenue provided an enclosed multi-level covered pedestrian space facing 52nd while reinforcing the asymmetry of the Special Fifth Avenue

15 *Plan for New York City, Manhattan* 4, The New City Planning Commission, MIT Press, Dec 1970. The introductory volume, *Critical Issues*, was written by William H. Whyte. Volumes 2 through 6 were devoted to each of the New York boroughs: Brooklyn, Queens, Manhattan, Staten Island, and the Bronx. *Plan for New York City* 1969, NYPL Digital Collections [https://digitalcollections.nypl.org/].

16 But also see the nearly contemporary *Urban Design Manhattan, A Report of the Second Regional Plan*, A Studio Book, Viking Press, New York, 1969. The Regional Plan Association, founded in 1922, focuses on the 31 county regions of New York, New Jersey, and Connecticut. The *Urban Design Manhattan* supplemented a 1966 regional plan, its emphasis was on improved transportation connectivity and related economic opportunities of built form density.

17 "The 48th Street Office Spine" *Plan for New York City, Manhattan* 4: 58-61. Notably, 48th St. is a crosstown street that marks the north end of the United Nations site and crosses Broadway just above Times Square. The study's plans and multi-level recommendations included cross town transit connections linking the proposed Second Avenue subway line to other north-south lines and emphasized incentivizing new development based on existing use patterns of office-commercial on the avenues with residential between them on the cross town streets, a recommendation that subsequently had meaningful application throughout Midtown Manhattan. The 48th St. study evolved into the Special Clinton District adopted in late 1974 not long after Williams had moved from OMPD to OLMD. The Special Clinton District is roughly located between West 41st and West 59th Streets west of Eight Ave. It primarily preserves and strengthens the residential character including maintaining lower scale side streets and a broad mix of incomes including Inclusionary Housing designations. More recent crosstown links appear to emphasize 42nd and 55th Streets. Recently, a small part of the long-planned Second Avenue subway was completed. [https://www1.nyc.gov/site/planning/zoning/districts-tools/special-purpose-districts-manhattan.page.].

18 Today both Fifth and Park Avenues, extending from East 59th Street to East 111th Streets, are Subdistricts within the Special Midtown District of 1982.

Fig. 9. Proposal for Grand Central Terminal, Marcel Breuer, ca. 1975.

Fig. 10. Jackie Onassis rallying for the preservation of Grand Central Terminal with Bess Meyerson, Philip Johnson, and Ed Koch, 1975.

District.[18] As Stephen Quick and I became more adept at working with lawyers and planners, we realized new opportunities. With incentive zoning, we invented the Through Block Connection, a much-needed privately owned public amenity in the form of mid-block pedestrian connections that could mitigate the exceptionally long 800-foot standard blocks of Manhattan.[19]

We also significantly reconfigured the massing of several buildings, improving them for both public and private interest, as in the case of the Olympic Tower, which we altered from an articulated building mass to a simple backdrop for Saint Patrick's Cathedral.

After a year or so, Alex Caragonne moved back to Texas, but Stephen Quick and I continued to enjoy contributing to the opportunities offered by the OMPD. We not only improved projects; we stopped a few that would have had severe negative impacts on their surroundings. The most dramatic and far-reaching of these went all the way to the U.S. Supreme Court. Penn-Central was the owner of Grand Central Terminal and the surrounding rail yards. The rail yards had long since been covered and built on, but Penn-Central still owned the property. Penn-Central and their architect, Marcel Breuer, went to the relatively new Landmarks Preservation Commission[20] with a proposal to use the remaining 13.5 FAR to build a 700-foot high office building over the landmarked Grand Central Terminal. The grandiose plan was rejected by the Landmarks Preservation Commission, an action that could be interpreted as a 'taking', that is, the condemnation of property without compensation, a deprivation of Penn-Central's property rights.

However, the City Planning Commission, working with the UDG and OMPD, had passed legislation permitting the transfer of development rights from a landmark to adjacent properties. The new legislation permitted Penn-Central to transfer the unused FAR from the Terminal site to Penn-Central's adjacent properties. Nevertheless, Penn-Central and their developer brought suit against New York City, challenging the legality of the Commission's ruling. The U.S. Supreme Court found that the legislation was part of an overall plan, not a singular act limited to one property. Therefore, the Court found in favor of New York City supporting the Commission and the transfer of development rights plan. This landmark ruling by the Supreme Court has been a boon to city planning and historic preservation throughout the United States.[21]

Stephen Quick and I were heavily involved in two other controversial projects. The first was an attempt by the United Nations Development Corporation (UNDC) to build an enormous three-tower complex with a 40,000-square foot footprint clustered around an equally large atrium. We were able to drastically reduce its scope with the Special United Nations Development District adopted on February 20, 1970. The second project was a proposal by Con Edison, developer Sylvan Lawrence, and their architect, SOM, to build a third slope-sided tower on Con Ed property within the as-of-right zoning envelope.[22] Two well-known SOM towers had already been built on West 42nd Street and West 57th Street, so the stakes were high. We were successful in rejecting the slope-sided tower by presenting a number of building configurations that demonstrated a project could be built that would be better in both planning and economic terms.

19 North of the original settlement area of Lower Manhattan, the typical New York City block was platted with exceptionally narrow and long blocks at approximately 200 by 800 feet. These 'Through Block Connections' are pedestrian ways that subdivide the 800-foot block length. Some are covered and skylit as are the gallerias and arcades of their late 19th century antecedents.

20 The Landmarks Preservation Commission had been created, in partial response to the recent demolition of New York's other magnificent railroad station, Penn Central (1910-1963, demolished 1963-1968).

21 Penn Central Transportation Co. v. New York City, 438 U.S. 104 (1978).

22 'As-of-right' means within the allowable zoning for that property including the FAR and other limitations and allowances determining the maximum shape.

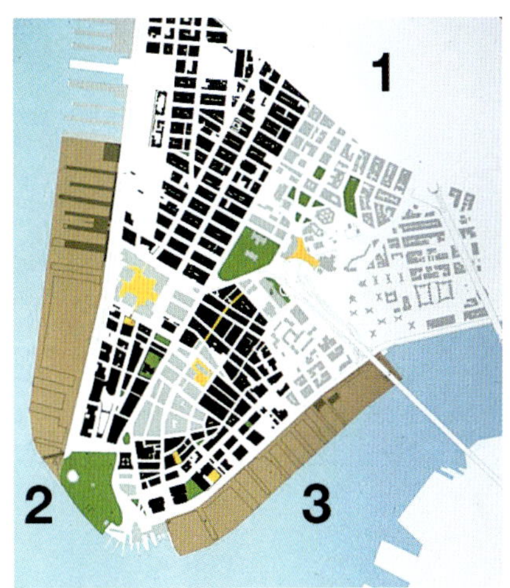

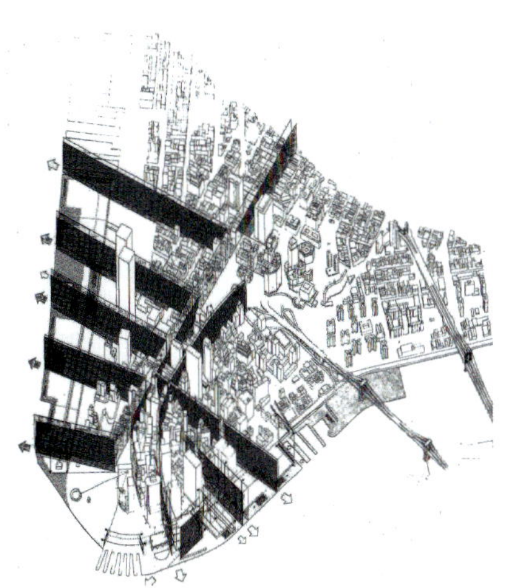

Fig. 11. Olympic Tower Proposal, OMPD, ca. 1968.

Fig. 12. Lower Manhattan Waterfront: Zoning Districts, OLMD, 1973.

Fig. 13. Lower Manhattan Waterfront: View corridors, OLMD, 1973.

Mayor's Office of Lower Manhattan Development

Given the success rate of OMPD with both the citizens and the architectural and development communities, in 1971 Lindsay appointed me Deputy Director of the Office of Lower Manhattan Development (OLMD) directed by Richard Weinstein.[23] Working with John West and others, we soon created a unified graphic format that identified all our work as that of the Mayor's Office, a format soon adopted by most of the other development offices.

John West became our senior urban designer. With his input and recommendations from Cornell faculty, we began to build a new staff around two recent Cornell undergraduates, Stephen Anderson and Frank Gilmore, and Rowe graduate student, Richard Baiter.[24] By 1971 the Mayor's urban design offices were receiving international notice. Inundated with resumes from around the world, we hired designers capable of thinking spatially and putting their egos aside.[25] The quality and quantity of work produced by OLMD increased dramatically. Following a presentation of the 1971 Lower Manhattan Implementation Plan, *The New York Times* architectural critic, Ada Louise Huxtable, declared that our work was "of a sophistication and complexity virtually without parallel". Quoting Jonathan Barnett's book title, we were establishing *Urban Design as Public Policy*.[26]

Following on the "1965 Master Plan for Lower Manhattan" by Conklin and Rossant with Wallace, McHarg, Roberts, and Todd, OLMD was working simultaneously on numerous projects: preservation of the historic U.S. Customs House;[27] design and planning of the Second Avenue Subway and Water Street;[28] Battery Park City; the South Street Seaport Museum; studies of the feasibility of special zoning district overlays for Greenwich Street, Tribeca, and the most complex, Manhattan Landing.[29] Despite their varied contexts and unique circumstances, these individual initiatives were seen as an integrated whole.

23 Lower Manhattan: the land area south of Canal Street and the Manhattan Bridge, including Tribeca: TriBeCa (Triangle Below Canal), now a trapezoidal area bounded by Canal St., West St., Broadway, and Chambers St. In the 1970s, a smaller triangular area was formed by the TriBeCa Artists's Co-op for filing legal documents related to planned zoning.

24 Richard Baiter was in the Rowe Studio group that executed the Buffalo Waterfront project, primarily in 1966.

25 Among these talents was Karl Frederick Du Puy (1942-2020), Dartmouth, U. Penn Architecture, Delft masters degree, who was with NYC UDG offices for eight years, then joined the faculty at the University of Maryland in 1977 where Du Puy taught studio as well as a required urban design lecture and seminar courses during his long teaching career.

26 Barnett (1974).

27 In cooperation with the New York Landmarks Conservancy, this was a building-specific project to find a reuse for the monumental Alexander Hamilton U.S. Custom House, 1902-07 designed by Cass Gilbert, now the National Museum of the American Indian–New York, a Smithsonian Institution. It is located at One Bowling Green at the northeast corner of Battery Park.

28 John West directed the Water Street study examining how best to connect the southernmost stations of the Second Avenue Subway in Water Street with the public realm and adjacent buildings.

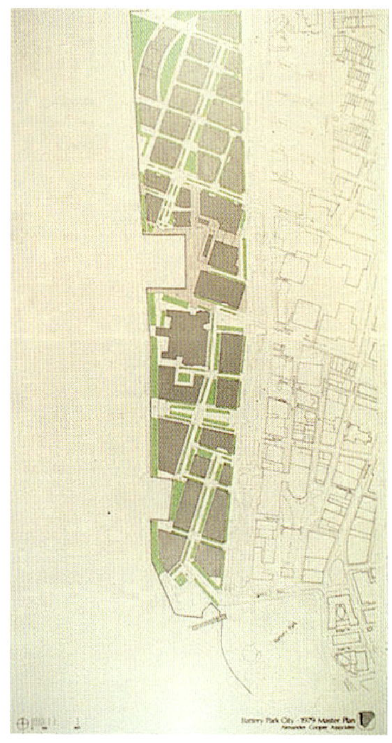

left, top to bottom:
Fig. 14. Perspective view of Lower Manhattan from the "1965 Master Plan for Lower Manhattan" by Conklin and Rossant with Wallace, McHarg, Roberts and Todd. Taken from "The Lower Manhattan Plan" by Wallace, McHarg, Roberts and Todd; Whittlesey, Conklin and Rossant; Alan M. Voorhees and Associates Inc., for the New York City Planning Commission, 1966.

Fig. 15. Rector Place, aerial view, Alex Cooper and Stan Eckstut, ca. 1973.

inset left to right:
Fig. 16. Urban Plan, Battery Park City, Alex Cooper and Stan Eckstut, ca. 1973.

Fig. 17. Model, Battery Park City, Alex Cooper and Stan Eckstut, ca. 1973.

Battery Park City

While Battery Park City was a New York State project, the land underwater out to the pier-head line belonged to the city. There had been numerous attempts to achieve a coherent plan for this newly created land along the Hudson River frontage of Lower Manhattan. However, all proposals dealt with the filled land as a separate and distinct entity from the historic pattern of streets initiated by the Dutch in the 1600s. The most recent scheme by Harrison & Abramovitz, Johnson/Burgee Architects was a mega-building: long, linear, and highly articulated with three huge towers at the southern end. In the 1960s the mega-building was popular among a certain *coterie* of architects and urban designers—Archigram in the UK, and O.M. Ungers, transplanted from Germany to Cornell as department head. Even some developers, including the Battery Park City Authority (BPCA), promoted this mono-scale of urban intervention.

For us, the mega-building scheme had three major problems. It would bring another 10-to-12 million square feet of office space into Lower Manhattan which, when combined with the 12 million square feet of the World Trade Center, would overwhelm the real estate market in that part of the city. Mega-building proposals also ignored the U.S. pattern of real estate development based on individual land parcels and zoning laws; few, if any mega-buildings could be built without government sponsorship. Lastly, as students of Rowe's, we were skeptical of the possibility of mega-structures to relate to the existing context.

Timing and the astute insight of Richard Weinstein came to our rescue. A new lease on the property was being negotiated. Weinstein suggested to BPCA Director Charles Urstadt that, since the land underwater belonged to the city, wouldn't it be appropriate for the city to write the zoning? Urstadt, possibly not realizing just how powerful zoning could be, agreed.

---

29 Special Battery Park City District, Dec. 1973; South Street Seaport Subdistrict is one of two sub-districts within the Special Lower Manhattan District that also included the Historic and Commercial Core delimited by Wall St., Broadway, Water St. and Whitehall St. It was intended to preserve the streets mapped for historic New Amsterdam and Colonial New York, and provide compatibility of new with old buildings; Greenwich Street is at least partially located in the Special Tribeca Mixed Use District, June 1976.

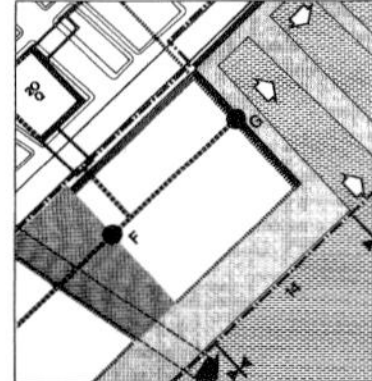

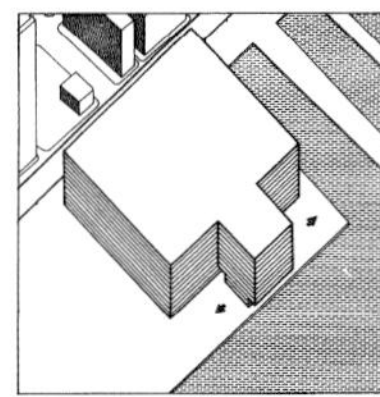

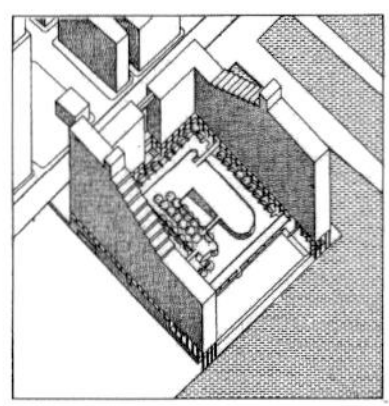

Weinstein, Ed Lampert, our legal counsel, and I walked back to the office, just elated: so ended the life of the mega-building. Finally, we could protect one of the experiential essences of Manhattan: the narrow streets that frame views of sky and water when looking either east or west, particularly the tip of Manhattan Island. First, we mapped no-build view corridors along historic streets from Broadway to the coastline of Lower Manhattan, including Battery Park City. At the same time, we also mapped a continuous promenade from Battery Park City to the South Street Seaport Museum located at Fulton Street and the East River water frontage. The design process of extending the streets and blocks of existing patterns was a standard technique used in Rowe's Studio to understand existing urban orders and how they might be extended or clarified. Now we were applying that technique for real. Battery Park was established as a sub-district with special zoning in December 1973.[30] Ultimately the BPCA hired the new architectural firm of two former Lindsay architect/urban designers, Alex Cooper and Stan Eckstut. The Cooper Eckstut plan clearly linked the new development to the rest of Lower Manhattan and became an icon for the new and emerging context-sensitive approach to urban design and development.[31]

inset:
Fig. 18. Manhattan Landing, Land Reclamation Study, OLMD, ca. 1973.

above, top to bottom:
Fig. 19. Manhattan Landing, Alternate Landfill Development, OLMD, ca. 1973.

Fig. 20. Manhattan Landing, detail: Land Reclamation Study, OLMD, ca. 1973.

Manhattan Landing

Manhattan Landing was to be the last filled land to be added to Lower Manhattan. Like Battery Park City, it would extend buildable area out to the pier-head line running from the Staten Island Ferry Terminal, at the southern tip of Manhattan, up to and beyond the South Street Seaport Museum to end slightly beyond the Brooklyn Bridge. Because of the projected need for future office space to serve Wall Street and the banking community, we were required to change the zoning, increasing both the density and the commercial square footage and lowering the residential footage.[32] Despite these challenges, Manhattan Landing successfully mimicked the dramatic spatial qualities existing in the Lower Manhattan core. It extended the existing street and block pattern of Lower Manhattan out to the water's edge. It created no-build historic street corridors. And it mapped a view corridor focused on the Statue of Liberty.

30 [https://www1.nyc.gov/site/planning/plans/pops/pops-history. page.]. Also see Latini, Antonio Pietro, *Battery Park City, New York: Principi e tecniche di Urban Design attraverso la storia di un modello*, Officina Edizioni, Roma, 2011.

31 The Battery Park City plan by Cooper Eckstut won a Progressive Architecture Citation award in 1984, as did the Duany Plater-Zyberk plan for Seaside, Florida. Significantly, both projects emphasized the traditional forms of adjacent city districts or regional towns.

32 Seigel, Max H., "Manhattan Landing Clears Last Major Government Hurdles", *The New York Times*, July 21, 1972: citing approval of the Board of Estimates.

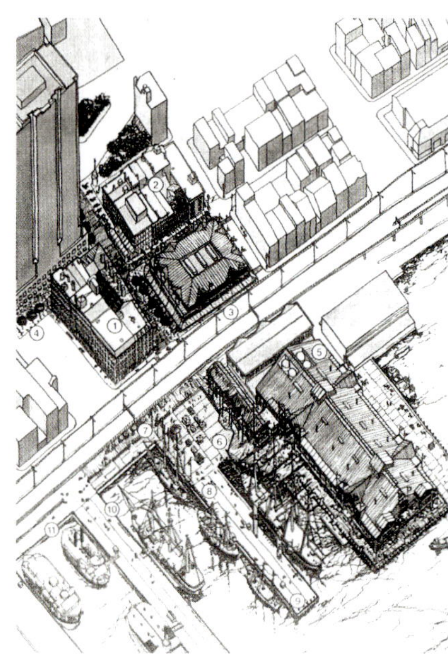

Fig, 21. Aerial View of South Street Seaport, ca. 1975.

Fig. 22. Axonometric, South Street Seaport Proposal, ca. 1973.

Fig. 23. South Street Seaport Bogardus building, corner of Front and Fulton, Beyer, Blinder, Belle, 1980.

The South Street Seaport

The South Street Seaport was to be the crown jewel of Manhattan Landing. In both its infancy and in our aspirations for it, the Seaport was much different from the commercialized environments nearby. The waterfront area was one of the oldest and still-vital mixed-use areas in the city. It included the wholesale Fulton Fish Market, sailors' hotels, various maritime operations, seamanship classes for Boy Scouts, wonderful book and print shops, all mixed in with the fishmongers, retail oyster bars, and two old restaurants: Sloppy Louie's and Sweet's, the latter opened in 1842. In the intervening years Sweet's claimed to have had only three managers, all in the family. All this rich New York City history was threatened by the pressures of the real estate market. When OLMD first got involved in the Seaport, it was a grassroots venture led mostly by old sailors and naval and ship historians.

The Mafia may or may not have been involved in the wholesale fish businesses, but the Seaport had been smart enough to put a person referred to as the "Capo di Capo of the Fish Market" on its board. The Director of the South Street Seaport Museum, Peter Sanford, introduced me to him.[33] Joe, as I will call him, invited me to join him for a 3:00 A.M. tour of the Fulton Fish Market. I felt like I was immersed in a Damon Runyon short story; this was raw New York. Joe introduced me as his good friend to everyone in the market. Joe's imprimatur made it possible to do the kind of surveys and studies necessary to establish the special zoning district needed to protect the future of the Seaport. We learned to be discreet about taking photos after I had a photographer colleague chased up Fulton Street by a fishmonger with a filleting knife.

OLMD did the initial master planning for the Seaport. It included connecting the buildings to the piers by closing Fulton Street from Water Street to South Street and a few ancillary streets as well. But most importantly, five blocks of historic buildings dating back to 1811 needed to be saved. Given the 1961 Zoning

33 The South Street Seaport Museum was founded in 1967 by Peter and Norma Stanford. In 1998 it was designated by Congress as one of several museums that make up America's National Maritime Museum. Through the years, the pier head line moved eastward beginning at Pearl Street, followed by Water St., Front St., and finally South Street. Attempts to create a successful 'festival marketplace' have had mixed results. The area was extensively damaged by Hurricane Sandy in 2012. (Wikipedia).

Resolution, the historic buildings were in a high-density commercial zone with an FAR of 12/15. The existing buildings had an FAR of only three or so, leaving them vulnerable to demolition in order to make way for much larger buildings. Weinstein approached David Rockefeller and asked if it might be possible to organize a consortium of Lower Manhattan banks to purchase the unused development rights over the five blocks of historic buildings. Even though the real estate market was depressed, the consortium of banks purchased the surplus development rights. Their action removed the development pressure on the five historic blocks. Eventually the financial market revived, and the banks sold most of the excess FAR to developers on designated receiver sites.

The OLMD master plan for the Seaport established design guidelines for all new construction. The guidelines included building elements that determined appropriate scale—not simply the building shape. One of the results of the guidelines is the building at the corner of Fulton and Front Streets by Beyer Blinder Belle, a 20th century edifice sitting comfortably in a 19th century context.[34]

Fig. 24. Offices of OLMD, ca. 1975.

Conclusions

Did the introduction of urban design into the planning processes of New York City in the Lindsay administration years have a positive impact on the city? That it did is hardly in doubt. Much of the groundwork that preserved and complemented the enduring character of New York was realized through the efforts and innovations made at that time. In Lower Manhattan alone, what has been realized? Not only the development of successful precincts such as Battery Park City and South Street Seaport discussed above, but also the Special Tribeca Mixed Use District of 1976 and numerous other projects and plans many of which were incorporated into the Lower Manhattan Implementation Plan[35] which won a *Progressive Architecture* award in 1974. Among the multiple projects gathered into the Lower Manhattan Implementation Plan and having a positive impact on the city, I think most particularly of the Greenwich Street Special Zoning District, the preservation of the U.S. Customs House, and the longer-term impact on an uptown portion of the Second Avenue subway that is now open. Special district zoning and the transfer of development rights that were so important to our accomplishments in New York City have become critical tools for planning nationwide in the U.S.

While it is too much to credit Colin Rowe directly with many of these successes, it is also clear that his direct engagement and interest in the IAUS, Eisenman-inspired study of the New York City 1961 Zoning Resolution showed to those of us working with him that Rowe's ideas were not only theoretical and critical, but also practical and achievable. Moreover, he had grounded us with a broad view of the development of cities over time: skepticism about supposedly rational and simple ideas imposed on urban complexity; and an interest in the possibility of the resolution of the old with the new. Colin Rowe helped us gain the confidence and certainty that more than one solution exists for any urban design problem we might face. These lessons allowed us to work creatively and successfully with a wide range of people from our own discipline and other disciplines and on a wide range of projects all focused on maintaining a city's quality in the flux that is, in the end, its reality.

34 The Fulton Street Fish Market and the surrounding area remained vital until 2005 when the Market moved to Hunters Point in the Bronx ending its nearly 200-year location at Fulton Street.

35 The nyc.gov web site that leads to "Zoning Districts & Tools: Special Purpose District: Manhattan", the names and areas of districts and sub-districts changed for numerous reasons over time. It appears that the "Lower Manhattan Implementation Plan" was later incorporated into the "Special Lower Manhattan District".

Grand Arsenal

The Koetter Kim Practice, a Paragon of Contextualism?

Steven W. Hurtt

Introduction: Context, Collision and Collage

The Koetter Kim urban design and architectural practice is inevitably and logically linked with Colin Rowe's impact on the field of urban design for multiple reasons. Fred Koetter was a student of note in the formative years of Rowe's urban design Studio at Cornell (1965–66). He shared the development and authorship with Rowe of *Collage City* (1970–73), and, with Susie Kim launched their professional practice the same year that *Collage City* was published (1978). Their practice achieved world renown specifically for its combined urban design and architecture.

Because the associated theories of Collision City, Collage City, and Contextualism would seem to have been fundamental to the Koetter Kim practice, several questions beg for attention. Summarily, how do the associated theories manifest in the work? And how might this have come about? To attempt answers, I note the development and emergence of the theories from the Studio, their entry into the literature, Fred Koetter's promotion of collision and collage and rumored reservations about contextualism. Then I examine nine Koetter Kim architectural urban projects from among the many in the Koetter Kim monograph (1979–95), with particular attention to the theoretical grounding provided to their practice primarily by *Collage City* and, surprisingly, more illustrative of Contextualism than either Collision or Collage.

It was at Cornell in the Rowe Urban Design Studio of 1966–67 that 'contextualism', 'collision city', and 'collage city' were incubated.[1] Our understanding of urban design was primitive. Reference material was scarce. Mainly, we were predisposed to think that an *in situ* or context-based understanding of buildings and spaces represented a superior form of architecture – urban design. That view was common among a handful of Cornell faculty and students who shared their knowledge of examples as a corrective critique of the building isolated from its physical context that was typical of architecture history classes. For the Urban Design Studio, Rowe gave no formal seminar or lecture class. He did suggest we look at "this or that". Otherwise, the Department of Planning offered numerous

frontispiece top to bottom:

Galerie d'Orleans, Paris.
Imperial Fora, plan, Rome.

Unter den Linden, Berlin.
Palazzo Chiericati, Vicenza.

Place des Vosges, Paris.
Plaza España, Vittoria Gasteiz, Spain.

Louvre Colonnade, Rue de Rivoli, Paris.
Imperial Fora, model, Rome.

1 Discussions about naming the evolving ideas as 'theory' took place between January 1966 and June 1967, primarily among Stuart Cohen, Fred Koetter, Tom Schumacher and me. Others, then in the Studio, might have contributed also. I remained in Ithaca and the Cornell orbit until June 1970 when subsequent discussions might have included at least Roger Sherwood, Michael Dennis, Jerry Wells, Don Duncan, Alex Caragonne, David Grahame Shane, and Larry Witzling, among others. Jim Tice prompted this essay with remarks on Koetter's reservations about Contextualism, see footnote 43.

courses. Those taken by many of us included John Reps' popular lecture course that had become *The Making of Urban America*, and an urban design seminar.

The Buffalo Waterfront project was underway. Rowe spoke of the extreme contrast between the traditional dense city and the sparse city posed by CIAM and evident in Modernist architecture and planning. He encouraged finding a reconciliation of these "trad" and "Mod" opposites. To do so, we were attempting to learn all we could about both, simultaneously. In the resulting crucible, we began to think the ideas being explored were developing into a theoretical alternative to Modernism with significant potential for the newly named and promoted field of urban design.[2] Possibly, we were on to something big—a theory of architecture as urban design radically different from what the CIAM crowd had so successfully promoted.

We talked about popularizing our developing theory, tossing around names for it. Tom Schumacher liked 'Juan Gris Roman', a self-conscious jest combining Rowe's interests in Cubism and Renaissance Rome. Fred Koetter favored either collision city or collage city. He found the complex, colliding urban geometries and buildings of European cities, such as those being drawn by Wayne Copper, a compelling critique of the more simplistic regularization of the colliding geometries of U.S. cities the Studio had been developing.[3] And collage had proved an intriguing technique of investigation and design inspiration.[4] Stuart Cohen and I promoted contextualism. We argued it would be intuitively understood and readily adopted whereas collision and collage, while appealing to an architectural intelligentsia, were too esoteric to achieve popular understanding and common use.[5] Robert Venturi's house for his mother had been recently published. I saw the Vanna Venturi house as raising the same challenges to Modernist orthodoxy in architecture as Rowe was raising about Modernism in our Studio.[6] Cohen and I drew further parallels between Rowe's articles that linked Modernist and traditional architecture and similar assertions by Venturi in *Complexity and Contradiction in Architecture* in 1966. Weren't both Rowe and Venturi rejecting the hegemony of Modernism and throwing open the doors to urban and architectural history and iconographies slammed shut by Modernism?

None of us in 1966–67 could have imagined the ensuing events. The dissemination of the related ideas of contextualism, collision city, and collage city. Or the ways they were embraced, critiqued, and misconstrued.

Arrival of Contextualism, 1971

Cohen and I described a proto-theory of *contexturalism* in our 1967 thesis. Rowe commented that the word should have been *contextualism*, and it was "Contextualism" that was introduced into the architecture literature by Schumacher in his 1971 article for *Casabella*, "Contextualism: Urban Ideals and Deformations".[7] Notably, Schumacher and Rowe had begun a convivial relationship when Schumacher was an undergraduate. Shortly after completing the graduate Studio, Schumacher was awarded a Fellowship to the American Academy in Rome, and Rowe spent the fall semester of 1969 at the Academy as well. Schumacher's article was grounded in our shared Studio experience and likely discussions with Rowe while in Rome. Schumacher's article put the

2 In the U.S., architectural historians turned their attention to cities in the early 1960s contemporary with the AIA promoting the study of urban design. See Handlin, Oscar, and Burchard, John ed., *The Historian and the City*, MIT and The President and Fellows of Harvard College, 1963; Mumford, Eric, *Defining Urban Design: CIAM Architects and the Formation of a Discipline, 1937–1969*, World Print, 2009. Mumford claims a first for Harvard's program, but it seems to have been in name only. Despite their intentions, neither Joseph Hudnut nor Josep Lluís Sert got support from other programs: see Pearlman, Jill, "Breaking Common Ground, Joseph Hudnut and the Prehistory of Urban Design", 117–29; and Marshall, Richard, "Josep Lluis Sert's Urban Design Legacy", 130–43 in *Josep Lluís Sert: The Architect of Urban Design, 1953–1969*, Mumford, Eric and Sarkis, Hashim, eds., with Turan, Neyra, Yale University and Harvard University Graduate School of Design, 2008. For Hudnut resistance came from the planning program for many years. Subsequently Gropius frustrated Sert's multidisciplinary effort with his insistence on a Bauhaus-based foundation. At Cornell 1962–1970 there was no required curriculum beyond Rowe's Studio. While urban design support courses were offered by planning faculty Stuart Stein, John Reps, K.C. Parsons, and Allan Feldt, students freely followed their interests in selecting courses, often making for a rich intellectual exchange.

3 Both more collisive and more regular geometries were related to Analytic and Synthetic Cubism.

4 Franz Oswald promoted the collage of known work into design projects as challenges to our thinking, and as checks on the dimensions and scale of our designs.

5 The Cohen-Hurtt argument proved correct about popular understanding while the Koetter argument became foundational to the extended critique he and Rowe developed in *Collage City* and widely appreciated by the architectural intelligentsia. See Hurtt, Steven, "Conjectures on Urban Form: The Cornell Urban Design Studio 1963–1982", *The Cornell Journal of Architecture* 2, Cornell University, Department of Architecture, 1983. At the beginning of the Cornell essay, I provided very short definitions of each of the terms remarking on their origin, meanings, and relationships.

6 I saw the composition of the Vanna Venturi house facade as similar to Mannerist facades Rowe was describing in history lectures. And its plan, section, and volumetric development as having Cubist qualities: partial figures suggesting larger wholes, and collagist references including child-like simplicities, vernacular, arch-typal, high-style, and Ancient and Renaissance Roman motifs. Venturi figures prominently in both *Collage City* and *As I Was Saying*, a big change from 1966–70.

7 Schumacher cited our 1967 thesis acknowledging Cohen and me for coining the term.

intuitively understood *contextualism* into the literature and associated what became Contextualism with Rowe and the Studio.[8] That association was reinforced a few years later when Cohen's article "Physical Context, Cultural Context: Including it All" was published in *Oppositions* in 1974.[9] Physical context suggested at least the immediate visual field; cultural context suggested an expansive range of considerations. "Including it All" was Robert Venturi's phrase adopted by Cohen. Venturi challenged the Modernist strictures against traditional architectonic, stylistic, ornamental, and iconographic forms as exclusive, as opposed to an inclusive revitalization of architectural forms and meanings. The Miesian 'less is more' had become 'less is a bore'. Venturi argued for a reengagement with a rich diversity of forms and iconographies from 'trad' to Pop, high-style, and vernacular. While Venturi's focus was broad, it was on architecture, not urban design, whereas Schumacher and Cohen clearly linked urban and architectural form. Schumacher had described Contextualism along the lines of the Rowe theme of the 'ideal' form that is 'deformed' by circumstances of site, time, or both. The title of Cohen's article provided the straightforward clarity of physical and cultural context. Articles by other Rowe Studio students, including David Grahame Shane in 1976, and William Ellis in 1979, primarily reinforced the emphasis on context and hence Contextualism, while secondarily referencing collision and collage.[10] In the same time frame, Rowe and Koetter were expanding on the meanings of collision and collage as they would appear in the chapters in *Collage City*.

Postmodernism, Contextualism, Rationalism

Contextualism was swept up in the various critiques of Modernism that had been emerging for several decades. In 1977 Charles Jencks wrote *The Language of Postmodern Architecture* and included Contextualism as one indicator of that critique.[11] Jencks acknowledged Contextualism as an important theory, but his narrow focus on contemporary matters of style diverted attention from the emphasis of Contextualism on the holistic environment, history, culture, and city. The prolific and influential Robert A.M. Stern initially misconstrued Contextualism similarly, noting three emerging theories as constituting Postmodernism: *contextualism, allusionism, and ornamentalism.*[12] Meanwhile a European critique of Modernism was developing. It emphasized an urban morphology and architectural typology quite parallel to the development of thinking in the Cornell Studio.[13] Bearing different names in different regions, Rationalism and La Tendenza among them, these were associated with Rowe and others presumed to be in the Postmodernist or Contextualist camps.[14] In 1978, a select group of European and U.S. architects participated in an exhibition, each submitting a plan and commentary on the development of Rome to be based on Nolli's 1748 plan of the city.

Arrival of Collage City *and* Roma interrotta

Collage City was published in 1978, *Roma interrotta* in 1979. Their nearly simultaneous publication compounded their presence in the literature. Rowe is correctly associated with both Contextualism and Collage City or Urban Collage. If Contextualism has had a greater presence in the architectural and urban design literature, it is partially because of timing: Contextualism arriving on the scene in 1971, *Collage City* not until 1978.[15]

8 Schumacher, Thomas, "Contextualism: Urban Ideals and Deformations", *Casabella* 359-360, 1971: 79-86. Apparently, Cohen and I had convinced some of our colleagues that 'contextualism' was an appropriate name for these associated ideas.

9 Cohen, Stuart, "Physical Context, Cultural Context: Including It All", *Oppositions* 2, MIT Press, Cambridge, MA, 1974.

10 Shane, Grahame, "Contextualism", *Architectural Design* 46 (11), 1976; Ellis, William, "Types and Context in Urbanism, Colin Rowe's Contextualism", *Oppositions* 18, MIT Press, Cambridge, MA, 1979.

11 Jencks, Charles, *The Language of Post-Modern Architecture*, Rizzoli, New York, 1977. And at least five updated editions, 1977–91.

12 Stern, Robert A.M.; Davidson, Cynthia, (ed.), *Architecture on the edge of postmodernism: collected essays, 1964–1988*, Yale University, New Haven, 2010. See especially, "After the Modern Movement, 1977 1978", 107 115. Judging from the arc of Stern's work to the present, he has increasingly embraced Contextualism in his practice. Also see the quite comprehensive Broadbent, Geoffrey, *Emerging Concepts in Urban Space Design*, Van Nostrand Reinhold Co. Ltd., London and New York, 1990: 253; Broadbent paraphrases Stern.

13 Léon Krier, Rob Krier, et al., 'Rationalism'; Aldo Rossi et al., 'La Tendenza', and investigations of 'type' by the Venice school and in Germany by Mathias Ungers. Rowe was partially responsible for Ungers becoming chair at Cornell resulting in a difficult time for Rowe caused by Ungers.

14 Younes, Samir, "Modern Traditional Architecture" in Sagharchi, Alirea and Steil, Lucien, *Traditional Architecture, Timeless Building for the Twenty-First Century*, Rizzoli, New York, 2013: 20-37. Rationalism was the most directly related of these movements.

15 Rowe, Colin and Koetter, Fred, *Collage City*, MIT Press, Cambridge, MA, and London, England, 1978: 186. In the acknowledgment Rowe says the text was written 1970–73, completed Dec. 1973, except for "minor emendations".

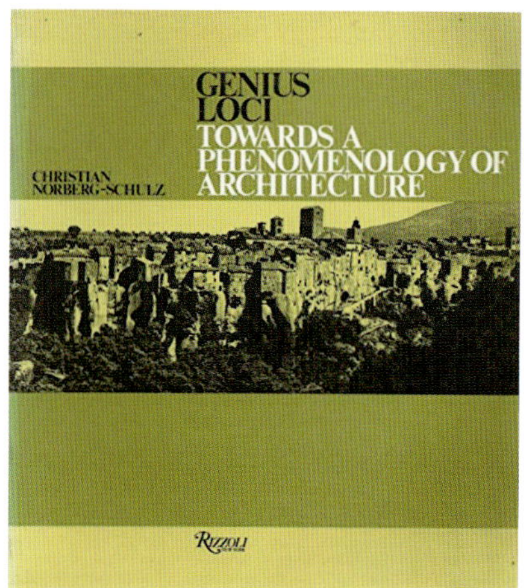

Fig. 1. *Genius Loci: Towards a Phenomenology of Architecture*, Christian Norberg-Schulz, 1980.

Rowe had begun exploring and presenting the collision and collage ideas developed with Koetter for *Collage City* beginning with a lecture in the fall of 1967, and at least another in 1970 using "Collage City" in the titles.[16] When Rowe and Koetter were further developing the ideas in 1970–73, they apparently decided against including Studio design work as illustrations. Fortuitously, shortly after *Collage City* was published, the Rowe team's submittal to the "Roma interrotta" exhibition was also published. It was readily interpreted as an extensive and superb illustration of the ideas described in *Collage City*. Additional power was given to the one-two punch of *Collage City* and "Roma interrotta" by the contrast between the Rowe team "Roma interrotta" submission and the other eleven entries. While the U.S. and European invitees indicated a transatlantic convergence of proto-contextual ideas,[17] the Rowe team submittal was singular in illustrating an alternative to Rome's 1748–1978 development that respected rather than disrupted Rome's traditional urban patrimony.[18] It uniquely assumed that the physical and cultural context was the *raison d'être* for the exhibition, even something of an extended elaboration of the Nolli Plan. Rowe had even written a text that linked an imagined historical and cultural context to the team's design of the physical context. The result was two elaborate compositions, one verbal, the other graphic. Both demonstrated the *bricoleur* of *Collage City* at work, one using remembered historical situations to weave a fictive history, the other using urban and architectural exemplars at hand and demonstrating collision and collage techniques to weave a fictive urban design plan. Both were quite believable.

Subsequently, primary team contributor Steven Peterson supplemented the figure/ground plan with his analytic "Urban Design Tactics" and followed that 1979 article in 1980 with "Space and Anti-Space" emphasizing well-defined public space, the 'figural void'.[19] These made the *Roma interrotta* scheme an excellent instrument of urban design instruction. And in 1981 Michael Schwarting published "The Lesson of Rome", likewise explaining ideas incubated in the Rowe Studio.[20] These 1971–81 publications provided a very complete and compelling critique of 'Mod' as opposed to 'trad' architectural urban forms and the promise of their reconciliation.[21]

Remarkably, with the near simultaneous publication of *Collage City* and *Roma interrotta*, it seemed the 1966–67 Studio discussions had come to fruition. *Collage City* expanded greatly on what began as Koetter's formal interest in collision and collage becoming, in chapters four and five, "Collision City and the Politics of *Bricolage*" and "Collage City and the Reconquest of Time". Combined with the other chapters that expanded on ideas Rowe had explored previously, and the "Excursus" chapter, the book is a thorough critique of Modernism. Meanwhile, Contextualism had become the popular term associated with that critique and understood as a design alternative to a strident Modernism. For Rowe and Koetter, the *psycho-cultural field* conveyed the idea of *physical and cultural context.*[22] What of any difference between the two? Only that *Collage City* posits a both/and dialectic that really does mean, as the title of Cohen's essay asserted, "Including it all".[23] And the "Excursus", framed as "atemporal and necessarily transcultural", is illustrated with a vast array of traditional, Pop, and *zeitgeist* imagery, even a huge offshore oil rig.[24] Contextualism, however inclusive, implies a more restrained and nuanced approach to *zeitgeist* imagery in most situations.

16 As Rowe describes his presence in Berlin in both *As I Was Saying: Recollections and Miscellaneous Essays* 2, *Cornelliana*, MIT Press, Cambridge, MA, and London, 1996: 4-5, and in *The Architecture of Good Intentions*, Academy Group Ltd., London, 1994: 6. In the latter he writes, "previous versions of this material were offered at a symposium sponsored by Mathias Ungers at the Technical University of Berlin as long ago as 1967…". It seems certain Rowe's first lecture mentioning the ideas of *collage* and *utopia* would have been Dec. 1967, shortly after the Studio student nomenclature discussions. Tice recalls a May 1970 Cornell symposium, "The Provincial City" and Rowe's lecture title as "Utopia or Collage City?"

17 The European invitees were Constantino Dardi, Antoine Grumbach, Léon Krier, Rob Krier, Aldo Rossi, Paolo Portoghesi, Piero Sartogo, James Stirling. The U.S. invitees were Romaldo Giurgola, Michael Graves, Colin Rowe, and Robert Venturi.

18 In an introduction to the *Roma interrotta* publication, Alan Chimacoff wryly remarked that, having had a year to develop their responses and many invitees well known to each other, it did not appear any of the twelve "avowed contextualists" had conferred. For example, Rowe and Stirling had been friends since their student days. Rowe had met the Venturis and written sympathetically about Robert Venturi (Yale Mathematics Building Competition). See Rowe, *As I Was Saying* 2, 1996: 79–102. Both Rob and Léon Krier reciprocated forewords and introductory essays with Rowe in contemporary publications. Rowe wrote "Revolt of the Senses" for Rob Krier's *Stadtraum* of 1979, published in English as *Urban Space*. Léon Krier later wrote the "Foreword" for *The Cornell Journal of Architecture* 2. In *As I Was Saying* 3, *Urbanistica*, MIT Press, Cambridge, MA, and London, 1996, Rowe notes of Rob and Léon Krier, that he "long regarded them both as quasi-allies". A related version of this American and European exchange and revaluation of the street is evident in the Venice Biennale of 1980–81 titled "The Presence of the Past", for which facades along a 'street' *Strada Novissima* were invited, submitted, and built, the effort orchestrated primarily by Robert A.M. Stern.

At the Interpretative Extremities

As intended, Contextualism communicated the idea with a single word that appropriately invited broad interpretation—both a strength and a weakness. Two books published in 1980 focused on context at the opposite extremes of scale. This seemed to cloud rather than clarify the meaning of Contextualism.[25]

Christian Norberg-Schulz argued for an expansive consideration. In *Genius Loci* he made the phenomenological argument for the existential affirmation of one's place in the world by sustaining meaningful form relationships between the new and the extant.[26] He argued for grounding new forms in a context extending from the immediate vicinity through cultural-form identities discerned locally, regionally, and beyond. The *genius loci* described by Norberg-Schulz includes much of the psycho-cultural field. Norberg-Schulz was amending his other books in which he had been describing and addressing numerous perceived shortcomings of Modern architecture. In his 1962 *Intentions in Architecture* he had written, "architecture is dependent upon a unifying creative process where the single components are usually transformed by the total context", adding that it "aims at creating an ordered physical milieu and a meaningful symbol-milieu", a phrasing both close to physical and cultural context and anticipating *Genius Loci*.[27]

Fig. 2. *Architecture in Context: Fitting New Buildings with Old*, Brent C. Brolin, 1980.

Brent Brolin took the opposite tack. Deeply disturbed by the deleterious impact of Modernism on the city, in his 1976 *The Failure of Modern Architecture*, he had already dismantled the numerous theories rationalized as the "Cultural Roots of Modern Architecture".[28] For his 1980 *Architecture in Context*. Brolin radically narrowed his focus. He took on the troublesome issue of how well or poorly a newer building maintained or detracted from the character of those in the immediate vicinity.[29] He carefully distinguished his approach from those of other people addressing the issue.[30] Brolin's effort was theoretically sound, sweeping in the range of examples demonstrating the compatibility of buildings from the past despite significant differences in era, style, size, and use. Turning to Modernist and Postmodernist examples, he attempted to fairly describe their compatibility with their context. His unconvincing effort was hampered in at least two ways. Despite his 1976 dismantling of Modernist rationales, he accepted CIAM-based Modernist strictures against figurative, iconic, or historic stylistic references. Perhaps unintentionally, this gave credence to the idea that concern for context might fetter creativity or lead to historicist 'dead ends'.[31] Second, his focus on facades excluded sometimes equally important contextual characteristics of urban morphology, building typology, and iconography. Brolin's effort can be seen as representative of many who similarly focused too narrowly on only the facade.[32]

One result seems to have been a contagious narrowing of discussions of Contextualism from the vast *psycho-cultural field* to the narrow visual field.[33] Wasn't imagining an architecture based on the goal of "reconciliation" or "amelioration", informed by the vast area and riches of the *psycho-cultural field* between the extremes, what Rowe and Koetter were suggesting?[34]

19 Peterson, Steven, "Urban Design Tactics", first written for *Architectural Design*, an issue devoted to *Roma interrotta* (1979) and Peterson, Steven, "Space and Anti-Space", *Harvard Architectural Review* (1980). Peterson Littenberg also received one of three Project Laureates in the Les Halles Design Competition of 1979. These are now available online at petersonlittenberg.com-Urban Design/UD and in Peterson, Steven and Littenberg, Barbara, *Space and Anti-Space: The fabric of place, city, and architecture*, ORO editions, Gordon Goff, San Francisco, 2020.

20 Schwarting, Jon Michael, "The Lesson of Rome," *Harvard Architectural Review* 2, Spring 1981.

21 Among early Studio efforts at 'trad'/ Mod reconciliation, see the 1966 Buffalo Waterfront project and the 1967 Harlem Redevelopment Project.

22 The 'psycho-cultural' was under discussion in the academic world about the time Rowe was first teaching in the 1950s at the University of Texas. See Stoddart, Curwen and Hession, Charles H., "The Psychocultural Approach to Social Science", *The Journal of Higher Education* 22, 6, Taylor & Francis, Ltd. Jun 1951: 310–320+344.

23 In the "Excursus" subtitled "Nostalgia-producing instruments" nothing seems off-limits whether "… 'scientific' and of the future, 'romantic' and of the past … offshore oil rigs … rocket launching … old Roman tombs … small town America, a Vauban fort, and the Las Vegas or any other strip so adored by the Venturis", see Rowe and Koetter, *Collage City*, 1978: 172–173.

24 Ibid.: "Excursus", *Collage City* (1978): 151.

25 Pittas, Michael and Ferebee Ann, ed., *Education for Urban Design*, Institute for Urban Design, Purchase, NY, H. Ross Publishing Co., Boston, MA, 1982.

A More Expansive Argument

Enter *The Cornell Journal of Architecture*. Three topical issues were published between 1981–87. Theoretical essays were illustrated with student work. Volume 1, 1981, focused on the complexities of the architectural plan;[35] Volume 2, 1982, on *Urban Design*; and Volume 3, 1987, on *The Vertical Surface*.[36] It was as if Cornell's faculty, students, and alumni were rallying to an expanding worldwide cause. These journals can be seen as revitalizing the body of knowledge necessary for making the traditional city with corridor streets,[37] defined urban spaces, buildings that complete the urban fabric, and designed landscapes that constitute the complementary elements of the entire city. Emphasis is, first, on the continuity of the urban realm; second on the hierarchic importance of spaces and buildings representative of the societal order;[38] third, on their related iconic/typological identity; and last on massing and facade composition. These are most of the qualities rejected by Modernist architecture but foundational to the Rowe and Koetter understanding of the city and, provisionally, a contextual approach to urban and architectural design.

Place, Preservation, and the Psycho-cultural Field

The sentiments of the *Journals* and the 1960–80s Studios were shared by many. Some had been creating legislative realities with financial incentives to preserve valued physical and cultural contexts. By the 1980s, national programs validating historic forms of urbanism and architecture had come to the fore. The National Trust for Historic Preservation was created in 1976 and its Main Streets Program initiated in 1977. Historic districts and associated guidelines and review boards were being established. And context-sensitive projects were increasingly in evidence and even earning design awards.[39] As Cohen wrote of the related design process, "contextualism refers to the design of buildings by *selectively choosing* to relate them to their immediate physical context *or to their cultural context—the history of a place*".[40] Indeed, during the 1970s, *contextualism*, the *psycho-cultural field*, and *place* had come to share overlapping meanings. Kevin Lynch, already known for his 1960 *Image of the City*, followed it in 1972 with *What Time is this Place?*[41] Lynch's title captured the essential conflict between preferences or allegiances to expressions of the *zeitgeist* or time versus the *genius loci,* or place. 'Place' typically would emphasize the *genius loci*, whereas, from the *psycho-cultural field* or the physical and cultural context, the architect-urban designer might selectively combine characteristics derived from both to achieve reconciliation or amelioration. In 1986, Roger Trancik, in *Finding Lost Space*, provided an excellent, well-illustrated summary of the 'Mod problem' and several approaches that seemed otherwise at odds: *figure/ground*, *linkage*, and *place*, each with case study proposals.[42]

Fred Koetter: "Contextualism?"

Apparently, while teaching Studios at Cornell and working with Rowe on *Collage City* ca. 1970–73, Fred Koetter asked his students and others about Contextualism, "What if you are in a bad neighborhood?" From this, some have wondered about the "curious omission" of the word *contextualism* from *Collage City*. As it seemed Koetter had reservations about Contextualism, did Rowe as well?[43] Most

26 Norberg-Schulz, Christian, *Genius Loci: Towards a Phenomenology of Architecture*, Rizzoli, New York, 1979 (trans 1980). Norberg-Schulz collaborated with Paolo Portoghesi in *Roma interrotta* writing that they studied the environmental history of the site, restored its ravines, and sketched an architecture evoking the steep and irregular ravine slopes—a contextual response?

27 Norberg-Schulz, Christian, *Intentions in Architecture*, MIT Press, Cambridge MA; George Allen and Unwin, Ltd., London; Universitetsforlaget, Oslo, 1965: 201. His words anticipate physical and cultural context, I did not yet know the book and doubt Cohen did either.

28 Brolin, Brent C., Chapter II, "The Cultural Roots of Modern Architecture", *The Failure of Modern Architecture*, Van Nostrand Reinhold Co., New York, 1976.

29 Brolin, Brent C, *Architecture in Context: Fitting New Buildings with Old*, Van Nostrand Reinhold, Co., New York, 1980.

30 For Brolin the jarring juxtaposition of Modernist buildings among older ones epitomized the broader issue. He emphasized the compatibility of adjacent buildings not the "large scale issues of urban design" acknowledging Rowe, Schumacher, and Colquhoun but explaining, "Configurations that seem integrated on a large-scale plan can easily fail to convince at the 1:1 scale of reality", Brolin (1980): 14. He briefly notes legitimate 'monumental' or 'civic' exceptions to compatibility, but emphasis on immediate adjacency overwhelms it. For useful purposes see his "Conclusion" (138-47), and "Appendix A" (148-50), "To the Architects: Some Common Questions About Designing in Context".

31 Pevsner, Nikolaus, "The Return of Historicism", *Journal of the Royal Institute of British Architects* 3: 68, 1961. Pevsner applied the term "historicist" in his less than substantive, very dismissive remarks on a collection of then recent works, declaring the approaches as leading to "dead ends".

32 For example see, Richard Meier's "Museum for the Decorative Arts, Frankfurt am Main, Germany", *Richard Meier Architect* 2, Rizzoli International Publications, Inc., New York, NY, 1991: 96–127. There is an extensive rationale of abstracting and applying the facade shapes and proportions of the earlier building to the new one, while the new addition is a very nice Modernist building, both are white, the proportions of windows, windowpanes, and wall to window are all related, but other figural characteristics are dominant. Consequently, the new building contrasts markedly with the old building.

33 As evident in academic, professional, design review, design guidelines, and journal descriptions.

34 Rowe used 'reconciliation' and 'amelioration' to describe the hoped-for and intended resolution of Mod/ 'trad' urban problem. Tice related Rowe differentiating amelioration as meaning an improved or better situation or result.

evidently, Rowe did not. Rowe likely encouraged the title of Schumacher's article "Contextualism: Urban Ideals and Deformation". And for *As I Was Saying* written in the 1990s, he wrote, "The word *contextualist*, so frequently used nowadays, probably first erupted in Cornell studio conversation—always very loud—between Tom Schumacher and Stuart Cohen".[44]

The relation of figure and field, Cubism, and the *collision* and *collage* phenomena had been part of Rowe's thinking and vocabulary for some time. It deeply affected the entire Studio, bringing to it the language of perception psychology—overlap, superposition, interpenetration, shared contour, collision and collage. Beginning in 1965, Koetter became an active participant in using that shared parlance and promoting it, primarily collision and collage. Rowe used the 'collage' analogy as early as 1967 to describe, if not rationalize, the impact of Modernism on traditional city form. The formal interest in collision and collage shared by Rowe and Koetter in 1965–70 no doubt deepened considerably during the writing of *Collage City* between 1970–73, resulting in the chapters "Collision City and the Politics of Bricolage" and "Collage City and the Reconquest of Time". Those chapters addressed a multiplicity of both longstanding and contemporary urban and architectural issues.[45] Contextualism, as essentially the same argument but with a quasi-independent presence in the literature, would have added nothing to the all-inclusive *psycho-cultural field*.[46]

Koetter's "bad neighborhood" remark was likely a poor choice of words born of a sincere anxiety. "Bad neighborhood" suggests economic and social impoverishment rather than an impoverished or vacuous *psycho-cultural field*—granted, the two often go together. But understood as a query about form-making, the question becomes: How can one achieve good contextual buildings when the psycho-cultural field offers little guidance? Quite possibly, Koetter was attempting to formulate an operational *theory of practice* as distinct from his thinking about the *theory of history and criticism* that is *Collage City*. Koetter was likely challenging his studio students and others, but also himself, with the broad question: Would one always be able to find adequate *matériel* in the context, in the *psycho-cultural field*, to guide new work? And would one be able to use it effectively? How might such a commitment limit or opportune practice? Koetter's anxiety is understandable.

The Koetter Kim practice: Grounded in and Launched from Collage City

Whatever reservations Fred Koetter or Susie Kim might have had about Contextualism, once they embarked together on professional practice, they dedicated themselves to an expansive exploration of the *psycho-cultural field* as a guide to decision making grounded in the thinking that went into *Collage City*. What had the grounding provided? Synoptically, a thorough critique of Modernism framed by a history of ideas. A few dozen specific urban exemplars drawn from 'trad' cities and presented as possibly useful general analogies. It is suggested that the 'trad' city provides a better guide to the making of the good city than does the 'Mod city'. But Mod architecture is not forsaken. Instead, something like a reconciliation or amelioration is imagined as an optimal possibility. But no demonstrations are provided. 'Nostalgias for both the past and the future' are seen as a fact of the human condition and illustrated with an expansive

35 Of the eight faculty or student authored essays, three demonstrate design responses to complex landscape and urban site conditions: Hodgden, Lee "Formal Gardens"; Dennis, Michael, "Architecture and the Post-Modern City"; Goehner, Werner, "Architecture as an Integral Part of the City", *The Cornell Journal of Architecture* 1, 1981. The essays explore *architectural promenade, poché* versus figural spaces; ideal type and deformations that accommodate geometrically complex urban sites and landscape limits and opportunities.

36 Most explicitly the illustrated essays: Schumacher, Thomas L., "The Skull and the Mask" and "Palladian Variations"; Goehner, Werner, "Viennese Facades Between 1890 and 1910"; Warke, Val K., "The Bay, Investigations in the Analysis and Synthesis of Elevational Phenomenon", *The Cornell Journal of Architecture* 3, 1987.

37 Representative of Modernist ideology, Le Corbusier railed against the 'corridor street'. Reclaiming the social-aesthetic-economic-functional value of the street has enlisted numerous contributors—Jane Jacobs of course, then: Anderson, Stanford, ed., *On Streets*, MIT Press, Cambridge MA and London, 1978; Jacobs, Allan B., *Great Streets*, MIT Press, Cambridge, MA and London England, 1993; Aurbach, Laurence, *A History of Street Networks: From grids to sprawl and beyond*, Pedshed Press, Hyattsville, MD, 2020.

38 Such as city halls, court houses, civic auditoriums, libraries, other government buildings, places of worship, service clubs, and associations.

39 In 1984 both Battery Park City and Seaside were awarded "Citations" by *Progressive Architecture* in its annual awards issue. While at the extremes of urban scale, both projects were notable for their design codes related to local and regional contexts.

40 Cohen, Stuart, "Contextualism: From Urbanism to a Theory of Appropriate Form," *Inland Architect*, May/June, 1987: 68–69. The italics are mine. More accurately, *'and/or* their cultural context'. Referencing only 'place' is too limiting, potentially excluding iconographies conveyed by buildings.

41 Lynch, Kevin, *What Time is this Place*, MIT Press, Cambridge, MA, 1972. Subsequently, the architectural journal *Places* was founded in 1983.

42 Trancik, Roger, *Finding Lost Space: Theories of Urban Design*, Van Nostrand Reinhold Co., New York, 1986. This book is an excellent, well-illustrated summary of the then-current theories, their integration, and application. Trancik was at Cornell, initially in the Landscape program not well connected to the departments of Architecture or Planning.

iconography in the "Excursus" of *Collage City*. Acceptance of these nostalgic iconographies results in the inclusive 'city of composite presence', a *Collage City*, not a reconciliation or amelioration. In the dialectical presentation that is *Collage City*, many possible choices are presented, but only one clear choice is made: the city is chosen over anti-city forms and forces.

Koetter Kim made that most fundamental choice as well—they chose the city. They must have known that, while they were projecting a practice grounded in *Collage City*, they were launching it into a world vastly different from the 'trad' city exemplars they intended to use to guide and even propel their practice. Likewise, they must have known that the architecture they might make in the future would not be informed by the nostalgic extremes of either iconoclasm or iconophilia. They most likely assumed that, having chosen the 'trad' city as their model, a logical cascade of urban and architectural choices would follow, not that these would be either obvious or easy. In a sense, they would be field-testing whether the views, propositions, and choices suggested by *Collage City* could be made viable in present-day practice given the increasingly difficult realities of the burgeoning 'Mod city' real estate development paradigms and new engineering and construction possibilities.

It is the results of that field test that Koetter Kim present and argue for in their monograph, *Koetter Kim and Associates: Place | Time*.[47] Their subtitle, *Place | Time* both introduces and disguises the complexity of their effort. It wraps most of the dialectical issues explored in *Collage City* into just one, place/time, to confront the fact that, for more than a century, our culture has favored *time* over *place*, *change* over *stasis*, *zeitgeist* over *genius loci*, and that this has been generally problematic for our culture, and particularly devastating to our cities. "Time" and "Place" are used as headings for essays that explain their thinking, looking back on a practice devoted to making the 'trad' city and a related architecture their lodestar, such that 'place' took precedence over 'time'.

In considering their projects, it is worth noting the ways Koetter Kim drew guiding lessons from *Collage City*, but decisively so, almost always making an architecture that would or could contribute to a 'trad' city form within the limits of the opportunities pursued and offered by their practice.[48]

43 Coeditor James Tice, a student of both Koetter and Rowe, prompted my reflection on the "omission" of Contextualism from *Collage City* in the email below (edited for clarity); *I think it would be interesting to examine the question, Why Colin, in* Collage City, *did not include contextualism as an idea. It is an extraordinary omission. I know that Fred [Koetter] was flip about contextualism not being such a good idea because you might find yourself in a bad neighborhood, but I think it goes much deeper than that. I would suspect that typology and contextualism often go hand in hand—is that logical? I wonder if arguments against contextualism also use a similar argument against typology? Conservatism? I think there is a notion that contextualism, in the end, defeats the "new" and winds up being an apotheosis of the status quo: harsh words, I know, but spending some intellectual investment in responding to these criticisms would be very helpful. These are important questions about contextualism that no one has adequately covered. And it would give you an opportunity to rebut high profile types like Steven Holl, Peter Eisenman, Frank Gehry, etc. Remember Rem Koolhaas said, "F... the context".*

I regret not asking Fred directly about his bad neighborhood comment related to Contextualism, but it had never seemed important until Tice suggested it should be addressed. Regarding Koolhaas and his "F... the context" remark, it was made regarding the seemingly impossible task of relating a huge building driven by the capitalist economy to the older, adjacent, and smaller buildings.

44 Rowe (1996/3): 2.

45 Additionally, Koetter could reasonably claim 'collision' and 'collage' to have originated with him in the Studio 1965–67. He quite likely promoted their further development in conversations with Rowe. The argument is more complex and esoteric than that of Contextualism. In 1966–70 he likely intuited their further development and more esoteric appeal to the architectural *intelligentsia*. Interestingly, despite the same ideas resonating in both texts, few of the word descriptions in *Collage City* appear in *Koetter Kim & Associates: Space|Time*. But parallels are readily found, for example, 'situation' in *Koetter Kim* equates to 'circumstance' in *Collage City*.

46 Most 'isms' in architectural discourse are more narrowly focused than Rowe's wide-ranging inclusive interests and ideas. Cohen and I assumed Rowe would be averse to any 'ism' as unnecessarily limiting and therefore never discussed with Rowe the idea of promoting the Studio ideas as Contextualism. We sensed disinterest or even discouragement. Schumacher's 1971 article was a delightful surprise.

47 *Koetter Kim & Associates: Place | Time*, Rizzoli International Publications, New York, NY, 1997.

48 The Koetter Kim practice did not include the opportunity to design major civic buildings such as Federal or County Court Houses, which quite likely would have yielded more iconic, figural, and possibly object buildings but with the same attention to the *psycho-cultural field* typical of their practice.

The Koetter Kim practice: Nine representative projects

Thirty-two projects are presented in the monograph, most executed between 1978–95, a few slightly earlier. The nine considered below span the scale range of the work, from small to large architectural projects followed by immense urban design plans. The sequence begins with those for which context is visual, immediate, and more architectural than urbanistic. It then moves through projects increasingly shaped by references to building typologies and related urban morphologies that can be seen as universal in relation to natural and urban environments and cosmologies. Contextual references drawn from the *psycho-cultural field* range from the quite literal to the ephemeral.

Fig. 3. *Koetter Kim & Associates: Place | Time*, 1997.

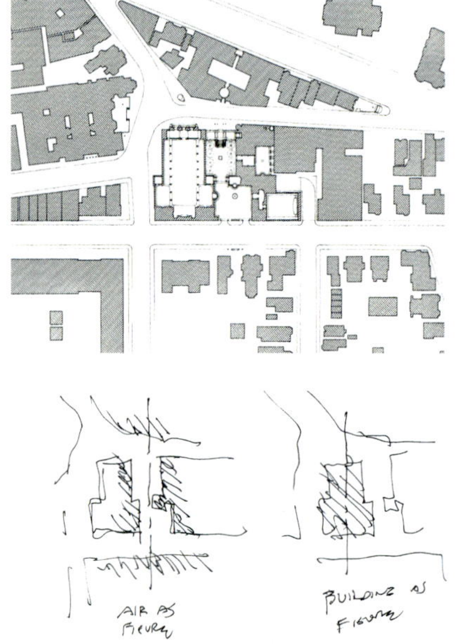

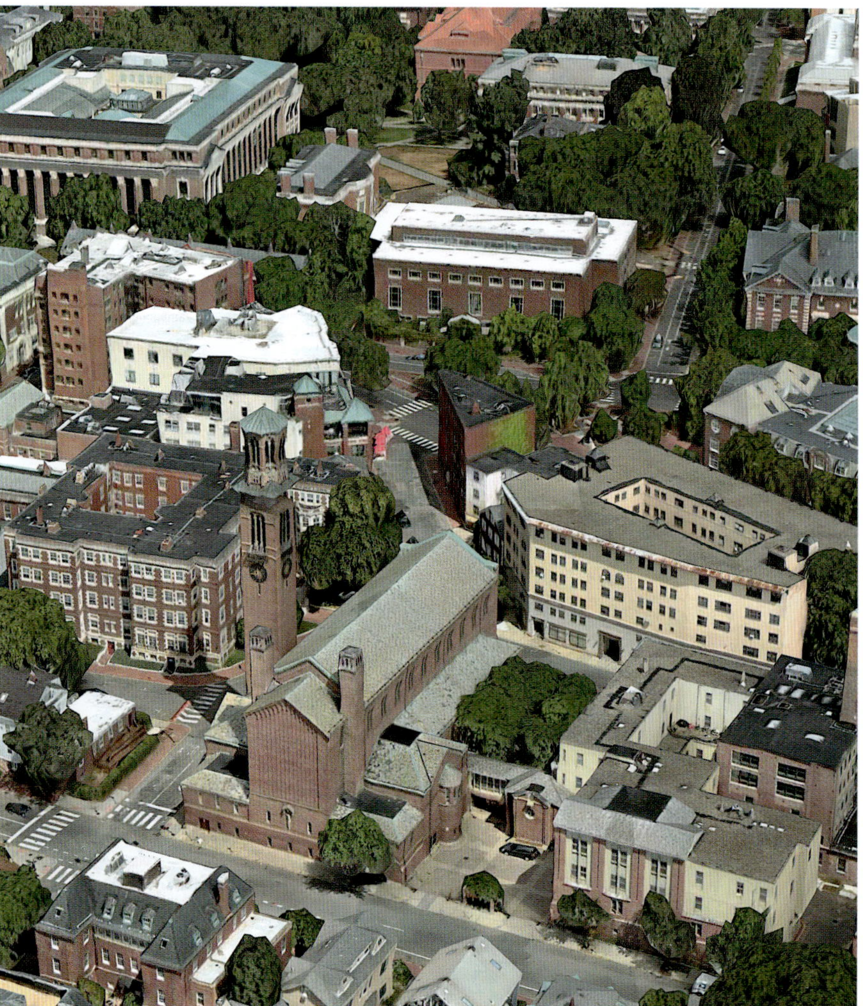

above:
Fig. 4. Ground level 'Nolli Plan'.

Fig. 5. Conceptual sketch: Air as figure; Building as figure.

inset:
Fig. 6. Aerial view.
Photo: Apple Maps.

Church of St. Paul, Cambridge, Massachusetts

This addition to a Roman Catholic Church demonstrates a high level of attention to the immediate context. First, to preserve a cherished pedestrian passage through the property: a diagram of the site describes space or "Air as figure" and "Building as figure", "irreducible protagonists in a debate".[49] Second:

> *When we examined the physical and material nature of the neighborhood, a largely brick precinct of the city, an attitude and a vocabulary of the situation began to form… . In the city, some buildings draw their strength not from conscious manipulation but from some other force related to the collective presence of the city—a tension between this presence and the individual building… a presence that is very difficult to secure… .*[50]

For the addition, Koetter Kim developed a refined use of brick related to both the existing church and the "material nature of the neighborhood" so that the church and addition would maintain the "anonymous but forceful collective presence" of the area. Third, the architectural forms of the addition include a small chapel that is, when viewed from the street, seen as figure against the ground of the rest of the addition and embraces the iconography of the church. Built in

49 As remarked about Sant'Agnese and Piazza Navona, Rowe and Koetter (1978): 77.

50 Koetter Kim (1997): 48.

inset:
Fig. 7. Pedestrian passage from Asbury Street. Photo: Lisa Abitbol.

Fig. 8. Pedestrian passage from Arrow Street. Photo: Lisa Abitbol.

right:
Fig. 9. St Paul's Parish, view at Bow Street. Photo: Lisa Abitbol.

1952 in a Romanesque style, the church conveys what Rowe had written elsewhere of U.S. architecture, that "there will sometimes be experienced a feeling of inextinguishable antiquity".[51] This quality, one that partially results from the comparatively stable iconography of the architectural forms of such institutions, is less readily communicated by Modernist architecture. This project is clearly grounded in the issues explored in *Collage City*, shaped by the physical conditions of the site and its cultural context. It demonstrates design choices made in favor of the local urban pedestrian network, of the *genius loci* of the neighborhood, and of the cultural iconography of the church.

51 Rowe, Colin, "Lockhart, Texas", *As I Was Saying: Recollections and Miscellaneous Essays* 1, MIT Press, Cambridge, MA, and London, 1996: 55–71; first published in 1957 in *Architectural Record.*

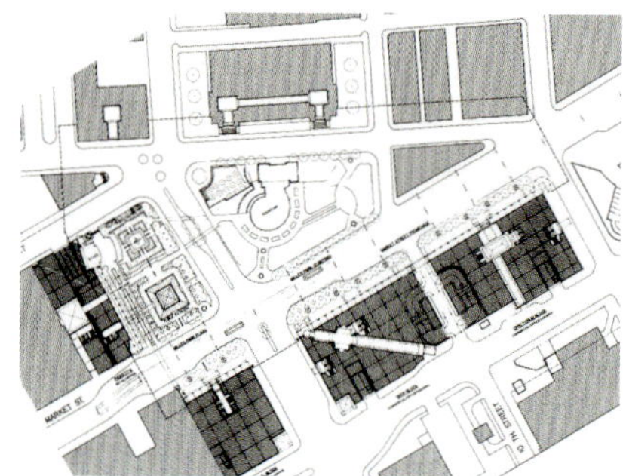

Miller Park Plaza, Chattanooga, Tennessee

In *Collage City*, it is the object/texture and solid/void antonyms that optimally characterize the 'trad' city made of a 'prevalent texture' of densely packed 'solids' that make the *res privata*, within which a few 'voids' are the all-important public spaces of the *res publica*. Complementing these are a few object buildings, or figural 'solids', independent of or erupting from the texture, and optimally a part of the *res publica*.

In downtown Chattanooga, the triangular Miller Park existed at the spatial juncture of what Koetter Kim saw as colliding grids. On the east side of the square stands a monumental, white, marble-clad 1932–1933 U.S. Courthouse and Federal Building that, combined with the park, creates a *res publica*. Along the street north and south of the courthouse, other buildings provide good continuous street definition. Likewise, the short side of a flatiron building provides enclosure at the south end of the park. But, if other buildings once provided enclosure on the west and north sides of Miller Park, that was no longer the case.[52]

Participating in a revitalization plan, Koetter Kim proposed colonnaded buildings intended to give "literal and continuous definition" along the street west of Miller Park. On the north side, they designed Miller Park Plaza, which includes a freestanding figural public pavilion on the northwest corner, and behind it a two-story colonnaded background building extending the width of the block. Incorporated into the colonnade is a small outdoor stage facing an audience area that is part of an intimate landscaped square. The look of the new buildings was to be "inspired by the existing historical buildings of the district", essentially late 1800s and early 1900s masonry-clad office and industrial buildings.[53] The brick red color of the new buildings and plaza avoids dissipating the presence of the white marble clad courthouse. While the architectonic language of the Koetter Kim buildings can be seen to derive from the local context as stated, they provoke other associations not mentioned. The boxy pavilion with its pyramidal

above:

Fig 10. 'Nolli' site plan.

Fig. 11. Federal Building and Courthouse (former U. S. Post Office and Courthouse). Photo by author.

Fig. 12. The EPB Building. Photo by author.

inset:
Fig. 13. Aerial. Miller Park at the center, Miller Park Plaza and Public Pavilion on the left, Federal Courthouse at the top, EPB Building lower right. Photo by Google Maps.

---

52 It appears that, then as now, the block to the southwest was a parking lot; facing into it on the south side an immense Modernist six-story TVA building, and on the west side a 'Brutalist' public library.

53 Koetter Kim (1997): 132.

Top to bottom, left to right:

Fig. 14. Miller Plaza. Google Street View.

Fig. 15. Colonnade, Miller Plaza. Photo by author.

Fig. 16. Miller Plaza, Public Pavilion. Photo by author.

Fig. 17. Colonnade, EPB Building. Photo by author.

roof and square lantern, its giant order pilasters and slightly vertical bays recall similarly sized and shaped Georgian, Federal, Greek Revival, and Italianate buildings that, like this one, aspire to grandeur with a simple Platonic form and simplified classical detailing.

Later in the work of Koetter Kim we find the idea of the 'resilient type'. Here at Miller Park Plaza three resilient architectural urban types are already present: the pedestrian-sheltering colonnade, the ideal figural public building, and the background linear building or, as described in *Collage City*, a 'potentially interminable set piece'.

The redevelopment was to be regulated by design guidelines that come close to being a required urban design code. The EPB Buildings captured the intended spirit of the guidelines in overall composition, material selection, and by not only gracing the entire length of the block facing onto Miller Park with a colonnade but also extending it around the corner for the length of the south facing block. Guidelines such as these are not mentioned in *Collage City*.[54] But Koetter Kim were fully aware of the developments and applications of such regulations. Whereas they never became a feature of Studio studies, they did become fundamental to the Koetter Kim practice.

54 Early Studio students seeking to understand historic urban forms had begun to discover that design guidelines and codes had regulated building form and materials for centuries. Rowe, in the late 1960s, agreed to have a group of Studio students study the impact of changes to the City of New York zoning code in league with the Institute for Architecture and Urban Studies (IAUS).

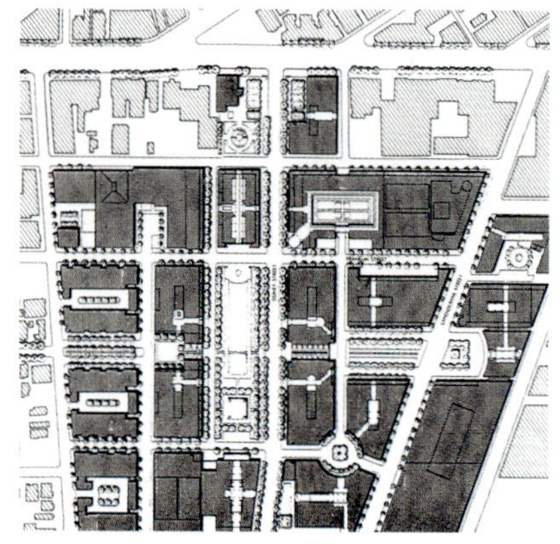

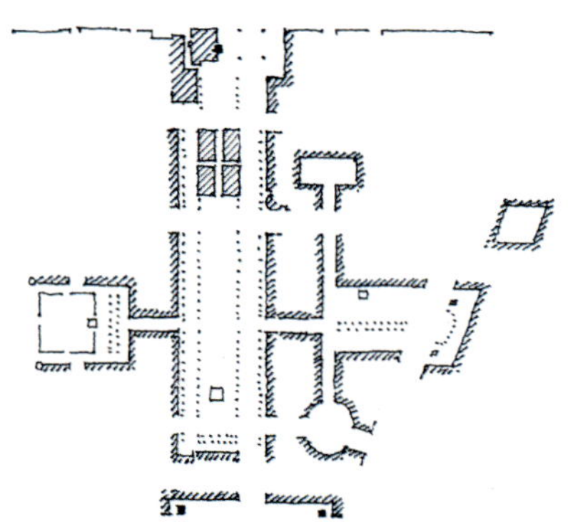

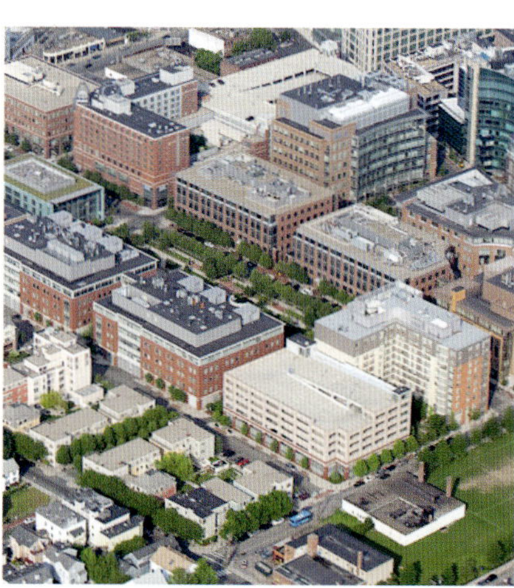

University Park, Cambridge, Massachusetts

The Koetter Kim remark on Miller Park applies equally to University Park, Cambridge and to many of the projects that followed:

> *The several building sites surrounding the park were to give literal and continuous definition to the space of the park… strong repetitive structures inspired by the existing historical buildings of the district… . Specific guidelines also identify important locations within the district, significant building entry locations, conspicuous points of visual focus, and areas of transition with respect to the surrounding city. Preferred modes of building expression, the nature of the street-defining wall, and the required finish materials are also informed by design guidelines.*[55]

The Koetter Kim description of University Park typifies the contextualist approach exhibited at Chattanooga, but for a larger site area in a less singular location:

> *Our general strategy was to reconnect the site to its surroundings by literally continuing the street pattern of the city through the site… we identified buildings of a size range, scale, and format related to the robust light-industrial building stock that was historically typical to that part of Cambridge… . Our challenge was to provide these buildings with an identity while maintaining the resilient qualities of the type.*[56]

The project is provided locational identity on Mass Ave by the 1893 Lafayette Square Firehouse with its remarkable hose tower and flanking public space. Aligned with them, Koetter Kim proposed: 1) a market building with an open

galleria, 2) a two-block-long by one-block-long common, framed by, 3) what in Studio parlance, were called background or liner or wall buildings to distinguish them from figural buildings such as the firehouse and proposed market building.[57]

Three qualities of the plan and buildings for this project, and their relation to one another, are found in *Collage City*. The first is seen in the attention to the weave of linked exterior with interior spaces inspired by the Nolli Plan. Second is the resilient type. In *Collage City*, the palazzo is the resilient type, both ideal and circumstantial, part of the "prevalent texture" of the *centro storico* of Rome. In both Chattanooga and Cambridge, it is the "robust light-industrial building" extracted from far less circumstantial evidence than the palazzi of Rome but similarly anchored in the past, evident in the present, and applicable for some time to come. And third, these resilient types, when extended for some distance, become, as described in the "Excursus", "potentially interminable set pieces".[58] The Koetter Kim buildings slightly elevate the "prevalent industrial type" to that of modest grandeur achieved with a two-story base, a two-story mid-section, and one attic story. The repetitive bays are relieved by subtle recessed multi-story framing of entry bays. These entry bays are asymmetric to each individual building but symmetric to the cross axis of the project. That axis connects the area of the neighborhood to the northwest, across the center of the common, to a courtyard on the opposite, southeast, side of the project.

opposite left:
Fig. 18. Proposed 'Nolli' Plan.

Fig. 19. Structure of open spaces.

Fig. 20. Figure/ground, proposed.

Fig. 21. Figure/ground, existing.

opposite inset left to right:
Fig. 22. Proposed market hall perspective beyond the landmark firehouse and public plaza at Lafayette Square, Mass Ave.

Fig. 23. Lafayette Square Firehouse. Photo: jjg/Cambridge Fire Department.

Fig. 24. Aerial, looking northwest. Photo by Google Maps.

Fig. 25. Aerial, looking northeast. Photo: Alex MacLean/Landslides Aerial Photography.

above top row:
Fig. 26, 27. University Park Commons, Auburn Street, cross-axial views. Photo: Lisa Abitbol.

Fig. 28. University Park Commons, Auburn Street cross-axis looking northwest. Photo by Apple Maps.

bottom row:
Fig. 29, 30, 31. Plaza, park, and colonnade at Auburn Street between Blanche and Landsdowne Streets. Photo: Lisa Abitbol.

55 Koetter Kim (1997): 132.

56 Ibid.: 31.

57 The market building with pedestrian passage was not built, but the building that replaced it does have a figural presence resulting from an architectural language different from all the other buildings.

58 Rowe and Koetter (1978): 160–63.

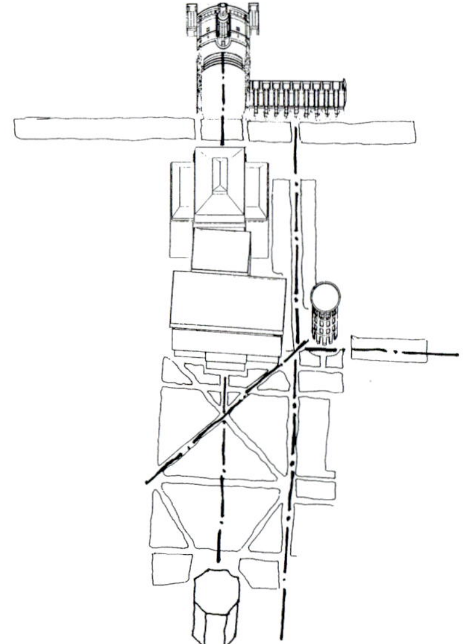

Plan projection of campus extension (top) and main quadrangle (bottom).

Syracuse University

One of the most useful books available to the early Studios was the encyclopedic *The American Vitruvius: An Architects' Handbook of Civic Art* by Werner Hegemann and Elbert Peets of 1922. The authors used the phrase "the grouping of buildings" for what we now call urban design. A subsection on "Educational Groups" is introduced by an essay, "The Development of the American College Campus". In the U.S., college campuses have often been the most highly developed examples of a contextual interaction between landscape, townscape, and buildings. Campus buildings can often be seen as playing both background and foreground roles, in whole or in part. This campus tradition was followed by Koetter Kim, jointly with Dennis and Clark, in "working on the definition of campus plan, building massing, and exterior envelope design" for the Syracuse campus, and manifest in two buildings.[59] The Shaffer Arts Building provides a round tower on a corner of the central campus quadrangle. It marks walkways that lead from that quadrangle along the two perpendicular faces of the building and toward campus expansion areas.

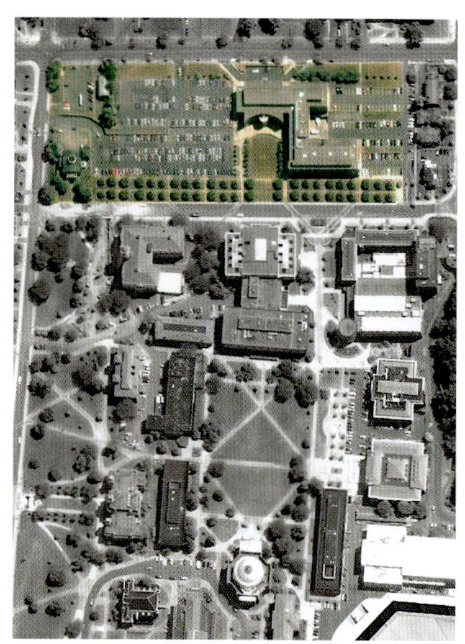

One of the walkways is toward the Science and Technology Center that, due to its location, is the first campus building built on a long city block across the street from the campus. To make the block be simultaneously of the city and of the campus, the city street remained open, but a campus-like landscape terrace was extended for the entire block facing the campus. Set back from the landscape terrace, the building forms a right-angle Z shape, such that a recessed court is on axis with the central east-west axis of the campus and faces back across the street to Slocum Hall, home to the School of Architecture. That facade is cupped to form a shallow arc and is decidedly figural. The other two wings of the Z are background surfaces that define the courtyard, the street, and space of the walkway area that connects with the central quadrangle. These legs of the Z diffuse attention with their repetitive bays. Here again is the resiliency of the type, a facade rooted in the architectonics of the classical but with no reference to the Classical orders, while in the facade of the shallow arc that partially defines the setback court, one sees Rowe's influence, not via *Collage City*, but through his descriptions of the compositional characteristics of Renaissance Mannerism.[60]

opposite top to bottom:
Fig. 32. Site plan: Science and Technology Center at top, Shaffer Art Building, lower right.

Fig. 33. Axial walks and vistas.

Fig. 34. Central campus. Google Earth, historic maps, 1984.

opposite inset:
Fig. 35. Exterior entry court, Science and Technology Center. Photo: Jeff Goldberg.

top to bottom:
Fig. 36. Shaffer Art Building at a corner of the central campus quad, view to the Science and Technology building beyond. Photo: maukinthewise.

Fig. 37. Street facade, Science and Technology Center. Photo: maukinthewise.

59 Koetter Kim (1997): 189–201. The associated architect responsible for the interior development of these buildings is noted as King, Lindquist of Philadelphia.

60 This curved, taut, facade certainly owes something to Rowe's special appreciation for Mannerist composition. It is interesting to compare these facades to those by Dennis and Clark (Michael Dennis) at Carnegie Mellon. Fred Koetter, Suzie Kim, Michael Dennis, and Colin Rowe shared a particularly close friendship for many years. Koetter and Dennis had both been students at Oregon where their friendship began. Subsequently they both taught at Cornell in the early 1970s and, as seen here, shared some professional practice experiences as well.

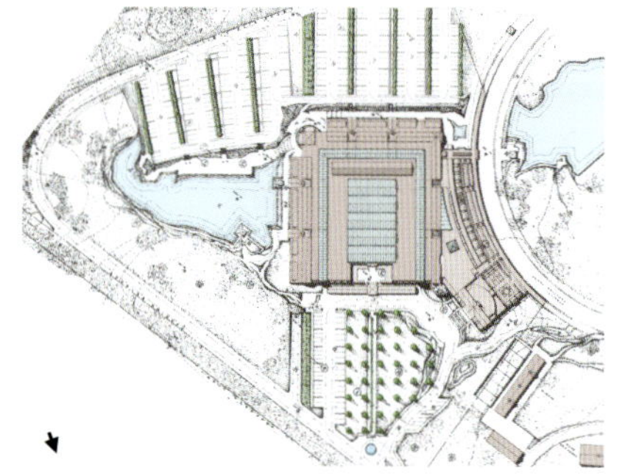

directly above:
Fig. 38. Site Plan.

top:
Fig. 39. Axial view 1998.
Photo: Shakeel Hossain.

Codex World Headquarters, Canton, Massachusetts

In the projects discussed so far, Koetter Kim found urban, architectural, and cultural resources on which to anchor, guide, and develop their work. Those projects are representative of a larger group for which similar urban and architectural resources were found in the immediate visual context. The Codex World Headquarters site offered a different challenge. It necessitated searching for guidance in more ethereal areas of the *psycho-cultural field*.[61]

Not quite a bland suburban corporate office park, it threatened to be that. While Koetter Kim found this troubling, the site is not without pre-existing assets and a history. Located in a rural landscape adjacent to a public nature preserve, the eleven-acre parcel had recently been a horse farm with a track and constructed water pieces. Not perfectly bucolic, it is also adjacent to a highway cloverleaf. Koetter Kim describe a naiveté brought to this encounter they later imagined advantageous:

> *...our first major buildings and our first building situated outside of the urban context... allowed us to approach the situation with a relatively unbiased eye... we automatically began to think of the Codex building as a form of urban development, grounding it in a similar physical and social understanding that we were developing within the city...*[62]

Although this description sounds casual, one nevertheless senses an anxiety about finding in the *psycho-cultural field* a superior rationale for this suburb of the city so building and site could:

61 This Codex building is now a Meditech Headquarters building.

62 Koetter Kim (1997): 57.

left to right:
Fig. 40. Arrival drive in 1988. Photo: Shakeel Hossain.

Fig. 41. Arrival drive in 2022. Photo: Lisa Abitbol.

Fig. 42. Arrival drive, entrance court, atrium entry. Photo by Google Maps.

Fig. 43. Entrance axis in 2022. Photo: Lisa Abitbol.

> *be imagined as a new kind of suburban settlement or suburban/urban community… the joint presence of two antagonistic suburban/rural New England landscapes: the still present grandeur of the classic New England primeval/agrarian countryside and the ever increasing spectacle of suburban sprawl… The larger Eurocentric traditions of dense form communities and the working farm villa were examined along with the related traditions of New England rural agriculture and industrial building patterns… the farm complex, villa, or industrial installation often served as urbanistic "seeds", gathering around themselves elements and activities of a true comprehensive community in compact form.*[63]

The resulting building has aspects of the ideal/circumstantial duality we know from *Collage City*. The ideal portion is centered by a nearly square skylit courtyard located on the entrance axis. Seen from the exterior, the glazing of the industrial skylight above the courtyard appears nearly continuous with the glazing of the upper stories of the front facade. The scale and regularity of this large symmetrical centerpiece is mediated by what Koetter Kim call "little buildings", some arranged along the entranceway, others reaching out to embrace the curve of the horse track. The ideal central atrium is wrapped by tall slab-like loft structures serving as generalized office or lab space, the same resilient type seen at Miller Park and University Park. Codex seems to have been the first project to bring this prevalent 19th century U.S. industrial building type to the sustained attention of Koetter Kim: in quick succession Codex 1983, Miller Park and Chattanooga 1984, University Park 1985, and soon to follow, the Immunex project in Seattle discussed below.[64] The light-industrial building is only one of the resilient types evident at Codex and indicative of a Koetter Kim frame of mind grounded on

63 Koetter Kim (1997): 57.

64 Among reasons for vertical stacking of floors for this industrial type was the mechanical transfer of water or steam power via vertical wood shafts that better resisted torque when vertical than horizontal. Electrical power distribution encouraged horizontal rather than vertical buildings.

At the entrance drive arrival court, building entrance, and in the atrium, 'little buildings' modify scale with variations on a 'resilient type' but the entrance axis aedicula has been removed.

left top to bottom:
Fig. 44. Aerial. Photo by Google Maps.

Fig. 45. Arrival and entrance aediculae in 1988. Photo: Shakeel Hossain.

Fig. 46. Garden aedicula in the central atrium. Photo: Lisa Abitbol.

inset:
Fig. 47. Skylighted entrance atrium and gathering court. Photo: Lisa Abitbol.

opposire top to bottom:
Fig. 48. Site plan, Immunex, Seattle.

Fig. 49. Projection of buildings onto site aerial. Photo: KKA/Aerolist.

Fig. 50. Aerial suggesting the vista over Elliott Bay to Mt Rainier. Photo: KKA/Aerolist.

the emphasis in *Collage City* on the atemporal as opposed to the temporal, thus the search for atemporal types. At Codex, the other resilient type is the atrium with its industrial skylight. In other projects the same type may be a linear space or passage. The root form is the early 1800s greenhouse that developed with sheet glass and wood frames shortly replaced with iron frames. There soon followed the magnificent 1851 Crystal Palace in London. Other related examples abound. They range in refinement from train sheds to the gallerias of Milan and Naples, and in the U.S. the still-extant 19th century urban arcades such as those in Providence 1828, and Cleveland 1890. For Koetter Kim, the type was associated with spaces intended to be shared with others.[65]

Immunex, Seattle

The landscape is primary in the psycho-cultural field of the next several projects. The site for the Immunex project is on Elliot Bay, Seattle's port on Puget Sound, and at the northern end of a previously industrialized waterfront. The site is the potential terminus of a developing linear park at the edge of the Bay linking the site with the city center. The Koetter Kim description of the site emphasized the landscape, the "combined presence of Queen Anne Hill and Magnolia Hill", that "define between them a shallow valley" and vistas to the southeast that include the active waterfront of Elliot Bay, with its constant ferry service, Seattle's downtown skyline, and, when visibility allows, a spectacular view of the snow-capped and seemingly close Mount Rainier. Maximizing these features, the Koetter Kim scheme provides an axial entrance *allée* arriving from the north. It parallels a long, narrow building and terminates on a pavilion serving as the social center of the complex. That focal pavilion marks a shift of the visual axis into the splayed green that opens to the south and a vista of Elliot Bay and toward Mt. Rainier. Barely mentioned is the vista to the west across the Sound to the Olympic Mountains. That vista partially explains the channels of space between the buildings east of the splayed green. Primary emphasis on the landscape is consistent with the culture of the Northwest and Seattle, where great value is placed on participating in and enjoying the views of the extraordinary landscape surrounding the fjord estuary of Puget Sound:

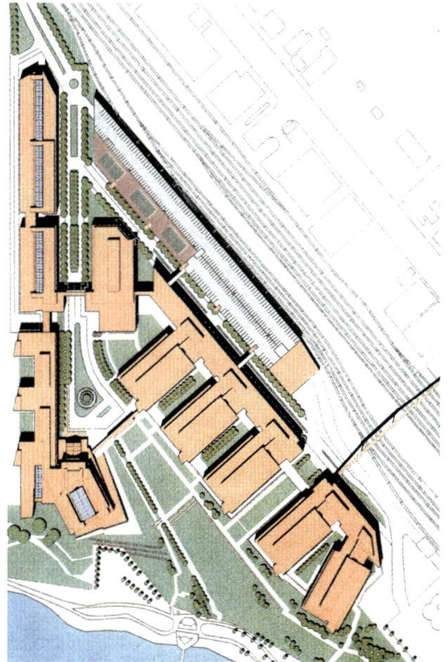

> *The powerful presence of Mount Rainier projected itself into the design process and helped determine the plan, the arrangement of buildings, the location and nature of gathering spaces… The mountain is a fact—to those in its presence it is as certain as gravity or the sun coming up in the east. It is a fact that defies the urges of indeterminacy and non-fixed meanings.*[66]

This is the kind of appreciation of landscape that is owed to Edmund Burke's 1757 *Philosophical Inquiry into Our Ideas of the Sublime and the Beautiful*, and, following on Burke, over a century of work by painters and writers like Thomas Moran and naturalists like John Muir who have contributed to our current regard for majestic landscapes that diminish the grandest efforts of humankind, even entire cities such as Seattle. Discussions of such landscapes are not found in *Collage City*. Others are. Most pointedly, "*The garden* as a criticism of the city and hence as a model city", illustrations of Baroque formal gardens, and the use of similarly grand ordering axes in the city.[67] While the sublime natural world and the rational Baroque version, whether garden or city, are formal opposites, both are sublime in their scale and majesty. But more influential than *Collage City* on Koetter Kim would have been their close personal association and travel with Rowe: his sensitivity to landscapes and related cityscapes commented upon by his travel companions and occasionally seen in his essays and letters.[68]

65 Variations on these several-story-high spaces, skylit with industrial-appearing skylights, can be seen throughout the Koetter Kim work, one of their 'resilient types'.

66 Koetter Kim (1997): 126. I surmise that "indeterminacy and non-fixed meanings" refers to Seattle's high-rise downtown area.

67 Rowe and Koetter (1978): 175.

68 Naegele, Daniel ed., *The Letters of Colin Rowe: Five Decades of Correspondence*, Artifice, London, 2016.

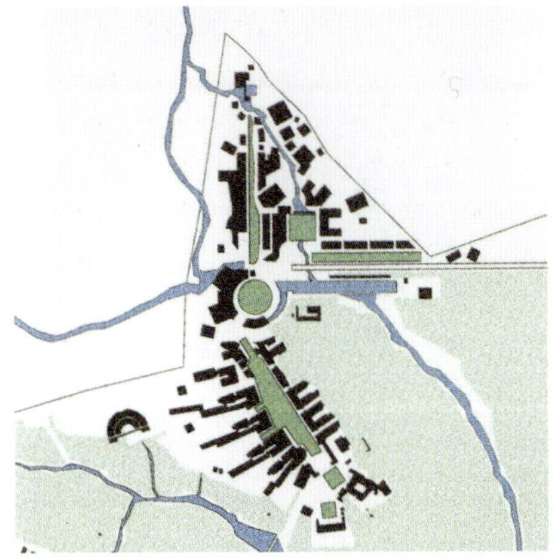

a

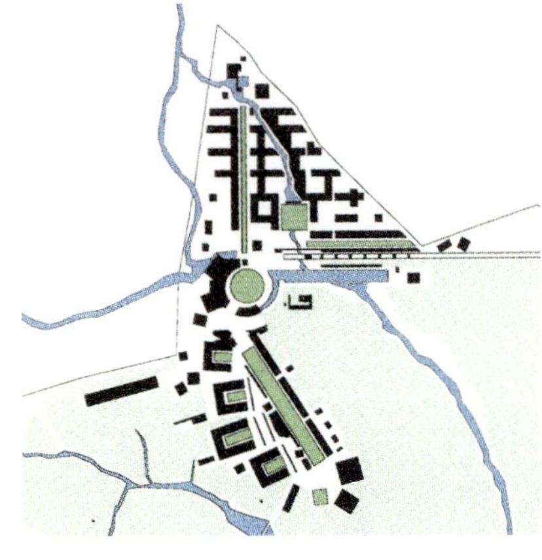

b

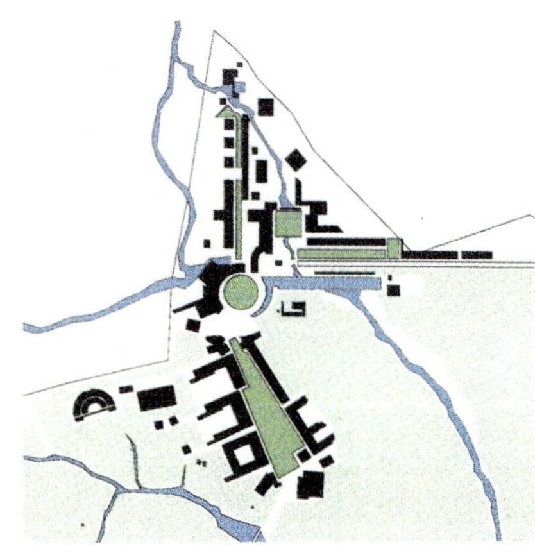

c

above, left to right:
Fig. 51 a, b, c. Alternate schemes share the same conceptual framework.

opposite:
Fig. 52. Framework diagram.

Fig. 53. General use patterns.

Fig. 54. Proposed plan.

Fig. 55. Model. KKA.

opposite below:
Fig. 56. A proposed 'stabilizing' figure: a solar collector atop a cistern and central gathering area. KKA.

Fig. 57. Section, solar collector and cistern.

ParcBIT Competition, Mallorca

The ParcBIT Competition site for a new town in Mallorca lies inland from the sea with long vistas to it. Backed up against two steep hills, the site includes several joined ridges with valleys between them. The Koetter Kim design is ordered primarily by environmental factors: first, water; second, contour; and third, prevailing breezes:

> *although surrounded by water and enjoying significant amounts of rainfall, Mallorca is presently an internally water-poor place. Most of the island's rainfall is not held on the land and simply runs into the sea... the essence of the situation ultimately had to do with water... a very small percentage of runoff... could easily deliver the required base water resources... a large cistern... could be fed from these runoff patterns and controlled by way of shock dams and holding ponds... distributed around the site for irrigation, domestic water use, and for heating/cooling... this newly secured water resource provides the foundation for a new kind of environment... oasis-like... a close and dramatic relationship between human habitation and its natural setting.*[69]

Little of this is immediately obvious. ParcBIT was intended to develop in service to a "new kind of community... combining economic with environmental concerns... a settlement that might embrace the highest levels of emergent electronically based communication technology", therefore requiring a structuring plan for buildings yet unknown.[70] Koetter Kim drew an analogy to the development of most cities. Buildings and building types change over time, but landform and public infrastructure remain relatively constant. Therefore, the watercourses, landforms, and urban spaces were projected as structuring constants across alternate schemes while depiction of buildings differed. In each scheme, blue lines indicate the capture and display of the all-important water elements. Water is channeled from the steep hillsides into the town and along the edges of its ridges. It converges on the central area marked by a cluster of regularly shaped spaces, one square, one circular, another a long thin rectangular pool. Otherwise, three long axial spaces lie along ridges generally parallel to the water features. They are strikingly regular in contrast to the irregularities of the landforms and

69 Koetter Kim (1997): 143–44.

70 Ibid.: 142.

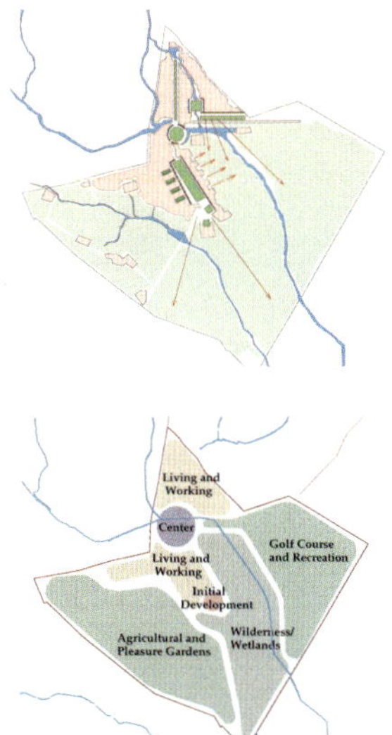

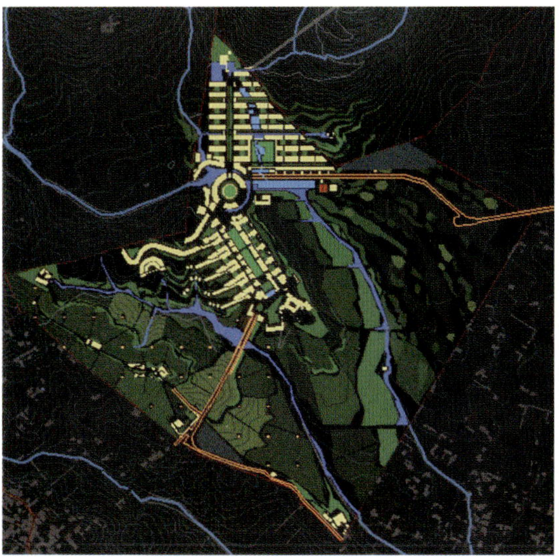

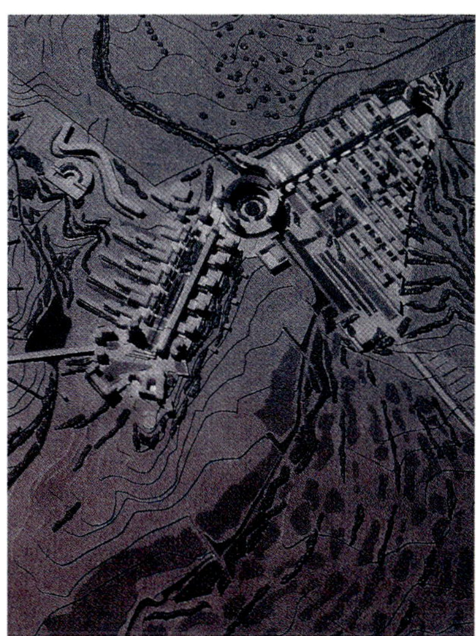

the various building forms gathered around them. Buildings, generally arranged perpendicular to the ridge lines, channel prevalent breezes.

Little in *Collage City* can be seen to have directly influenced the high level of attention to the natural environment that shaped ParcBIT. But just as the Studio interest in context extended to Robert Venturi, it also included the 1962–67 widely published development of Sea Ranch on the coast of California. The master plan and code for the landscape and buildings at Sea Ranch had been similarly shaped by contextual environmental considerations. Of related interest was Edmund Bacon's 1967 *Design of Cities* that included hill towns such as Todi and Siena as geomorphic urban types that cluster on hill tops and splay out along ridgelines and are experienced as having the "close and dramatic relationship between human habitation and its natural setting" that Koetter Kim sought to achieve at ParcBIT.

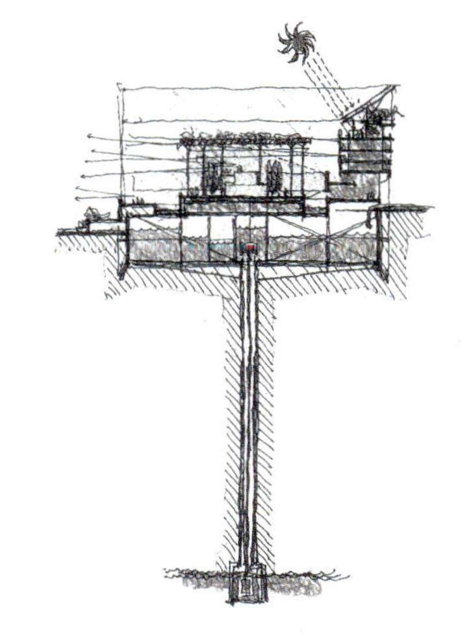

Notice that the composition for ParcBIT is *collisive*, displaying a formal interest shared by Rowe and Koetter. In contrast to a singularly centralized composition typical of a concentration of authority, a collisive urban form tends to result from a diffusion of authority resulting in "an accumulation of disparate ideal fragments" or "an amalgam of discrete enthusiasms". The compositional difference is explained in *Collage City* by comparison of the Versailles of Louis XIV with Hadrian's villa, and further by associating the Modernist utopias of Le Corbusier, CIAM, and Walter Gropius's "total design" with autocractic authority.[71] Given the choice of making an urban form with a single, formal center affirming the authority necessary to make ParcBIT a reality, Koetter Kim chose to provide a more polycentric and collisive order on behalf of its future population.

71 Rowe and Koetter (1978): 90–91.

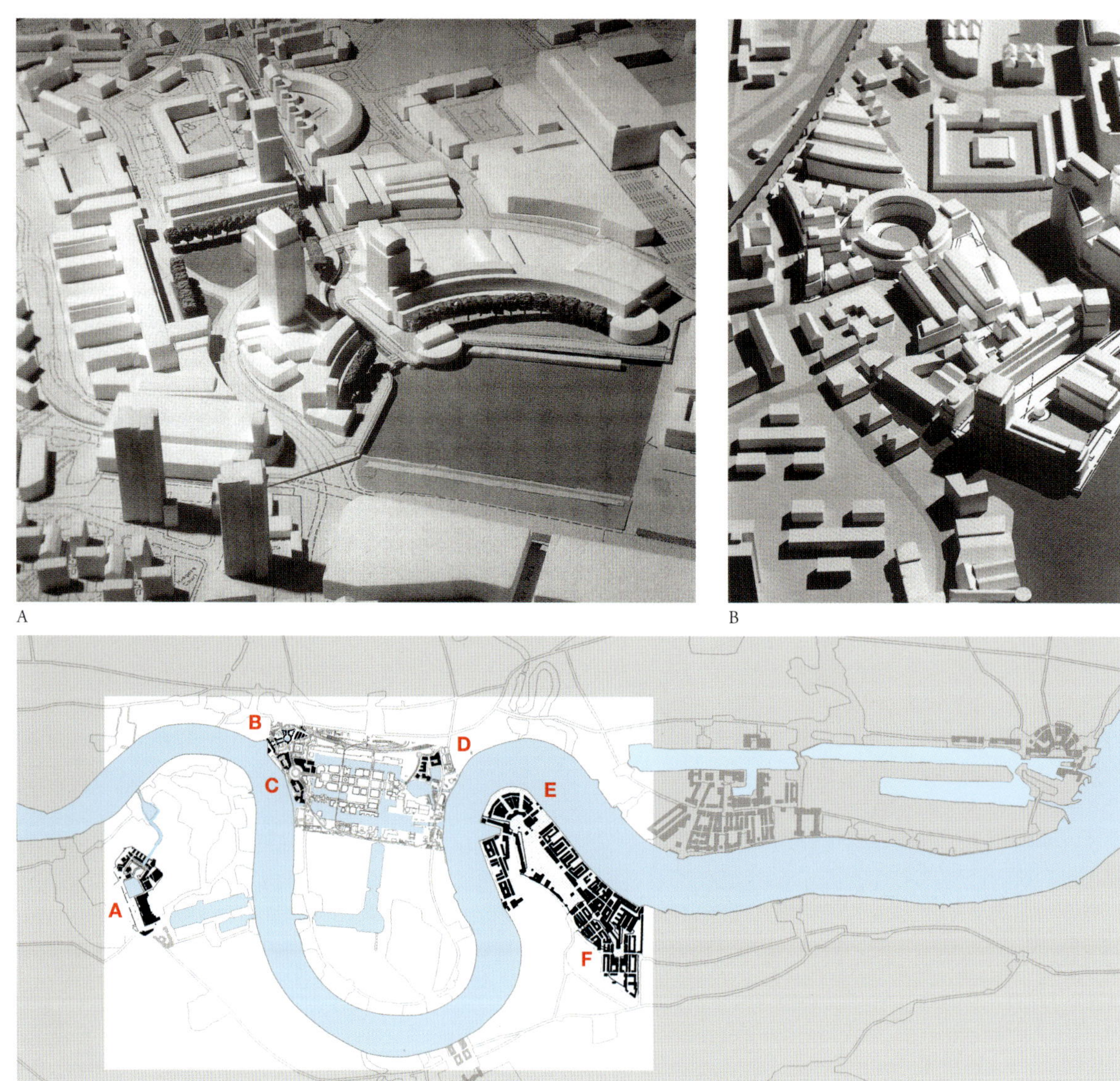

directly above:
Fig. 58. Composite of East London Docklands projects.

top row, left to right:
Fig. 59. A. Surrey Quays. KKA.

Fig. 60. B. Limehouse. KKA.

Fig. 61. C. Western Segment and Westferry Circus. KKA.

Fig. 62. D. Poplar Docks. KKA.

Fig. 63. E. and F. Greenwich at Blackwall Peninsula. KKA.

Docklands, East London

This vast redevelopment project includes five sites along the formerly industrialized area of the Thames River. In addition to the ordering presence of the river and the reshaped land-water forms that served as docks, the broad strategy informing these projects was derived from the historic urban pattern, the *psycho-cultural field* of central London. Rowe and Koetter acknowledge student David Grahame Shane whose "field analysis of central London" thesis is cited in *Collage City*.[72] It represented a design strategy for Koetter Kim:

> *Contrary to normal assumptions of comprehensive planning, such a strategy might imply a city of identifiable spots, or "nodes" if you will, situated within a matrix of less deterministic, erratic, or even chaotic interstices. Thus the city might evolve, across time, as a variable condition of interaction between these two conditions—spots and interstices, relative order and relative chaos.*[73]

C

D

E and F

Multiple schemes were typically developed for each site, some returned to years later with additional studies. From left to right in the plan are Surrey Quays, Limehouse adjacent to Westferry Circus and the flanking Western Segment, Poplar Dock, and lastly the Port Greenwich project that followed earlier studies for Blackwall Peninsula.[74] 'Spots of order' echoes *Collage City* descriptions of "Stabilizers" and further "that we are in the presence of a style of argument which is not lacking in universality... collisive fields and *interstitial debris*";[75] an "ideal of a conglomerate of independent parts";[76] or even, but not quite, the concluding notion of the "city of composite presence".[77]

For the Docklands, the buildings required are much bigger than the exemplars exhibited in *Collage City* that rarely exceed five stories, provide a constant height along street frontages, and are devoid of tall building. Compared to 'trad' city buildings, most Mod city buildings are wider, bulkier, and higher.[78] Koetter Kim are aware of the challenge: "the intrusion of large-scale built objects and insular activities into an ongoing urban setting... extremely jarring to the circumstantial and mosaic-like scale of the existing built surroundings".[79] What do Koetter Kim propose?

There are no clusters of tall buildings. Building heights will be regulated. A standard height is established at approximately six to eight stories with setbacks for several more levels—central Paris comes to mind. The opportunity for additional height is provided in two ways. A few stories may be encouraged or required to mark hierarchically important street corners, paired to imply gateways, or suggest axes. A few tall buildings, always singular, more tower-like than slab-like, are positioned to serve as focal points. Bulk is possibly the greatest concession to the Mod city. Some blocks are quite large and might be occupied by single buildings rather than the more optimal "variety of legible, small, contiguous, incremental building parcels that can combine in various ways", common to 'trad' cities.[80]

72 Rowe, Koetter (1978): 114. An analysis drawing titled, "Grahame Shane: field analysis of central London, 1971". This was the subject of David Grahame Shane's Cornell Urban Design thesis.

73 Koetter Kim, (1997): 71.

74 Ibid.: 70–99. At some level of consciousness, the new Docklands areas would resonate with memories of central London, the *psycho-cultural field* working its magic. Albeit the 'spots of order' while emphatic are sometimes less regular in shape than the 'stabilizing' squares of London.

75 Rowe and Koetter, (1978): 107.

76 Ibid.: 128.

77 Ibid.: 181.

78 Not considered in *Collage City* are the many compositional strategies City Beautiful era architects developed so that skyscrapers, towers, and high-rise buildings might comport with 'trad' city streets and blocks. Perhaps these strategies were best ignored by Rowe and Koetter lest their presence detract from the main line of argument. Reed, Jr., Henry Hope, *The Golden City*, Doubleday & Co. Inc., 1959: With devastating photo comparisons, Reed makes the point that 'trad' "American Renaissance" buildings enrich the experience of the street while Mod buildings impoverish it.

79 Koetter Kim (1997): 72.

80 Ibid.: 25.

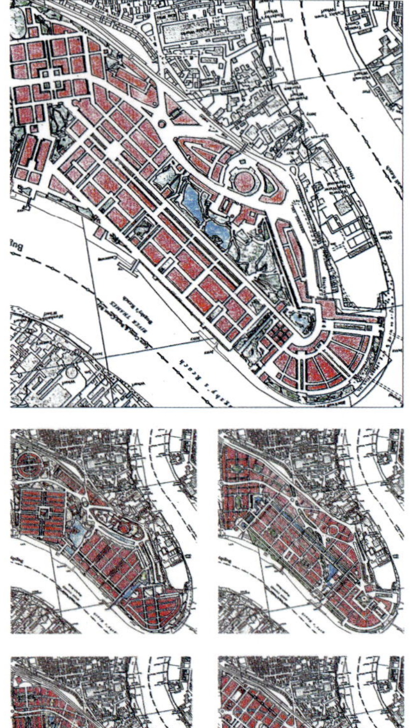

Fig. 64. Blackwall Peninsula, five alternate schemes.

Blackwall, East London

Blackwall is among the several Docklands projects. In describing their typical multi-scheme process, Koetter Kim expand our understanding of a design process that includes collage and is illuminated by reference to the bricoleur. In *Collage City,* Rowe and Koetter cite a Claude Lévi-Strauss description of the bricoleur as one who must:

> *make do with 'whatever is at hand', that is to say with a set of tools and materials which is always finite and is also heterogeneous because what it contains bears no relation to… any particular project, but is the contingent result of all the occasions there have been to renew or enrich the stock, the elements are collected or retained on the principle that 'they may always come in handy'.*[81]

For Rowe and Koetter, "the 'bricoleur' is more of a 'real-life' specification of what the architect-urbanist is and does than any fantasy deriving from 'methodology' and 'semantics'".[82] In their critique of contemporaneous models of architectural and planning theory and practice, the architect-bricoleur is posed against the architect-scientist. The architect-bricoleur is advantaged by analogies available from architectural and urban history, while the architect-scientist is hampered by the limited 'raw materials' of program and construction subjected to scientific principles, methods, and tools.[83] According to this argument, urban-architectural design work benefits far more from analogic knowledge than from the abstract principles of the physical and social sciences. The architect-bricoleur inserts things, 'collected or retained on the principle that they may always come in handy', into the context under consideration, as if making a collage. The resulting schemes, whether considered a composition or collision of forms, are then examined for what they offer as solution possibilities:

> *At Blackwall we created a series of initial options informed by various urban locations and models: Central Park (top), little cities (center left), the parks and canals of German models (Dusseldorf, etc., center right), collision (bottom left), and Manhattan (bottom right).*[84]

This collage process developed in early Rowe Studios. It created an enthusiasm for looking at historic examples, elevated the range of considerations underway, and increased our knowledge.

These conjectures typically produced a collision of forms that revealed things about the existing context and the item collaged into it. Alternative conjectured schemes commented on each other. Instead of one scheme produced laboriously with no assurance of certainty, numerous rapidly created schemes readily suggested further forms of transformation, reconciliation, amelioration, or possible *détente*, possibilities not readily found in other ways.[85] Greater certainty of final scheme selection is achieved through comparison of alternatives. This process encourages the architect as bricoleur to develop what Rowe, in another context, called "essential knowledge",[86] that of exemplary architecture that might 'come in handy' at some time.

Koetter Kim refined this process working with clients in the real estate investment development and construction industry. Square footage is among the most

---

81 Rowe and Koetter (1978): 102–103. They cite Lévi-Strauss, Claude, *The Savage Mind*, George Weidenfeld and Nicolson Ltd., London, 1966, New York, 1969.

82 Ibid.: 104.

83 Ibid.: 102–113.

84 Koetter Kim (1997): 81.

85 This process is common among Rowe Studio graduates in teaching and practice, but rare in architectural education despite test-fit of form 'solutions' imposed on a 'problem' having been described numerous times in design process literature. See for example: Jones, Christopher, *Design Methods: Seeds of a human future*, John Wiley and Sons Ltd., London, New York, Sydney, Toronto, 1970; Koberg, Don, and Bagnall, Jim, *The Universal Traveler, A Soft -Systems Guide to: Creativity, problem-solving, and the process of reaching goals*, William Kaufman, Inc., Los Altos, CA, 1972. Rowe, Peter G., *Design Thinking*, MIT, Cambridge, MA, 1987; Cross, Nigel, *Designerly Ways of Knowing*, Springer, 2006.

Fig. 65. Blackwall Peninsula, model. William T. Smith.

important measures in that industry. Koetter Kim maintained the same building bulk representing square footage as a constant across otherwise highly varied schemes. Rowe at some point remarked that, "Bankers know all about building types". And common enough to bankers and both the 'trad' and 'Mod city' were an expanding but limited group of resilient types. With these as constants, and similar street, block, and open space infrastructures, alternate schemes could vary extravagantly while a select group of types, and hence projected financing, could be seen as constants. While Rowe, the Studio, and *Collage City* held type in higher regard than program,[87] Koetter Kim applied the lesson that, over time, the city infrastructure and its buildings are more fixed, stable, and rigid than their associated uses or 'programs'. They expanded the fundamental idea of type, making urban situation types and resilient building types, to reconcile the seemingly irreconcilable program of large-scale real estate development and construction capabilities of 'our time' with 'trad' city forms.[88] And they brought a rigor to alternate schematic studies that far exceeded those of the Studio or were considered in *Collage City*.[89]

86 Caragonne, Alex, *The Texas Rangers: Notes from an architectural underground*, MIT Press, Cambridge, MA, and London, 1995: 33. The last of four brief points on architectural education includes both "essential knowledge" and "essential attitude". The source that Caragonne references is: "Memorandum, March 1954", Hoesli Archives, ETH, Zurich. In that memorandum prepared by Bernhard Hoesli and Colin Rowe in their earliest years of teaching, they state that architectural education requires both "certain principles" and "essential knowledge". Hoesli perhaps made the argument for "certain principles", primarily those rooted in the hard physical sciences, but secondarily extended to softer social and psychological sciences, including perception psychology, the last a common ground for Rowe and Hoesli. Rowe, skeptical of the soft sciences as opposed to culture, likely argued for "essential knowledge", a knowledge of exemplary architecture.

87 The late-1960s Studio was fond of Alan Colquhoun's essay, "Typology and Design Method", *Arena* 83, Jun 1967, later published in Colquhoun, Alan, *Essays in Architectural Criticism: Modern Architecture and Historical Change*, IAUS and MIT Press, Cambridge, MA, 1981: 43-50. Also see Rowe, Colin, "Program vs. Paradigm", *The Cornell Journal of Architecture* 2, 1983: 8-19. These essays rebut the presumed more scientific, analytic, problem analysis, programming approaches then being advanced. That the functional program did not determine architectural form seemed obvious to anyone who experienced a few semesters of architectural studio education and/or for anyone who had any experience of cities where building uses changed more frequently than the buildings.

88 Koetter Kim (1997): 21. See Koetter's general description of these "recurrent, transcultural, and location-related themes or situations within the city".

89 I saw this process when I visited the Koetter Kim London office in January 1990. Rough models were used as a means of simultaneously representing the same building volume in varied schematic urban design configurations.

left, top to bottom:
Fig. 66. Royal Crescent, Bath, England.
Photo by Google Maps.

Fig. 67. Logan Circle, Washington, D.C.
Photo by Google Maps.

Fig. 68. Radcliffe Camera, Oxford, England.
Photo by Google Maps.

Fig. 69. Monument Circle, Indianapolis, Indiana.
Photo by Google Maps.

inset:
Fig. 70. Colonnade and facade at Westferry Circus, unified facade of Buildings B-1, 2, and 3.
Photo by Keep Clicking.

opposite inset left to right:
Fig. 71. Westferry Circus. Photo by Google Maps.

Fig. 72. Westferry Circus, Building 3.
Photo: Dennis Gilbert.

A 'Resilient Urban Situation' Type

One among the various urban situation types that Koetter Kim adopted ought to be recognized for its versatility in combining cultural meaning, place making, and practical utility. In *Collage City* terms, it belongs to the category of 'stabilizer' and can be a 'void', a 'solid', or both. The 'void' version is known immediately by recalling the Royal Circus in Bath, England, or others such as Logan Circle in Washington, D.C., and Monument Circle in Indianapolis. Among 'solid' versions—the Radcliffe Camera at Oxford. And representing both 'solid' and 'void'—the Colosseum in Rome or the amphitheater in Verona. The shape of this 'resilient' urban form is stable, its character and size highly variable. Optimally, it can be at once an axis-mundi, omphalos, a defined and memorable space and place, a form that resolves colliding urban geometries, and, to some extent, converging vehicular traffic. Essential to its success is that the space-enclosing elements are more continuous than not and that traffic does not displace the celebration and pedestrian occupancy of either its center or its perimeter.

In the work of Koetter Kim, it appears first at University Park where it was initially intended to resolve a shift in urban street geometries. That circle, realized differently, nevertheless makes a memorable space and place. At the London Docks, several variations of the type are proposed. At Limehouse, a circus is both a solid and a void 'stabilizer'. In their final framework plan for Surrey Quays, the cousin of the circus, the crescent is the largest organizing space-defining figure. And one is realized in the Western Segment where the Westferry Circus existed as a problem and opportunity:

> *the site was dominated by a huge circus space, a double-decker roundabout with a large garden in the center of its upper level… we were to devise a design strategy for the inland frontage of this circus space.* [Our]… *framework diagram indicated a high degree of building surface continuity around the circus frontage…*[90]

Koetter Kim developed the massing strategy and design guidelines for the circus and adjacent buildings. Their frontage diagram shown in model form emphasizes enclosure approximately three-quarters of the circle, and paired vertical elements frame the one-quarter opening to the Thames. Three wide roads entering the double-decker roundabout made the aspired-to continuity of the vertical surface difficult to achieve. But so also, it appears, has departure from the facade guidelines. Otherwise, the as-built, one-quarter circle and lengthiest frontage designed by Koetter Kim demonstrates much of what could have been achieved to give even greater coherence and singularity to this 'spot' along the Thames. They provided a continuous unifying facade and covered colonnade along the street frontage for what is three attached buildings. Their portion is named B-3.[91]

In their schemes for ParcBIT, Koetter Kim suggested that the proposed circus, one of the three figural urban spaces, have, as its core, a large cistern. That cistern was then to be mounted by an enclosing perimeter and an elevated roof-structure fitted with solar panels. The resulting solid/void condition promised to have the quality described in the Excursus of *Collage City* as a 'stabilizer' and, like an amphitheater, be at once both a void and a solid. In the Koetter Kim work, this is among the closest linking of the idea of *genius loci* and its environmental reality with a form representing an integration of past, present, and futuristic iconographies. It is at once an axis mundi, omphalos, cistern, possible theater, central space, and symbol and actor in environmental sustainability—the visionary ambition that sponsored the competition.

above top to bottom:
Fig. 73. Roman amphitheater as a 'stabilizer', Verona. Photo: Google Maps.

Fig. 74. ParcBit solar collector and cistern. Photo by KKA.

Fig. 75. Westferry Circus, Docklands, London. Photo: John Miller.

Fig. 76. Princeton University Firestone Library, Nassau St. and Washington Rd. Photo: Jeff Goldberg.

Conclusion

We have seen that *Collage City* served as a theoretical grounding for Koetter Kim. It also provided overlapping operational models for practice: the architect-bricoleur who collects *matériel* that might be useful; a unique perspective on type in relation to context; design strategies for exploring type/context relationships through collision, collage, deformation, transformation and even *détente*, and a collection of illustrative exemplars. It also provided the dialectical presentation of opposing ideologies, among them: *genius loci* / *zeitgeist*, place/time, 'trad'/ Mod, memory/amnesia, iconophile/iconoclast, city/anti-city.[92] Dialectic presentation can provide clarity about possible choices, but such clarity little notes what is to be encountered with choices made: difficulties to be faced, challenges to practice, and possible outcomes. While Mod/'trad' was thoroughly critiqued in *Collage City*, and preferences implied, there was only one clear choice—Rowe and Koetter chose the traditional city.[93] So did Koetter Kim.

Choosing the city meant choosing the 'trad' city over the Mod anti-city. It meant Koetter Kim were taking a position opposed to the dominant forces then prevalent and that remain so. One might imagine the choice was political and moral, favoring forms encouraging democracy and sustainability, having understood the enduring social, economic, political, and environmental resiliency of 'trad' city patterns. If as we saw, Koetter had initial doubts about the consequences of choosing the city, and thereby choosing Contextualism, Koetter Kim exhibited no such doubts. Quite the opposite. Once that choice was made, Koetter Kim were unflinching in their resolve to follow the logic, to find the characteristics of the 'trad' city and of an architecture that would sustain it, seeking those characteristics in the psycho-cultural field: physical and cultural, local and cosmic.

Quite consistently, they sought to apply the most enduring urban morphologies of streets and blocks and urban spaces consistent with *Collage City*.[94] But the world of practice Koetter Kim were entering was not one structured by the customs of the previous centuries, related municipal codes, or the kinds of authority that resulted in most of the 'trad' city exemplars offered in *Collage City*. Thus, the high degree of difficulty overcome in their successes.

They made urban design the mainstay of their practice. Urban design considerations informed the architecture they proposed either through guidelines that were exceptionally specific and/or through their own architectural design work that illustrated those guidelines. Doing so, they addressed the big architectural questions of iconography, meaning, and the *zeitgeist* vs. *genius loci* dilemma, about which most guidelines are often deliberately mute or ambiguous to a fault.[95] And about which *Collage City*, in its entirely reasonable acceptance of both the iconophile and iconoclast, concludes by suggesting the accommodation of the iconographies of both the past and the future in the "city of composite presence": *Collage City* does not choose one over the other. But Koetter Kim did choose. Their evolving maniera, or architectural voice, avoids iconoclastic imagery, avoids pretensions about foreseeing, representing, or heralding the future, avoids Postmodernist collagist forms and witticism, and avoids stylistic specificity on both sides of the iconophile/iconoclast ledger. Their architecture is both enriched and constrained by allegiance to the architectonic language derived

90 Koetter Kim (1997): 91.

91 Ibid.: 72-76, 90-93. What appears to be one building is three with shared party walls. Koetter Kim was the architect for the corner building, B-3, at the intersection of West India Avenue with Westferry Circus, SOM for the other two.

92 Rowe, Koetter (1978): 83. In *Collage City* the mode of discussion is qualified speculation, 'if, then'. Argument favors both-and, not either-or; "debate in which victory consists in each component emerging undefeated", and might produce "a condition of alerted equilibrium", and of, "Cross breeding, assimilation, distortion, challenge, response, imposition, superposition, conciliation… "

93 Ibid.: 83–85. The choice of the city is made with reference to plans of the Athenian Acropolis and the Roman Imperial Fora which is unequivocally preferred.

94 See Koetter Kim (1997): 148–155, Ho Chi Minh City and Saigon South, New City Center.

95 For example, as a resilient type, the 'trad' base, middle, and top with a constant cornice height may comfort the iconophile and make the iconoclast irritable, but it is far too abstract a regulation to calm the extreme urges of either.

Fig. 77. Fred Koetter and Susie Kim. KKA.

from trabeated construction developed over millennia into the present, shaped by city form 'situation' opportunities, and explored within the typological limits of their work opportunities.[96]

Koetter Kim exhibit the attitude described by T.S. Eliot: "The progress of an artist is a continual self-sacrifice, a continual extinction of personality".[97] In stark contrast, what dominates the architectural press is a cult of personality linked to avant-garde formalism and to personal identity conflated with architectural identity, the opposite of Eliot's "progress of the artist".[98] Koetter Kim produced a body of work that tested the idea that the *psycho-cultural field* could provide the essential knowledge for a practice in our time that would not, as they feared it otherwise might, "obliterate the past".[99] The *Koetter Kim* monograph demonstrates how to practice architecture as a form of urban design that adds to our body of knowledge with a wide range of work that is a paragon of Contextualism.

96 Regarding architectural language, see Porphyrios, Demetri, *Classicism is not a Style*, St. Martin's Press, 1982. Regarding typological limits, there are few civic or religious programmatic opportunities.

97 Eliot, T.S., "Tradition and the Individual Talent", *The Sacred Wood*, Barnes and Noble, New York (1920) 1955: 53.

98 Rowe, Koetter (1978): 137. Rowe and Koetter make the point of an imbalance between "two distinct but interrelated formulations of Modernity. There is the formulation, dominant for the architect… described by the names: Emile Zola, H.G. Wells, Marinetti, Walter Gropius, Hannes Meyer; and there is the alternative… identified by the further names: Picasso, Stravinsky, Eliot, Joyce, possibly Proust ... poverty on the one side and richness on the other".

99 Koetter Kim, (1997): 21.

Evidence of an Argument

Blake Middleton

To appreciate Colin Rowe's impact on the last half century of urban design in the United States, and indeed internationally, one need look no further than to those who attended the graduate Urban Design Studio at Cornell University from 1963 to 1990. Many of these students have made notable contributions to the pedagogy of architecture and urban design as teachers; at least five became deans of major architecture schools. But it is in these students' subsequent careers and accomplishments as practicing architects, urban designers, or planners that one will find a remarkable record of achievement and positive impact in the built environment.[1]

Within their professional work can be found compelling "evidence of an argument": the testing and retesting of a profound conceptual problem that Rowe presented to successive Studio students. To paraphrase a former student, Rowe formulated the question as how to resolve two opposite propositions and manifestations: the antithetical and unresolved conflict between the traditional and Modern city.[2] The sensibility and conceptual approach instilled during their Cornell experience had, for many of these students, a profound, substantive and persistent influence as practicing architects. This began in the late 1960s with a group from the Urban Design Studio who, working in the public sector, helped give shape to planning policies in several U.S. cities. This group may be considered, somewhat loosely, as members of the "Early Period" of the Studio (1963–1977). Their advocacy for examining design problems through a formal framework—loosely defined as Contextualism—was slowly absorbed into design regulatory policies in many municipalities in the United States. As the Studio continued into its second decade, a growing number of Rowe's students joined the profession in practices large and small, many forming their own offices. The built work of architects of this "Late Period", those who graduated from late 1970s through the 1980s, has resulted in a distinguished body of realized urban design projects.[3] Through a selective overview of their work including urban master plans and other built projects, I hope to establish how students from both Studio periods continued to address the argument for reconciling the contradictory forces between the traditional city of streets, city blocks and public squares, and the Modern city of freestanding building types set in open space.

frontispiece:

clockwise:

Olympic Sculpture Park, Seattle, Weiss/Manfredi Architects, 2007. Photo: Ewan Baan.

Tokyo Midtown, SOM Architects, 2007. Photo: courtesy SOM / © Shinkenchiku-sha.

Coffee Plaza, Richard Meier and Partners, 2010. Photo: © Klaus Frahm/Artur images.

Millennium Tower Boston, Boston, MA, Handel Architects, 2017. Photo: Bruce Martin.

1 See Appendix: "Urban Design Studio Graduates and Thesis Topics – Cornell University 1963-1995" prepared by Blake Middleton.

2 Terrance Williams, UD graduate, made this insightful comment. He worked as Deputy Director for the Office for Lower Manhattan Development in New York City under the Lindsay administration.

3 The taxonomy and categorization of the work of the Urban Design Studio has a variety of definitions. Steven Hurtt in "Conjectures on Urban Form" identifies them as "The Early Years – Academic Modernism"; "Contextualism"; "Collision City"; "Collage City"; culminating in a "Retrospective-Prospective" of the period 1980-1983 when the article was written. Hurtt, Steven, "Conjectures on Urban Form: The Cornell Urban Design Studio 1963-1982", *The Cornell Journal of Architecture* 2, Fall 1983: 54-78. Grahame Shane has divided Studio periods into a tripartite "Three End Pieces" the periods of which are 1963-69, 1970-73 and 1973-80 which coincide with Rowe's evolving interests and writings in the study of urbanism. For simplification, and to avoid the schema of 'beginning, middle, and end', this author has divided the Studio development into "Early" and "Late" periods roughly at the mid-point of the attendance of the total graduates of the program (161 students).

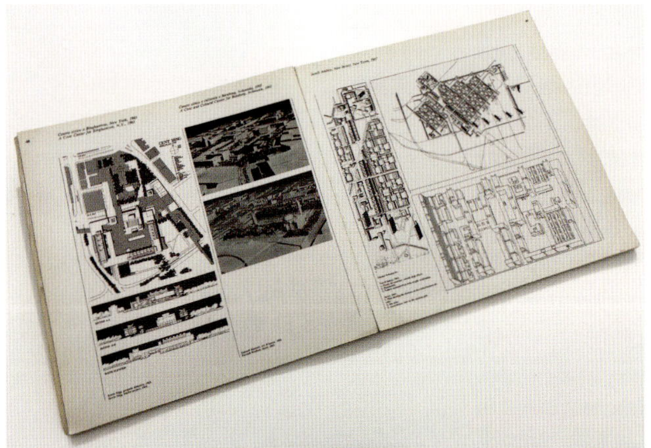

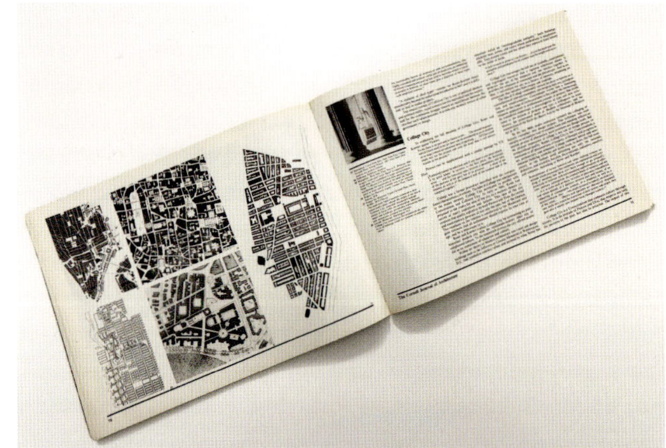

left to right:
Fig. 1. "The Combining of the Traditional City and the Modern City" by the author introduced 20 pages of graduate student projects and theses from the Cornell Urban Design Studio. The *Lotus* compendium did not include projects of Cornell's five-year undergraduate studios, nor reference the rigorous synthesis between history, theory, and design within the curriculum held in common to them both.

Fig. 2. "Conjectures on Urban Form" by Steven Hurtt presented an analysis and critique of the methods and conceptual approach of the Studio. Published in *The Cornell Journal of Architecture* 2, it correlated various projects with the evolution and theory of contextualism, collision city, and collage city.

To begin this evidentiary discovery process, we need to briefly examine the work of these professionals while they attended the Studio. The demonstration of the 'argument' can readily be seen in the publication of *Lotus,* 27 in 1980 and *The Cornell Journal of Architecture,* 2 in 1983 (Fig. 1, 2). Did this extensive display of the Urban Design Studio work with accompanying explanatory narrative open the minds of the design and planning profession in any meaningful way? The answer is somewhat elusive: there appears to have been little published criticism of the design work at that time. Those critics who had comments on the work would inevitably focus on the theory articulated in Rowe and Koetter's *Collage City* rather than the series of design studies produced in the Studio.

Few seem to have apprehended what the projects published in *Lotus* or the *Journal* represented; the Studio work was not the product of a specific theory, but rather, seen in its entirety, an iterative process. Rowe and his colleagues inductively tested these tactical approaches, which incrementally assimilated themselves in several of the hypotheses articulated in articles from Studio alumni or in *Collage City*. Others have commented on how the ideas oscillated between theory and its application in the Studio projects. While the work tended to narrow the focus on massing, spatial definition and connections, and typological manipulation (building program was often generalized) they were consistently—sometimes boldly—addressing the *tabula rasa* already created by the seriously misguided approach to urban highway interventions, slum clearance and mass public housing developments between 1950 and 1975.

If one peruses Rowe's graduate students' theses, they will find a remarkable collection of projects that tackled real problems of the day. Woven through this collection of over 147 bound books are found arguments for applying bulk zoning regulations, addressing the acute need for affordable housing, rebuilding vast areas devastated by urban blight, and, as the work progressed in the early 1980s, advocacy for urban plans of modest scale and localized ambitions. Central to the tactics Rowe encouraged was the argument of employing 'urban *bricolage*'. As it evolved in the Studio it was an initial approach for employing a formal framework to resolve complex urban planning problems. It was, and is still, a valid starting point for analytical urban design. It is not, however, an end in itself. The Studio design problems and thesis projects were in effect, especially in the Early Period, a running critique of the on-going, misdirected American urban renewal planning approach derived from pre-WWII European urban design theory of the Modern city.

To apprehend how the Urban Design Studio experience influenced these students' subsequent careers, we turn our attention from the Studio 'product' toward the context in which this training and research was conducted over twenty-five years of near-continuous interaction with Rowe. What was the structure of the curriculum that shaped their thinking and studio design experience? What was the demographic composition of this cadre of students? Where did they come from? And, with their graduate thesis work completed, what was the impact these individuals had on the practice of urban design and architecture?

The Cornell Curriculum

The 'origin story' of how the Urban Design Studio came into being credits Cornell Professor of City Planning John Reps as giving inspiration to Rowe for the nature of the program. Reps, active as Professor Emeritus until his death in 2021, had the following recollection:

> *Colin was at Cornell for one or two years before he went to Cambridge, England. During that time, I must have had lunch with him two or three times a week at the Faculty Club at the Statler. Colin's conversations on these occasions were not so much an exchange of ideas and opinions as an opportunity to sit and listen to the constant flow of ideas from him. I spent part of a sabbatical leave in London, and one day my wife and I drove to Cambridge to visit Colin. Perhaps that was the reason he sought me out after his return to Ithaca and after learning of his assignment as head of the graduate program in architecture [in 1962]. Apparently, he had been appointed to that position but had not been given any directions concerning the content of the curriculum.*
>
> *During the previous several years, beginning a year or two after my appointment in 1952, I had enjoyed some modest success in working with other colleges (and Architecture itself) to build joint degree programs. I explained all this to Colin, suggesting he should think about doing something similar. When he asked for suggestions, I pointed out Cornell had a world-famous Hotel School, and that he could develop (with their help) a design program concentrating on hotels and resort complexes. He shook his head. I then told him of the program in the business school that dealt with hospitals and public health. Would it not be possible for him to work with their faculty on design issues of large hospitals and other health facilities? He quickly waved that off. (It was only much later that I learned of his serious injury in military training and what must have been his many months in the hospital). Then I suggested that our planning program had achieved some success and recognition and that an urban design program would fill a large and important gap in what the College then had to offer. This struck a nerve immediately and Colin said (as I recall) "that's it"! The rest is history.*[4]

4 Reps's email to author, July 17, 2019. Grahame Shane has observed that Sir Patrick Abercrombie, a professor at Liverpool University where Rowe studied architecture, appears to have coined the term "urban design" in 1943.

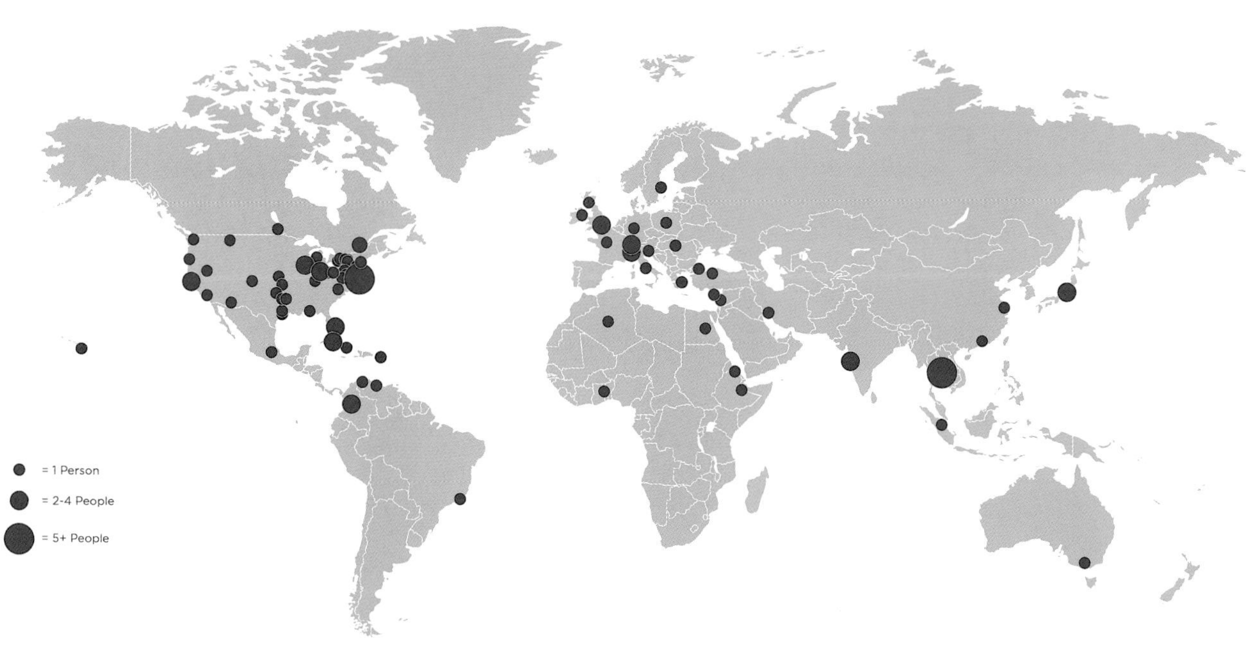

Fig. 3. Home Countries of Rowe's Students. Student cultural diversity in the Urban Design Studio was the norm, not the exception. For example, in addition to the author's classmates from different parts of the U.S., they hailed from Lebanon, Canada, Mexico, England, Ireland, Venezuela, Colombia, Japan, and Cuba. This cultural *mélange* was a formative part of the Studio education. Rowe would typically stimulate discussion and promote a deeper cultural appreciation about a given student's chosen site, city, and country. He would inevitably proceed to recite whole chapters about the history of the place and biographies of its famous personages—facts of which even the thesis student native to a given country had not been aware.

The structure that eventually evolved for the Urban Design Studio at Cornell may be summarized as follows: the curriculum would be a post-professional degree in architecture; to qualify for entry, typically students had to possess a professional degree in architecture, usually a Bachelor of Architecture.[5] Each student had to declare a 'major' and 'minor' field of study. 'Urban Design' was the major, a discipline wholly distinct from 'City Planning', which was a separate department in the College of Architecture, Art, and Planning. The first year typically would have studio design problems defined by Rowe. Course distribution requirements included history of architecture and architectural theory, which was taught by Rowe and various architectural history and design studio professors. For their minor, students often chose City Planning, which for a number of years would find them in Reps' seminal survey, that treated the history of city planning in the U.S. But students could also choose Art or History, or even Art History.[6] The second year of studio would involve thesis research and then a design proposal typically focused on a specific city. The thesis defense critiqued by Rowe and other advisors was typically an elaborate affair lasting several hours accompanied with large-scale, high-contrast plans and site models painstakingly crafted by the student that required several months of preparation.

5 In 1962, Cornell already had a professional five-year degree Bachelor of Architecture curriculum. Evidently the College of Architecture did not see any value adding a professional graduate program. The post-professional M. Arch. in Urban Design was likely intended to be a feeder program for Cornell undergraduates to continue on to graduate studies, which many did. Since the mid-2000s, Cornell has offered an M. Arch., a 3½ year professional degree, and transformed the post-professional graduate degree to a Master of Science in "Advanced Architectural Science", either three or four semesters duration, in "a critical framework for investigating pertinent design concerns, practices, and technologies in 21st century architecture and urbanism". The Urban Design program ceased around the time of this restructuring.

6 Middleton, D. Blake, "Introduction", Hurtt, Steven W. and Wells, Jerry A., "Preface", *The Cornell Journal of Architecture* 2, Fall 1983. In the 1960s it was three semesters for students with a B. Arch degree; this changed to four semesters in the 70s. Studio graduate students frequently attended courses on European intellectual history by Dominic La Capra or art history by Esther Dotson.

The Students

The program grew slowly but after a few years Rowe had about seven-to-ten new students each year.[7] This dropped to about five-to-six in the mid-1970s, perhaps owing to Rowe's sabbatical in Rome in 1976 and other diversions from the Ithaca campus. But as Rowe's position on urban design was more widely circulated with the publication of *Collage City* in 1978, the enrollment doubled to ten-to-twelve per year in the mid-1980s. Beginning in 1962, six first-year students were admitted to the program, all born outside the U.S. Three came from Bangkok and one each from Poland, India, and Egypt. The following year Hachiro Ishizu, from Hawaii, received the first M. Arch. in Urban Design. The program expanded further with nine students admitted in 1963, still mostly from outside the U.S. and again many from Asia. But this group also included Phillip Handler from Connecticut and a Swiss student, Erwin Nigg. Bernhard Hoesli, having returned to Zurich after his "Texas Rangers" days in Austin, may have connected Nigg to Rowe. Also linking this class to Rowe's own Texas days was Irving Phillips, a University of Texas graduate and his classmate, Jerry Wells, who arrived in 1965 to teach in Cornell's undergraduate program.

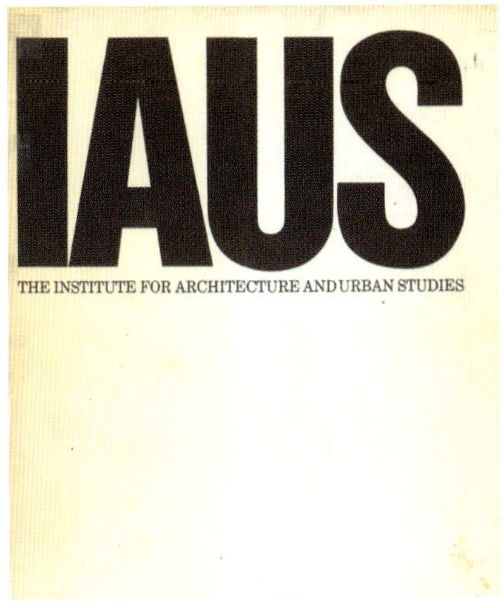

Fig. 4. Cover of Institute for Architecture and Urban Studies, *IAUS Curriculum Brochure*, ca. 1979. Suzanne Frank observes in her *IAUS: An Insider's Memoir*, that the intense collaboration between Peter Eisenman, Colin Rowe, and Arthur Drexler on "The New City" exhibition in 1966–67 at the Museum of Modern Art spawned the creation of the IAUS in New York City.

The diverse backgrounds of the Studio's members remained a distinctive feature throughout the next two decades. There would always be a mix of students from Asia, Africa, the Middle East and, in later years, Latin America. Naturally a European contingent was often represented but given Rowe's roots in England and strong ties to the ETH in Zurich, there were fewer from these locales than one might expect. Over the 28 years of Rowe's tenure at Cornell (1962–1990)[8] it is likely that 170–180 students attended his Studio; of these, approximately 161 students completed their graduate theses under his guidance.[9] Despite Cornell's location in upstate New York it is interesting to observe that just 26 students came from New Jersey and New York and only seven percent of all the students were from the New York metropolitan area. The Ivy League draw was strong but not overwhelming: those from the Northeast numbered 40. The East Coast bias is evident in that just over 13 percent of the students (22) came from west of the Mississippi. And four out of ten were from countries other than the U.S. (Fig. 3).

In a profession that continues to this day to be dominated by men, it is important to note that 17 women graduated from the program while Rowe was involved. The ratio in a typical class was probably smaller than other graduate programs at the time, but this may be attributed in part to the fact that it was a post-professional degree and therefore attracted fewer applicants. Many of the women who graduated from the Studio moved on to distinguished careers in the profession or academia. The first was Inthira Ittakasem from Thailand (1964) followed the next year by two others from her homeland, Kingkae P. Uathavikul and Supatra Assaret (1965). Others who attended the Studio include Isabelle Herpin from France (1970) and Miriam Gusevich (1979), Gladys Diaz (1982), and Maria Abrua-Garcia (1982), the latter all Cuban-Americans. The Studio was heterogeneous in the diversity of the student geographic background (though not especially so regarding racial diversity), particularly in the early 1960s and late 1980s. Almost every year there were one or more non-U.S. students. Close to half of all students posed a 'hometown' thesis project for themselves, which meant that each year at least several thesis projects focused on a city outside the

7 To reconstruct a comprehensive list of Studio attendees and when they graduated, The Fine Arts Library (FAL) was an invaluable repository of nearly all graduate thesis books for the College of Architecture. It was the only source available to the author to ascertain the graduates of—but not necessarily all those who attended—the Studio. At least ten graduates' thesis books are not on file in the FAL. The author wishes to thank librarian Martha Walker for her unfailing assistance in unearthing all the known Studio thesis books, and Aya Mears and Andrew Wang for preparing the preliminary database used here. Any omission or error in the final list is solely the responsibility of the author.

8 Rowe became Professor Emeritus at Cornell in 1990. While officially retired, he continued to lecture intermittently in Ithaca, taught in Rome in 1992, and served as a thesis advisor for a handful of students enrolled in the program.

9 A number of students attended initial Studios and perhaps other courses for the degree program, later transferring to another department or to another academic institution. Of the 161 students, several completed their course work and thesis, but did not receive a diploma.

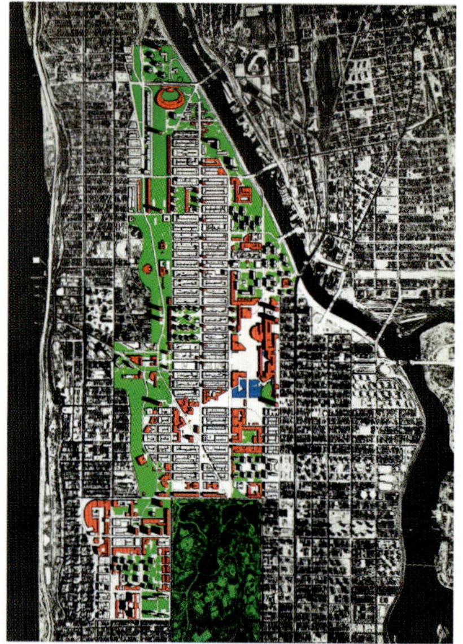
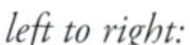

left to right:
Fig. 5. "The New City" site plan for the 1967 MoMA exhibition. The Cornell team, led by Rowe and Tom Schumacher with Jerry Wells and Fred Koetter, created a proposal for Harlem. Central to their design investigation was the question, "how to modify the existing grid plan to improve circulation, encourage the development of parks and new neighborhoods, and clarify the order implied by the terrain itself".

Fig. 6. Preparing the Harlem Redevelopment model for the 1967 MoMA exhibition. Colin Rowe (center), with (from left to right) Stephen Potters, Michael Schwarting, and Fred Koetter.

U.S. Inevitably this fostered stimulating and sometimes robust cross-cultural exchange between the students themselves, and, of course, with Rowe, who clearly relished and appreciated the diversity.

By the late 1960s, the complexion of the Studio had changed when more students matriculated from U.S. architecture programs. A watershed moment occurred when Rowe, with a handful of his Cornell students, became involved for several years with the Institute for Architecture and Urban Studies (IAUS) in New York City, which Peter Eisenman began in late 1967 (Fig. 4).[10] During this period President Lyndon Johnson's Great Society, the War on Poverty, and various urban renewal programs were ascendant. At the same time the efficacy of some federal policies dating from the New Deal in the 1930s were being deeply questioned on many fronts, in particular the wholesale eradication of existing 'traditional city' neighborhoods, replaced with new mass housing, usually of the high-rise, 'tower in the park' variety. As the ensuing decades would confirm, the net result was merely replacing old slum tenements with new 'towers in the parking lot' slums. Rowe and like-minded urbanists, critical of the 'scientific approach' of highway engineers, policy planners, and demographers defining zoning and urban planning, posited that perhaps the skills of architects trained in the art of city-making should be harnessed to promote positive change in renewing the desiccated neighborhoods of many cities.[11]

Impact on the Profession

In 1967, through an affiliation with the nascent IAUS, Rowe and his students raised the profile of the Cornell Urban Design program. One vehicle for this was an invitation by the Museum of Modern Art to participate in an "urban design demonstration" with other schools of architecture. This resulted in a design proposal for Upper Manhattan for the exhibition "The New City: Architecture and Urban Renewal" (Fig. 5, 6). While unabashedly an academic theoretical exercise for public consumption, the leaders of these design teams were at the same time being engaged directly as urban design consultants.[12]

10 Frank, Suzanne, *IAUS: An Insider's Memoir*, AuthorHouse, Bloomington, IN, 2011: 20-21.

11 Among Studio alumni/ae whose work has been influential in cities includes, foremost, Fred Koetter (1967), dean of Yale's School of Architecture for five years, who profoundly influenced the ideas developed in the Studio as an instructor alongside Rowe. With his partner, Susie Kim, he led Koetter Kim in Boston from 1978 until his death in 2017. It includes significant built urban projects in London, Ho Chi Minh City, and Chattanooga, TN. Others to recognize include Richard Cardwell (1966) of Cardwell Thomas Architects since 1980 specializing in urban institutional projects; Kaya Arikoglu (1976) who founded Arikoglu Arkitekt Ltd. in Adana, Turkey, has produced a number of large-scale mixed-use projects; Grant Mariani (1983), a partner at Robert A.M. Stern Architects, has designed large scale urban projects, especially in Asia; Derek Tynan (1983) has led DTA Architects in Dublin, specializing in institutional buildings that have received multiple awards; Paul Mortensen (1987) who since 2014 is Chief of Urban Design in the Montgomery County, Maryland Planning Department; Cheryl O'Neil (1987), partner at Torti Gallas; and Matthew Bell (1988) partner at Perkins Eastman in Washington, D.C.

Fig. 7. Lower East Side Master Plan, 1967. As part of the studies undertaken by the Cornell Studio in New York, Rowe and his students developed a series of designs addressing the "irresolute and ragged" periphery along the East River resulting from highway construction and New Deal Urban Renewal housing projects.

Shortly after establishing themselves in New York, another batch of Cornell students, along with some from the IAUS, were commissioned by the New York City Department of City Planning to work on several areas in Manhattan and the Bronx that were perceived as ripe for some 'new thinking' about urban renewal (Fig. 7). Michael Schwarting, a graduate student during this period, recounts that:

> *Steve Potters and I did our second year at the first year of the IAUS with Eisenman, with Colin visiting I think every other week. We were joined by John Stouman (from my undergrad class at Cornell) and Bill Ellis who came from Texas. We did the Kingsbridge Heights—Bronx Project for Lindsay's Urban Design Group. This task force of professionals, commissioned by the city through the IAUS, included Jonathan Barnett, Alexander Cooper, Jacquelin Robertson, et al.*[13]

Two other students from this group went on to influence planning policy in New York City. One graduate was Terrance Williams, who worked for five years as deputy director for Mayor Lindsay's Office for Lower Manhattan Development (OLMD) in New York City. The other was Stephen Quick, who worked for Robertson at the OLMD on the Fifth Avenue Special District. This team helped encourage development in Midtown Manhattan by reformulating significant changes to the ill effects of the 1961 Zoning Resolution that had promoted indiscriminate "towers in the plaza", which in turn eviscerated the traditional street continuity along 6th Avenue. Quick and his fellow designers also made the first proposal for resolving the dangerous traffic problem in Times Square by proposing the closure of several blocks of Broadway to form what eventually became the pedestrian-dominated Times Square we know today.[14]

Through some sort of professorial dispensation by Rowe, students in the New York program were relieved of the requirement to submit a thesis book, having met their course obligations through their work on these design studies and reports produced in New York.[15] Among the ten students who worked on the Urban Design Group contract for the NYC Planning Department, three were

12 In addition to the Cornell group led by Rowe, the Columbia team included Jaquelin T. Robertson, Richard Weinstein, and Jonathan Barnett, all of whom played a major role in Mayor John Lindsay's Urban Design Group. Princeton was represented by Peter Eisenman and Michael Graves. The MIT team was led by Stanford Anderson who also would be involved in various planning studies for New York City in the coming decade.

13 Jon Michael Schwarting and Stephen Quick emails to the author, September 2018. Schwarting completed his graduate degree in 1970 and, like Thomas Schumacher (1966), received a fellowship to study at the American Academy in Rome.

14 Both Williams and Quick went on to work on a variety of large-scale, private development projects in the U.S. and abroad, with offices in New York and Pittsburgh respectively.

15 In correspondence with them in September 2018, Schwarting, Quick, and Hammann confirmed they were conferred M. Arch degrees in Urban Design without a formal thesis book submission.

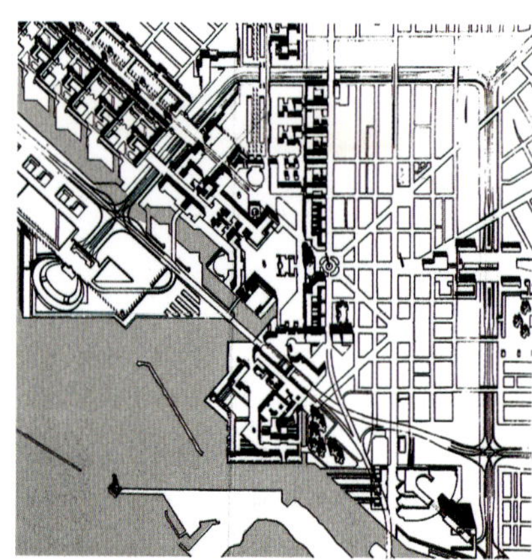

left to right:
Fig. 8. MUND Plan, site axonometric, 1971. Partly financed by the U.S. Government Office of Economic Opportunity, former Rowe students Donald Duncan and Art Valk of the Baltimore Planning Office, in collaboration with Cornell's Roger Sherwood and his undergraduate architecture students, produced much of the design work in the MUND publication. Sherwood's assistant was Norman Crowe, an Urban Design Studio graduate. Rowe had only an advisory role on this project. In an unusual arrangement, Sherwood had previously studied with Rowe while in the Graduate City Planning Program at Cornell.

Fig. 9. The Buffalo Waterfront Plan, 1966 was later exhibited in 1969 at the Albright Knox Art Gallery in Buffalo. Rowe's teaching method of encouraging small groups of students first focusing on local tactical design issues, followed by a group effort creating a composite overall concept was first applied in the Buffalo Waterfront project. This method was similarly applied to studies for Harlem, Bronx, and Manhattan's Lower East Side. Buffalo was perhaps the exemplar of the Studio 'Early Period'.

classmates who then proceeded to produce a master plan study for Baltimore. Having spent the previous year in New York with Rowe and inspired by their work on the various planning agency studies, Donald Duncan, Frederick Hammann, and Arthur Valk developed a joint thesis for downtown Baltimore and invited the Director of City Planning to Ithaca for their final thesis review. They were hired on the spot to work for the Baltimore Department of Planning. Over the course of five years, Valk, Hammann and Duncan were responsible for several major planning initiatives for the city. Hammann recalls: "We became part of a task force and helped develop the Baltimore inner city block redevelopment strategy, including the Upton Neighborhood Action Plan. This was the beginning of the War on Poverty, gearing up for Section 8 days by the mid-'70s and all that".[16] Through the agency of Valk and Duncan, Cornell students and faculty had further work directed to them by the Baltimore Department of Planning that facilitated community-engaged design proposals for the Model Urban Neighborhood Demonstration Corporation (MUND) (Fig. 8).[17] Duncan eventually became Director of Urban Design, retiring in the late 1990s after having made a career at the agency producing a number of planning initiatives, several of which were implemented.

It is important to note that these two sets of students of the Early Period of the Urban Design Studio—inspired by the experience of working in New York City with professional city planners, participating in the founding days of the IAUS, seeing the potential of urban design to positively shape city planning policy and even legislation to implement it—continued for five years or more working in the public sector. The mid-1960s was a time of optimism, of a belief that large-scale urban design initiatives could still make a difference, a time when political support for such programs, in particular for public housing, remained relatively robust.

The influence of the Studio on the profession can also be observed from the mid-1970s onward in how the idea of Contextualism was disseminated by those members of the Cornell and IAUS teams working with these city agencies, who then later had professional contact with planning departments around the U.S. The term was eventually adopted by community activists bent on preserving those parts of the traditional downtown that hadn't already suffered the ravages of misguided urban renewal. Steven Hurtt described Contextualism as "the derivation of form from its context. It depends upon and extends a pre-existing form

16 Hammann email to the author, September 2018. Section 8 is part of the Federal Housing Act of 1937, amended many times since, and is overseen by the U.S. Department of Housing and Urban Development. It provides rent assistance for low-income households.

17 The Baltimore Planning Commission, Department of Planning; Cornell University College of Architecture Art and Planning, *The* MUND *Plan*, 1970.

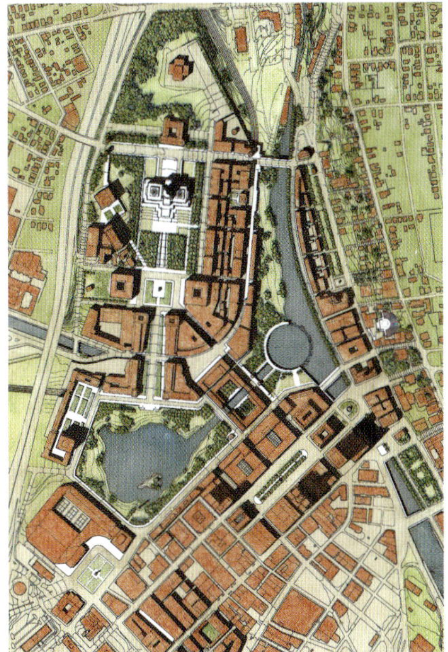

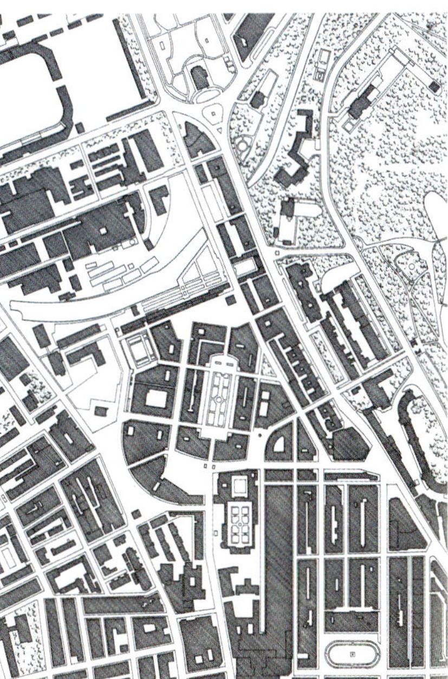

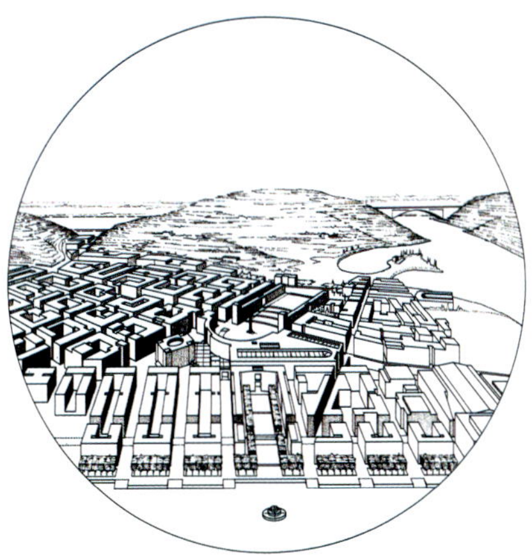

left to right:
Fig. 10. Providence, RI: Capitol District Development Strategy, Blake Middleton graduate thesis, 1980-81. Retaining some of the scale ambitions of earlier 'heroic' Studio tactics, but focused within a highly contoured area around the State Capitol, Rowe encouraged the author to explore a robust manipulation of landscaped open spaces—the "Splendid public terraces" and "The garden" as celebrated in *Collage City*—rather than relying solely on additional building.

Fig. 11. London: A Proposal for the Marylebone District, graduate thesis by Steven Fong, 1983. The ongoing investigation by Studio members of the irregular boundaries between urban grids, often topographically generated, can be easily traced in Fong's series of localized insertions. This thesis typified the studio "Late Period" favoring more modest scaled projects.

Fig. 12. Upper Manhattan Development Strategy, Michael Manfredi graduate thesis, 1978. This project is emblematic of the transition taking hold in the Studio in the late 1980s, using a broader graphic representation palette and increased use of traditional city building and space-making prototypes evident in the contemporary work of the Kriers, Peterson, Littenberg, et al., as well as Stirling and Wilford's museum designs.

order".[18] There were certainly benefits to this approach. Chief among its formal virtues, as it evolved into public policy in various cities, was reestablishing the primacy of street and square as spatial entities that should be preserved, reenforced or reconstituted. Where incorporated in zoning regulations, it was a way to ameliorate discordant building bulk adjacent to, or within, urban neighborhoods. In recent decades, contextualism has become deeply embedded in the *lingua franca* of public design review and the accepted standard by which a designer needs to advance a project through the regulatory process.

By the late 1970s federal funding through the Department of Housing and Urban Development (HUD), and therefore from many state agencies, began to shrink. The anti-urban bias of the Reagan administration, coupled with the recession of 1981–82, precipitated a dramatic reduction in federal funding for urban revitalization. The increasing disenchantment with urban renewal—especially following the urban riots of 1968—coincided with a gradual shift in the scale and type of problems in the Rowe Studio. The 'heroic' interventions in the early years of the Studio—exemplified by the Harlem and Bronx rezoning plans of 1968, the Buffalo Waterfront in 1966 (Fig. 9), the various Baltimore master plans—yielded to smaller scale thesis propositions from the early 1980s like that of Michael Manfredi's for Upper Manhattan (Fig. 12), by the author's project for Providence, RI (Fig. 10), or for the Marylebone district in London by Stephen Fong (Fig. 11). Hurtt and others have shown how Rowe's interest, and that of his students, recalibrated toward more discrete and contingent solutions yet still employing the *bricolage* tactic of creating spatial coherence through the recognition of the irregular and *ad hoc* in the local physical context.[19]

By 1986, a reviving economy and plummeting lending rates drew most graduates from the Studio "Late Period" into the private sector; the opportunity to gain experience in a design firm outweighed the offerings of working at planning or redevelopment agencies with far fewer job openings than a decade before. One

18 Hurtt (1983): 67.

19 Based on the evidence of Studio projects produced after 1980, one might take issue with Kenneth Frampton's observation in *Lotus* 27 (1980) that there was a "loss of direction and method within the Cornell school ... and a growing disbelief in the 'collage' approach". Frampton, Kenneth; Latour, Alessandra, "Notes on American Architectural Education", *Lotus international* 27, 1980: 31. The UD projects continued to explore the collage city and collision city concepts as outlined in Hurtt's article in *The Cornell Journal* 2. The influence of Rob and Léon Krier can also be easily detected.

above clockwise:
Fig. 13. Carleton College Weitz Center for Creativity by MSR Design, 2011. Located in Northfield, MN. Rockcastle's concept expands an existing warehouse-like building complex with a series of cubic volumes. Photo: Lara Swimmer.

Fig. 14. Weitz Center, site plan. The new addition creates a threshold into the complex while making a visual terminus to the main campus green several blocks distant, thereby linking the disparate campus clusters through a set of low-rise street blocks.

Fig. 15. College of Media Arts and Design, Drexel University, Philadelphia, MSR Design, 2013.

might also deduce a loss of faith in, and consequent disdain for, work at public agencies once perceived as agents of progress. *The Death and Life of Great American Cities* by Jane Jacobs in 1961, chronicled "the system" responsible for aiding and abetting the destruction of seemingly blighted but socially cohesive neighborhoods, was a touchstone for this perception.

Theory Applied

These trends during the 1980s—in national politics, in a profession questioning the efficacy of urban renewal (due in no small part to Rowe's theoretical critique beginning in 1960s) and in the Urban Design Studio's embrace of design problems more modest in scale—significantly affected the formative experience of students of the Late Period. This in turn would heavily influence both their design work as professionals and their agency in disseminating the theoretical approach of the Studio. There are approximately seventy Studio graduates from 1978 onward in this group. However, editorial limitations compel narrowing the selection to eleven alumni/ae whose work clearly exemplifies this focus on projects of significant and positive contextual impact.[20] Many represent the leadership of firms or agencies of varying size, whose practice is focused primarily on urban architecture. They exemplify a diversity of practices (large corporate firms to small non-profit organizations), of project types, or of site contexts ranging from dense urban centers to semi-rural landscapes. Arranged roughly chronologically by the year they completed their thesis in parentheses, the work of these designers demonstrates a variety of ways in which the conceptual underpinnings of the Urban Design Studio have been translated into built form or into urban design guidelines in the last two decades.

As a founding principal of MSR Design in Minneapolis, Garth Rockcastle (1978) has made several accomplished urban campus projects as well as work that creatively repurposes early or mid-20th century industrial buildings. A building addition at Carleton College's Weitz Center for Creativity makes a visual link to the main campus quadrangle several blocks away while establishing a gateway through the Center by juxtaposing different building volumes to emphasize the

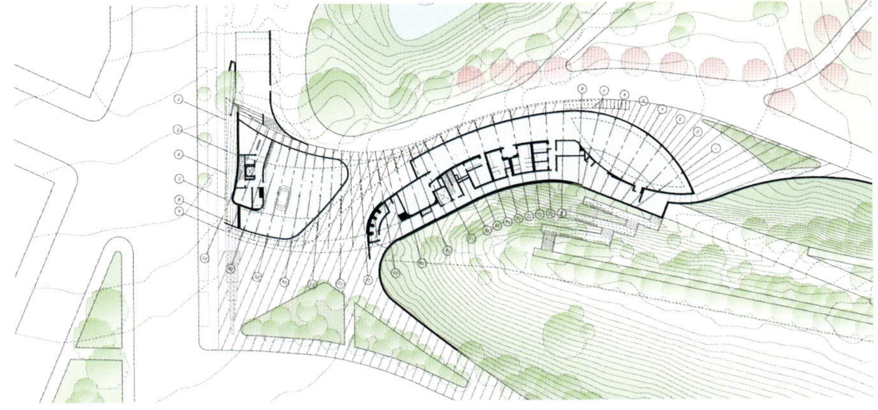

entrance (Fig. 13, 14). In a radical deconstruction and adaptive reuse of Robert Venturi's first major 'decorated shed', Rockcastle's team leaves the iconic exterior intact while opening the interior floors to create interconnected and flexible work space (Fig. 15).

Michael Manfredi (1980), with his partner, Marion Weiss, has developed a remarkable practice over the last 30 years producing work of powerful urbanity and sophistication. The Olympic Sculpture Park in Seattle (Fig. 18), along with the Brooklyn Botanic Garden Visitor Center (Fig. 16, 17), demonstrate a continuation of Rowe's interest in gardens and parks as *urbanistica* vital to the character and livability of cities. The firm's work on urban campuses illustrates a straightforward approach to urban space-making by reestablishing public street definition and private campus quadrangles such as the Barnard College project in New York (Fig. 19) or the Singh Center for Nanotechnology in Philadelphia (Fig. 20, 21) where the latter establishes a gateway into an urban campus without literally invoking the traditional 'gate'. These projects reveal a Rowe Studio obsession in that all are located at urban edges and all treat unresolved peripheries: a park entrance facing an avenue (Bronx), city grid meeting disconnected

top left to right:
Fig. 16. Brooklyn Botanic Gardens, Weiss/Manfredi Architects, 2012, site plan. Landscape and building become nearly indistinguishable: the structure serves as a gateway; the roof transforms from talismans of roof gables indicating 'front door'.

Fig. 17. Brooklyn Botanic Gardens, aerial view. Photo: Albert Vecerka/ESTO.

below left to right:
Fig. 18. Olympic Sculpture Park, Seattle, Weiss/Manfredi Architects, 2007. Use of landscape elements as equal players in the urban design 'toolbox' recalls Rowe's lament: "if only the landscapers knew that they had the solution to many of our urban problems...".
Photo: Ewan Baan.

Fig. 19. Barnard College Diana Center, Weiss/Manfredi Architects, 2011. From the historic entrance gate at Broadway, the wedge-shape design frames a clear sightline linking the central campus at Lehman Lawn to the lower-level historic core of the campus. Photo: Albert Vecerka/ESTO.

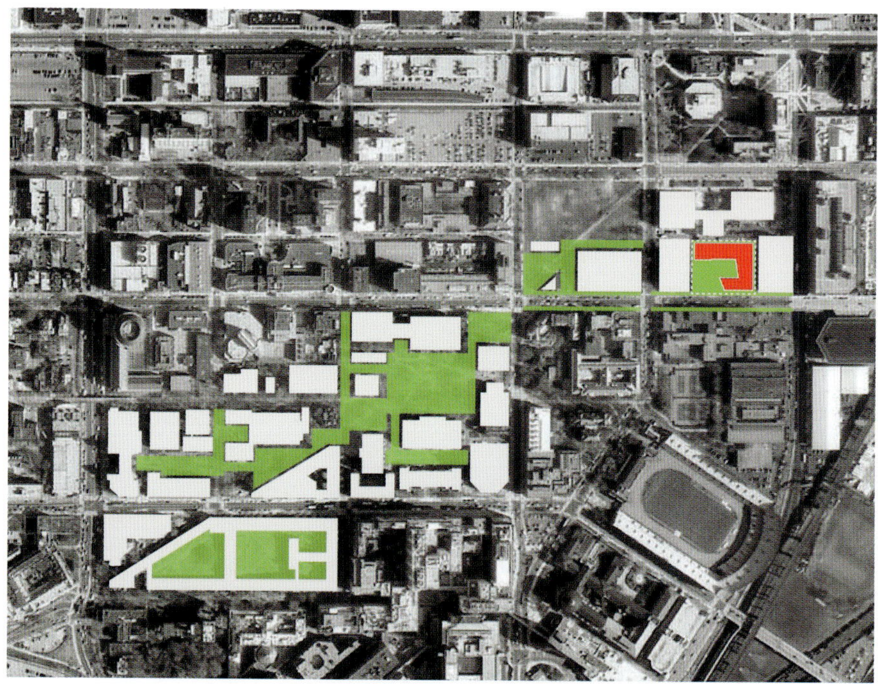

above left to right:
Fig. 20. University of Pennsylvania Nanotechnology Center, Weiss/Manfredi Architects, 2013, view of main entrance. Photo: Albert Vecerka/ESTO.

Fig. 21. Nanotechnology Center, site plan.

below clockwise:
Fig. 22. Woods Hole Oceanographic Institute Marine Mammal Research Building, University of Rhode Island, Ellenzweig, 2004-06, aerial perspective. The building complex unites previously disconnected campus areas

Fig. 23. Oceanographic Institute, site plan. The site leads to the water's edge, a defining element for the new campus structures.

Fig. 24. Oceanographic Institute, general view of builidng complex. Photo: Anton Grassl.

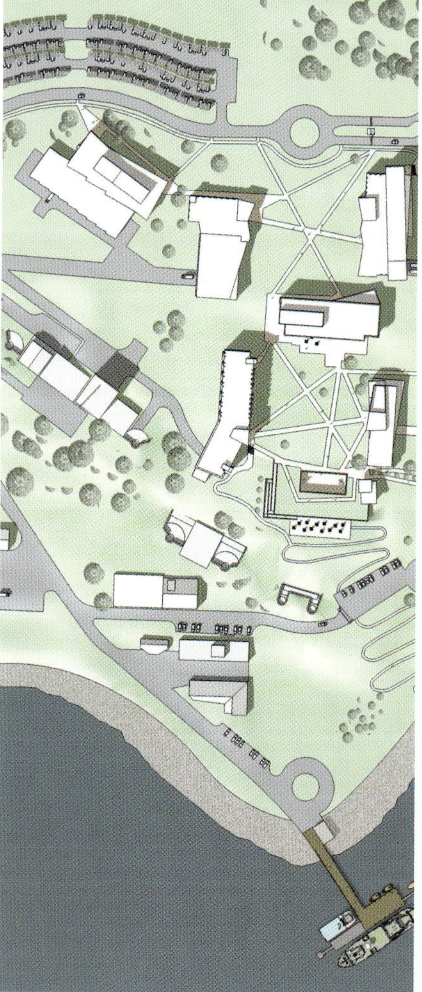

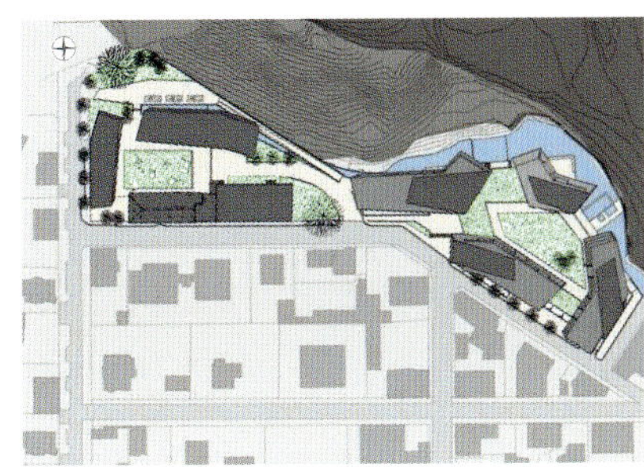

inset:
Fig. 25. Jewels of Salzburg, Hariri & Hariri Architects, 2014, aerial view. The complex forms both neighborhood edge and center and acts as a scale transition between low-rise residences at the peripheral city grid and the 'cliff-nymphaeum'.

above:
Fig. 26. Jewels of Salzburg, site plan. Buildings oscillate between figural objects and continuations of city texture.

Fig. 27. Jewels of Salzburg, courtyard view. The shear walls of the quarry are echoed in the varied building volumes.

waterfront bounded by highway and rail lines (Seattle), and campus buildings reestablishing street frontage while defining gateway spaces (Barnard College and University of Pennsylvania).

Three graduates from the 1980s have authored a significant body of built work, two of whom happen to be expatriates, not uncommon for many Rowe students. Shirine Boulos (1980), a Lebanese-American, is a principal at the firm Ellenzweig in Boston. She has designed a number of university campus master plans and completed several noteworthy urban laboratory buildings for Michigan State University, the University of Mississippi, and two rural campus complexes in New England. The latter, while in a distinctly non-urban setting, are noteworthy for their mastery of spatial definition in open terrain and their echo of the local vernacular while accommodating important extended landscape vistas (Fig. 22, 23 and 24).[20]

Mojgan Hariri (1983) is a partner with her sister, Gisue, at Hariri & Hariri in New York City. They are Iranian-Americans who have created, among their urban projects, an unusual mixed-use complex in Salzburg, Austria.[21] Set in a pocket-like neighborhood defined by stone escarpments, these buildings create a dramatic dialogue between the severe cliffs and the existing neighborhood of low-rise buildings. It is a refined demonstration that interprets the local context of topography as well as history. Deploying the power of small building fragments, it transforms a discarded industrial edge site with a unique publicly accessible open space surmounted by private residences (Fig. 25, 26 and 27).

As a studio Director at Kohn Pederson and Fox Architects, Jerri Smith (1981) has overseen several large urban projects including new campus buildings at the University of Michigan and Arizona State University. A recent project proposes

20 Women Studio graduates include Cristina Echeverria (1982), Cathleen Crabb (1984), Henrietta Cheng (1985), Travis Cloud (1985), Ann Cederna (1986), Cheryl O'Neil (1987), and Irene Mun (1989). In his first decade teaching at Cornell, Rowe was an advisor for several undergraduate women thesis students who have had notable careers including: Judith Wolin (B. Arch. 1968), Professor of Architecture at Rhode Island School of Design; Barbara Littenberg (B. Arch. 1971), for many years Professor of Architecture at Yale and Principal at Peterson/Littenberg Architects; Susie Kim (B. Arch. 1972), Principal of Koetter Kim Architects; and Judith DiMaio (B. Arch. 1974), Professor of Architecture at Notre Dame and earlier at Yale and Dean of New York Institute of Technology School of Architecture. Miriam Gusevich and Cederna have been for some years Professors of Architecture at Catholic University of America. Gusevich has designed several award-winning urban park plazas and memorials.

21 Both Gisue and Mojgan Hariri completed their B. Arch. degrees at Cornell with Rowe as a thesis advisor. Mojgan continued in the Urban Design Studio.

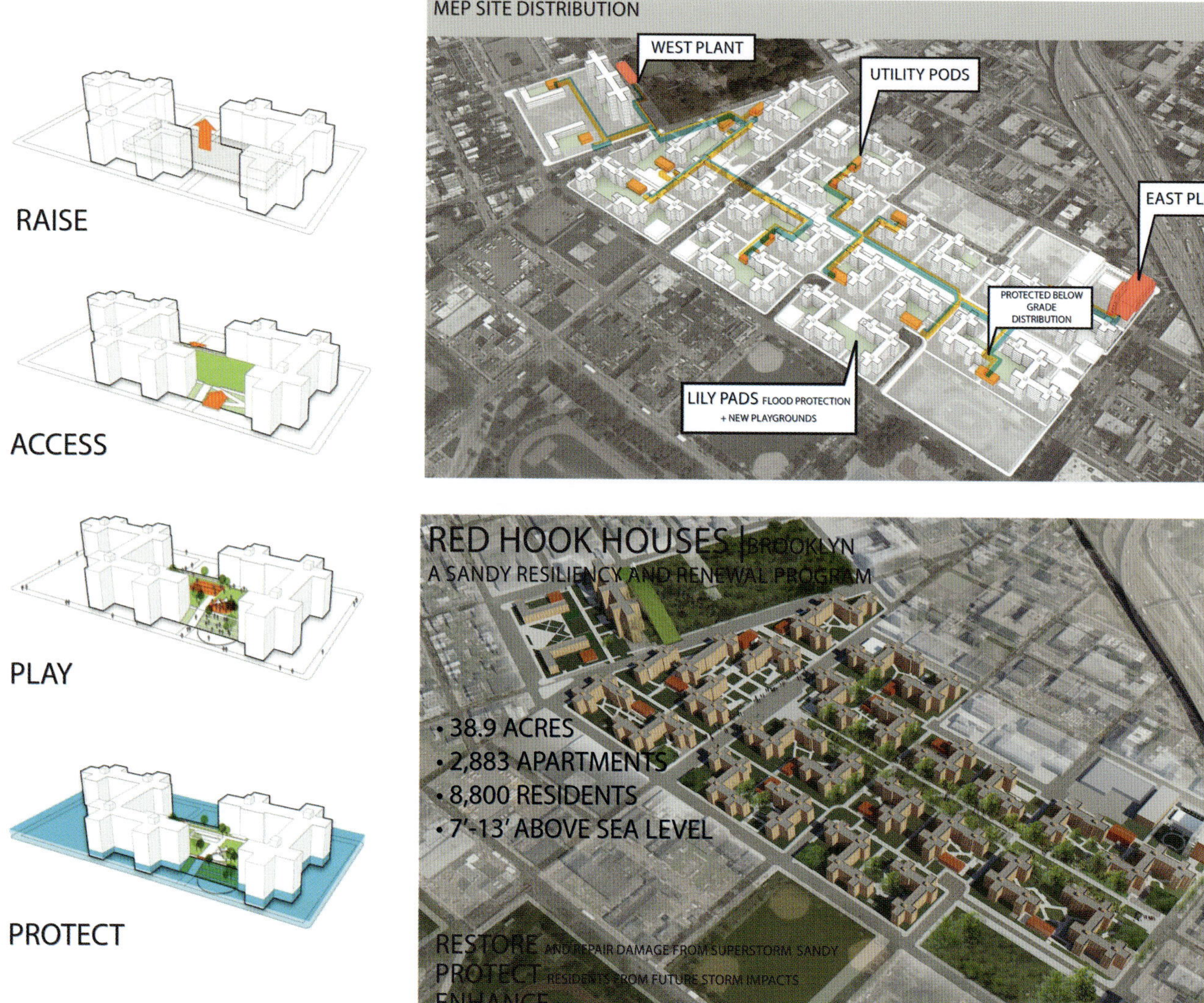

Fig. 28. (Hurricane) Sandy Resiliency and Renewal Program at Red Hook Houses, Brooklyn (NY), KPF Architects, 2017; plan overseen by Jerri K. Smith.

a massive renovation of Red Hook Houses, a quintessential late 1930s housing project in Brooklyn, NY, severely damaged from flooding from Hurricane Sandy in 2012. Smith's team authored a multidisciplinary 'resiliency and renewal' master plan that takes urban design to a new dimension. The plan replaces, improves, and provides new construction for resilient infrastructure and architecture on the 34-acre site. Hardening the site against future storms required building the critical new central plants for the complex above the flood plain. The plan not only integrates systems for mitigating future flooding and residential safety but also addresses past ills attendant to buildings detached from their streets with new landscape solutions (Fig. 28). The Red Hook project gives new and urgent meaning to 'urban renewal' through the imperative of 'urban resiliency', now a critical focus of all coastal cities in the era of climate change.

The author's experience over the last two decades, of designing five new buildings in the historic city center of Boston, offers a lesson in the power of what the author

22 The author completed his studio thesis in 1980, receiving his MArch degree in 1981. Gary Handel (Cornell BArch 1978) started his eponymous firm in 1994. 'Hybrid High-rise Buildings' refers to the complexity of function, form and finance of certain types of large-scale, mixed-use buildings.

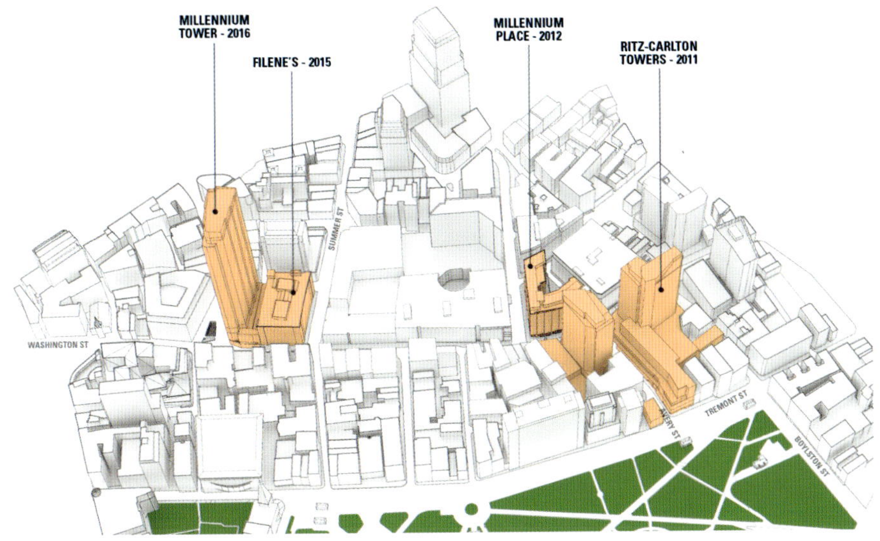

above clockwise:
Fig. 29. Transforming Washington Street, Boston, aerial perspective. Five buildings designed by the author over a 20-year period revitalized this pre-colonial, downtown district. The transformation of a neighborhood once called "The Combat Zone" into a 24-hour mixed-use community, a case study for the power of localized, strategically incremental redevelopment.

Fig. 30. Millennium Place, Boston, Handel Architects, 2001-2011. Constructed on failed urban renewal sites, a complex program of uses assembled in a composite building type re-establishes the street while forming a new visual 'hinge' at a critical intersection. The two towers frame an important link to Boston Common.

Fig. 31. Millennium Place, view on Washington St. with the 2011 addition of a 15-story masonry building evocative of early 20th century loft buildings contrasts with the stone and glass podiums of the 2001 complex. Photo: Gustav Hoiland.

Fig. 32. Millennium Tower, 2016, plaza view. Contextual fit for this high-rise at a key intersection in the Colonial-era district is established by a calibrated massing strategy. Photo: Bruce Martin.

and his partner Gary Handel have coined "Hybrid High-rise Buildings".[22] The transformation these interventions have had on the Midtown Cultural District is significant: reconstituting the street wall continuity without mimicking the prevailing early 20th century Neo-classicism; creating composite towers on podiums that adjust to contingent adjacencies; and, because of the complexity of multiple building uses, stimulating a dramatic increase in pedestrian—and economic—activity. The architectural expression for each building varies with the location and variegated character of the neighborhood (Fig. 29–32).

In an unusual example of long-term urban design advocacy, Thomas K. Davis (1983) has, since 1995, initiated and overseen several non-profit participatory organizations in Tennessee. This includes work with his students at the University of Tennessee, through the agency of Davis' Kingsport Regional Interactive Design Studio, to identify urban design issues and opportunities in Kingsport and nearby regions (Fig. 34). He is also a co-founder of the Nashville Civic Design Center,

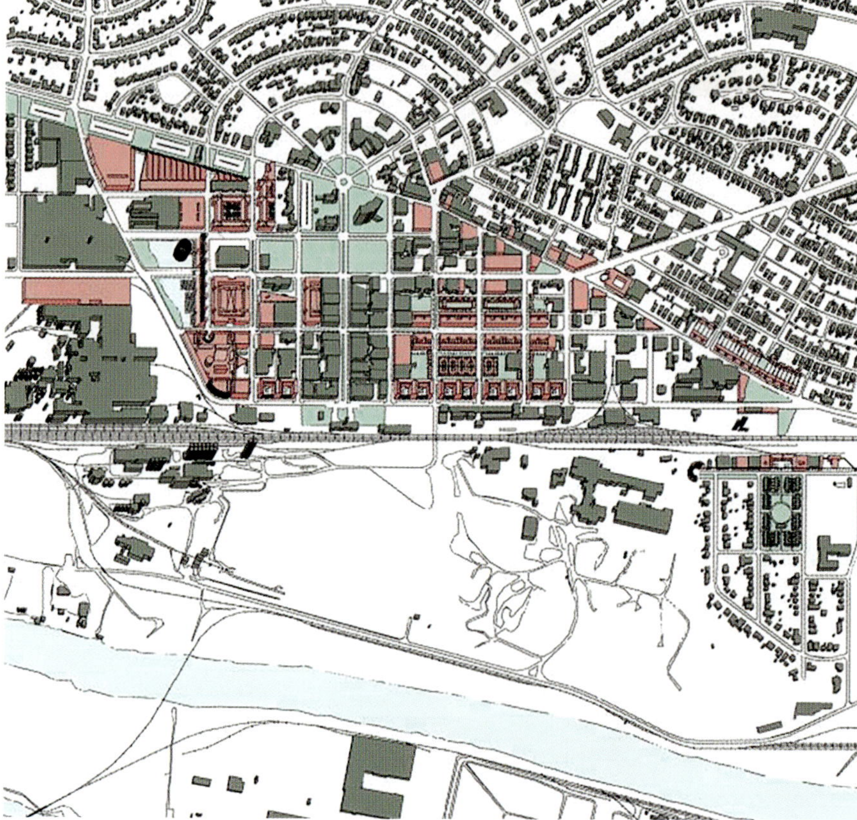

left to right:
Fig. 33. Nashville Micro-unit Student Housing, 2013. Each year since 2004, T. K. Davis's citizen participatory work with his students at the Nashville Civic Design Center addresses a pressing topic for the city and region.

Fig. 34. Kingsport Plan, 1998. With citizen and local planning agency participation, Davis's work with the Kingsport Regional Interactive Studio created a framework plan for future growth that integrated the 1927 John Nolen town planning concepts for an industrial city.

an independent think tank that has provided continuous outreach and advocacy for design issues facing Nashville to the present day (Fig. 33).

Mustafa Abadan (1984), a design partner at SOM in New York, has designed projects in Asia that emphasize linkages more to cultural context than any particulars of scale or building typology. Designing large-scale, mixed-use buildings is challenging enough; it is more so within zoning regulations that permit significant bulk on vast blocks in districts that have evolving and increasing density. This is partly a cultural preference valuing south daylighting and eschewing double loaded corridors for residential buildings for direct natural ventilation. The Tokyo Midtown Project appears to echo a bipartite palazzo-and-garden scenario: the clustering of towers around two linear courts (the palazzo) connected to the main street, which lead through the complex to a substantial five-acre open space (the garden) peripherally bound by the low-scale existing context (Fig. 35, 36, 37).

Brian Kelly (1987) was one of the last group of students to study with Rowe during his tenure at Cornell. Kelly has developed a specialty as a design consultant for campus master planning. In addition to projects for Harvard and Notre Dame, he has led a large-scale plan for Arizona State University in Tempe. This plan, encompassing over 40 acres, recreates components of the traditional quadrangle while adopting contemporary research and entrepreneurial co-location building prototypes (Fig. 38, 39).

clockwise:
Fig. 35. Tokyo Midtown, SOM Architects, 2007, aerial view. Mustafa Abadan's concept reclaims an eight-hectare site for public benefit. The master plan allocates 465,000 square meters of mixed-use development and includes a five-acre park. One of Toyko's tallest towers anchors a corner of the site while adjacent mid-rise buildings form 'foothills' inspired by traditional Zen gardens. Photos: courtesy SOM / © Shinkenchiku-sha.

Fig. 36. Tokyo Midtown, view of Center Plaza. For many Asian cities, post-WWII created zoning regulations valuing detached building massing over street-wall continuity. The SOM project reinforces urban space, adopting space defining priorities while respecting local zoning codes.

Fig. 37. Tokyo Midtown, view of Plaza Portal.

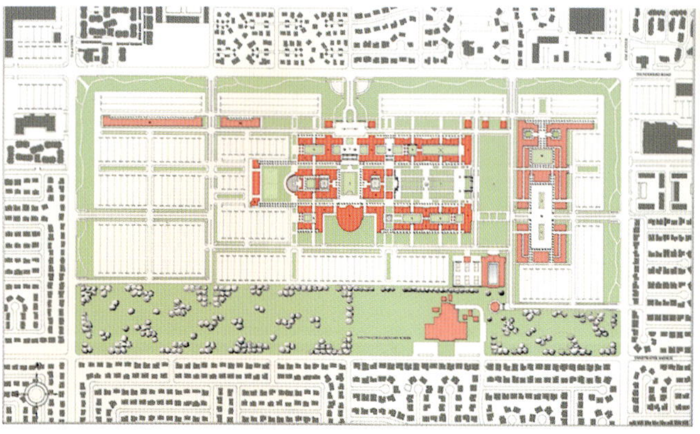

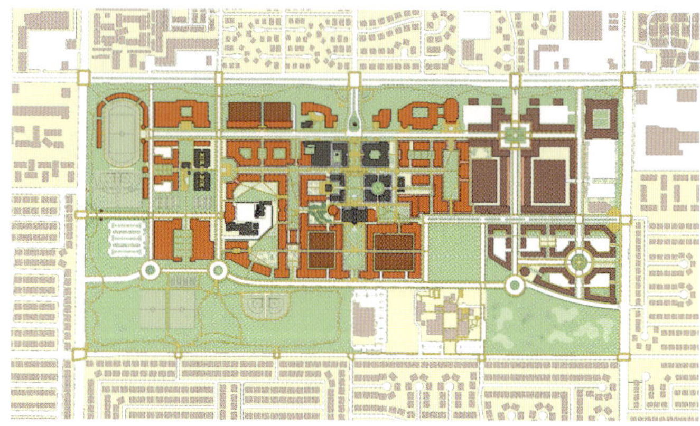

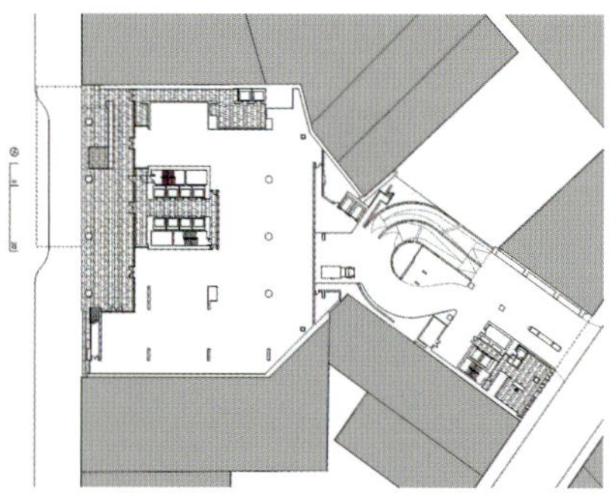

Bernhard Karpf (1988), a native of Stüttgart, has been a member of design teams at Richard Meier and Partners for a variety of iconic projects. He has overseen the design of two projects especially relevant to this overview: the Torre Cuarzo on the Paseo de la Reforma in Mexico City (Fig. 40, 41) and the Coffee Plaza Office Development in Hamburg (Fig. 42, 43). The former is a mixed-use project on an irregular site; it is another instance of a 'hybrid high-rise', in this case two towers joined by a parking garage podium imbedded within the party walls of the site. The Hamburg complex is situated in an open plaza opening to a canal forming a sculptural border to the development's expansive open spaces. The three buildings rise from an elevated plaza to delineate city blocks defining an oval tower set-piece to the park and canal buttressed with two smaller and normative buildings along the street wall.

This small sampling by no means fully represents the collective experience or influence of Urban Design Studio graduates on the profession. But overall, the work illustrates a persistent and skillful application of the lessons and theory absorbed from Rowe and his colleagues during the Late Period of the Studio. This is manifested in the manner in which building massing adjusts to context in ways that are either subtle or overt, in apparent opposition or cohesion, in how street space and pedestrian ways are developed as clearly defined spatial experiences, or in how urban developments of scale are connected into ever-evolving city fabric and historic memory. Of course the work also reflects the skill and sophistication of these individual designers, however much influenced by their Rowe Studio experience.

The Argument is Evident

The substantive—and lasting—legacy of the Urban Design Studio may be found in at least three ways. First is the dissemination of a method of teaching. For many studio members this started with their experience as teaching assistants in the Cornell undergraduate program and continued with astonishing frequency, as Alexander Caragonne amply demonstrated in *The Texas Rangers*, with graduates teaching at so many other schools of architecture and design.[23] Second is the institutionalization of Contextualism, primarily of the physical variety, in

23 Caragonne, Alexander, *The Texas Rangers: Notes from an Architectural Underground*, MIT Press, Cambridge, MA, and London, 1995.

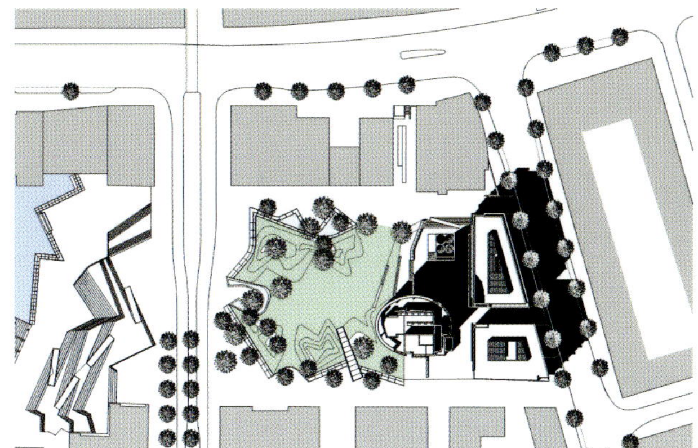

urban design policy in so many cities in the U.S. Third is in the professional design work of the graduates of the Studio. As one of his students aptly observed, Rowe introduced them "to the value of ambiguity and to the fact that there is never a single solution to any problem. Perhaps his most lasting gift ... was a design methodology that prepared [his students] to work flexibly at any scale whether furniture, architecture, or urban precinct, and in either public or private sectors".[24] Even within this necessarily abridged survey, the breadth and quality of these architects' work is a substantive and highly visible "evidence of an argument" initially postulated by Rowe and his colleagues in the early 1960s, which has subsequently been developed and refined over three decades by his students. It is a powerful and positive legacy, a fact of built form and urban design.

With this in mind, one cannot help but recall the Pirandello quip that Rowe was fond of quoting, "... a fact is like a sack—it won't stand up if it's empty". He employed it to say that arguments for an idea are only as good as the foundational facts and the theoretical organization deployed in support of the position one is taking. Rowe often omitted the second part of the Pirandello quote, germane to this overview, which goes on to say, "In order that it [the sack] may stand up, one has to put into it the reason and sentiment which caused it to exist".[25]

The ideas underpinning the work of the Cornell Urban Design Studio—for all their virtues and faults—have proven to be remarkably durable. The ongoing efforts of its alumni/ae, wherever they are practicing or teaching, continue to have a positive and lasting influence on the ceaseless evolution of the urban environment. The formal skills, appreciation for cultural context, and a cultivated receptiveness to local contingency these designers first developed in the studio—the 'reason'—bolstered by a faith in, and commitment to, an approach to urbanism fostered by Colin Rowe—the 'sentiment'—are indeed facts which continue to stand up over time.

opposite left to right:
Fig. 38. Arizona State University (ASU) Master Plan, commuter satellite campus, Thunderbird Road, Phoenix, by Brian Kelly and Max Underwood, 1987.

Fig. 39. ASU Master Plan mixed-use and sustainability update. Brian Kelly, with Ayers Saint Gross Architects, 2007.

opposite below top to bottom:
Fig. 40. Torre Cuarzo, Richard Meier and Partners, Mexico City, 2018, aerial view. This mixed-use building, is another example of a composite building conforming to an irregular site in a triangular block. Office and residential uses in separate towers, are linked to a common podium roof terrace. Photo: ©Roland Halbe Fotografie.

Fig. 41. Torre Cuarzo, Mexico City, 2018. Ground plan. Karpf's plan is reminiscent of the *hôtel particulier* typology studied at Cornell in the 1980s with a set of distinct organizing centering and recentering axes and rotations induced by the site geometry.

above left to right:
Fig. 42. Coffee Plaza, Hamburg, Richard Meier and Partners, 2010, view facing canal. Overseen by Bernhard Karpf the urban design on a former working waterfront district reveals a classic object/edge dialogue. Two seven-story office buildings reconstruct the street-wall. The detached oval-shaped thirteen-story tower is set on a low plinth overlooking the plaza and canal. Photo: © Klaus Frahm/Artur images.

Fig. 43. Coffee Plaza, site plan.

24 Terrance Williams comment relayed to the author.

25 Pirandello, Luigi, "Act 1", in *Six Characters in Search of an Author*, now in Bentley, Eric, ed., *Naked Masks: Five Plays by Luigi Pirandello*, E. P. Dutton and Co., Inc., New York, (1921) 1952: 230.

Students of the Graduate Urban Design Studio at Cornell University, 1963-1997

Thesis Date	Author Name	Birth Location, Year	Thesis Title	Cornell B.Arch
1963	Ishizu, Hachiro	Hawaii, 1936	Villa Savoye - A Search for its Iconographic Contents	
1964	Chongvatana, Anujit	Bangkok, Thailand, 1934	The Library and Administration Building of Chulalongkorn University Bangkok, Thailand	
	El Kholy, Mohamed Badr	Seberbai, Egypt, 1931	El Alamein Resort on the Southern Mediterranean Coast of Egypt - U.A.R.	
	Itthikasem, Inthira	Bankgkok, Thailand, 1937	Bangkok Air Terminal Building (Thailand)	
	Kasprzak, Gregory	Poland, 1932	Cornell University Science Center Ithaca, New York, USA	
	Koita, Taher Taiyebali	Bombay, India, 1939	A New Campus for the University of Bombay, India	
	Yomnak, Torpong	Bangkok, Thailand, 1937	The Commissioner's Office of Metropolitan Police (Thailand)	
1965	Assarat, Supatra	Bangkok, Thailand, 1938	Cheingmai University (Thailand)	
	Dluhosch, Eric	Czechoslovakia, 1927	Expansion of the Ohio University Campus & the Core of the City of Athens, Ohio	
	Gyllenstierna, Nils Elson	Stockholm, Sweden, 1938	New Town, Aalborg	
	Handler, Philip Stephan	Hartford, CT,1940	Charter Oak-Meadows Redevelopment Hartford, Conn.	1964
	Koluksuz, Ozcan Cetin	Istanbul, Turkey 1935	Redevelopment Plan for Konya, Turkey	
	Moeloek, Raysoeli	Sumatera, Indonesia, 1936	A Civic and Cultural Center for Bandung, Indonesia	
	Nigg, Erwin	Switzerland, 1936	Auxilary Campus for the University of Zurich	
	Phillips, Irving	Houston, TX	A Satellite Town	
	Uathavikul, Kingkae Pisitkasem	Thailand, 1939	Bangokok Redevelopment: Civic and Cultural Center	1963
1966	Elpidio, Olympio Fernando	Togo, West Africa	Central Accra Renewal Proposal	
	Makoto, Miki	Tokyo, Japan, 1939	Tokyo Urban Redevelopment	
	Oswald, Franz	Bern, Switzerland, 1938	Zurich Center '66	
	Prakalphakul, Tadapong	Bangkok, Thailand, 1937	The Development of the Chulalongkorn University, Bangkok	
	Schumacher, Thomas Lawrence	New York, NY, 1941	South Amboy New Town	1963
1967	Baiter, Richard Abbott	New York, NY, 1937	A Redevelopment Project for the Brooklyn Navy Yard	1963
	Cardwell, Richard Hugh	Seattle, WA, 1941	Seattle: A Project for the Redevelopment of the Denny Regrade Area	
	Chan, David Wing Kwai	N/A	Hong Kong Urban Redevelopment	1965
	Cohen, Stuart E.	Chicago, IL, 1942	Le Corbusier: The Architecture of City Planning (joint thesis)	1966
	Hurtt, Steven W.	Washington DC, 1941	Le Corbusier: The Architecture of City Planning (joint thesis)	
	Copper, Wayne	McKeesport, PA, 1942	Figure/Ground	1965
	Koetter, Alfred H. (Jr.)	Great Falls, MT, 1938	A Civic Center for Birmingham, Alabama	
	McBride, Richard Dale	Oklahoma, 1933	Urban Design for Dallas	
1968	de Vengoechea, Manuel R.	Bogota, Colombia, 1940	An Exercise in Urban Design: Santa Marta, Colombia	1965
	Duncan, Donald	San Francisco, CA, 1934	Baltimore Master Plan	
	Hammann, Frederick	Baltimore, MD, 1942	Baltimore Master Plan	1966
	Nichols, Larry D.	Texarkana, AK, (?)	Manchester New Hampshire: A Study in Urban Design	
	Potters, Steven	San Francisco, CA, 1941	Kingsbridge Heights - Bronx Master Plan	1966
	Schwarting, Jon Michael	Columbus, OH, 1943	Kingsbridge Heights - Bronx Master Plan	1966
	Stoumen, Jonathan A.	Philadelphia, PA, 1943	Urban Design Group in 2nd Year in NYC program.	1966
	Valk, Arthur	Durham, NC, 1942	Baltimore Master Plan	1966
1969	Caragonne, Alexander	Aldine, TX, 1935	Urban Redevelopment for San Antonio	
	Dobson, John (Jack)	N/A	NYC Rezone: A Proposal for Residential Zoning Reform	1965
	Garrison, Glenn L.	Paris, TX, 1938	West Side, Manhattan	
	Henderson, Philip T.	N/A, 1939	West Side, Manhattan	
	Pressman, Norman Ezra Philip	Montreal, Canada, 1939	An Urban Redevelopment Proposal for Hull, Quebec	
		Los Angeles, CA, 1944	NYC Rezone: A Proposal for Residential Zoning Reform	
	Sanford, Roswald (Randy)	Margaretville, NY, 1942	NYC Rezone: A Proposal for Residential Zoning Reform	1967
	Williams, Terrance	Coos Bay, OR, 1938	NYC Rezone: A Proposal for Residential Zoning Reform	
1970	Crowe, Norman A.	Pueblo, CO, 1938	Suburban Form: A Proposal for Syracuse, New York (joint thesis)	
	Tice, James T.	Dover, NJ, 1945	Suburban Form: A Proposal for Syracuse, New York (joint thesis)	1968
	Curtis, Paul A.	Cambridge, MA, 1943	SPQR: Southern Peninsula Queens Redevelopment	1966
	Herpin, Isabelle M.T.	Tours, France, 1944	Urban Design Study for Manhattan, Eastside	
	Mankowski, Leonard Edward	Stuenbenville, OH, 1937	An Urban Design Study of the City of Pittsburg	
	McCue, Thomas P. (III)	Syracuse, NY, 1944	Ontario Park Redevelopment Area (Rochester, NY)	
	Pannenborg, Frank	New York, NY, 1945	Logan Square Area, Philadelphia, PA	1965
	Peterson, Steven K.	Indianapolis, IN, 1940	University Avenue Urban Development	1965
	Richardson, Henry W.	Nsawam, Ghana, 1941	Spanish Harlem Study	1968
1971	Bekele, Assefa	Dire Dawa, Ethiopia, 1942	Baltimore: Development Strategies	
	Birkett, Bruce Tiffany	New York, NY 1945	Ithlan/Ithaca, Planned Growth of the Intermegalopolitan Region, An Alternative to Sprawl	1968
	Feinn, Harris C.	Tuscon, AZ, 1946	Baltimore: Development Strategies	1969
	Kreider, Jerry W.	Harrisburg, PA, 1946	Baltimore: Development Strategies	1969
1972	Kulkarni, Ashok V.	Bombay, India, 1938	Times Square: Development Strategies	
	Shane, David Grahame	London, England, 1945	Urban Patterns in London	
1973	McDonald, Arthur Walter	New York, NY, 1939	Urban Design Study: West 14th Street and Waterfront	
	Moor, Malcolm Douglas	Glasgow, Scotland, 1944	Northampton Central Area Redevelopment	
	Mueller, Joerg	Horgen, Switzerland, 1942	Urban Redevelopment for Basel, Switzerland	
	Vakalo, Emmanuel-George	Athens, Greece, 1946	Gardens of the Mind: An Anthology of Formal Gardens with Some Observations	1970
1974	Brown, Robinson Osborn	New York, NY, 1945	Contextualism in Modern Architecture: A Study of Prague, Czechoslovakia, 1919 - 1939	
	Chen, George Chuan Yi	Shanghai, China, 1949	Urban Design Study: Lower Manhattan West Side	
	Chmura, Jeffrey A.	Pawtucket, RI, 1948	Central Boston Redevelopment	
	Walluk, John Nils	Johnson City, NY, 1949	Urban Design Plan, Downtown Binghamton, New York	
1975	Kleinman, Martin	Brooklyn, NY, 1947	Urban Design Proposal for Brooklyn, N.Y.	
1976	Arikoglu, Kaya Sahin	Baltimore, MD, 1949	South Baltimore Development	
	Keep, Douglas T.	NJ, 1949	Syracuse Development Strategy	
	Muse, Stephen Alan	Washington D.C., 1950	Richmond Waterfront Strategy	
	Reibel, Gale Joseph	Louisville, KY, 1951	Downtown Cleveland Development Strategy	
1978	Christodoulou, Christakis L.	Nicosia, Cyprus, 1951	Lower Manhattan Development Strategy	
	Hunt, Anthony V.	Philadelphia, PA, 1952	A Redevelopment Proposal for Southwest and Lower Southeast Washington D.C.	
	Rockcastle, Garth Carl	Rochester, NY, 1951	Urban Synthesis: A Formal Strategy for Rochester, N.Y.	
	Tzerai, Ghebremichael	Corbaria (Eritrea), Ethiopia	Harlem Coast-Bronx Redevelopment	
	Yukutomi, Seiichi	Japan, 1945	An Urban Design for a Finger Lake City: Ithaca with Arboretum	
1979	Graves, Charles P. (Jr)	Atlanta, GA, 1952	Manhattan: A Measure	
	Gusevich, Miriam	Havana, Cuba, 1953	Urban Design: Quebec	1975
	Tregebov, Alan Jerome	Winnipeg, Canada, 1952	An Urban Design Proposal for Boston, MA: Back Bay and South End	1977
1980	Boulos, Shirine Souheil	Beirut, Lebanon, 1953	Beyrouth Centre-Ville/Bord de Mer	1978
	Chadwick, John Charlton	Sutton, Surrey, UK, 1950	The West End of London: An Urban Design Study	

Thesis Date	Author Name	Birth Location, Year	Thesis Title	Cornell B.Arch
1980	Griest, Darrell Bruce	Springfield, OH, 1955	Utica Development Strategy	
	Griffin, David Elder	Montreal, Canada, 1953	Montreal: Urban Design Alternatives	1978
	Manfredi, Michael	Trieste, Italy, 1953	Urban Design Strategies: A Study for the Northern Tip of Manhattan	
1981	Albin, Enrique	Mexico City, Mexico, 1954	The Magical City: An Urban Dream for the City of Mexico	
	Askew, John Emerson	Paterson, NJ, 1954	An Urban Design Strategy for Troy, New York	
	Middleton, David Blakeslee	Cambridge, MA, 1956	Providence: Capital District Development Strategy	1978
	Nealy, Craig Burton	Boston, MA, 1956	The Urbanization of Burlington, Vermont	1979
	Nichols, Robert	Princeton, NJ, 1954	West Philadelphia Development	1979
	Ohnishi, Shin-Ichiro	Tokyo, Japan, 1954	A Set-Piece Street for Manhattan	1980
	Rodriguez, Juan Manuel Robayo	Bogota, Colombia, 1946	Commentaries on Manhattan	
	Smith, Jerri Kay	Manhattan, KS, 1949	The Cincinnatti Waterfront	
1982	Abrue-Garcia, Maria J.	Camaguey, Cuba, 1956	An Urban Design Proposal for Miami Beach	
	Diaz, Gladys Margarita	Matanzas, Cuba, 1956	Downtown Miami, Florida: The Urbanization of an American City	1981
	Echeverria, Cristina Garcia	Maracaibo, Venezuela, 1954	Caracas: Urban Renewal From 1950 to 1980	
	Fong, Steven Tseun-Yi	Seattle, WA, 1952	London: A Proposal for the Marylebone District	1978
	Garcia, Jorge Luis	Havana, Cuba, 1956	Governors Island: Architecture and Urban Design	1981
	Sennyey, Esteban L.	Caracas, Venezuela, 1956	Cumana: An Urban Design Exercise	
	Tynan, Derek Edward	Dublin, Ireland, 1954	Dublin: The Park and the City	
1983	Alaskewic, Richard	Staten Island, NY, 1950	Contextual Additions: A Design Proposal for the St. George Waterfront	
	Davis, Thomas Kirby	San Francisco, CA, 1953	Holyoke, Massachusetts: An Urban Design Study	1977
	Dick, Jon Alexander	Imlay, NV, 1956	The Oneiric Reconnection: The City and the Lake, Ithaca, New York	
	Frederick, Douglas Brent	Wiesbaden, Germany, 1956	A Proposal for the Urban Design Strategy on Metz, France	
	Giardina, Michael R.	Bronx, NY, 1956	An Urban Design Proposal for the Fort Point Channel District, Boston	
	Hariri, Mojgan	Aghajari, Iran, 1958	Reconstruction of Quincy, Massachusetts	1981
	Marani, Grant Furio	Melbourne, Australia, 1953	Melbourne: The Garden and the City	
	Metsky, Richard J.	Newark, NJ, 1957	Urban Design Study: Lower Manhattan West Side	1981
	Mitsch, Lawrence Stephen	Scotia, NY, 1956	The Development of Vienna's Stubenring, Parkring, and Karlsplatz Areas	
	Schickel, Thomas Mindzenty	Ithaca, NY, 1950	Restructuring Tricentennial Philadelphia	1981
	Schwartz, Kenneth Alan	Rochester, NY, 1957	The Gianicolo in Rome: Gardens and the City	1979
1984	Abadan, Mustafa Kemal	Ankara, Turkey, 1958	Urban Design Study Interventions in Izmir, Turkey	1982
	Bumiller, Georg Heinrich	Landau, W. Germany, 1957	Karlsruhe - Park City	
	Crabb, Cathleen Ann	Chicago, IL, 1956	A Park with Edges: The Reconstruction of the Roxbury Area of Boston, Massachusetts	
	Milford, Christopher A.	New Haven, CT, 1957	Cultural Contextualism	1983
1985	Barnes, Elliott Le Roi	Los Angeles, CA, 1960	The Crenshaw Business Center	1983
	Cheng, Henrietta Wai Kwan	Hong Kong, 1960	San Francisco: A Proposal for the Misson Bay Area	1983
	Cloud, Travis Caroline	Illinois, 1953	Boston Waterfront	1983
	Dias de Carvalho, Raul Antonio	Niteroi, Brazil, 1951	Urban Design Proposal for W. Berlin	
	Kass, Spencer Roger	Philadelphia, PA, 1955	Trenton, New Jersey: Garden State Capital Development Plan	
	Monge, Jose Maria	Santurce, Puerto Rico, 1956	San Juan, Puerto Rico	1983
	Trelles, Jorge Luis	Havana, Cuba, 1958	Baroque Urban Design in the Late 20th Century - La Habana & Recent Urban Design Projects	
	Trelles, Luis E.	Havana, Cuba, 1956	Baroque Urban Design in the Late 20th Century - Key West & Recent Urban Design Projects	
1986	Cederna, Ann Terese	Michigan, 1960	Urban Design Proposal for Florence, Italy (Area of Santa Croce)	
	Janusz, Frank P.	Buffalo, NY, 1955	A New Urban Order for the Misson Bay & South of Market Districts, City of San Francisco	
	Ouahes, Rachid	Algeria, 1955	Algiers - Beaux-Algers: A Design for a Historical Continuity	
	Pohlman, Richard	Elmira, NY, 1941	Ordering the City of Objects	
	Zissovici, John E.	Oradea, Romania, 1950	Savannah: A Historical Exploration, Transformation & Application for a New Town in Holland	1974
1987	De Salvo, John Francis	Chicago, IL, 1961	Chicago: Urban Design Proposal, Chicago Riverfront Development	
	Devlaminck, Marc J-P.	Roubaix, France, 1957	An Urban Design Strategy in Lille, France	
	Hinders, Kevin	Dayton, OH, 1960	The Mausoleum of Augustus and the Monte Celio, Rome	
	Hinchman, Mark	Dallas, TX, 1960	The Plan of Chicago: An Urban Design	
	Kelly, Brian Paul	Denville, NJ, 1957	Rome: Via dei Fori Imperiali	
	Lee, Kenny	New York, NY, 1962	Clerkenwell, London: A Study of Urban Spaces	1985
	McWhorter, James Carey	Pensacola, FL, 1959	New Orleans: The Lower Garden District, "The Promenade Ridge"	
	Mortensen, Paul Robert	Seattle, WA, 1959	Urban Transformations in Boston's Northwest End	
	O'Neil, Cheryl	Newton, MA, 1956	Largo Argentina	1980
	Schmitt, Frederick John	South Amboy, NJ, 1960	Urban Design Proposal for Newport, RI: Redevelopment of a New England Waterfront	1983
1988	Bell, Matthew	New York, NY, 1959	Rome: Quartiere de'Banchi	
	Klamon, C. Andrew	St. Louis, MO, 1960	The Normative Urban Grid: A Proposal for the Upper West Side, New York	
	Weintraub, Mark	New York, NY, 1961	Chicago: A Plan for the Central Area	1984
1989	Hord, Carter	Memphis, TN, 1963	Manhattan: Object-Fabric	
	Karpf, Bernhard M.	Stuttgart, Germany, 1956	Skyscrapers - An Urban Speculation	
	McMahon, Edward T.	Mount Vernon, NY, 1958	Dialectic Images: Boston South End Proposal	
	Mun, Lee Siew (Irene)	N/A	Chinese City Planning Principles and their Application to a Site in Beijing	
	Tan, Peter Bu-hin	Alor Star, Malaysia, 1962	Georgetown, Malaysia: A Critique and Development Strategy	1986
1990	Berdini, Paolo	Rome, Italy, 1951	Borgo Pussino	
	Botwin, Jeffrey	New York, NY, 1965	Seven Mile Institute of Marine Biology	1988
	Epley, Robert Frederick	Portland, OR, 1965	Ladies Mile: The Historic District in the City	
	Role, Richard Branton	N/A	Rome: An Urban Design Proposal for the Aventine Hill	
1991	Hofman, Thomas C.	South Bend, IN, 1959	Urban Design Strategies & Building Typology Studies - King's Cross, London, England	
	Lu, Wen-ying	Taipei, Taiwan, 1963	Residential Square as a Model for Contmeporary Urban Design	
	Muller, Stuart Arnold	Chicago, IL, 1961	Haifa: Proposals for the Redevelopment of the Old City	
	Protopappas, Antonios	Limmasol, Cyprus, 1964	The Indeterminant – The Determinate: Morphallaxis of Cerameicus, Athens	
	Tai, Chei-Wei	Taiwan, 1959	Composite Buildings: A Case Study Federal Triangle Washington, D.C.	
	Wilson, Stephen G.	New York, NY, 1964	London is Streets and Squares: An Urban Design Proposal for The London Wall	
1992	McDonald, Debi L.	Dayton OH, 1957	Boston's Central Artery: North Station to South Station; date completed	1980
	Wang, Chun-Hsiung	Taipei, Taiwan, 1963	An Urban Design Strategy for the Expansion of Sun-Shar, Taiwan	
1994	Butz, Pamela	Wilmington, DE, 1962	Boston MA: I-93 Central Artery Suppression	1985
	Goodill, Robert	Erie, PA, 1960	Three Urban Design Projects	
1995	Adams, Edgar George (Jr.)	Philadelphia, PA, 1956	Richmond and the James: An Urban Design Proposal	1980
	Cheng, Chung-Hsien	Hong Kong, 1962	Skyscraper and the City, A Proposal For Hunters Point	
1997	Gnat, Richard Raymond	Milwaukee, WI, 1962	Proposed Design for a Museum of Contemporary Art in Chicago	

This list includes students who are known to have either a) a thesis book in the Fine Arts Library at Cornell University; b) completed their thesis but not their degree; c) received a degree without submitting a bound thesis for the F.A.L., or d) completed their degree after Rowe retired in 1990. Compiled with the generous assistance of Librarian Martha Walker, Cornell students Aya Mears and Andrew Wang, and Lorainne Capogrossi of Cornell AAP Alumni Affairs. Any error or omission is solely that of the Author. DBM.

MUSIC
RESTAURANT
BOTANICAL CONSERVATORY
TEA GARDEN
PRIVATE GARDEN
F I F T H · A V E.

Collage City: Theory into Practice

Matthew Bell

Collage City by Colin Rowe and Fred Koetter has frequently been cited as a highly influential critique of the Modern movement, with a particular focus on presumptions underpinning theories of urban form and the city. Like other writings by Rowe, it has enjoyed a strong following in academic circles with perhaps a less robust following in the profession. But, viewing it as a traditional 'treatise', both theoretical and practical, raises a series of questions. Is it possible to examine how it has functioned as a guide to design and repair the damage to cities brought about by urban renewal and theories of Modern urbanism? Do the examples and strategies outlined in *Collage City* offer a way forward for designers to create urban buildings and articulate urban space? Has *Collage City* been influential in the making of the complex tapestry of public and private buildings that comprise the city? And if so, aside from projects illustrated in the Rowe and Koetter book, what contemporary designers might be practicing in the manner described who are able to provide examples of *Collage City* realized?

frontispiece:
Roof plan, Rockefeller Center, rendering by John D. Wenrich.

Architects and Teachers

Over the course of his career as a professor of architecture, mainly at Cornell University, Colin Rowe developed a cadre of students who have taught or followed careers in the profession, and sometimes both.[1] Through teaching and practice, many of them have studied the problems of modern urbanism at various scales from the individual building to the entire city context and have extended the ideas described in *Collage City* as built examples of the treatise. The same can be said for others who have studied the Rowe and Koetter critique and related the models found in that text to their professional work, ranging from museums and civic and school/campus buildings to mixed-use retail and commercial complexes. Broadly speaking, Contextualism as a way of approaching the design of the city has been disseminated by many, from those close to Rowe, to others in related disciplines such as the city planning and preservation and adaptive reuse fields.

What follows is a survey of some of the most significant ideas of *Collage City* with particular attention to the examples offered in the book's last chapter, "Excursus." By way of several urban-architectural examples below, Excursus provides a

1 Fred Koetter and Michael Dennis belong to the earlier generation of Rowe students and associates, as do Steven Peterson and Barbara Littenberg of Peterson Littenberg Architects. Aside from distinguished academic careers, Peterson and Littenberg have been winners of notable international urban design competitions, most recently as finalists in the competition to rebuild Ground Zero after the terrorist attacks of 9/11. Koetter maintained a robust practice, taught for many years at Harvard, and served as dean at Yale. Dennis was a longtime Cornell faculty member and has spent the later part of his career at MIT and in practice. Other former students from that period, such as Stuart Cohen, have combined a career in teaching with an interest in the typology of the American house. Cohen has used his base in Chicago to engage scholarly and professional interests in the American house. Later generations of Rowe's students have also embraced the architect/professor model. Judith DiMaio was in practice with Kohn Pedersen Fox Associates and served as dean at the New York Institute of Technology (NYIT). Michael Manfredi of Weiss/Manfredi was also on the faculty at NYIT and is now engaged in significant public sector, institutional, and higher education practice. Jorge and Luis Trelles practice in Miami, taught at Notre Dame and the University of Miami, and have established an academic practice together, mostly focused on residential commissions but clearly pursuing many of the themes present in *Collage City*. The list here is quite long and I mention the people above as examples of where former associates, collaborators, and students have migrated in their respective careers but it is incomplete. For a more elaborate genealogy of Rowe's associates and former students, see Caragonne, Alexander, *The Texas Rangers: Notes from an Architectural Underground,* MIT Press, Cambridge, MA, and London, 1995.

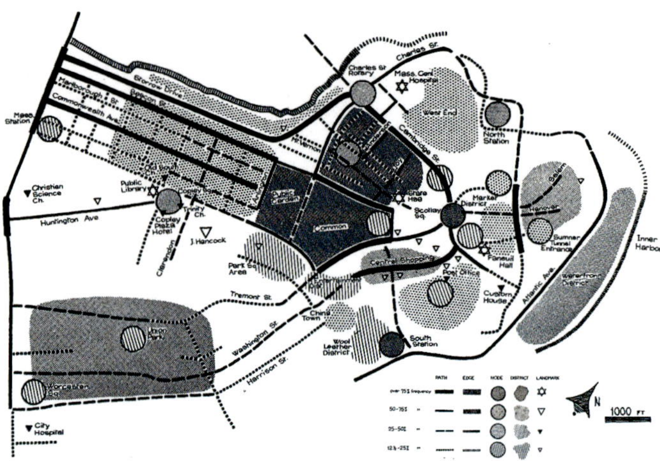

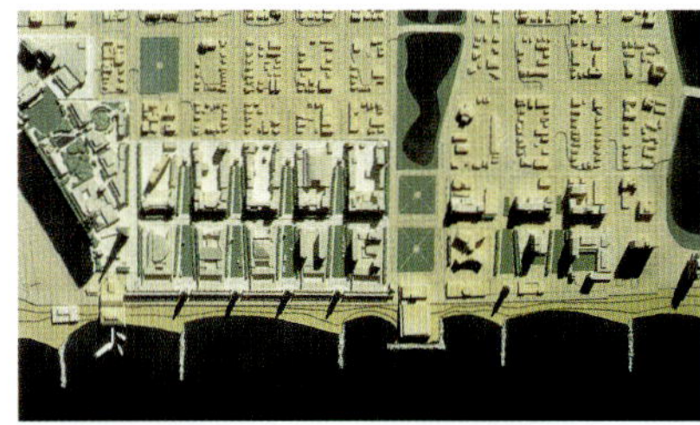

above left to right:
Fig. 1. Boston, figure/ground plan, ca. 1950.

Fig. 2. Boston, diagram from *Image of the City* by Kevin Lynch, 1960.

below top to bottom:
Fig. 3. Asbury Park, NJ, proposal by Koetter Kim.

Fig. 4. Seaside, FL, Duany Plater-Zyberk. The drawing is a hybrid of both figure/ground and landscape plan techniques.

taxonomy of sorts, which are intended as models useful in creating the 'good city'. These range from iconic buildings symbolic of either the past or possible future, to public places such as gardens and streets. They are introduced with the statement, "We append an abridged list of stimulants, a-temporal and necessarily transcultural as possible *objets trouves* in the urbanistic collage". My focus here is to examine the Excursus chapter in *Collage City* as an architectural treatise. I look at how the ideas it illustrates have been both broadly adopted in professional architecture and planning practice, and at how projects by Rowe's former students, as well as other colleagues and architects, illustrate the best practice approaches outlined in *Collage City*.

The Figure/Ground

Perhaps the most wide-reaching impact of *Collage City* and the Cornell School is the entry into common urban design usage of the figure/ground drawing as a tool to read, analyze, and manipulate city form. Evolved from sources such as the tourist maps found in the *Baedeker* guide books of the late 19th and early 20th centuries, the figure/ground assumes that one significant and fundamental way to understand city form is through the lens of *gestalt* psychology, always relating the part to the context of the whole (Fig. 1). The technique allows the designer to immediately grasp, in a very general sense, any design intention's impact on the city's overall form and fabric.[2]

The figure/ground technique permitted Rowe and his students to see the city as more than generalized schemas of nodes, landmarks, paths, edges, and districts, *à la* Kevin Lynch (Fig. 2) but instead as formal geometric compositions with identifiable morphologies that could be analyzed, manipulated, and thereby understood. As a critique of Modernism, the figure/ground revealed the paucity of well-defined urban space in that conceptual framework and the overall fixation of Modernist architecture's proposals—both built and unbuilt—as objects rather than as definers of space.

Widely adopted as a design tool, the figure/ground technique has helped to reveal city form and to provide a context for interventions from the scale of the

2 A common critique levelled at the Cornell approach is that the figure/ground does not explain all there is to know about any selected site or city context. To that Rowe once replied, "Well, no one ever said that it did, but it's not such a bad place to start".

Fig. 5. Texas A&M University, Master Plan, Michael Dennis & Associates with Barnes, Gromatzky, Kosarek. Like the Seaside drawing, the plan incorporates landscape elements as equal to buildings in defining spaces.

individual building to large plans of cities. For municipal city planning offices working with neighborhood groups, the figure/ground has become a common technique for showing the existing urban form as a way to demonstrate a concern for maintaining, infilling, and extending the character of their neighborhoods. In this case, the figure/ground assists those responsible for planning cities and towns in measuring the merits of development proposals and navigating the challenges of growth and change.[3]

Several important interpretative techniques emerged from the development of the figure/ground as a representational tool. First, the idea that larger 'readings' or fields can constitute a predominant geometry or orientation of a city's plan. Interventions may support the predominant reading of the field, such as the Koetter Kim project for the waterfront at Asbury Park , NJ (Fig. 3), or may strengthen or even introduce the geometry or orientation of another field. The Cornell figure/ground technique has also been highly influential in New Urbanist projects such as Seaside (Fig. 4) and can become elaborated and expanded as a technique for the rendition of city form.[4]

Second, the figure/ground may be used to identify patterns in the urban fabric, to identify and sort typologies, and to distinguish public buildings like schools and other civic institutions. Drawn accurately, a careful examination can reveal overall ordering relationships, such as the orientation of the various parts of a city's plan, inherent topographic characteristics, or the clustering of similar building types.

Third, as a technique, the figure/ground has also evolved over time, from the initial abstract, black-and-white renditions of the 1960s that excluded almost everything other than buildings, to more advanced descriptive possibilities that include landscape and distinctions between existing and proposed buildings. For example, the campus master plan for Texas A&M by Michael Dennis and Jeffrey Clark & Associates (Fig. 5) includes subtle distinctions in the drawing between

3 The widespread use of the figure/ground as a principal technique to understand city form by the planning profession is a particular area of impact for *Collage City*. A principal critique put forward by Rowe and Koetter was focused on the scientific or positivistic approach to city planning as practiced in the 1960s, with the city planner interpreting data to arrive at solutions. Form was the result of the scientific process, not something that *a priori* had intrinsic value. The situation of today seems reversed with good city form as a goal of many departments of city planning.

4 A minor 'cottage industry' has developed with scholars producing analytical studies and collections of such drawings both prior to Rowe and his followers and after. One early text that deploys such analytical techniques is Morini, Mario, *Atlante di storia dell'urbanistica,* Hoepli, Milano, 1963. It uses both figure/ground representations of historical cities and graphic conventions derived from Camillo Sitte. A later study using strictly the figure/ground technique is Graves, Charles P., Jr., *The Geneology of Cities* Kent State University Press, Kent, OH, 2009, by a former student of Rowe, including an impressive comparative compendium of figure/ground drawings of many cities.

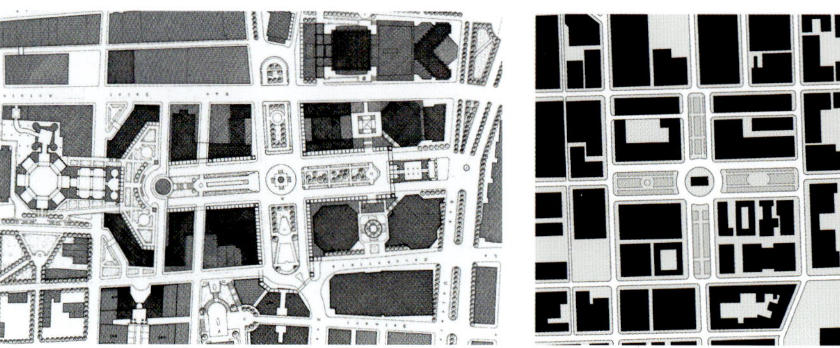

left to right:
Fig. 6. Piazza Ducale, Vigevano, Italy.

Fig. 7. Metro Tech, Brooklyn, NY, is an example of a new public space providing focus and generating value for redevelopment.

Fig. 8. Competition Cité International, Montreal, by Peterson Littenberg 'stabilizes' a portion of the downtown providing for a rich set of spatial relationships.

Fig. 9. Mt. Vernon Place, Baltimore, MD, is a unique cruciform shape conceived to memorialize the first president and generate real estate value.

existing and proposed buildings, articulating indications of the original campus, while indicating how the center of the campus is in-filled with new buildings of many different types and configurations.

Dennis's work in Texas also reveals how the setting, in this case the American Southwest, has transformed and advanced the technique itself. By combining the basic figure/ground technique with the addition and elaboration of color and landscape, so essential for an American context, the technique distinguishes several different levels of information with the inclusion of landscape elements that reinforce the major design intentions of the plan.[5] Building *and* landscape typologies are easily understood, including some that are proposed to complete fragmentary parts of the adjacent college town.

Stabilizers

The urban 'stabilizer' in *Collage City* takes the form of a clear, simple, and large figure, either a space or a large building or both, that provides order to the urban fabric, or is introduced as an identifiable space or object within an enclave or neighborhood. Typically, such an element possesses a coherent and simple geometry, and is a dominant space or building defining an urban district. Its presence asserts control over a larger field of urban fabric. Examples from *Collage City*

5 Rowe and his students tended to gravitate toward European cities for analytical lessons in complex readings of the figure/ground, although American cities with complex grid collisions and intersections were often the vehicle for design investigations.

Fig. 10. Silver Spring Civic Building and Veterans Plaza, Silver Spring, MD, by Machado and Silvetti provides a stable locus for an emerging part of the downtown.

include the Place des Vosges in the Marais quarter in Paris, France, Plaza Mayor in Vittoria, Spain, and Piazza Ducale in Vigevano, Italy (Fig. 6).[6]

Other examples not cited by Rowe and Koetter might include any English-style residential square such as those found in London (Grosvenor Square), Edinburgh (Charlotte Square), Boston (Louisburg Square), or Philadelphia (Rittenhouse Square) or similarly assertive buildings like the Palazzo Farnese in Rome, the Great Mosque at Cordoba, Spain, or a set of buildings such as the White Star, Cunard, and Royal Liver Buildings on the waterfront at Liverpool. Rockefeller Center in New York (*frontispiece*), with its mini-grid of streets, provides both the stable space (the plaza) and the stable object (the RCA Tower) in a unique and sophisticated interplay of figure and field, object and space.

In the American context, the Midwestern American courthouse and courthouse town, a favorite of Rowe's from his days teaching in Texas, is a familiar stabilizer in county courthouse towns across the U.S. from Ohio to the Pacific Ocean.[7] Typically the county courthouse sits in an open square that is simply an unbuilt portion of a continuously gridded city plan. Central to the square, it sits equidistant from all sides of the square with an assertive skyline above a centralized building plan. The interplay between grid and object, skyline and town, gives form and meaning to both the town fabric and the civic building. The fabric exists because of the courthouse and its definition in turn depends on the sides of the square in what is otherwise an undifferentiated grid.

The Metro Tech Commons by Perkins Eastman (Fig. 7) uses just such a strategy to regularize the surrounding fabric by making the central urban space the dominant form in the neighborhood. Thus stabilized, the role of other buildings and their relationship to the neighborhood are more easily understood. Likewise, the competition entry for the Cité Internationale in Montreal by Peterson Littenberg Architects (Fig. 8) inserts a figural space or stabilizer into the surrounding fabric, in this case a transformed version of Mount Vernon Place in Baltimore (Fig. 9). The remaining fragments of the neighborhood are unified and brought into a coherent whole via the presence of the stabilizer.

6 Michelangelo's design for St. Peter's and his proposed piazza, long a favorite of Rowe's, is an object version of a stabilizer within a square or rectangular plaza, radically different from later Baroque versions.

7 Rowe's fascination with the Midwestern courthouse town is chronicled in this essay about Lockhart, Texas. Rowe, Colin; Hejduk, John, "Lockhart, Texas", *Architectural Record* 121 (3), Mar 1957: 201-06.

A more recent example of a stabilizer might be the Civic Building and plaza in Silver Spring, Maryland, by Machado and Silvetti (urban design plan by RTKL), which anchors a multi-block redevelopment project and sets the basic framework for the balance of the mixed-use plan by defining an associated public space, and by extending its geometry to the adjacent canopy covering part of the plaza (Fig. 10).

Potentially Interminable Set Pieces

In contrast to the stabilizer, the potentially interminable set piece is a repetitive element that extends its presence by means of a repetitive bay or loggia, a backdrop, rarely deforming to accommodate incidental differences in context and supporting a setting. *Collage City's* examples include the Stoa of Attalos, Athens; the Palazzo Chiericati, Vicenza; Chester Terrace, London; the Louvre and Tuileries, Paris; and, the Procuratie Vecchie, Venice, any of which could be extended farther into the city fabric. As the name suggests, the potentially interminable set piece is seen as a backdrop or stage set, not too assertive by itself, but important as a datum or setting for a nearby figural building that likely hosts a celebrated civic or public function. And, although not exclusively so, the set piece is most often comprised primarily of a residential program, whether it is a large palace or groupings of blocks of apartments or flats.

Examples not mentioned by Rowe and Koetter might include Vasari's Loggia in Arezzo, Italy (Fig. 11), the Weissenhof Housing, and the Kiefhoek Housing Estate by J. J. P. Oud. Many of Alvar Aalto's library and civic center projects are composed of repetitive set piece elements paired with more figural stabilizer elements, typically the main reading room or assembly spaces. Although not typically located in urban contexts such an arrangement seems easily adaptable to denser settings.[8]

The Christian Science Center in Boston by I. M. Pei & Associates (Fig. 12) from the 1970s uses an urbanized version of Le Corbusier's monumental language at Chandigarh for the Colonnade Building, providing a repetitive set piece as backdrop for the historic 1894 Mother Church. Conversely, Kohn Pederson Fox's facade for the ABC News headquarters on the Upper West Side in New York uses surface to establish a repetitive bay in a fabric of small facade increments and articulates the wall with a sense of extreme flatness contrasted with literal and implied depth.

Two projects by Dan Solomon, the David Brower Center, Oxford Plaza in Berkeley, and 101 San Fernando in San Jose (Fig. 13), set distinct and simple patterns of repetitive facades on major streets albeit via distinctly different programs. The 101 San Fernando example is a residential infill project with layers of residential courtyards covering almost the entire city block with adjustments in the scale of street facades based on the external street hierarchy. The Brower Center occupies an important neighborhood corner, and is, in *Collage City* parlance, a stabilizer supported by a repetitive band of affordable housing, with Oxford Plaza using the housing block as a set piece to frame the academic building. Each project is large enough to be more than simply the infill of a few lots but rather, in terms of overall size and coordination of repetitive vertical

Fig. 11. Loggia, Arezzo, Italy, by Georgio Vasari is a classic example of the "potentially interminable set piece", the repetitive facade extends past the main square.

Fig. 12. Christian Science Complex, Boston, MA by IM Pei and Associates.

Fig. 13. 101 San Fernando Housing, San Jose, CA by Daniel Solomon and Associates, a repetitive facade-housing module.

8 *Maison redents* by Le Corbusier, clearly inspired by various phases of the Louvre, can also be understood, potentially, as set-pieces, although in Corbu's usage, they typically do not attempt to define discreet streets and pubic space, an obvious disadvantage in making urban fabric.

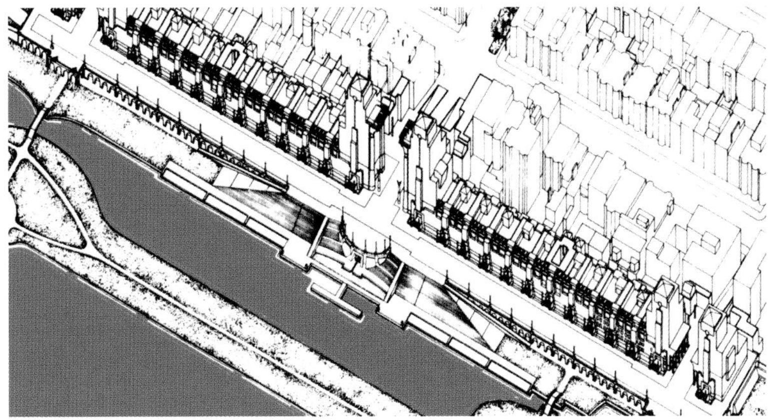

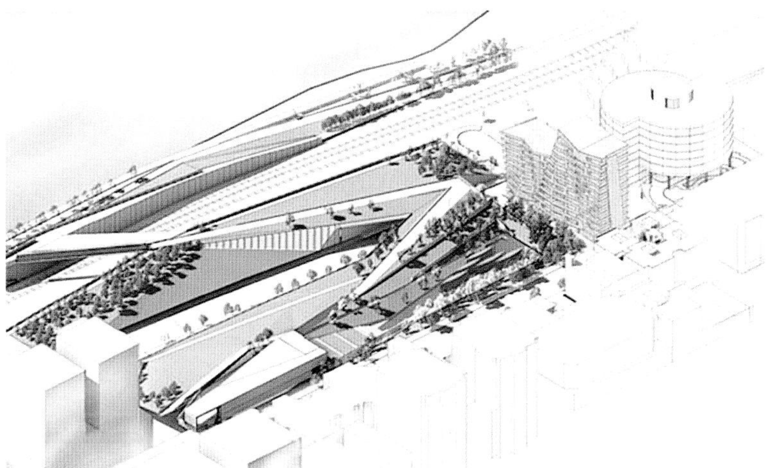

elements such as towers, balconies, etc., becomes a set piece for each neighborhood, large enough and repetitive enough to become a possible pattern to influence future redevelopment.

left to right:
Fig. 14. Storrow Terrace project, Boston, MA, by Koetter Kim, proposes a new front to the Charles River as both a potentially interminable set piece and "splendid public terrace".

Fig. 15. Brooklyn Heights Promenade, NY, as a "splendid public terrace".

Fig. 16. Art Museum Olympic Sculpture Park, Seattle, WA, by Weiss Manfredi; the public terrace overcomes a waterfront highway and railway line..

Fig. 17. Algiers Waterfront, cited in *Collage City*, ramps and terraces connect the main level of the city to the port. .

Splendid Public Terraces

Collage City identifies the public terrace or belvedere as an important element in the making and understanding of the city. In contrast to the free-flowing, shapeless space of the Modernist city, the public terrace provides a defined place for the city and landscape to be revealed and understood. Implicit is the idea that such prospects enable a sense of the totality of the urban scene, presenting the city as a work of art by obscuring local detail and incident via the distance and height of the terrace viewing point. Rowe and Koetter cite terraces specifically for viewing, such as the Pincio in Rome or Piazzale Michelangelo in Florence, as well as the monumental terraces and working waterfront examples in Algiers (Fig. 17) and the now-demolished Adelphi Terrace in London.

9 Prior to establishing his own firm with Marion Weiss, Michael Manfredi worked for several firms with a distinct focus on urban design such as Cooper Eckstut in New York.

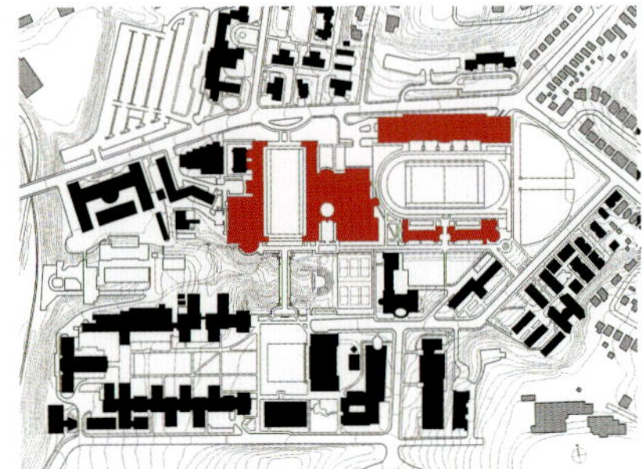

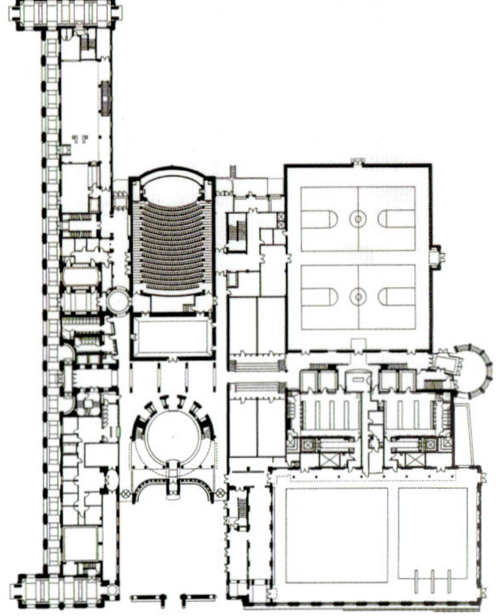

top to bottom:
Fig. 18. Campus plan, Carnegie-Mellon University, Pittsburgh, PA, by Dennis and Clark, uses a "composite building" strategy cited in *Collage City.*

Fig. 19. Building plan, University Center.

Fig. 20. Colonnade facing entry quadrangle, University Center.

inset:
Fig. 21. Entry court, University Center.

Other examples of the belvedere type include the Brooklyn Heights Promenade in New York offering outstanding views of Manhattan across the East River (Fig. 15), or in Barcelona, the Parc Guell by Antonio Gaudi. Washington, D.C., possesses several historic overlooks, such as Meridian Hill Park and the West Front of the U.S. Capitol facing the National Mall. The Storrow Terrace project in Boston (Fig. 14) is an example of splendid public terrace in the work of Koetter Kim.

The firm of Weiss Manfredi pursues a decidedly Modern adaptation of the public terrace idea at the Seattle Art Museum Olympic Sculpture Park (Fig. 16).[9] Envisioned as a new model for an urban sculpture park on an industrial site at the water's edge, the park-terrace navigates a challenging slope that separates two developing portions of the city: an up-slope urban neighborhood and a waterfront experiencing ongoing revitalization. The design establishes a continuous landscape terrace for art that capitalizes on views of the Seattle skyline and Puget Sound, while providing an urban connection for two areas of the city that had been previously separated.

The recently opened District Wharf (Fig. 25, 26), by Stan Eckstut and Hilary Bertsch of Perkins Eastman, at the old Southwest Waterfront in Washington, D.C., is a version of the industrial terrace or waterfront. Like Algiers, it is replete with a rich collection of entertainment, residential, commercial, and maritime uses recalling the traditional, if somewhat invented, history of the place.[10] Like many of the *Collage City* examples, the Wharf focuses primarily on the delineation and definition of public space with a variety of massing and facade approaches above the first few floors. Like Algiers, the Wharf deploys multiple levels of access along a waterfront promenade that supports pedestrian activity, maritime functions, and vehicular access.

Ambiguous and Composite Buildings and the Hôtel Particulier

In *Collage City* Rowe and Koetter identify the Parisian *hôtel particulier* as an ideal model to adapt to complex city fabric with its ability to conform to irregular sites and yet retain a clear notion of *parti* and distribution of program and circulation. For example, the Parisian Hôtel de Beauvais, with its stable figural center and malleable edges, allows adjustment to the complex geometry of its embedded urban site. Similarly, the 'ambiguous and composite building' also

10 Eckstut of Perkins Eastman has long hired former Rowe students in his professional endeavors and with Alex Cooper at Cooper Eckstut, designed one of the first post-war projects in the U.S. to extend the configuration and scale of the adjacent urban fabric at Battery Park City in Lower Manhattan.

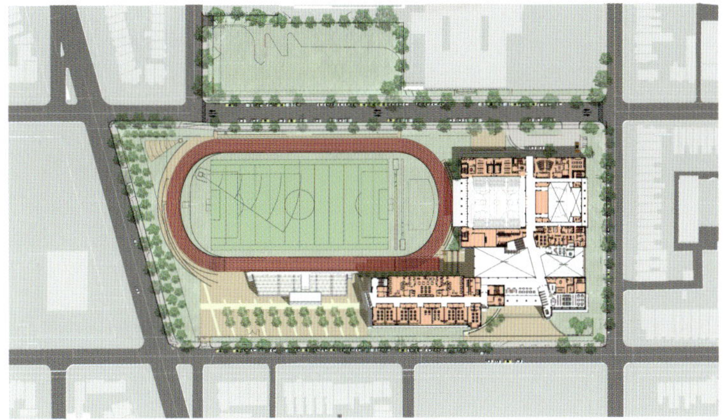

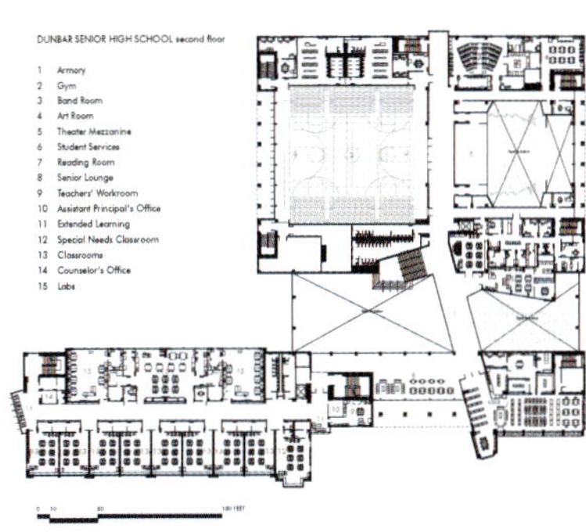

includes a complex internal program but is a composite of several distinct formal building types. Standing free of other buildings, its exterior edges adapt to different external urban conditions. These are contrasted by Rowe and Koetter with the Modernist figural object represented by Le Corbusier's Villa Savoye, a form that can only be seen as distinct and set apart.

The professional work of Dennis and Clark was developed largely in the realm of campus planning and university buildings. Dennis uses the combination of these two models, the *hôtel particulier* and the ambiguous and composite building. Taking lessons gleaned from his studies of the French *hôtel,* with its rich attendant circulations and hierarchies, Dennis is able to resolve the complex programmatic requirements that have evolved to serve higher education. Combined with the ambiguous and composite building, Dennis is enabled to respond to opportunities offered by the external formal order of the American campus—quadrangles, academic lawns, walks, and such.

The Dennis and Clark competition winning scheme for Carnegie Mellon University (Fig. 18) uses a rich interplay of both of these models. The University Center is a species of the ambiguous and composite building like the Hofburg in Vienna and the Residenze in Munich cited in *Collage City.* The Center building plan (Fig. 19) is composed of long, thin building elements (classrooms and labs) that mask the larger interior volumes. Each facade has a distinct role. The west facade (Fig. 20) provides a loggia along the entrance quadrangle to the campus. The north facade marks the campus entry. On the east facade the large gymnasium volume terminates the axis of the adjacent sports field, also treated as a courtyard. The south facade edges a primary campus walkway further defined by two dormitory buildings. Along this face is the primary entrance. It is marked by a small courtyard (Fig. 21) similar to the *cour d'honneur* that serves the *hôtel particulier*. The *cour d'honneur* not only addresses a major campus walkway but is intended to engage a new future quadrangle to the south. Like the composite buildings cited in *Collage City,* the Center's different exterior surfaces define each space and clarify its campus role.

Likewise, the recent rebuilding of Dunbar High School (Fig. 22–24), in Washington, D.C., by Perkins Eastman with Moody Nolan Architects, uses a composite building strategy to organize typologically different building/program

above left to righ:
Fig. 22. Campus plan, Dunbar High School, Washington, D.C., by Perkins Eastman and Moody Nolan Architects uses a "composite building" strategy.

Fig. 23. Entry facade, Dunbar High School.

below:
Fig. 24. Building plan, Dunbar High School.

Fig. 25. District Wharf, Washington, D.C., By Perkins Eastman.

Fig. 26. Master plan, District Wharf.

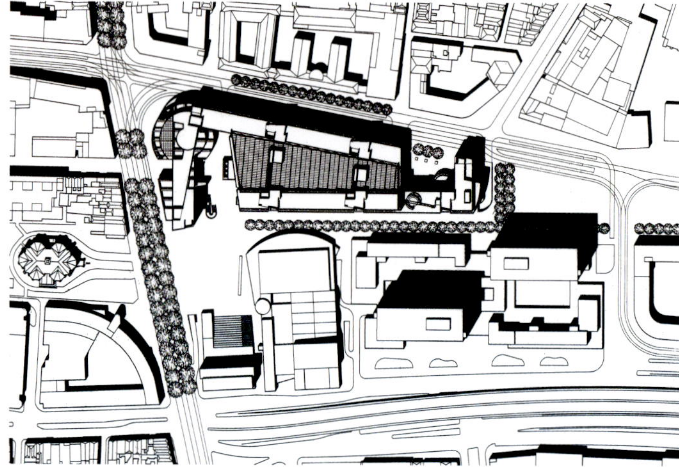

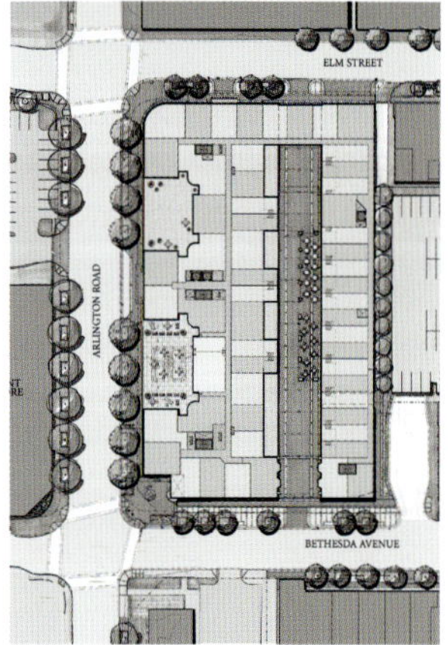

above:
Fig. 27. City Hall and Central Library at the Hague, Netherlands, by Richard Meier and Partners uses a composite building strategy.

Fig. 28. Site plan, City Hall, and Central Library at the Hague.

below:
Fig. 29. Pedestrian street, Bethesda Row, Bethesda, MD, by Torti Gallas and Partners.

Fig. 30. Site plan, Bethesda Row.

assemblages (a long classroom wing, a gym/pool complex and a library) around an enclosed, linear courtyard and exterior forecourt, while the building's exterior is adjusted to address diverse urban perimeter conditions, such as an existing park. Like the complex composite building, facade elements enjoy discrete local autonomy and organization, and are specific to the urban space onto which each of them faces.

The Hague City Hall and Central Library, by Richard Meier and Partners Architects (Fig. 27, 28), neatly deploys a composite building strategy with a more figural city hall element at the head of the block facing the plaza while the rest of the program is woven into the block via long wings and courtyards. Meier's project acknowledges two urban spaces, or *piazze,* one across from the Nieuwe Kerk and the other providing a receiving space at the end of an important downtown street, Fluwelen Burgwal. Although stylistically distinct, the building oscillates between figure and field, wall and object, and defines important urban spaces (Fig. 25).[11]

Torti Gallas + Partners, a New Urbanist architecture firm, uses thin residential building 'liners' and courtyards, à la the Hofburg in Vienna, to develop a composite building at Bethesda Row (Fig. 29, 30). It defines a small street or plaza spanning between two main streets and, like the Hofburg, poses a distinctly different character along each street frontage.[12] While located in a relatively straightforward urban grid, the sophistication of the approach completes the end of the block and responds differently between edge and center. The project also compares to the Uffizi in Florence, with its two built liners that define an urban space and connect one part of the city to another.

Memorable Streets, The Garden

In *Collage City,* the garden is introduced as an essential aspect of urban theory and practice in several contexts. First it is presented as a model for city form, both as structure (*allées* becoming networks of city streets and blocks, etc.) and in its more literal presence in the form of memorable public parks and places. Second, examples such as Hadrian's Villa are presented as precedents for the nesting and linking of adjacent ideal figures into complex formal ensembles

11 Bernhard Karpf, one of the Meier partners, was a Rowe student in the urban design studio and leads many of the firm's large-scale efforts.

including diverse forms of city fabric.

In a broader sense the strategy of using the garden as a model for urban form is perhaps most apparent in many New Urbanist proposals, from the radiating Baroque axes of the early plan for Seaside to the Olmsted-inspired redevelopment plan for the former site of Stapleton Airport, a brownfield development outside Denver, Colorado.

The winning competition entry for the Cité Internationale proposal in Montreal, by Peterson and Littenberg, relies heavily upon typologies of the Baroque garden of extended axes and formal points of resolution to collect and order the leftover fragments of an existing Montreal neighborhood (Fig. 8). The proposal brings a resolute hierarchy to a collection of urban fragments composed of vastly different building types and also influenced by a street infrastructure based upon suburban highway design. As a design process strategy, the deployment of the garden, absent a specific program, allows the designer to initially ignore the constraints of street design and program and to reveal linkages and sequences that are latent but not immediately apparent.

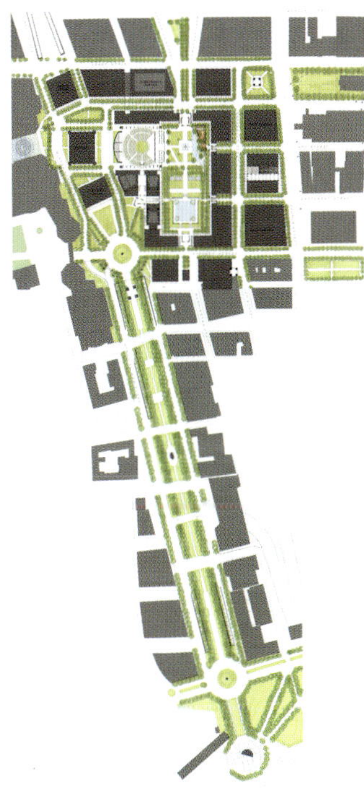

Fig. 31. Proposal for Ground Zero, Lower Manhattan, NY, by Peterson Littenberg; view down West Street towards the Statue of Liberty

Fig. 32. Proposed Master plan Lower Manhattan by Peterson Littenberg linking Ground Zero to Battery Park.

While not selected as the winning entry, the Peterson and Littenberg proposal for the rebuilding of New York's Ground Zero is a model example of the 'Memorable street and Garden' ideas (Fig. 31, 32). It proposes a walled urban compound based on the Palais Royale in Paris, as both public place and habitable wall, creating a strong sense of definition and enclosure for the sacred precinct of Ground Zero. The proposal uses nesting forms and typologies all connected via an urban garden linking lower Manhattan, Battery Park City, and the Ground Zero. Rendered like an *allée* of Baroque gardens linking nodal points, the formal strategy provides clear direction for organizing the city blocks and streets that surround the site and engages other important urban spaces with the former World Trade Center location. The transformed Parisian garden scheme establishes the perimeter of the new civic plaza while locating important connections to the adjacent street grid and other nearby important spaces by connecting them with memorable streets.

In a more general sense, the resurgence of the traditional street as an important element of city form is owed in part to the critique of Modern urbanism outlined in *Collage City*. Rowe and Koetter's examples of Fifth Avenue in New York, Princes Street in Edinburgh, and the Strada Nuova in Genoa, among others, have become an active and essential part of New Urbanist theory, supplemented by current advancements in transportation theory in areas such as mobility, sustainable streets, and "complete," multi-modal streets. The dissolution of the street, advocated by Le Corbusier among others, now seems to have been widely rejected in favor of the simple, well-defined street, hopefully one that is occasionally memorable.[13]

Nostalgia-producing Instruments

Rowe and Koetter introduce one of the more intriguing aspects of *Collage City* in the "Excursus" saying, "Finally, a quantity of *nostalgia producing instruments* which may be 'scientific' and of the future, 'romantic' and of the past, or which in different ways, may be simply elegant vernacular or Pop". They contend that

12 Torti Gallas and Partners, led by John Torti, is perhaps one of the most ardent synthesizers of New Urbanism and Contextualism, largely via its deep portfolio of projects of housing and mixed-use projects. O'Neill, Cheryl; Torti, John; Gallas, Thomas, *Torti Gallas + Partners Architects of Community*, Vendome, New York, 2017.

Fig. 33. Carré d'Art, Nimes, France, by Foster + Partners with the Roman Maison Carrée in the foreground.

Fig. 34. Harold Washington Library in Chicago, IL, by HBRA Architects.

the city requires imageable nostalgia in the form of important places and artifacts that memorialize the past and represent aspirations for the future. Perhaps operating as an exhibition of the author's erudition and eclectic interests, the list includes main streets, fortifications, rocket launch pads, and mysterious garden grottos (Bomarzo), all suggested as possible examples and models for consideration. One could perhaps add Terragni's unbuilt *Danteum*, which appears elsewhere in *Collage City*, to the list, as well as other designs produced under the influence of Italian architecture of the 1930s, as these often-combined images that simultaneously suggested nostalgia for both the past and future.[14]

In *Collage City* the idea of nostalgia is also produced to challenge the abstract aesthetics and functionalist rationale of the Modern movement, and the politics of utopia. Within the conceptual temporal frame suggested by *Collage City*, it is probably fair to say that some architects, due to their stylistic interests, produce work that speaks consistently to a nostalgia for the past, while others embrace nostalgia for the future, but rarely do architects do both. One thinks of the value that the traditional small town main street has for the Congress for the New Urbanism, along with the current generation of Classical architects—Robert Stern, Allan Greenberg and others—who base their practices on traditional architecture. Buildings like Hammond Beeby Babka's Harold Washington Library in Chicago (Fig. 34) embrace the past, at least in style and character, even

13 Anderson, Stanford ed., *On Streets,* MIT Press, Cambridge, MA, 1980, a collection of essays edited by Stanford Anderson, was published about the same time as *Collage City* and can be seen also as an early critique of Modern urban theory. It contains essays by several of the first generation of Rowe students such as Thomas Schumacher and William Ellis.

14 One of the myths of Modern architecture, surely, is that the new architecture does not rely on historical myth. Rowe addresses this in Rowe, Colin, *The Architecture of Good Intentions: Towards a Possible Retrospect,* Academy Editions, London, 1994. Even an architect like Terragni, who has been the subject of studies claiming his 'system' to be self referential, pursued a strong iconographic program in some projects, particularly the Danteum.

though the program is thoroughly contemporary.

Conversely, with buildings such as the Pompidou Center, Lloyds of London, and the Carré d'Art in Nimes (Fig. 33), architects Norman Foster and Richard Rodgers embrace a stylistic high-tech 'futuristic' imagery, and are examples of a nostalgia for "the 'scientific' and of the future...".[15]

The recent National Museum of African American History and Culture on the National Mall, designed by a consortium led by David Adjaye, Phil Freelon, and Max Bond, may also be a nostalgia-producing instrument via a massing based on an African woman's traditional hat (Fig. 35).

Cuban-born Miami architects, Jorge and Luis Trelles, of Trelles Cabarrocas Architects, students of Rowe in the 1980s, now practice in Miami, Florida, and have dedicated their careers to an idea or mythology (or nostalgia) of Florida. As first-generation Americans of Cuban descent, the firm's residential and commercial work interprets Florida as an exotic native Seminole culture, or as an original part of the Caribbean, creating a nostalgic iconography for an indigenous or Cuban culture long established elsewhere. The Casa Touret (Fig. 32), built on a site overlooking Biscayne Bay with a grand loggia, or porch, evokes the great houses of Havana, yet reveals a plan with a decidedly Modern sensibility. A competition entry by the same firm for a new bridge into Miami incorporates native

inset top down:
Fig. 35. The National Museum of African American History in Washington, D.C., by Freelon Adjaye Bond/SmithGroup.

Fig. 36. Casa Touret, Miami, FL, by Trelles Cabarrocas Architects.

right:
Fig. 37. Brickel Bridge competition entry, Miami, FL, by Trelles Cabarrocas Architects.

15 Rowe, Colin; Koetter, Fred, *Collage City*, MIT Press, Cambridge, MA, London, 1978: 172.

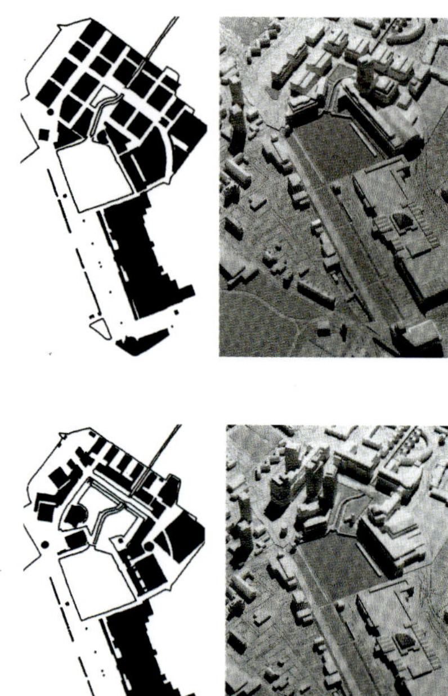

Fig. 38. *Atlantis* by Léon Krier, painting by Carl Laubin.

Fig. 39. London Docks project, various schemes by Koetter Kim.

Seminole imagery (Fig. 37). Like the Classical Munich of Leo von Klenze that is invoked by Rowe and Koetter, the Trelles Cabarrocas embraces the iconography of another time and place to make an association of culture and value through architectural form, albeit in a place where those associations strongly resonate.

Rowe and Koetter conclude the "Excursus" section with a "Commentary", illustrated with a series of paintings with invented architectural backgrounds ranging from Canaletto's invented views of the Grand Canal with Palladian buildings to Poussin's mythological and biblical scenes in pastoral settings. These views or *capricci* are fantasies conscripting objects from one place and time to another, intended to show, as a possibility, the "benevolent metropolis of loosely organized sympathies and enthusiasms" as opposed to an all-encompassing utopian city of a singular vision. Key to such a view (in *Collage City* illustrated by examples shown in the paintings of Canaletto and Marlow) is the cheek-by-jowl presence of the highly recognizable St. Paul's of London or the Palazzo Chiericati, Palladio's Basilica and his unbuilt version of the Rialto Bridge appearing all together in Venice, in a new and altered (ideally improved?) context. The unfamiliar, brought to the scene from elsewhere, and the equally familiar context enter into a new dialogue, one in which each exists as a critique of the other, resulting in yet a new, third creation. Perhaps at the city scale, a similar argument might be made about Peter the Great's converting a seaside swamp into a world-class modern city, St. Petersburg, based on his interpretation of Amsterdam, his experiences there having been reportedly transformative. Léon Krier's imaginary city of Atlantis (Fig. 38), a *tour de force* of Krier's architecture-making talents, uses a similar combination of diverse buildings presented in a perspective view and assembled to suggest a dramatic landscape and the provision of loosely defined

16 Credit is also due Carl Laubin, the illustrator of Krier's fantastical visions and a graduate of Cornell's undergraduate architecture program during the time of Rowe's tenure there.

public places.[16]

Bricolage and Collage as Urban Strategy

Another urban design strategy discussed in *Collage City* derives from the theories of Claude Lévi-Strauss. The *bricoleur* adapts the ad hoc nature of existing urban form by piecing together fragments using a limited palette of tools and making a new whole from disparate parts. For Rowe and Koetter, such a strategy can produce solutions that are both contemporary *and* adaptable to contingencies and complexities of Modernist urban settings. Fred Koetter and Susie Kim's studies for Boston (Chinatown, the Back Bay, and Storrow Terrace) (Fig. 14 and 40) were largely based on such approaches and eventually led to large-scale commissions in London during the real estate boom there in the 1980s and 1990s. In a series of built and unbuilt projects, Koetter Kim's work reorders the underlying and often fragmentary pieces of the urban landscape via the deployment of a precedent transformed to address the specifics of the site.

Fig. 40. Chinatown project, Boston, MA, by Koetter Kim.

Fig. 41. Miller Park, Chattanooga, TN, by Koetter Kim.

Projects for the unbuilt Surrey Quays, East London (Fig. 39) district of London propose transforming the fragments of that area into plazas and interior sequences to make completed urban blocks. New and developing parts of the city, such as old docks and waterfronts, become the locus for the complex collision or resolution of city grids and the concurrent nesting of ideal fragments (see Hadrian's Villa) often of contrasting building typologies or program. Interestingly, Koetter Kim's collage strategies often place high-rise buildings at important points or nodes to terminate axes or assert control over a field of lower-rise buildings and the fragmentary parts of the existing field of docks and waterways.

As the name implies, Collage City as a theory relies upon the acceptance and inclusion, via collage, of given conditions and using what is there in the context as the basis to make something new. Koetter Kim's Miller Park Plaza project and development in Chattanooga, Tennessee, located at the collision of two existing landscape/city grids, establishes a node through the marking of that location with a city square for activities (both stabilizers) (Fig. 41) and a pavilion for public activities. What was a mundane, yet typically American, collision of grids becomes elevated into a noteworthy place, with the shape of the square a reflection of that collision. Thus, a condition inherent to the American urban landscape is amplified and enhanced, providing a setting for the theater of present and future public life, affirming the city's history by celebrating that place in the city where its two most significant urban grids collide.

A more recent example of the *bricoleur-collage* strategy used at the scale of a city neighborhood is Handel Architects' design for the transformation of the Midtown Cultural District in Boston.[17] Using historic Washington Street as the main street or spine for the project, the plan nimbly adopts a variety of strategies, from repurposing Daniel Burnham's Filene's Department Store (set piece and composite building in one) to other infill projects by the same firm that serve at times as vertical urban markers at major crossroads or to extend the street wall at an appropriate scale. Structured around the initial inspiration of re-envisioning Washington Street as Nash's Regent Street in London, the irregular sites of Boston's colonial-era plan are resolved in a composite-hybrid building plan

17 Blake Middleton, FAIA, leader of Handel Architects' Boston projects, was a student in Rowe's graduate studio in the 1980s.

Fig. 42. Millennium Place, Boston, MA, by Handel Architects.

manner with stabilizer-like towers set on set piece urban street walls (Fig. 42).

Collage City and the Psycho-cultural Field

"Collage City and the Reconquest of Time" is the chapter just preceding the "Excursus," focusing on the city as a "didactic instrument," using Karl Popper's notion that society can never "start afresh" and "this means we must stand on the shoulders of our predecessors."[18] In their rejection of 'total design' and the politics of utopia, Rowe and Koetter see as a basis for the city, a dialectic between utopia and tradition in the form of the existing city, the idea that the good city has both continuity with the past and yet is equally capable of breaking or transforming old traditions in favor of new ones.

> *But, if Collision City, as so far discussed, has only incidentally betrayed an iconic intention, questions of symbolic purpose or function begin now increasingly to rise to the surface. ... Iconoclasm is and should be an obligation. It is an obligation to expurgate myth and to break down intolerable conglomerates of meaning. ...but permanently—and as one knows—such efforts can only contribute to another iconography.*[19]

For Rowe and Koetter, neither the 20th century notion of the *zeitgeist* (spirit of the age) nor the notion of the *genius loci* (spirit of the place) alone are sufficient conditions for the "reconquest of time." Instead *Collage City* presents the city as the place where complex cultural, political, and social aspirations are played out in built form over time, often by diverse or competing groups, but clearly the result of conscious choice. And, although the "spirit of the place" may assert an influence in the mind of the designer via the imperatives of climate, taste, or program, Rowe and Koetter also underscore the agency and importance of free will in the person of the architect or patron who transforms or makes the city based

18 Rowe and Koetter (1978): 118.

19 Ibid.: 119-20.

Fig. 43. Alys Beach, FL, by DPZ Architects and Town Planners.

on their insights, values or both. Those influences may be real or contrived. As cited in *Collage City* these include the importation of Greek ideals and building types by Karl Friedrich Schinkel to Berlin or Potsdam, or simply may be the fragments of a "tradition," such as the rustication visible in Luigi Moretti's decidedly modern Casa del Girasole, referencing the traditional Roman palazzo. Implicit in the argument is that the city made up of continuous, well-defined spaces of streets and blocks is uniquely capable of providing the setting for the display of values in built form. Without the texture/object dialectic, any capacity to absorb, communicate, value, and express ideas in the city becomes tenuous. As a result, the relationship between ideas and forms becomes fragile. Thus in *Collage City* the notion of the reconquest of time asserts the mutability of the iconic aspects of architecture. It recognizes that the approach of both the iconophile and the iconoclast can result in new iconographic intent, perhaps for distinctly different reasons.[20] For the iconophile, a nostalgic sense is preeminent. Such an approach is embodied in New Urbanist projects like Alys Beach in Florida by Duany Plater-Zyberk and based on, among other things, Caribbean and Dutch South African building types as well as other precedents. In the New Urbanist agenda, one sees a willingness to see myth reassembled in another place and time, reconquering and re-establishing an historical time as a new history and identity of place, and these established via the use of form-based codes and a thematic stylistic agenda. In the New Urbanist model, the iconography of place is specifically and consciously chosen.[21]

Polemic and Treatise

The Oxford English Dictionary traces the word "polemic" to the mid-17th century, via medieval Latin, from the Greek word *polemikos*, from "polemos" or war. Certainly, *Collage City* can be read, in much of the text, as an assault on some of the more dubious assumptions of Modern architectural theory, particularly its urban theory. Similarly, the OED traces "treatise" to Late Middle English from

20 Rowe and Koetter point out in *Collage City* that the iconoclast may possess a nostalgia for the future, or at least, break away from any 'tradition' as cultural pattern, expectation, style, or type and as such becomes a transitory pleasure but, if successful, it merely establishes a new iconography.

21 The iconophile/iconoclast aspect of late Modern architecture can be seen as an interpretation of the iconography of Le Corbusier's work, see Rowe and Koetter (1978): 118-149.

Anglo-Norman French *tretis*, from Old French traitier (see *treat*), the same base as "traitor" or "treatment".

This combination of both polemic and treatise is common throughout the history of architecture, although rarely is a work presented as an even balance of both. For Palladio's *Four Books of Architecture* the treatise aspect is expansive in discussions of proper techniques for building, etc., but it is also a polemic in favor of the rebirth of the architecture of the ancients as models for contemporary building. Many of the pre-Modern works considered to be treatises reside in the how-to genre, profusely illustrating construction techniques and how to raise mundane aspects of building to the higher level of architecture. Although largely a polemic, Le Corbusier's *Vers une architecture* of 1923 includes a small treatise toward the end entitled "Mass Production Houses", illustrated with large and small housing designs intended to show the way to solutions for the housing crisis of the time.

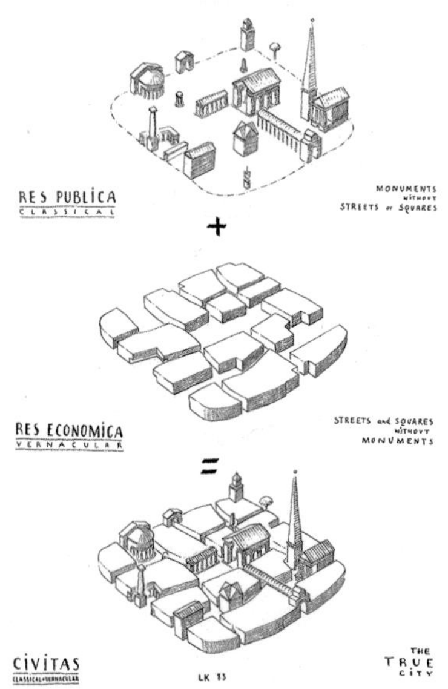

Fig. 44. "Res Publica + Res Economica = Civitas" by Léon Krier.

As a complex critique of the city of Modern architecture, *Collage City* is unique in its equally rich written and illustrated polemic, and, as a treatise it has been widely influential in specific techniques, such as the figure/ground and collage as methods to relate and weave parts of a city together. If the first five chapters of *Collage City* can be read as a polemic, then, like the works cited above, the two last chapters, "Collage City and the Reconquest of Time" and the "Excursus" in combination can also be read as an architectural treatise, with the concluding chapter providing a possible how-to guide for repairing the existing city after the tragedy of Modern urbanism.

Viewed as a treatise, can Rowe and Koetter be viewed as having been as influential as others concerned with the making of the city? Does it compare well to such contributors as Camillo Sitte, Daniel Burnham, or more recently, Léon Krier and the New Urbanists?[22] It may be too early to judge, but it is clear that many of the ideas and techniques proposed by the authors of *Collage City* have become common to the urban design and planning worlds and they have been used to understand, analyze, and adapt the city. These range from drawing techniques like the figure/ground to urban design parlance. Others, in related fields, from regulatory officials to individual designers, have also taken up the mantle of the rejection of the city of Modern architecture in favor of preservation, adaptation, collage, context, and continuity with the past. Certainly Contextualism has helped to expand the influence of the preservation movement, from initially focusing on individual buildings to a more encompassing concern with larger historic districts and landscapes, now common features of any historic city.[23]

As a treatise, the basic thesis of *Collage City* seems to be quite clear and simple. The city, well-made (stabilizers, set pieces, gardens, memorable streets, composite buildings, appropriate doses of iconographic intent and nostalgia, etc.), requires the continuum of city fabric to be legible, and *Collage City* is abundant with examples of each group, both in the text and in the Excursus. In any good city, the examples advocated by Rowe and Koetter ought to be present, unique to each place, and yet capable of making fabric, values, and memorializing history. It is interesting to compare Léon Krier's diagram of *Civitas* (Fig. 44) to an image that is among the first Rowe and Koetter display in *Collage City*—a drawing by

22 *Collage City* was published by MIT Press in 1978 but existed as a series of lectures and short articles beginning in the 1970s. Schumacher, Thomas, "Contextualism: Urban Ideals and Deformations", *Casabella* 359-60, "The City as an Artifact" Frampton, Kenneth, ed., Dec 1971: 79-86, were among of the first academic articles visiting the problems of modern urbanism. Taken in the context of architectural theory of the 1960s, it is clear that Rowe and Koetter were the first to take on the subject and offer a comprehensive critique of the Modernist city.

23 It is worth noting that the rise of Contextualism in the early 1970s more or less coincided with the rise of historic district designations across the United States. Although Charleston, South Carolina, is the first city to designate locally an historic district in 1931, by 1981 the National Trust for Historic Preservation noted 882 historic districts across the country.

Hans Kollhoff and David Griffin that Rowe and Koetter title, "City of composite presence" (Fig. 45). Krier's diagram is often used to illustrate how the *res publica* and the *res economic*a combine to make the traditional city or *Civitas.* The Kolhoff/Griffin drawing is a collage of (mostly) recognizable buildings, urban spaces, and complexes. It is cleverly composed yet not composed, the ultimate Aristotelian contingency in urban form. Conversely, the Krier paradigm is organized with a grid, locating each block in a clearly defined geometry, in this comparison a Platonic counterpoint.

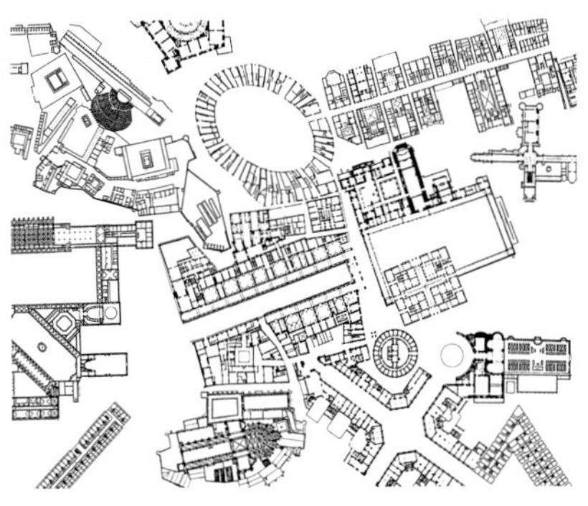

Fig. 45. "City of Composite Presence" by David Griffin and Hans Kolhoff.

Perhaps the good city, as advocated by Rowe and Koetter, is something akin to both, from the "City of Composite Presence" a sense of contingency and historic continuity, the ancient juxtaposed with the modern, adapted and transformed in the process, providing a model by which to design in the existing city. Krier's *Civitas* might be seen as an ideal (but not utopian) structure that could include the elements of the "Excursus": a combination of the two adopted as a model for new towns or suburbs. For in it, might not most of the items elucidated by *Collage City* be present as well?

As the 21st century struggles to recoup urban form devastated by 20th century architectural theory (and in some places the additional impact of war and destruction), the adaptability of the Rowe and Koetter treatise is set forth, not as specific model, but rather as generalizable strategies necessary to make the good city. These strategies range from abstract, conceptual tools, such as the figure/ground, to real precedents of building type, urban fabric, and iconography.

The numerous examples of architectural, urban design projects illustrated here, and realized after the publication of *Collage City*, offer ways to understand context, to design urban buildings, and to articulate open space, so as to support the complex tapestry of public and private buildings that comprises the city. *Collage City* continues to be widely influential in the conceptualization and realization of the good city.

Colin Rowe's Influence on the New Urbanism

Neal I. Payton

> *The ideal thing would be to have a* good *American suburb adjacent to a very concentrated Italian town. Then you'd have the best of both worlds.*[1]
>
> COLIN ROWE

frontispiece:
Aerial view of Seaside, 2007.
Photo: courtesy Alex Maclean.

With this oft-quoted quip, Colin Rowe admitted to a guilty pleasure. Despite a passion for and a career devoted to the pursuit of urbanism, particularly as experienced in historic European villages and towns, he also appreciated the convenience of the traditional city's antithesis, the American suburb, which allowed one-stop shopping, accessed via the automobile. Immediately preceding this remark, he had stated, "… here in Rome there are times, in fact every day, when I would prefer to get into an automobile and go shopping in a supermarket than go shopping around in all these little stores".[2]

It is safe to say that Colin's many years of life in Ithaca, and Austin, Texas, before that, had not transformed him into an apologist for the ever-expanding, suburban sprawl surrounding virtually every city in North America. His use of the word 'good' is evidence of that. Instead, his comment was a simple recognition that contemporary culture demanded an urbanism that was more varied and complex in its infrastructure and arrangement than he experienced in Rome at that time.

Colin was not alone in his recognition of the desirability of these two opposite forms of urbanism. One might argue that, at one level, the tens of thousands of Americans who visited Rome and Florence every year, or for that matter, Charleston, South Carolina, and Annapolis, Maryland, perhaps in lesser numbers, only to return to their charming suburban homes to wonder, "Why don't we build cities and places like that in America", echoed a similar sentiment, albeit with a bit more naivete. At a professional level, the leaders of the New Urbanism movement also recognized the dilemma inherent in Colin's desire for these two forms of urbanism to coexist. But the New Urbanists took this aspiration one step further. Rather than merely speculating, the New Urbanists offered a solution aimed at combining the best of both urbanisms, or if not the best, at least

1 From an interview with Colin Rowe as quoted by Richard Ingersoll, *Design Book Review* 17 Win 1989: 11-14 (emphasis mine). In the interview, Ingersoll asks, "Isn't the problem of the automobile, even if it was not the origin of the formal solutions of Modernism, still central in a current urban scheme?" On academic appointment in Rome and living in the historic center at the time, Rowe's response was, "… here in Rome there are times, in fact every day, when I would prefer to get into an automobile and go shopping in a supermarket than go shopping around in all these little stores. The ideal thing would be to have a good American suburb adjacent to a very concentrated Italian town. Then you'd have the best of both worlds".

2 Ibid.

Fig. 1. Aerial view of Seaside, 2007. Photo: courtesy Alex MacLean.

some of the best of both urbanisms. It ultimately became a project of regulatory reform that would result, it was hoped, in new suburbs that combined the spatial coherence and walkability of traditional urbanism with the scale and infrastructure necessary to accommodate the automobile.

Such an ambitious project required frequent check-ins by the participants to measure progress and to be critiqued, both by other like-minded designers as well as 'objective' outsiders. In 1999, shortly before his death, Colin Rowe participated in one such check-in. The event was a small conference at Seaside, the little town on the Florida panhandle that is to the New Urbanism movement what Rome is to the Renaissance (Fig. 1, 2). The conference, documented in the book *The Seaside Debates: A Critique of the New Urbanism*,[3] brought together many of the New Urbanism's preeminent designers. Along with several academic critics, including Colin, this group was to examine the movement's accomplishments and deficiencies, seven years after the first Congress for the New Urbanism in Alexandria, Virginia in 1992, and five years after the publication of the book, *The New Urbanism: Towards an Architecture of Community*,[4] and 14 years after Seaside itself broke ground. Each of the critics who participated were thought to be at least somewhat sympathetic to the aspirations of the New Urbanism, if not its accomplishments to date. However, a more significant reason for Colin's inclusion in the list of speakers was the recognition by the New Urbanism's founders of the enormous formal and intellectual debt they owed to his outpouring of scholarship and academic work.

If, in inviting Colin to the Florida panhandle, the New Urbanists were hoping for a pat on the back, they were no doubt disappointed. Colin did not seem particularly impressed by the work he saw presented. Though, to be fair, the attendees could be forgiven for imagining greater acceptance of their efforts, as two years earlier Colin had given a modicum of praise to Kentlands, a Duany Plater-Zyberk "traditional neighborhood development" in Gaithersburg, Maryland, stating:

> *It must have taken great patience and ability, even genius, to persuade the mortgage agencies, that not every resident wanted—or seriously needed—an enormous lawn back*

3 Bressi, Todd, ed., *The Seaside Debates: A Critique of the New Urbansim*, Rizzoli, New York, 2002. The presenters included Victor Dover, Raymond Gindroz, Douglas Kelbaugh, Elizabeth Moule, Elizabeth Plater-Zyberk, Stefanos Polyzoides, Brian Shea, and Daniel Solomon. The critics included, Warren Byrd, Judith DiMaio, Harrison Fraker, Jr., Allan Jacobs, John Kaliski, Donlyn Lyndon, Alan Plattus, Colin Rowe and Witold Rybczynski. Robert Campbell, who was the architectural critic for the Boston Globe, served as the moderator.

4 Katz, Peter, ed., *The New Urbanism: Towards an Architecture of Community*, McGraw-Hill, New York, 1994.

Fig. 2. Modified figure-ground plan of Seaside showing landscape as green (image courtesy of Duany Plater-Zyberk).

and front, that a house on a small site, close to a sidewalk, and with little more than a courtyard at back was once again—or had always continued to be, a viable possibility. But, with so much achieved—achievement of a very high order—one must now look for the next installment in the saga.[5]

While it is not clear that Colin was aware of his own influence on projects like Kentlands and other examples of the New Urbanism, it is impossible to review the ideology of the New Urbanism and the work of its founders and early devotees without seeing Colin's influence. This is the case despite the fact that none of the New Urbanism's founders—Andrés Duany, Elizabeth Plater-Zyberk, Stefanos Polyzoides, Elizabeth Moule, Daniel Solomon or Peter Calthorpe, were students of, or taught with, Colin at Cornell or elsewhere. Nor were any of the eleven members, of what Duany called the "original swarm",[6] among Rowe's students or former faculty colleagues.

It is not surprising that leading urban designers would emerge from the tutelage of many different academics and critics of post-war urban development. By the late 1980s, when the early New Urbanists were coalescing into a movement, critics of contemporary urban form-making were already numerous. In 1961, Jane Jacobs had written a powerful, if highly personal, critique of the single-use zoning and auto-centric street design that had become the norm in post-war North America. At the same time the 'pattern language' theories of Christopher Alexander provided specific spatial strategies for early New Urbanists to deploy. Léon Krier's models for the reconstruction of the European city were inspiring to a generation of fledging urbanists in the U.S. and Canada who had looked to these historic cities for ideas that might be transferable to North America, while Anthony Vidler, at Princeton, as well as the oft-published architect Aldo Rossi, inspired many of the founders' interests in typology as a way of understanding the interrelatedness of building types as constituent elements of the city.[7]

Of particular significance among the list of influential critics was Vincent Scully, who has been credited for inspiring Duany and Plater-Zyberk to look closely at the early 20th century American suburb for inspiration. As Duany writes about his wife and partner, Elizabeth Plater-Zyberk,

5 Rowe, Colin, "A Modest Proposal for a New Sub-Urbanism", *Harvard Design Magazine* 1, Cambridge, MA, Win–Spr 1977: 65.

6 Duany, Andrés, "Ground Zero of New Urbanism", in Thadani, Dhiru, ed., *Visions of Seaside*, Rizzoli, New York, 2013: 153. Duany refers to the 'original swarm' as Judy Corbett, Jaime Correa, Robert Davis, Victor Dover, John Massengale, Paul Murrain, Robert Orr, Neal Payton, Pat Pinnell, Shelly Poticha, and Dhiru Thadani.

7 Vidler, Anthony, "The Third Typology", *Oppositions* 7, Win 1977.

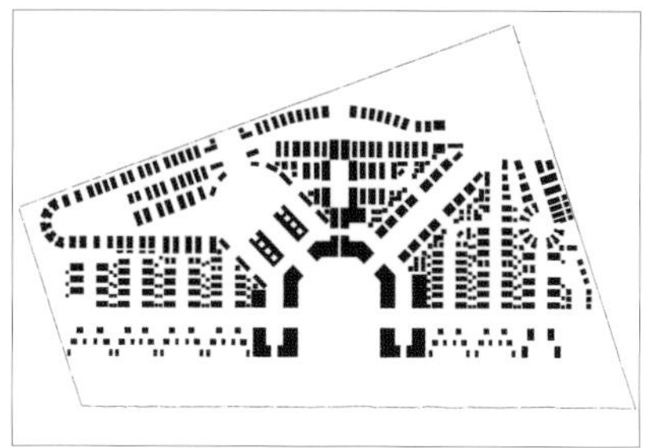

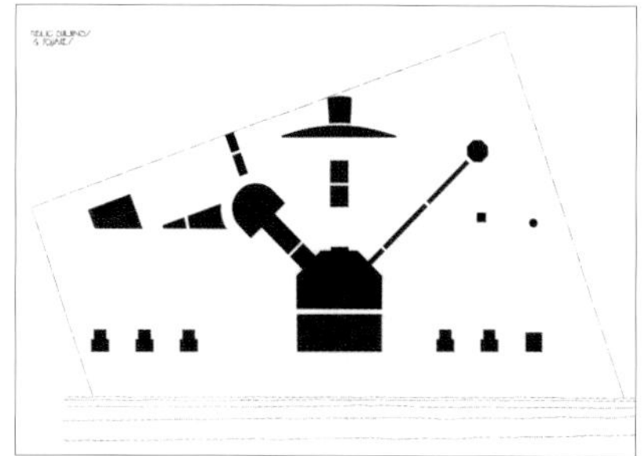

Her third great influencer [after her father, and her hometown of Paoli, [PA] *must have been Vincent Scully at Yale, with his enthusiasm for American architecture and an utter absence of prejudice against tradition, the vernacular or the historic city. This was unique among academics in the 1970s, so when we became enamored of porch-laden New Haven as students, Scully was supportive beyond what one could expect from a professor.*[8]

Among all these academics and practitioners, however, Colin's urban design pedagogy—most often characterized, albeit simplistically, by the figure/ground drawing—was unique in providing a design methodology with which to conceive a project as a complex urban experience. Represented most prominently by *Collage City*, which he co-wrote with Fred Koetter, his formal strategies (one might say, ways of conceiving and drawing urbanism) were also disseminated in the publications of the work of his Cornell Urban Design Studio, as well as in articles by his students in *The Cornell Journal of Architecture* and elsewhere,[9] and significantly in the book *Court and Garden*, by his colleague, Michael Dennis. Emmanuel Petit writes:

... the American contextualists [including the New Urbanists, among others] integrated concepts of town planning with the stylistic characteristics of traditional townscapes. For this they readily appropriated Rowe's figure/ground studies as the central technique of their new urbanism centered on the primacy of the street space ... Andrés Duany and Elizabeth Plater-Zyberk made themselves the principal codifiers and popularizers of the so-called New Urbanism and defended street-based town planning as a new civic art.[10]

It is not too far a stretch to assert that if Scully and Vidler, among many others, provided the theoretical gist for a new type of post-war urbanism, Rowe and his disciples provided the formal strategies for accomplishing the same. Evidence of this can be seen in the areas of design investigation that the New Urbanist founders had been pursuing as they coalesced their strategies into a movement. For example, having begun construction in 1981, the design of Seaside, Duany Plater-Zyberk's transformational project, started in the late 1970s and took several years to evolve. The plan as we know it, with its sequence of traditional urban spaces, did not begin to take shape until 1979, one year after the publication of *Collage City*, and immediately after a visit to Miami by Léon Krier who was lecturing on "A New Wave of European Architecture".[11] The little town is characterized by a figural central space serving as the locus of a radial street network and corresponding urban spatial sequence. Prior to coining the term "New Urbanism", Duany Plater-Zyberk referred to this type of project as a Traditional Neighborhood Development (TND). While its organizational framework seems to follow in the tradition of the City Beautiful movement, as handed down from the École des Beaux-Arts, its unique quality in the American suburban context of 1980 relied on one's ability to experience the spaces (the voids) between the individual buildings (the solids), as best understood in the figure/ground and reverse figure/ground drawings (Fig. 3, 4).

Today it can be imagined, though this would admittedly be a fiction, that the spatial sequence came first and then the buildings and streets were added to support the ensemble. The buildings not only frame the streets, they also frame the large and small spaces, the latter of which seem to have been the most important consideration. Roadways themselves, while not separate from the spatial

8 Duany, Andrés, "The Road to Seaside", in Thadani (2013): 61.

9 Among the most significant of these may be Schumacher, Thomas, "Contextualism: Urban Ideals and Deformations", *Casabella* 359-360, 1971: 79-86, and Copper, Wayne, "The Figure/Grounds", *The Cornell Journal of Architecture* 2, Fall 1983.

10 Petit, Emmanuel, "Rowe after Colin Rowe", in Petit, Emmanuel, ed., *Reckoning with Colin Rowe: Ten Architects Take Position*, Routledge, Abingdon, and New York, 2015: 7.

11 Duany, Andrés, "Evolution of the Seaside Plan", in Thadani (2013): 173.

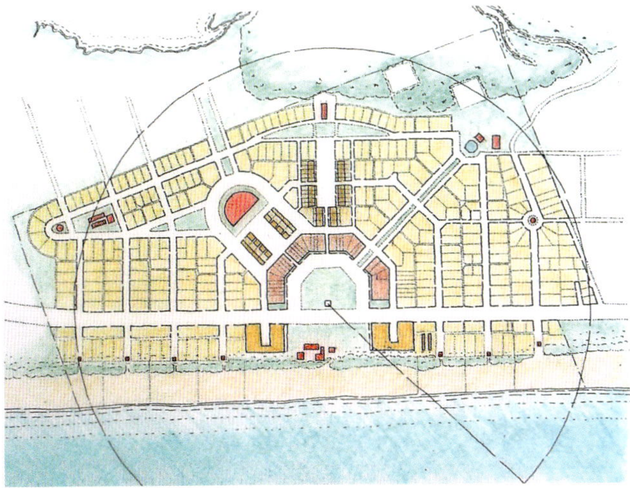

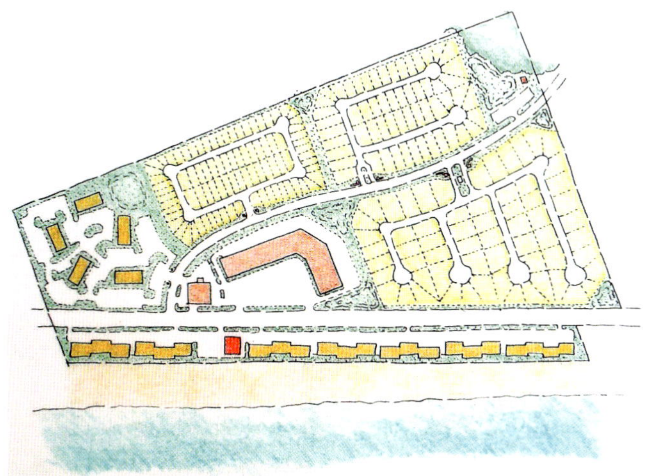

hierarchy, are secondary to the space-making method. This is a process that relies on figure/ground drawing popularized in the Cornell Studio as a design tool, specifically its ability to allow simultaneous readings of the solids or their opposites, the voids, as figural.

opposite:
Fig. 3. Figure/ground plan of Seaside (image courtesy of Duany Plater-Zyberk).

Fig. 4. Reverse figure/ground of Seaside (image courtesy of Duany Plater-Zyberk).

above:
Fig. 5 and 6. Plan of Seaside as designed compared to Seaside as it might have been under conventional zoning (image courtesy of Duany Plater-Zyberk).

While the basic organizational structure of Seaside, a radial grid, seems conventional enough, it was rather unconventional for its time (Fig. 5, 6). Indeed, conventional planning practice would have seen Seaside as having a set of pods, single-use or single-type housing precincts on cul-de-sacs, emanating from a collector street. Such a plan would have entailed a pod of apartment buildings scattered around parking lots, and then a pod of large-lot houses, and another of small lot houses. None of them would have connected, and no spatial sequences would have been apparent. This was not merely the result of planning fashion: separation of housing densities and types was inscribed in the land-use zoning regulations of the day.

Meanwhile across the country in Northern California, Daniel Solomon has credited the evolution of his professional perspective as well as his passion for urbanism rather directly to Colin Rowe, Fred Koetter, and Michael Dennis (Fig. 7, 8). He summarized his 1980s excitement thusly:

> *After reading* Collage City, *I felt like someone who had spent years on a Micronesian island listening to scratchy ukulele records suddenly finding himself in the middle of a von Karajan performance of the Ninth Symphony ... Never before* Collage City *had the fury of language been directed so magnificently at the failings of the Modernist city and the intellectual underpinnings of its tacit theory.*
>
> *For 181 pages ... an argument is constructed that says that all my professional colleagues of my generation and I had been breathing a colorless and odorless poison gas from the moment we entered architecture school. What we had breathed in was a lethal concoction of naive utopianism, pseudo-science, historical determinism, and cockeyed populism. The results were those very urban renewal, federal highway, and public housing programs that were tearing San Francisco and every other city in the world to bits. What it seemed to be*

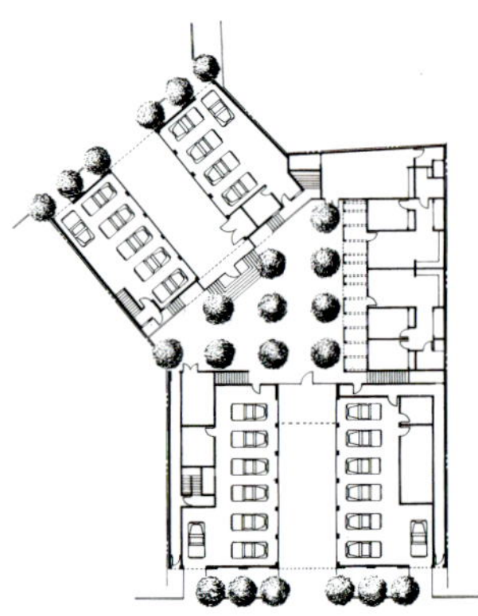

> *saying was that in my own little efforts of the past few years I was not alone and armed with a peashooter but that I had this giant with a mighty sword standing beside me.*[12]

It wasn't just *Collage City* that inspired Solomon. At around the same time, bootleg photocopies of Michael Dennis's manuscript about French *hôtel particuliers,* later to be named *Court and Garden,* was making the rounds in the architectural academy, and Solomon is effusive about the significance of this work:

> *The most clear and systematic explication of Colin Rowe's conception of architecture and the city in "healthy intercourse," is Michael Dennis' great book* Court and Garden ... *Dennis' book lays bare the secrets of generations of Parisian architects who brought about the most virtuosic mediations between the traditional city as the grand setting for civic life and the emerging complexity of building programs with specialized internal demands. The French Hotel, or large private aristocratic house and its shaping of the splendors of the public realm of Paris from the 17th century to the 19th, is a textbook for the Modern city.*[13]

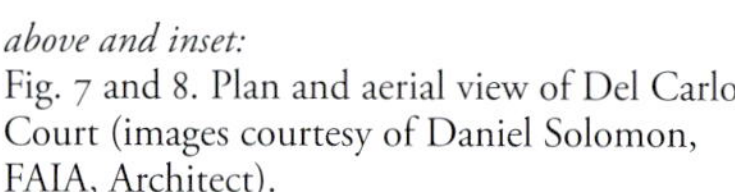

above and inset:
Fig. 7 and 8. Plan and aerial view of Del Carlo Court (images courtesy of Daniel Solomon, FAIA, Architect).

In Southern California another of the CNU's founders, Stefanos Polyzoides, was collaborating with his colleagues at the University of Southern California, James Tice and Roger Sherwood, on the book *Courtyard Housing in Los Angeles.* While Tice and Sherwood had been graduate students in the Cornell Urban Design Studio and Sherwood had been a faculty colleague of Colin's, Stefanos's connection was a vicarious one. His education included studying at Princeton, where he was exposed to Anthony Vidler's interest in typology and where he discovered the work and writings of Aldo Rossi. Thus, it is easy to see *Courtyard Housing in Los Angeles* as a blending of these two areas of interest. A casual look at the analytical drawings of the individual courtyard buildings displayed in the book reveals a fascination with the ambiguity of figural spaces and solids, which is to say that the city's composition can be read as a dialectic between solid and void (Fig. 9). In fact, the book would almost seem to represent an American, or at least a Los Angeles, version of *Court and Garden.*[14] While this may not have been the intention of the book, it seems reasonable to imagine that the drawings and the thinking they represent grow out of the same tradition. Importantly, this book would go on to inspire a substantial component of the work of Moule & Polyzoides (Fig. 10), Polyzoides's subsequent firm, particularly the firm's well-crafted block-scale projects, which include multiple buildings forming a sequence of well-defined spaces.[15]

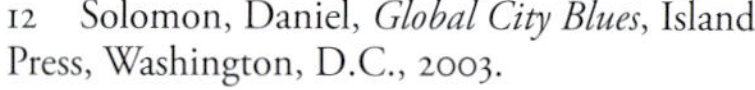

12 Solomon, Daniel, *Global City Blues*, Island Press, Washington, D.C., 2003.

13 Solomon, Daniel, "The Thirty Years' War: New Urbanism and the Academy", *Public Square: A CNU Journal,* Sep 27, 2017.

14 Tice has stated, "I can assert that although we were aware of Mike's book, there was never any attempt to emulate it in our book".

15 Interestingly, the City of West Hollywood, California, uses this book in determining historic preservation eligibility. Tice explains that historic preservation was one of Colin's important, if less noticed passions.

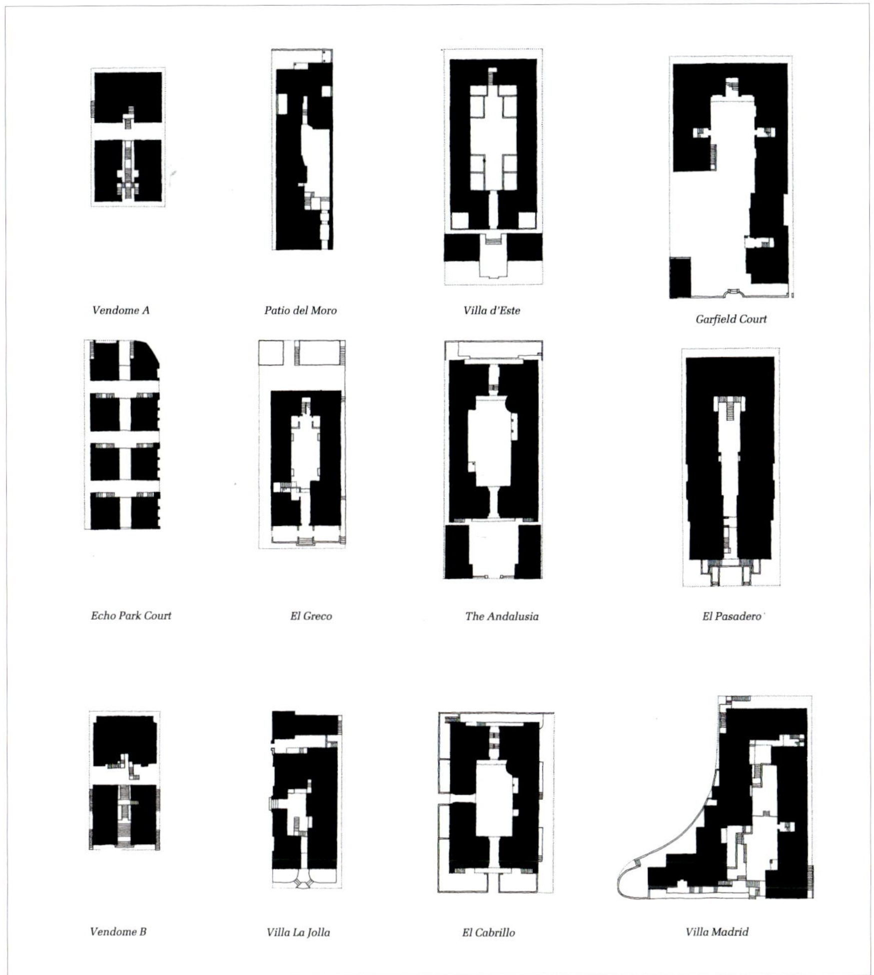

Fig. 9a, 9b. Typological array of courtyards from *Courtyard Housing in Los Angeles*, also showing book cover, by Stephanos Polyzoides, Roger Sherwood and James Tice. Photo: Julius Shulman. Drawing by J. Tice.

Each of these founders, Duany, Plater-Zyberk, Solomon, Moule, and Polyzoides, had been working either in the American suburb or low-density areas of the city, and each had been working more or less independently of the others, but they found that they had common ground for some sort of unified theory. They had each pieced together some version of the story as to what went wrong with the North American city in the years following World War II. In *Collage City,* Colin Rowe and Fred Koetter provided the unifying element, not the answers, but a template upon which to graft everything they had learned about public policy, development practice, traffic engineering, and every other subject that bears upon the act of city building.

Colin Rowe was by no means the first theoretician to discuss urban spatial form and equate it with the problems of the American city. However, most others had been looking almost exclusively at the center city. But Rowe in his teaching, and Rowe and Koetter in *Collage City*, provided the theoretical structure by which to look beyond the central city. They adroitly addressed the issue in a laser-like exposition of the problem:

> [By] *1930 the disintegration of the street and of all highly organized public space seemed to have become inevitable; and for two major reasons: the new and rationalized form of*

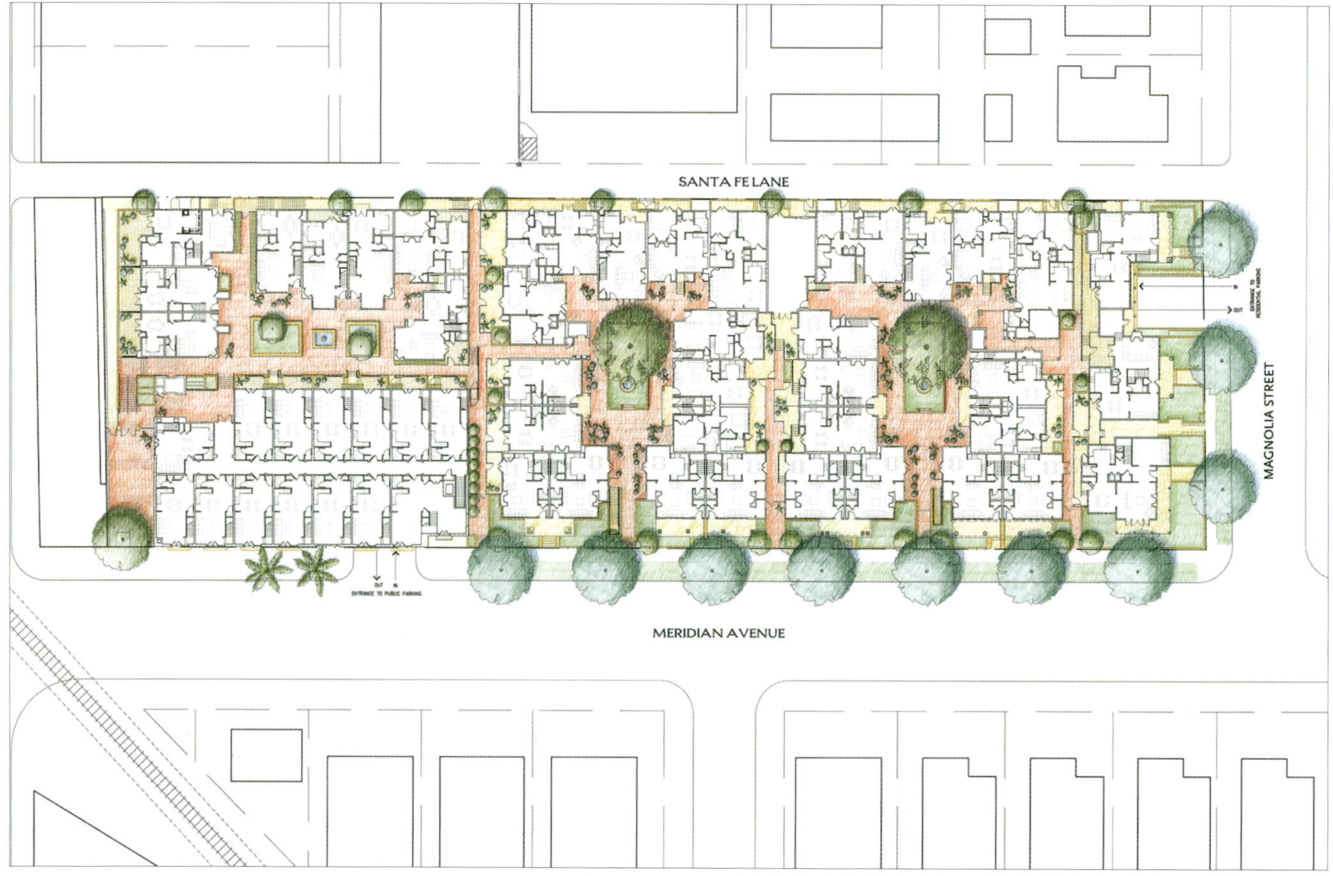

Fig. 10. Plan for Mission Meridian in Pasadena, CA one of Moule & Polyzoides block-scale projects (Courtesy of Moule & Polyzoides, Architects and Urbanists).

housing and the dictates of vehicular activity. For, if the configuration of housing now evolved from the inside out, from the logical needs of the residential unit, then it could no longer be subservient to external pressures; and if external public space had become so functionally chaotic as to be without effective significance, then … there were no valid pressures which it could any longer exert.[16]

And that is what the New Urbanists attacked, the paradigmatic America suburb. The New Urbanists understood that the public realm, as embodied in public space, was not a part of the suburban paradigm. The house was designed from the inside out, as Rowe and Koetter noted, with each sitting on a plot of land, spatially oblivious to its neighbors. And the street network was designed by traffic engineers at a super-block scale. While at one level this is the condition of every gridded street network, the scale of these typical suburban blocks and the width of the streets meant that they were designed to be experienced by automobile not by pedestrians. Thus, the requirement for spatial coherence related to the scale of the pedestrian, the requirement of making a public realm, was moot.

By the 1980s the American *zeitgeist* had produced a condition whereby both the city and the suburb were in need of reform. Reform of the city was the area of interest for most architects despite the challenges that the future New Urbanists could see: urban infill projects were almost non-existent, larger scaled redevelopment projects were still quite limited because of the difficulty in assembling a meaningfully sized parcel of land, and the massive public subsidies required

16 Rowe, Colin; Koetter, Fred, *Collage City*, MIT Press, Cambridge, MA, and London, 1979:56.

for infrastructure were lacking. The New Urbanists, as they would soon brand themselves, understood that the suburbs offered an important opportunity, not just for criticism, but for serious reform (Fig. 11). They also understood that by co-opting the design of the American suburb and claiming it as a proper domain for urbanists, they could have a positive impact on American urbanism. To do so they looked not to Rome but to traditional American towns as models to be emulated. The older districts of places like Alexandria, Charleston, Savannah, Boston, and New Orleans were studied with care. And of smaller and archetypal American towns, an article on Lockhart, Texas, and the archetypal county courthouse town as a particularly American manifestation written by Colin Rowe and John Hejduk three decades earlier, was also influential:

Fig. 11. Aerial view of American suburb.

> *... in the sharp light and the vacant landscape of the West architectural detail will seem to achieve an almost archaic clarity, so that the most-tawdry saloon or incrusted false facade may acquire a pretentious distinction, while whole towns founded no earlier than the [eighteen-] sixties can exude an Italian evidence of age. For these reasons, for the sympathetic traveler Utah will evoke memories of Tuscany; Virginia City, Nevada will appear a nineteenth-century Urbino; while such mining cities as Leadville, Colorado, Carson City, Nevada, or Globe, Arizona, will seem as unquestionable as Gubbio or Siena to have always occupied the land. Like the cities of Umbria, they are potent symbols of urbanity; and like these they become more definite, more surprisingly crystalline to the mind, by reason of the emptiness through which they are approached.*[17]

Now a project as grand as the New Urbanism, which promised nothing less than the wholesale transformation of the form of the American suburb, needed a proper advocacy structure, one that could codify the movement's expectations, and operationalize its strategies for systematically affecting regulatory change. To that end, the Congress for the New Urbanism was founded and modeled, at least in its operating methodology, directly on Congrés Internationaux d'Architecture Moderne (CIAM), albeit with a decidedly different social and spatial agenda. The formal agenda of the CNU combined the concept of figural space, as represented in the various incarnations of the figure/ground drawing, with an interest in the American suburban and small-town prototypes. Again, emulating CIAM, the creation of a charter was an assertion that New Urbanism wasn't merely a label given to the work of several like-minded urbanists, as would be well illustrated by Peter Katz's book, *The New Urbanism*. Instead, the Charter was an effort to draw a 'line in the dirt'.

It is easy to imagine that the arguments among the CNU's founders and early adopters that went into writing the charter were exhausting. But out of that tedium and disputation came a document consisting of a preamble and 27 statements of policy.[18] As a broad statement reflecting the views of a range of disciplines, it is perhaps dangerous to assign too much influence to this or that scholar, including Rowe. However, several assertions are certainly consistent with Rowe's point of view. For example, from the preamble:

> *We advocate the restructuring of public policy and development practices to support the following principles ... cities and towns should be shaped by physically defined and universally accessible public spaces and community institutions; urban places should be framed by architecture and landscape design that celebrate local history ...*[18]

17 Rowe, Colin; Hejduk John, "Lockhart, Texas", *Architectural Record* 121 (3), Mar 1957: 202.

18 The Charter of the New Urbanism has been published in various forms, but is most easily read online, [https://www.cnu.org/who-we-are/charter-new-urbanism.].

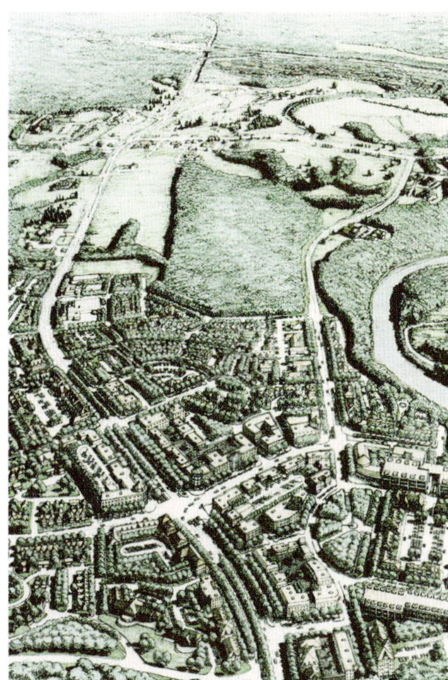

Fig. 12. Triptych of Albemarle County, VA (image courtesy of Torti Gallas + Partners).

The rediscovery of the figure/ground drawing in the Cornell Urban Design Studios, and in particular the fascination with Nolli's plan of Rome, acknowledged the importance of the building footprint to frame public space, including the internal public spaces of key institutions.

Among the policy statements, Principle #20 seems to clarify the preamble above by stating, "A primary task of all urban architecture and landscape design is the physical definition of streets and public spaces as places of shared use". This of course is a direct renunciation of CIAM and Le Corbusier's attack on the street[19] and an acknowledgement of the value of streets as spaces, as envelopments of space within which the public life of the city can transpire. It specifically acknowledges the reciprocity between buildings and streets as both figure and ground. Thomas Schumacher, one of Colin's influential students, argued as much in his essay for Stanford Anderson's groundbreaking collection of essays, *On Streets*.[20]

As well, Principle #21 states, "Individual architectural projects should be seamlessly linked to their surroundings. This issue transcends style". This assertion of a contextualist approach which, without reliance on style per se, refers instead to issues of plan, as evidenced in the figure/ground, as well as building massing and typology, is directly dependent on the arguments of both Schumacher in his article on Contextualism [21] and another of Colin's students, Stuart Cohen, and his article, "Physical Context, Cultural Context: Including it All".[22]

With the publication of the Charter, the New Urbanists had methodically staked out the terrain upon which they would operate. An important component of the CNU's agenda was the stipulation that New Urbanism would operate at a variety of scales, beginning with the region and moving to progressively smaller

19 In *Precisions: On the Present State of Architecture and City Planning*, Le Corbusier had made it his project to kill the street or *rue corridor*.

20 Schumacher, Thomas L., "Buildings and Streets: Notes on Configuration and Use", in Anderson, Stanford, ed., *On Streets*, MIT Press, Cambridge, MA, 1978: 133-50.

21 Schumacher (1971): 79-86.

22 Cohen, Stuart, "Physical Context, Cultural Context, Including it All", *Oppositions* 2, Jan 1974.

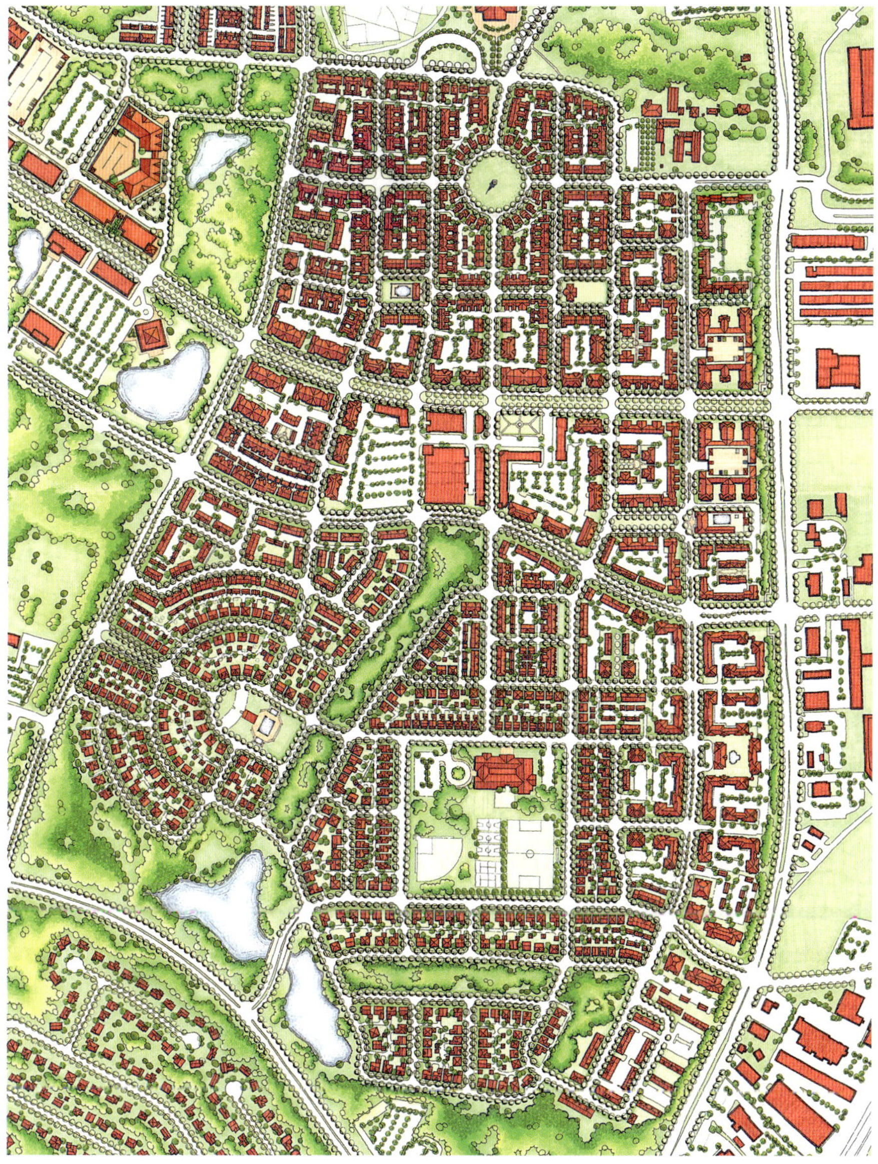

Fig. 13. Plan of King Farm (image courtesy of Torti Gallas + Partners).

increments, such as the neighborhood and the corridor, as well as the block and the building.

The significance of this cannot be overstated. They were taking the lessons of Krier, Rowe, Scully, Vidler and others and putting them into practice. Among other things, they did not cede the regional scale to the realm of the scientists or the technocrats.[23] Using the spatial methodologies of Rowe, and illustrating them with compelling depictions of urban life, the New Urbanists hoped to influence public policy at almost all scales. For example, for a study of Albemarle County, Virginia, Torti Gallas + Partners, created a triptych showing three views of an emerging neighborhood (Fig. 12). On the left is a view of existing conditions; in the middle is a view of how the area would likely grow under the existing regulatory regime; and on the right is a depiction of an alternative future

23 *The Regional Plan of New York and Its Environs*, Lewis, Harold M. and Orton, Lawrence M., 1931 was clearly another influence.

Fig. 14. Detail view, satellite image of King Farm.

showing an equal quantity of new development as the one in the middle, but arranged in a manner that preserves the landscape while providing figural public space, well-defined streets, and an enhanced public realm.[24]

At the same time and at the scale of the neighborhood, examples such as King Farm (Fig. 13), also by Torti Gallas + Partners, used several standard American builder prototypes of the kind produced by production builders to create figural spaces and well-designed streets and corridors.[25] In examples such as these, the New Urbanists attempted to re-establish a relationship between housing and urban form, recognizing that the configuration of individual house plans was still somewhat fungible, and with due care, these houses could support a particularly American form of urbanism (Fig. 13, 14).

For example, instead of locating garages in the front of the houses, they could just as easily be placed behind the houses in service alleys, thereby freeing up the fronts of the houses for porches that could serve as particularly gracious accouterments of urban life and provide 'eyes on the street' only if, of course, they were deep enough to accommodate furniture. With adjustments to the dominant suburban housing prototype such as these, as well as others—like insisting that house configurations on corner lots avoid the blank wall to the street and even be equipped with wrap-around porches on occasion—the New Urbanists recognized that the carefully modulated repetition of detached single-family houses could, in combination with slightly narrowed streets and town-like blocks, be the genesis for a uniquely American form of urbanism.

Perhaps most importantly, the New Urbanists were able to articulate this vision of community form to the real estate development community. A few of the enlightened early adopters of the new urbanism in the real estate industry shared the kind of vision and goals represented by Robert and Daryl Davis, the developers of Seaside, who had imagined a place that would provide for the creation of experiences similar to those they enjoyed as children. Joe Alfandre, who developed Kentlands, in Gaithersburg, Maryland, is representative of the early adopters who shared that kind of vision. Others would follow, including a few who, lacking the same altruism, saw a way to make significant profits. Increasingly, a number of developers were willing to risk investing in a new urban paradigm, one that placed an equal emphasis on both the single-family home and on community, and specifically a walkable community with attention to the public realm. Others, such as the St. Joe Company, at Watercolor, adjacent to Seaside, or the Walt Disney Company, at Celebration in Orlando, were large corporations. In all cases, they intuited there was a pent-up demand for the kind of alternative that the New Urbanists were promoting, and they could earn significant monetary returns by using this new paradigm for real estate developments.

At the same time, the work of Daniel Solomon and of Moule & Polyzoides, among others, was demonstrating the relevance of Rowe's pedagogy at the scale of individual buildings. Little moments, figural spaces, and pedestrian passages within infill buildings, as exemplified by Daniel Solomon's Fulton Grove Townhouses, in San Francisco, were being designed and built, and block-by-block, a strategy of framing streets and public spaces became apparent (Fig. 15).

24 This project by Torti Gallas + Partners was led by Neal I. Payton. The landscape architecture firm of Dodson Associates collaborated on the effort.

25 The initial design of King Farm was led by John F. Torti, whose connections with Colin were indirect, mostly through the summer architecture programs at The Catholic University of America, where he collaborated with Steven Hurtt and Thomas Schumacher, among others. However, Cheryl O'Neill was a senior designer on the effort and the Town Architect was Matthew Bell. As King Farm was built out over time, Robert Goodill was also heavily involved in its design. O'Neill, Bell, and Goodill were all protégés of Colin Rowe.

Fig. 15. Aerial view of Fulton Grove Townhouses, 1992. Photo courtesy of Daniel Solomon, FAIA, Architect.

With the commercial success of the New Urbanists in the suburbs, it wasn't long before other designers understood how the agenda could expand. It was shortly after the first CNU Congress that another track became evident, and in this case, it led back to the center city. While he was not one of the CNU's original founders, Ray Gindroz was an early ally of the movement. His interest in neighborhood preservation and in urban fabric, which predated the New Urbanism by a couple of decades, led him and his firm, Urban Design Associates, to redesign and revitalize public housing (or what is called social housing elsewhere in the world) under the Hope VI program of the U.S. Department of Housing and Urban Development. Taking the same New Urbanist principles that others had applied to the suburbs, Gindroz's efforts include the re-knitting of mixed-income, mixed-use neighborhoods back into the fabric of the city itself. The figure/ground drawing was once again the device by which one could understand how the physical plan impacted the social performance of the neighborhood.

The New Urbanist agenda also began to be applied to other settings, including neighborhoods for families stationed on U.S. military installations (Fig. 16, 17, 18). In an effort to improve retention of military recruits, each of the armed services identified quality of life issues as key. The physical design of its family housing, and the neighborhoods in which they sit, became of utmost importance. Torti Gallas + Partners took the lead in this area, advocating for and ultimately constructing neighborhoods around the nation. All are characterized by the creation of spatially defined streets and public spaces, a hierarchy of spatial sequences and even a mix of uses, completing the first mixed-use structure with housing over retail ever constructed on a U.S. military installation (at Fort Belvoir, Virginia).[26]

At the same time as these exercises in urban design were taking place, the Congress for the New Urbanism began to identify three branches of advocacy and focus:

26 The master planning for Fort Belvoir, including the effort to create the first mixed-use town center on military installations, was led by Neal I. Payton and John Torti.

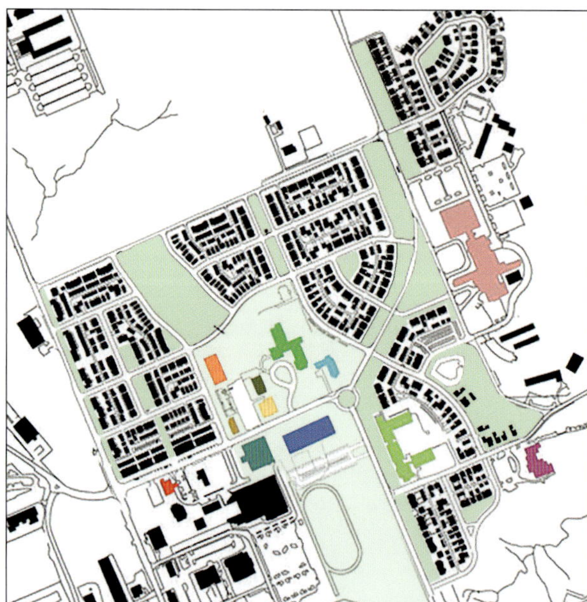

Fig. 16 and 17. Before (left) and after (right) figure/ground drawings of Fort Belvoir, VA (image courtesy of Torti Gallas + Partners).

1) process, particularly methods for including affected communities in the design and planning process; 2) physical design; and 3) public policy, i.e. the development of design criteria that evolves from physical design. Rowe's influence is most obvious in the second of these, specifically its two complementary components, building typology and public space design.

The first of these components included the assertion that building types should support urbanism. This included the recognition that the house can be thought of both from the inside-out and the outside-in. In this way, the New Urbanists thought of the suburban house and its accompanying setting as a bit like the French *hôtel* in an American context, albeit at a more competitive price point.

The second component emphasized street and public space design as the physical embodiment of the public realm. In fact, this issue of street design has been a major focus of the New Urbanists.[27] Early New Urbanism terminology such as 'context-sensitive' street design has given way to catchier and more accessible terms like 'complete streets', which are now in the lexicon of the traffic engineers. These terms evolved from the emphasis on the design of streets that could be appreciated as public spaces serving pedestrians and vehicles equally well. The idea of the street as the *rue corridor*, spatially defined by buildings that were formally subservient to the street, was not unique to Rowe's pedagogy, but it had its most profound evocation in the drawings that came out of Rowe's studios and in his writings, particularly *Collage City*.

Putting into practice Rowe's teaching required the synthesis of models of urbanism that could be measured and thus codified. For example, the New Urbanists placed an emphasis on creating an interconnected framework of 'capillary' streets and passages (gridded-networks) as opposed to 'dendritic' systems, where small neighborhood streets are in service to arterial highways, because these gridded networks allowed each of the corridors or thoroughfares to be smaller and more intimate, befitting a person on foot.

27 See for example: Massengale, John; Dover, Victor, *Street Design: The Secret to Great Cities and Towns*, John Wiley & Sons, Hoboken, NJ, 2014.

Fig. 18. View of ceremonial public space at Fort Belvoir, VA. Photo courtesy of Torri Gallas + Partners.

However, putting this point of view into practice, in the context of a bureaucratic system of traffic engineers and other 'experts' who were not necessarily conversant with Colin Rowe (nor had they traveled to Rome!) meant identifying and codifying how 'finely grained' a street network needs to be for it to be 'walkable'. For example, it was necessary to identify the minimum number of intersections per square mile necessary for a walkable urban environment—an indicator of the number of ways there are to go from point A to point B. At the same time, it was important to measure and codify appropriate proportions (width to height) of street sections and how they might fit different urban situations. While this kind of documentation can be found in Hegemann and Peets', *Civic Art*, the application of such urban design methodologies to a suburban setting was unheard of.[28]

So, while Colin was fighting an intellectual battle from thousands of feet in the air, the New Urbanists were fighting the same battle on multiple fronts, from the air and on the ground. They were directing an entire campaign: recruiting new troops, developing long and short-term benchmarks, and fighting everyday battles in the suburban trenches where they spent much of their time rooting out resistance. Among the examples of this trench warfare were the battles with fire departments over the size of curb radii at street intersections. While the New Urbanists wanted these radii as small as possible to make the intersections safer for pedestrians to traverse, the fire departments preferred them extra large to accommodate their super-sized emergency vehicles speeding around the same corners.

With all that the New Urbanists were taking on and accomplishing, it was thus surprising, even a bit disappointing, to some of those conference participants in Seaside that Colin did not rhapsodize about their work, especially when so much of it bore an obvious debt to his teaching. At least one participant surmised that Rowe might have felt a "sense of betrayal as he looked at some of the latest work of CNU's leaders. He saw his own influence over-simplified and trivialized and he was deeply troubled".[29]

28 Hegemann, Werner; Peets, Elbert, *The American Vitruvius: An Architect's Handbook of Civic Art*, The Architectural Book Publishing Company, New York, 1922.

29 Solomon (2017).

And yet, it might also be argued, that Colin's critique was far more matter-of-fact than pejorative. For example, in his critique of Seaside he stated:

> *I can see the principal problem of Seaside, sitting in this chair, looking out of the window over there. I am looking at a building that is on a diagonal to this building. If we think about what things want to be, that building over there is particularly anxious to be rectilinear in its nature. ... You can see that the piazza here was foolishly arranged so it is an octagon or something involving diagonals. Now that can be accommodated, I suppose, in a Garden City development, but I've always been brought up to despise Garden Cities. It cannot be accommodated in a small-town environment, and that is a genuine problem. I know that if I were to look through those windows, I would find then the problem of residual triangles all around, which can only be solved if you control many kinds of curvilinear Baroque apparatus, which do not belong to small town culture, nor Garden City culture, really. ... We are talking about forms.*[30]

It was not the idea of Seaside that bothered him, or its attempt to straddle the line between traditional European urbanism and the American suburb. Rather, his critique was technical in nature, and purely objective, i.e., it related to Seaside's formal composition in relation to the formal typologies of towns and garden cities well known to him.

Some have argued that Colin's critique was premature.[31] Seaside and other New Urbanist projects were simply too young and not fleshed out enough to have achieved the spatial complexity that may be observed in Nolli's rendered plan of Rome. After all, Rome itself was not built in a day. At the same time, even the New Urbanists' biggest defender, Andrés Duany, acknowledged one of the movement's shortcomings.

> *I do think that the design quality of the New Urbanism in general, is not as sophisticated as what was achieved in the Cornell school in its heyday when Colin was there. Whenever I run across a Cornell grad of that generation [I see that] there is a vocabulary and a series of strategies applied that have not yet been cross-bred into the New Urbanism. I don't know why that should be the case.*[32]

With the benefit of hindsight, some explanation for this shortcoming might be apparent. In their effort to dissect the constituent elements of the city, the New Urbanists, borrowing heavily from Léon Krier, identified two kinds of urban buildings: those ordinary buildings that constitute the city fabric and special, or civic buildings, that sit on hierarchically significant (symbolic) sites. But Colin never simplified things to that extent. His interests went beyond the rather simplified dichotomy of fabric and monument. He was also interested in what Daniel Solomon has called "buildings of a third kind".[33] Solomon was referring to the fact that choice of site is not always an option. As a result, some important and figural buildings sit on fabric sites, while there are some ordinary or everyday buildings that sit on symbolic sites, and these "buildings of a third kind" are not readily found in the monument/fabric diagram.

For example, Sant'Agnese is a church that sits on what the New Urbanists would clearly identify as a fabric site on the Piazza Navona in Rome. In their design for the facade, the church's architects, Borromini and Rainaldi, managed to properly

30 Rowe, Colin, "General Commentary", in Bressi (2002): 138.

31 Duany, Andrés, "Time is Urbanism", *Public Square: A CNU Journal,* Oct 6, 2017.

32 Duany, Andrés, "Presentation of projects", in Bressi (2002): 75.

33 Solomon (2017).

define the edge of the piazza, while using the facade to imply a complex spatial sequence appropriate to a public building and a symbolic site. And they do so within the space of ten feet (Fig. 19, 20).

Fig. 19. View of Sant'Agnese (image courtesy of Neal Payton).

Likewise, back in the U.S., Rowe observed buildings in Lockhart, Texas, other than the centrally focused courthouse, sitting within the Cartesian grid deserving of attention. Of these 'buildings of a third kind' he writes "… it becomes apparent that some of these buildings are not in themselves undemonstrative … the presence of three white-painted gables of unequal height and width soon demands attention". He continues by describing St. Mary's church:

> *… a building of orange brickwork relieved by brick of a yellow or deeper red and occasionally checkered, as for instance in the tower, with a pattern of greenish gray headers … St. Mary's is not so ambitious a building as the other, its details are less ambitious and more delicate, its modeling confident and distinguished, and its Gothic both lyrical and strangely firm, with something of the economy of a child's drawing of a church.*[34]

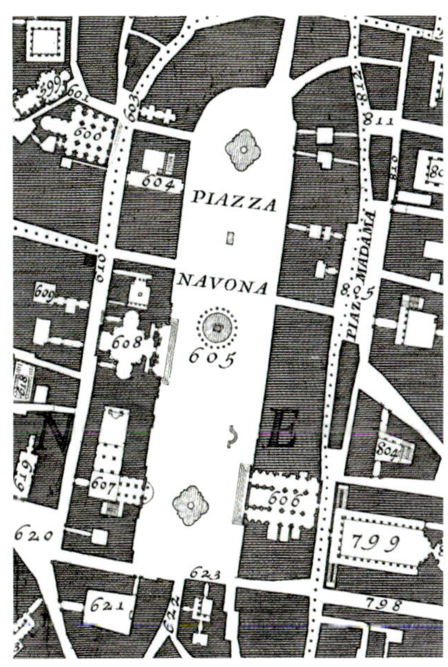

Fig. 20. Detail of Piazza Navona from Giambattista Nolli's Plan of Rome, 1748.

Léon Krier has written that he was "puzzled and almost angered by the fact that he [Colin Rowe] never developed a synthetic vision of his ideas. Why did he not turn these ideas into a major American and worldwide movement—like CIAM before him or New Urbanism, now"?[35] It is noteworthy that Krier did not view the New Urbanism itself as a stand-in, at least in part, for just such a Colin-inspired movement.

It may be surmised that New Urbanism's reductivism of the Cornell method is why Léon did not view New Urbanism as Colin's movement, and why Colin himself did not embrace it. It may also explain why so few of Colin's students have wanted to belong to the New Urbanist club, despite their sympathies for much of its agenda. New Urbanism's prescriptions, as seen in the Charter and in the many form-based codes authored by its practitioners, were perhaps seen as too simplistic, limiting the three-dimensional responses possible on any given site. Others may have shied away from the historic garb that was applied to many New Urbanist ventures, though card-carrying practitioners like Dan Solomon never followed the historicist's path. Still others may have simply been put off by the New Urbanism's early focus on the suburb, rather than the compact city.

In response to these reservations, it may be argued that this reductivism, eschewed by many of Colin's students, is part of the New Urbanism's success. The urban design strategies articulated by Colin provided for many urban designers—particularly those of us who were not schooled in Ithaca—a common language, both spoken and in drawing, with which to propose urbanism. More than anything this language taught us to recognize the destructiveness of the architectural object that stands indifferently, perhaps defiantly, in opposition to the fabric of the city.

When considering Colin's paradigm of the ideal urban arrangement, i.e., the American suburb adjacent to the concentrated Italian hill town, it might be argued that while many of Colin's students focused on evolving, if not perfecting, the concentrated Italian city, at least in academic exercises, the New Urbanists focused on making hybrids of these Italian villages, which is to say, both suburban and urban environments that are walkable and spatially coherent, yet with

34 Rowe and Hejduk (1957).

35 Krier, Léon, "Unresolved Encounters with Colin Rowe", in Petit, Emmanuel, ed., Reckoning with Colin Rowe, *Ten Architects Take Position*, Routledge, Abingdon, and New York, 2015: 83.

enough room in the middle of their blocks to park copious numbers of cars, and enough space on their streets to accommodate the apparatus of most American fire departments. And the American suburb offered, at least initially, the only locale for putting their theories into practice. They took the work where and when it came. Therefore, early on, the New Urbanists were focused on making good American suburbs that owed much of their spatial structure to historic European urbanism mixed with a bit of the archetypal American town, but with a scale and increment of construction, appropriate to what could be approved within a rigid regulatory environment that prescribed the opposite model, and by bureaucrats who were oblivious to the miasma of American suburban sprawl.

The overall success of this strategy can be seen in the hundreds of new suburban neighborhoods that include some measure of a mix of uses, in transformed public and affordable housing, in new street design paradigms, and in a revitalized discourse that includes such terms as 'great streets' and 'complete streets' when discussing issues of urban design and mobility. Other terms for which the New Urbanists can claim authorship include 'placemaking' and 'Transit-Oriented Development' (TOD) which are now used by local elected officials across North America. By codifying the rules learned by observing cities and towns from Rome to the American courthouse town, as well as performing detailed examinations of cities like Annapolis, New Haven, Charleston and Savannah, among others, and sharing the resulting information at conferences, in books and in casual conversation, the New Urbanists have put into practice an academic theory related to Colin Rowe. In this way, they have provided a heretofore unimagined relevance of Collage, Contextualism, and Figure/Ground to contemporary urban design problems.

It is tempting to measure the New Urbanism's success by the quantity of projects that bear its urbanist sensibilities, but that metric would do it a disservice because its most important contribution to urbanism has been its influence on otherwise stagnant, suburban-styled regulatory regimes across the continent, many of which went on to infiltrate center cities as well. An anecdote from Ray Gindroz is illustrative: "My partners and I have been working in inner cities for the length of our careers. Ninety percent of the time we have been told, 'You can't do that because …'. In the last five years, we've been hearing, 'Maybe you can'. And even, in some cases, 'Sure'. That is a fundamental change. That raises the stakes".[36]

Mixed-use zoning is no longer a rarity. 'Walkability' or 'walkable urbanism', terms whose meanings are very much linked to the urban spatial ideas that Colin taught for decades, are now built into the expectations of general or comprehensive plans around the nation. The macro-economic benefits to a neighborhood of walkable urbanism have been quantified and linked to higher land values and greater economic prosperity for that locale.[37]

Even the technocrats have gotten the message, as evidenced by a recent publication of the National Association of City Transportation Officials (NACTO) a group that heretofore had not been known for its advocacy of high-quality public spaces. NACTO's publication, *Urban Street Design Guide*, states that its prescriptions and guidelines are "based on the principle that streets are public spaces for

36 Bressi (2002): 138.

37 See, for example, Leinberger, Christopher B.; Hadden-Loh, Tracy, "Catalytic Development: (Re)creating Walkable Urban Places", Brookings Institution, May 2018. [https://www.brookings.edu/wp-content/uploads/2018/05/brookings-180420-catalytic-development-paper_may-2018-final.pdf].

people as well as arterials for traffic and transportation. This guide foregrounds the role of the street as a catalyst for urban transformation".[38]

As a result of their systematic approach to reform, the New Urbanists have seen successes well beyond what most of them had ever imagined. Rather than wringing their hands and lamenting the loss of public space in metropolitan areas across North America, they took on the institutional forces standing in the way of making better urbanism, whether in the suburbs or in concentrated city centers, and quite often they won their battles. They have transformed the way urbanism is thought about in North America in the present day by imposing a new (or old) way of insisting that the individual building does not only exist as private space, but that it can and should also be a constituent element of the urban realm. They did this by reconsidering the concept of zoning, moving it away from use and density only, and more toward form and spatial definition. The New Urbanists put into practice a contemporary method for making figural space.

Part of this transformation has been led, not by the architects and urban designers, but by organizations like the Congress for the New Urbanism, which includes traffic engineers, financiers, and government officials, as well as other organizations that were significantly influenced by the movement. Among this latter group is the Urban Land Institute (ULI), which has quantified higher returns on investment for 'urbanism' versus 'not urbanism'. The practices advocated for the suburbs, by the New Urbanists, have now been reapplied to the cities themselves. Battles like those waged in the suburbs have been successfully re-fought by the New Urbanists in the city.

The millennials have been quick to notice the rediscovery of urbanism. Like no other generation, they embraced immersive urban environments more by choice than circumstance. Even those residing outside of northeastern U.S. cities are living lifestyles that allow them to drive less than their parents. Many don't get their licenses until they are in their late teens or early '20s, in some cases eschewing car ownership all together. They walk, bike, ride transit, and use ride-sharing services. The highly employable among them are college graduates and choose the city they want to work in before they choose their jobs. Quality of life is measured not only in such things as amount of parkland, but in walkability. 'Walk score' is the new currency of urbanism. It impacts where folks want to live, and hence real estate values. Employers see that, as do real estate developers. Silicon Valley is decanting to the Mission Bay of San Francisco as well as other walkable areas around the Bay area (some of which are more suburban in their locale and density, but not in their walkability). Urbanism is winning, not only in the center city, but throughout the metropolitan areas of North America.

Some of the credit for this change in fortunes can be ascribed to the New Urbanists and by extension to Colin himself, though no doubt he'd deflect the credit as unwarranted because he would be reticent to accept the connection. So be it. If New Urbanism is guilty of having reduced or oversimplified some of Rowe's arguments, it did so in the spirit of making things better within the circumstances faced, within the means available, in the process of going from paper to reality, and most importantly, in the service of getting stuff done, a lot of stuff done.

38 National Association of City Transportation Officials, *Urban Street Design Guide*, Island Press, Washington, D.C., 2013: 3.

Beyond Dialectics: *Collage City* in the Contemporary Metropolis

Adolf Sotoca

> *Simply, the scientist and the* 'bricoleur' *are to be distinguished 'by the inverse functions which they assign to event and structures as means and ends, the scientist creating events ... by means of structures and the* 'bricoleur' *creating structures by means of events.'*
>
> CLAUDE LÉVI-STRAUSS

> *For, if we can divest ourselves of the deceptions of professional* amour propre *and accepted academic theory, the description of the 'bricoleur' is far more of a 'real-life' specification of what the architect-urbanist is and does than any fantasy deriving from 'methodology' and 'systemics'.*[1]
>
> ROWE AND KOETTER

The above quotation is one of the most critical statements in *Collage City.* It constitutes the grounding of Rowe's fierce criticism of the positivist approach to urban interventions in the city. As the central argument of the chapter "Collision City and the Politics of 'Bricolage'", it marks a turning point between two different parts of *Collage City:* the first, a brilliant analysis of the modern condition through a critique of utopia, time, and urban space; whereas the second part develops the concept of *Collage City* as an intellectual and design attitude toward urbanity and urban design.

This essay neither aims to account for nor paraphrase the many concepts and ideas that derive from Rowe's critiques; others who share first-hand knowledge of Rowe, many contributing to this book, are better authorities than me for that. This writing aims to identify and describe the very elements through which, following the terms of action of Rowe's *bricoleur*, the collage condition of the city is both legible and provides operational tools for its design. The focus here, as it is for Rowe, is to describe the physical and material condition that constitutes the urban world. This includes the usual matters of urban morphology, but extends to the more detailed levels that give urban areas their identities, their unique 'sense of place', and allow societies and individuals to assemble their urban experiences according to their own interpretations and values. Such an architectural

frontispiece:
Trieste Porto Vecchio, Manuel de Solá-Morales, 2001. The section as a sequence of urban episodes is here shown as an aerial view.

1 Rowe, Colin; Koetter, Fred, *Collage City*, MIT Press, Cambridge, MA, and London, 1978: 103-04, quoting Claude Lévi-Strauss *The Savage Mind.*

26

La atención a las cosas, el respeto a la cultura material, el filósofo Michel Foucault o el cineasta Víctor Erice nos dicen que el reclamo a las cosas no es sólo la reivindicación de lo físico puro, sino de nuestra mirada sobre la materia, nuestra preocupación y nuestro entendimiento, nuestro amor por las cosas.

Proyectar en la ciudad se inscribe para mí en este acto de atención. Operar en la epidermis urbana es un continuo atender a cómo están las cosas. Y a cuáles añadir, quitar o cambiar, y a cómo disponerlas mejor. No hay otra elección u otra inventiva que la incidencia en la estrategia de las cosas, de las cosas urbanas.

LA CIUDAD ES CUESTIÓN DE COSAS

La ciudad contemporánea no es más fea cada día: es cada día más rica. La pérdida de imaginación que tanto se lamenta, quizá no sea limitación objetiva, sino consecuencia de un gran defecto de información. Si para interpretar la forma de la ciudad contemporánea pretendemos reinventar un nuevo catálogo de espacios, los prototipos que creemos descubrir desaparecen al día siguiente. La cohesión formal propia de los buenos espacios convencionales o la relación biunívoca entre forma y materiales se produce hoy cada vez menos. Esto hace repetir a muchos que la ciudad se aleja, que es ya un artefacto agotado históricamente. Y, a veces, se llega a decir que se ha convertido en territorio virtual, informático y dinámico, pero sin lugar.

Al contrario: cada día hay más lugares. La extensión y la ocupación crecen exponencialmente.

También hay cada vez más contactos. Y cada vez más actividades, usos, construcciones, movimientos, áreas e imágenes urbanas. El número de objetos urbanos se multiplica y acostumbrarnos a esta multiplicidad exige abrir otras perspectivas.

Si los móviles de Alexander Calder pudieron ser metáfora del espacio como sistema de interdependencias en movimiento (la ciudad como sistema), y los collages de Georges Braque anticiparon las figuras de la ciudad hecha por superposición y yuxtaposición de fragmentos (mosaicos), Kasimir Malevich y, sobre todo, Joan Miró reconocieron el espacio como constelación de objetos, como campo de formas libres, como mesa llena de cosas.

La lista de las cosas urbanas podría quizá resultar tan diversa como, por lo menos, la de Borges. Pero si nos fijamos con atención, con devoción incluso, las escenas de la ciudad contemporánea sin coherencia visual ni significado aparente

1

2

3
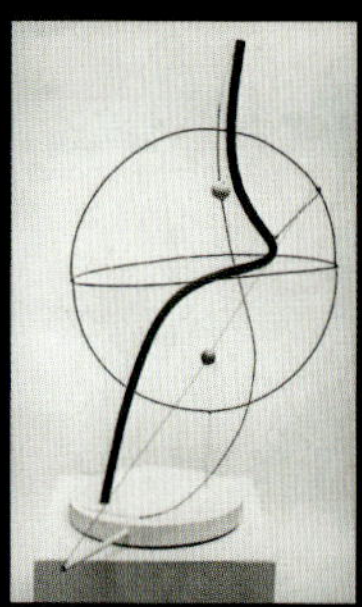

4

1 **Georges Braque,** *El pequeño provenzal*, **1913.**
2 **Joan Miró,** *L'addition*, **1925.**
3 **Alexander Calder,** *Un universo*, **1934.**
4 **Kasimir Malevich,** *Composición suprematista*, **1915-1916.**

"En cierta enciclopedia china" está escrito que "los animales se dividen en a) pertenecientes al Emperador, b) embalsamados, c) amaestrados, d) lechones, e) sirenas, f) fabulosos, g) perros sueltos, h) incluidos en esta clasificación, i) que se agitan como locos, j) innumerables, k) dibujados con un pincel finísimo de pelo de camello, l) etcétera, m) que acaban de romper el jarrón, n) que de lejos parecen moscas".[1]

1 BORGES, Jorge Luis, "El idioma analítico de John Wilkins", en *Otras inquisiciones*, Alianza Editorial, Madrid, 1997, pág. 158

son conjuntos fortuitos que, por la fuerza de su realidad material, adquieren interdependencia. Como en los bodegones pictóricos que disponen sobre una mesa cosas ajenas (una manzana, un jarro, un periódico, una tela), las cosas urbanas establecen entre sí relaciones directas, inmediatas. La ciudad es la mesa que las soporta y presenta esas cosas en su pura materialidad, como realidades identificables en sus diferencias, su posición relativa y sus mutuos reflejos. Reflejos que las refieren a un campo exterior, inmenso, polisémico.

Un pavimento, una fachada de cristal, un muro, una rampa o una perspectiva lejana interrumpida por obstáculos, un perfil contra el cielo en un patio cerrado, calles por terminar y descampados ocupados a medias por trastos provisionales, etc. Todas las gamas de situaciones banales, de tarjetas postales insignificantes, de repetidos espacios "periféricos", "inconexos" o "informales" son bodegones urbanos si los miramos con los ojos del pintor de caballete o del naturalista ensimismado. Son sintagmas del lenguaje de los lugares urbanos. El respeto por las cosas urbanas comporta el aprecio de rincones y vacíos, de ambientes, voladizos, barandillas, garajes, sótanos y tribunas, pórticos y almacenes, rampas y barandillas, pasajes, jardines y rejas, no como anécdotas de un paisaje, sino como formas urbanas que la arquitectura actual produce con frenesí aunque todavía sin nombre... Y quizá sea esta debilidad taxonómica la que impide reconocerlas en su materialidad, en su inquietante presencia.

Cruces y esquinas como lugares de referencia y de intercambio, rampas y huecos que combinan niveles distintos, incidencias intermitentes de túneles, puentes y vías férreas —componentes rígidos de la fluidez—, intervalos de aceras y paseos como soporte primario, o hileras de árboles o de coches aparcados sugieren una lógica de la ciudad física que opera por elementos diferenciados. Sin dejar de incluir los trazados regulares ni las continuidades de fachadas y los largos ejes de circulación, son los episodios truncados, los elementos dislocados, los espacios ambiguos y los objetos amontonados, y su transitoriedad en el espacio y en el tiempo, las características formales que hacen de nuestras ciudades territorios de cosas, campos de elementos.

La atención a las cosas urbanas es la que nos permite hacer de la "cantidad" urbana traducida en variedad el principal adjetivo del territorio metropolitano; masas de casas y edificios, barrios de oficinas, ilimitadas zonas de viviendas unifamiliares, ensanches abiertos sin programa, litorales marítimos en algarabía, parques industriales, centros comerciales, ciudades de vacaciones, grandes aparcamientos

DE COSAS URBANAS 27

Fig. 1. (above) and Fig. 2. (opposite). Visual essay of the city and the *bricoleur* from the preface of *A Matter of Things*, Manuel de Solá-Morales, 2008.

view of the city places the emphasis on physical form and 'urban materiality' without excluding the contributions of other disciplines. This seems to me a most needed discussion at a time in which urban identity is allegedly in crisis due to global urbanization and sprawl. Therefore, I will extend Rowe's ideas to our present day by comparing them to the positions of two urbanists who, between the early 1960s and today, have been reflecting on that urban materiality as well: Ludovico Quaroni and Manuel de Solá-Morales.

Bricoleurs of the City

Among the many references Rowe uses to illustrate his discourse, the city of Rome plays a predominant role.[2] Its *urbs* constitutes, in Rowe's view, an alternative to urban positivism, social engineering, and total design. Rome is the result of a specific topography and several successive and particular cultures and the physical remnants of its urban history result in one of "the most graphic examples of collisive fields and interstitial debris". As described by Rowe, the works of imperial and papal *bricolage* are intertwined with 19th century bourgeois interventions on the urban fabric, a compilation of rationally gridded fields, mostly corresponding to "state structure".[3] The Eternal City becomes the central case study whereby Rowe develops the three fundamental dialectics that sustain *Collage City*, namely, the dialectics of solid/void, object/texture and, ultimately, fragment/collision. And he does so by describing, both graphically and textually, significant urban episodes where the dialectics can be seen, the papal period being the most significant. When Rowe develops the concept of *bricolage*, he

2 Besides the many references to Rome in *Collage City* he also took part in the "Roma interrotta" exhibition, where he submitted a proposal for the Aventino-Palatino sector. Cerruti, Marisa, ed., *Roma interrotta*, officina edizioni, Roma, 1978.

3 Rowe and Koetter (1978): 107.

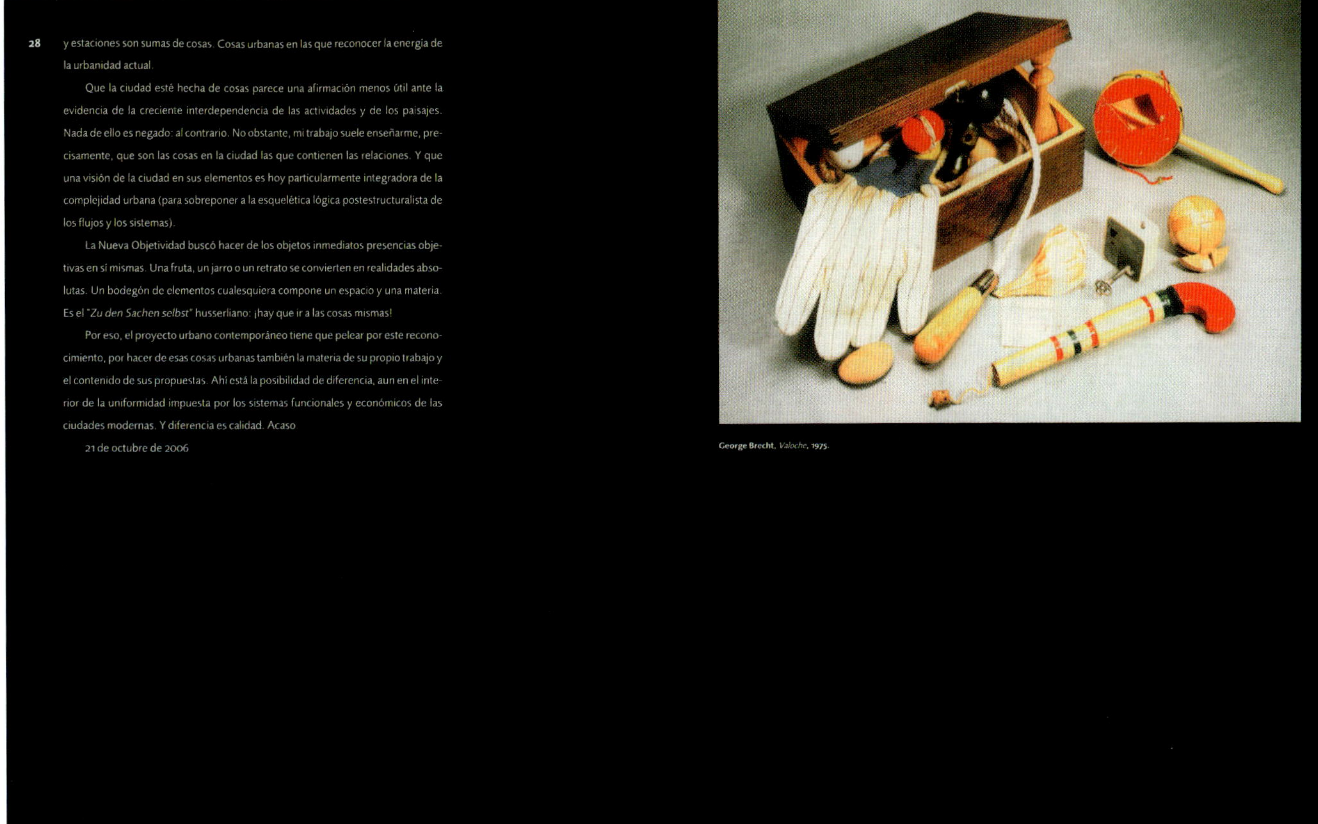

28 y estaciones son sumas de cosas. Cosas urbanas en las que reconocer la energía de la urbanidad actual.

Que la ciudad esté hecha de cosas parece una afirmación menos útil ante la evidencia de la creciente interdependencia de las actividades y de los paisajes. Nada de ello es negado: al contrario. No obstante, mi trabajo suele enseñarme, precisamente, que son las cosas en la ciudad las que contienen las relaciones. Y que una visión de la ciudad en sus elementos es hoy particularmente integradora de la complejidad urbana (para sobreponer a la esquelética lógica postestructuralista de los flujos y los sistemas).

La Nueva Objetividad buscó hacer de los objetos inmediatos presencias objetivas en sí mismas. Una fruta, un jarro o un retrato se convierten en realidades absolutas. Un bodegón de elementos cualesquiera compone un espacio y una materia. Es el "*Zu den Sachen selbst*" husserliano: ¡hay que ir a las cosas mismas!

Por eso, el proyecto urbano contemporáneo tiene que pelear por este reconocimiento, por hacer de esas cosas urbanas también la materia de su propio trabajo y el contenido de sus propuestas. Ahí está la posibilidad de diferencia, aun en el interior de la uniformidad impuesta por los sistemas funcionales y económicos de las ciudades modernas. Y diferencia es calidad. Acaso

21 de octubre de 2006

George Brecht, *Valoche*, 1975.

does so as a counter and alternative to the approaches so characteristic of positivism. The references to Rome provide an anthology of closed compositions and dialectics between ideal types and empirical context.[4] Strangely enough, Rowe does not refer in his writings and proposals to "Una città eterna. Quattro lezioni da ventisette secoli", the seminal text by Ludovico Quaroni that describes Rome in analogous terms to the ones used by Rowe. Quaroni, who had taught at MIT in the late 1950s and had some influence in British and American architectural educational institutions,[5] had built an urban narrative on Rome which is quite coincident to that of Rowe. Quaroni also describes the city as a result of conflicts that are legible through the collision of solids and voids. Quaroni's reading of cities is based on a contrast between what he refers to as "homogenous fabrics" and "urban emergences" seen to erupt from that fabric. As he cites examples from his childhood and adolescence:

> *walking along narrow alleys or contemplating whatever I could from the roofs, an interest began to grow inside me, fed by the walls and sun of Rome, for the relationship between 'grid' and 'emergences' that is, between all that gave its shape to the network of small streets and houses, and, in contrast, the monuments, full of dignity, towering above the grid, and standing apart from it even in their vertical surfaces. I have always known that my interest in the city does not lie in the houses, taken on their own, or in monuments outside their context, but in the amalgam, in the cocktail of monuments and larger or smaller houses, that is, in the 'grid' and 'emergences' as I like to call them, although in many cases the 'emergences' may be lower and smaller than the buildings making up the fabric.*[6]

4 Delbeke, Maarten, "Roma Interrotta. Barok Rome als een (post-)modernistisch model", *OASE* 86, 2011: 74-85.

5 Del Monaco, Anna Irene, "Emergence-urban fabric in the urban design of Ludovico Quaroni: morphology vs typology", L'architettura delle città. *The Journal of the Scientific Society,* Ludovico Quaroni 1-2, 2013: 161-85.

6 Interview of Quaroni by Manuel de Solá- Morales, "Ludovico Quaroni, Answers at Length", *UR, Urbanismo Revista* 7, Quaroni, Ludovico; de Solá-Morales, Manuel (1989): 2-17.

Fig. 3. Model for "Barene di San Giuliano" (Venice), Ludovico Quaroni, 1959. The proposal was drafted the same year that "Una città eterna: quattro lezioni da ventisette secoli" was published. The image shows how monumentality is achieved by the use of Modern architectural typologies. The dialectic emergence/fabric is also explicit in the urban layout.

Quaroni's identification of fabric/emergences can very well be regarded as synonymous with the object/texture dialectic present in Rowe's texts. However different their respective conclusions might be, especially when it comes to the politics of the city and its governance, their approach to reading city form, as well as their skeptical view toward positivism and totalitarian design approaches, are very much aligned. Their appreciation for the succession of events as foundations for city-intervention, a truly *bricoleur* procedure as explained in the beginning of this text, is explicitly acknowledged in the essay "Urbanisti Italiani",[7] in which Quaroni is portrayed as a figure whose work is that of the paradigmatic *urban planner* and becomes that of a *bricoleur*.[8]

Urban Dialectics

The tension between generic idealism and specific empiricism is the ideological grounding for the theories of both Rowe and Quaroni. While Rowe describes the "literal extension of total design into total management and total print out as a dubious and fruitless enterprise, unable to respond to fine grain association, immediate circumstance and vitality",[9] he also questions the critical adoption of what he calls populist empiricism. His proposal, a halfway between both, is that of, in the words of Lévi-Strauss, a "rational thinking at the level of the sensitive".[10] Quaroni, on the other side, works on generalizable solutions, not to make them generally valid, but in order to tend toward general and extensive aspects of the city: masses of development, systems of solidness and emptiness, or of vegetation and architecture, operational units, updating models for old neighbourhoods, centers, boulevards, and campuses.[11] On the operational field, the approaches of both Rowe and Quaroni rely on a common ground, namely the dialectics solid/void, texture/emergence, and fragment/collision.

7 Di Biagi, Paola; Gabellini, Patrizia, *Urbanisti Italiani: Piccinato, Marconi, Samonà, Quaroni, De Carlo, Astengo, Campos Venuti*, Editori Laterza, Roma–Bari, 1992.

8 "However, that obsession on the scientificity of urban-science prevented the theorist Aldo Rossi from understanding the no-method, empirical and synthetic, narrative and sincretic, of Quaroni.... The city is a human work or the art-work for excellence – between Claude Lévi-Strauss and Aldo Rossi; but the attitude of Lévi-Strauss is that of a 'bricoleur', a characteristic that Di Biagi and Gabellini (1992) assigned nonetheless to Quaroni: a temporal and spatial elaboration, vivid and collective, organic in the biological understanding of the term". Terranova, Antonino, "Entre Arquitectura y Urbanística. Un Paseo Por La Ciudad Eterna", in Quaroni, Ludovico, *Una ciudad eterna. Cuatro lecciones de veintisiete siglos*, Fundación Caja de Arquitectos, Barcelona, 2008: 7-19.

9 Rowe and Koetter (1978): 96.

10 Lévi-Strauss, Claude, *The Savage Mind*, University of Chicago Press, London, 1973.

Fig. 4. Weisbaden, figure/ground by Wayne Copper.

Solid/Void

As for the first dialectic, Rowe devotes a whole chapter of *Collage City* to the "Crisis of the Object and the Predicament of Texture". In it, he delves into the origins of the crisis of the object that took place during Modernity, when space, or void, came to be seen as prevalent over matter, or solid. Rowe suggested that the purpose of the spatial continuum was that of facilitating the ideals of freedom, nature, and spirit, thus becoming a widespread tendency to what amounts to a worship of limitless natural space as opposed to any framed and structured urban ambience. As a result, the pattern of the city has been transformed from continuous solid to continuous void. The remediation for such loss of urban legibility would be, as the "Excursus" chapter of *Collage City* suggests, a series of urban stimulants, "a-temporal and necessarily transcultural, as possible *objets trouvés* in the urbanistic collage".[12]

It is as if Quaroni had been building upon a similar set of stimulants. He sought an urban project methodology aiming for "diffuse quality" and based on a fabric able to bring to contemporary cities a permanent urban identity by introducing qualities of solid-void contrast, rhythm, colors or uses, making the city both beautiful and comfortable.[13]

If Rowe tested his ideas, strategies, and tactics in his proposal for the Buffalo Waterfront and later in "Roma interrotta", Quaroni finds in the proposal for San Giuliano, Venice, the ideal canvas for his compositional explorations. As Antonino Terranova describes, "In [the] San Giuliano project three big artifacts, eccentric crescents in the shape of circular segments, face the Venetian Lagoon and reflect themselves on the water, telling us that both the historical and contemporary city need to be presented with an equivalent symbolical meaning".[14]

11 A more detailed description of Quaroni's compositional repertoire, can be found in de Solá-Morales, Manuel, "Quaroni, a Distant Lucidity", *UR, Urbanismo Revista* 7, 1989: 37-46. Their description very much resembles the stimulants that Rowe lists in the "Excursus" of *Collage City:* "Ludovico Quaroni turns perhaps to two favourite solutions in order to group together the elements of residential fabric into formal units of larger dimensions, in scale with the urbanised territory: circles and links. Circles repeat themselves in Ludovico Quaroni's iconography as an almost inevitable constant element of his later projects, with the force of playing a protagonist role in the composition, but at the same time with a familiarity that detracts importance from the difficulty entailed in their development, thus turning them into an almost common geometry of urban forms".

12 Rowe and Koetter (1978): 151.

13 de Solá-Morales (1989): 39-41.

14 Terranova (2008): 9-10.

above:
Fig. 5. Government Center in Tunis, Ludovico Quaroni, 1965. The confrontation between the urban fabric of the old kasbah and the new intervention is legible from the aerial view. The display of voids in both fragments is of great interest, being the counterpart to the figure/ground plan of Wiesbaden.

opposite:
Fig. 6. Casilino (Rome), Ludovico Quaroni, 1964. The neighborhood serves as an interesting counterpart to Rowe's prescriptions found in "The present urban predicament". Despite its Modern architecture repertoire, archetypes suggested by Rowe—such as the garden, the display of long buildings, and the serial repetition of elements—are identifiable in the proposal.

Object/Texture

The proposal for San Giuliano is strongly determined by the will to cast visible and legible urban emergences onto the fabric. The symbolic meaning that Quaroni assigns to the residential buildings at San Giuliano is shaped through the dialectic fabric/emergences, which finds its equivalent in the object/texture dialectic so extensively developed by Rowe. For both authors, the texture/fabric of the city constitutes its very essence, the identity of the 'place'. While Rowe describes "the texture as giving energy to its reciprocal condition, the specific space: the ensuing square and street acting as some kind of public relief valve and providing some condition of legible structure",[15] Quaroni is, as described by Manuel de Solá-Morales, confident in the urban form as an observable cultural event and as a field for operative, practical project design. For Quaroni the fabric forms different parts within the overall body of the city, concerned with a preponderantly formal proposition. His general theory of urban form, the articulation of "fabrics" and "emergences", denotes in itself the scale of attention he propitiates.[16] The varying relation between forms of urban growth and forms of development is what creates the variety and beauty of each part of the city and every city itself.[17] The city seen as a collage of fragments finds its legibility in the contrast among the textures that are so characteristic of urban fabrics. And it is precisely in the relation among fragments, in how the dialectic fragment/collision takes place, where Rowe and Quaroni differ the most.

Fragment/Collision

Even though both Rowe and Quaroni coincide in understanding the city as a succession of political struggles and, furthermore, both conclude that conflicts are drivers for urban intervention, they attribute significantly different meanings

15 Rowe and Koetter (1978): 63.
16 Quaroni and de Solá Morales (1989): 2-17.
17 de Solá-Morales (1989): 39-41.

to the third dialectic, that of fragment and collision. For Rowe, the confrontation of fragments provides the opportunity for objects to be conscripted out of their context.[18] Such collisions of urban forms is thought of as a collage, both as a collage technique and in the way a collage conveys meaning and accommodates a range of possibilities; as the reading belongs to the observer, there is the freedom to assign new meanings. And, just as with a pictorial collage, change of context changes meaning, that is, different figures potentially mean different things in relation to one another as well as to their background or context. Therefore, it frees formal poetics from the burden of historical meanings, or in the words of Rowe, "a means of permitting us the enjoyment of utopian poetics without our being obliged to suffer the embarrassment of utopian politics".[19] *Collage City* is an operational method deriving its virtue from its irony because, as a technique for using things while simultaneously disbelieving in them, it is also a strategy that can allow utopia, or fragments of a utopia —thus representing it— to be dealt with as image. We may assert that historical time is, for Rowe, freed from its linear imperatives and, therefore, is allowed to rearrange itself according to experiential schemata.[20]

Quaroni, in contrast, conceives time as a cumulative series of episodes that, however unequally relevant, shape the urban materiality of the city. Present time is seen, therefore, as an actual episode of an *axis mundi* in which its historical significance is legible. In "Una città eterna: Quattro lezioni da ventisette secoli",[21] Quaroni argues that the city would live in the history of its figure/ground, a history that would be defined as a process that includes the conflicts between societies and between buildings. The diverse plays of urban fabrics that characterize any city, showing the various cultural episodes that the city has gone through is

18 "It is suggested that a collage approach, an approach in which objects are conscripted or seduced from out of their context, is–at the present day–the only way of dealing with the ultimate problems of either or both utopia and tradition". Rowe and Koetter (1978): 144.

19 Ibid.: 149.

20 That particular understanding of time is explicitly stated by Rowe in the text accompanying the proposal for the Aventino–Palatino–Circo Massimo sector for "Roma interrotta" (1978). The design, which might be understood as a heterotopic revisiting of Giambattista Nolli's map of 1748, is a remarkable piece of work that discloses Rowe's stand put forth in *Collage City:* "Instead, as one of the goals is to extract from Nolli a Rome that could have been and was not, we have invented a history that it could have been and it was not. However, in the same way as things and within the limits of the mind of the Nolli, we have tried to make a plausible Rome, a city that belongs to the category of those impossible but reliable". In the text accompanying the proposal Rowe accounts for the succession of events that confirm the urban history of this part of the city. Cerruti (1978).

21 Quaroni, Ludovico, "Una città eterna. Quattro lezioni da ventisette secoli", *Urbanistica* 27, 1959: 66-67.

Fig. 7. Ludovico Quaroni (1911-1987).

Fig. 8. Casilino (Rome), Ludovico Quaroni, 1964.

a legible code of a wider political understanding of societies. And Quaroni, in an optimistic stance that he will abandon later on in his life, affirms that urban projects have a high political meaning and transformative capacity, "projects define pieces of the city, heterogeneous and significant, enough to involve urbanistic options".[22] In describing his proposal for the Casilino neighborhood in Rome, he accounts for the themes and topics that define the struggle of the urban project:

> *It was considered that the whole life would take place above all within the open spaces left between the two winding buildings: a street life since the space between the two buildings was wide and lively, like an avenue, in this way allowing for the construction of gardens, children's playgrounds, tennis courts, small open-air theatres, and so on: practically the whole of community life, something which no-one has ever bothered to try out. But the project was rejected because, being as it was a compact composition, it would have been badly received by the concessionaires of the works who each had their own laws, rules and habits, with no one above them to impose a model, a scheme, a form of development. And how can anything good ever be achieved for the city if we have done away with all specific personal responsibilities by delegating and expecting decisions to be taken left, right and centre, so that it is later impossible to find anyone responsible for a badly developed work?*[23]

In this passage, a direct connection between urban composition and the political model is seen. It is in this connection that both Quaroni and Rowe ask themselves about their respective approach to the city and their ability to properly respond to the contemporary city.

The Contemporary City

In *Collage City* and "Una Città Eterna", Rowe and Quaroni respectively build their theory based on the analysis, either synchronically or diachronically, of existing cities (with Rome the main case study for Rowe and "the one" for Quaroni).

22 de Solá-Morales (1989): 39.

23 Quaroni and de Solá-Morales (1989): 11.

Fig. 9. Torresana (Terrassa, Barcelona), Manuel de Solá-Morales, 2004.

Fig. 10. Manuel de Solá-Morales (1939-2012)

However, both authors are aware of the need to make their views operational for the actual challenges that contemporary urbanization faces. Again, the dialectic, in this case between the historical city and the contemporary metropolis, is the method they both use to confront their theories with the challenge of reality.

The main concern for Rowe is that of perception-comprehension; in the Modern city with its abundant and continuous open space and proliferation of objects located in such a diffuse manner that, the resulting multiplication of 'in-between' spaces becomes so great as to no longer offer a perceptual basis for orientation. Rowe asserts the difference between the traditional and the Modern city in saying:

> *while limited structured spaces may facilitate identification and understanding, an interminable naturalistic void without any recognizable boundaries will at least be likely to defeat all comprehension. ...For, if the appreciation or perception of object or figure is assumed to require the presence of some sort of ground or field, if the recognition of some sort of however closed field is a prerequisite of all perceptual experience and, if consciousness of field precedes consciousness of figure, then, when figure is unsupported by any recognizable frame of reference, it can only become enfeebled and self-destructive.*[24]

The remedy proposed by Rowe consists of a series of prescriptions that, being further elaborations of the *Collage City* dialectics, he presented in "The Present Urban Predicament":[25] visual evidence and constitution of the traditional city; central void-figure, stable and obviously planned; the scrutiny of long, skinny buildings operating rather more as special cases than as parts of a general system; and finally, the garden, which may comprise yet another prescription for overcoming object fixation. Despite Rowe explicitly stating that "in an age, allegedly, of optional latitude and pluralist intention, it should be possible at least to plot some kind of strategy of accommodation and coexistence"[26] between what he variously calls the traditional or classical city, and in contrast with it,

24 Rowe and Koetter (1978): 64-65.

25 Lecture first delivered at the Royal Institution of London in 1979. Rowe, Colin, "The Present Urban Predicament", in *As I Was Saying: Recollections and Miscellaneous Essays* 3, Caragonne, Alexander, ed., MIT Press, Cambridge, MA, and London, 1995: 165-220.

the Modern or contemporary city. Rowe illustrates his prescriptions with reference primarily to examples from traditional cities; for example, the Galleria Uffizi, the Munich Residenz, the Palais Royal, and, above all, the vast catalogue of architecture in Rome.

As for Quaroni, he acknowledges urbanization as the image of a new sociopolitical paradigm, materialized in the phenomenon of urban sprawl on the peripheries of metropolitan areas. Architects are faced, in his view, with the challenge of finding new methodological directions, not so much in order to control urban morphology, but so as to implement the efficient infilling of the diffuse, heterogeneous, and incoherent urban environment of sprawl.[27] For Quaroni, city centers are not only a closed reality but an open heritage that must be reinvented in the contemporary city, updating them and, maybe, posing contradictions. In the relations between the historical and the contemporary landscapes, the phenomenology of the city-region needs to be created as an allegorical memory of the Baroque city through the reinterpretation of its historical compositional devices, such as crescents, circuses, and squares.[28]

That task had already begun shortly after the publication of "Una Città Eterna". In 1963, Quaroni was working on the design of the Turin Civic Center development and the Casilino residential area in Rome. As described by him, the urban composition for the residential neighborhood of Casilino dealt with similar concerns and categories as those vindicated by Rowe. Quaroni writes of it,

> *The first draft, drawn up to test the restrictions of the main client, that is, the Town Hall, still suffered from my old tendencies towards an architecture of free and non-rectilinear, non-parallel, volumes: a first and rough scheme foresaw winding buildings, although without spirals. Special care had been put, somehow, on the spatial effects obtainable from these lines which slowly moved away or came closer, fragmenting themselves repeatedly, creating streets or piazzas, or something comparable to them .... The buildings were higher in the third draft which consisted of six arms of buildings several stories high, wrapping and unwrapping themselves around the elongated area, leaving open, like a garden, the site facing Primavera street. ... There were thus two totally external spaces drawing a beautiful curve offering good day-lighting possibilities, with an area that changed from light to shade, depending on the time of day, this being the great virtue of curves.*[29]

Manuel de Solá-Morales, a young Catalan architect, who would later become one of the leading figures of European urbanism, was working side by side with Quaroni at that time. In later years he would repeatedly refer to the influence of Quaroni on his thoughts, as well as acknowledging the influence of Rowe on post-Modern urbanism. In 1995, almost 40 years after "Una Città Eterna" and 20 years after *Collage City*, de Solá-Morales wrote, "Ideas of the city as a mosaic or 'collage', such as those put forward, for example, in the excellent book by Colin Rowe, are good morphological paradigms for analysis", but then he continues, "However, to say that the whole city is made of different pieces ends up by being tautological if we do not say how to make another piece, or how to change faulty parts, or how to create new mechanisms in the juxtapositions".[30] He will take on the discussion and will devote much of his activity, as theorist and practitioner, to seeking strategies for urban interventions in the spatially continuous contemporary city that Rowe found so worrisome.

26 Rowe and Koetter (1978): 66.

27 de Solá-Morales (1989): 41, Terranova (2008): 9-10.

28 Terranova (2008): 9-10.

29 Quaroni and de Solá-Morales (1989): 9-11.

30 de Solá-Morales, Manuel, "Città tagliate. Appunti su identità e differenze", in *I racconti dell'abitare: Un seminario, una mostra,* Abitare, Segesta, Milano, 1994: 184-89.

Again, as described before in this text, the role of time in the urban experience is a critical element in comparing the approaches of Rowe and Quaroni and de Solá-Morales: time is sequential and cumulative to Quaroni and de Solá-Morales, whereas for Rowe the conception of date is of minor importance. However relevant this different approach might be for the three authors, we may find continuities between them in terms of the themes they deal with and the dialectical methodology present in all their writings. De Solá-Morales, by bringing to the present time the three dialectics present in both Rowe and Quaroni, would reinterpret them and make them operational strategies for urban development in contemporary metropolises. The fragment/collision dialectic would be solved by de Solá-Morales by his "section-cities" strategy; solid/void confrontation would give way to the "interesting distance" balance; and finally, object/texture would find integration in "collective spaces".

Fig. 11. Alexanderplatz proposal, Manuel de Solá-Morales, 1990 © Manuel de Solà-Morales Archive.

Void as an "Interesting Distance"

In line with Rowe's diagnosis on the difficulty of legibility in Modern cities, de Solá-Morales accepts that the classical sense of place has vanished in those areas where the solid in the solid/void dialectic has become discontinuous as the prevailing condition due to the morphology of the contemporary metropolis. However, de Solá-Morales identifies a different and specific spatial quality in these peripheral areas; it is characterized by the abundance of "expecting" spaces, which, on the other hand, are indifferent to architecture, whether figure-object or not. The quality of such landscapes lies in the fact that the ubiquitous presence of empty space weakens the presence of uses, activities and the architectures immersed in them. And because neither "difference" nor "repetition"[31] has been consciously used as a compositional device, the dominant role played by this continuously flowing space appears to be the condition of our contemporary peripheries.

In that sense, de Solá-Morales states that the specific spatial condition of peripheries, the ones we conventionally regard as spontaneous and unplanned, are in fact planned using a system of distances between built objects, or rather distances between the location and site planning of building compounds devoted to diverse uses and activities. The spaces between them may be determined by chance, but the location and site planning of building compounds is determined by access for users to diverse activities, or access to favorable advertising possibilities. And such location strategies typically disregard any kind of general composition or formal rationale. Instead, the rationale is a system of distances based on territorial logic: determining locations for building compounds particular to the economic exploitation of topographies or seeking preeminent views, and, most importantly, measured distances to nearest infrastructure, to accessible facilities, to environmental assets, and to neighbors. The system is not based on the perception and comprehension of space, but on presumptions of functionality based on distances related to time and mobility, that is, "access".

Designing and planning the outskirts of contemporary metropolises may rely, according to de Solá-Morales, on the interplay of these "interesting distances" and on the diversity of situations that arises from them. His view is that the void in peripheries should not necessarily be considered as areas to be planned as gardened pieces of land evoking more or less naturalistic green spaces. And that such

31 Used by Manuel de Solá-Morales in the meaning that the French philosopher Gilles Deleuze gives to the terms. Deleuze, Gilles, *Différence et répétition* (5. éd.), Presses universitaires de France, Paris, 1985.

areas may be left devoid of figurative formal content, while their abstract value as distance should be acknowledged. The "interesting distances" would, therefore, be regarded as the main driver in the composition of the urban form of the periphery. The aesthetics, architecture, and landscape, in their own autonomy and efficiency, need to include these empty spaces as far as they are considered as "interesting distances", critically chosen for their figurative capacity and their environmental and scenic rationality.

Here we can draw a parallel with Rowe's argument regarding the relational capacity of the *poché* concept,[32] that is, *poché* as a conceptually solid matrix assisting the legibility of adjacent spaces or major architectural episodes. The matrix of distances in contemporary peripheries could potentially become a similar device for reading a series of major architectural episodes, for either building compounds or significant public spaces. Using distances as a decoding tool consists of finding multilateral relations among them in which movement and "cinematic deepness" will allow simultaneous perceptions of architectural sequences. It might be that—contrary to the conception that voids, whether urban, peripheral, or external, are potential plots for landscape—they should not be treated as works of architecture because this has already been shown to lead towards hyper-design and tedium. Rather, peripheral voids are the stage for minimum or maximum distances. As de Solá-Morales states, "in fact they [peripheries] are full of them, but no consideration is given to the overall interest in these distances. Yet in urban space, interesting distances are filled with purpose in terms of the positive separation between a whole range of different objects".[33]

Collective "Objects"

Once the relational network among objects is devised, the question about the ontology of the object still remains. Alternative to denouncing the disintegration of the architectural building, so characteristic in Rowe's critique of Modern architecture, both Quaroni and, more specifically, de Solá-Morales, suggest the concept of "emergence" as indicative of social construct. If much of Rowe's criticism of the Modern city and the crisis of the architectural object points out that "the demolition of public life and decorum reduces the public realm, the traditional world of visible civics to an amorphic remainder" and that, even though "the public realm has shrunk to an apologetic ghost, the private realm has not been significantly enriched",[34] then de Solá-Morales proposes a new category, which transcends the dialectic between public and private domains and finds in the 'in-between' its denominator: collective spaces.[35]

In his view, the terms of private and public are not useful at the present time because the spaces where we build our community sensibilities are in the "collective spaces" of hotels and restaurants, shopping malls or suburban hypermarkets, and amusement parks and sport-fields with their engulfing parking lots. These are the significant places in our daily lives. Most of these new spaces are located in metropolitan outskirts that today, are inevitably, the true social centers of cities for many, perhaps most, of the 'urban' population whether dwelling in the realm of the city, the suburb, or its sprawl. Architects and planners are faced with the challenge of designing such intermediate spaces, the majority of which are free of the rhetoric of formal representation. They are understood as neither

32 "Frankly, we had forgotten the term, or relegated it to a catalogue of obsolete categories and were only recently reminded of its usefulness by Robert Venturi. But if *poché*, understood as the imprint upon the plan of the traditional heavy structure, acts to disengage the principal spaces of the building from each other, if it is a solid matrix which frames a series of major spatial events, it is not hard to acknowledge that the recognition of *poché* is also a matter of context and that, depending on perceptual field, a building itself may become a type of *poché*, for certain purposes a solid assisting the legibility of adjacent spaces. And thus, for instance, such buildings as the Palazzo Borghese may be taken as types of habitable *poché* which articulate the transition of external voids". Rowe and Koetter (1978): 78-79.

33 de Solá-Morales, Manuel, "Territori privi di modello", in Neri, Raffaella, ed., *Il centro altrove: Periferie e nuove centralità nelle aree metropolitane*, (Ente autonomo La Triennale di Milano), Electa, Milano, 1995: 171-73.

34 As literally described in "Crisis of the Object: Predicament of Texture", where the authors reason that the disintegration of object questions the very definition of public and private realms. Rowe and Koetter (1978): 63-65.

35 The term is widely defined by de Solá-Morales in the article "Public Spaces / Collective Spaces", published in the newspaper *La Vanguardia*. de Solá-Morales, Manuel, "Espacios públicos / Espacios colectivos", *La Vanguardia*, 12 May, 1992.

public nor private. Neither are they understood as only objects for advertising and profit. But rather, they are considered stimulating parts of the multiform, urban-to-sprawl matrix.

For de Solá-Morales, the most challenging thing to overcome is the traditional view of former public spaces as models for expression of the quintessential attributes of a cohesive society and, consequently, the prime form of the social expression of that which is public. The fact is that, on the contrary, the contemporary periphery of the metropolis is the place where the collective must be social too. Under this new paradigm, the quality in the individual realm is required if, when semantically shared by the collective, it is going to turn out to be the meaningful aesthetic of the community. And it may be the case that, in our cities, the spaces of an ambiguous and amorphous nature are the ones that are going to play a more and more significant role in everyday social life.

Therefore, de Solá-Morales suggests that undertaking programs of 'urban beautification', 'peripheral monumentalization' or 'engineered environmentalization' based on an obsolete iconic understanding of 'public' spaces, may lead us to apply outdated strategies to the make-up of urban peripheries. Such attitudes may possess the great virtue of establishing the aesthetic importance of works of urbanization, but from a more ambitious approach to our present task, they do not have a great future. The necessary cohesion between public and private has to be practiced to the extent required by the delicacy of the urban and social fabric, where "emergences" do not simply belong to the realm of the public but to new collective buildings where the actual social activity and associated meaning is found. That would necessarily lead us to a new urban ontology and related semiotics. In such an ontology the relation between fragments ought to go beyond collision and, instead, look for design strategies able to build narratives based on qualitative correlation rather than on confrontation.

"Cut Cities"

The new semiotic needed is what de Solá-Morales names "cut cities".[36] A 'cut', which one may interpret as a 'section', strings the several and diverse fragments of the city together. While a fragment is a piece concept, a section is a sequential idea of experience, of time continuity in the spatial discontinuity. The city as a collage is a good morphological paradigm for analysis. De Solá-Morales argues, however, that, as with so many analogies, it is brilliant in concept and of operational value for the dense central city but of dubious operational value for relating the dense central city to the sparse perimeter. The section, on the contrary, makes the fragment less important because it accepts it naturally and binds it with others perceived as sequential episodes, as if a casting of the experience of the 'cut'. The section 'cut' synthetizes all spatial and functional components of the city, as it implies we are to simultaneously think of ground plane, of the multiple levels revealed by the section, of the section-elevation, of topography, territory, and use.

By "cutting cities" we are able to represent the continuities of the fragmentary peripheral condition, more so nowadays, when hybrid suburb forms seem to be the shared territory common to most citizens, "it is most interesting to understand the lengthwise section cut of the cities, from the periphery to the city

36 Note from the author: the original article "Città tagliate: Appunti su identità e differenze" was included in its English version in: de Solà-Morales i Rubió, Manuel; Frampton, Kenneth; Ibelings, Hans, *A Matter of Things*, NAi, Rotterdam, 2008. The term "Città tagliate" was translated to English as "Cut Cities", thus losing some of its technical meaning, as the article referred mostly to the "section" as a graphic device and strategy for urban design. Here the term "cut" is faithfully kept in the title, although "section" or "section cut" is used for the rest of the text.

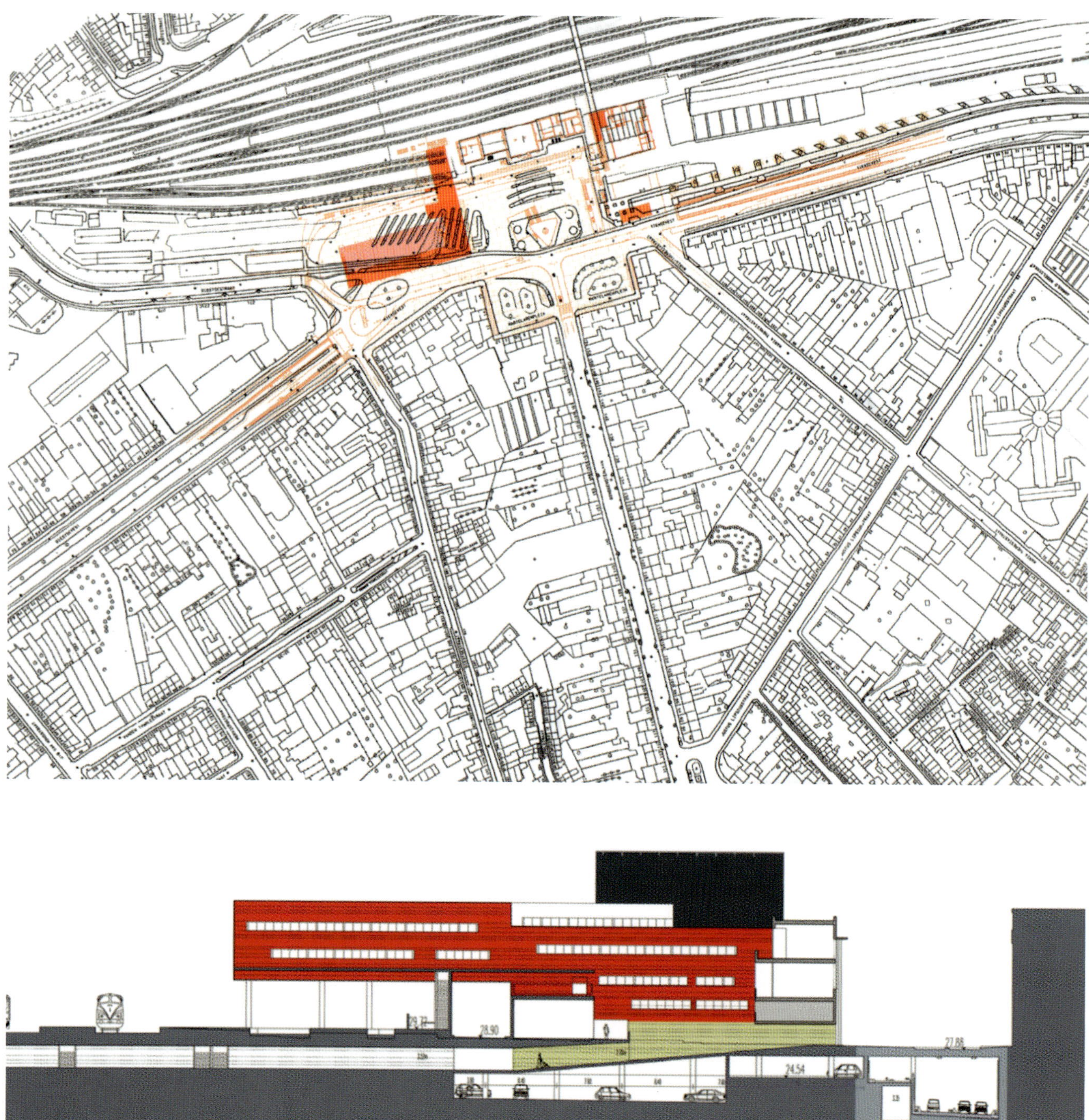

Fig. 12. Stationsplein, urban plan (Leuven, Belgium), Manuel de Solá-Morales, 2002. A true paradigm of collective space, the building gathers several programs and a diverse set of relations with public space and infrastructure.

Fig. 13. Stationplein, section through car park.

Fig. 14. Stationsplein, view of the station square, showing context of historic buildings with new intervention at center (2021 Google Earth).

center".[37] The highways that enter the cities cut them from outside-in, letting us imagine how the different parts of the city are linked in a vaguely intended sequence of "interesting distances".

In my view, if malleable images of the urban periphery are now part of our aesthetics, perhaps it makes sense to devise socially and architecturally positive planning proposals for these phenomena without the need, as de Solá-Morales suggests, to "mend" or "monumentalize" what exists. A new thinking is needed, a reflection on how to integrate buildings, empty spaces, and access routes by designing the place and landscape simultaneously. The "collage city" of Rowe is, indeed, a powerful tool in understanding and offering a range of possible strategies for ameliorating the increasingly fragmentary condition of our contemporary cities. However, if we are to intervene operationally in the contemporary urban periphery, we may be able to extend its true meaning using the knowledge of the peripheral condition that we have gained since Rowe's ideas were first published in *Collage City* in order to further develop operational tools of analysis and design that he suggested. First, the overabundance of shapeless peripheral spaces demands a new metric in the solid-void relationship which may use the interesting distance as an operational tool. Second, the many new graphic tools at hand today might redefine the way we are empowered to think about the contemporary built environment. Lastly, the design of collective spaces as "emergences" from the peripheries of 'in-between' locations—ambiguously neither public nor private—may be an approach more in line with our contemporary experience of metropolitan spaces. These might be suitable ways to build upon Rowe's concepts in discussions of the changing urban condition.

37 de Solá-Morales et al. (2008): 177-78.

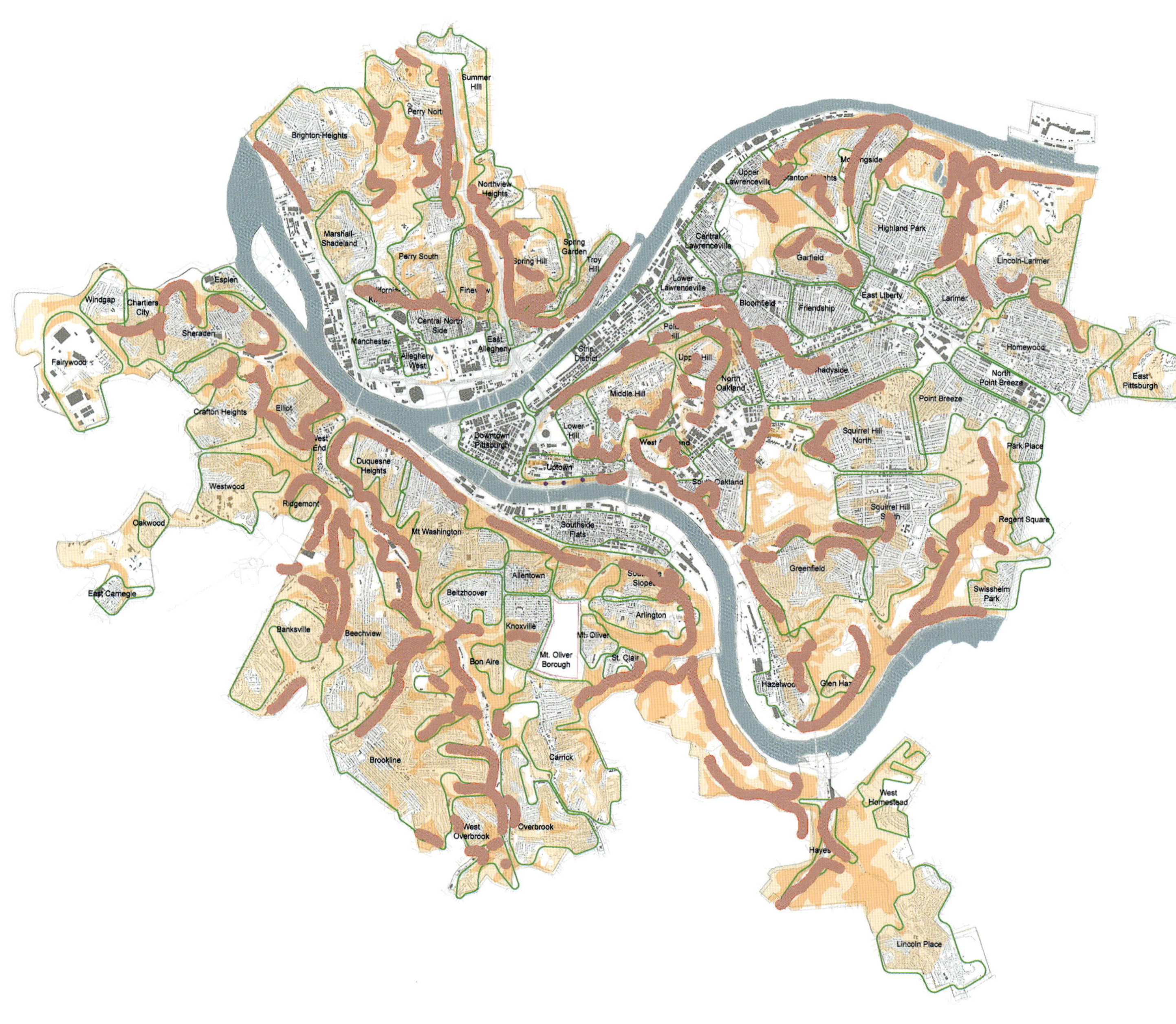
Summer Hill
Brighton Heights
Northview Heights
Marshall-Shadeland
Perry South
Spring Garden
Spring Hill
Troy Hill
Esplen
Windgap
Chartiers City
Sheraden
Central North Side
Manchester
Allegheny West
East Allegheny
Fairywood
Crafton Heights
Elliot
West End
Duquesne Heights
Westwood
Ridgemont
Oakwood
East Carnegie
Banksville
Beechview
Mt Washington
Downtown Pittsburgh
Lower Hill
Uptown
Middle Hill
Strip District
Southside Flats
Allentown
Beltzhoover
Knoxville
Mt. Oliver Borough
Mt. Oliver
Arlington
St. Clair
Bon Aire
Brookline
Carrick
West Overbrook
Overbrook
Upper Lawrenceville
Central Lawrenceville
Lower Lawrenceville
Garfield
Highland Park
Bloomfield
Friendship
East Liberty
Larimer
Lincoln-Lemington
Homewood
North Oakland
Shadyside
Point Breeze
North Point Breeze
East Pittsburgh
Squirrel Hill North
Park Place
Regent Square
Greenfield
Swisshelm Park
Hazelwood
West Homestead
Hays
Lincoln Place

Coding Urban Morphology: Urban Form as Pattern and Character of Place

Stephen Quick

Editors' Note: This essay recounts one example of an increased appreciation for the topological landscape of a city that achieved legislative protection through adoption of zoning that recognizes specific settlement patterns related to equally specific landscape topographies, and proposes that urban form which defines the character of place become a new zoning category. The author was a student in the Rowe Urban Design Studio, participated with fellow studio students in the Institute for Architecture and Urban Studies (IAUS) study of New York City Zoning, followed by several years working in the Urban Design Group with the Department of City Planning during Mayor John Lindsay's administration. These experiences found that Rowe, rather surprisingly and counter to his expectations, was deeply interested in "Urban Design as Public Policy" and its implementation through a combination of legal restrictions and incentives. These experiences with Rowe were fundamental to the exceptional success of the form-based zoning described in this essay.

Introduction

Anyone who has visited Pittsburgh is struck by its dramatic topography and its equally dramatic development patterns, its hemmed-in downtown, the monumentally scaled industrial development along its floodplains, and the clustering of its residential development tucked in its small valleys and ravines, surmounting its hilltops, and slung along the slopes of those hills as well. Pittsburgh's 19th century industrial development drove a booming economy that saw the natural environment primarily in exploitive terms and despoiled it. The post-1960s decline of Pittsburgh's economy, and changes in both that economy and views about the natural world, are bringing about a shift in cultural values that a recent conflict over the potential development of Pittsburgh's hillsides brought into focus.[1]

Surrounded by the Appalachian Mountains, Pittsburgh shares a regional culture that has traditionally viewed natural resources as commodities to be used primarily for the support of industrial production and daily living. Pittsburgh's hillsides[1] were stripped bare of their trees in the 19th century for fuel and construction. Historically, natural or physical beauty has not been a prevalent value and

frontispiece:
Hillside Development Zones. Pittsburgh is located at the confluence of the Allegheny and Monogahela rivers forming the Ohio River. The river valleys and steep hillsides give the city its unique identity. In this diagram, the reddish brown represents the steep hillsides.

1 Pittsburgh's "hillsides" are technically "slopes" created by the erosive action of the region's rivers; however, they are colloquially referred to as hillsides by local citizens.

hillsides are still viewed by many as obstacles meant to be topped and graded so they can be put to economic use.

Today these once-stripped hillsides are covered with trees and, along with Pittsburgh's three rivers, are increasingly understood to be among the city's primary assets. While celebrated by artists and writers, little acknowledgement of the civic value of these tree-covered hillsides had been recognized by local citizens and government; only since the late 20th century has this attitude begun to change. Pittsburgh's ranking as "the most livable city" by the *Places Rated Almanac* in 1985 surprised everyone, including most Pittsburghers.[2]

Pittsburgh's distressed economy and search for development opportunity recently brought focused attention to the two conflicting perceptions of the value of these hillsides. Some civic leaders and developers believed that economic development of the city's remaining greenfield sites, mostly its distinctive hillsides, would draw new residents, invigorate the economy, and spur investment throughout the city. In 2004, a large-scale residential development was proposed for a highly visible hillside site in view from downtown that would jeopardize the Mount Washington hillsides, one of the city's iconic landscapes. Public resistance to such development led to a Department of City Planning-sponsored study, examining the feasibility of limiting development on the city's steep hillsides resulting in a 'Hillsides Study'.

This essay describes a portion of the study, titled "A Physical Investigation of Pittsburgh's Hillsides", with emphasis on the urban design conditions and recommendations that led to new hillside zoning. It also proposes that a city's physical assets embodied in its patterns of community-accepted physical development—its urban form—can and should be integral to future zoning law similar to the increased acceptance of form-based codes.

The Situation

Economic stress, caused by disinvestment and population loss, created a competitive disadvantage for Pittsburgh. The region's economy has been in decline since the late 1960s. The loss of the steel industry in 1982 and the decline from the third-largest corporate headquarters city in 1980 with sixteen of the Fortune 500 firms down to today's eight has had its effects.[3] The city's population dropped from its 1950 peak of over 750,000 to around 300,000 today.[4] While the public is increasingly aware of the need for both economic and environmental sustainability, most Pittsburghers believe jobs still take precedence over all other issues.

Economic research found that Pittsburgh's hillsides provide little tax value for two reasons.[5] First, there is little assessed value differential between hillside and flatland development or between adjacency and access to open space throughout the city because, with Pittsburgh's hilly topography, most sites have views and, with the city's high percentage of tree cover, visual or physical access to open space is readily available. Second, the Hillsides Study found that for hillside properties, the city government incurs high infrastructure, maintenance, and public safety costs. Due to narrow streets and low densities, it is costlier to install and maintain infrastructure, collect refuse, and reach persons and property in need

2 Anon. "Pittsburgh Called Best Place to Live", *Pittsburgh Post-Gazette*, Feb 28, 1985.

3 Nixon, Alex, "Fortune 500 Lists 8 Pittsburgh Firms", *Trib Total Media*, Jun 4, 2014.

4 The city's population bottomed out around 2010 and there are only now slim indications that population growth has begun to occur. Pittsburgh's growth rate at a negative 8.6 percent between 2000-2010 is far below the country's average for large-sized cities at a positive 10.9 percent let alone the 9.7 percent experienced by all metro areas.

5 Farber, Stephen, "Economic Report to the Hillsides Steering Committee", University of Pittsburgh, 2004.

Fig. 1. Hillsides are form-givers to the city's neighborhoods and its commercial core.

of emergency services. With undermining and poor soils, most of the hillsides are slide-prone and, therefore, the annual cost to keep streets open due to slides adds to the annual cost of hillside snow and ice removal.

At the time of the Hillsides Study, zoning had been ineffective in regulating most of Pittsburgh's development because public demand for regulation had been low and previous political leadership had been eager for investment in new development. Even today, most mid-size and large development projects, whether developer or corporate sponsored, are subsidized by public investment through the sale of city-owned land, tax increment financing, or tax credits. Without population growth, there is little demand for private investment.

Although Pennsylvania's zoning enabling legislation contains strong aesthetic language, the State's court system has consistently upheld property rights over aesthetic concerns. Aesthetic zoning has not been supported in Pennsylvania, unlike western states where scenic views of mountains, green space, and bodies of water have achieved acceptance as scenic preservation features of zoning ordinances.[6]

In early 2004, a developer was poised to purchase property from the Urban Redevelopment Authority of Pittsburgh to build several large multi-unit buildings as a planned unit development on a publicly-owned hillside site known as the "Saddle" on Mount Washington. Neighborhood opposition was vocal and

6 Research for the Hillsides Study identified over 15 examples of hillsides ordinances, districts, overlays, and preservation regulations based on the aesthetic value of views, vistas, and landscapes in western states, including Arizona, California, Colorado, Idaho and Utah; one in Ohio; and none in Pennsylvania.

influential, but the development was to be as-of-right and not in need of variances or public subsidies. Some city leaders and developers were pushing to build on the hillsides—seeing them as an economic development opportunity. Attractive housing with spectacular views was seen as a catalyst to draw new residents, invigorate the economy, and further spur investment throughout the city. Hillsides are the last greenfield sites in Pittsburgh, highly visible and desirable for their views of downtown.

The Challenge

Pittsburgh's Department of City Planning wanted to stop the proposed development by rezoning the hillsides as designated open space; however, the department had not been able to develop a cogent legal rationale for the taking and the city had no money to purchase hillside properties.

Realizing the need to find a solution, the planning director formed a volunteer task force, the Hillsides Committee, to seek and recommend solutions. With the assistance of The Heinz Endowments, funds were secured to commission the Hillsides Study led by the firm of Perkins Eastman. Fearing developer opposition, the planning director imposed requirements that the study's recommendations must be economically justifiable and legally defensible if challenged in court.

To compound an already complex situation, Pittsburgh's official zoning map contained (and still does) many 'paper' streets located on steeply sloping hillsides seeming to signal an intention for their development. Fortunately, the economic market and the city's former suburban-oriented zoning, a result of the wave of 1960s and 1970s ordinances favoring larger lots and four-sided setbacks, kept hillside development at bay over the years.

Perkins Eastman and the Hillsides Committee developed a multidisciplinary team and a four-pronged collaborative approach. Ecological, economic, legal, and urban design issues, guided by a unifying theme, were investigated by four teams whose reports comprised the Hillsides Study:[7]

- The ecological investigation, performed by the Studio for Creative Inquiry, based in the work of the 3 Rivers 2nd Nature team at Carnegie Mellon University covered geology, forestation, plantings, and the current status of infrastructure systems available on the hillsides.
- The economic research, performed by the head of the Economics Department at the University of Pittsburgh, concentrated on the fiscal impact of hillside development, the cost/benefit of building on hillsides, and the benefits of open space and associated property values.
- The legal investigation, performed by a former Pittsburgh city solicitor, researched the implications of patterns of urban form as legal precedent and Pittsburgh's ability to regulate development specific to hillsides.
- The urban design (physical) investigation, performed by the urban design staff in Perkins Eastman's Pittsburgh office, studied the topological and building

7 The 2004 Hillsides Study is a compendium of four separate reports, each prepared independently: "A Physical and Ecological Investigation of Pittsburgh's Hillsides" by the ecological team; the "Economic Report to the Hillsides Steering Committee"; the "Legal Report to the City of Pittsburgh Hillsides Steering Committee: Land-Use Controls for Hillside Preservation in the City of Pittsburgh"; and the "Physical Investigation of Pittsburgh's Hillsides" by the urban design team. The urban design team subsequently published a summary of the physical investigation in 2007 titled "Zoning, Urban Form and Civic Identity: The Future of Pittsburgh's Hillsides" for local distribution and for awards submissions.

development patterns on hillsides, where hillside development did and did not occur, development anomalies that raised public opposition, and the relationship of slope angle to settlement types and locations.

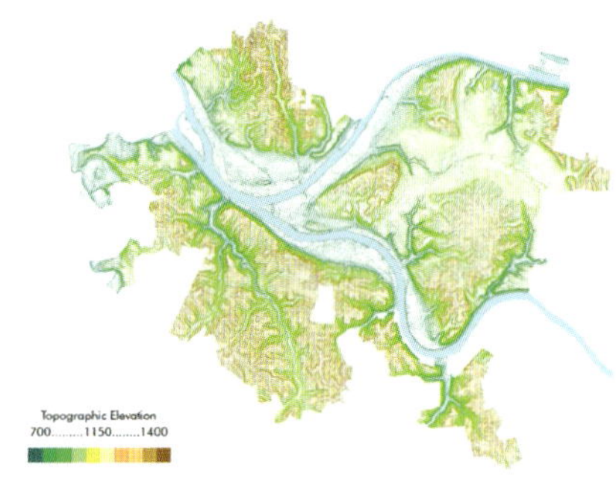

Fig. 2. Pittsburgh's topological landscape.

Geographic and historic research, along with investigation of best practices, was conducted by the urban design team using GIS, interpretive mapping, photography, and on-site observations. Internet-based research included surveying hillside ordinances researching U.S. approaches to development controls and regulatory features. Overlaying building footprints at each degree of slope resulted in the definitive clustering of place-making hillside settlement patterns. The place-making patterns became the basis for determining where and how buildings should occur on hillsides. Anomalies, those elements or features that are out of place and out of character, were analyzed to help understand what should, and should not, be encouraged. General planning and design principles were formulated and tested on three hillside sites that displayed the hillside settlement pattern types. The process was iterative and context-based. Patterns and critical place-making characteristics were challenged, and then further researched and observed in order to clarify their underlying structure and unique attributes.

The unifying theme of these investigations was that urban identity is a resource. In a global economy a city can no longer rely on standard planning formulas to ensure its citizens' wellbeing and prosperity. Cities must distinguish themselves in the competitive marketplace, and assets and public valuations cannot necessarily be measured by economic and population growth alone. Quality of life, opportunity choices, livability, a balance between work and family, a diversity of people and ages, and distinguishable qualities of place are but a few of these new measurements. For Pittsburgh, this means a recognition that its rivers and hillsides are essential to its sense of place and identity. A city's unique character is more than the sum of its parts, and a distinctive and coherent city form is one of a city's most important assets.

Tentative Conclusions

The ecological study of the Pittsburgh region found a landform that strongly and clearly directed patterns of settlement and growth related to specific landscape configurations, which made important contributions to Pittsburgh's urban identity.

The economic study demonstrated that the cost/benefit of maintaining roads and infrastructure on hillside sites was negative. That is, the tax benefits were significantly less than the costs of city obligations to development infrastructure and maintenance.

The legal investigation found that precedents are one of the fundamentals of zoning and land use planning, and that use and building envelope patterns are familiar and accepted standards of zoning. In fact, it is the long-term, self-determination and historic continuity recorded as land use and embodied in use and envelope controls that give such precedents their legitimacy. More broadly, urban form is similarly composed of familiar and accepted patterns (although zoning law has not recognized or validated them as yet).

Fig. 3. Distinctive bluffs and terraces.

While simple in statement, both the initial reasoning and these tentative conclusions were developed slowly over the tenure of the study. For example, a case could not be made for the hillsides' natural historic environmental value because the overwhelming majority was found to be second-growth forest. Neither could a special case be made for the hillsides' present-day ecological value because these values are no different from those in other wooded areas of the city. Lastly, opposition to proposed dense development of hillsides, based only on surveying public preference, could not gain legal standing because of its assumed subjective nature.

Only when the urban design team began to understand the relationship between zoning criteria and recognizable urban patterns was significant progress made. As a working thesis, the team's eventual conclusion was that an empirical analysis of urban form as pattern and the role of its various components, such as hillsides, could provide a useful tool for regulating development. Because it could be empirically based, the courts should not hold the reasoning to be subjective or aesthetically biased. The more recognizable the pattern—its clarity, consistency, and repetitiveness—the more likely it would be accepted into zoning regulations.

Analysis: Patterns of Urban Form at Three Scales

The urban design study identified recognizable patterns and features of urban form that resulted from Pittsburgh's geographic and settlement history, including the unique development patterning of its hillsides. Hillside natural and urban form was found to have influence at three scales:

- City Scale: Citywide natural and built patterns that contribute to Pittsburgh's character and the role of hillsides in creating those urban forms.

- Hillside Scale: Settlement and development patterns specific to the hillsides that document their built form and open space patterns.

- Parcel Scale: Site and building patterns related to property platting specific to hillsides.

City Scale Patterns

Patterns at the City Scale take two forms: natural form and built form. The strongest influence has been the natural geography where the geologic forces that created Pittsburgh's eroded, or 'carved', landscape shaped the city's settlement patterning, particularly that of its hillside development. The adaptation of built form to this topological landscape created Pittsburgh's distinctive urban form. Once the bottom of a vast inland sea, the area that became Pittsburgh rose to become the great flat Allegheny Plateau that was later scored by rivers and streams eroding deep valleys into the soft sedimentary rock. Today the bluffs and terraces on which much of Pittsburgh is built show the shifting courses of the rivers over time. They give the city many of its distinctive features creating natural rooms, corridors, terraces, and a variety of slopes and bluffs.

A significant part of the city is formed of 'bluff' slopes, consisting of 20 percent of its land area and ranging in height from 40 to more than 400 feet. These bluffs have slopes that typically vary from 15 percent to more than 25 percent grade and sometimes reach close to 50 percent. Most are eroded compound forms and, in some places, are interrupted by small, flatter terraces. Pittsburgh's distinctive hillsides are these bluff slopes at 25 percent grade and greater.

Most of the city sits below the Allegheny Plateau in proximity and orientation to the city's three rivers. Flatland development occurs on the floodplains and on sloping ground up to around 15 percent, which is true for the river plains and valleys as well as the plateau. Hillside development begins on slopes above 15 percent and levels off at a 25–27 percent slope, with very little development occurring above 27 percent. This has resulted in an overall urban form with distinctive development patterns and physical attributes.

Settlement began at the confluence of the rivers, then spread along the riverbanks for easy access to water transportation. As the population increased, settlement spread to nearby lower plateau areas, mostly to the east between the two rivers. In the 20th century the streetcar and later the automobile opened expansion into all areas of the city. Because of steep slopes, the southern portion of the city developed later. Hillsides were mined and logged for their commodity resources and, consequently, given little intrinsic value. Those greater than 25 percent were the last areas to be settled, if at all.

Commercial development is concentrated at the confluence of the rivers, and remains the center of the city. Industrial uses claimed the flatlands along the rivers' edges and expanded linearly from the confluence. Residential uses are generally

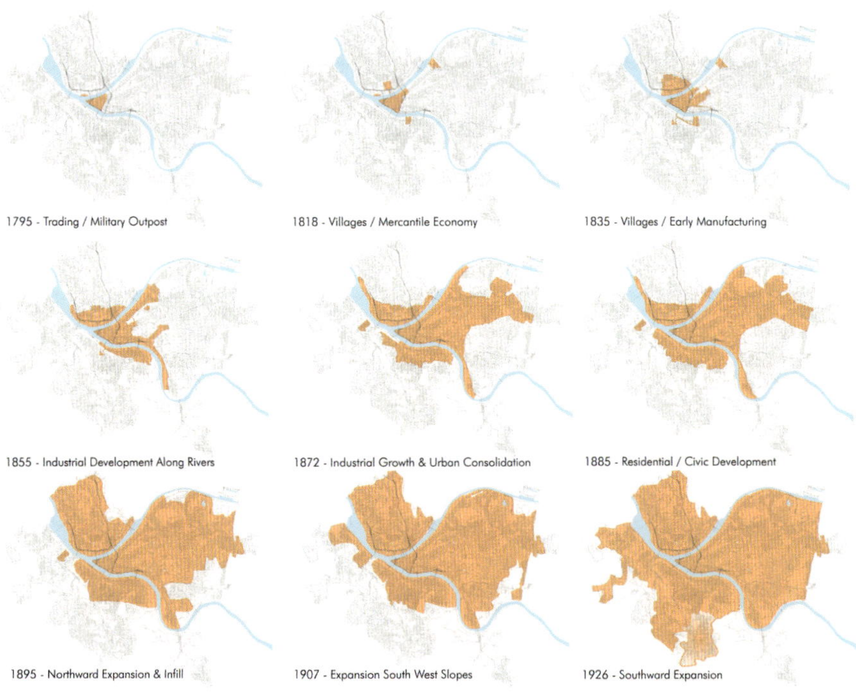

Fig. 4. Historic settlement patterning.

found on the plateaus and terraces high above the rivers as an attempt to escape the smoke and pollution of former heavy industry.

Pittsburgh's 90 neighborhoods are typically bounded by steep hillside slopes that separate one from another. Because buildable flatland is limited, built form tends to tightly cluster, forming 'islands' of development between the slopes. Neighborhood street patterns form mosaics as they respond to the local topography rather than to an applied regular geometry. Each is different and often culturally distinctive.

Natural form and settlement created many features of Pittsburgh's physical character that are best described by its spatial patterning and order, open spaces, texture, and by the resultant pathways that maintain connection.

Because the tops and bottoms of the slopes tend to be well-defined, they form the 'floors' and 'walls' of spatial rooms. Narrow tributaries are connective 'hallways' linking the plateaus to the river terraces. The steep bluffs form the strongest walls. Thresholds of natural valley openings and newly constructed tunnel and bridge portals connect the urban fabric of the city. Views and vistas are bounded by hillside walls; views are short-ranged, often dramatic, and omnipresent. River valley and major tributary hillsides are highly visible, while steep slopes and crests provide dramatic views of downtown and river terrace development.

Most of Pittsburgh's open spaces are the steep, wooded, and ungroomed forested hillsides that occur in continuous ribbons. Only their edges are accessible, and natural vegetation contrasts with both built form and the formal quality of the city's designated park open spaces. The natural landscape and tree covered areas

left to right:
Fig. 5. Neighborhood identity.

Fig. 6. Rooms created by topography.

exceed 40 percent of the city's land area and dominate the built form of the city, except for the pockets of large footprint and tall structures along the river edges and in the commercial cores.

Limited flat land resulted in Pittsburgh's large buildings congregating on the rivers' flood plains, in downtown at their confluence, and along seams created by the tributary watercourses throughout the city. Their large-grain texture is in distinct contrast to the fine-grain texture of the neighborhoods, with hillside buildings having the smallest footprints due to limited land and soil instability. The open spaces, which include the hillsides, form a third and distinct texture. This interplay throughout the city results in strong edges and seams.

Paths follow the natural contours and the watercourses, typically located parallel to contours and rivers. River flatlands and large tributary valleys contain the city's major arterials that feed into the central commercial core. This is similar to a hub-and-spoke typology, but distorted by the natural topography. Neighborhood internal paths are often disjointed and differ from one neighborhood to the next.

Hillside Scale Patterns

While the geomorphic qualities of the hillsides influence citywide development patterns, the intermediate scale of the hillsides presents a more complex relationship of topography, development, and open space. Topography informs where buildings can most easily be built and sets the development pattern through plats and infrastructure. Context patterning is most discernable and understood at this intermediate scale.

Fig. 7. Large grain texture along the rivers and fine grain on the plateau.

Four development pattern types were observed: No Development, Developed Edges, Ribbon Development, and Grid Development.

Each has a distinct relationship to the natural landscape and represents a well-established pattern of development. Each was analyzed for inherent characteristics and mapped on a citywide basis to confirm shared characteristics. No judgment was made regarding their appearance qualities; their long-time community acceptance made appearance a moot issue. The urban design team and the Hillsides Committee interest was in the appropriateness and feasibility of continuing the existing patterns.

Common to all four types are two qualities: a distinctive relationship to the natural landscape and a well-established pattern of development already in place.

Natural, unchanged hillsides with no development. These hillsides often form edges to the river valleys and provide a natural backdrop to the built environment. Mostly cliffs and inaccessible wooded hillsides, they are usually the steepest slopes, 25 percent and greater, and the most unstable. These hillsides typically comprise large parcels with few owners. Most of them are in public ownership with a few designated as parks and open space. They do not support active recreational activities, but may contain paths and steps. Infrastructure, including roads and streets, is minimal or non-existent.

Development occurring at the crests of ridges, the toes of slopes, or both. The natural landscape occupies the area between the crests and toes. These undeveloped open spaces may be thin at times, but discernable, as development stops at the transition to a steeper slope. Trees, occasionally interrupted by tops of buildings, form the skyline at the crests. A street or open space at the top of a steep slope, along a crest or ridge, frequently offers vistas or views accessible to the public.

Parcels at the tops and bottoms of the slopes are typically platted for small scale residential uses. Roads may traverse these slopes, but they are often undeveloped, narrow, and without sidewalks.

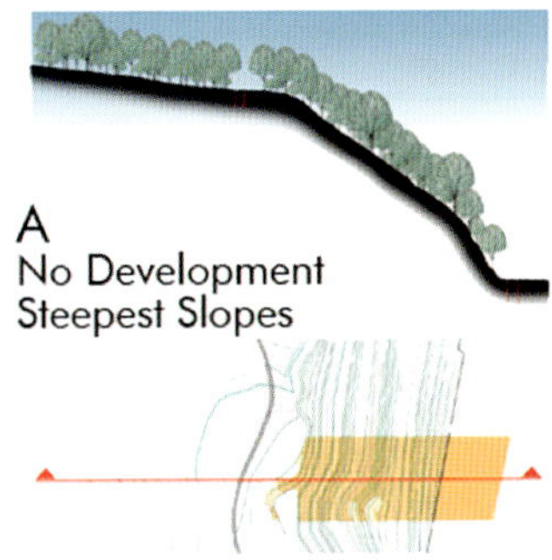

Development along streets that diagonally connect crests and toes. Ribbon Development occurs when terraces are wide enough and long enough to support both roads and buildings built along at least one side of the roadway, not necessarily as continuous development. Sometimes Ribbon Development extends along a terrace until the land reaches a steeper slope where development stops. Ribbon Development divides the hillsides into two, and sometimes three, bands or corridors alternating between structures and open space. There may or may not be Developed Edges at the top or bottom of the slope. Ribbon Development typically occurs on slopes of 25-to-40 percent, with the roadway incline less than 15 percent. Street widths are narrow. These corridors are referred to by their street names, not by the names of the neighborhoods at the top or bottom of the same hillsides. Rectangular parcels run perpendicular to the street and frequently extend from the flatter roadway terraces into the steeper slopes away from the street. Buildings on the upper side of the street are built into the slope and are typically taller and more visible than buildings that extend down the slope as these are often masked by trees. Building footprints are small and compact. Utility infrastructure is typically not available in the sloped areas above or below the ribbons.

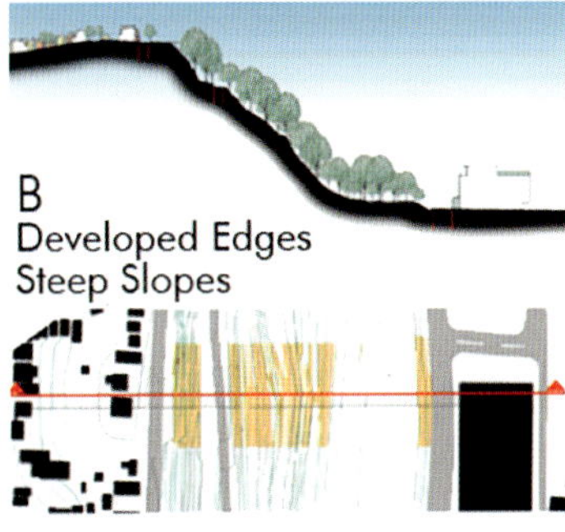

Extensions of the urban grid up or down the hillsides. Grid Development occurs similarly to that of a flat plateau neighborhood, but recognizes that outcroppings and prominent natural features render some parcels unbuildable. Grids are traditional, that is regular and orthogonal, or combinations of ribbons very close to one another as extensions of an established neighborhood pattern. Grids occur on hillsides of slopes between 15 and 25 percent where the contours are fairly equally spread and the street slope is minimal along the contours. Streets and platted parcels, even if they are unbuildable, are typically present throughout this slope pattern. Most buildings are single-family detached residential structures. Grid Development is fully served by utility infrastructure.

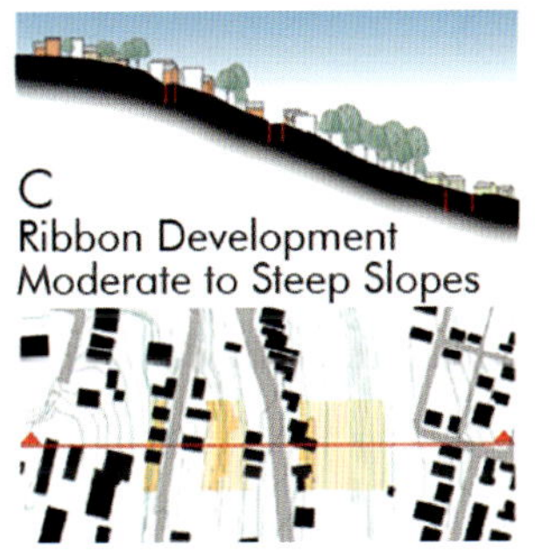

Parcel Scale Patterns

Fig. 8. Four distinctive patterns characterize hillside development.

Pittsburgh's riverfronts and hillsides are parceled and typically privately owned. Customarily, development on the slopes has been residential with a small footprint. Other occasional uses are neighborhood-serving: recreation, schools, religious buildings, and cemeteries. Open space is typically not a designated use; rather, it consists of the unbuildable rear yards in private ownership or city-owned land.

Hillside properties have distinctive qualities not found in other areas of the city, such as differently proportioned parcels, smaller-scaled structures, and retention of the natural landscape on the unused portions of properties. Parcels are deep and narrow, usually 20-to-25 feet wide, which differentiates them from typical lots on flatlands. Structures are set close to the street and utilities, often with no front yard setback. Typically, there is only one building per parcel with small side yards that create narrow spaces between buildings. Although side yards are small, the buildings appear to be set within the landscape. Streets are narrow,

Fig. 9. Ribbon pattern along Allegheny River Boulevard.

and most houses do not have garages; cars park straddling the sidewalk. Some streets have no sidewalks.

Hillside buildings are urban in character with simple massing, solid walls, and foundations that meet the ground. Individuality is expressed through color, building materials, and architectural features such as gables and porches, but within a context of simple volumes with flat surfaces. Typical structures are narrow, with building width averaging between 15-to-20 feet with footprints between 600 and 1,000 square feet. Building volumes are small and simple, and proportionally about three-quarters the size of flatland structures. Buildings are vertical in orientation, with rooms stacked over one another to conserve land and energy, no higher than two to three and one-half stories, and below the tree line.

Four types of building anomalies were observed: tall, wide, scattered, and stepped or 'cascading' buildings. On hillside sites, buildings have high visibility and their impact is significantly greater than similar buildings on flat land.

Tall buildings can occur anywhere on hillsides, but most often at the crests and toes of slopes. They visually block the continuity of the natural vegetation or rise above ridgeline trees, breaking the hilltop's natural horizontal plane.

Wide buildings are extended low-rise buildings, such as attached townhouses, a fairly new building type on hillsides. They disrupt scale, block views of natural vegetation, and disrupt the continuity of the natural landscape. In other neighborhoods and urban settings, townhouses are low-impact housing, but they are high-impact structures in the smaller-scale hillside context. Visually, they are like tall buildings set onto their sides.

Fig. 10. Houses on the South Side slopes.

Scattered buildings occur randomly and exhibit poor patterning qualities that do not constitute a continuous built fabric. Stand-alone residences occur because of either a desire for privacy or as remnants of disinvestment. Their infrastructure needs are costlier to provide and maintain, and they contribute to ecological discontinuity.

Stepped or cascading buildings are found at slope crests, where they may appear as two or three-story buildings facing the street, but extend many basement floors below, stepping down the slope. Visually they are like tall buildings that disrupt the natural continuity of the hillside's contours and vegetation.

Synthesis: Recommendations

The study's recommendations, and later those adopted by the Hillsides Committee, provide general principles for hillside development and detailed building and site recommendations at the city, hillside, and site scales to reinforce the four hillside development patterns.

City Scale Recommendations

Hillsides provide the backdrops, the settings, and the boundaries between pockets of development and make a significant contribution to urban form identity. They need to be protected from development that dilutes this role.

The natural and green landscape should remain continuous and unbroken. Create ecological landscape corridors around and among the concentrations of built form by planting additional trees to infill between buildings and strengthen hillside

Fig. 11. South Side slopes.

Fig. 12. Narrow hillside parcels and buildings.

edges. Build within the tree line or tree canopy at slope crests and ridges to maintain continuity of the city's treetop horizon. On city-owned land, maintain open space around portals and valley openings so their visual impact is enhanced.

Strengthen the contrast between the built and natural landscapes by adding to and completing Developed Edges and Ribbon Development and discourage scattered development. Revise the zoning ordinance to define districts by pattern type and regulate only the critical features for each district, which should result in clearer patterns of urban form to distinguish one hillside district from another. Design review of hillside development requires rigor.

Hillside development demands tighter controls and should be subject to a higher standard of design massing than typical city land. Consider adopting the following:

On all slopes 25 percent and greater, require:

- a development impact analysis
- submission of site and building plans for design review
- a maintenance bond to guarantee completion of vegetation plan

Remove 'paper' hillside streets and parcels from the zoning map to discourage development in hazardous or undesirable locations, including those with predictably high maintenance costs to the city.

Prioritize infill development on flatland parcels by government agencies and private development receiving public subsidies as public policy.

Reinforce the built fabric of the city and strengthen the differentiation of built form from natural open space in order to relieve pressure to build on the hillsides and acknowledge the landscape value of hillsides.

Hillside Scale Recommendations

Build only where hillside development patterns can be reinforced.

Encourage development where it strengthens the patterns of:

- Developed Edges of crests and toes
- Ribbon Development
- Grid Development

Encourage infill and projects along Developed Edges to sustain and reinforce neighborhood fabric that is consistent with local density and building configuration patterns. Maintain lot sizes and dimensions based on the prevailing neighborhood pattern by discouraging lot consolidation. On slopes greater than 15 percent, allow only residential uses as-of-right, restrict residential uses to one or two unit buildings, and prohibit multi-family structures.

Control development based on slope steepness.

0% to 15%	Hillside controls are not needed. These slopes should be treated as flatland and fully serviced by city infrastructure.
15% to 25%	Control Grid Development to specific building pattern types and respect good engineering practices to minimize erosion and landslides. Encourage infill development.
25% to 40%	Control steep-slope development carefully due to high visual impact. Require moderate engineering solutions for all parcels to minimize erosion and landslides.
Above 40%	Discourage or not allow development to avoid very high visual impact and highly unstable soils or solid rock requiring extreme engineering solutions, including terracing of hillsides and extensive cut-and-fill measures.

If new streets are created at tops of slopes, locate them between parcels and the crest to create a public edge at these landslide-prone locations. Maintain the hillside brow in a natural condition when viewed from below, which means discouraging structures that appear to be perched on the edge. Set buildings back at least 100 feet from edges of slopes that are 25 percent and greater for safety reasons.

Consider limiting all new hillside development to locations where infrastructure is available. All new hillside development should be built no farther than 100 feet from existing infrastructure, located at the front lot line to minimize hillside disturbance. Do not extend street and utility infrastructure beyond existing locations.

Fig. 13. Hillside development is distinct from other urban patterns.
Photo: Bruce Emmerling/pixabay.

Parcel Scale Recommendations

Continue the practice of setting buildings set into, not onto, the landscape.

As policy, maintain existing parcel widths to discourage larger buildings, and, where parcel consolidation has been approved, encourage multiple buildings rather than a single, large structure. Retain side yard setbacks even if they are minimal to assure openings between buildings.

Strive to preserve the natural shape of the land when grading, especially at the horizon line of crests where balanced cut-and-fill terraces are most noticeable. Regulate the maximum area of allowable site disturbance and locate on-site stormwater retention below slope crests. Open space should remain natural to the greatest extent possible and the majority of the site should remain tree-covered. Ban clear-cutting below the structure to enhance views for property owners. Instead, encourage planting on the slope side of the building to allow for controlled views out, yet screen and soften the architecture; in general, 50 percent screening of a building's downslope view facade(s) is recommended. Restore tree density in locations where site disturbance has occurred during construction. Private rear yard space on downhill sides can be provided by small yards, terraces, or decks. Control site lighting to mask the light source when viewed from lower slopes and do not allow light spread beyond the property line. Prohibit open parking areas for more than two cars.

Respect historic hillside building conventions by keeping buildings small and at hillside-scale by controlling footprint size, height, and width. Maintain the sense of structural verticality by orienting building massing with the narrow faces toward views and at right angles to the contour lines; likewise, stepping and pole-supported structures, horizontal building configurations, and excessive decking should be discouraged. Along with simple flat facades and architectural expressions of dwelling units within the building envelope, these simple massing gestures will maintain the hillsides' building character.

Conclusions

Testing the Recommendations

Three test sites, which exhibited combinations of the four hillside settlement patterns, were selected for detailed study to determine how the pattern types would influence the built and natural form and to test the application of the recommendations.

The patterns demonstrated that strong edges, created by development or by preserving natural features, accentuate and reinforce the contrast between the natural and built environments. New development can serve to strengthen the built form of Developed Edges, Ribbon Development, and Grid Development patterns. Where appropriate, maintaining the continuity of both open space and development is a beneficial outcome of this process. Developed Edges and Ribbon Development patterns clearly define where open space should be preserved.

The test sites demonstrated that there is an abundance of buildable parcels of the three steep-slope development pattern types as mostly infill sites on vacant and platted parcels or sites where previous development had been abandoned: this alleviated the Department of City Planning's concern over whether legislating hillside development would curtail development. Pittsburgh's hillsides, if and when developed, will preserve and strengthen Pittsburgh's urban form identity.

Legal Finding

The legal investigation confirmed that physical development prototypes (patterns) are a legitimate basis for regulation. Pittsburgh's zoning and enabling legislation requires that zoning regulations "be made with reasonable consideration, among other things, to the topography and character of the district, with its particular suitability for particular uses, and with a view to conserving the value of buildings and encouraging the most appropriate use of land throughout such city".[8] The legal report concludes that "the enabling legislation invites regulations that respect these distinct prototype characteristics and are designed to preserve them".[9]

Outcome of the Hillsides Study

The recommendations of the Hillsides Study were adopted by the Hillsides Committee in their report, "Opportunities for Hillside Protection", and conveyed to the Department of City Planning in early 2005. The Department prepared hillsides zoning legislation, largely based on the urban design study's recommendations, and presented it to the City Planning Commission several months later. New hillside legislation creating a Hillsides (H) District was adopted by City Council in fall of 2005 and subsequently mapped.

Simultaneously with the new Hillsides District legislation, the City Council designated a large portion of Mount Washington as a significant and highly visible hillside facing downtown, as a public park, thus removing this developer-sought, city-owned land from future development, the plan that had initiated the current study in the first place.

8 Fox, Cyril A., "Legal Report to the City of Pittsburgh Hillsides Committee: Land-Use Controls for Hillside Preservation in the City of Pittsburgh", University of Pittsburgh, 2004.

9 Ibid.

South Side pattern development

South Side Slopes

□ Study Site
■ Developed Edges
□ Ribbon Development
■ Grid Development

South Side development strategy

□ Study Site
■ Open Space
■ Vacant Parcels
--- Pedestrian Circulation

Urban Form as a New Zoning Category

Land uses form patterns of the built environment and, over time, become accepted on a localized basis and even cherished when new development threatens change. These patterns of use-form, while universal and observed around the world, maintain a general equilibrium yet slowly adjust to economic, social, and physical condition pressures. They are evolutionary indicators of local cultural norms and values.

When approved as an official zoning map, these use-form patterns are legally recognized as the primary component of a city's long-range comprehensive plan. As regulatory devices, the two mainstays of zoning have been land use and massing, both parcel-specific. Zoning recognizes urban form indirectly by acknowledging area-specific districts, such as use and historic districts, that value context and place.

Urban form provides the same type of coherent framework on a city-wide basis just as land use and massing do for parcels. It is an idea that encompasses the broader perspective of place and recognizes that place-based physical patterns define communities and cities that are unique. Urban form exists but is often not observed; typically, we only understand its value when anomalies disrupt its patterns.

A shared understanding of place includes a comprehension of its physical attributes that result from interactions over time between geography, environment, technology, economy, and culture, and that differentiate one locale from another. It is a rethinking of zoning that moves beyond individual property to consider and value the broader physical-cultural context and civic identity that the Hillsides District legislation represents.

Fig. 14. Buildable sites were identified for all hillside development patterns.

Urbanism at Ground Zero: The Attempted *Colin*-ization of Lower Manhattan

Barbara Littenberg

Colin Rowe often expressed ambivalence about the physical form of New York City—the urbanism was simplistic and fundamentally monotonous, the blocks were too long and repetitive (at least there was Broadway), there were few public spaces of any quality (Rockefeller Center being the notable exception), and residential squares were few and far between. It was not the place he chose to settle after his retirement from Cornell University, although it had been considered briefly. London, Boston, or Washington, D.C., were far more intriguing options, partly because of their perceived superior urbanism, or perhaps, for the conversation of friends and acquaintances. He had lived on the Upper East Side during his work with the Institute for Architecture and Urban Studies in the 1960s, and he had visited the city on countless occasions. Lower Manhattan, which, during his lifetime, was a predominately commercial district, probably did inspire in him the same awe of its extraordinary physical being that was experienced by other Europeans from Le Corbusier in the 1930s to Prince Charles today.

Fig. 1. Aerial photograph of iconic Lower Manhattan.

frontispiece:
Model view of the Peterson Littenberg final design showing the relationship between the Public Garden and West Street Boulevard. Model photo: Jock Pottle.

I really can't say with certainty what Colin Rowe's reaction to the design efforts to rebuild the World Trade Center site, after the tragic events of September 11, 2001, might have been, although I have often pondered the question. Given the myriad stakeholders involved with the rebuilding—governors, mayors, interstate agencies, community boards, real estate developers, business associations, the AIA, and most prominently, committees formed on behalf of survivors, family members of victims, and rescue workers—Colin would have been highly skeptical that urban design, as he taught it and loved it, would have had a voice in such a process. It would have seemed to him an impossible, hopeless undertaking—he would have been right.

However, it proved not to be the complex makeup of constituent groups that undermined urban design in Lower Manhattan in the wake of 9/11. Instead it was the fundamental struggle that played out between two conflicting viewpoints: one put forward by advocates for finding a solution based on the idea of appropriate city form and the other by proponents of the redemptive power of iconic architecture that derived its justification from Modernism. The site would be entangled in what Colin Rowe in his article "The Present Urban Predicament" described as the ongoing struggle, "object versus context". He attributed this conflict to 200 years of architectural theory which placed "enormously high premia upon the building as an isolated object", and from the 1920s onward, the Modern movement, "following suit in its rejection of frontality and facade, and the preoccupation with a building's manifestation in three-dimensional form".

In response to the iconic object building, Colin advocated a theory of Contextualism, which posited that good urban design allows for the inclusion of exemplary architecture when embedded in the urban fabric. This generated a debate between Contextualists and Modernists, and urbanists and expressionists, that continues unabated. In 2002, during the World Trade Center rebuilding process, the two theoretical positions intersected and vied for the authority to determine which viewpoint would dominate the process to rebuild. As of 2020, 20 years later, neither has prevailed: there is neither a coherent assembly of inspirational objects, nor a vital complex based on a continuous and coherent urban context.

What follows is a cautionary tale: whether it would have been possible for urban design, a distinct discipline located somewhere between architecture and planning, to be effective in influencing the outcome of the massive civic, symbolic, and economic undertaking to rebuild the World Trade Center site. It recounts the experiences of Steven Peterson and Barbara Littenberg, and gives the background for their design proposals for that site, including their earlier Lower Manhattan Urban Design Plan of 1994 that is the source of their understanding of the World Trade Center rebuilding problem. It affirmed their belief that any viable solution should engage the entire fabric of Lower Manhattan and that in order to move forward with a proposal, Manhattan, as an example of enduring city form, was to serve as the model for its own reconstruction, interpreted and extended as idea and typology.

The 1994 Urban Design Plan for Lower Manhattan

The stock market crash of 1987 was a major disaster for the city of New York, severely impacting its crucial financial industry, general prosperity, and real estate markets. Lower Manhattan, site of the original 1624 settlement and storied historic core and physical home to Wall Street, was especially affected (Fig. 1). The terrorist bombing of the World Trade Center in 1993, resulting in six deaths and over 1,000 people injured, further threatened its future and tragically prefigured the disaster to come. The Port Authority of New York and New Jersey, owners of the site, had been haunted by issues of security from terrorism ever since. Despite its glorious architectural quality and iconic skyline image as the prototypical world metropolis, Lower Manhattan's future as a viable office district seemed grim, with a persistent commercial vacancy rate of 28 percent.

In 1994, seven years before 9/11, Lower Manhattan was still staggering from the effects of the 1987 financial crash and the lingering real estate crisis. To help analyze the situation, the Battery Park City Authority commissioned Steven Peterson, principal of Peterson Littenberg Architects (PLA), to undertake an urban design and public space study of possible improvements to Lower Manhattan. The resulting Lower Manhattan Urban Design Plan was supported by extensive documentation, having been developed with representatives of public agencies, and

Fig. 2. Lower Manhattan Urban Design Plan, 1994, before/after.

presented to community leaders and government officials in conferences and public meetings. Richard Kaplan, of the J. M. Kaplan Fund, videotaped PLA's two public presentations of the plan and the videotape was then circulated over the next year. The project was chosen by *Progressive Architecture* magazine for an Urban Design Award in its January 1995 edition.

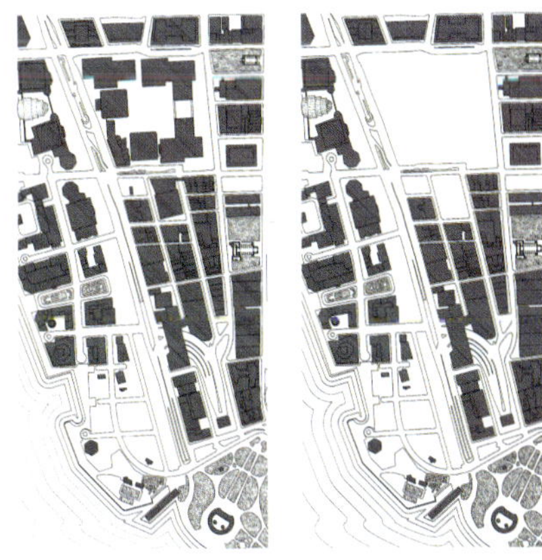

Fig. 3. Lower Manhattan and World Trade Center site plan before/after attack of 9/11/2001.

Urban Design and Architecture after 9/11

Soon after the 9/11 attack on the World Trade Center, Peterson Littenberg were asked to participate in the planning for rebuilding, serving as consultants to the Lower Manhattan Development Corporation (LMDC), the new state agency created to coordinate that effort. Specifically, Alexander Garvin, Vice President of Planning, Design, and Development, asked us to provide a range of alternative design strategies for the site to be presented to any and all interested parties. While the underlying urban design deficiencies of Lower Manhattan identified in the 1994 urban design study still remained when the 9/11 attack occurred, the district now faced an unprecedented major design challenge: its voided center changed the scope, nature, and complexity of the overall problem. Now the task was to bring forward and pursue the goal of reintegrating the surrounding urban fabric while simultaneously establishing an appropriate place to memorialize the tragedy. Our various proposals for the World Trade Center site maintained and extended the following urban ideas put forward in the 1994 plan:

1. Urban context is necessary for making place

Good urbanism, as manifest in the great cities of Western Europe, has an ineffable quality that elicits positive, visceral responses without the need of analysis or explanation—you know it when you see it. To create good urbanism anew, and extend it in Lower Manhattan, the solution needed to be founded on the tactics, techniques, and evaluative criteria of urban design.

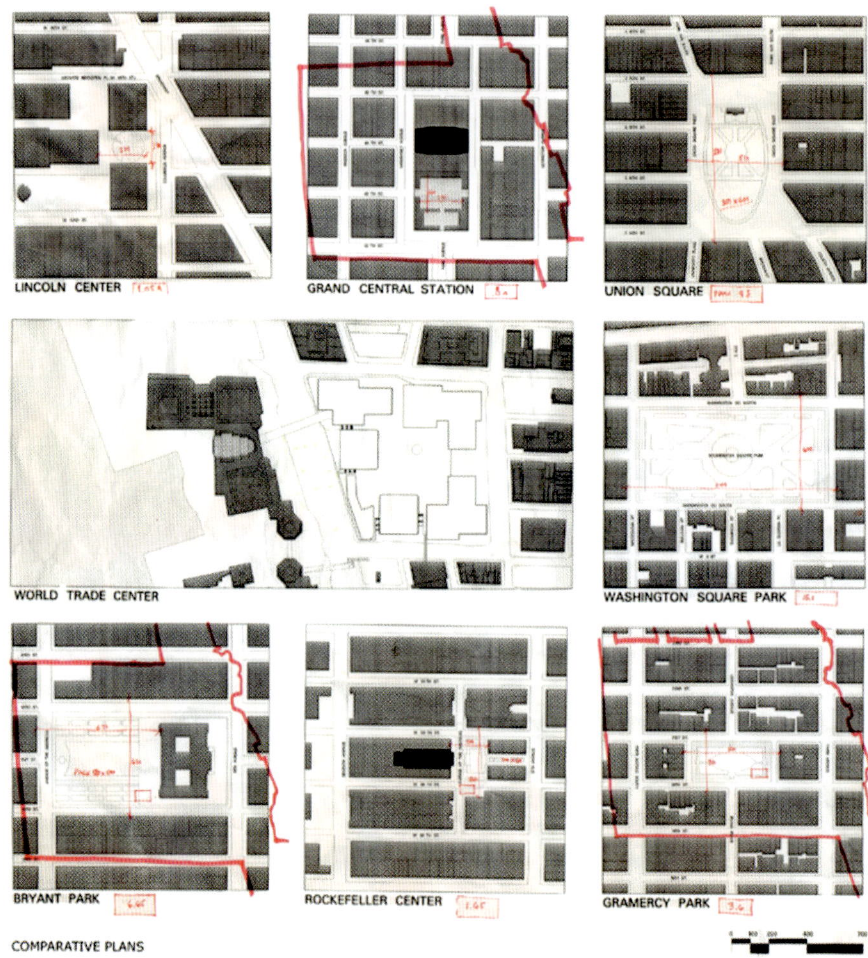

inset:
Fig. 4. Chart of New York City public spaces: clockwise, Lincoln Center; Grand Central Station; Union Square; Washington Square; Gramercy Park; Rockefeller Center; Bryant Park; and NY Public Library, compared to the World Trade Center site outlined in red. The NY public space comparisons and the model of Lower Manhattan were made for the AIA, New York New Visions group by Jerri Smith's team at Kohn Pedersen Fox.

inset opposite:
Fig. 7. Matrix chart of diverse urban site solutions with differing grid resolutions and open space locations.

2. Urban form and architecture exhibit different temporalities

The rate of change for an urban structure is different than that of individual works of architecture. Lower Manhattan dramatically illustrates the capacity of an enduring 17th century urban plan to allow for the continued renewal of individual architectural elements. Its history of constant rebuilding demonstrates that each new building replacement can be successfully incorporated into a relatively stable urban fabric and need not be prefigured by an entirely new future city plan.

3. Urban form is the framework for architecture

Urban design is a distinct and important discipline that is both connected to and independent of architecture. A successful urban plan promotes multiple opportunities for architecture by determining its placement within a larger group form.

Ironically, the ill-fated site was de-urbanized twice—losing its urban fabric once through urban renewal to clear the site for the construction of the World Trade Center in 1973, and then again in the terrorist attack of 9/11. The resulting empty World Trade Center site (Fig. 3) presented an opportunity to restore the city at street level and remediate the failings of the prior Minoru Yamasaki superblock design. It was our belief that the redeployment of the lost building area should reestablish the site's connections to the surrounding urban life by providing public spaces, streets, and parks. The idea of rebuilding the world's tallest building

Orthogonal Grids Orthogonal Squares Diagonal Grids Diagonal Squares Footprint Squares Fulton Linear Park Courtyard Blc

in the immediate aftermath of the attack seemed preposterous: why provoke another attack with an overt act of hubris?

To investigate and explain the planning issues related to the World Trade Center site, simple comparisons were made: a drawing showed the size of seven well-known New York City public places and their surrounding city blocks at the same scale. These are then inscribed with the red outline of the World Trade Center site in order to understand its actual size (Fig. 4). The simple insertion of a model such as that of Rockefeller Center, to scale, into the site model (Fig. 5, 6) that equaled the lost 10 million square feet, produced an incredulous reaction: it both implicitly criticized the original Yamasaki design of the World Trade Center, and showed that a normative, exemplary urban model for its replacement was feasible. Although the World Trade Center is technically 16 acres, the actual urban void from building face to building face, including the space of West Street and adjacent lost properties to the north and south, measured 34 acres. This analysis was intended to de-objectify the site in people's minds and to open up possible strategies for consideration that included engaging and relating to areas of the adjacent city beyond the immediate site boundaries to ameliorate previously identified failings.

Eighteen alternative designs were generated with plan drawings and massing-models to demonstrate a broad variety of feasible arrangements that would both respond to the new program and also re-urbanize the site's connectivity with its context. Those designs are organized typologically in the matrix chart (Fig. 7) according to predominant street and space orientation. They are characterized for simplicity as 'orthogonal' and 'diagonal'. All had a major memorial space, some as large as Union Square, some located within the original 16 acres, while still others created a memorial place by reclaiming space over West

Fig. 5. Empty World Trade Center site model after 9/11.

Fig. 6. Rockefeller Center model inserted into the site replicating the same 10 million square feet of lost World Trade Center building area.

Fig. 8. Peterson Littenberg, Memorial Park project included in the first public presentation, July, 2002.

Street and south of Liberty Street. At this early stage, many configurations were plausible because the 'footprints' of the Twin Towers, erased by the severity of the impact, were not yet imprinted in the public imagination as sacrosanct. We explored in plan and model: ranges of street and block patterns; the means of engaging urban adjacencies; the dimension and number of the proposed urban blocks; etc. Each reconnected the site to the adjoining neighborhood fabric by virtue of the continuation and resolution of all contiguous streets in addition to Greenwich and Fulton Streets.

All the alternatives contained the required replacement program that included ten million square feet of commercial space, 600,000 square feet of retail space, and 600,000 square feet for hotels. Unfortunately, the 'program' was fixed by a stipulation in the property insurance policy to 'rebuild in kind'. The absurdity of this precondition precluded the possibility of substituting any alternative uses for the lost space, although it was universally agreed that a genuine mix of housing, cultural, and institutional uses, along with retail and office space, would constitute a far superior replacement. Allowing a change of program would have remediated some of the failures of the district identified in the 1994 plan by creating a 24-hour neighborhood with its resultant street life and amenities, and would have added resilience to the cyclical commercial real estate market during downturns. Unfortunately, the dictates of money ruled the day. The original program was to hold, with the addition of memorial elements that were to be financed separately.

First Public Presentation

Of all the schemes we developed, two, Memorial Park and Memorial Boulevard, were included in the first of six plans presented by the LMDC to the public in July 2002, in a town hall-style meeting, "Preliminary Urban Design Study", held at the Javits Convention Center. The LMDC had intended to narrow down the alternate designs to three, which would be developed for a second presentation to the public the following September, with a final design to be selected by the end of the year.

Fig. 9. Peterson Littenberg, Memorial Promenade project included in the first public presentation, July, 2002.

Memorial Park (Fig. 8) one of the 'diagonal' schemes, joins new replacement buildings with the World Financial Center also damaged from the attack with a major urban park by reclaiming space over West Street. The park exploits the natural grade change on the site to attach directly to the upper, primary level of the World Financial Center and Winter Garden, obviating the need for the 1973 enclosed walkway bridges. Bounded by the east-west extension of Fulton and Cortlandt Streets, the park is oriented on the grid established by West Street and a reconstituted Greenwich Street, both laid out parallel to the Hudson River shoreline.

Four new towers stand as sentinels around the park, two of which are paired around an entry to an arcaded retail center. In the northeast corner of the site, an additional park is located on the orthogonal grid across from St. Paul's Chapel. A major tower (possibly iconic, height unknown) is placed on Church Street, logically located closest to the Wall Street business center and transportation hubs. It is oriented to the normative uptown grid in order to mark the site on the skyline from long distances.

CELEBRATING 200 YEARS

NEW YORK POST

SPORTS EXTRA

THE BIG DOWNTOWN REBUILDING DEBATE

New Yorkers' shock verdict

TWIN TOWERS II

CITY VOTES ON WTC DESIGNS: PAGES 8-9

Fig. 10. *New York Post*, July 18, 2002, declares: "Twin Towers II" - Memorial Promenade (Fig. 9) – "overwhelming favorite" after the Town Hall presentation.

In order to achieve both a two-sided Greenwich Street and a precisely formed public space, the Memorial Park design necessitated building on the southern tower footprint. Meanwhile public and political consensus coalesced around the idea that the original footprints were to remain as sacred markers never to be built upon. As a consequence, although Memorial Park was included in the public event, it was effectively eliminated from further consideration as an urban design strategy.

The second scheme, Memorial Promenade (Fig. 9) one of the 'orthogonal' schemes, established a new grid with an urban street and block pattern that followed the orientation of the World Trade Center superblock; therefore, it easily accommodated the 200-foot by 200-foot World Trade Center tower footprints that are shown in the plan as two urban parks. Greenwich Street shifts its orientation in a triangular space at the north edge of the site, joins West Broadway,

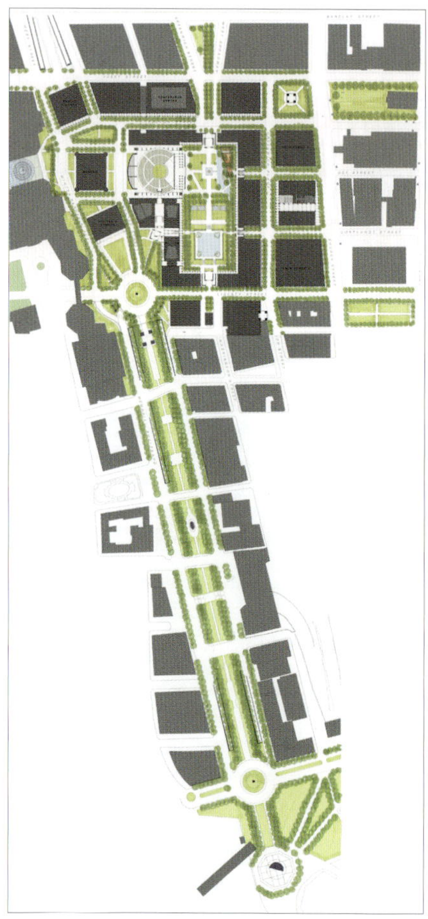

inset:
Fig. 11. Peterson Littenberg project for the "Innovative Design Study" the final "Master Site Plan Competition", December 18, 2002 - September 17, 2003.

opposite inset:
Fig. 12. Peterson Littenberg model looking down on the Public Garden precinct, surrounding elevated roof gardens, and the new Twin Towers. Model photo: Jock Pottle.

and extends south, connecting to Washington Street, thereby eliminating the diagonal altogether. The southern portion of Greenwich Street terminates in the proposed shopping galleria that is entered alongside the footprint of the southern tower. This street arrangement proved to be an interesting, and ultimately useful, discovery that was carried over to our final proposal.

Memorial Promenade used as precedent the Champs-Élysées in Paris, an idyllic vision of the Elysian Fields dedicated to those fallen in war. Repurposing West Street as a boulevard created a new spatial focus joining Battery Park City to the original city center with a common central amenity. It also provided places for community memorials that could be sponsored by victims such as firefighters, police, business co-workers, ethnic communities, etc., which would be in addition to a collective memorial projected for the main site. Given the technical difficulty of reoccupying the 'bathtub', or enormous excavation in the center of the site—which did in fact take a decade to achieve—this idea was intended to serve as a more immediate emotional salve, while alleviating some of the planning pressures on the site.

The scheme's massing created twin towers, axially aligned with the footprint of the northern tower. They contained at their base a cruciform galleria for the new retail center. The thematic recapitulation of the two lost towers suggested

a possible heroic architecture that resonated with the public, while the promenade itself was also a distinctive feature. Memorial Promenade was deemed by the *New York Post* the "overwhelming favorite among the six proposals", outpacing its competitor (Memorial Park) by a 2:1 ratio in the public opinion surveys, with a 43.7 percent approval rating, in part due to the proposed new twin towers (Fig. 10).

Public and Press Reaction

However, the choice to depict the six unattributed proposals with a uniform graphic technique—one plan and one model photo from the same viewpoint for each—backfired. If the intent had been to focus on distribution of building mass and land use while intentionally avoiding architectural expression, that intent was not forcefully explained. This provided an opening for immediate backlash from the architectural *cognoscenti,* most notably *The New York Times* architecture critic Herbert Muschamp and *New York* magazine critic Joseph Giovannini. Both columnists mounted campaigns soliciting schemes from their favorite star architects. A number of these designs were published the following September. The core argument was that these designers would presumably satisfy the need for "visions ... worthy of our grief and hope", to supply the "redemptive power of wonder". *The New York Times* lead editorial (influenced by Muschamp) contended

above:
Fig. 13. View down proposed West Street Boulevard, looking south toward Upper New York Bay, Ellis Island, and the Statue of Liberty. Color watercolor rendering by Michael McCann.

below:
Fig. 14. The staged development of Park Avenue north of Grand Central Station, 1888, the precedent for reconstruction of the World Trade Center site.

that the public would never be satisfied with any redevelopment that contained as much commercial space as was previously on the site, thereby challenging the Port Authority to relinquish rights to the real estate it had controlled.

The LMDC reacted to this editorial criticism by changing course and issuing an open Request for Qualifications from architects and planners to participate in a limited design competition, thereby restarting the process. The selection of the participants was to be made in consultation with a high-profile outside advisory panel. Of the firms chosen to compete, and despite enjoying international architectural repute, none of them, even remotely, espoused an urban point of view. Those firms among the qualified applicants that had urban design reputations were unfortunately passed over. Predictably, large architectural extravaganzas ensued, confirming Colin Rowe's perception of the Modernist era bias favoring the 3D architectural object over the urban fabric—the object would appear to win the day, thereby disrupting the LMDC's thoughtfully developed urban design methodology.

Plans in Progress: Innovative Designs for the World Trade Center Site

Peterson Littenberg Architects were automatically included among the seven finalists selected as part of the continuing work for the LMDC. We maintained the position that a coherent urban design plan was necessary for the site, and that any memorial design should reside in a distinctly public realm, immutably part of the continuous city—public space, garden, amphitheater, boulevard— a public

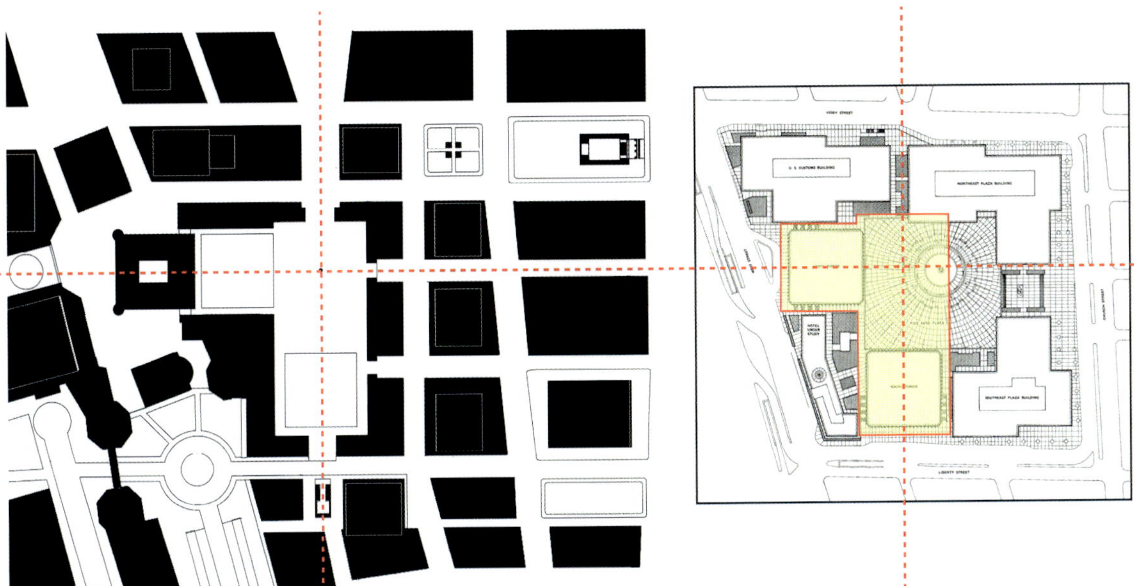

space with the stature of Central Park, Washington Square, or Park Avenue. A secular building would be, by definition, subject to temporality, i.e. obsolescence, change of occupancy, owner renaming, and reinterpretation as an alternative symbol. The simple, self-evident limitation of a commercial office building's capacity to be an eternal sacred symbol of the tragedy seemed obvious.

The final design plan (Fig. 11) was developed from the Memorial Promenade scheme that had been deemed the best and most popular in the previous public presentation. It maintained the orthogonal grid plan as the basis of the urban solution and kept the boulevard idea intact. The tower footprints are united in a dedicated public garden precinct, enveloped and protected by the new construction, which is massed in concentric layers moving up and out from this epicenter (Fig. 12). A mile-long sequence of public spaces was conceived to stretch through the site from City Hall Park into the new St. Paul's Square, through the Public Garden, continue down the boulevard to Battery Park to reveal the landmarks in New York Harbor—Ellis Island, the Statue of Liberty, and the bay beyond (Fig. 13). This innovative urban ensemble, embodying civic qualities, would be on a grand scale worthy of both Manhattan as a world city and as a tribute to the tragic attack. Lower Manhattan's historic past would be woven into its street pattern as an experience laden with symbolic meaning.

The implementation strategy of the plan used as a precedent the initial development of Park Avenue (1870–88) extending north from Grand Central Station (Fig. 14). In that case the former grade-level railroad tracks were covered over with a new elevated avenue intersected by the established grid of east-west streets to clearly delineate prestigious development parcels. The concept we provided was a strategy to achieve the phasing and redevelopment of the World Trade Center site as shown in the model of the memorial precinct (Fig. 15). The Public Garden could be achieved as an independently constructed element with its own history, narrative, and defining surfaces; and it could be actualized prior to the commercial build-out of the rest of the site, which would occur in accordance with market demand.

inset:
Fig. 15. The Public Garden Precinct (in yellow) is drawn on the World Trade Center plan to show how the relationship between the original twin towers is maintained.

below:
Fig. 16. *Public Garden* precinct containing the tower footprints and memorial museum surrounded by streets with future building sites. Model photo: Jock Pottle.

Fig. 17. Sectional model of 2,800 seat commemorative amphitheater leading down to the Memorial Museum on the north tower footprint. Model photo: Jock Pottle.

above:
Fig. 18. View of St. Paul's Square located at the north end of Greenwich Place. The tower at its center marks the northeast entry to the underground shopping concourse and mass transit. Watercolor rendering by Michael McCann.

below:
Fig. 19. Sectional perspective through the Public Garden, Greenwich Place with underground pedestrian shopping concourse below, PATH trains, and subway.

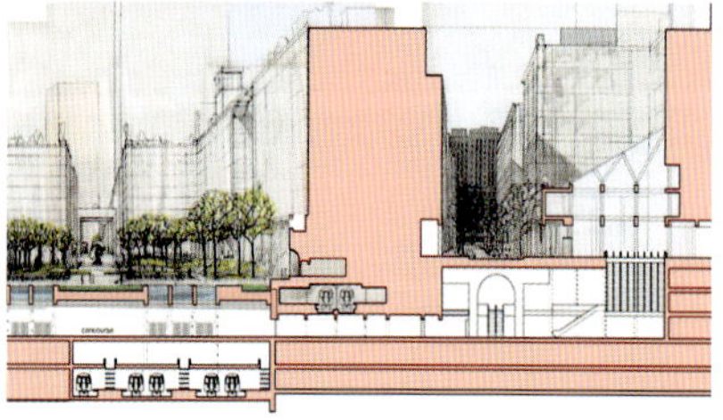

In the plan, the destroyed World Trade Center tower footprints are inscribed in the garden, the south footprint as a memorial reflecting pool, the north footprint as an amphitheater containing 2,800 seats, each dedicated to a victim (Fig. 16). The space of the theater, defined by a semi-ruined enclosing wall, allows the visitor to understand the vastness of the collapsed building's one-acre floor plate. A new Memorial Museum is located immediately beneath the amphitheater and is entered via a new building opposite the Winter Garden, an existing important public space. The exhibition progresses down to bedrock and the slurry wall, still miraculously holding the river at bay. Franz Koenig's sculpture of the world, *Sphere,* which, like the slurry wall, survived the attack, reoccupies its position in the former entry plaza where it had united the two towers (Fig. 17). Also revealed in the garden is a fragment of the Hudson River's original shoreline. This commemorates the place where George Washington landed for his inauguration as first President of the United States. He had proceeded to St. Paul's Chapel, located on the edge of the site, to pray before the inaugural ceremony took place nearby.

The 'sacred' public garden needed to be a protected, quiet, and meditative space, coexisting with, but distinct from, the 'profane' day-to-day city activity. This is achieved by lowering the garden from street level through the thickness of the demising urban 'wall', a Janus-like element that establishes two distinct faces, one to the garden, one to the city, as seen in cross-section (Fig. 18). Entry portals, aligning with and extending the surrounding street grid, form thresholds to the garden, transitioning from one state of mind to another. The tower in the newly created St. Paul's Square (Fig. 19) marks the northeast entry to the underground transportation network and retail concourse (Fig. 20).

The program accommodates eighteen individual development parcels. The shallow depth footprints that surround the 'garden wall' are appropriate for schools, cultural institutions, and housing that are programmatically necessary for the activation of a vibrant street life. The building height is limited to ten floors, where roof gardens are located to serve sky lobbies for the larger sites whose

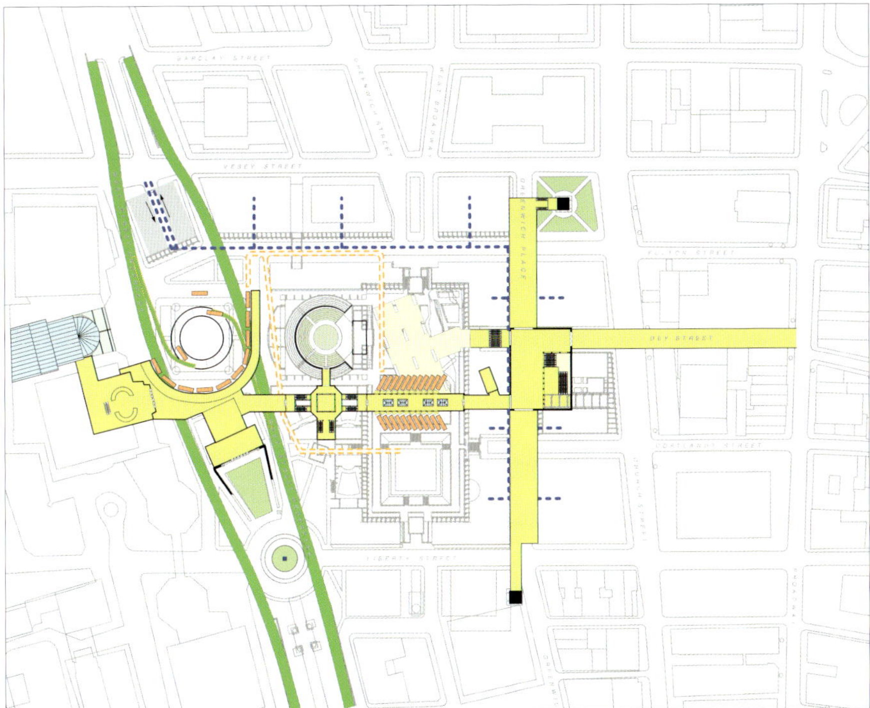

Fig. 20. Below-grade plan of the pedestrian network (in yellow) linking the lower lobby of the World Financial Center East to the transportation hub on Broadway and the north/south shopping concourse under Greenwich Place.

dimensions are calibrated to receive standard floor plate office buildings. The paired main towers, seen from the Hudson River (Fig. 21), are positioned in the plan to 'checkerboard' with the other proposed tall buildings to optimize open views from each, mimicking the staggered arrangement of the original World Trade Center towers.

Normative two-sided retail streets, Fulton Street to the north and Liberty Street to the south, are established through the site to promote street continuity from one side of the Manhattan waterfront to the other. Fulton Street connects the Winter Garden of the World Financial Center to South Street Seaport, while Liberty Street, the primary entry to Battery Park City, leads east to the center of the financial district. Connecting them north to south is Greenwich Place, a new retail street that is the extension of lower Greenwich Street, now terminating at the proposed St. Paul's Square. Along it are located entryways into the Memorial Garden via two portals, one each at the termini of Dey and Cortlandt Streets, spatially extending them into the site from the east. With this plan, the two primary goals for the site are achieved: a re-urbanization of the site that reconnects it to the surrounding city by extending the urban fabric into the future, and the World Trade Center footprints memorialized as a genuine, sacred, and public place.

Context versus Object – A Comparison

A comparison of the Peterson Littenberg plan with Daniel Libeskind's winning design dramatically illustrates Colin's construct of the struggle between object and context represented in these two fundamentally different approaches to the nature of architecture and the city and their underlying assumptions about

Fig. 21. Skyline with new Twin Towers showing their staggered placement relative to the World Financial Center in Battery Park City.

urban form (Fig. 22). Comparing the plans and models of both demonstrates that the Libeskind project is primarily about the individual architectural object, consisting of freestanding expressive elements in a continuous undefined free space. The Peterson Littenberg project is primarily about the common urban context, creating continuity of group form—the integrated, continuous fabric of defined public space.

Libeskind's buildings are manifest as multiple autonomous extrusions that come to the ground uninterrupted by bases or street walls, unlike the typology common to Manhattan's tall buildings. Libeskind's buildings have arbitrary setbacks and shifts in geometry assuring non-associations between their individual pieces, and complete independence of each object from the surrounding streets, thereby avoiding definition of any enclosed urban space. Paved paths pass through random empty plazas with the casualness of country roads. No two-sided streets or continuous street walls are formed to create the requisite street spaces needed to generate vitality and interactive energy. The diagonal of Greenwich Street, a hoped-for restoration of the urban context, reverberates in the shaping of building masses and open spaces, deliberately provoking unresolved urban collisions. Compositionally, the solution emphasizes a single symbolic tower on West Street, the "Freedom Tower", as a typically freestanding, Modernist object.

The Peterson Littenberg proposal is radically different in plan and massing, above all by insistently responding to and creating a new urban context and fabric within which the future buildings would be built. Orthogonally arranged in plan, it adheres to, extends, and resolves the city grid by forming two-sided, precisely defined street spaces, maintaining the essence of city form and establishing a permanent public realm. The towers and their positions in the scheme are also based on a very different viewpoint from the singular iconic tower approach taken by Libeskind. The plan reprises the symbolic idea of the Twin Towers, forming the coordinates of a square space above the street. The horizontal street elements

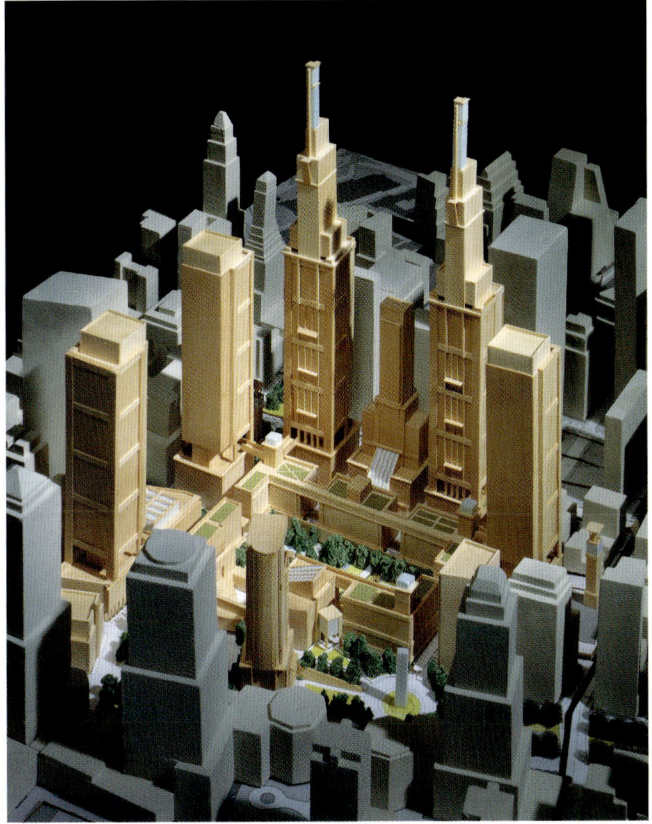

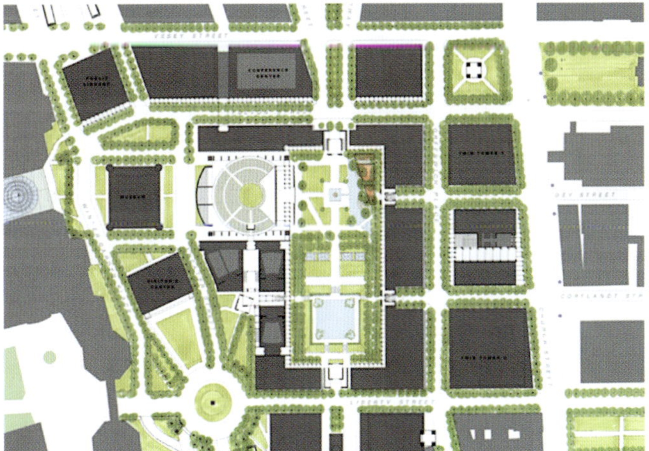

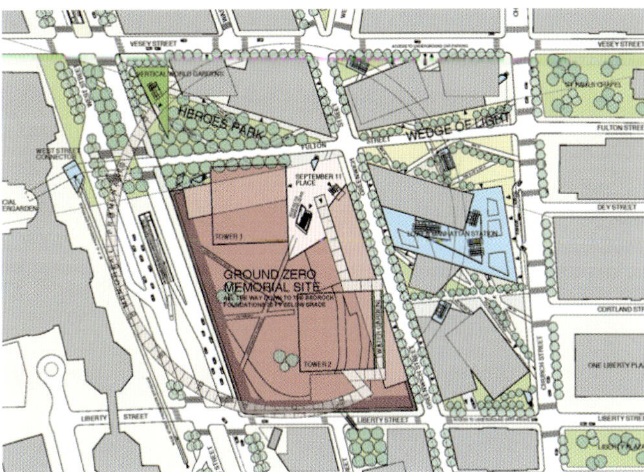

below create a unique intimate city fabric, not unlike Rockefeller Center. These features integrate with the traditional city grids on its boundaries to create a singular sense of place that weaves together interior and exterior spatial sequences. The careful compositional arrangement, of both the horizontal street elements and the vertical towers, balances the countervailing needs of the object and the context resulting in a complete urban fabric that heals the urban wound wrought on the World Trade Center site and its surroundings.

Fig. 22. Projects compared: Peterson Littenberg, left, and Libeskind, right.

Fig. 23. Model view looking north from Battery Park showing the Peterson Littenberg proposal integrated with the surrounding city form. Model photo: Jock Pottle.

An Appraisal

In the end, neither heroic Architecture nor City has succeeded in making an appearance at Ground Zero. The two adjacent towers between Church and Greenwich Streets, now completed, look like unrelated speculative office buildings. They create no coordinated presence on the site, despite being built simultaneously by a single developer employing two talented 'signature architects'. The "Freedom Tower" is a staid, bi-laterally symmetrical cenotaph with a 20-story windowless, bomb-resistant, concrete base clad in ornamental glass and surrounded at the street level by security bollards and check points. Attesting to the fragile temporality of assigning commercial architecture a memorial role, the intended symbolic tower has already been demoted, renamed the prosaic, "One World Trade Center". It looms inertly and mute over the memorial pools that constitute the world's largest inaccessible manmade 'water feature'.

Minimal lip-service was paid to the urban planning intentions of the LMDC. The only indications of the continuities of Greenwich, Liberty, and Fulton Streets are curbs and paving; the necessary urban street walls are left unformed and interrupted. Mechanical barriers and 24-hour manned guard posts prohibit normal traffic onto or through what remains delineated as Port Authority property. Liberty Street, the honorific entrance to Battery Park City, is blocked off; the blocks to its south side, where the demolished Deutsche Bank once stood, are occupied by new one-story secured garage entrances to underground parking with landscaped pedestrian walkways on the roof.

The two most honorific structures, the organic, bony Oculus and PATH transportation hub, the singular vanity achievement of the Port Authority costing an outrageous four billion dollars, and the slanted, boxy Memorial Museum, were placed for their own maximum prominence, but resulted in the visual disruption of the site. The Oculus competes for attention with the memorial pools and museum, while repelling its neighbors with its spiky thrusts. The museum building is slanted on the site like a temporary utility shed or a theme park ride entry. Its placement in the master plan between the pools, intended to connect them, actually blocks their simultaneous viewing from the site entrance.

The World Trade Center footprints, so venerated from the outset of the planning process, are difficult to locate because they lack any spatial presence in the third dimension. All told, the rebuilding of the World Trade Center site marks a triumph of architectural indifference and planning disunity, where each mismatched piece is oversized in scale and extravagantly articulated, seemingly designed in competition with its neighbors in an attempt to draw attention to itself as the most effective symbol of remembrance and resolve.

In the end, the architectural merit of each individual element is not the real problem; the real problem is the lack of coordinated relationships among them that a master plan should have provided. In other words, after 20 years of often contentious, intense planning, there is no evidence of a coherent overall composition, no concept of a master design plan.

This brings us back to Colin Rowe's postulation of the Modern "predicament" of object versus context, architecture versus city, individual versus collective. It is not inconsistent to imagine that he would have appreciated and preferred the Peterson Littenberg solution in that it integrated architecture within the framework of a new urban fabric and juxtaposed many collaged references, melding them together on the site—a sequestered public garden, a boulevard bracketed by obelisks, a Greek theater inside a reconstructed ruin, a recapitulation of matching twin towers, a new urban square to extend St. Paul's churchyard, monumental gateways to the memorial precinct, a contextual re-weaving of streets and blocks through the site, a coordinated placement of towers—in the Modernist sense—to frame space in the sky above a roof garden datum (Fig. 23 and *frontispiece*). Our proposals for rebuilding the World Trade Center site were intended to demonstrate the positive attributes of urban design's multifaceted capacities—creating a variety of unique places that visibly accommodated the various conflicting program requirements for the site in different ways, while also extending Lower Manhattan's legendary, characteristic forms of urbanism and architecture, as Colin might well have expected.

V. Diagnosis / Prognosis

If it is possible to believe with Le Corbusier that between "belief and doubt it is better to believe", then it might also be possible to assume that matters are not quite so desperate as they are often said to be, that neither physics envy nor Zeitgeist worship, object fixation nor stradaphobia is irremediable, and that exacting analysis with a distinctly more varied diet may yet effect a cure.

The Present Urban Predicament, The Cornell Journal of Architecture 1, 1981.

Finally I have come to understand why, in the nineteenth century, one went to spend the summer (if one could afford it) at a German spa, surrounded by good German forests … the heat and humidity have been completely intolerable … . Well, all this is to tell you that, having contemplated the immediate future scenario as envisioned by The Times, *I am as of right now, become an ecological partisan. …you see, it must be a matter of forests, and forests, and forests. Acid rain … is destroying forests in Canada …in Germany. The forests in Tennessee, Alabama, the Carolina's, etc. are said to be wilting. And, as one reads, the worst offender must be Brazil. … So, maybe, I am becoming messianic, which I don't think is my temperament; but, all the same, I am convinced that some great climatological catastrophe is about to impend … as the polar ice caps melt … levels of the ocean will rise and you know all the rest of that story … A New Ice Age which can happen very quick—and this is likely to destroy everything in which, during my lifetime, I have taken pleasure and delight.*

Letter to Dorothy Rowe, August 12, 1988.
Naegele, Daniel (ed), *The Letters of Colin Rowe: Five decades of correspondence.*

Rowe masterfully diagnosed the root causes of the Modernist city's afflictions. As prognosis, he offered alternatives: ignore the afflictions putting the city and civilization at risk; or change behaviors to "effect a cure".

The afflictions are summed up as: physics envy, stradaphobia, object fixation, "*zeitgeist* worship", techno-determinism, and a belief in historical inevitability, all inhibiting and all causing paralysis. He and Koetter use antimonies in *Collage City* to make the complexity of the city readily understandable: object/texture, solid/void, Acropolis/Forum, space/time, hedgehog/fox, *zeitgeist/genius loci*, iconoclast/iconophile, futurist/antiquarian, and many more. From these and attendant examples, an urban morphology emerges that values the traditional city of streets, blocks, and squares. Rowe and Koetter enrich the morphological with the metaphorical: the city as museum, the city as theater, and city as instrument of instruction. Total design was anathema. Authoritarian controls limited freedoms of debate and activity. To be preferred is the democratic process of competing powers and the entertainment of alternative ideas, the classic liberalism of John Stuart Mill, resulting in a multivalent city, 'the city of composite presence' described analogically as 'collage city'.

How did Rowe come to his diagnosis/prognosis? Among the following essays, a psychobiography maps Rowe's life, geographically and intellectually, illuminating how his ideas emerged, developed, and changed over time. Rowe initially embraced Modernist architecture and believed in it. But possessing an analytical mind and skeptical temperament, faith gave way to doubt. Experiencing 'trad' cities likely fortified his readings of Western cultural history and he came to find early 20th century polemics wanting. He saw the totalitarian propositions of Le Corbusier, Patrick Abercrombie, and Frank Lloyd Wright as utopian, their proponents having imbibed a millennialist crisis/salvation cocktail, a secular Parousia, stirred with eschatological hallucinations.

Rowe was dismayed by the paradox of architects simultaneously imagining themselves heroes and saviors changing the course of history, while slavishly obeying the dictates of that same history. As a result, architects sacrificed their responsibility, demurring to presumptions of historical inevitability. He used the RCA building in Rockefeller Center to personify the schizophrenic American architect: Yankee Pragmatist in the boiler room, Transcendental Poet in the Rainbow Room—nothing in between. Rowe was amused and alarmed by *zeitgeist*-inspired futures, fantasies of society's technocratic perfectibility, and the concomitant totalitarian tendencies in Modernist thought that threatened the liberal traditions he believed essential to open, democratic societies.

Despite his prognosis, Rowe retained a strain of optimism captured in the concluding essay. We are cautioned against the insularity of the professions and the hermeticism of the academy. We are reminded of the human condition characterized by the hedgehog and the fox. We are encouraged to remember that there is no one optimal solution, but many possible and good solutions worth pursuing. We are called to a global awareness of the problems facing the planet and humanity. Finally, we are admonished to elevate common sense, to recognize that any responsible path forward should be guided by reason not faith, in the words of Léon Krier, by choice not fate.

The Timeliness of Rowe's Legacy

Elio Piroddi

frontispiece:
Aerial view, Urbino, Italy.
Photo: Giorgio Simi.

Collage City *potrebbe apparire, in questa Collana, come un «a parte»: perché affronta questioni che sembrano molto più generali oppure molto più particolari – secondo come le si prende – di quelle trattate nei volumi precedenti.*

In realtà il suo interesse sta proprio nell'ampiezza di oscillazioni dell'osservazione critica, nel modo disinvolto di svagare da problemi di fondo a problemi di margine, e viceversa; con tocco leggero sui primi e attanagliando i secondi; con distaccata eleganza e deliberata malvagità; con spericolata o prudente, secondo il rischio, volontà dissacrante.

Il fatto è che questo abile procedimento, sostenuto da un infaticabile abuso di intelligenza porta alla scoperta di situazioni architettoniche che, anche se sono già state identificate e studiate da altri, vengono ricollocate in una trama di relazioni intricate, attraverso la quale baluginano implicazioni complesse.

Così, per esempio, la questione del fallimento dei grandi programmi urbanistici, rilevato come esito della contraddizione tra ideologia e prassi tipica del nostro tempo, ma subito dopo proiettato nell'insinuazione di quanto sia antica e inoppugnabile l'incapacità umana di trasformare uno spazio che vada al di là della dimensione individuale. Oppure la questione del bricolage, *spiegato come rappresentazione inclusiva e composita di una realtà pluralistica, ma anche suggerito come ritorno agli incontrollabili impulsi dell'ispirazione e all'istrionica duttilità del genio.*

Nell'alternanza continua tra analisi su fatti sicuri e proiezioni su induzioni incerte, il panorama si allarga e svela contrasti che non appaiono nelle vedute più nette ma parziali in cui la problematica dell'architettura è generalmente ritagliata.

Per questo, più che un «a parte», Collage City *può essere considerato come un «complementare» dei volumi già apparsi in questa Collana. Il suo testo apparso qualche anno fa in una prima stesura succinta, pubblicata da una rivista britannica, è stato infatti il primo avvertimento tangibile e intelligente della profonda crisi di contenuti e di linguaggio attraverso la quale oggi l'architettura sta passando.*[1]

Collage City might appear as an 'exception' in this series of books because it tackles matters that seem to be either more general or more specific—depending on how one looks at them—than those treated in the previous volumes.

Actually, its relevance lies precisely in the broad range of its critical observations and in its easy way of going from general issues to peripheral issues and vice versa. Touching lightly on the former and seizing the latter, with distant elegance and deliberate wickedness, with either reckless or careful, depending on the risk, subversive intention.

The fact is that this skillful proceeding, supported by a tireless abuse of intelligence, leads to the discovery of architectural situations that, even if they have already been identified and studied by others, are relocated in a weave made of intricate connections, through which complex implications glimmer.

This is the case, for instance, of the question dealing with the failure of large urban programs. This is presented at first as the outcome of the contradiction between ideology and praxis that is typical of our time, but, immediately after, it is projected over the insinuation of how the human inability to transform space beyond the individual dimension is ancient and indefeasible. Or the question of *bricolage,* which is explained as an inclusive and composite representation of a pluralistic reality but also suggested as a way of returning to the compulsive urge of inspiration and to the histrionic suppleness of the genius.

In a situation in which the analysis of sure facts and projections based on uncertain inductions continuously alternate, the panorama broadens and reveals contrasts that do not appear in the clearer but partial views into which architectural issues are generally partitioned.

That is why, rather than an 'exception', *Collage City* may be considered as a 'complement' to the volumes that have been already published in this book series. Its text, which appeared a few years ago as a first succinct version published by a British review, was in fact the first tangible and intelligent warning of the deep crisis of contents and of language through which architecture is struggling today. (Trans.: APL)

1 De Carlo, Giancarlo, [presentation], in Rowe, Colin; Koetter, Fred, *Collage City*, Il Saggiatore, Milano, 1981: third of cover.

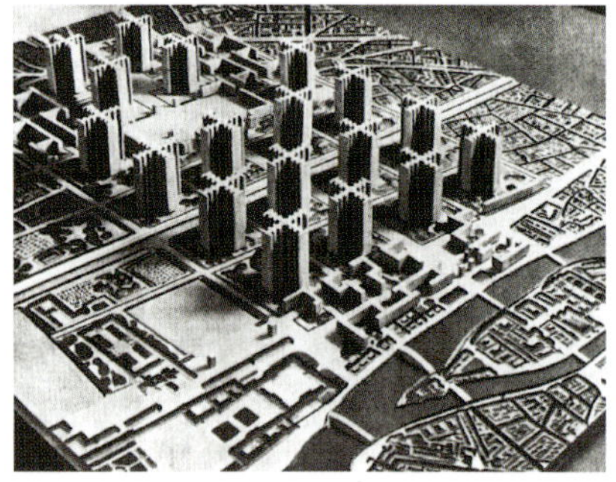

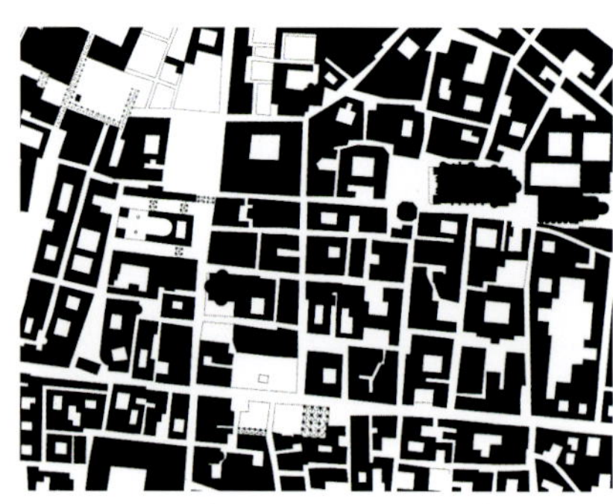

top to bottom left to right:
Fig. 1. La Défense, Paris, ca. 1970.

Fig. 2. Plan Voisin, Paris, Le Corbusier, 1925.

Fig. 3. Stuyvesant Town – Peter Cooper Village, New York, 1942-47.

Fig. 4. Demolition of Pruit-Igoe towers, St. Louis, 1971.

Fig. 5. Figure/ground of Saint-Dié, France, Le Corbusier, 1945, Wayne Copper, 1967.

Fig. 6. Figure/ground of Parma, Italy, Wayne Copper, 1967.

1. De Carlo in his presentation of Collage City

"Rather than an 'exception', *Collage City* may be considered as a 'complement' to the volumes that have been already published in this book series. Its text", De Carlo writes in the presentation of the book, above, "was in fact the first tangible and intelligent warning of the deep crisis of contents and of language through which architecture is struggling today".

Whether an 'exception' or a 'complement', the work of Rowe is placed on the edge of an ideal circle which, according to De Carlo, was centered on overcoming the contradictions between the "expressive nature" and the "scientific aspiration" of urbanistics which aim was a "theoretical and operative renewal", placing urbanistics alongside the human sciences (sociology, economics, etc.), "tending to become a human science itself". This was quite a different goal from the one that the authors of *Collage City* had in mind when writing and, most importantly, illustrating, their book.

2. Some samples to understand the meaning of the discussion

To look more closely into the merits of the arguments made in *Collage City*, we can begin by considering some text excerpts and proposing some brief observations on each individual chapter. We will proceed without any pretense of being exhaustive or offering objective criticism, our sole purpose being to pick up on what surfaces as the hues and tonality of this book.

For example, in the "Introduction" of *Collage City* one can read: "the city of modern architecture ... has not yet been built ... it has remained either a project or an abortion".[2] So the argument goes while discussing the Plan Voisin:

left to right:
Fig. 7. Versailles, 17th century, Pierre Patel. 1668.

Fig. 8. Hadrian's Villa, Tivoli, Italy, 2nd century AD, model, Italo Gismondi, ca. 1935.

Fig. 9. Unité d'Habitation, Marseille, France, Le Corbusier, 1946.

Fig. 10. Uffizi Corridor, Giorgio Vasari, Florence, Italy, 1560 81.

> *For, while the city of Ludwig Hilberseimer and Le Corbusier, the city celebrated by* CIAM *and advertised by the Athens charter, the former city of deliverance, is every day found increasingly inadequate, apparently its very expediency guarantees its adulterated and all-devouring growth.*[3]

Images follow of *La Défense* and of the infamous demolition of Pruitt-Igoe towers in St. Louis, and the text concludes with, "then we are obliged to think again. Which is what the present essay is all about".[4]

The chapter which follows, "Utopia: Decline and Fall?", is a long and, in its way, ironic dismissal of utopian 'classics' (Fourier and companions). The argument is against Futurism, "a sort of romantic front edge of Hegel"[5] made even more extreme by Nietzsche, and concludes with a full-on attack on the "modern" of Le Corbusier (Plan Voisin), Gropius, Mies, etc., and with the following epilogue: "we must recognize and can speak of utopia's decline and fall".[6]

2 Rowe, Colin; Koetter, Fred, *Collage City*, Il Saggiatore, Cambridge, MA, and London, England, 1978: 2.

3 Ibid.: 6.

4 Ibid.: 8.

5 Ibid.: 30.

6 Ibid.: 31.

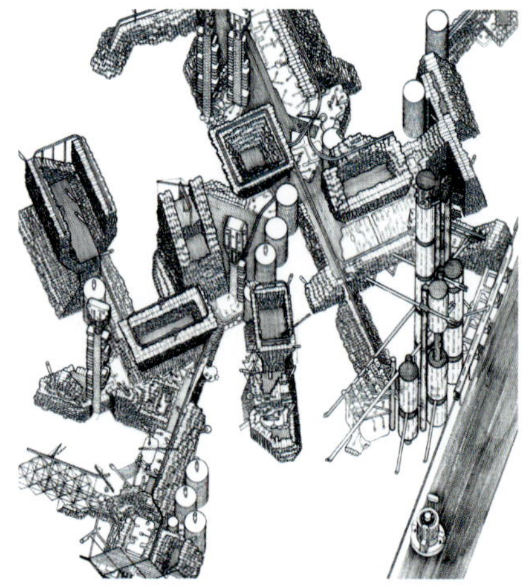

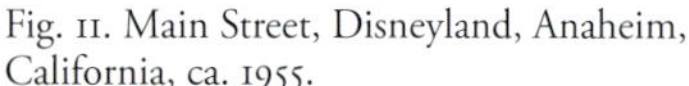

Fig. 11. Main Street, Disneyland, Anaheim, California, ca. 1955.

Fig. 12. Plug-in City, Archigram, 1964.

inset:
Fig. 13. The Acropolis, Athens, 5th century BC, detail of painting, Leo von Klenze.

In the chapter "After the Millennium", the discussion opens with "the 'parousia' of modern architecture, a bundle of eschatological fantasies".[7] Reflecting on its drifts, "... slowly it began to appear that something had gone wrong. Modern architecture had not, *ipso facto*, resulted in a better world",[8] whether "science-fiction" inclinations (Archigram and Superstudio) or the so-called Disney world, Venturi-style.

In the chapter "Crisis of the Object: Predicament of Texture", the key to the reading can be found in two illustrations which synthesize the object-versus-texture concept—figure/ground plans of Le Corbusier's project for Saint-Dié and of the historic center of Parma, Italy.[9] These are preceded by criticism of Corbu's project for Saint-Dié. In discussing it, the observation is that: "... the city of modern architecture become a congeries of conspicuously disparate objects is quite as problematic as the traditional city which it has sought to replace".[10] As is evident in the following pages,[11] the image of Harlow's New Town market flaunts its bleakness. On this point, we allow ourselves reservations. Although we generally agree with the concept, as with those like us who have always supported the relevance of the "form-texture" against the object oriented "bric-à-brac" philosophy, we cannot but notice that the comparison between Saint-Dié and Harlow is not historically fair.

However, whatever the opinion of the reader, it is indisputable that, as we continue reading the following chapters, the depth and, therefore, the fascination

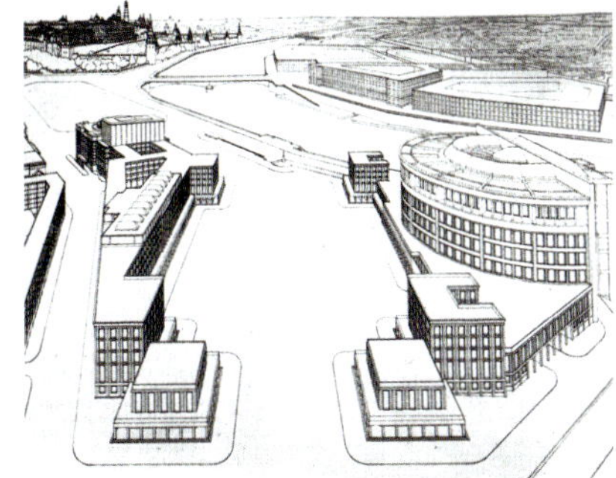

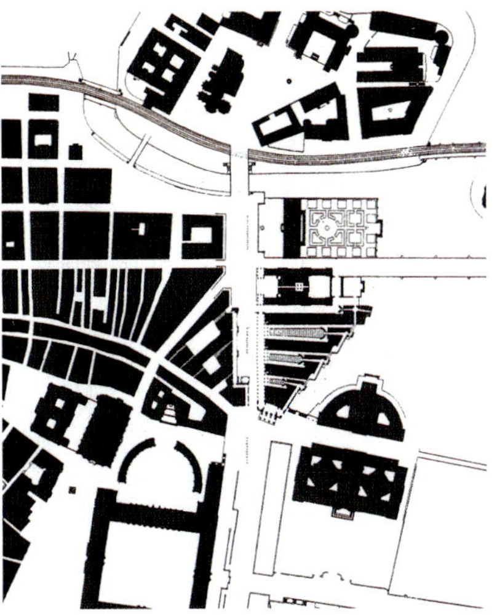

inset:
Fig. 14. Imperial Rome, ca. 4th century AD, model, Italo Gismondi, ca. 1935.

right:
Fig. 15. Palace of the Soviets, Moscow, competition, Auguste Perret, 1922.

Fig. 16. New Chancellery, Stockholm, project, Gunnar Asplund, 1922.

of this book grows. This is not so much thanks to the rigor of the arguments, rather it is because the assertive style of the first part gives way to the evidence provided by visual documents, exactly as the titles of the following two chapters state: namely on *bricolage* and on the *reconquest of time*. The examples used are of an extraordinary appropriateness and, to state it plainly, beauty.

Using the dialectical contrast of Vasari's Corridor and Le Corbusier's Unité, the samples of Perret's Palace of the Soviets and Asplund's Royal Chancellery, the Acropolis and the Roman Forum, Versailles and Hadrian's Villa, Imperial Rome and Baroque Rome, Haussmann's Paris and Vienna with its Ring, the meaning of *bricolage* and the *reconquest of time* emerge with a power, and also emotion, that has no equal when compared with other architectural treatises. Up to the final statement in the chapter that is a self-irony for collage and seems to apologize to utopia.

> *Which is to say that, because collage is a method deriving its virtue from its irony, because it seems a technique for using such things and simultaneously disbelieving in them, it is also a strategy which can allow utopia to be dealt with as image, to be dealt with in fragments without our having to accept it in toto, which is further to suggest that collage could even be a strategy which, by supporting the utopian illusion of changelessness and finality, might even fuel a reality of change, motion, action and history.* [12]

7 Ibid.: 32.
8 Ibid.: 33.
9 Ibid.: 62-63.
10 Ibid.: 58.
11 Ibid.: 60-62.
12 Ibid.: 149.

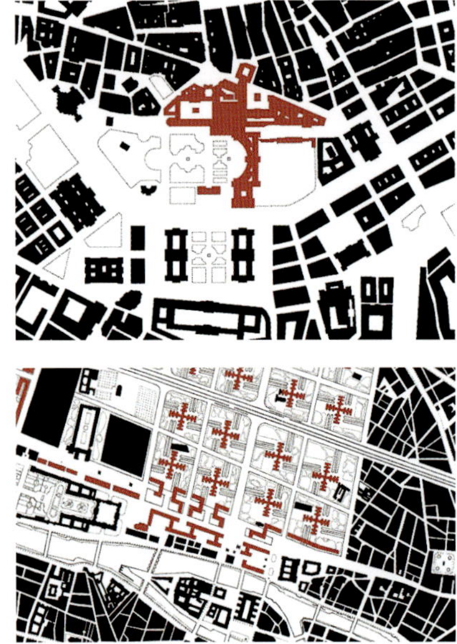

left top to bottom:
Fig. 17. Figure/ground, Ringstrasse, Hofburg Palace highlighted, Wayne Copper.

Fig. 18. Figure/ground, Plan Voisin, Le Corbusier, 1925, detail, drawing by Stuart Cohen and Steven Hurtt, 1967.

Fig. 19. Gropiusstadt, Berlin, Germany, ca. 1970.

Fig. 20. Bobigny, Paris, France, ca 1969.

inset:
Fig. 21. Venice with Palladian buildings, capriccio, Canaletto, ca. 1750.

3. The un-timeliness of Colin Rowe with respect to contemporaneity (?)

Then, we find the "Excursus"—arguably the best part of the book—with its urban themes that are still topical today, despite the fact that the examples are dated.

The question mark at the end of the title of this section will perhaps disappear during the development of our argument. For the time being, it is there because we are questioning why the "Excursus" seems to have deliberately avoided confrontation with the contemporary city: with the city that had already been built or was *in nuce* during those years —*Collage City* is dated 1978— and was already showing or anticipating the "bleakness" which De Carlo writes about in presenting the Italian edition. Given that examples of "collage city" could be found also in the contemporary city. Among them, the works of Kahn, the Internationale Bauausstellung Berlin (IBA-Berlin) and subsequently the "critical reconstruction" by Hans Stimmann that is completed by the new Chancellery—perhaps not-so-accidentally echoing Kahn.

A possible answer or reason for the exclusion of examples selected from the contemporary city could lie in the fact that these examples were becoming more and more rare and were destined to succumb to the quickly spreading and atrophic mass-produced building (see Berlin's Gropiusstadt, *nomen omen*) where the aesthetic intentionality that plays as the bass in the ideal score of *Collage City* was completely absent. Thus, a renunciation. Or, the sense that contemporaneity could not provide valid examples. Or that, in any event, one would be dealing with *élite* cases.

However, it does not seem that the missing confrontation with contemporaneity can be attributed to the fact that Rowe, in a Krier fashion, would subscribe to returning to the antique. We don't believe this both because this would be

inconsistent with the attitude of the ideal reconciliation between utopia and tradition that pervades the book; and because the book's philosophy does not imply at all that urban architecture has to give in to senseless historicist replicas. The "historicism" in *Collage City* appears to us much deeper.

On this point, we agree with the idea that the core problem of urban design does not lie in the language of the "object", but rather in that of the city that, like an "unstable surface", needs rules. Rules that do not exclude eclecticism and diachrony but only proscribe aphasia and de-contextualization.

Thus, and despite our initial reservations, we consider that the work of Rowe and Koetter remains timely, if by this we mean its continuing historical and didactic relevance. And we believe that its *epistemic* roots—from Popper to Lévi-Strauss—its antinomies—objects/texture, solid/void, Acropolis/Forum, imposition/bricolage, space/time, hedgehogs/foxes—and the perfect pertinence of the apparatus of the references—particularly those of the Excursus and the samples from Vasari, Perret, Asplund, Palladio, Canaletto, etc.—are still to be considered cornerstones of urban morphology and of the theory of designing the city considered as a work of art.

clockwise:
Fig. 22. *Le Boulevard de Montmartre, Matinée de Printemps*, Camille Pissarro, 1897.

Fig. 23. IBA Berlin Master Plan, Josef Paul Kleihues, 1987.

Fig. 24. Federal Chancellery, Berlin, Schultes Frank Architekten et al., 2001.

Urbanistics
notes towards an
intellectual biography of
1938-
1978.
Parachutisti Colin
1
Liverpool
Warburg
Yale
Lecorbusier:
St. Die & Stirling
Texas London
New York
2
London
IAUS 1968-69
IID 1970
London
3
Buffalo
Roma Interrotta
Guitar
Maxxi
Trajan
CORNELL 63-80
Washington
4
Rowe = Ro

Urbanistics: Notes Towards an Intellectual Biography of Colin Rowe

David Grahame Shane

frontispiece:
Collage: Urbanistics; Colin Parachutisti 1938-1978.

Colin Rowe would have appreciated that the "Rowe/Rome" conference of 2014 took place in the elegantly renovated lecture hall of Roma Tre University, housed in Rome's 19th century former slaughterhouse. Rowe himself transformed and changed over time, constructing and refining his intellectual and conceptual apparatus in response to his changing circumstances. His three-volume *As I Was Saying* edited by Alex Caragonne[1] created a unifying meta-historical narrative seen from his retirement in Washington, D.C. In the 1990s, looking back on his long career he described a dense, Proustian network of characters and events mapped by Caragonne in his *Texas Rangers*[2] as a vast spreadsheet of interactions and influences covering six pages. The narrative that follows draws deeply on this network diagram, chronicling Rowe's movements and interactions until 1978 in three phases. The description of each phase first concentrates briefly on the people, place, and time. A second section traces the construction of Rowe's spatial and cultural imaginary, his shifting intellectual world view.

There can be little doubt that the single most formative experience of the young Rowe was his time with Rudolf Wittkower at the Warburg Institute. This time was crucial to the formation of his personal aesthetic, his appreciation of utopia, transparency, perspective, rational proportion, and the shifting meaning of symbolic elements. There he also learned of the necessity of ideal and deformation, the contextual impacts of temporal and spatial local distortions. He initially focused on an architectural construct that could include both Palladio and Le Corbusier, linking classicism and Modernism. He ignored the rich urban design and planning tradition of Liverpool University, whose professor Patrick Abercrombie guided the rebuilding of London after WWII.[3] Belatedly he turned to the urban dimension, attempting unsuccessfully to adapt Wittkower's diagrammatic analyses to Le Corbusier's Saint-Dié with his students Robert Maxwell and James Stirling. Later with the Texas Rangers he began to unpack the centrality of the Wittkovian geometry into the landscape, studying Le Corbusier's League of Nations competition entry. He continued this process to recoup the traditional, classical city via Camillo Sitte. From this hybrid base Rowe constructed a new, sublime, meta-historical, reflexive apparatus of the "city as museum" outlined in *Collage City* and "Roma interrotta".[4] Such a three-phase progression is a useful device, but belies the complexity of classical and Modern continuities and contradictions that made Rowe's intellectual struggle so difficult and dynamic in the period between 1938–78:

1 Rowe, Colin, *As I Was Saying. Recollections and Miscellaneous Essays* 3, *Urbanistics*, Caragonne, Alexander, ed., MIT Press, Cambridge, MA, and London, 1996.

2 Caragonne, Alexander, *The Texas Rangers: Notes from an Architectural Underground*, MIT Press, Cambridge, MA, and London, 1995: 347-53.

3 Foreshaw, Joseph Michael; Abercrombie, Patrick; Latham, Charles; London County Council, *County of London Plan*, Macmillan & Co., London, 1943. And Abercrombie, Patrick, *Greater London Plan*, University of London Press, London, 1944.

4 Cerruti, Marisa, ed., *Roma interrotta*, officina edizioni, Roma, 1978; Rowe, Colin; Koetter, Fred, *Collage City*, MIT Press, Cambridge, MA, and London, 1978. See also Rowe, Colin, "In Conversation with Charles Jencks", 1975, Artnet video [https://www.youtube.com/watch?v=L-n_8ymrqgdE]. Lecture text in Rowe (1996/2): 65-73, shown at 2014 conference.

Editor's Note: All collages by D.G. Shane.

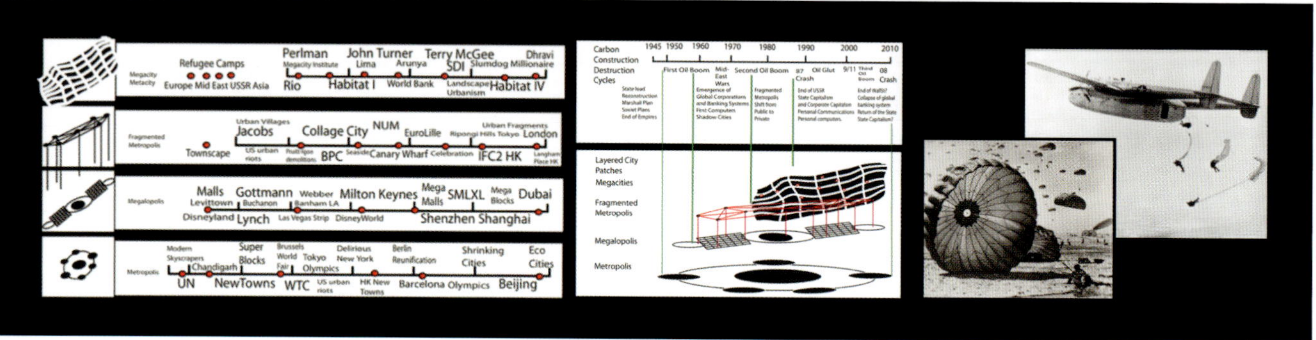

Collage 1: Colin Parachutist, Collage City in Post-modern timelines.

Phase 1: British Origins: Liverpool and the Warburg Institute, London
Phase 2: Yale, University of Texas at Austin, Cornell, Cooper Union, Cambridge
Phase 3: Cornell UD, the IAUS New York, the IID London, Roma interrotta

This study will see Rowe's war-time training as a paratrooper[5] as a metaphor for his ability to jump into multiple and complex situations throughout his lifetime, crossing the Atlantic several times. Rowe had a resilience and capacity to recover and react to the tumultuous European reconstruction after WWII. At the same time he witnessed the accelerated suburbanization of America in rural-urban networks as the country emerged as a dominant world power. This study seeks the basis for his strength and resilience through examining Rowe's transatlantic trajectory before the publication of "Roma interrotta" and *Collage City* both in 1978.

Phase 1 begins in 1938 with journeys from home to Liverpool, then to Scotland and London. *Phase 2* started with the first Atlantic crossing to Yale in 1951 and then across America to California and Mexico 1952–53, finally landing in Texas in 1954. After a brief three-year stay in Austin, the journey continued via semesters at the Cooper Union and Cornell in 1957–58. Then Rowe returned to England for a four-year stay in Cambridge University before settling down at Cornell in Ithaca in 1963. In *Phase 3* Rowe established the Cornell graduate Urban Design Studio. Thereafter he continued to travel to conferences in Europe, including in Berlin with O. M. Ungers in 1967,[6] and in 1968 co-founded the Institute for Architecture and Urban Studies (IAUS) in New York with Peter Eisenman. Rowe took his first Cornell sabbatical in Rome in fall 1969. In 1970, he participated in Alvin Boyarsky's International Institute of Design (IID) Summer Session in London, presenting a first draft of *Collage City*. In *As I Was Saying* Rowe described three periods of the Cornell UD Studio: the first involving Contextualism, the second "dark" period of crisis 1970–72 involving the gestation of *Collage City* with Fred Koetter, leading to a late period, 1974–90, when students explored the collagist strategy of "Roma interrotta". In retirement Rowe settled in London, but following the deaths of Stirling and Boyarsky, he moved to Washington, D.C. where he completed his retrospectives, *As I was Saying*, and *The Architecture of Good Intentions*.[7]

5 Riedijk, Michiel, "The Parachutist in the China Shop", *Oase* 79, "The Architecture of James Stirling, 1964 – 1992", Nov 2009: 43-50.

6 Ungers, O[swald] Mathias, "He Who Did Not Understand the Zeitgeist", in Petit, Emmanuel, ed., *Reckoning with Colin Rowe: Ten Architects Take Position*, Routledge, Abingdon, and New York, 2015: 65-72.

7 Rowe, Colin, *The Architecture of Good Intentions: Towards a Possible Retrospect*, Academy Editions, Academy Group Ltd., London, 1994.

Collage 2: Wath upon Dearne, Yorkshire/Hitler in Munich.

Phase 1. British Origins 1938–51: Liverpool University and Warburg Institute, London

Rowe was born in Rotherham in 1920 and brought up in the small coal-mining town of Wath upon Dearne in South Yorkshire, midway between the industrial cities of Doncaster, Rotherham, and Barnsley. His father was a schoolteacher who, after WWII, with the nationalization of the coal industry, became a senior manager in the local National Coal Board. Countryside and rural villages surrounded the heavily industrial cities and smaller, industrial mining towns, forming an agri-urban-industrial mixture of high contrasts, dominated by the working-class miners and their unions. His friend, the architect and teacher Tony Eardley, a few years his junior, was born in the same town and attended the same, new, selective, state Wath Grammar School, founded in 1924. Eardley recounted that students took two languages; he thought French and German in Rowe's case. Eardley also believed, based on a story told by Rowe's younger brother David, that Rowe in 1938 went on the Wath Grammar School's summer bicycle tour in Germany. This tour included Munich in July when Hitler opened *Haus der Deutschen Kunst*, with its infamous "decadent art" exhibition of Modernist art.[8]

8 Eardly, Anthony, email communication and meeting 2015.

Collage 3 + 4: Liverpool faculty, Warburg, Wittkower, Panofsky, Cassirer, Yates.

Spatial Imaginary 1: Wittkower, Utopia, Saint-Dié, Maxwell, and Stirling

On a scholarship at Liverpool University starting in 1938, Rowe received an education that still included the Classical orders and morphologies, as well as Beaux-Arts variations extending to American Modernism and Erich Mendelsohn's Art Deco. This range represented an English Neoclassical and Empirical tradition, with an appropriate character, or 'style for the job', serving the British Empire. Robert Maxwell, who arrived a year later, described the disruptive power of Rowe's radical teenage advocacy of Le Corbusier and his discovery and promotion of Wittkower's writings on Palladio and Mannerism.[9] Maxwell recounts their friend Thomas (Sam) Steven's discovery of Italian architectural magazines with Terragni's geometric and Moretti's collagist designs. Maxwell and Rowe ended up as classmates in 1944 when the studio project was to design a department store. Maxwell described Rowe's approach as an Italian double-height ground floor with mezzanine that maintained the street with a Miesian grid facade forming a cube in the center and a roof-top Corbusian villa modeled on Villa Savoye. Maxwell illustrated his own design that fulfilled this shared program. Maxwell's descriptions bring out the intensity of the young group's belief in a Modernist utopia of geometry, transparency, and layered variations (in the midst of war).[10] Rowe, away on military service, missed Wittkower's lecture on Michelangelo at Liverpool in 1943, but probably saw his and Fritz Saxl's exhibition on "British Art and the Mediterranean" on display at the school in 1944.[11]

---

9 Maxwell, Robert, "Rowe's Urbanism in Collage City: A Triumph for Common Sense", in Marzo, Mauro, ed., *L'architettura come testo e la figura di Colin Rowe*, Marsilio, Venezia, 2010: 154-69.

10 Maxwell, Robert, *The Time of My Life: in Architecture*, Artifice Books, London, 2017: 28-33.

11 Benelli, Francesco, "Rudolf Wittkower e Colin Rowe: continuità e frattura" and Mazzucco, Katia, "L'incontro di Colin Rowe con Rudolf Wittkower e un'immagine del cosiddetto 'metodo warburghiano'", in Marzo (2010): 96-111, 72-95.

12 Saxl, Fritz; Wittkower, Rudolf, *British Art and the Mediterranean*, Oxford University Press, London and New York, 1948.

13 Warburg, Aby, *Bilderatlas Mnemosyne – The Original* (Ohrt, Roberto; Heil, Axel), eds., Haus der Kulturen der Welt and The Warburg Institute), Hatje Cantz, Berlin, 2020. [https://warburg.sas.ac.uk/archive/bilderatlas-mnemosyne].

14 Bing: [https://www.hkw.de/en/programm/projekte/2020/aby_warburg/bilderatlas_mnemosyne_start.php] and for Cassirer: [https://www.hkw.de/en/programm/projekte/veranstaltung/p_171827.php].

Wittkower and Saxl prepared a book[12] based on this exhibition while Rowe was their student at the Warburg (1945–47). They traced the arrival of classical forms and theories in Britain. The exhibition, like the panels from the Aby Warburg *Bilderatlas Mnemosyne* exhibition in Hamburg (1927–29) pioneered a meta-historical, mind-mapping approach to cultural and artistic history.[13] They employed a comparative method contrasting visual, photographic collages to bring out similarities and differences in designs over time. Warburg worked with Gertrud Bing, a student of the German philosopher Ernst Cassirer, to create a library as a giant memory device. Like the exhibition, the library traced the 'living history' of mutations of symbolic forms in different iterations.[14] For Warburg, the perfection, mathematical clarity, and transparency of Renaissance utopian classical beauty, epitomized by Raphael, inevitably intertwined with the mystical, mythical, pre-modern sciences of the Middle Ages, or the distortions of more recent popular culture.

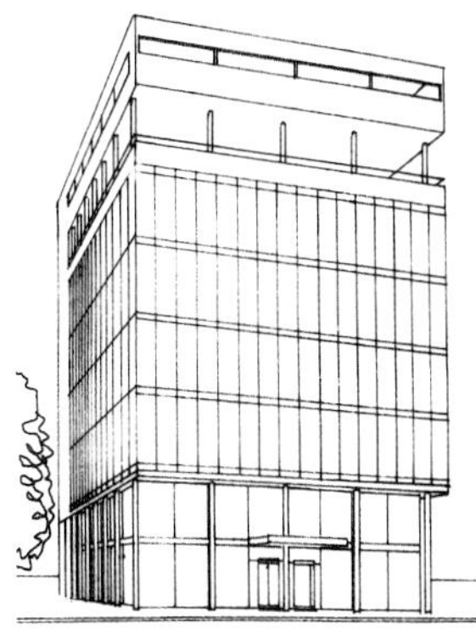

Fig. 1. Student Project, Liverpool University; Department Store, Robert Maxwell, ca.1944.

It is easy to see the appeal of the Warburg method for the student Rowe, who possessed a photographic memory with an intense, quick, visual intelligence. Through Wittkower he absorbed the Warburg lessons: the bipolar system with its checks and balances, and its symbolic continuities and discontinuities.[15] Wittkower diagramed a fundamental *9-square grid schema* as a recombinant grid system in Palladio's corpus.[16] Rowe followed Le Corbusier's leap, connecting Modernism to Michelangelo and Mannerism, presented in *Towards A New Architecture* (1927).[17] Rowe collaged the 9-square grid onto Le Corbusier's villas in his 1947 *The Architectural Review* (*AR*) article, much to Wittkower's dismay.[18] This 9-square schema, a simple organizing and sorting device, became a key spatial, analytical diagram in Rowe's later development. Rowe considered that Wittkower knew "nothing" of Modernism.[19] In 1947, his teacher reviewed a new translation of Camillo Sitte, rejecting it as a neo-picturesque distortion and critique of Le Corbusier's "mechanical utopianism". This anticipated Rowe's reaction to the Townscape of the 1951 Festival of Britain.[20]

Rowe's thesis fitted well within Wittkower and Saxl's argument, testing their hypothesis that Inigo Jones was preparing an architectural treatise based on Palladio. Rowe had difficulty accessing archives while he also worked part-time in Sir Patrick Abercrombie's office.[21] He could easily have looked at Jones's classical urban projects and their utopian, proportional, and theatrical scenographic backgrounds. He could have seen, for instance, Jones's 1632 design of Covent Garden for the Earl of Bedford with its false church facade blocking the main axis. John Summerson, in *Georgian London*, described this as London's first planned "new town" initiating an incremental system of "Great Estates" grid developments in West London.[22] Through Margaret Whinney's Warburg research, Rowe could also have known of the project attributed to Jones for a vast, 9-square, multi-courtyard Palace of Whitehall modeled on Versailles that the architect planned for Charles I.[23]

Summerson described how Jones based his Covent Garden plan on the Medici new port of Livorno. From east to west the Covent Garden estate layout had a clear theatrical scenography. The constricted front layer entry street led to the wide middle layer of the 300 x 450 ft main square dominated by the Doric church portico. In the back layer, a street grid of the same dimensions, lined with Dutch

15 Benelli (2010); Centanni, Monica, "Per una iconologia dell'intervallo. Tradizione dell'antico e visione retrospettiva in Aby Warburg e Colin Rowe" and Semerani, Luciano, "Introduzione a Colin Rowe e all'architettura come testo", in Marzo (2010): 58-71, 12-29; Marchi, Alessandro, "Città ideali", in Marchi, Alessandro; Valazzi, Maria Rosaria, eds., *La Città Ideale: L'utopia del Rinascimento a Urbino tra Piero della Francesca e Raffaello*, Electa, Milano, 2012.

16 Rowe (1996/2): 14-23.

17 Le Corbusier, *Vers une architecture*, Editions Crés, Paris, 1923 (English edition, Etchells, Frederick, trans., Architectural Press, London, 1927).

18 Rowe, Colin, "The Mathematics of the Ideal Villa: Palladio and Le Corbusier compared", *The Architectural Review*, CI (603), Mar 1947: 101-04. Benelli (2010); Mazzucco (2010); Ponte, Alessandra, "Woefully Inadequate: Colin Rowe's Composition and Character", in Marzo (2010): 30-47; Vidler, Anthony, "Reckoning with Art History: Colin Rowe's Critical Vision", in Petit (2015): 40-55.

19 Naegele, Daniel, ed., *The Letters of Colin Rowe: Five Decades of Correspondence*, Artifice, London, 2016. Accessed online as "The Letters of Colin Rowe: Five Decades of Correspondence", Architecture Books, 2, 2015. [https://dr.lib.iastate.edu/handle/20.500.12876/10160] also Rowe (1996/1): 21.

20 Wittkower, Rudolf, "Camillo Sitte's 'Art of Building Cities' in an American Translation", *The Town Planning Review* 19 (3/4), Sum 1947: 165.

21 I owe this information to a conversation with David Rowe during the days of the Rowe Rome conference 2014. I thank Nicholas Boyarsky for giving me access to Alvin Boyarsky's copy of Colin Rowe's Warburg Master's thesis. For Abercombie: Dehaene, Michiel, "Urban Lessons for the Modern Planner: Patrick Abercrombie and the Study of Urban Development", *The Town Planning Review* 75 (1), 2004: 1-30.

22 Summerson, John, *Georgian London*, Pleiade Books, London, 1945.

23 Whinney, Margaret D., "John Webb's Drawings for Whitehall Palace", *The Volume of the Walpole Society* 31, 1942-3: 45-107.

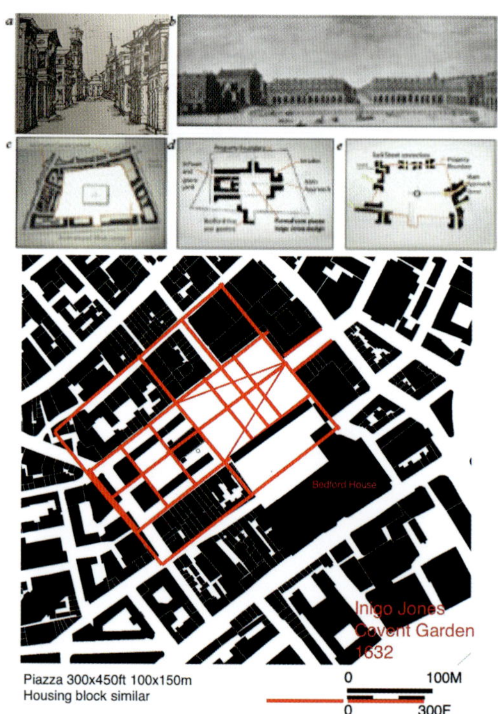

Collage 5 + 6: Renaissance Utopia, Urbino, Vicenza, Inigo Jones, Covent Garden; Shane analysis.

rowhouses, completed the picture. A minor north-south axis bisected the main square facing the Earl's back garden. Each subsequent London estate had the same set of urban elements, creating an urban system of idealized fragments, separated by 'chaotic' interstices. Later Victorian engineers exploited the interstices, often hidden streambeds, for their sewers, telegraphs, railways, and boulevards.[24]

At Chatsworth,[25] Rowe could also have seen Jones's drawings for the Royal Masques and theatrical performances at the court theater.[26] These demonstrated Jones's familiarity with Serlio's three classical urban scenes: the tragic, the comic and the satyric (or village in the countryside). Richard Krautheimer[27] associated these with the three Ideal City, utopian Renaissance perspectives from Urbino from the 1470–80s.[28] Scholars are uncertain, but now link these images with Piero della Francesca and Francesco di Giorgio (and the mathematician Luca Pacioli). The mathematics and proportional construct of Renaissance perspective, the recombinant system of the New Science, controlled everything seen as outlined by Erwin Panofsky at the Warburg.[29] These urban perspective studies were perhaps commissioned in connection with the Ducal *studiolo* with its masterful *trompe l'oeil* intarsia panels.[30] Jones—and Rowe—certainly knew of Palladio's perspectival representation of this Renaissance utopia on the stage of the Teatro Olimpico in Vicenza (1580–85).

Rowe well understood that Modernist utopian projects also inherited this Renaissance monocentric, mathematical, and perspectival idealism from Vicenza as in Le Corbusier's City for Three Million (1922) and Plan Voisin (1925). The City for Three Million involved an enormous grid of super-blocks and geometrical highways meeting at a skyscraper core raised on a service podium. This central business district (CBD) contained shopping arcades, four railway terminals, and parking garages tucked below an airport on the roof, with four cruciform office

24 Greater London Council, The Parish of St. Paul Covent Garden, (Survey of London), 36, Athlone Press, University of London, London, 1970.

25 Wittkower wrote to gain Rowe access to the Burlington Collection of Palladian drawings held at the Duke of Devonshire's Chatsworth country estate. Benelli (2010).

26 Harris, John; Orgel, Stephen; Strong, Roy C., *The King's Arcadia: Inigo Jones and the Stuart Court; A Quatercentenary Exhibition Held at the Banqueting House, Whitehall, from July 12th to September 2nd, 1973*, Art Council of Great Britain, London, 1973: 146-48.

27 Krautheimer, Richard, "The Tragic and Comic Scenes of the Renaissance; the Baltimore and Urbino Panels", *Gazette des beaux-arts* XXXIII (VI), (1948): 327-46; Idem, "Le tavole di Urbino, Berlino e Baltimora riesaminate", in Millon, Henry A.; Magnago Lampugnani, Vittorio, *Rinascimento da Brunelleschi a Michelangelo: la rappresentazione dell'architettura*, Bompiani, Milano, 1994: 233-57.

28 Chastel, André, "Les 'vues urbaines' peintes et le théâtre", Bollettino del Centro Internazionale di Studi di Architettura Andrea Palladio di Vicenza, XVI, (1974): 141-44.

29 Panofsky, Erwin, *Perspective as Symbolic Form* (Wood, Christopher S., trans.), Zone Books, New York, (1929) 1997: 19-66; and Castelli, Patrizia, "La citta ideale di Federico da Montefeltro: geometria e matematica discipline senza retorica", in Marchi and Valazzi (2012): 41-61.

30 Marchi (2012): 83-99, 105-27, 238, 282-89.

towers attached. In the 1925 Paris International Exhibition, Le Corbusier presented these utopian spaces in a circular diorama. It was attached to the back of the pavilion of Amédée Ozenfant's magazine, *L'Esprit Nouveau*, the building itself a sample housing unit from the *immeuble villa* of the proposed city machine.[31]

Le Corbusier, like Ozenfant, was deeply impressed by Mussolini, Marinetti, and Italian Fascism, and the state-based dream of rapid modernization.[32] In the Athens Charter (1934–37), Le Corbusier laid out the Modernist urban design principles for the segregation of the "Four Functions": Residential, Work (as CBD or Industrial), Recreational, and Transportation in separate, spatial enclaves (there was also a 'miscellaneous' category).[33] In Le Corbusier's version the result was a horizontal metropolis based on the automobile with a distinctive set of urban elements: collective housing in large blocks of apartments; a single central skyscraper business district; an industrial district; a musem quarter; and parkland, often arranged after the 1930s in a linear sequence along a large, axial highway, as in the case of Le Corbusier's 1945–51 plan for Saint-Dié.[34]

Rowe, like many of his generation, closely studied Le Corbusier's Saint-Dié plan as a fragment of a mathematical, utopian model manipulating urban elements. But the project was impossible to understand from Le Corbusier's *Oeuvre Complète* of 1946.[35] The problem was that the position of the central municipal tower shown in the published plan differed from the position shown in the published perspectival drawings. Le Corbusier was unable to make up his mind whether to allow the deep space of the long (2000 ft/600 m) old main street to go up to the cathedral in the north of town. The plan showed the municipal tower blocking the main street axis, while the perspective showed the street running clear to the cathedral. When the tower blocked the main street, Le Corbusier showed a smaller, 9-square layout of small public buildings forming a square forecourt (150 ft/45 m). When off the main street, the tower blocked the view from the parallel, raised, pedestrian bridge looking towards the cathedral's flank. But a plan from 1945–47 showed the tower in this western position with small-scale modern public buildings in front making an east-west plaza, so a pedestrian had to turn around the tower to get to the cathedral, completing a picturesque *promenade architecturale*.[36]

Le Corbusier's perspectives saw the project from south to north in a clearly layered system, each layer being about 600 ft/180 m deep. The industry belt and riverside park formed the front layer of *redent*-like linear factories. Then, an assortment of smaller-scaled, picturesque, village-like buildings nested in their local grid marked the middle layer; a commercial street-like armature of two linear buildings, a community building (theater), and a low, spiral-shaped museum. This cluster was approached by pedestrian ramps along the east-west axis from the Unité-like housing mega-blocks set in open parkland. The state apparatus of a municipal tower, a police station, and the cathedral formed the third, back layer of symbolic urban elements set in parkland, allowing sublime views into the Vosges Mountains and along the east-west highway in the river valley. The two long (2000 ft/600 m) north-south view corridors for pedestrians, 200 ft/60 m apart, created a 9-square formation crossing the three east-west layers.[37] After WWII Le Corbusier promoted his unbuilt Saint-Dié plan as the epitome of the Modernist city and its functionalist space, the "Heart of the City".[38] The

31 Difford, Richard, "Infinite horizons: Le Corbusier, the Pavillon de l'Esprit Nouveau dioramas and the science of visual distance", *The Journal of Architecture*, RIBA, 14 (3): 295-323.

32 Brott, Simone, "Architecture et révolution: Le Corbusier and the fascist revolution", *Thresholds* 41, 2013: 146-57. [https://direct.mit.edu/thld/article-abstract/doi/10.1162/thld_a_00106/56641/Architecture-et-revolution-Le-Corbusier-and-the?redirectedFrom=fulltext].

33 Le Corbusier, "CIAM's 'The Athens Charter'", in *Le Corbusier, The Athens Charter* (Eardley, Anthony, trans.), Grossman, New York, (1933) 1973. According to Antonio Latini, it is Eardley's view that there was a draft of the Athens Charter approved by CIAM members on the island of Patris in 1933, and that Le Corbusier radically altered it for publication in 1937.

34 McLeod, Mary, "St. Dié: A 'Modern Space Conception' for Post-war Reconstruction", in Cohen, Jean-Louis, ed., *Le Corbusier: An Atlas of Modern Landscapes*, MoMA, New York, 2013: 193-97. As a graduate student I was commissioned by Rowe to contact Wayne Copper about his figure/ground drawings.

35 Le Corbusier; Jeanneret, Pierre, *Oeuvre Complète, 1938-1946* Boesiger, Willy, ed., Editions Girsberger, Zürich, 1946.

36 Rowe, Colin, "The Present Urban Predicament: Some Observations", (lecture delivered at The Royal Institution, London in 1979), *The Architectural Association Quarterly* 11 (4), and Rowe (1996/3): 204. Also see McLeod (2013): 193-97.

37 Given the information available in *Oeuvre Complète* of 1946, this 9-square analysis was impossible in the 1940s. In any case the scale jump from a Corbusian villa to Saint-Dié was difficult. In the 1960s Bernhard Hoesli successfully applied Rowe's analytical apparatus to highlight the tension between deep and shallow space in the three urban layers. But Hoesli did not find a restraining, perimeter geometry for the 9-square grid in the CBD. Hoesli did note that Le Corbusier positioned two Unité blocks closer to the river to try to strengthen the enclosure of his civic podium, thus reinforcing the depth and drive of his aerial perspectival axis to the Vosges Mountains. Hoesli, Bernhard, "Commentary", in Rowe Colin; Slutzky, Robert, *Transparenz*, Birkhäuser, Basel, 1997: 57-83.

38 Mumford, Eric Paul, *Defining Urban Design: CIAM Architects and the Formation of a Discipline*, 1937-69, Yale University Press, New Haven and London, 2009; Maxwell (2010); McLeod (2013): 193–97; Shane, David Grahame, "The Revival of the Street: Birth and Decline from Renaissance to Today", *Lotus international* 24, 1979; Idem, "The Street in the Twentieth Century", *The Cornell Journal of Architecture* 2, 1983: 20-39; Marchi, Leonardo Zuccaro, *The Heart of the City: Legacy and Complexity of a Modern Design Idea*, Routledge, London, 2017.

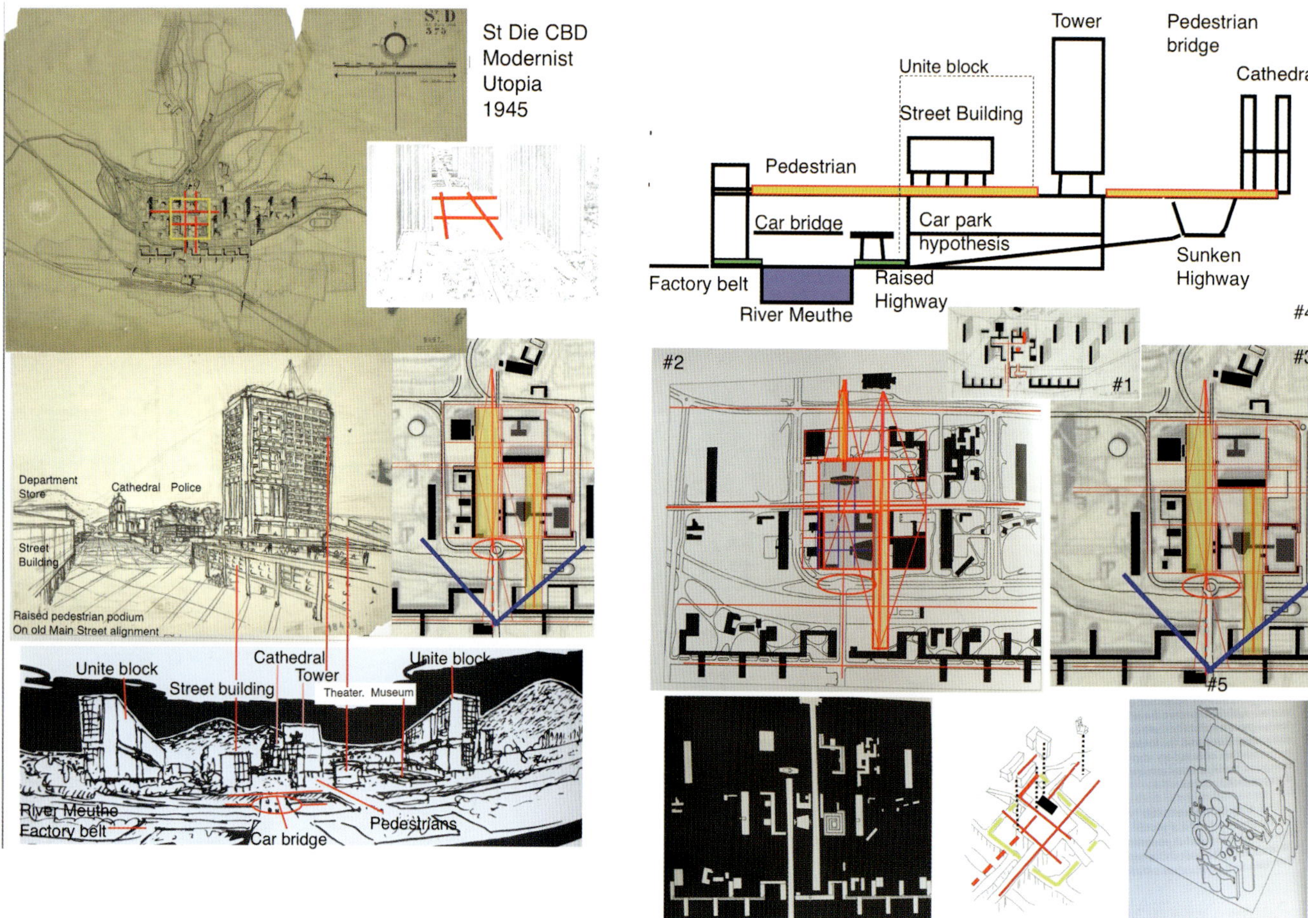

Collage 7 + 8: Corbusier, Saint-Dié, Modern Utopia, Urban Elements.

International Congress of Modern Architecture (CIAM) held its first post-war meeting, CIAM 6, in Bridgwater, outside Bristol, in 1947. There, Le Corbusier showed the Saint-Dié plan, and again at the later CIAM 8 in Hoddesdon, 1951, when Sigfried Giedion, Ernesto Rogers, Josep Luís Sert, and even Le Corbusier, all spoke about the ideal of Mediterranean public space, democracy, and the classical tradition. Rowe did not attend. Two of the editors of *The Architectural Review* (AR) were present, Morton Shand, Stirling's future father-in-law, and J. M. Richards (both members of the British MARS planning group) beside CIAM founders and Cornelis van Eesteren. Rowe wrote for Nikolaus Pevsner, the third editor of AR, who saw Le Corbusier and Gropius as 'Pioneers of the Modern Movement', bringing the logical clarity of iron and steel structural grids to architecture, along with the transparency of glass, exemplified by Joseph Paxton's Crystal Palace for the Great Exhibition in London (1851).[39]

Pevsner saw in Rowe's "mathematics" a link to the Modernist transparency that Rowe would later describe with Slutzky as "literal". In seeking independence of Wittkower, Rowe had landed in a difficult position. The eccentric owner of *AR*, Hubert de Cronin Hastings, had employed Pevsner as a refugee scholar to research the Picturesque as a nationalistic key to the British character. For Pevsner, who had admired Hitler's attempt to define Germanic culture, the picturesque led to a long series of *County Guide* books defining "Britishness" in contrast to

39 Pevsner, Nikolaus, *Pioneers of the Modern Movement: From William Morris to Walter Gropius*, Faber and Faber, London, 1936.

the cosmopolitan Warburg tradition.[40] For Hastings, English villages, pubs, and landscaped gardens, along with Italian hill towns with cobbled streets represented the best of the Picturesque tradition, a style *AR* promoted as "Townscape", illustrated by Gordon Cullen.[41] Wittkower's review of the new translation of Sitte's *Town Planning According to Artistic Principles* pointed out the many inaccuracies in the text, distorted to meet Townscape principles. In addition, Wittkower emphasized that, despite Le Corbusier's characterization of Sitte as a lover of the "donkey's path", Sitte also valued classical urban design spaces and their perspective control as in Piazza San Marco in Venice.[42]

Wittkower's strong reaction to both the Corbusian "mechanical" utopia and the emerging British Townscape movement anticipated Rowe's later polarized rejection of the Festival of Britain exhibition of 1951.[43] Rowe, through the Warburg, knew of Ernst Cassirer's *The Platonic Renaissance in England* that highlighted the Cambridge school of Neo-Platonists in the age of the scientist Francis Bacon.[44] These scholars combined science and art, myth and magic, chemistry and alchemy, mathematics and proportion in a hybrid system.[45] The Neo-Platonic classical tradition for Wittkower included Picturesque landscape elements derived from Nicolas Poussin, epitomized by the shifting "Et in Arcadia ego" readings described by Warburg scholar Erwin Panofsky.[46] Lord Burlington and William Kent had collaged these elements around Burlington's Neo-Palladian 'villa rotunda' at Chiswick House in 1729, initiating the British, Anglo-Chinese landscape tradition.[47]

After Rowe studied at the Warburg, he worked for Abercrombie, wrote for Pevsner at the *AR*, and he began to teach at Liverpool University (1948-51). There he tutored his two friends Maxwell and Stirling on their thesis projects.[48] Maxwell chose to design a Warburg Institute containing a library, exhibition hall, lecture theater, classrooms, and offices in a U-shaped building. Asymmetrical wings housed each function with an entry, art gallery, and exhibition hall between. This long north-south block, at right angles to the street, aligned sideways with the front courtyard of the British Museum. Nicholas Hawksmoor's St. George's Bloomsbury stood isolated in a new plaza. Its facade faced south to Bloomsbury Way wrapped with new gardens behind the new Warburg.[49] Maxwell admitted it was an impossible site and on graduation he enrolled in Liverpool's Civic Design course where he wrote a dissertation on Sitte's *Town Planning According to Artistic Principles* and the English Garden City tradition.[50] Later he worked for the Civic Design professor, William Holford, and for Casson-Conder, the architects of the 1951 Festival of Britain. Then he designed the riverfront facade addition of the Festival Hall for Sir Leslie Martin at the London County Council (LCC).[51]

Stirling recounted that Rowe at Liverpool used Wittkower and Saxl's oversize *British Art and the Mediterranean* as a teaching tool, spreading it out on the floor or a low table. Under Rowe's supervision, Stirling's thesis manipulated humbler versions of Le Corbusier's Saint-Dié plan, layering the urban elements of a new town civic center on a flat, gridded ground plane with a recessed, 9-square, civic plaza. A long administration building, a hotel, and courtyard of shops formed the back wall of the project. A garden axis, the civic plaza with underground parking, and municipal tower formed the middle layer, as at Saint-Dié. The front plane beside the street consisted of smaller buildings, including the post office,

40 *Visual Planning and the Picturesque: Nikolaus Pevsner*, Aitcheson, Matthew, ed., Getty Publications, Los Angeles: 1-5.

41 de Wolfe, Ivor, *The Italian Townscape*, 1963; and Cullen, Gordon, *Townscape*, Architectural Press, London, 1961.

42 Wittkower (1947): 17.

43 Banham, Mary; Hillier, Bevis, *A Tonic to the Nation: The Festival of Britain 1951*, Thames & Hudson, London, 1976.

44 Cassirer, Ernst, *The Platonic Renaissance in England* (Pettegrove, James P., trans.), Thomas Nelson and Sons, London, (1933-34) 1953. Rowe still employed this text in 1971-72 for teaching purposes.

45 Cassirer stressed the mutability of forms, shapes, patterns, and relationships, retained in the perspective of a formidable memory system. Warburg worked with Cassirer's ex-student Gertrud Bing, who later became the director of the Institute in London, befriending the British scholar, Frances Yates. Yates, Frances, *The Art of Memory*, The University of Chicago Press, Chicago, 1966.

46 Panofsky, Erwin, "'Et in Arcadia ego' et le tombeau parlant", *Gazette des beaux-arts* 80 (19), Jan 1 1938: 305, later in *Meaning in the Visual Arts: Papers in and on Art History*, Doubleday, Garden City, NY, 1955.

47 Wittkower, Rudolf, "English Neo-Palladianism, the Landscape Garden, China, and the Enlightenment", *L'Arte* 6, 1969: 18-35.

48 Crinson, Mark, *Stirling and Gowan: Architecture from Austerity to Affluence*, Yale University Press, New Haven, 2012: 29-44.

49 Maxwell (2016): 38-42.

50 I am grateful to Celia Maxwell Scott for sharing a copy of the drawings of the Warburg thesis design and Liverpool Civic Design Master's thesis on Sitte. Rowe (1996/3): 343-44. Rowe returned to the Warburg Institute theme at Pitigliano at Cornell with Paolo Berdini in 1985 (Rowe (1996/3): 57-62).

51 Maxwell (2016): 46-49.

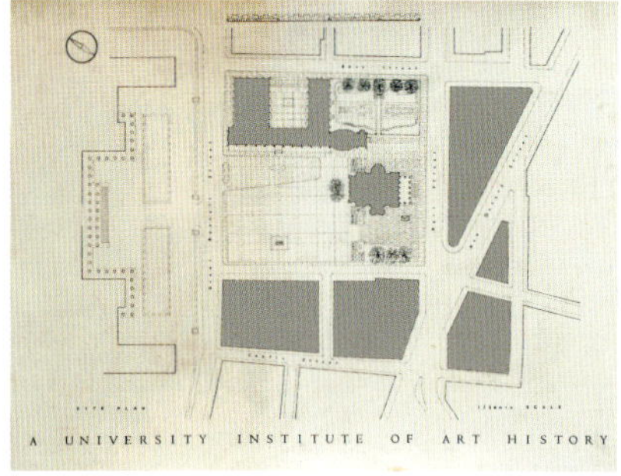

Fig. 2. Thesis: Warburg Institute perspective and site plan by Robert Maxwell, Liverpool University, ca. 1948-49.

theater, cinema, and police station and the subject of his thesis, a "community building". This building, like Maxwell's, had a hybrid program: a lecture hall, meeting rooms, a cafeteria, and rooftop gymnasium, all raised on *pilotis*, and articulated against a three-dimensional framework, with two internal courtyards. Maxwell, an excellent draftsman, drew two key perspectives of the recessed pedestrian plaza for his friend.[52]

Rowe, in supervising his two friends' theses in Liverpool (1948–49), tested the urban apparatus and elements of Modernism in both the central city (Maxwell) and the new town (Stirling). In the city center, demolishing the city block and isolating the church posed a problem with the rear of the church facing the front of the British Museum. Stirling had more freedom to arrange his urban elements in a classical, formal landscape as alternative to the Scandinavian Modern new towns of the Abercrombie Plan being built on austerity budgets around London.

Rowe had met the Canadian landscape architect Christopher Tunnard at the Warburg (who attended CIAM 6 in 1947).[53] Perhaps Tunnard's landscape gardens, disciplined, Modern, theatrical, and yet free-form and Picturesque, inspired Rowe and his students' plantings. Tunnard taught city planning at Yale, at first embracing the landscape promise of the automobile and American suburbia (like Giedion) but later shifting to a much more critical and classical stance. He anticipated Rowe's later intellectual trajectory. Rowe asked Wittkower's support for a Fulbright as he planned to research classical proportional systems: the work of McKim Mead and White, and in Chicago, Frank Lloyd Wright (under Henry-Russell Hitchcock at Yale).[54]

In Phase 1 Rowe initially concentrated with Wittkower on the geometry of the Palladian building as a singular object, leading to his analysis of the Corbusian villas, breaking a Modernist convention that separated the classical tradition from Modernity, extending Warburg's comparative thesis to Modern architecture. His analytical apparatus focused on the geometry, proportions, and mathematics of the individual building in three dimensions, incorporating Le Corbusier's "five points" of Modern architecture and the *promenade architecturale*. He turned a blind eye to contemporary Abercrombie's City Planning and Civic Design at Liverpool (established 1909). He ignored the fragmented, multi-cellular fabric of Georgian London and tradition of the British Neo-Palladian urbanism even as he worked for Abercombie, the master planner of the Green Belt and post-war London. Teaching Maxwell and Stirling in Liverpool, Rowe did attempt to apply the Wittkovian diagram method at an urban scale in Stirling's new town center thesis, following his analysis of the monocentric Saint-Dié CBD and the presence of its 9-square grid. Like Wittkower, Rowe rejected British Townscape and its micro-scaled, neo-picturesque interpretation of Sitte, studied by Maxwell in the Liverpool Civic Design course.

Phase 2. 1951–63: Yale, Texas, Cornell, Cooper Union, Cambridge

Escaping from the Townscape Festival of Britain in London (1951), Rowe went in the autumn with a Fulbright Fellowship to study at Yale with Henry-Russell Hitchcock, whom he had first met at the Warburg. Rowe honored Hitchcock as a historian who understood the continuity of the classical tradition in the

52 Vidler, Anthony, *James Frazer Stirling: Notes from the Archive*, Yale University Press, New Haven and London, 2010: 44-75.

53 Tunnard, Christopher; Reed, Henry Hope, *American Skyline: The Growth and Form of Our Cities and Towns*, Mentor Books, New York, 1956; Tunnard, Christopher; Pushkarev, Boris, *Man-made America: Chaos or Control? An Inquiry into Selected Problems of Design in the Urbanized Landscape*, Yale University Press, New Haven and London, 1963; and Giedion, Sigfried, *Space, Time and Architecture: The Growth of a New Tradition*, (The Charles Eliot Norton Lectures for 1938-1939), Harvard University Press, Cambridge, MA, 1941.

54 Benelli, Francesco, "Rudolf Wittkower e Colin Rowe: continuità e frattura", in Marzo (2010): 96-111.

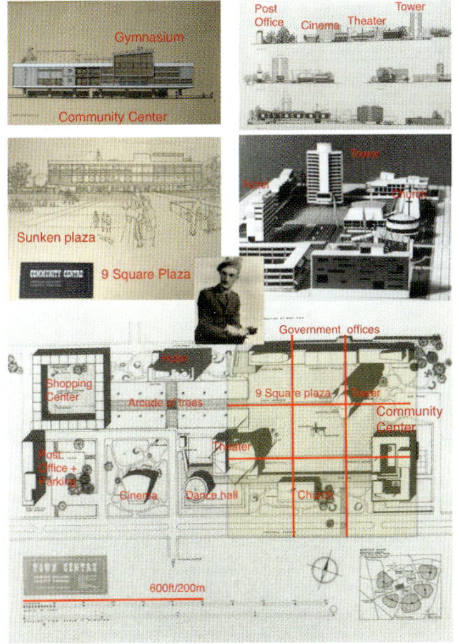

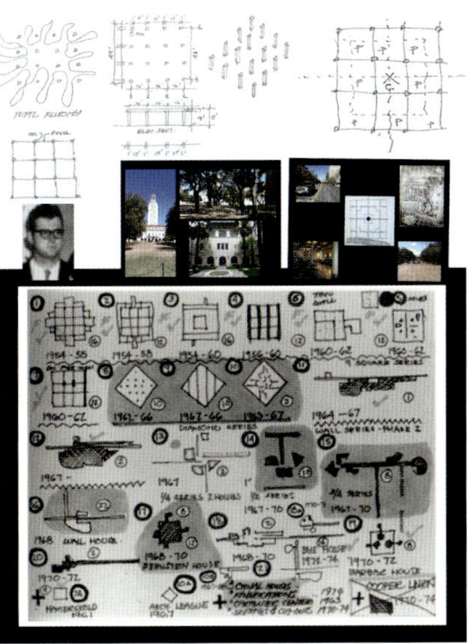

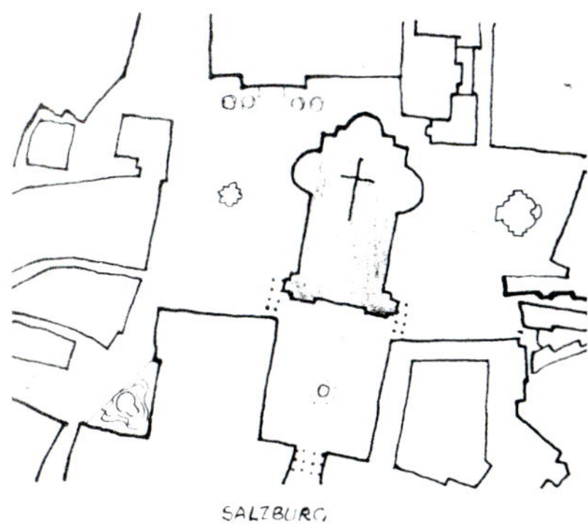

Fig. 3. Sketch of Salzburg Cathedral, after Sitte, by Robert Maxwell.

Collage 9 + 10: Stirling, Liverpool Thesis, 9 Square Grid Variations, Hejduk, Austin, Texas.

Industrial Revolution and Modernism. Hitchcock had just published his *Painting Toward Architecture,*[55] connecting Cubism, abstraction and Modern architectural space, citing György Kepes's phenomenal transparency and the role of visual memory.[56] Rowe wrote home about Josef Albers' classes as "simply the best thing going". His rigorous geometry of squares, aligned about a single center, created an ambiguity about front and back, in color fields, and layered, spatial matrices.

Rowe also described driving up and down the East Coast with Hitchcock, including visiting Philip Johnson's Glass House in New Canaan, Connecticut. Yale, in New Haven, stood in the midst of the Boston to Washington East Coast corridor, containing 32 million people in a new urban model, extending 400 miles/700 km, that Jean Gottmann described in *Megalopolis.*[57] With its sprawling private housing developments, this was very different from Le Corbusier's CIAM vision and from the compact metropolitan urban design model of Abercrombie (1943–45) in London, with its green belt, new towns, and population of eight million. After Yale, Rowe took a year off and drove across America with the transportation engineer Brian Richards, whom he knew from Liverpool. On his way back Rowe met Jean Bangs Harris, the wife of Harwell Hamilton Harris the dean of the architecture school at the University of Texas, Austin, who offered him a teaching post. Later Rowe taught briefly at the Cooper Union, Cornell, and then Cambridge, England.[58]

Spatial Imaginary 2: Texas, Slutzky, League of Nations, Analytic Cubism, and Contextualism

Rowe, while in Texas, continued to seek a new, reflexive Modernity that could combine Modern utopian elements with a critical reading of classical history, continuing research begun at the Warburg.[59] Alex Caragonne described how Rowe and Bernhard Hoesli proposed a restructured curriculum that emphasized drawing and analysis in the first year. Hoesli's first year layered single-point perspective and framed axonometric drawings of Cubist masterpieces proved an enduring

55 Hitchcock, Henry-Russel, *Painting Towards Architecture*, Duell, Sloan and Pearce, New York, 1947. Rowe (1996/2): 11-43.

56 Arnheim, Rudolf, *Art and Visual Perception: A Psychology of the Creative Eye*, University of California Press, Berkeley, 1954.

57 Gottmann, Jean, *Megalopolis: The Urbanized North Eastern Seaboard of the United States*, Twentieth Century Fund, New York, 1961.

58 Naegele (2016): 16; Rowe (1996/1): 25-26.

59 Rowe, Colin, "Neoclassicism and modern architecture", *Oppositions* 1, 1973: 1-26, (written in 1956-57).

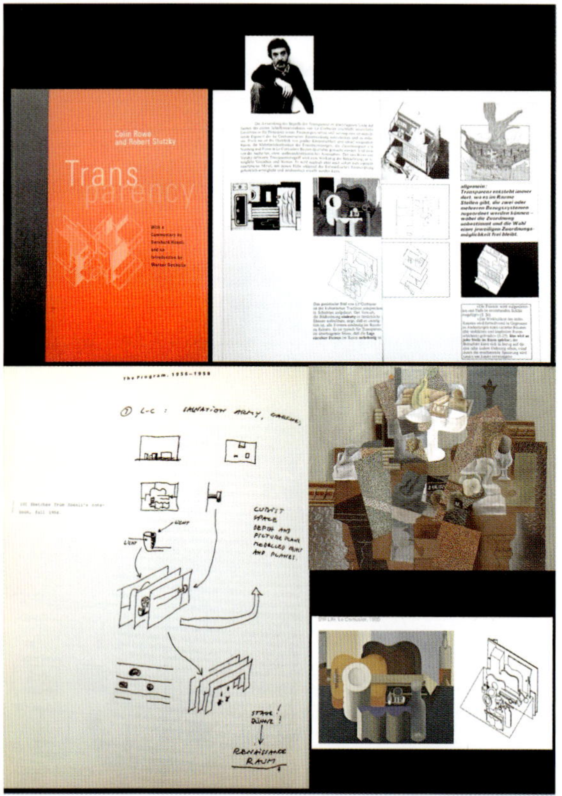

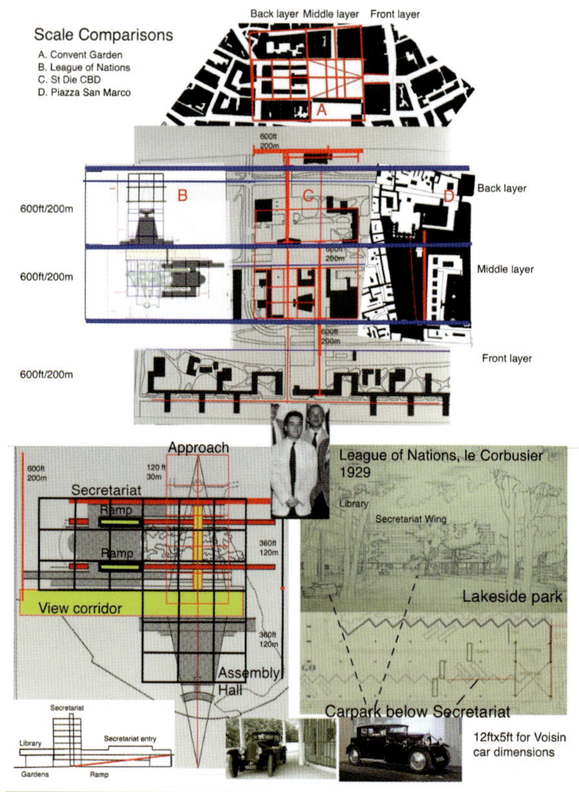

Collage 11 + 12: Texas, Hoesli, Cubism, Layering, Scale Comparisons, League of Nations, Transparency 1, Slutzky.

teaching tool.[60] Robert Slutzky, a painter whom Rowe had met at Yale, added his Cubism-inspired reading of the ambiguous interplay of Modernist deep and shallow, flattened space.[61] John Hejduk's 9-square grid expanded on the Wittkower and Rowe diagram creating innovative exercises for first year, with their flexible, interspersed, flat panels making figural enclosures.[62] In sophomore year more technical requirements at a building scale followed. Junior year added an urban component before thesis in the final year.

Writing with Slutzky, Rowe reinterpreted many of the urban questions unanswered in Liverpool and London by studying Le Corbusier's monumental League of Nations project from 1929, sited on a remote suburban promontory overlooking Lake Geneva.[63] Here Rowe and Slutzky made a great refinement of the conceptual and geometric construct Rowe had brought from London. His spatial imaginary lost its Wittkovian autonomy and became more open to local site disturbances in context and landscape. Le Corbusier disposed his urban elements with great precision, taking account of the landscape, a task made easier by the absence of streets. In place of streets, Le Corbusier planned grand visual axes, one to the blank facade of the largest symbolic element, the meeting hall. Another cross-axis stretched from the entry court before the meeting hall out to the right along the facade of the secretariat building across the lake to Mont Blanc. Le Corbusier mirrored and flipped over the perspective cone of the approach axis to shape the auditorium of the assembly hall, creating an unmarked central point where the three perspective cones overlapped.

---

60 Caragonne (1995): 220-21. The entire school program: 154-331. Rowe (1996/1): 43.

61 Ockman, Joan, "Form without Utopia: Contextualizing Colin Rowe", *Journal of the Society of Architectural Historians* 57 (4), (1998): 448-56; and also Ponte (2010).

62 Moneo, Rafael, "The Work of John Hejduk or the Passion to Teach; Architectural Education at Cooper Union", *Lotus international* 27, 1980: 65-85.

63 Rowe, Colin; Slutzky, Robert, "Transparency: Literal and Phenomenal, Part I", *Perspecta* 8, 1963, later in Rowe, Colin, *The Mathematics of the Ideal Villa and Other Essays*, MIT Press, Cambridge, MA, and London, 1976: 159-83, (written in 1955-56); Idem, "Transparency: Literal and Phenomenal, Part II", *Perspecta* 13-14, 1971, later in Rowe (1996/1): 73-106, (written in 1956).

The two mirrored perspective cones both included 9-square grids, as did the layout of the H-shaped secretariat and library building on a cross-axis. This *tour de force* of geometry and elegant Mannerist massing, blocking, and opening view corridors demonstrated for Rowe and Slutzky Le Corbusier's 'phenomenological' conceptual approach. This involved a complex reading of plan, landscape, urban elements, sequencing, and view corridors in the visitor's imagination and memory. In Frances Yates's and Warburgian terms, it involved a classical system of memory, with niches and enclaves as symbolic markers representing various functions and associations along the ideal route, the sculptural *promenade architecturale*.

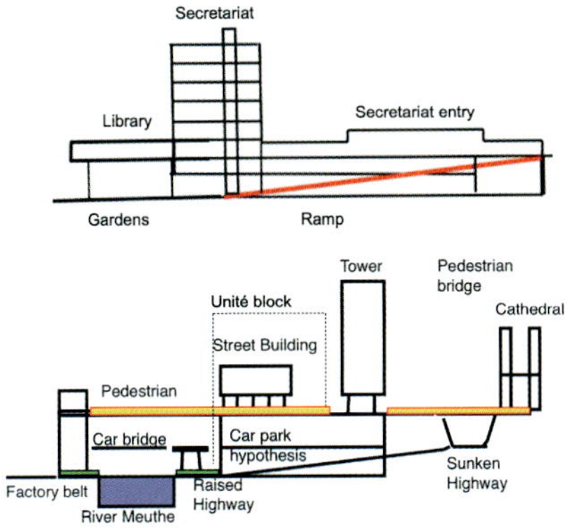

Fig. 4. Le Corbusier: analagous sections showing lower level car parks, from top to bottom: League of Nations competition and project for Saint-Dié.

The symbolic power of the geometric diagram, as in Wittkower's reading of Palladio, drove this interpretation, making an unflattering comparison with Gropius' Bauhaus with its "literal" transparency of a bridge across a street and of transparent corners. The tripartite layering at Geneva, as later in Saint-Dié, went from an entry axis to a middle Mannerist block and smaller scale Picturesque field, opening out to a monumental scale set against sublime vistas. In the classical tradition of Tony Garnier, the symbolic mass of the giant sculptural composition of the assembly building dominated the site. Around this core the scheme wove five urban elements together in a classical hierarchy: armatures of landscaped visual axes, the secretariat courtyard and long office arm, the plaza in front of the assembly building, the park landscape, and the parking below.

The five urban elements overlapped in three 9-square spatial figures in the Rowe and Slutzky plan diagram. But each retained its own integrity, setting up a desired conceptual ambiguity, the key to a phenomenological reading based on Kepes' theories. As Sébastien Marot[64] pointed out, this reading in plan could be augmented by a phenomenological reading in section, in which the landscape of the site sloping down to the lake, as described at length by Le Corbusier, formed yet another layer. Marot argued that the platform of the secretariat building's approach would have floated out on its *pilotis* over the park, allowing a literal transparency from the parking undercroft to views of the lake as shown by Le Corbusier's perspectives. The two cross-axes of the 9-square grid of the middle zone led down to and up from a 98-space car park below the secretariat. Cars drove along the approach, through the trees, and to the entry concourse, returning to turn into the secretariat courtyard. There, ramps led down two floors below the building, revealing the driver's vista out into the landscape of lakeside park and mountains.

The problem for the 'transparency' analysis was that, unlike Picasso's Cubist *L'Arlésienne* (1912) there was no virtual vertical axis, about which the spatial figures could rotate and re-integrate in the viewer's memory, as in the many silhouettes outlined in the fragmented Cubist portrait cited by Giedion.[65] At the League of Nations, in Geneva, the controlled theater of the classical, linear sequence approaching the blank assembly hall facade stood on one level, with a shallow side space for administration. This was the important symbolic scenario leading to a sublime release down the visual corridor to Mont Blanc. Below lay an alternative reality of car park and picturesque gardens. The visitor had to integrate the fragmented fields from two levels, the classical above, the car park and landscape below, making a new reality. From a classical perspective the 'transparency' article greatly refined the symbolic elements incorporated in the urban design

64 Marot, Sébastien, "Extrapolating Transparency", in Marzo (2010): 112-35.

65 Marot (2010): 114 and Giedion (1949): 426.

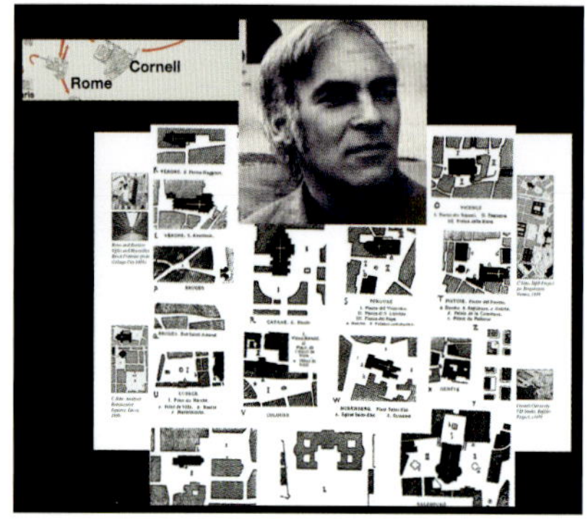

Collage 13: Boyarsky, Thesis, Camillo Sitte, Cornell.

apparatus; the focal object, the void of perspectival approach avenue with side screening. The construct handled blocking, symmetry and asymmetry, mirroring and proportional systems. But there was no vertical integration and no marker on the assembly hall forecourt designated as the central hinge point of the design, obliterating the vertical axis.

The Le Corbusier archive, now online, shows that the same sectional problem, highlighted by Marot, was also present in the plan for Saint-Dié.[66] It was not immediately clear from the *Oeuvre Complète* that the Saint-Dié pedestrian civic plaza stood on the roof of a vast car park by the river that clearly connected to the hillside by the cathedral. A 1945 drawing showed three entrances to the car park, one below the shopping street, another below the department store, and another at the north by the police station. In the *Oeuvre Complète* plan, Le Corbusier sank the flank roads and back road by the cathedral in cuttings and elevated the road beside the river over winding pedestrian paths. This implied that the high pedestrian bridge leading from the old town crossed the elevated road by the river at about 30 ft/10 m. The municipal tower blocked the cathedral vista. At the rear of the municipal tower, another pedestrian bridge at the same level led to the cathedral from the main street axis that was also raised on the parking podium level. Underneath the podium, the parking level would have had a view south out to the river, industrial belt, remains of the old city, and mountains beyond.

In "Transparency: Literal and Phenomenal" Rowe extended Wittkower's classical, conceptual, geometric device beyond a single villa into a building complex, with the potential reading of the city and landscape together in a fragment beyond the ideal 9-square grid. In this hybrid Texas framework, Rowe and Hejduk saw Lockhart, Texas, as an ideal, symbolic representation of American agri-urban Jeffersonian democracy, with its courthouse set in a central square surrounded by shops, churches, and social buildings.[67] A small grid of streets and a landscape of farms surrounded this civic core. Lockhart became in this symbolic cultural interpretation a variation of the classical model of the Italian Renaissance. Hejduk at Cooper turned the 9-square grid into a cube, with rotations around a vertical axis, extensions, wall houses, mobile habitats, and finally symbolic operatives, his symbolic urban "actors". As Hejduk recounted in diagrams, he began the experiments with the rotation of the Diamond Houses and Wall Houses unfolding the flat panels out from the Mannerist 9-square grid exercises of Texas.[68]

After Texas, at Cooper and then Cornell, Rowe also began to open up his closed classical approach to different spatial fields, offering opportunities to reconsider the grid, the rotation of elements, and fragmentation in the city.[69] Boyarsky's Master's research amplified this intuition, returning to Sitte to show how urban designers could bury figural objects, even centrally planned buildings, in the fabric of the city adjacent to figural voids, regular and irregular. Sitte advocated 'turbine' piazzas for new developments with closed corners.[70] Sitte also showed how the wide-open Modern spaces of the Vienna Ringstrasse could be reinhabited by blocks of apartments, squares and new streets, switching code from Modernism. Sitte argued that the figural public voids were an expression of the life of the local community. In Sitte's micro-contextual analysis of Viennese medieval squares and church placements, the classical figure was warped and transformed by the

66 Online archives of the Fondation Le Corbusier, "Urbanisme, Saint-Dié, France, 1945", [https://www.fondationlecorbusier.fr/en/work-architecture/projects-urban-planning-saint-die-france-1945/].

67 Rowe, Colin; Hejduk, John, "Lockhart, Texas", *Architectural Record* 121 (3), Mar 1957: 201-06; now in Rowe (1996/1): 55-71.

68 Hejduk, John, *Masque of Medusa: Works 1947-1983*, Rizzoli, New York, 1985: 37-38, 283.

69 Schrijver, Lara, "Utopia And/Or Spectacle? Rethinking Urban Interventions Through the Legacy of Modernism and the Situationist City", *Architectural Theory Review* 16 (3), 2011: 245-58.

70 Boyarsky, Alvin, "Camillo Sitte: 'city builder'", thesis presented to the Faculty of the Graduate School of Cornell University for the Degree of Master of Regional Planning, (1959). Typescript copy in black folder: [AA SHELFMARK: 711.4:92SIT BOY (RARE-STORE)]. I am grateful to Nicholas Boyarsky sharing the copy in the Alvin Boyarsky library.

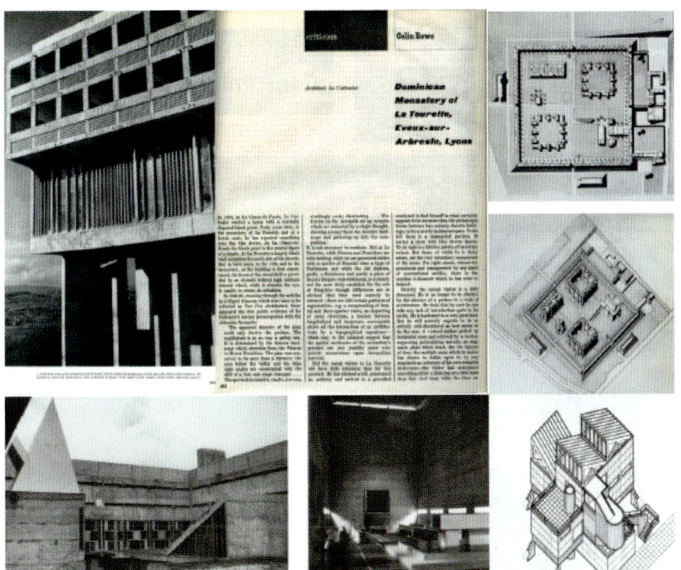

Collage 14 + 15: La Tourette, Scroop Terrace, Cambridge, Stirling and Gowan, Churchill College, Leicester Labs, Peter Cook, Plug In City.

local, much as Saxl and Wittkower traced the transformation of classical forms from Italy to England following Warburg.[71]

After Cornell, during his short Cambridge four-year stay,[72] Rowe struggled with the three-dimensional "masterpiece"[73] of Le Corbusier's La Tourette monastery with its figural void of a three-sided courtyard of monks' cells hovering on *pilotis* over a series of shared spaces, refectory, chapter room, etc. Then corridors descend on the sloping landscape below to the base of the church, a discrete object building that ambiguously forms the fourth side of the monastic figure.[74] He next wrote of Stirling and Gowan's monumental Churchill College proposal with its vast figural void of a courtyard containing five figural objects as "The Blenheim of the Welfare State".[75] Meanwhile, beginning in 1957, Stirling and Gowan collaged fragments from British industrial vernacular and Modernist architectural history in their Leicester Laboratory (completed 1963).[76] The Lab dominated a neighboring park landscape through its strong vertical axis, expressed through ramps and neatly tailored staircases and elevator shafts in the tower. The building presented different profiles from different perspectives, like Picasso's *L'Arlésienne,* combining literal and phenomenal transparency around a compressed, involuted circulation spine, ascending through the building's sectional space.

In Phase 2, Rowe, with Slutzky, Hoesli, and Hejduk in Texas, refined his analytical apparatus, further removing the binary block between classical and Modern architecture, allowing both the old city texture and landscape to play a role in the composition. The analysis of the League of Nations with Slutzky opened the Wittkovian diagram out into the landscape, while ignoring the parking undercroft, as pointed out by Marot. The analysis isolated the different urban elements. Mirrored and coordinated on the upper floor, a mega-structural geometry dissolved into a transparent system of *pilotis,* which in the undercroft faced the gardens. Rowe, in his contextualist Cornell Studio work, following the encounter with Boyarsky, attempted to break this binary code, relating the

71 Sitte, Camillo, *City Planning According to Artistic Principles* Collins, George; Collins, Mary Crasemann, trans., *Columbia University studies in art history and archaeology*, Wittkower, Rudolf, ed., Random House, New York, (1889) 1965. Also Wittkower (1947): 164-69.

72 Saint, Andrew, "A History of the Department", Cambridge School of Architecture website, 2006 [https://www.arct.cam.ac.uk/aboutthedepartment/aboutthedepthome] and Eisenman, Peter, "The Rowe Synthesis", in Marzo (2010): 48-57; Idem, "Bifurcating Rowe", in *Petit* (2015): 56-61. On Rowe's discomfort at Cambridge, where Prof. Lesley Martin did not appoint him to a college. I am indebted to Nicholas Bullock who was a Cambridge student in the period, personal communication 2015. Also Schrijver (2011). Rowe's "Utopia" article was originally published in the student magazine *Granta* 63, Jan 24, 1959: 20-26, 41, later in Rowe (1996/2): 134-42. Michael Spens, personal communication, 2007.

73 Rowe (1996/3): 3.

74 Rowe, Colin, "Dominican Monastery of La Tourette, Eveux-sur-Arbresle, Lyons", *The Architectural Review*, Jun 1961: 400-10. Also Rowe, (1976): 185-203.

75 Rowe, Colin, "The Blenheim of the Welfare State", *Cambridge Review*, Oct 1959; now in Rowe (1996/1): 143-51.

76 Boyarsky, Alvin, "Stirling 'Dimostrationi'", *Architectural Design* 38, Oct 1968: 454-58. Stirling also taught at Cambridge.

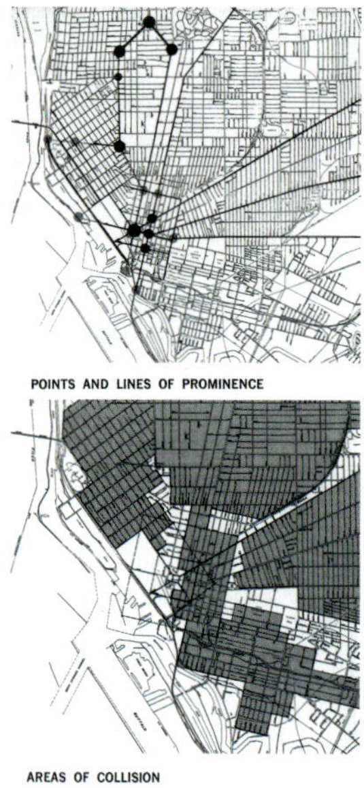

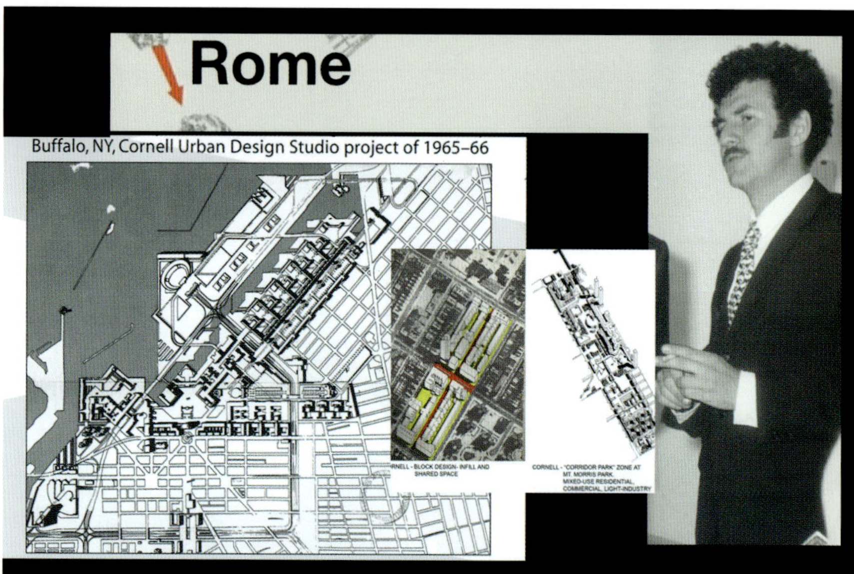

Fig. 5. Buffalo Waterfront, diagrams by Franz Oswald.

Wittkovian geometric diagrams to the old city geometry and lakeside landscape, as in the later fragmentary Buffalo diagrams. Schumacher's Contextualism article described exactly this confrontation between systems and feedback in terms of classical response and distortion often involving rotations and scale shifts. The later MoMA Harlem project provided an example of this system, inserting towers in the 200 x 600–800 ft standard Manhattan grid, while making parks and public buildings at grid collisions. The Buffalo Waterfront project looked back to the Corbusian mega-scale of Saint-Dié with a mile-long mega-building and 800 foot square blocks of housing lining the waterfront from the old CBD.

Phase 3. 1963–78: Cornell, Berlin, New York, London, and Rome

Returning to Rowe's paratrooper trajectory, again crossing the Atlantic offered a release from the constrictions and crisis of Cambridge academia, as Rowe went to teach at Cornell in 1962 and was later offered a tenured position there. Rowe taught two undergraduate history lecture courses, fall semester Renaissance, and spring semester Modern Architecture.[77] Professor John Reps, the author of *The Making of Urban America*,[78] suggested that Rowe teach a graduate urban design course since Sert had started a course at Harvard in 1960 (Kahn's Civic Design course at Penn was even earlier). Reps had studied planning at Liverpool and knew of that Civic Design course.[79] The Cornell program began with a few, mainly foreign students. Early Studios dealt with the suburban expansion of Ithaca towards its new airport.[80] But Rowe's extensive network of friends soon funneled students to the program. By 1966 Fred Koetter had come from the University of Oregon (via Hodgden and Boyarsky). Franz Oswald had come (via Hoesli) from the Eidgenössische Technische Hochschule, Zürich (ETH), and the office of O.M. Ungers. Tom Schumacher transitioned from the Cornell undergraduate to the graduate program. The following year, Schumacher's classmate, Wayne Copper, catalogued historic and Modern city plans as figure/grounds for his thesis.[81]

During this period Rowe's Cornell UD Studio worked on two commissioned, group projects: the first for Buffalo (1966 later exhibited in the Albright Knox

77 Rowe, Colin; Satkowski, Leon, *Italian Architecture of the 16th Century*, Princeton Architectural Press, New York, 2002; and Rowe, Colin, *The Architecture of Good Intentions: Towards a Possible Retrospect*, Academy Editions, Academy Group Ltd., London, 1994.

78 Reps, John William, *The Making of Urban America: A History of City Planning in the United States*, Princeton University Press, Princeton, 1965.

79 Mumford (2009): 104, 148.

80 Handler, Philip, (Rowe's first teaching assistant in the UD program) personal communication, 2013.

81 Copper, Wayne, "The Figure/Grounds", *The Cornell Journal of Architecture* 2, 1983: 42-53; and Schumacher, Thomas, "Contextualism: urban ideals and deformation", *Casabella* 359-360, 1971: 79-86.

Gallery in 1969); the second for Harlem in MoMA's first Urban Design Exhibition (1967). Meanwhile Rowe in 1968 founded the Institute for Architectural and Urban Studies (IAUS) in New York with Peter Eisenman, his former student at Cambridge. After this tumultuous start of the UD studio, Rowe took his first sabbatical in Rome in 1969, having been instrumental in inviting O. M. Ungers (Stirling's friend) to become the chairman of the department at Cornell. It seemed that he had made a good start at creating a new Modernity that combined with historical precedents and that he had found a new companion in Ungers. But Rowe still harbored growing doubts about the role of the utopian vision of Modernism, whereas Ungers in 1970–71 investigated American utopian settlements. Ungers also spent much of the school's budget inviting all the aging Team X members to come to teach in Ithaca throughout the year. As Rem Koolhaas[82] described, Ungers was in crisis after the student revolt at the Free University of Berlin in 1968, just as Rowe was in crisis about the role of Modernism in the midst of the Civil Rights and anti-Vietnam War demonstrations in Ithaca. It took Rowe three years to absorb the double impasse of Ungers's arrival and the loss of the IAUS in New York to Eisenman in 1969. In *As I Was Saying* this was his "dark period" at Cornell.

In this dark period, Rowe attended Boyarsky's first International Institute of Design (IID) Summer Session, with Stirling and Brian Richards as critics working on an alternative design for Covent Garden London, then threatened with demolition by the Greater London Council (GLC) masterplan. This proved a cathartic experience for Rowe, who, very early on, presented his ideas for *Collage City* there in 1970. After teaching the Urban Design Studios at Cornell for seven years, Rowe contrasted the American "Collision City" of grids to a "Collage City" of Cubist overlaps and interpenetrations using Oswald's diagrams of Buffalo.[83] Reyner Banham, in the same conference, spoke about Los Angeles, previewing a chapter from *Los Angeles: The Architecture of Four Ecologies* (1971),[84] anticipating Venturi, Scott Brown, and Izenour's *Learning from Las Vegas* (1972).[85] Boyarsky presented his "Chicago à la carte"[86] lecture using vintage postcards of Chicago to

opposite inset:
Collage 16: Colin, Cornell Urban Design, 1963–70, MoMA, Corb, Contextualism, Schumacher.

inset:
Collage 17: IAUS 1968–69, *Five Architects*, New York.

82 Koolhaas, Rem, "'But Most of All, Ungers': Berlin Stories", in Ungers, Oswald Mathias; Koolhaas, Rem, (with) Riemann, Peter; Kollhoff, Hans; Ovaska, Arthur, *The City in the City: Berlin; A Green Archipelago*, Hertweck, Florian and Marot, Sebastien, eds., Lars Müller Publishers, Zürich, (1977) 2012: 44-45; Idem (in conversation with Florian Hertweck and Sébastien Marot), "Ghostwriting", in Ungers et al. (2013): 131-43; Idem, "Being O.M.U.'s Ghost Writer", in *Petit* (2015): 87-97.

83 Rowe, Colin; Seligmann, Werner; Wells, Jerry, *Buffalo Waterfront project*, (exhibition catalogue), Albright-Knox Art Gallery, Buffalo, NY, 1969. Oswald confirmed that he drew the analytical drawings later for the exhibition: personal conversation, Bern, Switzerland. The Buffalo Waterfront studio project dated from 1966-67. Middleton, Blake, "Studio Projects", *The Cornell Journal of Architecture* 2, 1983: 88-91.

84 Banham, Reyner, *Los Angeles: The Architecture of Four Ecologies*, Pelican Books, Harmondsworth, 1971.

85 Venturi, Robert; Scott Brown, Denise; Izenour, Steven, *Learning from Las Vegas*, MIT Press, Cambridge, MA, 1972.

86 Boyarsky, Alvin, "Chicago à la carte", *Architectural Design* 40 (12), Dec 1970: 595-622.

Collage 18: IID London 1970, Collage City Lecture, Chicago, Boyarsky.

illustrate how the grid of the Modernist, layered city-machine exploited the agricultural territory of the Great Plains, reaching even into the Rocky Mountains. Other Liverpool graduates such as Robert Maxwell (praising the Picturesque landscape) and Sam Stevens also attended, as well as Archigram members, plus Cedric Price (an ex-Cambridge graduate), stimulating Rowe. Archigram also brought a younger international generation including Bernard Tschumi, Coop Himmelblau, and Superstudio.[87]

Rowe, without Koetter, after 1973, continued his Urban Design Studio and by 1976 had begun to develop a non-Corbusian, urban vocabulary, switching code to figural voids, as shown in the "Urban Precedents" research (1974) made up entirely of historic city centers by Klaus Herdeg and Michael Dennis. After Koetter left Cornell in 1973, Dennis often taught in the Studio. The Studio work was indebted to the contemporary Rationalist revival: to Aldo Rossi and his 'Analogous City' drawings.[88] Rowe wrote the introduction to Rob Krier's *Stadtraum* in *Theorie und Praxis* in 1978,[89] marking the return of the street and facade to urban design. Blake Middleton described how Rowe again attracted another cohort of students to rival those of the 1960s, who could work to combine high-rise and high-density perimeter blocks in schemes that built towards the return of the street, as in the Rowe team's "Roma interrotta".[90] The chronicle of this essay finishes in 1978. But, in 1978–90, many studio projects contained street and square, ideal fragments as described in *The Cornell Journal of Architecture,* 2, edited by Blake Middleton, and Rowe's "Urbanistics" in *As I Was Saying.*

Spatial Imaginary 3: Collage City and Roma interrotta

In *As I Was Saying,* Rowe wrote, "I returned [from Rome] in January 1970 to an entirely different body of students. A great cultural event had occurred. But the students were not at all hostile. Simply they had determined that the *Zeilenbauen* were not their *thing*; and, from then on, it was the trad city and trad city blocks". In the case of my own "Covent Garden Urban Patterns in London"[91] thesis, the "trad city" strategies included pedestrianization, as in Copenhagen (1963), micro-incisions, micro-insertions, new small squares (with underground parking) and creative (read Archigram) historic, mixed-use,

87 Sunwoo, Irene, ed., *In Progress: The IID Summer Sessions*, Architectural Association Press, London, 2016. Also Marjanovic, Igor, "Drawing Ambience", in Marjanovic, Igor; Howard, Jan, *Drawing Ambience: Alvin Boyarsky and the Architectural Association*, University of Chicago Press, Chicago, 2014.

88 Braghieri, Gianni, *Aldo Rossi: Works and Projects*, Gili, Barcelona, 1991: 50-57; and *The Analogous City Map*, 1976. [https://www.researchgate.net/publication/280530086_The_Analogous_City_The_Map].

89 Krier, Robert, *Stadtraum in theorie und praxis*, Kramer, Stüttgart, 1975; Shane, David Grahame, "Theory vs Practice", (review of Krier's book), *Architectural Design* 46 (11), 1976: 680-84.

90 Middleton, Blake, "Disseminating an Idea", in this volume.

91 Shane, David Grahame, "Urban Patterns in London", M. Arch. thesis, Cornell University, 1972.

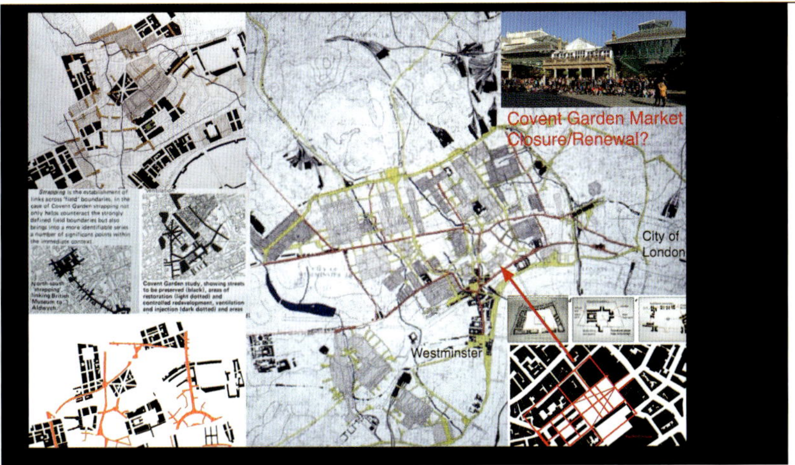

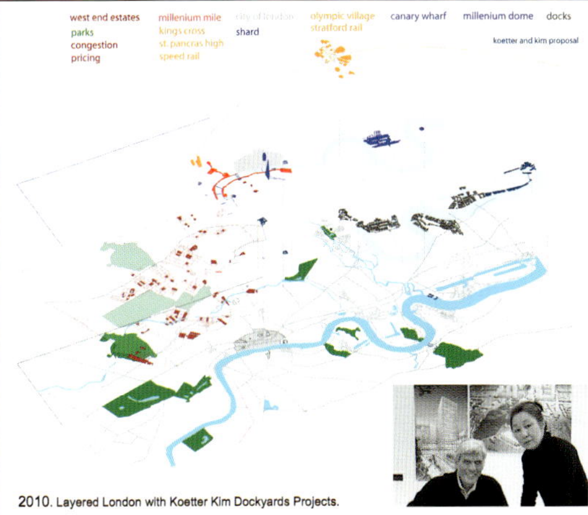

Collage 19: Shane Thesis, Covent Garden IID 1970.

Fig. 6. Shane analysis: Layered London Dockland Plans, Koetter/Kim; photo of Fred Koetter and Suzie Kim.

hippy-style preservation-renovations. The thesis developed at the IID 70 had worked with the Covent Garden Community against the GLC mega-structural masterplan.[92]

By 1975, when Rowe and Koetter had developed design strategies for *Collage City*, Rowe argued with Charles Jencks at Peter Cook's Artnet Conceptual Architecture Conference that, "if you don't have utopia then the city becomes a species of museum".[93] Rowe also spoke in very Warburgian terms of the necessity of collage, memory, and the renewal of tradition through its betrayal in code shifts for innovation. Rowe's Renaissance lecture series at Cornell in the early 1970s included ideal cities and the vast scale of Baroque garden layouts as precedents for later Beaux-Arts city planning. Rowe still emphasized the virtues of Le Corbusier's domestic architecture in his Modern Architecture lecture series, even his utopian urban ideals. Yet by 1970 these lectures had a highly developed contextual critique of Le Corbusier's dream, beginning to reintegrate a historical and symbolic dimension, loosely linked to Warburg and Wittkower. This contextual history included many of the later illustrations of *Collage City*, like the 1922 Asplund competition entry for the Stockholm Royal Chancellery, featured among Wayne Copper's 1967 thesis drawings.

The Urban Design Studio continued to produce Harlem and Buffalo-like large scale masterplans, while Rowe and Koetter puzzled about how to create a new hybrid design construct. Tom Schumacher's "Contextualism: Urban Ideals and Deformations" in *Casabella* in 1971 had raised the studio profile and provided a clear explanation of Rowe's 1960s urban design strategy.[94] Previous urban elements remained as traces of past life-forms, each with their symbolic core. In this fluid, multi-scalar, multi-functional, multi-centered, symbolic construct, urban designers could operate without a masterplan, mixing and matching narratives and urban fragments.

Urban design now occupied an ambiguous and precarious position in the process of facing the complexity of the city without a master plan, with a collage of multiple centers and many, fragmented actors with different spatial imaginaries and symbolic priorities. These ranged from garden cities to hyperdensity.

92 Shane, David Grahame, "Contextualism 1; Covent Garden", *Architectural Design* 42 (4), 1972: 229.

93 Rowe, Colin, "In Conversation with Charles Jencks", 1975, at Artnet video, [https://www.youtube.com/watch?v=Ln_8ymrqgdE]. Lecture text in Rowe (1996/2): 65-73.

94 Schumacher, Thomas L. "Contextualism: Urban Ideals and Deformations", *Casabella* 359-360, 1971: 79-86.

Arlesienne 1912

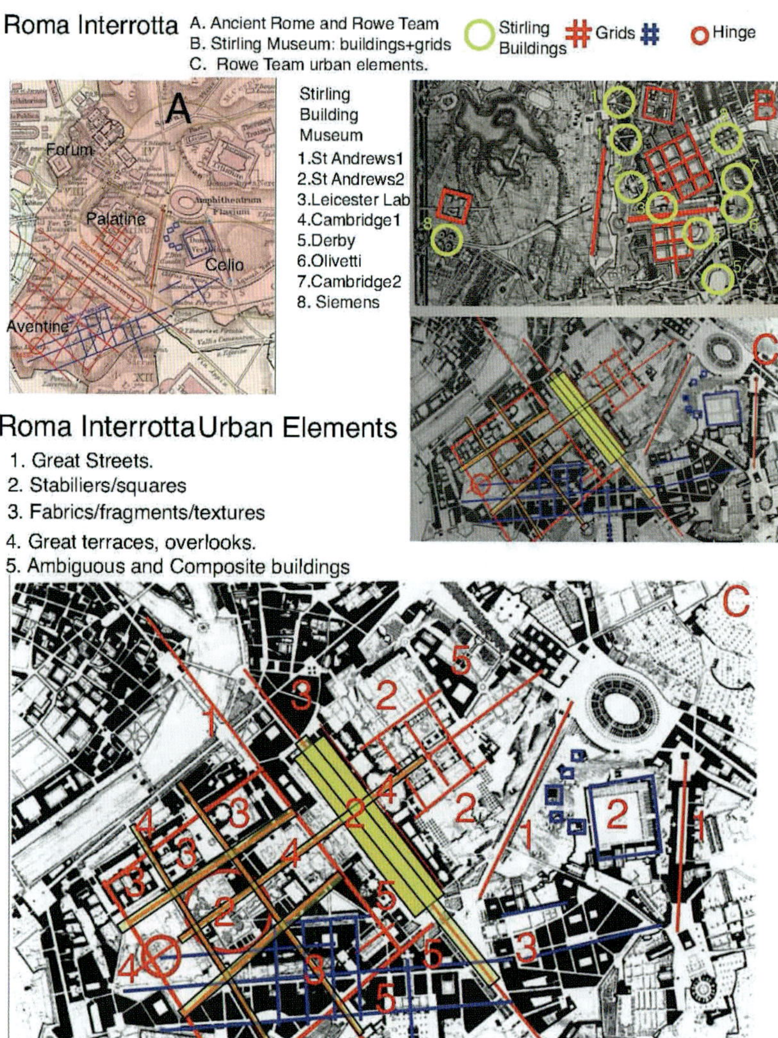

above left:
Collage 20: Picasso's *L'Arlesienne, Roma interrotta.*

inset:
Collage 21: *Roma interrotta:* Urban Elements, Rowe, Stirling.

From his classical base in Ithaca, Rowe sought to create a new synthesis of Modernism and Contextualism, ideal and deformation, in a meta-city of geometry and memory.

In the "Roma interrotta" panel, the Rowe team of Peter Carl, Judith DiMaio, and Steven Peterson explored this new meta-city dimension at a vast scale. Using many of the elements appearing in *Collage City*, they created a hypothetical city-museum. Rowe's meta-history included an enormous palace by Valadier for Napoleon's son, the King of Rome, who in reality died in infancy. The palace had extensive Baroque gardens covering most of the Palatine Hill and a splendid terrace looking south across the 2000 ft/600 m long axis of the Circus Maximus in the valley below to the Aventine Hill. There, extensive gardens climbed up the central axis to a circular terminus in a botanical garden. Rowe also created another terrace on the Aventine for a series of smaller, pre-existing palaces and churches overlooking the Tiber. On the third hill to the east, the Celio, the team placed small object buildings on the slopes looking down on the Via Sacra. This

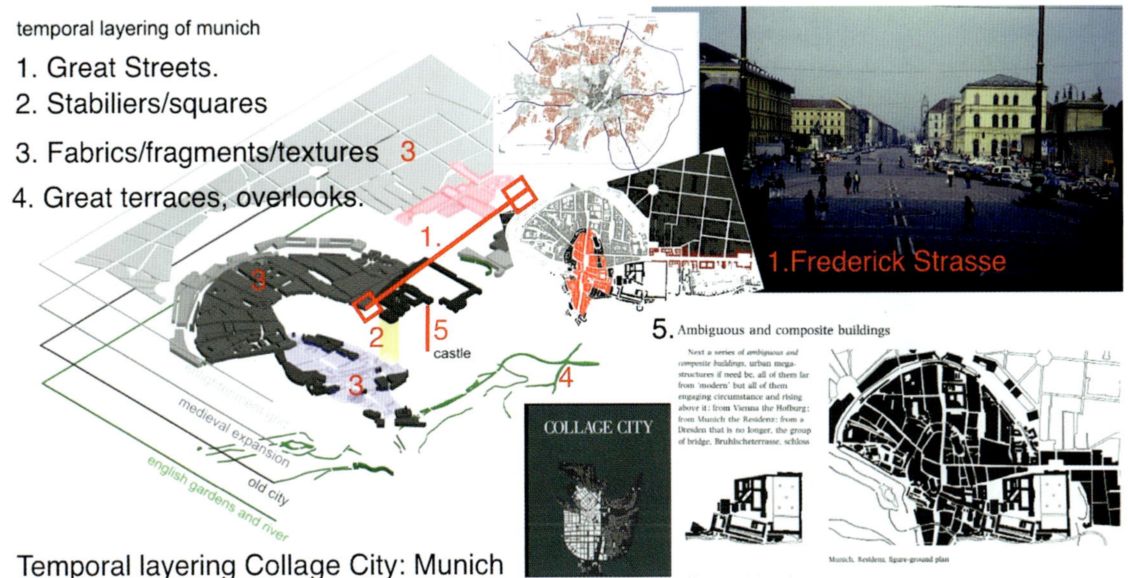

Collage 22: Shane analysis, Rowe and Koetter, *Collage City*, layers/elements, Munich.

"memorable street" became an *allée* of trees overlooked by the huge, hilltop memorial hall based on Terragni's unbuilt Fascist *Danteum* (1938). The Danteum backed onto another 'memorable street' from the Colosseum to Santo Stefano. Various triangular parks and wedge-shaped interstitial void spaces handled the awkward junctions between fragments. The Danteum was the only reference to Modernity, since Rowe's meta-historical commentator decried Modern urbanism in all its aspects.[95]

Marco Biraghi argued that Stirling and Wilford's "Roma interrotta" panel was truer to *Collage City*, since each fragment of their city represented a Stirling project, built or unbuilt, and together they formed an ironic collage city museum of Stirling buildings.[96] Each fragment was distinct and clearly articulated three dimensionally in the landscape, while some iconic buildings formed hinges between elements. In addition, each fragment had an interior, gridded geometry, the largest being a 9-square grid based on Runcorn New Town Housing (1967–76).[97] The Stirling-Wilford panel also included a series of competition entries for Düsseldorf and Cologne (1975) playing with the circular voids inside the solid rectangular box of Karl Friedrich Schinkel's Altes Museum in Berlin.[98] The partners threaded pedestrian paths from the city fabric into the closed center, making it porous, the void becoming a cylinder inside the 9-square box as in the 1977 Stuttgart Neue Staatsgalerie (completed in 1984). Rowe considered this Stirling's 'masterwork' and proposed that his friend's ashes should be placed in a niche in the cylindrical courtyard there.[99]

In contrast the Rowe team used five urban elements listed by Rowe and Koetter in *Collage City* including: "Memorable streets", "Stabilizers" (idealized, regular spaces or solids), "Potentially interminable set pieces" (repetitive morphologies creating fragments with a recognizable pattern), and "Splendid public terraces" (magnificent overlooks from which all the fragments could be seen from above and integrated into a conceptual map). There is no mention by Rowe's fictive narrator of Wittkovian geometrics as the elements are distributed at various

95 Stirling team: 68-75; Rowe team: 42-49; Peterson, Steven, "Urban Design Tactics": 76-81, all in Graves, Michael, ed., "Roma Interrotta", *Architectural Design* 49 (3/4), 1979 Academy Editions, London, republished as Graves, Michael, ed., "Roma Interrotta", *AD Profile 20*, 1979. Rowe considered the smaller scaled, more diverse Celio Hill the best "where I began celebrating the lines of the old garden of the Villa Mattei ... we were elegantly lucid". Rowe (1996/3): 153.

96 Biraghi, Marco, "Colin Rowe and James Stirling: from Collage City to Roma interrotta", in Marzo, 2010: 136-145.

97 Pearman, Hugh, "The naked and the demolished: the scandalous tale of James Stirling's lost Utopia", *Flashbak*, Dec 1, 2010. [http://hughpearman.com/the-naked-and-the-demolished-the-scandalous-tale-of-james-stirlings-lost-utopia/]; and Chatel, Guy, "Facts and Figures", *Oase* 79, "The Architecture of James Stirling, 1964 – 1992", 2009: 52-61.

98 Shane, David Grahame, "Cologne in Context", *Architectural Design* 46 (12), Dec 1976: 685-87; Scalbert, Irénée, "James Stirling", *Oase* 79, "The Architecture of James Stirling, 1964–1992", Nov 2009: 34-42.

99 Rowe (1996/3): 358.

Collage 23 + 24: Ungers, Cornell Exhibition UD X 2, 1970–78.

scales across the landscape. The scheme operated chiefly as a polycentric system in plan powered by the meta-historical narrative. It seemed almost as if Rowe had returned to his origins in Yorkshire, with fantasy classical palaces and gardens replacing the now shuttered coal mines in an elaborate, agri-urban, botanical landscape. The team appeared to abandon the intellectual rigor of the "Mathematics of the Ideal Villa" and to continue the opening up of the Rowe-Slutzky layered spatial apparatus of the League of Nations toward the landscape.

In *Collage City* the authors reserved a special place for a fifth urban element: "Ambiguous and composite buildings" that operated at multiple historical levels and architectural scales. One such example was the Munich Royal Residenz that linked to the medieval fabric, the new state street grid, and English Garden. The Rowe and Slutzky reading of the Le Corbusier League of Nations analysis also tried to tie contradictory fields together. The co-authors of *Collage City* cited 1830s Munich as their ideal urban model. Here each phase of development could be read as an ideal fragment, from medieval core with castle and cathedral to later medieval rings and a new street of state offices. Later, a Greek Revival grid for the bourgeoisie extended the city beside the English Gardens, as the Residenz added long arms embracing the river valley. State museums and a miniature Crystal Palace represented culture and industry.

The multi-scalar layering of the "Ambiguous and composite buildings" infects all the elements distributed across the "Roma interrotta" landscape in the museum city construct. As in the analysis of Le Corbusier's Saint-Dié and League of Nations, even of Palladio's and Corbusian villas, there is here a rigorous geometric substructure layered beneath the rhetorical urban actors populating Rowe's complex meta-history. Rowe's team operated at three scales. They created a huge 9-square grid on the Aventine Hill. They shuffled the front, middle, and back layers of the Corbusian Saint-Dié schema to suit the site. The three western squares of the 800 ft/240 m mega-block system bracketed pre-existing palaces and churches on cliffs facing the Tiber. The central 2400 ft/730 m long axis of the 9-square grid extended the central axis of Giuseppe Valadier's palace from the Palatine Hill. This axis rotated the huge 2000 ft/600 m dimensions of the Circus Maximus up the Aventine Hill to form one gigantic geometric figure terminating in the circular botanical garden. It marked the hinge point with a subsidiary, rotated Manhattan street grid (800 ft/240 m x 200 ft/60 m). This slid, as an underlay, beneath the three eastern squares of the Aventine 9-square mega-figure. The subsidiary Manhattan-style grid linked diagonally to the main axis of the Celio, where a micro-scaled, Sitte-esque village fan layout broke the axial drive on the difficult sloped terrain.

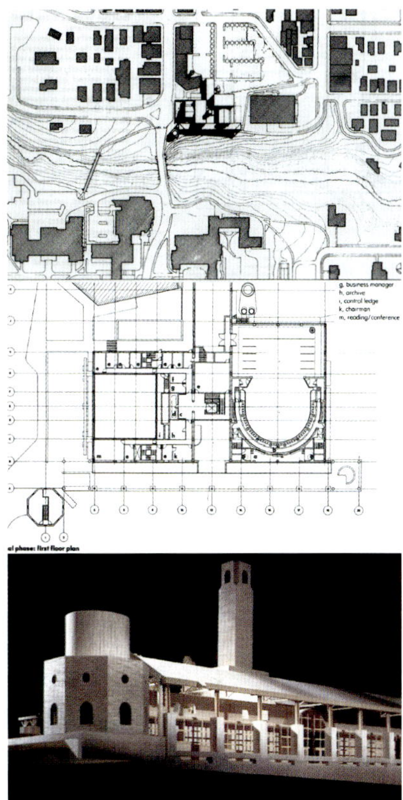

Fig. 7. Cornell Performing Arts Center, Stirling Wilford, 1981-89.

The basic geometrical diagram remained very simple, involving the integration of only three interpenetrating grid fields. There was the enormous 9-square mega-grid atop the Aventine Hill four times the size of the Stirling and Wilford figure. But unlike an axial, frontal, Corbusian 9-square, this grid was ambiguous. One reading of the 9-square layered in from the Tiber. Another reading layered in from the Palatine Hill with a largely landscape, central axis. A third reading drew on the rotated Manhattan scale grid that leaked out of the mega-figure to populate the Celio. The center of the 9-square mega-grid was void and in a classical Beaux-Arts scheme would have held the circular (domed?) coordinating figure. But the circular botanical garden shifted up the Aventine Hill to become the Manhattan hinge. In place of the central point Rowe's meta-historical, omniscient voice of the Warburgian memory theater narrator moved in to play the integrative role.

Rowe and Slutzky in their "Transparency" article used Picasso's *L'Arlésienne* portrait with its vertical integrating axis as their Cubist reference, following Giedion. It is instructive to substitute Picasso's *Guitar* (1912) for *L'Arlésienne*. This cardboard sculpture was so important to him that he carried it from studio to studio, eventually bequeathing it to the MoMA at his death in 1973. There it remained in pieces in an envelope for thirty years until its rediscovery by Professor Christine Poggi in 2003 and subsequent exhibition.[100] One sheet at the front tilted forward to make the tabletop. Another back layer showed the silhouette of the right-hand-side back of the guitar. A folded, intermediate layer created a box-like rectangular volume with an open front, its edge folded out to make the front silhouette of the guitar body. A long, thin, folded piece of cardboard shot down into this box representing the guitar neck and tuning pegs (a deep space slot?). At the center of the void of the box, a cylinder rose to the level of the front of the guitar representing the circular hole in the front of the guitar body. Here, literal and phenomenal transparency came together as the space of the opening in the non-existent guitar front plane pierced back into the box forming the cylinder. Le Corbusier, in his Purist phase, drew and copied this mysterious transparency and guitar cylinder constantly, but was never able to achieve the same clarity and impact. Hoesli's layered, hyper-rational exercises in Austin also missed this essential, three-dimensional ambiguity of the circular figure.

100 Umland, Anne, (curator), "Picasso's Guitars 1912-1914", Museum of Modern Art, New York (Feb 13 – Jun 6), 2011.

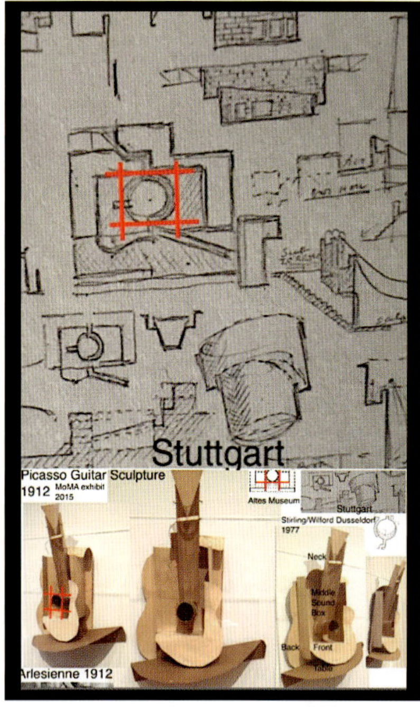

Collage 25: Picasso's *Guitar*, Neue Staatsgalerie, Stuttgart.

The cylinder in the guitar layers represented an absent, but still desired, center, a ghostly, ambiguous, phenomenal presence. The Rowe team's return to the system of classical fragments and layered, incremental growth, like Stirling and Wilford's memory of the circle in the square from the Neoclassical Altes Museum, at first glance seems to reject the Modern ideal of literal and phenomenal transparency. But like Picasso's *Guitar*, while these were recognizable as classical figures, the hope was that they might also be the team's way to make a new, more porous city space that still retained memory traces of the old city. This hope is clearest in the Rowe team's retention of the 9-square grid and multiple landscapes running as threads through the topography of their site, connecting palaces and squares, culminating in the displaced circular botanical garden as a hinge.

It is easy to contrast the two Cornell Urban Design Studios of the 1970s after Ungers set up a rival program in 1969.[101] But with hindsight, both studios engaged in a vision of the fragmentary historic city including ruins, Rome for Rowe, Berlin for Ungers (and New York for Koolhaas). Both Cornell professors sought a combinatory system between old and new fragments that formed around ideal typologies and morphologies, with chaotic interstices. Both studios sought new forms of public space for the public nodes in their systems. Rowe called this "collage or collision city" in his first public lecture at the IID in 1970. Oswald Mathias Ungers and Rem Koolhaas would call their fragmentary recombinant system the "city in the city" in their publication of the Cornell 1976–77 Berlin Summer School and later in their book, *The City in the City, Berlin: A Green Archipelago*.[102] Both systems relied enormously on the landscape to absorb their Rationalist fragments. A collagist monument to both programs exists at Cornell in Stirling and Wilford's Performing Arts Center (1981–89)[103] built at the College Town entry to the campus, beside one of Ithaca's gorges. Here the building's blank street facade directed visitors to an arcade overlooking the gorge leading to side entries to an enclosed, square courtyard, a miniature opera house auditorium, and a clock tower.

In Phase 3, Rowe, at Boyarsky's IID Summer Session 70, and Koetter, in 71, confronted a mega-structural proposal involving the demolition of Inigo Jones's Neo-Palladian Covent Garden for a buried highway in Central London. The Covent Garden project involved the reintroduction of the Georgian scaled street and square system, as well as the surrounding boulevards descended from Haussmann's Paris. In the subsequent years, they tried to move beyond the binary. They created a new Modern city-museum: a multi-scalar, multi-nodal, multi-geometric system of urban fragments, both ancient and Modern that still cohered as a humanistic environment through conceptual cues to a collective memory, like Picasso's *Guitar*. As in the MoMA Harlem project, or in Battery Park City, this new apparatus could accommodate towers, or new public buildings and squares, at difficult interstitial junctions often related to topography or landscape. As Rowe described the meta-history of the team's imaginary historic fragments, elements from urban history recurred at multiple scales as a system of fragments across the landscape, coordinated by a hidden mega-scale geometry relating back to a Wittkovian diagram cued to a Warburgian memory theater.

101 Shane, David Grahame, *Recombinant Urbanism: Conceptual Modeling in Architecture, Urban Design and City Theory*, Wiley, Chichester, 2005; Suh, Yehre, "Rowe x Ungers: Untold Collaborations on the City", Thomas Memorial Exhibition, Cornell, 2010, [http://urbanterrains.com/project/rowe-x-ungers-exhibition/].

102 Ungers et al., *The City in the City, Berlin: A Green Archipelago*, Lars Müller, Berlin (2012) 1977.

103 Warke, Val K., "Stirling: Cornell", *The Architectural Review* CLXXV (1046), Apr 1984: 28-34, republished online as "Ithaca's campus infrastructure by James Stirling", [https://www.architectural-review.com/archive/ithacas-campus-infrastructure-by-james-stirling].

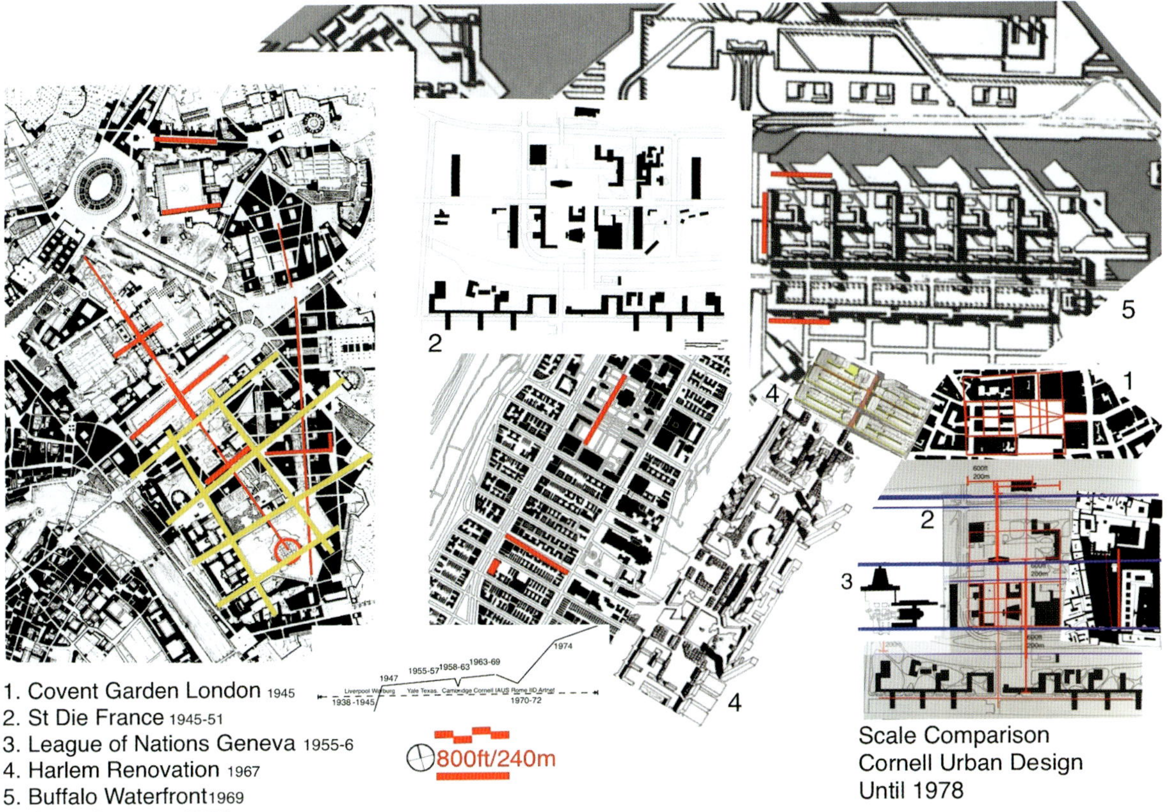

Collage 26: Cornell Urban Design, Scale Comparisons until 1978.

Conclusion: Surveying Rowe's 40-year Trajectory.

The initial question asked was how could Rowe survive the many migrations and shifting worlds of his first 40 professional years? It would seem that Rowe operated on three basic codes that gave him stability. One was a strand of classicism and the Neoclassical tradition that initially attracted him to Wittkower and the Warburg, representing a long strand in European culture. This strand found many representations in multiple morphologies, but was always controlled by a geometric sense of proportion in plan and perspective. In urban terms, this strand descended from the Renaissance, Palladio, Inigo Jones, etc. to American small towns planned around a figural void with symbolic buildings.

Modernism and its various utopian ideals formed the second strand in Rowe's stabilizing triad. This Modernism could also take many forms, but in urban terms it meant a concentration on Le Corbusier's projects, from The City of 3 Million to the League of Nations and on to Saint-Dié. Rowe carried over Wittkower's emphasis on the geometric plan diagram, even as he attempted with Slutzky, to accommodate the layering and fragmentation of Cubism. This breaking apart of the Modernist figural object into a field of idealized plan figures produced patches that the authors still hoped could be integrated around a virtual, absent center, by an informed sympathetic observer. Versions of Contextualism, as in Oswald's geometric plan diagrams for the Buffalo group project, still maintained the fiction of potential, conceptual integration, descended from Wittkower.

The third feature of Rowe's stabilizing triad was an imaginary third space for new hybrid spatial ordering systems. This imaginative space embraced continuity and change, it enabled Rowe as a paratrooper to see various cultural productions as recombinant symbolic systems that could take on new meanings, forming meta-histories rich in potential, new symbolic intermediaries following Warburg. In urban terms, this space could encompass the Modernist layering of Le Corbusier's League of Nations or the Neoclassical restructuring of Munich. But most importantly this space allowed complex, open, hybrid systems that embraced both earlier systems and the landscape, as in "Roma interrotta".

Here Rowe articulated his meta-historical project based on a copious flow of information, true and false, creating his version of the meta-city of information based on *Collage City*. All the "Roma interrotta" designers operated in this imaginary, informational space with their own narratives, as demonstrated by Stirling's rival version of his personal museum city. In both examples, picturesque landscape and topography gave an extended space and freedom for formal juxtapositions and quantum leaps of imagination.

Between 1938 and 1978, Rowe switched his urban spatial apparatus or code at least three times. Different codes dominated in different periods as Rowe adapted his trajectory. Initially an unstated presupposition involved a rejection of the Georgian city he inhabited every day in Liverpool or London, epitomized here by Covent Garden with its (300 x 450 ft/90 x 140 m) main square and mirrored grid. Rowe's *Phase 1* Apparatus involved a commitment to the Modern utopia, in the form of Saint-Dié with its mega scales, that continued into the 'contextual' Buffalo mile-long mega-building and (800 x 800 ft/210 x 210 m) public squares. The following *Phase 2* Apparatus involved questioning the Modern with Slutzky in Texas, searching for reflexive Modernism in Cubism that could open up the closed formula of Wittkower's Palladian 9-square in Le Corbusier's League of Nations. This led to early 'contextualism' at Cornell with Boyarsky and Sitte. The third *Phase 3* Apparatus, with Koetter, involved the rediscovery of the Neoclassical city that had been hiding in plain sight. Like the Picasso *Guitar*, it allowed for the hybridization of Apparatus 1 and 2 in a new meta-city formulation including landscape. Rejecting utopia for a time and returning to the classical allowed Rowe to articulate the city as a museum, leading to the multi-centered, meta-historical Apparatus 3 of "Roma interrotta" with its multiple scales: Sitte-esque village, Manhattan grid, and 1-mile-by-1-mile mega-block.[104]

In the new collage, ideas about landscape, classical memory, comparisons and contrasts played additional roles derived from Warburg, Wittkower, and later from Stirling, Slutzky, Schumacher, and Koetter. The new norm of street and square, with the insertion of commercial towers, was to prove enormously successful as a new global morphology. Cooper and Eckstut's 1979 plan for Battery Park City showed the commercial potential of these ideas in New York City, creating a new town in town, an idealized fragment, complete with Rector Place.[105] With the same developer, Koetter and Kim, in association with SOM, would show the power of these ideas as a regenerative source in the project for Canary Wharf in East London's abandoned docklands.[106] This set a global trend for large scale capitalist developments. In the last 40 years, such form-based urban design codes and ideas have become the staple of large corporate offices such as SOM,

104 Sitte-esque style village (300 x 450 ft/100 x 150 m); the Manhattan grid (600-800 ft/260 m x 200 ft/70 m); mega-block scale (1 mile x 1 mile/1.6 km x 1.6 km).

105 Gordon, David L. A., *Battery Park City: Politics and Planning on the New York Waterfront*, Gordon and Breach, Amsterdam, 1997: 65-77.

106 *Koetter Kim & Associates: Place/Time* (Koetter, Fred; Plattus, Alan; Rowe, Colin) Rizzoli, New York, 1997.

Collage 27: "Roma interrotta" at Trajan's Market 1978, and MAXXI 2014.

KPF, NBBJ, and AECOM. This is especially evident in rapid growth areas like Asia, associated with the neo-liberal spatial turn for wealth investment in cities.[107] While the revitalization of the city centers was to be welcomed, the problem of agency, who controlled the city growth, still dogged the *Collage City* ideal, as few enlightened urban princes remained in the landscape of Modern capitalism.[108]

It is not so surprising that Rowe identified with Rome as a site that had also endured many traumas with multiple codes. Rome had emerged from many triumphs and failures, growth spurts and shrinkages, with ruins from every age, ranging from the tribal to Imperial, from the medieval to the Renaissance papacy, from the creation of the Italian nation state to the EU and UN. The chaotic and fragmented nature of the city's government, dominated by privately elected popes for centuries, demonstrated one of the difficulties of the *Collage City* model. Also its relationship to the automobile displayed the old city center's charms and problems. Similarly the city as a museum could easily become a tourist trap, especially as the meta-historical narrative, the theater of memory loved by Rowe, became amplified in the meta-city of new media, the internet, and handheld devices. All were symptoms of the shift of the city towards information, image, and vast, recombinant, memory structures and systems imagined by Warburg.

It was entirely appropriate following Rowe's meta-historical theme of constant renovation and continuity that the "Roma interrotta" was displayed in Trajan's Market in 1978. Located beside the Forum, the market, as a multi-level interior street, a Roman mall connecting to the Campus Martius, had been converted into a museum. Archaeologists had found that later inhabitants rolled the head of the emperor's enormous statue through the underground sewers of the market to clean out the detritus. It was also appropriate that the 2014 recreation of "Roma interrotta" was housed in Zaha Hadid's new, futuristic MAXXI Museum, a part of Rome's 21st century meta-city renovations. Rowe, as he wrote his reflexive comments in retirement for *As I Was Saying,* anticipated this contemporary meta-historical universe. Like Hadrian in his Villa, Colin Rowe displayed for our pleasure his own virtual memory palace, a Rowe-Rome hybrid, an associative place of collective and personal treasures both inside and outside of time.

107 Harvey, David, *A Brief History of Neoliberalism*, Oxford University Press, Oxford and New York, 2005; Soja, Edward W., *Postmodern Geographies: The Reassertion of Space in Critical Studies of Cities and Regions*, Verso, London, 1989.

108 Oechslin, Werner, "Working with Fragments: The Limitations of Collage", *DAIDALOS* 16, 1985: 16-30; Bunschoten, Raoul, "Collage City: A Masquerade of Fragment Utopias", *DAIDALOS* 16, 1985: 31-42; Secchi, Bernardo, "Collage City", in Marzo (2010): 146-53.

The Best of Both Worlds: Rowe's "Dialectic Liberalism"

Antonio Pietro Latini

The disposition of mankind, whether as rulers or as fellow-citizens, to impose their own opinions and inclinations as a rule of conduct on others, is so energetically supported by some of the best and by some of the worst feelings incident to human nature, that it is hardly ever kept under restraint by anything but want of power; and as the power is not declining, but growing, unless a strong barrier of moral conviction can be raised against the mischief, we must expect, in the present circumstances of the world, to see it increase.[1]

JOHN STUART MILL

The ideal thing would be to have a good American suburb adjacent to a very concentrated Italian town, then you'd have the best of both worlds.[2]

COLIN ROWE

frontispiece:
Figure/ground of the center of Rome (lower left) and its South-East hinterland. North is left (courtesy of Rachele Passerini).

What is Colin Rowe's most important legacy in urbanistics?[3] As is evident after reading the essays that precede this text, the wide range of his work allows for multiple legitimate opinions. Many authors have discussed Rowe's inclusive reasoning based on dialectic pairs. In what follows, I argue that Rowe's most important urbanistic legacy is his synergic combination of dialectical reasoning and his uncommon inclination towards liberalism.

Neither dialectic comparisons in the visual arts nor liberal thinking are new in Rowe's conceptual context, of course, but his specific position is not a simple matter of echoing the current debate. Liberalism has had a long history of supporting architecture and urbanistics up to the present and, considering its inclusive nature, it is therefore not surprising that attitudes are multiple and sometimes contradictory. Examining the relevant character of Rowe's stance in comparison to his close and distant cultural surroundings may contribute to a better understanding of both. Documents, either unpublished or not yet well known, shed light on both Rowe's dialectic attitude and his liberal frame of mind. Moreover, deriving conclusions that are implicit in these sources could benefit the predicament of present-day urbanistics.

1 Mill, John Stuart, *On Liberty*, Batoche Books, Kitchener, (1859) 2001: 17.

2 [Ingersoll, Richard], "Dialogue: Colin Rowe", *Design Book Review* 17, Win 1989: 12; also in Rowe, Colin, *As I Was Saying: Recollections and Miscellaneous Essays* 3, "Urbanistics", (Caragonne, Alexander, ed.), MIT Press, Cambridge, MA, and London, 1996: 325.

3 The term 'urbanistics' is drawn from the title of the third tome of Rowe's *As I Was Saying*. I use it here as a rough equivalent of the Italian *urbanistica* in its traditional sense. It is meant to include urban design as well as urban planning, studies and related theories. 'Urbanistics' does not imply a selection or an ideological preference for the traditional, compact city as the term 'urbanism' seems to do. I believe that the legacy of Colin Rowe, certainly for the aspects that will be considered in this text, is of special relevance not only for design in a strict sense but for planning as well as for policy issues. Rather than trying to be an essay in urban design historiography, this text is a biased attempt of *critica operativa* in the sense that, it seems to me, emerges in Berdini, Paolo, "Confronti inaspettati: osservazioni sulla retorica comparata di Colin Rowe", in Monica, Luca, *La critica operativa e l'architettura*, Edizioni Unicopli, Milano, 2002. On this basis, however, my argument proposes here an opinion rather dissimilar to Berdini's.

Dialectics

In the appendix is a transcription of the reading list of the Cornell Urban Design Studio of Spring 1969, likely based on references mostly provided by Rowe and compiled by Fred Koetter.[4] Two aspects seem particularly relevant: the comparison with the list of books recommended by Rowe and Bernhard Hoesli to the students of the academic year 1954–55, in Austin,[5] and the rich set of references included in the 1969 list.

Comparing the two bibliographies despite the differences in time and educational levels, while not a minor circumstance, is meaningful nevertheless. Only a few texts appear in both reading lists: *Art and Visual Perception* by Rudolf Arnheim, *Towards a New Architecture* by Le Corbusier, and *Principles of Art History* by Heinrich Wölfflin.[6] And in his volume dedicated to the Texas Rangers, Alexander Caragonne indicates that only one of these books was selected by Rowe and not by Hoesli: Wölfflin's book on the dialectical categories. Regardless of any uncertainty, this is a significant fact.

Rudolf Wittkower, Rowe's advisor at the Warburg Institute, had had Wölfflin as his professor in Munich for one year before moving back to Berlin to study with Adolph Goldschmidt. Despite the relatively short period of direct contact, Wölfflin must have affected Wittkower and not in a minor way, as the adoption of the comparative method is one of the major aspects of both Wölfflin's and Wittkower's legacy.[7]

Although Wölfflin was not the only one to use the comparisons and dialectic method in art history research and teaching,[8] he was the one who fostered a widely shared adoption of this comparative binary system. He adopted the comparative dialogue method in his teaching, in *Renaissance und Barock* (1888) and, in an extensive form, in *Kunstgeschichtliche Grundbegriffe* (1915), published in English as *Principles of Art History* (1932). This lineage would reach Rowe as confirmed by a number of in-depth studies and by Rowe himself.[9]

The interpretative system of dialectical conceptual pairings radically affected Rowe. As is well known, Rowe's scientific itinerary is rich with dialectical pairs. Christopher Wren provides the first couple—natural and customary beauty—for the epigraph of Rowe's first published essay, "The Mathematics of the Ideal Villa",[10] and from the date of that publication forward, dialectical pairings are plentiful in Rowe's texts. "A reintroduction of Wölfflinian strategies", comparing diachronic pairs of eminent architectures, is among the purposes of Rowe's last projected book, *Bramante to Scamozzi and Beyond*, as we infer from his letter of September 1995 to Ernst Gombrich.[11]

Rowe's reasoning develops around pairs, and temporary sympathies for one of the two elements of the pair are often evident, but he never seems to fully adopt the one over the other. In fact, Rowe's positions are ambiguous and contradictory: endorsements and condemnations are rarely absolute. Commonly, dialectic poles are introduced to articulate an argument, and various reciprocities as antitheses, as analogies, as derivations, or as complements are presented: ideal type and context, figure and ground, space and object, acropolis and forum,

4 I owe this document, which deserves a much more accurate analysis than the one possible here, to Prof. James Tice, who was a student of Rowe in that year. During this period, the Urban Design Graduate Studio was co-taught by Rowe and Koetter. While the substantial paternity of this document must be ascribed to Rowe, Koetter and the whole group of faculty and students might have contributed. As described by Jim Tice in a private exchange of messages on this subject, "some faculty contributed to our class conversations and likely their references are included in the list (Hodgden, Herdeg, Sherwood, Seligmann). In other words, there was a culture of readings to which the entire Cornell program was attuned and at least some of this made its way onto the 'reading list'. In hindsight, it may be why Colin did not sign the reading list as being issued by 'him' alone. So, if anything, the list was a 'joint project' but it was unquestionably driven primarily by Colin ...". While supporting my thesis, this is a further confirmation that, as I conjectured in my other essay in this volume, faculty and students gathered around Rowe would work as a "creative group".

5 Caragonne, Alexander, *The Texas Rangers: Notes from an Architectural Underground*, MIT Press, Cambridge, MA, and London, 1995: Appendix 7.

6 If the texts added in pen by Jim Tice, contributed by faculty and classmates, are considered, *The Modulor* by Le Corbusier and *Geometry of Art and Life* by Matila Ghyka are in both lists, too.

7 Benelli, Francesco, "Seeing and Reading: Metodi analitici di Rudolph Wittkower per l'articolo su Leon Battista Alberti del 1940", in Bulgarelli, Massimo, ed., *Leon Battista Alberti e l'architettura*, Silvana Editore, Cinisello Balsamo, 2006: 556-67; Idem, "Rudolph Wittkower e Colin Rowe. Continuità e frattura", in Marzo, Mauro, ed., *L'architettura come testo e la figura di Colin Rowe*, Marsilio, Venezia, 2010.

8 Benelli (2010) and Benelli, Francesco, "Rudolf Wittkower versus Le Corbusier: A Matter of Proportion", *Architectural Histories* 3 (1), 2015: 8, 1-11. I would consider Worringer's dual perspective of abstraction and empathy as a further example of this epistemological approach, possibly deriving from Alois Riegl, from the Nietzschean interpretation of Greek tragedy and from Hegel. Gombrich, Ernst, "Hegel and Art History", *Architectural Design* 51 (6/7), 1981: 3-9. Worringer, Wilhelm, *Abstraction and Empathy: A Contribution to the Psychology of Style*, International Universities Press, New York, (1908) 1953.

9 Rowe, Colin, *The Mathematics of the Ideal Villa and Other Essays*, MIT Press, Cambridge, MA, and London, 1976: 16. Also, Berdini, Paolo, "Introduzione", in Rowe, Colin, *La matematica della villa ideale e altri scritti*, Zanichelli Editore, Bologna, 1990; Berdini (2002); Vidler, Anthony, "Mannerist Modernism: Colin Rowe", in *Histories of the Immediate Present: Inventing Architectural Modernism*, MIT Press, *(cont)*

literal transparency and phenomenal transparency, Palazzo Farnese and Palazzo Borghese, Parma and Saint-Dié, Unité and Uffizi, precedent and invention, program and paradigm, program and archetype, engineer and *bricoleur*, Mannerism and Modern Architecture, Neoclassical and Modern Architecture, Renaissance and Modern Movement, Renaissance and Baroque, character and composition, Palladio and Le Corbusier, Claude and Poussin, utopia and freedom, hedgehog and fox...

Some of these pairs are metaphors for others. Steve Hurtt has indicated the binomial ideal type/context as a sign of many other pairings that develop in the course of Rowe's writings.[12] This evolution does not, however, produce a shift from one conceptual position to its opposite: rather, eventually both conditions can and should arguably coexist in an articulated, rich and motivated synthesis: a "dialectical inter-animation".[13] The process from "Mathematics" to "Urbanistics", which I tried to trace in another essay of this volume, is not one of replacement of the one with the other; rather it is a process of incremental inclusion. Therefore, the *urbanist* Colin Rowe is the same author who wrote "Mathematics", the ideal reference of the English neo-Palladian, the passionate interlocutor of Louis Kahn and the critical mentor of the 'white' New York Five. As Emmanuel Petit has pointed out, "it is remarkable and perplexing that, in the United States, both the formal experiments out of the (neo-) avant-garde and the neoconservative attitudes toward the city, could each be traced back to Rowe and his entourage".[14]

Rarely are the dialectical couples antagonist 'either-or' propositions; almost always they are 'both-and' indications of inclusion. The synergy "concentrated Italian town" and "good American suburb" that I refer to at the beginning of this essay is an explicit example of this inclusive, liberal attitude. After all, isn't the dialectic co-presence of the combination of possible alternatives and their synergies an implicit legitimization of both? Doesn't it provide room for a productive argument? Doesn't it reveal the willingness to accept different opinions? Isn't it a sign of a preference for multiplicity rather than singularity, for inclusion rather than exclusion, and, therefore, to leave an opening for a different possibility: a proposition for a solution that is not anarchist but plural, searching for a—partial—control of complexity?

"Rather Textbook"

Recently, Daniel Naegele has published a memoir dedicated by Rowe to the otherwise little known Countess Lilian Priuli-Bon, who we understand is a protagonist in Rowe's early years as a young scholar in London during the late 1940s.[15] Besides being a vivid account of some of Rowe's social dynamics in that period, this text provides encouragement to my conjecture. With the introduction of the experience-directed Countess Priuli, yet another pair materializes in Rowe's dialectical world: she seems perfect for the prominent role of counterpart to the scholarship-directed "Rudy" Wittkower, Rowe's official advisor. As the scholarly Wittkower personifies the spirit of abstract 'mathematics', the experience-educated Priuli-Bon seems to embody Rowe's conceptual attitude towards inclusion of both the abstractions of 'mathematics' and 'experience' of concrete realities.

(cont) Cambridge, MA, and London, 2008: 61-105, as well as the essays: Centanni, Monica, "Per una iconologia dell'intervallo: Tradizione dell'antico e visione retrospettiva in Aby Warburg e Colin Rowe"; Mazzucco, Katia, "L'incontro di Colin Rowe con Rudolf Wittkower e un'immagine del cosiddetto «metodo warburghiano»; Marzo, Mauro, "Postfazione"; and Benelli (2010), all in Marzo (2010).

A tempting hypothesis, deserving further study, might consider Rowe placing himself in the formalist lineage of Fiedler, Hildebrand, and Wölfflin, as represented by Mundt in a text—one of the few articles—included in the 1969 Cornell Urban Design Studio reading list. Considering Rowe's inclusive attitude however, this legacy would combine with both Panofsky's conceptual and Worringer's psychological traditions in one whole aesthetic, as in the auspices of Mundt's representation. Mundt, Ernest K., "Three Aspects of German Aesthetic Theory", *The Journal of Aesthetics and Art Criticism* 17 (3), 1959: 310.

10 Rowe, Colin, "The Mathematics of the Ideal Villa. Palladio and Le Corbusier compared", *The Architectural Review* CI (603), Mar 1947: 101-04; also in Rowe, Colin, *The Mathematics of the Ideal Villa and Other Essays*, MIT Press, Cambridge, MA, and London, 1976: 1-27. Also, my other text in this collection.

11 Naegele, Daniel, ed., *The Letters of Colin Rowe: Five Decades of Correspondence*, Artifice, London, 2016: letter of September 1995 to Ernst Gombrich. The book, published posthumously, is Rowe, Colin; Satkowski, Leon, *Italian Architecture of the 16th Century*, Princeton Architectural Press, New York, 2002.

12 Hurtt, Steven, "Conjectures on Urban Form: The Cornell Urban Design Studio 1963-1982", *The Cornell Journal of Architecture* 2, "Urban Design", (Middleton, D. Blake, ed.), Fall 1983: 67. Hurtt has highlighted this couple while emphasizing that, in *Collage City*, "'ideal type' and 'context' are variously seen as signs of: Utopia and Tradition; Theatre of Prophecy and Theatre of Memory; order and disorder; ... permanent reference and random happening; tragic and comic; the 'rational' and the relative; the possibility of the general and the recognition of the specific; the empiricist reacting to site and the idealist concerned with normative condition; archetype and accident; local concession and a declaration of independence; ... the overtly planned and the genuinely unplanned; of the public and private, of the state and the individual".

13 Deyong, Sarah; Babe, J. Craig, "Colin Rowe's double-edge", in De Vos, Els; De Walsche, Johan; Michels, Marjan, eds., *Theory by Design: Architectural Research Made Explicit in the Design Teaching Studio*, ASP, Bruxelles, 2013: 131-36.

14 Petit, Emmanuel, "Rowe after Colin Rowe", in *Reckoning with Colin Rowe: Ten architects take position*, Routledge, Abingdon and NY, 2015: 5, 13.

15 Rowe, Colin, "Excursus on Contessa Priuli-Bon", (Naegele, Daniel, ed.), *AA Files* 72, 2016: 68-72.

A clue is particularly relevant to understand Priuli's symbolic role. In Wittkower's chapter "The Break-Away from the Laws of Harmonic Proportion" which refers to the epistemological break in the development of 18th century taste, the influential historian had stated his well-known critique: "It was, however, in England, that the whole structure of classical æsthetic was overthrown from the bottom".[16] Priuli's reaction to this charge is summarized by Rowe as follows:

> *[Priuli] felt that everything could not be so circumscribed, that there must be eruptions from outside; and thus she was disturbed by the negative interpretation of English and Scottish aestheticians considered responsible for this 'break-away': William Hogarth, David Hume, Edmund Burke, Lord Kames, Richard Payne Knight, Archibald Alison. She found that this was an inadequate presentation, felt without compassion and understanding, an example of what she used to call 'rather textbook'.*[17]

The role of the whole tradition of British Picturesque liberalism is under scrutiny here. Like Wittkower, Priuli—Rowe goes on—was "highly responsive to the concepts of musical ratio, mathematical law and harmonic proportion; but ... she also knew the exigencies of a dissenting attitude, the insistencies of what today we would call the *romantic* revolution".[18]

What impact can we infer that Lilian Priuli-Bon—or, rather, this almost mythological Wittkower/Priuli dualism—had on Rowe's attitude? Noticeable, if we are allowed to believe what he declares in his posthumous text: "And it was in this context of positive-negative, yes-no, figure-ground reaction that, I believe, being inspired by her, I wrote that ambiguous article ... 'The Mathematics of the Ideal Villa'."[19]

I cannot say I see evidence that the inclusive attitude, the predilection "of working to minimize the violence of ideological collision"[20] embodied by Priuli's character, had already surfaced in "Mathematics" therefore making it "ambiguous". However, this attitude is clear in Rowe's intellectual development, as confirmed by his production in subsequent years. Thus, Rowe's reference in the epilogue of his text is hardly an overstatement. Out of his mentors, including two principal ones—Wittkower and Hitchcock—plus Ms. Jean Murray Bangs Harris, "[his] principal teacher must have been Lilian Priuli-Bon, whose lesson was less *singular* than those of the three others".[21]

Liberalism

The reading list that developed in the Cornell Urban Design Studio is, by itself, of great interest for its strong multi-disciplinary content. Included in it are books of theory, criticism and history of architecture and urban design (Bacon, Banham, De Zurko, Hitchcock, Hudnut, Kaufmann, Le Corbusier, Scott, Sitte, Summerson, Whittick, Zevi), studies of the psychology of form and perception (Arnheim, Attneave, Beardslee, Gibson, Wertheimer), aesthetics (Berenson, Chambers, Fitch, Gilbert and Kuhn, Gray, Heyl, Jarret, Pepper, Rawlins), essays on history and philosophy of art (Bahr, Fiedler, Hildebrand, Hulme, Kubler, Lewis, Mundt, Panofsky, Poggioli, Venturi, Wilensky, Worringer, and Cassirer, Langer, and Bell, Fry, Stokes, Scott[22]) and of various other historical kinds (Hughes, Tuveson), theory of scientific thought and method (Medawar, Northrop, Pólya),

16 Wittkower, Rudolf, "Principles of Palladio's Architecture-II", *Journal of the Warburg and Courtauld Institutes* 8, 1945: 100.

17 Rowe (2016): 71.

18 Ibid. (My italic).

19 Ibid.

20 Ibid.

21 Ibid. (the italics is in the original). Rowe's Lilian Priuli might seem a fictitious character and this "Excursus" could very well, at least partly, be the fruit of Rowe's notoriously fervid *historiographical* imagination, just like the story supporting the "Roma interrotta" project described in Judy DiMaio's text in this collection. However, Matt Bell who was in close contact with Rowe while both lived in Washington, D.C., confirms that Rowe was referring to the actual, Countess Priuli, very active in London's cultural panorama at the time. Lilian Priuli-Bon was the author of a monograph on Sodoma: Priuli-Bon, Contessa [Lilian], *Sodoma*, George Bell and Sons, London, (1900) 1908.

22 Vidler (2008): 62, refers to Bell, Fry, Stokes, Scott as both recipients and promoters of Wölfflin's legacy in England.

anthropology (Lévi-Strauss), sociology (Mannheim), music (Craft, Stravinsky), film (Eisenstein), and even, ironically, a book about the legendary football coach of the Greenbay Packers, Vince Lombardy.

Philosophy texts are a conspicuous part of the list. It includes books by the most important authors of contemporary liberal thought: liberal understood as pluralistic, anti-totalitarian, free from preconceptions, catholic. Here is a selection of the authors: Jacques Barzun, Carl Lotus Becker, Isaiah Berlin, Clarence Crane Brinton, Norman Cohn, José Ortega y Gasset, Frederick August Hayek, Karl Popper, Judith Nisse Shklar. Some of these are also frequent references in Rowe's writings.

In the early years of constructing his cultural-intellectual background, Rowe could count on both a solid production by liberal thinkers and a relation between architecture and liberalism much stronger than in the subsequent decades. Rowe could build on this base to develop the fertile Whig, radical middle-ground cultural tradition, to which he was certainly not extraneous. The Spanish liberal philosopher José Ortega y Gasset, for instance, was a main reference for President Josep Lluís Sert opening remarks at CIAM 8 in July 1951, likely one of the most important acts of the Modern Reform.[23] And, the following month, Ortega y Gasset was invited along with Martin Heidegger to participate in the second Colloquium in Darmstadt, dedicated to "Man and Space". It was at this Colloquium that Heidegger delivered his famous lecture "Bauen, Wohnen, Denken" (Building, Dwelling, Thinking). José Ortega y Gasset presented an important contribution entitled "Der Mythus der Menschen hinter der Technik" (The Myth of Men behind Technique).[24] As Tony Vidler notes: "José Ortega y Gasset [was] an author whose newly translated works [Rowe] had consumed with a passion".[25]

Rowe's special attention to the tradition of liberalism and to the related issues may have been reinforced in the Austin, Texas period. Although seen from a different perspective, liberty—along with regionalism—must have been a concept dear to Dean Harwell Hamilton Harris as well, as indicated by his Eugene, Oregon 1954 conference on "Regionalism and Nationalism in Architecture".[26] In the didactics of the Texas Rangers, the question of positive and negative liberalism appears. Alex Caragonne refers to Hoesli's reflections on "freedom from" and "freedom for" and to "extended discussions and debates" about Ortega's *Revolt of the Masses* among the young Austin faculty. This is taken from Hoesli's notes, vaguely Kantian: "... we must remember what freedom means if it is to enrich, to enlarge the possibilities of human experience. It is not so much *freedom from* but *freedom for*. Freedom to be free to do what one must".[27]

Even the renewed attention for and the shift towards urbanistics and the centrality of space—in both Rowe's thinking and the Modern Reform discourse—lend themselves to be interpreted using this line of reasoning, if one is allowed to believe what Bernhard Hoesli has submitted:

> *It may be that attention to space is the expression of an open society where plurality is accepted and recognized, where contradiction is not only tolerated but held in esteem as inherent in the* condition humaine *and where dialog is an indispensable technique for mutual advancement.*[28]

23 Modern Reform is an inclusive label that I use here for those cultural and disciplinary positions mostly emerging during the early post-WWII years as an evolution of the orthodox Modern Movement as Townscape, post-WWII CIAMs, including Team 10, organic architecture, regionalism, new empiricism, neo-liberty... A renewed attention for individuality and multiplicity, for cultural history and tradition, for the uneven nature of space and the relevance of place, context, region, and geography, for existing cities and anonymous architecture are common features and, although in different degrees, contrary to the following Postmodern inclinations, the engagement in an anthropocentric project of progress is shared as well.

24 The proceedings of the *Darmstädter Gespräch*, held on August 4 to 6, 1951, were published the following year. Bartning, Otto, ed., *Darmstädter Gespräch: Mensch und Raum*, Neue Darmstädter Verlagsanstalt Gmbh, Darmstadt, 1952. Heidegger, Martin, "Building, Dwelling, Thinking", in *Poetry, Language, Thought*, Harper & Row, New York, 1971: 145-61 (orig. *Vorträge und Aufsätze*, 1954). Ortega y Gasset, José, *Meditazione sulla tecnica e altri saggi su scienza e filosofia*, Mimesis, Milano, 2011. This text, originally in German, has been translated in Italian, Spanish and French. No English version seems to be yet available.

25 Vidler, Anthony, "Up Against the Wall: Colin Rowe at La Tourette", *Log* 24, Win-Spr 2012: 12; Idem, "Reckoning with Art History: Colin Rowe's Critical Vision", in Petit (2015): 48.

26 Harris, Harwell Hamilton, "Regionalism and Nationalism in Architecture", *Texas Quarterly* 1, Feb 1958: 115-24, now in Canizaro, Vincent B., *Architectural Regionalism: Collected Writings on Place, Identity, Modernity, and Tradition*, Princeton Architectural Press, New York, 2007: 57-64.

27 Caragonne (1995): 234. (My italics).

28 Hoesli, Bernhard, "Addendum (1982)", in Rowe, Colin; Slutzky, Robert, *Transparency*, (Hoesli, Bernhard, ed.), Birkhäuser, Basel, 1997: 96, reprinted as "Transparent form-organization as an instrument of design", in Petit (2015): 132.

Dialectics, Liberalisms and Townscape

Liberalism in the English tradition had an important role in the founding of Townscape, the movement originated and developed by *The Architectural Review*, the most influential British architectural magazine. In its original version, the inaugural, eponymous article "Townscape"[29] was written by Hubert de Cronin Hastings, owner and co-editor of the *Review*, under the pseudonym of I[vor] de Wolfe. It is exemplary for both its extensive reference to dialectical pairs and its passionate dedication to the meanings and ideals of liberalism, illustrated with a wealth of arguments and examples. The whole case is organized around a dialectic couple: rational liberalism and radical liberalism or "freedom from" and "freedom for" in Hoesli's terms. Hastings specifies:

> *The one looks to found the social structure upon the basis of the unanimity ultimately predictable of all individual minds in virtue of the ultimate identity of reason; the other seeks the higher social organization in the differentiation of the individual from the mass. One cultivates the universal, the other the particular. The pattern and the atom philosophy.*[30]

As in Rowe's recurrent theoretical and rhetorical structure, the pair "rational" and "radical" liberalism generates further couples: France and England as ideal cultural cradles of the two attitudes; Voltaire and Rousseau, Ludwig II of Bavaria and Wilhelm Humboldt, as assertors of the two positions; equality and independence, rationality and individualism, leveling intellectualism and anti-intellectualist reaction, conformity and complexity, smoothness and irregularity, as their ideals and consequences.

Beautiful and picturesque are both means and aesthetic outcomes of these couples in the disciplinary realm of the visual arts. International Style and *genius loci* are the current embodiment of those alternative attitudes. And since the Modern Reform with its renewed attention to place and geography can be interpreted as the antithesis to an *a-topic* International Style, one is encouraged to associate the latter with the "rational" declension and the former with the "radical" one. For Hastings, radical liberalism, representing the true spirit of English culture, is the conceptual source to support, via the intermediation of landscape architecture—specifically in its 18th century English Picturesque legacy—a new form of architecture and urban design: Townscape.

The Picturesque tradition, then, is not just a stylistic component of what a few years later, on the occasion of his 1955 Reith lectures, Nikolaus Pevsner would indicate as the "Englishness of English Art". In fact, the following year, Pevsner's lectures were made into a book, dedicated to Hastings, and a few pages of the chapter "Picturesque England" were dedicated to the "relation of picturesque gardening to liberty" with plenty of references.[31]

Wittkower, in a later, 1969 text in which "English Neo-Palladianism, Landscape Garden, China, and the Enlightenment" are considered in their combination, has shown that the conceptual connection between freedom and "the creation of a national taste and a national style" was present in the early development of the English Landscape movement.[32] This connection had already been made

29 De Wolfe, I[vor], "Townscape: A Plea for an English Visual Philosophy Founded on the True Rock of Sir Uvedale Price", *The Architectural Review* CVI (636), Dec 1949: 354-62. Its title allows us to consider this as the inaugural text of the 'movement' although several other signs of the same disciplinary attitude had already appeared in *The Architectural Review*, including the fundamental: The editor, "Exterior Furnishing or Sharawaggi: The Art of Making Urban Landscape", *The Architectural Review* 95, 1944: 2-8. Both "Townscape" and "Sharawaggi" were actually written by Hubert de Cronin Hastings.

30 De Wolfe (1949): 358.

31 Pevsner, Nikolaus, *The Englishness of English Art*, Frederick A. Praeger, New York, 1956: 166-67, 178.

32 Wittkower, Rudolf, "English Neo-Palladianism, the Landscape Garden, China, and the Enlightenment", *L'Arte* 6, 1969: 18-35.

explicit in the 1712 essay *A Letter Concerning the Art, or Science of Design*, written by Anthony Ashley-Cooper, third Earl of Shaftesbury, while residing in Italy. Hastings reminds us that Shaftesbury can be considered the founder of the Landscape movement.

Furthermore, both Wittkower and Pevsner before him[33] argue how "Liberty" is actually the flag under which the classicism of Neo-Palladianism and the romanticism of the English garden, both surfacing in the early decades of the 18th century, especially within the circle of Richard Boyle, Earl of Burlington, could find a synergic composition despite their apparently antipodal aesthetic inclinations.

According to Hastings, the "regional development of the International Style"[34] and the *de facto* reconciliation between Modern Architecture and the outstanding values of the traditional city can rely on the "contemporary message" of the Picturesque philosophy. This question, implicit in the dynamics of the reevaluation of vision and phenomenology in urban design of those years, was to remain one of the fundamental problems of the whole Modern Reform as well as a recurring topic in Rowe's writings and in the production of his students.

In order for this rhetorical device to represent the contemporary scene in a form that is functional to Hasting's argument, when it is projected into the disciplinary field, the original ideological pair takes the format of two systems of three components each. The Grand Manner of the Latin and French tradition, i.e. the axial planners of continental Europe, is contrasted at first with the English Landscape movement, broadly taken. This movement is further divided between the early group of the "Race of the Improvers", William Kent, Capability Brown, and Humphry Repton, and the later literary intelligentsia, Uvedale Price and Richard Payne Knight. It is the latter which fully embodies the Picturesque reaction to the continental state of the art and is the proposed model for a translation from landscape to urban settings, through the action of Townscape.[35]

The Modern corresponding analogy is rather confused. The "rational or classic or crystalline" Le Corbusier—classic and therefore, one is led to infer, analogous to the Grand Manner—is nevertheless "said to be still in a Lancelot Brown phase"—thus analogous to the first phase of the cultural revision—but at the same time inclined to the "re-establishment of the unified, the universal, the ideal picture". Despite these uncertain correspondences and whatever interpretation one is inclined to adopt, in Hasting's view the dualism between Le Corbusier and the "romantic" or "organic" Wright is to be overcome and resolved by the unprecedented and rooted at once "English or Radical" movement which, as we would expect, is able to simultaneously reject and embody both Corbusier's and Wright's inclinations.[36]

The Question of the 'Whole'

In the foundational text of Townscape, the necessary evolution of Functionalism is interpreted, as it will be in Harris' contribution above, as the result of the conceptual axis between freedom and the plural essence of space—context-region. This is a *vexata quaestio* of the Modern Reform and of the post-WWII CIAMs that will eventually lead to a renewed relevance and acceptance of the role of *locus* in

33 Pevsner, Nikolaus, "The Genesis of the Picturesque", *The Architectural Review* XCVI (575), Nov 1944: 139-46.

34 De Wolfe (1949): 354-55.

35 It is perhaps worth further examining the fact that in "Townscape" Hastings proposed this distinction between the two phases of the English landscape movement whereas in "Sharawaggi", published five years before, he refers to a "Picturesque Theory" which "evolved on this island early in the eighteenth century" therefore apparently making no distinction: 3.

36 De Wolfe (1949): 362.

both its topographic and anthropologic forms. This restored *episteme* is embodied both in Rowe's special version of contextualism and in the positions of Critical Regionalism, the latter sharing the concerns for placelessness and the unintended consequences of globalization as anticipated by Paul Ricoeur's "Universal Civilization and National Cultures".[37] And yet free from the underhanded implications of *Kunstgeographie* beguilements,[38] it is, in fact, engaged in a search for "interstices" towards "Liberty" in the sense proposed by Abraham Moles.[39]

In Hastings—and by synecdoche the Townscape movement—and Rowe—and perhaps by analogy Rowe's acolytes—liberalism is mainly a recognition of some room for freedom and, at the same time, of an obligation in the field of form, be it a cultural claim of specificity and/or a pure quest for an appropriate good *Gestalt.* Most of the residual normative character of both positions resides in this morphological realm. Therefore, the analogy between design and politics, as it is presented by Hastings, seems to rely on a purely conceptual association—an "essential concordance"[40]—between ideology and an inclusive phenomenology extended to all senses.

Although Hastings relates the Picturesque and implicitly, by analogy, Townscape to *laissez-faire*[41] and elects the imperative of "Be[ing] Thyself" as central to his philosophy, the implication is far from anarchy. While here individual freedom does not seem to be tied to what "one must", as in Hoesli, some organizational system is nevertheless considered necessary. It should proceed in the direction of complexity rather than abstraction: "as a departure from conformity, as a means of differentiation in the biological sense—of achieving, that is, *an increase in complexity,* or organization, equivalent to that which occurs when differentiation takes place in the embryo and the organs appear".[42] Hence, freedom seems not only a possibility but also a necessity.

Therefore, freedom in urbanistics is both an asset and a liability. On one hand, it is the ability to avoid the shortcomings of the "Bauhausians"—"They have no tolerance of accident"[43]—and to understand the relative, "contextualized" relevance of form.[44] On the other hand, the Picturesque approach carries an inherent "inability to see wholes"—the very same inadequacy that Wittkower had attributed to Sitte—which is interpreted as a weakness.[45]

But if the lack of an all-encompassing vision is lamented as the grudgingly accepted shortcoming of a multiple, picturesque reality and the fastidious tradeoff of a liberal attitude, some form of normative reference cannot be avoided, as Hastings had anticipated in "Sharawaggi", despite the limited reliance on rationality:

> *[W]e should not be led to draw from this the totally false conclusion that picturesque effect can be obtained merely by letting every building owner do as he likes; that is, that the right effects will happen, if you don't worry about planning. A policy of visual laisser-faire is nearly always fatal.*[46]

How should one proceed then, even if the goal is just to control the "field of vision"? The ability to turn to a "paradigmatic" method, to use Rowe's terms, to a deeper awareness of the disciplinary dynamics and products might be essential.

37 Ricoeur, Paul, "Civilisation universelle et cultures nationales", *Esprit* 29 (10), 1961. Trans.: Ricoeur, Paul, "Universal Civilization and National Cultures", *History and Truth*, Northwestern University Press, Evanston, 1965, now in Canizaro (2007): 42-53. Tzonis, Alexander; Lefaivre, Liliane, "The Grid and the Pathway: An Introduction to the Work of Dimitris and Suzana Antonakakis", *Architecture in Greece* 15, 1981: 164-78; Frampton, Kenneth, "Toward a Critical Regionalism: Six Points for an Architecture of Resistance", in Foster, Hal, ed, *The Anti-Aesthetic: Essays on Postmodern Culture*, Bay Press, Port Townsend, WA, 1983: 16-30.

38 Béchard-Léauté, Anne, "Questions de méthodes chez Nikolaus Pevsner et Erwin Panofsky: deux nouvelles monographies", *Perspective. Actualité en histoire de l'art*, 1/2013: 168-75.

39 Moles, Abraham, "The Three Cities", in Hill, Anthony, *Data: Directions in Art, Theory and Aesthetics*, New York Graphic Society Ltd., Greenwich, CT, 1968: 191; Frampton, Kenneth, "Prospects for a Critical Regionalism", *Perspecta* 20, 1983: 149; Idem, "Ten Points on an Architecture of Regionalism: A Provisional Polemic", *Center* 3, "New Regionalism", 1987: 20-27.

40 De Wolfe (1949): 356.

41 Ibid.: 358.

42 Ibid.: 358. (My italics).

43 "Sharawaggi": 7.

44 "Sharawaggi": 5. "Uvedale Price, perhaps the first man in history to reveal that an object may be 'ugly' in itself and yet *in a suitable context* may have aesthetic possibilities". (My italics).

45 "... the essential characteristic of that visual philosophy [Picturesque] was: namely (to put it negatively first) a dislike which amounts to an inability to see wholes or principles and an incapacity for handling theory". De Wolfe (1949): 362. In the previous page de Wolfe insists on the "urge" of making a rather elusive "new kind of whole", "through the cultivation of significant differences". Analogously Wittkower had stated: "[Sitte] cannot see and interpret [the town] as an entirely integrated whole—an interest which for us lies at the heart of town-planning". Wittkower, Rudolf, "Camillo Sitte's 'Art of Building Cities' in an American Translation", *The Town Planning Review* 19 (3/4), Sum 1947: 164. The question of the "whole" as search for coherence rather than homogeneity is not new, of course. See for instance Burnham, Daniel H., "White City and Capital City", *The Century Magazine* 63, Feb 1902: 619-20.

46 "Sharawaggi": 5.

> *The question arises, how is the true radical–for whom theory and rule of thumb, reason and revelation are taboo–to operate? With what* principia, *and from what base? Unrooted in principle where and in what is he to root himself? The answer is one, it seems to me, that architectural journalism (for one) should inwardly digest.* On precedent. *Meaning on the accumulating examples of* individual *experience, whose function is to train first the creative faculty, then to provide exemplars from which to depart.*[47]

The 'precedent' method—analogous to the English case-based legal system—is the reliable basis for a design activity founded on the fundamental principles of liberalism. This applies to both Hastings and Rowe, who would dedicate some illuminating reflections on this subject.[48] And, regardless of their different ideological stances, it will be the same for a conspicuous number of theorists and designers, mainly relying on the rediscovered discourse of typology which would follow.[49]

The Asymmetrical Nature of Hedgehog and Fox

It should be evident, by now, that the reference to Hastings and Townscape is actually meant to explore Rowe. And through Rowe's legacy, the uncertain destiny of urbanistics. There is no doubt that the ideological dynamics produced by the Townscape creative group and by the creative group that forms around Rowe in the 1960s have relevant common ingredients.[50] All of them share a similar devotion to freedom as a generating concept and for its urban design outcomes.

In fact, regardless of Rowe's occasional broadsides against "the insufferable tedium of Townscape, the dreary accumulation of public house chi chi, and the insipid neo-Regency aesthetic with which we have been blanketed since the war"[51] and even though for Rowe and Koetter "in application, townscape was surely less defensible than it was as an idea",[52] an interpretation of Townscape and Rowe in terms of antithetical positioning seems neither justified nor heuristically revealing. Likewise, it seems impractical to look for some form of derivation from Townscape to Rowe or a direct overlap of one with the other. Rather, the assertive, engaging, and influential development and divulgence of the Townscape architecture argument, and the more problematic, intellectual and inclusive rhetorical construct of Rowe and his circle, both seem to be expressions of the same cultural *milieu*. Both are promoters of the long process of the still incomplete Modern reform. Both engaged the architectural and urban design debate during the early post-WWII decades, which owes a great deal to the reemerging liberal thought of those years.

Several things divide the Hastings I have tried to highlight and the Rowe that we are getting to know (including through the common effort collected in this book). To different degrees, Hastings, Rowe, and the whole Modern Reform share a common awareness that even a liberal approach needs a suitable regulating system. Such a system can be based on a complex set of logical or metaphoric connections of the design project with both specific history (precedent) and geography (context and region). But Rowe does not interpret the epistemological break with the recent and remote past in its totalitarian slant towards an all-inclusive, standardizing common project of the future, as an irreparable, though necessary, loss.

47 De Wolfe (1949): 362. (The emphasis on both "On precedent" and on "individual" is mine).

48 Rowe, Colin, "Program vs. Paradigm", *The Cornell Journal of Architecture* 2, "Urban Design", (Middleton, D. Blake, ed.), 1983: 9-19, now in Rowe, Colin, *As I Was Saying: Recollections and Miscellaneous Essays* 2, "Cornelliana". (Caragonne, Alexander, ed.), MIT Press, Cambridge, MA, and London, 1996: 7-41; Rowe, Colin, "Letter to the editor", *Harvard Design Magazine* 5, 1986, now ibidem: 367-70.

49 To mention some of the best known: Argan, Giulio Carlo, "On the Typology of Architecture", *Architectural Design* 33, Dec 1963, or. 1962: 564-65; Colquhoun, Alan, "Typology and Design Method", *Arena* 83, Jun 1967, later in *Perspecta* 12, 1969, also in *Essays in Architectural Criticism: Modern Architecture and Historical Change*, MIT Press, Cambridge, MA, and London, 1981; Vidler, Anthony, "The Third Typology", *Oppositions* 7, Win 1977, also in Delevoy, Robert L., ed., *Rational Architecture Rationnelle: The Reconstruction of the European City*, Archives d'Architecture Moderne, Bruxelles, 1978.

50 A well-rounded account on the controversial analogies between Townscape and *Collage City* is in Aitchison, Mathew, "Who's Afraid of Ivor de Wolfe?", *AA Files* 62, 2011: 34-39 and a rich comparison between de Wolfe's "Townscape" and *Collage City* is in Macarthur, John, "Appropriation", in *The Picturesque: Architecture, Disgust and Other irregularities*, Routledge, London and New York, 2007: 176-232, where there is also a thorough argument on Rowe's picturesque inclinations ("Rowe is more, not less, picturesque than de Wolfe": 224).

51 Rowe, Colin, "Connell, Ward and Lucas", *Architectural Association Journal* lxxii (808), Jan 1957: 163.

52 Rowe, Colin; Koetter, Fred, *Collage City*, MIT Press, Cambridge, MA, and London, 1978: 36.

The similarity between Hastings' dialectic poles, rational and radical liberalism, and those presented by Isaiah Berlin in his well-known lecture on "Two Concepts of Liberty", delivered almost a decade later, in 1958, is evident. This has some relevance for the argument made here, regardless of the abundance of precedents.[53] When Hastings wrote his article in the 1940s, his references were classical liberals such as Locke, Humboldt, Rousseau, whereas Rowe's disciplinary architecture which came together in the following decades was mostly supported by the insights of Isaiah Berlin and Karl Popper.[54]

In one of his late-1990s letters, Rowe refers to Berlin as "part of a block of Jewish criticism, anti-determinism and free will to which I subscribe".[55] In fact, the two show some interesting analogies. Berlin is a champion of both liberalism and dialectic pairs but also of ambiguity in the sense used by Rowe to define his "Mathematics", or while listing the ingredients for "making safe the city".[56] As Edmund Fawcett points out in his review text on *Liberalism*:

> *Berlin had a dramatist's gift of personalizing ideas and for bringing them alive in paired opposites. Thinkers he disagreed with particularly attracted him. A child of the Enlightenment, Berlin was fascinated by anti-Enlightenment thought. Conflict preoccupied him, and conflict was easiest to dramatize digitally, in twos, on or off, black or white. As writer and lecturer Berlin grasped the irresistibility of the neat contrast. He divided political thinkers into hedgehogs with one idea and foxes with many. He split liberalism's biggest totem into negative liberty (good) and positive liberty (bad).*[57]

More than for his standing on liberalism, Berlin seems to influence Rowe's arguments for dialectic analogies projected onto the realm of form. This specific architectural inclination seems to be confirmed by the reading of both "Collision City and the Politics of 'Bricolage'", the chapter of *Collage City* where Berlin's dialectic couple hedgehog/fox is introduced and discussed,[58] and Rowe's 1987 Walter Gropius Lecture at Harvard where Berlin's pair is applied again to a wide set of architects and projects.[59] The morphological field seems the prevailing ground of impact of Berlin's ideas on Rowe's theoretical construct although it is obvious that, as Rowe and Koetter assert: "those ... who relate everything to a single central vision, one system less or more coherent or articulate, in terms of which they understand, think and feel—a single, universal, organizing principle in terms of which all that they are and say has significance" are an adequate metaphor of positive (rational) liberalism whereas "those who pursue many ends, often unrelated and even contradictory, connected, if at all, only in some *de facto* way, for some psychological or physiological cause, related by no moral or aesthetic principle" aptly represent the projection of negative (radical) liberalism.[60]

While the evocative power of the hedgehog and the fox is such that Berlin's influence on Rowe's conceptual development does not need further emphasis here, the impact of Karl Popper (b. 1902) seems somehow more multi-faceted and complex. Popper was a close friend of Ernst Gombrich (b. 1909), whom Rowe (b. 1920) in turn was familiar with from the years of his studies at the Warburg.[61] Although the bibliography provided to the Cornell students of 1969 includes only Popper's *Open Society* (published in 1945, the year Popper returned to London

53 This dialectical pair had been treated on several occasions before: by Kant, Green, Bosanquet, de Ruggero, Plamenatz. Ricciardi, Mario, "Berlin on Liberty", in Crowder, George; Hardy, Henry, eds., *The One and the Many: Reading Isaiah Berlin*, Prometheus Books, Amherst, NY, 2007: 135. For a thorough discussion on these two concepts of freedom: Carter, Ian, "Positive and Negative Liberty", in Zalta, Edward N., ed., *The Stanford Encyclopedia of Philosophy*, (Sum) 2018, who adds Norberto Bobbio as a further precedent, closer in time. [https://plato.stanford.edu/entries/liberty-positive-negative/]. The several versions of Berlin's conference/text can be found in "The Isaiah Berlin Virtual Library" [http://berlin.wolf.ox.ac.uk/published_works/tcl/index.html].

54 Berlin and Popper, together with Ortega y Gasset, are among the references that are used for the epigraphs of chapters of *Collage City*. Ortega is quoted at the beginning of "Crisis of the Object: Predicament of Texture": 50; Berlin in "Collision City and the Politics of Bricolage": 86. With Ortega and Popper begins "Collage City and the Reconquest of Time": 118. Berlin and Popper appear, together, in Rowe's letters collected by Naegele. Letters to Boyarsky of December 5, 1964, to Davidson of mid-October, 1994, to McDonald of August 2, 1997. Naegele (2016).

55 The group to which Rowe refers includes also Karl Popper and Ernst Gombrich. Letter of August 2, 1997 to Arthur McDonald. Naegele (2016): 521.

56 Rowe and Koetter (1978): 117.

57 Fawcett, Edmund, *Liberalism: The Life of an Idea,* (2nd ed.), Princeton University Press, Princeton and Oxford, 2018: 318-19.

58 Rowe and Koetter (1978): 91-93. Berlin introduced the hedgehog-fox interpretation couple in an article published in its earliest version in 1951. Berlin, Isaiah, "Lev Tolstoy's Historical Scepticism", *Oxford Slavonic Papers* II, 1951: 17-54. Here is the *incipit*: "There is a line among the fragments of the Greek poet Archilochus which says: 'The fox knows many things, but the hedgehog knows one big thing.' Scholars have differed about the correct interpretation of these dark words, which probably mean no more than that the fox, for all his cunning, is helpless before the hedgehog's one defence. But, taken figuratively, the words can be made to yield a sense in which they mark one of the deepest differences which divide writers and thinkers, and, it may be, human beings in general. For there certainly exists a chasm between those, on one side, who relate everything to a single central vision, one principle, one system less or more coherent or articulate, in terms of which they understand and think and feel—a single, universal, organizing principle in terms of which alone all that they are and say has significance—and, on the other side, those who pursue many ends, often unrelated and even contradictory, connected, if at all, only in some *de facto* way, for some psychological or physiological cause, related by no moral or aesthetic principle; these last lead lives, perform acts, and entertain ideas that are centrifugal rather than centripetal, their thought is scattered or diffused, moving on many levels, seizing upon the essence of a vast variety of experiences and objects for what they are in themselves, for *(cont.)*

from his 'exile' in New Zealand), *Logic of Scientific Discovery*, *Poverty of Historicism* and the collection *Conjectures and Refutations* recur throughout Rowe's texts.[62]

Popper first appears, I believe, in Rowe's "Addendum 1973" to "The Architecture of Utopia".[63] Not only do a few main *topoi* of Popper's legacy support some of the fundamental aspects of Rowe's conception of architecture but they also provide Rowe with the basis for overcoming the deadlock that a radical application of Popper's ideas would have brought to design.

All the fundamental references are there. Firstly, the refusal of the deterministic bias of historicism and of the ineluctability of *Progress*, implying a substantial irrelevance of individual actions, works, in fact, as a multiplier of perspectives. Further, isn't the system of conjectures and refutations adopted in the Cornell Urban Design Studio, that Hurtt indicates as "the basis for a process that accepts, even demands, hypothesis as a point of departure in problem solving", analogous to the well-rooted, evolutionary, trial and error process, in design?[64] Therefore, while historical determinism is rejected, history becomes the fulcrum of individual projects, the reference of micro-utopias, relying on traditions rather than on the *Tradition:* an essential tool in Rowe's theoretical network for structuring, communicating, improving, explaining.[65]

Moreover, the adoption of a strategy of "piecemeal engineering" over "utopian engineering"[66] is not only the sign of a shrewd realism but also a sign of a preference for a multiple, 'collaged' reality able to overcome the primacy, even the desirability, of all-inclusive wholes as the highest, much longed-for, but unachievable goal. Finally, if the open-society model is adopted and abstract comprehensive totalitarian planning rebutted, the future, and the future of the city as a part of it, must be not only incremental but also plural. Both process and product are affected by this condition. Hence, the fox's approach liberates the project from being dependent on an all-inclusive theory; the piecemeal improvement strategy overturns the problem of the 'whole' that had burdened, one way or another, both Wittkower's interpretation of Sitte and the supposed shortcomings of the Picturesque (and Townscape?) suffered by Hastings.

"The Architecture of Utopia" is a rejection, perhaps partially induced by Rowe's reaction to the deterministic environment of the school run by Leslie Martin, of the totalitarian impositions of utopian urbanism. With the eclipse of the basic principles of freedom, despotic urbanism generates a geometrically rigid environment where variety is excluded, and differences are disregarded. As Rowe would write in the "Addendum 1973", written more or less at the time when *Collage City* was taking shape:

> *Utopia, because it implies a planned and hermetically sealed society, leads to suppression of diversity, intolerance, often to stasis presenting itself as change, and, ultimately, to violence. Or, more specifically: if Utopia proposes* the achievement of abstract goods *rather than* the eradication of concrete evils *then it is apt to be tyrannical: this since there can far more easily be consensus about concrete evils than there can be about abstract goods. Such is the Popperian message, which, supported as it is by a critique of determinism and a developed theory of the nature of investigation, remains hard to refute and which, very largely, continues to be ignored.*[67]

(cont.) their own sakes, without, consciously or unconsciously, seeking to fit them into, or exclude them from, one unchanging, all-embracing, sometimes self-contradictory and incomplete, at times fanatical, unitary inner vision. The first kind of intellectual and artistic personality belongs to the hedgehogs, the second to the foxes ...".

59 This conference in which a further analogous couple, talent and ideas, derives from hedgehog and fox, is available in two versions. Rowe, Colin, "Talent and ideas: A conference", *Lotus international* 62, 1989: 6-17; Idem, "Ideas, Talent, Poetics: A Problem of Manifesto", in Rowe (1996/2): 277-354.

60 Rowe and Koetter (1978): 86.

61 The relation between Rowe and Popper is treated in two recent essays: Kömez Dağlioğlu, Esin, "Karl Popper's Architectural Legacy: An Intertextual Reading of *Collage City*", *METU JFA (Middle East Technical University Journal of the Faculty of Architecture)*, 33 (1), 2016: 107-19, which by providing a revealing intertextual reading of Popper's and Rowe's essays dispenses me from a detailed illustration of similarities and derivations, and Deyong, Sarah, "Colin Rowe, Karl Popper and the Discipline of Architecture", *journal of visual culture* 15 (3), 2016: 372-76. For the relation between Gombrich and Popper: Gombrich, Ernst H., "Personal Recollections of the Publication of *The Open Society*", in Jarvie, Ian; Pralong, Sandra, eds., *Popper's Open Society After Fifty Years: The Continuing Relevance of Karl Popper*, Routledge, London and New York, 1999; later in Popper, Karl, *The Open Society and Its Enemies*, Routledge, London and New York, 2002: xvii-xxix.

Vardan Azatyan has described the cultural aspects of the intense friendship between Ernst Gombrich and Karl Popper, certainly influential in Rowe's thinking, and their indebtedness to Frederick Hayek: Azatyan, Vardan, "Ernst Gombrich's Politics of Art History: Exile, Cold War and *The Story of Art*", *Oxford Art Journal* 33 (2), 2010: 127-41.

62 Popper, Karl R., *The Open Society and Its Enemies*. [I. The Spell of Plato. – II. The High Tide of Prophecy: Hegel, Marx, and the Aftermath], Routledge & sons, London, 1945; Idem, *The Poverty of Historicism*, Routledge & Kegan Paul Ltd., London, (1944-45) 1957; Idem, *The Logic of Scientific Discovery*, Basic Books, New York, (1934) 1959; and the collection: Idem, *Conjectures and Refutations: The Growth of Scientific Knowledge*, Routledge & Kegan Paul Ltd., London, 1962.

63 Rowe, Colin, "The Architecture of Utopia", *Granta* LXIII (1187), Jan 24, 1959: 20-26, 41; Rowe (1976): 205-23.

64 Hurtt (1983): 55.

65 Rowe and Koetter (1978): 122.

66 Popper, Karl, "The Poverty of Historicism, II. A Criticism of Historicist Methods", *Economica*, New Series, 11 (43), Aug 1944: 122.

67 Rowe (1976): 215. (My emphases).

An unresolved question remains. Isn't facilitating collective goods by excluding individually generated disturbances, in fact, the original, statutory goal of urbanistics? The projected shortcomings of populisms, that Rowe and Koetter would highlight, are implicit in this circumstance.[68] Rowe's synthesis reads: "how to designate specific evil without at least *some* theory of general good?"[69] The closing of the "Addendum" anticipates the solution that *Collage City* would further stress:

> ...*it should only be said that* some *affirmation of a limited Utopia remains a psychological obligation. Utopia, in any developed form, in its post-enlightenment form, must surely be condemned as a monstrosity; but, while always a flagrant sociological or political nightmare, as* a reference *(present even in Popper), as* a heuristic device, *as* an imperfect image *of the good society, Utopia will persist—but should persist as possible* social metaphor *rather than probable* social prescription.[70]

This is the escape that we are offered by Rowe from the Popper-induced stalemate: a ploy that, although alluring, remains a mere *escamotage*. And this is a plausible reason why, I suspect, "Popper makes no distinction between utopia as metaphor and utopia as prescription".[71] Is this Utopia—an elected 'natural' repository of ideas of general goods—when taken as a "heuristic device" and as a "social metaphor", liberated from its tendency to seek its totalitarian, all-inclusive ambition and to impose universal laws and generalizations to a combination of multiple desires? Is it a generous offering, a prodigal allowance, or an imposing constriction? Is an *open* utopia believable? Open to all, that is, and not to the privileged few?

The answer to the question might be embodied in the asymmetrical nature of the inclinations of the fox and the hedgehog, since the former is allowed to include the latter but not vice versa. To use an example illustrated by Rowe and Koetter, a "stabilizer" has direct and easily perceivable geometries and an immediately sensed order, and it is well received in the plural realm of inclusion. Whereas, a single central vision, a coherent system, a universal all-inclusive ambition, is intolerant of contaminations, hard to defend by pure consensus, and therefore conceptually fragile. At the same time, as a point of principle, a plural attitude cannot afford to *eradicate* its contrary: not only is it welcoming by character, but also its construct relies on the presence of the *other*. In fact, a limited regularity—a number of partial, localized regularities—are germane components of a composite whole. Open vs. closed, flexible vs. rigid, soft vs. hard, understanding vs. resolute: isn't this a question of inclusion vs. exclusion? By default, a dialectic inclination cannot be but inclusive.

Serving the Devil

A 1944 letter by John Maynard Keynes to Friedrich August von Hayek—two champions of liberalism, the latter an early mentor of Popper—about Hayek's book *The Road to Serfdom*,[72] lends support to the fundamental question in dealing with liberalism and freedom: the difficulty of achieving an equilibrium between anarchy and despotism. The letter is a review of what is possibly Hayek's best-known book and the question of planning is one of the major issues raised, namely, where to draw the line between individual freedom and public control.

68 Rowe and Koetter (1978): 97-98.

69 Rowe (1976): 216.

70 Ibid.: 216. (My emphases).

71 Rowe and Koetter (1978): 123.

72 Keynes, John Maynard, "To Professor F. A. Hayek 28 June 1944", *The collected writings of John Maynard Keynes. Vol. 27: Activities 1940–1946, shaping the post-war world employment and commodities*, (Moggridge, Donald Edward, ed.), The Macmillan Press Ltd., Cambridge, UK, 1980: 385-88. Hayek, Friedrich A. von, *The Road to Serfdom*, University of Chicago Press, Chicago, 1944.

> *I come finally to what is really my only serious criticism of the book. You admit here and there that it is a question of knowing where to draw the line. You agree that the line has to be drawn somewhere, and that the logical extreme is not possible. But you give us no guidance whatever as to where to draw it. In a sense this is shirking the practical issue.*[73]

We know that Hayek strives for a minimum of planning while Keynes looks at "the middle course".[74] But Keynes' counter-proposal, seeking moderate planning, is not convincing either, based as it is on a commonly shared "moral position" and exactly because of the "important section [of people] who could almost be said to want planning not in order to enjoy its fruits but because morally they hold ideas exactly the opposite of [Hayek's], and wish to serve not God but the devil".[75]

The achievement of common goods, whether concrete or abstract, is a commendable goal, indeed. This applies to urbanistics as much as to any other field of communal life. In the reality of current urbanistics, some individual actions are encouraged or simply allowed, some are discouraged, most are prohibited by regulations. Making axiological distinctions between actively promoting goods (prescriptions) and inhibiting evils (proscriptions), as Popper proposes and Rowe endorses—just as separating a benign utopia as metaphor and a malignant one as prescription—seems a dangerous, although very common, rhetorical expedient.

At present, prohibition seems the most common currency, and despite some slogan consensus, the supporting rationales are frequently uncertain and the consequences often dire on both inhabitants and environments. Differential prohibition planning "to serve the devil" is a recurrent, although disguised rule of the game. And while the declared objective is always some form of public interest, it seems that the negative implications of arbitrary prohibitions are at least as severe as those of undue allowances. Thus, in the current climate of "rational liberalism", the fundamental question of Alexis de Tocqueville's "tyranny of the majority" remains applicable and unresolved.

One of the main problems of totalitarian democracy occurs where stronger constituencies—by numbers or by power—groups, associations, classes, castes who are "energetically supported" by some good or bad intentions—"feelings" in Mills's words—impose on others "their own opinions and inclinations". Relief might be found in the inclusive dialectic generated by some form of radical liberalism as argued for by Hastings. But confronted with the problem of the need for generating synergies, and avoiding the irreparable disruption of common goods by individual actions, we are left with the singular device of the redeeming power of planning, again as referred to by Hastings—the design dimension of planning, one is led to suppose—or direct design, as indicated by Rowe and Koetter.[76] Both propositions—we, as designers, must admit—are pleasing but overly vague.

The Boundaries of Freedom

The way the agenda of Townscape emerges in the writings of its protagonists is highly commendable. In fact, it is deeply rooted in the history of urban design and has been authoritatively and successfully carried forward up to the present

73 Keynes (1980): 386.

74 Ibid.: 386.

75 Ibid.: 387.

76 "For, surely, the job is that of making safe the city (and hence democracy) by large infusions of metaphor, analogical thinking, ambiguity; and, in the face of a prevailing scientism and conspicuous *laissez-aller*, it is just possible that these activities could provide the true *Survival Through Design*." Rowe and Koetter (1978): 117.

day. Yet since it is often a form of conditional and contained 'liberalism', it is not so radical after all. This is not just because it relies on arbitrary planning and design scenarios but because its pluralism seems to be limited to the realm of architectural design, the form of buildings and urban spaces, and it is resistant to variations in the realm of settlement typology. That's likely why *The Castles on the Ground*,[77] the 1946 book by James Maude Richards, one of the most representative editors of the *Review*, was bound to be "an apotheosis of English suburbia for which some have never forgiven him"[78] and a target of friendly fire; and why Richards himself felt the need to make multiple distinctions in the introduction to the second, 1973, edition of that book;[79] why "Outrage" and "Counter- attack", flag issues of the *Review* against the worst aspects of post-WWII planning, in their "prophecy of doom", anticipate the subsequent and present concerns about both "suburban sprawl" and the blur of "the distinction between places", and express a desire for "compactness", "towns", "villages", and "hamlets".[80] Ultimately, that is why the Townscape rhetoric and Gordon Cullen's captivating drawings forestall the mostly recent and current propaganda that compares suburbs that are ugly, monotonous, chaotic, to urban centers that are good looking, rich, diverse, and frequently old.

This is how Townscape's, and certainly Hastings's, rhetoric develops. The 1971 project for Civilia, possibly the last important contribution by Ivor de Wolfe, is a new manifesto echoing the "Townscape" article in some of its conceptual references. After more than twenty years, it is a "genuine high-density city" presented as "the end of the sub urban man".[81] Civilia is illustrated, in fact, through the pictures of a three-dimensional *collage city*, combining selected Modernist models, but its description is neither clear in its actual feasibility—due to the lack of two-dimensional plans—nor convincing in terms of overall aesthetic quality or habitability.

In fact, Townscape had provided a systematic and alluring support to the anti-suburban and anti-growth crusades. While based on a different mix of rationales than those of Townscape, these crusades had been passionately pursued for decades, starting with the reaction coming from the alliance of intellectuals and gentry opposed to the occupation of the countryside by the wave of the middle and working class in 1920s England. These objections would evolve into recurring aesthetic alarms and into the current environmentally-concerned talk often accompanied by a certain authoritarian tendency.[82] It is no wonder that these rather elitist positions seemed to find greater conceptual support in a regime of "enlightened autocratic control" than in one of "dull democracy" as claimed by Thomas Sharp who was another protagonist of Townscape in the early thirties.[83]

Rather than offering, or at least looking for, good-design tools applicable to the new forms of settlement emerging during the post-WWII years and multiplied today, these conservative positions appear to have harbored a prejudicial conviction that a positive response to that design challenge was either impossible or unsuitable. The shortcomings of their nostalgia for the past is not in their appreciation for well-tested and successful models. It is rather in their *a priori* exclusion of any positive alternative or complementary model which seems yet another form of the hedgehog syndrome: while multiplicity is accepted and promoted at the building scale, it is refused and demonized at the settlement scale.

77 Richards, J[ames] M[aude], *The Castles on the Ground: The Anatomy of Suburbia*, The Architectural Press, London, 1946.

78 Banham, Reyner, "Revenge of the Picturesque: English Architectural Polemics, 1945-1965", in Summerson, John, ed., *Concerning Architecture: Essays on Architectural Writers and Writing Presented to Nikolaus Pevsner*, Allen Lane, London, 1968: 265.

79 Richards, J[ames] M[aude], "Introduction: 1973. The more things change...", in *The Castles on the Ground: The Anatomy of Suburbia*, John Murrary, London, 1973.

80 Nairn, Ian, ed., "Outrage", *The Architectural Review* CXVII (702), Jun 1955: 365; and Idem, "Counter-Attack", *The Architectural Review* CXX (719), Dec 1956: 355.

81 De Wolfe, Ivor, "Towards a Philosophy of the Environment", *The Architectural Review* CXLIX (892), "Civilia: The End of Sub Urban Man", Jun 1971: 327-34; de Wolfe, Ivor, ed., *Civilia: The End of Sub Urban Man: a Challenge to Semidetsia*, The Architectural Press, London, 1971.

82 Bruegmann, Robert, "The diagnosis: Three campaigns against sprawl", in *Sprawl: A Compact History*, The University of Chicago Press, Chicago and London, 2005: 113-66.

83 Sharp, Thomas, *Town and Countryside: Some Aspects of Urban and Rural Development*, Oxford University Press, London, 1932: 217-19, 224; Erten, Erdem, "Thomas Sharp's collaboration with H. de C. Hastings: the formulation of townscape as urban design pedagogy", *Planning Perspectives* 24 (1), Jan 2009: 29-49.

In this context, Rowe's mentioning "a good American suburb adjacent to a very concentrated Italian town" as offering the possibility of having the best of both worlds is the basis for a liberal revolution. Rowe's statement implies that "good suburb" is a possible, legitimate category and a postulate for a post-Fordist urbanistics. This is such an outstanding statement to provoke passionate reactions such as the one proposed by Monica Centanni which can be taken to represent a widely shared feeling among urban design insiders: "The refined scholar's elegant and brilliant lightness however leads towards the drift of *reactionary* indifference and risks the theory of a plan for a fractured world, articulated on *non-modular dichotomies*."[84]

"Non-modular" translates "*incomponibili*" in the Italian original which means incompatible, unable to be composed together. The analogy with what I mentioned above regarding the asymmetrical nature of the inclinations of the fox and the hedgehog is evident: while a world accepting 'good suburbs' is able to welcome and actually needs 'compact towns', the current, ideal, exclusive world of 'compact towns' rejects any other settlement type, as if compact town and suburb are necessarily either/or, mutually exclusive: a proposition in which one is good, the other is bad. Isn't it at least a peculiar conceptual overturn that commonly in the contemporary political and disciplinary discourse composing the two settlement types in a both/and, dialectic, liberal manner as Rowe suggests, is considered "reactionary"?

If we accept that Robert Stern has succeeded, hands down, in proving that plenty of good—American and not only American—suburbs have been, and therefore are in fact, possible,[85] what if hyper-city, arcadia and intermediate types can all be good and compoundable? What if it is just a question of good design, to use Rowe's argument? Banning any of them on the basis of presumed inherent malignant features is not only an aesthetic deprivation but, I would argue, a form of *unsustainable* social exclusion due to the proven economic rent-generating effects of prohibition policies:[86] those which select growth-curbing (proscription) over growth-guiding (prescriptions) tools. And while attributing to Rowe a development of his thought such as this would be a mystification, when I associate his referring to the inclusive dialectic of concentrated town and good suburb with the long list of liberal thinkers in his reading list, I recognize an implicit, fundamental urban design legacy.

It is hard to believe that Rowe's deployment of authoritative liberal thinkers was merely meant to legitimize a stylistic *pastiche*. Rather, it seems to suggest his openness to a multiplicity of design generators and to a plurality of methodological perspectives and reminds me of his predilection for a collage of micro-utopias over the Procrustes, abstract, one-type-fits-all choices of urban form that dominate our contemporary debate.

Thus, for example, having to deal with good and pluralist, designed suburbs—the "good American suburbs"—how should we interpret Rowe's 1997 "modest proposal for a new sub-urbanism"?[87] He proposed an eclectic multiplication of compact and cozy hill-towns—and one must assume each to be a masterfully

84 Centanni (2010): 228. (My italics).

85 Stern, Robert A. M.; Fishman, David; Tilove, Jacob, *Paradise Planned: The Garden Suburb and the Modern City*, Monacelli Press, New York, 2013.

86 During the most recent years, literature proving that planning restricting growth generates economic rent, aggravates the affordability crises, and is by far the most important factor in social inequalities is substantial. Among the most significant contributions: Gyourko, Joseph; Molloy, Raven, "Regulation and Housing Supply", in Duranton, Gilles; Henderson, J. Vernon; Strange, William C., eds., *Handbook of Regional and Urban Economics* 5, Elsevier, Amsterdam, 2015: 1289-337; Ikeda, Sanford; Washington, Emily, "How Land-Use Regulation Undermines Affordable Housing", Mercatus Center at George Mason University, Nov 2015; Rognlie, Matthew, "Deciphering the Fall and Rise in the Net Capital Share: Accumulation or Scarcity?", *Brookings Papers on Economic Activity*, 2015: 1-6; Moroni, Stefano, "Interventionist responsibilities for the emergence of the US housing bubble and the economic crisis: 'neoliberal deregulation' is not the issue", *European Planning Studies*, Apr 6, 2016; Romem, Issi, "Paying For Dirt: Where Have Home Values Detached From Construction Costs?", *Buildzoom*, October 17, 2017. [https://www.buildzoom.com/blog/paying-for-dirt-where-have-home-values-detached-from-construction-costs]; Glaeser, Edward; Gyourko, Joseph, "The Economic Implications of Housing Supply", *The Journal of Economic Perspectives* 32 (1), 2018: 3-30; Hsieh, Chang-Tai; Moretti, Enrico, "Housing Constraints and Spatial Misallocation", May 7, 2018, [https://faculty.chicagobooth.edu/chang-tai.hsieh/research/growth.pdf].

87 Rowe, Colin, "A Modest Proposal for a New Sub-Urbanism", *Harvard Design Magazine* 1, Win/Spr 1997: 64-67.

designed projection of a Calvino-esque "invisible city". However, rather than Rowe winking at the idea of a deck of cards or a palette—a number of masterfully designed options—from which to pick, this seems a friendly if ironic challenge to the narrow-minded rhetoric of the omnipotent contemporary policies. For, if Rowe's disgust with "the remorseless suburban landscapes of the present day"[88] must be genuine and more than justified, I am inclined to see the alternative strategy—"... a constellation of minitowns, apprehensible as distinct communities, adjacent but not contiguous, gridded but not completely identical in plan ..."[89]—as a generously inflected and quick-witted reminder of the 1729 Dr. Jonathan Swift's *Modest Proposal* pamphlet.[90]

The constellation of minitowns is conceptually amusing and able to pretend both a *laissez-aller* approach and the exercise of the libido but oblivious of the experienced complex realities of our metropolitan settings: in fact, "rather textbook". So, the legacy that ultimately remains is Rowe's equally candid preference for "modest rather than heroic, intellectually vacant rather than throbbing with the protesting integrity of blind conviction"[91] choices over the "violence of ideological collision".[92]

The Present Urban Design Predicament

Townscape and Rowe share a positive predilection for a world made of harmonious variety: a regulated freedom, a sort of projection in urban forms of Leibniz' *diversitas identitate compensata*—harmony as variety compensated by identity—as highlighted by Rosario Assunto.[93] This has been a recurring aesthetic value in urban design at least since Leon Battista Alberti and enlisting Picturesque landscape architecture, Marc-Antoine Laugier, romantic eclecticism, medievalism, Raymond Unwin, and all the contextual inclinations of the Modern Reform since the post-WWII years.[94] It is the celebration of the composition of a multiplicity—according to the diversity of people, *pro hominum varietate*[95]—and the rejection of the uniformity of one solution that is presumed good for all.

The New Urbanism movement (NU), possibly the most important event in the history of urban design since the late 20th century, seems to develop along these lines, at least in some respects. Neal Payton has explored its multifaceted debt to Rowe's legacy in this volume. It is in large part the positive development of the application of the values of evolutionary design, of harmony and of post-Fordist variety to the basic principles of the project of modernity. This is not limited to the guided diversity induced and enhanced by form-based codes, at least in their original, aesthetic-focused spirit. One of New Urbanism's major cultural and disciplinary products, the "transect", is evidence of a liberal, plural, mindful awareness.[96] It is analogous to the wild-to-metropolis sequence of the Townscape tradition as well as of the previous Patrick Geddes' "valley section", and somehow of the 1954 Team 10's Doorn manifesto and of Ian McHarg's *Design with Nature*.[97] It shows an active awareness of the multiple natures of human settlements from rural to urban core, each legitimate and consistently organized around its specific rules. Thus, the liberal, inclusive design attitude applied to the realm of diverse and harmonious building styles, in the programmatic underpinnings of New Urbanism extends to urban types as well!

88 Ibid.: 65.

89 Ibid.: 67.

90 Swift, [Jonathan], *A Modest Proposal for preventing the Children of Poor People From being a Burden on Their Parents or Country, And for making them Beneficial to the Publick*, S. Harding, Dublin, 1729. I am grateful to Jim Tice for providing this insight.

91 Rowe (1997): 67.

92 Rowe (2016): 73.

93 Piro, Francesco, *Varietas identitate compensata. Studio sulla formazione della metafisica di Leibniz*, Bibliopolis, Napoli, 1990; Assunto, Rosario, "Alla ricerca della teoresi perduta", in *La Città di Anfione e la Città di Prometeo: Idea e poetiche della città*, Editoriale Jaca Book, Milano, (1983) 1997: 73-89.

94 Laugier, Marc-Antoine, "Of the embellishment of cities", in *An Essay on the Study and Practice of Architecture...*, Stanley Crowder and Henry Woodgate, London, (1753) 1756: 234-57; Unwin, Raymond, "Of Buildings, and how the Variety of Each Must Be Dominated by the Harmony of the Whole", in *Town Planning in Practice: An Introduction to the Art of Designing Cities and Suburbs*, T. Fisher Unwin Ltd., [reprinted by Princeton Architectural Press, New York, 1994]: 360-74.

95 Assunto (1997): 80.

96 Duany, Andrés, "Introduction to the Special Issue: The Transect", *Journal of Urban Design* 7 (3), 2002: 251-60; Talen, Emily, "Help for Urban Planning: The Transect Strategy", *Journal of Urban Design* 7 (3), 2002: 303-07; Duany, Andrés; Brain, David, "Regulating as If Humans Matter: The Transect and Post-Suburban Planning", in Ben-Joseph, Eran, ed., *The Code of the City: Standards and the Hidden Language of Place-Making*, MIT Press, Cambridge, MA, and London, 2005: 293-332.

97 Nairn (1956): 356; Geddes, Patrick, "The valley section from hills to sea", (lecture given to the New School of Social Research, New York, 1923), in Tyrwhitt, Jaqueline, "Introduction", in Geddes, Patrick, *Cities in Evolution*, Oxford University Press, New York, 1950: xv-xxviii; Geddes, Patrick, "The Valley Section (or Profile)", in Geddes (1910) 1950: 163-67; Smithson, Alison, ed., *The Emergence of Team 10 out of CIAM*, AAGS Theory and History Papers, 1, London, 1982: 33-34, 38-41; Vv. Aa., "Doorn Manifesto", (CIAM Meeting 29-31 January, 1954), in Ockman, Joan, *Architecture Culture 1943–1968: A Documentary Anthology*, Columbia Books of Architecture, Rizzoli, New York, 1993: 181-83; McHarg, Ian, *Design with Nature*, The Natural History Press, Garden City, NY, 1969.

As Andrés Duany and Emily Talen explain in one of the foundation documents of the proposed system: "No desire for a particular type of development is categorically 'wrong'; it is just in the wrong Transect location".[98] Since transect zones are not bound to be composed in rigid sequence, this is in fact an urban-rural collage, relying on a masterful internal coherence. Then, to make the inclusive and liberal awareness of their position clear—sensitive to the multiplicity of contexts and regions, one would assume—they confirm: "there is no *one* transect—there are in fact many transects, each specific to local building traditions and a variety of other locally derived nuances of urban form".[99] Doesn't this qualify as the optimal basis for a much-needed update of Rowe and Koetter's *collage city* at the regional scale?

However, the higher the expectations, the more painful the disillusion. Despite New Urbanism's numerous attempts to reject a cookie-cutter drift at the architectural scale, which must be recognized, praised and encouraged, both a deeper reading of this Duany-Talen text and of some of the other original descriptions of the transect, along with the mounting discursive activities, suggest an uncertain attitude towards the regional scale. Disenchantment occurs because T3s, the lower-density and, contrary to sprawl, orderly and designed "Sub-Urban" zones, with their codes meant to generate "*good* American suburbs", seem limited in scope and recognition to be just marginal infills. While their description appears open to multiple interpretations, when projected on many actual urban fringe conditions where the distinction between infill and greenfield is blurred—a great pretext for prohibition—it is clearly stated that low-density interventions require a large minimum acreage.[100] On one hand, this implies the amassing and use of large areas of pristine land. On the other, it excludes *de facto* multiple and direct interventions, gives to large developers the monopoly of residential production while banning the possibility of a short production chain, and interdicts the implementation of healthy lean-urbanism principles and procedures where they are most needed: in the existing diffused city.

Any possibility of positively dealing with the complexity of the actual form of contemporary metropolitan areas in their fine-grained components is actually denied. Why is this large acreage demanded? Aren't morphological regulations sufficient tools to guarantee coherence in a small-parceled and heterogeneous setting? At this point a New Urbanist discourse increasingly maintaining that T3 zones are, in fact, not sustainable, regardless of their design quality, does not surprise.

The New Urbanist position that gradually emerges is rather equivocal in its development. While originally, policies that *allow for* and *encourage* "traditional"—i.e. compact—developments in an otherwise "suburban nation", enabling plural and inclusive scenarios, were claimed, more recently and with growing resoluteness, policies that *proscribe* anything but a vague compact, mixed-use, walkable world, regardless of specificities, are required. What was once a fox-inclined, liberal disposition is gradually morphing into a hedgehog-driven, control maniacal drift.

It is unfortunate that possibly the most revolutionary insight of urbanistics in the last several decades is being crippled by such a bias. And to avoid any misunderstandings, this prejudice is not regrettable because it seems to imply a preference for the model of the walled city, originated at the dawn of the second

98 Duany, Andrés; Talen, Emily, "Making the Good Easy: The Smart Code Alternative", *Fordham Urban Law Journal* 29 (4), 2002: 1454.

99 Duany, Andrés; Talen, Emily, "Transect Planning", *Journal of the American Planning Association* 68 (3), Sum 2002: 256.

100 Duany and Talen, "Making the Good Easy", (2002): 1463.

millennium, over the model of the sometimes green-belted garden city invented at the sunset of the same millennium. It is untimely because it is oblivious to the circumstance that, despite all their unmatched allure, neither the precedent of the "very concentrated Italian town" nor that of the "good American suburb", while both remaining extraordinary models, offer sufficient guidance for the challenges of the current millennium.

—

Then, if turning to the declared antagonist party: the alternative, less structured and yet promising Landscape Urbanism (LU), one finds no relief, for both NU and LU, despite their opposite interpretations of the *status quo* and their antipodal appearance, are analogously competing for the same well-intentioned but conservative, slightly reactionary and despotic goal of binding a concentration of resources, attention, and opportunities in areas that have plenty of attention and resources and are given the monopoly of opportunities, while disregarding and depriving of significant chances to the *sub*-ordinate, leftover, and marginal areas.

Landscape Urbanism, while able to detect the necessary realms of urban design engagement, including those beyond the ideal and often administrative walls of the supposedly contained city, has for long remained focused on a learned and esoteric filling-in of residual areas or in the decorative upgrade of the image of well-consolidated urban realities. Charles Waldheim, founder of the movement, "saw Landscape Urbanism, like landscape architecture, as an interstitial design discipline, operating in the spaces between buildings, infrastructural systems, and natural ecologies".[101] With a similar attitude, James Corner focuses on processes of "unbuilding, removal and erasure"[102] and if his attempt of dialectically combining urbanism and landscape induces a moderate excitement, the promise of a replacement, rather than an integration, of "aesthetic" by "ecology" is rather depressing and raises some legitimate suspicions.[103] Because if Olmsted's Riverside is just one of the many and diverse combinations of the urbanism/landscape dialectic, excluding such "exemplar from which to depart" from our conceptual horizon—if only as primitive models from which to evolve and adapt to the actual reality of dispersal—is an unforgivable conceptual waste. Yet, in the most promising product of the recent debate, finally dealing with the *Infinite Suburbia* of the immediate present, Alan Berger envisions a destiny of "wastebelt", "wastewater" areas, "energybelts", "wetbelts", "drossbelts" for the "not-so-smart greenbelt" and suggests that "both existing form-based codes and zoning that privileges the building of objects over designing for dynamic ecological processes are diminished".[104]

And since this vision of a *de facto* lesser future for the *extra moenia* is increasingly echoed by a large part of the current urban design discourse, a center-centric bias, no matter if one or many centers, excludes the possibility of exploring all typological options and expanding our potential to design the unprecedented, multiple forms of the contemporary open city. As a consequence, either the city increasingly becomes a high-class commodity, where "draconian planning regimes"[105] are imposed and growth is obstructed, or growth happens regardless, without any design guidance.

101 Shane, Grahame, "The Emergence of 'Landscape Urbanism': *Reflections on* Stalking Detroit", *Harvard Design Magazine* 19, Fall 2003/Win 2004: 4; Waldheim, Charles, "Landscape as Urbanism", in *The Landscape Urbanism Reader*, Princeton Architectural Press, New York, 2006: 35-53.

102 Shane (2003–04): 5.

103 Corner, James, "Terra Fluxus", in Waldheim (2006): 24.

104 Berger, Alan M., "Belting Future Suburbia", in Berger, Alan M.; Kotkin, Joel; Balderas Guzmán, Celina, eds., *Infinite Suburbia*, Princeton Architectural Press, New York, 2017: 541.

105 Berger, Alan M.; Kotkin, Joel; Balderas Guzmán, Celina, "Introduction", in Berger et al. (2017): 10.

In the meantime, in many of the insiders' yearnings, the promising collage city of inclusion is replaced by a unified model: one of exclusion from both a typological and a social point of view. Despite its stylistic eclecticism, this upcoming model is conceptually analogous to the city imagined by the naive functionalism of the early Modern Movement. While the latter's rhetoric concentrated on a mechanical program and narrow-minded disregard of both the more complex system of human needs and desires and the relevance of different contexts, the current unified propaganda often concentrates on a rather simplified and internationalized environmental agenda in which human beings are programmatically marginal.[106] Emerging and non-conforming settlement types, the spontaneous and disorderly *pavillionaire,* and the incoherent and episodic metropolitan fringe are psychologically repressed. The consequence is not only a persistent disciplinary inability to guide the current regional dynamics but also the 'protection' of the current state of crisis and the prohibition of any form of regeneration and densification. While the problem of the 'whole' could be finally overcome, from a stylistic point of view, by a *harmony-variety balance* facilitated by a growing appreciation of form-based coding, it reemerges because of the deliberate exclusion of the out-of-growth-boundary "middle landscape",[107] which is neither certified compact city nor pure farmland.

Neoliberal Urban Design

> *The idea of Non-Plan never went away. It continued as a kind of underground river. Recently, it has resurfaced. Is this because we are once again surrounded by people who think that planning is the answer to everything and who believe that they alone know the way we should all live?* [108]

This question might well apply to the present urban predicament. It appears in Paul Barker's 2000 introduction to a republished 1969 text proposing an "experiment on freedom" that he had written together with Reyner Banham, Peter Hall, and Cedric Price.[109] It was valid both in 1969 and in 2000; certainly not isolated in its impatience with the impositions of planning if one thinks of the multiple variations of this attitude provided by Guy Debord, Robert Goodman, Henri Lefebvre, or Turner and Fichter, and, most recently, Marco Romano, among many,[110] and it is certainly still applicable to the present condition.

While some important current trends, just like the Modern Movement orthodoxy, seem overly seduced by the allure of a substantial total planning-design combination, some other equally energetic and controversial tendencies have developed under the standard of neoliberalism: the total non-design as celebrations of self-organizing complexities. And if to support action, complexity is a concept on which both Landscape Urbanists and New Urbanists look with some justified insistence, either as background or as a cherished goal, for others a similar awareness of complexity seems a sufficient justification for a rhetoric of abstention.

A special interpretation of Rowe's legacy combined with the tradition of Non-Plan and supported by Hayek's free-market economics has generated original and rather tantalizing theoretical results. But despite the soundness of all its conceptual provisions, significant doubts remain regarding the field of application

106 For an *ante-litteram* critique of the current "environmental crisis" talks, one should re-read the precious, evergreen *incipit* to Rowe, Colin; Koetter, Fred, "Collage City", *The Architectural Review* CLVIII (942), Aug 1975: 66, partially reported below.

107 Rowe, Peter G., *Making a Middle Landscape*, MIT Press, Cambridge, MA, 1991.

108 Barker, Paul, "Thinking the Unthinkable", in Hughes, Jonathan; Sadler, Simon, eds., *Non-Plan: Essays on Freedom Participation and Change in Modern Architecture and Urbanism*, Architectural Press, Routledge, London and New York, 2000: 6.

109 Banham, Reyner; Barker, Paul; Hall, Peter; Price, Cedric, "Non-Plan: An experiment in freedom", *New Society* 13 (338), 20 Mar 1969: 435-43.

110 Debord, Guy, *The Society of the Spectacle*, Bureau of Public Secrets, Berkeley, CA, (1967), 2014; Sadler, Simon, *The Situationist City*, MIT Press, Cambridge, MA, and London, 1998; Schrijver, Lara, "Utopia and/or Spectacle? Rethinking Urban Interventions Through the Legacy of Modernism and the Situationist City", *Architectural Theory Review* 16 (3), "The Right to the City", 2011: 245-58; Goodman, Robert, *After the Planners*, Simon and Schuster, New York, 1972; Turner, John F. C.; Fichter, Robert, *Freedom to Build: Dweller Control of the Housing Process*, Macmillan, New York, 1972; Lefebvre, Henry, *The Production of Space*, Blackwell, Oxford and Cambridge, (1974) 1991; Romano, Marco, *Liberi di costruire*, Bollati Boringhieri, Torino, 2013.

of this 'liberal' attitude, and on the fundamental question of how liberal—i.e. plural, inclusive, open, catholic—neoliberalism is.

In his analysis of the projections of neoliberalism on architecture, Douglas Spencer has indicated its major tools—"folding, complexity or parametricism"[111] among them—, conceptual components, and underlying rationales:

> *Among the fundamental truths that neoliberal thought has constructed are those that state that individuals can achieve only a narrow and very limited knowledge of the real complexities of the world; that the planning of society by individuals is, consequently, an untenable proposition; that the economic market is better able to calculate, process and spontaneously order society than the state is able to; that the competition between individuals facilitated by equality of access to the market is a natural state of affairs; that the job of the state is to intervene to ensure the conditions of possibility that sustain the operation of the market and to ensure that individuals are rendered adaptable and responsive to these conditions; that its truths are a guarantee of liberty.*[112]

The recognition of the complex nature of the world is a diagnosis difficult to dismiss, optimal antidote against simplistic prescriptions. It is certainly older than Hayek, whom this recent wave of designers often refers to, than the 1938 Colloque Walter Lippmann and the 1947 Mont Pelerin Society. And while Hayek masterfully supports his argument with the evidence of complexity and the promise of spontaneous order, and offers a very topical warning against the effects of an enduring pseudo-science, the implications of complexity go back to the fundamental insights of Jules Henry Poincaré and therefore the whole thing is not just an *affair* depending on economics. And, to different degrees, this has certainly long affected architecture.[113] However, the question of how to deal with complexity from a design-planning point of view remains unresolved. For if it is evident that looking for and imposing total solutions is a risible and at the same time gloomy pretension, the contrary idea of a complete dismissal becomes similarly totalitarian and unrealistic.

To begin with, the arena of this liberal attitude should be clarified because, while the dispute on the architectural *how* is a congenial battlefield for the current epiphenomenal debate, the discussion on the urbanistic *where* is rather contradictory, episodic or hesitant. Barker's conceptual development is significant in this direction. In his 2000 commentary he specifies: "Non-Plan, however, was never against some kinds of negative planning (for example: this land shall not be built on); the trouble, so often, lay—and lies—with would-be positive planning." [114]

Here is an interesting analogy with the Popper-Rowe distinction mentioned above and, despite first intuition, also in this case, the different attitude towards positive and negative planning, although widely shared in the disciplinary discourse, is not convincing at all and it is actually rather concerning. This is because in current urbanistics the "eradication of concrete evils" that is supposed to justify negative planning—one would dare to simplify as zoning—embodies the 'structural' issue of the attribution/denial of development rights. And although this is often hidden behind a veneer of ecological concern, in many cases the proscription "this land shall not be built on" in fact doesn't defend land that is actually dedicated to agriculture, pristine nature or beautiful landscapes but protects a

111 Spencer, Douglas, *The architecture of neoliberalism: how contemporary architecture became an instrument of control and compliance*, Bloomsbury Academic, New York, 2016: xiii.

112 Ibid.: 2.

113 Alexander, Christopher, "A City is Not a Tree", *Architectural Forum* 122 (1), Apr 1965: 58-61; Venturi, Robert, *Complexity and Contradiction in Architecture*, Museum of Modern Art, Doubleday, Garden City, NY, 1966; Kroll, Lucien, *The Architecture of Complexity*, Batsford, London, 1986; Jencks, Charles, *The Architecture of the Jumping Universe: A Polemic: How Complexity Science Is Changing Architecture and Culture*, Academy Editions, London, 1995. Also, Gell-Mann, Murray, *The Quark and the Jaguar: Adventures in the Simple and in the Complex*, W.H. Freeman & Company, New York, 1994; Taylor, Mark C., *The Moment of Complexity: Emerging Network Culture*, University of Chicago Press, Chicago, 2001.

114 Barker (2000): 7.

less noble *status quo*—often land that has already been partially built on—and a network of differential privileges, "to serve the devil".

At the same time, the "achievement of abstract goods" that is often questioned together with its support of positive planning—I think of rules of form—has to do with the 'minor' issue of the morphological quality of the places in which we live and its impact on human wellbeing and happiness. Here is again the question of the boundaries of freedom. For mainstream and most official urbanistics, designers should be allowed to fiddle with the aesthetics of buildings (the 'how') as long as they don't threaten the system of generation and distribution of economic rent (the 'where').

Meanwhile, the tendency to protect the prerogatives of centers against any alternative scenario has been rock solid for a long time. In fact, the defense of the uniqueness of the 'very concentrated town' vs. the contamination by the 'suburb', however 'good', is only one variation of it. If one is allowed to go back to the architect and urbanist by far most referred to by Rowe, in his Plan Voisin, studied by Cohen and Hurtt in their often-mentioned and seldom-read thesis partly published in this volume, Le Corbusier would erase and replace most of the very center of Paris with the revolutionary forms of his *ville contemporaine* instead of building it somewhere else, also in consideration of the need to protect the "immense" real estate values involved and the opportunity to inflate them.[115] So, the matter was and is not just center against peripheral suburb; it was and is center, metropolitan center, rather than compact town, against any possible alternative or substantial competition. The analogy with the hardly-liberal current urban planning business seems rather evident to me.

Then, it is significant that Peter Hall, promoter with Barker of the Non-Plan initiative mentioned above, after a few years from that publication, would write a landmark text on the social implications of urban containment policies: a prescient critique of the contemporary growth-management strategies.[116]

Nonetheless, acknowledging that 'unlimited' space is an ideal as anthropologically relevant and worth consideration as the 'enclosed' space of the higher Western tradition, as Banham, another of the authors of "Non-Plan" in that same period, was describing,[117] does not imply that we are exempted from the responsibility for some form of design guidance and some synergic accord other than urban growth boundaries.

—

The recent tradition of neoliberalism applied to the management of human habitats seems either to concentrate on apparently free architectural forms or to assign an often modest and contained right to develop to the episodic interaction between administrations and powerful real estate entrepreneurs. The latter case is *en vogue* since the mid-1980s at least, but despite being labeled as neoliberal urbanistics, it is actually relying on a differential deregulation that is limited to selected areas in an otherwise starched *milieu* of prohibition policies: an often authoritarian, discretionary, and uneven economic-rent-generating attribution of rationed and concentrated development rights.

115 Le Corbusier, *The City of To-morrow and its Planning*, Dover Publications Inc., New York, (1929) 1987: 294-95. Marco Romano has highlighted Le Corbusier's dedication of his *Ville Radieuse* plan to "l'Autorité". To be true, a few years before, 1915, in his *Sulla conservazione della bellezza di Roma e sullo sviluppo della città moderna*, Marcello Piacentini was proposing for Rome: "Let the old city be the way it is, let's build the new city somewhere else". Neither propositions were actually implemented except for excellent episodes as Rome's EUR. Also, Townscape's "Civilia", mentioned *supra*, was planned as a high-density city, placed in a well-connected brownfield in the English Midlands.

116 Hall, Peter, *The Containment of Urban England*, Allen and Unwin, London, 1973; Idem, "The Containment of Urban England", *The Geographic Journal* 140 (3), Oct 1974: 386-408.

117 Banham, Reyner, "Environmental management", in *The architecture of the well-tempered environment*, The Architectural Press, London, and The University of Chicago Press, Chicago, 1969: 18-28.

In both cases of pseudo-freedom applied to architectural form and urban planning, a meta-authorial, computer-generated *Reklamearchitektur* might well work as the appropriate tool for our current, deceiving marketing culture. Thus, while neoliberalism in its current embodiment does not seem actually liberal from the point of view of the structural allocation of resources and of the production of a typologically and socially inclusive multiplicity, it is not so liberal after all, from either a methodological or stylistic point of view.

When contemporary architecture "grounds its own principles and practices" upon "spontaneous orders, self-organization, complexity and cybernetics"[118] not only is it not free in its design decisions strictly speaking, which may be a good thing, but it also limits the targeted realm of freedom to an interstitial symbolism often relying on a veneer of futurist high-tech. As is revealed in an interview between Peter Eisenman and Patrick Schumacher,[119] while the recognition of human settlements as complex adaptive systems is a necessary background and the interpenetration of spatial orders "picked up from Colin Rowe"[120] is an effective analytical and generative conceptual tool, neither the question of the position of the authorial presence in the decision process nor the parametric simplification of that complexity are convincingly 'free': it seems that freedom of individualism and freedom of populism, as described by Rowe and Koetter,[121] are replaced by an esoteric form of stochastic fortuity that is, in fact, largely predetermined. As Schumacher makes clear elsewhere, parametric design looks at "reestablishing *strong urban orders and identities* on the basis of its adaptive and evolutionary heuristics".[122] Here, Rowe and Koetter's Popperian prophecy applied to Superstudio's apparently 'natural' but in fact totalizing, hypertech work, could perhaps use a replica: "And what to say about this? That such poetry may seduce but can seldom convince: that insistence upon total freedom is to deny the small approximate freedoms which are all that, historically, have been available and are probably all that we can ever anticipate?"[123]

And while the idea of a "radical free-market urbanism that doesn't produce the current garbage spill of deregulated urban development"[124] is an especially captivating goal, its production is hardly direct or automatic: it is rather naively conditional, in fact: "So I'd love to promote a radical free-market urbanism, but that would only work if all the architects who are hired also bring their versatile engagement with market contingencies in under the spell of parametricism's methodology."[125]

Schumacher's insight of "a hegemonic style ... that is able to deliver a legible order via local rules without imposing an overarching global order"[126] seems worth more than a simple reflection. One is stimulated to wonder what the aesthetic nature of that style might be. Is it the outcome of a perishable high-tech flaunting digital omnipotence or is it a free-collage, citizen-driven style as, for instance, in MVRDV's Almere-Oosterwold? And while the latter proposition allows for a moderate, yet uncommon enthusiasm in a *milieu* of despotic inclinations and urban boundaries, doesn't it confirm the need for some aesthetic guidance and encouraged synergy, nevertheless?[127] Because if it is true that the anonymous architecture chosen as a model by our Reformist tradition was an efficacious remedy against the repressive stiffness of the International Style, one does not need an in-depth study to verify the desolation caused by our global, location restricted, and morphologically free-wheeling contemporary settlements.

118 Spencer (2016): xiii, 40.

119 Schumacher, Patrik, "I am trying to imagine a radical free-market urbanism", (interviewed by Eisenman, Peter), *Log* 28, Sum 2013: 39-52.

120 Ibid.: 49; Lynn, Greg, "New variations in the Rowe Complex", *ANY* 7/8, 1994: 38-43, later in Idem, *folds, bodies and blobs: collected essays*, La Lettre Volée, [Bruxelles], 1998: 199-236; Petit, Emmanuel, "Spherical Penetrability: Literal and Phenomenal", *Log* 31, Spr/Sum 2014: 31-39; Giamarelos, Stylianos, "Calling Rowe: After-lives of Formalism in the Digital Age", *Footprint* 22, "Exploring Architectural Form: A Configurative Triad", Spr/Sum 2018: 89-102.

121 Rowe and Koetter (1978): 97-99.

122 Schumacher, Patrik, "Free-Market Urbanism. Urbanism beyond Planning", in Verebes, Tom, ed., *Masterplanning the Adaptive City: Computational Urbanism in the Twenty-First Century*, Routledge, London and New York, 2014: 118. (My italics).

123 Rowe and Koetter (1978): 47.

124 Schumacher (2013): 50.

125 Ibid.: 51.

126 Schumacher (2014): 119.

127 Van Straalen, Fennie M.; Witte, Patrick; Buitelaar, Edwin, "Self-Organisation in Oosterwold, Almere: Challenges with Public Goods and Externalities", *Tijdschrift voor Economische en Sociale Geografie* 108 (4), 2017: 503-11.

With limited exceptions, one has to believe that as Spencer has argued, during the last several decades, the neoliberal, free market attitude is making architecture "an instrument of control and compliance".[128] The uneven configuration of democracy, with its recurrent tyrannical political majorities, is replaced by the subtle despotism of the unequal power of market forces. The involuntary synergies of "total design and total non-design both equally total",[129] although differently shaped than in Rowe's panorama, are still present, conceptually flawed, and increasingly worrisome.

—

The current urban design discourse would do well to be equally interested in a multitudinous wealth of settlement possibilities, both experienced and potential, including but not limited to the "Italian very concentrated town" and the "good American suburb", and look for settlement rules that are flexible, able to maximize their necessary synergies and, yes, their aesthetic quality. The attendance to an "infinite suburbia" inclusive of a conflation of "hard-boiled eggs", "fried eggs", and "scrambled eggs", to use the effective metaphor proposed by Cedric Price, another author of the "Non-Plan" article, and revived by Grahame Shane,[130] is likely to be, with any luck, the major challenge of the next several decades.

Suburbia in its twofold 'fried' and 'scrambled' appearances should not be any longer regarded as an inferior, illegitimate, misplaced city—and I would add, no longer be 'protected' as it is. Rather, *especially in its scrambled form*, it could be a valid alternative field for those processes of densification that are presently spoiling other neighborhoods, often full of decor. Extrapolating Marco Romano's compelling argument, up zoning, while allowing for additions on existing buildings or their replacement with larger ones, is "in fact conceived to consolidate the privilege of those who already own a home".[131]

In order to adequately explore this concept, as Sébastien Marot has proposed—and exactly because Marot's insight that "[t]he century of expanding cities has passed" if far from being either true or desirable—one might undergo a process of Rowe-inspired phenomenal-transparency: a deep, multi-layered reading, conscious of the complexity of the case, with "Aristotelian balance".[132] And if indeed "the allied Design and Planning fields need a new intellectual framework",[133] infinite suburbia, while inclusive, should be neither *infinite* in the sense of undifferentiated nor *sub*-urban, in the sense of being an inferior receptacle of undesirable uses. From this perspective, it is impossible to pursue any decent urbanistics if some of the best eggheads of current urban design exclude either, on one hand, the actual nature of polymorphic cities or, on the other hand, the need to provide all of their multiple components with a good, people-friendly *Gestalt*.[134]

Urban Design and the Legacy of Colin Rowe

In claiming a naive, mechanical functionalism on the one hand and abstraction on the other as primary design drivers, and in disregarding the complex variety of different cultural and geographical situations, the rhetoric of the orthodox Modern Movement made apparent the shortcomings of its reductionist attitude. Liberalism, in its several manifestations in the post-WWII years, was the

128 Spencer (2016).

129 Rowe and Koetter (1978): 100.

130 Shane, Grahame, "The Emergence of Landscape Urbanism", in Waldheim, Charles, *Landscape Urbanism Reader*, Princeton Architectural Press, New York, 2006: 55-67.

131 Romano (2013): 107. (My translation).

132 Marot, Sébastien, "Coda", in *Sub-Urbanism and the Art of Memory*, Architectural Association, London, (1999) 2003: 83-87.

133 Berger et al. (2017): 11.

134 "Despite all the evidence showing that the world's most prevalent and rapidly growing form of urbanization will be suburbia, the fields of Planning, and especially Design, still lack a robust, unbiased intellectual and theoretical platform to examine and debate it. ... The allied Planning and Design fields have proved unable to significantly shape suburbia, which has continued unabated and in forms primarily driven by economic policies, some consumer preferences, speculation, tax policies, and lax government regulation. ... A truly 'back to the city' future, as imagined by retro-urbanists, seems highly unlikely short of imposition of draconian planning regimes." Berger et al. (2017): 10. Also, Viganò, Paola, "The Horizontal Metropolis", in Berger et al. (2017): 552-69.

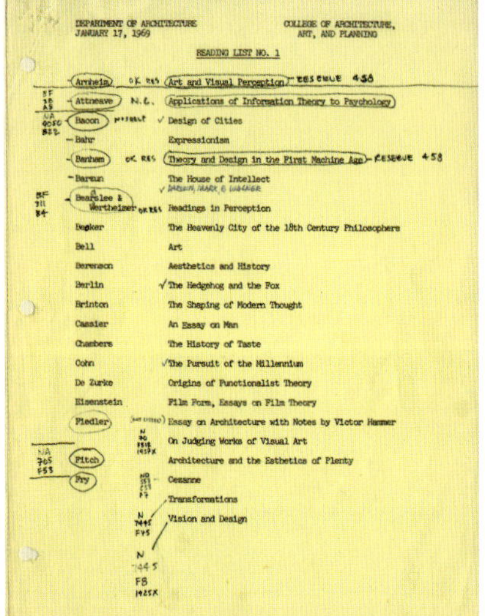

DEPARTMENT OF ARCHITECTURE
JANUARY 17, 1969

COLLEGE OF ARCHITECTURE,
ART, AND PLANNING

READING LIST NO. 1

Arnheim	Art and Visual Perception
Attneave	Applications of Information Theory to Psychology
Bacon	Design of Cities
Bahr	Expressionism
Banham	Theory and Design in the First Machine Age
Barzun	The House of Intellect
Beardslee & Wertheimer	Readings in Perception
Becker	The Heavenly City of the 18th Century Philosophers
Bell	Art
Berenson	Aesthetics and History
Berlin	The Hedgehog and the Fox
Brinton	The Shaping of Modern Thought
Cassier	An Essay on Man
Chambers	The History of Taste
Cohn	The Pursuit of the Millennium
De Zurke	Origins of Functionalist Theory
Eisenstein	Film Form, Essays on Film Theory
Fiedler	Essay on Architecture with Notes by Victor Hammer
	On Judging Works of Visual Art
Fitch	Architecture and the Esthetics of Plenty
Fry	Cezanne
	Transformations
	Vision and Design

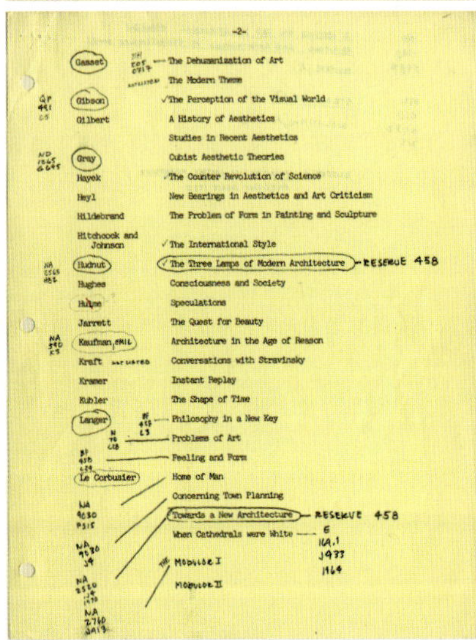

-2-

Gasset	The Dehumanization of Art
	The Modern Theme
Gibson	The Perception of the Visual World
Gilbert	A History of Aesthetics
	Studies in Recent Aesthetics
Gray	Cubist Aesthetic Theories
Hayek	The Counter Revolution of Science
Heyl	New Bearings in Aesthetics and Art Criticism
Hildebrand	The Problem of Form in Painting and Sculpture
Hitchcock and Johnson	The International Style
Hudnut	The Three Lamps of Modern Architecture
Hughes	Consciousness and Society
Hulme	Speculations
Jarrett	The Quest for Beauty
Kaufman	Architecture in the Age of Reason
Kraft	Conversations with Stravinsky
Kramer	Instant Replay
Kubler	The Shape of Time
Langer	Philosophy in a New Key
	Problems of Art
	Feeling and Form
Le Corbusier	Home of Man
	Concerning Town Planning
	Towards a New Architecture
	When Cathedrals were White

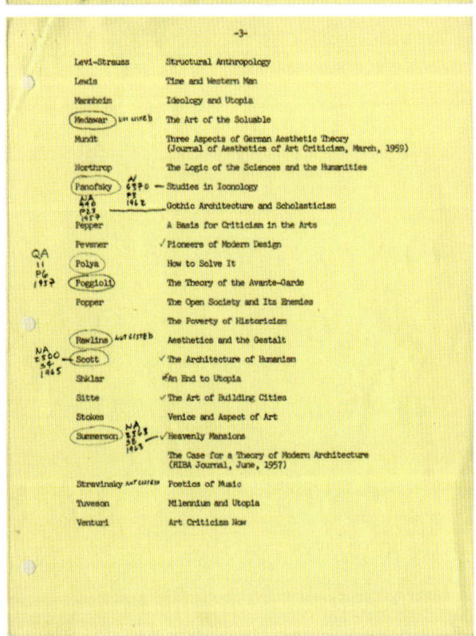

-3-

Levi-Strauss	Structural Anthropology
Lewis	Time and Western Man
Mannheim	Ideology and Utopia
Medawar	The Art of the Soluable
Mundt	Three Aspects of German Aesthetic Theory (Journal of Aesthetics of Art Criticism, March, 1959)
Northrop	The Logic of the Sciences and the Humanities
Panofsky	Studies in Iconology
	Gothic Architecture and Scholasticism
Pepper	A Basis for Criticism in the Arts
Pevsner	Pioneers of Modern Design
Polya	How to Solve It
Poggioli	The Theory of the Avante-Garde
Popper	The Open Society and Its Enemies
	The Poverty of Historicism
Rawlins	Aesthetics and the Gestalt
Scott	The Architecture of Humanism
Shklar	An End to Utopia
Sitte	The Art of Building Cities
Stokes	Venice and Aspect of Art
Summerson	Heavenly Mansions
	The Case for a Theory of Modern Architecture (RIBA Journal, June, 1957)
Stravinsky	Poetics of Music
Tuveson	Milennium and Utopia
Venturi	Art Criticism Now

left and right:
Fig. 1. Reading list of the Cornell Urban Design Studio of Spring 1969. (Handwritten notes by James Tice also in Spring of 1969).

quintessential tool used to gently prod, from within, the Modern Movement away from its despotic and arrogant inclinations towards an aporetic, inclusive, humanistic perspective by means of history, reasoning, and irony. This was, in fact, meant to be achieved without compromising, and actually reinforcing, the anthropocentric ideal of the project of modernity.

Multiplicity has been a challenge for the project of modernity for more than half a century at least. Despite more than fifty years of post-Fordism awareness, urban design seems not to have fully metabolized the legacy of the Modern Reform carried on by Colin Rowe ever since the post-WWII years. The practical effects of these shortcomings are dire for both habitats and dwellers.

During the last several decades, the theories and policies of the design of human settlements seem to have sought a new formula of standardization and internationalization, albeit in forms different from those proposed by the orthodoxy of the Modern Movement. The resulting multifaceted scenario shows examples of senescent avant-gardism and unlikely-happy degrowth canonizations. Most of all, a sterile diatribe has emerged between the anarchic disengagement of pieces of *Reklamearchitektur* immersed in undifferentiated and/or episodic landscapes and the millenarian zeal of the good-intention, one-type-fits-all prescriptions of a generic compactness, walkability, and mixed-use. One would hope to see these axioms replaced by a less pretentious, less imposing, and likely more rewarding idea of completeness, variegated inclusiveness, and aesthetic pleasure.

On one hand the theories of an epiphenomenal avant-garde reveal the actual realm and scale of present regional and global challenges but provide no support to policies and design processes aimed at producing design complexity and continue generating noisy aphasias. On the other hand, a consolidating retro-urban tradition, while well aware and highly conversant with the centrality of design logic, invests in an agenda of imposing often superficial and generic recipes into the disciplinary discourse where the dimension of the efforts and the sincerity of the good intentions of the true-believer lead to unintended and unprecedented social and affordability crises.

In the meantime, geography, topography, and typology proceed towards a condition of iconic irrelevance in the disciplinary activity of urban design. While exhibited in statements, they increasingly disappear both in design products and in the most 'progressive' policies. The barely achieved cosmopolitanism of regional cultures and context sensitivity is increasingly replaced by a renewed standardization of chaotic forms that yet conform to an internationalism of either a hyper tech or a superficially traditional appearance.

How is it possible that the wealth of disciplinary intelligence that the current discourse exhibits cannot find a more positive collaboration, a common project, a fertile harmony of diversities? All too often, a stance that takes into consideration both thesis and antithesis is held as radical in a *milieu* where only one of the two is considered legitimate and the other non-sense, or retro, or uninformed, or criminal. Shouldn't we promote a healthier dialectic dynamic, one that is more productive than the ones offered by the present urban design predicament? Shouldn't we focus on a positive alternative to the current default of the anarchy of solipsistic buildings? Shouldn't it be recognized that the dimensions and variety of today's settlements cannot be understood as if they are the walled city of the second millennium, and that these multiple settlements are worth some design effort and some good *Gestalt*, nevertheless?

Although defining Colin Rowe as a liberal might be no more than an effective abstraction, a substantial component of liberalism in his complex intellectual construct cannot be minimized.[135] Rowe's liberalism, cultured, structured, argumentative, "quasi-eclectic",[136] shows his ability to collect and make available to the urban project apparently contradictory components in a cultural system that was, in those years of the second half of the 20th century, coming together with extraordinary effectiveness. Perhaps, that is why the creative group that formed around the figure of Colin Rowe in those fertile 1960s and went on growing for almost forty years and more, whatever the interests of its various members, was able to make so many useful contributions to the development of design and make them available for many different situations, up to the present day.

Rowe not only stabilized the axiology of 'place' and 'context', as is widely recognized, but also brought to the service of urbanistics those prospects of dialectic composition and liberalism which neither design theories nor regional and urban policies seem to have yet fully metabolized. Rowe's profoundly liberal and dialectical attitude in urbanistics is the most original and fertile aspect of his contribution, often indirectly disseminated through his 'school', to the discourse of urbanistics, theory and practice. It is a precious contribution to a discipline that is naturally *dirigiste*, often single-minded, and, nowadays again disturbingly inclined towards a renewed pseudo-scientific, totalitarian dogmatism of "good intentions".

Today, as many times in the remote and recent past, urbanistics is called upon to contribute to the solution of a combination of substantial, often conflicting problems: affordability, environmental degradation, the satisfaction of the many different needs and desires of our human neighbors, both present and future, to name a few. Pursuing these multiple goals with the liberal and inclusive attitude that I learn from Colin Rowe's legacy seems to me more promising than threatening environmental cataclysms should humanity refuse to urgently comply to the specifications of a generic *status-quo* utopian counter-utopia.

> *It may be presumed that a crisis exists; but it must also be insisted that the peddling of crisis by the architect begins to become an objectionable platitude, that it is now one of those retarded gambits of criticism which any sense of obligation should feel obliged to avoid.*[137]

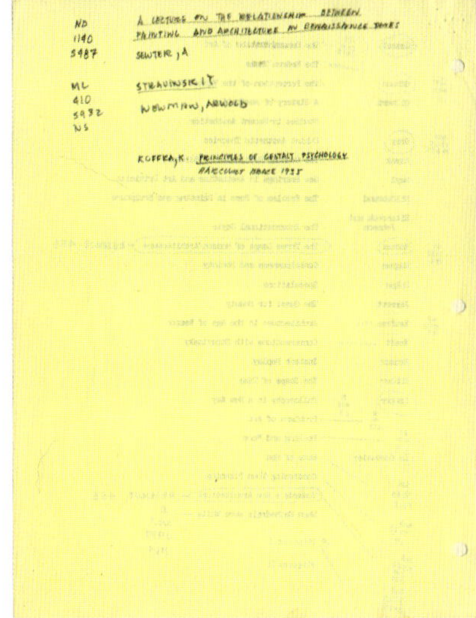
ND 1140 5487
SEWTER, A
ML 410 5932 N5
STRAVINSKI, I
NEWMAN, ARNOLD
KOFFKA, K. PRINCIPLES OF GESTALT PSYCHOLOGY
HARCOURT BRACE 1935

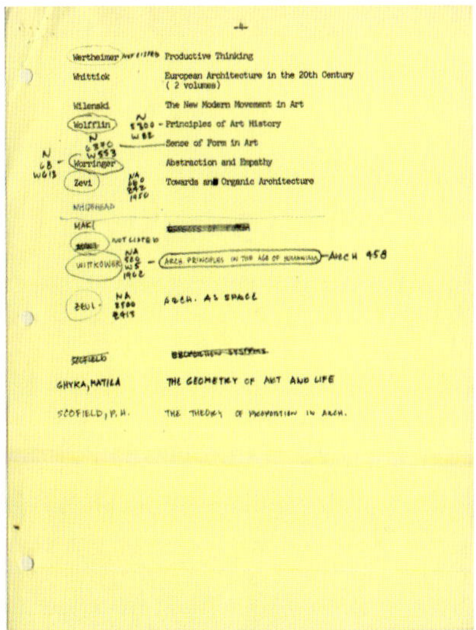
-4-
Wertheimer — Productive Thinking
Whittick — European Architecture in the 20th Century (2 volumes)
Wilenski — The New Modern Movement in Art
Wolfflin — Principles of Art History
Sense of Form in Art
Worringer — Abstraction and Empathy
Zevi — Towards an Organic Architecture
WITTKOWER — ARCH. PRINCIPLES IN THE AGE OF HUMANISM — ARCH 458
ZEVI — ARCH. AS SPACE
GHYKA, MATILA — THE GEOMETRY OF ART AND LIFE
SCOFIELD, P. H. — THE THEORY OF PROPORTION IN ARCH.

---

135 Fernández-Galiano, Luis; Ingersoll, Richard, "Epitafios para un liberal: Colin Rowe, 1920-1999", *Arquitectura viva* 68, (1999): 112.

136 Engel, Braden R., "Ambichronous historiography: Colin Rowe and the teaching of architectural history", *Journal of Art Historiography* 14, Jun 2016: 7.

137 Rowe and Koetter (1975): 66.

Postscript:
I am grateful to Grahame Shane for his providential suggestion to substantially revise this text and for the precious references he provided. No words are adequate to explain how much I owe to the friendship, patient mentorship, and generous insights of Steve Hurtt and Jim Tice: much beyond the scope of these pages. Both have provided fundamental ideas and challenges. Steve has meticulously revised and discussed the language and the concepts of my texts innumerable times. If now they are much less obscure than they used to be, it is certainly his merit. This essay is dedicated to them.

Appendix

This is a transcription of a reading list of the Cornell Urban Design Studio of Spring 1969. As the title confirms it is: (on the top left) DEPARTMENT OF ARCHITECTURE. JANUARY 17, 1969. (on the top right) COLLEGE OF ARCHITECTURE, ART, AND PLANNING. (lower center) READING LIST N. 1

In the original document, references appear with the last name of the author and the title, only. They are completed here with all missing information. When different editions are available, reference is to the last edition prior to 1969. A previous date of publication in English is in parenthesis.

The sequence is maintained as it appears in the original typewritten document. References added by hand by James Tice at about the same time of issue of the document are indicated with an asterisk.

Besides integration of information, changes from the original document include minor misprints.

Arnheim, Rudolf, *Art and Visual Perception: A Psychology of the Creative Eye*, University of California Press, Berkeley, CA, 1954.

Attneave, Fred, *Applications of Information Theory to Psychology: A Summary of Basic Concepts, Methods, and Results*, Holt, New York, 1959.

Bacon, Edmund, *Design of Cities*, Viking Press, Inc., New York, 1967.

Bahr, Hermann, *Expressionism*, F. Henderson, London, 1925.

Banham, Reyner, *Theory and Design in the First Machine Age*, (2nd ed.), Praeger, New York, (1960) 1967.

Barzun, Jacques, *The House of Intellect*, Harper & Row, New York, (1959) 1961.

* Barzun, Jacques, *Darwin, Marx, Wagner: Critique of a Heritage*, (2nd ed.), Doubleday, Garden City, NY, (1941) 1958.

Beardslee, David Cromwell; Wertheimer, Michael, *Readings in Perception*, The University Series in Psychology, D. Van Nostrand, Princeton, NJ, (1958) 1965.

Becker, Carl L[otus], *The Heavenly City of the Eighteenth Century Philosophers*, (Yale University. William L. Storrs Lectures), Yale University Press, New Haven, (1932) 1942.

Bell, Clive, *Art*, Putnam Capricorn Book, Capricorn Books, New York, (1913) 1958.

Berenson, Bernard, *Aesthetics and History*, Doubleday, New York, (1948) 1965.

Berlin, Isaiah, *The Hedgehog and the Fox: An Essay on Tolstoy's View of History*, Weidenfeld & Nicolson, London, (1953) 1967.

Brinton, [Clarence] Crane, *The Shaping of Modern Thought*, Spectrum Book, Prentice-Hall, Englewood Cliffs, NJ, 1963.

Cassirer, Ernst, *An Essay on Man: An Introduction to a Philosophy of Human Culture*, Yale University Press, New Haven, (1944) 1962.

Chambers, Frank Pentland, *The History of Taste: An Account of the Revolutions of Art Criticism and Theory in Europe*, Columbia University Press, New York, 1932.

Cohn, Norman Rufus Colin, *The Pursuit of the Millennium: Revolutionary Messianism in Medieval and Reformation Europe and Its Bearing on Modern Totalitarian Movements*, (2nd ed.), Harper Torchbooks, Academy Library, Harper & Row, New York, (1957) 1961.

De Zurko, Edward Robert, *Origins of Functionalist Theory*, Columbia University Press, New York, 1957.

Eisenstein, Sergei, *Film Form: Essays in Film Theory*, (Leyda, Jay, ed. and trans.) Harcourt Brace, New York, (1949) 1969.

Fiedler, Conrad, *Essay on Architecture*, [with notes by Victor Hammer], privately printed by Carolyn Reading, Lexington, KY, 1954.

Fiedler, Conrad, *On Judging Works of Visual Art*, (2nd ed. rev.), University of California Press, Berkeley, CA, (1949) 1957.

Fitch, James Marston, *Architecture and the Esthetics of Plenty*, Columbia University Press, New York, 1961.

Fry, Roger, *Cézanne, a Study of His Development*, (2nd ed.), Noonday Press, New York, (1927) 1960.

Fry, Roger, *Transformations: Critical and Speculative Essays on Art*, (2nd ed.), Doubleday Anchor Books, Garden City, NY, (1926) 1956.

Fry, Roger, *Vision and Design*, Meridian Books, World Pub., Cleveland, New York, (1920) 1969.

Ortega y Gasset, José, *The Dehumanization of Art and Other Essays on Art, Culture, and Literature*, Princeton University Press, Princeton, NJ, (1948) 1968.

Ortega y Gasset, José, *The Modern Theme*, Harper, New York, (1931) 1961.

Gibson, James J[erome], *The Perception of the Visual World*, Houghton Mifflin, Boston, 1950.

Gilbert, Katharine Everett; Kuhn, Helmut, *A History of Esthetics*, (rev. and enl. ed.), Thames and Hudson, London, (1939) 1956.

Gilbert, Katherine Everett, *Studies in Recent Aesthetic*, University of North Carolina Press, Chapel Hill, 1927.

Gray, Christopher, *Cubist Aesthetic Theories*, Johns Hopkins Press, Baltimore, 1953.

Hayek, Friedrich A[ugust] von, *The Counter-Revolution of Science: Studies on the Abuse of Reason*, Free Press of Glencoe, London, (1948) 1964.

Heyl, Bernard Chapman, *New Bearings in Esthetics and Art Criticism: A Study in Semantics and Evaluation*, Published for Wellesley College by Yale University Press, New Haven, (1943) 1957.

Hildebrand, Adolf von, *The Problem of Form in Painting and Sculpture*, G.E. Stechert & Co., New York, (1907) 1945.

Hitchcock, Henry-Russell; Johnson, Philip, *The International Style*, W.W. Norton, New York, (1932) 1966.

Hudnut, Joseph, *The Three Lamps of Modern Architecture: Lectures Delivered at College of Architecture and Design, University of Michigan, May 12-16, 1952*, University of Michigan Press, Ann Arbor, 1952.

Hughes, H[enry] Stuart, *Consciousness and Society: The Reorientation of European Social Thought, 1890-1930*, Vintage Books, New York, (1958) 1961.

Hulme, T[homas] E[rnest], *Speculations: Essays on Humanism and the Philosophy of Art*, Routledge & Paul, Humanities Press, London and New York, (1924) 1965.

Jarrett, James L[ouis], *The Quest for Beauty*, Prentice-Hall, Englewood Cliffs, NJ, 1957.

Kaufmann, Emil, *Architecture in the Age of Reason: Baroque and Postbaroque in England, Italy, and France*, Dover Publications, New York, (1955) 1968.

Craft, Robert, *Conversations with Igor Stravinsky*, Doubleday, Garden City, NY, 1959.

Kramer, Jerry, *Instant Replay: The Green Bay Diary of Jerry Kramer*, Signet, New York, (1968) 1969.

Kubler, George, *The Shape of Time: Remarks on the History of Things*, Yale University Press, New Haven, 1962.

Langer, Susanne K[atherina], *Philosophy in a New Key: A Study in the Symbolism of Reason, Rite, and Art*, New American Library, New York, (1942) 1958.

Langer, Susanne K[atherina], *Problems of Art, Ten Philosophical Lectures*, Charles Scribner's Sons, New York, 1957.

Langer, Susanne K[atherina], *Feeling and Form: A Theory of Art*, Charles Scribner's Sons, New York, 1953.

De Pierrefeu, François; Le Corbusier, *The Home of Man*, Architectural Press, London, 1948.

Le Corbusier, *Concerning Town Planning*, Yale University Press, New Haven, (1947) 1948.

Le Corbusier, *Towards a New Architecture*, (Etchells, Frederick, ed.), Architectural Press, London and Praeger, New York, (1927) 1965.

Le Corbusier, *When the Cathedrals Were White*, McGraw-Hill, New York, (1947) 1964.

* Le Corbusier, *The Modulor: A Harmonious Measure to the Human Scale, Universally Applicable to Architecture and Mechanics*, (2nd ed.), MIT Press, Cambridge, MA, (1948) 1968.

* Le Corbusier, *Modulor 2, 1955. (Let the User Speak Next) Continuation of The Modulor, 1948*, MIT Press, Cambridge, MA, (1955) 1968.

Lévi-Strauss, Claude, *Structural Anthropology*, Harper Torchbooks, Basic Books, New York, 1963.

Lewis, [Percy] Wyndham, *Time and Western Man*, Beacon Press, Boston, (1927) 1957.

Mannheim, Karl, *Ideology and Utopia: An Introduction to the Sociology of Knowledge*, Harcourt, Brace, and World, New York, (1936) 1968.

Medawar, P[eter] B[rian], *The Art of the Soluble: Creativity and Originality in Science*, Penguin Books, Harmondsworth, (1967) 1969.

Mundt, Ernest K., "Three Aspects of German Aesthetic Theory", *The Journal of Aesthetics and Art Criticism* 17 (3), 1959: 287-310.

Northrop, F[ilmer] S[tuart] C[uckow], *The Logic of the Sciences and the Humanities*, Meridian Books, New York, (1947) 1959.

Panofsky, Erwin, *Studies in Iconology: Humanistic Themes in the Art of the Renaissance*, Harper & Row, New York, (1939) 1967.

Panofsky, Erwin, *Gothic Architecture and Scholasticism*, Meridian Books, New York, (1951) 1957.

Pepper, Stephen C[oburn], *The Basis of Criticism in the Arts*, Harvard University Press, Cambridge, MA, 1945.

Pevsner, Nikolaus, *Pioneers of Modern Design: From William Morris to Walter Gropius*, (rev. ed.), Penguin Books, Harmondsworth (Middlesex), (1936) 1960.

Pólya, George, *How to Solve It: A New Aspect of Mathematical Method*, (2nd ed.), Doubleday Anchor Books, Garden City, NY, (1945) 1957.

Poggioli, Renato, *The Theory of the Avant-Garde*, Belknap Press of Harvard University Press, Cambridge, MA, 1968.

Popper, Karl R[aymond], *The Open Society and Its Enemies*, (5th ed.), Princeton University Press, Princeton, NJ, (1945) 1966.

Rawlins, F[rancis] I[an] G[regory], *Aesthetics and the Gestalt: a Collection of Essays and Other Writings*, Nelson, Edinburgh, 1953.

Scott, Geoffrey, *The Architecture of Humanism: a Study in the History of Taste*, Charles Scribner's Sons, New York, (1914) 1969.

Shklar, Judith N[isse], *After Utopia: The Decline of Political Faith*, Princeton University Press, Princeton, NJ, (1957) 1969.

Sitte, Camillo, *The Art of Building Cities: City Building According to Its Artistic Fundamentals*, Reinhold Pub., New York, 1945.

Stokes, Adrian (Piper, John, ill.), *Venice: An Aspect of Art*, Lion and Unicorn Press, London, (1945) 1965.

Summerson, John, *Heavenly Mansions and Other Essays on Architecture*, W.W. Norton, New York, (1949) 1963.

Summerson, John, "The case for a theory of modern architecture", (Lecture given at the RIBA on May 21st), *Royal Institute of British Architects Journal* 64, Jun 1957: 307-13.

Stravinsky, Igor, *Poetics of Music in the Form of Six Lessons*, Vintage Books, New York, (1947) 1959.

Tuveson, Ernest Lee, *Millennium and Utopia: A Study in the Background of the Idea of Progress*, Harper & Row, Publishers, New York and London, (1949) 1964.

Venturi, Lionello, *Art Criticism Now*, (Lectures Delivered March 12, 13, 14, 19, 20, 1941, at the Johns Hopkins University), Johns Hopkins Press, Baltimore, 1941.

Wertheimer, Max, *Productive Thinking*, (Wertheimer, Michael, enl. ed.), Harper, New York, (1945) 1959.

Whittick, Arnold, *European Architecture in the Twentieth Century*, C. Lockwood, London, 1950.

Wilenski, R[eginald] H[oward], *The Modern Movement in Art*, (new and rev. ed.), Faber, London, (1926) 1965.

Wölfflin, Heinrich, *Principles of Art History: The Problem of the Development of Style in Later Art*, Dover, New York, (1932) 1956.

Wölfflin, Heinrich, *The Sense of Form in Art: A Comparative Psychological Study*, Chelsea Pub., New York, 1958.

Worringer, Wilhelm, *Abstraction and Empathy: A Contribution to the Psychology of Style*, International Universities Press, New York, (1940) 1967.

Zevi, Bruno, *Towards an Organic Architecture*, Faber & Faber, London, 1950.

* Wittkower, Rudolf, *Architectural Principles in the Age of Humanism*, Random House, New York, (1949) 1965.

* Zevi, Bruno, *Architecture as Space: How to Look at Architecture*, Horizon Press, New York, 1957.

* Ghyka, Matila C[ostiescu], *The Geometry of Art and Life*, Sheed and Ward, New York, 1946.

* Scholfield, P. H., *The Theory of Proportion in Architecture*, Cambridge University Press, Cambridge, UK, 1958.

* Sewter, A[lbert] C[harles], *A Lecture on the Relationship between Painting and Architecture in Renaissance and Modern Times*, (Delivered to the Manchester Society of Architects, February 13, 1951), A. Tiranti, London, 1952.

* Newman, Arnold; Craft, Robert; Steegmuller, Francis; Stravinsky, Igor, *Bravo Stravinsky*, World Pub., Cleveland, 1967.

* Koffka, Kurt, *Principles of Gestalt Psychology*, Harbinger Book, Harcourt, Brace & World, New York, (1935) 1963.

Charisma and Insight: Urban Design in the Concurrency of Times

Franz G. Oswald

frontispiece:
Untitled (No. 8), Robert Slutzky, 1978.

His striking charisma and his innovative insights enabled Colin Rowe, 1920–1999, architect and teacher, to create a lasting legacy. He reinvented the *architecture of the city* and the contemporary *architectural history of the city* for himself and for all architects following in his footsteps. His love of dialogue captivated his students and colleagues. His distinctive aura displayed in his erudite references to people, places, and events was always present, along with an irrepressible wit and inspired creativity accompanied by a critical mind—all of which created opportunities for exploring alternative realities of unexpected dimensions. This is the basis for my contribution to "Rowe Rome 2014: Urban Design and the Legacy of Colin Rowe" as it relates mostly to the early period of Colin's influence at Cornell University.[1]

In the early 1960s, urban design education still was an emerging academic discipline; its teaching at Cornell University was just beginning. Thanks to Colin there was an exceptional approach to design issues in the chosen context of a city or part of a city in the U.S. Urban design was conceived as a forum for designing within the built form of a city, as a way of thinking about the city and its architecture as a form of living within society. Examples of that approach are evident in the project for Buffalo Waterfront (1965–66) and Zurich City Centre (1966), which were developed at that time (Fig. 1A, 1B, and Fig. 1C, 1D).

WWII: *Tabula Rasa, Change of Paradigms, Re-Inventions*

In 1945 the European self-destructive upheavals of WWII ends. A long period of peace begins. The next year, at the age of 26, Colin Rowe continues his studies with Rudolf Wittkower at the Warburg Institute. His basic education had been at the School of Architecture in Liverpool and since 1942 he had served in the infantry of the British Army.

What kind of influence can the historic events of that period have had on a young person like Colin Rowe?

1 The first "Rowe Rome 2014" conference, session "Colin Rowe and the Futures of Urban Design".

Fig. 1a and Fig. 1b. ZH '66, Proposal for Zurich City Center, Franz G. Oswald, 1966.

The answers to that question can only be speculations. In the face of destruction, misery, and impoverishment around the time of 1945, human existence could be imagined as either at the end of history or at its beginning. Perhaps, out of necessity, the ambivalence of these times becomes a driving force of creativity that turns increasingly into reality, particularly in Great Britain. For intellectuals guiding reconstruction and the renewal of European culture, the U.S. offered the invigorating calm of exile or, perhaps at least, a welcome climate for new utopian thinking.

Already in 1944–45, Karl Popper had published "The Poverty of Historicism"[2] and, in 1945, *The Open Society and its Enemies*. These two works are revelations, particularly for Colin Rowe. Only two years later, in 1947, his ground-breaking essay "The Mathematics of the Ideal Villa" appears in print. It is considered the first theoretical foundation for his design teachings. In "Transparency: Literal and Phenomenal", 1955, together with Robert Slutzky, he enlarges his argument substantially by addressing dimensions of spatial perception. By 1964–65 these works by Karl Popper, Colin Rowe, and Robert Slutzky offer the framework for teaching urban design at Cornell. They serve as the starting point for the discussions about the socio-political and esthetic-historical basis for the design of the city.

Contributions by others played out at the same time. These include the works of Team X (1953–1981), a group of architects owing allegiance to the Congrès Internationaux d'Architecture Moderne (CIAM) that sharply criticized the dogmatic representatives of the 'classical modern', most of all Le Corbusier. In 1960 Buckminster Fuller caused a sensation with his provocative drawing of Dome over Manhattan, presenting a new concept of the city. The book by Kevin Lynch, *The Image of the City*, is the result of a five-year study of Boston, Jersey City, and Los Angeles. One year later, in 1961, it is followed by writer and activist Jane Jacobs's *The Death and Life of Great American Cities*, a scathing critique of 1950s

2 Popper first publishes "The Poverty of Historicism" as an article in 1944-45 and later he publishes it as a book in various languages beginning in 1954 including English in 1957.

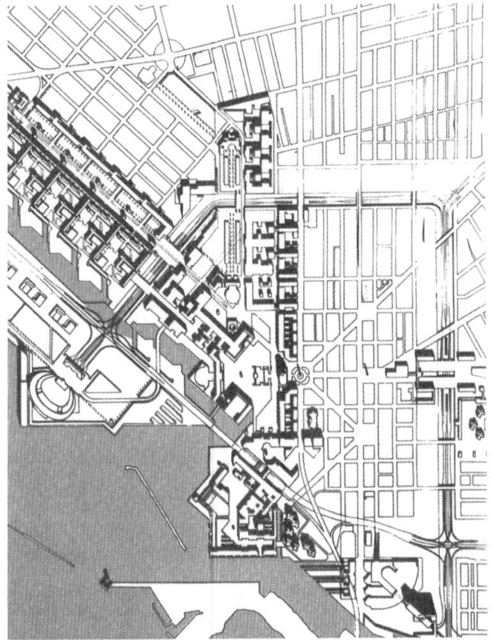

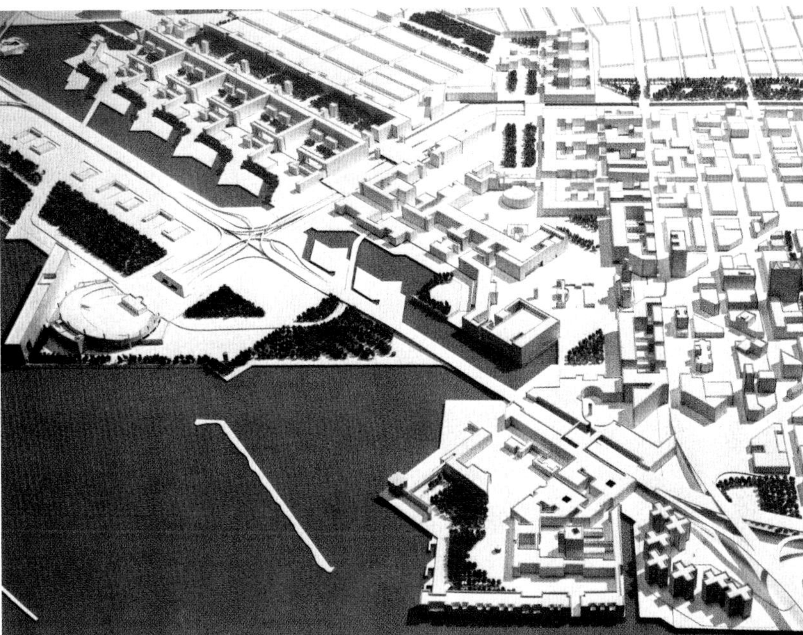

Fig. 1c and Fig. 1d. Buffalo Waterfront, 1969, by the Urban Design Studio, under the direction of Colin Rowe, with Werner Seligman and Jerry A. Wells. Students include: Richard A. Baiter, Richard H. Cardwell, David W. K. Chan, Wayne W. Copper, Harris N. Forusz, Alfred H. Koetter, Makoto Miki, Elpidio F. Olympio, Franz G. Oswald.

urban planning policy. And in 1960 Marshall McLuhan publishes *Understanding Media: The Extensions of Man*, a milestone of contemporary media theory.

These publications helped provide the context and intellectual subject matter for the early studies in the Urban Design Studio at Cornell. The evolving discussion was reoriented in 1965 by two widely regarded texts: "A City is not a Tree" by Christopher Alexander (1965) and *Complexity and Contradiction in Architecture* by Robert Venturi (1966).

In a period of only 30 years—from 1914 to 1945—Modern society, architecture, and city culture were first constructed and then completely destroyed. The two decades after the end of WWII can be characterized as reconstruction and experimentation. After 1945 the literal *tabula rasa* of the war was mirrored in the *tabula rasa* of imagination. Indeed, away from a horrid totalitarian past, humankind turned to an open future full of hope. The time after 1945, on one hand, presents itself as an intensive period of reconstruction; on the other, it remains an empty page in regard to the designing of architecture and the city.

Now the time had come for experiments in thinking and acting. With the demands for a change of paradigm, the blank page offers the space for the reinvention of symbols, reproductions, advancements and new discoveries. The production of architecture and of the city everywhere gains intensity and diversity in form, with the provenance of place and time from history and, not least, in the methods of production of the human habitat.

All this was anticipated in Ithaca in the 1960s. No one doubts the seriousness of this mission by Rowe's generation or the person of Colin Rowe himself. Upon entering the stage of architectural discourse, he explains his thoughts on architecture using his charisma to convey his insights, making them accessible by

Fig. 2. Caricature of Isaiah Berlin, social and political theorist, philosopher and historian of ideas. Sketch by David Levine, ca. 1978.

linking the present with the past and in so doing revealing their historical roots and contemporary meaning and potential. Thanks to his methods in the Studio he succeeds in applying exemplary methods and ideas that reform theory and teaching in urban design.

The Hedgehog and the Fox, the Fable as a Compass

Maybe the younger Colin Rowe and the older Sir Isaiah Berlin never met face to face (Fig. 2). *The Hedgehog and the Fox*, the famous masterly essay of Tolstoy's view of history, was written by the older man. The younger man makes it the obligatory reading for the Urban Design Studio. It seems that, at the slightest provocation, he refers to the fable. In the course of time the animals become both grave warnings and delightfully stimulating companions for the teacher and his students to explore intellectual dialectics—without calling them out as such. The pair, fox and hedgehog, embody, by way of metaphor, the dialogue and dilemma, and the wisdom of any dialectical argument, also represents the ambivalence that is typical for the creative architect.

The dilemma unfolds during the exploration and creation of form. It is insignificant if the goal is merely a concrete or an abstract form without content. At some stage, the plight of a decision arises from the complex course of emotions, thoughts and the workflow of matter, knowledge or thematic raw materials. It is a question of which direction or into which condition the actual product should be realized, whether it should be changed, abandoned, finished, or revoked. Design work knows no pity and often requires momentous decisions, particularly as it concerns not only the architect but others who enjoy or suffer the consequences.

The importance of a design decision varies according to the scale of the object and the persons involved. For a piece of jewelry, the dilemma can be solved in a discussion between the jeweler and the client. But for a single house, things already become more complicated. More people are involved, they may speak different languages and have different fantasies, they may or may not choose to become involved in the drama as it unfolds.

But what about the creative process in designing a city, regardless of its size? First, we have to ask the question: How do we want to define a city? Is the city a big house as postulated by Leon Battista Alberti? Or is the city simply a pragmatic aggregate of innumerable smaller and bigger structures scattered far and wide? Which institutions, buildings, and landscapes should be provided; why, what for and for whom? According to which rules will the inhabitants live together? Will they be able to shape their own fate and the fate of the city or will they be held captive by it?

In designing and building a city and its architecture, the architect has to ask all these questions and more. They concern persons and things, but also concepts, actions, processes, and products as they manifest themselves when people live together in a city. The architect has to recognize the dilemma and find a way out of it.

This is where the fable, passed on from Archilochus in the 7th century BC, comes in; the fox knows many things, but the hedgehog knows one big thing. The biography of a city and its architecture can take two different directions; to put it radically, it can be the tyranny of the big thing or the chaos of the many. If we believe in the big thing as the only right and allowable form we have to sacrifice freedom. If, contrariwise, we believe in many things we open the way for anarchy. History has taught us that neither the one nor the other leads to peace and happiness or to beauty. How must we therefore handle architectural design?

The fox and the hedgehog meet. They talk to each other and come to a mutual agreement. Both want to live and thrive, neither of them wants to impose his own justice or injustice on the other. They arrange for their next meeting and, as before, go their separate ways, maybe looking forward to a later fruitful encounter.

The wisdom of the fable mirrors for us, in a most human way, the traits and histories of animals. In creative design, and in the teaching of urban design, the fable's wit and canny irony lead to many questions. For example: which animal do I want to play in any given situation, which animal is my opponent going to play and how can any ensuing dilemma be resolved to be mutually beneficial?

The fable offers a huge insight and advantage—that teaching and practice do not have to be overshadowed by tedious and, as a rule, rather useless declarations and discussions of superficial value judgements. The insight has been put in a nutshell. In other words, the fable serves as a compass in the choice of direction for one's own work and actions. The fox and the hedgehog teach us an old humanistic wisdom about the importance of freedom and responsibility. As a compass, the fable offers an open and undogmatic direction in architectural design, enabling everyone to exercise freedom of choice and to accept responsibility for doing so.

Colin Rowe: Urban Design in the Concurrency of Times

Looking back, we may be justified in interpreting the beginning of Colin Rowe's Cornell Studio as a turning point in the practice of architecture and the teaching of urban design, acknowledging that it had far-reaching consequences. My experience of those earlier times and their importance for me today lead to two questions: How can the beginning of an architectural process in design be shaped? How does a work begin that is intended for the architectural interplay at multiple scales: house, city, and landscape?

Our first design task in 1965–66 is typical of the Cornell studio. It is set in an unbuilt, empty neighborhood on the inner edge of a small town. There is no program, no specific goals, no specification of functions or requirements concerning the outcome. The only sure thing was perplexed stupefaction on the part of the students!

Faced with the unfamiliar gaps we try to understand how we might cope with the void. Before, architects had been taught how to excel with the help of the history of architectural styles, esthetic doctrines, and models of Modernity. With regard to the building of a city we had been led to believe that the goals and procedures of building a city were based on secure knowledge and scientific fact, without ever knowing for sure what precisely constituted a fact. So it seemed clear how the new design had to be determined.

But now, at the beginning, there is a void, no word, no dogma, no law. As a painter is provoked by the white canvas, the architect is challenged by the empty city plan. The void itself becomes the topic and focus of thinking. The void does not set any limits to architectural fantasies of designing the city, for housing, gardens, warehouses or parks on fallow land. What are we talking about if we are talking about void? Is it a void in a landscape, somewhere on earth, on a map, or the void in our own consciousness?

A void is not nothingness, but a space in the mind for imagining a new part of the city, one that is integrated into the context rather than provoking discordance.

The imagination of the integrated city shows familiar traits. Among them is the knowledge that the city represents the cohabitation of human societies. It is contradictory and ambiguous, at the same time a living organism and a solid structure. Without regard to size, density, dimension, or position in a landscape, it presents itself equally well as an open entity and as a closed entity.

The designing of a city relates to the anatomy, physiognomy, and the metabolism of the city, its landscape and its history. Architecturally the city can be a fragment of an imagined but unfinished entity or an entity consisting of fragments. The city shows as many faces as there are histories about the individuals and societies that evolved in that place and continue to live there or have left traces of their existence.

For the discussion of these topics the 1965–66 Cornell Studio offered two conceptual groupings:

- Concepts about the perception of form: figure/ground; transparency, phenomenal and literal; levels of scale of the objects.

- Concepts for the production of form: space and volume; field and boundaries; line and net; density and scale.

I want to restrict my remarks to the concepts for the production of form. They are defined as twin notions of diversity and ambiguity in order to clarify the interaction of competing concepts.

Space and Volume

We are indebted to Adolf Loos for his insight that, after the skin and clothing, a building is the third layer of protection of the human body. The analogy of the human body and its clothing with the building as an extension can be developed even further. A hat, a coat, a shoe are perceived and used according to climate, time of the year, days of festivities or work. In other words, according to accumulated wisdom, custom and skill, a piece of clothing and a building are given their particular texture and form. Depending on the number of inhabitants or the volume of a building, forms result that are symptomatic of considerate or aggressive intervention.

Field and Boundary

The twin concepts of field and boundary deal with concrete and abstract phenomena. They are a great challenge in urban design as their outlines and proportions are rarely defined at the beginning. A field is the surface, delineated by a line within a larger area. It also is the stage for any kind of activity. The boundary is the closed contour of a surface. It also means a line of division between inside and outside, front and back. It both divides and connects; it means separation and coexistence simultaneously. The transitions can be sharp or fluid.

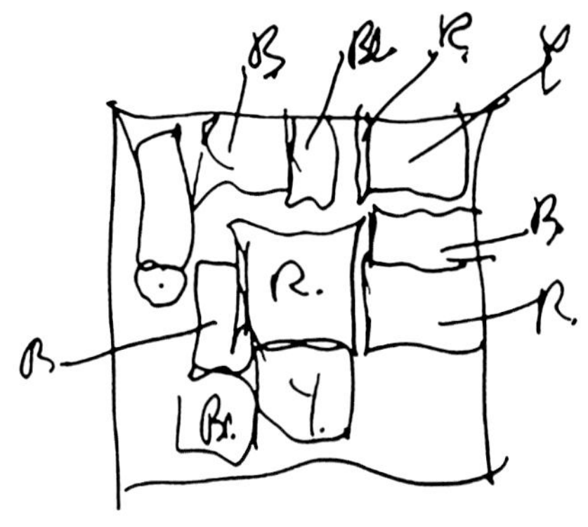

Fig. 3. Sketch for *Sauce Hollandaise,* Robert Slutzky, 1958/74.

Line and Net

The line is a moving point. Crossing lines and their points of intersection result in the creation of the net. Lines cross fields and boundaries, divide them into aggregates of smaller units and connect them into aggregates of bigger units. They represent the smallest and the largest orders in space and time (Fig. 3). In respect to architecture, line and net are the precursors of inside and outside, light and dark. In respect to the metabolism of architecture, they represent the flow and stock of goods and energy. To use Loos's analogy of the anatomy and metabolism of the human body, lines and nets make it possible to directly compare it to the anatomy and metabolism of house, city, and landscape.

Density and Scale

Density and scale are interrelated. Density is the variable proportion of the mass of a body and its volume. Scale is defined by points and by units of surface, volume, and time. Generally speaking substances expand with rising temperature and their density decreases and vice versa. Scales serve as instruments to observe the transformation and dynamics of living beings or objects in their context, to define and project them.

This dynamic is of particular relevance for the architect. The number of people, houses, and building elements can either increase or decrease. The patterns of volumes and spaces show countless variations in form, size and location, but also in time and duration.

Anchored to the soil, the orders of cities and their landscape, of houses and gardens seem immobile. But they rather resemble a flock of birds or a shoal of fish. They stay together for shorter or longer periods, regroup, and finally move on or rest at single points. The arrangements of cities, houses, and their related landscapes follow similar patterns. But the dimensions of time differ greatly, as cities exist for differing reasons and for much longer periods of time.

How can we design the project of the future town and its use of resources in the context of an existing city? For this we can rely on scales, the units of politico-economic and administrative organizations of people, territories, and resources. Scales are defined quantitatively. Low scales present the basic units and high scales are aggregated from low scales.

The map of Wiesbaden 1900, Germany, can be understood against this background. It serves as a synopsis of the four concepts used in the late 1960s for the production of form in the Urban Design Studio at Cornell (Fig. 4).

Fig. 4. Wiesbaden 1900 Germany; synopsis of four concepts.

I would like to express what has so far only been assumed or implied, that the 'concurrency of times' was the preeminent characteristic of the Urban Design Studio. It is presumed that the intentionally set void of the first design task mirrored the existential experience of the architect and teacher, Colin Rowe. The manner in which the beginning of the design was staged reproduces his insights gained from living through the war and its chaos. It relates to the rediscovery of history and, not least, provides insights into his personal anguish and the reinvention of his own existence, including the ironical mask of the hedgehog and the fox.

The fiction of the void offers the teaching architect a creative impulse for the new teachings in urban design, and, to his younger colleagues, a new view of building, open and available to all in the concurrency of times. The new teachings turn out to be an ironic revolt against the blind belief in progress and its obsolete architecture of the *tabula rasa*.

This was clearly and coherently manifest in the composition of the work-stage at Cornell University. It consists of two components: on one side the studio for design and discussion and on the other, the lecture hall for lessons and discussions parallel to the studio. I have a vivid memory of the brilliant and inspiring presentations devoted to Renaissance, Baroque, and Neoclassicism in the architecture of Italy, France, England, and German-speaking Europe. Unforgettable are the explanations and 'walks' in the parks and gardens from the same epochs, and the continuous, clever, and ironical references to the work and person of Le Corbusier. Only later would I comprehend why the works of Corbu keep reappearing at the center of our attention, in spite of all their paradoxes and flaws. Our attention is captured by the deeply felt humanism that is embodied in the works of the preeminent architect of an outdated Modernity.

I consider the work-stage and its components at Cornell to be a model. It offers a think tank in architecture which results from the interplay of house, city, and landscape. And it survives.

Postscript: The Concurrency of Times in the Urban Age and Wiesbaden 2020

Today, the concurrency of times is permanently present, but in a different way from the epoch of the 1960s to 1980s. In academic forums or public debate reference is often made to historic experiences if this stimulates media entertainment. For this purpose, there is an innumerable amount of reproduced images, floods of data, and constructions from the past. We instantly move from here to there, visit each other virtually, regardless of distance. We are here and there at the same moment in time.

Concurrency of times does not primarily mean the borrowing of articles or lifestyles from different epochs. It means the synchrony in one place of people and artifacts of different origin, languages, materials, images and myths. It is the spatial vicinity of differing everyday lives or the clash of existences, individual or collective, unknown to each other, foreign, in the Urban Age; a name derived from the statistical assessment that more than half of the world's population is living in urban settlements since 2015–16. Concurrency of times, together with density and informality, characterizes these settlements. So we have to ask ourselves how, in relation to urban design, we may understand this characteristic, unfamiliar, but also a fundamental factor in creating identity.

For human bodies, concurrency of time implies that physical boundaries are suspended by aggregates of sensors, screens, loudspeakers, microphones, and more. I, myself, or my counterparts, are directly present and can be addressed without inhibiting distances or other barriers. The preconditions for visual and acoustical perception are secured. At every point of time and from any location an encounter can take place or can be interrupted. However, the traditional interplay of spatial distance and material cover or between body and space, noted by Loos, is abolished. The interplay occurs between turning on and turning off or between searching and finding. It can be initiated from locations that are moving permanently and automatically, self-directed or externally controlled. In addition, these locations can move at different speeds in the form of a capsule or a bubble for humans. These conditions are familiar and belong increasingly to

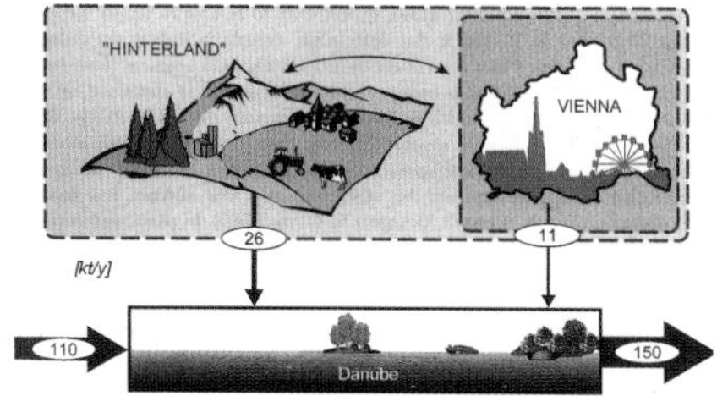

Fig. 5. Regions depend on their hinterland; interrelations between the two make up urban systems.

everyday life. Against this backdrop are set the vital design questions concerning the Urban Age:

What does concurrency of time mean in the here and now in relation to the city as a form of social cohabitation? Is the city tantamount to a dictatorship of technological systems?

As is well known, the required connections can be set up automatically, controlled and serviced without human intervention. So new questions arise: what does the architecture of a city look like under the conditions of concurrency? How is the architecture of the city under the conditions of concurrency related to living in a landscape, a neighborhood, to buildings, materials, work place, and not least, how is it related to the emergence and dying of other living things, animals or plants on the planet?

I do not know the answers, but I share my concerns with others. They are related to the "global village" as described by Marshall McLuhan in *Understanding Media* published in 1966.

Wiesban 2020 in Light and Darkness (Fig. 6) illustrates the urban system of today. It is the global jump in scale of urban living in relation to the density of inhabitants, together with other forces of technology from the 20th century, that makes concurrency possible.

Wiesbaden 2020 is the image of the city in the 21st century. City life is not restricted to local or regional aggregates of human settlements. It is a system of networks that overlaps countries, continents, and oceans. It is a system of points and their connections, including the human body. Radically simplified, it is the internet of things. The connections and their points of intersection are organized on levels of scale: megalopolis, metropolis, cities, and medium to small towns. The direct hinterland, close and distant landscapes are included. They all communicate through variable media and at variable frequencies. The communication is, however, controlled by central agencies, private or public. Because of the often contradictory interests of the major actors, communication is either reinforced or blocked.

Wiesbaden 2020 represents the actual relationship between the city and its hinterland in global dimensions. The term 'hinterland' (Fig. 5) is used according to the theory of site for land use by Johann Heinrich von Thünen (1783–1850). He was a farmer, a German, a snazzy dresser, and an amateur economist who was interested in appropriation economics. Inspired by Adam Smith and creating his model before industrialization, von Thünen was interested in the natural laws that govern rural land use, that is, the best way for farmers of different goods to locate their farms within a boundless landscape so that they could maximize their profits.

He is the author of the model christened the 'isolated state'. The central city, where goods are sold and exchanged, is located centrally within an isolated state. It is self-sufficient and there are no external influences. The isolated state is surrounded by unoccupied wilderness.

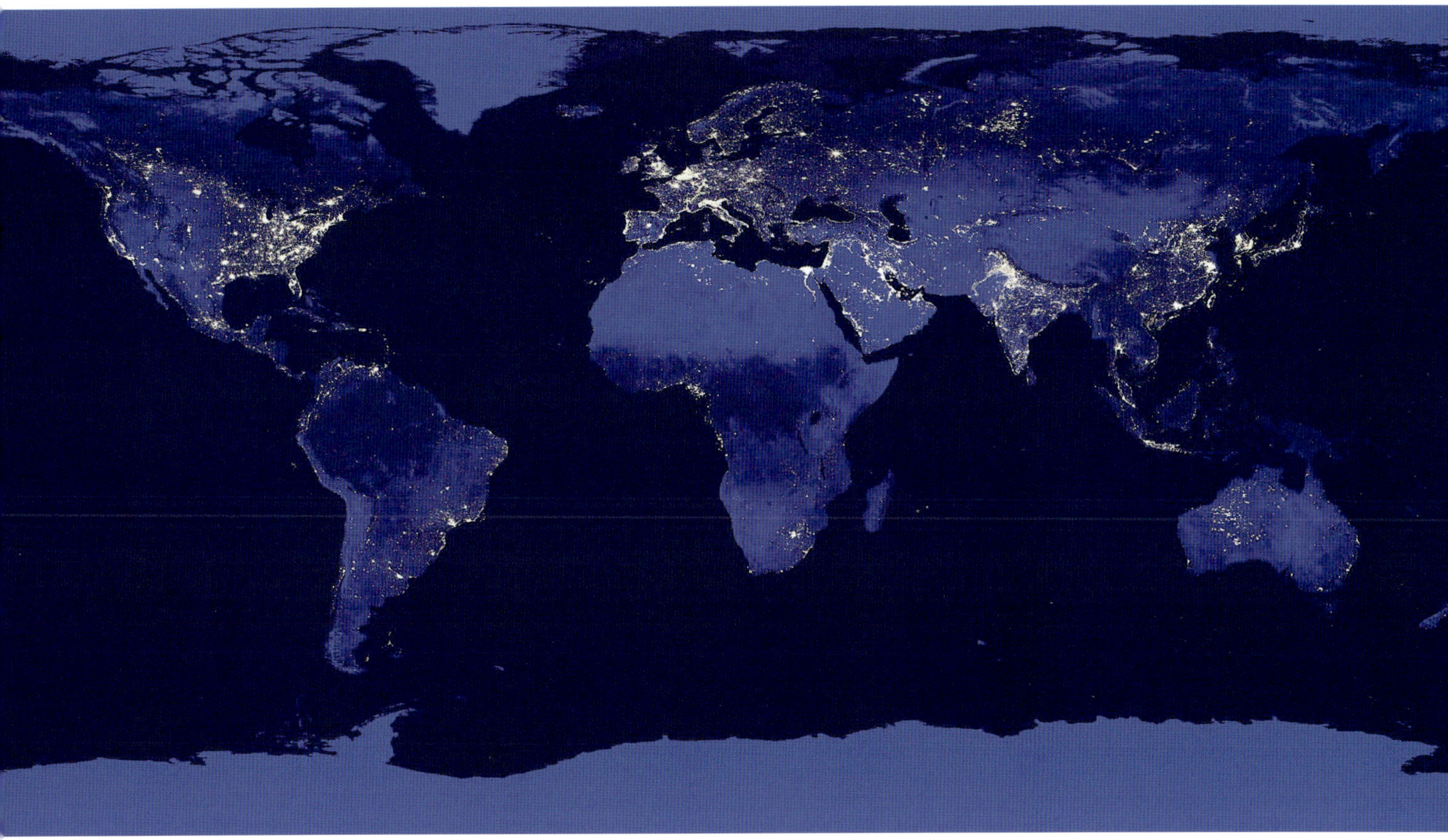

Fig. 6. *Wiesbaden 2020, in Light and Darkness,* original image courtesy of NASA.

Similar conditions as they were presumed to be in von Thünen's model for his time are mirrored by Wiesbaden 1900. But by the middle of the 19th century, isolation and wilderness have strongly decreased because of the development of national states and the building of railroads until they reach the state shown in the illustration Wiesbaden 2020. Urban life today is radically different from those times. In the 21st century pure isolation and wilderness are definitely non-existent globally. Unless they serve as political tools of oppression.

Planet Earth consists of permeable and interwoven layers forming innumerable scales and spheres. They shape the landscapes, the hinterland, on which the urban system depends. Humans use the urban systems with their interplay of hinterland and city in their attempt to keep the spheres of the earth living and liveable.

Following the model for Urban Design at Cornell in 1965–1966, I postulate that it is not the destruction of cities that causes the sense of emptiness in our design tasks, it is the destruction of the hinterland on urbanized Planet Earth. To use an aphorism I learned working in Africa: the building of a city starts in its hinterland and with the planting of trees.

For me charisma and insight, heightened by the courage to abandon conventional modes of thinking, are the legacy of the architect and teacher, Colin Rowe. Thinking about Colin I realized that embedded within his legacy lies a hidden responsibility for the later-born.

Acknowledgments

Given the subject matter of this book, the relation of text and image was supremely important. As the co-editors, both of us have reviewed the content of the book as coequals. In the early stages however, individual interests and experiences came into play. Thus, Tice assumed primary responsibility for the overall look of the book and the page layouts. A select few of our contributors provided preliminary layouts. Hurtt accepted primary text editing responsibility. While part of the co-editing team, Latini focused his attention primarily on footnote and bibliographic issues.

We are deeply grateful to the other twenty-three essayists whose work is found here. Beyond their individual contributions, their combined patience, endurance, understanding, and generous good humor over several years made the endeavor not only possible but rewarding for the editors. Initially, a much shorter text with far fewer illustrations, was imagined. As the book's scope expanded, so did our ambition and the time required to achieve it.

Among our contributors, Antonio Pietro Latini deserves special mention. The idea for this book was his. Early on, he provided guidance on scope and content. He was one of its co-editors, until, due to teaching responsibilities as a distinguished professor in China, he found it imperative to formally withdraw from that role. Without his encouragement and labors—especially in organizing the series of international conferences that proved pivotal— the book would not have been realized. The two essays he contributed serve as an indication of his commitment to the idea of the book. For all these reasons we are especially grateful to him.

We thank all those who provided the venues and support for the series of Rowe/Rome conferences devoted to Colin Rowe's urban design legacy:

Università Roma Tre Architettura (2014)
Ordine degli Architetti PPC di Roma e provincia; Casa dell'architettura (2015)
Facoltà di Ingegneria della Sapienza Università di Roma (2016 and 2017)
The School of Architecture, Planning, and Preservation, University of Maryland (2019)

Many people provided editorial assistance. Our work with one of them came about due to the passing of one of our initial contributors, Terry Williams, who died in 2021. He had very nearly completed his essay. It was just short of a final edit. Terry had relied on his former coworker and close friend, John West, for recalling and verifying factual details. John likewise helped us with final edits and footnotes while maintaining an exacting eye on the original text.

In the early years of the project, Peter Hetzel, teacher and architect, willingly read and commented on materials sent to him for review with a record turnaround time. Most importantly, he introduced us to many nuances of editing, style guides, and the mechanics of publishing. In that same vein but more recently, Michael Dennis has provided good-humored prodding and hard-nosed advisory directives, all advice followed as best we could. True to form, and over the long years we have known him, he has always generously shared his knowledge of teaching, professional practice, and scholarship.

Associate Professor Virginia Cartwright at the University of Oregon and Carol Hurtt, read and commented on nearly every essay. They caught grammatical errors and often improved phrasing that helped with the clarity of the writing. Virginia also provided commentary on the substance of topics. About accuracy of content, Allan Ceen, Director of Studium Urbis in Rome, provided historical accounts that aided us with the essays gathered in the book's section focused on Rome.

Our first professional copy editor Claudia Kousolas reviewed texts, further educated us about editing protocols, and helped build a preliminary style guide. As we approached the last editing phase, Evie Anderson provided expert manuscript editing of the text of all the essays.

Finally, we would like to thank Meridith Murray for her exacting attention to the indexing. Of course, any errors or omissions are the sole responsibility of the co-editors.

Our contributors typically provided both text and graphic materials. Many contributors, designers all, were involved with graphic layouts. With eyes on the entire book, Gretchen Leary, our initial graphic designer, suggested alternate layout schemes. The basic graphic structure of book was determined by James Tice who assisted Gretchen with composing the imagery for each essay. When other responsibilities made it impractical for Gretchen to continue, Pablo Mandel, graphic designer and consultant with our publisher, ORO Editions, was enlisted. We owe a very large debt of gratitude to Pablo for the skill and finesse he brought to the final phases of the layout and look of the book. We thank all these designers for their contributions during the long campaign of producing this book.

As the number of images increased so did the challenges associated with them. Good friend Christopher Pullman and his friend, photographer Lisa Abitbol, went the 'extra miles' for current photos of Boston area Koetter Kim projects. Richard Bosch, Cornellian and architect, provided superior knowledge and assistance in accessing images, tracking sources and credits, occasionally inventing graphics, and always casting his 'eagle eye' on images, text, and captions. Richard also built an enormously helpful website for us devoted to the entire collection of book images. Virginia Cartwright constructed a digital dossier and table by which to track illustrations, captions, and credits. Our gratitude for the help provided by both Richard and Virginia is immeasurable.

Vincent J. Buonanno generously allowed us free access to his premier collection of historic Italian prints through the Brown University Library website, "The Theater that was Rome". Carl Laubin, a Cornellian, volunteered his exquisite portrait of Rowe. To us, it is as if Colin is musing on some of his favorite architectural and urban settings—waiting to see if the book itself measures up to these icons. We were pleased to make Carl's painting the very first image encountered in the book.

We thank the editorial staff at ORO Editions, Applied Research and Design Publishing, Goff Books, and particularly Gordon Goff and Jake Anderson, for their patience, understanding, advice, and support.

Special thanks are due to the assistance provided by the Cornell University Library staff to Blake Middleton in compiling a list of Urban Design Studio degree recipients under Rowe. A more comprehensive list is attached as an appendix to Middleton's "Evidence of an Argument" essay. It also includes those who attended the Studio but did not receive a degree. We too are grateful for the support of Cornell Librarian Martha Walker for her help and advice.

Brad White, Program Director at The Driehaus Foundation; Dawn Jordon, Dean at the University of Maryland; Stefanos Polyzoides, Dean at the University Notre Dame; J. Meejin Yoon, Dean at Cornell University and Annalisa Maione, Director of Cornell in Rome; and others at the University of Oregon have provided support for this project in numerous ways.

Together, in addition to the above, we think it important to acknowledge the special circumstances at Cornell that allowed us to benefit from the rich intellectual environment created by the following faculty and fellow students with whom we interacted most extensively: Alex Caragonne, Stuart Cohen, Norman Crowe, Michael Dennis, Klaus Herdeg, Lee Hodgden, Bernhard Hoesli, Fred Koetter, Franz Oswald, Steven Peterson, John Reps, Tom Schumacher, Werner Seligmann, Jon Michael Schwarting, John Shaw, Roger Sherwood, Stuart Stein, Jerry Wells, and Larry Witzling.

A note about the "Oregon connection": Colin Rowe was the Inaugural Pietro Belluschi Fellow at the University of Oregon in 1995. During his visit to the campus, he taught a seminar and delivered public lectures in Eugene and Portland. Below is an excerpt from his letter on January 21, 1994, in response to his nomination:

> *... let me take a little time to say that I have always enjoyed the happiest of relations with by products and products of the University of Oregon. And I think of Alvin Boyarski, a former student of mine at Cornell, and of Lee Hodgden, a former colleague of mine at Texas. And then, as Oregonians who came to me as students, I can only cite a galaxy of brilliance: Barry Borak, Rick McBride, Roger Sherwood, Fred Koetter, Terry Williams, Don Duncan, Norman Crowe, all of whom I regard as extended family. And then James Tice, my highly regarded student at Cornell, Don Genasci, whom I knew in London, Rick Mather, my London neighbour up the road, and—of course—Michael Dennis, now at M.I.T. In fact it sometimes seems to me that, all by myself, I could hold a little convocation of my Oregon connection.*

Rowe might similarly have remarked of "extended families" resulting from his appointment as Kea Distinguished Visiting Professor at the University of Maryland in 1978; his several year-long visiting positions at the University of Notre Dame's Rome Program in the 1980s; and annual reunions of sorts for many of these family members at the The Catholic University of America's summer programs from the mid-1970s through the 1980s, and instigated by John McDermott.

Our special thanks are due to Colin's brother, David Rowe, who graciously exchanged his many pleasant accounts of Colin's life and times. Carol Hurtt and Virginia Cartwright deserve the largest measure of credit and thanks for their helpful comments on virtually every aspect of the book, unwavering support, empathy, near limitless patience, and attention to burdensome miscellaneous matters otherwise being ignored by us. It is standard form that we thank them last, but they are, in a real sense, first and the most deserving.

Benefactors/Donors

Benefactors

Cornell University
Driehaus Foundation
University of Maryland
University of Notre Dame

Donors

Virginia Cartwright
Carol Hurtt and Steven W. Hurtt
Blake Middleton
Barbara Littenberg and Steven K. Peterson
James T. Tice

Supporters

Matthew Bell
Richard Bosch
Judith DiMaio
Peter Hetzel
Brian Kelly
Neal Payton
Stephen Quick
David Grahame Shane
Jon Michael Schwarting
Dhiru Thadani

Author Biographies

Matthew Bell
FAIA, FCNU Principal, Perkins Eastman, Professor, School of Architecture, Planning, and Preservation, University of Maryland
Matthew Bell was a student of Colin Rowe's in Notre Dame's Rome Studies program in 1980–81; in the graduate studio at Cornell in 1985–87; and taught with Rowe at the Cornell program in Rome in 1988. At the University of Maryland since 1989, he has led the urban design pedagogy and public initiatives and advised award-winning student teams in the ULI/Hines Urban Design and Development Competition. He has served as President of the Neighborhood Design Center, as Director of the NE Region of the Mayor's Institute on City Design, and sits on D.C.'s Historic Preservation Review Board. With Perkins Eastman, he leads large-scale architectural and sustainable urban design and campus planning and has garnered professional awards for master plans and residential, civic, and educational projects.

Stuart Cohen
FAIA, Cohen & Hacker Architects LLC
Professor of Architecture Emeritus, University of Illinois Chicago
Stuart Cohen is a practicing architect and a Fellow of the American Institute of Architects. He is professor of architecture emeritus at the University of Illinois, Chicago, and is the author of four books on Chicago's historic residential architecture. His writing and work was recognized in 2018 by an Arthur Ross Award from the Institute for Classical Architecture and Art and in 2019, along with his partner Julie Hacker, he received the Society of Architectural Historians' Award for Excellence in Design, Academics, and Scholarship. He is the recipient of the Chicago Chapter of the American Institute of Architects 2021 Lifetime Achievement Award. He recently published *Frank L. Wright and the Architects of Steinway Hall: A Study in Collaboration.*

Thomas K. Davis
FAIA, Professor of Architecture
University of Tennessee Knoxville
Thomas K. Davis received a Bachelor of Architecture in 1977 and his Master of Architecture in 1983, both from Cornell University. He was a Fulbright Scholar in Italy from 1983–1984, as well as the recipient of the NIAE Traveling Fellowship at the American Academy in Rome. Davis taught architecture at Syracuse University from 1984–1994. Since 1994, he and his students have worked on

urban architecture projects for Kingsport, TN as well as Nashville, receiving in 2016 a national Collaborative Practice Award from the ACSA. From 2004–2008, Davis served as Design Director at the Nashville Civic Design Center. He was a co-recipient in 2016 with Marleen Kay Davis of the AIA Tennessee Samuel Morgan Lifetime Service Award for Contributions to Architecture in the Public Realm.

Michael Dennis
Professor Emeritus MIT
Michael is the founder of Michael Dennis & Associates. Their award-winning work has been published nationally and internationally. He is the author of *Court & Garden, Architecture & the City, Elements and Principles of Planned Towns*, and, forthcoming, *The Venetian Facade and Carnegie Mellon University: Campus Planning & Architectural Design*. He was the Director of the post-professional Architecture and Urbanism Program at MIT, teaching Urban Design and Urban Design Theory. He taught at Cornell, Kentucky, Princeton, Rice, Harvard, and Columbia. Distinguished teaching posts include: University of Virginia, Yale University, Architecture at the University of Michigan, and Notre Dame. In 2011 he was awarded the CNU Athena Medal for contributions to urbanism.

Judith DiMaio
FAIA, RIBA
Judith DiMaio, FAIA, RIBA, is a licensed architect and a renowned educator. DiMaio holds a M. Arch from Harvard, a B. Arch from Cornell, and a BA from Bennington College. In 2013, the AIA elevated DiMaio to its prestigious College of Fellows. She is Dean Emerita at NYIT's School of Architecture and Design, and was an associate professor at Yale's School of Architecture and director of the major in Architecture. DiMaio has been a distinguished professor at numerous universities, and an invited lecturer at Magdalen College, Oxford. She was awarded both the Rome Prize in Architecture and the Colin Rowe Residency by the American Academy in Rome. DiMaio's newly launched consultancy, *Close Reads*, offers her expertise to architecture and design firms, institutions, and cultural organizations.

Roberto Einaudi
Architect, Artist
Roberto Einaudi, B.Arch. Cornell University, 1961; M.Arch. MIT, 1962, worked with Louis I. Kahn and has practiced in Africa, Middle and Far East, the U.S., and Europe, including designs for new cities. In 1986, he founded the Cornell Program in Rome, directing it until 1992. Studio Einaudi has designed museums (Capitoline Museum, Museo dei Gessi, Rome), exhibitions, archeological sites (Roman Imperial Fora, Ancient Roman Theater Naples), restoration historical buildings (American Academy in Rome, Villa Aurelia), and urban sites (Venice historical center, athletic facilities central Naples). He contributed to *La lezione di Pier Luigi Nervi* and the critical re-edition of *Aesthetics and Technology in Building by Nervi*, and he edited and translated *Roma Moderna* by Italo Insolera. He writes and draws about dreams, family history, the poets Keats and Shelley, and Virginia Woolf.

Charles P. Graves, Jr.
Professor Emeritus Kent State University
Charles P. Graves received a Bachelor of Architecture in 1975. 1977–1979 from the University of Kentucky. Graves studied with Colin Rowe, graduating with a

Master of Architecture in Urban Design from Cornell. Then, Graves moved to Manhattan and worked with architects Stephen Potters and Elton Becket. In 1985, he began teaching architecture as an Assistant Professor for the ETH Zürich. In 1987, he followed up teaching at the College of Architecture and Environmental Design, Kent State University. Graves was awarded two Graham Foundation Grants, one to produce his thesis, "Manhattan: A Measure," and one to author his book, *The Genealogy of Cities*. Graves retired from the CAED, Kent State in 2018, is presently a professor emeritus, and practices architecture and photography. His website, *Looking @ Cities* [https://lookingatcities.info/] is devoted to the study of the Urban Fabric.

Kevin J. Hinders
Architect & Urbanist
Associate Professor, School of Architecture, University of Illinois Urbana Champaign
Kevin Hinders was a student of Colin Rowe's in Notre Dame's Rome Studies program in 1980–81, and in the graduate studio at Cornell in 1985–87. In 1985, Matt Bell and Hinders had the unique opportunity to live with Rowe at his home. Rowe mentions this as an extension of their education in his 'salon'. Early in his career, he taught at The Catholic University of America, Arizona State University, and Washington University. He joined the faculty at the University of Illinois Urbana Champaign in 1990. In 2014, he created the *Chicago Studio*, an urban design and professional practice studies program. His work is at all scales of architecture and urban design. It has included master plans for the University campus, its research parks, and 'Campustown 2000'.

Steven W. Hurtt
Professor Emeritus, School of Architecture, Planning, and Preservation, University of Maryland
After BA and MFA professional degree architecture studies at Princeton, Hurtt joined the Cornell Rowe Studio, 1966–67. Co-writing a thesis with Stuart Cohen, they are credited with coining Contextualism to describe the ideas developing in the Studio. At Notre Dame, 1973–90, he taught in the Rome Studies program in 1978–79, and again in 2009 and 2011–13. While dean at Maryland in 1990–2004, the school's graduate offering expanded from Architecture to include Planning, Preservation, a National Center for Smart Growth, and, subsequently, Real Estate Development and a PhD in Urban & Regional Studies and Design. Service and practice included Hurtt-Kenrick Architects, PC 1984–90, CNU Board, JAE editorial board, and, in 1990–2019, campus planning for U. Maryland, and occasional consulting for College Park and with Thadani Architects + Urbanists.

Brian Kelly
Professor of Architecture, School of Architecture, Planning, and Preservation, University of Maryland
Brian Kelly received his professional degree at the University of Notre Dame and his post-professional degree in Urban Design from Cornell University. He teaches at the University of Maryland, where he also serves as Associate Dean for Development and Faculty Affairs. His professional expertise is in campus planning. Kelly is a watercolorist and he regularly leads groups of architecture students to study in Italy. Kelly's creative work has been shown in a traveling exhibition

titled "Lines of Inquiry: The Architectural Drawings of Brian Kelly" (www.linesofinquiry.com).

Antonio Pietro Latini
Independent Scholar, Jinshan Distinguished Professor, Jiangsu University
Antonio Pietro Latini is an independent scholar based in Rome, Italy, Registered Architect of the Order of Rome, and Full Member of the Istituto Nazionale di Urbanistica. As a Fulbright Fellow and Fulbright Scholar, he taught in several universities in the U.S., Italy, and China. Among them, he was Jinshan Distinguished Professor at Jiangsu University and Kea Distinguished Professor at the University of Maryland. He studied architecture, urban planning, restoration, urban design, and business management at Sapienza, Columbia, and INSEAD. He is currently a Candidate for a Doctor of Philosophy in Architecture at the University of Oregon. He authored *Battery Park City, New York* and co-edited the trilogy *La progettazione urbana.*

Barbara M. Littenberg
Architect, Urban Designer
Barbara M. Littenberg is a practicing architect. She is co-founder of Peterson Littenberg Architects and Urban Design. She was Adjunct Associate Professor of Architecture at Yale University. Her firm acted as Urban Design consultants to the Lower Manhattan Development Corporation which was the public authority charged with rebuilding the World Trade Center Site following the tragic attack of 9/11. She has recently co-authored *Space & Anti Space, The Fabric of Place, City, and Architecture.*

Blake Middleton
FAIA FAAR
Blake Middleton, FAIA, FAAR, is a founding partner at Handel Architects. His work has pioneered innovative approaches to sustainable design and urban living in urban cores around the world. These include precedent-setting high-rise Passive House and mixed-use projects, adaptive reuse of historic buildings, mass timber construction, and an array of institutional and civic buildings. Blake has taught and lectured widely, and his work has won distinction from AIA, SARA, CNU, and the Urban Land Institute. He received his B. Arch. and M. Arch. in Urban Design from Cornell and is a Fellow of the American Academy in Rome, the Urban Design Forum, and the American Institute of Architects.

Franz Oswald
Professor Emeritus, ETH Zürich (Eidgenössische Technische Hochschule)
At the ETH, Oswald has been the Director, President, or Program Leader of the Institute for Local, Regional and National Planning (ORL); Salzburg Congress of Urban Planning and Development (SCUPAD); the Future Cities Laboratory, ETH Singapore (SEC), Curricula Reform Expert, Addis Ababa University. His practice, since 1974, has focused on urban housing projects, participatory workshops, and city development, primarily in Germany, Israel, and Switzerland. Awarded projects include Deutscher Betonpreis für Wohnen der Zukunft, IBA-Emscher Park, Bottrop. Preservation of Historic Buildings, Kanton Bern, Wohnsiedlung Bleiche Worb. Bern. Selected publications are *"NETZSTADT - Designing the Urban"*, with P. Baccini (2003); *"neue urbanität – das verschmelzen von stadt und*

landschaft", with N. Schueller (2003); *"Grassroots Urbanization. Building New Town Communities in Ethiopia"* with Z. Cherenet, W. Assefa, B. Staehli.

Neal Payton
FAIA, FCNU
Neal Payton, FAIA, FCNU, is a senior principal at Torti Gallas + Partners. He directs the firm's office in Los Angeles, which has a focus on the public realm. His work transforms urban environments into socially and culturally diverse, walkable, and economically vital communities. He has led multidisciplinary teams in the creation of visionary, yet implementable, master plans and form-based codes for the redevelopment and revitalization of declining urban centers, brownfields, and vast areas of aging inner suburbs. Neal has served on the faculties of architecture at several universities, including The University of Virginia, Rice University, Washington University in St. Louis, and The Catholic University of America. He holds a B. Arch from Carnegie Melon University and a M. Arch from Syracuse University.

Steven K. Peterson
Architect and Urban Designer with Peterson / Littenberg Architects, New York City
1964: Colin Rowe is Peterson's undergraduate thesis critic at Cornell University.
1968: Peterson returns to Cornell from Chicago to study with Rowe in his graduate Urban Design Studio.
1977: Peterson is asked by Rowe to collaborate on the final design of the Nolli Plan sector for *Roma interrotta*, in Rome.
1999: At Rowe's memorial service Peterson postulates that the sum of Colin Rowe's work and writings constitute a standard model to understand and design urban form.
2020: Essay on *Roma interrotta plan* is published in Peterson and Littenberg: *SPACE & ANTI SPACE, The Fabric of Place, City, and Architecture.*

Elio Piroddi
Professor of Urban Design, Sapienza, Università di Roma
Elio Piroddi is professor of Urban Design at Sapienza and the founder and director of Centro Studi "Futuri della città". As a designer of published buildings, public housing neighborhoods, and plans, he is also winner of design competitions, major awards of which include the IN/ARCH national prize in 1969. He is currently advisor of the Municipality of Rome for the new Comprehensive Plan. He has taught in universities in Italy, the US, and Africa, directed national research groups on urban planning and morphology, and promoted and coordinated national and international congresses. He is the author of essays and books on planning in Italy, urban history, urban morphology, and rules of urban re-composition. His work has been recognized to be of "historical value" for Architecture and Urban Planning and kept in the Central State Archive.

Stephen Quick
FAIA
Steve is an urban designer, architect, and educator. He has practiced as a principal in Pittsburgh since 1980 in his own firms, today with Civic Design and Planning LLC, and previously with Perkins Eastman. Steve's work as a professional has focused on urban design, environmental and economic development strategies, community design, and the design and construction of buildings

throughout the northeast. As an educator and researcher at Carnegie Mellon University, Steve has taught design studios and seminars that integrate urban design and architecture, performance and systems-design, civic engagement, and design management. His research through CMU's Remaking Cities Institute has focused on community and transportation design, design and data communication, and smart city infrastructure with collaborating computer science, robotics, and engineering researchers.

Jon Michael Schwarting

Professor of Architecture, New York Institute of Technology

Schwarting is an architect, urban designer, and professor. He studied Architecture and Urban Design at Cornell University and received a Rome Prize Fellowship from the American Academy in Rome. He has taught at Cooper Union, Columbia, Penn, Yale, Cornell, and Syracuse. He has lectured and published articles on architecture. He was an Associate with Richard Meier and practiced with partners since 1975. Work has been exhibited and published internationally. He received numerous grants. He has directed the restoration of the 1931 Aluminaire House since 1987. He has served on the Board of the Architectural League of NYC, Van Alan Institute and is Trustee Emeritus of the American Academy in Rome. He is the author of *Rome: Urban Formation and Transformation* (2017).

David Grahame Shane

Professor of Architecture Emeritus, Columbia University

Grahame Shane studied at the Architectural Association, London (AA Dipl 1969), Cornell M.Arch (Urban Design 1972), and PhD in Architectural and Urban History (1978) with Colin Rowe and Chris Otto. He taught at the AA for Alvin Boyarsky, Bennington College, and Columbia in the 1980s; in Urban Design since 1991. He lectured widely and published in Europe, the U.S., and Asia. He authored *Recombinant Urbanism: Conceptual Modeling in Architecture, Urban Design and City Theory* (2005) and *Urban Design Since 1945; a Global Perspective* (2010), and co-edited "Sensing the 21st Century City: Close-Up and Remote" (2005). His article "Gardens as Public Space; A Century of Continuity and Change in the Greater Bay Area" is in *The Emerging Public Realm of the Greater Bay Area* 2022.

Adolf Sotoca, PhD

Architect and Urbanist, Professor Serra Hunter, UPC_BarcelonaTECH

Guest Professor, Luleå Tekniska Universitet

Adolf Sotoca has taught urbanism at UPC_BarcelonaTECH since 2002, and is former Chair Professor at Luleå Tekniska Universitet, Sweden. He has also been Visiting Associate Professor at University of Illinois at U-C, USA, among others. He leads studios, theory courses, and seminars focused on the materiality of the City in a wide range of scales. He is researcher of several internationally funded programs and author of a vast number of publications. Professor Sotoca is principal of CSArquitectes, an acknowledged Barcelona-based firm. Adolf Sotoca is particularly interested in Colin Rowe's conception of time and texture, which he frequently brings to his scholarship. See more on www.adolfsotoca.com.

Dhiru Thadani

Architect, Artist, Urban Designer

Dhiru A. Thadani is an architect, urban designer, author, and educator who has been in practice since 1980 and has worked internationally. He has been the principal designer of new towns and cities, urban regeneration, neighborhood revitalization, and infill densification. Dhiru was born in Bombay, India, and moved to Washington, D.C., in 1972 to study architecture. During his fifty years in Washington, D.C., he has taught, practiced, and strived to place architecture and urbanism in the public eye. He is the author of *The Language of Towns and Cities: A Visual Dictionary,* (2010); *Visions of Seaside: Foundations, Evolution, Imagination,* and *Built & Unbuilt Architecture*; (2013); *Reflections on Seaside: Muses, Ideas, Influences, and New & Future Projects,* (2021); and *Washington Drawings: Abe to Zoo,* (2022).

James T. Tice

Architect, Professor Emeritus, Department of Architecture, University of Oregon

Tice is an award-winning architect and urban designer. He graduated from Cornell with a B. Arch (1968) and M. Arch (1970) in Urban Design under Colin Rowe, then studied at the American Academy in Rome. At the UO since 1991 he taught at USC, Notre Dame (Rome), and Columbia. Lecturing widely and authoring essays on architectural education, he has also co-authored *Courtyard Housing in Los Angeles*; *Frank Lloyd Wright: Between Principle and Form*; and *Giuseppe Vasi's Rome*, the exhibition and catalog. His co-authored websites include: the *Nolli Map Website*; *Giuseppe Vasi's Rome*; and *Images of Rome*. He received the UO Outstanding Research Career Award in 2014. His "Mapping Rome", [https://mappingrome.com/], focuses on the urbanism and cartography of Rome.

Jerry A. Wells

Architect, Professor Emeritus, Department of Architecture, Cornell University

Wells began teaching at Cornell in 1965, often teaching in the Rome Program. He served as department chair 1980–1989 and initiated *The Cornell Journal of Architecture*. Wells earned his B. Arch in 1959 at the University of Texas, beginning a life-long friendship with Colin Rowe. He studied at the ETH in Zurich, 1960–62. He has served on the Fulbright Committee, the National Screening Committee for Architecture, NAAB Board, JAE Editorial Committee, and the AIA Architects in Education Committee. In partnership with Fred Koetter, he won the 1970 "Brighton Beach Housing Competition", Brooklyn, NY, and the 1974 "Broadway East Housing", Kingston, NY. His "Shenandoah House" received a Progressive Architecture award in 1997 and was exhibited at MoMA.

Terrance 'Terry' Williams (1938–2015),

FAIA The Catholic University of America, Professor Emeritus

Terry Williams was among the Rowe Studio students responsible for executing a NYC and IAUS contract assessing a new zoning code, one of several efforts related to creating multiple local urban design offices in the city during the Lindsay Administration. Terry subsequently became deputy director of the mayor's office of Lower Manhattan Development and led visionary projects including creation of the South Street Seaport, and rezoning Tribeca and the Theater District. In private practice, he led the design team for Shahestan Pahlavi in Tehran, Iran, and Sanaa University in Yemen for I.M. Pei, and for many years, also led his own practice, The Williams Group. He later served as campus architect for the University of Virginia, then joined The Catholic University of America faculty.

Illustrations

Every effort has been made to contact copyright holders, but should there be any errors or omissions, the publisher would be pleased to insert the correct acknowledgement in any subsequent edition of the book.

Abbreviations for Frequently Used Sources:

Collections, Museums

(INITIALS) ARCHIVE: author's collection

HERM: State Hermitage Museum, Saint Petersburg

LVR: Louvre, Paris

MET: Metropolitan Museum of Art, New York

MoMA: Museum of Modern Art, New York

NGA: National Gallery of Art, Washington, D.C.

NPG: National Picture Gallery, London

MAXXI: Museo nazionale delle arti del XXI secolo, Rome

VJB: Collection of Vincent J. Buonanno (Brown University Library)

Books, Projects, Exhibitions, Cartography

AWS(1-3): *As I Was Saying: Recollections and Miscellaneous Essays* (3 vols.) Colin Rowe, Alex Caragonne, ed., 1996

BG: *Baedeker* travel guides

BWF: "Buffalo Waterfront Project", Albright-Knox Gallery, NY, 1969

CC: *Collage City*, Colin Rowe, Fred Koetter, 1978

CG: *Genealogy of Cities*, Charles Graves, 200

DPZ: Duany, Andrés and Plater-Zyberk, Elizabeth: *The New Civic Art*, 2003; *Towns and Town-Making Principles*, 2006

FUR: *Forma Urbis Romae*, Rodolfo Lanciani, 1901

FURR: *University of Oregon Forma Urbis*, digitally remastered, 2014

HP: *The American Vitruvius*, Hegemann and Peets, 1922

KK: *Koetter Kim and Associates: Place |Time*, 1997

LC ( ): *Oeuvre Compléte*, Le Corbusier, (seven volumes), with volume-years in parentheses

LT: *Édifices de Rome Moderne*, (three volumes), Paul Marie Letarouilly, 1840–55

MST: *Main Street*, Carole Rifkind, 1977

NCTY: "The New City: Architecture and Urban Renewal", MoMA, 1967

OLMD: Office of Lower Manhattan Development, 1966 ca.

OMPD: Office of Midtown Planning and Development, 1966 ca.

QL: *Quattro Libri*, Palladio, (four volumes), 1570

ROM: *La Pianta Grande di Roma*, Giambattista Nolli, 1748, digital remaster, University of Oregon 2004 ©

RIT: *Roma interrotta*, *Architectural Design* special issue, 1979

STA: *Space, Time and Architecture*, Sigfried Giedion (1948 ed. unless otherwise noted)

STT: *City Planning According to Artistic Principles*, Camillo Sitte, 1889

TXR: *Texas Rangers*, Alex Caragonne, 1995

WC: "The Figure/Grounds", Wayne Copper, 1967

WTT: *Architectural Principles in the Age of Humanism*, Rudolph Wittkower, 1949

Journals, Websites, Videos

AD: *Architectural Design*, 1979 (*Roma interrotta* issue unless otherwise noted)

AM: Apple Maps

ANET: *Art Net.* Issue 1, (video) Charles Jencks, 1975

AR: *The Architectural Review* (1947 unless otherwise noted)

CAS: *Casabella* (359-360, 1971 unless otherwise noted)

CJA1: *Cornell Journal of Architecture*, 1, 1981

CJA2: *Cornell Journal of Architecture*, 2 "Urban Design", 1983

GE: Google Earth

GM: Google Maps

IAUS: *Institute for Architecture and Urban Studies*

Book Cover

P. Mandel and J. Tice

Photo from the estate of Thomas Schumacher; courtesy of Patti Sachs; Nolli Map, detail, University of Oregon, 2004.

Foreword

13: *Rowe Interrotto*, Carl Laubin, 102cm x 148cm, oil on canvas, 2002, collection of Eve Happold

I. Colin Rowe & Urban Design 34: ANET

The Colin Rowe Model of Urban Form: 'Just How to Make a City' (S.K. Peterson)

SP ARCHIVE: 36; 41.3; 44.5; 45.6; 46.7; 47.8; 48.9; 49.10; 50.11, 12; 51.13; 52.14; 53.15, 16; 55.17; 56.18; 57.19

Other: 38.1a, 1b: GE; 38.1c: Photo, Pierre Selim, Wikimedia Commons; 40.2a: R. Feymann; 40.2b: R. Jägals; 43.4a: Manhattan Post Card Pub., ca. 1939; 43.4b: The Frick Collection

Colin Rowe: The Rediscovery of the City (M. Dennis)

MD ARCHIVE: 60; 63.2, 3; 65.10; 67.15, 16, 17; 73.29, 30, 31; 75.35

Other: 62.1: M.R.G. Conzen, 1960; 63.4: ROM; 63.5: S. Muratori, 1963; 64.6, 7: *Die Grosstadt*, O. Wagner, 1911; 65.8: *City of the Future*, E. Henard, 1910; 65.9: Dubai Center, anon.; 66.11: LC (1910–29); 66.12: *Bauen für die Weltgemeinschaft*, K. Schwarz, 2016; 66.13: CJA2; 66.14: M. Wagner 1942; 68.18: City of Boston Archive, Photo, Zack, 1930; 68.19: City of Boston Archive 1960s; 69.20: S. Minsk, K. Lynch, J. Meyer, 1962; 69.21: A. Le Pautre, 1654; 69.22: QL; 69.23: LC (1910-29); 70.24, 25: CJA2; 71.26: RIT; 71.27: *Stadtraum*, R. Krier, 1975; 72.28: L. Krier, 1976; 74.32: R. Krier, 1989; 74.33, 34: R. Krier, 1991

From "Mathematics" to "Urbanistics" (A.P. Latini)

76: JT ARCHIVE; 79.1: AR, 1947; 80.2: WTT; 81.3: *Poem of the Right Angle*, Le Corbusier, 1955; 82.4: *Parentalia*, C. Wren, 1750; 83.5: *Castles on the Ground*, J.M. Richards, P. Angus, 1947; 86.6: *Gardens in the Modern Landscape*, C. Tunnard, 1938; 86.7: AR(1955); 86.8: AR, 1956; 86.9: *Townscape*, G. Cullen, 1961; 88.10: Lockhart, TX, Herronstock Photoshelter; 88.11, 89.12: TXR; 93.13: SH ARCHIVE; 93.14: STT; 95.15: *Towns and Buildings*, S.E. Rasmussen, 1949; 96.16: "Urban Precedents", M. Dennis and K. Herdeg, 1974; 96.17: WC; 97.18: VJB

The Legacy of Colin Rowe and the Figure/Ground Drawing (C. Graves)

CG ARCHIVE: 98; 109.18, 19; 110.21, 114.28, 116.33

Other: 100.1: *Ueber Fühlen und Wollen: Eine Psychologische Studie*, C. Ehrenfels, 1887; 100.2: *The Psychologist* 25, J. Pind, 2012d; 101.3: *Composition with Lines*, 1917 P. Mondrian; *Fox Trot*; *Lozenge Composition with Three Black Lines*, 1929 P. Mondrian; *About Two Squares*, El Lissitzky, 1922; 101.4: *Art and Visual Perception*, R. Arnheim, 1954; 102.5: HP; 102.6: *The Anatomy of the Village*, T. Sharp, 1946; 102.7: *Design in Town and Village*, H.M. Stationary Office, London, 1953; 103.8: *Saper Vedere L'architettura*, B. Zevi, 1948; 103.9: *Town Design*, F. Gibberd, 1953; 104.10: *Townscape*, G. Cullen, 1961; 104.11: ROM; 105.12a: *Image of the City*, K. Lynch, 1960; 105.12b: *Guide of Paris*, G. Debord, 1955; 105.12c: Golden Lane, A. and P. Smithson, 1952; 105.d: *Plug in City*, Archigram, 1966; 105.12e: *City Helix*, K. Kurokawa, 1961; 105.12f: *Ville Radieuse*, Le Corbusier, 1934; 106.13a: TXR; 106.13b: WC; 107.14: CJA2; 107.15a: Royal Collection Trust RCIN 912284 and plan, C. Graves; 107.15b: SDUK and WC; 108.16, 17; 109.18: CJA2; 109.19: RIT; 110.20, 22, 23, 24: CJA2; 111.25: *Italian Gardens of the Renaissance*, Shepherd and Jellicoe, 1925; 111.26: AWS(2); 112.27a: L. Krier, 1971; 112.27b: *Formal Structure in Indian Architecture*, K. Herdeg, 1977; 112.27c: Dennis, Clark & Associates, TAMS, 1992; 112.27d: KK, 1985; 112. 27e Z. Hadid, 1978; 112.27f: *Suprematism No. 58*, K. Malevich (Wikipedia Commons) 1916; 112.27g: Z. Hadid, 1990; 112.27h: R. Koolhaas, 1994; 112.27i: *The Figural City / West L.A.* 2012; 113.27j: *X-Urbanism: Architectuand the American City*, M. Gandelsonas, 1999; 114.29: *Space Syntax*, B. Hillier, et. al, 1998; 114.30: *Schwarzpläne*, 2014; 115.31: *Open Street Map*, 2014; 115.32: *Points+Lines*, S. Allen, 1999; 116.33: 116.34: KK; *Manhattan Timeformations*, 1994; 117.35: BG Deutschland, 1896; 177.36: ROM

Type and Transformation (J.T. Tice)

JT ARCHIVE: 118; 125.9, 10; 126.11; 128.16, 17; 129.18, 20; 133.27; 135.31; 136.32; 137.34; 138.36, 37; 139.39

Other: 121.1: *Classification of Species*, H. Winkles, 1851; 121.2: *Encyclopedie ou Dictionanaire raisonné*, Diderot and d'Alembert, 1765; 122.3: WTT; 122.4: *Précis des leçons d'architecture donnees à École polytechnique*, J.N.L. Durand, 1802; 123.5: P. Zygas, 1986; 123.6: LC (1946-52); 124.7: "Mayan Plan Transformations", R. Sherwood, 1968; 124.8: HP; 126.12: *Architektonisches Alphabeth*, J.D. Steingruber, 1773; 127.13: *On Growth and Form*, D. Thompson; 127.14: *Art and Illusion*, E.H. Gombrich, 1959; 128.15: *Liberation*, M.C. Escher, 1955; 129.19: Photo: E.J. Marey, 1884; 130.21: *Formal Structure in Indian Architecture*, K. Herdeg, 1967; 130.22: *Arcades*, J.F. Geist, 1983; 131.23: "Galloping Horse and Rider", E. Muybridge, 1870; 131.24: H. Edgerton MIT Archive, 1937; 132.25: *Temples by the Water*, P. Klee, 1927; 132.26: *Strada Nuova*, Univ. Genova, 1968; 133.28a: *Tratato di architettura*, Francesco di Giorgio Martini, 1497; 133.28b: *Architecture in Italy, 1400-1600*, L.H. Heydenreich and W.A. Lotz, 1974; 134.29: Photo: A. Bertozzi; 135.30: CC; 136.33; 137.35: VJB; 138.38: H. Edgerton MIT Archive, 1938

Inland Architect and Contextualism: A Commentary (S. Cohen)

E. Bacon, *Design of Cities*, 1967: 140; 143; 144; 147:

The Influence of Colin Rowe on My Urbanism and Architecture (D.A. Thadani)

DT ARCHIVE: 148–159 © inclusive

Three Stage Sets in Search of a City: An American Perspective (J.T. Tice)

JT ARCHIVE: 160; 162.1; 163.5; 164.7; 166.12; 167.16; 168.20

Other: 162.2: MET; 162.3: Architectural Drawings, Vv.Aa, 2011; 163.4: MET; 163.6: Rijksmuseum; 164.8: MET; 164.9: Currier & Ives, New York, 1870; 166.10, 11: *Palladio*, J. Ackerman, 1974; 167.13, 14, 15: VJB; 168.17, 18: *Design of Cities*, E. Bacon, 1967; 168.19: VJB; 169.21: "Inigo Jones's Stage Architecture and Its Sources", J. Peacock, 1982; 169.22: Photo: George Cserna; 170.23: MST; 170.24: Photo: C.P. Cushing, 1872, by permission; 170.25, 26: MST; 172.27: STA; 172.28: H.D. Nichols, L. Prang &

Co. Publisher; 172.29: Riverside Historical Museum, 1868; 173.30: *Portfolio of Views*, C.D. Arnold, 1893; 173.31, 32, 33: Chicago Historical Society, ca. 1893; 174.34: *Campus: An American Planning Tradition*, P.V. Turner, 1984; 174.35: "Palace of Fine Arts", C.C. Cooper, 1915; 174.36: *The Architecture and the Gardens of the San Diego Exposition*, M. Winslow, 1915; 175.37: *Plan of Chicago*, Burnham and Bennet, 1909; 175.38: Benjamin Franklin Parkway, C. Finley & Co., 1925; 176.39, 40: *Washington on View*, J. Reps, 1991; 176.41: *Washington, D.C. Garden Stories*, G.I. Parkyns, ca. 1795; 177.42: Times Square 1953, archival photo; 177.43: Rockefeller Center, Inc., ca. 1939; 177.44: Photo: Dave Beckerman, 1994; 178.45: Photo: Turismo Roma, IG giorgioteti; 179.46: AM; 180.47: Merrit Parkway, Postcard, A. Kleban & Sons, 1938; 180.48: Courtesy of Park Commission, New York in STA(1967); 181.49: Promotional poster, ca. 1930; 181.50: *The Disappearing City*, Frank Lloyd Wright, 1932; 182.51: Google Arts & Culture; 182.52: Photo © Museum Associates/LACMA, ca. 1965; 183.53: Le Corbusier, 1945, 18413. "FLC-ADAGP; 183.54: STA (1967) Photo: Robert D. Harvey, 1953; 184.55: "Mulberry Street", Detroit Publishing Co. Wikimedia Commons, ca. 1900; 185.56: Disneyland, Upjohn Co. ca. 1955; 185.57: Photo: Wallace Litman, ca. 1971; 186.58: Las Vegas News Bureau, ca. 1970; 186.59: *Progressive Architecture*, C. Moore (attrib.) ca. 1965; 186.60: "Learning from Levittown studio", Yale University, ca. 1970; 187.61: Photo by permission: Luke Sharrett; 187.62: Photo by permission, Alamy, Paul Schutzer; 187.63: Photo: Craig Wolfe; 188.64: Los Angeles County Museum of Art; 189.65: NGA; 189.66: Whitney Museum of American Art

II. Pedagogy 190: ANET

Colin Rowe: My Personal Recollections (J.A. Wells)
192: CJA1; 197: Sibley Dome, Cornell University Archive

The 1967 Cohen-Hurtt Master's Thesis (abridged) (S.W. Hurtt)
SW & SC ARCHIVE: 200; 215.21; 217.23; 218.24; 219.25
Other: 204.1: *Holy City of the New Jerusalem*, J. Goltzius, 1646; 205.2: Isaac Newton, J. Vanderbank, 1725; 205.3: René Descartes, F. Hals, 1649; 205.4; *Auguste Comte*, J. H. Hoffmeister, 1851; 205.5: G.W.F. Hegel, Bollinger engraving after J.C. Xeller, ca. 1825; 206.6: Photo: P. Halsman, 1935; 207.7: "Le Panorama, 1900", *Librairie d'Art*; 208.8: *La Ville Radieuse*, Le Corbusier, 1934; 208.9: LC (1910-1929); 209.10: *Le Plus Excellents Bastiments de France*, Du Cerceau, 1576; 209.11: J.N.L. Durand, *Recueil et Parallèle: L'Architecture*, 1799-1801; 209.12: *Histoire de l'Architecture*, A. Choisy, 1899; 209.13: LT; 210.14 *Still Life*, 1920, Charles-Édouard Jeanneret-Gris, MoMA; 212.15: Plan of Paris, M. Turgot, 1739; 213.16: Plan of Paris, P. Patte, 176; 213.17: Art Carrousel, N. Wolpert, 1900; 213.18: Rue de Castiglione, W. Price, 1831; 214.19: Ideal City, V. Scamozzi, 1615; 214.20: LC (1910-1929); 216.22: Plan of Paris, Turgot, 1739; 220.26: LC (1910-1929); 221.27: *La Ville Radieuse*, Le Corbusier, 1934; 224.28: WC; 225.29: New York Public Library, 1866

Contexualizing Contextualism (B. Kelly)
BK ARCHIVE: 226
Other: 230.1: SC & SH ARCHIVE; 231.2: CJA2; 232.3: MoMA; 234.4: CJA2; 235.5, 237.6; 238.7: BG, 1927; 239.8: WC; 240.9; 241.10; 242.11: CJA2
Buffalo and Beyond: The Cornell Urban Design Studio, Theory and Practice, 1962–1988 (S.W. Hurtt)
244: CJA2; 250.1, 251.2: New York Heritage Digital Collection; 252.3a; 253.3b; 254.4a; 255.4b: BWF: 256.5; Fairchild Aerial Surveys, 1933; 256.6: *Harper's Weekly*, 1877; 257.7: Composite image, *Collage City*, *Cornell Journal of Architecture* 2, *As I Was Saying* 3; 258.8: *The Radiant City*, 1933/1967; 259.9: HP; 259.10: *Townscape*, G. Cullen, 1961; 260.11:*The Theory of the Avant-Garde*, R. Poggioli, 1968; 261.12: *Mont Sainte-Victoire*, P. Cezanne,1902–04, Philadelphia Museum of Art; 261.13: *The Portuguese*, G. Braque, 1911–12, Kunstmuseum, Basel, Switzerland; 261.14: *Bouteilles et Couteau*, J. Gris, 1912, Kröller-Müller Museum, Otterlo, Netherlands; 262.15: *Pan-American Exposition*, C.E. Pelz, 1901, Harvard Map Collection; 262.16: BM ARCHIVE; 263.17: *Château de Chantilly*, Honoré Daumet, 1875, Wikimedia Commons; 263.18; 264.19; 20: CJA2; 264.21: WC ; 266.22: GM; 266.23: SC & SH ARCHIVE 266.24: AM; 267.25: CJA2; 268.26, 27: CJA2; 270.28: Cornell University Archive; 270.29: *Grandes Compositions Exécutées*, G. Gromort, 1910; 271.30: CJA2; 272.31: AWS(2) and "Milan Triennale Catalogue", 1987; 273.32, 33: CJA2

Disseminating an Idea: The Cornell Journal of Architecture 2 (B. Middleton)
BM ARCHIVE: 283; 289
Other: 274: JT ARCHIVE; 276a: BWF; 276b: *Design of Cities*, 1967; 276c: NCTY; 276d: CAS; 276e: AD 1979; 276f: CC; 277a *The Mund Plan*, 1970; 277b Oppositions 4; 277c: *Architecture Rationelle*, 1978; 277d: *Urban Space*, 1979; 277e: AD; 278a: "Urban Precedents", 1974; 278b: "The Paris Architectural Center", 1977; 278c: "The French Hôtel Plans", 1974; 278d: *Court & Garden*, 1986; 279a: "Gotham City", 1976; 279b: "The Urban Villa", 1978; 279c: *Delirious New York*, 1978; 279d: *Modulus*, 1979; 280a: *Precis* 1, 1979; 280b: *Perspecta* 16, 1980; 280c: "The Provincial City", 1970; 280d: AD (Collage City) 1979; 280e: CC; 281a "Roma interrotta", 1978; 281b: AD (*Roma interrotta*) 1979; 281c: *Harvard Architectural Review* 1, 1980; 281d CJA1, 1981; 281e: *Lotus International* 27, 1980; 282: *Design Quarterly* 113-114, 1980; 284a, b, c: CJA2; 285d, e, f, g: CJA2; 286a: TXR; 286.b AWS (1, 2, 3); 287a: *ANY*, 1996; 287b: IUAV, 2009; 287c: *Reckoning with Colin Rowe*, 2015; 287d: *Letters of Colin Rowe*, 2018; 288a: Photo: Barbara Morgan; 288b: Photo: Creative Commons; 288c: Photo, Nancy Lassalle/Eakins Press

Reflections on Colin Rowe, Three Decades Hence (T.K. Davis)
TD ARCHIVE: 290; 294.4, 5; 296.6, 296.7; 297.8; 298.9; 299.10; 300.11; 303.13; 304.14d; 305.15; 306.16; 307.17
Other: 294.1: Photo: Valerie Bennett; 295.2, 3: L. Krier; 296.6: Plan, S. Chase, 1853; 302.12: Map Kingsport, TN, J. Nolen, ca.1919

Teaching Urban Design and the 'Reconquest of Time' (K. Hinders)
KH ARCHIVE: 310; 312.1; 314.3; 317.4; 321.5; 324.6a; 325.6b; 327.7; 328.8; 329.9; 330.10
Other: 313.2: Photo, Mike Bohlmann, protomaker.io

III. Rome 332: ANET

Colin Rowe: Rome and Cornell (R. Einaudi)
LT: 335-339

Rome: A Study in Urban and Architectural Formation and Transformation (J.M. Schwarting)
JS ARCHIVE: 340; 343.4; 347.19, 20; 348.21; 349.22; 350.23; 351.24; 352.25; 353.26; 354.27; 355.28; 356.29; 357.30; 358.31; 359.32
Other: 343.1: Servius Tulius, 1527; 343.2: Map of Rome (Augustan), 1517; 343.3: T. di Bartolo, 1414; 344.5: Ideal City, Fra Giocondo, 1511; 344.6: Sforzinda, Filarete, ca. 1464; 344.7: Palmanova, V. Scamozzi, 1593; 344.8 Leonardo da Vinci ca.1487; 344.9: Photo: Adonovan0, Wikimedia Commons: 344.10: San Pietro, Vatican Library ca. 1560; 344.11: *Grandes Compositions Exécutées*, G. Gromort, 1910; 344.12: Sforzinda, Filarete ca. 1464; 344.13: Archival photo; 344.14: *Ten Books on Architecture*, Vitruvius, 1st century BC; 344.15: Sforzinda, Filarete, ca.1464; 344.16: QL; 345.17: *Ideal City*, School of Piero della Francesca ca. 1480; 346.18: VJB; 360.33: SC & SH ARCHIVE; 360.34: Prudential Center, TAC, ca.1959; 360.35: Euralile Project, OMA, 1988; 360.36: *Garden Cities of Tomorrow*, E. Howard, 1902; 360.37: Radburn, NJ, Stein, et. al ca. 1929; 360.38: DPZ 1985; 361.39: *James Stirling: Buildings and Projects 1950–1974*, 1974; 361.40: Stuttgart Rail Yards, Gerkan, Marg, and Partners ca. 1995

The Micro-Urbanism of Rome (J.T. Tice)
JT ARCHIVE: 362; 364.1; 366.4; 367.5; 368.7; 370.10, 11; 371.14; 372.16, 17, 18, 20; 374.21; 375.22; 376.26; 377.27, 28, 29; 378.30, 31; 379.34, 36; 381.38a, 38b, 39, 40; 382.41; 383.44, 45, 46; 384.47; 385.48
Other: 365.2: ROM and FURR; 365.3: VJB; 368.6a: Wikimedia Commons; 368.6b, 6c: VJB; 369.8a–l; VJB; 370.9: VJB; 370.12: G.B. Falda 1676; 371.13, 15: VJB; 373.19, 375.23a–e, 376.24, 376.25: LT; 376.25: Vatican Library, Codex Chigi P. VII, 9, c. 46; 378.32: VJB; 378.33: Dudley P. Allen Fund, L. Cruyl, The Cleveland Museum of Art, 1665; 379.35: Wikimedia Commons, Livioandronico; 380.37: VJB; 382.42: Galleria Nazionale d'Arte Antica, Roma, 1685; 382.43: Photo: Saiko

Rome: The Lost and Unknown City (Roma Ignota e Perduta) (J. DiMaio)
JD ARCHIVE: 409.76; 410.78
Other: 386: Emma Hart, R. Cosway, ca. 1775; 388.1: ROM; 388.2: MAXXI; 388.3: ROM; 388.4: RIT; 389.5: HERM; 390.6: NGA; 390.7: LVR; 390.8: Museo di Roma 1874; 391.9: Peterhof Palace and Gardens, Photo: anon; 391.10: Towneley Hall Art Gallery and Museum, 1782; 391.11: Museo di Roma, 1656; 391.12: British Museum 1777; 392.13: The Altes Museum, Berlin 1850; 392.14: Casa di Goethe, Rome 1787; 392.15: *A Collection of Designs for Household Furniture and Interior Decorations*, G. Smith, 1808; 393.16: NPG, London ©, by permission; 393.17: Scottish National Portrait Gallery for Dawe 1860; 393.18: Museo e Gipsoteca, Possagno, Italy ca. 1799; 394.19: Bündner Kunstmuseum, Chur, Switzerland; 394.20: Thorvaldsen Museum, Copenhagen; 394.21: NPG; 394.22: Blanton Museum of Art, Austin; 394.23: Bayerischen Staatsgemäldesammlungen, Munich; 394.24: Alte Nationalgalerie-Staatliche Museen, Berlin; 394.25: Venizelos Mansion, Athens; 394.26: NPG; 394.27: NPG; Keats-Shelley Memorial House, Rome; 395.28: The Tate, London 1889; 395.29: ROM; 396.30: Photo: Museo Civiltá Romana; 396.31: MAXXI; 396.32: Photo: J. Bondono; 397.33: Private collection 1818; 397.34: Musée Nationale des Châteaux de Malmaison et Bois-Préau, Malmaison; 397.35: Private collection, Paris; 398.36: ROM; 398.37: Museo di Roma, 1779; 398.38: Instituut Collectie Nederland, early 17th century; 399.39: SMB, Kupferstichkabinett, Berlin ca. 1841; 399.40: Photo: Architas; 400.41: The Bowes Museum, Barnard Castle, County Durham 1689; 400.42: Rijksmuseum, Amsterdam ca. 1764; 400.43: MAXXI; 400.44: Schloss Weimar, Stiftung Weimarer Klassik und Kunstsammlungen, Weimar: 401.45: Sir John Soane's House and Museum, London, Photo: D. Moore; 401.46: LVR; 401.47: Château de Versailles; 401.48: NGA; 401.49: Accademia Nazionale di San Luca, Rome; 402.50: Museo del Prado 1630; 402.51: ROM; 403.52: Private collection, 19th century; 403.53: Calcografia Nazionale, Rome; 403.54; Birmingham Museum and Art Gallery, Birmingham, England; 404.55: Photo: anon; 404.56: Photo: F. Bourgouin; 404.57: *Italian Gardens of the Renaissance*, Shepherd and Jellicoe, 1925; 404.58: P.M. Letarouilly, *Le Vatican et la basilique de Saint-Pierre de Rome*, 1882; 405.59: Private collection, 1689; 405.60: Roma, the Pincio, Casina Valadier, Blick auf Valadier Häuslein, anon. postcard, ca. 1910, A. Sorocchi-Milano-Roma No. 4688-7; 405.61: ROM; 406.62: NPG; 406.63:

Ruins of the Palace of the Emperor Diocletian at Spalato in Dalmatia, R. Adams, 1764; 406.64: British Library; 407.65: Peterhof Palace, Saint Petersburg; 407.66, 67: HERM; 407.68: Baltimore Museum of Art, Baltimore; 407.69: Private collection; 407.70: N. Boylston, Museum of Fine Arts; 408.71: C. Percier, 1786-90, Bibliothèque de l'Institut de France, Réunion des Musées Nationaux, Paris; 408.72: Art Institute Chicago; 408.73; National Galleries Scotland; 408.74: *Italian Architecture 1750 - 1914*, C.L.V. Meeks, 1966; 409.75: MET; 410.77: Anon., zonageografia. deascuola.it; 411.79: Photo: *Art in Vista Guide Viterbo*; 411:80: Photo: *Awesome Aviaries*; 411.81: Photo: A.F.E. Bernhard; 412.82: Bibliothèque Nationale de France 1801; 413.83: Musei Civici, Padova, Italy; 413.84: Hamburger Kunsthalle, Hamburg, Germany; 413.85: LVR; 413.86: Städel Museum, Frankfurt; 413.87: Private collection; 413.88: LVR; 414.89: MET; 414.90: Biblioteca di Archeologia e Storia dell'Arte (BiASA), Palazzo Venezia, Rome 1800; 415.91: Photo: M. Bell, by permission; 415.92: *Italian Villas and Their Gardens* by E. Wharton, 1904

IV. Praxis 416: ANET

The Impact of Colin Rowe on New York City (T.R. Williams)
418: OLMD, 1973; 419.1, 420.2, 3: NCTY; 420.4; 421.5, 6: Proposed plan of Upper East and West Sides of Manhattan, Urban Design Group, 1968; 422.7: Fifth Avenue Special Zoning District Plan, OMPD, ca. 1968; 423.8: NYC Planning Commission, 1969-1970; 424.9: Proposal Grand Central Terminal, M. Breuer and H. Beckhard, 1968; 424.10: Photo: Mel Finkelstein/NY Daily News Archive 1975; 425.11: Olympic Tower Proposal, OMPD, ca. 1968; 425.12, 13: Lower Manhattan Waterfront: Zoning Districts, OLMD, 1973; 426.14: "The Lower Manhattan Plan" by Wallace, McHarg, Roberts and Todd; Whittlesey, Conklin and Rossant; Alan M. Voorhees and Associates Inc., NYC Planning Commission, 1966; 426.15: Rector Place, aerial view, StreetEasy.com anon; 426:16, 17: Battery Park City, A. Cooper and S. Eckstut, ca. 1973: 427.18, 19, 20: Manhattan Landing Land Reclamation Study, "Lower Manhattan Waterfront" OLMD, 1975; 428.21: Aerial view of South Street Seaport, 1975, Courtesy of philip.greenspun.com; 428.22: "Lower Manhattan Waterfront" OLMD, ca. 1973: 428.23: Photo: Paul Warchol, 1980; 429.24: NCTY

The Koetter Kim Practice, a Paragon of Contextualism? (S.W. Hurtt)
SH ARCHIVE: 430; 442.11, 12; 443.15, 16, 17
Koetter Kim ARCHIVE: 439.3; 440.4, 5; 442.10; 444.18, 19, 20, 21, 22, 23; 446.32, 33; 448.38; 451.48; 452.51 a, b, c; 453.52, 53, 54, 55, 56, 57; 454.58, 59, 60; 455.60, 61, 62, 63; 456.64; 457.65; 459.74
Other: 434.1: *Genius Loci*, C. Norberg-Schulz, 1980; 435.2: *Architecture in Context*, B. C. Brollin, 1980; 440.6: AM; 441.7, 8, 9: Photos L. Abitbol; 442.13: GM; 443.14: GM; 444.24: GM, Street View; 444.25: Photo: A. McLean/Landslides; 445.26, 27, 29, 29, 30, 31: Photos: L. Abitbol; 446.34: GE; 446.35: Photo: J. Goldberg;
447.36, 37: Photos: maukinthewise; 448.39, 40: Photo: S. Hossain/MIT/Dome; 449.41: Photo: L. Abitbol;
449.42: GM; 429.43: Photo: L. Abitbol; 450.44: GM;
450.45: Photo: S. Hossain; 450.46, 47: Photo, L. Abitbol;
451.49, 50: Photo: KKA/Photo: Aerolis Photographers;
458.66, 67; 68, 69; 70; 459.71: GM; 459.72: Photo: D. Gilbert; 459.73: GM; 459.75: Photo: J. Miller; 459.76: Photo: J. Goldberg; 461.77: Photo: KKA

Evidence of an Argument (B. Middleton)
BM ARCHIVE: 462; 466.3; 471.10; 477.29, 30; 482; 483
Other: 464.1: *Lotus International* 27 1980; 464.2: CJA2; 467.4: IAUS, 1979; 468.5: NCTY; 468.6: Photo: Stephen Potters; 469.7: CJA2; 470.8: *MUND Plan*, R. Sherwood, U.S. Government Office of Economic Opportunity, 1970; 470.9: BWF; 471.11, 12: CJA2; 472.13: Photo: Lara Swimmer; 472.14: Weiz Center site plan 2011; 472.15: MSR Design 2013; 473.16: Weiss/Manfredi Architects, 2002; 473.17: Photo: Albert Vecerka/ESTO; 473.18: Photo: Ewan Baan; 473.19, 474.20: Photo: Albert Vecerka/ESTO; 474.21: Nanotech Center, site plan 2013; 474.22: Shirine Boulos, Ellenzweig, 2004-06; 474.23: site plan; 474.24: Photo: Anton Grassl; 475.25, 26, 27: Jewels of Salzburg, Hariri & Hariri Architects, 2014 aerial view; 476.28: KPF Architects, 2017; 477.31: Millennium Place, photo: Gustav Holland; Photo: Bruce Martin: 477.32; 478.33, 34: T.K. Davis; 479.35, 36, 37: Photos: courtesy SOM/©Shinkenchiku-sha; 480.38: Arizona State University, Master Plan, B. Kelly and M. Underwood, 1987; 480.39: ASU Master Plan update with Ayers Sainte Gross Architects, 2007; 480.40: Photo: ©Roland Halbe Fotografie; 480.41: Richard Meir and Partners; 481.42: Photo: ©Klaus Frahm/Artur images; 481.43: Richard Meier and Partners

Collage City: Theory into Practice (M. Bell)
484: Rockefeller Center, Inc.; 486.1: CJA2; 486.2: *Image of the City*, Kevin Lynch, 1960; 486.3: KK; 486.4: DPZ, 1985; 487.5: Dennis & Associates with Barnes, Gromatzky, Kosarek, 1992; 488.6: Piazza Ducale, Vigevano, Italy, milanodavai.com; 488.7: Perkins Eastman/Steve Amiaga 1992; 488.8: "Cité International Competition", Peterson Littenberg, 1991; 488.9: DT ARCHIVE; 489.10: Photo: Anton Grassl/ESTO; 490.11: Arezzo, *G. Vasari*, C. Conforti, 1993; 490.12: Wikipedia/Creative Commons; 490.13: Daniel Solomon and Associates 2000; 491.14: KK; 491.15: Photo: Ezequiel Rodriguez Baudo; 491.16: Weiss Manfredi 2007; 491.17: Photo: Compagnie des Arts Photomécaniques; 492.18, 19, 20, 21: Dennis and Associates, 1992; 493.22: Perkins Eastman and Moody Nolan Architects; 493.23: Photo: Joseph Romeo; 493.24: Perkins Eastman and Moody Nolan Architects; 493.25: Photo: Andrew Rugge/Perkins Eastman; 493.26: Perkins/Eastman; 494.27: Photo: Richard Bryant/Arcaid Images; 494.28: Richard Meier & Partners; 494.29, 30: Torti Gallas and Partners 2008; 495.31, 32: Peterson Littenberg 2002; 496.33: Photo: James Morris; 496.34: HBRA Architects 1991; 497.35: Freelon Adjaye Bond/Smith Group 2016; 497.36, 37: Trelles Cabarrocas Architects 2008; 498.38: courtesy Carl Laubin; 498.39, 40; 499.41: KK; 500.42: Millenium Place, Boston, Handel Architects, Photo: Bruce Martin; 501.43: Alys Beach, FL, DPZ, Photo: STUDIO 10 Eight/Shuttercock; 502.44: "Res Publica + Res Economica + Civitas", L. Krier; 503.45: "City of Composite Presence", D. Griffin and H. Kollhoff

Colin Rowe's Influence on the New Urbanism (N.I. Payton)
NP ARCHIVE: 521.19
Other: 505, 506.1: Photo: Alex MacLean; 507.2; 508.3; 508.4; 509.5, 6: DPZ; 510.7, 8: Daniel Solomon, Architect; 511.9a: drawing, J. Tice; : 511.9b: *Courtyard Housing in Los Angeles*, S. Polyzoides, R. Sherwood, J. Tice, 2nd ed. 1992 Cover Photo: Julius Schulman; 512:10: Moule & Polyzoides; 513.11: GM; 514.12; 515.13: Torti Gallas + Partners 2008; 516.14: GM; 517.15: Daniel Solomon, 1992; : 518.16, 17; 519.18: *Architects of Community: Torti Gallas + Partners*, J.F. Torti, et. al, 2017; 521.20: ROM, detail

Beyond Dialectics: Collage City in the Contemporary Metropolis (A. Sotoca)
524: Trieste Porto Vecchio, Manuel de Solá-Morales; 526.1, 2: "A Matter of Things", Manuel de Solá-Morales 2008; 528.3: Barene di San Giuliano, L. Quaroni, 1959; 529.4: WC; 530.5: Government Center, Tunis, L. Quaroni, 1965; 531.6: Casilino, Rome, 1964, Photo: GE; 532.7: L. Quaroni, portrait archive; 532.8: Casilino, Rome, L. Quaroni, Model 1964; 533.9: Model, Torresana, Barcelona, 2004, M. de Solá-Morales; 533.10: M. de Solá-Morales, portrait archive; 535.11; 536.12, 13: M. de Solá-Morales archive; GE: 537.14

Coding Urban Morphology: Urban Form as Pattern and Character of Place (S. Quick)
"Hillsides Study": 540; 541.1; 545.2; 546.3; 548.4; 549.5, 6; 550.7; 551.8; 552.9; 553.10; 554.11, 12; 558.14
Other: 556.13: Photo, Bruce Emmerling/pixabay

Urbanism at Ground Zero: The Attempted Colin-ization of Lower Manhattan (B. Littenberg)
BL ARCHIVE: 560; 561.1; 563.2, 3; 564.4; 565.5, 6; 565.7; 566.8; 567.9; 568.11; 569.12 (Model Photo, J. Pottle); 570.13 (Perspective, Michael McCann); 571.15; 571.16 (Model Photo, J. Pottle); 571.17 (Model Photo, J. Pottle); 572.18 (Perspective, Michael McCann); 572.19; 573.20; 574.21 (Model Photo, J. Pottle); 576.23 (Model Photo, J. Pottle)
Other: 567.10: *New York Post*, July 18, 2002; 570.14: Photo Park Ave, 1888; 575.22: Model photo J. Pottle, and drawings by Peterson Littenberg and Office of D. Liebskind

V. Diagnosis/Prognosis 578: ANET

The Timeliness of Rowe's Legacy (E. Piroddi)
581: Photo: Giorgio Simi; 582.1: Photo: Bretwa, Wikipedia; 582.2: Plan Voisin, 1925; 582.3: NY State Archives 1947; 582.4: *Creating Defensible Space*, O. Newman, 1966; 582.5, 6 WC; 583.7: *Versailles*, Pierre Patel, 1608; 583.8: Hadrian's Villa, 2nd century, model by I. Gismondi, 1935; 583.9: *Le Corbusier Le Grand*, Phaidon Press, 2008; 583.10: AM; 584.11: Memories of Upjohn in Disneyland; 582.12: *Plug-in City*, Archigram, Peter Cook ca 1964; 584.13: Neue Pinakothek, Munich; 584.14: Museo della Civilità di Roma; 585.15: CC; 585.16: WC; 586.17: WC; 586.18: SC&SH Archive; 586.19: Photo: Andrea Kasiske, 1962; 586.20: Photo: Lyna 1962 astudejaoublie.blogsport.com; 586.21: Galleria Nazionale di Parma; 587.22: Private collection; 587.23: IBA Berlin Master Plan, J. P. Kleihues, IBA Berlin, 1987; 587.24: Federal Chancellery, Berlin, Schultes Frank Architeken et. al, courtesy PERI Group:

Urbanistics: Notes Towards an Intellectual Biography of Colin Rowe (D. G. Shane)
DGS ARCHIVE: 588; 590.+1; 591.+2; 592.+3,4; 594.+5, 6; 596.+7,8; 599.+9, 10; 600.+11, 12; 602.+13; 603.+14, 15; 604.+16; 605.+17; 606.+18; 607.+19; 608.+20, 21; 609.+22; 610.+23, 24; 612.+25; 613.+26; 615.+27
Other: 593.1: Figures: Project, R. Maxwell, 1944; 598.2: Thesis, Warburg Institute, R. Maxwell, 1948-49; 599.3: Sketch, R. Maxwell, (after Sitte); 601.4: Le Corbusier, League of Nations and Saint-Dié, D.G. Shane; 604.5: BWF; 607.6: "Layered London", Photo: Fred Koetter and Susie Kim; 611.7: Cornell Performing Arts Center, Stirling Wilford, Archival Photo of Model, 1981-89

The Best of Both Worlds: Rowe's 'Dialectic Liberalism' (A.P. Latini)
612: "Figure/ground Rome and its hinterland", courtesy Rachele Passerini;
640.1, 641.2: JT ARCHIVE

Charisma and Insight: Urban Design in the Concurrency of Times (F.G. Oswald)
FO ARCHIVE: 646.1a, b
Other: 644: *Untitled (No. 8)*, Robert Slutzky 1978; 647.1c, 1d: BWF; 648.2: Isaiah Berlin, *The Undefeated*, David Levine, ca. 1978; 651.3: *Sketch for Sauce Hollandaise*, R. Slutzky, 1958/74; 652.4: WC; 654.5: *Regions depend on hinterland*, J. H. von Thünen, ca. 1826; 655.6: *Wiesbaden 2020 in Light and Darkness*, courtesy of NASA, 2020

Index